MARITIME HISTORY SERIES

Series Editor

John B. Hattendorf, *Naval War College*

Volumes Published in this Series

Pietro Martire d'Anghiera, et al.
The history of travayle in the West and East Indies (1577)
Introduction by Thomas R. Adams,
John Carter Brown Library

Willem Ysbrandsz. Bontekoe
Die vier und zwantzigste Schiffahrt (1648)
Introduction by Augustus J. Veenendaal, Jr.,
Instituut voor Nederlandse Geschiedenis, The Hague

Josiah Burchett
A complete history of the most remarkable transactions at sea (1720)
Introduction by John B. Hattendorf,
Naval War College

Alvise Cà da Mosto
Questa e una opera necessaria a tutti li naviga[n]ti (1490)
bound with:
Pietro Martire d'Anghiera
Libretto de tutta la navigatione de Re de Spagna (1504)
Introduction by Felipe Fernández-Armesto,
Oxford University

Martín Cortés
The arte of navigation (1561)
Introduction by D. W. Waters,
National Maritime Museum, Greenwich

John Davis
The seamans secrets (1633)
Introduction by A. N. Ryan,
University of Liverpool

Francisco Faleiro
Tratado del esphera y del arte del marear (1535)
Introduction by Timothy Coates,
Brown University

Gemma, Frisius
De principiis astronomiae & cosmographiae (1553)
Introduction by C. A. Davids,
University of Leiden

Tobias Gentleman
Englands way to win wealth, and to employ ships and marriners (1614)
bound with:
Robert Kayll
The trades increase (1615)
and
Dudley Digges
The defence of trade (1615)
and
Edward Sharpe
Britaines busse (1615)
Introduction by John B. Hattendorf,
Naval War College

William Hacke
A collection of original voyages (1699)
Introduction by Glyndwr Williams,
Queen Mary and Westfield College, University of London

Marine architecture:
or Directions for carrying on a ship from the first laying of the keel
to her actual going to sea (1739)
Introduction by Brian Lavery,
National Maritime Museum, Greenwich

Pedro de Medina
L'art de naviguer (1554)
Introduction by Carla Rahn Phillips,
University of Minnesota

Thomas Pownall
The administration of the colonies (4th ed., 1768)
Introduction by Daniel A. Baugh, Cornell University,
and Alison Gilbert Olson,
University of Maryland, College Park

St. Barthélemy and the Swedish West India Company:
A selection of printed documents, 1784-1814
Introduction by John B. Hattendorf,
Naval War College

John Seller
Practical navigation (1680)
Introduction by Michael Richey,
Royal Institute of Navigation

Shipbuilding Timber for the British Navy:
Parliamentary papers, 1729-1792
Introduction by R. J. B. Knight,
National Maritime Museum, Greenwich

Jean Taisnier
A very necessarie and profitable booke concerning navigation (1585?)
Introduction by Uwe Schnall,
Deutsches Schiffahrtsmuseum, Bremerhaven

Lodovico de Varthema
Die ritterlich un[d] lobwirdig Rayss (1515)
Introduction by George Winius,
University of Leiden

Gerrit de Veer
The true and perfect description of three voyages (1609)
Introduction by Stuart M. Frank,
Kendall Whaling Museum

Isaak Vossius
A treatise concerning the motion of the seas and winds (1677)
together with
De motu marium et ventorum (1663)
Introduction by Margaret Deacon,
University of Southampton

A Complete History of the Most Remarkable Transactions at Sea
(1720)

by Josiah Burchett

A Facsimile Reproduction with
an Introduction by

JOHN B. HATTENDORF
Ernest J. King Professor of Maritime History
Naval War College

Published for the
JOHN CARTER BROWN LIBRARY
by
SCHOLARS' FACSIMILES & REPRINTS
DELMAR, NEW YORK
1995

SCHOLARS' FACSIMILES & REPRINTS
ISSN 0161-7729
SERIES ESTABLISHED 1936
VOLUME 489

Published by Scholars' Facsimiles & Reprints
Delmar, New York 12054-0344, U.S.A.

New matter in this edition
© 1995 Academic Resources Corporation
All rights reserved

Printed and made in the United States of America

The publication of this work was assisted by a grant from the
National Endowment for the Humanities,
an agency of the Federal government

Reproduced from a copy in,
and with the permission of,
the John Carter Brown Library
at Brown University

The text and maps reproduced in this work
have been reduced from their original sizes

∞ The paper used in this publication meets the minimum requirements
of the American National Standard for Information Sciences—
Permanence of Paper for Printed Library Materials Z39.48—1984.

Library of Congress Cataloging-in-Publication Data

Burchett, Josiah, 1666?-1746.

A complete history of the most remarkable transactions at sea :
(1720) / by Josiah Burchett; a facsimile reproduction
with an introduction by John B. Hattendorf.
p.   cm. —
(Maritime history series)
(Scholars' Facsimiles & Reprints ; vol. 489)
"From the earliest accounts of time to the conclusion of the last war with
France ... and other maritime occurences that have happened among all
nations which have flourished at sea, and in a more particular manner of
Great Britain from the time of the Revolution in the year 1688 to the
aforesaid period"—Facsim t.p.
Originally published: London : Printed by W. B. for J. Walthoe, 1720.
With a new introd.
Includes bibliographic references.
ISBN 0-8201-1489-8 (alk. paper)
1. Naval history.
I. Hattendorf, John B.
II. Title.
III. Series: Maritime history series (Delmar, N.Y.)
D27.B94   1995
359'.009—dc20   95-2179
CIP

Introduction

Josiah Burchett's *A Complete History of the Most Remarkable Transactions at Sea* was the first general naval history published in the English language. As such, it holds a special place in the study of naval history.

There is no doubt that Josiah Burchett was one of the most knowledgeable men of his time in naval affairs. He held the post of Secretary of the Admiralty, the key administrator of the Royal Navy, for forty-eight years from 1694 to 1742, longer than any other person. An understanding of the range and depth of his knowledge may be gained, perhaps, from the telling comment made in 1700 by the anonymous pamphleteer who wrote that "whoever conns the ship of the Admiralty," as its nominal head, "the Secretary is always at the helm of the Admiralty: he knows the reaches, buoys and shelves of the river of Parliament and knows how to steer clear of them all. He is the spring that moves the clockwork of the whole board, the oracle that is to be consulted on all occasions."[1]

Josiah Burchett lacked the personal eminence that Samuel Pepys achieved when he held the same office from 1673-79 and 1684-89, but much of Pepys's stature today stems from the literary importance of his diary and from the decisive role he played in establishing many administrative methods for the Admiralty. While never having the same aura about him, Burchett, nevertheless, did have vast knowledge. Therefore, his writing has a special authority and is founded on insight that deserves consideration. Yet, because of Burchett's official position, both readers and historians have tended to discount the value of his book, assuming that as a civil servant his object must have been to obscure the facts rather than to clarify them. This contrast in views is a feature of the book that makes it even more interesting for modern research.

INTRODUCTION

BURCHETT: A BIOGRAPHICAL SKETCH[2]

The family name of Burchett, and its cognates Burkit, Burkett, Byrchett, and Birchett, was not an uncommon one in southeastern England in the seventeenth century. The names of Josiah Burchett's parents and the exact place of his birth are not known. There is a clue in the coat of arms that appears on the monument to the memory of his first wife. The same coat of arms is also on the frontispiece portrait in *A Complete History*. These link him to the arms granted in 1589 to one Thomas Byrchett of Rye, Sussex, whose children were born in Goudhurst, Kent. Tradition links the future Admiralty Secretary with Sandwich in Kent, but no other evidence in church or other records has been found to confirm this. At Burchett's death in 1746, he was said to have been about eighty. Thus, he must have been born about 1666.

Documents directly relating to Josiah Burchett first occur when he was a clerk in the service of Samuel Pepys, who was also associated with the borough of Sandwich. Burchett seems to have entered Pepys's employ about 1680.[3] He sailed with Pepys and Lord Dartmouth on the Tangier expedition in 1683-84[4] and he probably became one of Pepys's clerks upon his return in May 1684.

In the years that followed, Burchett became Pepys's favorite young clerk. In 1686 alone, Burchett went on twenty trips from London to Windsor, helping Pepys prepare for audiences with King James II. By the mid-1680s, Burchett had become a confidante and companion as well as a virtual member of Pepys's household. All this ended in 1687, when Burchett apparently strayed from Pepys's strict rules and Pepys peremptorily dismissed him after more than seven years of service.[5] Today, one finds the three earliest of Burchett's extant letters are those he wrote to Pepys in 1687,[6] denying a charge that he had accepted bribes while he had been in Pepys's employment, seeking his forgiveness, and asking for reemployment.

Sometime later, Pepys must have forgiven Burchett. Burchett's later career suggests that Pepys may have indirectly had an influence. In the end, on the directions that Pepys left for his own funeral in 1703, Pepys's executor gave Burchett a mourning ring valued at 15 shillings.[7]

INTRODUCTION

Failing to reinstate himself with Pepys in 1687-88 or to get Pepys's direct recommendation for further employment, Burchett eventually found some temporary work with one of Pepys's associates. Burchett's new employer was William Hewer, who had also been one of Pepys's former clerks and would eventually be the executor of Pepys's estate. Finally in September 1688, Burchett entered naval service on board the 46-gun ship HMS *Portsmouth* under the command of Captain George St. Lo. With this appointment, Burchett found a new avenue for preferment. Finding favor with the Earl of Dartmouth, commander in chief of the fleet, who was himself then quarreling with Pepys, Burchett moved on to become a member of Dartmouth's retinue on board the 70-gun, flagship HMS *Resolution*. There, he worked under Dartmouth's private secretary, Phineas Bowles. Shortly afterwards, following William III's landing at Torbay at the end of the year, Bowles attached himself to Dartmouth's successor, Admiral Arthur Herbert.

On 8 March 1689, William III appointed Herbert as First Lord of the Admiralty and Bowles became Admiralty Secretary. Burchett soon followed to serve as an Admiralty clerk under Bowles. With the Earl of Torrington's resignation in January 1690, the Admiralty Commissioners dismissed Bowles and replaced him with James Southerne. During these changes, Burchett remained at the Admiralty and came to know Admiral Edward Russell, who soon became Burchett's patron.

In June 1691, Burchett resigned his Admiralty position and reported on board Russell's flagship, the 100-gun HMS *Britannia*. He remained on board through 1692 and, most likely, he was present at the battle of Barfleur.[8] In July 1693, Burchett rejoined the Admiralty Office, probably serving as Chief Clerk in July and August 1693.[9] During the overlapping period of 4 July 1693 and 18 August 1694, Burchett also served as Deputy Judge Advocate of the Fleet, following Samuel Pepys's tenure in that position. About 24 April 1694, Burchett left the Admiralty again to serve as Russell's secretary, going with the fleet to the Mediterranean and remaining with Russell until November 1695.[10] This time, however, Russell was in a very powerful position, acting as both fleet commander and First Lord of the Admiralty. Russell went on to serve as First Lord for nearly five years, from 2 May 1694 through the end of the war and on into 1699.

INTRODUCTION

Meanwhile in London, William Southerne retired and the duties of Admiralty Secretary passed to William Bridgeman, a clerk of the Privy Council. As First Lord, Russell was concerned that he had his own man in office who would be willing to send him confidential information. Russell privately asked Bridgeman to include this sort of advice in his regular reports from London, noting that "among the common business of the office, you might now and then mix affairs worth knowing."[11]

With wartime operations creating ever more business for the Admiralty board, the Commissioners decided to take up a suggestion that Bowles had made upon leaving office four years before. They appointed two joint-secretaries to deal with the wide range of wartime business in coordinating Admiralty policy and administration. Disappointed by Bridgeman's failure to keep him fully informed of "affairs worth knowing," Russell used the opportunity to have Burchett appointed joint-secretary along with William Bridgeman. The Admiralty appointed Burchett on 26 September 1694, but the news did not reach him with the fleet at Cadiz until early November. Sailing with the first homeward convoy, Burchett joined the English Ambassador in Portugal, John Methuen. With the fleet of English and Dutch merchant ships, they arrived at Spithead on 11 January 1695.

Taking up his duties, Burchett was, at first, the junior secretary. Bridgeman continued to sign all letters and commissions through the spring and summer of 1695. Bridgeman had already begun a wide-ranging reorganization of the Admiralty office, creating new filing systems that advanced the work Pepys had started in 1673. Working with Burchett, Bridgeman continued to build this system. With this change also came the abolition of fees from the issue of commissions, warrants, and other documents and the establishment of a salary for the secretaries. Burchett and Bridgeman were each paid £800 a year. By the autumn of 1695, Burchett began to share fully in all the business required.

From 1696 onwards, Bridgeman's health slowly declined. By the end of the war, he had, for all practical purposes, ceased to work and finally resigned his office in June 1698. From 24 June 1698 until May 1702, Burchett was the sole Admiralty secretary. In this role, he had to deal with the entire range of business involved in paying off the fleet and reducing the Navy at the end of the Nine Years' War. With that barely

INTRODUCTION

completed, he had to turn around and administer the build up for the War of the Spanish Succession.

In May 1699, Admiral Russell, now the Earl of Orford, resigned and left Burchett without the direct support of his long-time patron. The new Board of Admiralty Commissioners contained only two members who had served in the earlier Board, Sir George Rooke and Sir Robert Rich, the latter of whom died by the end of the year. Given the very political nature of Burchett's appointment, clearly tied to Russell, it is remarkable that Burchett retained his office. Just as remarkable is the fact that Burchett survived further changes in the leadership of the Admiralty. These included many organizational as well as political transitions: The change from Admiralty Commissioners to the appointment of the Earl of Pembroke as Lord High Admiral in 1701, followed by the appointment of Queen Anne's consort, Prince George of Denmark, to that same post from 1702-1708, and then the return of Pembroke in 1708-9, before the placement of the office in commission again in November 1709 with Orford as First Lord and, finally, a total change of Admiralty commissioners in 1714.

Burchett showed that the position of Admiralty secretary was one for a knowledgeable civil servant rather than for a temporary political appointee. Under the earlier system, each major change would have brought a change in the Admiralty secretary. Yet, Burchett weathered them all, clearly exemplifying the new role of civil servants and the independence of the administrative machinery of government.

Burchett was Lord Pembroke's sole advisor during the five months of his tenure as Lord High Admiral in 1701. Without a board of commissioners, Burchett was, often, the only authority at the Admiralty. The weakness of this situation was apparent and on Prince George's appointment, a new body was created, The Lord High Admiral's Council, to deal with the situation. Prince George was also Generalissimo of All her Majesty's Land forces and, in addition, Lord High Admiral. With these two posts, he directly exercised the constitutional authority of the Crown over the armed forces. This represented certain political difficulties. At least for the Admiralty, the Prince's Council served as a check on the potential growth of royal authority. Simultaneously, it was a practical advisory council to a man in poor health who had limited

INTRODUCTION

experience in directly administering a department of state.[12] During the first three years of Prince George's tenure, Burchett joined George Clarke, the Prince's private secretary, as joint Admiralty Secretary. Here, however, Burchett was the senior secretary, a fact recognized by the fact that the Prince paid Burchett an additional £200 per year. While Burchett attended to the regular, day-by-day business of the Admiralty, Clarke was often absent from London on other aspects of the Prince's business. In 1705, the Prince abruptly dismissed Clarke who had voted against the Court nominee for Speaker of the House of Commons. For the next thirty-five years, from 25 October 1705 until 29 April 1741, Burchett remained the sole Secretary of the Admiralty.

Burchett, himself, stood for election to Parliament in 1705. As a Whig and member of the "Court group," he was elected in May 1705 as one of three members representing the borough of Sandwich. He remained a member until 1713, when the property ownership requirements of the Qualifications Act of 1711 prevented him from standing in the 1713 election. During the 1710-13 period, Burchett had been one of fifteen or so government officials in Parliament.[13]

With his first wife's death in October 1713, Burchett received an inheritance that would have satisfied the property requirement, but he did not return to Parliament until 1721. He then remained a member for twenty years until May 1741. At the age of about seventy-five, he lost in an election in which three other candidates stood against him.

Upon Clarke's dismissal in 1705, the Admiralty Commissioners created a Deputy Secretary to help handle the load of business. Filled by John Fawler from 1705 to 1714, the office remained vacant until 1728. It was vacant again in 1741, when Burchett at age seventy-five, was in uncertain health. At that point, the Deputy Secretary's post was left vacant and Thomas Corbett became Joint Secretary with Burchett. On 14 October 1742, the Admiralty Commissioners petitioned the Crown to retire Burchett with a pension equivalent to his former salary.

In 1742, Josiah Burchett retired with his third wife to the property that he had inherited from his first wife at Hampstead. Four years later, he died there on 2 October 1746, leaving two daughters and a son from his earlier marriages. He left no large estate or any group of

INTRODUCTION

private papers. His principal legacies are the documents in the Admiralty papers and his published books.

WRITINGS

Memoirs of Transactions at Sea.

Burchett's first published naval writing[14] was his *Memoirs of Transactions at Sea during the War with France; beginning in 1688 and Ending in 1697... .*[15] Burchett explained modestly in the preface that when he "undertook the following work, it was not with design to make it Publick, but rather to refresh my own memory, when anything contained therein might have escaped its reach." Published by Edward Jones, who served as the Queen's Printer until 1706, the work is very clearly based on the official reports received in the Admiralty, and not on any other less authoritative material. For example, as one historian has reported, Burchett's account of Vice Admiral Sir John Nevill's 1696 campaign in the West Indies follows Nevill's report "almost word for word in many passages."[16] His aim was clearly to record, in terse narrative form, the facts of English naval operations during the Nine Years' War, providing authoritative information on the dates, basic instructions, and events involved in naval battles and operations, avoiding the administrative issues and policies lying behind the operations. There is probably some truth in his prefatory statement. He faced a great range of daily administrative details. Perhaps, he did not always remember the details he read, from day to day, in the multitudinous reports of what happened at sea.

Alone of Burchett's writing, the *Memoirs* were translated and published on the continent.[17] Like many other widely read English books in the period, it was translated into French, but published in Amsterdam. In this case, however, it was published by a firm that specialized in music and had only a very short list of works in military or political history.

INTRODUCTION

A Critic of the Memoirs.

Among the events that Burchett described was the ill-fated expedition to the West Indies commanded by Commodore Robert Wilmot.[18] This alone, among all the controversial events of the war, sparked an immediate public comment on Burchett's work. Colonel Luke Lillington, the commander of the land forces in Wilmot's expedition against the French in western Hispaniola, took immediate offense at Burchett's account and published a pamphlet attacking it.[19] Seeing Burchett's account as slanderous, Lillington wrote in his preface:

> Tho' Writing of Books is something remote to the profession of a Souldier, yet as the World has found out new ways of offending us, viz., by Pen and Ink instead of weapons, it becomes us to be able by all sorts of Arms to defend our selves.[20]

Attacking Burchett directly, Lillington declared:

> ... Mr Burchett, who undertaking the part of a historian, which I perceive he is but indifferently qualified for, has forc'd me to this method, by giving himself the liberty to publish such particulars of the voyage of Captain Wilmot, as I must say he can have no good authority for.[21]

Continuing, Lillington expressed a fundamental distrust in allowing a civil servant to write history:

> If Clerks and Secretaries come to write Journals of other mens Actions, those Actions are very much at their mercy, and those men too. He can never be duly qualified for such an Authoritative Relation as is required in such a case who was not on the spot, nor concerned in the action, unless he had the particulars from those men.[22]

Lillington then went on to give a detailed account of the action, as he recalled it. It provides much detailed information and seems to have been

INTRODUCTION

well enough received to have been reprinted at least once.[23] Despite the apparent accuracy of many of his details, the tone of Lillington's account shows violent hatred toward the Navy and particularly Wilmot, who had died in September 1695 during the expedition's return passage. Explaining his difficulties, Lillington attacked Wilmot in vivid terms, detailing his drunkenness and rude manners, concluding:

> Let any man judge what a Task I had, that was tyed to a man that had neither Courage to answer himself as a gentleman nor Manners to behave himself as a Man, but that I was obliged to bear ill treatment of a man of his temper, without any possible Method of Redress.[24]

Summarizing his argument on the final page, Lillington wrote:

> This unhappy voyage, made so by the treachery and covetousness of the sea officers, but particularly of the commodore, who having his private interest only in his Eye, regarded neither his Commission, his Instructions, the Rules of War, and the Laws of Arms, the Square of Division: nor indeed did he keep any measures, but such as were the Dictates of his Avarice and Pride.
>
> How Mr Burchett came to his Account, how he came to give it any credit as to abuse all the rest of the people concerned with it, are Questions he would do well to answer, before he can obtain the reputation of an impartial and careful Historian.[25]

Burchett's Justification.

Lillington's criticism was something that Burchett could not ignore. In a pamphlet reply, *Mr Burchett's Justification of his Naval-Memoirs*, he clearly took the high ground with a moderate tone. "I shall not be influenced by the Method Colonel Lillington has taken, for I am well assured it will be in my power to keep my own Pen within the Rules of decency,"[26] Burchett wrote. Replying to Lillington's charge that his history had no authentic documents to support it, Burchett clearly showed his sources. Using more than fifteen pages, Burchett printed two

INTRODUCTION

letters from Wilmot, one in March and another in July 1695, with a variety of other information.

Starting his detailed refutation of Lillington's charges, Burchett noted that he had intended no direct reflection on Lillington. He had taken great care "to mention nothing of the land service than was absolutely necessary to make the other intelligible."[27] Admitting one mistake, Burchett noted that he had misread the documents and had confused Colonel Lillington with his brother, Major Lillington.[28] Turning his pamphlet into a commentary on current naval and military practices, Burchett skillfully took up each issue that Lillington raised. He then dealt with them broadly, in a series of questions and general observations, avoiding an attack on Lillington, but providing some insight into the issues. In concluding the pamphlet, Burchett raised some serious questions on the value of such expeditions:

> How great the charges hath been of our Foreign Expeditions, but more especially to the West Indies, and what little benefit to the Nation hath reaped therefrom is too well known. This is a matter of great consequence to the Publick, as it calls for the most severe Consideration, what measures may be taken to render such Expeditions (when such there must be) more beneficial for the future.[29]

Concluding his examination of past experience, Burchett wrote something that seems quite remarkable for a civil servant to set down in print. "In fine, I cannot recollect that one beneficial service hath been performed in America for many years past," Burchett declared, "either by our Squadrons or Land Forces; at least not any that hath in any measure been answerable to the Expence and other misfortunes."[30] Yet, Burchett clearly reflected the current views on English strategy in the War of the Spanish Succession. At the time he was writing, the number of English warships in the West Indies in 1704-05 was at a low point and there was clear resistance to undertaking such expeditions.

In his concluding pages,[31] Burchett enumerated the practical considerations that affect the success or failure of such expeditions.

INTRODUCTION

A Complete History.

Burchett's next publication (reproduced in facsimile here) appeared in 1720 from the press of J. Walthoe, a prominent father and son printer who were in business from 1683 to about 1733. *A Complete History* appeared when Burchett was about sixty years of age and sixteen years after he had published the *Memoirs of Transactions at Sea*.

In his new book, Burchett took clear advantage of his official position and brought attention to the possible uses of British naval power:

> ... far from disturbing Europe with such pursuits [of power], are only watchful of its Repose, and employ that awful Strength you are possessed of to no other purpose, than to preserve a Ballance among its Princes as is absolutely necessary to its Peace, and reduce to Reason those who, by their boundless Ambition, would involve it in War and Desolation.[32]

This note echoed recent British foreign policy.[33] Linking it even more closely to official policy, Burchett dedicated the volume to King George I, added an allegorical painting by Thornhill, and printed a statement of Burchett's royal license and privilege. This reserved the rights for the sole printing, publishing, and distributing of the book for fourteen years, signed in the King's name by the Secretary of State for the Southern Department, James Craggs.[34]

The new volume bore a similar title to the first work, *A Complete History of the most remarkable Transactions at Sea*, but as its subtitle suggested, it was a much expanded work.[35] As Burchett's title makes clear, his intention was to provide a general overview of world naval history as a preface to a more detailed study of English naval affairs from 1688 to 1712, the period of which he had direct knowledge. Just half the volume, 407 of 800 pages, Books One through Three, is devoted to general naval history while the 168 pages of Book Four are devoted to the period 1688-1697 and the 225 pages of Book Five to the period 1698 to 1712.

INTRODUCTION

Book Four.

Clearly the origin of the book is found in Burchett's 1703 *Memoirs of Transactions at Sea*, reproduced almost *verbatim* in Book Four.[36] In this version, it varies, as Burchett described it, "but very little from what hath already been written thereof, yet it is now put into such a Dress, and such Amendments have been made therein, as it is hoped, may render it much more agreeable to the Reader."[37] A close comparison of the texts of Book Four with the 1703 version, confirms Burchett's claim. He divided the text into chapters, copy-edited it, and made stylistic changes, but changed very little of substance. Most changes are on a very small order, correcting the spelling of place names or spelling out numbers instead of using figures.[38] For example, in the 1703 account of a West Indian expedition, he replaced "300 Whites and 200 Negroes" with "three hundred Whites and two hundred Blacks."[39]

In a very few places, he amended some comments. For example, in describing Lord Dartmouth's movements in October 1688, Burchett deleted the personal aside that he had published in his 1703 book that noted "in execution whereof I had the Honour to accompany his Lordship, as I did several years before in his expedition for the demolishing of Tangier in Barbary."[40]

In another case, where he described Admiral Sir Francis Wheeler's operations in the Mediterranean, Burchett mentioned Wheeler returning with the Dutch and English ships of War to join with the Spanish Squadron and together annoying the enemy. Burchett removed from the 1720 work a comment he had made about joining "the few Spanish Ships (and those rotten ones too) which that Nation call their Armada and with their invincible Assistance"[41] annoy the enemy. In the same chapter, Burchett modified a sentence that in the 1703 work had originally read:

> The Rear-Admiral knowing the Danger, but not being able timely, or effectually, to forewarn them of it, stood away directly through the Streights ... .[42]

In the 1720 edition, the same sentence read:

INTRODUCTION

> The Rear-Admiral foreseeing the Danger, was not able timely to give them notice of it, but stood away directly through the Streights ... .[43]

It appears that wherever Burchett was aware of an error of fact in the 1703 booklet, he took care to correct it in the 1720 version. Simultaneously, he followed his general principle of having a very terse narrative description.

In another example of Burchett's corrections in the 1720 *History*, he altered his account of Sir John Nevill's West Indian expedition. In the 1703 *Memoirs*, Burchett had taken care to follow carefully Nevill's report. In the *History*, he added a bit of additional information and expressed an opinion that he had not stated previously. In his revised account, Burchett clearly implied that Nevill had received information from St. Thomas that the French Admiral Pointis was then laying off Cartagena, and that if Nevill had promptly sailed to attack him there, instead of sailing to Jamaica, he might have caught and defeated him off Cartagena.[44]

With these examples in mind, it is too simple to say that Burchett merely reprinted his earlier work. While this is largely the case, the *Memoirs* appear again in *A Complete History* in a slightly revised version. In evaluating the two versions for modern scholarship, one must modify John Ehrman's opinion, which until now has been completely unquestioned, that for King William's War one should normally cite the *Memoirs* rather than *A Complete History*.[45] While Book IV of *A Complete History* is Burchett's fullest, corrected, and final statement, the two versions bear detailed examination and comparison in terms of the precise research issue at hand.

Book Five.

At the end of the War of the Spanish Succession, Burchett felt that it would be useful to record the events of that war as something

INTRODUCTION

"very worthy as well to be more universally known to the present Age, as to be communicated to Posterity." Believing himself

> furnished with Materials for such an Undertaking which could not be in the Possession of any other Person, I have imposed on my self that Task, and in the Performance thereof, borrowed many of those Hours which were no more than necessary for the Preservation of my Health.[46]

Burchett's account of the naval side of the War of the Spanish Succession employs the same technique as that for the Nine Years' War: a terse narrative summary based on the official Admiralty records, giving the essential facts on the naval operations, fully printing the Admiralty's basic instructions to commanders for their major actions, and generally avoiding personal characterizations as well as the technical, administrative, and logistical background.

Books One to Three.

After completing his revision of Book Four and writing Book Five, Burchett then turned to writing the general survey of naval affairs that would preface his detailed study of the 1689-1714 period. No other study existed in English as an example to follow or to use as the basis for a "revisionist approach". Over the last century, scholars have generally ignored this section of the book, uncritically accepting the judgment of Sir John Knox Laughton, who wrote in the 1880s:

> For this very extended undertaking Burchett's studies and opportunities had in no way fitted him; and the pages in which he attempted the ancient and foreign history have no value whatever; his chapters on earlier English history, and even on the Dutch wars, are little better, and of his volume of 800 pages rather more than half is thus worthless. The last half has, however, an exceptional value.[47]

INTRODUCTION

While scholars have tended either to ignore or to denigrate Burchett's approach to naval history for this period, it is illuminating to try to relate it to the main trends in British historiography in the early eighteenth century. This was a watershed period for writing history in England, with the first successful attempts to write broad narratives, moving away from disjointed biographical sketches and focusing on the secular events in social, cultural, and political affairs.[48] The most famous histories of the time were Clarendon's *History of the Rebellion* (1702-1704) and Bishop Burnet's *History of his Own Time* (1724-1734). In this type of historical writing, Burchett's achievement in identifying a single strand of secular historical development and following it through from ancient times to the present was an *avant garde* contribution to the literature. He was very much in line with a new trend in creating a narrative chronology from ancient times to the present, placing English history within a broad chronological context.

There were no professional historians, as such, who were writing these works, and the writers of history were only just beginning to turn to manuscript materials as the basis for their research. In the same period, men such as Robert Harley began to amass manuscript and book collections, suggesting the emphasis on such materials. There was no public access to official government papers, although some scholars did get occasional access to some of them. Thus, Burchett's use of the official Admiralty papers at this early stage is particularly important, and he shared also with Clarendon and Burnet their use of personal experience as a source.

Within the general context of writing of this period, Burchett's subject of naval history had clear, political implications. Historians seem to have tied virtually everything published in England during this period to partisan politics, and one can make a case that Burchett was an establishment Whig, linking his official position with the use of history as a literary tool to promote the Navy's foreign policy, political, and commercial interests.

One of the most intriguing issues surrounding the first three books of Burchett's history is the suggestion that it might have had some relationship to the history of the navy that Samuel Pepys's had long planned. Pepys's *Naval Minutes*[49] is filled with notes to himself on topics

INTRODUCTION

in naval history and there are repeated references in his correspondence to undertaking such a project.[50] Clearly Pepys was thinking about doing a history while Burchett was in his employ, and Burchett would have had an opportunity to hear Pepys mention it or to observe that some of his fellow clerks were copying historical materials. No evidence has yet been found to prove that Burchett was among the clerks employed in this work, although it is known that other clerks such as Hewer, Hayter, and Gibson were.[51]

Burchett appears not to have attempted any serious work on pre-1688 naval history until after he had completed Book Five. Thus, one can estimate that he was researching the material for the first three books sometime between 1713 and 1719. The question arises then about whether Burchett had access to any of the materials that Pepys had collected. Although Pepys died in May 1703, the 3,000 volume Pepysian Library was not moved to Cambridge until July 1724. In the interval, it was maintained by Pepys's nephew, John Jackson. It is possible that Burchett might have had access to it at that time. However, the fact that Burchett had so little detail on naval operations during Pepys's period in office would suggest that he did not make much, if any, use of the library.[52]

Sources For Books One, Two, and Three.

Burchett was clearly carving out a new area of historical studies by concentrating on naval affairs. The margins of his pages are full of notes to the traditional sources that one would expect: The Bible, Thucydides, Caesar, Polybius, Dion. Cassius,[53] and for English history, William Camden. In his preface, however, he makes clear that besides these sources, he relied on several other lesser known works, mentioning particularly[54] the works written in Latin by Ryves[55] and Morisotus[56] for early maritime affairs. He supplemented these, he wrote, with Coutrarini[57] and Gratiani[58] on the Battle of Lepanto, Famiau Strada[59] on the Duke of Parma's actions between the Spanish and Antwerp on the Scheldt. Interestingly, he took his account[60] of the Duke of Buckingham's 1626 expedition to the Isle of Ré from an original

INTRODUCTION

manuscript. Burchett had earlier owned, but lost or misplaced, the original manuscript diary kept by Buckingham's secretary, Sir William Beecher. In searching for it, Burchett had apparently publicly advertised for information on its whereabouts. In response to this, he received another manuscript from a clergyman in Cambridge and used it in the book.

Besides the question of sources, the final chapters of Book One, Chapters X-XII, contain a useful summary of the legal question on the Dominion of the Sea, as seen from the early 18th century.[61] In this section, Burchett provides an authoritative geographical definition of the boundaries of the British Ocean[62] that many later writers, such as Lediard, Colliber, Entick and Campbell, repeat in their books.[63] Burchett also contributes to perpetuating a common historical error relating to this subject, exaggerating the £501 15s. 2d. that the Earl of Northumberland took from Dutch fishermen in the North Sea in 1636. In reporting the figure as £30,000, Burchett was following some other early authors, not having readily available to him Northumberland's manuscript journal that was in the State Papers, not the Admiralty Papers that Burchett supervised.[64]

Thomas Lediard as Critic.

A Complete History seems to have been immediately accepted and highly regarded as an authoritative work, appearing in all the major library collections of the time. At the same time, it created little comment. No critical pamphlets appeared immediately and no commentary has yet been found in either the Dutch or English press or in the surviving correspondence of the period. The first challenge to its authority came fifteen years later with the publication of Thomas Lediard's *The Naval History of England*.[65]

Born in 1785, Thomas Lediard apparently began his career as an attaché in the English embassy at Hamburg from which joined the staff of the Duke of Marlborough in 1707 for his journey to Altranstadt for conferences with Charles XII of Sweden. Later, he served as secretary to the English envoy, Sir Cecil Wych, at Hamburg and was deeply involved with the Hamburg Opera. While in Germany, he produced several

INTRODUCTION

works, including a grammar and works for opera.[66] After returning to England about 1732, he settled in Smith Square, Westminster, where he first wrote his *Naval History* and then went on to write a biography of the Duke of Marlborough[67] and the continuation of Paul de Rapin de Thoyras's *History of England* as well as other works.[68]

By the time Lediard published his *Naval History*, there had been some changes in English historiography, and it was more in vogue to look at English history alone, rather than as a continuum of ancient history. Like Burchett before him, Lediard employed the available authorities, one of whom was Burchett himself. In his research, Lediard had run across Colonel Lillington's 1704 pamphlet, and used it extensively to criticize Burchett, noting:

> And Indeed, as these reflections of the Colonels were published in the year 1704 and Mr Burchett did not publish his larger *Naval History* until the year 1720, in which he has again inserted the Relation, which the Colonel has so severely treated it has been the Wonder of many others, that he should not have either endeavoured to refute the Colonel's Reflections or amended his Relation. But, I hope he had his sufficient Reasons, with which he has not thought fit to acquaint the World, doing neither.[69]

Only two weeks after Lediard's *History* appeared, Burchett placed a notice in both the *Daily Courant* and in the *St James's Evening Post* for 12 March 1735 objecting to Lediard's assertion and drawing notice to the fact that he had refuted Lillington's allegations immediately. In the following issue of those papers, Lediard replied on 15 March that he would be glad to do Burchett justice if someone would provide him a copy of Burchett's *Justification*. Burchett apparently tried to reply immediately and forwarded a copy of his pamphlet through a mutual acquaintance. Lediard's notice, however, continued to appear in a subsequent issue of the newspaper, irritating Burchett, who on 24 March, placed another notice asking Lediard to cease publication of his letter. This exchange of notices created a controversy in itself and led to publication of an anonymous pamphlet, *An Appeal to the Publick; or Burchett and Lediard Compar'd*.[70] The result is an interesting and

INTRODUCTION

detailed comparison, but a far from impartial one. The author very clearly favors Lediard's book and fails to appreciate either Burchett's pioneering contribution to naval history or his effective rebuttal of Lillington. The pamphleteer does indirectly show how Lediard effectively built on Burchett to create a revised, corrected, and expanded work.

ILLUSTRATIONS IN *A COMPLETE HISTORY*

Alone among his works,[71] Burchett illustrated *A Complete History* with a portrait, a painting, and eight charts, all of which connect Burchett and his history with the leading figures of his day in these areas.

The Portrait.

George Vertue engraved the portrait in an oval frame, "Josiah Burchett, Esqr. Secretary of the Admiralty of Great Britain and Ireland," showing his family arms. Curiously, while the engraver clearly signed this piece, it is not included in the published list of Vertue's works.[72]

A Catholic, Vertue was born in London in 1684, and about the age of thirteen was placed with a French artisan in London who engraved arms. Returning home after three or four years, Vertue studied drawing and then worked under Michael van der Gucht for seven years, engraving copper plates for him. Through this connection, Vertue came into the mainstream of engraving in England, as van der Gucht had come from Amsterdam in the 1680s and had earned a great reputation by doing the illustrations for Clarendon's *History of England*.

Moving into self-employment, Vertue came to the attention of Lord Somers who employed him to engrave a print of Archbishop Tillotson. This work became the foundation of his reputation. Moving on in 1711 to join Sir Godfrey Kneller's painting academy, he began to engrave portraits from the work of Kneller, Dahl, Richardson, Jervas, Gibson, and others. With the accession of George I in 1714, Vertue produced large portraits of the King and other members of the royal family that were shown at Court. As early as 1713, Vertue began to work

INTRODUCTION

on a history of the arts in England, and through this work gained the patronage of Robert Harley, Earl of Oxford, and Heneage Finch, Earl of Winchelsea. Through the latter, he became engraver to the Society of Antiquaries. He engraved several *Almanacks* for the University of Oxford as well as the portraits of the Kings of England for Rapin's *History of England*. Remaining a Roman Catholic throughout his life, he died in 1756, and was buried in the cloisters of Westminster Abbey. After his death, Horace Walpole purchased his research collections, publishing part of them, before they passed to the British Museum.

For this volume, Vertue took the likeness from a portrait of Burchett painted by James (or sometimes Jacques) Maubert, although this fact is not stated on the engraving. Born, possibly in Ireland, in 1666, Maubert first studied under Gaspar Smitz in Dublin, but was highly influenced by the work of Godfrey Kneller and Michael Dahl. He specialized in small portraits of British poets. Maubert died in London in 1780. The original of this portrait of Burchett was, in 1994, owned by the Admiralty and on loan to Concourse Hall, Ministry of Defence, London.

Painting.

The allegorical painting shows Neptune presenting the globe and foreign peoples presenting gifts of bounty and a crown to a seated Britannia, with a warship in the background. It was engraved for this volume by Gerard van der Gucht, the son of Michael van der Gucht. Born in London in 1696, where he also died in 1776, he was a student of Louis Cheron. He started his career by engraving for publishers, and this piece is an example of that work, however, he soon abandoned it to go into the business of selling paintings and works of art. A brother, Jan or John, continued as an engraver and caricaturist, collaborating with William Hogarth and reproducing Sir James Thornhill's paintings of St. Paul.

This painting has been attributed to John Thornhill, the son of Sir James Thornhill (1675-1734), whom Queen Anne had earlier employed to decorate the royal palaces. He worked in the chapels of Oxford Colleges, including All Souls, Queens, and New College, and at

INTRODUCTION

some of the best-known country houses, including Blenheim Palace, Easton Neston, Wimpole, and Chatsworth, but his most famous works with a maritime theme are those in the dining hall for Greenwich Hospital, now the Royal Naval College. With Sir Godfrey Kneller, he was a founder of an academy of painting.

John Thornhill carried on his father's work and became well known for his maritime painting. Most active from 1730 to 1760, he succeeded his father as painter to the Court, remaining in that role until 1757. This allegorical painting is a very early example of his work.

The Charts.

Burchett commissioned Herman Moll to prepare eight charts for the volume:

Page 41: A Chart of the Mediterranean Sea according to Mons Berthelot,[73] &c.

Page 48: A Chart of the Sea Coast of Naples, Sicily, Greece and the Archipelago Islands &c., According to Monsr Berthelot and the History of the Most Remarkable Transactions at Sea &c.

Page 253: A Chart of the East Indies. With the Coast of Persia, China also the Philippina, Moluca and Sunda Islands &c.

Page 265: A Chart of the West Indies or the Islands of North America in the North Sea.

Page 299: A Chart of the Baltick or East Sea, Gulf of Finland &c.

Page 322: A Chart of the Sea Coast of Great Britain and Ireland.

Page 407: A Chart of the Channel between England & France and also Part of the Coast Sands and Banks between England and Holland.

INTRODUCTION

Page 575: A Chart of the Sea Coast from England to the Streights [with an inset of:] The City and Harbour of Cadiz.

Born in the Netherlands, Herman Moll had come to England about 1681 and established himself in London at Devereux Court, between Temple Bar and St Clement's Church off The Strand. In 1681, he contributed maps to Jonas Moore, *New System of Mathematicke*. From that time onward, he began engraving and publishing several atlases, maps, and globes in London, also contributing maps and charts to books. Among them was the best general Atlas of the period, *The World Described* (London, 1720). Jonathan Swift seems to have copied from Moll the geographically correct parts of the imaginary maps he used in *Gulliver's Travels*, ironically referring to Moll in *Gulliver* as "my worthy friend."[74]

INTRODUCTION

Suggestions for Further Reading

For further biographical information on Josiah Burchett, see:

G.F. James, "Josiah Burchett, Secretary to the Lords Commissioners of the Admiralty, 1695-1742," in *Mariner's Mirror*, 23 (1937), 477-497.

For the various aspects on the background, substance, and circumstances surrounding Burchett's tenure as an administrator in the Admiralty, see:

Daniel A. Baugh, *British Naval Administration in the Age of Walpole* (Princeton, 1965).

Daniel A. Baugh, ed., *Naval Administration 1715-1750*. Publications of the Navy Records Society, volume CXX (London, 1977).

John Ehrman, *The Navy in the War of William III 1689-1697: Its State and Direction* (Cambridge, 1953).

R.J.B.Knight, "Civilians and the Navy, 1660-1832," in *Sea Studies: Essays in honour of Basil Greenhill CB,CMG, on the occasion of his retirement* (Greenwich, 1983), pp. 63-70.

R.D. Merriman, ed., *The Sergison Papers*. Publications of the Navy Records Society, volume LXXXIX (London, 1950).

R.D. Merriman, ed., *Queen Anne's Navy: Documents Concerning the Administration of the Navy of Queen Anne, 1702-1714*. Publications of the Navy Records Society, volume CIII (London, 1961).

N.A.M. Rodger, *The Admiralty* (Lavenham, Suffolk, 1979).

INTRODUCTION

F.B. Wickwire, "Admiralty Secretaries and the British Civil Service," *Huntington Library Quarterly*, 28 (1965), pp. 235-254.

For a study of English historiography in this period, see:

Laird Okie, *Augustan Historical Writing: Histories of England in the English Enlightenment* (Lanham, Md., 1991).

For further information on Herman Moll, see:

J.N.L. Baker, "The Earliest Maps of H. Moll," *Imago Mundi*, 2 (1937), p. 16.

Dennis Reinhartz, "Herman Moll, Geographer: An Eighteenth Century View of the American Southwest," in Dennis Reinhartz and Charles C. Colley, eds., *The Mapping of the American Southwest* (College Station, TX, 1987), pp. 18-36.

Dennis Reinhartz, "Herman Moll's West Indies Map of 1715," in Forbes E. Smiley, ed., *English Maps of North America 1675-1715* (New York, 1987).

Dennis Reinhartz, "Additions to the Gulf and Indies maps of Herman Moll," *The Map Collector*, 43 (Summer 1988), pp. 27-30.

Henry Stevens, *The World Described in Thirty Large Two-Sheet Maps by Henry Moll, Geographer* (New York, 1952).

David A. Woodword, "English Cartography, 1650-1750," in Norman J. W. Thrower, ed., *The Compleat Plattmaker: Essays on Chart, Map and Globe Making in England in the Seventeenth and Eighteenth Centuries* (Los Angeles, 1978), pp. 159-193.

INTRODUCTION

NOTES

1. *Remarks on the Present Condition of the Navy, And particularly the Victualling ... In a letter from A Sailor to a Member of the House of Commons* (1700), p. 7. Quoted in R.J.B. Knight, "Civilians and the Navy, 1660-1832," in *Sea Studies: Essays in honour of Basil Greenhill, CB, CMG, on the occasion of his retirement* (Greenwich, 1983), p. 65; also G.F. James, "Josiah Burchett, Secretary to the Lords Commissioners of the Admiralty, 1695-1742," in *Mariner's Mirror*, 23 (1937), 477-497 at p. 487; John Ehrman, *The Navy in the War of William III, 1689-1697: Its State and Direction* (Cambridge, 1953), p. 561; F.B. Wickwire, "Admiralty Secretaries and the British Civil Service," *Huntington Library Quarterly*, 28 (1965), pp. 235-254 at p. 245; N.A.M. Rodger, *The Admiralty* (Lavenham, Suffolk, 1979), p. 53.

2. Except where noted, this section is based on G.F. James, "Josiah Burchett."

3. J. C. Sainty, *Admiralty Officials, 1660-1870. Office Holders in Modern Britain*, IV (London, 1975), p. 113, citing R.G. Howarth, ed. *Letters and Diary of Samuel Pepys* (London, 1932), p. 181.

4. Burchett, *Memoirs of Transactions at Sea During the War with France; beginning in 1688 and ending in 1697* (London, 1703), p. 12.

5. Arthur Bryant, *Samuel Pepys: The Saviour of the Navy* (Cambridge, 1942), pp. 148, 177, 214, 219, 268, 296, 360.

6. Bodleian Library, Rawlinson MSS A.189, fos. 1, 7, 20.

7. J.R. Tanner, ed., *Private Correspondence and Miscellaneous Papers of Samuel Pepys, 1679-1703, in the Possession of J. Pepys Cockerell* (London, 1926), vol. 2, pp. 314-318.

8. Thus, the text below in *A Complete History*, pp. 439-451, 461-476, may be partially based on personal observation in the fleet.

9. Sainty, p. 113, citing letters signed in PRO, ADM 2/384.

10. Thus, pp. 495-514, below, may be partially based on personal observation.

11. Quoted in Rodger, *Admiralty*, p. 48.

12. John B. Hattendorf, *English Grand Strategy in the War of the Spanish Succession: A Study of the English View and Conduct of Grand Strategy, 1702-1712* (New York, 1987), pp. 32-35.

13. Geoffrey Holmes, *British Politics in the Age of Anne* (London, 1967), pp. 180-181.

14. The Catalogues of the British Library and the Bodleian Library contain several poems attributed to J. Burchett, e.g., *The Ark, a Poem, in imitation of Du Bartas (1714); For Patie and Roger, Strife and Envy since the fall of man: To Mr Allan Ramsay,* (1716) but none of these have been clearly connected to the Admiralty Secretary.

15. Josiah Burchett, *Memoirs of Transactions at Sea during the War with France; beginning in 1688 and Ending in 1697. Most humbly Dedicated to his Royal Highness Prince George of Denmark, Lord High Admiral of England and Ireland, and*

INTRODUCTION

Generalissimo of all her Majesty's Forces &c. ([London] in the Savoy: Edward Jones, 1703).

16. R.D. Merriman, ed., *The Sergison Papers.* Publications of the Navy Records Society, vol. LXXXIX (London, 1950), p. 287.

17. *Mémoires de tout ce qui s'est passé de plus considérable sur Mer, Durant la Guerre avec la France Depuis l'an 1688, jusqu'à la fin de 1697. Par Mr. Burchett, Sécrétaire de l'Amirauté.* A Amsterdam aux Dépens d'Estienne Roger, Marchand Libraire, chez qui l'on trouve un Assortiment général de tout sorte de Musique. MDCCIV [1704], 362 pp.

18. *Ibid.*, pp. 305-321; Reprinted below, pp. 531-537.

19. *Reflections on Mr Burchett's memoirs or, Remarks on the Account of Captain Wilmot's Expedition to the West Indies* [by] Colonel Luke Lillington, Commander in Chief of the Land forces in that Expedition (London, 1704).

20. *Ibid.*, preface unpaginated.

21. *Ibid.*

22. *Ibid.*

23. The John Carter Brown Library holds two copies, each in a different state. Shelf Number D704 L729. The differences between the two are (1) the presence of a page number on p. 9; (2) the catchword on p. 87 either *sion or eight;* (3) the presence of an errata slip.

The errata slip notes:
    p. 104 line 4 for one mortar read two mortars.
    p. 105 line 7 for six pieces of cannon read three pieces of cannon; for four saker read three saker.

Copy 2 in the John Carter Brown Library also contains a list of errata in manuscript:
    p. 59 line 1 read Machaneel [Manchioneal] Bay line 25 read Machaneel [Manchioneal] Bay.
    p. 118 line 18 for 133 read about 140 pieces of cannon
    p. 137 line 17 for arrived at Jamaica the 23rd of July read 27th July.
    p. 157 line 8 for three companies read five.
    p. 157 line 11 for 200 men read 130 private men.

24. *Ibid.*, p. 41.

25. *Ibid.*, p. 171.

26. *Mr Burchett's justification of His Naval-Memoirs in Answer to Reflections made by Col. Lillington, On the Part which relates to Cape François and Port de Paix. With Some Short observations on Our West India Expeditions* ([London] In the Savoy: Edward Jones, 1704), p. 3.

27. *Ibid.*, p. 23.

28. This error was corrected in the 1720 text below; see the reference to Major Lillington on p. 536, line 30.

29. *Ibid.*, p. 149.

INTRODUCTION

30. *Ibid.,* p. 153.

31. *Ibid.,* pp. 153-166.

32. Burchett, A *Complete History,* Dedication, p. A2.

33. For a general survey of British foreign policy on this period, see Basil Williams, *Stanhope: A Study in Eighteenth Century Diplomacy* (Oxford, 1932), pp. 353-383, and Ragnhild Hatton, *George I: Elector and King* (London, 1978), chap. VIII, pp. 211-242.

34. James Craggs (1686-1721) had been secretary to General James Stanhope in 1708-11, cofferer to the Prince of Wales, 1714-17, and Secretary of State from 15 March 1718 until his death 16 February 1721.

35. Josiah Burchett, Esq. Secretary of the Admiralty, *A Complete History Of the most Remarkable Transactions at Sea, From the Earliest Accounts of Time To the Conclusion of the Last War with France. Wherein Is given an Account of the most considerable Naval-Expeditions, Sea-Fights, Stratagems, Discoveries, and Other Maritime Occurrences that have happen'd among all Nations which have flourished at Sea: And in a more peculiar manner of Great Britain, from the time of the Revolution, in the Year 1688, to the aforesaid period. Adorn'd with Sea-Charts adapted to the History. With an exact Index of the names of all the Places where any considerable Battel has been fought, in any part of the World. In Five Books* (London: Printed by W.B. for J. Walthoe in the Temple Cloysters, and J. Walthoe, junior, against the Royal Exchange in Cornhill, MDCCXX [1720].)

36. Burchett, *A Complete History,* pp. 407-575.

37. *A Complete History,* Preface, [p. 1].

38. Contrast, for example, *Memoirs,* pp. 158-159, with *A Complete History,* pp. 472-473.

39. Contrast *Memoirs,* p. 320 with *A Complete History,* p. 537.

40. Contrast *Memoirs,* p. 12 with *A Complete History,* p. 411.

41. Contrast *Memoirs,* p. 203 with *A Complete History,* p. 491, line 18 from bottom.

42. Burchett, *Memoirs,* p. 209.

43. Burchett, A *Complete History,* p. 493, last line.

44. Merriman, *Sergison Papers,* p. 289.

45. John Ehrman, *The Navy in the War of William III, 1689-1697: Its State and Direction* (Cambridge, 1953), p. 680.

46. *Complete History,* Preface.

47. Sir John Knox Laughton, "Josiah Burchett," in *Dictionary of National Biography* (London, 1886), vol. VII, pp. 291-92.

48. Laird Okie, *Augustan Historical Writing: Histories of England in the Enlightenment* (Lanham, Md., 1991). pp. 4-5.

49. J. R. Tanner, ed., *Samuel Pepys's Naval Minutes.* Publications of the Navy Records Society, vol. LX, (London, 1926).

INTRODUCTION

50. Tanner, ed. *Private Correspondence,* vol. 1, pp. ix, 15, 109, 134, 145, 201; vol. 2, p. 232.

51. Information from Dr. C.S. Knighton. A careful search for evidence of Burchett's handwriting in the Pepysian MSS at Magdalene College, Cambridge, particularly MSS 2869-79, might possibly reveal something further.

52. Burchett had written to Pepys asking him to return material in June 1700. Tanner, *Private Correspondence,* vol. 1, p. 354. For things that Pepys had already returned, see J.P.W. Ehrman, "The official Papers Transferred by Pepys to the Admiralty by 12 July 1689," *The Mariner's Mirror,* 34 (1948), pp. 000.

53. Cassius Dio Cocceianus.

54. The following authors are mentioned in the text on the third page of the unpaginated Preface.

55. Sir Thomas Ryves (1583?-1652), *Historia Navalis* (London: Thomas Harper, 1629); *Historia Navalis Antiqua* (London: Robert Barker, 1633).

56. Claude Barthélemy Morisot (1592-1661), *Orbis Martimi rerum in mazi et littoribus gestarum generalis historia* (Pivione [Metz]: Petrum Palliot, 1643).

57. Probably, Giovanni Contarini (1549-c. 1603), *Historia delle cose successe dal principio della guerra mossa da Selim Ottomano a Venetiani* (Venetia: Francesco Rampazetto, 1572).

58. Antonio Maria Grazianii, Bishop of Amelia (1537-1611), *De Bello Cyprio Libri Quinque* (Rome: Alexandrum Zanettum, 1624); *De Bello Cyprio: The History of the War of Cyprus. Written originally in Latin. With a new map of the island.* Translated into English by Robert Midgley [1655?-1723]. (London: J. Rawlins, c. 1687).

59. Famiano Strada (1572-1649), *De Bello Belgico Decas Prima ab Excessu Caroli V. Imp. Usque ad Initia Prafecturae Alexandri Famesij Parmae ac Placentiae Ducis III.* (Antwerp: Jean Cnobbaert, 1635); *De Bello Belgico Decas Secunda ab Initio Prafecturae Alexandri Famesij Parmae ac Placentiaeque Ducis III. An. MDLXXVII usque ad An. MDXC* (Antwerp: Ionn. Cnobbari, 1648).

English translations: Famianus Strada, *De Bello Belgico: The History of the Low Countrey Warres: Written in Latine by Famianus Strada; in English by Sir Robert Stapylton, Kt.* (London: H. Moseley, [c. 1650]); *The Siege of Antwerp. Written in Latin by Famianus Strada, Englished by Tho: Lancaster* (London: H. Moseley, 1655).

60. Burchett, *A Complete History,* pp. 371-379.

61. See below, pp. 22-39. Also, Thomas Wemyss Fulton, *The Sovereignty of the Sea: An Historical Account of the Claims of England to the Dominion of the British Seas* ... (Edinburgh and London: William Blackwood, 1911; Millwood, NY: Kraus Reprint, 1976), pp. 521-22.

62. Burchett, *A Complete History,* pp. 28-29.

63. Samuel Colliber, *Columna Rostrata or, a Critical History of the English Sea Affairs* (London: Samuel Robinson, 1727); Thomas Lediard, *The Naval History of England* (London: John Wilcox, 1735); John Campbell, *Lives of the Admirals* (London:

INTRODUCTION

J.& M. Pemberton, 1742-44); John Entick, A *New Naval History, or, compleat view of the British Marine* ... (London: R. Manby, 1757).

64. Burchett, A *Complete History*, p. 379; Fulton, pp. 309, 311n. In 1911, Fulton cited Northumberland's journal as State Papers, Domestic, cccxxxii.

65. Thomas Lediard, *The Naval History of England from the Norman Conquest in the Year 1066 to the Conclusion of the Year 1734.* (London, 1735).

66. Thomas Lediard, *Grammatica Angliana Critica, oder Versuch zu einer volkommen Grammatic der englischen Sprache* (Hamburg, 1726); *Eine Collection verschiedener Vors-stellungen in Illuminationen* ... (Hamburg, 1730).

67. Thomas Lediard, *The Life of John, Duke of Marlborough* (London, 1736; 2d ed., 1743).

68. Paul de Rapin-Thoyras, *The History of England as well Ecclesiastical as Civil, done into English from the French, with large and useful notes (and a summary of the whole)* ... *by N. Tidal.* (London, 1732).

Thomas Lediard, *The History of the Reigns of William III and Mary, and Anne, in continuation of the History of England by Rapin de Thoyras* (London, 1737).

Thomas Lediard, *The German Spy, in familiar letters ... written by a Gentleman on his travels to his Friend in England* (London, 1738).

69. Lediard, *Naval History*, p. 708.

70. *An Appeal to the Publick: or, Burchett and Lediard Compar'd. being an Impartial and just Parallel between Mr Burchett's* Compleat History of the Most Remarkable Transactions at Sea, &c., *and Mr Lediard's* Naval History of England, in all its Branches, &c., *grounded upon plain incontestable Matters of fact and referring to the respective Pages and Passages in each History. To which is added a short view of the late Advertisement Controversy, between Mr Burchett and Mr Lediard, with the occasion of it: The Whole being a proper supplement to both these histories. By a Lover of Truth and a friend to Both these authors.* (London, MDCCXXXV [1735]).

71. However, the 1704 French translation of *Memoirs*, but not the original English edition, did include a frontispiece showing a typical naval battle.

72. Horace Walpole, A *Catalogue of Engravers who have been born, or resided in England* ... *From the MSS of Mr George Vertue, to which is added An account of the life and work of the latter* (Strawberry Hill, 1763).

73. This is probably F. Berthelot, cartographer of two 1695 charts.

74. David A. Woodword, "English Cartography, 1650-1750," in Norman J.W. Thrower, ed., *The Compleat Plattmaker: Essays on Chart, Map and Globe Making in England in the Seventeenth and Eighteenth Centuries* (Los Angeles, 1978) p. 192.

GEORGE R.

GEORGE, by the Grace of God, King of *Great Britain*, *France*, and *Ireland*, Defender of the Faith, &c. To all to whom thefe Prefents fhall come, Greeting. Whereas Our Trufty and Well-beloved *Jofiah Burchett*, Efq; hath humbly reprefented unto Us, that he hath with great Care and Pains compiled a Work entituled, *A Compleat History of the moft Remarkable Tranfactions at Sea, from the earlieft Accounts of Time to the Conclufion of the laft War with* France. *In five Books*. And hath therefore humbly prayed Us to grant him Our Royal Privilege and Licence for the fole printing and publifhing the faid Hiftory; We are gracioufly pleafed to condefcend to his Requeft, and do therefore hereby give and grant unto the faid *Jofiah Burchett* Our Royal Licence and Privilege for the fole printing and publifhing the faid Hiftory compiled by him the faid *Jofiah Burchett*, for and during the Term of fourteen Years, to be computed from the Day of the Date hereof. Strictly charging prohibiting, and forbidding all our Subject within our Kingdoms and Dominions to reprint or abridge the fame, either in the like, or any other Volume or Volumes whatfoever, or to import, buy, vend, utter, or diftribute any Copies of the fame, or any part thereof reprinted beyond the Seas, during the faid Term of fourteen Years, without the Confent and Approbation of him the faid *Jofiah Burchett*, his Heirs, Executors, Adminiftrators, and Affigns, by writing under his or their Hands and Seals firft had and obtained, as they and every of them offending herein, will anfwer the contrary at their perils; whereof the Mafter, Wardens, and Company of Stationers of Our City of *London*, Commiffioners and Officers of Our Cuftoms, and all other Our Officers and Minifters, whom it may concern, are to take due Notice, that ftrict Obedience be given to Our Pleafure herein fignified. Given at Our Court at St. *James*'s the 20th Day of *November* 1719, in the Sixth Year of Our Reign.

By His Majefty's Command,

J. CRAGGS.

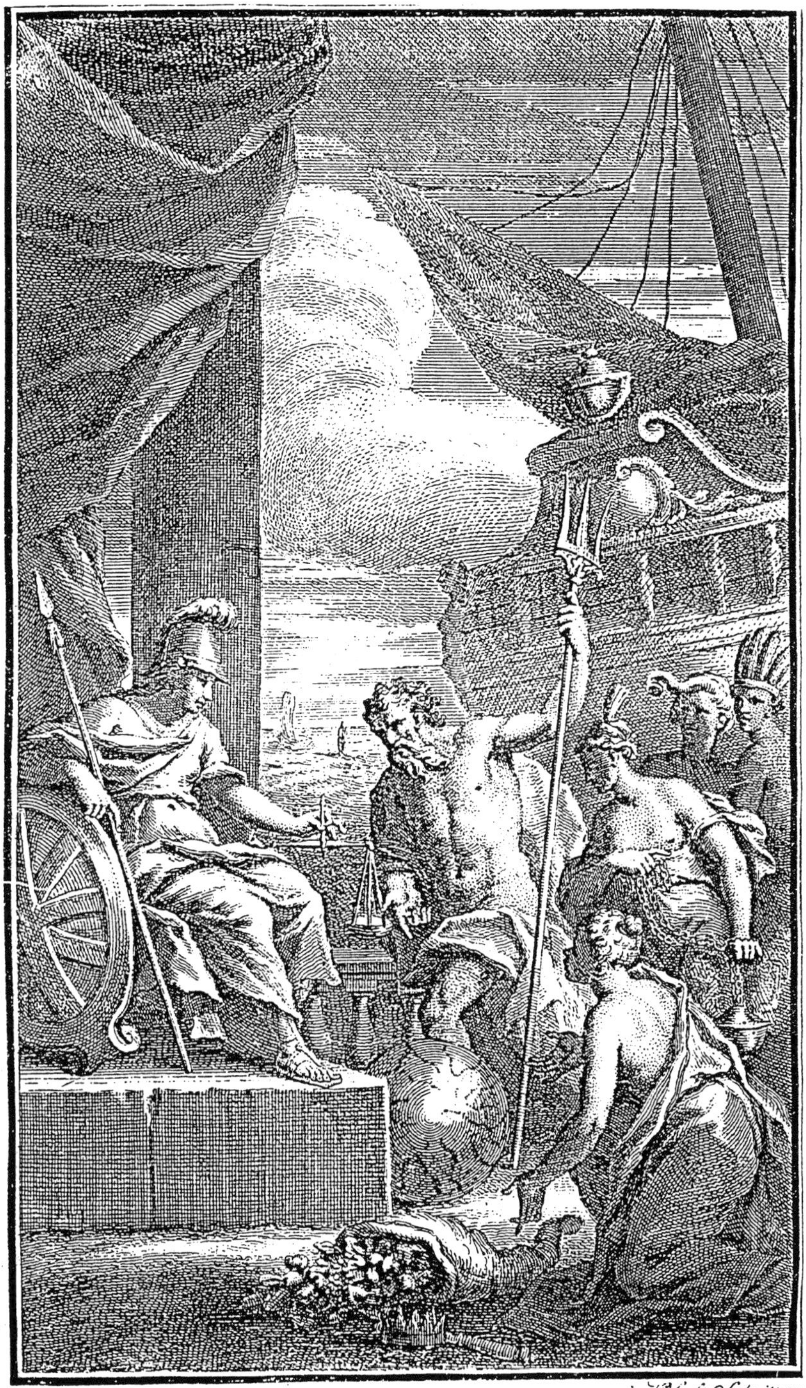

J. Thornhill Inv. et Del. | Gucht Sculpsit

Josiah Burchett Esq.
Secretary of the Admiralty of Great Britain and Ireland.

A Complete History

Of the most REMARKABLE

TRANSACTIONS

AT

SEA,

FROM THE

Earliest ACCOUNTS of TIME

To the CONCLUSION of the

LAST WAR with FRANCE.

WHEREIN

Is given an ACCOUNT of the most considerable

Naval-Expeditions, Sea-Fights, Stratagems, Discoveries,

AND

Other MARITIME OCCURRENCES that have happen'd among all *NATIONS* which have flourished at SEA:

And in a more particular manner of *GREAT BRITAIN*, from the time of the REVOLUTION, in the Year 1688, to the aforesaid *Period*.

Adorn'd with SEA-CHARTS adapted to the *History*. With an exact *INDEX* of the Names of all the Places where any considerable Battel has been fought, in any Part of the World.

In FIVE BOOKS.

By *JOSIAH BURCHETT*, Esq;
SECRETARY of the ADMIRALTY.

Hæ TIBI erunt artes————————Virg.

LONDON:
Printed by *W. B.* for J. WALTHOE in the *Temple Cloysters*, and J. WALTHOE *Junior* against the *Royal Exchange* in *Cornhill*. MDCCXX.

TO THE
KING.

SIR,

THE Employment I have the Happiness to enjoy in Your Majesty's Maritime Service, and the Subject of the following Sheets, have embolden'd me, with the utmost Humility, to lay my self and them at Your Royal Feet.

They

DEDICATION.

They contain, Sir, *An Account of Remarkable Transactions at Sea from the first Ages to the present Times*; and as Your Majesty's Kingdom of *Great Britain* must necessarily make the most considerable Figure therein, so do its Naval Actions, those especially since the happy Revolution, furnish out great part of the ensuing History, and, in this respect, by much the more valuable, in that it exhibits to Your Royal View the gallant Behaviour of great Numbers of Your Majesty's Subjects, yet living, who, in fighting for the Preservation of Religion, Laws, and Liberty, have given a glorious Earnest how ready they will always be to expose their Lives in Defence of Your Sacred Person and Dignity.

As this Your Kingdom, Sir, hath in all Times been remarkable for its Naval Power, so is that Power so much augmented since the beginning of the Reign of Your Majesty's Royal Predecessor, and Great-Grandfather, King *James* the First, that it hath not been equalled in any Age or Nation.

For if we look back to the most flourishing Maritime Potentates of old, as *Tyre*, *Athens*, *Carthage*, or even *Rome* itself, when in her most flourishing State, we shall find them fall so very short of Your Majesty's Naval Strength, as not to admit of any Comparison; and among the Moderns, which of them is there that it doth not greatly exceed?

So

DEDICATION.

So vast indeed is that Part of Your Majesty's Power, that were it possible for you, Sir, to be influenced by other Principles than those of the most consummate Justice, and of being actuated by the lawless Desire of Universal Sway, instead of a generous Love of Liberty, and a noble Ambition of Patronising it throughout the World, and *Britain* should, under Your Majesty's Influence, launch forth her utmost Strength on the Seas, what Alliances could be entered into, what Confederacies formed, sufficient to withstand so mighty a Force?

But You, Sir, serenely content with those Dominions which Heaven, and the Consent of willing Nations have called you to Rule, far from disturbing *Europe* with such Pursuits, are only watchful for its Repose, and employ that awful Strength you are possessed of to no other purpose, than to preserve such a Ballance among its Princes as is absolutely necessary to its Peace, and reduce to Reason those who, by their boundless Ambition, would involve it in War and Desolation: So that, in Your Majesty's Hands, this Power resembles that which is invested in a ministring Angel over the Elements, who doth not make use of it to lay waste the World, and destroy Mankind at pleasure, but to procure the Good of the Whole, by the Punishment of particular Nations that are guilty; which yet he forbears to inflict, unless repeated Provocations force him, unwillingly, thereunto. And

DEDICATION.

And as Your Majesty doth thus piously endeavour to establish a lasting Tranquillity among others, so is Your Tenderness towards Your own Subjects without Example; insomuch that it hath been abundantly extended even to those who, regardless of their Duty to God, and You their rightful Sovereign, were unhappily wrought upon to appear openly in Arms against Your Royal Person and Government.

Long may Your Majesty preside, in this Your high Station, over the Interests of *Europe*, and when late, very late, You shall cease to labour here on Earth, not only for the Happiness of the People of these Your Kingdoms, but the Universal Good of Mankind, and ascend to the Possession of an Immortal Crown, may that You leave behind flourish for ever on the Heads of Your Illustrious Offspring. Which is the ardent Prayer of,

May it please Your Majesty,

Your Majesty's most Dutiful,

and most Obedient

Subject and Servant,

J. Burchett.

PREFACE.

ALTHOUGH I might very reasonably have been excused from the trouble of any part of the following Work, since the publick Station I am honoured with hath called for the much greater part of my Time, yet when I considered that the Transactions of our Nation on the Seas, during the two long and expensive Wars with *France*, were Matters very worthy as well to be more universally known to the present Age, as to be communicated to Posterity, and that I was furnished with Materials for such an Undertaking which could not be in the Possession of any other Person, I have imposed on my self that Task, and, in the Performance thereof, borrowed many of those Hours which were no more than necessary for the Preservation of my Health.

Reasons for undertaking the Work.

What happened remarkable at Sea between us and the *French* during the first of the aforemention'd Wars, I published some Years since; but upon reviewing the same, when I set about writing an Account of the last War, I thought it might not be improper to put them together; and though the material Circumstances of the former, as being Matters of Fact, vary but very little from what hath been already written thereof, yet is it now put into such a Dress, and such Amendments have been made therein, as, it is to be hoped, may render it much more agreeable to the Reader.

When I had compleated these two Parts, which compose the Fourth and Fifth Books of the ensuing History, I began to reflect that, among the numerous Subjects which have been treated in

the

PREFACE.

the *English* Tongue, (wherein scarce any in any part of Learning hath been left untouched) no one hath hitherto undertaken to collect somewhat of a *Naval History*, or general Account of Wars on the Sea; whereof both ancient and modern Times have been so productive, that I know not any Subject which affords more ample Circumstances. And this I the rather admired at, for that, about fourscore Years since, there were published in *Latin* two such Histories as I have mentioned, the one written by our Countryman Dr. *Ryves*, Advocate to King *Charles* the First, and the other by *Morisotus*, a *French* Lawyer, which, however, have escaped the Diligence of our Translators, who very often search into all Languages for Matters not altogether so worthy their Trouble as these would have been. But since no such Account hath ever appeared in our Tongue, I judged it would be a Subject not unacceptable, should I set my self about a Work of that Nature, and deduce a Narrative of the most remarkable Naval Wars, and Maritime Transactions, which have happened from the first Use of Shipping to the time of the Revolution, where the Account I had already written begun; and accordingly I have endeavoured to perform it in the three first Books of the following Work.

The first of the before-mentioned Authors published what he had written in several Parts, and at different Times, but I do not find he carried it farther than the Year 960, when King *Edgar* reigned in *England*. The other, indeed, brought it down to his own Time, *viz*. the Year 1642.

These two learned Men having gone before me on this Subject, it would have been Presumption not to have made use of their Labours; so that wheresoever it was found necessary, or for the Advantage of the Reader, a liberty hath been taken of following them, yet not so closely, but that, upon consulting thoroughly the Originals from whence they drew their Materials, many Mistakes have been rectified which their Inadvertency had led them into, especially that of the *French* Gentleman, notwithstanding his Publisher assures us that the Work had passed the Revision of two great Criticks, appointed by Cardinal *Richelieu*, besides that of several other learned Men.

They have both of them, but chiefly *Morisotus*, been guilty, in some places, of handling too lightly Matters of Importance, and in dwelling too long on things of less Note, which Errors I have endeavoured to avoid, especially the former.

Authors, among others, who have been consulted.

Those things I have been the most particular in (but without fear of the last mentioned Imputation) are, among the Ancients, the Naval Events of the *Peloponnesian* War, from *Thucydides*; the Siege of *Tyre* by *Alexander the Great*, from *Curtius* and *Arrian*; the Battel, off of *Cyprus*, between *Demetrius* and *Ptolemy*, with the former's War on the *Rhodians*, from *Diodorus Siculus*; the Sea-Fight between the *Romans* and *Carthaginians*, in the first *Punic* War, off of *Heraclea Minoa*, (which I esteem the most accurate Relation, of that kind, extant in all Antiquity) from

PREFACE.

from *Polybius*; *Cæsar*'s Expedition to *Britain*, from his own Commentaries; and the Battel of *Actium*, from *Dion. Cassius*. And, among the Moderns, the Battel of *Lipanto*, from *Contrarini* and *Gratiani*; the great Exploits on the *Scheld* between the Duke of *Parma* and the People of *Antwerp*, from *Famian Strada*; the *Spanish* Invasion from Mr. *Cambden*; and the Duke of *Buckingham*'s Expedition to the Isle of *Rhé*, from a Manuscript Journal, which, since the Loss of a very curious one I had in my Possession, was, on my publishing an Advertisement concerning the same, kindly communicated to me by a Reverend Divine of *Cambridge*. Most of which Affairs, besides very many others, have been either superficially run over, or else left entirely untouched, by Dr. *Ryves* and *Morisotus*.

The before-mentioned Authors are those to whom the most Obligations have been owing; but as the handling so general a Subject must unavoidably have requir'd the making use of many more, besides other necessary Assistances, I might here present the Reader with a long Catalogue of them, and have filled my Margin with Quotations, which, in my opinion, tend more to Ostentation, than any real good purpose; not but that in some particular Cases their Names are mentioned in the Narration. I shall therefore only acquaint you, that, in the first three Books, the same liberty as before-mentioned hath been taken with the rest of the Authors there hath been occasion to consult, nay often their very Words have been followed; and where any of the Ancients have been well turned into our own Tongue, as particularly *Polybius* and *Justin*, seeing it could not be pretended to set them in a better Light than the ingenious Gentlemen who last translated them have done, their Version hath, in a great measure, been observed.

As most Princes, and States, whose Dominions have bordered on the Sea, did, more or less, even in early Ages, furnish themselves with Shipping, as well for the Defence of their Coasts and Traffick, as to extend their Conquests; so have they, from time to time, augmented their Naval Force, in proportion to what they found others do who were nearest Neighbours to them. Thus *Rome*, when she was much annoyed by the *Carthaginians*, deemed it absolutely necessary to prepare a floating Power to repel them, between whom many bloody Battels were fought, as had been before, when the *Athenians* and *Lacedæmonians* contended, and since between other States and Potentates.

Of Fleets in ancient Times.

The Tyrants of *Sicily* have been famous for their Fleets, but more especially those of *Syracuse*. There were often Naval Battels between the Republicks of *Venice*, *Genoa*, *Pisa*, and others, but more especially the former and the Turks. The *Saracens* with their Fleets encountered the Christians when they attempted to recover the Holy Island; and the Governments of *Algier*, *Tunis*, and *Tripoli* have for a long time had their Ships of War; nay even the Emperor of *Morocco* wanteth not his Rovers, which frequently have molested the Trading Subjects of other Princes.

As

PREFACE.

As the Kings of *England* thought it necessary, from time to time, to encrease their Maritime Strength, the *French*, and the States-General of the United Provinces have augmented theirs, especially in latter Days; but of those Princes, or Governments, who have been most formidable at Sea, from the remotest Times of Navigation, I shall be as particular as possible in the ensuing History, and will therefore confine my self in this Preface to what doth more immediately relate to the Royal Navy of *Great Britain*.

On what Services the Ships of the English Navy have been employed in the two last Wars.
Various have the Services been which necessarily required the Use of our Fleets, and Squadrons, but more especially in Times of so great Action as the two last Wars. Many of our Royal Ships have been employed in the *Mediterranean* Sea, not only to protect the *Spanish* Monarchy from the Attempts of the *French*, but afterwards to assist in establishing his present Imperial Majesty on the Throne of that Kingdom, when *Great Britain*, together with her Allies, maintained, at an incredible Expence, as well of Treasure as Blood, a long War not only with the *French* King, but with that part of *Spain* also which adhered to the Interest of his Grandson *Philip*, who is now in Possession of the Crown.

While great part of our Warlike Ships were thus ranging about the *Mediterranean*, no small Numbers have been employed in the *British* Chanel, as well as on the Coasts of *America*, *Portugal*, and other foreign Parts: Besides which, others were, at the same time, made use of in convoying our Trade to *Turky*, *Newfoundland*, *Russia*, the *Baltick* Sea, and to our remote Governments and Plantations, insomuch that the Ships of War of *Great Britain* have been constantly traversing not only our own, but almost all the other known Seas, so that the Number of Officers, and Men established on them, have sometimes amounted

The Expence of the Fleet of England in time of War.
to Fifty Thousand, the Expence whereof (supposing them to be continued in Service thirteen Lunary Months) for Wages, and Victuals, together with the Wear and Tear of the Ships, the former and latter being commonly estimated at thirty Shillings a Man a Month each, and the other at twenty, amounts to two Millions, six hundred thousand Pounds; not but that, as Circumstances of Affairs would admit thereof, divers of the Ships have from time to time been paid off, and laid up in the several Harbours, for easing, as much as might be, this very great Charge. And, besides what may be absolutely necessary for the

The necessity of Supplies of Money to pay off Ships, for easing the publick Charge.
many other pressing Affairs of the State, if sufficient Sums of Money could be hereafter provided, for the timely paying off the Officers and Men of such Ships whose immediate Service may be dispensed with, or whose Conditions are such as to require considerable Repairs before they can be longer employed, the Expence of the Government would in that Particular be very much lessened.

Although this Nation hath been, even in remote Times, famous for its Strength at Sea, were it to be compared with that

of

PREFACE.

of other Princes and States; yet could we look back, and view those Shipping which were heretofore made use of in our Maritime Wars, what a vast Disproportion would there appear between them and those which composed our Royal Navies two Centuries past, (I mean not as to the Number of the Ships and Vessels, but their Magnitude) and much more so, were they to be compared with our present floating Castles?

King *Edward* the Third, when he crossed the Seas in order to lay siege to *Calais*, had indeed a very great Number of Ships, but most of them were furnished by the Sea-Port Towns of the Kingdom, and some from *Spain*, *Ireland*, *Flanders*, and other Parts.

Comparison of our present Navy with those of former Times.

The whole Number, as it appears by a Record in the famous *Cottonian* Library, amounted to seven hundred thirty eight, and the Mariners on board them to fourteen thousand nine hundred fifty six, each of whom were allowed after the Rate of 4d per *Diem*; but of these there were no more than twenty five Ships of the King's own, carrying about four hundred and nineteen Seamen, which, at a Medium, was not above seventeen to each; and throughout the whole, taking one with another, there were not many that had above twenty six Men; not but that those which were furnished by the Maritime Ports were larger than the King's own Ships, especially those of *London*, *Sandwich*, *Dover*, *Dartmouth*, *Plimouth*, *Bristol*, *Southampton*, *Newcastle*, *Lynn*, *Yarmouth*, *Harwich*, *Ipswich*, and *Colchester*. But besides the Mariners, there were transported in this Fleet the Land-Forces which his Majesty had occasion to take with him for carrying on the aforesaid Siege of *Calais*.

From this it may be gathered what the Maritime Power of this Nation was in those Times; for even then, before, and afterwards, the greatest part thereof was composed of Merchant-Ships furnished by the Sea-Ports; yet the Strength we could in those Days launch on the Salt Water was much superior to that of our Neighbours. But when our Princes, in After-Aages, turned their Thoughts towards providing, and establishing a Royal Navy, the same hath, by degrees, not only been much encreased in Number, but in the Magnitude of the Ships also; but more especially in the Reign of King *Charles* the Second; and in like manner the trading part of the Nation did from time to time very much encrease the Dimensions of their Shipping, insomuch that in the first of the aforemention'd Wars with *France*, several of them were taken into the Publick Service, some of which were capable of carrying 70, 60, and 50 Guns. And that the Reader may be informed to what a prodigious Bulk the Navy of *Great Britain* is at this time swelled, I have underneath inserted the Number of Ships of which it is composed, with the Guns established on each of them, wherein there is not any regard had to Fireships, Bomb-Vessels, Storeships, Sloops, Yachts, Hoys, or other smaller Embarcations, which amount to no less than fifty.

The

PREFACE.

The Strength of the ROYAL NAVY.

The Strength of the Royal Navy of Great Britain.

	Guns		Nº.	
Of	100	—	7	
	90	—	13	
	80	—	16	} 125 of the Line of Battel.
	70	—	23	
	60	—	19	
	50	—	47	
	40	—	23	
	30	—	9	
	20	—	25	
			182	

Which 182 Ships will require 9940 Guns, exclufive of thofe neceffary for others of lefs Dimenfions.

Thus hath the Navy of *Great Britain* encreafed, and that very confiderably too, fince the Year 1573, at which time it ftood thus, *viz.*

What our Navy was in 1573.

	Guns.		Nº.	
Of	100	—	1	
From	88 to 60	—	9	} 59 of the Line of Battel, as they might be reckoned in thofe Days.
From	58 to 40	—	49	
From	38 to 20	—	58	
From	18 to 6	—	29	
			146	

Great care ought to be taken of the Ships while in Harbour.

Moft of the Ships of our prefent Royal Navy, efpecially thofe of the larger Rates, being, in time of Peace, laid up at the feveral Ports, the greateft part of them at *Chatham* and *Portfmouth*, and others at *Deptford, Woolwich, Sheernefs*, and *Plimouth*, it is of the utmoft Importance that all poffible care fhould be taken for their Safety in all Particulars, but more efpecially that the Places where they are thus harboured, and principally the River *Medway*, and *Portfmouth*, fhould be always kept in fuch Condition of Defence as that they may be fecure from any Attempts of an Enemy.

And fince thefe our floating Bulwarks are, like other Machines, fubject to decay, how abfolutely neceffary is it that the utmoft care fhould be taken in the keeping their Hulls in a conftant good Condition? The like regard fhould alfo be had to the Pre-

Care ought to be taken in preferving Timber.

fervation and Well-husbanding not only that useful Timber which the Nation now affordeth (efpecially that of Compafs and Knee) for building Ships, but in having conftant Nurferies thereof, toward fupplying what may from time to time be expended. Nor

a   is

PREFACE.

is it of less Importance that greatest care should be taken of the publick Woods abroad, but more especially of those large and valuable Trees in and about *New England*, most proper for Masting Ships of the greatest Magnitude.

Having thus informed you of the Strength of our Royal Navy, it may not be improper to add thereunto the following Account of the Charge of building a Ship of each Rate, and furnishing her with Masts, Yards, Sails, and Rigging, together with a Proportion of eight Months Boatswain's and Carpenter's Sea-Stores, as near as the same can be estimated, *viz.*

Guns.	*l.*
For a Ship of — 100	35553
90	29886
80	23638
70	17785
60	14197
50	10606
40	7558
30	5846
20	3710

The Charge of building a Ship of each Rate.

Thus, according to the Number of Ships we have of the aforesaid Rates, the Charge of Building, Rigging, and furnishing them with Stores, as aforesaid, amounts to 251197*l.* besides which, there is the Expence of their Ordnance, and Gunner's Stores.

And here it may be observed, that supposing forty thousand Men, Officers included, are employed at Sea one whole Year, or thirteen Lunary Months, the Charge thereof, accounting each of them one with another, at 4*l.* a Month, (which is for Wages, Victuals, and the Wear and Tear of the Ships) is not above 431975*l.* less than what may be sufficient to build and rig as many Ships as *Great Britain* now hath, from the First to the Sixth Rate, inclusive, and to furnish them with Boatswain's and Carpenter's Stores; nor have I herein accounted for the Charge of Tenders, and other incident Expences towards the manning a Fleet.

Besides which there is the ordinary Expence of the Navy, in which is included the Salaries and Contingencies of all the Naval Officers on shore; the Charge of the Officers and Workmen employed in the Dock-Yards, and Rope-Yards; Moorings, and ordinary Repairs of the Ships while lying up in Harbour, with the Wages and Victuals of the Warrant-Officers and their Servants, and of the Men born on Ships of the largest Dimensions, together with Pensions to those Officers who are superannuated, and Half-Pays to others while unemployed, the Charge whereof is more or less, according to the Number of Men made use of at Sea; for as in time of great Action the ordinary Estimate of the Navy seldom amounts to more than 175000*l. per Annum*, so in Peace, supposing there are not above ten thousand Men in Pay,

The ordinary Expence of the Navy.

Preface.

it comes to near 225000*l.* for when fewest Ships are employed, the ordinary Expence of those lying up in Harbour doth consequently encrease proportionably, both as to the Wages and Victuals of the Warrant-Officers and Men born on them for their Security, their Moorings, necessary Repairs, and other Particulars.

The extraordinary Repairs of the Navy. But over and above the Charge of the Ordinary of the Navy, there are other expensive Works necessarily to be performed, which are more properly termed the extraordinary Repairs thereof; and those are the rebuilding of Ships, and giving a good Repair to others lying up in Harbour; the building of Houses in the Yards for the Reception of Stores, when others are decayed, or shall not be found capable of containing them, and the repairing of Store-houses, Docks, Wharfs, Officers Houses, and several other Particulars, as well in the Dock-Yards as Rope-Yards, and the like extraordinary Expences as to the Office of Victualling His Majesty's Navy, both in Town, and at the several Ports.

Let us, in the next Place, consider how this our Royal Navy may be rendered most useful to the Nation, for if every Circumstance be not timely, and effectually provided for, so as that the Ships, or a sufficient Number of them, at least, may be always in a Readiness, upon any pressing occasion, the publick Service must inevitably suffer.

The Magazines ought to be replenished. In the first Place, therefore, it is absolutely necessary that the Naval Magazines should be constantly kept well replenished with Timber, Plank, Cordage, Hemp, Tar, and all other Things proper for equipping forth a Royal Fleet, at least with such Species as are not the most liable to decay.

Care ought to be taken in the well fitting Ships. It is likewise no less necessary that the Master-Builders at the Dock-Yards, and those Officers employed under them, should carefully, and conscientiously apply themselves towards the well fitting His Majesty's Ships, when there shall be occasion for their Service, as well as in the giving them proper Airings and Repairs while they lie at their Moorings in Harbour; nor ought they to be less careful when any Ships return into Port, in order to their being refitted; for it is demonstrable that, where the same is well performed, such Ship will be capable of doing the Government twice as much Service as another possibly can, which is hurried out of Port without being thoroughly searched into, since, in such case, she must necessarily come sooner in, and will, doubtless, require much more time, as well as Expence, to put her into a good Condition, than it might have done, had her chief Ailments been at first remedied.

I say it highly behoves the Master Shipwrights, and the proper Officers under them, to be very circumspect in these Particulars; and though it must be owned that in times of great Action, when the Pressingness of the Service requires the utmost Dispatch in the putting Ships into the Sea, there cannot be so much time allowed as may be necessary for making a thorough

Search

PREFACE.

Search into the Defects of thofe which are fitting out, or others coming into Port to be refitted, yet as, in the firft Cafe, all poffible care fhould be taken to infpect into, and repair their chief Ailments while they lie in Harbour, (I mean fuch as, if not timely taken in hand, may foon render them in a worfe Condition) fo, in the latter, the Commanders of His Majefty's Ships, and the fubordinate Officers, but more efpecially the Mafter Carpenters, ought carefully to inform themfelves of the Complaints they make while at Sea, that fo they may be able to acquaint the Mafter Shipwrights of the fame, and they to apply proper Remedies; for, without thefe Precautions, a Ship may be fent out again with fome flight Works done unto her, without difcovering the principal Defects fhe complains of, and thereby be conftrained, to the no fmall Difappointment of the Service, to return into Port, even in a worfe Condition than when fhe departed from it, as hath been before obferved.

It is no lefs incumbent on the Officers of the Dock-Yards, as well as thofe of the Rope-Yards, to fee that the feveral Species of Stores, delivered into His Majefty's Magazines be, in all refpects, anfwerable to the Contracts made with the principal Officers and Commiffioners of the Navy, whether the fame be Canvas, Hemp, Tar, Cordage, Timber, Plank, or any other Species, and that the Rigging, Anchors, Cables, and all other Materials be well wrought up; for as the faid Commiffioners of the Navy, nay even the Surveyor himfelf, cannot perfonally infpect into all things neceffary to be done to the Hulls of the Ships, fo are they much lefs able to view the various forts of Stores delivered into the feveral Yards, or to fee that they are well husbanded; wherefore as this Truft doth more immediately lie in the Officers of the Yards, fo ought they themfelves, and not by their Inftruments, if it can by any means be avoided, to look carefully thereinto, and rather to have a greater regard to the Good of the Publick, than if they were tranfacting Affairs for the Advantage of their own Families. *Care ought to be taken of the Goodnefs of the Stores.*

Nor ought there to be lefs Caution ufed by the proper Officers of the Yards in the converting of, and applying the refpective Species of Stores to their neceffary Ufes, but more efpecially Timber and Plank; for if Care and Judgment go hand in hand therein, unneceffary Wafte may be prevented, and thereby great Sums of Money faved. *Converting Timber, &c. to proper Ufes.*

Having faid thus much relating to the Navy itfelf, let us, in the next Place, confider the Circumftances of the Seafaring Men of *Great Britain*; a Race of People, who, as they are the moft valuable becaufe the Fleets wherein they ferve are our chief Defence, fo, confequently, the greateft care ought to be taken to treat them in fuch manner as that it may encourage their Encreafe, aud leave them as little room as poffible for Complaints of Hardfhips. *Touching the Seafaring People of Great Britain.*

I do heartily wifh that fome fuch Methods could be come at as might effectually contribute hereunto; for as they are a Body
of

PREFACE.

of brave People, subjected to greatest Dangers, not only from an Enemy, but on many other Accounts, so may they with good Usage be easily wrought upon, and induced, with uncommon Chearfulness, to look Death in the Face on all occasions; wherefore since they are so intrinsically valuable in themselves, all that is possible should be done towards rendering the Publick Service easy to them.

If some other Method, I say, could be found out to bring them into the Service of the Crown, when there shall be occasion, than that which hath for many Years been practised, of forcing great Numbers thereinto, as it would, doubtless, be much more agreeable, so might it induce Numbers of young People to betake themselves to a Seafaring Life, who now rather shew a total Dislike thereunto; but until such Methods can be luckily come at, either by a general Regiftry, which, besides the Encouragements, should carry with it some Penalties also, (for a voluntary one it hath been experienced will not answer the purpose) or some other way less grievous than Pressing, it may not be altogether improper to admonish Gentlemen who shall be hereafter employed in raising Men for the Fleet, to cause them to be treated with all possible Tenderness and Humanity, that so they may be induced with the greater Chearfulness to expose their Lives in the Service of their Prince, and Country, when they shall be brought to face an Enemy.

It must be acknowledged that no Seafaring People whatever have the like Advantages with those of *Great Britain*, more especially as to their Pay, and Provisions; and if some such Regulations could be made as might prevent their being imposed *Abuses of Landladies and Ticket-buyers.* upon by their Landladies, as they themselves term them, and others who concern themselves in purchasing their Tickets at a most unreasonable Discount, the Service of the Crown might be yet much more comfortable to them and their Families.

The Inconveniencies of Impressing Seamen. The present Method of impressing Men for the Royal Navy, is not only attended with great Inconveniences to the Men themselves, but it also causes no small Interruption to Trade; for very often when there hath been occasion for considerable Numbers of Men to serve in the Fleet, it hath been found necessary to put almost a total Stop, for some time, to the proceeding of all outward-bound Merchant Ships and Vessels; whereas if some Measures could be taken, by a Regiftry, as aforesaid, or other*Regiftring of Seafaring Men.* wise, so as to come at the certain Knowledge of every Seaman, or Seafaring Man in the Kingdom, together with their Ages and Descriptions, and that such an Account were from time to time kept compleat, as the same shall vary, either by Death, or other Circumstance, at a particular Office to be established for that purpose, the Lord High-Admiral, or the Commissioners for executing that Office, might not only be constantly informed what Numbers of such People are Inhabitants in the Nation, but an Account might likewise be kept, from time to time, which of them are employed as well in the Publick Service, as that of

the

Preface.

the Merchants, and when they shall be discharged either from one or the other: Besides, it might be so provided for, that when such a Number of them have been employed a certain Time in the Service of the Crown, they should have Licence to enter themselves on board of Merchant Ships, and when they have so served a limited Time, be obliged to go on board the Ships of the Royal Navy, when there shall be occasion for them. Somewhat of this kind, if rightly set on foot, would be of singular Use, especially in time of War; for as the Government would not be put to Trouble and Expence, as now, in raising Seamen, so would not the Merchants be at a Loss for a sufficient Number at all Times to carry on their Trade. And in time of Peace, when the Crown will not have occasion for very considerable Numbers of Seamen, they may be more at liberty to employ themselves otherwise.

As this is a thing of such a Nature as to require no small Application to render it effectual, I have only hinted at it here; but if it shall at any time be judged proper to put it in Practice, and it shall please God to bless me with the Continuance of Life and Health, I will most readily contribute all I am able towards the establishing what, in my humble Opinion, may so much tend to the Good of my Country.

This being said with regard to the Seafaring People of the Nation, let us now consider, in as brief a manner as may be, somewhat of the OEconomy of the Navy, and what Officers are under the Direction of the Lord High-Admiral, with respect as well to the Military as the Civil Administration of his Office, and to set forth, as much as may be consistent with a Preface, the Nature of their several Employments. *Relating to the OEconomy of the Navy.*

First then, That Officer who is next and immediately under the Lord High-Admiral, (I mean in his Military Capacity) is the Vice-Admiral of *Great Britain*, and next to him the Rear-Admiral, the annual Fee of the former being 469*l*. 5*s*. 8*d*. and of the latter 369*l*. 4*s*. 3*d*. Both these Officers are appointed by Commissions under the Great Seal, the former of whom at this time is *James* Earl of *Berkeley*, and the latter *Matthew* Lord *Aylmer*; but heretofore such Powers have been granted by the Lord High-Admiral, and also by the Commissioners for executing that Office. *Vice, and Rear-Admiral of Great Britain.*

The Lord High-Admiral grants his Commission to such Person as His Majesty thinks fitting, by which he is appointed Admiral and Commander in Chief of the Fleet for the Expedition whereon it is designed; and he, when out of the *British* Channel, appoints all Officers, as Vacancies happen, either by Death, or otherwise, who at the end of the Expedition are confirmed by the Lord High-Admiral, or Commissioners of the Admiralty, in case there doth not appear any reasonable Objections thereunto. *Admiral of the Fleet.*

The Officer thus appointed to Command the Fleet is empowered by the Lord High-Admiral, or the Commissioners for managing

PREFACE.

Power to the Admiral of the Fleet and others to hold Courts Martial.

naging that Office, to hold Courts Martial, for trying Offenders, and, in the Absence of the Judge-Advocate of the Navy, or his Deputy, to appoint some Person to act as such. The same Power is also given to inferior Flag-Officers, who command Squadrons appointed for particular Services, to make Officers, and to hold Courts Martial, with this difference only, that if the Officer so commanding is a Vice-Admiral, he hath only a Warrant authorising him to hold such Courts, but if a Rear-Admiral, he hath a Commission appointing him Commander in Chief, as well as a Warrant for his so doing. Nay, in the Absence of a Flag-Officer, the Commander of a private Ship hath been empowered by Commission to hold such Courts, and directed by Warrant to try particular Cases, and Commanders junior to him required to assist thereat; but the Commission by which he is appointed Commander in Chief is limited to a certain Number of Days.

Lord High-Admiral empowered to act by Deputy.

The Lord High-Admirals being empowered by their Patents to execute the Duty of their Office either by themselves, or Deputies, they have heretofore, when employed themselves at Sea, (as the Duke of *York* did in the Reign of King *Charles* the Second) appointed such Persons as they deemed most proper to do their Duty at home, and required all subordinate Officers to be obedient to the Commands of those so deputed.

Principal Officers and Commissioners of the Navy.

The principal Officers and Commissioners of the Navy are appointed by particular Patents under the Great Seal; and when the King approves of any Person recommended, the Lord High-Admiral issues his Warrant to the Attorney General, in His Majesty's Name, to prepare a Bill, for the Royal Signature, to pass the Seals, constituting the said Person a principal Officer and Commissioner accordingly.

By the OEconomy of the Navy formerly, none other were esteemed principal Officers and Commissioners than the Treasurer, Comptroler, Surveyor, and Clerk of the Acts; but since the Revolution they have been all termed so in their Patents, not but that the four before-mentioned preside at the Board, and any three of the whole Number (the Treasurer excepted in Matters relating to Mony) are a *Quorum*.

But the multiplicity of Business, especially during the two last Wars with *France*, made it absolutely necessary to add a considerable Number of Commissioners to assist the principal Officers, insomuch that there was one particularly appointed to assist the Comptroler in that Branch of his Office which relates to the Treasurer's Accounts, another in those of the Stores, and a third for examining into the Accounts of the Victualling. There was also another Commissioner appointed for some time to assist the Clerk of the Acts, but that Officer hath been for several Years discontinued, and in his stead there is at this time an Assistant allowed only, at the Salary of 300*l*. *per Annum*.

There were also, during some part of the War, two Surveyors of the Navy, but there being at this time only one, an extraordinary Instrument is allowed him, with a Salary of 150*l*. *per Annum*;

PREFACE.

num; and in like manner upon reducing the Number of Commissioners of the Navy, (for in time of War there were several who had no particular Branches assigned them) an Assistant is allowed to the Comptroler of the Victualling Accounts, with a Salary of 300*l.* a Year; so that, besides the Treasurer, Comptroler, Surveyor, and Clerk of the Acts of the Navy, and the Comptrolers of the Treasurer's, Storekeeper's, and Victualling Accounts, there is but one more principal Officer and Commissioner at the Board, who, together with the said Comptroler of the Victualling Accounts, (besides their respective Duties as Commissioners) and another Gentleman added to them, (who hath not the Title of a Commissioner of the Navy) are appointed to manage the Business of sick and hurt Seamen, as well as that of Prisoners at War, and Transportation of Forces, which in time of great Action were performed by particular Commissions.

Besides the aforementioned principal Officers and Commissioners of the Navy residing in Town, there is one who has his Residence at *Chatham*, another at *Portsmouth*, and a third at *Plimouth*, whose Business is more immediately to inspect into the Affairs of the Yards there, and the Conduct of the Officers belonging thereunto; but, when in Town, they have the same Right of sitting and acting at the Board as any the other Members thereof. *Commissioners residing at the Dock-Yards.*

There are also, under the Direction of the Lord High-Admiral, Commissioners for managing the Affairs of Victualling His Majesty's Navy, who are constituted by a joint Commission, by virtue of a Warrant from the Office of the Lord High-Admiral, in the King's Name, to the Attorney General, authorising him to prepare a Bill to pass the Seals, in the same manner as for the Patents to the principal Officers and Commissioners of His Majesty's Navy; and as the Officers of the respective Dock-Yards and Rope-Yards are (under the Lord High-Admiral) more immediately subject to the Inspection and Directions of the Navy Board, so have the said Commissioners of the Victualling Officers under them at the principal Ports, as well as Agents abroad, when the Service requires the same. *Commissioners for Victualling the Navy.*

The Judge of the High Court of Admiralty, who is Lieutenant, as well as Council to the Lord High-Admiral, in all Matters relating to the Civil Law, is appointed by his Warrant to be his Advocate in the said Court, by which he is directed to prepare a Bill, to pass the Seal thereof, constituting the Person, who shall be agreed on, Judge of the said High Court of Admiralty, in which Employment the said Officer is generally confirmed by a Patent under the Great Seal of the Kingdom; and the Authority given to the said Judge by his Commission, or Patent, is as follows, *viz.* *Judge of the High Court of Admiralty.*

1. To take Cognizance of, and determine all Causes whatever that are Civil and Maritime, *viz.* all Contracts, Offences, Complaints, &c. that do any ways concern Shipping; as also

b

PREFACE.

so Injuries, Extortions, and all Civil and Maritime Dealings whatsoever, between Merchants and Owners of Ships, or Vessels employed within the Jurisdiction of the Admiralty of *England*, or between any other Persons had, committed, or contracted, not only upon the Sea, or in publick Rivers, but also in fresh Waters, Rivulets, Havens, Creeks, and all Places overflowed, and within the Flux and Reflux of the Sea, or high Tide of the fresh Waters; as also on the Shores or Banks of the same, below the first Bridge towards the Sea, within the Kingdoms of *England* and *Ireland*, and the Dominions thereunto belonging, or in any other Places beyond the Seas.

2. To receive Appeals from inferior Courts of Admiralty, and to inhibit their Proceedings in Causes depending before him.

3. To arrest Ship, Persons, and Goods, in Cases of Debt, or other Forfeitures, provided the Persons and Goods be found within the Jurisdiction of the Admiralty.

4. To enquire, by Oath of honest and lawful Men, into all things which by the Laws or Customs of the Court used to be enquired into; and to punish, fine, or imprison Contemners of his Jurisdiction, according to the Laws and Customs of the Admiralty, or the Statutes of the Realm.

5. To look after the Conservation of the publick Rivers, Rivulets, Havens, and Creeks within the Jurisdiction of the Admiralty, as well for the Preservation of the Navy, as other Ships, and also of the Fish; and to punish such as make use of Nets which are too narrow, or other unlawful Engines, or Instruments for Fishing.

6. To judge and determine of Wrecks at Sea, and also of dead Bodies found within the Jurisdiction of the Admiralty, according to the Statute concerning Wrecks, and of the Office of a Coroner, made in the third and fourth Years of *Edward* the First, and the Statute about Goods coming to *England* being plundered at Sea, in the twenty seventh Year of *Edward* the Third.

7. To judge of Cases of *Maheim, (i.e. Maim,* or Loss of Limb) and to punish the Delinquents.

8. To depute and surrogate a Substitute, or Substitutes, and to revoke all such Deputations at pleasure, and to hold his Place *quam diu se bene gesserit.*

Inferior Officers in the High Court of Admiralty.

The Lord High-Admiral hath also an Advocate in the said High Court of Admiralty; and as the King hath also an Advocate General therein, so hath the High-Admiral a Proctor; besides whom there is a Register, and a Marshal.

Judge Advocate of the Navy, and his Deputy.

The Lord High-Admiral doth, by his Commission, appoint a Judge Advocate of the Navy, for the more regular holding Courts Martial, and trying Offenders; and the said Judge Advocate hath a Deputy, to assist him in the Execution of the Business of his

Preface.

his Office, who is appointed in the same manner.

There is likewise a Councellor for the Affairs of the Admiralty and Navy, as to Matters relating to the Common Law, to whom the Lord High-Admiral, or the Commissioners of the Admiralty, and the Navy Board refer such Matters as are proper for his Consideration and Advice; and the said Councellor is allowed an Assistant, who solicits, and manages, by Directions from the Admiralty and Navy Boards, all things relating to those Offices respectively, which are proper for his Cognizance. *Councellor to the Admiralty and Navy, and his Assistant.*

As the Lord High-Admiral is the principal Wheel by which all Matters relating to the Royal Navy have their Motion, so are the principal Officers and Commissioners of the Navy next and immediately under him, I mean as to what relates more particularly to the OEconomy thereof on shore. To them he issues his Orders for the building, repairing, fitting out, and paying off, and laying up in Harbour His Majesty's Ships; and as to the Victualling the Ships in Sea Pay, from time to time, they do, in pursuance of his Orders, send Directions to the Commissioners particularly appointed to manage that Branch of the Navy. *Lord High-Admiral directs the building Ships, &c.*

Towards the end of each Year, the Lord High-Admiral doth, by his Memorial to the King in Council, humbly pray His Majesty to declare the Number of Men necessary to be employed in his Service at Sea the next Year, which being done, Estimates are prepared, and laid before His Majesty in Council, for his Royal Confirmation, of the Charge of their Wages, and Victuals, and of the Wear and Tear of the Ships wherein they may be employed; and the Navy Board are directed by the Lord High-Admiral to consider, and propose to him how, in their opinion, and that of the Commissioners for Victualling the Navy, the Provisions for the said Men may be most properly distributed at the several Ports, which being approved of, Directions are sent to the said Commissioners of the Navy accordingly, and by them to the Commissioners for Victualling. *Lord High-Admiral moves the Crown for a Declaration of the Number of Seamen each Year.*

The Lord High-Admiral doth also, by Letter to the Master-General of the Ordnance, desire him to cause Guns, and Gunner's Stores to be put on board His Majesty's Ships which are from time to time ordered to be fitted out for Service, and for the taking them on shore again, and placing them in His Majesty's Magazines, when such Ships are ordered to be discharged from farther Service; and the like he doth when any Ships come into Port to be refitted. *Ships are supplied with Guns, &c. by Letter from the Lord High-Admiral to the Master of the Ordnance.*

The Lord High-Admiral doth by his Warrants to the principal Officers and Commissioners of the Navy, direct them to cause all Officers to be entered in His Majesty's Dock-Yards and Rope-Yards, as also all standing Officers on board His Majesty's Ships, such as Pursers, Gunners, Boatswains, and Carpenters; but the Masters, Chyrurgeons, and Cooks are, by the Authority they have received from the Lord High-Admiral, appointed by their own peculiar Warrants. And as to all Flag-Officers, Captains, *In what manner Officers of the Yards and Ships are appointed.*

b 2 and

PREFACE.

and Lieutenants, they are commission'd by the High-Admiral, or Commissioners of the Admiralty, without passing through the Hands of the Navy Board; and the Chaplains, Volunteers, and Schoolmasters of Ships, are immediately appointed by the Lord High-Admiral, or Commissioners of the Admiralty, by Warrants directed to the Captains of the said Ships, as are Midshipmen extraordinary, but no Person is admitted as such, who hath not before served as a Lieutenant.

Navy Board, and Victuallers have Power to make Contracts,

Both the principal Officers and Commissioners of the Navy, and the Commissioners for Victualling, have Power from the Crown to make Contracts for all Naval Stores and Provisions necessary for the Publick Service. But since the enumerating the several Branches of the Instructions to one and the other, together with those to the Officers of the Dock-Yards, Rope-Yards,

but

&c. would be a Work much too large for a Preface, I shall only touch on one thing more relating to this Head, which is, that

cannot perform any considerable Work without the High-Admiral's Approbation

before either of those Boards give Orders for the Performance of any considerable Work, or Buildings, they prepare, and lay before the Lord High-Admiral, or Commissioners of the Admiralty, Estimates of what the Charge of such Works may probably amount unto, and if the same are approved of, Orders are issued for their being performed accordingly.

Vice-Admirals at home and abroad.

The Lord High-Admiral also appoints his Vice-Admirals as well in the Maritime Countries of these Kingdoms, as in His Majesty's foreign Governments and Plantations, and this by Warrants to the Judge of the High Court of Admiralty to issue Commissions under the Great Seal of the said Court, by which they are empowered, I mean the Vice-Admiral abroad,

Powers given to a Vice-Admiral

1. To proceed on, and determine (with the Assistance of the Judge of the Admiralty, who with the Registers, and Marshals, are appointed by the Lord High-Admiral) all Civil and Maritime Causes.

2. To make Enquiry into, by a Jury, according to ancient Laws and Customs, the Goods and Chattels of all Traitors, Pirates, Murderers, and Felons, trespassing within the Jurisdiction of their Vice-Admiralties, together with the Goods, Debts, and Chattels of their Accessories and Accomplices, and of Felons *de* Sea, Fugitives convict, attainted, excommunicated, and out-lawed: But such Goods and Chattels of Pirates ought not to be proceeded against and condemned, until they have been in the Possession of the High Court of Admiralty, or the Vice-Admiralty Courts abroad, for the space of one Year and a Day, which time is allowed to such Persons who pretend a Right to them to put in their Claims.

3. To enquire into all Goods of Ships that are *Flotson, Jetson,* or *Lagon,* and all Shares, Treasure found, and to be found, and *Deodands*; and also all Goods found in the Seas, Shores, Creeks, and within the fresh Waters, on Places overflowed by the Sea.

To

PREFACE.

4. To inspect into Anchorage and Ballastage, as also all Royal Fishes, such as Sturgeons, Whales, Porpusses, Dolphins, Grampusses, and, in general, all large Fishes, and to hear, and determine in the same, either by themselves, their Lieutenants, or Deputies, and to levy, collect, and preserve whatever is adjudged, mulcted, or forfeited, for the Use of the King, (when those things are reserved by the Crown to its own Disposal) or the Lord High-Admiral.

5. To arrest Ships, Goods, and Persons within the Jurisdiction of their Vice-Admiralties, according as the case shall require, and conformable to the Maritime and Civil Laws, upon any Applications, or Complaints that shall be made to them; and to compel Persons to appear, and answer in their Courts, and to punish, mulct, or imprison those who refuse so to appear.

6. To put in Execution all Laws, Orders, and Customs for the Preservation of the Ports, Rivers, and Fishes within the District of their Vice-Admiralties.

7. To take away all Nets that are too scanty, and all unlawful Engines and Instruments for catching Fish, and to punish those who use them.

8. To proceed in Judgment on Bodies found dead on the Water, and to appoint Deputies, and other Officers, for the better inspecting into, and management of the Matters committed to their Charge; with a Proviso that nothing shall infringe the Rights of the High Court of Admiralty of this Kingdom, and any Person, or Persons, who shall think themselves agrieved by the Sentence of their Court, their appealing to the aforesaid High Court of Admiralty.

9. They hold their Places, as Vice-Admirals, with all the Profits and Perquisites belonging thereunto, during pleasure; and they are enjoined to transmit in every Year, if demanded, between the Feasts of St. *Michael* the Arch-Angel, and All-Saints, an exact Account of all their Proceedings, and of what doth remain in their Hands, pursuant to the aforesaid Directions in their Commissions, which, in default thereof, are to become void, as those are also to the Vice-Admirals at home.

And since several Disputes formerly happened between the Vice-Admirals, and the Judges of the said Courts, in relation to their respective Authorities, the late King *James*, when Lord High-Admiral, in the Reign of his Brother, determined the same in the manner following.

1. That the Vice-Admiral (as he is authorised by his Patent) should proceed solely in the Exercise of Jurisdiction in the Matters following, *viz.*

To

PREFACE.

Disputes between the Vice-Admirals and the Judges of the Vice-Admiralties reconciled by the Duke of York, when High-Admiral.

>To enquire *per sacramentum proborum & legalium hominum, de omnibus & singulis quæ de jure, statutis, ordinationibus, vel consuetudinibus, Curiæ Principalis, Admiralitatis Angliæ, ab antiquo inquiri solent vel deberent.* That is, of all and singular those Things which by the Law, Statutes, Ordinances, or Customs of the High Court of Admiralty of *England*, are, from ancient Times, wont, or ought to be enquired into upon the Oaths of good and lawful Men.
>
>To take Possession, and have the Custody of all Goods wrecked, whether *Flotson, Jetson,* or *Lagon*, and all Goods of Felons and other Offenders forfeited or found in that Vice-Admiralty; as also of all pecuniary Mulcts, and Fines inflicted within the same, and the Forfeitures of all Recognizances, and all other Admiralty Droits and Perquisites, and to dispose of the same to the use of the Lord High-Admiral, giving him a particular Account thereof.
>
>To use the Seal committed to his Custody in all Writs and Proceedings which concerned the Exercise of his Jurisdiction,
>
>To receive the Profits of Anchorage, Lastage, and Ballasting of Ships with Sand within his Vice-Admiralty, if the same should not be especially granted to some other Person, and to be responsible for the same.

2. And as for the Power of the Judge, it was determined as follows;

>That he should proceed alone in all Matters of Instance whatsoever between Party and Party; as to the giving Oaths to all Witnesses; to decree Compulsories against such as should refuse to appear; to grant Commissions for Examination of Parties, Principal and Witnesses; to take all manner of Recognizances before him, and, as need should require, to declare the same to be forfeited; and to order all such things as might be requisite to be decreed, and done, concerning any Suit or Matter depending in Court before him for the concluding thereof; and at last to give and pronounce Sentence definitive, as the Merits of the Cause should require.
>
>That he, by Deputation from the Vice Admiral, should alone take Cognizance of, and determine all Contracts made beyond the Seas to be performed here, and of those which should be made here to be expedited beyond the Seas, and this, notwithstanding the Power thereof was particularly mentioned in the Patent to the Vice-Admiral.
>
>That as to all Matters of Office (saving to the Vice-Admiral the Power to enquire *per sacramentum & legalium hominum de omnibus & singulis, &c.* before-mentioned,

PREFACE.

and faving alfo to him the Collecting, and Cuftody of all thofe Things which belong to him by his Patent) the Judge fhould have Power to impofe Fines upon Offenders, commit them to Prifon for not Payment of thofe Fines; to examine, and commit any Perfon taken and apprehended upon Sufpicion of Piracy, and to proceed to the Adjudication of Goods forfeited and confifcable (faving to the High Court of Admiralty the Right of proceeding againft all fuch Ships and Goods for which any Perfon fhould put in his Claim there, and fuch, as being of very great Value, are there to be adjudged, as it hath always been accuftomed) which are to be feized, and taken into Poffeffion by the Vice-Admiral, who was to give Intimation thereof to the High Court of Admiralty, and, after Condemnation thereof, to difpofe of the fame, and to be accountable to the Lord High-Admiral, as directed by his Patent.

And that there might be a right Underftanding between the Vice-Admiral and the Judge, (admitting the Exercife of the Judicial Proceeding in, and fentencing of all Caufes depending in Court to belong only to the Judge, as aforefaid) the Vice-Admiral was at liberty, at his pleafure, at any time to fit with the Judge in Court, in regard he might oftentimes be efpecially concerned in fome Matters of Office depending in the faid Court, and that the appointment of the Courts fucceffively fhould be with his Knowledge, and Approbation. And that if the Judge fhould not keep Courts, and do thofe things which are fitting to be done by his Place, the Vice-Admiral might then, or his Deputy, keep fuch Courts, and judge, and receive the Judge's accuftomed Fees.

The Lord High-Admiral, having made thefe Regulations between the Vice Admirals and the Judges of thofe Courts, he thought it fitting alfo to eftablifh certain Articles, and to enjoin the then Judge of the High Court of Admiralty ftrictly to comply therewith, that fo due care might be taken in the miniftring of Juftice, and that with difpatch, in regard the fame was fo abfolutely neceffary upon the Score not only of the Subjects of this Kingdom, but of thofe of its Allies alfo; which Articles were as follows, *viz.* *Inftructions given by the Duke of York, when High-Admiral, to the Judge of the Admiralty.*

1. That he fhould be very careful and intent in the preventing all Delays, and Subterfuges whatfoever in Judicial Proceedings, and, with particular Application, give all poffible difpatch to Foreigners in their Suits, and to Seamen, ferving in Merchant Ships about their Wages, efpecially when they fhould be found entangled with dilatory Exceptions, or Appeals.

PREFACE.

peals. And that if he found any Defects in the Constitution, or Abuses in the Practice of the Court, which could not be remedy'd otherwise than by His Majesty's Authority, he should, upon considering thereof with the Advocate to the Lord High-Admiral, represent the same to him, in order to the obtaining such farther Regulations as to His Majesty should be thought fitting.

2. That he should, as much as in him lay, preserve the Respect and Reverence that ought to be in a Court of Justice, where Foreigners, among others, might have frequent Applications to make, and effectually to repress all insolent Speeches, and indecent Behaviour, which could not but raise in the Apprehensions of Strangers both a Scorn to that Court, and a Prejudice to all the Judicial Proceedings in the Kingdom.

3. That he should lay before him an exact Table of the Fees usually paid for any Monition, Warrant, Decree, Sentence, Instrument, Copy, Exemplification, or any other Act, or Thing whatsoever, payable to himself, as Judge, or to the Register, Marshal, or any other Person belonging to the Court, which Table was to be attested under the Hands of the Advocate and Proctor to the Lord High-Admiral, and those of the most ancient Practitioners in the High Court of Admiralty, that in case it should appear such Table had in it nothing differing from the Table approved by his Predecessors, Lords High-Admiral, he might confirm the same under his Hand and Seal, and take such farther Measures as might effectually restrain all Exactions, and Demands not justifiable by the said Table.

4. To survey, with all possible Exactness, all the Records and Writings in the Possession of the Register of the Court, and, with the Advice of his Advocate, to cause them to be digested in such a Method, and deposited in such safe and convenient Places, as might best preserve them from Damage or Embezilment. And that in every long Vacation he should set aside some time to visit the said Registry, with the Assistance of the Advocate and Proctor to the Lord High-Admiral, and to give Orders to the Register of the Court for the fair transcribing, and careful digesting the aforegoing Year's Records, so as that the same might be most ready, and most useful to Posterity.

5. Once in every Year he was to call all the Vice-Admirals to account, on Oath, in the High Court of Admiralty, as had been accustomed, for such Droits and Perquisites as should have come the preceding Year into their Hands, and effectually to proceed to the pronouncing their Commissions void, in case any of the said Vice-Admirals should neglect, or refuse to give in their yearly Accounts at the time accustomed. Nor was he, in any case, to content himself with the Oaths of their Proctors, Solicitors, or Servants, unless it

should

PREFACE.

should appear unto him that any of the said Vice-Admirals had exercised their Office by one or more Deputies, in which Case he was to admit of his or their Oaths, and of the Accounts so exhibited; provided the Court were satisfied that his or their Deputation was legal, sufficient, and not revoked at the time of his, or their accompting. And in case it should so happen that any of the said Vice-Admirals, or their Deputies, could not conveniently attend to give in his, or their Accounts personally in Court, he was then, with the Consent of the Advocate and Proctor to the Lord High-Admiral, to issue out a Commission, in the usual form, to such Persons of known Worth and Quality, as might receive their respective Oaths and Accounts in any convenient Place within their Jurisdictions.

Lastly. He was to endeavour to inform himself, from the aforesaid Vice-Admirals, and by all other Methods in his Power, what Lords of Mannors, and what Corporations within their respective Jurisdictions, should either by Violence usurp, or, under Colour of Grant, or Prescription, challenge to themselves the Rights and Droits of the Admiral, and from time to time to acquaint him therewith, that due Course in Law might be taken to rescue the ancient Rights and Royalties of the Office from being altogether swallowed up by Encroachments, and Usurpations.

The aforementioned Powers delegated by the Lord High-Admiral to the Vice-Admirals, are much the same as those granted to him by the Crown, so far, I mean, as they relate to those particular Branches of his Office; and when the King doth not reserve to himself the Rights and Perquisites of Admiralty, the High-Admiral's Fee, or Salary, is no more than three hundred Marks a Year, which he receives out of the Exchequer; but when he doth not enjoy those Perquisites, his Salary is 700*l. per Annum*, which Perquisites are as follows, *viz.* *The Fee, and Salary of the Lord High-Admiral.*

All Goods, Debts, and Chattels of Traitors, Pirates, Murtherers, and Felons, and of their Accessaries and Accomplices; as also of all Felons *de se*, Fugitives, Convicts, attainted, excommunicated, and out-lawed Persons, within the Limits of his Jurisdiction. *The Perquisites of the Lord High-Admiral.*

All Goods that are found on the Surface of the Sea, as also Jetson and Lagon, Treasures, Deodands, and Derelicts, together with all lost Goods, Merchandizes, and Chattels found in the Sea, or thrown out thereof; and all casual Goods found upon the Sea, or its Shore, Creeks, Coasts, or Sea-Ports; as also upon fresh Waters, Havens, publick Rivers, Rivulets, Creeks, or other Places overflowed, lying beneath the Flux and Reflux of the Sea, or Water at full Tide, or upon the Shores, or Banks of the same, from the first Bridge towards the Sea.

PREFACE.

Also Anchorage of foreign Ships upon the Sea, or in Havens or publick Rivers, or near the Shores, or Promontories of any of the same.

All Royal Fishes, *viz.* Sturgeons, Whales, Porpusses, Dolphins, and Grampusses; and, in general, all other Fishes of an enormous Thickness or Fatness, which have by ancient Right, or Custom, belonged to the Office of High-Admiral.

All Fines, Mulcts, Forfeitures, Amerciaments, Redemptions, and Recognizances whatsoever that are forfeited; and all pecuniary Punishments for Transgressions, Offence, Injuries, Extortions, Contempts, and all other Crimes whatsoever, inflicted, or to be inflicted in any Court of Admiralty.

Perquisites to the Lord High-Admiral discontinued. These Perquisites, among others, were always enjoyed by the Lord High-Admirals, until the Year 1673, when the Duke of *York*, afterwards King *James* the Second, surrendring his Patent, King *Charles* the Second appointed several of the great Officers of State to execute the Employment, but with a very limited Power; for His Majesty reserved to himself the Disposal of all Employments, as well as the Droits of Admiralty, and the said Droits, or Perquisites, have continued in the Crown ever since; for when his Royal Highness Prince *George* of *Denmark* was appointed Lord-High-Admiral, and *Thomas* Earl of *Pembroke* and *Montgomery*, both before and after him, although both one and the other had the Grant of all such Perquisites in their Patents, yet by Deeds of Gift they reinstated them in the Crown, and they have from time to time been applied towards defraying the publick Expences.

Other Perquisites to the Duke of York, when Lord High-Admiral. I also find by the Records in the Office of Admiralty, that, besides the Perquisites mentioned in the Patent to the Prince of *Denmark*, King *James*, when Duke of *York*, and Lord High-Admiral, had several others annexed to his Office. For in the Year 1660 he rented out the publick Chains, by which Ships were moored in the River of *Thames*, to *Thomas Elliot* Esq; by a Lease of fourteen Years, at 600*l. per Annum*, the said *Elliot* obliging himself to keep them in good Repair.

His Royal Highness also rented out all Sea Weed, Minerals, Sand, Gravel, and Stone lying between high, and low Water Mark, over all *England* and *Wales*, the River of *Thames* excepted, at 400*l. per Annum*.

He had also a Duty on all Ferries on Navigable Rivers, or Arms of the Sea below the last Bridge; and in the Year 1665 he made a Grant of all the Ferries in *Ireland* to Sir *Maurice Berkeley*; and in former Times the Lord High-Admiral had Duties on Lighthouses and Beacons.

He had likewise the one tenth part of all Merchant Ships, Vessels, and Goods taken from an Enemy, either by Ships of War, or Privateers, and appointed Commissioners to demand and

recover

PREFACE.

recover the same, and his Advocate, and Proctor in the High Court of Admiralty to assist them therein.

As to the present Extent of the Jurisdiction of the Lord High-Admiral, or Commissioners for executing that Office, it is over Great Britain, Ireland, and Wales, with the Dominions and Islands of the same; as also New England, New York, East and West Jerseys, Jamaica, Virginia, Barbadoes, St. Christopher's, Nevis, Monserat, Bermudas, and Antegoa in America, and Guinea, Binny, and Angola in Africa, with the Islands and Dominions of the same; and all and singular other Plantations, Dominions, and Territories whatsoever in Parts beyond the Seas, in the Possession of any of His Majesty's Subjects. *Extent of the Lord High-Admiral's Jurisdiction.*

When War is declared against any Prince, or State, the Lord High-Admiral, by his Memorial to the King in Council, prays that he will be pleased to direct the Advocate for the Office of High-Admiral in the Court of Admiralty, to prepare, and lay before His Majesty, for his Royal Approbation, the Draught of a Commission, authorising him the said Lord High-Admiral, to empower the High Court of Admiralty in the foreign Governments and Plantations, to take Cognizance of, and judicially proceed upon all, and all manner of Captures, Seisures, Prizes, and Reprizals of all Ships and Goods seised, and to adjudge, and condemn the same, according to the Course of the Admiralty, and Law of Nations; as also all Ships and Goods liable to Confiscation, pursuant to the respectives Treaties with His Majesty, and other Princes and States. *Relating to the Condemnation of Prizes at home and abroad.*

The Lord High-Admiral also humbly desires His Majesty's Directions in Council to his Advocate General in the High Court of Admiralty, and to the Advocate to the Office of High-Admiral in the said Court, to prepare, and lay before His Majesty a Commission, authorising him the said Lord High-Admiral to to issue forth Letters of Marque and Reprizals, to those he shall deem fitly qualified, to seize the Ships or Vessels belonging to the Prince against whom War is declared, his Vassals and Subjects, or any within his Countries and Dominions, and such other Ships, Vessels, and Goods as are, or shall be liable to Confiscation, pursuant to Treaties between His Majesty, and other Princes, States, and Potentates. And, by like Directions of the King in Council, the Lord High-Admiral's Advocate in the Court of Admiralty prepares, for his Royal Approbation, Instructions to Commanders of Merchant Ships to whom such Letters of Marque, or Reprizals shall be granted, the Substance of which Instructions are as follows, viz. *Relating to Letters of Marque, or Reprizals.*

1. They are empowered to seize all Ships of War, and other Vessels whatsoever, as also the Goods, Merchandizes, Vassals, and Subjects of the Prince, or State against whom War shall be declared; as also all other Ships and Vessels that may have contraband Goods on board; but to take care that not any Hostilities be committed, nor Prize taken, within *Instructions to the Commanders of private Ships of War.*

C 2

PREFACE.

within the Harbours of Princes and States in Amity with his Majesty, or in Rivers, or Roads within the reach of their Cannon.

2. To bring such Prizes as they take either to some part of this Kingdom, or to carry them to any of his Majesty's foreign Colonies and Plantations, where there are Courts of Admiralty, as it may be most convenient for them, in order to their being legally adjudged. And here it may not be improper to observe, that there is no other Appeal from the said Courts of Admiralty abroad, with relation to Prizes, than to a Committee of his Majesty's most honourable Privy Council, particularly appointed to hear and determine therein.

3. They are to produce before the Judge of the High Court of Admiralty, or the Judges of the Admiralty Courts in the foreign Governments, three or four of the principal Persons who belonged to the Prize, that so they may be examined, and sworn, touching the Interest and Property of such Ships, Goods, and Merchandizes; as also to deliver to the Judge all Papers found on board such Prize, and to produce some Person who can make Oath that those Papers were actually found on board at the time of Capture.

4. To take care that not any thing belonging to the Prize be embezzeled, before Judgment be given in the High Court of Admiralty, or by the Courts abroad, that the said Ship, Goods, and Merchandizes are lawful Prize; and not to kill any Person belonging to such Ship in cold Blood, or to treat them otherwise than according to custom in such cases.

5. They are forbid to attempt, or to do any thing against the true meaning of any Article, Articles, Treaty, or Treaties depending between the Crown of *Great Britain* and its Allies, or against the Subjects of such Allies.

6. It is declared lawful for the Captors, after Condemnation, to sell, or dispose of such Prizes, with the Goods, and Merchandizes on board them, such only excepted as by Act of Parliament ought to be deposited for Exportation.

7. They are required to aid and assist any Ship or Vessel of his Majesty's Subjects that may be attacked by the Enemy.

8. Such Persons who shall serve on board Merchant Ships with Commissions of Marque or Reprizals, are in no wise to be reputed, or challenged as Offenders against the Laws of the Land.

9. The Merchants or others, before their taking out such Commissions, are to deliver in Writing, under their Hands, to the Lord High-Admiral, or Commissioners for executing that Office, or the Lieutenant, or Judge of the High Court of Admiralty, an Account of the Name and Burthen of the Ship, with the Captain and Owner's Names, her Number of Guns, and Men, and for how long time she is Victualled.

PREFACE.

10. The Commanders of such Ships are to hold a constant Correspondence with the Secretary of the Admiralty, and to give an Account of the Designs or Motions of the Enemy's Ships, as far as they can discover, or be informed thereof, as also of their Merchant Ships and Vessels, and whether bound, either out, or home.
11. They are restrained from wearing the King's Colours, commonly called the Union Jack, and Pendant; but, besides the Colours born by Merchant Ships, they are allowed to wear a Pendant, together with a red Jack, with the Union Jack described in a Canton at the upper Corner thereof next the Staff.
12. They are required, upon due notice given them, to observe all such other Orders and Instructions as his Majesty shall think fit to direct.
13. It is also farther declared, that those who violate these Instructions shall be severely punished, and be obliged to make full Reparation to Persons injured.
14. Before Letters of Marque, or Reprizals are issued, it is required that Bail be given in the High Court of Admiralty, before the Judge thereof, in the Sum of 3000*l.* if the Ship carries about a hundred and fifty Men, and if a lesser Number 1500*l.* to make good any Damages that shall be done contrary to the Intent, and true Meaning of their Instructions, and (in case the whole of the Prizes is not given to the Captors) to cause to be paid to his Majesty, or such Person as shall be authorized to receive the same, the full tenth part of the Prizes, Goods, and Merchandizes, according as the same shall be appraised, as also such Customs as shall be due to the Crown.

When his Majesty in Council hath approved of the aforementioned Draught of Instructions, and Commissions, and that the latter have passed the Great Seal of the Kingdom, they are register'd in the High Court of Admiralty, and the Lord High-Admiral issues out Warrants to the Judge of the said Court, to grant Letters of Marque, or Reprizals, in his Majesty's Name, and his own, under the Great Seal of that Court, who annexes thereunto the proper Instructions, and takes Bail, as aforesaid.

The Lord High-Admiral doth also, by his Warrant, will and require the High Court of Admiralty, and the Lieutenant, and Judge of the said Court, as also the Courts of Admiralty abroad, to take Cognizance of, and judiciously proceed upon all, and all manner of Captures, Seisures, Prizes, and Reprizals of all Ships and Goods taken from the Enemy, and to adjudge and condemn all such Ships, Vessels, and Goods, whether taken by Ships of War, or those which have Letters of Marque or Reprizals; as also such other Ships, Vessels, or Goods, as may be liable to Confiscation, pursuant to the respective Treaties between his Majesty, and other Princes and States; and if the Crown doth

The Lord High-Admiral empowers the Courts of Admiralty to try Prizes.

PREFACE.

doth grant to the Captors the whole of the Prizes taken by them, a Declaration is issued, by which the Shares of the said Prizes is directed to be divided as follows, *viz.*

Shares of Prizes, when the Crown grants all to the Captors.

To the Flag-Officer, when there is any such concerned in the Capture, $\frac{1}{8}$th part of the whole, and to the Captain $\frac{2}{8}$ths; but if there is not any Flag-Officer who hath a Right to a Share, then the Captain is to have } $\frac{3}{8}$ths.

To the Maritime Captain, if any, Lieutenants of the Ship, and Master } $\frac{1}{8}$th.

To the Marine Lieutenants, if any, Boatswain, Gunner, Carpenters, Masters, Mates, Chirurgeon, and Chaplain } $\frac{1}{8}$th.

To the Midshipmen, Carpenter's Mates, Boatswain's Mates, Gunner's Mates, Corporal, Yeomen of the Sheats, Coxwain, Quarter-Master's Mates, Chirurgeon's Mates, Yeomen of the Powder Room, and the Serjeant of the Marines } $\frac{1}{8}$th.

To the Trumpeters, Quarter-Gunners, Carpenter's Crew, Steward, Cook, Armourer, Steward's Mate, Cook's Mate, Gunsmith, Coopers, Swabbers, Ordinary Trumpeters, Barber, Able Seamen, Ordinary Seamen, Volunteers by Warrant, and Marine Soldiers, if any, } $\frac{2}{8}$ths.

And where there are no Marine Officers or Soldiers on board, the Officers and Soldiers of Land Companies, if any, have the like Allowance as is appointed for them. But in case any Officers are absent at the time of Capture, their Shares are to be cast into the last Article.

Vice-Admirals have no Authority over Captains of Ships of War.

I have before recited the Powers given to a Vice-Admiral of one of his Majesty's foreign Governments, by which some of them have been led into an Opinion that they are thereby invested with Authority to command, and controul all things done on the Seas within the limits of the said Vice-Admiralties, nay even to wear a Union, or Jack Flag (the same which is born by the Admiral of the Fleet) on board his Majesty's Ships appointed to attend thereon, and to displace the Officers of such Ships, and appoint others in their room: But far are they from having any such Authority; for, by the same parity of Reason, any Vice-Admiral of a Maritime County in *Great Britain* (their Powers being alike) may lay a Claim to the exercising Maritime Jurisdiction within the limits of his Vice-Admiralty, and of placing, and displacing Officers of Ships of War at his pleasure, when they happen to come within his reach.

Admiralty Jurisdiction obstructed abroad.

It is but too obvious how much the Jurisdiction of the Office of High-Admiral hath been infringed and obstructed in his Majesty's foreign Governments and Plantations, by some who have assumed to themselves an Authority which was never intended them,

PREFACE.

them, and is, indeed, inconsistent with the Nature of their Office, either as Governor or Vice-Admiral; and this little regard shewn to Admiralty Jurisdiction hath frequently occasioned no small Disorder and Confusion; for while the Governors endeavour to wrest the whole Authority to themselves, the Provincial Judges, under such Umbrage, very much perplex, if not entirely over-rule the Proceedings of the Courts of Admiralty; and till some effectual Methods shall be taken to restrain the Governors herein, there is but little hopes of such a good Harmony between them, the Commanders of his Majesty's Ships appointed to attend on their Governments, and the Officers of the Courts of Admiralty, as were to be wished, and is absolutely necessary.

This being said, let us, in the last Place, take notice of some Particulars relating to the Laws and Customs of the Sea, as far as the same do more immediately relate to our own Country. *Relating to the Laws and Customs of the Sea.*

First then. As the Kings of *Great Britain* have an inherent Right in the Persons, and to the Service of their natural born Subjects, especially Mariners, and Seafaring People, so may they consequently restrain them from serving any foreign Prince or State, or by their Royal Proclamation recal them, when in such Service; for such Right would be to little purpose, were it not attended with means to compel; and the Lord High-Admiral, by virtue of the Authority he derives from the Crown, may, and doth require the Commanders of our Ships of War to demand such Seafaring Men from foreign Ships, and upon refusal, (which is a palpable Injury to the Prince whose Subjects they are) to take them by force. And as this is an undoubted Right of all Maritime Princes whatsoever, so hath it been a Custom of long Continuance. *The King may restrain Seamen from serving other Princes.*

2. The Right of searching Ships of a common Friend, and the taking Subjects, or Goods of an Enemy out of them, is a Matter which hath not hitherto been fully determined by the Law of Nations. The Party in Hostility alledges that, for his own Preservation, he hath a Right to seize the Persons and Goods of an Enemy, and that he ought not to be interrupted therein by a Neuter; whereas, on the other hand, the Neuter insists on a Liberty of Trade allowed by the Law of Nations, especially in carrying Goods not useful in War; and that Liberty would be, indeed, destroyed, if the Right to visit were made use of for committing Spoil and Rapine. But as the searching of Ships hath been often stipulated in Treaties, because otherwise it might occasion Disputes, and even War between Princes; so is there a Necessity for making such Provision, because the Variety of Cases cannot admit of any general Determination by the Law and Consent of Nations. But where there is not any *Searching Ships of a common Friend by a Prince in War.*

Signi-

Preface.

Signification published by a Prince in War, restraining the Ships of another Prince, or State, their being employed in the Service of him with whom he is in actual Hostility, and thereby a Caution given to a Friend, there is no just reason for seizing the Goods, or Persons found on board such Neutral Ships, provided they are Freighters, or Passengers, and that the Loading is not Utensils of War, but the Goods of Merchants; for hereby the Pretence of the Safety of the States being concerned in it is excluded, which Safety is the principal reason of such Search; and this being secured, liberty of Trade hath been mutually permitted by Enemies, in regard of the common Benefit accruing therefrom to Mankind; insomuch that when Persons or Goods are seized in the manner before-mentioned, Satisfaction ought to be made to the Prince to whom the Persons so seized are Subjects.

Ships of a Neutral Prince may be detained.

3. Yet Ships belonging to the Subjects of a Neutral Prince may be detained by another in actual War, if they have Goods on board proper for the Service of that Prince, or State with whom he is in Hostility, in case the Masters of such Ships produce not Passes to shew that they are bound to the Port of an Ally. Nay, it is a received Opinion, that if upon failure of a legal Proof that they do actually belong to the Subjects of that Prince from whose Dominions they shall pretend to have come, they may, although actually bound to some Port of an Ally, as aforesaid, be proceeded against, and condemned as lawful Prize.

Transporting Powder, &c. to Infidels.

4. By the Civil, as well as Common Law, the transporting of Powder, or Warlike Instruments to Infidels, is prohibited; but yet those Laws are become void by common Usage and Practice; and although by the Statute of the 12th of King *Charles* the Second, the supplying Powder, Muskets, &c. is admitted to be lawful, by way of Merchandize, the Crown may, by virtue of that Statute, prohibit the same when there shall be a just, and necessary occasion so to do, and if taken, they are by the Law of Nations confiscable: Nay, even by Treaties between one Prince and another, Provision is made that no Warlike Implements shall be carried by Neutrals for the Supply either of one or other who are in actual War.

About Ships re-taken.

5. Admitting that *England* and *Holland* were in Confederacy against *France*, and a *Dutch* Ship to have been plundered, and afterwards left by the *French*, but recovered by some of the Subjects of *England*, and forcibly taken from them by those of the States-General, and being afterwards brought into some Port of *England*, is claimed by a Lord of a Mannor, in Right of his Royalty, such Ship is neither a Perquisite of Admiralty, nor doth she belong to the Lord of the Mannor, but ought to be restored, upon paying Salvage

to the Persons who recovered her, by those who had the Property when seized by the *French*.

6. Although the Vice-Admirals of the Maritime Countries of Great Britain have a Power to take into their Possession all Ships and Vessels derelicted, wrecked, or driven upon the Shores within their Districts, yet have they not any manner of Right or Interest to detain Prizes brought in by the Ships of War of this Kingdom, or by Ships which have private Commissions. And all Wrecks of the Sea are of the same Nature as Strays, Treasure-Trove, and Things found on the Land, which, if no rightful Owner appears to claim them in a Year and a Day, belong to the Crown, or such Person who derives from it. And here it may be observed, that ancient Records, beyond Memory, recite a Custom of dividing Wrecks, and all other Casualties, taken within the Precinct of Vice-Admirals, as follows, *viz.* " One Moiety " to the Lord High-Admiral; and in consideration that " Vice-Admirals had no Fees for holding their Courts, the " other half was divided thus. To the Vice-Admiral, Judge, " and Under-Officers two Parts, and the other to the Re- " gister and Marshal. These Casualties were, by order of " the Vice-Admiral, to be appraised, and sworn to by ho- " nest Men, and the said Vice-Admirals to transmit to the " Lord High-Admiral an Account thereof at *Lady-day* and " *Michaelmas* every Year. *Touching Wrecks of the Sea, &c.*

How Wrecks &c. were anciently divided.

7. Before the Crown was pleased, as an Encouragement to the Captains, Officers, and Companies of Ships of War, and of Ships with Letters of Marque, to grant the entire Property of all Prizes to them, and even after such Grant, the Method of proceeding to the Condemnation of such Prizes hath been thus. The Captors transmit to the Judge of the High Court of Admiralty all Papers found on board them, whereupon the Proctor to the Crown, in the said Court, takes out Monitions, to call all Persons pretending Interest in the Ships and Goods, to shew Cause why the same should not be condemned as lawful Prize; which being done, the Proprietors, on the other hand, put in their Claim, according to the regular Course, and thereupon, after a full Hearing, the Ship is either cleared or condemned, upon Proof legally and judicially made; and after such Adjudgment in the High Court of Admiralty, no Claims can be admitted otherwise than before the Lords of Appeals, who have often heard such Cases, and reversed the Judgment. But if their Lordships decree a Restitution, and the Claimers to pay the Expences of the Law, they, and not the Court of Admiralty, ought to adjudge the same to be paid. And as to the Trial of Prizes in the *West-Indies*, it was, in the beginning of the Reign of King *William*, proposed by Sir *Charles Hedges*, then Judge of the High Court of Admiralty, as also by his Majesty's Attorney and Solicitor General, that the Lord *The Method of trying, and condemning Prizes at home and abroad.*

Preface.

Lord High-Admiral, or Commissioners of the Admiralty, should (as they are at this time) be invested with the like Power in *Ireland*, and all the foreign Plantations, as they had in *England*; as also that a Clause might be inserted in their Patents, empowering them to give Authority to the respective Vice-Admirals there, or the Judges of those Courts, to take Cognizance of Prizes. Besides which, an Article was added to the Instructions to the Commanders of Privateers, giving them liberty to carry their Prizes to any Place where there should be a Court of Admiralty, whereby, and by the Vice-Admirals their taking out Patents under the Great Seal of the High Court of Admiralty, they were sufficiently empowered to condemn Prizes in their respective Courts.

A Prize taken in Port.

8. In case a Prize is actually taken in Port, the Captor hath a Right to no more than the Crown, or the Lord High-Admiral shall think reasonable, the same being a Perquisite of Admiralty, if the Crown doth not reserve it to itself.

An English *Ship of War retaken before carried into Port,*

or

after two Years in the Enemy's Possession.

9. If a Ship of the Royal Navy of *Great Britain* happens to be taken by an Enemy, and is retaken by another *British* Ship of War before she can be carried into Port, or the Enemy's Fleet, the Captors have a Right to no other Reward than what the Crown shall think fit.

10. If a *British* Ship, or a Vessel of War, happens to be taken by an Enemy, and to be re-taken after she hath been upwards of two Years in their Possession, there is no legal Course of returning her into the Service of the Crown, otherwise than by buying her, when condemned, of the Commissioners for Prizes, when such a Commission is subsisting, or of the Captors, when the whole is given unto them by the Crown.

A Merchant Ship retaken by a Ship of War.

11. If a Ship or Vessel, belonging to the Subjects of *Great Britain*, is retaken from an Enemy by any of our Ships of War, the Owners ought to pay one eighth part for Salvage, without any regard to the time she was in the Enemy's Possession, which Salvage, or part thereof, as the Crown hath thought fit, hath been bestowed on those who retake the Ship; but in strictness the whole is a Perquisite of Admiralty, when the Crown doth not reserve the same to itself.

The releasing a Ship after she is taken.

12. If the Captain of a Ship of War of *Great Britain* seizes any Ship or Vessel of an Enemy, and releases her after taking out part of her Loading, he is guilty of an high Misdemeanour, and Breach of Trust, and may be punished for the same in the Court of Admiralty, by a Court Martial, or in the Exchequer, and the Offender may be incapacited, fined, or imprisoned: Nay the Punishment may be Death at a Court Martial, or if tryed by a Commission of *Oyer* and *Terminer*, according to the sixteenth Paragraph of the Statute of the thirteenth of King *Charles* the Second. But as to the Trial in the Exchequer, it must be by Information, where

the

Preface.

the Offender incurs the Penalty of 500l. together with the Loss of his Share, according to the Privateer Act. Yet if a Ship is taken from an Enemy, and she shall appear to be so disabled by the Captors, as that they shall have no hopes of bringing her into Port, she may be justifiably ransomed.

13. The Lord Warden of the Cinque Ports hath no Right to Wrecks, if chased on shore within his Jurisdiction by Ships of War, or Privateers; nor hath he a Power exclusive to the Lord High-Admiral in the *Downs*, or any other Place, which is esteemed the usual Rendezvous, Road, Harbour, or Station of Ships of the Royal Navy; not but that he hath Admiralty Jurisdiction within the Limits of the Cinque Ports; but how far those Limits extend hath not been decided, though often disputed. And although there be a concurring Jurisdiction, yet the Lord Warden may have an exclusive Right to wrecked Goods taken up within the Limits of the aforesaid Ports: But if such Goods happen to be taken up by Officers under the Lord High-Admiral, the Lord Warden ought to sue for them in the High Court of Admiralty. And when any Droits are seized by the Officers of the Cinque Ports within their Limits, and happen afterwards to be wrested from them by the Officers of the Admiralty, or Ships of War, they ought to be restored to the Officers of the Cinque Ports; but by no means is it proper for the Lord High-Admiral to order Commanders of Ships of War to assist in the Execution of the Warrants of the Lord Warden, because it derogates from his own Authority and Jurisdiction.

The Right of the Warden of the Cinque Ports as to Wrecks, &c.

14. If an Enemy's Ship is chased by a *British* Ship of War, and strikes to her, but happens to be taken and possessed by any Ship of War belonging to a Prince or State in Alliance with his Majesty, which lies fairly in the way, and such Prize is brought into any Port of *Great Britain*, a Warrant should issue out of the High Court of Admiralty to arrest her at the Suit of the Crown; but if she is carried into *Holland*, or any Place in Alliance with his Majesty, the Commissioners for Prizes (when such a Commission is subsisting) should have notice of it, and they, and the Captors, prosecute for the King's, and their own Interest therein, before the Admiralty, where the Prize is carry'd in.

A Ship striking to a British Ship of War, but taken by one of an Ally.

15. When a Dispute happens between a Vice-Admiral of one of the Maritime Counties of this Kingdom, and a Lord of a Mannor relating to Wrecks, a Suit ought to be commenced in the High Court of Admiralty, in order to condemn the Goods as a Perquisite of the Lord High-Admiral, which will oblige the Lord of the Mannor to produce his Title; and the Lord High-Admiral's Proctor is the proper Person to concern himself in, and manage that Affair.

Dispute between a Vice-Admiral and the Lord of a Mannor about Wrecks.

16. If during War a Vessel be fitted out as a Privateer in an Enemy's Dominions, and is manned with *English* Men,

Englishmen serving on board the Ships of an Enemy.

PREFACE.

with a Commission from the Enemy, such Persons, if taken, ought to be punished as Traitors, but if no Commission can be produced, their Crime will be adjudged Piracy.

Letters of Marque, or Reprizal, granted in time of Peace.

17. Letters of Marque, or Reprizals (which are as effectual as any others) have been often granted in time of settled Peace, and are allowed by the Law of Nations; for as they do not depend on the Civil Law, so whensoever a Prince, or any of his Subjects have received Damage from another Prince, or from his Subjects, and satisfaction having been demanded, the same hath been refused, or unreasonably delayed, such Letters of Marque or Reprizals may be granted, without Violation of the Treaties subsisting between such two Princes.

Persons serving in Ships under the Commission of the late King James to despoil the People of England.

18. In the Year 1692, the then Attorney and Solicitor General declared it to be their Opinions, that any Persons, Subjects of *England*, who should take Commissions under the late King *James*, to seize any Ships or Vessels belonging to *English* Subjects, and, by virtue thereof, should plunder and rob them, and commit Outrages as Pirates, they might be proceeded against according to the Statute of the twenty eighth of *H.* 8. Ch. 15. by Commission under the Great Seal, to be directed to the Lord High-Admiral, or his Lieutenant, or Deputy, and such others as should be named therein. They also conceived the same to be Treason within the Statute of the twenty fifth of *Ed.* 3. as being an actual levying War against the Crown of *England*, and the Offence to be the same as if Persons, by Commission of the like Nature, had landed in *England*, and committed open Hostilities upon the Subjects thereof.

A Person killed by accident upon saluting.

19. If any one belonging to a Merchant Ship, coming under the Stern of a Ship of War to salute, happens, by firing a Shot into her, to kill any Person, he is to be tried at an Admiralty Sessions, but in the mean time may be admitted to Bail.

A Person condemned by a Court Martial for Mutiny,

20. If a Court Martial condemns any Person for Mutiny, the said Court hath Power to award Execution, even in the narrow Seas; but if they submit the Time and Place to the Lord High-Admiral, his Pleasure ought to be signified therein. And if a Court Martial awards a Fine to the use of the Chest at *Chatham*, the Trustees being thereby invested with it, the same cannot be remitted. Likewise if a Court Martial gives Sentence of Death in the narrow Seas for a Crime committed in remote Parts, although the Intention of the Act be to prevent hasty Executions, yet, if the Commander in Chief gives Orders for its being done, the purpose of the Statute is answered.

for Crimes committed in remote Parts.

How Marine Officers and Soldiers may be tried for Crimes committed.

21. As to the Regimented Maritime Officers and Soldiers, they cannot, for Offences committed on shore, be punished by a Court Martial of Sea Officers, although they receive their

Commis-

PREFACE.

Commissions from, and are under the immediate directions of the Lord High-Admiral; but they may be tried and punished by a Warrant from the Crown, directed to their chief Officer, or any other appointed by such Warrant, according to the Articles of War for Land Soldiers; and for Offences at Sea, they may be tried at a Court Martial, as Sea Officers and Mariners are.

22. By the Act for regulating the Navy, or Ships of War, a Person deserting from a Ship whereunto he belongs, may be tried for the said Offence, although the Ship from which he so deserted be paid off and discharged; for the Act doth not make any Distinction, or limit the Jurisdiction given by it. And as there are severer Punishments in the aforesaid Act than what are ordained in the Sea Laws, which are principally for the Government of Merchant Ships, so without such a particular Act, Offenders of this kind might escape unpunished. *Deserters from his Majesty's Ships.*

23. The Number of Officers of which a Court Martial is to consist is not limited by the Act, in Cases which are not capital; but in capital Cases such Court should not consist of less than five Captains. *Number of Officers to make a Court Martial.*

24. If Persons serving at Sea are sentenced to Death by a Court Martial, and the Crown shall afterwards extend Pardon to them, a Court Martial may be summoned, where the Criminals pleading the said Pardon, the Court may decree them to be discharged; but this hath been frequently done in a general Pardon, or a particular one under the Great Seal, or under the Royal Signet and Sign Manual. *The pardoning of Persons condemned by a Court Martial.*

25. A Court Martial, held according to the Statute of King *Charles* the Second, hath Power to incapacitate, in Cases where the manner of Punishment is not expressly and positively directed by the said Act, but left to the Discretion of the Court; and Officers so incapacited ought not to be employed again without Directions from the Crown. *A Court Martial may incapacitate Officers.*

26. Any Person in the Service of the Crown who shall give false Intelligence of the Enemy's Fleet, or any Foreigner doing the same, may be prosecuted as a Spy by a Court Martial; and a Native, not in the Service, may be articled against in the Court of Admiralty, and be fined and imprisoned, *Punishment for false Intelligence.*

27. No Prisoner at War is subject to any Action for what he doth by virtue of the Commission of that Prince whose Subject he is. *A Prisoner at War.*

28. In case a Person belonging to one Ship is accidentally killed on firing Guns, as a Salute, from another, and the Widow of the Person so slain, after Trial at an Admiralty Sessions, designs to prosecute elsewhere for Damages, it ought to be in her own Name, by way of a Civil Action: But the Maritime and Civil Laws will, in such case, allow *A Person accidentally killed on firing of Guns.*

Damages

PREFACE.

Damages against those through whose Neglect or Carelessness the Accident happened; and if it cannot be fixed on particular Persons who are responsible, the Master and the Ship will be liable.

The Master of a hired Ship cannot be tried by a Court Martial.
29. The Master of a Merchant Ship hired by Charter Party to carry publick Provisions, or Stores, cannot, for breach thereof, be tried at a Court Martial, because he is not in actual Service or Pay in the Fleet as a Ship of War.

A Prisoner for High Treason.
30. A Prisoner against whom a Bill is found for High Treason, for Crimes committed on the Seas, cannot be admitted to bail.

An Action in the Court of Admiralty against a Sea Officer. Rescuers of deserting Seamen.
31. If an Action, either Civil or Maritime, be commenced against any Sea-Officer in the High Court of Admiralty, and he gives in bail, it ought not to interrupt his going to Sea.
32. Those who rescue deserting Seamen, ought for their Offence to be tried at an Admiralty Sessions, Information upon Oath being first made; and they may be committed by Warrant from the Court of Admiralty.

A Prize taken by a Captain of a Privateer who alters his Ship.
33. If a Master of a Merchant Ship takes out a Letter of Marque, and, being in foreign Parts, meets with a Ship more fit for his purpose, and with her takes several Prizes by virtue of the said Letter of Marque, those Prizes will, upon Trial, be condemned as Perquisites of the Admiralty, but some Allowance be made to the Captor for his Service.

Treasonable Words spoken at Sea.
34. If any Person belonging to a Ship of War speak on board such Ship treasonable Words against the Government, they may be tried and punished by a Court Martial, for offending against the nineteenth Article of the Statute of King *Charles* the Second.

How Pirates or Robbers are tried at home.
35. When Piracies, or Robberies are committed on the Seas, and the Offenders are taken, they are tried at an Admiralty Sessions, by a Commission of Oyer and Terminer under the Great Seal, at which Trials some of the Judges of the Common Law assist; and if the Lord High-Admiral, or the Commissioners for executing that Office, are present in Court, he, or they preside, otherwise the Judge of the High Court of Admiralty, who, in either Case, gives Sentence.

Pirates Goods are Perquisites of the Admiralty.
36. All Ships and Goods taken from Pirates are Perquisites belonging to the Lord High-Admiral, in case the Crown doth not reserve them to itself, whose Advocate and Proctor ought to proceed against them in the Court of Admiralty, and obtain Sentence for Condemnation.

Pirates may be tried abroad.
37. If Pirates are taken abroad, and carried to any of his Majesty's Foreign Governments, they may be properly and legally tried by the Admiralty Courts there, by virtue of a Commission under the Great Seal empowering the proper Officers of such Courts to do the same.

38. If

Preface.

38. If a Merchant Ship, after her being taken, and legally condemned as good Prize, be bought by the Subjects of another Prince, she is not seizable by the Law of Nations; or if seized, she ought to be restored to the Purchasers; but if she shall not be condemned, those who buy such Ship have no Right to her. *A Prize bought by the Subjects of another Prince.*

39. If Vessels be taken by Pirates, Sea-Rovers, or others who have not lawful Commissions, they can have no just Property in them; and if retaken, they ought to be restored to their Owners, upon due Proof of their Title to them. *Vessels taken by Pirates.*

40. If the Lord High-Admiral suspects that any Ship belonging to his Majesty's Subjects is going on an unjustifiable Design, he may, before she is permitted to proceed, cause the Judge of the High Court of Admiralty to take sufficient bail of her Owners for the good Behaviour of her Master and Men; and even the Judge himself may cause her to be detained, if, upon Information, he shall deem it reasonable. *A Ship suspected may be stopp'd from proceeding.*

41. If a Warrant is issued out of the High Court of Admiralty for arresting a Merchant Ship or Vessel, and Resistance is made, upon the Application of the Persons entrusted with the said Arrest to the Commander of one of his Majesty's Ships of War, he ought to assist them in the Execution. *A Warrant issued for arresting a Ship.*

42. All Sentences in Civil and Maritime Cases in the Plantations are, upon Appeals from thence, to be determined by the High Court of Admiralty here, and upon failure of Justice in the said Court, the final Determination is in the Court of Delegates. But in the Case of Prizes, the Appeal lies directly from the Courts of Admiralty in the Plantations to the Lords of the Council, as hath been already observed. *Sentences in Civil and Maritime Cases in the Plantations.*

43. If the Jurisdiction of the Admiralty should be infringed in any of his Majesty's foreign Governments by the Courts of Common Law, in Cases purely cognizable in the Courts of Admiralty, in which those Courts of Judicature have no Right to prohibit, the Parties aggrieved ought to seek Remedy by an Appeal to his Majesty in Council. *Infringement of Admiralty Jurisdiction by Courts of Common Law.*

44. If Murder be committed on shore in any of his Majesty's Dominions, by any Person belonging to a Ship of War of *Great Britain*, the same cannot be enquired into by a Court Martial, nor can the Offender be otherwise tried than by Common Law. *Murder committed on shore.*

45. If any Officer belonging to a Ship of War of *Great Britain* shall conceal on board the said Ship any of the publick Stores committed to his Charge, he ought to be tried for the same at a Court Martial; but if the said Stores shall be embezzeled, and carried on shore, then he must be tried for his said Offence by Common Law. *Concealment, or Embezzelment of Stores.*

Lastly.

PREFACE.

An English Seaman taken in the Ship of a foreign Prince.

Lastly. If any Seaman, a Subject of *Great Britain*, shall enter himself into the Service of any foreign Prince or State, and be taken in such Service by the *Algerines*, or others, they have not any Right to expect their being reclaim'd by the Crown, as Subjects of this Nation.

CONTENTS.

CONTENTS.

BOOK I.
Containing a general Account of those People who have flourished at Sea in all Ages.

CHAP. I.
Of the Origine *of* Navigation *and* Invention *of* Shipping. Page 1

CHAP. II.
Of the Improvements in Navigation, and Naval Affairs, by the Ægyptians, Phœnicians, *and* Assyrians. p. 3

CHAP. III.
Of the Greeks, *and those among them and the Neighbouring Nations who held the Dominion of the Sea, according to* Eusebius's *Catalogue.* p. 6

CHAP. IV.
Of the Navigations and Naval Power of the Hebrews *under* David *and* Solomon. p. 8

CHAP. V.
Of the Corinthians, Ionians, Polycrates *the Tyrant of* Samos, *the* Persians, Athenians, Lacedæmonians, Massilians, Tyrrhenians, Spinetans, *and* Carthaginians. p. 10

CHAP. VI.
Of the Naval Power of the Romans. p. 12

CHAP. VII.
Of the Cilicians, Veneti *of* Gaul, Goths, Saxons, Saracens, *and* Normans. p. 14

CHAP. VIII.
Of the Venetians, Pisans, Genoese, Portuguese, Spaniards, *and* Dutch. p. 16

CHAP. IX.
Of the Swedes, Danes, Muscovites, Turks, French, *and* English. p. 18

CHAP. X.
Of the Dominion of the Sea in general. p. 22

Contents.

Chap. XI.

Of the Right of the Kings of Great Britain *to the Sovereignty or Dominion of the* British *Seas.* p. 28

Chap. XII.

Of the Boundaries of the British *Seas, the Extent of the Sea-Dominion of the Kings of* Great Britain, *and the Right of the Flag; with some Observations on the Use of the Term* the British Seas *in Treaties.* p. 34

BOOK II.

Containing an Account of the most remarkable Naval Transactions throughout the World, from the Expedition of the *Argonauts* to the Dissolution of the *Roman* Empire by the Irruptions of the barbarous Nations.

Chap. I.

Of the Naval Wars of the Grecians, *from the Expedition of the* Argonauts *to the breaking out of the War with the* Persians. p. 41

Chap. II.

Of the Naval Wars of the Grecians, *from the breaking out of the* Persian *War to the Defeat of the* Persians, *and burning their Fleet at the Promontory* Mycale. p. 48

Chap. III.

Of the Naval Wars of the Grecians *in* Sicily *with the* Carthaginians, *then in Alliance with the* Persians. p. 57

Chap. IV.

Of the Naval Wars of the Grecians, *from the Defeat of the* Persians *at* Mycale, *to the Victory obtained over them by* Cimon *at* Eurymedon, *and the Peace that ensued thereupon.* p. 59

Chap. V.

Of the Naval Wars of the Grecians, *from the Peace with* Persia *after the Battel of* Eurymedon, *to the beginning of the* Peloponnesian *War.* p. 63

Chap. VI.

Of the Naval Wars of the Grecians, *from the beginning of the* Peloponnesian *War, to the great Expedition of the* Athenians *against* Sicily. p. 69

Chap. VII.

Of the Naval Wars of the Grecians, *from the great Expedition against*

Contents.

against Sicily *by the* Athenians, *to their utter Defeat in that Island by the* Syracusans. p. 77

Chap. VIII.
Of the Naval Wars of the Grecians, *from the Overthrow of the* Athenians *in* Sicily, *to the Victory obtained over them by* Lysander *the* Spartan *General at* Ægospotamos, *and the End of the* Peloponnesian *War.* p. 85

Chap. IX.
Of the Naval Wars of the Grecians, *from the end of the* Peloponnesian *War, to the beginning of the* Macedonian *Greatness under King* Philip. p. 92

Chap. X.
Of the Naval Wars of the Grecians, *from the beginning of the* Macedonian *Greatness under King* Philip *to the Death of* Alexander *the Great.* p. 96

Chap. XI.
Of the Naval Wars of the Grecians, *from the Death of* Alexander *the Great, to the Reduction of* Macedonia *to the Obedience of the* Romans. p. 105

Chap. XII.
Of the Naval Wars of the Carthaginians, *from the Foundation of their City, to their first War with the* Romans; *wherein are also contained those of the* Syracusans. p. 113

Chap. XIII.
Of the Naval Wars of the Romans, *from their first vigorous Application to the Sea in the first* Punic *War, to the Conclusion of the said War.* p. 119

Chap. XIV.
Of the Naval Wars of the Romans, *from the Conclusion of the first* Punic *War, to the end of the second.* p. 129

Chap. XV.
Of the Naval Wars of the Romans, *from the end of the second* Punic *War, to the beginning of the first* Triumvirate. p. 142

Chap. XVI.
Of the Naval Wars of the Romans, *from the beginning of the first* Triumvirate, *to the Death of* Julius Cæsar. p. 152

Chap. XVII.
Of the Naval Wars of the Romans, *from the Death of* Julius Cæsar, *to the Battel of* Actium, *and the Establishment of the Empire by* Augustus. p. 164

Contents.

Chap. XVIII.
Of the Naval Wars of the Romans, *from the Establishment of the Empire by* Augustus, *to the Dissolution thereof by the Irruptions of the barbarous Nations.* p. 174

BOOK III.

Containing an Account of the most remarkable Naval Transactions of all Nations that, since the Ruin of the *Roman* Empire, have been considerable at Sea; and, among them, of the *English* down to the Revolution in the Year 1688.

Chap. I.
Of the Naval Wars of the Goths. p. 183

Chap. II.
Of the Naval Wars of the Saracens. p. 188

Chap. III.
Of the Naval Wars of the Normans. p. 193

Chap. IV.
Of the Naval Wars of the Venetians, *from the Foundation of their Republick to the time of the League of* Cambray. p. 197

Chap. V.
Of the Naval Wars of the Venetians, *from the Conclusion of the League of* Cambray, *to the present Times.* p. 225

Chap. VI.
Of the Naval Wars of the Genoese, *containing those they were engaged in with the* Pisans, *and with the* Venetians. p. 238

Chap. VII.
Of the Naval Wars of the Genoese, *containing those they have been engaged in with other Nations besides the* Pisans *and* Venetians. p. 244

Chap. VIII.
Of the Naval Wars of the Portuguese. p. 253

Chap. IX.
Of the Naval Wars of the Spaniards. p. 265

Chap.

CONTENTS.

CHAP. X.
Of the Naval Wars of the Dutch.   p. 282

CHAP. XI.
Of the Naval Wars of the Swedes.   p. 299

CHAP. XII.
Of the Naval Wars of the Danes.   p. 305

CHAP. XIII.
Of the Naval Wars of the Muscovites, and of the Turks. p. 308

CHAP. XIV.
Of the Naval Wars of the French.   p. 309

CHAP. XV.
Of the Naval Wars of the English, from the first known Times of Britain, to the Norman Conquest.   p. 322

CHAP. XVI.
Of the Naval Transactions of the English, from the Norman Conquest, to the end of Queen Mary I.   p. 329

CHAP. XVII.
Of the Naval Transactions of the English, during the Reign of Queen Elizabeth.   p. 342

CHAP. XVIII.
Of the Naval Transactions of the English, from the beginning of the Reign of King James I. to the breaking out of the first Dutch War in 1652.   p. 368

CHAP. XIX.
Of the Naval Transactions of the English, from the breaking out of the first Dutch War in 1652, to the Revolution in 1688. p. 380

BOOK IV.

Containing an Account of the Naval Transactions of the English from the Revolution in 1688, to the Peace of Ryswick in the Year 1697.

CHAP. I.
The Proceedings of the English Fleet upon the Preparations made in Holland, till the Prince of Orange his landing in England. p. 407

Contents.

Chap. II.
Admiral Herbert's *engaging a* French *Squadron on the Coast of* Ireland, *with an Account of what happened in that Kingdom, and of Admiral* Russell's *carrying the Queen of* Spain *to the* Groyne.
p. 415

Chap. III.
Vice-Admiral Killegrew's *Proceedings, from the Time of his sailing to the* Mediterranean, *to that of his Return to* England. p. 422

Chap. IV.
An Account of the Earl of Torrington's *engaging the* French *Fleet off of* Beachy. p. 425

Chap. V.
An Account of the joint Admirals (Sir Richard Haddock, *Mr.* Killegrew, *and Sir* John Ashby) *their Proceeding with the Fleet to* Ireland, *and Return from thence.* p. 428

Chap. VI.
Sir Cloudesly Shovell's *Proceedings on the Coast of* Ireland *with a Squadron under his Command.* p. 431

Chap. VII.
Admiral Russell's *Proceedings in the* Soundings *in search of the* French *Fleet; with what happened till the* Reduction *of* Ireland. p. 433

Chap. VIII.
Captain Lawrence Wright *sent with a Squadron of Ships to the* West-Indies; *with an Account of what happened in those Parts during the Time of his Command, and that of Captain* Ralph Wren. p. 451

Chap. IX.
An Account of Admiral Russell's *engaging the* French *Fleet off of* La Hogue, *and of what happened till the Time of his coming on shore.* p. 461

Chap. X.
Sir Francis Wheler's *Proceedings with a Squadron and Land Forces, to and from the* West-Indies. p. 477

Chap. XI.
The Proceedings of Mr. Killegrew, *Sir* Cloudesly Shovell, *and Sir* Ralph Delaval, *joint Admirals of the Fleet in the* Chanel *and* Soundings; *and of Sir* George Rooke *his falling in with the* French *Fleet in* Lagos Bay. p. 480

Chap. XII.
An Account of Sir Francis Wheler's *Proceedings to the* Mediterranean, *to the Time of his unfortunate Loss, and what happened afterwards.* p. 490

Chap.

Contents.

Chap. XIII.
Admiral Ruſſell's *Proceedings with the Fleet in the* Chanel, *with an Account of the Attempt made on* Breſt, *and other French Towns.* p. 495

Chap. XIV.
An Account of Admiral Ruſſell's *Proceedings with the Fleet in the* Mediterranean, *to the Time of his Return to* England. p. 504

Chap. XV.
An Account of Sir George Rooke's *proceeding with a Squadron of Ships as far as the Bay of* Cadiz, *and of his Return to* England. p. 524

Chap. XVI.
Attempts made by John *Lord* Berkeley *on ſeveral of the* French *King's Ports.* p. 526

Chap. XVII.
Captain Robert Wilmot *ſent with a Squadron of Ships and Land Forces to the* Weſt-Indies, *with an Account of his Proceedings.* p. 531

Chap. XVIII.
An Account of the ſpeedy getting together a Squadron of Ships when the French *deſigned to make a Deſcent from* Dunkirk; *with Sir* George Rooke's *Proceedings in the* Chanel *and* Soundings p. 537

Chap. XIX.
John *Lord* Berkeley's *Proceedings with the Fleet in and about the* Chanel, *and of ſeveral Attempts made on the* French *Coaſts.* p. 546

Chap. XX.
Rear-Admiral Benbow's *Proceedings with a Squadron of Ships appointed to cruiſe againſt thoſe of* Dunkirk. p. 549

Chap. XXI.
Rear-Admiral Nevil's *Proceedings to and in the* Weſt-Indies, *with an Account of his engaging a* French *Squadron, and of Mr.* Meeſe *his taking* Petit-Guavas. p. 551

Chap. XXII.
An Account of Monſieur Ponty's *coming with a* French *Squadron to* Newfoundland *while Sir* John Norris *was with a Squadron of* Engliſh *Ships there.* p. 559

Chap. XXIII.
An Account of the Engagement in the Soundings *between a Squadron of* Engliſh *Ships, and that commanded by Monſieur* Ponty. p. 572

Chap.

Contents.

Chap. XXIV.

Sir George Rooke, *Admiral of the Fleet, his Proceedings to and fro in the* Soundings; *with those of Vice-Admiral* Mitchel *in the same Place.* p. 564

Chap. XXV.

Rear-Admiral Benbow's *Proceedings in the* Soundings, *and before* Dunkirk, *being the last Expedition of the War; with Observations on the whole, and a Comparison of the Losses* England *and* France *sustained in their Naval Force during this War.* p. 569

BOOK V.

Containing an Account of the Naval Transactions of the *English,* from the Year 1698, to the Year 1712.

Chap. I.

Rear-Admiral Benbow's *Proceedings in the* West-Indies. p. 575

Chap. II.

Vice-Admiral Aylmer *sent with a Squadron to the* Mediterranean; *Captain* Andrew Leake, *and, after him, Captain* Stafford Fairborn *to* Newfoundland, *and Captain* Thomas Warren *to* Madagascar, *to treat with the Pirates there.* p. 581

Chap. III.

An Account of Sir George Rooke's *Proceedings in the* Baltick, *for reconciling the Kings of* Denmark *and* Sweden. p. 582

Chap. IV.

An Account of Sir George Rooke's *Proceedings with the Fleet in and about the* Chanel, *and the Naval Preparations of the* French. p. 585

Chap. V.

Vice-Admiral Benbow's *Proceedings in the* West-Indies, *and particularly of his engaging a Squadron of* French *Ships in those Parts, till the time of his Death, when the Command devolved on Rear-Admiral* Whetstone. p. 590

Chap. VI.

An Account of Sir William Whetstone's, *Captain* Hovenden Walker's, *and Vice-Admiral* Graydon's *Proceedings in the* West-Indies p. 599

Chap.

Contents.

Chap. VII.
The Earl of Pembroke, *Lord High-Admiral, sends some Ships to bring the Effects of the* English *Merchants from* Cadiz, *upon Suspicion of a War: With the then Naval Preparations of the* French. p. 607

Chap. VIII.
Sir John Munden's *Proceedings for intercepting a Squadron of French Ships bound to the* Groyne, *and thence to the* West-Indies. p. 611

Chap. IX.
The Establishment of six Marine Regiments; with some Observations thereupon. p. 615

Chap. X.
An Account of Sir George Rooke's *Expedition with the Fleet, and the Land Forces under the Duke of* Ormond, *to* Cadiz; *and of the successful Attempt made on the Ships of War and Galleons at* Vigo. p. 619

Chap. XI.
Captain John Leake's *Proceedings with a Squadron of Ships at* Newfoundland. p. 631

Chap. XII.
An Account of what was done by Captain Bazil Beaumont *while at the Head of a Squadron employ'd against the* French *Ships at* Dunkirk. p. 635

Chap. XIII.
A Relation of Sir George Rooke's *Proceedings with the Fleet in and about the* Chanel. p. 640

Chap. XIV.
An Account of Sir Cloudesly Shovell's *Proceedings with a considerable part of the* English *and* Dutch *Fleet in the* Mediterranean. p. 646

Chap. XV.
What Damages were done by the violent Storm in the Year 1703; *and of Rear-Admiral* Beaumont *before* Dunkirk *and* Ostend. p. 656

Chap. XVI.
An Account of Sir George Rooke's *carrying to* Lisbon *the Arch-Duke of* Austria; *and of his Proceedings afterwards to, and engaging the* French *Fleet in the* Mediterranean. p. 662

Chap. XVII.
An Account of Sir John Leake's *relieving* Gibraltar, *and destroying several* French *Ships.* p. 681

f   Chap.

Contents.

Chap. XVIII.

Sir Cloudesly Shovell's *Proceedings in the* Mediterranean, *when appointed joint Admiral of the Fleet with the Earl of* Peterborow *and* Monmouth; *the Landing the King of* Spain *at* Barcelona, *and the Reduction of that important Place.* p. 684

Chap. XIX.

Sir John Leake's *Proceedings on the Coast of* Lisbon *and in the* Mediterranean, *(the Earl of* Peterborow *and* Monmouth *continuing still Admiral of the Fleet, and General of the Forces in* Spain) *and of the Relief of* Barcelona *when besieged by the* French; *as also of the yielding up of* Carthagena *by the* Spaniards; *the taking of the Town and Castle of* Alicant, *and the Surrender of* Yviça *and* Majorca. p. 689

Chap. XX.

An Account of Sir William Whetstone's *Proceedings in the* West-Indies; *with what happened afterwards while Commadore* Kerr, *Sir* John Jennings, *and Mr.* Wager *commanded in those Parts, and particularly of the taking of a Galleon, and other Ships by the latter; as also of the taking another Galleon, and several* French *Ships while Mr.* Littleton *commanded them.* p. 697

Chap. XXI.

Sir Thomas Hardy's *Proceedings in and about the* Soundings, *till order'd to the* Mediterranean; *as also of some of our Ships being taken in their Passage from the* Downs *Westward, and others in the* Soundings. p. 716

Chap. XXII.

The Lord Dursley's *Proceedings with a Squadron in the* Soundings, *and of several* French *Ships taken during his Lordship's Commanding there.* p. 720

Chap. XXIII.

Sir John Norris *sent with a Squadron for intercepting some* French *Ships of War, and Merchant Ships with Corn from the* Baltick. p. 726

Chap. XXIV.

Sir Cloudesly Shovell's *Proceedings to, in, and from the* Mediterranean; *with the beating of our Army in* Spain. *The unsuccessful Attempt on* Thoulon *by the Duke of* Savoy, *and the bombarding of that Place soon after; together with the Loss of Sir* Cloudesly Shovell, *and several of our Ships on the Islands of* Scilly. p. 728

Chap. XXV.

Rear-Admiral Dilkes *his Proceedings while he commanded in the* Mediterranean; *as also of the Loss of* Lerida. p. 734

Chap.

CONTENTS.

CHAP. XXVI.

An Account of Sir Stafford Fairborn's *Expedition to the River* Sherrant; *as also of his Proceedings with a Squadron off of* Ostend, *when part of our Army laid siege to that Place; and of what was done by Sir* Thomas Hardy *in the* Soundings. p. 737

CHAP. XXVII.

A Relation of Sir George Byng's *Proceedings Northward after a Squadron of* French *Ships that sailed from* Dunkirk, *with the Pretender, and a Body of Land-Forces which were intended to land in* Scotland. p. 740

CHAP. XXVIII.

Sir John Leake's *Proceedings with the Fleet in the* Mediterranean. *His landing the Queen of* Spain *and Troops at* Barcelona. *The Surrender of* Sardinia; *as also the taking of the Town and Castle of* Mahon, *while Sir* Edward Whitaker *was at the Head of a Squadron, with the Forces under the Command of General* Stanhope, *and the Pope's owning* Charles *the Third King of* Spain. p. 749

CHAP. XXIX.

Sir George Byng's *Proceedings while he commanded in the* Mediterranean, *with the unsuccessful Attempt made to relieve* Alicant *by the Fleet, and the Troops under the Command of General* Stanhope. p. 756

CHAP. XXX.

Sir Edward Whitaker *his Proceedings while he commanded in the* Mediterranean, *and what was done in those Parts by Vice-Admiral* Baker: *Together with an Account of Admiral* Aylmer's *Proceedings with the Fleet at home; and of the Expedition to, and Reduction of* Port Royal *in* Nova Scotia. p. 761

CHAP. XXXI.

Sir John Norris *his Proceedings while he commanded in the* Mediterranean; *with an Account of the Attempt made on* Cette *and* Adge, *on the Coast of* Languedoc, *and the beating of the* Spanish *Army near* Saragossa. p. 768

CHAP. XXXII.

The unsuccessful Expedition against Quebec, *with a Squadron under the Command of Sir* Hovenden Walker, *and a Body of Troops commanded by General* Hill. p. 775

CHAP. XXXIII.

Sir Hovenden Walker's *Proceedings with a Squadron in the* West-Indies; *with an Account of the Attempts made by the* French *on our Governments of* Antegoa *and* Montserrat; *as also an Account of the terrible Hurricane at* Jamaica. p. 781

CHAP.

Contents.

Chap. XXXIV.

An Account of Sir Thomas Hardy's *Proceedings off of* Dunkirk, *and in the* Soundings; *as also of the delivering up of* Dunkirk *when Sir* John Leake *commanded the Fleet.* p. 786

Chap. XXXV.

Vice-Admiral Baker's *Proceedings while he commanded a Squadron on the Coast of* Portugal. p. 790

Chap. XXXVI.

Sir John Jennings *his Proceedings while he commanded in the* Mediterranean *till the Cessation of Arms: As also his carrying the Emperor from* Barcelona *to* Vado, *and the Empress to* Genoa. *The People of* Barcelona *declare War against* Philip, *and after they are constrained to submit, are inhumanly treated. His carrying the Duke and Duchess of* Savoy *to their Kingdom of* Sicily. *With a Comparison between our Naval Loss and that of the* French *during this War.* p. 793

A COMPLEAT

HISTORY

Of the moſt Remarkable

TRANSACTIONS at SEA.

BOOK I.

Containing a general Account of thoſe People who have flouriſhed at Sea in all Ages.

CHAP. I.

Of the Origin of Navigation, and Invention of Shipping.

IT is highly probable that in few Centuries after the Creation the Continent of the Earth, if not the Iſlands, was as univerſally inhabited as now it is; and that the Deluge occaſioned no conſiderable Alteration in the Terraqueous Globe; but that its Land, Seas, and Rivers were, in a very great Meaſure, the ſame as at this time. This Suppoſition being allowed, it will not be unreaſonable to conjecture that, in the earlieſt Ages of the World, the Uſe of ſmall Embarcations, ſuch as Boats, and other Veſſels neceſſary for paſſing Rivers, was known to Mankind, ſince without them

The firſt Uſe of Embarcations.

Before the Deluge.

them it would not have been possible for the Posterity of *Adam* to have taken Possession of the different Parts of the Earth which God had allotted for their Habitation. If that Knowledge had not been necessary for carrying on this great Design of Providence, *the inhabiting of the Earth*, and we were to suppose, with the Heathens, that the People of each Country were *Aborigines*, and produced out of the several Soils wherein they dwell'd, we cannot reasonably imagine they could long continue ignorant of some Materials proper to waft them on the Water, such as Floats of Rushes, Wood, or the like, to the Use of which they must needs have been soon induced, by observing the Quality of the Water in bearing up things of that kind, which the swelling of Rivers, or other various Accidents, might have forced thereinto.

For inhabiting the World.

By Floats of Rushes, Wood, &c.

To suppose the Use of so small a Part of Navigation before the Flood, will in no wise be derogatory from the Account given thereof in Scripture, nor leave room for objecting, that if it was so early known, it would in fifteen or sixteen Ages have been improved to such Perfection, as that the rest of Mankind might have been as well able to build capacious Vessels, and secure themselves therein from perishing, as *Noah* and his Family: for tho' Man's Advances in Knowledge are usually attained by an equally gradual Progression; yet unforeseen Accidents do oftentimes give Rise to an Invention which the Study of many Ages would not have arrived to. The Inhabitants of *America*, upon the Discovery of that Continent about two hundred Years since by the *Spaniards*, were found to have the Knowledge of such a Navigation as is above described, in small Boats, or Canoos, in the Management whereof they were even more dextrous than the *Europeans*. With the Use of these they had probably been acquainted some thousand Years; but they were no less surprized at the Sight of the *Spanish* Ships, and as totally ignorant of the Structure of such great Bodies, as we may reasonably believe the Contemporaries of *Noah* were with respect to his Ark.

Reasons of no greater Progress.

Instances in the Americans.

In Process of Time the Wickedness of Men grew to such a Height, that the Divine Wisdom thought fit to destroy them from the Face of the Earth; only *Noah* being a just Man, perfect in his Generation, and walking with God, found Grace in his Eyes, and received his Directions for building an Ark of *Gopher*-Wood, 300 Cubits long, 50 Cubits broad, and 30 Cubits high, for the Reception and Security of himself and Family, with those Creatures which were ordained to live, when the Waters should prevail upon the Earth. To this immediate Interposition of God then are we to attribute the Invention of Shipping, as we are to his concurring Providence those Improvements which have been since made therein, and the Perfection it is arrived to at this time. Not many Years after the Flood, there was occasion for the Descendants of *Noah* to put in practice all they had learnt in this Art from their common Father, in order to their arriving at the respective Countries assigned them for their Possession; for in the Days of *Peleg*, who was born a hundred Years after the Waters were dried up, the Scripture tells us the Earth was divided by the Families of the Sons of *Noah*, and, in particular,

Noah's Ark the Original of larger Vessels.

Invention and Improvement of Shipping.

By Noah's Descendants.

Peleg.

lar, that to the Sons of *Japheth* were allotted the Isles of the *Gentiles*; by which are meant not only the Continent of *Europe*, the Northern Parts of *Asia*, and *Asia Minor*, but all the Islands of the *Mediterranean* and *Ægean* Sea. *Kittim*, a Grandson of *Japheth*, is particularly said by *Josephus* to have settled in *Cyprus*, from whence, says he, not only all Islands in general, but most maritime Places are in the *Hebrew* Tongue called *Kittim*. Now of these Islands it is impossible they could have taken Possession without Vessels for Transportation.

<small>Japheth.</small>
<small>Kittim.</small>

CHAP. II.

Of the Improvements in Navigation and Naval Affairs by the Ægyptians, Phœnicians, and Assyrians.

IN the sacred Writings we have no more Footsteps of the Progress of Navigation till the time of *Solomon*, wherefore we must now have recourse to profane History. Heathen Antiquity doth generally attribute to the *Ægyptians* the Invention of Arts and Sciences, and among them that of Navigation: But as the *Greek* and *Roman* Authors were unacquainted with the Writings of *Moses*, we need not wonder at their ascribing that Honour to those who were but Improvers of it; however, we may from thence reasonably conclude that the *Ægyptians* did indeed make considerable Discoveries therein. Their Situation was as advantagious as possibly it could be for the Advancement of this Knowledge, for all the Eastern Shores of their Country were washed by the Red Sea, and the Northern by the *Mediterranean*. *Isis*, who reigned in *Egypt* with her Husband *Osiris*, about the Year of the World 2230, and afterwards engrossed a considerable Part of the Worship of the *Pagan* World under the different Names of *Isis*, *Cybele*, and *Ceres*, among other her Inventions is said to have first taught the Use of Sails. She was thought also, in a peculiar manner, to preside over the Sea, whence it became a Custom for such as had been saved from Shipwreck, to have the Circumstances of their Adventure represented in a Picture, which was hung up in her Temple, as an Acknowledgment of their Obligation to her for their Deliverance; in like manner as is practised at this Day in Popish Countries at the Shrines of their Tutelary Saints. *Tacitus* says the *Suevi*, a People of ancient *Germany*, worshipped her in the Form of a Ship: And as there are now in the Hands of the Curious, *Ægyptian* Medals struck by the Emperor *Julian* the Apostate, wherein she is placed in a Ship, so are there also several Figures where she is represented with one in her Hand. *Pliny* tells us the first Ship which was seen in *Greece* was that in which *Danaus* came thither from *Ægypt*, before which time, says he, only Floats were used, invented by King *Erythras* among the Islands of the Red Sea. To these might be added many other

<small>Navigation farther improved.</small>
<small>1. By the Ægyptians.</small>
<small>Isis.</small>
<small>Suevi.</small>
<small>Danaus.</small>
<small>Erythras.</small>

4   *Of People who have flourished*   Book I.

other Authorities, but thus much will suffice to shew that Heathen Writers have given to the *Ægyptians* the Honour of this Invention.

But tho' their Situation was equally commodious for navigating both to the East and West, yet they seem to have been more particularly intent on the former, and made frequent Voyages to the Southern Coasts of *Arabia*, *Persia*, *India*, and *China*, as well on account of Wars as Traffick, especially after the famous Expedition of *Sesostris*, one of their Kings *, to those Countries, who with a numerous Army reduced the In-land Parts to his Obedience, while his Fleet from the Red Sea, consisting of about 400 Ships, subdued the maritime Coasts.

Sesostris.

These People, the *Ægyptians*, were willing probably to resign the Western Navigation to the *Phœnicians*, who, by reason of their Neighbourhood and Intercourse with them, imitated and at length far exceeded them in this Art. The *Phœnicians* were the first who attempted to sail by Night, and applied the Knowledge of the Stars to Navigation, which they improved to the carrying on a vast Trade to *Greece*, and other Parts of the *European* as well as *African* side of the *Mediterranean*. Their capital Cities, *Tyre* and *Sidon*, were for many Ages the most flourishing *Emporiums* of *Asia*. It was to Colonies of the former that [a] *Byzantium*, the Grecian [b] *Thebes*, [c] *Leptis*, [d] *Byrsa*, and [e] *Utica*, owed their Foundations. These People were so hardy as to venture out on the *Atlantic* Ocean, where they built [f] *Gades*, made several Settlements along the Western Coast of *Spain*, and sailed as far as the *Cassiterides* Islands, whither, after their first Discovery, they made frequent Voyages for Lead and Tin; which they carried into the *Mediterranean*, and gained immense Riches by those useful Commodities. By the *Cassiterides*, most learned Men are of Opinion were understood, in those Times of remote Antiquity, our *British* Islands, or at least as much of them as was known; which 'tis supposed were the Islands of *Scilly*, and Western Parts of *England*, as *Cornwall*, *Devonshire*, and *Somersetshire*, where those Metals are in such great Plenty.

2. By the Phœnicians, &c.

Who build
[a] Constantinople,
[b] Stives,
[c] Tripoli in Barbary,
[d] Carthage,
[e] Biserta,
[f] Cadiz.

And discover the Cassiterides, or British Islands.

When the *Phœnicians* had once adventured out of the *Mediterranean*, they, not content with their Discoveries in *Europe*, sailed southward in the *Atlantic* Ocean, along the Shores of *Africa*, and built several Towns on that Coast. Their Reputation for maritime Affairs induced several Princes of other Nations to employ them in their Service: They were of great Use to the *Assyrian* and *Persian* Emperors in their Naval Wars with *Greece*, and other Countries; and *Herodotus* tells us, that *Neco*, King of *Ægypt*, after he had laid aside his Project of cutting a Canal from the *Nile* to the Red Sea, sent out some *Phœnicians* to make Discoveries; who sailing from that Sea, launched into the Southern Ocean, where, when *Autumn* came on, they landed in *Libya*, sowed Corn, and stayed till it was ripe, whence, having got in their Harvest, they departed; and when they had been absent two Years, arrived the third in *Ægypt*, by way of the [g] Pillars of *Hercules*: They reported, says he, what who-

And Atlantic Ocean.

Employed by Pharoah Neco.

[g] *Streights of Gibraltar.*

---

* Vid. Diod. Sic. p. 28, 29. *a Ship* 280 *Cubits long.*

so will may believe for me, that, in their Passage about *Africa*, they had the Sun on their Right Hand; and in this manner, he goes on, was *Lybia* first known. Which, by the by, is an ample Testimony that the Cape of *Good Hope* was known, and doubled by the Ancients, and that too, long before the Time of *Hanno* the *Carthaginian*, whom we shall have occasion hereafter to mention in his proper Place. *Cape of* Good Hope.

These People were not less powerful in a Naval Force, than expert in Navigation, being reckoned in the List *Eusebius* has given us of those Nations who usurped the Dominion of the Sea; and *Quintus Curtius* says of the City of *Tyre*, that for a long time it held in Subjection not only the neighbouring Seas, but those also wheresoever its Fleets were sent. Whence a *Tyrian* Sea became a proverbial Expression for any Sea possessed in such a manner, as that a free Navigation in it was not allowed without the Consent of the Lord, or Proprietor thereof. That City in a short time eclipsed the Glory of *Sidon*, of which it was at first a Colony, and continued in a flourishing Condition several Ages, its Inhabitants abounding in the Wealth and Riches of the then known World, till they drew upon themselves the Displeasure of *Nebuchadnezzar* King of *Babylon*, who after a Siege of thirteen Years took the City, and levell'd it with the Ground. Tyrians, &c. Old Tyre *destroyed,* by Nebuchadnezzar;

The *Tyrians* who were saved from this Destruction, rebuilt their City in a neighbouring Island, about a Mile from the Shore, which soon acquired the Reputation of the ancient *Tyre*, and at length exceeded it. It continued in this Prosperity till the Time of *Alexander the Great*, who, after a Siege of seven Months, utterly destroyed it, and sold 30000 of its Inhabitants into Slavery. and New Tyre by Alexander.

There is no doubt to be made that the *Phœnicians* had a considerable Sea Force, as hath been alledged; otherwise they could not have established the several Colonies we are assured they did, and have dispossessed the Inhabitants of those Places they chose to settle in: But the first Naval Armament we read of in History, is that of the *Assyrians* under their Queen *Semiramis*. That Princess being engaged in an Expedition for adding *India* to her Empire, caused to be built in *Bactriana*, an Inland Province of her Dominions, two thousand Vessels with brazen Beaks, which were formed in such manner as to be carried in Parts Over-land by Camels to the River *Indus*, where they were to be joined together and made use of. Though this Fleet was thus numerous, we cannot conceive any great Idea of its Force, the Vessels of which it consisted being doubtless but very small, since they were carried Over-land in the manner before-mentioned. The King of *India*, to oppose these Preparations, had gotten together upon the same River 4000 Vessels, formed of a kind of Reed which grew there in great Plenty. These numerous Fleets came at length to an Engagement, wherein the *Assyrians* obtained the Victory, sinking a thousand of the other's Vessels; but passing the River, they were brought to a Battel ashore, wherein they received a total Defeat from the *Indian* King, and *Semiramis* was obliged to return precipitately into her own Dominions. But we must not omit, Assyrians *first made Naval Armaments.* Semiramis invades India. Her Naval *Victory:* But beaten at Land, *retires.*

omit, for the Honour of the *Phœnicians*, that they were of the Number (and probably the greatest part) of those who were employed on board *Semiramis*'s Fleet, the rest being *Syrians*, *Ægyptians*, *Cypriots*, and *Cilicians*, with other the maritime Inhabitants of *Asia Minor*, as far as the *Hellespont*.

CHAP. III.

Of the Greeks *in general, and those among them and the neighbouring Nations, who held the Dominion of the Sea, according to* Eusebius's *Catalogue.*

<small>3. By the Greeks.</small>

FROM *Ægypt* and *Phœnicia* the *Greeks* learned the Lessons of Navigation, and challenged to themselves the Honour of several Improvements therein. They seem to have applied themselves more to the making it serviceable in War than Traffick, or voyaging to distant Countries to make Discoveries, and confined their Navigation to the *Mediterranean* Sea; out of which we do not read they so much as once ventured before the Time of *Colæus* the *Samian*, 600 Years after the Expedition of the *Argonauts*, and then no farther than to *Tartessus*, at the Mouth of the River *Bætis*, the modern *Guadalquivir*, where St. *Lucar* now stands.

<small>Their Naval Armaments.</small>
<small>Argonauts.</small>
<small>Tartessus.</small>

<small>4. By the Cretans.</small>
<small>Minos *reduces the* Carians, &c.</small>

In the early Ages of *Greece* the maritime People of it, and those of the neighbouring Islands in the *Ægean* Sea, together with the *Carians* and *Phœnicians*, practised Piracy, and committed Depredations on that Sea and the adjacent Coasts; till *Minos*, King of *Crete*, fitted out a considerable Fleet, with which he soon reduced them. This Prince became so considerable as to make himself absolutely Master of the *Grecian* Sea, that is, that part of the *Ægean* which is between *Crete* and *Græcia propria*, reducing to his Obedience the Islands *Cyclades* situate therein, planting Colonies in them under the Conduct of his Sons, dispossessing their piratical and temporary Inhabitants, and keeping a constant Force cruising against the Rovers, for the safe Conveyance of his Revenues arising from those Islands to *Crete*. He is said to be the first who fought a Naval Battel, (in the *Mediterranean* it must be meant) and is placed at the Head of *Eusebius*'s Catalogue of those who were celebrated for their Dominion at Sea; whom we shall here mention in the order that Author has transmitted them to us.

<small>*and* Cyclades.</small>
<small>Plants Colonies.</small>

<small>His Naval Battels.</small>

The *Cretans*, under the Successors of *Minos*, maintained the Reputation at Sea which that Prince had acquired for about 175 Years; when the *Lydians*, or *Mæonians*, a People of *Asia Minor*, became celebrated for their Naval Dominion, and continued so for about 120 Years. To them succeeded the *Pelasgi*, a People of *Greece*, whose Credit lasted 85 Years. After them the *Thracians* ruled at Sea for 89 Years, whose Successors in that Power were the *Rhodians*, with whom it remained, according to our Author, 23 Years.

<small>5. By the Lydians, &c.</small>
<small>Pelasgi.</small>
<small>Thracians.</small>
<small>Rhodians.</small>

Next

Next to these are placed the *Phrygians*, who had Dominion of the Sea 25 Years, about the Time of *Lycurgus*, and were succeeded by the *Cypriots*, who held it 23. They are followed by the *Phœnicians*; but as *Eusebius* mentions not how long they were powerful at Sea, so was it, in my Opinion, wisely omitted; for as they were remarkable a great while before any in this List mentioned, so do they deserve a much higher Place in it. *Phrygians. Cypriots. Phœnicians.*

The *Ægyptians*, continues the Author, possessed the Seas under their Kings *Psammis* and *Bocchoris*, who reigned a little before the Beginning of the Olympiads. These were succeeded by the *Milesians*, the People of *Miletus*, a considerable City of *Ionia*; the Time of whose Superiority is likewise omitted: But *Stephanus de Urbibus* says, the City of *Naucratis* in *Egypt* was built by them when they were Masters of the Sea, which was about the Time of *Romulus*. A Colony of that People also founded *Sinope* in *Paphlagonia*, upon the *Euxine* Sea, which became a City of great Trade, and, as *Strabo* says, had the absolute Dominion of that Sea as far as the *Cyanean* Islands, that is, to the Mouth of the *Thracian Bosphorus*, or inner Streights of *Constantinople*, where those Islands lie. *Ægyptians. Milesians. build Naucratis, and Sinope.*

The *Carians*, a People of *Asia Minor*, are the next who are here celebrated for their Sea Dominion; after whom the People of *Lesbos*, an Island of the *Ægean*, obtained the supreme Power; which they held for 69 Years; and were succeeded in it by the *Phocæans*, the Inhabitants of *Phocæa*, a City of *Æolis*, about the Time of the *Babylonish* Captivity, with whom it continued 44 Years. A Colony of theirs, in the Time of *Tarquinius Priscus*, came into the Mouth of the *Tyber*, entered into Amity with the *Romans*, and thence went into *Gaul* and built *Massilia*, the modern *Marseilles*. *Carians. Lesbians. Phocæans, built Massilia.*

The People of *Naxos*, one of the *Cyclades* Islands, next obtained the Dominion of the Sea, which they possessed 10 Years, at the time *Cambyses* was King of *Persia*, when it fell to the Inhabitants of *Eretria*, a City of the Island *Eubœa*, and with them remained 7 Years. *Naxians. Eretrians.*

The last in this Account of *Eusebius* are the People of *Ægina*, an Island in the Gulf between *Athens* and *Peloponnesus*, whose Naval Power lasted 20 Years, till *Darius*, the Successor of *Cambyses*, sent his Embassadors to demand Earth and Water of the Cities of *Greece*, at which time the *Æginetans* submitted to his Authority. We are not however to suppose that they were not after this Masters of a Sea Force; for we find that in following Times, by reason thereof, and their Neighbourhood to the *Athenians*, they became so obnoxious to those People, that they cut off the Thumbs of all such as they took Prisoners, to disable them for further Service at Sea. *A barbarous Cruelty! which tho' committed under the specious Pretence of the publick Profit, is by* Tully, *in his Book of Offices, wherein he handles that Subject, very justly condemned.* But of these things more at large, when we shall come to treat of the *Grecian* Affairs in particular, which will furnish out a considerable Part of the ensuing History. *Æginetans. Athenians, their Cruelty.*

CHAP.

Chap. IV.

Of the Navigations and Naval Power of the Hebrews under David and Solomon.

Navigation of the Jews.

WE are not to imagine that the Naval Dominion of the People in the foregoing Catalogue was so extensive as to reach all over the *Mediterranean*: for, on the contrary, excepting that of the *Cypriots*, *Phœnicians*, and *Ægyptians*, we have reason to believe it reach'd not farther than in and about the *Ægean* Sea; for during the time that their Succession to each other takes up, we are assur'd there were other Nations more considerable at Sea, both in Number and Strength of Ships, than 'tis probable most of the forementioned were. About the time the *Pelasgi* are celebrated for their Superiority, we read of the great Fleets of *David* and *Solomon*, which, under the Conduct of the *Phœnicians*, carried on in the *Mediterranean*, from the Port of *Joppa*, the Trade to *Tarshish* for those Princes, as they did likewise in the *Red* Sea and *Indian* Ocean to *Ophir*. Also between the Time that the Dominion of the *Phocæans* and *Naxians* is placed, we learn from *Thucydides* that the *Corinthians* and *Ionians* were considerable at Sea, and immediately after them *Polycrates*, Tyrant of *Samos*, a noted Island of the *Ægean*, was very potent in that Sea, and reduced several of its Islands to his Obedience, whom therefore 'tis to be wonder'd *Eusebius* has omitted in his Account. Of these we shall take notice in the order we have mention'd them.

Fleets of David and Solomon.

Corinthians. Ionians. Samians. (Polycrates vide post.)

David's Riches.

The Scripture gives us an Account of the immense Wealth *David* had amassed together for the building of the Temple, who in his Instructions to his Son *Solomon*, says he had prepared for that purpose an hundred thousand Talents of Gold, a thousand thousand Talents of Silver, and of Brass and Iron without Weight; and in another Place, he, to induce the People to contribute to the Charge, tells them the particular Use for which part of it was designed, *viz.* three thousand Talents of the Gold of *Ophir*, and seven thousand Talents of refined Silver to overlay the Walls of the Houses; besides which he had the *Onyx*, and all manner of precious Stones in Abundance.

How disposed.

We cannot reasonably suppose all his Wealth was designed for this End, but that there was a very considerable part made use of to defray the necessary Expences of his Government; yet *Josephus* assures us that he left behind him more than any Prince of the *Hebrews*, or of any other Nation ever did; and this appeared from the great Treasure *Solomon*, in an unusual Strain of Magnificence, buried with him in his Sepulchre, which on two several pressing Emergencies of the State, was, about 1300 Years afterwards opened, and out of it were taken the first time 3000 Talents, and the next likewise a very great Sum. The same Author tells us of the particular Intercourse *David* had with *Hiram*, King of *Tyre*, and 'tis also

His Sepulchre.

Confederacy with Hiram.

CHAP. IV.　*at Sea in all Ages.*　9

also plain from him that he had Ports in the *Mediterranean* Sea; so that we cannot any other way account for his immense Riches, than by concluding that he did, as well as his Son *Solomon*, send out his Fleets to *Tarshish* and *Ophir*, to import to him the Wealth of those Countries. But we need not depend on Conjectures in this Matter; for *Eupolemus*, an ancient Author quoted by *Eusebius*, expressly says that he built a Fleet at *Achanis*, a City of *Arabia*, (the *Ezion Geber* of the Scripture) which he sent, with several expert Miners on board, to *Urphen*, an Island abounding in Gold, from whence they brought to *Judæa* great Quantities thereof. *His Fleet, &c.*

This *Urphen* is concluded by the Learned to be the same as *Ophir*; but where that *Ophir* was, they are much divided in Opinion. *Josephus* says 'tis the same as was in his time called *The Land of Gold*. Some have thought it to be the *Aurea Chersonesus* of *Ptolemy*, the *Peninsula* of *India* beyond *Ganges* of the Moderns. *Ortelius* tells us, that in *Vatablus*'s Bible printed by *Robert Stephens*, 'tis said to be the Island *Hispaniola* in *America*; that *Postellus*, *Goropius*, and *Arias Montanus* were of Opinion it was the Kingdom of *Peru*; but it doth not in the least appear probable to him that it was any Part of *America*; for that, besides the vast distance of that Continent from *Judæa*, we never find it produced Elephants, which it must have done to have been the *Ophir* of *Solomon*, from whence we read his Ships brought him Ivory. Indeed his Opinion seems by much the most likely to be true, who believes it to be the Eastern Coast of *Africa*, particularly that Part of it which is now called *Sofala*, a Country abounding in Gold Mines, and whose Inhabitants are said by the *Portuguese*, who discovered it to the *Europeans* in these latter Ages, to have Chronicles written in their own Tongue, wherein mention is made of *Solomon*'s being supplied every third Year with Gold from thence. *A Digression concerning Ophir. Sofala.*

To confirm this Conjecture of *Ortelius*'s, may be added what modern Travellers relate of a People of the neighbouring Island of *Madagascar*, term'd *Zaffe Hibrahim*, that is, the Race of *Abraham*, and those of a small Island adjacent called the Isle of *Abraham*, that they observe the *Jewish* Sabbath, and give not only a faint Account of the Creation of the World and Fall of Man, but also some broken Passages of the sacred History concerning *Noah* and *Abraham*, *Moses* and *David*. Which People differing thus in Religion from the neighbouring Inhabitants on every side, who are all Pagans, are doubtless the Descendants of some of the *Hebrews* who either settled there, or suffered Shipwreck in the time of this Intercourse between *Judæa* and those Countries. *Madagascar, &c.*

Authors do not much more agree in their Sentiments about *Tarshish*, some believing it to be *Tarsus* in *Cilicia*, some the City of *Carthage*, and some the *Mediterranean* Sea in general. Others think it was the *Tartessus* of profane Authors, with which Opinion, in part, concurs that of the learned Monsieur *Huet*, who says *Tarshish* was a general Name for all the Western Coast of *Africa* and *Spain*, and in particular the Country about the *Guadalquivir*, very fertile in Mines of Silver; at the Mouth of which River (the *Bætis* *And Tarshish. (Vide ante.)*

C

Bætis of the Ancients) the City of *Tarteſſus* ſtood. But to return from this Digreſſion.

Solomon's Navigation

Solomon, according to the ſingular Prudence with which he was endued from Heaven, improved the advantagious Circumſtances his Father left him in, to the aggrandizing his Kingdom, and increaſing the Wealth of his Subjects. To this purpoſe he took care to culti-

and Confederacy with Hiram.

vate the Friendſhip *David* had begun with *Hiram*, King of *Tyre*, and gave him twenty Cities in the Land of *Galilee*. By his Aid and Aſſiſtance he brought into a regular Order the Sea-Force of which his Father had laid the Foundation, and became very intent

His Sea-Ports, Ezion-Geber.

on purſuing the gainful Voyages to *Ophir* and *Tarſhiſh*. The Port for the firſt was *Ezion-Geber* on the *Red Sea*, and for the latter *Joppa* in the *Mediterranean*. To *Ezion-Geber the Scripture tells

* Vide ante. Achanis, and Ioppa.

us he went himſelf, and to *Joppa*, which was almoſt in the Neighbourhood of *Jeruſalem*, 'tis very probable he did the ſame, to give the neceſſary Directions for thoſe Expeditions, and encourage his People by his Preſence and perſonal Concern in the Preparations. From

The Imports of his Fleets, &c.

thoſe Countries we read they brought him Gold and Silver, with precious Stones, Almug-Trees, and Ivory; and that the Weight of Gold which came to him in one Year on his own Account, beſides what he had of the Merchants, of the Kings of *Arabia*, and the Governours of the Country, was 666 Talents. After the Death of this great Prince, the inteſtine Diviſions of his Kingdom, which was rent in two, admitted not of any Opportunity for cultivating their Naval Affairs, which from thence forward totally declined, notwithſtand-

Jehoſaphat.

ing the Efforts *Jehoſaphat*, one of Succeſſors, made in vain to revive them.

Chap. V.

Of the Corinthians, Ionians, Polycrates *the Tyrant of* Samos, *the* Perſians, Athenians, Lacedæmonians, Maſſilians, Tyrrhenians, Spinetans, *and* Carthaginians.

The Navigation of the Corinthians.

WE come next in order to the *Corinthians*, who, as *Thucydides* tells us, firſt changed the Form of Shipping into the neareſt to thoſe in uſe in his time; that at *Corinth*, 'twas reported were made the firſt Gallies of all *Greece*; and that they furniſhed themſelves with a conſiderable Navy, ſcoured the Sea of Pirates, and by their Traffick both by Sea and Land mightily encreaſed the Revenue of their City.

Ionians.

After this, continues he, the *Ionians* in the times of *Cyrus*, and of his Son *Cambyſes*, got together a great Navy, and making War on *Cyrus*, obtained for a time the Dominion of that Part of the

Polycrates.

Sea which lieth on their own Coaſt. Alſo *Polycrates*, who in the time of *Cambyſes* was Tyrant of *Samos*, had a ſtrong Navy, wherewith

with he subdued divers of the Islands, and among the rest, having wone *Rhenea*, consecrated the same to *Apollo* of *Delos*. He was so considerable, we learn from *Herodotus*, as to be able to assist *Cambyses* with forty Gallies of three Tire of Oars, towards the Reduction of *Ægypt*, and at the same time to keep at home a sufficient Force for the security of the Islands, and asserting his Dominion of the Sea.

His Gallies, &c.

About this time we find the *Persians* began to make a great Figure in Naval Power, as did their Rivals therein the *Athenians* and *Lacedæmonians*, of whom we shall defer what we have to say till we come to handle the *Grecian* Sea-Affairs at large, wherewith those of the *Persians* are intermixed.

Persians. Athenians. Lacedæmonians.

'Twas in the time of *Cyrus* that, upon the occasion of the Successes of *Harpagus*, his Lieutenant in *Ionia*, the Colony of *Phocæans* before mentioned left their City, and after several Adventures settled near the Mouth of the *Rhosne* in *France*, and built * *Massilia*. These we are now to consider under the Name of *Massilians*, who derived from their Ancestors an Aptitude for Naval-Affairs, and in a short time grew considerable therein, so that to reduce the growing Power of these strangers in those Seas, the *Tyrrhenians* and *Carthaginians* associated themselves, and with a Fleet of one hundred and twenty Sail, engaged that of the *Massilians* of not above half the number, off of the Island of *Sardinia*; who after a long and doubtful Battel, wherein several Ships were sunk and taken on both sides, were at length forced to yield with the loss of thirty. This discouraged them for the present, but in after times they renewed their application to Sea-Affairs with great diligence, and became a very flourishing and powerful People. They planted several Colonies upon the Coasts of *Gaul*, *Italy* and *Spain*, and were amongst the earliest who adventured upon long Voyages out of the *Mediterranean*, *Euthymenes* having advanced Southward in the Ocean as far as the *Ægnator*, and *Pytheas* having sailed Northward, and made great Discoveries along the Coast of *Europe*, both of them Natives of *Marseilles*.

Massilians.

* *Marseilles.*

Beaten by the Carthaginians, &c.

Euthymenes.

Pytheas.

In these parts of the *Mediterranean* had flourished for some Ages the *Tyrrhenians*, (People of the Modern *Tuscany*) who from the Dominion they for a long time held therein, imposed on that part of it which is adjacent to the South and West Coasts of *Italy*, the Name of the *Tyrrhene* Sea. While they were Masters on that side of *Italy*, there ruled in the *Adriatick* the People of *Spina*, (a Town on the Southermost Mouth of the *Po*) who maintained their Sovereignty there for many Years, and flourishing in Wealth consecrated to *Apollo* of *Delos* the Tenth of their Maritime Revenues, which contributed not a little to the immense Riches of that Temple.

Tyrrhenians.

Spinetans.

The *Carthaginians* were now very considerable in Naval Affairs, wherein they had been improving themselves from the very Foundation of their City; following herein the Genius of the *Tyrians* from whom they descended. They, by degrees, made themselves Masters not only of all the Northern Coast of *Africa*, from *Ægypt* to the Pillars

Carthaginians.

Their Naval Conquests

Pillars of *Hercules*, and of a great part of the Western Coast of that Continent, but also the Islands *Sicily*, *Sardinia*, *Corsica*, *Majorca* and *Minorca*, together with the Kingdom of *Spain*, and arrived at such a degree of Wealth and Power, as to be able for a long time to contend with the *Romans*, not only for the Dominion of the Sea, but that of the World itself: The Naval Wars between which People, will in the proper place of this History be particularly treated of. The Foundation of the *Carthaginian* Greatness, was the vast Commerce they carried on to all the parts of the then known World; to the discovery of much of which they were very instrumental, having sent out several Adventurers on that Errand. *Pliny* tells us, that *Hanno*, in the flourishing times of *Carthage*, sailed round *Africa* from *Gades* (i. e. *Cadiz*) to the end of *Arabia*, and published an Account of his Voyage, as *Himilco* did of his likewise, who was sent at the same time to make Discoveries along the Coast of *Europe*.

and Commerce.

Chap. VI.

Of the Naval Power of the Romans.

Romans.

THE *Romans*, as Sir *Henry Savil* hath observed in his excellent Annotations upon *Tacitus*, notwithstanding their City was so commodiously situated for Maritime Affairs, being not above fifteen Miles from the *Tyrrhene* Sea, upon a River of a convenient Breadth, yet seem to have wholly neglected all Naval Concerns for some hundred Years after the Building of *Rome*; which is by many assigned as one principal Cause of the continuance of that State so long in Integrity, and free from that Corruption, which some Systems of Politicks pretend is occasioned by a Traffick at Sea, and Intercourse with Foreigners But at length having reduced all *Italy* to their Obedience, and observing that their Coasts lay exposed to the Depredations of the *Carthaginians*, who held uncontested the Dominion of the Sea derived from their Ancestors, they became sensible of their Error, and determined diligently to apply themselves to Naval-Affairs, having before, as *Polybius* informs us, not any Vessels with Decks, or long Ships, or so much as a Passage Boat, but what they borrowed. As for Gallies with five Tire of Oars, so serviceable in War, they had no manner of Notion of them, till by accident one of those of the *Carthaginians* ran ashore near *Rhegium*, in the Streight of *Messana*, which being seized by them served as a Model to build by. This Work they immediately set about, and the Men they were to employ having never been at Sea, they caused Banks to be erected on the Shore, in the same order as in the Gally, and thereon exercised them in the use of their Oars, how to dip, and how to recover them out of the Water. But to say truth, the Assertion of *Polybius*, that this was the first time these People adventured to Sea, can by no means be reconciled with what

Their Naval Affairs.

Their first Pattern for their Gallies, &c.

Their Fleets.

CHAP. VI.   *at Sea in all Ages.*   13

what is by all the *Roman* Authors alledged on occasion of the *Ta-* *In the Taren-*
rentine War some Years before, namely that there being an ancient *tine War.*
Treaty with the *Tarentines*, that the *Romans* should not pass with
their Ships beyond the Promontory of *Lacinium*; the *Duumvir* (*a Cape Ri-*
nevertheless going with a Fleet of ten Ships to survey the Coasts of *zuto.*)
Magna Græcia, went into the Gulph of *Tarentum*, beyond that
Promontory; where four of the Ships were taken, one sunk, and
he himself slain by the *Tarentines*: From which it is plain, that the
Romans had used the Sea long before. It is certain, that in the time
of the first *Punick* War, they were more than ordinarily intent on *First Punick*
Naval Affairs, and made most considerable Advances therein; for *Po-* *War.*
lybius tells us, they in the 5th Year of that War, fitted out one hun-
dred Gallies with five Tire of Oars, and twenty with three. *Lucius*
Florus increaseth the whole number to one hundred and sixty, which
Fleet, says he, within sixty Days after the Wood was cut down in the
Forest, rode at Anchor on the Sea: Of so wonderful dispatch must they
be who would be Sovereigns of the World. In the 9th Year *Regulus*
sailed to *Africa* with three hundred and fifty Gallies. The Consuls
Æmilius and *Fulvius* had three hundred and sixty four Ships of Service in the same War, which number can hardly be matched again in
the *Roman* State for many Years after. In the second *Punick* War *and second*
we find one hundred and sixty, and two hundred, or not much above. *Punick War.*
Against *Antiochus* King of *Syria* they fitted out but eighty, and the
like at other times in their more flourishing Condition. Altho' the
highest number beforementioned of three hundred sixty four Ships
seem not to be so very considerable, yet such, and so great was the
Fleet, by reason of the Quality of the Ships, that not only the *Gre-*
cian, but even the *Persian* Power, which covered the Sea with one *The Fleets of*
thousand and two hundred Sail, could not in *Polybius*'s Opinion *Pompey*,
stand in any Competition therewith for Strength. After *Polybius*'s
time, *Pompey* had not above two hundred and seventy to reduce
the Pirates; but in the Civil War he commanded six hundred long
Ships compleatly manned and stored. And *Augustus*, after he had *Augustus*.
forced *Sextus Pompeius* out of *Italy*, had six Hundred long Ships
of his own, besides seventeen which fled with that *Pompey*, and the *Mark Antho-*
Navy of *Mark Anthony*; who soon after at the Battle of *Actium* *ny*.
furnished five hundred Ships of War, where *Augustus* had but two
hundred and fifty; and this was the greatest Sea Force the *Romans*
were ever Masters of; for as to what we read of one Thousand six *Sylla and*
Hundred Sail with *Sylla* out of *Asia*, and a Thousand with *Ger-* *Germanicus*.
manicus in *Germany*, and such like, we are not to understand them
to be other than Transport Vessels.

After the Conclusion of the Civil War, *Augustus* having for the
Security of the Empire disposed his Legions in the most advanta- *Augustus's*
gious manner by Land, established also for its Guard by Sea two sta- *Stationary or*
tionary Fleets in *Italy*, one at *Misenum*, (the northernmost of the two *Guard Fleets*
Promontories that shoot from the Gulph of *Naples*) to protect *at Misenum*
and keep in Obedience *Gaul*, *Spain*, *Africa*, *Ægypt*, *Sardinia*,
and *Sicily*; and the other at *Ravena* in the *Adriatick*, to de- *and Ravenna*.
fend and bridle *Illyricum*, *Greece*, *Crete*, *Cyprus*, and *Asia*. He
had

in the Euxine *and* Red Sea.

had also in the *Euxine* Sea a Fleet of forty Sail, for the Security of the Countries adjacent thereto, with another of a hundred and thirty on the *Red Sea*, for the Protection of *Ægypt* on that side, and of the Trade to *Arabia* and *India*. Beside these, which remained as the ordinary Defence of the Empire, *Tacitus* tells us that *Augustus* sent the beaked Gallies which were taken at the Battle of *Actium*, and very well manned, to remain at [b] *Forum Julii* for the Security of the neighbouring Coast of *Gaul:* And in several of the Provinces were also the proper Gallies of those Countries. The Emperor *Claudius* having reduced *Britain* into the Form of a *Roman* Province, also added the *British* Fleet for the Guard of *Britain* and the Isles adjacent; and not only by Sea, but also upon the great Rivers which bounded the Empire, several Squadrons were maintained, as the *German* Squadron upon the *Rhine*, and those of the *Danube* and *Euphrates* upon those Rivers.

([b] Frejus in Provenæ.)

In the British Seas,

and on the Rhine, &c.

CHAP. VII.

Of the Cilicians, Veneti *of* Gaul, Goths, Saxons, Saracens, *and* Normans.

Naval Affairs of the Cilicians, Cypriots, and Pamphylians. ([a] Streights of Gibraltar.)

IN the times next preceding the Subversion of the *Roman* Commonwealth by *Julius Cæsar*, were formidable at Sea the Pirates of *Cilicia*, who being joined by great Numbers of *Syrians*, *Cypriots*, and *Pamphylians*, with many of the Inhabitants of *Pontus*, rendered themselves for a considerable time Masters of the *Mediterranean*, from *Syria* to the [a] Pillars of *Hercules*, and defeated several *Roman* Officers who were sent against them.

They assist Mithridates.

In the Wars between the *Romans* and *Mithridates* King of *Pontus*, they espoused the Part of that Prince, (who indeed first set them to work) and did him important Services. The long Continuance of those Wars, and the intervening Civil War between *Marius* and *Sylla*, gave the *Cilicians* a favourable Opportunity to increase their Numbers and Strength, which they did not fail to improve, and in a short time grew so powerful, that they not only took and robbed all the *Roman* Ships they met with, but also ravaged many of the Islands and maritime Provinces, where they plundered above four hundred Cities, extending their Depredations even to the Mouth of the *Tyber*, from whence they took several Vessels loaden with Corn. Their Force consisted of above a thousand Ships, of an excellent Built for Celerity, stored with all kind of Arms for their Piratical Expeditions, manned with hardy and expert Seamen and Soldiers, and conducted by vigilant and experienced Officers; so that they were now grown so considerable, as it became a Work of great Importance to the *Romans* to subdue them, though then almost arrived at the highest Pitch of Power their State ever attained to. No less a Person than *Pompey* was chosen

Make Depredations on the Romans.

Their Navy.

CHAP. VII.   *at Sea in all Ages.*   15

for the Reduction of them, with a Commission giving him the supreme Command of all the Sea within the Pillars of *Hercules*, and of the Land for fifty Miles from the Shore, with Power to take what Number of Ships and Troops he thought fit, and six thousand *Attick* Talents, that is, above a Million of our Money, without Account. Thus, with the Assistance of fifteen inferior Admirals, whom he disposed with their Squadrons in several proper Stations in the *Mediterranean*, himself sailing about and giving the necessary Orders, he in few Months cleared the Sea of the Pirates, to many thousands of whom he extended Mercy, and assigned them Habitations in the inland Parts of *Cilicia*. *Pirates destroyed and suppressed by Pompey.*

In few Years after we find the [b] *Veneti*, a People of ancient *Gaul*, to be very considerable in the Ocean, where they had great Numbers of Ships, and carried on a Trade to *Britain*. These People, as we learn from *Cæsar*, exercised a Dominion on the Sea that washes their Coast, exacting Tribute of all such as navigated therein, it being an open and tempestuous Sea, with few Ports of which they were Masters. *Veneti of Gaul. ([b] Those of and about Vannes in Bretagne.) Their Naval Force*

They gave *Cæsar* more trouble to subdue them than any of the rest of *Gaul*, their Naval Force obliging him to build a numerous Fleet of Ships on the *Loire*, and make a general Levy of Seamen from the remotest Parts of his Government. The *Veneti*, for their Defence, made great Preparations, and by their Aid from *Britain* and the Northern Coasts of *Gaul*, got together a Fleet of two hundred and twenty Ships, compleatly manned and furnished with all kinds of Arms: But at length coming to an Engagement, they were totally defeated by means of a Stratagem the *Romans* made use of, who with Scythes fixed to the end of long Poles, cut to pieces their Rigging, and deprived them of the Use of their Sails, whereon they greatly depended; which Victory was followed by the entire Reduction of that People to the Power of *Cæsar*. *subdued by Cæsars Stratagem.*

In the declining Times of the *Roman* Empire, the *Goths* of several Denominations leaving their Habitations in the North, came down in Swarms to the *Roman* Frontiers, and at length penetrating them in several Places, got down to the Shores of the *Mediterranean*, and providing themselves of Fleets, grew very powerful there, and crossing over to *Africa*, possessed themselves of its Coasts on that Sea, in all Parts whereof they committed great Depredations, and maintain'd long Naval Wars with the *Roman* Emperors. *The Goths. Their Naval Wars and Depredations.*

About the same times the *Cimbri* and *Saxons*, who inhabited the Country now called *Denmark*, and the North-West Parts of *Germany*, employed very numerous Fleets of small Ships on the *German* Ocean, on which frequently embarked great Multitudes of those then barbarous Nations, and made Descents on the Coasts of *Flanders*, *France*, and *Britain*, and committed many Disorders on the interjacent Seas; till invited by the Inhabitants of the Southern Parts of *Britain* to aid them against their Countrymen of the North, at length the greatest Number of them settled and established themselves there. *The Saxons and Cimbri (i. e. Cambrians.) Invade Britain, &c.*

About

The Saracens *with a Naval Force*

take Cyprus, Rhodes, &c.

Syracuse,

Barbary,

Spain,

Capua, Genoa, &c.

Beat the Venetians, &c.

About two Centuries after this, the *Saracens*, originally of *Arabia*, became a formidable Nation, and very potent at Sea. They soon extended their Conquests over *Syria* and *Ægypt*, and sailing from *Alexandria* with a numerous Fleet, took the Islands of *Cyprus* and *Rhodes*, and passing into the *Archipelago*, seized and plundered many of the Islands there. From thence they went into *Sicily*, took *Syracuse*, spoiled the Sea-Coasts, burnt and destroyed the inland Country, and at length with immense Multitudes overran all *Barbary*, from *Ægypt* to the Streights of *Gibraltar*; when passing over into *Spain*, they reduced it wholly to their Obedience, except *Asturia* and *Biscay*. Breaking into *Italy*, they took *Capua* and *Genoa*, and laid waste all the adjacent Coasts. A very considerable Fleet of the *Venetians* which was sent out against them, they engaged off *Sicily*, and took or destroyed the most part of it with great Slaughter. By the prosperous Condition of their Sea Affairs chiefly, they at length arrived to such a Height of Power, as that their Dominions at one time extended from the Gulph of *Persia* to the Bay of *Cadiz*: And of the Numerousness of their Fleets we may well judge by that wherewith *Muhavias*, one of their celebrated Leaders, invaded and took *Cyprus*, which consisted of *seventeen hundred* Sail.

Note.

The Norman *Fleets infest the* Ocean, Mediterranean, Flanders, France, *&c.*

Toward the Decline of the *Saracen* Power, the *Normans*, a People of *Norway*, left their frozen Habitations, and infesting the Ocean and Mediterranean Seas with numerous Fleets, render'd themselves formidable to all maritime People. They cruelly ravaged and laid waste the Coasts of *Flanders*, *France*, *Spain*, and *Italy*; and at length obliged the *French* to assign them a Country to settle in, the same that is now from them called *Normandy*.

CHAP. VIII.

Of the Venetians, Pisans, Genoese, Portuguese, Spaniards, *and* Dutch.

Venetians.

Their Original,

Situation,

and Naval Affairs.

Possess'd Candia,

MUCH about the time of the *Saxons* before-mention'd Settlement in *Britain*, was founded the City of *Venice* on a Cluster of Islands at the bottom of the *Adriatick*, by the principal Inhabitants of *Aquileia*, *Padua*, and the neighbouring Cities of that part of *Italy*, who retired with their Effects into those Islands, before uninhabited, to avoid the Fury of *Attila*, King of the *Huns*, then laying waste the Country with an Army of 500000 Men. Their Situation and the Necessity of their Affairs soon obliged them to an Application to Naval Concerns, wherein they had very good Success, and in a short time grew potent at Sea. They possessed themselves of several Ports in *Greece* and *Syria*; and for the good Services rendered by their Fleet to Christendom in the Holy War, the Island *Candia* was given to them as a Reward. They were also

Masters

CHAP. VIII. *at Sea in all Ages.* 17

Masters of *Cyprus* for many Years, and for some Ages enjoyed all *Cyprus, &c.* the Trade to *Ægypt, Syria, Arabia, Persia,* and *India*; the Com- *Their ancient* modities of which latter Countries were brought over-land to *Aleppo Commerce,* and *Damascus,* and thence to *Scanderoon,* and other Ports of *Syria.* They had long Wars with the Republick of *Genoa,* their Ri- *War with* val in Naval Power and Commerce; and after many sharp Con- *Genoa,* flicts gained the Superiority over them they still maintain. The modern Discovery of the Passage to *India* round *Africa* by the *Portuguese,* deprived *Venice* of the Benefit of its rich Trade, but it *Trade, &c. at* nevertheless continues to this time a very flourishing Republick, is *this Day.* Mistress of a considerable Naval Force, and is one of the strongest Barriers of Christendom against the Power of the Turk.

The People of *Pisa* in *Tuscany,* after the Declension of the Em- *The Pisans* pire, made themselves Masters of a Naval Force, and by means thereof subdued *Sardinia,* took *Carthage,* seized several Ports in *reduce Sardi-* *Sicily,* and with a Fleet of three hundred Gallies reduced the Islands *Carthage,* of *Majorca, Minorca,* and *Yvyça.* They resisted the *Saracen Sicily, &c.* Power very vigorously, and in some Engagements worsted them; *resist the Sa-* but having been long at Variance with the *Genoese,* they at length *racens,* obtained the Superiority, by a great Defeat given them near the *but subdued* Isle of *Malora,* off of *Leghorn,* which the *Pisans* never re- *by the Ge-* covered. *noese.*

After the Dissolution of the *Roman* Empire, when *Genoa* erected *The Genoese* itself into a Republick, her Inhabitants very industriously applied themselves to augmenting their Commerce, and increasing their Naval Force. In a short time they possessed themselves of the Islands *reduced Cor-* of *Corsica* and *Sardinia,* but the *Saracens* being then very formida- *sica and Sar-* ble, made a considerable stand against them. In *Syria* their Fleet *dinia,* reduced most of the Maritime Towns to their Obedience; and in *Coasts of Sy-* *Spain,* whither, as we have before observed, the *Saracens* had *ria* spread themselves, they took *Almeria* and *Tortosa,* with several *and Spain,* other Sea Ports, as also the Island of *Minorca,* with great Slaughter *Almeria and* of the Infidels. They were also Masters of *Chios, Lesbos,* and *Tortosa,* many other Islands in the *Archipelago,* together with *Theodosia Minorca,* (now *Caffa*) in *Little Tartary*; by which great Acquisitions they *Chios,* became so considerable as to rival the *Venetians* in their Trade and *Lesbos. &c.* Naval Power, and maintained long Wars with them on that account, *Caffa.* but were at length forced to yield to the superior Genius of that Re- *But are re-* publick: And of all their foreign Possessions they retain now on- *duced by the* ly the Island of *Corsica.* *Venetians,* *Corsica.*

The *Portuguese* discovering the Navigation to *India* by the Cape *Portuguese.* of Good Hope, as hath been observed, occasion'd the great Decrease *Their Navi-* of the *Venetian* and *Genoese* Naval Power and Commerce; the *gation to the* Chanel of the rich *India* Trade, then the chief Support of those *East Indies,* Commonwealths, being turned quite another way. The *Portuguese* thus becoming the most considerable People at Sea, they discovered *Possess the* and took Possession of the Islands of *Azores, Maderas,* and Cape *Azores, Ma-* *Verde,* with others of less Note in the Ocean, established them- *deras, Isles of* selves in the most advantagious Places for Trade all along the Coast *Cape Verde,* of *Africa,* and made several Settlements in *Arabia, Persia,* and *and Coasts of* *India.* *Africa, Ara-* *bia, Persia,* *India.*

D

India, subduing many of the Maritime Provinces, and entirely reducing to their Obedience several of the *Indian* Islands. They likewise in *America* peopled the Coast of *Brazil* with Colonies of their own, about nine Years after the first Discovery of other parts of that Continent in 1492, by *Christopher Columbus*, a *Genoese*, in the Service of the King of *Spain*.

Brazil, &c. in America.
Columbus.

From that time are we to date the Naval Power the Kings of *Spain* were for many Years Masters of, the reducing of the Countries discovered, planting in them Colonies of *Spaniards*, and improving them by Trade, obliging that Nation to apply themselves to Sea Affairs. The Accession of the Crown of *Portugal*, and the Dominions thereto belonging, was a mighty increase of the *Spanish* Power both by Sea and Land, which happened under *Philip* the 2d, and then it was that he, aiming at Universal Empire, and knowing the best step towards it was the subduing to his Obedience those who were most to be feared at Sea, fitted out that formidable Armada, which *English* Valour, and the Anger of Heaven utterly destroyed.

Spaniards.
Original of their Naval Power.

Philip the 2d's Armada.

Then had lately risen up, under the auspices of Queen *Elizabeth*, the Republick of the United Provinces, who made an early Application to Naval Affairs, and, by quick Advances, became one of the most considerable Powers that ever flourished at Sea. From the King of *Spain*, and his then Subjects the *Portuguese*, they took many of the *Indian* Islands, destroyed most of their Colonies, and supplanted them in the best part of their Trade, and at this time they enjoy the most extensive and advantagious Commerce of any Nation of the World, not excepting even *Great Britain* itself, to which they are well able to be either a useful Ally or formidable Enemy; and, on account of their Naval Strength, bear almost as considerable a Weight in the Balance of Power in *Europe* as any of the Princes in it.

Dutch.

Their Naval Force, &c.

Chap. IX.

Of the Swedes, Danes, Muscovites, Turks, French *and* English.

THERE are not any People better furnished with Materials for Shipping than the *Swedes*, their Country abounding not only with useful Timber of all kinds, but with numerous Mines of the best Iron in the World, and producing great Quantities of excellent Tar and Hemp. In the War that *John* the 3d King of *Sweden* had with *Denmark*, he is said to have maintained a Fleet of seventy large Ships, besides several small ones, on Board of which were 18000 Men. The ordinary Naval Strength of that Kingdom is reckon'd to consist of about forty Ships of War, the greatest number carrying from fifty to one hundred Guns, most of which, in time of Peace, lye

Swedes.
Their Naval Stores.
Fleets, &c.

up

CHAP. IX. *at Sea in all Ages.* 19

up at *Carelscroon*, a fine Harbour in the Province of *Bleking*, very well fortified. *Carelscroon Harbour.*

The Kings of *Denmark* are Masters of a great number of Islands, and a large extent of Country along the Ocean, especially since *Norway* was annexed to that Crown, and have for many Ages had a considerable Sea Force, of which the Histories of our own Nation can bear good Testimony. In the Year 1564, the *Danes* obtained a signal Victory over the *Swedish* Fleet, and took their Admiral Prisoner, together with his Ship called the *Nonsuch*, mounted, as 'tis said, with two Hundred Guns: And it is related, that *Christian* the 3^d, upon the Instances of the *French* King *Henry* the 2^d, aided the *Scots* with a Fleet of a Hundred Sail, manned with 10000 Men, against the *English*. The King of *Denmark* is said now to have in the *Bason* of *Copenhagen* six and thirty Ships of the Line of Battle, fifteen or sixteen Frigates, eight or ten Fireships, and some Bomb Vessels, and he exercises a Dominion on a part of the *Baltick* Sea, levying a Toll on all Merchant Ships that pass into it by the *Streight* of the *Sound*, which he commands by the Castle of *Cronenburg*. *Danes. Their Sea Force. Beat the Swedes. Fleets at Copenhagen, &c. Cronenburgh Castle.*

The Naval Forces of these two Potentates of *Denmark* and *Sweden* is pretty near an Equality for deciding their frequent Differences; but the Preservation of the Peace of *Europe*, oftentimes obliges *England* and *Holland* to interpose with their formidable Fleets, and put an end to their Quarrels. *Balance of Power.*

But within these few Years is risen up in those Parts of the World a new Naval Power, that of *Muscovy*, which in a short time is arrived to that Perfection which the *Dane* and *Swede* have been so many Ages acquiring, and this entirely owing to the unwearied Industry, and even Personal Labour of the present *Czar*: a Prince of a vast and enterprizing Genius, who is wholly bent on improving the advantagious Situation of his large Empire for Trade, and cultivating the Manners of his before barbarous Subjects, by the Introduction of the learned Sciences, and the Arts of War and Commerce. What will be the event of the Accession of so great a Power by Sea and Land, in the Hands of a Prince, Master of so wide a Dominion, peopled with such infinite Multitudes, and what Alterations in the Affairs and Interests of *Europe* it may occasion, I leave to the Politicians to discuss, and proceed in the next place to the Naval Affairs of the *Turks*. *Muscovites Naval Force, owing to the present Czar.*

That People, as Sir *Paul Ricaut* tells us, abound with all imaginable Conveniencies for a Sea Power, having all sorts of Materials fit for Navigation, as Cordage, Pitch, Tar, and Timber, within their own Dominions, which are easily brought to *Constantinople*, with little or no risque from their Enemies. For Timber, the vast Woods along the Coasts of the Black Sea, and parts of *Asia*, at the bottom of the Gulph of *Nicomedia* supply them; Pitch, Tar, and Tallow are brought to them from *Albania* and *Walachia*; Canvas and Hemp from *Grand Cairo*. Their Ports are several of them convenient for erecting both Ships and Gallies: The *Arsenal* at *Constantinople* hath no less than one hundred thirty seven Chambers *The Turks have the Conveniencies of all Naval Stores. Ports and Arsenals,*

D 2 for

for Building, where so many Vessels may be on the Stocks at the same time. At *Sinopoli, Midia,* and *Anchiale,* Cities on the Black Sea, are other Arsenals; and in many Parts of the *Propontis,* the *Hellespont,* and the *Bosphorus,* are such Ports and Conveniencies for Shipping, as if all things had conspir'd to render *Constantinople* happy, and not only capable of being Mistress of the Earth, but formidable in all Parts of the Ocean. These Advantages the Turks for many Years made use of, and were very potent at Sea; but their ill Success against the *Venetians* in the last Age has very much decreased their Naval Force; so that they have not for many Years past been able to equip above one hundred Gallies, which together with some Ships of War, and the Auxiliaries from *Tripoli, Tunis,* and *Algier,* tho' (compared with that of some other States) it may appear a considerable Number, yet, happily for Christendom, it is in no degree proportionable to the Power that Empire has by Land, and its natural Advantages to enjoy the like by Sea.

but their Naval Power

abated by the Venetians;

now not equal

to their Land Force.

It was but in the last Age, under the Ministry of the great Cardinal *Richelieu,* that *France* took any Steps toward attaining a considerable Power at Sea. Before his time the *French* are not ashamed to confess they had so few Ships, and those so ill equipped, that they were but of very little Importance; and that they were therefore obliged, with no less Dishonour than Expence, to borrow or hire Ships of foreign Nations to defend them from their Enemies. To remedy this Defect, that Minister laid out great Sums of Money for building in *Holland* several Ships of War, and for clearing many of the Sea Ports in the *Ocean* and *Mediterranean,* and erecting Naval Magazines. His Conduct herein was diligently pursued by his Successor in the Ministry, Cardinal *Mazarine,* but more especially by the late *French* King, who with unwearied Application carried on his Design of being Master of a good Naval Force, and at length obtained it, but not without the Assistance of a neighbouring Court, lull'd in a supine Security by his Artifices; who, if they would not endeavour to quell the growing Power of so formidable a Neighbour, at least should not industriously have furnished him with Weapons for their own Destruction. Which false Step in the Politicks this Nation has more than once had reason to repent, as will appear in the Sequel of our History.

The French owe their Naval Power

to the Cardinals Richlieu

and Mazarine

and our Court's Supineness.

Note.

And now we are at length come home to *Britain,* the Queen of Isles, and Mistress of the Ocean; for we may justly pronounce her to be at this time the Possessor of a much greater Naval Power than any other Nation does, or ever did enjoy. Of this the Reader will have been already convinced, from the Account of the State of our Navy in the Preface to this Work; so that here there will not be occasion to say any thing more, than to take notice of the vast Increase thereof during the last Century, which will be very conspicuous, if we compare with the present the Naval Force in the times of Queen *Elizabeth* and King *James* the First. The Merchant-Ships of the Kingdom were then esteemed the principal Part of our maritime Power, of which in the twenty fourth Year of Queen *Elizabeth* were reckoned one hundred and thirty five, many of them

The English Naval Power, how far encreased

Since Q. Elizabeth, &c

of

of five hundred Tuns each; and in the beginning of King *James*'s Reign 'twas computed there were four hundred, but those not of so great Burthen. As to the Ships of War belonging to the Crown in the time of the first of these Princes, their Number was thirteen, to which eleven were added by the latter, the Names whereof we shall here set down from Sir *Walter Raleigh*, as thinking it not improper to give place in this Work to a List of the Royal Navy of *England* in those times of its Minority. They were these.

Navy of England.

Temp. Eliz & Jac. 1.

Under Queen Elizabeth.

The *Triumph*,
The *Elizabeth-Jonas*,
The *White Bear*,
The *Philp* and *Mary*,
The *Bonadventure*,
The *Golden Lion*,
The *Victory*,
The *Revenge*,
The *Hope*,
The *Mary-Rose*,
The *Dreadnought*,
The *Minion*,
The *Swiftsure*.

Added by King James *the* I.

The *Anthilope*,
The *Foresight*,
The *Swallow*,
The *Handmaid*,
The *Jennet*,
The *Bark* of *Boulogne*,
The *Aid*,
The *Achates*,
The *Falcon*,
The *Tiger*,
The *Bull*.

From this general View of the People who have in all Ages been most considerable in Naval Affairs, and the several Instances of their Exercise of a Dominion on the Sea, it will be no improper Transition to pass on to the Proof of that Claim the Kings of *Britain* make to the Dominion of the *British* Seas; and preliminary to that, to discuss the Question, whether the Sea be capable of private Dominion, and can have particular Proprietors? This Argument hath, to the Honour of our Nation, been long since most accurately handled by that Prodigy of Learning Mr. *Selden*, in a [a] Treatise professedly written thereon; to which there cannot any thing well be added. But having in the Perusal of some Papers of the *Cottonian* Library met with a Dissertation on the same Subject, wherein the Argument is reduced to a narrow Compass, I could not dispense with my self from communicating the Substance of it to the Reader, which I shall do in the two following Chapters.

[a] Mare Clausum.

Chap. X.

Of the Dominion of the Sea in general.

Touching the Dominion of the Sea.

THE Truth of this Proposition, *That the Sea is capable of private Dominion, and can have particular Proprietors,* is, saith my Author, in itself so clear, that there needeth not any great Pains to illustrate it: For (besides that the general Practice of Time hath familiarized the Notion hereof to us, and made it evident by way of Fact) it must be acknowledged that to exempt the Sea from the Jurisdiction of proprietary Lords, would have no other Effect than the giving a Liberty to Mankind at their Pleasure to become Pirates, and thereby render them in no better a Condition than the Fishes of the Sea, the larger whereof devour the less.

Propriety in the Sea prov'd by Arguments.

1. Ex Necessitate.

Wherefore, although some there are who have attempted to prove that every Part of the Sea, and the Shores thereof, are equally publick to all Men, without Distinction of Bounds, or severed Interest; yet the irresistible Argument of Necessity *(quæ dat, non accipit legem)* which gives, not receives Law, may save any Man the labour of confuting an Assertion which doth so inevitably subvert the very Frame of human Society, which cannot subsist without Order; nor can there be any Order where Interests are confounded, and where Command and Obedience are left arbitrary and undetermin'd.

2. Ex Lege.

Before I enter on the Title of our own Princes to the Propriety of the Seas of *Great Britain*, I shall first touch upon the general Right of others to those Parts of the Sea which approach their several Territories; and in as brief a manner as may be, produce Authorities from the *Law Divine, Natural,* and *Civil,* to prove this their Claim justifiable from the Creation.

Dominion of the Sea proved 1. From the Divine Law. Gen. 1. 26.

We find, by undeniable Proof, that the Stamp of Sovereignty was by God himself set upon Man at the time of his Creation. *Let us make Man in our Image, after our Likeness, and let them have Dominion over the Fish of the Sea, and over the Fowl of the Air, and over the Cattel, and over all the Earth.*

And this was afterwards accordingly exercised by divine Ordinance, not only over all other Creatures and Works of God, but also among Men themselves in the narrow Room of two, of three, of an House, of a Nation. This farther appears from the Terms *Noah* used when he branded *Canaan*, and said, *Cursed be* Canaan, *a Servant of Servants shall he be unto his Brethren.* Thus the Masters of Families, the Tops of Kindreds, the Founders of Nations, being endued and qualified from the beginning, not only with Names of Honour, but Power of Direction and Command, Sovereignty upon the numerous Propagation of Mankind dilated itself by God's Appointment over Multitudes of Places and Nations, according to the Blessing given in the plural Number by *Isaac* to his Son, *Let People serve thee, and Nations bow down to thee.* So that we can

Gen. 9. 25.

Gen. 27. 29.

can trace the Footsteps of Sovereignty beyond the times of *Nimrod*, even from the first Intention of God to give Man Being.

No reasonable Man can suppose that the Title and supreme Power of Princes is to be generally held an Usurpation contrary to divine Institution, when he shall find that to be the Father of Kings is singled out by God himself as the most eminent of his worldly Blessings; for so God speaking unto *Abraham*, tells him, *That Kings should go out of him*; and of *Sarah*, *That Kings of the People should arise from her*: From whence it is evident, that as in Proportion of Dignity the divine Law makes not all Men alike, nor in gross esteemeth them all at an even rate or worth, as not intending equal Capacities to all Men, but that some should be qualified for Government, and others adapted for Subjection and Obedience: so, likewise, for Distinction of Proprieties in all things real and personal, it cannot be doubted but that *Meum* and *Tuum*, Terms of Severalty, began to be in use as soon as there were several Persons to claim several Interests; for certainly *Cain*'s *Sheaf* was not properly *Abel*'s, nor the *Fat of Abel's Sheep Cain*'s. That which was the Father's was not in Propriety the Son's, much less a Stranger's; for *Isaac* received his Father *Abraham*'s Goods by way of Gift, who disposed of some other Parts thereof, as best liked him, to the rest of his Children. Nor were the Kinsmen's Goods those of the Uncle; for though *Lot* lived under the Tuition of *Abraham*, yet saith the Text, *And* Lot *also who went with* Abraham *had Flocks, and Herds, and Tents*. As to the Goods of *Bera* King of *Sodom*, *Abraham* disdain'd a thred, even to a Latchet of a Shoe. And as for the appropriating of real Possessions and Inheritances, if we doubt whether the Divisions of Lands or Countries made by the Sons of *Noah* were made by divine Ordinance, (of whom the Scripture saith, *By these the Isles of the Gentiles were divided in their Lands*, &c.) Yet we shall find presently after, that it was not only the Act of God himself to disperse Mankind over several Parts of the Earth, *(The Lord scattered them abroad upon the Face of all the Earth)* and to allot different Habitations for several Nations and Families to dwell in, but that he also set out the Land of *Canaan* by Bounds to the Posterity and Tribes of *Israel*; and, more than all this, inflicted a Curse upon him who should remove the Mark-Stone of his Neighbour, so to encroach upon or confound the proper Interest of another Man. In fine, seeing that Law, which, as St. *Paul* saith, was written in the Heart of Man at his Creation, and was afterwards published by *Moses* to the *Israelites*, commandeth not only the honouring of some Persons above others, but forbiddeth Stealth, and generally all indirect taking or coveting what is another Man's, it inevitably followeth, that to throw down this Inclosure by making all things common, and annihilating particular Interests, is at once to raze three express Commandments out of the Decalogue, and to confound that which God by his primary and divine Law would have distinguish'd. And therefore since these Words, *Subdue the Earth*, are not to be understood, as that all Men in common were to be Lords alike of every Part thereof, it cannot be conceived

Gen. 17. 6.
Gen. 17. 16.

Gen. 4. 3,4,5

Gen. 25. 5,6.

Gen 13. 5.

Gen. 10. 5.

Gen. 11. 8.

Vide Joshua, *ch.* 13, 14, 15, &c.

Deut. 27. 17.
Rom. 2. 14, 15.

Exod. 20. 17.

Gen. 1. 28

Gen. 1. 26. conceived that the Words immediately following, *Have Dominion over the Fishes of the Sea*, should give equal Interest and Propriety in every Part of the Sea to all Men without Distinction; for every Man must confess that Stealth and Injuries done on the Sea, are equally as much against Justice and divine Precept, as those done upon the Land; and therefore those Princes whose Territories border upon any part of the Sea, have the same relation to Justice and Order as well on the one as on the other, and may with equal Authority of divine Law hold and enjoy the Sovereignty of the same, as of those Territories and Countries which properly belong unto their Crowns; for the Pre-

1 Cor. 14. 40. cept of the Apostle, *which willeth all things to be done honestly and in order*, being general, comprehendeth Actions to be done as well at Sea as on Land; which without the supreme and binding Power of Princes, cannot possibly be effected. And since that Interest which Time hath given to Kings and others in several Parts of the Earth is not held injurious to divine Law, surely it cannot be proved that the Propriety which Princes claim by the like Act of Time in any Part of the Sea, is by the same Law less justifiable; nor is it to be conceived why Rivers and Inlets of the Sea should admit Proprietary Owners, who have an exclusive Interest both in the Shores, the Passage, and Fishing within the same, and all this warranted by divine Law, as is not deny'd; and yet that Princes and others may not have the like Propriety in the Seas neighbouring upon their Territories.

2. *From the Laws of Nature and Nations.*

Thus then the Dominion of the Sea being warranted by divine Ordinance, it may seem unnecessary, though natural or civil Law should aver the contrary, to vouchsafe them Answer. But yet because some have endeavour'd to make the *Law of Nations*, or the *particular Law of Nature* the main Platform from whence to batter the Power of Princes on this Quarter, as supposing it to lie naked and indefensible against the Strength of that Law, which (as they say) hath left the Sea and every part thereof indifferently common to all Men, I shall make it appear that, even by the Law of Nature, this Claim and Right of Princes is without all danger of being forced. For first, seeing that which by the Strength of natural Reason hath been successively observed and assented to by all People, is properly termed the Law of Nature, it can never be satisfactorily proved that this imaginary Parity and Community of Things hath ever had that large Acceptance among Men, as that at any time it could procure universal Consent to give it Passage: For besides that we have in divine Story express Words to justify the contrary, as hath been already shewn; and that all succeeding Histories of Time generally disclaim any such *Anarchy*, or confused Commission of Power or Properties, and that we our selves see it disavow'd by the universal Practice of of our Times, it cannot but give ample Satisfaction in this Point,

The Americans, &c. observe the Rules of Propriety.

that even those Men who are only guided by the Strength of natural Reason (as are the Nations of late discover'd in Parts of the World not yet civilized) maintain Severalty in Dominion, and Propriety in Territory, House and Seed Plots, and even in Rivers and Seas, as far as their Power can extend, and gain them the Mastery.

And

CHAP. X.   *at Sea in all Ages.*   25

And more than this; though we grant the main and fundamental Ground work whereon this common Claim is raised, to be found, *viz.* That Nature at first did not distinguish several Interests and Proprieties in Things created, yet it followeth not, that by Apprehension, Occupation, mutual Agreement, or Constitution of Men, those things could not be appropriated, which by Nature were at first left without Owner; and that an acquired Right could not be gotten by Time, which was not settled in the Beginning. For we are to consider that although the Law of Nature be immutable, as touching the General, and that no Law of Man can make that lawful which is prohibited by the Law of Nature; yet it followeth not that in the Particular it may not suffer Alteration, and that those things which are permitted, or left at large by that Law, may not by positive Laws and human Constitutions be restrained or ascertained, especially such as are, in the Language of the Schools, said to be *Juris Naturalis negativè, quæ possunt uni potiùs quam alteri ex causâ concedi*; that is, negatively of the Law of Nature, which may on certain Accounts, Reasons, or Occasions, be granted to one Person rather than another. *How Proprie- ty is founded.*

The Sea then being of this kind of things, *(Quæ jure Gentium nullius sunt)* which by the Law of Nations belong to no private Person, it must necessarily follow, that Princes, by an acquir'd Right of Occupation, Concession, or other Titles, may claim some Parts thereof, as properly subject to their Dominion of Sovereignty, without violating the Law of Nature, or of Nations. For (I may add) *Quod nullius est, id ratione naturali occupanti conceditur,* i. e. That which has no Owner does, by natural Reason, become the Propriety of him who first seizes it, *Inst. l. 2. l. de Rerum divis. §. litorum.*

I pass on therefore to the Civil Law, which though it bind *Contrahentes* only, that is, such as are Parties thereunto; and so we who disavow it, are no way compellable to observe it; yet out of it a Multitude of Quotations are mustered up, to make good this pretended Right of common Interest in all Parts of the Sea alike, which seem to stand in full Opposition to what I have before asserted, and with some Colour of Reason, till we consider when and by whom those Laws were first compiled; for in those times the *Roman* Emperors reputing themselves as common Fathers of the whole World, and that all Nations of that vast Empire were to them as of their Houshold and Family; and *Rome* her self being accordingly termed *communis Patria*, the common Country, it might very well stand with Justice and Reason, that Fellow-Citizens and Subjects should partake alike of the Commodities of the Sea, without any Mark of Difference, or Inequality of Interest; but from thence to conclude that the Emperors themselves were utterly debarr'd from having Propriety in any Part of the Sea, is to afford them less Power therein than that great Lawyer *Pomponius* alloweth to the *Prætor*, an under Officer, whose Words are, *Quamvis quod in litore publico, vel in mari extruxerimus nostrum fiat; tamen decretum Prætoris adhibendum est, ut id facere liceat.* Although what we build on the publick Shore, or in the Sea, may become ours, *From the Civil Law.*

Pomponius, l. quamvis D. de adquirend rer. dominio.

E

ours, yet the Decree of the *Prætor* must be obtained to make it lawful to do the same. So that there remained a disposing Power in the *Prætor*, and consequently a Sovereignty superior in the Emperor; which Sovereignty upon better reason may be claimed by absolute Kings and Princes in their several Seas, than by the Emperors of *Rome* over the *whole Ocean*, as well in respect to the Protection they afford to those who pass within the Limits of their Command, as of their many Years Prescription, whereby their Claims by length of time are settled and confirmed. And therefore now, when several Parts of that Empire are devolved to proprietary Lords by just and lawful Titles, to give notwithstanding all Men a common Interest in every Part of the Sea, and to put the Reins of Power over the same equally into the Hands of all Men, were not only injuriously to take away that which of right appertaineth to Princes, but also to dissolve the Bands of Order and Justice, which when once growing uncertain by whom or on whom to be exercised, forsakes the World, and gives place to all Violence and Confusion.

In Consideration whereof, later Civilians, of greatest Note and Learning, have been forced to acknowledge, that Seas, as well as the Land, have their peculiar Lords and Owners, and this even by the Law of Nations. *Videmus* (saith *Baldus*) *de jure gentium in mari esse distincta dominia, sicut in terrâ aridâ*; that is, We see that by the Law of Nations there are distinct Dominions on the Sea, as well as on the dry Land. Nor is thus much confessed in general only, but some of them descend to more Particulars: As first for the Proportion of Extent, *Bartholus* assigns an hundred Miles of Sea (if the Breadth will carry it) to every Territory from the Main. Next, over this Proportion they not only give proprietary Lords Power, but in mannerly Terms tie them to undergo the Care of Protection. *Maris protectio ad omnes pertinet, sive principes sive populos, pro rata parte illius portionis quæ ad illos propius accedit, i. e.* All Princes and States have belonging to them the Protection of such Portion of the Sea as lies next to their Dominions. And lastly, they enforce a Right of Jurisdiction upon Princes in the Sea, which they cannot put off without renouncing those their Territories upon which the Sea coasteth. For first, *Insulæ in mari proximæ adjacentes, & mare ipsum, ad centum usque milliaria, pro territorio districtuque illius regionis cui proximè appropinquat, assignatur*; that is, The nearest adjacent Islands, and the Sea itself, as far as a hundred Miles, are assigned for a Territory and District to that Country to which they lie nearest. And then *Jurisdictio territorio tanquam accidens materiæ necessariò tenaciterq; cohæret; i. e.* Jurisdiction does as necessarily and tenaciously cohere with Territory, as Accident with Matter. So that if in the Sea there be distinct Dominions, and this Distinction express'd in a demonstrative Certainty, and in this Certainty Power given to Princes, both of Protection and Jurisdiction, what can be in effect more said, or more desired, for that Claim of Jurisdiction which Princes make in these our Days, to those Seas which wash the Coasts of their Kingdoms? For as Protection, by the Civil Law, draweth after it

Power

[margin notes: Baldus. Bartholus. L. 1. Cæs. de Classi. lib. 11. tit. 12. Per l. Insul. de Jud. & l. Cæs. de pub. & Bartolus quâ supra. Per l. fin. de jurisd. & Bartol. ad l. inter eos. De acquirend. rer. domin.]

CHAP. X. *at Sea in all Ages.* 27

Power to impose Taxes and Tributes, which in justice those who are protected ought to pay towards the Maintenance of their Protection, at least to acknowledge a Right of Power or Superiority in the Protector; so to Jurisdiction is *incompatibly* requisite the Power of Coercion by Mulct, Confiscation, corporal or capital Punishment, to restrain the Neglect or Breach of such Laws as are prescribed, the Institution thereof being altogether vain and fruitless, where there wanteth Authority to enforce Observance and Execution. Insomuch as within this large Extent of Sovereignty, even the particular Power (so stiffly by some controverted) of restraining the Passage *Propriety of* and Fishing within some Parts of the Sea, upon just occasion, is ne- *Passage,* cessarily comprized and included: For since the Sea bordering upon any Country is in the Nature of a Territory (as hath been before shewn) and that therein Princes by the Civil Law have a Right to impose and establish Laws, not only Enemies offering open Violence, but all others who shall refuse Obedience to such Orders and Conditions as by the rightful Owners are reasonably prescrib'd, may, by warrant of the Civil Law and Reason, be prohibited from passing within the same, until they shall regularly conform themselves. And as for the point of Fishing; whereas some object that therein *and of Fishing* not any one can have more Property than another, for that Fishes in the Sea are as the Birds in the Air, which cannot be appatronated, by reason of the Uncertainty of their Possession, being, as the Law saith, *properly his that catcheth them (Volucres piscesq;* Inst. l. 2. de *jure gentium fiunt capientium:)* yet it hath been allow'd to be §. Feræ. warranted by the same Law, that *Qui venandi aucupandique gratiâ alienum fundum ingreditur, potest a domino fundi, si is præviderit, prohiberi ne is ingrediatur, i.e.* The Owner of any Ground may prohibit the Entry of any Person who would go upon it, in order to fish or fowl. And therefore, by the same reason, he who is a proprietary Lord of any bounded Part of the Sea, as annexed to his Crown, may lawfully prohibit Strangers from entering within the Limits of his Command, to take such Fish as are therein, the Maxim of the Law being, that *Quæ non differunt ratione, non differunt juris dispositione*, where the Reason is the same, so likewise is the Disposition of the Law. And this they may the rather do, for that Fishing, by the express Words of the Law, is acknowledged to be among the Regalities.

Yet although every Part of the Sea is not to all Men indifferently common, it cannot be denied but that it ought to be communicable, as created by God for the sake of Commerce, and the Convenience of Mankind; but so communicable, that it ought to be upon those fair Terms offered by *Moses* to the King of the *A-* Numb. 21. 22. *morites*, viz. *We will go by the King's High-way; Sell us Meat* Deut. 2. 27, *for Money, that we may eat; Give us Water for Money, that* 28. *we may drink.* At least there ought to be an Acknowledgment of the Owner's supreme Right, and a Conformity in the Passengers to established Laws and Orders.

E 2 CHAP.

CHAP. XI.

Of the Right of the Kings of Great Britain to the Sovereignty or Dominion of the British Seas.

Kings of Great Britain their Dominion of the Sea.

HAVING thus made it evident from the Law Divine, Natural and Civil, that the Sea is capable of private Dominion; proceed we next to shew that the Kings of *Great Britain* have an exclusive Propriety of Dominion in the British Sea, both as to the Passage through and Fishing within the same. For this there are so many evident and irresistible Proofs, as that no private or publick Person whatsoever, can produce better or more ample evidence to support and convey the right of his own Inheritance or any other thing he enjoyeth, than they can do for their Claim on this behalf; which may be made good by many irrefragable Arguments drawn, 1. From Prescription. 2. From the Common Law of this Realm. 3. From Ancient Records thereof. 4. From Authentick History. 5. From Treaties and Acknowledgments of other Princes. 6. From continued Possession and Disposition. And 7. From the Example of other Kingdoms and States; but here for Brevity's sake we shall retain only those Arguments that are deduced from Prescription, referring the Reader for the rest to the forementioned Work of *Selden*, who hath made use of them all.

Prov'd from Prescription.

All that part of the Ocean which environs the Island of *Great Britain* is known in general by the name of the British Ocean, which is divided according to the Quarters of the World, into four Seas.

Division of the British Ocean.

1st. On the South is the *British* Ocean, properly so called; part whereof is that commonly termed the Channel flowing between *England* and *France*.

2dly. On the East is the *German* Ocean, otherwise called the *North Sea*.

3dly. On the North is that anciently known by the several names of the *Hyperborean*, *Deucaledonian* and *Caledonian* Ocean, now the *Scotch Sea*. And

4^{thly}. On the West is that anciently called the *Nergivian* Ocean, (in which lies *Ireland)* that part whereof which flows between *England* and *Ireland*, being commonly called the *Irish Sea*, and the rest now swallowed up in the general name of the *Western* or *Atlantick* Ocean. Over the *British* Ocean the Kings of *England* have by immemorial Prescription callenged Sovereignty: For (omitting to deduce the Title to it which the *Saxon* Kings, by their becoming Masters of the Country, derived from the *Britains*; who on the *Romans* abandoning their Conquest, again succeeded to that right they had been in Possession of from remotest Ages) it can be proved, that divers of our said *Saxon* Kings have been in the absolute and actual Fruition of the entire Dominion of those Seas, of whom *Egbert* the 1st who called himself King of *England* in the Year 840,

Egbert.

provided

provided himself with a strong Navy for the maintenance thereof, as *Alfred* did thirty or forty Years after.

Edgar had a very numerous Fleet, which he divided into several Edgar. Squadrons, and employed to guard the Seas and secure the Coasts, assuming to himself the Title not only of King of *England*, but of all the Kings of the Islands, and of the Ocean lying round about *Britain*, as appears by an old Charter of his among the Patent Rolls of *Edward* the 4th.

Ethelred being invaded by *Swane* King of *Denmark*, caused of Ethelred. every three hundred and ten Hides of Land a Ship to be built, which rendezvouzing at *Sandwich*, made the greatest Navy which had been known in this Isle to that time.

Knute the *Dane* took the like care (as did his Successors of the Knute. *Danish* Race after him) to preserve the Seas of the Kingdom in their former Estate, without admitting any of the Neighbouring Princes to have any Dominion in any part thereof; and so they remained in the time of *Edward* the Confessor, until the Conquest made by *William* Duke of *Normandy*, when the same Rights the William the preceding Princes were possessed of devolving to him, passed on to 1st. his Successors; who tho' they were for almost a Century and a half Lords of both Shores of the Channel, and so could not possibly have any others so much as to pretend to a share with them in the Dominion of that part of the *British* Sea, yet did not found their Right thereto on that Circumstance of their being Lords of both Shores, but possessed it as an inseparable Appendant unto the Crown of *England*, and *by Reason* and *in Right of the said Kingdom*. For in the time of *Edward* the 1st, who held not a Foot of Ground in *Norman-* Edward the *dy*, the Sovereignty of the Kings of *England* over the narrow Sea 1st. was not only challenged by him, but was also acknowledged by all other Neighbouring Nations to be his due *from times beyond all Memory*; as particularly appeareth by the Record of the said King *Edward* the first, in the thirtieth Year of whose Reign, *Anno Dom.* 1303. when *Philip* the Fair, the *French* King, sending forth certain Gallies and other Ships in aid of the *Flemings* against *Guy* Earl of *Flanders*, and Marshal of *Namure*, unto *Zurickzee*, under the Command of *Reyner Grimbaltz*, a *Genoeze*, creating him by his Commission his Admiral, and he, by virtue of his said Commission, beginning to exercise Sovereign Jurisdiction in the narrow Sea, then called, even by the *French* themselves, *La mier d'Engleterre*, the Sea of *England*, and in *Latin*, *Mare Angliæ*; complaint was thereupon made both to the King of *France* and to the King of *England*, and certain Commissioners or Auditors, as the Record calleth them, were appointed by both Kings, to hear and redress such Remonstrants wrongs as had been done to the Passengers on the said Seas, to which *to the Kings* Auditors the several Agents of divers Nations preferred a Bill of Com- England, 30 plaint or Remonstrance (in the *French* of those times) to the pur- Ed. 1. *An.* pose following, *viz.* 1303.

To you the Lords Commissioners, deputed by the Kings of England and France, to redress the Damages done to their Subjects by
Sea

Sea and Land in time of the late Peace and Truce, do most humbly Remonstrate the Procurators of the Prelates and Nobles, and of the Admiral of the English Seas, and of the Communities of Cities and Towns, as also of the Merchants, Marriners, Messengers, Inhabitant-strangers, and of all others belonging to the Kingdom of England, and other Territories subject to the said King of England; as likewise the Inhabitants of other Maritime Places, viz. Genoa, Catalonia, Spain, Germany, Zeeland, Holland, Frizeland, Denmark and Norway, and many other places of the Empire; that whereas the Kings of England, by right of the said Kingdom, have from time to time, whereof there is no Memorial to the contrary, been in peaceable Possession of the Sovereignty of the English Seas, and of the Islands situate within the same, with Power of Ordaining and Establishing Laws, Statutes, and Prohibitions of Arms, and of Ships otherwise furnished than Merchant Men use to be, and of taking Security, and giving Protection in all Cases where need shall require, and of Ordering all other things necessary for the maintaining of Peace, Right and Equity among all manner of People, as well of other Dominions as their own, passing through the said Seas, and the Sovereign Guard thereof; and also of taking all manner of Cognizance in Causes, and of doing Right and Justice to High and Low, according to the said Laws, Statutes, Ordinances and Prohibitions, and all other Things, which to the exercise of Sovereign Jurisdiction in the places aforesaid may appertain. And whereas [a] A. de B Admiral of the said Sea, deputed by the said King of England, and all other Admirals deputed by the said King of England, and his Ancestors formerly Kings of England, have been in peaceable Possession of the said Sovereign Guard, with Power of Jurisdiction, and all the other Powers beforemention'd, (except in case of Appeal and Complaint made of them to their Sovereigns the Kings of England in default of Justice, or for evil Judgment) and especially of making Prohibitions, doing Justice, and taking security of good Behaviour from all manner of People carrying Arms on the said Sea, or sailing in Ships, otherwise fitted out and arm'd than Merchant Ships use to be, and in all other Cases, where a Man may have reasonable cause of suspicion towards them of Piracy, or other Misdoings. And whereas the Masters of Ships of the said Kingdom of England, in the absence of the said Admirals, have been in peaceable Possession of taking Cognizance, and Judging of all Facts upon the said Sea between all manner of People, according to the Laws, Statutes, Prohibitions, Franchises and Customs. And whereas in the first Article of the Treaty of Alliance, lately made between the said Kings at Paris, the words following are set down, viz. First of all it is agreed and concluded between us the Envoys and Agents above-mention'd, in the Names of the said Kings, that they shall be to each other for the future, good, true and faithful Friends and Allies, against all the World (except the Church of Rome) in such manner that if any one or more, whosoever they be,

against Grimbald the French Admiral.

[a] *Coke Inst. l.4. c.22. says his name was De Botetort.*

be, shall go about to interrupt, hinder or molest the said Kings in the Franchises, Liberties, Privileges, Rights or Customs of them, an other Kingdoms, they shall be good and faithful Friends, and aiding against all Men living, and ready to die, to defend, keep and maintain the above-mention'd Franchises, Liberties, Rights and Customs, &c. And that the one shall not be of Counsel, nor give Aid or Assistance, in any thing whereby the other may lose Life, Limb, Estate or Honour. And whereas Monsieur Reyner Grimbaltz, Master of the Ships of the said King of France, who calls himself Admiral of the said Sea, being deputed by his Sovereign aforesaid, in his War against the Flemmings, did (after the above-mention'd Alliance was made, and ratified, and against the Tenor and Obligation of the said Alliance, and the Intention of those who made it) wrongfully assume and exercise the Office of Admiralty in the said Sea of England above the space of a Year, by Commission from the said King of France, taking the Subjects and Merchants of the Kingdom of England, and of other Countries, passing upon the said Seas, with their Goods, and did cast the Men so taken into the Prisons of his said Master the King of France, and by his own Judgment and Award did cause to be deliver'd their Goods and Merchandizes to Receivers, establish'd for that purpose in the Sea Ports of the said King, as Forfeit and Confiscate to him; and his taking and detaining the said Men with their said Goods and Merchandizes, and his Judgment and Award on them as Forfeit and Confiscate, hath pretended in Writing to justify before you the Lords Commissioners, by Authority of the aforesaid Commission for the Office of Admiral by him thus usurped, and against the general Prohibition made by the King of England in places within his Power, in pursuance of the third Article of the before-mention'd Alliance, containing the Words above written: This Article being in the Record ommitted, it is therefore necessary for the understanding of this second Plea of Monsieur *Grimbaltz* concerning the Prohibition, to observe, that it was by the said Article agreed, That neither of the contracting Parties should give any Aid or Assistance to the Enemys of the other, nor suffer the same to be given in any manner of way in any of their Territories or Places within their Power, and that they should forbid the same to be done, on pain of Forfeiture of Body and Goods in the Offenders; which King *Edward* having accordingly forbid on his part, Monsieur *Grimbaltz* pretended that all such as, after that Prohibition, relieved the *Flemings* by Merchandize or otherwise, were to be esteemed as Enemies, of whatsoever Nation they were; and that he having taken none but the Persons and Goods of such, conceived himself to have Permission so to do by virtue of the foresaid Prohibition, whereby the King had in effect declared (as he interpreted it) that he would not take it for an Injury to himself, during that Alliance and Prohibition, although the *French* should fall upon any of their Enemies in his Dominion, or which is all one here, though they should be taken in his Sea by the *French* King's Officers. And hath therefore required that he may be be acquitted and abſolved of the ſame, to the great Damage and Prejudice of the ſaid King of England, and of the Prelates, Nobles and others before-mention'd; wherefore the ſaid Procurators do, in the names of their ſaid Lords, pray you the Lords Commiſſioners beforemention'd, that due and ſpeedy delivery of the ſaid Men, Ships, Goods, and Merchandizes, ſo taken and detain'd, may be made to the Admiral of the ſaid King of England, to whom the Cognizance of this matter doth rightfully appertain, as is above-ſaid, that ſo, without Diſturbance from you, or any elſe, he may take Cognizance thereof, and do what belongs to his aforeſaid Office; and that the aforeſaid Monſieur Reyner may be condemned, and conſtrained to make due ſatisfaction for all the ſaid Damages, ſo far forth as he ſhall be able to do the ſame; and in default thereof, his ſaid Maſter the King of France, by whom he was deputed to the ſaid Office; and that after due Satisfaction ſhall be made for the ſaid Damages, the ſaid Monſieur Reyner may be ſo duly puniſhed for the Violation of the ſaid Alliance, as that the ſame may be an Example to others for time to come.

King of England's Dominion,

This Acknowledgment (as my Author hath truly obſerved) is poſſibly the moſt remarkable Authority of Antiquity of the like Nature which any Prince can produce; by which it appeareth that the Kings of *England* had then been by Preſcription of Time immemorial, in the actual Poſſeſſion of the Sovereign Dominion of the narrow Sea, both in preſcribing Laws, granting of ſafe Conducts, keeping of the Peace, and judging of all kind of Perſons and Actions, as well their own Subjects as Strangers, within the ſaid Sea; and that this Dominion does inſeperably belong to the Kings of *England (par raiſon du dit Royaume,* ſays the Record)

and his Admiral's Juriſdiction

by right of the ſaid Kingdom; and that, under the ſaid Kings, their ſeveral Admirals were to judge of all Facts, and Perſons within the Sea aforeſaid, from whom lay no Appeal, but only to their Sovereign Lords the Kings of *England*; and that in the Abſence of the ſaid Admirals, the Maſters of the King's Ships were to be Judges as aforeſaid: As alſo that the Kings of *France*, who of any other might beſt pretend a Right, could not juſtify ſo much as the making of an Admiral, but only a Maſter of his Navy in theſe Seas: And thus is the Claim of the Kings of *England* to the Dominion of this Part of the *Britiſh* Sea made good by the unanimous Acknowledgment of divers neighbouring Nations, viz. *Italy, Spain, Germany, Zeeland, Holland, Frizeland, Denmark, Norway,* and others.

in the narrow Seas

Seeing therefore that although, in the caſe of Preſcription, it is ſufficient for him who is in Poſſeſſion to ſtand upon the affirmative without farther Proof; yet having this general Confeſſion, and Acknowledgment from abroad, to ſecond and fortify our Right, we may confidently affirm, that our pretenſions to this Sovereignty over the narrow Sea is not a bare Aſſertion, and Uſurpation of our own, but the evident Work of Time, and of that Continuance too, that we are not able to aſſign how, and when it began; but that we have ever had and enjoy'd the ſame for many hundreds of Years, without ſo much as any pretended Claim of other Kings or Nations.

And

CHAP. XI. *at Sea in all Ages.* 33

And as for the other Parts of the *British* Ocean, it must needs *and British* follow, in reason, that if the *French* King, a Neighbour within *Ocean.* view, who might perhaps have Colour to claim an Interest of Dominion in the narrow Sea, half Seas over, was, notwithstanding, debarr'd from any Right thereunto, much more must any other Pretenders be foreclosed from having a Title to those Parts of our Seas, which for the most part have no opposite Neighbours within many hundreds of Leagues. But yet, for further Satisfaction herein, to make it appear that the Ancestors of our Kings were, and esteemed themselves Lords in fact of every Part of the surrounding Ocean; the Commission granted by *Edward* the III. to *Geffrey de Say*, in the tenth Year of his Reign, by the Addition of the word *Circumquaque*, or round about, manifestly expresseth the Resolution of that time; so much of which Commission as serveth for our purpose is as followeth, " *Rex dilecto & fideli suo Galfrido de Say,* Edw. III.'s " *Admirallo Flotæ suæ navium ab ore aquæ Thamisiæ versus par-* Commission to " *tes occidentales, Salutem. Cum nuper vobis, &c. Nos adver-* Say. " *tentes quod Progenitores Nostri Reges Angliæ Domini Maris* " *Anglicani circumquaque, & etiam defensores contra hostium in-* " *vasiones ante hæc tempora extiterint, & plurimum Nos tæderet* " *si honor Noster Regius in defensione hujusmodi nostris (quod ab-* " *sit) depereat temporibus, aut in aliquo minuatur, &c. Manda-* " *mus firmiter injungendo, quòd statim visis præsentibus, &* " *absque ulteriore dilatione, naves portuum prædictorum, & alias* " *naves quæ jam paratæ existunt supra mare teneatis, &c.* That is, " The King to the trusty and well-beloved *Geffrey de Say*, Ad-
" miral of his Fleet of Ships from the Mouth of the River *Thames*
" Westward, Greeting. Whereas lately, &c. We taking into our
" Consideration that our Progenitors, the Kings of *England*, have
" been in times past Lords of the *English* Sea *round about*, and also
" Defenders thereof against the Invasion of Enemies; and for that it
" would be very grievous to us to have our Royal Honour in Defence
" thereof lost, or suffer any Diminution in our Time, (which God
" forbid) &c. We strictly charge and require you, that immediately
" upon Sight of these Presents, and without any further Delay, you
" do put to Sea with the Ships belonging to our Ports, aforesaid,
" and such other Ships as are now ready, &c.

And for further Proof of the Right of our Kings to the Sovereignty of the Seas round about, they have successively constituted Admirals and Governours, as well over other Parts of our Seas, as *Commissions* in the Chanel between us and *France*. In ancient Times there *to English* were for the most part two, and sometimes three Admirals appointed *Admirals* in the Seas of *England*, all of them holding the Office *durante beneplacito*, and each of them had particular Limits under their Charge and Government. The first was Admiral of the Fleet of Ships from the Mouth of the *Thames* Northward, *viz.* to the Northward of *of the North,* *Scarborough*; and so was *William Ufford* in the fiftieth Year of *Edward* the III, and divers others before and after him.

The second was Admiral of the Fleet from the Mouth of the *Thames* Westward, *viz.* to the furthest Part of *Cornwall*, and so *of the South,*

F to

to the utmost Verge of *Ireland*; as was *Geffrey de Say* before mention'd, *William Montague* in the forty ninth of *Edward* the III, and many others before and since their Times.

of the Cinque-Ports.

And, besides these Admirals, we find that the Cinque-Ports have had theirs likewise; for so was *William Latimer* in the seventh of *Edward* the III. who is styled in the Record, *Admiralis Quinque Portuum*; and sometimes we find all these centered in one Man; for Sir *John Beauchamp*, Earl of *Warwick*, was in the thirty fourth of *Edward* the III, called Admiral of all the Fleets to the Southward, Northward, and Westward. But for the Style of *Admirallus Angliæ*, it was not frequent before the Reign of *Henry* the IV, in whose eleventh Year *Thomas Beauford*, Brother to the King, had that Title given him, which was afterwards used in all Commissions granted to the succeeding Admirals.

[b] *De Botetort, says Coke, Instit. l. 4. before cited.*

Yet some few there were who had the same Style given them before, though very sparingly, and with Intermission; for [b] *A de B*, in the time of *Edward* the I, was called *Admirall de la Mier d'Engleterre*, Admiral of the Sea of *England*, as appeareth by the Record before quoted at length. And *Richard* Earl of *Arundel*, in a Proclamation directed to the Sheriffs of *London*, requiring all Mariners to attend him at *Southampton*, is called *Admirallus Angliæ*, in the eleventh Year of *Richard* the II. So likewise was the Earl of *Rutland* in the nineteenth Year of the said King: Not but that those other before-mention'd, who were only call'd Admirals of all the Fleets, &c. had as absolute Jurisdiction and Power over the Parts of the Seas assigned to their Charge, as any other who had more ample Titles. And it may be moreover observed, that there was a Style above that of the Admiral of *England*, which was, *Locumtenens Regis super mare*, or the King's Lieutenant-General of the Sea; and so was *Thomas* Earl of *Lancaster*, Son to *Henry* the IV. Nay before that, in the eleventh Year of *Richard* the II, *Richard* Earl of *Arundel* had the like Title given to him. So far for my fore-mention'd Author.

Chap. XII.

Of the Boundaries of the British *Seas, the Extent of the Sea Dominion of the Kings of* Great Britain, *and the Right of the* Flag; *with some Observations concerning the Use of the Term,* The British Seas, *in Treaties.*

The Limits of the British Seas.

HAVING thus set before the Reader the most considerable of the Arguments, by which the Title of the Kings of *Britain* to the Sovereignty and Dominion of the *British* Seas may be made good from Prescription; it will be proper in the next Place to give some Account of the Extent of those Seas. Their Boundaries on the

CHAP. XII. *at Sea in all Ages.* 35

the East are the Shores of those Countries opposite to *Great Britain* on that side, *viz. Norway, Denmark, Germany,* and the *Netherlands,* by these Limits including that Part of the *British* Seas called the *German* Ocean, or North Sea. On the South they extend the opposite Shores of *France,* to those of *Spain* as far as Cape *Finisterre,* and to a Line drawn from that Cape, in the same Parallel of Latitude, to their Boundary on the West hereafter mention'd; thus taking in that Part of the *British* Seas which consists of the Chanel, the Bay of *Biscay,* and part of the *Atlantick* Ocean. For the West and North, if from the before-mention'd imaginary Line extending from Cape *Finisterre,* a Line be drawn, in the Longitude of twenty three Degrees West from *London,* to the Latitude of sixty three Degrees, and thence be drawn another, in that Parallel of Latitude, to the middle Point of the Land *Van Staten* in *Norway,* we may esteem these to be proper Boundaries of the *British* Seas on those Quarters, thereby taking in, to the West, that Part of them which consists of part of the *Atlantick* Ocean, and the *Irish* Sea, or St. *George*'s Chanel; and, to the North that called the *Caledonian* Ocean, or *Scotish* Sea: And tho' the same Boundaries on the East and South, *viz.* the Shores of the opposite Countries, are also the Limits of the Sea Dominion of the Kings of *Great Britain* that way; yet, to the West and North, does that Dominion extend very much farther than the fore-mention'd Boundaries of the *British* Seas on those Quarters. For tho' (as Mr. *Selden* says) the vast Western and Northern Ocean (stretching out to so great a Latitude as to reach, on the one hand, the Shores of *America*; and, on the other, those of *Greenland,* and Parts utterly unknown) cannot all be called the *British* Seas, yet hath the King of *Great Britain* most ample Rights on both those Seas, beyond the Bounds of the *British* Name: As he most certainly has, even as far to the West, as *Newfoundland* and the adjacent Parts of North *America,* by virtue of first Invention and Occupancy thereof by *Sebastian Cabot* for *Henry* the VII, and of a more full Possession and Occupancy by Sir *Henry Gilbert* for Queen *Elizabeth:* And, to the North, as far as the Shores of *Greenland,* by virtue of the same Title of first Invention by Sir *Hugh Willoughby* for *Edward* the VI, and of the full Occupancy thereof, and the Discovery of the Use and Profit of those Seas in the Whale-Fishery, by the *English Muscovy*-Company, for Queen *Mary* and Queen *Elizabeth.* However within the Limits before laid down, ought ever to be required (and forced in case of Refusal) from all Ships or Vessels that the *British* Ships of War meet with on those Seas, the striking their Flag and lowering their Topsail; or, where they have no Flag, the lowering their Topsail only, in Acknowledgment of his Majesty's Sovereignty therein.

and

The Extent of the Sea Dominion of Great-Britain.

This Custom of striking the Flag, or Topsail, has prevailed in the *British* Seas, likewise, by Prescription of Time immemorial, having been ever attendant on the Dominion thereof; and so is to be looked upon, not as an honorary Salute or Ceremony, but as an absolute Sign of the Acknowledgment of the Right of that Dominion.

The Duty of striking the Flag, &c.

F 2

Its Antiquity.
Anno 1200.

nion. For the Antiquity of it, we have an ancient and ample Testimony in that memorable Record of King *John*, entitled, *The Ordinance at Hastings*, from the Place where it bore Date, in the second Year of his Reign, *Anno* 1200. By that it is declar'd, **That if the Lieutenant of the King's Fleet, in any Naval Expedition, do meet with on the Sea any Ships or Vessels, laden or unladen, that will not vail and lower their Sails at the Command of the Lieutenant of the King, or the King's Admiral, or his Lieutenant, but shall fight with them of the Fleet, such, if taken, shall be reputed as Enemies, and their Ships, Vessels and Goods be seized and forfeited as the Goods of Enemies, notwithstanding any thing that the Masters or Owners thereof may afterwards come and alleadge of such Ships, Vessels and Goods, being the Goods of those in Amity with our Lord the King: And that the common Sailors on board the same shall be punished for their Rebellion with Imprisonment of their Bodies at Discretion.**

Salutes paid to the English Flag

During the long Series of Years between that and the present Time, this Usage hath met with but very little Opposition, the Flag of *England* having been duly respected, not only within the Bounds of the *British* Seas, but without; some Instances whereof, in the former Part of the last Century, I shall here set down.

at Uleckery in Norway,

About the sixth Year of King *Charles* the I.'s Reign, Sir *John Pennington* then wearing an inferior Flag, and being at *Uleckery* in *Norway*, a Fleet of *Dutch* Ships struck to him in that Harbour.

Dunkirk,

In the Year 1636, in the first Voyage the Earl of *Northumberland* made, who was then Lord High Admiral, the *Happy Entrance*, a Ship of his Fleet, meeting the *Spanish* Fleet, of about twenty six Sail, between *Calais* and *Dunkirk*, (whither they were then carrying Money and Men) obliged them on their own Coast to take in their Colours.

Helvoet Sluice.

In the same Ship, and in the same Year, Sir *George Carteret* carried the Earl of *Arundel*, our Ambassador, to *Helvoet Sluice*, where *Van Trump*, the *Dutch* Admiral, was then riding at an Anchor, who took in his Flag, although Sir *George* wore none himself, and saluted with seven Guns; but in regard he was in a Harbour of the States-General, he hoisted it again.

Fayal,

In the Road of *Fayal*, one of the *Azores* Islands, a *French* Ship of War struck to one of ours, and kept in her Flag while ours was in Sight.

Lisbon,

A *French* Ship of War coming out of the River of *Lisbon*, struck her Topsails to Sir *Richard Plumbly*.

Dunkirk,

The Admiral of *Holland*, at the Blockade of *Dunkirk*, in 1635, always struck his Flag to any of our Ships of War which came within Sight.

Cadiz,

A Squadron of *English* Ships which came from the Coast of *Sailey* in *Barbary*, being in *Cadiz* Bay, and the Duke of *Maqueda*, Admiral of *Spain*, being then going forth to Sea with a Fleet, they both mutually struck and saluted; and the same was done between

Sir

Sir *Robert Manfel*, when going to *Algier*, and *Don Frederick de Toledo* the then *Spanish* Admiral.

When Sir *John Pennington* carried Duke *Hamilton* into *Germany*, in the Year 1631, the *Dutch* Ships which he met with in the *Baltick* Sea, made no Difficulty of striking to our Flag; and even the *Dutch* Admirals when in the Mediterranean have struck to our *English* Ships of War. Baltick, Mediterranean.

This Salutation, or Respect, as we have said, due by Right of the Sovereignty of the Sea, has been accustomed by Prescription of Time immemorial, and hath met with very little Interruption. So much as was, happened from the Republick of the United Provinces, about the times we have been above speaking of, but with very ill Success to them: whose Opposition thereto, and unreasonable Claim to the Community of the Sea against the *British* Sovereignty therein, was so far sufficient to bar the Prescription in either Case, that it occasioned a solemn Acknowledgment of our Right in both, by their Treaty with *Oliver Cromwell* in the Year 1653, the thirteenth Article whereof runs thus: This Right solemnly acknowledg'd by the Dutch, &c. in 1653.

" *Item*, The Ships and Vessels of the said United Provinces, as
" well Ships of War, and fitted out for repelling the Force of Ene-
" mies, as others, which shall, in the *British Seas*, meet with any
" of the Ships of the State of *England*, shall strike their Flag, and
" lower their Topsail, in such manner as hath been ever observ'd in
" any time past, or under any former Government whatsoever.

Since that time due Care hath been taken in most of the subsequent Treaties with the States General to insert an Article concerning the Duty of Striking, as was the tenth Article of the Treaty of 1662, the nineteenth of that of *Breda* in 1667, and the fourth of that in 1673, which last, because it is so full and express to our Purpose, and that therein is ascertained how far to the Northward and Southward the said Duty is required to be paid, I shall here set down. 662, 667. 1673.

" The aforesaid States General of the United Provinces, in due
" Acknowledgment, on their Part, of the King of *Great Britain*'s
" *Right to have his Flag respected* in the Seas hereafter-mention'd,
" shall and do declare and agree, that whatever Ships or Vessels
" belonging to the said United Provinces, whether Vessels of War
" or others, or whether single, or in Fleets, shall meet in any of
" the Seas from Cape *Finisterre* to the middle Point of the Land
" *Van Staten* in *Norway*, with any Ships or Vessels belonging to
" his Majesty of *Great Britain*, whether those Ships be single or
" in greater Number, if they carry his Majesty of *Great Britain*'s
" Flag or Jack, the aforesaid *Dutch* Vessels or Ships shall strike their
" Flag, and lower their Topsail, in the same manner, and with as
" much Respect, as hath at any Time, or in any Place been for-
" merly practised towards any Ships of his Majesty's of *Great*
" *Britain*, or his Predecessors, by any Ships of the States General,
" or their Predecessors.

It

Observations on the Use of the Term, The British Seas, in Treaties made by our Nation.

It is since these times likewise that it hath become necessary, in those Articles of Treaties of Peace wherein are ascertain'd the Places where, and Times when such Peace shall take effect, to take care that the Seas belonging to *Great Britain* be express'd by the Name of the *British* Seas, as was done by the Treaty of Peace which *Cromwell* made with *France*, by the Treaty with *Holland* in 1667, and by the Treaties of *Ryswick* and *Utrecht*. Where it hath happened otherwise, as in the Treaty with *France* at *Breda*, in 1667, and some others, it is to be looked on as a great Omission, and a sort of tacit Departure from the Right of *Britain* to those Seas, by neglecting so fair an Opportunity of asserting it, in giving them their proper Name of the *British Seas*. Of this we find the Minister who negotiated with *France* the Treaty for a Suspension of Arms in 1712, was very well aware, as well as the *French* Minister with whom he concluded the same. The latter had inserted in the Draught *(les Mers qui entourent les Isles Britanniques)* the Seas which surround the *British* Isles, and cited the foresaid Treaty of *Breda* as a Precedent. The *British* Minister shewed him that, before that Treaty, the Expression had always run *Maribus Britannicis*, particularly in the Treaty with *Cromwell*; and that the Error committed in that of *Breda*, had been rectified in that of *Ryswick*; and notwithstanding the other's Endeavours to retain his Words, by entering into the Dispute of Sea-Dominion, and otherwise, he peremptorily insisted on having them razed out, and altered according to his Mind. This, as it appears by the Treaty, was accordingly done in the latter Part of the third Article, but in the former Part of it, happened to be unluckily omitted, although in that Place most of all necessary. For there instead of saying (as it appears by what is above-said was intended) that " the Ships, Goods, " and Effects which shall be taken in the Chanel, *the British*, and " North Seas, after the Space of twelve Days, to be reckon'd from " the signing of the said Suspension, shall reciprocally be restored " on both sides:" The Words, *the British*, are left out, and so the Agreement runs for only such as should be taken in the Chanel and North Seas. This very Omission was it that occasioned the Loss of a Merchant-Ship called the *Favour*, taken, after twelve Days from the Date of the Treaty, by a *French* Privateer, in the Latitude of fifty three Degrees, and about eighty or a hundred Leagues *W. N. W.* of *Ireland*, and condemned in *France* as Prize, as also of some other Ships in the like Case; for their Owners claiming the Benefit of the said third Article, the late Queen, by reason they were not taken within the Limits of the Chanel, or of the North Seas, according to the Letter of the said Article, could not interpose for their Restitution, although they were taken many Leagues within the Western Limits of the *British* Seas.

Treaty of Breda,

an Omission therein

to be rectified. Here we might enlarge on the Impropriety of particularly mentioning the Chanel with the *British* Seas, as if it were not a Part of them, as is done towards the Close of the Article above-mentioned, and in some other Treaties; and in observing how much better it it would be to include all the Seas surrounding *Great Britain* under the general Name of the *British Seas*, as is done in the Treaties of *Ryswick* and *Utrecht* ; but it is now time to put an end to this long Digression, and return to the Pursuit of our Design.

Having thus deduced from the first Ages of the World to our own Times, a general Account of the People who have flourished at Sea, we shall from thence select such as have made the most considerable Figure among them, and enter into a particular Detail of their Naval Affairs, which shall be the Subject of the following Books.

Pag. 41.

10 20 40 60 80 100
eagues of Great Britain

BLACK SEA
MANIA
Thracian Bosphorus
Constantinople
lipoli Marmora
Lampsacus
Hellespont
Troy
Antandrus
ANATOLIA
Phocæ
Fochia
Smirna
Ephesus
Miletus

ASIA MINOR

CARMANIA

Stramille Satalia Aiazzo
Candelor Scanderoon
C. Luzymedon
Seleucia Antiochia
Rhodes P. Penice Tarsus
Prom. Calycadnus
C. S. Pisano Carpasia
Salomen Nicosia
CYPRUS I. Famagosta Tortosa
Tripoli
C. de Gata Gibel
Damasenes
Sidon
Tyrn
LEVANT
Cæsaria
Joppa
Gaza

Pharus
Alexandria
Naucratis Damiata
Grand Cairo
EGYPT

A COMPLEAT

HISTORY

Of the most Remarkable

TRANSACTIONS at SEA.

BOOK II.

Containing an Account of the most remarkable Naval Transactions throughout the World, from the Expedition of the *Argonauts* to the Dissolution of the *Roman* Empire by the Irruptions of the barbarous Nations.

CHAP. I.

Of the Naval Wars of the Grecians, *from the Expedition of the* Argonauts, *to the breaking out of the War with the* Persians.

THE People who first occur to us to be particularly considered are the *Grecians*, in regard they are the most ancient of those whose Affairs afford fit Matter for *Naval History*. Under this Denomination we are to comprehend not only the Inhabitants of *Greece*, but also those of the Islands of the *Ægean* Sea, and of the Coasts of *Asia Minor*, where the *Grecians* planted Colonies, without excluding even the People of *Sicily*. Among the *Greeks*,

Grecians.

Argos

Mengrelia. Argonauts. Jason, &c. About the Year of the World, 2714. Before Christ, 1234. Before the building of Rome 484.

Argos is said to be the first who built a long Ship, from whom she was likewise called *Argos*, and the Persons who made use of her to *Colchis* derived the Name of *Argonauts*. *Jason*, a Prince of *Thessaly*, was the Person under whose Conduct this Expedition was undertaken, wherein he was accompanied by *Castor* and *Pollux*, *Hercules*, *Telamon*, *Orpheus*, and others of the most considerable Quality in *Greece*. Their Design was in Quest of the *Golden Fleece*, by which Name it is generally thought was understood either a great Treasure carried to *Colchis* by *Phryxus*, or else the Gold Mines of that Country. Whatsoever it was, *Jason* met with all the Success he expected, by the Assistance of *Medea*, Daughter to *Æetes*, King of the Country, whom he carried off with him to *Greece*, and married.

Hercules goes against Troy.

After *Jason's* Return, *Hercules*, with several of the *Argonauts*, undertook an Expedition to *Troy* against King *Laomedon*, who had barbarously violated the Law of Nations, by putting to Death the Agents *Hercules* had sent to him on some publick Affairs; and on their Arrival they levelled with the Ground that City, which had been but newly built.

Minos King of Crete. A. M. 2730. Dædalus improves Navigation.

The next Naval Naval Armament among the *Greeks*, was that of *Minos* King of *Crete*, against the Pirates of the *Ægean* Sea, of whom in the preceding Book. To what we have there said of him may be added his Expedition to *Sicily* on account of *Dædalus*, who had escaped thither with part of his Fleet. *Dædalus* was a noble *Athenian* of great Quality, and the most extraordinary Genius of that Age for the Mechanicks, who happening to kill his Sister's Son at *Athens*, fled to *Crete*, and there entring into the Service of *Minos*, put his Naval Affairs in the most flourishing Condition they had ever yet been, by making several very considerable Improvements in the Use of Masts, Yards and Sails; for the *Grecians* before his Time depended chiefly on their Oars, having very little Knowledge of the Management of Sails. Here he became a Party in some criminal Intrigues, for which *Minos* threw him into Prison, from whence escaping with part of the Fleet aforesaid, it gave Rise to the Fable of his flying with Wings from *Crete* to *Sicily*. In that

Flies to Cocalus King of Sicily.

Country he was received into the Protection of *Cocalus*, who refusing to deliver him up to *Minos*, there ensued a long and bloody War between those Princes, wherein at length *Minos* was slain; to revenge the Death of whom, the *Cretans* fitted out a great Fleet,

The Cretans invade Sicily,

and repaired again to *Sicily*. So intent were they on the Prosecution of this Quarrel, that they passed over in such great Numbers as to leave their Country almost uninhabited. On their Arrival in

besiege Camicus,

Sicily they laid siege to *Camicus*, the Royal Seat of *Cocalus*, but having spent five Years before it, were obliged to raise the Siege. Then embarking their Forces in order to return home, they met with such furious Tempests, that despairing ever of seeing their Country again, they put into the Gulph of *Tarentum*, and landing there

settle in Italy.

took up their Habitations in *Italy*. On this occasion the Inhabitants of *Greece*, properly so called, to whom the *Cretan* Wealth and Power had long appeared formidable, observing the great Fertility,

CHAP. I. *Dissolution of the* Rom. *Empire.*

tility, and commodious situation of that Island, now not only undefended, but almost uninhabited, sent over numerous Colonies, and took Possession thereof, from which time it was reckoned among the *Grecian* States, and, as such, in few Years after contributed its Quota of eighty Ships, under the Command of *Idomeneus* and *Merion* for the *Trojan* Wars.

The Greeks possess Crete.

Idomeneus and Merion.

In the beforementioned Expedition of *Hercules* to *Troy*, *Hesione*, the Daughter of *Laomedon*, was forcibly carried off from thence, and married to *Telamon*. *Paris*, her Nephew, being sent to *Greece* to demand her, found means of getting into the good Graces of *Helena*, Wife of *Menelaus* King of *Sparta*, and carried her away with him, whereby he at the same time gratifyed his Love, and made Reprizal for the injury his Country had received from the *Greeks*. They, under the conduct of their several Princes, to revenge this Violence, got together at *Aulis*, a Town of *Bœotia*, a Fleet of one thousand two hundred Sail; to such a degree were their Naval Affairs by this time improved; one great means whereof was the commodious situation of the Country, all the Sea Coasts abounding with Necks of Land, and Promontories jutting out into the Sea, which not only formed large and secure Harbours, but afforded the most convenient spots of Ground for building Cities, as needing but very slight Fortifications for their defence, and having the Sea open either for Wars or Commerce.

Hesione and Helen's Rape.

Expedition of the Greeks against Troy. A.M. 2756.

Homer in his Iliad, reckoning up the number of Ships that were sent from the several parts of *Greece* upon this Expedition, attributes to each of the *Bœotian* Ships one hundred and twenty Men, and to those of *Philoctetes* fifty Men each, thereby intimating, as *Thucydides* thinks, the Burthen of the largest and smallest Ships. So that if we estimate them at a Medium to carry eighty five Men apiece, the whole number on Board the one thousand two hundred Ships will amount to one hundred and two thousand; all whom, except the Princes, and some few others of chief Authority, served both as Mariners and Soldiers. These Ships, we are to observe, were according to the Built of those times, open and without any Deck, wherein if there was found occasion, upon meeting with Pirates or otherwise, to come to an Engagement, they fought only from the Head and Stern, as from a Retrenchment, the waste being entirely taken up with the Rowers. There was not any thing considerable transacted at Sea during the time of this Siege, for the *Grecian* Ships were not only not proper for War, but if they had been ever so much so, the Enemy they had to deal with would not have afforded them any opportunity for the use of them: So that as soon as the Troops were disembarked, the Ships were hawled on shoar, and secured with a Trench and Rampier, from whence they were launched again, as occasion offered, either for getting in Provisions from the Neighbouring Islands, or taking Prizes on those Coasts for the support of the Army before the Town.

Their Ships not proper for Naval Fights.

The Wars being ended, and great part of the Fleet returned to *Greece*, there happened such strange Revolutions in that Country, as might render the *Grecians* themselves objects of Pity even to the poor

Strange Revolutions in Greece after their War with Troy. poor remains of the *Trojans* they had reduced. For to say not any thing of *Agamemnon* and *Menelaus*, who suffered more from their own People than the Enemy had from them, there were but few, if any, of the principal Persons who were not tossed about by Tempests, and being at length thrown on Foreign Countries, died far from their native Land. *Diomedes* and *Philoctetes* were driven to different parts of *Italy*. Some came to untimely ends by the Sword, and many perished by Shipwrack. As for *Ulysses*, the fates seemed to inflict a double portion of Revenge on him, for the principal share he had in the Destruction of *Troy*; for after the various Afflictions he had undergone in his long wandrings about the Sea, returning to his Country, he was slain by his Son *Flegonus*, whom he had by *Circe*. So that upon the whole, that numerous Army, and great Fleet of one thousand two hundred Ships, seem to have occasioned as much Destruction to *Greece* as they carried to *Troy*.

After this *Greece* enjoying for many Years a profound Peace, it *Greek Colonies.* became so overstocked with People as that it was found necessary to send out Colonies to Foreign Parts. The first of them was that *Ionians. A. M. 2906.* of the *Ionians*, a People of *Athens*, who passing over into *Asia Minor* and the Islands on that side, invited by the richness of the Soil, and the goodness of the Climate, they there settled themselves, and building therein twelve Cities, gave the Country the name of *Ionia*. Those Cities in process of time, on account of their extraction from the same Original, united into one Common Wealth, and relying on their great Strength by Sea and Land, had the courage to wage War with the most Potent Princes of those Ages. Some *and Peloponnesians.* time after this Expedition of the *Ionians*, the *Peloponnesians* sent out numerous Colonies to the Westward, who planted themselves in *Italy*, and there built *Crotona, Tarentum*, and other very considerable Cities; so that from them all the Southern parts of *Italy* had the name of *Magna Græcia*.

As yet the *Greeks* were unacquainted with the Art of Naval War, and seemed chiefly intent either on the improving their Trade, or the Propagation of their Name and Power, by the swarms of People sent out, as abovementioned, to Foreign Countries. But above four hundred Years after the taking of *Troy*, the *Corinthians*, on occasion of their Wars with the People of *Corcyra*, did, as I may presume to say, invent this Art, and fitted out a Fleet not only furnished in a much more warlike manner than any in the preceding *Corinthians first Inventors of large Gallies.* times, but also consisting of Vessels of a different and stronger form, that is, of Gallies with three Tire of Oars, which were at this time first built by *Aminocles*, a Citizen of *Corinth*; for before their Gallies had no more than thirty, or at the most fifty Oars, all in the same rank, or height from the Water.

The Island *Corcyra* (now *Corfu*) in the time of the *Trojan* War was inhabited by the *Phæaces*, who are celebrated by *Homer* in his *Odysses* for their skill in Sea Affairs. These People, about two Cen-
Phæaces inhabiting Corcyra dispossest by the Corinthians. turies after, were dispossessed by a Colony the *Corinthians* sent thither, who built the City *Corcyra*, and imposed likewise that name on the whole Island. The *Corcyræans* treading in the steps of the
Phæaces,

CHAP. I. *Dissolution of the* Rom. *Empire.* 45

Phæaces whom they had turned out, and of the *Corinthians* from whom they drew their Origine, did, from their very first Settlement, apply themselves to Naval Affairs, and in Confidence of their Abilities therein, had several rude Skirmishes at Sea with their Founders: But the *Corinthians* now engaging them with these their new invented Gallies, did by a total defeat reduce them to Obedience. This Battel is not remarkable either for the number of the slain, or of the Ships sunk or taken, nor for the great conduct wherewith it was managed on either side, nor the fame or renown of the Commanders, but only for that it is celebrated by *Grecian* Writers as the first Naval Battel in their Country; for as to what we have before said of *Minos*, from *Pliny*, that he was the first who fought with Ships, it is meant of his Expedition against the Pirates, wherein he may not be properly said to have fought any set Battel, but that he had only Skirmishes and single Engagements, as occasion offered. *The Corintho-Corcyræans reduced by their Founders.*

Next after the *Corinthians*, the *Ionians*, as hath been mentioned before, became the most considerable at Sea, and (those of the Islands especially) relying on their great Naval Force, set at Defiance the Threats and Power of the most flourishing Monarch of *Asia* at that time. Of the twelve *Ionian* Cities before taken notice of, *Samos* and *Chios* were situate in two Islands of the same Names. Against these *Crœsus*, King of *Lydia*, preparing a great Armada, it is said that *Bias* (celebrated for his Wisdom among the seven Sages of *Greece*) happening at that time to come to the Court of *Sardes*, the King asked him, *What News from* Greece? *Sir*, said he, *the Islanders intend to invade you with an Army of ten thousand Horse. Heaven cannot favour my Wishes more*, replied the King, *than for those Islanders to venture themselves on the Continent, and think to attack me with Land Forces. True*, said *Bias*, *and what more does your Majesty think the Islanders desire than to get you, whose Arms have ever been employed ashore, on their own Element, the Sea, to which they have been always accustomed, and wherein their whole Strength and Power consists?* Struck with the Force of Truth, the King took this able Minister's Advice, and put a stop to his Naval Preparations, but could not withstand the impetuous Motions of his restless Ambition, which hurried him on to turn his Arms against the rising Glory of *Cyrus*, King of *Persia*; but with this fatal event, that he did, as the delusive Oracle had foretold, overturn a flourishing Kingdom, but it was his own, not that of the Enemy, as he had fondly interpreted it; and thus he became one of the greatest Examples of mortal Frailty, and the Instability of human Affairs. *The Ionians. Crœsus intending to invade 'em. Is disswaded by Bias. Crœsus overcome by Cyrus.*

Mean while the *Ionians* daily increasing the Reputation of their Naval Arms, held for some time the uncontested Dominion of the Sea, and looked with the same Eyes of Indifference on the Power of *Cyrus* as they had before on that of *Crœsus*, although by this time he had subdued almost all *Asia* to his Obedience. This they thought they might do with the more Impunity, for that the *Persians* had not hitherto so much as set foot on the Salt Water; but long they did not triumph in this Success, for some new Commotions

tions in *Persia* requiring the Presence of *Cyrus* there, he committed the *Ionian* War to the Care of his General *Harpagus*, who in a short time reduced, either by Force, or Treaty all the *Ionian* Cities on the Continent. The first Town he took among them was *Phocæa*, whose Inhabitants being driven out, they put to Sea, and after various Adventures, settled at *Marseilles*, as we have related in the foregoing Book.

Cyrus being dead, he was succeeded in the *Persian* Throne by *Cambyses*. In his Time flourished *Polycrates*, the celebrated Tyrant of *Samos* before-mention'd, who was Master of a hundred large Ships, besides a great Number of Gallies with three Tire of Oars.

The *Lesbians* coming to the Aid of their Friends of *Miletus* with all their Force, *Polycrates* overcame them in a Sea Fight, and took as many Prisoners as served him to draw a Ditch round the Walls of *Samos*. After this he subdued many more Islands and Towns on the Continent, and indeed invaded all his maritime Neighbours without any Difference, having established this for a Maxim with himself, that he gratified his Friend more by restoring what he had taken from him, than if he had not taken any thing away. So great was this Prince's Success, that *Amasis*, King of *Ægypt*, his Friend and Ally, suspecting that such an uninterrupted Course of Prosperity must have some disastrous End, wrote to him, and desired he would make some certain Change therein, by chusing out the thing he set the greatest Value on, and so to make it away as that he might never more enjoy it. To comply with this Advice, he went on board one of his Ships, and threw into the Sea his Signet, which was an extraordinary rich Emerald set in a Ring of Gold: But it so happened that the next Day a Fisherman taking a very large Fish, presented it to the King, as only worthy of it, in which, when it was cut up, was found the Royal Signet. *Amasis* hearing this, took such Assurance that unfortunate must be the End of this prodigious Success, that he immediately renounced his Friendship and Alliance, lest he should be involved in the same Calamities, which he thought must necessarily fall upon him.

When *Cambyses* was raising his Forces for an Expedition he had undertaken to reduce *Ægypt*, *Polycrates* desired him underhand to send to him for some Supplies, who doing so, he picked out such of his *Samians* as he thought most ripe for Rebellion, and embarking them on board his Gallies, sent them accordingly to *Cambyses*, at the same time desiring him not to let any of these People come back. The *Samians*, nevertheless, upon the Conclusion of that War, found Means to withdraw themselves from *Cambyses*, and went to *Lacedæmon* to crave Aid of that State against the Tyrant, whose Power was now grown so formidable to the rest of *Greece* that it was easily granted; and the *Corinthians* likewise entered into the same War. The *Lacedæmonians* coming with a great Fleet to *Samos*, besieged the City, but endeavouring to storm it, were repulsed with some Loss; and having in vain spent forty Days in the Siege (so valiantly was it defended by *Polycrates*) they then returned home to *Peloponnesus*. This their Departure, some reported, was procured

CHAP. I. *Dissolution of the Rom. Empire.* 47

procured by *Polycrates*'s coining a great Quantity of Leaden Money, which he covered over with Gold, and distributed among the Enemy's Officers. Some time after, *Orætes* the King of *Persia*'s Vice-Roy at *Sardes*, and Successor of *Harpagus* in that Government, finding himself reproached at Court, for that he had not yet annexed *Samos* to the King's Dominions, which lay so near to his Province, and so easy, as his Enemies alledged, to be reduced, did by all means compass the Destruction of *Polycrates*, and became the Instrument of an unfortunate End to him whom *Amasis* had so violently suspected. This *Orætes* knowing *Polycrates*'s Ambition to become Master of *Ionia*, and the Islands, he sent to acquaint him that he was not ignorant of the commendable Ambition he had to possess himself of those Provinces he so well deserved; but that hearing he had a present Occasion of a Supply of Money, and knowing that his own Destruction was determined by his Master *Cambyses*, if he would receive him into his Protection, he should have half of the King's Treasure which he had in Possession, whereby he might not only attain his Ends in *Asia*, but even the Sovereignty of all *Greece*. *Is circumvented by Orætes,*

Polycrates with great Joy received the Message, being very avaritious; and to make sure Work of it, first sent over *Mæandrius* his Secretary. *Orætes* knowing him to be a cunning and circumspect Man, filled several Chests with Stones, and covering them at the top with Gold, thereby deceived him. *Polycrates* was dissuaded by all his Friends from going over, notwithstanding which, and many Omens and Presages of ill Success, he embarked with a slender Retinue to secure this Treasure, and going up the River *Maander* as far as *Magnesia*, was there seized by *Orætes*, and nailed to a Cross. *and crucified.*

As for *Cambyses*, tho' he did not himself do any thing very remarkable at Sea, yet was he the occasion of that great Accession of Naval Power to the succeeding Kings of *Persia*, which enabled them to give so much Disturbance to the *Grecian* Affairs. In his before-mention'd Expedition to *Ægypt*, he by the way reduced to his Obedience the *Phœnicians*, so long celebrated for their Naval Strength and Knowledge; and having subdued *Ægypt*, was desirous to add *Carthage* to his Empire, giving it in charge to the *Phœnicians* to conquer that City: But they desired to be excused from embruing their Hands in the Blood of their own Relations, it being a Colony of theirs who first founded that City, as well as many others both within and without the Mediteranean, as we have mentioned in the first Book. From the Account there given of these People, we shall not at all wonder that, chiefly in Confidence of their great Abilities at Sea, the Kings of *Persia* ventured to wage a Naval War with *Greece*, then near arrived to her most flourishing Condition. *Cambyses reduces the Phœnicians, &c.*

Chap. II.

Of the Naval Wars of the Grecians, *from the breaking out of the* Persian *War, to the Defeat of the* Persians, *and the burning their Fleet at the Promontory* Mycale.

<small>Persians war against the Grecians. Sub Anno Mundi 3400. Aristagoras deserts the Persians,</small>

THIS War was principally occasioned by the *Athenians*, who now first began to be Masters of a Naval Force. About this time *Aristagoras*, Tyrant of *Miletus* in *Ionia*, having abdicated his Government, on account of some Mismanagements for which he feared to be expelled by the *Persians*, he withdrew to *Sparta*, and represented to *Cleomenes*, then reigning there, the Hardships of *Miletus* and the other Colonies of *Ionia*, which groan'd under the *Persian* Yoak. The great Courage and Power of the *Grecians* he artificially set off to be yet much greater than it was, at the same time expressing himself very contemptibly of the *Persian* Strength, and shewing how easy a Task it would be for *Greece*, but more especially the *Spartans*, to drive out of the *Lesser Asia* so weak an Enemy, who, in comparison of them, were totally ignorant of the Art of War. But *Cleomenes* was too wise a Prince to hearken to these Delusions of an Exile, and engage in so hazardous and unnecessary a War; who despairing of Success at *Sparta*, repaired to *Athens* to involve that City in his Misfortunes. On his Arrival there, an Assembly of the People being called, he made use of the same Arguments as he had to *Cleomenes*, adding further, how reasonably the *Ionians* might expect Assistance from *Greece* in general, but most of all from the *Athenians*, as being their particular Colony. Scarce had he ended his Speech, but they decreed War against *Persia*, and immediately fitted out a Fleet of twenty Sail for *Ionia*, where landing their Troops, they marched a few Miles up into the Country, and surprized and burnt *Sardes* the Capital of *Lydia*. The News whereof coming to *Darius*, then keeping his Court at *Susa*, he made a solemn Vow to be revenged on them, and ordered one of his Attendants who stood by, every time he sat down at Table, to cry out, *Sir, remember the Athenians.* Nor were his Threats in vain, for soon after, with a great Fleet, of which the *Phœnicians* made up the best part, he presently reduced, as it were on his way, *Lesbos, Chios,* and other Islands of the *Ægean,* who soon rising in Rebellion, as usually newly conquered Countries do, there ensued that memorable Fight between the *Persians* and Islanders at *Lada,* which was the most considerable that had been hitherto fought at Sea, from the beginning of the World to this time. *Lada* was a small Island lying off *Miletus*: Near this the two Fleets came to an Engagement, that of the *Ionians* consisting of three hundred Gallies, and the *Persians* of double the Number. The Battel was fought with great Courage and Resolution on both sides; on the one for Glory and Honour, on the other for their Lives and Liberties;

<small>flies to Cleomenes.</small>

<small>Athens declares War against the Persians,</small>

<small>and burn Sardes.</small>

<small>The Sea-Fight off Lada.</small>

berties; these encouraged with the Desire of Conquest, and those animated with Despair, the last Refuge in Rebellion. The *Persians* notwithstanding their great Superiority, had gone near to have been defeated, but that the *Samians*, who were in the Right Wing (such was the Disposal of their Fleets in those Times) quitted the Fight, on what Occasion is uncertain, and so left the Center exposed to the Fury of the Enemy. Thus the remaining Part of the Fleet being surrounded on all sides by such unequal Numbers, and seeing themselves treacherously deserted, were only intent on selling their Lives as dear as they could, and died bravely in the Bed of Honour. This Victory was followed by the immediate Surrender and Sacking of *Miletus*, in Sight of which it was obtained: And *Samos*, *Chios*, and other neighbouring Islands were cruelly ravaged and laid waste by the insulting Conquerors. *The Persians beat the Islanders, sack Miletus, Samos, Chios, &c.*

And now *Darius* had nothing left to do, but to pursue his Revenge against the *Athenians*, and the rest of *Greece*; to which Purpose, early the next Spring, he deputes *Mardonius*, to whom he had lately given his Daughter in Marriage, to reduce it to his Obedience. He, on his Arrival on the Coast, took upon him the Command of the Fleet, consisting of the Sea-Force of *Cilicia*, *Cyprus*, *Ægypt*, and *Phœnicia*, (on the Ships and Sailers of which last he principally relied) and there embarking a considerable Body of Troops, having appointed the rest of the Land-Army to meet him at the *Hellespont*, he set sail for that Place, where receiving them on board, he made the best of his way for *Greece*. In his Passage thither, coasting about the Mountain *Athos* (now Cape *di Monte Santo*) he met with such a violent Tempest, as proved the entire Destruction of this Expedition, three hundred Ships, and twenty thousand Men perishing therein. *Mardonius* himself made a shift to escape, but was in a short time recalled, as a Person not fit to be entrusted with the Management of the War, which was committed to the Care of *Datis*, a *Mede*, and *Artaphernes* the King's Nephew. *But bending their Force against the Athenians, their Fleet is destroyed by Tempest.*

These Generals having gotten together a very numerous Army, came down to the Sea Coasts of *Cilicia*, where they found a great Number of Vessels, of a peculiar Built for the Transportation of Horse, which *Darius* had ordered the maritime People of the *Lesser Asia* to get ready for this Expedition. Embarking the Troops, they set sail with a Fleet consisting of six hundred Gallies, besides Transports, and reducing most of the Islands *Cyclades* in their way, landed safely in ª *Eubœa* with an Army of above a hundred thousand Men. There in few Days they had *Eretria* surrender'd to them, and thence passing over into *Attica*, were met on the Plains of *Marathon* by *Miltiades* the *Athenian* General with a Body of chosen Troops. Who should have seen both Armies ranged in order of Battel, would have thought them a vastly unequal Match, that under *Miltiades* not amounting to above eleven thousand Men, but they indeed full of Courage and Bravery. On the Signal for the Charge, the *Athenians* rushed on with such incredible Fury and Precipitation, as disordered the Enemy on the very first Shock, and at length entirely routed, and put them to flight. They retreated *They equip a new Fleet, &c. ª Now Negroponte. But at Marathon are beaten by the Athenians, A. M. 3459.*

H

in great Confusion toward their Ships, but were so closely pursued by the *Athenians*, that they again engaged them as they were em-

and their Fleet again destroyed. barking. Some of their Ships they took, and some they set on fire; and the whole Coast was a Scene of Slaughter and Destruction. In this Action is deservedly celebrated the Behaviour of *Cynægirus*, an *Athenian* Captain, who, as a Gally full of *Persians* was putting off

The noted Valour of Cynægirus. from the Shore, catched hold of the Rudder with his Right Hand to prevent their Escape, which being presently lopp'd off, he seiz'd it with his Left, and losing that too, fastned his Teeth in it, and expired; that so it might appear that even Rage and Fury prompted him to attempt what his Valour could not perform for the Service of his Country.

The Persians arm anew. Upon this ill Success, by Sea and Land, the *Persian* Generals made the best of their way back to *Asia*; and *Darius*, on the News of their Defeat, immediately began new Levies for another Army, and gave Orders for fitting out a Fleet: But in the midst of these

Darius's Death. Preparations he died, and was succeeded in the Throne by his Son *Xerxes*. He, either to revenge his Father's Disgrace, or through a real Ambition of adding *Greece* to his Dominions, carried on the Preparations with great Vigour, and was entirely bent on prosecu-

The Ægyptians rebel against Xerxes, but are reduced. ting the War; but just at the same time *Ægypt* rising in Rebellion, he thought it necessary first to extinguish that Flame, and invading the Country with a great Force by Sea and Land, he, in the first Year of his Reign, reduced it to his Obedience, and imposed such hard Conditions on the *Ægyptians*, as he thought should leave them little room to rebel again. Having thus settled *Ægypt*, he turned his Thoughts wholly to the Reduction of *Greece*, and resolving to compass it, if human Power possibly could, he spent three whole Years in his Preparations, and at length, in the fifth of his Reign, set out from *Susa* with the greatest Army that ever the World knew, at the same time having ready on the Coasts a very formidable Sea-Force, which consisted of a Fleet of four thousand and two hundred Sail, twelve hundred of them Gallies with three Tire of Oars, and the rest of them from fifty to thirty Oars each. Of these the largest carried two hundred and thirty Men, and the least about eighty, as well Soldiers as Rowers: The whole Fleet having on board in all about five hundred and eighty thousand Men. The first Effort of

The Persians come to Mount Athos. this mighty Naval Force was against the Mountain *Athos*, a very high Promontory of *Macedonia*, jutting out into the Sea between the Gulphs of *Strymon* and *Singus*, join'd to the Continent by a Neck of Land about a Mile and a Quarter over, and is now known by the Name of Cape *di Monte Santo*, as before observed. And because the Fleet under *Mardonius* had met with such a terrible

Xerxes makes an Island of the Peninsula. Disaster in doubling this Cape, *Xerxes* gave order for cutting a Chanel through the *Isthmus*, which was in a short time perfected, so as to admit of two Gallies a-breast to pass through.

There was a great Ambition among the Ancients of making Islands of *Peninsula*'s, as was more than once attempted by the Kings of *Ægypt* in cutting the *Isthmus* of *Suez*, and by *Nero* in that of *Corinth*, which had some Shew of Profit and Advantage;

but

CHAP. II. *Dissolution of the* Rom. *Empire.* 51

but this, since they might safely enough have gone round the Cape, was only a most foolish Vain-gloriousness, and unseasonable Ostentation of prodigious Power, to little or no Purpose, the Chanel in a short time growing dry, and leaving scarce the Foot-steps of so stupendous a Work.

The Land Army being now arrived near the Sea Coast, *Xerxes* gave Orders for laying a Bridge over the *Hellespont*, which being shattered and broken down by tempestuous Weather, he commanded the Heads of the Workmen to be cut off, the Sea itself to be whip'd with three hundred Stripes, and a Pair of Fetters to be thrown into it, in token of its future Subjection. He then made two Bridges of Gallies, so well anchored, and secured to each other, that they resisted the Violence of the Weather, and the whole Army passed over in seven Days and Nights, the Troops on the one, and the Slaves and Carriages, with the Baggage on the other. The Army being now arrived in *Europe*, his next Care was to take a Review of his Naval Force, to which Purpose he went on board a Ship magnificently fitted for his Reception, where sitting on the Deck under a Golden Canopy, he sailed about and viewed the whole Fleet, frequently asking *Demaratus* the *Spartan* King, then in Exile, and with him, if 'twas possible for any Mortal to be more happy than himself. *Themistocles* was at this time the Man who bore the most considerable Sway in *Athens*, being a Person of very extraordinary Abilities, and who had from his Childhood given his Country great Hopes of his Courage and Conduct. While he was yet very young, he was the principal Occasion of the War with the *Æginetans*, who had, without any manner of Necessity, complied with the *Persian* Demands of sending Earth and Water, in acknowledgment of their Subjection; in which War the *Æginetans* were entirely worsted, and quite left their Dominion at Sea. *Themistocles* wisely foreseeing the Storm that was gathering in *Persia*, persuaded the *Athenians* to build those Ships against the *Æginetans*, for which they should have future Occasion against the *Persians*: He made it likewise his Business, upon all Occasions, both publickly and in private, to induce his Countrymen to apply themselves to Sea Affairs, and look upon a Naval Force as the most effectual Means of obtaining both Safety and Power. Pursuant to this wholsome Advice, the *Athenians*, after the Battel of *Marathon*, built two hundred Gallies of three Tire of Oars, and when *Xerxes* was now advancing against them, and they consulted the Oracle of *Delphos* thereupon, they received for answer, that they must trust to their wooden Walls. *Themistocles*, who was of a most ready Wit on such Occasions, told them the meaning of the Oracle was, that their Shipping must be their Safe-guard; that their Country did not consist in their Walls, but their People, that the City of *Athens* was wheresoever they themselves were, and that they had much better trust their Safety to their Fleet, than the Town, which was very little able to endure a Siege. The *Athenians* accordingly transported their Wives and Children, with their most valuable Effects, to some of the neighbouring Islands, and put themselves,

Lays a Bridge o'er the Hellespont.

Themistocles's Character,

Persuades the Athenians to subject the Æginetans,

and to fight the Persians by Sea.

H 2 with

with their Ships, under the Conduct of *Themistocles*, to fight for their Country.

The Persian Fleet shattered by Tempest.

The *Persian* Fleet was by this time got to the Height of Mount *Pelion*, not far from *Attica*, and having lain all Night at Anchor off of that Place, about Day-break it began to blow very hard at North, and soon encreased to such a Tempest, as four hundred of the stoutest Ships were sunk in few Hours, and all their Companies lost, together with a great Number of Transports, and other small Vessels; so that the Fleet was lessened by a third Part before it came in Sight of the Enemy.

Themistocles in the mean time observing the great Obstruction the the publick Service met with from the mutual Grudgings and Resentments of the *Grecians*, persuaded them to sacrifice their private Animosities to the common Safety, and join unanimously in the Defence of their Country; of which as the *Æginetans* were a part, he likewise prevailed with them, notwithstanding their late Variance, to add their Naval Force to that of the *Athenians*; and also, pursuant to a general Resolution of *Greece*, sent to *Gelon*, King of *Sicily*, offering to enter into an Alliance with him, and desiring his Aid against the *Persians*.

King Gelon refuses to aid the Athenians.

Gelon was one of the most powerful Princes of that Time, both by Sea and Land, and was able to furnish out a greater Number of Ships than all *Greece*, having maintained a long War against the *Carthaginians*, and given them several notable Defeats at Sea. When the *Athenian* Ambassadors mentioned the Alliance, he lent a willing Ear to the Proposal, and promised to assist them with Men, Money, and Provisions, together with a Fleet of two hundred Gallies, and even with his own Person, but all this upon Condition he might be constituted Generalissimo of the *Grecians*, otherwise he could afford them no Aid, nor at all concern himself in their Affairs. They refused the Conditions, as too unreasonable, and unbecoming the Dignity of *Athens*, to whom, as the rest of *Greece* had committed the Care of the Sea, they thought it would be dishonourable for them to yield that Preheminence to a *Sicilian*, and so returned from this unsuccessful Errand.

The Athenian Fleet at Artemisium

The *Grecians* being thus denied all foreign Aid, had only their own Force to rely on, and having gotten together a Fleet of one hundred and eighty Gallies, repaired to *Artemisium*, not far distant from *Pelion*, where the *Persians* met with the afore-mention'd Misfortune. This *Artemisium* was situate at the Mouth of the Chanel which flows between *Eubœa* and the main Land of *Greece*, and was a dangerous Station for any Fleet to continue in, by reason of the sudden and violent Gusts of Wind which frequently came down from the Mountains both of the Island and the Main, and for that the Tides were so uncertain, as to ebb and flow not only seven times a Day, (as the Ancients imagined) but were as variable as the Wind itself, and often came with Currents as rapid as if they fell from a steep Mountain. *Themistocles*, nevertheless, chose this Place to fight the Enemy in, as being the most proper on several Accounts;

under Themistocles's Conduct.

CHAP. II *Dissolution of the* Rom. *Empire.* 53

counts; first, for that it was the readiest Passage into *Greece* for all Ships coming from the *Hellespont*, and also because there, by reason of the Narrowness of the Streight, the Enemy could not make use of the Advantage of their great Superiority, not having room to extend their Fleet, or fight with more Ships than themselves. Nor were the *Persians* at the same time ignorant of *Themistocles*'s prudent Conduct in this Matter, for which reason they detached two hundred Gallies to sail round without the Island, and come at the other End of the Streight astern of the *Athenians*, that so they might hem them in on both sides. To perform this Service, they made choice of the ensuing Night, when having gotten about half way the length of the Island, there arose so furious a Storm of Wind, Rain, Thunder, and Lightning, as not one of the whole Number escaped, but were all swallowed up in the Ocean, and not a Man of their Companies saved. *Many of the Persian Gallies destroyed by Tempest.*

This was a second Blow from Heaven on *Xerxes*'s Fleet, but the *Persians* entirely ignorant of what had happened, put themselves the next Morning in a Posture for Fight, expecting every Moment when the two hundred Gallies should make a Signal of their attacking the Rear of the *Grecian* Fleet. The *Athenians* as ignorant as the Enemy of what had befallen them, kept their Station in the Mouth of the Streight, as before-mentioned, where the two Fleets came to an Engagement, which lasted, with almost equal Loss on both sides, till Night parted them. The next Day they both prepared for renewing the Fight, when, as a damp to the *Persian* Courage, the Bodies of their Countrymen came floating down the Chanel in such Numbers as clogged their way, and checked the Stroke of their Oars: However, they at length joined Battel again, and with much the same Success as before. The Day following the *Grecians* were reinforced with fifty three Gallies from *Athens*, and by them had the News of the Shipwreck of the *Persians* as they were going about the Island, which gave them new Courage and Resolution. Mean while the *Persians*, highly incensed at the Resistance they met with from so inconsiderable a Force, and likewise fearing the Resentments of *Xerxes*, for their making so tedious a Business of getting through the Chanel to *Greece*, now offered the *Athenians* Battel the third time, who advancing a little way without the Streight, there waited the Enemies Motions. The *Persians* disposed their Fleet in a half Moon, in order to encompass the *Athenians*, who doubting they should fare the worse if they suffered them to continue in that Posture, bore down speedily with Design to break them. The *Grecians* never gave greater Proofs of their Courage and Bravery than at this time; but as much as they excelled in Valour and maritime Skill, so much did the *Persians* in the Number and Nimbleness of their Ships. At length, after a long and obstinate Engagement, wherein great Numbers were slain, and many Ships sunk and taken on both sides, the Fleets both drew off, but the Victory remained to the *Persians*, the *Greeks* retiring hastily out of the Chanel, and leaving the Coasts open to them to make their Descent as they pleased; and at the same time that they obtained this Success *Three Sea Engagements near Euboea; in the last whereof the Persians are victorious,*

gain the Pass at Thermopylæ,

A. M. 3470. and destroy Athens.

* *Now Coluri in the Gulph of Engia.*

Artemisia's Advice to Xerxes.

The Grecian Fleet at Salamis.

Themistocles endeavours to prevail with the Confederates to fight at Sea.

cess at Sea, *Xerxes* with his Army gained the Pass of *Thermopylæ*, *Leonidas* King of *Sparta*, being first slain, who so valiantly defended it.

Having thus opened his way into *Greece*, he fell down into *Attica* with his vast Army, and miserably harrassing the Country, entered *Athens*, which he entirely burnt and destroyed, without sparing even the Temples of the Gods. Having staid there a few Days, he received Intelligence from the Deserters that the *Athenians* had retreated from *Eubœa* to the Island * *Salamis*, and were there gathering together new Forces, whereupon he repaired on board the Fleet, where was held a general Council in his Presence, to deliberate on the further Naval Operations, and whether they should venture another Engagement with the *Grecians*. The Kings of *Tyre* and *Sidon*, who accompanied *Xerxes* in this Expedition, were first asked their Opinions, who both declared themselves for another Battel; but when it came to the turn of *Artemisia*, Queen of *Halicarnassus*, to speak, (who out of Duty to *Xerxes*, whose Tributary she was, had not only join'd him with five large Gallies, but done very considerable Services for him, as well at *Artemisium* as elsewhere, insomuch that the *Athenians* offered a great Reward for any Person who should bring her in alive or dead) she enlarging somewhat on the aforesaid Services rendered by her to the King, gave her Opinion, which she supported with many powerful Arguments, that it would be most expedient for his Majesty to lay aside the Thoughts of any farther Operations at Sea, and march directly with his Army into *Peloponesus*, the Consequence of which would be the breaking all the Measures the Enemy had taken as a collective Body, and force them every one to shift for themselves, when they would fall an easy Conquest to his Majesty's Arms.

Having taken all their Opinions, the King was much inclined to that of *Artemisia*, but it was in Fate that the *Persians* should be beaten at *Salamis*, and, according to the Majority of Voices, it was resolved to fight the Enemy there. At this Place the *Grecians*, with a Fleet of three hundred and eighty Gallies, lay ready to receive them, when suddenly there was a Rumour spread through the Fleet, that *Xerxes* was advancing with all the Land Army into *Peloponesus*, which struck such a Damp into the *Grecians*, that all of them, except the *Athenians*, were against another Engagement. On this Occasion *Themistocles* was extremely industrious in going about to every one, solliciting and pressing them to fight, but more especially to *Eurybiades*, the *Spartan* Admiral, who commanded in chief, praying and beseeching him not unadvisedly to ruin his Country, and with his own Hands make a Breach in those Walls the Oracle had commanded them to trust to; telling him withal, that if they staid at *Salamis*, Glory and Honour and Victory attended them, but if they departed, it would be to the sure and inevitable Destruction of *Greece*. This Advice was most true, but the Weight of it was much lessen'd, in that *Themistocles* having no Country to lose, it was thought he might more readily consent to the hazarding that of others; it being continually objected to him, that it was

not

CHAP. II. *Dissolution of the* Rom. *Empire.* 55

not going at all upon equal Terms for them to fight for a Country in the Hands of the Enemy, and a City that had not Being, while *Sparta*, and *Argos*, and *Peloponnesus* were left defenceless, and exposed an easy Prey to the Invader. *Themistocles* being thus repulsed and reproached, he bethought himself of a Stratagem equally hardy and doubtful, but from which, if it succeeded, he could gain nothing less than immortal Honour. He sends a trusty Messenger to the *Persian* Admirals, who, with all Professions of his Friendship, was to tell them, that the *Grecians*, afraid of the Power they had so lately felt, were determined the next Morning to fly; that now all the Force of *Greece* was united in one Place, and might be cut off at one Blow; that they should by no means permit their Enemies to escape out of their Hands; and if they let slip this Opportunity, it might be long enough before Heaven would afford them such another. This was not more wisely concerted on one hand, than indiscretely believed on the other; for the *Persians*, that they might not have any thing to do in the Morning, disposed every thing for the Attack at Midnight, and block'd up the Streights of *Salamis*, that so there might be no Possibility of Escape. The King placed himself on an Eminence on the Shore, there to see the Fight, and animate his People to behave themselves well; and the *Grecians* now finding themselves almost surrounded by the Enemy, became valiant out of pure Necessity, and engaged with great Ardour and Alacrity. The *Athenians* had to deal with the *Phœnicians*, who were of greatest Reputation for Sea-Affairs among the Enemy, and the *Spartans*, not so remarkably expert therein, were opposed to the *Ionians*. In this Battel the *Persians* are said even to have outdone themselves in Feats of Gallantry and Bravery, and the rather, for that they fought under the Eye of their Prince, whom, with their Fellow-Soldiers of the Land Army, they had to be witness of their good or ill Behaviour, all the Hills and rising Grounds along the Shore being covered with *Xerxes*'s Troops, where himself, as we have said, was on an Eminence from whence he might best behold the Fight. But the *Grecian* Valour was insuperable, insomuch that the two Fleets joining Battel, that prodigious Multitude of *Persian* Ships, although disposed in the most advantagious manner, were very soon disordered, and fell foul on one another, the *Grecians* bearing down on them in a firm and unbroken Order. This was in a great measure owing to *Themistocles*, by whose Advice it was that the *Grecians* deferred attacking the *Persians* with the Beaks of their Ships till the time the Land *Breeze* came up, when going on right afore it, they were carried against them with great Violence, while at the same time those of the Enemy were rendered almost useless, because, having the Wind in their Teeth, they could not oppose Beak to Beak, but received the Shock of the *Grecians* on their Bow or their Broadside.

There fell in this Battel, almost at the beginning of it, *Ariamenes* the *Persian* Admiral, a Person of great Valour, and Brother to *Xerxes*, whose Body floating in the Sea, amongst many others, was taken up by *Artemisia*, and presented to the King to be Royally interred.

Themistocles deceives the Persians.

The Sea-Fight at Salamis.

The Persian Fleet beaten,

and Ariamenes, their Admiral, slain.

Xerxes leaves Greece.

terred. The Fight continued till late in the Evening, when many thousands of the *Persians* being slain, the few Remains of their vast Multitude retired in Confusion into the Port of *Athens*. *Xerxes* immediately call'd a Council on the present Emergence, and, pursuant to the Resolutions taken therein, made the best of his way, by long Journies, to the *Hellespont*, where finding his Bridges broken down by bad Weather, he passed over in a Fisher-Boat, and landing in *Asia*, repair'd first to *Sardes*, and then to *Susa*, his capital City, for fear of any Commotions the News of this Defeat might occasion there.

Artemisia's Valour.

In this Engagement Queen *Artemisia* performed Wonders, insomuch that *Xerxes* said, his Men were turned Women, and the Women become Men, thereby reproaching especially the Behaviour of the *Phœnicians*, who so far degenerated from the Naval Glory of their Ancestors, that they were the first who began to fly; and such of these as he himself particularly observed performed not their Duty he immediately sent for and executed.

Precedency in Valour given to the Æginetans,

In a general Assembly of *Greece*, when it came to be considered who had behaved best in the Fight, the *Lacedæmonians*, although they well knew not any of their own Body had performed ought that was extraordinary in it, yet because the *Athenians*, who had so particularly signalized their Valour in that Day, should not run away with the Glory so justly due to them, prevail'd to have it ordered, that the Heralds should make publick Proclamation, that of the People of *Greece* in general the *Æginetans*, and of particular Persons *Amynias*, had deserved best of their Country in the late Fight at *Salamis*. For this Preference given to the *Æginetans* there

and Amynias,

was no Shadow of Pretence, and as for that of *Amynias*, it was because he was the first Captain who boarded the *Persian* Admiral, and slew him with his own Hand, which although a very gallant and honourable Action, yet, alas! how infinitely does it fall short

tho' due to Themistocles;

of the Merit of the great *Themistocles*, born for the Defence and Preservation of *Greece!* He was a Man possessed of every good Quality which could render him eminent in the Service of his Country, but so peculiarly excelled in the Knowledge of Sea Affairs, that he derived to himself the Sirname of *Naumachus*, or the Naval

his Encomium.

Warrior. He needed now no longer to complain that the Trophies of *Miltiades* would not let him sleep, having atchieved greater Actions than he, and being himself to be esteemed as a more noble Pattern for Imitation to Posterity. His Courage, Conduct, and good Fortune it was which extorted from the *Persians* the unwilling Confession, that they were not any longer able to cope with the *Grecians* at Sea, as appeared not long after when they retreated from the Island *Samos* to the Promontory of *Mycale*, in *Ionia*, to have recourse to the Protection of the Land Army that was left by *Xerxes* to keep those Parts in Obedience; where declining a Naval Fight, they haled their Gallies ashore, fortified them with a Trench and a Rampire, and

The Persians beaten by Land, and their Fleet destroyed.

joined the Army. Upon this the *Athenians* likewise landing, engaged the whole Force, and entirely defeating them, returned to the Sea-Coasts, where they forced the *Persian* Fortifications, and burnt their Fleet.

CHAP.

CHAP. III.

Of the Naval War of the Grecians *in* Sicily *with the* Carthaginians *then in Alliance with the* Persians.

WHILE these things were transacting in *Greece*, there fell out a bloody War between *Carthage* and *Sicily*; for *Xerxes*, so soon as he had come to a Resolution of invading *Greece*, sent an Embassy to the *Carthaginians*, offering to enter into an Alliance with them against the *Greeks*, which they readily enough consented to, and it was agreed, that at the same time as *Xerxes* passed over into *Greece*, the *Carthaginians* should make a Descent in *Sicily*. The Negotiation was carried on with so much Secrecy, that the *Sicilians* had not the least Suspicion of the Designs against them; and no sooner were the *Persian* Ministers dispatched, but the *Carthaginians*, at a vast Charge, made Levies of foreign Troops in *Italy*, *Liguria*, *Gaul* and *Spain*, at the same time raising great Numbers in the City of *Carthage*, and in *Numidia*. At length having, as well as *Xerxes*, spent three Years in their Preparations, they had got together an Army of three hundred thousand Men, and a Fleet of five thousand Sail, two thousand whereof were long Ships, the rest Victuallers and Transports. The Command of this Fleet and Army they committed to *Amilcar*, who, when Advice came of *Xerxes*'s Arrival in *Greece*, repaired on board, and made sail for *Sicily*. When he was got about half Seas over, he met with so violent a Storm, that all the Transports which carried the Horses and Baggage perished in it, and 'twas with Difficulty he escaped with the rest to *Himera*, a Sea-Port of *Sicily*. Having on his Arrival there disembarked the Troops, he formed two Camps, one for the Land Army, the other for the Sea, in which latter making a proper Receptacle for the Ships, he haled them ashore, and secured them therein with a very deep Trench, and a Rampire of great Height. The People of the Town having received considerable Loss in a Sally they made for interrupting the Works, dispatch'd frequent Messengers to implore the Assistance of *Gelon*, King of *Syracuse*, who, as we have before observed, had lately denied Aid to his Kindred *Grecians* on the Continent: But that which through Envy and Emulation he refused to them, he did not think fit to do to those of *Himera*, who were his near Neighbours, and who, he knew, would, without his Assistance, be entirely ruin'd.

A Prince of his Penetration easily observed that the *Carthaginians* had no better Grounds for a War against *Himera* than *Syracuse*, and that it arose more from a favourable Conjuncture than any good Reason; that, in reality, it was the Dominion of *Sicily* was aspired to by a foreign Nation, and the Destruction of *Himera* a Step only to the Accomplishment of their Design: But as to the Convention of the *Persians* and *Carthaginians* to make their Descents in *Greece* and *Sicily* at the same time, he entertained not the

A War between Carthage and Sicily; the former aided by the Persians.

The Carthaginians besiege Himera.

Gelon King of Syracuse assists the besieged.

least

least Suspicion of it. Whatsoever was the Occasion, he thought a Flame broke out so near him was not to be neglected, and so, with all imaginable Expedition, marched with an Army of five and fifty thousand Men toward *Himera*, near which Place finding the *Carthaginians* straggling about, and plundering the Country, he slew great Numbers of them, took ten thousand Prisoners, and forced the rest to retire with Precipitation into the Camp. The next Day, as he was viewing from a rising Ground the Posture of the Enemy, espying their Naval Camp, he began to consider if, by any means, he could burn the Ships. While he was ruminating on this Design, it luckily happened that some of his Troops who had been on the Patrole, brought in a Courier going from *Amilcar* to the City of *Selinus*, whose Inhabitants the *Carthaginians* had drawn in to side with them. The Letters found about him imported the Desire of *Amilcar* that, on a certain Day appointed, the *Selinuntians* would join him with their Body of Horse; on which same Day was to be performed a great Sacrifice to *Neptune*. The Night before *Gelon* sends out a Body of Horse with Orders to them to take a Compass round the neighbouring Mountains, and getting into the Road from *Selinus* at break of Day, to present themselves at the Naval Camp of the *Carthaginians*, where *Amilcar* was then to be, as if they were the Horse expected from *Selinus*. In the mean time he orders some Scouts to place themselves on the top of an Hill which overlooked the Enemy's Camp, who as soon as the Troops were received into it, were to make a Signal, himself at the same time waiting the Event at the Head of the rest of the Army in order of Battel. On the Approach of the Horse beforemention'd to the Naval Camp, they were joyfully let in by the *Carthaginians*, who being ignorant of the Deceit, congratulated their good Fortune, which, in some sort, they thought, made amends for their Disaster at Sea, by the Fidelity of their Allies on shore; when immediately *Gelon*'s Troops drew their Swords, and fell upon them, slew *Amilcar* as he stood at the Altar assisting at the Sacrifice, and killing all they met, set fire to the Ships. *Gelon* in the mean time having received the Signal of their Success, and advancing with the whole Army to support them, was met by the *Carthaginian* Troops, who not knowing what had happened in the Naval Camp, came out of theirs to engage him. They fought very obstinately, and a prodigious Slaughter was made on both sides, when on a sudden the *Carthaginians* beholding the great Smoke that arose from the Ships, and hearing the News of *Amilcar*'s Death, became dispirited, and throwing away their Arms, betook themselves to flight. *Gelon* detached part of his Army to pursue them, with positive Orders to give no Quarter, and accordingly they committed a merciless Slaughter, while himself moved on with the rest to the Naval Camp, where he found *Amilcar* killed, and the Fire raging throughout in so terrible a manner, as 'twas hardly safe for the Conquerors themselves to abide within it. Thus were two thousand Ships of Force, vast Numbers of Transports, with the General himself, the Flower of the Army, and all the Sailors and Rowers, in a Moment of Time destroyed. Only twenty of the Ships, which

Amilcar

Amilcar had the Day before sent out on some necessary Services, escaped the Flames, and even they, in their return, all perished in a Storm, insomuch that but a few Soldiers, who saved themselves in Boats, were left to carry the dreadful News to *Carthage*. *Gelon* having thus successfully settled the Affairs of *Sicily*, and finding from the Examination of the Prisoners of Quality, that this formidable Invasion was originally projected in *Persia*, thought fit now to offer, of his own accord, that Aid he had before refused to Entreaties, and determined to repair to the Assistance of *Greece* with a Fleet of five hundred Ships; when, as he was just ready to sail, some *Corinthian* Merchants arriving at *Syracuse*, brought the News of the great Victory the *Grecians* had obtained at *Salamis*, and the shameful Flight of *Xerxes* into *Asia*; and 'twas afterwards understood that on the same Day *Gelon* forced the *Carthaginian* Camp, *Leonidas*, King of *Sparta*, dy'd bravely fighting against *Xerxes* in the Pass of *Thermopylæ*. All these things happen'd in the Year of the World 3470, and from the building of *Rome* the 273ᵈ, which 'tis thought proper to mention, because thro' the whole Course of the History, till we come to our own Times, we shall hardly find any Year so remarkable as this, for such extraordinary Actions, in different Parts of the World.

Leonidas's Death.

A. M. 3470.

CHAP. IV.

Of the Naval Wars of the Grecians, *from the Defeat of the* Persians *at* Mycale, *to the Victory obtained over them by* Cimon *at the River* Eurymedon, *and the Peace that ensued thereupon.*

IF we return from *Sicily* to *Athens*, we shall next find flourishing in that City *Cimon*, the Son of that *Miltiades* who gave the *Persians* the memorable Defeat at *Marathon*. This Gentleman, in his younger Years, was of such a Turn of Mind that, with all his Tutors could do, he could never be brought to learn Musick, Rhetorick, or any of the softer Arts of *Athens*, but at the same time was most peculiarly formed by Nature for Action, and Dexterity in Affairs. As he was perfectly well seen in the whole Art of War, so had he so thorough a Knowledge of Sea Affairs, that, with respect to this Particular, he may be said almost to have snatch'd the Laurel from the Brows of *Themistocles* himself. He gave a singular Specimen of his future Glory this way, while he was yet very young, when, as *Themistocles*, on account of the *Persian* Invasion, was haranguing the People, and persuading them, by forsaking the City and Country of *Attica*, to trust themselves and their Fortunes to the Sea, and they stood in Amazement at the Proposal, this Youth, with a brisk and pleasant Countenance, in sight of all the People, marches

Cimon the Athenian his Character.

His Skill in Naval Affairs.

I 2

marches up to the Citadel with a Bridle in his Hand he had taken off his Horse, and consecrates it to *Minerva*, the Goddess who assumed the peculiar Protection of that Place, thereby calling Gods and Men to witness that this was not a time for them to depend on Horsemanship, or a Land-Force, but to follow the Advice of *Themistocles*, and trust to their Ships for their Safety. Thereupon, having paid his Devotions to *Minerva*, he embark'd with the rest of his Countrymen on board the Fleet, where in the Fight at *Salamis* he behaved with remarkable Courage and Gallantry, and acquired to himself the Love and Esteem of all his Fellow Citizens; many of whom came to him and advised him to betake himself early to publick Business, and begin to think of doing somewhat worthy of his Father *Miltiades*, and the Field of *Marathon*. Pursuant to their Advice, he soon after enter'd into publick Employments, wherein he was welcomed by the universal Congratulation and Applause of the *Athenians*, who not long after (*Themistocles* being then on the Decline in their Favour) conferred upon him the most important Charges of the Commonwealth.

Is sent with the Athenian *Fleet to join that of* Lacedæmon.

After the Battel of *Platæa* with *Xerxes*'s General, *Mardonius*, which gave a total Overthrow to the *Persians*, and entirely ruin'd their Affairs in *Greece*, *Cimon* was sent out with the *Athenian* Fleet to join that of the *Lacedæmonians* under *Pausanias*, who commanded in chief. In this Expedition his Behaviour was entirely agreeable to what he had promised at his first coming into Affairs, and he drew the Eyes of all People upon him, by the punctual Care he took of his Men, their exact Discipline and Order, and the constant Readiness they were in for Service. At length finding out *Pausanias*'s Inclination to the *Persian* Interest, and the unnatural Intrigues he had enter'd into against his native Country, he immediately sent Advice thereof to the *Spartan Ephori*, and besieged *Pausanias* himself in *Byzantium*; who escaping thence, *Cimon*, in his Return to *Athens*, took especial care to open the Trade of the *Ægean*, by clearing it of Pirates, by whom it was much infested at that time; an Action highly acceptable not only to *Athens*, but to all *Greece*. He mightily increased his Reputation by a particular piece of good Conduct, whereby he rendered the *Athenians*, before very potent at Sea, perfectly Masters of it. For although the *Athenian* Confederates had willingly paid their Tax according to Agreement, yet, when they found the Seat of War far enough removed from them, they did not with the same Readiness contribute their Quota's of Men and Ships; whereupon the former Generals of *Athens* exacted a punctual Compliance by such Rigorous Methods as made their Government odious. *Cimon* went quite another way to work, so as not to make the Conditions uneasy to any one; for from such as desired their actual Attendance might be dispensed with, he took their several Proportions in Money, and Ships unmann'd; and then bringing the *Athenians*, by easy and gentle Methods, and a few at a time, to betake themselves to the Sea, soon manned the whole Fleet with them only; and they, thus supported by the Money of their

Cimon renders the Athenians *Masters of the Sea.*

Confe-

CHAP. IV. *Dissolution of the Rom. Empire.* 61

Confederates, who mean while enjoyed their Repose at home, became their Masters, and deprived them of Liberty.

The *Athenians*, now sollicited by *Amyrtæus*, a Prince of *Ægypt*, who had revolted from the *Persian* Government, repaired thither with a great Fleet, and maintained a dangerous War there for six Years. *Artaxerxes*, who sate on the Throne of *Persia*, dreading the *Athenian* Arms, sent *Megabyzus* to *Lacedæmon*, with great Sums of Money, to endeavour if by any means he could prevail with the *Spartans* to come to a Rupture with *Athens*, and invade *Attica*, that so they might have Work enough on their Hands at home: But the *Lacedæmonians*, although they were grown sufficiently jealous of the rising Power of *Athens*, yet at this time had they such a Reverence for the Treaties subsisting between them, that they would by no means hearken to the Proposal, and *Megabyzus* returned without doing any thing. The Money the King had assigned to be placed among the *Lacedæmonians*, he now applied towards carrying on the War in *Ægypt* against the *Athenians*, the Management whereof he committed to another *Megabyzus*, Son of that *Zopyrus* who recovered *Babylon* to *Darius*. This General entering *Ægypt* with a vast Army, gave the *Ægyptians* Battel, and entirely defeating them, forced the *Grecians* out of the City of * *Memphis* (of which they had been in Possession some time) into *Byblus*, on an Island of the *Nile* called *Prosopitis*, and there laid close siege to them, who so well defended themselves, that they held out eighteen Months. The *Athenian* Fleet lay in the River before the Town, but the *Persians* at length turned its course, and drained the Chanel, so that the Ships now remaining useless, the *Athenians* set fire to them, and surrendered the Place, on Condition they might be permitted to march in Safety to *Cyrene*. Arriving there, they, at several times, got home, but in as miserable a Condition as if they had suffered Shipwreck; and as one Misfortune generally falls on the Neck of another, the *Athenians* having sent fifty Gallies to their Relief, on a Supposition they were still in *Byblus*, these, utterly ignorant of what had passed, entered *Mendesium*, one of the Mouths of the *Nile*, and landing the Troops they had on board, they were all cut to pieces by *Megabyzus*, while the *Phœnician* Fleet which lay near attacked the Gallies, and entirely destroyed them. Such was the End of the *Athenians* six Years War in *Ægypt*, from which if they had been so wise as to have taken warning, and contenting themselves with their own, had withdrawn their Desires from foreign Acquisitions, especially far distant ones, this Misfortune in *Ægypt*, though so severe, had not been unuseful to them; but by knowing no bounds to their good Fortune, and affecting an Extent of Empire beyond the Abilities of their City to maintain, they at length brought their flourishing Republick to Ruin.

But to return to *Cimon*. He was the Person amongst all the *Grecians* who most effectually weakned the *Persian* Power; and so closely did he pursue them, that he would not let them take breath, or put their Affairs in any manner of Posture. For after the Death of *Pausanias*, the *Athenians* having obtained, through his Conduct, the

Athens maintains War in Ægypt against the Persians.

The Ægyptians and Athenians beaten by Artaxerxes.
* *New Grand Cairo.*

Athenians burn their Ships,

and

others are destroyed by the Persians.

Cimon reduces the Grecian Cities in Asia.

Beats the Persians at Eurymedon,

and

destroys their Fleet.

the supreme Command at Sea, they sent him out at the Head of a considerable Fleet, with which passing over to the *Lesser Asia*, all the *Grecian* Cities upon the Sea-Coast immediately came in, and the rest which were garrison'd by the *Persians* he took, partly by Storm, and partly by managing Intelligence within their Walls, so that he entirely freed all the Coast from *Ionia* to *Pamphylia* from the *Persian* Yoke. Then having notice that the *Persian* Generals were encamped with a Body of Troops on the Sea-Coast, and supported by a considerable Fleet, which lay in the Mouth of the River * *Eurymedon*, he made the best of his way thither with two hundred Gallies, and came in upon the Enemy at break of Day; who, surprised at so unexpected an Attack, deserted the Ships in Confusion, and joined their Army on shore. The whole Fleet consisted of six hundred Sail, two hundred whereof were taken, and of the rest the greatest part sunk, or entirely disabled, very few of them escaping. *Cimon*, flushed with this Success, immediately lands his Men, and encourages them with the Assurance of Victory, but more by his own Example, to engage the Enemy, which they did with great Fury, and were received by them with equal Warmth. The Fight was very obstinate, and continued long doubtful, wherein many of the bravest *Athenians*, and among them not a few Persons of Quality, were slain; but at length the Enemy received a total Defeat, and a furious Slaughter was made among them.

A. M. 3481.

The Persians agree to hard Terms of Peace.

Thus did *Cimon* gain two entire Victories by Land and Sea in few Hours; to render which fully compleat, he repairs with the Fleet, the same Day, to a neighbouring Port, where he had notice that eighty Sail of *Phœnicians* were arrived to the Assistance of the Enemy, not knowing any thing of their Defeat; but they seeing the *Grecians* coming down upon them, and yet reeking with Blood and Sweat, suspected the Fate of their Allies, and in Despair presently submitted to the Conqueror. These Successes so broke the Spirit of the *Persian*, that he was glad to treat on any Terms, and to comply with this hard Condition, *That not any of his Land Forces should come within fifty Miles of the* Asiatick *Coast of the* Grecian *Sea, nor any of his Ships of War beyond the* Cyanean *Islands on the one side, nor the* Chelidonian *Islands on the other:* So that he was hereby excluded from the *Propontis*, the *Ægean*, the *Cretan*, *Carpathian*, and *Lycian* Seas, from the Mouth of the *Thracian Bosphorus*, where lie the *Cyanean* Isles, to the sacred Promontory (now Cape *Celidonia*) in *Lycia*, off of which are the *Chelidonian* Islands before-mention'd.

---

* *The River on which now stands* Candelora *in the Gulf of* Satalia.

CHAP.

CHAP. V.

Of the Naval Wars of the Grecians, *from the Peace with* Persia *after the Battel at* Eurymedon, *to the beginning of the* Peloponnesian *War.*

CIMON, in his Return from *Pamphylia*, (upon Advice sent him that part of the scattered Remains of *Mardonius* his Army had seized on some Places in the *Thracian Chersonesus)* sends in the Fleet to *Athens* to refit, and with only four Gallies repairs thither, where he finds the *Thracians* joined with the *Persians*, and ready to receive him. But attacking them with great Vigour, he took thirteen Ships from them, and in a short time wholly subdued the *Thracians*, drove out the *Persians*, and entirely reduced the Country to the Obedience of *Athens*. Thence he proceeded to the Island *Thasus*, the Inhabitants whereof had revolted from the *Athenians*, and defeating them, took thirty three Ships, and had their capital City yielded to him at Discretion. Being recalled to *Athens*, he for some time endeavoured to calm the civil Dissensions of his Country; and finding the *Athenians*, at the Instigation of *Pericles*, hotly bent on a Rupture with *Sparta*, thought it best to divert the Humour, if possible, by a foreign War. To this end he prevails to have a Fleet fitted out of two hundred Gallies, with which making Sail towards *Asia*, he detached sixty of them to *Ægypt*, while himself repaired with the rest to *Cyprus*, where meeting with the *Persian* Fleet, he gave them a signal Overthrow; and having sailed round the Island, and taken by Force, or Treaty, all the Sea-Port Towns, he began to turn his Thoughts towards the War in *Ægypt*. For *Cimon's* Schemes were not calculated for small Matters, but aimed at nothing less than the total Subversion of the Power of *Persia*. Besides that, as he knew the Genius of the *Athenians* to be peculiarly adapted for War, he thought it both more honourable, and more easy for them to be engaged in one with *Persia* than *Greece*; and it was, perhaps, some farther Incitement of his Hatred to the *Persian* Name, to observe the singular Honour and Respect wherewith *Themistocles* was received by the King, when he retired in Exile into *Asia*. That Prince indeed entertained a mighty Value for *Themistocles*, as knowing his great Abilities, and relying on his Promises of being at the head of the Expedition he intended against *Greece*, wherein he therefore assured himself of certain Success; but he, either dreading the Courage, Conduct, and constant good Fortune which attended *Cimon*, especially in Naval Affairs, his own peculiar Talent, or distrusting his own Abilities declined with his Fortune, or else (what we should the rather believe) abhorring the Thoughts of being engaged in so unnatural a Design, poisoned himself, that so since he could not with Honour acquit himself of his Promise, he might, in some sort, of his Duty to his Coountry; and his

Death

and Cimon *dies.*

Death was followed soon after by that of *Cimon*, just as he was going with the Fleet from *Cyprus* to *Ægypt*.

It may be said of him, that even after his Death he was fatal to the *Persian* Power. For having signified his Desire to his Friends, who assisted him in his last Moments, that his Body might be carried to *Athens*, and there interred, the Fleet accordingly preparing to return home, fell in, off of *Cyprus*, with a Naval Armament of *Persians* and *Phœnicians*, which had been, with great Expedition, sent out against the *Athenians*. The *Persians*, whether they were ignorant of *Cimon*'s Death, or, if they knew it, assuring themselves of Advantage over the *Athenians*, being destitute of their General, prepared for the Fight with great Readiness and Alacrity. The *Athenians*, on the other side, were encouraged with the Remembrance of their late Successes, and exhorting one another to render this their melancholy Return to *Athens* memorable to future Ages, for their Behaviour in this Battel, engaged the Enemy with extraordinary Courage and Resolution. They fought very obstinately on both sides, and for a long time with various Success, till the *A-*

The Athenians *beat the* Persian *and* Phœnician *Fleets near* Cyprus.

thenians knowing themselves much the better Seamen, and yet making their Art subservient to the present Occasion, broke their own Line, as finding that of the *Persians* otherwise impenetrable, and engaging them separately, although they were without any supreme Commander, they acquitted themselves of all the Parts of Soldiership and maritime Skill, with as much Dexterity and Readiness, as if *Cimon* had been present to dispence his Orders amongst them, and be witness of their Behaviour. At length their Skill and Courage prevailed, for breaking the Enemy's Line, they sunk, or took all the *Persian* Ships, but the *Phœnicians*, being good Sailors, saved themselves by flight. They did not think it safe to follow them too far, for fear of losing Company with the Admiral's Ship, which having his Corpse on board, did not interfere in the Fight, but mutually making Signals to give over the Chace, they bent their Course towards *Athens* with the sorrowful News of *Cimon*'s Death, but that well tempered with the Joy of this Victory.

Pericles *incites the* Athenians *against the* Spartans.

While these Things were transacting abroad, *Pericles* was very busy at home in sowing the Seeds of Dissension between the *Athenians* and *Spartans*, who had been growing ripe for a Quarrel ever since the Battel of *Platæa*. The *Lacedæmonians* looked with an envious Eye on the Glory the others had obtained in that Battel, as well as in the Sea Fights of *Artemisium*, *Salamis*, and the River *Eurymedon*, wherewith they were indeed themselves elated to a great degree, and reducing most of the Islands of the *Ægean*, together with many Towns on both sides the Continent at *Potidæa*,

[b] Scutari.
[c] Constantinople.

Sestos and *Abydos*, *Perinthus*, [b] *Chalcedon*, and [c] *Byzantium* itself, seemed to aim at nothing less than to be Sovereign Umpires of *Greece*. They had an old Grudge boiling in their Minds, which, tho' now and then laid asleep for a time, could never be thoroughly forgotten. For at the time of *Xerxes*'s Invasion, it was agreed by the common Consent of all *Greece*, that as the *Lacedæmonians* should have the supreme Direction of Affairs by Land, so the *Athenians*

CHAP. V. *Dissolution of the Rom. Empire.* 65

nians should command at Sea; but when Matters came to an Extremity, the *Lacedæmonians* would needs preside in both, or else, they pretended, they would act on their own bottom, and let every one shift for themselves. As this was not a time to contend, the *Athenians*, through the Prudence and Moderation of *Themistocles*, submitted for the publick Good without any Resistance: But when the Fears of the *Persians* were over, they readily enough laid hold of any Occasion for Dispute. This was more especially observable after *Pericles* (who was set up in Opposition to *Cimon*) came to the Management of Affairs, when under Colour of assisting their Confederates, or one Pretence or other, there happened frequent Skirmishes and Quarrels, wherein several fell on both sides. The *Lacedæmonians* accidentally meeting with a Squadron of *Athenian* Ships, engaged them, and came off Conquerors, when soon after the *Athenians* reinforcing their Fleet, another Engagement ensued, wherein they doubly repaid themselves for their former Loss. There were not any Endeavours used to compose these Differences till six and thirty Years after the Fight at *Salamis*, when a Truce of thirty Years (called the Peace of *Eubœa*) was concluded between them, and such Places as had been taken were mutually restored on both sides.

Their mutual Jealousies,

and Quarrels.

A Peace concluded.

Six Years after this Treaty a War broke out between the *Athenians* and *Samians*, on account of *Priene*, a City of *Ionia* belonging to the *Milesians*. With these the *Samians* disputed it, and gaining a considerable Advantage over them, the *Milesians* sent a Deputation to *Athens*, with loud Complaints against their Enemies; which would, nevertheless, have had but little effect upon the People, had they not been well supported by *Pericles*, at the Instigation of *Aspasia*, a fair Mistress of his. This Lady was a Person of very great Beauty, and of such extraordinary Wit and Eloquence as would not have ill become Men of the highest Dignity in the Common-Wealth, insomuch that on that account even the great *Socrates* was one of her Admirers; and *Pericles*, himself an excellent Orator, is said once to have pronounced to the People, as his own, a very fine funeral Oration, entirely of her composing. She was a Native of *Miletus*, and so effectually sollicited the Cause of her Countrymen, that War was immediately denounced against the *Samians*. *Pericles* proceeding towards *Miletus* with forty four Sail, fell in with the *Samian* Fleet, consisting of seventy, and gave them an entire Defeat, pursuing them to the very Port of *Samos*, which he entered after them, and laid siege to the City. Receiving soon after a considerable Reinforcement from *Athens*, he left Part of the Fleet and Troops to carry on the Siege, and with sixty Gallies repaired to a proper Station for meeting the *Phœnicians*, who he was informed were coming to their Relief. When this great Detachment was made, the Person who commanded in *Samos* took the Advantage of *Pericles* his Absence, and in a very successful Sally sunk or took several of the *Athenian* Ships, and recovered the Harbour; so that having an open Sea for fourteen Days, they imported all their necessary Provisions. But *Pericles* returning with the Fleet,

A Quarrel between the Athenians and Samians.

Aspasia.

Pericles beats the Fleet of Samos.

The Samians take and burn several Athenian Ships.

K

Fleet, which was by this time augmented with forty Ships from *Athens*, and thirty from *Chios* and *Lesbos*, again invested the Town by Sea and Land; when the *Samians*, encouraged by their former Success, made another Sally, but were repulsed with great Loss, and at length, in the ninth Month of the Siege, surrendering the Place, they were obliged to demolish their Walls, deliver up their Shipping, pay a great Sum of Money to defray the Charge of the War, and to give Hostages for Performance of the Articles.

Pericles takes Samos.

We have before observed that the Truce between the *Athenians* and *Lacedæmonians* was concluded for thirty Years, but their Animosities grew to such a Height, as not to admit of so long a Delay from Action, so that they committed frequent Depredations on one another, both by Sea and Land, and in so hostile a manner too, as that it wanted nothing but the Name of an open War. It was during the time of *Cimon*'s Exile that these things happened; but when he was recalled, he brought Matters to an amicable Accommodation between them. For although when he was obliged to submit to the Ostracism, one of the things which carried the most considerable Weight was, that in all his Discourses to the People he seemed to be too great a Favourer of the *Spartans*, yet as he was a thorough honest Man, a Lover of his Country, and very constant in the Pursuit of his own Measures, as soon as he returned to *Athens*, he persuaded the People (notwithstanding all the Opposition *Pericles* could make) to maintain their Peace with *Sparta*; which during his Life they inviolably observed; but no sooner was he dead, than they were prevailed upon by the young and hot-headed Statesmen who were then in the Administration, to come to an open Rupture with them, wherein they mightily weaken'd each other with mutual Slaughters, and sheathed in their own Bowels those Swords which had been so often dyed with the Blood of the *Medes* and *Persians*.

The War between Athens and Sparta

renewed on Conon's Death.

This War was commonly reputed to have deduced its Rise from the People of *Corinth* and ^d *Corcyra* on this Occasion. The *Corcyræans* resolving to chastise the Inhabitants of *Epidamnus*, (afterwards called *Dyrrachium*, and now *Durazzo*) a Colony of theirs who had thrown off their Allegiance, the *Corinthians*, on pretence of their being the original Founders of both People, interposed in the Quarrel with a Naval Force. It consisted of seventy five Sail, and that of the *Corcyræans* of eighty, which meeting each other off of ^e *Actium*, in *Epirus*, they came to an Engagement, wherein the *Corinthians* were defeated, with the Loss of fifteen Ships. Although, with respect to the Force which met on both sides, there was a considerable Slaughter, yet was not this Battel so remarkable on that account, as for the Place it was fought in, and the Consequences which ensued thereupon. For the first, because it was there that *Augustus*, some Ages after, gained a signal Victory at Sea over *Anthony* and *Cleopatra*, which confirmed to him the Dominion of the World: And for the latter, because it was generally supposed to be the Grounds of, and furnished the Pretence to that long and dangerous Quarrel between the *Athenians* and *Lacedæmonians*, which is called the *Peloponnesian* War, and is the Subject of *Thucydides*'s History.

^d *Corfu.*
The chief occasion of the War.

^e *C. Figalo.*

The Corcyræans beat the Corinthians at Sea.

CHAP. VI. *Dissolution of the* Rom. *Empire.* 67

History. For the *Corinthians*, in order to revenge the Disgrace they had received at *Actium*, having gotten together a Fleet of much greater Force than the former, the *Corcyræans* began to fear they should not be able to cope with them alone, and therefore sent to the *Athenians*, desiring to enter into an Alliance with, and receive Aid from them against their Enemies. The *Corinthians*, on the other hand, prayed Assistance of the *Lacedæmonians*, who were the most powerful People of *Greece* by Land, as the *Athenians* were at Sea. At *Athens*, in pursuance of the Counsels of *Pericles*, they had been long ready for a Breach, and only wanted to be furnished with a good Pretence for it, while at the same time the *Lacedæmonians* knowing that, since the Death of *Cimon*, there was not any one at *Athens* who nourished pacifick Dispositions toward them, were equally inclined to come to a Rupture. The only Obstacle that remained was the forementioned Truce, which, as we have said, was to have continued for thirty Years, but there were yet no more than fourteen elapsed. It was agreed by that Treaty, *That neither the* Lacedæmonians *nor* Athenians *should prosecute any War with the Confederates of either Side: As also that it should be lawful for either Party to assume, as Confederates, any People who were not expressly comprehended in the said Treaty.* *The Corcyræans aided by the Athenians, and the Corinthians by the Lacedæmonians.*

Now the *Corcyræans* at that time had entered into no Engagements on either Side, but stood Neuter in the Quarrel, insomuch that the *Athenians* might, they thought, receive them as Confederates, and, according to the Law of Nations, protect them when so received, without any Infraction of the Treaty on their Part. This the *Corinthians* deny'd they could lawfully do, unless it had been before the War broke out between them and the *Corcyræans*. However if they broke with the *Corinthians*, the Case was plain they consequently did the like with the *Lacedæmonians*, as being included in the same Treaty with them. The Affair was controverted in an Assembly of the People at *Athens* for two Days both by the *Corinthian* and *Corcyræan* Ambassadors, when at length the former departed, as leaving the matter at an Uncertainty, and affording time for the *Athenians* fully to consider of the matter. On their Return home, the *Corinthians* immediately made Sail with a Fleet of a hundred and fifty Gallies for *Corcyra*, off of which Island they found the *Corcyræans* ready to receive them.

The Fleets on both Sides were divided, as Land Armies, into a main Body and two Wings. In the Right of the *Corcyræans* were ten *Athenian* Gallies under the Command of *Lacedæmonius*, Son of *Cimon* lately deceased; which the *Corinthians* no sooner perceived, than, pursuant to the Advice of the *Spartans* they had on Board, they began to alter their Order of Battel, and strengthen their Left Wing with the most considerable Force they had, to oppose to the *Athenians*; when presently the Signal for Battel being displayed, they engaged each other with great Fury. Laying their Broadsides together, there was no room for acting those Parts of their Naval Art which consisted in rushing on each other with the Beaks of their Ships, or brushing off their Oars, and the like, but they fought obstinately *The* Corinthians *beat the* Corcyræans.

K 2 nately

nately Hand to Hand from their Decks, and sometimes boarding one another, there was an incredible Confusion among them, and a prodigious Slaughter on both Sides. In the mean time the *Athenians* disposed themselves so as to support the *Corcyræans* wheresoever they were obliged to give way, so far forth as their bare Presence would do it in terrifying the *Corinthians* from prosecuting their Advantage, but without striking a Stroke, as by their Instructions they were strictly forbid to do, unless it were in case of absolute Necessity. And now the *Corcyræans* prevailed so against the Left Wing of the Enemy, where were the *Megareans*, that they obliged twenty of their Ships to quit the Line in the utmost Disorder, and pursued them to the Promontory *Cheimerium*, where they ran them ashore.

are overcome by the help of the Athenian Fleet,

The *Corinthians* taking the Advantage of the Absence of those Ships that follow'd the Chace, immediately attacked the Centre of the *Corcyræans*, and with very good Success, when the *Athenians* now finding them prest hard, prepared to assist them, yet not so as they might seem the Aggressors; but at length the *Corcyræans* betaking themselves to Flight, the *Corinthians* followed them very close, and took several of their Ships, with great Numbers on Board, all whom they put to the Sword, without so much as giving Quarter to a Man. Now was the Time the *Athenians* thought, or it never would be, for them to interpose, and accordingly they charged the *Corinthians* with great Vigour, and after an obstinate and bloody Dispute, tore out of their Hands that Victory they had otherwise entirely gained. This Battel, with respect to the Numbers that were engaged in it, was in no wise comparable to those of the *Persians* at *Salamis* and *Eurymedon*, but was by much the most considerable that had been yet fought between *Grecians* and *Grecians*, whether we consider the Number, or the Destruction both of Men and Ships; for on the part of the *Corcyræans* there were no less than seventy Gallies sunk or taken, and the *Corinthians* lost thirty; and great Numbers of Men were slain on both Sides, when at length the Night parting them, left the Victory doubtful. Some Hours after the Fight, there arrived a Squadron of thirty Gallies from *Athens* to reinforce the former ten, which encouraging the *Corcyræans*, they went off to Sea next Morning, and offered the *Corinthians* Battel. They knowing of the Arrival of the *Athenians*, kept their Station, resolving not to come to an Engagement, if they could possibly avoid it, but dispatched a Messenger to the *Athenian* Admirals, (not accompanied with a Herald, because they would not seem to treat them as Enemies) mildly to expostulate with them on the Injuries they had received, and know the Reason of their Violation of the Truce. The *Athenians* replied that they had not done them any Injury, nor could possibly be accused of Infraction of the Treaty on their Side; that they did not come thither with an hostile Design against them, but only to defend their Confederates; and that if they would go to any other Place than *Corcyra*, or against any other People than the *Corcyræans*, they should by no means be their Hindrance. The *Corinthians* having received this Answer, immediately put themselves in a sailing Posture, and passing pretty near the

which is held a Breach of the Peace.

Corcy-

Corcyræan Fleet, very handsomely saluted the *Athenians* as they went by, and made the best of their Way home. On their Arrrival *whereupon* there, the *Corinthians*, by their Ministers in all the Cities of *Greece*, made loud Complaints of this Behaviour of the *Athenians*; and at *Lacedæmon*, without any long canvassing the matter, they came to a Resolution that the Truce was broke, and that War should be de- *Sparta declares War against Athens.* creed against *Athens*, which was accordingly put in Execution without Delay, and is by Authors term'd the *Peloponnesian* War.

CHAP. VI.

Of the Naval Wars of the Grecians *from the Beginning of the* Peloponnesian *War, to the great Expedition of the* Athenians *against* Sicily.

THE Reason of the *Spartans* coming so suddenly to the afore- *Principal Causes of the Peloponnesian War.* going Resolves, without that more than *Spanish* Deliberation which usually attended their Councils, was not this Injury done to the *Corinthians*, as was commonly believed, but the Consideration of the exorbitant Power the *Athenians* were arrived to at Sea; for passing by older matters, they reflected on the great Glory they had so lately gained in reducing with their Fleet the Island of *Samos* to their Obedience, and that in so short a time, as occasion'd a common Saying, that *Pericles* had done as much in nine Months against *Samos* as *Agamemnon* had in ten Years against *Troy*. If to the Con- *Jealousies of the exorbitant power of Athens.* quest of *Samos* they should add that of *Corcyra*, and to *Corcyra Corinth*, what would be the Event, (they consider'd,) but that the Liberties of all *Greece* would be trampled under Foot, and they must submit to be Slaves to the *Athenians* instead of the *Persians*. Nor were they ignorant how very intent the *Athenians* were at this time in advancing their Naval Affairs to a yet greater Height; for if any considerable Person happened to fall under the Censure of the Publick for any Misdemeanour, or otherwise, the Punishment now assigned for it was, that he should build a Gally for the State at his own Charge, or two, according to the Circumstances of the Crime, or the Quality of the Offender: And now they thought by the Accession of the *Corcyræans*, who, next the *Corinthians*, were most considerable at Sea, the *Athenian* Naval Power would receive it's last Hand, and be too fully compleat for them ever to cope with hereafter, if they did not now attempt it. Indeed *Pericles* and the People of *Athens* was equally fond of this Confederacy with *Corcyra*, but with very different Views. The People out of a vain Notion of adding it to their other Acquisitions, and by that means of extending their Conquests to *Carthage*, *Sicily*, and *Italy*, from which latter it was not above a Day's Sail: But *Pericles*, because of its Naval Force, and its convenient Situation for prosecuting his Designs in the *Peloponnesian* War, wherein he was so deeply engaged. Thus

Year of the World, 3519. *Before Chrift*, 429. *Of the Building of Rome*, 322.
The Allies of Athens and Lacedæmon.

Thus, according to *Thucydides*, fifty Years after the *Perfian* War, and fourteen after the Treaty of *Eubœa*, broke out the *Peloponnefian* War between *Athens* and *Lacedæmon*, wherein, on one Side or other, almost all the rest of *Greece* was engaged. With the *Lacedæmonians* enter'd into Alliance all the People of *Peloponnefus*, except the *Argives* and the *Achæans*, who stood Neuter; though, amongst these latter, *Pellene* declared for them in the beginning, and the rest came in afterwards; and without the *Isthmus*, the *Megareans*, *Phocians*, *Locrians*, *Bœotians*, *Ambraciots*, *Leucadians*, and *Anactorians*, who were each to contribute their Quota, some of Horse, and some of Foot, and some of Shipping, of which they proposed to have five hundred Sail, besides what they could procure out of *Italy* and *Sicily*. On the *Athenian's* Side were the *Chians*, *Lesbians* and *Platæans*, the *Meffenians* of *Naupactus*, most of the *Acarnanians*, with the *Corcyræans* and *Zacynthians*; as also the maritime People of *Caria*, those of *Doris*, *Ionia*, *Hellefpontus* and *Thrace*, and in general of all the Islands of the *Ægean*, except *Melos* and *Thera*. Of these the *Chians*, *Lesbians* and *Corcyræans* furnished Shipping, the rest Land Forces and Money.

The Peloponnefians invade Attica.

The *Peloponnefians*, on an appointed Day, came to their general Rendezvous in the *Isthmus* of *Corinth*, from whence, under the Conduct of *Archidamus*, King of *Sparta*, they made an Irruption into *Attica*, and haraffing the Country for that Campaign, at length retired into their Winter Quarters. In the mean time the *Athenians* sent out a Fleet of a hundred Sail under the Command of three Admirals, who coasting about to the West of *Peloponnefus*, were there join'd by the *Corcyræan* Fleet, consisting of fifty Gallies, and with their united Forces making a Descent in *Elis*, laid that Province waste; while another Squadron of thirty Ships ravaged other maritime Places, plundered *Thronium* and *Solion*, two *Corinthian* Towns, and took the City *Aftactus*, together with the Island *Cephalenia*. On their return to *Athens* the People solemniz'd the Funerals of those who were first slain in this War, and *Pericles* was made choice of to celebrate their Memory in an Oration suitable to the Occasion. He, when *Archidamus* was the next Summer again fallen into *Attica*, with a Fleet of a hundred Sail passed over to *Epidaurus*, and spoil'd the adjacent Country, when repairing to *Troezen*, *Helias* and *Hermione*, he did the same, and then returned to *Athens*, by that time the Enemy had quitted the Frontiers.

The Athenians haraſs the Coaſts of Peloponneſus.

Mutual Miſchiefs done by the Lacedæmonians and Athenians.

At Sea this Summer the *Lacedæmonians* made an Attempt on the Island *Zacynthus*, (the modern *Zant*) where landing, they ravaged the Coasts and repaired home; and a Squadron of twenty Sail of *Athenian* Gallies, under the Command of *Phormio*, was sent to cruize in the *Sinus Criffæus*, (now the Gulph of *Lepanto*) to intercept all Ships going to, or coming from *Corinth*. Six Gallies were also sent over to *Caria* and *Lycia*, to fetch Money from the Confederate Cities there; but *Melefander*, the Commander in chief, landing in a Port of *Lycia*, which was in the contrary Interest, was slain by the People, with a considerable Number of his Attendants; and those of *Potidæa*, who, at the Instigation of the *Corinthians*, had

had revolted from the *Athenians* at the beginning of the War, were now, after a long Siege, reduced to their Obedience.

The third Year the *Peloponnesians* forbore to enter *Attica*, making *Bœotia* the Seat of the War; and *Cnemus*, the *Corinthian* Admiral, came to an Engagement with *Phormio* near the Mouth of the *Crissæan* Gulph. His Squadron consisted, as we have said, of twenty Sail, and that of the *Corinthians* of forty seven; but the *Athenian* Valour prevailed over their Enemy's Numbers, who having had twelve Gallies sunk in the Fight, made an ignominious Retreat to *Patræ* and *Dyme*, two Ports of *Achaia*. The *Peloponnesians* blamed their Admirals, in that they had not taken due Care for the Disposal of their Fleet, but placed those who were least acquainted with Sea Affairs against the *Athenians*; and to regain their lost Credit, they reinforced their Fleet with a strong Squadron, of of which *Phormio* having notice, he sent likewise to *Athens* for more Ships and Men, without which he could not hope for Success. They accordingly dispatched to him twenty Sail, with Orders to repair to *Crete* against the People of *Cydonia*, where having executed his Instructions, and destroyed the adjacent Country, he returned to his former Station near the Mouth of the Gulph of *Crissa*, where meeting with the *Peloponnesian* Fleet of seventy seven Sail, they joined Battel; but being not able to withstand the great Superiority of the Enemy, they were defeated, and forced to retire in Confusion. The Remnant of the *Athenian* Fleet, by the help of their Oars and Sails, made a shift to get into the Port of •*Naupactus*, and the Enemy closely pursuing them, they there prepared to give them a Reception. One of the *Athenian* Gallies being just ready to enter the Port, and having one of *Leucadia* almost on board of her, tacking suddenly about, came against her with so great a shock as she immediately sunk. This Action somewhat disturbed the *Peloponnesians*, who were now crouding into the Port after the *Athenians*, but so eager were they to render their Victory compleat, that many of them heedlessly ran aground on the Shelves. In the midst of this Disorder and Confusion the *Athenians* attack the *Peloponnesians* with great Fury, and in their turn become Conquerors, taking six Gallies. However, they erected Trophies on both sides, the *Athenians* at *Naupactus*, because they had repulsed the Enemy from thence, and the *Peloponnesians* at *Rhium*, for that there they had sunk some of the *Athenian* Gallies. Before the Fleets were laid up, *Cnemus* and *Brasidas*, the *Peloponnesian* Admirals, at the Instigation of the *Megareans*, resolved to make an Attempt on the *Piræus*, the Port of *Athens*, as being very slenderly fortified, and as ill guarded. To this Purpose a Body of Seamen were sent by Land from *Corinth*, each with his Oar in his Hand, to *Nisæa*, the Sea Port of *Megara*, where they embarked on board forty Gallies; but their Hearts failing them as to the Enterprize of the *Piræus*, and the Wind withal being contrary, they contented themselves with falling upon three Guardships which lay under *Budorus*, a Fort on the Cape of *Salamis*, which was next *Megara*. These they took, and, landing in the Island, committed

The Potidæans reduced by the Athenians.

The Athenians beat the Corinthians at Sea,

but are beaten by the Peloponnesians.

• *Lepanto.*

The Athenians beat the Peloponnesians at Naupactus.

what

what spoil they could, and then reimbarked. The Beacons fired by the People of the Island, had given notice to the *Athenians* of the Enemy's Approach, who immediately launching their Gallies, repaired on board in great Numbers, and leaving a sufficient Garrison in the *Piræus*, made the best of their way to *Salamis*; when the *Peloponnesians* finding they had taken the Alarm, returned to *Nisæa*, as the *Athenians* soon after did to *Piræus*, where they erected some new Fortifications, and had it better secured against the Surprize of an Enemy.

The Peloponnesians break into Attica.

In the fourth Year of this War *Archidamus* with the *Peloponnesian* Army again broke into *Attica*; and all the Island of *Lesbos*, except *Methymna*, declared for the *Lacedæmonians*. To punish this Treachery the *Athenians* dispatched a considerable Fleet under the Command of *Cleippides*, on whose Arrival before *Mitylene*, the Capital of that Island, the Townsmen made two Sallies, wherein they were repulsed with Loss, and *Cleippides* laid close siege to the Place: Mean while a strong Squadron under *Phormio* ravaged the

Athenians ravage Laconia.

Coast of *Laconia*, and thence repairing to *Acarnania*, plundered *OEnias*.

Lacedæmonians ravage Attica.

In the beginning of the fifth Year the *Lacedæmonians*, with their Allies, under the Conduct of *Pausanias*, the Son of *Plistonax* entered *Attica* with Fire and Sword, burning and destroying the Fruits of the Earth, and whatsoever they had left untouched in their former Incursions, insomuch that they were themselves obliged to quit the Country for want of Provisions, being disappointed of the

Mitylene seized by the Athenians.

Supplies they expected from *Lesbos*. There the *Athenians* had by this time seized *Mitylene*, put to Death most of the Inhabitants, razed their Walls, taken away their Shipping, and totally subdued the

and Platæa submits to the Lacedæmonians.

Island. The People in *Platæa*, worn out by a long Siege, surrendered themselves to the *Lacedæmonians* at Discretion, two hundred of whom they put to Death, and all the *Athenians* among them were sold into Slavery, and the Town itself given for one Year as an Habitation to such *Megareans* as had been expelled their City by Faction, after which it was razed to the Ground, and the Land set to Farm. While these things were doing at *Platæa*, there happened a great Sedition in *Corcyra*, whither at one and the same time were invited both the *Athenian* and *Peloponnesian* Fleets, the Commons espousing the Interest of the former, and the chief Men that of the latter. The two Parties had several bloody Disputes within the City, and with various Success, until *Nicostratus*, who lay with twelve *Athenian* Gallies at *Naupactus*, upon Notice of the Disturbance, timely arrived to the Assistance of the Commons, and reduced the Power of the Nobility. Soon after came the *Peloponnesian* Fleet, consisting of fifty Sail, under the Command of *Alcidas*,

Skirmishes at Sea between the Peloponnesians and Athenians.

with which the twelve *Athenian* Gallies before-mention'd, and those of the *Corcyræans* had several sudden and tumultuary Skirmishes; but Affairs had soon turned again in favour of the Nobility, had not *Eurymedon*, the *Athenian* Admiral, arrived with a Fleet of sixty Sail to support the *Plebeians*. *Alcidas*, fearing the Superiority of the *Athenians*, he with great Dexterity and Dispatch conveyed

CHAP. VI. *Dissolution of the* Rom. *Empire.* 73

veyed his Gallies over the narrow *Isthmus* of *Leucas*, to prevent meeting the Enemy's Fleet, which he had Advice was then coming about that *Peninsula* (now the Island St. *Maure*) to give him Battel, and repaired himself by Land to *Peloponnesus*. The *Corcyræan* Nobility thus abandoned by the *Lacedæmonians*, were exposed to the Fury of the Commons, who committed a merciless Slaughter among them, and polluted with their Blood even the Temples where they had taken Sanctuary. *Eurymedon* having thus settled them in the Government, repaired on board the Fleet, and left the Island, after whose Departure such of the Nobles as had made their Escape seized on the Forts belonging to *Corcyra*, on the Continent of *Epirus*, and frequently crossing the Streight, committed Depredations in the Island with great Success, and at length being not able, after a long Sollicitation by their Agents at *Lacedæmon* and *Corinth*, to obtain any Assistance from thence, they mustered up all their Force, and with some auxiliary Soldiers passing over into the Island, on their landing set fire to their Boats, and possessed themselves of the Hill *Istone*, which they fortified, and from thence made frequent Incursions on the Commons, untill in the seventh Year of the War *Eurymedon* coming over from *Pylus*, besieged and took them Prisoners, and delivered them to the People, who barbarously murthered them to a Man.

A great Slaugter at Corcyra.

The latter end of this Summer the *Athenians* sent a Fleet of twenty Men of War, commanded by *Laches*, to *Sicily*, under Pretence of aiding the People of *Leontium* against the *Syracusans*, but in reality to prevent the *Peloponnesians* receiving Supplies of Corn and other Provisions from thence, and, if possible, to obtain the Dominion of that Island. Upon their Arrival, by the Assistance of the People of *Rhegium*, on the opposite Shores of *Italy*, they made a Descent upon the *Æolian* Islands, (now those of *Lipari*) which were in Confederacy with *Syracuse*, and ravaging such of them as were inhabited, returned to *Rhegium*.

The Athenians make a Descent on the Æolian Islands.

The next Campaign the *Peloponnesians* intended to open with some notable Exploit in *Attica*, but were deterred from entering the Country by the frequent Earthquakes which then happened there: Mean while the *Athenians* fitted out two strong Squadrons, one of thirty Sail, under the Command of *Demosthenes*, to cruise about *Peloponnesus*, and infest the Coasts, the other of sixty, commanded by *Nicias*, to reduce the Island [b] *Melos*; which not being able to effect, they spoiled the Country, and repaired to the Coast of *Bœotia*; where landing, they defeated the People of *Tanagra* in an Engagement ashore, and then ravaged the Coasts of the *Locri Opuntii*, their next Neighbours. In *Sicily*, this Summer, the *Athenians* being, by an unexpected Assault of the Enemy, forced from *Himera*, repaired a second time to the *Æolian* Islands, where they found *Pythodorus* arrived from *Athens* with a few Ships, expecting to be followed in a short time with a Fleet of sixty Sail, under the Command of *Sophocles* and *Eurymedon*.

The Athenians fit out two Squadrons, and do Mischief in Peloponnesus.

[b] *Milo.*

L   The

The Peloponnesians invade Attica,
and take Messana in Sicily.

c Navarino.
The Athenians seize Pylus,

and destroy the Lacedæmonian Ships, &c.

They seize Methon,

d Regio.
and beat the the Fleet of Syracuse.
e Messina.

They sentence their Admirals.

The seventh Year of the War, the *Peloponnesians* began, according to Custom, with an Irruption into *Attica*, under the Conduct of *Agis*, the Son of *Archidamus*. In *Sicily* the Campaign opened with the taking of *Messana*, then in the *Athenian* Interest, by a Squadron of ten Gallies of *Syracuse*, and as many of the *Locri Epizephyrii*, in *Italy*, their Allies. *Eurymedon* and *Sophocles* being detained by contrary Winds on the Coast of *Peloponnesus*, surprized and fortified c *Pylus*, a Town of *Messenia*, that lay very opportunely for infesting the Frontiers of *Laconia*, and left *Demosthenes* with a Squadron of five Sail to cruise thereabouts for the Security of the Place, and Annoyance of the Enemy.

The *Lacedæmonians* immediately upon Advice thereof, as well knowing the Importance of that Town in the Hands of the *Athenians*, withdrew their Army out of *Attica*, and recalled their Fleet from *Corcyra*, in order to retake it. At the same time the *Athenian* Fleet having Notice of *Demosthenes*'s Danger, returned from *Zacynthus* to his Relief, and coming before *Sphacteria*, an Island at the Mouth of the Harbour, whereon the *Lacedæmonians* had landed a Body of Troops, endeavoured to force them to a Battel, which not being able to effect, the next Day they attacked the Ships there, of which they sunk several, took five, and had like to have seized and carried off to Sea most of the rest which lay nearer the Shore, but were repulsed by the superior Numbers of the *Lacedæmonians*: However they blocked up the Island so closely, that the Enemy, after having undergone great Streights, were at length all obliged to surrender Prisoners of War. The *Athenians* then strongly fortifying *Pylus*, repaired with their Fleet, loaden with Spoils, to the Eastern Coast of *Peloponnesus*, and landing near *Crommyon*, a Town belonging to the *Corinthians*, at the bottom of the *Sinus Saronicus*, (now the Gulf of *Engia*) plundered the adjacent Country, and departing thence, seized on *Methon*, a Place situate between *Epidaurus* and *Troezen*, which they environed with a Wall, and left a Garrison in it to infest the Inhabitants of those Towns.

In *Sicily* the *Athenian* Fleet off of d *Rhegium*, (near which was its Station for the Security of that Place) came to an Engagement with the *Syracusans*, and defeated them, pursuing them into the Harbour of e *Messana*, which City they invested by Sea and Land. The People of *Leontium*, whether now grown jealous of the *Athenian* Power, or really become weary of the War, sent back the *Athenian* Auxiliaries, and made a Peace with the *Syracusans*, the Terms whereof were approved by the *Athenian* Admirals; which Proceeding of theirs was so condemned by the People at *Athens*, whose Designs were levell'd at the Subjection of the whole Island, that a Sentence of Banishment passed on two of them, and *Eurymedon*, the third, narrowly escaped with a great Fine, it being laid to their Charge (tho' falsely 'tis supposed) that having so fair an Opportunity of establishing the *Athenian* Power there, they had suffered themselves to be bought off.

Next

CHAP. VI. *Dissolution of the* Rom. *Empire.* 75

Next Year the Exiles of *Lesbos* seized upon *Antandrus*, a City *The Exiles of* of *Mysia*, opposite to that Island, under the Mountain and Forest of *Lesbos seize* *Ida*, which affording excellent Materials for Shipping, they resolved *drus.* to fit out a Fleet there to annoy the Island, from whence they had been expelled by the *Athenians*. They in the mean time meditating greater Matters, with a Fleet of sixty Sail, commanded by *Nicias*, made a Descent on the Island *Cythera*, (now *Cerigo*) lying *The Atheni-* off *Laconia*, and carried *Scandea* at the first Assault. Then taking *thera, and o-* *Cythera*, the chief Town, they transported its Inhabitants elsewhere, *ther Places.* and leaving good Garrisons in both Places, passed over to *Argia*, where they burnt and destroyed the Country about *Asine* and *Helias*, and from thence proceeding to *Troezen* and *Epidaurus*, did the like there. By Land, the *Athenians* failed in an Attempt on *Megara*, but surprized *Nisæa*, the Sea Port of that Place, which was also the chief Arsenal of the *Lacedæmonians*; but soon after lost it to *Brasidas* the *Spartan* General.

About the same time *Demodocus* and *Aristides*, who commanded a Squadron in the *Hellespont*, defeated the *Lesbian* Exiles, and took *Lesbian Ex-* *Antandrus*. *Lamachus*, who was joined in Commission with the *iles defeated.* two former, going with a Squadron of ten Sail to *Heraclea*, on the *Euxine*, and unadvisedly entering the *Calex*, which there falls into the Sea, the Ships were all sunk in the Mouth of that River by the *Athenian* Impetuosity of the Current, but most of the Men saved, with whom *visedly lost,* he repaired over-land to *Chalcedon*. This Misfortune to the *Athe-* *and other* *nian* Affairs was followed by several others; for in *Bœotia* almost *Misfortunes.* all those under the Command of *Hippocrates* were, together with their General, slain at *Delium*, a Town on the Confines of *Attica*. The Forces also commanded by *Demosthenes*, which had made a Descent near *Sicyon*, were forced to their Ships with considerable Loss: And at the same time *Brasidas* had *Amphipolis* in *Macedonia* *Several Ships* surrendered to him, a Town belonging to the *Athenians* in those *revolt from* Parts. The Cities also about the Mountain *Athos* revolted from *the Atheni-* them to the *Peloponnesians*, particularly *Thyssa*, *Cleone*, *Acrothon* *ans.* and *Olophyxus*; as did also several of the People of *Grestonia*, *Bizaltia* and *Eidonia*; and as *Brasidas* also took *Torone* by Treachery, and *Lecythus* by Storm, so *Scione* opened her Gates to him.

The *Athenians* began the ninth Year with a publick Decree for the Reduction of *Scione*, and fitted out a Fleet for that Purpose, when soon after came Advice that *Mende*, a Town in the *Peninsula* *Mende also* of *Pellene*, had revolted to the *Lacedæmonians*; whereupon a Fleet *recovered by* of fifty Sail was sent out under the Command of *Nicias* and *Nico-* *them.* *stratus*, who soon taking *Mende*, put to Death the Authors of the Revolt; and *Scione* was also, after a short Siege, surrendered to them.

The tenth Year of this War *Cleon*, who commanded in chief for *Cleon with* the *Athenians*, upon Advice that *Brasidas* had left *Torone* but slen- *the Atheni-* derly garrisonned, repaired with a Squadron to the Port of *Colophon*, *ans* near that Place, and thence having detached ten Sail to *Torone*, with Orders to seize the Haven, and use their best Endeavours to
L 2 enter

enter the Place on that side, disembarked the Troops, and marched himself at the Head of them toward the Town, as if he intended to invest it by Land; which the Inhabitants endeavouring to prevent, with their whole Force drawn to oppose him, the *Athenians* from the Ships, by this time got into the Harbour, entered without Opposition, and opening their Gates to their Fellow-Soldiers, presently rendered themselves Masters of the Town, making the Women and Children Slaves, and carrying the Men Prisoners to *Athens*.

take Torone.

The ill Success of the *Lacedæmonians* at *Pylus*, together with the Loss of the Island *Cythera*, and other Misfortunes, had so broken their Spirits, that they became very desirous of a Peace, to which the *Athenians* were now the more disposed, that they might be at leisure to prosecute their Designs upon *Sicily*. A Peace was accordingly concluded between them for fifty Years, in the Negotiation whereof *Nicias* having had a principal Hand, it was called the *Nicæan* Peace. The *Lacedæmonians*, in a Treaty for a Cessation of Arms preliminary thereto, consented to an Article that it should not be lawful for them to make use of any Ship of War on any Occasion whatsoever, but should only sail in Merchant Ships, and those too of a very small Burthen; which was a Condition the most dishonourable the *Spartan* Common-wealth ever made, and was little expected by their Confederates would have been ever condescended to.

A fifty Year's Peace concluded,

This Peace, concluded for fifty Years, continued in force but ten, if a Peace may be said to have at all subsisted between those People, which, tho' not directly in their own Persons, was every Day violated in those of their Confederates comprehended therein; as though they were less guilty of Perjury and Breach of Treaty in giving Aid to those their Confederates, than if they had carried on the War in their own Names.

but soon violated by several who were included therein.

The six following Years were mostly spent in a War between the *Lacedæmonians* and *Argives*, which latter, after they had maintained it some time, aided by their Allies the *Eleans* and *Mantineans*, were supported by the *Athenians*, in pursuance of a League entered into with them for a hundred Years, through the Management of *Alcibiades*.

Athens supports the Argives against the Lacedæmonians.
Alcibiades.

CHAP.

CHAP. VII.

Of the Naval Wars of the Grecians, *from the great Expedition of the* Athenians *against* Sicily, *to their utter Defeat in that Island by the* Syracusans.

THE good Fortune of the *Athenians* was now arrived to too great a Height for them to bear it with Moderation, having not only obtained the absolute Dominion of the Sea, by *Sparta*'s resigning all Pretensions that way, but increased their Reputation to a prodigious Degree by the Surrender of the *Spartans* at *Pylus*. It was remember'd that at *Thermopylæ* indeed the *Lacedæmonians* were beaten and cut to pieces, to a Man, by the *Persians*; but the *Athenians* were the only People upon Earth to whom they had delivered up their Arms, surrender'd their Persons, and received Peace from, on dishonourable and ignominious Terms. The Fame of these things, and Terror of the *Athenian* Name, soon passed into *Italy*, and reached even *Carthage* itself; nor did they make any Secret of it, that they had some great Designs in view to the Westward, to facilitate the Execution whereof, they thought it absolutely necessary first to possess themselves of *Sicily*, a rich and populous Island, and Mistress of a great Sea Force, the Accession of which would be a vast Advancement to their Affairs. This Design had been projected almost ever since the Conclusion of the *Persian* War, but vigorously and effectually to prosecute it, by transporting a sufficient Power to so distant a Country, (as *Sicily* appear'd to the Navigators of those Times) they had not any Opportunity till now, when having gotten their Hands somewhat clear of the *Lacedæmonians*, who were deeply embroil'd with the *Argives*, at the same time a fair Pretence offered for their Expedition to the aforesaid Island, the *Egestans*, a People in the Western Parts thereof, having by their Ambassadors prayed their Assistance against the *Selinuntians* and *Syracusans*, who had made an Irruption into their Territories, and laid waste the Country.

At this time the two Men who bore the most considerable Sway in *Athens* were *Nicias* and *Alcibiades*, Persons of very different Characters. The first somewhat advanced in Years, of great Experience, and consequently very wary and cautious, who considered that tho' the Affairs of the Common-wealth were now in a very flourishing Condition, yet they were not enough confirmed to admit of such hazardous Undertakings, and would frequently thunder out like an Oracle, that fatal was the End of all Wars which were not grounded on Necessity. The other was young, rash, bold and turbulent, of prodigious Parts, cultivated with Learning, (he having been a Disciple of *Socrates*) and adorned with an Eloquence equal to the greatest Orators of his Time. These Advantages, joined with his noble Birth, the Glory of his Ancestors, and his

great

great Riches, which he employed in Donatives, publick Shows, and all sorts of Munificence, together with the Reputation he had already gained in military Affairs, easily gained him the favour of the People, and he being violently inclined to this Expedition as well as themselves, by an Oration he made on the Subject, set them so on fire that there was no room left for them to hearken in the least to the wholsome Advice of *Nicias:* And accordingly the War was resolved on. The Management of it was committed to three Generals, *Alcibiades* the Promoter of it, *Nicias* who was against it, and *Lamachus,* one of the most considerable men of the City, in *Alcibiades's* Interest. A Fleet of a hundred and thirty Sail was immediately fitted out, so magnificently furnished both by the Publick, and the respective Officers, that they seemed rather going to celebrate a Triumph than to meet an Enemy: And their Levies as well for Sea as Land were quickly completed, both young and old crouding to be enroll'd in this Service.

Alcibiades prevails for a War against Sicily.

In the mean time the soberer sort of Citizens prayed indeed for its Success, but were in pain for the Event, and seemed to forebode it would have no good one, sending heavy Curses at *Alcibiades* for sacrificing (as they said) his Country to his own Luxury and Ambition; and as for the *Grecian* Cities, their Confederates, they looked on it more as an Ostentation of their Riches, and what they were able to do, than a real Design against an Enemy.

A. M. 3535.

It was now the seventeenth Year since the Beginning of the *Peloponnesian* War, when all things being in readiness, and the Troops embarked, to the Number of five thousand, the Fleet made Sail for *Corcyra,* where arriving, they found the auxiliary Fleet ready to join them, consisting of above two hundred Ships.

The Athenian *Fleet sails for Sicily.*

In the mean time the News of these Preparations having reached *Sicily,* it was variously received, some entirely disbelieving it, and looking on it only as a State Trick of the Nobles to terrify and amuse the People, others that it was a thing not improbable, and as it was very possible, ought by no means to be neglected. *Hermocrates,* a Man of great Abilities, and one of the first Rank in *Syracuse,* having at length certain Advice of the truth of it, communicated the matter to an Assembly of the People, and advised them to lay aside their Animosities, and heartily unite in defence of the Publick, at the same time exhorting them not to be discouraged with too great Apprehensions of the Enemy, for that it very rarely happened that such numerous Forces, at so great Distance from home, met with Success, but, on the contrary, generally came to a disastrous End. Then enlarging on their own Strength and Power, he put them in mind of what they might expect from others, and advised them to send Ambassadors to desire Aid of the *Peloponnesians* and *Carthaginians,* the former the old Enemies of *Athens,* and the latter already alarmed at the rising Power of that City, and therefore ready to lay hold of any Opportunity to crush it.

Tarentum, &c. *refuses to join with the* Athenians.

The *Athenian* Fleet had by this time crossed the *Ionian* Sea, and came before *Tarentum,* whose Inhabitants would not permit any Intercourse between the Ships and the Town, not so much as for a

Market

CHAP. VII. *Dissolution of the* Rom. *Empire.* 79

Market, nor would they, without much difficulty, afford them leave to water. The like Treatment they received from most of the other Cities in those Parts, tho' all of *Grecian* Original, they declaring they would not be any ways instrumental in the Invasion of *Sicily*, but observe a strict Neutrality on both sides. Frustrated of their hopes of these Cities, they repair'd to *Rhegium*, and fell to deliberate on their further Proceedings, in which what first offered to their Consideration was, where they should make their Descent; but in that they could not come to a Determination, 'till the Return of the Ships they had detached before them from *Corcyra* to the *Egestans*, about the Money those People had engaged to provide for Payment of the Army, most of which Charge was to be defrayed by them. These Ships brought Advice that there was not any Money provided, nor were the People in a Capacity to raise any, or comply with the least Part of their Engagement, having imposed on the Ministers the *Athenians* had before sent to treat with them, by making a false Shew of their Wealth, artificially exposing to their view the Riches of their Temples, and Plate borrow'd from the neighbouring Cities. On the Riches of these People they had so much depended, that this News caused a mighty Consternation among them, and the Generals now taking into Consideration the present State of Affairs, *Nicias* was of Opinion that the whole Fleet should repair toward *Selinus*, against which they were chiefly set forth, and if the *Egestans* would furnish them with Money, according to the Agreement, that then they should deliberate on their further Proceedings, but if not, they determined to require Maintenance for the sixty Gallies which were fitted out at their request, and either by force, or composition, to bring the *Selinuntians* and them to a Peace: After this to pass along and alarm the Enemies Coast, and having thus made a Shew of the *Athenian* Power, and their readiness to help their Confederates, to return home. *Alcibiades*'s Sentiments were, that it would be very dishonourable for so considerable a Fleet to return home without having performed any thing suitable to the greatness of the Preparations; that he thought it therefore best to sound the Minds of the *Siculi*, and solicite them to revolt from the *Syracusans*, which if they could not prevail with them to do by fair means to force them to it by foul; that they should make choice of some well fortified Town to land the Troops at, with a Harbour for the Reception and Security of the Fleet; but if no such could be found in the Hands of their Friends, that they should seize on some one, either by force or fraud, where they might securely view the Situation of Affairs, and take their Measures accordingly. As for *Lamachus*, he advised, that they should go directly to *Syracuse*, the Capital City, while the Troops were yet fresh and vigorous, and the People there under consternation; for that an Army was always most terrible before the Enemy recollected their Spirits, and made the danger familiar to them. Such was his Opinion, he said; but if they could not come into that, he acquiesced in what *Alcibiades* had proposed, as thinking it highly proper that something should be attempted. It was accordingly resolved to pursue *Alcibia-*

des's

The Syracusans appoint three Generals.

des's Design, and endeavour to bring over some of the *Sicilian* Cities to their Party: Mean while the *Syracusans* appointed three Generals for the management of the War, *Hermocrates, Sicanus*, and *Heraclides*, who with all expedition had got together an Army, and received into Confederacy with them the People of *Himera, Messana, Selinus*, the *Geloi*, and most of the *Siculi*.

One of the *Athenian* Admirals continued with a strong Squadron near *Rhegium*, to influence those Parts, while the other two repaired with sixty Sail towards *Syracuse*, detaching ten Ships before them into the Haven of that City, to give notice to the *Leontines* residing there of their Arrival to settle the Affairs of *Leontium*, which had almost ever since the forementioned Treaty, been at ill terms with *Syracuse*. The Fleet coming off *Catana, Alcibiades*, partly by persuasion, and partly by force, brought the People of that place to embrace the *Athenian* Interest, but failed in his Attempts to do the like with those of *Messana*, and other Cities thereabouts; whereupon the Squadron being recalled from *Rhegium* came into the Harbour of *Catana*, where a Camp was also formed on shore.

Catana joins with the Athenians.

Alcibiades called home, flies to Peloponnesus.

Now arrived a Gally from *Athens*, with Orders from the State for *Alcibiades* to repair home, and take his Trial for the Crimes he was charged with, of having prophaned the Mysteries of *Ceres* and *Proserpine*, and been concerned in defacing the Statues of *Mercury* throughout the City. He, whether apprehensive of the Power of his Enemies, or really conscious of his Guilt, fled first to *Italy*, and thence to *Peloponnesus*, where receiving Letters of safe Conduct from *Sparta*, he repaired thither, and was taken into great Trust and Friendship, assuring them that he would make them amends by his future Services for all the Mischief he had done them whilst he was their Enemy. His Advice to them was first to send Succours to the *Syracusans*, secondly to come to an open Rupture with the *Athenians*, and thirdly to fortify *Deccleа*, a Town in *Attica*, and place a strong Garrison in it, which by reason of its near Neighbourhood to *Athens* would extremely annoy that City.

The Advice of Alcibiades to the Lacedæmonians.

Lamachus and *Nicias* now dividing the Fleet into two Squadrons, took a different Course about the Island of *Sicily*, soliciting the maritime Cities to take part with them, which having prevailed with some of them to do, and received Supplies of Men and Provisions, they re-assembled their whole Force to undertake the Siege of *Syracuse*, in order whereto they repaired first to *Thapsus*, a Peninsula within few Miles of that place, from whence the Land Forces marched to *Epipolæ*, an Eminence that overlook'd the City of *Syracuse*, which they fortified with very strong Lines, to cut off the Communication of the Place on the Land Side; not but that the *Syracusans*, to interrupt the Works, made frequent Sallies, in one of which *Lamachus* was killed. The sole Command was now devolved upon *Nicias*, when *Gylippus*, whom the *Lacedæmonians* had sent at the head of a considerable Force to aid the *Syracusans*, arrived in *Sicily*, and landing at *Himera*, there haled his Gallies ashore, and marched over land to *Syracuse*; but before he reached the place *Consilus*, the *Corinthian* Admiral, who was sent on the same Errand,

The Athenians prepare to attempt Syracuse.

Lacedæmonians, &c. come to the Aid of Syracuse.

rand, was already arrived, and encouraged the Townsmen to a vigorous defence, and not to hearken to an accommodation. By the Accession of all this force the Enemy became greatly superior, and therefore there were dispatched to *Nicias* ten Ships with a considerable Sum of Money, and two other Persons were join'd in Commission with him, in the room of *Alcibiades* and *Lamachus*. These were *Eurymedon* and *Demosthenes*, the latter of whom was first sent out on the Coast of *Laconia* with a Fleet of sixty Sail.

By the Persuasions of *Gylippus* the *Spartan*, *Consilus* the *Corinthian*, and *Hermocrates* their own General, the *Syracusans* were prevailed with to try their Fortune on the salt Water. That City is situate on a Neck of Land jutting into the Sea, of which it takes up the whole Space, and the Land about it lies so as to form two Havens on the North and South Sides thereof, of which the latter is the great one, and the former the less. In the Bottom of the great Haven lay the *Athenian* Fleet, and in the same, but under the Protection of the Town, the *Syracusans* had thirty five Gallies, having a much greater Number in the little Haven on the other Side, where was their Arsenal. The Entrance of the great Haven was very narrow, and the *Athenians* having possessed themselves of the Promontory of *Plemmyrium*, which guarded the Passage, the *Syracusans* were at a loss how to bring in their Gallies from the other Haven. They nevertheless resolved to attempt it, and the two Fleets came to a sharp Engagement in the Mouth of the Haven, wherein the *Athenians* beginning to give way, the *Syracusans* crouded in so fast, and in such Disorder, that they fell foul of one another, in which Confusion the *Athenians* again attacked, and totally routed them, sinking eleven of their Gallies. During the heat of this Engagement, while the *Athenians* upon *Plemmyrium* were wholly taken up in viewing it, *Gylippus* took a Circuit round the Head of the Haven with a Body of chosen Men, entered the Outworks without Opposition, and forced the *Athenians* from the rest with great Precipitation: For which success ashore the *Syracusans* erected a Trophy on *Plemmyrium*, as the *Athenians* did near their Camp, on account of their Victory by Water. But the loss of the *Athenians* was by much the greatest; for in the Fortification at *Plemmyrium* they kept most of their Stores of War, and a great deal of the Publick Money, which was all taken by the Enemy, who now commanding the Entrance of the Haven, they could receive no Supplies of Provision, or ought else for the Camp, or Fleet, but what they were oblig'd by Fight to obtain a Passage for.

The Haven being at length open for the *Syracusans*, they sent out twelve Gallies, under the Command of *Agatharchus*, to intercept a Convoy of Stores and Provisions they had Advice was coming to the *Athenians* from *Rhegium*, and the Parts adjacent, falling in with which, they destroyed most of them, and thence repairing to *Caulonia*, they burnt near that place a considerable Quantity of Timber which the *Athenians* had there framed for building their Gallies. Soon after a light Skirmish happened in the Haven about some Piles the *Syracusans* had driven down before their old Harbour, that

that so their Gallies might ride in Security from any Assault of the *Athenians*; who thereupon brought to the place a large Hulk, fortified with wooden Turrets, and covered against Fire, from whence they sent out Men in their Boats, who fastening Ropes to the *Piles*, they in that manner forced them up; and some of them their Divers sawed asunder at the bottom. In the mean time the *Syracusans*, from the Harbour, and the *Athenians*, from the Hulk, shot at each other, till at length the greatest part of the Piles were gotten up: But almost as fast as they were removed, the *Syracusans* drove down others.

Their Success in gaining the Works at *Plemmyrium*, beforementioned, was looked on to be so considerable as all *Sicily* inclined to their Side, except the *Agrigentines*; yet were there after this several other slight Engagements between the *Syracusans* and *Athenians*, wherein sometimes the one and sometimes the other had the Advantage. At length, in pursuance of the Advice of *Ariston*, a Corinthian, and a very expert Seaman, the *Syracusans* shorten'd the Heads of their Gallies, and made them lower, with Beaks of a great Thickness, which they also strengthened with Rafters fastened to the Sides of the Gallies, both within and without; and with these they offered the *Athenians* Battel, who prepared to engage them with eighty Sail, having the rest of their Naval Force in the Bottom of the Haven. At a proper Distance from that Part of the Fleet which lay there, they placed two large Hulks, with a sufficient Space between them for a Gally conveniently to pass through, that so such as should be hard pressed in the Fight might retire to a Place of Security. The *Athenians* were superior to the Enemy both in the Number and Nimbleness of their Ships, and the Skill, Dexterity and Discipline of their Seamen, all which as they would almost have ascertained a Victory in the open Sea, so were they of little Use now they were shut up in a Haven, and wanted Sea-room to exert themselves. They fought several Hours with various Success, till at length, about Noon, *Ariston* advised that the *Syracusans* might take their Repast upon the Strand, and not go up into the Town as usual, who accordingly rowed suddenly astern towards the City, and there dined on the Shore. The *Athenians* looking upon this as a Retreat from the Battel, landed at leisure, and among other Business prepared for their Repast, as little expecting to fight any more that Day; but the *Syracusans* returning aboard, came down again towards them, when they in great Tumult, the most Part having not taken any Food, embarking disorderly, went out to meet them, and again they engaged each other. The *Syracusans* fighting, as they had before determined, with their Gallies Head to Head with those of the *Athenians*, and being provided with Beaks for the Purpose, did great Execution among them; and they were also greatly annoyed by the Darters from the Decks, but much more by those *Syracusans* who going about in small Boats, passed under the Oars of their Gallies, and coming close to the Sides of them, threw their Darts at the Mariners. The *Syracusans* vigorously prosecuting these Advantages, at length obtained the Victory, and forced the *Athenians*

The Syracusans *pursuing* Ariston's *Advice,*

Beat and spoil the Athenian *Fleet.*

CHAP. VII. *Dissolution of the* Rom. *Empire.* 83

nians to retire between the two Hulks beforemention'd to their Harbour, closely pursuing them thither; nay they had entered after them, had they not been prevented by a Contrivance of the *Athenians*, who having hung from the Yard Arms prodigious Weights of Lead, cast into the Form of Dolphins, they, as the Gallies approached near enough, let them down with great Violence, and by this means sunk one of the *Syracusan* Gallies which ventured too far, and so disabled another that they took her with all her Men.

In this Battel the *Syracusans* having sunk seven *Athenian* Gallies, spoiled as many, and taking and killing great Numbers, they retired and erected a Trophy on the Shore, promising themselves from this Success soon to bring the War to a Conclusion; but in the midst of these their Hopes, *Demosthenes* and *Eurymedon* arrived to the Assistance of the *Athenians*, with a Fleet of seventy three Sail, having on Board five thousand Soldiers, with three thousand Slingers and Darters. Notwithstanding this, the *Athenians* began to grow weary of fighting at Sea, and endeavour'd to gain some Outworks of the Town on the Land Side, but being repulsed in the Attempt with great Loss, *Demosthenes* and *Eurymedon* declared themselves for returning to *Athens*, but *Nicias strongly* opposed it, as well for the Infamy which, as he said, would attend so dishonourable a Retreat, as for that they should be charged, as the former Generals were, with having been corrupted with Money from performing their Duty. *The Athenians receive a Re-inforcement.* *Demosthenes and Eurymedon's Advice, opposed by Nicias.*

The *Syracusans* having Intelligence of these Debates, became yet more bold, attacked the *Athenian* Camp by Land, and with their Gallies closely blocked up the Mouth of the Haven, and thence provoked the *Athenians* to fight. *Heraclides*, a Youth of Quality, who had the Command of one of the *Syracusan* Gallies, came up very near to the *Athenians*, and in all Probability had been taken, but that *Poliuchus*, to whom he was related, came with ten Gallies to his Relief; and the *Syracusans*, anxious for the Safety of *Poliuchus*, resolved, if possible, to force the *Athenians* to a general Engagement, in order whereunto they manned out seventy six Gallies, disposing at the same time several Bodies of Land Forces along the Shore, to prevent the Enemy's Escape. The *Athenians*, though there was a great Consternation among them, being much fitter to flee than to fight, yet were they obliged, in their own Defence, to withstand the Enemy, and prepared to receive them with eighty six Gallies. Both Fleets were now disposed in order of Battel: To *Eurymedon* was given the Right Wing of the *Athenians*, to whom was opposed *Agatharchus* by the *Syracusans*. *Euthydemus* had the Command of their Left Wing, and had to do with *Sicanus* in the Right of the *Syracusans*, in whose Center was *Pythes* a *Corinthian*, as was *Menander* in that of the *Athenians*. The Signal for engaging being displayed, *Eurymedon*, relying on his Superiority of numbers, advanced with his Division, in order to surround that of the Enemy opposite to him, and was at length got so far from the Center, that the *Syracusans* cut off his Retreat, and forced him into a Cove surrounded with their Troops, where endeavouring to land and fight his Way through, he was slain, with great Numbers of his *The Syracusans beat the Athenian Gallies.*

M 2

his Men, and all his Ships fell into the Hands of the Enemy. The News of this Misfortune drove the *Athenians* almost to Despair, so that being now less able to resist the Fury of the *Syracusans*, they were soon forced to retire in so great Confusion, that they split several of their Gallies against the Rocks, and ran many of them aground. As they were landing their Men near the Place where *Gylippus* lay with the Troops, *Sicanus*, one of the *Syracusan* Admirals, filled an old Hulk with Faggots, and other combustible Matter, and setting fire to it, sent her afore the Wind toward the *Athenian* Gallies; but they took such effectual Care to keep her off, that his Design had no Effect; mean while they got the better of the *Syracusan* Troops ashore under *Gylippus*, and forced them to retire into the Town.

The Athenians have the better on shore.

In this Engagement the *Athenians* are said to have lost thirty three Gallies, and the *Syracusans*, thus encouraged, were meditating greater Matters, for they began to reflect what Glory they should acquire to themselves, not only among the *Greeks*, who would be universally obliged to them for freeing them from the Usurpations of *Athens*, but also among other Nations, if they could not only withstand, as they had hitherto done, but likewise totally destroy so powerful a Fleet and Army, which they resolved, if possible, to compass. To this End, they placed in the Mouth of the Haven, which was there about a Mile over, such a Number of Gallies, Head and Stern together, as took up the whole Space, and thus deprived the *Athenians* of all Means of Escape, unless they could force their way through. *Nicias*, finding himself under a Necessity of attempting to break this Chain, embarked the Seamen and Troops on board a hundred and ten Gallies, in order thereunto, resolving, if they succeeded, to repair home, but if they should be repulsed, to disembark again, set the Gallies on fire, and make the best of their way by Land to some confederate City in *Sicily*. They attacked the *Syracusans* with great Vigour, and were as warmly received by them, so that never was any Battel fought with greater Obstinacy and Fury on both sides, and considering the Narrowness of the Space there was not room for retreating and attacking again, but the Gallies lay close with their Broadsides together, so that the Men fought hand to hand as if they had been engaged on shore: And besides the Nature of the Place which made it necessary so to do, *Nicias*, to prevent the Enemy's making use of the Barks of their Ships so effectually as they had done in the former Engagement, ordered a Number of grappling Irons to be flung out of each of his Gallies, in order to bring them with their Broadsides to those of the Enemy, and so elude the Stroke of the Beaks; but to hinder the Success of this Stratagem, the *Syracusans* covered their Gallies with Hides, in which the grappling Irons taking no hold, easily slipped off. In this Engagement the Valour of the *Syracusans* far exceeded either their Art or their good Fortune. They laid the *Athenian* Gallies aboard, and pouring in Numbers of Men, committed great Slaughter among them, and at length forced them back, in the utmost Disorder, to their old Station. *Demosthenes* would have again attempted

Disposition of the Syracusan Gallies in the Mouth of the Haven.

The Athenians resolve to force their Passage.

Nicias's Stratagem eluded.

ed, the next Morning, to force the *Syracusan* Line with sixty Gallies which yet remained in good Condition, but the Seamen were so dispirited with their former ill Success, that they unanimously refused to go aboard; upon which the Generals came to a Resolution to decamp the next Night; mean while the *Syracusans* made another Attempt on the *Athenian* Gallies, some of which they took and carried off, others they burnt: And having Intelligence of the Enemy's Design to retire by Land, seized all the Passes, in order to cut off their Retreat. *Eurymedon* was already slain in the Engagement at Sea, and *Nicias* and *Demosthenes* were only remaining, who having thus lost all their Fleet, left their Dead unburied, and their Wounded to the Mercy of the Enemy, and fled with Precipitation, but after making several fruitless Attemps to escape, surrender'd themselves Prisoners at Discretion, together with the whole Army under their Command, whereupon they were both put to Death, and the Men either condemned to the Mines, or sold into Slavery.

and all the Athenian Gallies taken, or burnt.

And being also overcome on shore, surrender.

CHAP. VIII.

Of the Naval Wars of the Grecians, *from the Overthrow of the* Athenians *in* Sicily, *to the Victory obtained over them by* Lysander, *the* Spartan *General, at* Ægos-potamos, *and the end of the* Peloponnesian *War.*

WHEN the News of this terrible Disaster reached *Athens*, they would give no Credit to it, but having it soon confirm'd beyond Contradiction, they were filled with Terrour, Amazement and Despair, fearing nothing less than that the victorious Enemy would immediately repair to their City and level it with the Ground; and these dismal Apprehensions were the more increased, for that they had neither a Fleet, an Army, nor Money.

The People of Athens much terrified.

In the mean time the *Peloponnesians*, under the Command of *Agis*, laid waste the Country about *OEta*, raised great Contributions among the *Thessalians*, and received into their Protection the Islands *Eubœa* and *Lesbos*, which now revolted from the *Athenians*; who in the midst of these Misfortunes, made a shift to fit out twenty Gallies. These were no sooner got out into the Gulph, than they fell in with *Alcamenes*, one of the *Lacedæmonian* Admirals, just then come out of *Cenchrea*, a Port of the *Corinthians*, and defeated them in two Engagements, in the latter of which he was slain; but *Alcibiades*, now in the *Spartan* Service, soon revenged his Death, by procuring the Revolt of *Chios* and *Clazomenæ* from the *Athenians*, which was soon after followed by that of the *Milesians*, and a League Offensive and Defensive was struck up between the

The Peloponnesians mischief the Athenians.

Lacedæmonians beaten at Sea.

Places revolt from Athens.

Lace-

Lacedæmonians and *Tiſſaphernes*, one of the *Perſian* Governours of the *Leſſer Aſia*. In Purſuance of which, the *Lacedæmonian* Fleet being increaſed by the Acceſſion of ſeveral Ships of his, reduced to their Obedience the Cities of *Teos*, *Lebedus*, and *Eræ*.

A little before theſe things were done in *Ionia*, a Squadron of twenty ſeven Sail from *Athens*, which cruiſed off *Leucadia*, fell in with the Enemy's Fleet coming from *Sicily*, having on board *Gylippus*, with the Troops returning from that Iſland, and chaſed them into the very Port of *Corinth*. The *Athenians* alſo, near *Boliſſus*, defeated the Fleet of *Chios*, and, in conſequence of that Victory, recovered the whole Iſland, fifteen hundred of whoſe Inhabitants they embarked on board the Fleet, made ſail for *Miletus*, and inveſted that Place, and ſoon after laid ſiege to *Samos*: But about the ſame time ſeven *Athenian* Ships falling in with *Aſtyochus*, off *Cyme*, they were all taken, or deſtroyed.

The Athenians have the better at Sea, and take Chios, but afterwards loſe ſome Ships.

The *Lacedæmonians* now began to grow jealous of *Alcibiades*, by means of *Agis*, whoſe Wife he had debauched, and he becoming as weary of them, retired to *Tiſſaphernes*, inſinuated himſelf into his Favour, and was ſoon after reconciled to the *Athenians*, who putting him at the Head of their Fleet, their Affairs would ſoon have flouriſhed again, had they not fallen out among themſelves about altering the Form of their Government. However an end was at length put to theſe Diſſenſions, by the Power of *Alcibiades*, and the Enemy's coming before *Piræus* with a Fleet under the Command of *Hegeſandridas*, when they embarked on board the Ships in a very diſorderly manner, and going out to engage them, off *Eretria*, received a ſignal Overthrow, loſing two and twenty Sail. This Misfortune, together with the Revolt of *Byzantium* and *Eubœa*, brought the *Athenians* to an Agreement among themſelves, as knowing their Affairs would be otherwiſe entirely ruined; and accordingly the *Oligarchy* was aboliſhed, and the Government of the People again ſet up, who immediately paſſed a Decree that *Alcibiades*, and thoſe who were in Exile with him, ſhould be called home.

Alcibiades reconciled to the Athenians.

The Athenians beaten at Sea near Eretria.

Thraſylus, on the Coaſts of *Aſia*, coming from *Samos* to *Lesbos*, *Mindarus*, the *Peloponneſian* Admiral, to avoid meeting with him, repaired with the Fleet under his Command toward the *Helleſpont*, touching by the way at Cape *Sigeum*: And there being at *Seſtos*, within the *Helleſpont*, two and twenty *Athenian* Ships, which upon notice of the Enemy's Approach, by the Fires made in the Watch-Towers along the Coaſt, were at break of Day making toward *Elæus*, juſt without the Mouth of that Streight, that ſo they might have room to eſcape, if the Enemy ſhould not paſs by without diſcovering them, they were no ſooner in ſight, than the *Athenians* crouded from them with all the Sail they could make, and got ſafe to *Lemnos*, except the four ſtern-moſt of the Squadron, one of which ſplit againſt the Rocks, two others were ſunk, and the fourth was burnt near *Imbros*: And now *Thraſylus*, who lay before *Ereſus* in *Lesbos*, hearing of the Enemy's Departure for the *Helleſpont*,

An Action in the Helleſpont between the Athenians and Lacedæmonians;

CHAP. VIII. *Dissolution of the Rom. Empire.* 87

pont, raised the Siege of that Place, and repaired to the Assistance of the *Athenians*, who in his way received into his Protection some Ships of that Republick, to which the *Lacedæmonians* were giving Chace, and took two of their Gallies: And now he thought it proper, if possible, to bring them to an Engagement, which he effected after spending five Days in Preparations for it. The *Athenian* Fleet sailed along not far from *Sestos*, while the *Peloponnesians* came down the *Hellespont*, on the other side, near *Abydus*, and when they were opposite to each other, they drew up in a Line of Battel, the *Lacedæmonians* stretching along the *Asiatick* Shore from *Abydus* to *Dardanus*, and the *Athenians* along the *European* from *Didacus* to *Arrhiana*. In the Right of the *Lacedæmonians* were the *Syracusans*, and their Left was commanded by *Mindarus*. *Thrasylus* had the Left Wing, and *Thrasybulus* the Right of the *Athenians*, which latter, in the beginning of the Fight, was worsted by the *Peloponnesians*, and almost forced ashore near *Cynos-sema*. *Thrasylus*, in the Left Wing, not only defeated the *Syracusans* which were opposed to him, but also the *Lacedæmonians*, whom he drove into the Mouth of the *Pydius*, and some under the Protection of *Abydus*, taking two and twenty Ships, but with the Loss of fifteen of the *Athenians*; and this Victory over the *Lacedæmonians* was of very great Importance, for that it raised the dejected Spirits of the People, and put new Life into their Affairs. *wherein the Athenians have the Advantage.*

Not long after another Engagement happened near *Abydus*, which had lasted from Morning till Night, and was still dubious, when *Alcibiades* arriving with eighteen Sail, soon put the Enemy to flight, although *Pharnabazus*, the *Persian* Governour of *Hellespontus*, came down to their Assistance by Land, and did what he could to cover the Ships as they lay under the Shore. The *Athenians* not only recovered their own Gallies they had lost in the last Fight, but took thirty of the Enemy's, and erected a Trophy; and *Alcibiades*, after this Victory, went to visit *Tissaphernes*, who now, to recover the good Opinion of the *Peloponnesians*, whose Cause he had seemed for some time to abandon, seized on his Person, and confined him, but he luckily escaping in few Days, got again on board the *Athenian* Fleet, with which he went in Quest of the Enemy, then riding in the Port of *Cyzicus*. With twenty of his best Ships he broke through the *Peloponnesian* Fleet, pursued those who abandoned their Ships and fled to Land, and made a great Slaughter of them, among whom fell *Mindarus* himself; and the taking of all the Enemy's Gallies, together with the Surrender of *Cyzicus*, which had receiv'd a *Peloponnesian* Garrison, was the Reward of the Victory. *Alcibiades*, after this, ravaged the Coasts of the *Lesser Asia* with his Fleet, won several Battels, and being every where a Conqueror, reduced those Cities which had revolted, took others, and united them to the *Athenian* Government. Thus, having vindicated the ancient Glory of his Countrymen by Sea, and crowned the same with several Victories by Land, he returned to *Athens*, where he was impatiently expected by the whole City. In these Engagements he had taken two hundred Ships, and a very great Booty from the Enemy. *Alcibiades routs the Peloponnesian Fleet.* *Alcibiades goes to Tissaphernes.* *The Peloponnesians beaten at Cyzicus, and that Place taken,* *and Alcibiades being flushed with other Successes, he returns to Athens.*

nemy, and People of all Ages and Conditions went out to meet this triumphant Army, admiring the Gallantry of all the Soldiers in general, but especially of *Alcibiades*, a Person who was of himself so considerable a Weight in the Balance, that he subverted a most flourishing Government, and again restored it by his own Power, Victory still attending him, whatsoever side he espoused, and Fortune seeming not so much his Mistress as his Slave. Him they therefore received not only with human, but divine Honours; so that 'tis difficult to say whether they more contumeliously expelled, or more honourably recalled him: And those very Gods they brought to congratulate his Return, to whose Execrations they had before devoted him. Such was the Reception of *Alcibiades*, who never knew a Medium either in the Displeasure or Affections of the *Athenians*.

The Lacedæmonians make Lysander their General.
While this happened at *Athens*, the *Lacedæmonians* made *Lysander* their General both by Sea and Land, and *Darius*, the second King of *Persia* of that Name, constituted his Son *Cyrus* Governor of *Ionia* and *Lydia*, who assisted the *Lacedæmonians* with Men and Money, and put them in hopes of retrieving their Affairs. *Lysander* entered upon his Office with great Pleasure on this account, and receiving from *Cyrus* a Month's Pay for the Troops and Seamen, repaired on board the Fleet, consisting of eighty Sail, then lying at *Ephesus*.

Alcibiades offers Lysander Battel off of Ephesus.
Alcibiades was near that Place with the *Athenian* Fleet, with which he offered the Enemy Battel, but they declining it, and his Presence being at that time necessary at *Clazomenæ*, to fix that City in his Country's Interest, which was then in disorder, and wavering in its Fidelity, he left the Command of the Fleet to *Antiochus*, with positive Orders not to come to an Engagement with the Enemy on any account whatsoever. But so far was he from complying, that with two Gallies he stood in for *Ephesus*, and at the very Mouth of the Harbour used the highest Provocations possible to draw out the Enemy. *Lysander* at first sent out a few Ships to give him Chace, but the whole *Athenian* Fleet then advancing to the Relief of the two Gallies, he also drew up his in good order, and gained an entire Victory, fifteen *Athenian* Gallies being taken, and such great Numbers slain, (among whom was *Antiochus* himself) that the *Athenians* received a greater Blow by this single Defeat, than they gave the Enemy in all the former Engagements.

The Athenians routed at Sea in the Absence of Alcibiades.
This threw the whole City into such a Despair, that they immediately created *Conon* their General in the room of *Alcibiades*; for they concluded that they owed this Defeat not so much to the Fortune of War, as to the Treachery of their Commander, whom they supposed to resent his former ill Usage more nearly, than he did the late Honours they had loaded him with: That the reason why he was so successful in the last Campaign, was only to let the Enemy see what a General they had despised, as also to sell his Victory so much the dearer to his Countrymen: And indeed his intriguing busy Genius, joined to his irregular way of living, made every thing which was said of him be believed. Thus, fearing

CHAP. VIII. *Dissolution of the* Rom. *Empire.* 89

fearing to be insulted by the People, he voluntarily retired a second time into Banishment. *Alcibiades retires into Banishment.*

Conon, considering with himself what an extraordinary Person he succeeded, equipped the Fleet with all imaginable Application, but wanted Seamen, for the strongest and ablest of them were killed in the last Expedition. To supply their room, Boys and old Men were obliged to go into the Service, and thus they made up the Complement of Men, but still their Naval Force was deficient. Such feeble Adversaries gave the Enemy no great Trouble, for in an Engagement or two which happen'd soon after, they cut off, or took Prisoners, such great Numbers, and gave them so entire an Overthrow, that, in respect of the Slain and the Captives, not only the *Athenian* Government, but their very Name seemed to be extinguished. For *Callicratidas*, being appointed to succeed *Lysander* in the Command of the *Peloponnesian* Fleet, he not only totally routed *Conon* at Sea, and forced him to retire to *Mitylene*, but again engaging, defeated him a second time in the Harbour of that Place, obliged him to hale ashore his Gallies under the Protection of the Walls, and shut him up in the Town; and falling in with *Diomedon*, who was coming with twelve Sail to his Relief, he took ten, the other two narrowly escaping. *Conon the Athenian Admiral twice beaten by Callicratidas.*

In this terrible Exigence of the *Athenian* Affairs, for want of Men, they were obliged to give the Freedom of their City to Foreigners, Liberty to their Slaves, and Impunity to condemned Criminals. Thus were the late Lords of *Greece* forced to fill up their Army, and endeavour to defend their Liberty. However, they were once more resolved to try their Fortune by Sea; and so great was their Courage, that they who, a little before, had despaired of their Lives, now entertained certain Hopes of Victory. Their Fleet made sail for the Islands *Arginusæ*, lying off Cape *Malea*, between *Lesbos* and the Main, to which Place *Callicratidas* was come with the best part of the *Peloponnesian* Force, consisting of a hundred and twenty Sail, having left *Eteonicus* to carry on the Siege of *Mitylene*. *Callicratidas* was frequently advised not to hazard a Battel with the *Athenians*, who had with them two hundred and fifty Gallies, but constantly answered that he was resolved either to conquer or die. He took upon himself the Command of the Right Wing, and placed *Thrason* of *Thebes* with the *Bœotians* in the Left. To him, in the Right of the *Athenians*, was opposed *Protomachus*, having in his Rear *Thrasylus*, *Lysias*, and *Aristogenes*. *Aristocrates* was in the Left, supported by *Diomedon*, *Pericles* (the Son of the great *Pericles*) and *Erasinides*, in like manner. As soon as the Signal was displayed for engaging, *Callicratidas* firmly believing, as the Oracle had declared, that he should not survive the Fight, he with the first Shock of his Gally sunk that of *Naucias*, and having done great Execution among the Sails, Yards, and Rigging of others, and swept off the Oars of several, at length attacked that of *Pericles*, who fastening her close with grappling Irons, there ensued a bloody and obstinate Dispute between the Companies of each Gally, wherein *Callicratidas*, after having received *Callicratidas again engaging the Athenian Fleet, is slain,*

N ceived

ceived many Wounds, and revenged them by the Slaughter of Numbers of the Enemy, fell over board, and was lost. The *Peloponnesians* being now without their Admiral, soon began to give way, and at length fled before the Enemy to *Chios* and *Phocæa*, leaving seventy Sail in Possession of the *Athenians*; and *Eteonicus*, who lay before *Mitylene*, having Advice of this Misfortune, raised the Siege, set fire to his Camp, and marched over-land to *Methymne*. *Conon*, thus freed from the Enemy, drew down his Gallies, and went out to meet his Countrymen, who, after mutual Congratulations, repaired to *Samos*, there to lay up the Ships, and take their Winter-Quarters: And thus ended the twenty fifth Year of the War.

and the Peloponnesian Fleet routed at Arginusæ.

In this Fight at *Arginusæ* the *Athenians* having had five and twenty Ships destroyed, and lost great Numbers of Men, and the Admirals having, as it was alledged, neglected the Care of the Wrecks, and the taking up the dead Bodies for Interment, *Thrasylus*, *Calliades*, *Lysias*, *Aristocrates* and *Pericles* were condemned to Death, who suffered accordingly, *Protomachus* being slain in Fight, and *Aristogenes* went into voluntary Banishment.

The Athenian Admirals sentenced to Death, and executed.

Early the next Spring, at the Request of *Cyrus*, and the other Allies of the *Lacedæmonians*, *Lysander* was appointed to succeed *Callicratidas* in the Command of the Fleet, who repairing first to *Rhodes*, and thence to the *Hellespont*, laid siege to *Lampsacus*, and took it in a short time. On the News of the Loss of this Place, the *Athenians* repaired with a Fleet of a hundred and eighty Sail to *Sestos*, and there taking in Provisions for a few Days, went to the *Ægos*, a small River of the *Thracian Chersonesus* which falls into the *Hellespont*, over against *Lampsacus*, where then lay the Enemy's Fleet. The *Athenian* Admirals were, besides others, *Conon* and *Philocles*, which latter was he who advised, in an Assembly of the People, that the Prisoners which should be taken in this War might have the Thumbs of their Right Hands cut off, to prevent their carrying a Spear, or handling an Oar again, as had been formerly done to the *Æginetans*. When the Fleets came opposite to each other, there was not the first Day any Offer of Battel on either side, but the second both Parties were in full Expectation of coming to an Engagement: When *Lysander* observing the Enemy's Fleet to lie on an open and harbourless Coast, and understood from Deserters that by Night they kept neither Watch nor Ward, he resolved on some more than ordinary Enterprize.

Lysander made Admiral of the Peloponnesians, who takes Lampsacus.

Alcibiades, who had made choice of this Country to spend the time of his Banishment in, hearing the *Athenian* Fleet was at *Ægospotamos*, went down to the Sea-Coast to pay a Visit to the Admirals, where observing the Insecurity of the Place, which had no Works to defend it, and that they did not appoint Guard-ships, nor keep due Watch, according to the Rules of War, and that *Lysander*, a wise and vigilant Enemy, was so near them on the other side, frequently admonished them, both in publick and private, of the Danger they were in, but meeting with nothing else than Reproaches, and being told that no heed ought to be given to the Advice of an Exile, he with Grief took his leave of them, only saying,

The Athenian Gallies come to Ægospotamos.

that

that he was either entirely unacquainted with the Art of War, the Enemy they had to deal with, and the General who commanded them, or the River *Ægos* would soon be more remarkable for the Destruction of the *Athenians*, than ever *Syracuse* had yet been.

Lysander, pursuant to the Resolutions he had taken, gave out Orders as if he would engage the Enemy early the next Morning, and directed the Men should take their Repast by break of Day, repair all on board, and there keeping strict Order and Silence, hold themselves in Readiness for Action at a Moment's Warning. Next Day the *Athenians* advanced, according to Custom, and used all possible Provocations to bring *Lysander* to an Engagement, who sent out several Boats to hover at a Distance from the Enemy, with Orders not to go too near, nor by any means be provoked to engage. When Evening came on, the *Athenians*, weary of continuing in that Posture, retired again, and disembarked their People, but *Lysander* would not let a Man leave his Ships till the Boats he sent out returned with Advice of the Enemy's Landing. This he continued to do for four Days successively, omitting nothing which could confirm the Enemy in an Opinion of his Fear, and Inability to cope with them. The *Athenians* having spent the fifth Day in provoking the *Peloponnesians* to fight, and retiring again towards Evening, *Lysander* sent out his Boats, as usual, with orders to see the Enemy landed, and then with all Expedition to return, and as soon as they were in sight, make a Signal. In the mean time he went about to all the Ships of the Fleet, exhorting the Commanders to keep a good look-out for the Signal, and as soon as it was discovered, to make the best of their way toward the Enemy, telling them, that now was the time to revenge the Cause of their Country on the *Athenians*, and put a final Period to this seven and twenty Years War. This he had no sooner done, than the Boats appeared in sight, making the appointed Sign of the Enemy's Landing, and immediately the Fleet bore down with all the Expedition Sails and Oars could make, and having soon crossed the Streight, came suddenly upon them, where they found some of the Gallies haled ashore, and others yet remaining in the Water, but in both Places without Defence, or Security. *Conon* being the first of the *Athenians* who descryed the Enemy, made what haste he could to get his Men aboard; but they were so dispersed, that he was forced to make off with eight Ships, with which he escaped to *Evagoras*, King of *Cyprus*, and reserved himself for his Country, in Expectation of better Times. The rest of the Fleet *Lysander* took, with most of the Men, part of whom he killed on the spot, and the remainder the next Day; among which Number was *Philocles*, who being asked by *Lysander* what Punishment he thought he deserved for being the Author of so barbarous a Counsel as that abovementioned, replied, *I submit to you*, Lysander, *as a Conqueror, but know no reason I have to acknowledge you as a Judge*, and immediately offered his Neck to the Stroke of the Sword, so that *Lysander* having put to Death with *Philocles* three thousand *Athenians*, and destroyed their Camp, he returned in Triumph to *Lampsacus*

The Fight at Ægospotamos.

The Athenians totally routed by Lysander.

Lysander razes the Walls of Piræus, and takes Athens. *sacus*, from whence he made sail for *Athens*, besieged and took the City, and levelled the Walls of the *Piræus* with the Ground. In a general Assembly of the *Lacedæmonians* and their Confederates, it was warmly debated whether the City should not be entirely demolished, many being for extinguishing the very Name of the *Athenians*, and destroying the Town by Fire: But the *Spartans* opposed this Motion, saying, that they would by no means be guilty of putting out one of the Eyes of *Greece*. This Fight at *Ægospotamos*, and the taking of *Athens*, in Consequence of it, happened, according to *Polybius*, nineteen Years before the sacking of *Rome* by the *Gauls*, which was in the last Year of the Reign of *Darius Nothus*, King of *Persia*, seven hundred and seventy eight Years after the Destruction of *Troy*, and in the Year of the *World* 3545.

A. M. 3545.

Chap. IX

Of the Naval Wars of the Grecians, *from the End of the* Peloponnesian *War to the Beginning of the* Macedonian *Greatness under King* Philip.

The Athenians obliged to deliver up their Ships.

THE *Athenians*, besides the Demolition of the Walls of the *Piræus*, were obliged to deliver up all their Ships, and to receive thirty of their own Citizens to manage the Affairs of their Republick, which Governours were no sooner elected, than they shewed themselves true Tyrants, destroying the wretched Remainders of the City with Sword and Rapine, insomuch that because *Theramenes*, one of their own Number, expressed some Dislike to these their Proceedings, they sacrificed him to their Revenge. Upon this the Inhabitants daily fled out of the City, so that all *Greece* was filled with *Athenian* Exiles; and at length even this very Relief was denied to those miserable Wretches; for the *Lacedæmonians* published an Edict, by which they prohibited any of their Cities to receive them, insomuch that they were forced to betake themselves to *Thebes* and *Argos*, where they not only lived in Safety, but entertained some hopes of freeing their Country.

A very severe Decree against the Athenian Exiles.

Thrasybulus, a Person distinguished by his Valour, as well as noble Extraction, was one of this Number, who considering that some vigorous Effort ought to be made for the Recovery of the publick Liberty, though it carried never so much Danger with it, and having gathered these Exiles into a Body, seized upon *Phyle*, a Castle on the Frontiers of *Attica*: And some Cities commiserating the Condition of these Fugitives, favoured the Undertaking. *Ismenias*, the chief Magistrate of *Thebes*, tho' he durst not publickly support them with his Arms, yet he privately supplied them with Money; and *Lysias*, the *Syracusan* Orator, but then in Banishment, sent five hundred

The Exiles seize upon Phile, and are assisted by others.

hundred Men, whom he maintained at his own Expence, to assist towards the retrieving that Country, which had been the common Parent of Eloquence and Learning. The Tyrants were worsted in a Battel, when suspecting the Treachery of the Inhabitants yet remaining in the City, they forced them to quit it, and sent for Soldiers to *Lacedæmon*, to defend them; Who arriving, they took the Field again, and came to another Battel with *Thrasybulus*, wherein *Critias* and *Hippolochus*, two of the fiercest Tyrants, lost their Lives, the rest being oblig'd to retire to *Eleusis*, and ten Men were appointed in their room to administer the publick Affairs. *Pausanias* was sent from *Lacedæmon* to put an End to these Disturbances at *Athens*, who taking Compassion on the miserable Refugees, restored them to their native Country, and obliged the ten Tyrants, who had in all Respects imitated their Predecessors, to leave the Town, and herd with their Brethren at *Eleusis*. By this means the City in little time began to recover Breath, when the Tyrants, who were no less enraged at the Restoration of these Exiles than their own Banishment, got together another Army against them, but being invited to a Treaty, under Pretence that the Government was to be restored to them, they were all put to death. Thus the *Athenians*, who, in these publick Convulsions, had been dispersed all over *Greece*, were at last united again into one Body, and least the Remembrance of former Transactions should disturb the publick Tranquillity, every Man obliged himself by Oath to bury what was past in Oblivion. In the mean time the People of *Thebes* and *Corinth* sent their Ambassadors to *Lacedæmon*, to demand their Share of the Spoils and Booty taken in the late War, since they had equally run all the Risques of it; but being rejected, although they did not indeed declare open War against the *Lacedæmonians*, yet seemed they so much to resent this Indignity, that it might be easily judged what they intended.

The Tyrants of Athens beaten.

The Athenian Exiles restored to their native Country.

The Tyrants put to Death, and Athens begins again to flourish.

The *Lacedæmonians*, like the rest of Mankind, who the more they possess still covet the more, not content that their Forces were doubled by the Accession of *Athens*, began to affect the Dominion of all *Asia*. They had already supplied *Cyrus* with Aid against his Brother *Artaxerxes*, *Darius*'s Successor in the Throne of *Persia*, chosen *Dercyllidas* General for this Expedition, and corrupted *Tissaphernes* to embrace their Interest, when *Conon*, then living in Exile in *Cyprus*, was appointed by *Artaxerxes* to succeed *Tissaphernes* in the Command of the *Persian* Fleet. The *Lacedæmonians* understanding this, dispatched Ambassadours to *Hercynion* King of *Ægypt*, to assist them with some Ships, and obtained of him a hundred Gallies, and six hundred thousand Bushels of Corn. Great numbers of Recruits were also sent them by their other Allies, but still they wanted an able General to head these Forces, and oppose to so experienced a Commander as *Conon*; to fill which Posts the Confederates unanimously pitched upon *Agesilaus*, at that time King of *Lacedæmon*; but the *Lacedæmonians* had a long Debate whether they should entrust him with it, by Reason of an Answer they had received from the Oracle at *Delphos*, which forewarned them that

The Lacedæmonians affect the Dominion of Asia.

Conon commands the Persian Fleet.

Agesilaus appointed General for the Lacedæmonians.

their

their Republick would go near to be destroyed when the Kingly Government halted, for *Agesilaus* was lame of one Leg: But at last they came to this Resolution, that it was better for the King than the Kingdom to halt. Thus *Agesilaus* was sent with a formidable Army into *Asia*, where he performed many signal Exploits, and like a Tempest, carried all before him, as *Conon*, at the Head of the *Persian* and *Athenian* Fleet, did, at the same time, on the Coasts of *Laconia*, and the Parts adjacent. *Agesilaus* before his Departure substituted *Pisander* to command at Home, who got together a great Fleet, and resolved to hazard the Fortune of War; while on the other Hand *Conon* used no less Care to order every thing for the best Advantage against the first Opportunity that should offer for a Battel; and indeed both the Commanders shewed a mutual Emulation upon this Occasion. As for *Conon*, he did not so much regard the Interest of the *Persians* as that of his own Country; and as he had unluckily proved the Author of the *Athenians* Ruin when their Affairs were declining, so was he ambitious to be their Restorer, and to retrieve his native Country by one single Victory, which by the fatal Casualties of War he had undone. As for *Pisander*, besides the Relation he bore to *Agesilaus*, he was a generous Emulator of his excellent Qualities, and took all imaginable Care that he might not fall short of his great Performances, or, by an Oversight committed in one fatal Moment, destroy a State that had acquired its present Splendour with the Expence of so much Blood and Time. Off of *Cnidus* the two Fleets came to an Engagement, which held for some time with great Obstinacy, till at length *Pisander* lost his Life, bravely fighting in the midst of his Enemies, when the *Lacedæmonians* fled, leaving fifty Ships in Possession of the *Athenians*. *Conon* passed over to *Laconia*, where having ravaged the Coasts, and laid the Country in Ashes, he repaired to *Athens*, and was received with all possible Demonstrations of Joy, but he grieved more to see the City so burnt and demolished by the *Lacedæmonians*, than he rejoyced at its Restauration, after it had suffered so long by the Enemy: However, partly with the Booty he had gotten, and partly with the Help of the *Persian* Army, he repaired all that the Fire had destroyed. Thus, by a Fatality peculiar to this City, *Athens* as it had been before burnt by the *Persians*, so now it was rebuilt by their Hands; and as it suffered the same hard Treatment from the *Lacedæmonians*, so it was repaired out of their Spoils.

A Character of Conon

and Pisander.

The Persian *and the* Athenian *Fleets beat that of* Lacedæmon *at* Cnidus, *and* Conon *ravages* Laconia, *and repairs to* Athens.

Athens *once more gets the Dominion of the Sea.* Thebes, Corinth, &c. *declare against the* Lacedæmonians.

This Victory at *Cnidus* was so compleat that it again restored to the *Athenians* the Dominion of the Sea; and it was followed by the coming over to them of the *Ionians*, with the People of *Hellespontus*. At the same time the *Thebans*, *Corinthians* and *Argives* openly declared against the *Lacedæmonians*, and the People of *Rhodes* having forced a Squadron of *Peloponnesian* Ships from thence, revolted to the *Athenians*, receiving *Conon* with his Ships into their Port, during whose Continuance at that Island, a Squadron of *Lacedæmonian* Ships, loaden with Corn from *Ægypt*, supposing it to be still in their Interest, entered the Port, and fell into his Hands. The Revolt of *Rhodes* was soon after followed by that of *Chios*, *Teos*,

CHAP. IX. *Dissolution of the* Rom. *Empire.* 95

Teos, Mitylene, Ephesus and *Erethræ*, whence sprung up several other Wars, the *Lacedæmonians* yet bearing up against their Enemies, as the *Arcadian, Bœotian, Theban*, first and second *Lacedæmonian*, and *Tegeatic* Wars, which were the Names imposed on them either by the *Lacedæmonians* themselves, or the People who were engaged against them.

In Aid of the *Thebans* the *Athenians* fitted out a Fleet of sixty Sail, under the Command of *Timotheus*, with Orders to cruise about, and infest the Coasts of *Peloponnesus*, who off *Corcyra* fell in with the like Number of the Enemy's Ships commanded by *Nicolochus*, and totally routed them. To wipe off this Disgrace *Mnasippus* was sent out at the Head of another Fleet, but increased it with his own Destruction, for he received a signal Overthrow from the *Athenians* under the Command of *Stesicleus*, and was himself slain. Some time after this *Spodriades* having, at the Instigation of *Cleombrotus*, King of *Lacedæmon*, made an Attempt to seize on the the *Piræus*, the *Athenians* highly exasperated at such a Proceeding during a Cessation of Arms, attacked the *Lacedæmonian* Fleet, under the Command of *Pollis*, between *Naxos* and *Paros*. In this Engagement *Pollis* made great Havock in the Left Wing of the Enemy led by *Cedon*, whom he slew with his own Hand; but *Chabrias*, who commanded in the Right of the *Athenians*, advancing seasonably to their Relief, charged the *Lacedæmonians* with great Fury, and having made a terrible Slaughter, put them to Flight, not but that considerable Numbers were killed of his own Side, whose dead Bodies he caused to be carefully taken up and interred, well remembring the Fate of some of the preceding Admirals for Neglect charged on them in that particular.

The Athenians aid the Thebans by Sea.

The Lacedæmonians beaten at Sea.

They are beaten a second time, when they attempted Piræus.

Not long after the *Athenians*, under the Conduct of *Timotheus*, the Son of *Conon*, obtained another Victory over the *Lacedæmonians* near *Leucas*; and, off *Corcyra*, falling in with a Fleet of Ships, which *Dionysius*, the Tyrant of *Sicily*, had sent to their Aid, he took nine of them with great Numbers of Slaves, by the Sale whereof they got sixty Talents, and on the other Side of *Greece* they also invested *Torone* and *Potidæa*, both by Sea and Land, which they took after a short Siege. When the *Greeks* had waged Civil Wars amongst themselves for a considerable time, with various Success, they came all to a general Peace, except the *Lacedæmonians*, who being utter Enemies to the *Messenians*, could by no means be reconciled. At this time *Tachus*, King of Ægypt, maintaining a War against *Artaxerxes*, committed the Care of his Land Army to *Agesilaus* the *Lacedæmonian* beforementioned, and of his Fleet to *Chabrias* the *Athenian*; but in the midst of these Preparations *Agesilaus* died, as did also *Artaxerxes* himself, who was succeeded in the *Persian* Throne by *Ochus*.

The Athenians beat the Lacedæmonians, and the Fleet of Sicily.

Torone and Potidæa taken.

Peace among the Greeks, except the Lacedæmonians. A.M. 3586.

Ochus succeeds Artaxerxes.

CHAP.

Chap. X.

Of the Naval Wars of the Grecians, *from the Beginning of the* Macedonian *Greatness under King* Philip, *to the Death of* Alexander *the Great.*

The growing Greatness of Macedon.

FROM these intestine Feuds and Divisions, with which the *Grecians* (those properly so called) mutually harassed and weakened each other, began now to creep up in the World the before contemptible and obscure Name of the *Macedonians*, whose Country, more anciently called *Æmonia* and *Emathia*, was bounded on the North with *Thrace* and *Illyricum*, on the West with the *Adriatick* and *Ionian* Seas, on the East with the *Ægean*, and on the South by *Epirus* and *Græcia propria*. These People, in process of time, what by the Valour of their Kings, and their own Industry, having conquered their Neighbours first, and then whole Nations and Countries, extended their Empire to the remotest Parts of the East. After a Succession of several Kings, the Crown of *Macedonia* at length devolved on *Philip*, the Father of *Alexander* the Great, who while he was yet very young, and his Brother sate on the Throne, was sent to *Thebes* as an Hostage, in which City, famous for the Severity of its Discipline, and in the House of *Epaminondas*, that most excellent Philosopher and General, he received his first Education.

Philip of Macedon beats the Thessalians, &c.

Upon his Accession to the Crown he lay under no small Difficulties, for several Nations declared War against him; But he managed his Affairs with great Dexterity, and being not long satisfied with acting on the Defensive, attacked even his Neighbours who had not given him any Provocation. He fell unexpectedly upon the *Thessalians*, and defeated them, by whom, nevertheless, and the *Thebans*, he was constituted *Generalissimo* in the sacred War against the *Phocenses*, who had seized and plundered the Temple of *Apollo* at *Delphos*.

A. M. 3593.

These he totally routed in a Battel by Land, and by that Action acquired a very great Reputation among all People, who extolled him as the Revenger of Sacrilege, the Asserter of sacred things, and the only Person that had demanded a just Reparation for that Offence which ought to have been punished by the united Forces of all Mankind. But presently after, as if he had resolved not to be outdone in Sacrilege, he plundered and seized those very Cities that had chosen him for their General, that had fought under his Command, and now came to congratulate him upon the Success of his Arms. He sold the Wives and Children of all without Distinction, nor spared he so much as the Temples, or the very Images of the Gods, publick or private. From hence, as if he had performed some honourable Exploit, he marched into *Chalcidica*, where having managed the War with the same perfidious Methods, and killed or taken the principal Persons by Treachery, he added that whole Province to his Kingdom; After which he seized upon the Gold Mines in

adds Chalcidica to his Kingdom, and is guilty of great Rapine.

Thessaly,

Thessaly, and those of Silver in *Thrace*; and that he might leave no manner of Violence or Rapine unpractised, he began to set up the Trade of Piracy. Then, under Pretence of arbitrating their Differences, having killed two *Thracian* Princes, and plundered their Country, he returning toward *Greece*, seized the Pass of *Thermopylæ*; and, contrary to the most solemn Engagements given to the *Phocenses*, laid waste their Country with Fire and Sword.

After this he reduced the *Dardanians*, and besieging *Byzantium* by Sea and Land. Having exhausted great Part of his Treasure, he had recourse again to Piratical Depredations on the Sea, and seizing upon, and rifling a hundred and seventy Merchant Ships, he made a shift to relieve his pressing Necessities, and then turned his Arms against the *Scythians*, whom he overcame by Stratagem; which done, he returned, and opened the War he had so long dissembled against the *Athenians*, with whom at last he came to the Decision of a Battel; and tho' the *Athenians* were much superior to the *Macedonians* in Number, yet were they forced to submit to their Valour, which had been hardened and confirmed by so long a Series of Wars: And that Day put a final Period to the Liberties of *Greece*. *commits Piracies, and conquers the Scythians.*

overcomes the Athenians, and is made Generalissimo of Greece.

Philip artfully concealed his Joy for this important Victory, and would not suffer himself to be called the King, but the Generalissimo of *Greece*. This Title he had confirmed to him by the Suffrages of all the Cities, represented by their Deputies assembled at *Corinth*; in which Assembly it was resolved, under his Conduct, to enter into a War against *Persia*. Pursuant whereunto, early in the Spring, he sent over into *Asia* three of his chief Commanders, *Parmenio*, *Amyntas*, and *Attalus*, intending soon after to follow in Person; but in the midst of his Preparations he was assassinated by *Pausanias*, an abused noble *Macedonian*, as he was celebrating the Nuptials of his Daughter. *A. M. 3612.*

Wars designed against Persia.

He was succeeded by his Son *Alexander*, a Prince the very reverse of his Father; for he carried on his Wars not by Artifice and Stratagem, but by open Force; was kind and beneficent to his Friends, merciful and generous to his Enemies, free and open in all his Actions, and unknowing how to dissemble. With a Character contrary to this *Philip* laid the Foundation for the Conquest of the World, which *Alexander*, with these Qualifications, most gloriously accomplished, who being, by the States of *Greece* then assembled, constituted Generalissimo against the *Persians*, crossed the *Hellespont* with his Fleet, obtained a Victory at the River *Granicus*, and thence marching on towards *Miletus*, took in most of the Towns in his Way; and having also reduced that Place to his Obedience, thought fit to send back the Fleet, which met him there, to *Greece*; and thence proceeding into *Syria*, he sate down before the City of *Tyre*. But before we come to the Siege of that Place, we must not omit observing that *Alexander*, as soon as his Troops were embarked, was at the very Sight of *Asia* inflamed with incredible Ardour, insomuch that he erected on board the Fleet twelve Altars to the twelve Gods, whereon offering Sacrifice, he implored their Assistance in this his Undertaking; and when they drew near to the Continent, he first hurled a Dart *Alexander succeeds his Father Philip.*

His Successes.

Invades Asia.

Dart at the Shore, signifying thereby it was an Enemy's Country, and, in a dancing Posture, leap'd from the Ship in his Armour, when sacrificing again, he prayed that those Countries might freely receive him for their King. Which Custom of sacrificing on these Occasions, and denouncing War by the throwing of a Dart, we find also in Use among the *Romans*.

After *Alexander* had obtained the great Victory over *Darius* at *Issus*, *Amyntas* a noble *Macedonian*, who had before revolted to the *Persians*, thought fit also to desert them, and with four thousand *Grecians* under his Command, who had escaped thence, came to *Tripolis*[a], and thence passed over into *Cyprus*, there to wait a proper Opportunity to proceed to *Ægypt*, a Country equally in Enmity with *Darius* and *Alexander*, and there to set up for himself. On his landing in *Ægypt* the Natives joined his Forces, and drove the *Persian* Garrisons out of all the Cities, except *Memphis*, which the *Persians* having valiantly defended for a considerable time, they at length sallied out with their whole Force on the Besiegers, whom they entirely defeated, killing great Numbers, and amongst them *Amyntas* himself.

[a] *Tripoli in Syria, and Ægypt.*

In the mean while *Aristo*, the *Macedonian* Admiral, came to an Engagement with the *Persian* Fleet in the *Hellespont*, and obtained a signal Victory, so that now all the lesser *Asia*, together with *Syria* and *Phœnicia*, except *Tyre*, was subdued to the Obedience of *Alexander*; the Inhabitants of which City sent him, by their Ambassadors, a golden Crown of a considerable Weight, under Pretence of congratulating his great Victories: which he very kindly received, and told them that he designed to make them a Visit, in order to perform his Vows to *Hercules*. But the Ambassadors insinuating that he might do it much better in the old Town, where the more ancient Temple stood, and withal desiring him not to come within their new City, he was so highly incensed thereat, that he threaten'd to level their Town with the Ground, and to that Purpose immediately drew down his Army to the Sea Coast. The City of *Tyre* was built in an Island about four Furlongs distant from the Continent, the Space between which and the Town lay open to the South West Winds, which used to drive in a great Sea thither, and so rendered *Alexander*'s Design of joining it to the Land a Work of extreme Difficulty. There was also another Obstacle to the Siege, no less than this, to wit, that the City taking up the whole Space of the Island whereon it stood, its Walls were washed on every Side by the Sea, which was also very deep there, so that there was no fixing of Ladders, or raising of Batteries but on board Ship; Besides *Alexander* had not at this time any Ships there; or if he had, upon their approaching the Walls they might have been easily forced back with missive Weapons. Nor could the Machines that might have been raised on Board them do much Execution, by reason of the Agitation of the Waves. The *Tyrians* having resolved to abide the Extremities of a Siege, placed their Engines upon the Ramparts and Towers, deliver'd out Arms to their Youth, and set their Artificers at Work in making all Instruments of War necessary for their Defence.

The Macedonian Fleet beats that of Persia.

Alexander affronted by the Tyrians, brings his Army against it.

The Situation of Tyre.

CHAP. X. *Dissolution of the* Rom. *Empire.* 99

Alexander gave Orders for the Men to begin to work on the intend- *He begins to join the Island to the Continent.* ed Causeway, for which they were in no want of Materials, having Stone in Abundance from the Ruins of old *Tyre*, and Mount *Libanus* supplying them with Timber for it, as also for Boats and Towers. The Work was advanced to a stupendous Height under Water before it reached the Surface of it, for the further they went the deeper was the Sea, and swallowed the greater Quantity of Materials; but the *Tyrians* at length perceiving how far it was carried on, came out *The Tyrians interrupt his Works, and kill many of his Men.* in Boats to view it, and did great Execution among the Workmen with their Darts and Arrows. They also landed some Troops at a little Distance from the Camp, where they cut to pieces most of those who were employed in carrying the Stone; and *Alexander* thinking it a Diminution of his Glory to lye so long before a Town, committed the Care of the Siege to *Perdiccas* and *Craterus*, advancing himself with a flying Camp toward *Arabia*.

In his Absence the *Tyrians* bethought themselves of this Stratagem: *The Tyrians Stratagem.* They took the largest Ship they had, loaded her all abaft with Stones and Ballast, that so her Head might be raised the higher; and besmearing her with Brimstone and Sulphur, sailed her, with a brisk Gale of Wind, close up to the Causeway, when throwing themselves into their Boats they set fire to her, and before any Help could arrive, the Towers, and other Works that *Alexander* had caused to be made on the Causeway, for Defence of the Workmen, were all in Flames. The *Tyrians*, at the same time, threw from their Boats flaming Torches, Firebrands, and other combustible matter, into the upper Stages of the Towers, insomuch that many People were miserably burnt to Death, and the rest throwing down their Arms leap'd into the Sea, whom the *Tyrians*, being more desirous to preserve alive than to kill, took up, having first disabled them with Blows while in the Water. Nor was the Fire their only Enemy, for the same Day a violent Storm of Wind drove in the Sea with such Fury as loosened the Cement of the Materials, which being washed away, the Stones were soon forced asunder by the Weight of the Waves, and on their giving Way, down came all the Superstructure, so that by the time *Alexander* returned from *Arabia*, there were scarce any Traces left of so stupendous a Work.

He immediately set about erecting a new Causeway, which was *Alexander's Works destroyed by Fire and Tempest.* carried on with its Head toward the South West, to break the Sea that tumbled in from thence, the former having lain sideways toward that Quarter, and was consequently more exposed to the Force of the Waves. He also allowed it a much greater Breadth, that so the Towers, which were erected in the middle, might be out of the Reach of the Enemy's Darts and Arrows: And the better to effect this Work, they threw into the Sea a great Number of tall Trees with all their Branches on; Upon these they laid Stones, and upon them Trees again, which they covered with Earth to bind them together: Over this they laid another Pile of Stones and Trees, and covered the whole again with Earth. While this was doing the besieged were equally vigilant for their Defence, and left not any thing unpractised that might hinder the carrying on of the Works, wherein

O 2   their

their Divers were of singular Use to them, for plunging under Water, with grappling Irons, Hooks, and other proper Instruments, they laid hold of the Branches of Trees which stuck out from the rest of the Materials, and by main Force drew with them the Trees themselves, insomuch that the Foundation failing, the Stones and other Materials fell in, and by this means they destroyed all that part of the Causway which was furthest advanced.

Again destroyed by the Tyrians.

As *Alexander* was full of Perplexity at the slow Progress made in this Work, and undetermined whether he should continue or raise the Siege, the Kings of *Aradus* and *Byblus*, hearing he had reduced their Cities to his Obedience, together with the rest of *Phœnicia*, withdrew themselves from the *Persian* Fleet, and came over to him, bringing with them likewise the *Sidonian* Ships, amounting in all to eighty Sail; and about the same time arrived ten Gallies from *Rhodes*, three from *Soli* and *Mallus*, ten from *Lycia*, with one great Gally from *Macedonia*; and soon after, upon Advice of *Alexander*'s Success, the Kings of *Cyprus* went over to him to *Sidon* with their Fleet, consisting of a hundred and twenty Sail, to all of whom he freely extended his Royal Pardon, since they continued no longer in the *Persian* Interest than till they had an Opportunity to revolt. Having thus gotten together a sufficient Naval Force, he went on board, and took upon himself the Command of the Right Wing, accompanied with the Kings of *Cyprus* and *Phœnicia*, except *Pythagoras*, who was with *Craterus* in the Left. The *Tyrians*, tho' Masters of a potent Fleet, yet durst they not venture the Decision of a Battel, but disposed their Gallies around the City under cover of the Walls; nevertheless *Alexander* attacked some of them, of which he sunk three, and the next Day came to an Anchor very near the Walls, which he battered on all sides with his Machines, especially with the Rams prepared for that purpose. The Besieged used all possible Diligence in repairing the Breaches, and began to raise another Wall within, to which they might retire when the outermost should be beaten down: But now they were hard pressed on all sides, the Causway was advanced within Javelin shot of the Walls, they were close blocked up with the Fleet, and attacked at the same time both by Sea and Land: Besides, *Alexander* caused several Gallies to be laid two and two in such manner as that they were joined together astern, by means of Stages thrown across, whereon were placed great Numbers of chosen Landmen, who were thus rowed toward the Town, being secured from the Enemy on the Walls by the Prows of the Gallies which served them as a Parapet. About Midnight the King caused them to advance in this manner to surround the Walls, and give a general Assault, so that the *Tyrians* began now to be in the utmost Despair, when of a sudden there arose a furious Storm, in which the Gallies fell foul of one another with such Violence as forced their Cables, and tore the Planks asunder on which the Stages were laid, which drew down with them the Stages, Men, and all into the Sea, with a dreadful Noise, for the Tempest was so fierce, that it was impossible to govern the Gallies linked together in that manner; and in this Confusion the Soldiers inter-

The King of Aradus, and others revolt to Alexander.

He again attempts Tyre with a Fleet. His Designs

frustrated by a Storm.

interrupted the Seamen, as they did the Soldiers. However, the obstinate Efforts of the Rowers tore the Gallies, as it were, out of the Jaws of the Sea, and they at length got under the Shore, but for the most part extremely disabled. In the mean while thirty Ambassadors from *Carthage* arrived at *Tyre*, who made frivolous Excuses, instead of promising those great Succours which were expected from thence. The *Tyrians*, though frustrated thus of their greatest Hopes, yet kept they up their Courage, and sent their Wives and Children to *Carthage*, that so they might with more Resolution undergo whatsoever should happen, when they had so secured what was most dear to them. Not any thing was left uncontriv'd or unattempted which could contribute to their Security, and, as Necessity is the Mother of Invention, besides the ordinary Methods, they found out new Arts to defend themselves. To annoy the Ships which approached the Walls, they fixed grappling Irons, Hooks and Scythes to long Beams, then placing their Machines, which were made in the Form of Cross-Bows, they put into them great Beams, as if they had been Arrows, and shot them at the Enemy, so that many were crushed to pieces with their Fall, others miserably mangled by the Hooks and Scythes, and the Gallies themselves received considerable Damage. They had also brazen Targets, which they took red hot from the Fire, and filling them with burning Sand, or boiling Mud, threw them down from the Walls on the Besiegers. The *Macedonians* dreaded nothing so much as this, for if, through any Defect of their Armour, the burning Sand came at the Flesh, it immediately penetrated to the Bone, and stuck so fast as not to be removed; so that the Soldiers throwing down their Arms, and tearing off their Cloaths, remained defenceless and exposed to the Enemy's Shot.

Ambassadors arrive at Tyre from Carthage.

The Tyrians very much annoy Alexander's Men.

This so vigorous a Defence very much discouraged *Alexander*, insomuch that he once again deliberated on raising the Siege, and going on to *Ægypt*: But considering it would be a great Blemish to his Reputation, which had been more serviceable to him than his Arms, to leave *Tyre* behind him, as a Monument that he was to be overcome, he resolved to make the last Effort with his whole Fleet, on board of which he embarked the Flower of all his Troops. The main Body he ordered to lie before the Haven, looking towards *Ægypt*, leaving thirty of the smallest Ships to block up that called the Gate of *Sidon*; two of which latter being taken by the *Tyrians*, it gave such an Alarm to the rest, that *Alexander*, hearing the Outcries of the People, caused the Fleet to advance toward the Place whence the Noise came. The Admiral Gally, with five Tire of Oars, came up first singly, which the *Tyrians* no sooner perceived, than they detached two to attack her. Against one of these she ran with all her Force, and grappled her close, but not till she had first received a rude Shock from her Beak: Mean while, the other *Tyrian* Gally was bearing up against the contrary side of the Admirals, when another of *Macedon* came upon her with such Violence, as tossed her Pilot from the Poop headlong into the Sea. By this time several more of the *Macedonian* Ships arrived at the Place, where

He makes another Effort against Tyre.

where was also the King himself in Person, when at length the *Tyrians*, with very great Difficulty, disengaged their grappled Gally, and retired towards the Town with their whole Fleet, *Alexander* following them close in the Rear; and tho' he was not able to enter the Gate, being repulsed with Showers of Arrows from the Walls, yet he took or sunk most of the Ships.

A general Assault on the City.
After this he gave his Troops two Days rest, and then causing the whole Fleet to advance with all the Machines for a general Assault, he mounted one of the Towers himself, exposing his Person to the utmost Danger, in the most adventrous manner his Courage ever prompted him to; for being presently known by the Richness of his Armour, and other Ensigns of Royalty, he became in a Moment the But of all the Enemy's Shot. There he performed Wonders to be admired of all Mankind, killing first with his Javelins many of those who defended the Walls, and advancing nearer, he tumbled several down into the Town, and many into the Sea, some with his Sword, others with his Target, for the Tower from whence he fought almost touched the Wall. By this time all the principal Defences were beaten down by the battering Rams, the Fleet had forced its way into the Harbour, and several of the *Macedonians* had possessed themselves of the Towers abandoned by the *Tyrians*,

The City taken, and a great Massacre of its Inhabitants.
so that they being hard pressed on all sides, some fled to the Temples to implore the Assistance of the Gods, others shut themselves up in their Houses, and prevented the Fury of the Conqueror by a voluntary Death, while divers sallying out among the thickest of the Enemy, resolved to sell their Lives as dear as they could: But the greatest Number got up to the Roofs of the Houses, and thence threw down Stones on the *Macedonians*, or whatever came next to hand, as they entered the Town. *Alexander* gave Orders that all should be put to the Sword, except such as had taken Sanctuary in the Temples, and that they should fire the Houses: But notwithstanding this Order was published by Sound of Trumpet, there was not a Man among the *Tyrians*, who bore Arms, which would condescend to take Refuge in the Temples, where were found only Women and Children, the Men planting themselves at the Doors of their Houses, in Expectation every Moment of being sacrificed to the Rage of the Soldiers. The *Sidonians* indeed, who attended *Alexander* in this Siege, saved many of them, who entering the Town with the *Macedonians*, and remembering their Affinity to the *Tyrians*, whose City and theirs owed their Origine to the same Founder, they privately conveyed great Numbers of them on board their Ships, and transported them to *Sidon*.

Many Tyrians saved by the Sidonians.
There were no less than fifteen thousand saved by this pious Fraud from the Fury of the Conqueror, by whom what a dreadful Slaughter was committed, may be guessed by the Numbers cut to pieces only on the Ramparts of the Town, which amounted to six thousand. But the King's Anger was not yet pacified, for after the Troops were weary of killing, he caused, in cold Blood, two thousand *Tyrians* to be nailed to Crosses along the Sea-shore; a dreadful Spectacle even to the Conquerors themselves! To the Ambassadors of *Carthage*

CHAP. X. *Dissolution of the* Rom. *Empire.* 103

thuge he extended his Pardon, on account of the Sacredness of their *Alexander pardons the Ambassadors from Carthage.*
Character; but at the same time declared his Intentions of War against their City, so soon as his more important Affairs would give him leave. Thus was the City of *Tyre* taken in the seventh Month of the Siege, of whose ancient Glory in maritime Affairs we have already sufficiently spoken in the foregoing Sheets.

From hence *Alexander* repaired to *Gaza*, ordering *Hephestion* along the Coast of *Phœnicia*, and to meet him with the Fleet at that Place, where he received Advice that *Amphoterus* and *Egilochus*, with a Navy of a hundred and sixty Sail, had reduced to his Obedience all the Islands between *Greece* and *Asia*, where, in the Reduction of *Chios*, they had taken twelve *Persian* Gallies of three Tire of Oars each, with all their Equipage, and that *Aristonicus*, Tyrant of *Methymne*, arriving at the same Place, which he thought yet in the Hands of the *Persians*, was there taken Prisoner. *Alexander*, having made himself Master of *Gaza*, he hastened onwards *Ægypt*, having first dispatched *Amyntas* with ten Gallies to *Macedonia* for Recruits, and the *Ægyptians*, who had long groaned under the *Persian* Tyranny, joyfully received him into their Kingdom, where, between the Lake *Mareotis* and the Sea, he founded a new City, eighty Furlongs in Circumference, which he named from himself, *Alexandria*, and transplanting thither the Inhabitants of several neighbouring Places, render'd it a very populous and flourishing Emporium. The Government of *Ægypt* he committed to *Æschylus* of *Rhodes*, and for the Security of the Mouths of the *Nile*, he ordered a Squadron of thirty Sail under the Command of *Polemon*; when sending Instructions to *Amphoterus*, Admiral of the Fleet, to repair to *Crete*, and having settled that Island, to apply himself diligently to clear the Sea of Pirates, for the Security of Navigation, he marched on himself with his victorious Army toward the *Euphrates*, where defeating *Darius* again, who was soon after slain by the Treachery of his own Subjects, he became sole Possessor of the Empire of *Persia*. *Alexander taking Gaza, proceeds to Ægypt, and is received by the Ægyptians.*

Builds Alexandria.

He again defeats Darius,

After this, he subdued the *Hyrcanians*, *Mardi*, *Cedrosians*, *Paropamisadæ*, *Scythians*, *Arians*, and *Indians*, as far as the *Ganges*, and on the Banks of the River *Hypalis* erected Altars to the Twelve Gods, each of them fifty Cubits high, as a Monument to Posterity of his Expedition in those Parts. Marching thence, he encamped on the Banks of the *Acesine*, and the Fleet which he had ordered to be built, with design of visiting the Ocean, being now ready on that River, consisting of a thousand Sail, he, before his Departure, founded the Cities *Nicæa* and *Bucephala*; when embarking his Troops, he fell down the said River to that Place where it meets with the *Hydaspes*, and there found the *Sobians* drawn up to oppose him with an Army of forty thousand Men. Landing his Troops, he immediately drove them into their City, which, in Despair, they set fire to, and burnt themselves and their Effects. As *Alexander* was in one of his Barges, taking a View of the Citadel of this Town, which was situated where the *Acesine* and *Hydaspes* fall into the *Indus*, as hath been before observed, he narrowly escaped being drowned, *and subdues others.*

He founds the Cities Nicæa and Bucephala, overcomes the Sobians, ed, the Confluence of all those Rivers causing a very rapid Current there, in acknowledgment of which Deliverance, he raised an Altar to each River, whereon having sacrificed, he went on toward the Country of the *Oxidracæ,* and setting down before their chief City, was dangerously wounded. No sooner was he cured than he pursued his Voyage down the River *Indus* to the Ocean, where he built several Cities on the Coasts, as Monuments of his Glory. He gave Orders to *Nearchus* and *Onesicritus,* who were most skilled in Navigation, to take the strongest and best built Ships of the Fleet, and penetrate as far into the Ocean on that side as they could with Safety, and then return to him either up the same River *Indus,* or the *Euphrates;* the former of whom (as *Plutarch* tells us in the Life of *Alexander)* having coasted along *Arabia, Æthiopia,* and *Lybia,* came about to the Pillars of *Hercules,* and returned through the Mediterranean to *Macedonia.*

is dangerously wounded.

sends some Persons to discover the Indian Ocean,

Early the next Spring setting fire to most of his Ships which would have been useless in his Return, he erected Altars on an Island in the Mouth of the *Indus,* around which, as the Goal of his Race, and the Limits of his Empire, he caused himself to be rowed in one of his nimblest Gallies, when making Libations to *Neptune,* he threw the golden Cups he made use of in that Ceremony into the Sea, and erected an Altar to him and the Goddess *Tethys,* praying for a safe Return: Then having distributed among his Friends the Governments of *India,* he set forwards towards *Babylon* by Land, receiving Advice in his way that Ambassadors from *Carthage,* and the other Cities of *Africk,* as also from *Spain, Gaul, Sicily, Sardinia,* and some Cities of *Italy,* attended his Arrival: But he was no sooner come to *Babylon* with design, as one would think, to celebrate the Convention of the whole Universe, than at one of his publick Entertainments, Poison (as some have supposed) was given him, of which in few Days he died, in the thirty third Year of his Age, and thirteenth of his Reign. Thus fell *Alexander,* not by any hostile Attempt, but the treasonable Contrivances of his own Subjects, or, as others have related, of a Debauch.

burns his Ships in Indus,

dies at Babylon by Poison. Year of the World, 3625. Before Christ, 323.

His private Memoirs.

It appeared from his private Papers, containing Minutes of what he intended to do, which after his Death were read in a publick Assembly of the principal Officers of the Army, that he designed to have given Orders to the People of *Phœnicia, Syria, Cilicia,* and *Cyprus,* to get ready a Fleet of a thousand Gallies, larger than those of three Tire of Oars then commonly used, for an Expedition against the *Carthaginians,* and other maritime People of *Lybia, Spain, Italy,* and *Sicily,* purposing to reduce to his Obedience the whole Coast of *Africk* as far as the Pillars of *Hercules,* and all the Mediterranean Sea: And for the Reception and Entertainment of so great a Fleet, he intended to make convenient Harbours, with well furnish'd Naval Arsenals, in the Places most commodiously situate for that purpose.

A fit Successor was wanting to so great a King, and so excellent a Captain, but the Weight of Empire was too great for any other single Person to bear: However, for the present, *Perdiccas* was

made

made choice of to manage the Affairs of the Army, who, to remove such as might be jealous of his Power, as well as to make the Kingdoms he distributed pass for free Gifts of his own, divided the Provinces of the Empire among the chief Commanders. To *Ptolemy* was given *Ægypt* and *Africa*, and to *Laomedon Syria* and *Phœnicia*, *Antigonus* had *Lycia* and *Pamphylia*, with the Greater *Phrygia*; and *Leonatus* the Lesser *Phrygia* and *Hellespontus*. *Cassander* was sent to *Caria*, and *Menander* to *Lydia*, and *Cappadocia* and *Paphlagonia* fell to *Eumenes*, as *Media* did to *Pithon*. *Lysimachus* had the Government of *Thrace*, and the neighbouring Countries on the *Euxine* Sea, but in the Eastern Provinces and distant *Indian* Acquisitions the former Deputies were still retained. Not long after which, as if so many Kingdoms, and not Governments, were divided among themselves, they made themselves Kings instead of Governours, and acquired great Wealth and Power, which they left to their Posterity.

The Division of Alexander's Empire.

CHAP. XI.

Of the Naval Wars of the Grecians, *from the Death of* Alexander *the Great, to the Reduction of* Macedonia *to the Obedience of the* Romans.

WHILE Affairs went thus in the East, the *Athenians* and *Ætolians* carried on the War, which they had begun in *Alexander*'s Life-time, with great Vigour and Diligence, the Occasion whereof was this. *Alexander*, in his Return from *India*, had dispatched Letters into *Greece*, commanding all the Cities to recall their Exiles, except only such as were guilty of Murder; which Letters being read in the Presence of all *Greece*, then assembled at the Olympick Games, occasioned great Commotions, because several had been banished their Country not legally, but by the Factions of the great Men; who now began to apprehend that, if they were restored, they would soon come to have a greater Interest in the Government than themselves. For this Reason many of these Cities openly murmured, and gave out, that they would defend their Liberty by Force of Arms. The chief Promoters of this Insurrection were the *Athenians* and *Ætolians*, which when *Alexander* came to understand, he ordered his Allies to furnish him with a thousand Gallies to carry on the War in the West, resolving with a powerful Army to level *Athens* with the Ground; whereupon the *Athenians* raised an Army of thirty thousand Men, and, with two hundred Ships, made War upon *Antipater*, to whose Share the Government of *Greece* fell; but finding that he declined the Hazard of a Battel, and covered himself within the Walls of the City *Heraclea*, they closely besieged him. *Leonatus*, who had the Government

The Athenians and Ætolians carry on a vigorous War against Alexander and Antipater.

P   ment

ment of *Hellespontus* and *Phrygia Minor*, advancing with all Expedition to his Relief, was himself slain; but *Antipater*, by the Accession of these Forces, judging himself a Match for the Enemy, who had now raised the Siege, he left *Heraclea*, and marched his Troops into *Macedonia*, whence he advanced to *Athens*; which, after a short Siege, was surrendered to him, he obliging the *Athenians* to change the Government of the People to that of the Few, and to receive a Garrison of *Macedonians* into *Munychia*. On the Death of *Antipater*, the *Macedonians* were divided into two Factions, one of which was for *Cassander*, the other for *Polyperchon*, in the Interest of the former of whom were the great Men of *Athens*, and in that of the latter the Commons; but *Cassander* prevailed, and possessed himself of that Kingdom, having paved his way to the Throne by the Murder of *Aridæus*, Brother to *Alexander* the Great, and his Wife *Eurydice*, and of *Olympias*, *Alexander*'s Mother.

Antipater takes Athens.

Cassander gets the Kingdom of Macedon.

By this time there had fallen of the Successors of that Prince *Polyperchon*, *Craterus*, *Perdiccas*, and *Eumenes*, the rest taking part either with *Antigonus* or *Ptolemy*, the Demands of the latter of whom, and of his Confederates, *Cassander*, *Lysimachus*, and *Seleucus*, were, that an equal Dividend should be made both of the Provinces, and of the Booty taken since the Death of *Eumenes*, but *Antigonus* refused to have any Sharers with himself in the Profits of the War: And that he might have an honourable Pretence on his side to break with them, he gave out that he was resolved to revenge the Death of *Olympias*, who was slain by *Cassander*, and to deliver the Son of his Prince, and his Mother from the Imprisonment they were kept in by him; whereupon *Ptolemy* and *Cassander* entered into a League with *Lysimachus* and *Seleucus*, and carried on the War with all imaginable Vigour both by Sea and Land. *Ptolemy* at this time possessed *Ægypt*, with *Cyprus* and *Phœnicia*, and the greater part of *Africk*. *Macedonia* and *Greece* were under *Cassander*'s Government; and as for *Antigonus*, he had *Asia*, with most part of the East, having lately dispossessed *Seleucus* of the Government of *Babylon*, and the adjacent Provinces he had made himself Master of. After several bloody Battels fought with various Success, they came to a Treaty, that each should retain the Provinces he had; that *Alexander*'s Son by *Roxane*, when at Age, should be made King; that *Cassander* should be Captain General of *Europe*, and that the *Grecians* should live after their own Laws: But this Agreement was not long kept, for each of them endeavoured, under any Pretence, to enlarge the Bounds of his Dominions, and this with the less Restraint, for that shortly after *Cassander* not only took off that Son of *Alexander*'s, for whom they pretended themselves Administrators, with his Mother *Roxane*, but also his natural Son *Hercules*, and *Arsine* the Mother of that Son likewise.

War breaks out between Antigonus, Ptolemy, &c.

Cassander kills Alexander's Relations.

Under Pretence of enforcing the Execution of that Article of the foresaid Treaty, relating to the Freedom of *Greece*, *Antigonus* fitted out a formidable Fleet at *Ephesus*, where were also got ready

CHAP. XI. *Dissolution of the Rom. Empire.* 107

a considerable Body of Troops to be embarked, the Command of all which he committed to his Son *Demetrius*, with Instructions to procure to all the Cities of *Greece* their ancient Liberties, and first to begin with *Athens*, wherein *Cassander* maintained a strong Garison. When the Land-Forces were all on board, and the Fleet was ready to sail, *Demetrius* thinking it necessary, for some particular Reasons, to keep secret, as long as possibly might be, the Place he designed first to repair to, he delivered out to the respective Captains a sealed Paper, with Orders, if they kept Company together, not to open the same, but if they should happen to be separated by bad Weather, or any other Accident, then to break it open, and steer their Course to the Place therein directed. This Circumstance we learn from *Polyænus* in his Book of Stratagems, and is the first Instance in History of the Use of a sealed Rendezvous, though probably it might have been often enough used before, being what common Reason must necessarily dictate on such Occasions, however *Polyænus* happen'd to think it worthy of a Place in his Work. Arriving with the Fleet at the *Piræus*, he took it by Assault, and in few Days obliged *Demetrius Phalereus*, who commanded for *Cassander* in *Athens*, to withdraw his Troops thence; and having restored that Place to its ancient Government and Liberties, and also reduced the Fortress of *Munychia* and City of *Megara*, he received further Instructions from *Antigonus* to cause Deputies to be chosen by the several Cities of *Greece*, that they might meet together, and transact what was necessary for the publick Peace and Safety, and to repair himself with the Fleet to *Cyprus*, and use his best Endeavours to reduce that Island, where *Ptolemy* maintained a considerable Force both by Sea and Land.

Demetrius immediately made sail Eastward, and calling in at *Rhodes*, endeavoured to prevail with the People of that Island (who then made a great Figure in the Mediterranean) to break with *Ptolemy*; but they desiring to be left at liberty to remain Neuter, it was the Ground of *Antigonus*'s future Resentments against them. From thence *Demetrius* proceeded to *Cilicia*, where receiving a Reinforcement of Men and Ships, his Strength now consisted of fifteen thousand Foot, and four hundred Horse, above a hundred and twenty Gallies, and fifty three large Ships of Burthen, with which passing over to *Cyprus*, he landed his Troops not far from *Carpasia*, a Town on the North-East side of the Island; and there drawing his Gallies ashore, which, as well as his Camp, he secured with a strong Retrenchment, he made Incursions into the adjacent Country, and surprized *Carpasia*, with *Urania*, another neighbouring Town; when leaving a sufficient Body of Troops for the Defence of the Camp and Shipping, he marched toward *Salamis*, near which Place he was met by *Menelaus*, *Ptolemy*'s Governour of the Island, with an Army of five and twenty thousand Foot, and eighteen hundred Horse, with whom engaging, he gave him a Signal Overthrow, and obliged him to retire into the City, where *Menelaus* put himself in the best Posture of Defence he was able, and immediately dispatched Messengers to *Ægypt*, with Advice of the Loss he had sustained

Demetrius sent with a Fleet and Army to Greece.

Athens restored to its Liberty.

Demetrius proceeds to Cyprus.

Antigonus his General beaten in Cyprus.

P 2 in

Salamis besieged.

in the late Battel, and desiring speedy Succours to be sent to his Relief. *Demetrius*, on the other hand, immediately invested the Place, and prosecuted the Siege with the utmost Vigour, having brought over with him, in abundance, all necessary Instruments and Utensils for that purpose; and for the more speedy Reduction of the Place, he here invented that Engine called the *Helepolis*, a Machine of prodigious Bulk, not unlike those battering Rams which were covered with Shrouds, but vastly bigger, and of far greater force, containing several smaller Engines out of which Stones, and other missive Weapons, were cast. With this, the battering Rams, *Demetrius his Machines burnt.* and other Machines, he had very much ruined the Walls, when the Besieged found means to set them on fire: However, he was not discouraged with this Loss, but carried on the Siege with the utmost Application.

Ptolemy with a Fleet comes to the Relief of Menelaus.

Ptolemy, understanding what Straits *Menelaus* was reduced to, was now arrived at *Paphos*, where having encreased his Force with all the Ships of the Island, he advanced to *Citium*, about five and twenty Miles from *Salamis*, with a hundred and forty well appointed Gallies, the biggest of which had five Tire of Oars, and the least four, and was followed by above two hundred Transports, which had on board ten thousand Men, From hence *Ptolemy* dispatched a Courier to *Menelaus*, with Orders to send out to him with all speed, if it could possibly be done, sixty Gallies which were in the Port of *Salamis*, by the Accession of which his Fleet would be increased to two hundred Sail, and with that Number he doubted not to be able to deal with the Enemy. *Demetrius* having Intelligence of this Design, left part of the Army before the Town, and embarked a Body of chosen Troops on board his Gallies, each of which he furnished with a Machine for throwing missive Weapons, to be fixed on their Prows; and being thus well provided, he came about to the Entrance of the Port of *Salamis*, where, just out of Javelin-shot, he anchored with his whole Fleet, making choice of this Station, as well to prevent the sixty Gallies in the Harbour from coming out, as for that he reckoned it an advantagious Place to wait and engage the Enemy. But as soon as he found *Ptolemy*'s Fleet was nearer approach'd, he left *Antisthenes* with ten Gallies of five Tire of Oars to keep that Station, and block up the Harbour, on each side of the Entrance whereof, which was narrow. He also ordered some Troops to take Post near thereto, that they might be at hand to assist and receive into their Protection the Seamen, in case they should be obliged, by any ill Success, to retire to the Shore. This done, he advanced himself to meet the Enemy, having with him a hundred and eight Gallies, the largest whereof were of seven Tire of Oars, and the least of four. In the Left Wing were seven *Phœnician* Gallies of seven Tire of Oars, and thirty *Athenian* Gallies of four, commanded by *Medius*; besides which, he ordered in that Wing, wherein he intended to fight himself, ten Gallies of six Tire of Oars, and as many of five. In the Centre were disposed the smallest Ships under the Command of *Themison* and *Marsias*; and the Right Wing was led by *Hegesippus* of *Halicarnassus*,

Demetrius prepares to encounter him.

CHAP. XI. *Dissolution of the* Rom. *Empire.* 109

nassus, and *Plistias* of *Cos*. *Ptolemy* was making the best of his Way by Night toward *Salamis*, in Hopes of being join'd by the Ships in the Port before the Enemy could come up, but being surprized at Break of Day with the Sight of their Fleet coming down in Order of Battel, he immediately disposed his Ships to receive them, ordering the Transports with the Troops aboard to keep at a convenient Distance. A. M. 3642.

The two Princes now having at stake their Lives, their Glory and Honour, were both eager to engage, when immediately from *Demetrius*'s Gally was hoisted a gilt Shield, as a Signal for Battel, which was presently answered by the like Signal on *Ptolemy*'s Side: And now the Trumpets sounding a Charge, and the Men setting up a loud Huzza, they first bestowed Showers of Arrows and Darts at each other, and then advancing nearer, the Gallies rushed against each other with the utmost Fury and Violence, and with the Shock wiped off alternately whole Sides of Oars. Some of them were transfixed by others with their Beaks, when tacking about, they charged Stern to Stern, and some falling with their Broadsides together, were mutually boarded with great Slaughter. Numbers of Men in getting up the Sides of Gallies were either slain with Spears from above, or with missive Weapons swept off into the Sea; and thus the Engagement lasted many Hours with great Obstinacy, and various Success. *Demetrius* was in a Gally with seven Tire of Oars, and placing himself on the Deck fought with singular Courage and Resolution, doing wonderful Execution among the Enemy, not only with Javelins but his Spear, while they threw whole Showers of Darts at him, which, with great Dexterity, he avoided, or received on his Buckler; and of three Persons who were more particularly active against him, one he killed on the Spot, and dangerously wounded the other two. His Behaviour was so gallant, and every little Advantage he prosecuted so vigorously, that at length he entirely broke the Enemy's Right Wing, and put them to Flight, as well as their main Body; not but that *Ptolemy* performed all the Parts of a valiant and able Leader, and was so well sustain'd with the Gallies of greatest Force, and the chosen Men he had with him in that Wing, that he got the better of *Demetrius*'s Right which was opposed to him, and forced them to retire in Confusion, with the Loss of several Ships sunk and taken, with all their Men. Flushed with this Success, he little doubted of the like in the other Part of the Fleet, but when he advanced, and found his Right Wing and main Body entirely broken, and flying before the Enemy in Disorder, who gave them close Chace, he withdrew to *Citium*. *Demetrius* as soon as he had forced the Enemy to give Way, and made himself Master of several of their Ships, committed the main Body of the Fleet to the Charge of *Neon* and *Burichus*, with Orders to give Chace to the flying Ships and take up the Men that were swimming about, and repaired himself with the rest, and the Gallies he had taken, to the Port where were his Land and Naval Camps. During the Heat of this Engagement, *Menelaus*, who commanded in *Salamis*, gave Orders to *Menœtius* to take upon him the Command of the sixty Gallies in that Harbour, and fight his Way out to join *Ptolemy*, who accordingly

A Fight between the Fleets of Ptolemy and Demetrius.

Ptolemy beaten at Sea.

Menœtius forces through Demetrius's Gallies at Salamis.

4

cordingly executed his Orders, and obliged the ten Gallies *Demetrius* had left there, to retire under the Shore to the Protection of the Land Forces: But happening to arrive too late to have a Share in the Engagement, they all returned to *Salamis*.

The Damage done to Ptolemy's Fleet.

Such was the Event of this Naval Battel, wherein forty of *Ptolemy*'s Gallies were sunk, and all their Men drowned, eighty more, being very much shatter'd, were taken, together with most of the Transports, which had on Board them eight thousand Men; and all this with no other Loss than the disabling twenty of *Demetrius*'s Gallies, yet not so much, but that, with the necessary Care, they were put into a Condition for Service again. *Ptolemy* giving up *Cyprus* for lost, made the best of his Way for *Ægypt*, while *Demetrius*, in the mean time, improved his Success by the Reduction of all the Towns of the Island, where he took above sixteen thousand Foot Soldiers, and six hundred Horse, which he incorporated among his own Troops. He dispatched a Gally with some Persons of Quality to give an Account of, and to congratulate *Antigonus* on this Victory, who thereupon put on a Regal Diadem, and from that time forward took to himself the Title of King, with which he likewise honoured his Son *Demetrius*. *Ptolemy*, nothing the humbler for his late Losses, wore also a Diadem, and caused himself to be proclaimed King; and, in Imitation of these, *Seleucus* and *Cassander*, together with *Lysimachus* usurped the same Title: And now *Antigonus* recalling his Son from *Cyprus*, got together a vast Army in *Syria*, with which rendezvousing at *Gaza*, he marched toward *Ægypt*, ordering *Demetrius* to coast it along with the Fleet, to act in Concert with him, as Occasion should offer; but *Ptolemy* had made so good Preparation for his Reception, both by Sea and Land, by placing strong Garrisons in the Frontier Towns toward *Syria* (where he had also ready a flying Camp to harrass the Enemy) and well guarding the Mouths of the *Nile* by considerable Numbers of Ships, that *Antigonus* was obliged to return to *Syria* with his Army and Fleet, from this fruitless Expedition.

Demetrius conquers Cyprus.

Antigonus takes the Title of King, as did Ptolemy, &c.

Antigonus attempts Ægypt in vain,

prepares to go against Rhodes.

The next Year he thought fit to prosecute his Resentments against the *Rhodians*, which Republick was at this time Mistress of a great Naval Force, and its Government was so wisely administer'd, that all the neighbouring Kings and Princes courted her Friendship. The *Rhodians* knowing what vast Advantages would accrue from such a Conduct, cultivated Friendships with all the Princes and States where their Interests could be any Ways concern'd, carefully avoiding to send Aid to any, or at all to interfere in the Wars wherein any of them happened to be engaged, and so fairly maintained a Neutrality, that they were highly esteemed on all Sides. By this means having enjoyed a long Peace and flourishing Commerce, they had acquired prodigious Wealth and Power, insomuch that, at their own Charge, they took upon them, for the Service of *Greece* in general, to fit out a formidable Fleet to scour the Sea of Pirates, which they effectually did; not but that they had at the same time their own particular Advantage, by providing for the Security of their Trade. During all the Contentions between the Successors of *Alexander*

The Rhodians scour the Sea of Pirates.

CHAP. XI. *Dissolution of the* Rom. *Empire.* 111

auder, they had behaved themselves with the greatest Caution, so as not to give Offence to any, but in their Hearts were most inclined to favour *Ptolemy,* as being Master of that Country from which they received the greatest Advantages in their Trade; which Inclination of theirs *Antigonus* taking notice of, endeavoured to prevail with them to abandon the Friendship of his Enemy, and, when the Expedition against *Cyprus* was first resolved on, desired by his Ministers that they would aid his Son *Demetrius* with Men and Ships for that Service, which they refusing, he sent a Fleet against them, with Orders to the Admiral thereof to seize all the Merchants that traded to *Ægypt,* with their Ships and Effects. This the *Rhodians* not suffering him to do, he accused them as having begun Hostilities, and drawn upon themselves a just War, threatening withall to lay Siege to their City; but they endeavoured to divert this Tempest by decreeing extraordinary Honours to *Antigonus,* and by a solemn Embassy humbly prayed that he would not force them to a War with *Ptolemy,* contrary to the Faith of their Treaties subsisting with him, and the Law of Nations; notwithstanding which he peremptorily insisted on his Demands, and sending *Demetrius* with a strong Force to invest the place, they let him know that they should be ready to assist his Father against *Ptolemy* whensoever he pleased. He not satisfied with this, demanded a Hundred of their most considerable Men as Hostages, and Leave to enter their Harbour with his Fleet; but the *Rhodians* suspecting he designed to surprize them, resolved to sustain the War, and prepared for their Defence.

but not favouring Antigonus

he sends Demetrius *against* Rhodes.

Demetrius, on the other hand, was no less diligent in his Preparations for the Siege, having got together a Fleet of two hundred Gallies, an hundred and seventy Ships of Burthen, and Transports, on board all which were forty thousand Men; and he had also a thousand Ships belonging to Free-booters, or private Adventurers, who followed him for the sake of the Pillage of so rich an Island. With this Force advancing to *Rhodes,* he invested the Town by Sea and Land, and planted a great Number of Machines against the Walls; mean while the *Rhodians* were not negligent, but defended themselves with incredible Bravery, and, in several successful Sallies, destroyed his Machines with Fire. He nevertheless pushed the Siege with all imaginable Vigour, invented several Engines for annoying the Enemy, and at length found out and caused to be made one of a most enormous Magnitude, being nine Stories high, which required above three thousand strong Men to move it: From his peculiar Genius in the Invention of which Engines, and the Use he made of them, he was sirnamed *Poliorcetes,* or the Besieger of Towns.

The Rhodians *prepare for their Defence.*

Rhodes *is invested by* Demetrius.

A prodigious Engine made by Demetrius.

The Siege had now lasted almost twelve Months, for the *Rhodians* having all along kept their Communication open to the Sea, (*Demetrius* not being able to make himself Master of the Harbour,) received frequent Supplies from *Ptolemy* and other confederated Princes, and, at length, after many ineffectual Attempts for bringing matters to a Composition, (for which several Cities and States had interposed their good Offices,) *Antigonus,* from the Advices his
Son

Son sent him of their most obstinate Defence, despairing of reducing them, gave him private Instructions to come to an Agreement on any reasonable Terms. He waited a proper Opportunity to do this with a good Grace, which soon offered; for although *Ptolemy* had acquainted them by Letter that he would send them a Re-inforcement of three thousand Men, and a Supply of Corn, yet he at the same time advised them, if they could gain any good Terms, to come to a Composition with *Antigonus*, of which *Demetrius* having Advice, he made Use of the Ambassadors of the *Ætolians*, who were come to be Mediators, to open the Matter, and so at last a Peace was concluded on these Conditions, that the City of *Rhodes* should receive no foreign Garrison, but should enjoy all its Revenues; That the *Rhodians* should aid *Antigonus* in his Wars on all Occasions, except against *Ptolemy*; and that, for the Performance thereof, they should deliver up an hundred Hostages, such as *Demetrius* should make Choice of, excepting those that had gone through the Offices of State.

A Peace concluded with the Rhodians.

Having concluded this Treaty, he pursuant to further Instructions from *Antigonus*, crossed the *Ægean*, and repaired to *Aulis*, a Port of *Bœotia*, to perfect the Work he had begun of restoring the Liberty of *Greece*, which *Cassander* now ravaged with a powerful Army. There landing his Troops, he marched against *Cassander*, and obliged him to retire beyond the Pass of *Thermopylæ*, recovering all the Country he had over-ran, and restoring all the Cities to their Freedom as he passed; after which, he, in a general Assembly of the *Grecians* at the *Isthmian* Games, so far prevailed as to be constituted Generalissimo of *Greece*, in the same manner as *Philip* and *Alexander* had been; but while these things were doing, he received Advice that *Ptolemy*, *Seleucus*, and the other confederated Princes were marching against his Father with their united Forces, upon which he went over into *Asia*, and there joining Battel with the Enemy, *Antigonus* lost his Life therein, but he saved himself by Flight.

Demetrius proceeds to the restoring Liberty to Greece.

Antigonus slain in Asia.

Then repairing on board his Fleet, he laid waste the *Chersonesus*, had *Athens* again surrender'd to him, defeated the *Lacedæmonians*, and possessed himself of the Kingdom of *Macedon*, putting to Death *Alexander* the Son of *Cassander*. He also invaded *Thrace*, subdued the *Bœotians*, and having made himself Master of *Thebes*, declared War against *Pyrrhus*, King of *Epirus*, who had seized on Part of *Macedonia*, to whose Aid considerable Forces were sent by *Seleucus*, *Lysimachus*, and *Ptolemy*, the latter of whom also fitted out a formidable Fleet, which advancing toward *Greece* struck a mighty Terrour along the Coasts; and the *Macedonians* revolting to *Pyrrhus*, *Demetrius* thought it time to provide for his Safety by Flight; wherefore laying aside his Ensigns of Royalty, he, in mean Attire, and with a slender Retinue, withdrew to the City *Cassandria*, from whence repairing to *Thebes*, he passed over into *Asia*, where being taken by *Seleucus*, he died in Prison, leaving his Son *Antigonus*, to whom *Demetrius* the younger succeeded in the Throne of *Macedonia*. After him reigned *Antigonus-Doso*, *Philip*, and *Perseus*, in successive

Demetrius recovers Athens, beats the Lacedæmonians, and possesses Macedon.
A. M. 3655.

Demetrius flies to the City of Cassandria.

He is taken, and dies in Prison.

successive Order, under which last the Kingdom of *Macedonia* was *subdued by the Romans.* subdued by *Paulus Æmylius*, and reduced into the Form of a Roman Province.

CHAP. XII.

Of the Naval Wars of the Carthaginians *from the Foundation of their City to their first War with the Romans; wherein are also contained those of the* Syracusans.

WHILE the *Macedonian* Kingdom was in its most flourishing Condition, the *Carthaginian* and *Syracusan* Commonwealths were also very potent, and in great Reputation, being esteemed a Match not unequal even for *Alexander* the Great, in case he should have turned his Arms that Way. We have already taken some Notice of the *Syracusans*, and other People of *Sicily*, on Occasion of the War the *Athenians* carried into that Island, and shall relate what happened after the memorable Defeat of that People there, when we have first premised something concerning the Origine and Exploits of the *Carthaginians*.

Elissa, (more celebrated under the Name of *Dido*,) a Daughter *Dido builds* of the King of *Tyre*, flying from her Brother *Pygmalion*, then on *Carthage.* the Throne, who had murthered her Husband *Sichæus*, first came, accompanied with great Numbers of *Tyrians* of Quality, to the Island *Cyprus*, and thence to the Coast of *Africa*, where she purchased as A. M. 3080. much Ground of the Inhabitants as an Ox's Hide would encompass, which she ordered to be cut out in small Thongs, and so obtained a much larger Extent than she had seemed to desire, for which Reason the Place was afterwards called *Byrsa*. In a short time great Numbers of Men flocking thither from the neighbouring Countries out of Hopes of Lucre, to sell their Commodities to these Strangers, took up their Habitations with them, and by their Multitudes soon made the Resemblance of a City; mean while the Inhabitants of *Utica* dispatched Ambassadours with Presents, as being of Consanguinity with them, and advised them to build a City in that Place where they first settled: Nay the *Africans* themselves were desirous of keeping these new Guests among them. Thus by an universal Consent of the Natives the Foundations of *Carthage* were laid, as Authors have related, and a yearly Tribute assigned them for the Ground on which it was built; and their Affairs becoming soon in a flourishing Condition, *Hiarbas* King of the *Mauritanians*, demanded *Elissa* in Marriage, threatening to carry Fire and Sword into their Territory, in case he was refused that Princess: That Princess retained so inviolable a Respect for the Memory of her former Husband, that she could not be prevailed with to condescend to a second Love, but erecting a Pile of Wood in the furthermost Part of the

Q City,

City, as if she designed to appease the Manes of *Sichæus*, previous to a new Marriage, offered several Sacrifices, and then ascending the Pile with a drawn Sword in her Hand, she, in this Posture, told the People she was going to her Husband as they had advised her, and immediately stabbed her self.

Dido kills her self.

This City of *Carthage* was built an hundred and eighteen Years before *Rome*, and the Valour of its Inhabitants soon render'd it very famous, whose first Efforts abroad were in *Sicily*, where they fought with Success a long time; but removing the Scene to *Sardinia*, there they lost the Flower of their Army, and, after a bloody Dispute, were totally defeated. Enraged at these Losses, they sentenced their General *Maleus* (under whose Command they had conquered great Part of *Sicily*, and performed several noble Exploits against the *Africans*) with the Remainder of the Army that were left alive, to Banishment; who transporting his Troops to *Africa*, besieged and took the City, and punished the Authors of his said Banishment: However being not long after accused of a Design to make himself King, he was put to Death.

The first Exploits of the Carthaginians.

But many Years before this *Maleus*, the *Carthaginian* Power was grown very formidable, witness the potent Fleet and Army they sent to *Sicily*, in Concert with *Xerxes*, when he undertook an Expedition against *Greece*: Which consisting of five thousand Sail, and three hundred thousand Men, the Ships were all destroyed, and the Men killed, together with *Amilcar* their General, by *Gelon* King of the aforesaid Island, as we have before related. Notwithstanding the Greatness of this Loss, they were not discouraged, but with a new Fleet and Army again invading *Sicily*, they received a signal Defeat at Sea from *Hieron*, King of *Syracuse*, who flushed with this Success, sent his Fleet against the *Tyrrhenians* (a People that very much infested the Seas of *Sicily* with their Piracies and Depredations) wherewith he ravaged the Island *Æthalia*, (now *Elba*) and all the Coasts of the *Tyrrhenians*, made a Descent on *Cyrnus*, afterwards known by the Name of *Corsica*, when attacking *Æthalia* again, he reduced it to his Obedience, and returned to *Syracuse* loaden with Spoils.

The Carthaginian Fleet and Army defeated by Hieron. Hieron his Successes.

After the Overthrow of the *Athenians* in *Sicily*, the People of *Segesta*, who had espoused their Cause against the *Syracusans*, called over the *Carthaginians* to their Aid, and they accordingly sent to them a Fleet under the Command of *Hannibal*, the Grandson of that *Amilcar* who was slain by *Gelon*. He soon took and destroyed the Cities of *Selinus* and *Himera*, and returning to *Carthage*, was received with great Demonstrations of Joy, the Senators themselves coming out to meet him; but after his Departure from *Sicily*, *Hermocrates*, Admiral of the *Syracusan* Fleet, re-established the Remainder of the Inhabitants of those Places in the Ruins of their Cities, and encouraged them to re-build them, which they immediately set about, and gained considerable Advantages over the *Carthaginian* Confederates. To revenge this Dishonour, *Hannibal* was joined in Commission with *Himilco* the Son of *Hanno*, and placed at the Head of another Fleet, who detached forty Gallies before them

Hannibal sent to aid those of Segesta.

CHAP. XII. *Dissolution of the* Rom. *Empire.* 115

to the Coast where they intended their Descent, designing soon to follow with their whole Force; but the *Syracusans* falling in with the forty Gallies off of *Eryx*, sunk fifteen of them, the rest escaping by favour of the Night. The two Generals hereupon repaired with the rest of the Fleet to *Agrigentum*, where landing their Troops, they laid siege to that Town, during which *Hannibal* died of the Plague; and *Himilco* (after several successful Engagements, wherein he in some sort revenged the Death of his Collegue on the *Silicians*) finding the contagious Distemper raging more fierce, and that the Flower of his Troops were destroyed, returned to *Carthage*, where he put an end to his Life, in a Fit of Despair and Rage that he had been thus forced to abandon *Sicily*, which he was so near reducing to the Obedience of *Carthage*. *The Syracusans destroy several Gallies of Carthage.*
Trepano del Monte.
The Carthaginians return by reason of the Plague.

His Successor in the Generalship was *Maleus* beforemention'd, to whom succeeded *Mago*, who was the first of the *Carthaginian* Captains that introduced among them any thing of a strict and regular Discipline. He having subdued most of the Islands on the *African* Coast, was succeeded by *Asdrubal* and *Amilcar*, his two Sons, who treading the same Paths of Glory their Father had done, were Heirs to his Greatness and Bravery, as well as to his Fortune. They were both joined in Commission for the Management of the War in *Sardinia*, where *Asdrubal* was desperately wounded, and died, leaving the Command of the Army to his Brother *Amilcar*. The general Lamentation which was made for him in the City (he having passed through eleven Dictatorships, and four Triumphs) made his Death as remarkable as it was glorious, and hereupon the Enemies of *Carthage* took fresh Courage, as if the Genius of that Republick expired with their General. The People of *Sicily* had recourse for Aid to *Leonidas*, Brother to the King of *Sparta*, on which ensued a bloody War, which was carried on for a long time, both by Sea and Land, with various Success, till at length *Amilcar* was slain, leaving three Sons, *Himilco*, *Hanno*, and *Gisco*. Of these *Himilco*, being constituted General for the *Carthaginians* in *Sicily*, he defeated *Dionysius*, Tyrant of *Syracuse*, in several Engagements by Sea and Land, but lost the greatest Part of his Army afterwards by the Plague, upon which he returned to *Carthage*, where through Grief he laid violent Hands on himself. *Mago subdues several Islands.*
Asdrubal slain at Sardinia.
Amilcar slain.
Himilco beats Dionysius of Syracuse, but kills himself.

The *Carthaginians* being forced out of *Sicily*, *Dionysius* considered that so great an Army lying at home without Action, might endanger the Repose and Tranquillity of his Kingdom; wherefore he transported them to *Italy*, as well to keep them perpetually employed, as to enlarge the Bounds of his Dominions. He first built in *Sicily* Gallies with five Tire of Oars, and made also a maritime Arsenal near *Syracuse*, wherein were a hundred and sixty Houses for the Reception of his Naval Stores, with all necessary Conveniences for building and fitting his Ships; and making War upon those *Grecians* which inhabit the opposite Shores of *Italy*, he defeated them, attacked most of the neighbouring People, and reducing the Country of the *Rhegians*, together with the *Locri Epizephyrii*, intended to join his Arms with the *Senonian* Gauls, who had *Conquests made by Dionysius.*
His Arsenal near Syracuse.

Q 2

had lately burnt *Rome*, and afterwards to try his Fortune for the Conquest of all *Italy*; but, in the midst of these Designs, he was forced to return home, where *Hanno*, the *Carthaginian* General, was laying waste his Dominions. *Hanno* was found guilty of some treasonable Contrivances against the State, for which he suffered Death, and *Dionysius* becoming odious to his People, by his Pride, Ambition, and Cruelty, was at length slain by his own Subjects, and his eldest Son, of the same Name, set up in his room; who being in a short time expelled *Sicily*, was received by the *Locrenses*, with whom reigning tyrannically six Years, he was at length driven out of their City by a Conspiracy, and returned to *Sicily*; where having *Syracuse* surrender'd to him by Treachery, he slew *Dio*, to whose Courage and Conduct was owing his Defeat in a Sea-Fight off *Leontium*, and his Expulsion from the Kingdom. Becoming every Day by his Cruelty more hateful to the People, he was again exposed to a new Conspiracy of the Citizens, headed by *Icetes*, Prince of the *Leontines*, assisted by *Timoleon* the *Corinthian*, by whom being forced into Banishment, he retired to *Corinth*, where he lived, in extreme Poverty and Indigence, to a very advanced Age.

Timoleon placing a Garrison of *Corinthians* in the Citadel, *Icetes* was so enraged at it, that he called *Mago*, the *Carthaginian* Admiral, to his Assistance, and with a Fleet of a hundred and fifty Sail, entered the Haven of *Syracuse*: However, *Mago* being apprehensive of a Reconciliation between them, and fearing that by the *Sicilians* and *Corinthians*, under a Shew of Friendship, he might be deluded to his Destruction, he returned with his Fleet to *Carthage*. *Timoleon*, after his Departure, having considerably the Advantage, brought *Syracuse* entirely to his Obedience; which being exhausted of great Numbers of its Citizens by the long Wars, he re-peopled with *Corinthians*, and putting to Death, or expelling the Tyrants in most of the Cities of *Sicily*, restored the greatest part of that Island to its ancient Liberty. The *Carthaginians* having, on account of some Misbehaviour, nailed to the Cross the Body of *Mago*, who had laid violent Hands on himself, got together from *Africk*, *Spain*, *Gaul*, and *Lyguria*, an Army of seventy thousand Men, with a Fleet of two hundred Gallies, and a thousand Victualling Ships and Transports, which they sent under the Command of *Hannibal* and *Bomilcar* to *Sicily*, in order to extirpate all the *Grecians* out of that Island; but they being totally defeated by *Timoleon*, *Gisco*, the Brother of *Hanno*, was substituted in their room. This Success of *Timoleon*'s Arms had such an Influence on the *Carthaginians*, that, soon after *Hanno*'s Arrival in *Sicily*, they sent him Instructions to make Proposals of Peace, which was at length agreed to, on these Conditions. That the *Carthaginians* should quit all Pretensions to any part of *Sicily* beyond the River *Lycus*, which was to be their Eastern Boundary in that Island; that they should not for the future support any of the Tyrants there; and, lastly, that such of the *Carthaginians* as had their Effects at *Syracuse* might be permitted to settle there with their Families.

Timolion

CHAP. XII. *Dissolution of the Rom. Empire.* 117

Timoleon dying, *Agathocles*, a Person of very mean Extraction, attempted to get into his Hands the Government of *Syracuse*, but failing in his Design, withdrew in Banishment to the *Murgantines*, then at War with the Inhabitants of that City, who elected him *Prætor*, and afterwards made him their General. In this War he took the City of the *Leontines*, and besieged the *Syracusans*, who implored the Assistance of *Amilcar*; which Leader laying aside the Animosity which his Nation bore them, sent the desired Relief; so that at one and the same time an Enemy defended them with all the Zeal and Affection of a Citizen, and a Citizen attacked them with all the Fury of an Enemy. But *Agathocles*, by his Artifices, bringing over *Amilcar* to his Interest, they came to a Composition, wherein it was agreed, that *Agathocles* should not only return to *Syracuse*, but be made *Prætor*. The Death of *Amilcar*, whose Conduct in this Affair was highly disapproved by the *Carthaginians*, furnished *Agathocles* with a specious Pretence to make War on them, whose first Engagement was with *Amilcar* the Son of *Gisco*, and the *Carthaginian* Fleet entering the great Haven of *Syracuse*, was forced ignominiously to retire from thence, when an *Athenian* Gally falling in with them, they took, and barbarously cut off the Hands of all her Company. Thence steering for *Messana*, they were overtaken, off *Catana*, by a furious Tempest, wherein many of their Ships were forced ashore, which fell into the Hands of *Agathocles*'s Soldiers; and *Amilcar*, soon after landing his Forces on the South side of the Island, encamped in the *Geloan* Plains, where *Agathocles*, twice joining Battel with him, was as often defeated, and the victorious *Carthaginians* advancing to *Syracuse*, sate down before that Place.

Agathocles, finding he was neither equal to them in Number of Men, nor provided with Necessaries to sustain a Siege, but above all that his Allies, offended with his violent Behaviour, had abandoned his Interest, he resolved to move the Seat of the War into *Africa*. A most bold and astonishing Undertaking it was, that he who was not able to keep his own Ground at home, should be so sanguine as to attempt a War abroad, and that the Conquered should have the Hardiness to insult the Conquerors. Having landed his Army in *Africa*, he ordered all his Ships to be set on fire, that, since all hopes of Flight were taken away, his Troops might be sensible they must either conquer or die. He was presently met by *Hanno* with an Army of thirty thousand Men, whom he entirely defeated, killing with him three thousand on the spot; whereupon advancing further with his Troops, he encamped within five Miles of the City of *Carthage*; and to make up the Measure of the *Carthaginians* Misfortunes, there now came Advice of the entire Loss of their Army and General in *Sicily*. For *Agathocles*, upon his extraordinary Successes in *Africk*, dispatching *Nearchus* with two Gallies to *Syracuse* with Advice thereof, they in five Days reached that Port, and as they were entering the Haven, some of the *Carthaginian* Ships, which lay before the Town, attacked them, at which the People being alarmed, they came down in great Numbers on the

the Strand, manned out their Ships, and, fighting the Enemy with great Courage and Resolution, rescued the two Gallies, and brought them safe in; besides which, they gained a very considerable Advantage over them ashore. *Amilcar*, nevertheless, pushed the Siege with all possible Vigour, but being unfortunately taken Prisoner, he was carried into the City, and delivered up to the Populace, who put him to Death, his Army at the same time receiving a signal Overthrow. This Misfortune to the *Carthaginians* was not only attended with the Revolt of several of the *African* Princes, who now took part with *Agathocles*, but the Loss of several of the maritime Towns; which Tyrant having now got sufficient Footing in *Africa*, and thinking his Presence necessary in *Syracuse*, still besieged by more Forces the *Carthaginians* had sent thither since the Death of *Amilcar*, he left the Command of the Army to his Son *Archagathus*, and repaired to *Sicily*, where he no sooner arrived, than all the Cities of the Island, having heard what noble Exploits he had performed in *Africa*, strove who should first throw themselves under his Obedience, so that entirely expelling the *Carthaginians* thence, he became absolute Master of the whole Country.

Amilcar taken Prisoner, and murdered in Syracuse.

Agathocles makes himself Master of Sicily, and returns to Africa.

Upon his Return to *Africk*, he found the Soldiers revolting against his Son, because he had delayed the Payment of their Arrears; and so dissatisfied were they, that he found it necessary to secure his Person by embarking for *Syracuse* in the same Ships which had just brought him from thence; whereupon his Army capitulated with the *Carthaginians*, and surrendered themselves, first killing *Agathocles*'s Sons, whom they had taken as they were endeavouring to escape with their Father. After this, the *Carthaginians* sent new Commanders into *Sicily* to prosecute the War, with whom *Agathocles* concluded a Peace upon reasonable Conditions; and having thus rid himself of the *Carthaginians* again, and subdued all *Sicily* to his Obedience, he, as if he had been too strictly confined in the narrow Limits of an Island, transported his Army into *Italy*, after the Example of *Dionysius*, and took several Cities there; but a most violent Distemper seizing on him, and his Son and Grandson taking up Arms against each other for the Crown, obliged him to return to *Sicily*, where he soon after died.

Agathocles flies to Syracuse.

Peace between Agathocles and the Carthaginians.

Agathocles dies.
A. M. 3662.
Pyrrhus aids the Sicilians,

About this time *Pyrrhus*, King of *Epirus*, was engaged in a War against the *Romans*, and being implored by the *Sicilians* to come to their Assistance against the *Carthaginians*, he arriving at *Syracuse*, took several Cities, and joined the Title of King of *Sicily* to that of *Epyrus*. He defeated the *Carthaginians* in several Battels, but some time after his Allies in *Italy*, by their Deputies, acquainting him that they were not able to make head against the *Romans*, and that if he delayed to relieve them, they should be soon necessitated to surrender, he resolved, if possible, first to finish the War in *Sicily* by one decisive Battel with the *Carthaginians*, and accordingly fought, and entirely routed them; but, notwithstanding his great Successes, he immediately quitted *Sicily*, and fled like one conquered, for which reason all his Allies deserted his Interests, and revolted from him, so that he lost the Kingdom of *Sicily* in as short a time

and routs the Carthaginians in Sicily.

a time as he had acquired it; and the same ill Fortune attending him in *Italy*, he was constrained at last to return to *Epirus*.

Pyrrhus was a Prince of vast Projects and Designs, as may be judged, among many other Instances, from the extravagant Fancy, as *Pliny* tells us, he once entertained of laying a Bridge over from *Greece* to *Italy*, in order to march his Army into that Country. The Place where he designed to build it was in the Mouth of the *Adriatick* Gulph, to reach from *Oricum*, (now *Val del Orso*) a City of *Epirus*, a few Miles South of *Apollonia*, to *Hydruntum* in *Italy*, (now *Otranto*) where it is about fifty Miles over; but it being a very deep and tempestuous Sea, and the Distance so great, he found it impossible to put his Project in Execution. He was certainly one of the greatest Instances of good and bad Fortune which History affords; for as in his Prosperity every thing fell out above his Expectation, witness his Victories in *Italy* and *Sicily*, and so many Triumphs over the *Romans*; so now, when the Wheel turned about, this same Fortune destroyed the Work of her own Hands, and increased the Loss of *Sicily* with the Ruin of his Navy at Sea, an unsuccessful Battel with the *Romans*, and a dishonourable Retreat out of *Italy*. After he had quitted *Sicily*, *Hieron* was constituted chief Magistrate of the Island, who behaved himself with so much Moderation, that all the Cities, by unanimous Consent, made him their Generalissimo against the *Carthaginians*, and afterwards their King.

Pyrrhus, a Prince of vast Designs.

Pyrrhus his Navy ruined at Sea.

Hieron chief Magistrate of Sicily

A. M. 3675.

Chap. XIII.

Of the Naval Wars of the Romans, *from their first vigorous Application to the Sea in the first* Punick *War, to the Conclusion of the said War.*

THE *Romans* having about this time reduced all *Italy* to their Obedience as far as the Streights of *Messana*, there they stopt a while, as *Florus* expresses it, like a devouring Flame which has raged through a whole Forest, till the Course of a River falling through it, has a little stayed its Fury. Here having within their View a rich and flourishing Island, which seemed, as it were, cut off from *Italy*, they, since they could not join it by Land, determined to annex it to their Dominions by force of Arms; for attempting whereof, there offered a very specious Pretence; for just at that time, the *Mamertines*, a People in the Northern Parts of the Island, who were besieged in *Messana* by *Hieron*, King of *Sicily*, implored their Assistance, and complained of the *Carthaginians*, their late Allies, who now joined with *Hieron* against them; which People, as we have already observed, aspired to the Dominion of this Island, as well as the *Romans*; and, indeed, the principal Motive

The Romans have a Design on Sicily.

Motive to this War was their exorbitant Power, they having not only subdued *Africa*, but made themselves Masters of many Places in *Spain*, together with *Sardinia*, and all the adjacent Islands on the Coast of *Italy*; so that the *Romans* had reason to look on their Neighbourhood with an Eye of Jealousy, being, as it were, now surrounded by them. And knowing that they had Designs on *Italy* it self, they foresaw how formidable they would grow by the Accession of all *Sicily* to their State, which, unless they interposed to prevent it, by assisting the *Mamertines*, they perceived would certainly fall into their Hands: For since *Messana* would soon be theirs, *Syracuse* could not then be long able to withstand them, the Territory of which two Places contained a principal Part of the Island. Maturely considering these things, and that it would by no means be safe for them to abandon those of *Messana* in this Juncture, and permit the *Carthaginians* to be Masters of a Post which might prove, as it were, a Bridge to convey them into *Italy*, the Senate passed a Decree for War, which was confirmed by an Ordinance of the People: And *Appius Claudius*, one of the Consuls, was ordered to conduct an Army forthwith into *Sicily* to the Relief of *Messana*.

The Romans declare War against Carthage.

Year of the World, 3685. Of Rome, 488.

With a small Fleet consisting of Ships belonging to the *Locrenses*, *Tarentines* and *Neapolitans*, (for the *Romans* had then none of their own) he, with much danger and difficulty, passed the Streights, but so successful he was, that he raised the Siege of *Messana* in a short time, and after that defeated both *Hieron* and the *Carthaginians*, in two several Battels. These Victories frightening *Hieron* into Obedience, he entered into a Treaty of Peace and Friendship with the *Romans*, who vigorously prosecuting the War against the *Carthaginians*, now ventured to Sea with a Fleet of their own, consisting of a hundred Gallies of five Tire of Oars, and twenty of three: Their wonderful Diligence and Success in building whereof, and their Method of instructing the People to use their Oars, we have related in the first Book. After they had sufficiently exercised themselves ashore, in the manner there described, they embarked on board the Fleet, and went out to put what they had learn'd in Practice, at which time *Caius Cornelius*, who was General at Sea, was absent on an Expedition to *Messana*, with seventeen Ships under his Command, to give Directions for the Reception and Security of the Fleet; during whose Continuance there, an Occasion seemed to present for the surprizing of *Lipara*, one of the *Æolian* Islands, to which Place he therefore repaired with his Ships; but *Hannibal*, who commanded the *Carthaginian* Fleet, then lying at *Panormus*, (now *Palermo*) having Intelligence of his Design, detached a strong Squadron after him under the Command of *Boodes*, who blocked him up in the Harbour of *Lipara*, and forced him to surrender with all his Ships. Yet not long after this Adventure of *Cornelius*, it wanted but little that *Hannibal* himself had been taken in the like Snare; for receiving Advice that the *Roman* Fleet was at Sea, and cruising on the Coast of *Italy* not far off, he, with fifty Gallies stretched a-head of his Fleet, to view, and be himself a Witness of their

The Romans defeat Hieron and the Carthaginians.

The Roman Fleet block'd up at Lipara by Hannibal.

CHAP. XIII. *Dissolution of the* Rom. *Empire.* 121

their Number and Posture; but the *Romans* happening to be nearer than he was aware of, surprized him with their whole Fleet in Order of Battel, in which Rencounter he lost the greatest Part of his Squadron, and escaped narrowly himself, when every Body despaired of his Safety. The *Romans* after this made the best of their way for *Sicily*, and receiving Advice of the Defeat of *Cornelius*, sent immediately for *Duilius*, who then had the Command of their Land-Forces in the Island: But while they attended his coming, having Intelligence that the Enemy's Fleet was at hand, they prepared to engage them. Their Vessels not being built with extraordinary Art, and they finding them to be somewhat unwieldy in working, it came into their Thoughts to help this Defect by some Invention which might be of Use to them in Fight: And then was devised that Machine called the *Corvus*, which was framed after this manner: They erected on the Prow of their Gallies a round Piece of Timber of about a Foot and a half Diameter, and near twelve Feet long, on the Top whereof they had a Block or Pully. About this Piece of Timber they framed a Stage or Platform of Boards, four Feet broad, and about eighteen Feet long, which was well framed and fastened with Iron. The Entrance was longways, and moved about the foresaid upright piece of Timber, as on a Spindle, so that it could be hoisted up within six Feet of the top; and about this was a sort of Parapet Knee high, which was defended with upright Bars of Iron sharpened at the ends, towards the top of each of which there was a Ring, by which Rings it was slung, and by help of the Pully hoisted and lower'd at Pleasure. With these Machines they attacked the Enemy's Gallies sometimes on their Bows, and sometimes on their Broadsides, as Occasion best served; and whenever they thus grappled, if they happened to swing Broadside to Broadside, they entered from all Parts; but in case they attacked them on the Bow, they entered two and two by the help of this Engine, the foremost defending the fore part, and those which followed the Flanks, keeping the Boss of their Bucklers level with the top of the Parapet.

Hannibal's Fleet routed.

Romans invent an Engine to grapple the Carthaginian Gallies.

Duilius, leaving the Land Army to the Conduct of the Colonels, hastened aboard the Fleet, which he found waiting the Motions of the Enemy in this Posture. Upon his Arrival, he received Advice that they ravaged the Country on the Coast of *Mylæ*, (now *Melazzo*) whereupon he made the best of his way with the whole Fleet to encounter them. The *Carthaginians* greatly rejoiced when they descried the *Romans*, and with a hundred and thirty of their Ships stood off to Sea towards them, whom they held in so great Contempt, that, without any Order of Battel, they advanced with their Prows directly upon them, depending on certain Victory.

The Carthaginian Fleet overcome by Duilius.

The *Carthaginian* Fleet was commanded by *Hannibal*, whose own Gally was of seven Tire of Oars, the same which formerly belonged to *Pyrrhus*, King of *Epirus*; but approaching nearer, they became greatly surprized at the Sight of the *Roman* Engines, and stood some time in Suspence at the Novelty, having never before seen the like. However, the headmost, by the Boldness of their Attack,

R

Attack, made it appear how little they valued them: But the *Romans* grappling with them by the Help of their Machines, entered with ease, and came to fight hand to hand upon Deck, as on firm Ground. Some of the *Carthaginians* were slain, others yielded upon Quarter, frighted at the extraordinary Effect of this new and wonderful Invention, insomuch that they lost of those which came first to engage, thirty Ships with their whole Companies, of which Number the Admiral-Gally was one, *Hannibal* himself making his Escape in a small Boat, after having performed the Duty of a gallant and able Leader. At length the rest of the Fleet came up, but when they perceived the Defeat of their first Squadron, they held it not safe to tempt their Fortune too far, being not a little surprized at the Sight of those new Engines. However, having greatly the Advantage in the Lightness of their Ships, they used their best Skill, by nimbly rowing round them, to attack them with most Safety: But when they observed that which way soever they approach'd, those Machines were still traversed, and opposed to them, they were at length compelled to yield the Honour of the Day to the *Romans*, retiring with the Loss of fifty of their Ships, three thousand Men being slain, and seven thousand taken Prisoners. Immediately hereupon the *Romans* landed their Forces in the Island, marched to the Relief of *Egesta*, which was straitly pressed by the Enemy, which having raised, they from thence, in a Breath, marched to the Attack of *Macella*, and took it by Assault.

Egesta relieved, and Macella taken by the Romans.

These Successes were so unexpected at *Rome*, that the Senate decreed *Duilius* unusual Honours; for, besides his obtaining the Glory of the first Naval Triumph, he was ever after attended from Supper with Musick and Flambeaus, as if the Celebration of his Victories was to last his whole Life-time; and a Pillar was also erected to him in the *Forum*, adorned with the Beaks of Ships, on the top whereof was placed his Statue. *Hannibal*, being thus defeated at Sea, returned with the Remainder of the Fleet to *Carthage*, and after he was reinforced with more Ships and able Officers, he put to Sea for *Sardinia*, where he was no sooner arrived but he was surprized in Harbour by the *Romans*, who took many of his Ships, which Misfortune begat a Mutiny in the Remainder of the Army, who seized on his Person and crucified him. *Lucius Cornelius Scipio*, and *C. Aquilius Florus*, being now Consuls, they, at the Head of a considerable Fleet, forced the *Carthaginians* to retire, and ravaged the Islands of *Sardinia* and *Corsica*, which were still in the *Carthaginian* Interest. They took *Albia*, a Sea-Port of *Sardinia*, where they celebrated very honourably the Funeral of *Hanno*, the *Carthaginian* Admiral, who was slain bravely fighting in the Defence of that Place, and returning victoriously to *Rome*, they were also honoured with a Naval Triumph, after which they erected a Temple to the Gods which preside over Tempests, in Remembrance of their being delivered from a great Storm off of *Corsica*.

Honours decreed to Duilius.

Hannibal surprized at Sardinia, and crucified.

Success of the Romans.

The *Romans*, encouraged by the good Success they met with in their first Naval Battels, looking upon themselves to be already Masters of *Sicily*, resolved to carry the War into *Africa*, and attack the Enemy

CHAP. XIII. *Dissolution of the* Rom. *Empire.* 123

Enemy at home, that so they might find Employment in the Defence and Preservation of their own Country, while they were sollicitous to contest for the Mastery of *Sicily*. To this purpose they assembled a Fleet of three hundred and thirty Sail, with which repairing to *Messana*, they left Orders for the Management of Affairs there, and standing along the Coast of *Sicily*, having doubled the Promontory of *Pachinus*, (now Cape *Passaro*) they stretched away towards *Ecnome*, where their Land-Forces then were, in order to pass directly over to *Africa*. The *Carthaginians* resolved to oppose this Design with their utmost Power, and arriving with a Fleet of three hundred and fifty Sail off *Heraclea Minoa*, offered the *Romans* Battel, who accepting it, disposed their Fleet into four Divisions. The two Consuls, *M. Attilius Regulus*, and *L. Manlius*, were in the two Admiral-Gallies in the Front of their distinct Squadrons, each of them just a-head of their own Divisions, and a-breast of the other, the first Fleet being posted on the Right, and the second on the Left, making two long Files, or Lines of Battel: And whereas it was necessary to give a due Space between each Gally to ply their Oars, and keep clear one of another, and to have their Heads or Prows looking somewhat outwards, this manner of drawing up did therefore naturally form an Angle, the Point whereof was at the two Admiral-Gallies, which were near together; and as their two Lines were prolonged, so the Distance grew consequently wider and wider towards the Rear. In this manner were the first and second Divisions disposed. The third was drawn up Front-ways, in the Rear of the first and second, and so stretching along from Point to Point composed a Triangle, whereof this third Line was the Base. Their Vessels of Burthen, which carried their Horses and Baggage, being placed in the Rear of these, were, by the Help of small Boats, provided for that purpose, towed after them. In the Rear of all was the fourth Division, drawn up likewise in Rank, or Frontways, parallel to the third; so that the whole formed a Triangle, of which the *Area* was void, and the Base contained what we have already mentioned. In this Figure were they disposed for all that could happen, nor would it have been an easy matter to have broken them; and when the *Carthaginians* had observed how they were drawn up, they then determined after what manner to form their Battel: Accordingly they dispos'd their Fleet into four Divisions, and drew it out into one long File, that part of the Right of this Line stretching a great way out into the Sea, as if they intended to surround the *Romans*; the fourth Division, which was the Left of the Line, keeping close under the Shore, disposed in form of a *Forceps*, or Pair of Pincers. *Hanno* was on the Right with the first Division, having with him all the nimble and best rowing Vessels of the Fleet, being such as were proper to attack and retreat, and for their Lightness could row round the *Romans*. *Amilcar* was to have had the Command of the Left Wing, but removed into the Centre, which consisted of the second and third Divisions, where he devised a Stratagem which shewed him an Officer of no small Experience. The *Romans* having observed that the *Carthaginians*, by spreading their

The Roman *and* Carthaginian *Fleets prepare for Battel.*

In what manner the Roman *Fleet was drawn up.*

How the Carthaginians *formed their Battel.*

R 2 Fleet

The Fight between the Romans and Carthaginians. Fleet to so great an Extent, were by that means but thinly drawn up, they therefore attacked them in the middle of their Line; but the *Carthaginians*, pursuant to the Orders they had received, immediately retreated, with design to separate the *Romans*, and put them in disorder by the pursuit, who accordingly pressed on after them. The first and second Divisions were those which engaged in the Pursuit of the *Carthaginians*, who feigned to fly; and thus the *Roman* Fleet became disjoined, the third Division remaining with the Baggage in a Tow, and the fourth keeping their Post in the Rear of all. Now when the *Carthaginians* judged the first and second Divisions to be sufficiently distanced from the rest, the Signal was given from *Amilcar's* Gally, whereupon that Part of their Fleet which was chased by the *Romans* immediately tacked, and made head against them. The Battel now grew warm every where, and although the *Carthaginians* had the Advantage in the Lightness and ready Working of their Gallies, whether it were to advance or retreat, as Occasion required, which they performed with great Readiness and Facility, nevertheless the *Romans* lost not their Assurance of Success in the end, finding themselves better Men when they come to the Sword's Point, and having great Trust in their Engines, wherewith they grappled and boarded the Enemy. *Hanno*, who commanded the Right of the Line, and was at a good Distance from the Place where the Battel began, bore down, and attacked the fourth Division of the *Romans*, where he succeeded so well, as to reduce them to the last Extremity: Mean while, that Squadron of the *Carthaginians* which was posted on the Left under the Shore, ranged themselves into a Front, and turning their Prows upon the Enemy, charged the third Division which had the Guard of the Baggage and Horse Ships; whereupon the *Romans* casting off the Ships they had in a Tow, received the *Carthaginians*, and fought them with great Bravery.

Three Naval Battels at the same time. Now might be seen three Naval Battels fought at one and the same time in three several Places; but the Parties engaging being of equal Strength, it happened, as for the most part it doth in the like Adventures, that Fortune gave the Victory to that side for whom she first began to declare; so that *Amilcar*, not being able to sustain the first Shock of the *Romans*, was beaten, and betook himself to flight; *Manlius* towing away such of his Ships as he had taken. In the mean while *Regulus* perceiving the great Danger the fourth Division was in, and the Vessels which carried their Equipage, advanced to their Relief with the second Division, which remained yet entire; whereupon the *Romans*, in that fourth Division, now well-nigh vanquished, observing with what Bravery he attacked *Hanno*, took heart, and renewed the Battel; insomuch that he seeing himself assaulted from all Quarters, both in Front and Rear, and that *Regulus*, contrary to all Expectation, had thus come up and joined the Fleet, by which means he was in danger of being quite surrounded, yielded the Day to the *Romans*, and flying, got off to Sea. At the same time *Manlius*, who was now returned from the Chace, observing that the third Fleet of the *Romans* had been forced under the Shore by the Enemy's Left Wing, where they

held

CHAP. XIII. *Dissolution of the* Rom. *Empire.* 125

held them surrounded, came up to their Relief, and was seconded by *Regulus,* who had now rescued the fourth Division and Baggage Vessels, and left them safe. And indeed this Part of their Fleet was in great Danger, and had been lost e'er this, if the *Carthaginians,* frighted at their new Engine, could have had Resolution to attack them, but they barely contented themselves to force them on upon the Shore, and there to keep them beset, not daring to attempt or approach them, for fear of being grappled by their *Corvi.* In short the *Carthaginians* were quickly surrounded by the *Romans,* who routing them, took fifty of their Ships with their Equipage, very few, either of Soldiers or Seamen, escaping. Such was the Success of these three Battels fought in one Day, in all which the *Romans* were Victors. They lost but twenty four of their own Gallies, and those perished against the Shore; but of the *Carthaginians* above thirty were destroyed. On their Side not a Ship was taken, but of the *Carthaginians* sixty three. *The Carthaginians routed.*

The *Romans,* after this Success, having first repaired and equipped the Ships they had taken from the Enemy, and well refreshed their Army, set Sail for *Africk,* and when the Van of their Fleet had gained the *Promontory Hermæa* (now *Cape bona)* they there lay by, and attended the coming up of the rest of the Fleet, by which being joined, they stood along the Coast, till they came up with *Clupea,* where they made their Descent, drawing up their Gallies in the Port, which they secured with a Ditch and Palisade, and laying Siege to the Town, made themselves Masters of it in a short time. Having left a good Garrison for Defence of the Place, and the Country about it, they marched further up with their whole Army to forage and spoil, in which Expedition they plundered and destroyed many noble Buildings, took much Booty of all sorts of Cattel, and at least twenty thousand Prisoners, which they brought down to their Ships; and this they performed without any Opposition. Receiving Orders from the Senate that only one of the Consuls should continue in *Africk* with a competent Strength to prosecute the War, and the other return back to *Rome* with the rest of the Army, *Regulus* remained with forty Ships, fifteen thousand Foot, and five thousand Horse, and *Manlius* returned along the Coast of *Sicily* to *Rome* with the rest of the Army, carrying with him many Prisoners. *The Romans sail for Africa. Romans take Clupea, and do great Mischief.*

The Senate, not long after, received the unwelcome News that the *Carthaginians,* being reduced almost to Despair by the hard Conditions offered them by *Regulus,* (without which no Peace could be obtained) had sent to *Lacedæmon* for *Xantippus,* a most experienced General, and that under his Conduct they had killed thirty thousand *Romans,* taken *Regulus* alive, with fifteen hundred others, and closely besieged in *Clupea* two thousand Soldiers, who alone escaped from the Battel. Upon this Advice they immediately dispatched to Sea the Consuls *Servius* and *Æmilius,* with a Fleet of three hundred and fifty Gallies, who, by that time they reached the Height of Cape *Hermæa* beforementioned, fell in with the *Carthaginian* Fleet, which they entirely routed, taking a hundred and fourteen Gallies with *The Romans beat the Carthaginians off of Cape Hermæa.*

with all their Equipage; from whence proceeding on to *Clupea*, they raised the Siege of that Place, received their Troops on board, and shaped their Course back to *Sicily*; but being well advanced on their Way, they were surprized, off of *Camarina*, with so dreadful a Tempest, that the Losses and Hardships they sustained were without Example and beyond Expression: So terrible it was that of three hundred and seventy odd Sail that composed their Fleet, fourscore only escaped Shipwreck, the rest either foundering in the Sea, or were lost against the Rocks, insomuch that the Coast was covered with dead Bodies, and the Fragments of Ships.

The Romans suffer extremely in a Tempest.

The *Carthaginians*, upon this Misfortune of the *Romans*, were of Opinion that they should now be a Match for them at Sea, so that conceiving Hopes of recovering *Sicily*, they sent thither *Asdrubal*, with a Fleet of three hundred Sail, a great Army, and a hundred and fifty Elephants; who would certainly have made himself Master of the Island, had not the *Romans*, with wonderful Celerity, fitted out a hundred and twenty Gallies to join the eighty that escaped Shipwreck, with which Force they took *Panormus* by Assault, the most important Place the *Carthaginians* held in the whole Island. Encouraged by this Success they sailed the next Year toward *Africa*, with Design to make a Descent there, but found the Coasts so well guarded by the *Carthaginians* that they could not effect their Purpose; and being unacquainted with the Coast, they were got down so far Southward as the lesser *Syrtis*, or the *Flats*, where falling among the Sands, the Gallies stuck fast, and there remained till the Flood lifted them off, when, with great Difficulty and Hazard, throwing their Lumber over-board, they made a Shift to escape. From thence they stood away for the Coast of *Sicily*, and got into the Port of *Panormus*, but steering their Course homeward, they, by a Storm in the Streight of *Messana*, (where, by a blind Obstinacy, they were embayed) lost above a hundred and fifty of their Ships. These Calamities induced them to quit all farther Attempts, at Sea, and totally to rely on their Land Armies; but continuing not long in this Resolution, they fitted out a Fleet of two hundred Sail, which they sent to *Sicily* under the Consul *C. Attilius*, who investing *Lilybæum* (now *Marsala*) lay a whole Year before that Place, which, notwithstanding the *Roman* Fleet, *Hannibal*, the Son of *Amilcar*, succoured with a Body of Troops, and a great Supply of Provisions, with only fifty Gallies.

Asdrubal sent with a Fleet to Sicily.

The Romans take Panormus, and proceed to Africa.

their Gallies on the Syrtis in Danger.

and lost in the Streights of Messana.

Hannibal succours Lilybæum.

The next Year the *Romans* were re-inforced with ten thousand Men under the Command of the Consul *Clodius*, with which they thought of nothing less than surprizing *Adherbal*, the *Carthaginian* Admiral, and that not one of his Ships should escape out of their Hands, but were themselves surprized when they saw *Adherbal* near [b] *Drepranum*, in a Posture ready to give them Battel. He bravely sustained the Charge of the whole *Roman* Fleet, thrice as numerous as his own, and managed his Gallies, which were of an excellent built, with utmost Dexterity, they being manned by most expert Seamen, who were well acquainted with the Coast and Depth of Water, while the *Romans*, destitute of this Advantage, either run aground

[b] *Trepano del Valle.*
A Sea Fight between the Romans and Carthaginians.

on

CHAP. XIII. *Dissolution of the* Rom. *Empire.* 127

on the Sands, or were lost against the Rocks; and oftentimes endeavouring to grapple the *Carthaginians* with their Engines, or transfix them with their Beaks, they artfully retired to Shelves, and dangerous Places, whence the *Romans* could not possibly escape; so that the Consul observing the Distress of his Fleet, he with about thirty Gallies stood away toward *Lilybæum*, leaving ninety three with the *Carthaginians*, and very few of the Men that were thrown on the Shore escaped. This Loss of the *Romans* was followed by one no less in the same Year; for the other Consul, *Junius*, receiving Orders from the Senate to go with a great Convoy of Provisions to the Army before *Lilybæum*, as he was performing that Service, *Carthalo*, a *Carthaginian* Captain, encountered him with a hundred Sail, took several of the Barks, and so harassed the Consul, that he was obliged to retire to an open harbourless Coast, where, in a violent Storm, not one of his Ships escaped, nor was there so much saved as a whole Plank of all his Squadron, which consisted of sixty Sail.

The Romans lose many Gallies to the Carthaginians.

The Romans shipwreckt in a Storm.

The *Romans*, after so great Losses by Sea, resolved to content themselves with keeping Possession of what they had in *Sicily*, and to defend the Coasts of *Italy*; and the Garrison of ᶜ *Eryx*, a Town in the westermost Parts of *Sicily*, made a brave Defence against the *Carthaginians*, who besieged it two Years, while the Fleet that they kept at Sea for Defence of the Coasts, not only prevented the Enemy's making Descents in *Italy*, but chased them as far as the Island *Æginurus* (now *Zimbala*) on the Coast of *Africa*, and there entirely defeating them, took a great Booty, which however they did not long enjoy, being forced by a Storm into the *Syrtis*, where they were almost all shipwrecked; and this deprived the Consuls *Fabius* and *Buteo* of an expected Triumph. The *Romans* however took Courage, and since the publick Treasury was now exhausted, many private Persons joined, some two, and some three together, for building and equipping a Gally at their own Charge, according to the Model of a *Rhodian* Gally that was taken from the *Carthaginians* before *Lilybæum*: So that every one lending a helping Hand to the Work, they, in a short time, fitted out a Fleet of two hundred Sail. The *Carthaginians* having Advice of this, sent out *Hanno* to *Sicily* with two hundred and fifty Gallies, and a considerable Number of large Ships of Burthen, well provided with all Necessaries, who was ordered to convey a Supply of Provisions into the Town of *Eryx*, (which was possessed by the *Carthaginians*, as was the Citadel by the *Romans*,) and having lighten'd his Gallies, to join the Forces under *Amilcar Barcas*, with whom he was to act against the *Romans*; but *Lutatius* the Consul being informed of *Hanno*'s Arrival on the Coasts of *Sicily*, and suspecting his Design, he took on board the Choice of his Land Forces, and sailed to *Ægusa*, (now *Favagnana*) where he resolved to wait and give the Enemy Battel, notwithstanding the Wind was against him, and consequently favoured them, for that by so doing he should engage with *Hanno* only, and the Troops that embarked with him, whose Fleet was encumber'd with Stores and Provisions. It was not long before the

ᶜ *Trepani del Monte.*

The Carthaginians defeated, but the Romans suffer by Tempest.

The Romans contribute towards building a Fleet.

the Enemy were descry'd coming down with a flown Sheet, whereupon he stood out of the Port, and drawing into a Line of Battel made directly towards them; for his Seamen being in good plight, and well exercised, they surmounted all Difficulties, and advanced in a regular Order. In fine, the *Carthaginian* Ships, being very much pester'd, were but in an ill Condition for fight, so that the Controversy was soon decided, the *Romans* routing them at the first Encounter. Fifty of their Gallies were sunk and seventy taken with all their Men aboard; and when the News of this Defeat reached *Carthage*, though it surprized, yet did it not humble them, for they would willingly have continued the War, could they have found means to sustain it, but of that they had no Prospect; for while the *Romans* continued Masters at Sea, there was no Way whereby to succour and support their Forces in *Sicily*: Wherefore they dispatched full Powers to *Amilcar Barcas*, their General in that Island, to act in this Conjuncture as he should judge most conducive to the Welfare of the Commonwealth, who thereupon sent Ambassadors to the Consul to treat about a Peace, and the following Project was offered.

The Carthaginians worsted on the Coast of Sicily.

"That there should be a good, firm, and lasting Peace and Friendship between the *Romans* and *Carthaginians* upon these Conditions. The *Carthaginians* shall entirely evacuate *Sicily*. They shall not make further War upon *Hiero*, nor the *Syracusans*, nor their Allies. That they shall deliver up all the *Roman* Prisoners Ransom-free, and pay to the *Romans*, within the Space of twenty Years, [d]two thousand and two hundred *Euboic* Talents of Silver, and that this Treaty shall be valid and good if the People of *Rome* shall approve and ratify the same.

A Project for Peace, which was, with some Alterations, concluded.

[d] *That is, according to Thomasius, 385000 l. Sterling.*

These Articles were forthwith forwarded to *Rome*, but the People not being entirely satisfied, ten Plenipotentiaries were sent to *Sicily*, with Instructions, when they had thoroughly informed themselves of the State of Affairs, to determine on the Place what should appear to them reasonable, who shorten'd the time for Payment of the Money to ten Years, and would, besides, have a [e] thousand Talents more paid down, and an Article added that the *Carthaginians* should evacuate the Islands between *Italy* and *Sicily*. After the Conclusion of this Treaty, *Lutatius* returned to *Rome*, and celebrated a Naval Triumph, as his Prætor *Q. Valerius* also did, in consideration of the Share he had in the Victory, by commanding the Fleet after *Lutatius*'s Wounds confined him to his Bed. And further, in Regard of the great Importance of this Victory, Medals were struck in Honour of *Lutatius*, having a Quinquereme, or Gally of five Tire of Oars, encompass'd with a Civic Crown, composed of oaken Leaves, as a Token that the Lives and Safety of his Fellow-Citizens were owing to his Courage and Conduct. Thus determined the War that was waged between the *Romans* and *Carthaginians* for the Mastery of *Sicily*; which, as it had continued full four and twenty Years, so was it one of the most memorable that History hath recorded, they having once fought at Sea with five hundred Gallies, comprehending both Fleets, and afterwards with few less than seven

[e] 175000.

Observation on the Naval Strength of Rome and Carthage.

or

hundred. The *Romans* loſt, during this Conteſt, either by Tempeſt, or taken by the Enemy, ſeven hundred Ships, and the *Carthaginians* five hundred; ſo that if People were ſurprized at the Naval Battels of *Antigonus*, *Ptolemy*, and *Demetrius*, they had much more Cauſe of Admiration at the Account of theſe ſtupendous Tranſactions. And if, by comparing theſe with the Fleets wherewith the *Perſians* waged War againſt the *Greeks*, and the *Athenians* and *Lacedæmonians* among themſelves, we conſider the Difference between the *Roman* Gallies, which were all of five Tire of Oars, and theirs, which had but three, or leſs, we ſhall find that there was never before ſuch a mighty Force brought together on the Sea. All which Obſervations *Polybius*, (whom we have cloſely followed in the Deſcription of this War,) concludes with this fine Remark, " That from hence " it will become manifeſt it was not owing to Fortune, or Accident, " (as ſome *Grecians* believ'd,) that the *Romans* now began to aim " at the Dominion of the World, and at length accompliſhed their " End, but that they were led thereunto by the moſt likely and pro- " bable Meaſures Reaſon could ſuggeſt, after having acquired, by " being ſo long engaged in ſuch and ſo great Affairs, a thorough " Knowledge and Experience of their Abilities to compaſs their " Deſign.

C H A P. XIV.

Of the Naval Wars of the Romans *from the Concluſion of the firſt* Punic *War to the End of the ſecond.*

THE *Romans* were now in peaceable Poſſeſſion of all *Sicily*, except a ſmall Part of it which was enjoy'd by *Hieron*, their Ally, and maintain'd a good Correſpondence with the *Carthaginians* for ſome time, till ſeveral Merchants, tempted by private Gain, were found to have ſupply'd Proviſions by Sea to ſome of the Enemies of the *Carthaginians*, who, however, upon making Complaint thereof received due Satisfaction; but a ſhort time after a Body of Troops in the Pay of *Carthage*, retiring in Diſcontent to *Sardinia*, invited the *Romans* to take Poſſeſſion of the Iſland, and receive them into their Protection. This favourable Opportunity of acquiring a Country ſo commodiouſly ſituated, and with ſo little Trouble too, they could not find in their Hearts to forego, but reſolved to make themſelves Maſters of it, and to declare War againſt the *Carthaginians*, if they ſhould attempt to diſturb them, who not being in a Condition to oppoſe theſe Proceedings, were obliged to ſtifle their Reſentments.

The Romans take Sardinia. Reduce the Coaſts of Liguria. now

Two Years after the *Romans* reduced the Coaſts of ⁕ *Liguria*, together with the Iſland of *Corſica*; whereupon enſued diverſe Battels with the *Ligurians* and *Corſicans*, together with ſome *Sardinians*, who joined with them, they having been all underhand ſollicited to revolt by the *Carthaginians*, who were glad of any Opportunity to

⁕ *the Republick of Genoa, and take Corſica.*

S find

find Employment for the *Romans,* and to weaken them by little and little, while they took Breath themselves, and prepared for another War; but the *Romans,* nevertheless, defeating their Enemies in several Engagements, remain'd Masters of both the Islands, and the whole Coast of *Liguria.*

[b] Croatia, Bosnia, and Dalmatia.

About this time died *Agron,* King of [b] *Illyricum,* after having made several Usurpations on his Neighbours, the *Epirots* and *Grecians,* which, his Widow, *Teuta,* continued with the same tyrannical Disposition. She surprized *Phœnice,* the Capital of *Epirus,* with a Fleet, and permitted her Subjects to rob and plunder all the Ships they met with on those Seas, by which Depredations they wholly interrupted the Commerce of *Italy* and *Greece* on that Side. The *Romans,* wearied with the daily Complaints the Merchants made to them, dispatched Ambassadors to Queen *Teuta,* by whom they desired her to put an End to those insupportable Violences of her Subjects, but notwithstanding she condescended to admit them to an Audience, she treated them with great Pride and Disdain, and told them that though she would take Care for the future that no publick Injuries should be done to the People of *Rome* by the *Illyrians,* yet was it not the Custom of Princes to forbid their Subjects to make their particular Profits of what they met with in the open Sea. The youngest of the *Roman* Ambassadors, highly incensed hereat, reply'd, with some Heat, that it being the Custom of the *Romans,* to make themselves publick Reparation for Injuries done in particular, and to yield Succour to those who received them, they would therefore soon use their Endeavours, with the Will of Heaven, to oblige her to change that Princely Custom; which Answer so provoked her, that, without Regard to the Law of Nations, she barbarously caused him to be murthered; and, instead of putting an End to these Violences, fitted out, early the following Spring, a considerable Fleet against the *Grecians,* which separating into three Squadrons, at one and the same time laid Siege to [c] *Corcyra,* [d] *Dyrrachium,* and [e] *Issa.*

Teuta, Queen of Illyricum, *reduced by the* Romans.

[c] Corfu.
[d] Durazzo.
[e] Lissa.
A. M. 3722.

The *Romans,* resolving to revenge this inhumane Usage of their Ambassador, set out a Fleet against the *Illyrians* of two hundred Sail, under the Command of *Cn. Fulvius,* one of the Consuls, and sent over the other Consul *Posthumius* at the Head of an Army of twenty thousand Foot, and two thousand Horse, which struck such a Terrour into them, that, in few Days, *Demetrius* of *Pharia,* who commanded, surrendered the Place to the *Romans,* who presently raised the Siege of *Dyrrachium* and *Issa*; and they having soon after reduced [f] *Apollonia* and *Nutria,* immediately thereupon all the Places the *Illyrians* possessed in *Greece* revolted to them, which they willingly received into their Friendship and Protection, and assisted them with forty Ships of War to secure them against the future Insults of their Enemies. The Queen hereupon retired to a strong Place called [g] *Rhizon,* and being now sufficiently humbled, obtained Peace of the *Romans* on these Conditions, " That she should " pay a yearly Tribute, such as the Senate should think fit to im- " pose; That she should relinquish entirely her Interest in *Illyricum,* " except some few Places; and that she should not navigate beyond " [h] *Lissus*

[f] Spinarza *in* Albania.

[g] Risine *in* Dalmatia.

CHAP. XIV. *Dissolution of the* Rom. *Empire.* 131

"*Lissus* with above two Vessels, and those to be unarmed." Thus the *Romans* being already Masters of *Italy*, and the Islands between that and *Africa*, began to extend their Conquests to this other Part of *Europe*, taking Care to keep a good Understanding with the *Grecians*, to whom, upon this Occasion, they sent an Ambassy, to acquaint them with the Motives which induced them to undertake this War against the *Illyrians*, lest otherwise they should take umbrage thereat; whereupon ensued a Treaty of Friendship and Alliance between them, and the Consul *Fulvius*, at his Return to *Rome*, was honoured with a Naval Triumph.

^h Alessio in Albania, at the Bottom of the Golfo del Drino.

A Treaty between the Romans and Grecians.

About this time the *Istri*, a People between *Italy* and *Illyricum*, at the Bottom of the *Adriatick*, practised Piracy on that Sea, and having seized and plundered several Ships bound with Corn to *Rome*, a Fleet was sent against them, whereby they were subdued, but not without considerable Loss; and *Pub. Cornelius Scipio*, one of the Consuls, who commanded on the Expedition, had the Honour of a maritime Triumph.

The Romans subdue the Istri.

After the *Romans* had reduced all *Illyricum*, they committed the Government thereof to *Demetrius* of *Pharia*, in Consideration of several great Services he had render'd them during the Continuance of the War; but he finding them taken up with a Quarrel against the Gauls, and that *Hannibal* was cutting out Work for them in *Spain*, by the Siege of *Saguntus*, put to Sea, with a Fleet of fifty Ships of War, ravaged the Islands *Cyclades*, set himself up for King of *Illyricum*, and having put to Death those whom he suspected to be in the *Roman* Interest, placed Garrisons in all the fortified Towns, particularly securing *Dimalum*, the Place of greatest Importance in the Country, and shut himself up with six thousand of the choicest of his Troops in ⁱ *Charia*, situate in an Island of the same Name. The *Romans*, to reduce this Traytor, sent over several Armies, but were not able to bring the War to a Conclusion, till the Consulship of *Livius Salinator*, who passing over with an Army, attacked *Dimalum* so vigorously, that it surrender'd in seven Days; which struck such a Terrour through all *Illyricum*, that the greatest Part of the Country returned to its Obedience, and submitted to the *Roman* Consul, who then re-imbarking his Troops, sailed toward *Pharia*, wherein *Demetrius* was; and arriving with his Army by Night on the Coast, he landed most of his Troops, directing them to conceal themselves in the Woods and hollow Ways, and, by Break of Day, he made Sail towards the next Port with twenty Gallies only, and came in Sight of the Town. *Demetrius* observing, and contemning their Number, marched out with Part of the Garrison to oppose their landing, and thereupon the Battel began, which was fought with great Obstinacy, Supplies of Men being constantly sent from the Town to sustain their Fellows, insomuch that by Degrees all the Garrison marched out. Mean while the *Romans* advanced who had landed by Night, covering themselves in their March in the best Manner they could, and having gained an Eminence between the Town and the Port, they cut off the Enemy's Retreat. Upon this the rest of the Gallies coming up, *Demetrius*'s Troops were presently put to Flight, and he

Demetrius of Pharia sets up for King of Illyricum.

ⁱ Lesina a Town and Island in the Gulph of Venice part of the Republick of Ragusa.

Demetrius defeated by the Romans.

S 2

he himself getting on board some Vessels he had placed in a neighbouring Creek to serve him in such an Exigence, made his Escape into *Macedonia*. The Consul presently possessed himself of the Town, which he demolished; and having settled the Affairs of the Kingdom, returned to *Rome*, where he obtained a magnificent Triumph, and acquired the Reputation of a wise and gallant Leader.

The second Punick War. A. M. 3731.

While the famous *Hannibal*, at the Head of fifteen thousand Foot, and twenty thousand Horse, forced his way through the *Pyrenæan* Mountains, and the *Alps*, reputed till then impassable, and descending into *Italy*, filled that Country with Terror and Amazement, the *Carthaginians* thought they could never have a fairer Opportunity to attempt the Recovery of *Sicily*. To this purpose they first fitted out a Squadron of twenty Gallies to cruise about the Island, and plunder the Coasts, which in crossing over met with a furious Storm that drove them on the Shore, where they fell into the Hands of King *Hieron*; who understanding by the Prisoners that they were suddenly to be followed by another Squadron of thirty five Sail, which were to endeavour to surprize *Lilybæum*, and prevail with the old Allies of the *Carthaginians* to revolt from the *Romans*, and declare for them, he advertised the *Roman* Prætor thereof, and having well provided for the Defence of *Lilybæum*, received with great Bravery the *Carthaginians*, they fighting but carelesly, as thinking themselves secure of Victory, insomuch that, at the first Charge, he took seven Gallies, with seventeen hundred Men on board, and put the rest to flight. The Consul *Sempronius* arriving soon after, he entirely secured that Island, and possessed himself also of the Town and Island of [k] *Melita*, which had hitherto been in the Hands of the *Carthaginians*.

The Carthaginians attempt to recover Sicily.

The Romans beat the Carthaginian Fleet,

and take Miletus from them.
[k] *Malta.*

The next Year *Asdrubal*, the *Carthaginian* General in *Spain*, not thinking himself able to cope with *Scipio*, who commanded there for the *Romans*, passed over to *Africk*, and made great Levies of Troops, with which, and forty Ships of War, he soon after returned to *Spain*, resolving utterly to expel the *Romans* thence: when *Scipio*, finding himself inferior to them by Land, embarked his choicest Troops on board his Ships, with which sailing to the Mouth of the [l]*Iber*, he surprized the *Carthaginian* Fleet, taking five and twenty Sail, and forcing the rest to secure themselves by flight; and then disbarking his Troops, he made himself Master of all that Coast, and attacked, and carried the Town of [m] *Honosca*. Marching on to [n] *Carthago Nova*, he burnt the Suburbs of that Place, laid waste all the neighbouring Country, and made himself so formidable, that above a hundred different Nations revolted to him from the *Carthaginians*; nor was it long e'er the [o] *Baleares* Islands submitted to him; all which, what by his Address and obliging Behaviour to the *Spaniards*, (to whom he restored their Children which *Asdrubal* had kept as Hostages) and what by means of a Reinforcement of thirty Gallies, and eight thousand Men sent from *Rome*, he entirely secured in the *Roman* Interest; and at the same time *Cn. Servilius Geminus*, who had the Government of *Sicily*, with the other Islands neighbouring to *Italy*, kept in awe the Coasts of *Sardinia*

[l] *River* Ebro.
Scipio beats Asdrubal at Sea, and many Nations revolt.
[m] *Suppos'd to be* Villa Joysa *near* Alicante.
[n] Carthagena.
[o] Majorca, Minorca, *and* Yviça

CHAP. XIV. *Dissolution of the* Rom. *Empire.*

dinia and *Corsica*, taking Hostages for their Fidelity. Passing over to *Africk*, he made a Descent, and ravaging the open Country, got a great Booty: But divers of his Men advancing in Disorder too far, fell into Ambuscades, by which he lost about a thousand. Having punished some of his Officers for Neglect of Duty in this Affair, he reimbarked his Troops, and returned to *Sicily*: and not long after *Sardinia* revolting, T. *Manlius* was sent over thither, where landing his whole Force, as well Seamen as Soldiers, he came to a Battel with the Islanders, whom he defeated, and took thirteen thousand of them; nor was it long e'er he overthrew twelve thousand *Carthaginians*, who were sent to aid them, of which above three thousand became his Prisoners, among whom were *Asdrubal* the General, with *Hanno* and *Mago*, the next principal Officers. By this good Success *Sardinia* was entirely subjected to the *Roman* Yoke, as was now almost all *Spain*, by the Victories which the two *Scipio*'s obtained over another *Asdrubal*, the Brother of *Hannibal*, who was at the same time laying *Italy* waste. *The Inhabitants of Sardinia revolting, are overcome by the Romans; as also the Carthaginians.*

As *Sicily* was the original Occasion of these Wars, the *Carthaginians*, who had gained a great Victory at *Cannæ*, resolved again to attempt the Conquest of that Island, while the vanquished *Romans* should, they hoped, find enough to do to defend the Walls of their City. To this purpose they equipped at the same time two Fleets, one of which attacked the Territories of *Hieron*, who had continued a faithful Ally to the *Romans* ever since his first Treaty with them. *Gelon*, the Son of this Prince, revolted from his Father, and declared for the *Carthaginians*,; but his Treason and Impiety were soon punished with Death. The other Fleet repaired to *Lilybæum*, where landing the Troops, they made a great Progress in those Parts, having brought over to their Interest the common People; and while these things were doing *Hieron* died, being in the ninetieth Year of his Age, leaving *Hieronymus*, the Son of *Gelon*, to succeed him in the Throne; for whom, because he was but fifteen Years old, he had appointed twelve Persons to administer Affairs, till he should come to Years of Discretion. One of these, to ingratiate himself with the young King, represented to him that at that Age it was not fit for a Prince to be under Tuition, whereupon he discarded the rest of his Guardians, retaining this Person as his first Minister; but following the Steps of his Father *Gelon*, he preferred the Friendship and Alliance of the *Carthaginians* to that of the *Romans*, and concluded a Treaty with them, that, after they had expelled the common Enemy out of the Island, the River *Himera*, which almost equally divides *Sicily* in two Parts, should be the Boundary of their respective Territories; but by his imprudent Administration, and his abandoning himself to his Pleasures, he soon alienated the Minds of his Subjects from him, and was shortly after assassinated at *Leontium*. *The Carthaginians attempt to recover Sicily. Hieron dies, and Hieronymus succeeds him. Hieronymus assassinated.*

The People of *Syracuse* themselves had all along been in the *Roman* Interest, but at length, by the Artifices of *Hippocrates* and *Epicides*, being brought over to the *Carthaginian* Party, they drew upon themselves the Resentments of the *Romans*, who sent *Marcellus*

Marcellus sent to besiege Syracuse.

cellus to besiege them by Sea and Land with a Fleet of sixty five Gallies, and a considerable Land Army. This City continued long impregnable, by means of the wonderful Machines which *Archimedes*, the great Mathematician, invented for the Defence of the Place, with some of which he threw Stones of a prodigious Weight upon the *Roman* Ships, with such Exactness, that they seldom or

Archimedes very much annoys the Romans.

never missed doing terrible Execution; and with other Machines, and from Loop-holes in the Walls, which he invented on this Occasion, he discharged whole Showers of Arrows at a time on the Gallies. But the most admirable Engine of all was one he made of an immense Magnitude, somewhat after the manner of a Swipe, or Draw-Bridge, which also threw out great Beams of Timber, and large Stones, and having first clear'd the Prows of the Gallies, the Men retiring all astern to avoid the Destruction they made, immediately thereupon the Person who managed the Machine let fall a large grappling Iron, fastened to a strong Chain, with which seizing the Prow of the Vessel, he let down the Counterpoise of the Machine, (which was balanced, as we have said, after the manner of a Swipe) and so raised the Vessel upright on her Poop in the Air, when by means of a certain Pully and Rope, disengaging the grappling Iron, down fell the Gally, which violently plunged in the Waves. After this manner were several of the *Roman* Vessels sunk; so that *Marcellus* despairing of reducing the Place by Force, resolved to do it by Famine, and to that purpose turned the Siege into a close Blockade, both by Sea and Land. Leaving *Appius* to command there, he himself advanced with a third Part of the Troops, and took in *Pelorus* and *Herbesus*, plundered *Megara*, and cut to pieces a great Number of *Syrusans*, who had found means to escape out of the City in order to join the *Carthaginians* under *Himilco*: Who having landed near *Heraclea* with fifteen thousand Foot, three thousand Horse, and twelve Elephants, seized that Place, as presently after he did ᵖ*Agrigentum*, and causing several Cities to revolt from the *Romans*, he threw a Supply of Provisions into *Syracuse*, to which Place *Marcellus* returning, he found there *Bomilcar*, the *Carthaginian* Admiral, with a Fleet of fifty five Gallies, who upon Advice that the *Roman* Fleet was advancing against him, and that it consisted of double his Strength, stayed not for better Intelligence, but made the best of his way back to *Carthage*.

The Siege turned into a Blockade.

Appius takes Pelorus, Herbesus, &c.

ᵖ *Gergenti.*

Bomilcar returns to Carthage.

Marcellus makes a general Assault.

Now was at hand the Celebration of the Feast of *Diana*, on which Festival *Marcellus*, as he was viewing the Works on an Eminence whence he could look into the Town, saw the People within crowned with Garlands, and revelling in Mirth and Wine; whereupon he resolved to make a general Assault the ensuing Night, and accordingly possessed himself of that part of the Town called *Epipolæ*, which being seated on a Hill, overlooked all the rest of the City, and offering to the Soldiers, as a Reward to their Valour, the Plunder of *Tycha* and *Neapolis*, two other Divisions of the Place lying next to that they had taken Post in, they immediately attacked and carried them also; so that there now remained only the *Achradina*, an Island in the Enemy's Hands, the latter of which

being

CHAP. XIV. *Dissolution of the* Rom. *Empire.* 135

being gained in few Days by Intelligence from within, *Achradina* presently surrendered, and thus, after three Year's Siege, was the City of *Syracuse* taken. This long Defence of it was chiefly owing, as we have said, to *Archimedes*, for whom, nevertheless, *Marcellus* entertained so great an Esteem, that he gave the strictest Orders for sparing his Person. But when the Place was taken, a Soldier coming in to plunder his House, and asking him hastily who he was, his Application was so intense on some Geometrical Figures he had drawn on the Ground, that he did not answer him to the purpose, but with great Earnestness begged him to stand out of the way, and not deface the Figures, whereupon the Soldier, eager to secure his Plunder, immediately kill'd him, to the great Grief of *Marcellus*, who very honourably interr'd him, and bestow'd singular Favours on his Relations.

Syracuse taken. A. M. 3736.

We should be wanting to the Subject we are treating of, as well as to the Respect due to the Memory of this great Master of the Mechanicks, should we omit giving an Account of the famous Ship it is said he built for *Hieron*, King of *Syracuse*, which we cannot better do, than in this Place. It was so extraordinary a Piece of Workmanship, that one *Moschion* wrote a particular Treatise concerning the same, the Substance whereof *Athenæus* has preserved to us in the fifth Book of his *Deipnosophistæ*. For the building of this Ship (he tells us) there was cut down on the Mountain *Ætna* so much Timber as would have made sixty ordinary Gallies: Besides which, the Wood for Tree-nails, Ribs, and Knees was procured from other Parts of *Sicily*, and from *Italy*; and Materials for Cordage were fetched from *Spain* and the River a *Rhodanus*, as were other Necessaries from various Places. King *Hieron* having hired a Number of Shipwrights, and other Workmen for this Service, placed *Archias*, a *Corinthian* Architect, over them, but all under the supreme Direction of *Archimedes*, and exhorting them diligently to carry on the Work, he, to encourage them thereto, would be whole Days present at their Labour. The Number of Men employed was three hundred Master-Workmen, besides their Servants, who in six Months time built the Ship up to the half of its design'd Heighth, and as the several Parts were finished, they covered them with Sheet-Lead, to preserve them from the Injuries of the Weather. When it was brought thus forward, *Hieron* gave Directions for removing it into the Sea, and that the rest of the Work should be perfected afloat; but how to get this vast Pile into the Water they knew not, till *Archimedes* invented the Engine called the *Helix*, by which, with the Assistance of very few Hands, he drew the Ship into the Sea; where, in six Months more, she was entirely compleated, and driven full of large Nails of Brass, many of ten Pound weight, and others of fifteen, which were let into the Timbers by large awger Holes, to rivet them well together, and cover'd on the outside with pitched Cloaths, over which were nailed Plates of Lead. The Ship had twenty Tire of Oars, and three Decks, to the lowest whereof, next the Hold, there was a Descent by several Pair of Stairs. The middle Deck had on each side of it fifteen Apartments for Dining,

A Description of the famous Ship of Hieron King of Syracuse.

a *Rhoine.*

each

each furnished with four Couches, such as they used to lie on at their Meals; and on the same Deck was also the Place for the Accommodation of the Mariners, whereon were fifteen Couches, and three large Chambers for Men and their Wives, each having three Beds, next which was the Kitchin for the Poop, the Floors of all which were paved with *Mosaick* Work, wherein was represented the whole Story of the Iliad; and suitable to so rich a Floor was the Workmanship of the Cielings and Door to each Apartment. On the upper Deck was a Place for Exercises, and a fine Walk, wherein were several Garden-Plots furnished with Plants of all kinds, which were watered by Leaden Pipes laid to them from a great Receptacle of fresh Water; where were also several Arbours of Ivy, and Vines set in Hogsheads of Earth, whose Roots were watered in like manner as the Plants. Next to these was an Apartment devoted to the Pleasures of Love, the Pavement whereof was of *Agate*, and other the richest Stones that were to be found in *Sicily*: The Roof was of *Cyprus*-Wood, and the Doors of Ivory and the Wood of the *Almug*-Tree. It had three Beds in it, and was richly adorned with Pictures, Statues, and drinking Vessels of exquisite Workmanship. Adjoining to this was a Room for Retirement and Conversation, which was furnished with five Couches, and wainscoted with Box, with Doors of the same Wood; within this there was a Library, and in the Cieling thereof a fine Clock, made in Imitation of the great Dial of *Syracuse*; as also a Bagnio, with three Cisterns of Brass, and a Bath which held forty Gallons, adorned with the Gems called *Tauromenites*. There were also a great Number of Cabins for the marine Soldiers, together with twenty Stables for Horses, ten on each side the Deck, with good Accommodation for the Horsemen and Grooms. In the Forecastle was the Receptacle for fresh Water, made of Planks, well lined with Cloath and Pitch, which held two hundred and fifty three Hogsheads; and near that was a Well, lined with Sheet-Lead, which being kept full of Sea-Water, nourished great Numbers of Fish. From the Ships sides there jutted out, at a proper Distance from each other, several Beams, whereon were made Places for keeping Wood, as also Ovens, Kitchins, Mills, and other necessary Offices; each of which Beams was supported on the outside by a carved Image of nine Feet high: And the whole Ship was very handsomly painted. It was also furnished with eight wooden Towers, two in the Forecastle, two in the Poop, and the rest in the Midships: From each of which there jutted out two Beams, whereon was raised a Breast-work, full of Loop-holes, from whence an Enemy might be annoyed with Stones. Each Tower was full of those, and other missive Weapons, and constantly guarded by four Soldiers compleatly armed, with two Archers. On this upper Deck there was also raised a Stage, with a Breast-work round it, whereon was placed a Machine invented by *Archimedes*, which would fling Stones of three hundred Pound Weight, and Darts of eighteen Feet long, to the Distance of a hundred and twenty Paces; round which Machine were hung, by Chains of Brass, a kind of Curtains, composed of large Cables, for its Security. The Ship

was

was furnished with three Masts, and each of them with two Engines for throwing Stones, from whence also large Iron Hooks, and Dolphins of Lead were to be flung into an Enemy's Ship. It was also fortified with an Iron Palissade all round, to prevent an Enemy's boarding, and had grappling Irons in a Readiness in all Quarters wherewith to seize, and bring to, such hostile Vessels as it might be engaged with. Sixty Soldiers, compleatly armed, kept continual Guard on each side of the Ship, and as many at each of the Masts, and their respective Engines. Their Round-tops were of Brass, wherein was constant Watch kept, by three Men in the Main-Top, and two in each of the other, to whom, in case of Action, Stones were to be conveyed in Baskets by the help of certain Tackle for that purpose, and they were to be supplied with Darts and Arrows by Boys appointed to that Service. The Fore and Mizen Masts were without Difficulty procured in *Sicily*, but a Main-Mast of proper Dimensions was hard to be got, till at length one was found in the Mountains of *Britain*, which was brought down to the Sea by *Phileas*, an Engineer of *Tauromenium*. The Ship was furnished with four Anchors of Wood, and eight of Iron. And tho' it was of so vast a Depth, its Pump, by a Device of *Archimedes*'s, was managed by one Man. She was at first called the *Syracuse*, but when *Hieron* thought fit to send her to *Ptolemy*, he named her the *Alexandria*. She had several Tenders to accompany her, one whereof was a Gally called the *Cercurus*, and the rest Fisher-boats, and other small Vessels. Her whole Company consisted of an immense Multitude, there being in the Forecastle alone six hundred Seamen, always in Readiness to execute such Orders as should be given; and the Power of punishing all Faults and Misdemeanours done on board her was committed to the Captain, Master, and Master's Mate, who gave Sentence according to the Laws of *Syracuse*. There were put on board her sixty thousand Bushels of Corn, ten thousand Barrels of Salt-Fish, twenty thousand Barrels of Flesh, and as many Bales of Goods and Necessaries, besides all the Provisions for her Company. But at length *Hieron* finding that all his Harbours were either very dangerous for a Ship of so vast a Burthen, or else not capable at all to receive her, (as 'tis reasonable to believe not any of them were) he came to a Resolution of presenting her to *Ptolemy*, King of *Ægypt*, as hath been before observed, to whom she was accordingly sent, being towed in Safety to *Alexandria*. This *Ptolemy*, surnamed *Philopator*, was, as *Athenæus* also tells us, already possessed of two Ships of extraordinary Dimensions of his own building, one of which had forty Tire of Oars, and was four hundred and twenty Feet in length, and in breadth fifty seven: Its height from the Keel to the Bulk-head of the Forecastle was seventy two Feet, and to the Poop Lanthorn seventy nine and a half. When the King made an Experiment of her Sailing, she carried above four thousand Rowers, four hundred Seamen, and two thousand eight hundred and fifty marine Soldiers, besides a great Number of other People between Decks, with a vast Quantity of Provisions. The other was a Ship he built

The extraordinary Dimensions of two Ships of Ptolemy Philopator, King of Ægypt.

to take his Pleasure in on the *Nile*, which was three hundred Feet in length, and forty five in breadth, and the height of the Stern was fifty eight Feet and a half. She was of a Built different both from a Gally and a Ship of Burthen, being peculiarly formed for the River, with a broad flat bottom, and was furnished with several fine Apartments and beautiful Ornaments suitable to the Magnificence of the *Ægyptian* Kings; for a more particular Description whereof, I refer the curious Reader to the forementioned Author, and return to the Prosecution of the *Roman* Story.

Sicily reduced to a Roman Province. — *Syracuse* being taken, in the manner we have related, all other Cities of *Sicily* presently surrender'd to the *Romans*, and the whole Island was now reduced into the Form of a Province; when *Marcellus* returning to *Rome*, he celebrated both a Triumph and an Ovation, the first for his Victories obtained over the *Carthaginians*, and expelling them out of *Sicily*, the latter for having brought that Island to Obedience.

Philip of Macedon enters into a Treaty with Hannibal. — After the fatal Battel at *Cannæ*, wherein the *Romans* received so entire a Defeat, and lost seventy thousand Men, *Philip*, King of *Macedon*, hoping to take Advantage of their Misfortune, entered into a Treaty of Alliance with *Hannibal*, engaging to assist him with his whole Force to conquer *Italy*. His Ambassadors who were sent on this Errand happened to be intercepted by a Squadron of *Roman* Ships which were cruising on the Coast of *Calabria*; and *M. Valerius*, who was Admiral and Commander in chief of the Fleet, made such a good Disposition thereof in all Parts, that the *Macedonian* could not bring his Designs to take effect. For altho' *Philip*, in Execution of his Treaty, did put to Sea with a Fleet of three hundred Sail of small Ships, and Transports with Troops on board, he advanced no farther than *Apollonia*, into which Place the *Roman* Prætor having thrown a timely Reinforcement of Men, the Inhabitants made so successful a Sally on the *Macedonians* who lay before the Place, that they forced them to retire with the utmost Precipitation; the King himself, who with much Difficulty escaped, making the best of his way to *Macedonia* by Land, having first set fire to all his Ships.

Philip forced to retire from Apollonia.

The Romans make an Alliance with the Ætolians, and take Zacynthus, &c. ᵗ Zante. — The *Romans*, to prevent any more Disturbance from that Quarter, and to find him Diversion at home, made an Alliance with the *Ætolians* jointly to carry on the War against him; to which Purpose the Consul *Lævinus* repairing with a Fleet to *Corcyra*, sailed thence and reduced the Island ᵗ *Zacynthus*, and taking also *OEnias* and *Naxus* from the *Acarnanians*, *Philip*'s Allies, sequester'd them in the Hands of the *Ætolians*. This War was very successful in the Beginning, but the *Romans* abating by degrees in the vigorous Prosecution thereof, *Philip* and the *Ætolians* made a separate Peace, nor could all the Endeavours of the Proconsul *Tuditanus*, who arrived presently after with a Fleet of thirty five Gallies, make it void: But *Philip* soon after signifying his Desires to come to an Accommodation with the *Romans*, at length, by the Mediation of the *Epirotes*, a Treaty of Peace was concluded between them at *Phœnice*.

Philip and the Ætolians make a separate Peace; as

Philip soon after did with the Romans.

While

CHAP. XV. *Dissolution of the* Rom. *Empire.* 139

While *Marcellus*, after he had gained the Battel at [f] *Numistrum*, was driving *Hannibal* from Place to Place, the *Carthaginians* left no Stone unturned in order to make themselves Masters of the Citadel of *Tarentum*, having already possessed themselves of the Town; but *Livius*, who held that Fortress for the *Romans*, was in no pain for any thing they could do, provided he were but supplied with Provisions. This both Parties knew, and were equally diligent the one to perform, and the other to prevent; so that both their Fleets happening to meet, which were pretty equal in Strength, they engaged with such Fury, that presently coming Broadside to Broadside, the Men fought Hand to Hand as if they had been on shore. The two Admiral-Gallies happened to fall together, in one of which was *Quintius* the *Roman* Admiral, and in the other *Nicon*, a *Tarentine*, who commanded for the *Carthaginians*. These maintained the Fight with incredible Fury on both sides, but at length *Quintius* being slain by *Nicon*, as he was exhorting his People bravely to do their Duty, the *Roman* Courage began thereupon to droop; whereas, on the other hand, the *Carthaginians*, encouraged by that Success, renewed the Charge with such Fury, that they took, sunk, or drew ashore almost all the *Roman* Gallies. The Ships laden with Provisions for the Garrison at *Tarentum*, hovering in the mean time at a Distance, and seeing the Day lost, timely secured themselves by getting off to Sea, and escaped into the nearest Ports they could make which were in the Hands of the *Romans*: And *Livius*, the Governor of *Tarentum*, soon after retaliated the Loss of the *Roman* Gallies on the Besiegers.

About the same time *M. Valerius Messala*, another *Roman* Admiral, with a Fleet of fifty Gallies, made a Descent in *Africk*, not far from *Utica*, and marching up into the Country without Resistance, brought aboard a vast Booty, with a great Number of Prisoners, who informing him that the Enemy had assembled a very numerous Army to be transported into *Spain*, and thence to pass into *Italy*, he dispatched Advice thereof to the Senate, and took such prudent Measures as utterly defeated the Enemy's Designs

Claudius Nero, the Pro-Prætor, who had been just before sent to *Spain* with twelve thousand Foot and a thousand Horse, embarked on board fifty Gallies of five Tire of Oars, and having landed the Troops, he invested [t] *New-Carthage* on the Land-side, and, with the Assistance of the Fleet, presently made himself Master of the Place by Storm, wherein he found such a vast Booty as enriched the whole Army: And in the Harbour were taken no less than a hundred and fourteen Merchant-Ships, with all their Cargoes. There was a great Contention between two private Men, one a Soldier, the other a Seaman, for the Reward of a mural Crown, each alledging he had first scaled the Wall, insomuch that the Decision thereof was brought before *Scipio*, who contented both, by allowing that each of them mounted the Wall at the same time, and bestowed both on the one and the other a mural Crown, (the Recompence among the *Romans* for such Services) which was a Circle of Gold, with something

[f] Nicastro in the further Calabria.

A Sea-Fight between the Romans and Carthaginians.

The Roman Fleet destroyed.

The Romans make a Descent in Africa.

[t] Carthagena.

The Romans take New-Carthage.

A Contention between two private Men.

T 2

thing of a Resemblance of the Battelments of the ancient Walls set round it, of the same Metal.

A second Descent in Africa.
u Castle Gallipa.
The Carthaginians beaten at Sea.

Not long after *M. Valerius* sailed over again to *Africa* with a hundred Gallies, and landing near " *Clupea*, plundered all the adjacent Country; when eighty three belonging to *Carthage* appearing on the Coasts, he got his People on board with all Diligence, and charged them with such Fury, that he took eighteen, sunk several, the rest, with difficulty, escaping the same Fate. Next Year *Lævinus* the Pro-consul, Admiral of the *Roman* Fleet, making a Descent in the Territory of *Utica*, ravaged the open Country up to the Gates of that City, and having advanced almost to *Carthage*, returned victoriously on board with his Spoils. In his way home he fell in with seventy *Carthaginian* Gallies, and engaging them, sunk four, took seventeen, and put the rest to flight; when going on to *Lilybæum*, he repaired from thence to *Rome* with a great Convoy of Corn, without so much as meeting with one Ship of the Enemy's in his Passage.

Lævinus ravages the Country about Utica,
and
beats the Carthaginians at Sea.

Young *Scipio*, the Son of *Publius Scipio*, who was killed in *Spain*, being now made Consul, was wholly bent on carrying the the War into *Africk*; but it was with Difficulty the Senate came into this, nor did they allow him more than thirty Vessels of War for his Expedition. However, he asked leave to raise Volunteers, and receive what Contributions he could procure toward fitting out a Fleet suitable to his Project; which being granted, most of the young Gentlemen of *Rome* disposed themselves to follow his Fortunes; and the *Roman* Allies furnishing him with Seamen, Sails, Cordage, and Provisions, and being permitted to fell Timber in the publick Forests, he used such wonderful Dispatch, that in five and forty Days after they were taken in hand, his Ships were compleatly built, rigged, and in Condition for Sea-Service. The News of these Preparations very much alarmed the *Carthaginians*, who were already sensibly afflicted for the Loss of eighty Ships, laden with Corn and other Provisions, going to *Hannibal* to enable him to carry on the War in *Italy*, which were all taken by *C. Octavius* off of *Sardinia*.

Young Scipio prepares for Africa.

Scipio made *Sicily* the chief Seat of his Preparations, from whence when he was almost ready to proceed, he detached *Lælius* with the old Fleet of thirty Sail over to the Coast of *Africa* to learn the Posture of the Enemy, upon whose Return he made sail from *Lilybæum* with his whole Force, consisting of an Army of five and thirty thousand Men, and a Fleet of fifty two Gallies, four hundred Ships of Burthen, and many other Vessels of different sorts. Passing over in Safety, he landed his Troops at the ᵛ *Fair-Promontory* in very good order, and at the first Appearance of his Fleet the People on the Coast were so dismayed, that they all retired up into the Country; nay at *Carthage* itself the Alarm was so great, that the Gates were shut, and the Citizens mounted the Ramparts. As soon as they were a little recovered from their Surprize, they sent out five hundred Horse to view the Enemy, against which *Scipio* detached a Party of his Cavalry which cut them to pieces; and then giving

ᵛ Cape Bona.
He lands in Africa, and beats the Carthaginian Horse.

Lælius

CHAP. XIV. *Dissolution of the* Rom. *Empire.* 141

Lælius Orders to repair with the Fleet to *Utica*, he advanced thither himself with the Army, where he was joined by *Massanissa* King of *Numidia*, whom *Syphax* had dispossessed of that Kingdom. *joined by King Massanissa.*

The *Carthaginians*, being joined by *Syphax*, had by this time increased their Forces to eighty thousand Foot, and thirteen thousand Horse, upon Advice of which *Scipio* not only made a Shew as if he were disposed to hearken to the Cessation of Arms which the Enemy had proposed, but entered on a Treaty for that Purpose, sending with his Commissioners some of his ablest Soldiers, in the Habit of Slaves, to view the Camp. His Curiosity being thus satisfied, he broke off the Treaty, and suddenly set Fire to their Coverings of Mats, Reeds, dry Boughs, and the like; which they not suspecting, but thinking it came by Accident, were cut in pieces in the midst of the Hurry, and Confusion, to the Number of forty thousand Men, and six thousand were taken Prisoners. This News coming to *Carthage*, they immediately dispatched Orders to *Hannibal* to abandon all his Projects in *Italy*, and repair to the Relief of his native Country; and getting together another Army, they joined Battel again with *Scipio*, but lost ten thousand Men, and failed in their Design of raising the Siege of *Utica*. Indeed *Scipio* advancing with Part of his Troops to take Possession of * *Tunes*, the *Carthaginians* seized six of his Gallies; and soon after they raised a third Army as numerous as either of the former, but that was defeated by *Lælius* and *Massanissa*, while *Scipio* lay before *Utica*. In this Battel *Syphax* being taken, he was sent Prisoner to *Rome*, and soon after the *Carthaginians* obtained a Suspension of Arms, in order to a Treaty of Peace; but a Fleet of thirty Gallies, and two hundred Ships of Burthen, that were coming to *Africk* under *C. Octavius*, and were separated by a Storm, being plundered by the *Carthaginians*, and they having also ill used the Ambassadour, *Scipio* sent to complain of this Proceeding, and these Conferences were soon broken off. *Hannibal overcome, and returns to Carthage. Scipio beats the Carthaginians. * Tunis. The Carthaginians beaten a third time. The Treaty of Peace broken off.*

The Government of *Africk* being continued in *Scipio*, in quality of Proconsul, he had the Honour, not long after, of defeating *Hannibal* himself in an obstinate and bloody Battel, wherein the *Carthaginians* had twenty thousand Men slain, and as many taken Prisoners, whereupon *Hannibal* persuaded his Countrymen to beg Peace; and Ambassadors being immediately dispatched to *Rome* for that purpose, the People empowered *Scipio* and ten others to conclude the same, which was at last agreed to upon these Articles; "First, that the "*Carthaginians* should enjoy all their Territories in *Africk*, but "that the *Romans* should hold *Spain*, with all the Islands of the "*Mediterranean*. Secondly, that all Rebels and Deserters should "be delivered up to the *Romans*. Thirdly, that the *Carthaginians* "should give up all their Ships of War, except ten Gallies of three "Tire of Oars, with all their Elephants, and tame no more. "Fourthly, that it should not be lawful for them to make War out "of *Africk*, nor even within it, without leave from *Rome*. Fifthly, "that they should restore to *Massanissa* all that had been taken "from him. Sixthly, that they should find Money and Corn for *Scipio beats Hannibal in Africa. Articles of Peace between the Romans and Carthaginians.*

"the

"the *Roman* Troops, till the Ratification of the Treaty should ar-
"rive from *Rome*. Seventhly, that they should pay ten thousand
"*Euboick* Talents of Silver, in equal Proportions of two hundred
"at a time, in fifty Years: And eighthly, that they should give a
"hundred Hostages for Performance of these Articles to be such as
"*Scipio* should make choice of, none of them younger than four-
"teen, nor elder than thirty Years." The *Carthaginians*, in Execution of this Treaty, delivering up their Ships, *Scipio* caused them to be carried a little way out to Sea, where, within Sight of *Carthage*, they were all set on Fire, to the Number of five hundred; a Spectacle as dismal to the *Carthaginians* as if their City it self had been in Flames. After this *Scipio* repaired with the Fleet to *Lilybæum*, and thence passing over to *Italy*, went on to *Rome*, where he celebrated a magnificent Triumph, and was honoured with the Sirname of *Africanus*, being the first of the *Romans*, who received a Title from the Nation he had conquered. Thus ended the second *Punick* War in the Year of the World 3750, and from the building of *Rome* 553.

The Fleet of Carthage burnt.

Chap. XV.

Of the Naval Wars of the Romans *from the End of the second* Punick *War to the Beginning of the first Triumvirate.*

The War with Philip King of Macedon.

THE *Romans*, by the happy Conclusion of this War, were now a little at leisure to hearken to the *Ætolians*, who complained of King *Philip* of *Macedon*'s perfidious Dealings since their late Treaty with him, against whose Encroachmens the *Athenians*, and most of the People of *Greece*, did also at the same time prefer Complaints; whereupon a Fleet, with a sufficient Number of Land Forces, were presently dispatched to their Relief; by whose Valour the Tyrant, after several Defeats, was compelled to restore all *Greece* to their ancient Liberties, and obliged to pay an annual Tribute to the Conqueror.

Philip defeated.

The War with Antiochus King of Syria.

Hannibal, just as the late Treaty between *Rome* and *Carthage* was on the point of concluding, withdrew, out of *Africa*, (being jealous the *Romans* would make the Delivery up of his Person a new Demand on his Countrymen) and applied himself to *Antiochus* King of *Syria*, who at this time was making great Preparations against the People of *Rome*. *Acilius Glabrio* was first sent to oppose him, and had the Fortune to give him several Defeats; when *Cornelius Scipio*, the *Roman* Admiral, engaging with his Forces at Sea, under the Command of *Hannibal*, entirely ruined the Fleet; which Victory being immediately followed by another as signal at Land, the effeminate Prince was contented to purchase a Peace at the Price of

Antiochus's Fleet beaten.
A. M. 3754.

CHAP. XV. *Dissolution of the* Rom. *Empire.* 143

of almost half his Kingdom. By one of the Articles of the Treaty, it was provided, that he should deliver up all his Ships of War, with their Rigging and Naval Stores; that he should not possess above ten covered Ships, nor those to have more than thirty Oars apiece, and that he should not, on any Occasion, navigate on this side the Promontory [a] *Calycadnus*, unless it were to send a Vessel either with the Tribute he was to pay, or Ambassadors, or Hostages, to *Rome*.

[a] *The Cape near which* Scalimute *is* Natolia *stands about sixty Leagues wide of* Scanderoon.

The victorious *Romans* had scarce concluded their publick Rejoycings on Account of the late Success, when the Death of King *Philip* of *Macedon* presented them with an Occasion of a more glorious Triumph, whose Son, *Perseus*, succeeding, resolved to break with the Senate, and apply'd himself wholly to the raising Forces, and procuring other Necessaries for a War. Never were greater appearances in the Field than on both sides, most of the considerable Princes of the World being engaged in the Quarrel; But Fortune still declaring for the *Romans*, the greatest Part of *Perseus*'s prodigious Army was cut off by the Consul *Paulus Æmylius*, and the King obliged to surrender himself into the Hands of the Conqueror. The Consul having settled *Macedonia* as a *Roman* Province, and dismantled some Cities of *Epirus*, embarked on board a Ship that belonged to *Perseus*, of an extraordinary Magnitude, having no less than sixteen Tire of Oars, with which, loaden with the Spoils of *Macedonia*, he put to Sea, and in few Days arrived at *Rome*, where he was received with the greatest Demonstrations of Joy, and celebrated a splendid Triumph, wherein *Perseus*, and the Princes his Children, walked in Chains before his Chariot.

The War with Perseus, *King of* Macedon; *and the Reduction of that Kingdom to a Roman Province.* A. M. 3781.

But *Rome* could not think her self secure, amidst all these Conquests, while her old Rival *Carthage* was yet standing; so that a Pretence was soon found to begin the third *Carthaginian* War, which was their being in Arms against *Massanissa*, an Ally of the *Romans*, though they had therein sufficient Justice on their side: And War being accordingly proclaimed, both the Consuls were sent with a full Resolution utterly to destroy the City. The *Carthaginians* affrighted at the *Romans* Preparations, immediately condemned those that had broken the League, and most humbly offered any reasonable Satisfaction; but Answer was returned them that they should enjoy all as formerly, provided they sent three hundred Hostages of the chief of the City within thirty Days to *Sicily*, and complied with what the Consuls should further command them. They desiring nothing more than Peace, sent their Children as Hostages within the limited time; and the Consuls landing at *Utica* soon after, they dispatched Commissioners to wait on them, and know their Pleasure. *Censorinus* commended their Diligence, but demanded all their Arms, which, without any Fraud, were delivered up; and now these unhappy People imploring Mercy, with many Tears, and all humble Submission, desired to know their last Doom. The Consuls told them they must quit their City, for that they had special Orders to level it with the Ground, but that they might build another any where within their own Territories, so that it were not within ten Miles of the Sea, which severe Command they received with all the

The third Punick War.

The Consuls sent to destroy Carthage.

Concern

The Carthaginians enraged at the Demands of the Romans. Concern and Rage of a despairing People, and resolved rather to abide the utmost Extremities than abandon, or yield to the Ruin of their ancient Seat and Habitation.

The Consuls were very backward in opening the War, as not doubting but to make themselves easily Masters of the City, now in this naked and defenceless Condition; but they found themselves mightily disappointed; for the Inhabitants, animated with a Spirit of Rage and Fury, prepared for the most obstinate Resistance, both Men and Women working Day and Night in making of Arms. Where Iron and Brass were wanting they made use of Gold and Silver; and the Women parted with their Hair to supply the want of Tow or Flax. They made *Asdrubal* their General, who had already in the Field a good Army, and when the Consuls opened the Siege, they met with such notable Resistance as greatly discouraged them, and increased the Resolution of the Besieged. *Martius* commanded the Fleet, and *Manlius* the Land Forces that were employed before the Place. The *Carthaginians*, in a vigorous Sally, were near making themselves Masters of *Manlius*'s Camp, but were at length repulsed by the singular Courage and Bravery of *Scipio*, the Grandson, by Adoption, of him that conquered *Hannibal*, who was then only a Tribune in the Army. As *Martius*'s Fleet lay at Anchor off the Town, the Besieged filled a number of Boats with Faggots, and other combustible Stuff, and when the Land Breeze came up, set them on Fire, and sent them among the *Roman* Ships, most part of which they destroyed.

Most Part of the Roman Fleet set on Fire.

The following Year *Calpurnius Piso* was sent to command the Land Forces, and *L. Mancinus* at Sea, who endeavouring to take in *Hippargetes*, a Town between *Carthage* and *Utica*, was twice defeated, and forced to retire to *Utica*; which News the *Romans* received with great Concern, and the before named *Scipio*, then petitioning for the Office of Ædile was chosen Consul, tho' under Age, and had the War of *Africa* committed to him. He, arriving at *Utica*, received the Charge of the Fleet from *L. Mancinus*, whom he sent back to *Rome*, and finding it impossible to reduce *Carthage* but by Famine, he made strong Lines of Circumvallation and Contravallation on the Land side to cut off its Communication that way, and the Harbour being on the west side of the City, which was situate on a Neck of Land jutting into the Sea, he resolved also to prevent the passing of their Ships to and from thence, by building a Causeway from the Continent to the Point of the Neck of Land, which he effected with great Expedition, making it ninety six Feet broad at Bottom, and twenty four at the Top. The Besieged looked at first with great Contempt on this Design, as thinking it impracticable, but finding it far advanced, they were under a terrible Consternation; and, with prodigious Labour and Diligence (the Women and Children assisting in the Work) they dug another Harbour on the East side of the City; and with the Materials of their old Ships, they, with wonderful Celerity, built fifty Gallies of three Tire of Oars, some of five, and several other Vessels of different Kinds, amounting in all to a hundred and twenty, and this with so much

The Romans twice defeated.

Scipio endeavours to reduce Carthage by Famine.

The Carthaginians build a Fleet with great Expedition.

CHAP. XV. *Dissolution of the* Rom. *Empire.* 145

much Secrecy that the Besiegers were not in the least apprized thereof. When the Port was opened, and the Fleet sailed out, it struck such a Terrour among the *Romans,* that if the *Carthaginians* had attacked them, they had probably destroyed their whole Fleet; but it being in Fate that *Carthage* should be taken, they contented themselves with only sailing out, and returning into the Port. The *Romans* had now not only Notice, but Time to prepare for an Engagement, which they did for three Days together, when the *Carthaginians* again sailed out of the Port, and came to a Battel with them. At first the light Vessels of the *Carthaginians,* by their sudden attacking and retreating again, extremely annoyed the Enemies Gallies that were not so nimble; but at length Fortune began to declare for the *Romans,* and the others retreated with such Precipitation, that the light Vessels getting soonest to the Mouth of the Harbour, so crowded it that there was no Entrance for the Gallies; upon which the Battel began again, and lasted with great Obstinacy till late at Night, when the *Carthaginians* at length got into the Harbour with most of their Ships, leaving some in the Hands of the *Romans.* The next Day *Scipio,* with several Machines, made an Assault at the Quarter of the City called *Cothon,* and that with such Success as to demolish good Part of the Wall; and, in few Days after, marching in at the Breach, took Post there. He then set Fire to the City in three Places, but the Besieged, notwithstanding, disputing every Inch of Ground with incredible Obstinacy, it was six Days before he had reduced the whole. Those who were in the the *Byrsa,* or Citadel, surrendered to him, on Promise of their Lives, of which Number was *Asdrubal* himself; whose Wife hearing he had submitted to ask his Life of the *Romans,* set Fire to the Temple of *Æsculapius,* and first killing her three Childen, leapt with them into the Flames. Then was this magnificent Place laid in Ashes, being four and twenty Miles in Compass; nay so large it was that the burning of it continued seventeen Days; and this was the fatal End of one of the most renowned Cities of the World, both for Command and Riches, and of the third and last *Punic* War, which happened in the fourth Year after it began, being the 607th Year of the City of *Rome,* and of the World 3804.

The Carthaginian Fleet beaten.

Carthage taken and destroyed by Scipio.

A. M. 3804.

The Destruction of *Carthage* was presently followed by that of *Corinth,* and the Dissolution of the Republick of *Achaia:* And not long after * *Numantia* was taken and razed, a flourishing City of *Spain:* However this did not deter the People of the *Baleares* Islands from drawing upon themselves the Anger of the *Romans,* by their Piratical Depredations on the adjacent Seas, which they infested for a considerable time, plundering all Ships passing that way. When they descry'd the *Roman* Fleet advancing toward them, they, in Hopes of a great Booty, charged them at first very vigorously, throwing vast Numbers of Stones amongst them with their Slings, in the Use of which they were remarkably dextrous: But when they came to be more closely engaged, and felt the Smart of the *Roman* Javelins, and that the Beaks of their Gallies were amongst them, they fled to their Coves and lurking Places with the utmost Precipitation,

A. M. 3818. * Soria *in Old* Castile.

The Pirates of the Baleares *reduced by the* Romans; *as were those of* Cilicia.

U

tion, putting the *Romans* to the trouble of searching them out; and they were, at length, totally subdued by *Q. Metellus*, who commanding on this Expedition, was honoured with the Sirname of *Balearicus:* Nor was it long e'er *M. Antonius*, in Quality of Pro-Prætor, subdued the Pirates of *Cilicia* that infested the Seas, who returning to *Rome* celebrated an Ovation.

The Mithridatick *War.*

About this time *Mithridates*, King of *Pontus*, became very formidable; for having conquered the *Scythians*, and made himself Master of *Cappodocia, Paphlagonia* and *Galatia*, he began to think himself a Match for the *Roman* Power, who, by their Ambassadors, demanded that he should quit *Paphlagonia*, and restore it to its former Condition. Soon after a War began between *Mithridates* and *Nicomedes*, King of *Bithynia*, for the Province of *Cappadocia*, wherein the *Romans* assisted the latter, and *Tigranes* King of *Armenia* the former. In the first Battel the *Romans* and *Nicomedes* received a notable Defeat, and lost *Phrygia* and *Mysia* to the Con-

The Romans *beaten and massacred.*

queror, who caused a general Massacre to be made of all the People of *Rome* throughout the lesser *Asia*. The *Rhodians* were the only People that spared them, which they not only did with great Generosity, but armed their Fleet for the Protection of those that had fled thither, among whom was *L. Cassius* the Proconsul of *Asia*. *Mi-*

Mithridates *goes with his Fleet against* Rhodes.

thridates repairing with his Navy to *Rhodes*, they put out to Sea to receive him, but he being considerably more numerous, and attempting to surround them, they retired again into the Port, whereupon he invested the Place, but the *Rhodians* being encouraged by two or three successful Sallies, determined to hazard a Naval Battel, under the Conduct of *Damagoras*. Their Success was equal to their

The Rhodians *overcome* Mithridates *at Sea.*

Resolution, for coming to an Engagement, they boarded, and kept Possession for some time of *Mithridates*'s own Gally, of five Tire of Oars, and having sunk and disabled several, retreated with one of three Tire into the Harbour. The next Day a violent Storm forced *Mithridates*'s Ships ashore against the Rocks, and Walls of the Town, some of which the *Rhodians* took, some they sunk, and others they set fire to, taking four thousand Prisoners. The Besieged fancied the Goddess *Isis* interposed in their Favour; for that *Mithridates* having caused a large Machine, in Form of a Tower, to be raised upon the Decks of two Gallies joined together, and placed the same against the Walls near the Temple of *Isis*, from which terrible Execution was done by numerous Darts, Arrows, and other missive Weapons, at length, all of a sudden, without receiving any Damage

Mithridates *raises the Siege of* Rhodes.
Delos *taken by* Mithridates.

from the *Rhodians*, it fell to pieces, whereupon *Mithridates* raised the Siege, and retired to *Patara.*

Soon after, by his Admiral *Archelaus*, he took the Island *Delos*, together with a considerable Number of Ships belonging to the Place, and an immense Sum of Money consecrated to sacred Uses, whereby *Critias*, for his Service therein, acquired such a Share of the King's Favour, that he obtained the supreme Government of *Athens*. The *Achæans, Lacedæmonians* and *Bœotians* all submitted to *Mi-*

The Romans *beat his Fleet off* Eubœa.

thridates: but off of *Eubœa*, his Fleet, under the Command of *Metrophanes*, was defeated by *Brutius Surra*, Lieutenant to *Sentius*,

Prætor

CHAP. XV. *Dissolution of the* Rom. *Empire.* 147

Prætor of *Macedonia*. In the mean time *Sylla* was sent from *Rome* with an Army to carry on the War against him, who now having expelled from their Dominions the Kings of *Bithynia* and *Paphlagonia*, Allies of the *Romans*, took up his Residence at *Pergamus*, while one of his Sons of the same Name ruled *Pontus*, and the *Thracian Bosphorus*, and *Ariarathes*, another Son, was subduing *Thrace* and *Macedonia* with a great Army; and his Admiral *Archelaus* ranged the Seas with a considerable Fleet, with which he reduced the *Cyclades* to his Obedience, together with the Islands ^c *Cythera* and ^d *Eubœa*; and as all the maritime Places from *Athens* to *Thessaly*, through the Influence of the *Athenians*, revolted to him, so was *Brutius* also defeated by Land, and forced to abandon his Camp. *The Cyclades, &c. are reduced by Mithridates.* ^c *Cerigo.* ^d *Negroponte.*

This was the State of Affairs in *Asia* and *Greece* when *Sylla* came out on this Expedition, who meeting with *Archelaus* at the River *Cephisus* in *Bœotia*, obtained an entire Victory over him, and thereupon consecrated a Trophy to *Mars*, *Venus* and *Victoria*, when advancing against *Dorilaus*, another General of the Enemies, he engaged him with like Success; and gathering together the useless Arms and Machines that were left in the Field of Battel, and the Enemies Camp, caused a Pile to be made of them, to which he set fire with his own Hand, devoting them to the infernal Gods and *Mars*. *Sylla beats Archelaus and Dorilaus.*

While *Sylla* was thus successful abroad, he met with but ill Treatment at Home, being, by the Faction of *Marius*, adjudged an Enemy to the *Roman* People, who razed his House, confiscated all his Effects, and sent the Consul *Valerius Flaccus* to succeed him in the Management of the *Mithridatick* War. Notwithstanding this, *Sylla* retained the greatest Part of the Army with him, and passing over to *Asia* forced *Mithridates* to sue for a Peace, which he granted him on these Conditions; that the Forces under *Archelaus* should be delivered up to the *Romans*, and all Prisoners of War and Deserters restored to them; that his Troops should evacuate all the Towns in *Asia* which had been in Possession of the *Romans*, and that he should enjoy only his hereditary Kingdom of *Pontus*, entirely abandoning *Pamphylia*, *Bithynia*, *Nicomedia* and *Cappadocia*; that he should pay down two thousand Talents, and deliver up his whole Fleet, which consisted of seventy Gallies. *Sylla adjudged an Enemy to Rome, but forces Mithridates to sue for Peace*

Articles of Peace between the Romans and Mithridates.

In this manner was the *Mithridatick* War laid asleep for a short time: And *Sylla*, leaving only two Legions in *Asia*, advanced with the rest of his victorious Army towards *Italy*, that he might prosecute his Resentments against the opposite Faction there, and carry on the Civil War. L. *Murœna*, whom he left in *Asia*, being greatly ambitious of the Honour of a Triumph, laid siege to *Comana* the richest City in *Mithridates*'s Dominions, who advancing with great Expedition to the Relief of the Place, was defeated, but made up the Rupture again in the Terms of the former Treaty. This was called the second *Mithridatick* War; and the third fell out soon after, occasioned by the same L. *Murœna*, who entered with his Troops into *Cappadocia*, under Pretence of assisting *Ariobarzanes*, King of that Country, he having complained of the Devastation of his Territories by the Enemy. *Mithridates*, that he might be the more A. M 3868.

The Occasions of the second and third Mithridatick Wars.

U 2 able

Mithridates leagues with Sertorius.	able to deal with the *Romans*, made a League with *Sertorius*, who had seized on *Spain*, that so his Enemies might find Diversion in the West, while he was making his utmost Efforts in the East.

    Sertorius was an experienced Officer, who had passed through several of the most considerable Employments, and flying from the Cruelties which *Sylla* exercised in *Italy*, escaped to *Africk*, whence passing into *Spain*, he maintained the War there for some time; but being at length expelled thence, joined himself to the Pirates of *Cilicia*, who at this time very much infested all Parts of the Mediterranean, and by their Assistance made himself Master of the Island

c Yviça.	c *Pityusa*, forcing from thence the *Roman* Garrison under *Mannius*.
The Strength of the Pirates of Cilicia.	Several Sea-Port Towns, and many Islands fell into the Hands of these Pirates, and great Numbers of People, invited by the Hopes of rich Plunder, joined with them against the *Romans*, so that at length they possessed no less than forty Cities, and their Fleet consisted of above a thousand Sail, which were skilfully disposed of in Squadrons in the most convenient Stations, and Naval Magazines erected in several Places. They took two *Roman* Prætors, and *Julius Cæsar*, then a youth, fell into their Hands, as he was going to *Rhodes* to prosecute his Studies, as did several other Persons also of the most considerable Quality: Nor through the whole Mediterranean Sea, from *Gades* to *Syria*, or the *Hellespont*, was there a Place free from their Depredations. *Sertorius* did not long keep Possession of *Pityusa*, being defeated in an Engagement at Sea by *C. Annius*, and daring not to trust himself on any of the neighbouring Coasts, he was tossed about on the Sea for some Days, till at
d Streights of Gibraltar. e Guadilquivir.	length passing through the d Streights of *Gades*, he landed in the furthermost Parts of *Spain*, where the e *Bætis* falls into the Ocean, and there meeting with some Sailors, who told him fine Stories of the Fruitfulness and agreeable Climate of two Islands in the *Atlantick* Ocean, (probably the *Maderas*) he was very much inclined to quit his tumultuary warlike Life, and retire thither to spend the rest of his Days in Peace. But hearing the *Cicilian* Pirates, who
f People of Fez.	had now deserted his Interests, had attacked the f *Maurusians*, he crossed over to their Assistance, where he had no sooner settled their
g Portuguese.	Affairs, but the g *Lusitanians*, by their Ambassadors, desired his Presence in *Spain*. Returning thither, he defeated *Cotta* in a Sea-Fight
h Tariff in the Streights of Gibraltar. Sertorius beats Cotta, &c. by Sea.	near h *Mellaria*, as he soon after did on shore *Phidias* the Prætor, killing two thousand of his Men, overthrowing also *Metellus* himself, and his Lieutenant *Aquilius*, whom the Senate had sent against him. They then committed that War to *Pompey*, but had nevertheless gone near to have lost the whole Country, if *Lucullus*, having in view the Command of the Forces against *Mithridates*, had not taken more than ordinary Care, in causing Supplies of Money to be sent to *Pompey* for Payment of the Troops, fearing, if he returned to *Rome*, he might, by his Interest with the People, supplant him in his intended Expedition. *Sertorius* had already, as we have observed, made a League with *Mithridates*, and was about to put in Execution the great Projects concerted between them, when the

Roman

CHAP. XV. *Dissolution of the* Rom. *Empire.* 149

Roman Generals procured him to be taken off by one of his own Party, who stabbed him as he was at Supper.

Mithridates being ignorant of what had happened to his Ally, and resolving on some notable Expedition, sacrificed, according to the Religion of his Country, a white Horse to *Jupiter* the Warrior, and threw a Chariot into the Sea, as sacred to *Neptune*; which done, he marched into *Paphlagonia*, and invaded *Bithynia*; *Cotta* the *Roman* Prætor retiring before him, whom he pursued to [i] *Chalcedon*, and defeated him, killing three thousand of his Men under the Walls of that City. Breaking the Boom the *Romans* had laid cross the Mouth of the Harbour, his Fleet entered, and burnt sixty of their Ships, with ten beaked Gallies which the People of *Cyzicus* had sent to their Assistance. From thence he went on to *Cyzicus*, and invested it by Sea and Land; where placing together two large Gallies, he raised a Tower upon them of equal Height with the Walls, which he caused to be mounted by a Number of chosen Men, with design to enter the Town from thence; but being bravely repulsed by the Besieged, was forced to rise from before the Place, whence he proceeded with the Fleet toward the Island [k] *Paros*, sending his Army toward *Lampsacus*, which *Lucullus* coming up with at the River *Granicus*, entirely cut off. Upon Intelligence that thirteen Gallies of the King's were going to *Lemnos*, *Lucullus* immediately went in quest of them, with whom engaging, he slew their Admiral at the first Charge, took the Ship he fought in, and forcing the rest to retire to *Portus Achæorum*, near *Sigæum*, there they all fell into his Hands, together with *Martius* a *Roman* Officer, whom *Sertorius* had sent to the Enemy. *Mithridates* then leaving an Army of ten thousand Men, and fifty Sail of Ships near *Lampsacus*, made the best of his way to *Pontus* by Sea, but met with such a violent Tempest that he lost no less than forty of his Ships, and with great difficulty escaping in a small Fisher-boat, he, at length, contrary to all Expectation, got safe to *Heraclea*. *Lucullus*, upon his Successes by Sea and Land, dispatched a Gally to *Rome*, adorned with Laurel, in token of his Naval Victory, with Letters to the Senate, giving an Account of his Proceedings, when advancing to *Bithynia*, and from thence to *Pontus*, he fought several times with various Success, but at length, in the midst of his great Designs against the Enemy, was recalled to *Rome*, and *Mithridates*, encouraged by his Removal, fell upon the *Roman* Officers who were left to command the Troops, whom he defeated, and again reduced all *Cappadocia* to his Obedience.

While these things were doing in *Asia*, M. *Antonius*, Father of the *Triumvir*, having fought unsuccessfully at Sea with the *Cretans*, in the Interest of *Mithridates*, the *Romans* sent *Q. Metellus* against those People, who destroyed all their Sea-Force, and laid the Island waste with Fire and Sword. He defeated also *Lasthenes* and *Panares*, Admirals of *Cydon*, the Capital of *Crete*, which Place he took, together with *Gnossus*, *Lyctus* and *Erythrea*; and having entirely reduced the Island to the *Roman* Obedience, and settled it in Peace, was honoured with the Sirname of *Creticus*. The before-mention'd
M. *An-*

Sertorius murdered.
A. M. 3877.

i *Scutari, over against Constantinople.*

Mithridates successful against the Romans.

k *Pario.*
Mithridates his Army cut off by Lucullus, and his Fleet taken.

Mithridates his Ships lost in a Tempest.

Lucullus recalled to Rome, and Mithridates reduces Cappadocia.

Metellus destroys the Fleet of Crete, and reduces the island.

M. Antonius, who had been sent some time before this against the Pirates of *Cilicia*, made some ineffectual Attempts against them, in which he was once defeated by them in a Skirmish, and had the Mortification to see his Men who were fallen into their Hands, hung up on the Yard-Arms, and carried in that manner to *Crete*; to succeed whom, the *Romans* sent *P. Servilius* against these Pirates at the Head of a considerable Number of stout Ships, who dispersed and put them to flight in several Engagements, and landing a Body of Troops, attacked their Nests ashore, which were several strong Cities of *Cilicia* and Parts adjacent. He took and destroyed *Phaselis* and *Olympus*, full of their Spoils and Plunder, and also made himself Master of *Isauria*, their capital City, from whence he had the Title of *Isauricus*; which Success of *Servilius* obliged them to quit the Sea for some time, and separate into their several Countries, where they retired to Mountains and inaccessible Places; but not long after, with a great Accession of Strength from all Parts, they covered the Sea with their Fleets.

Hereupon *A. Gabinius* laid a Bill before the People for *Pompey*'s having the Government of the Sea from the ¹ Streights of *Gades* to *Syria* and *Pamphylia*, and from *Ægypt* and *Libya* up to the *Euxine*, in order to put an end to the Piratic War; and withal proposed that he might be assisted with fifteen Persons of Senatorian Rank, as his Lieutenants, to be of his own chusing; and that there should be issued to him from the publick Treasury such a Sum of Money as he should think necessary for defraying the Charge of the Expedition. *Pompey* having received this Command from the People, notwithstanding it was violently opposed by the Senate, got his Ships, Men and Provisions ready with incredible Dispatch, the Fleet consisting of two hundred and seventy Sail, and to cut off all Retreat from the Pirates, he made a Disposition of his Officers in this manner. The Coast of *Spain* within the Pillars of *Hercules* he committed to *Tiberius Nero*, and *Manlius Torquatus*; the Seas of *Gaul* and *Liguria* to *M. Pomponius*, and those of *Africk*, *Sardinia*, and *Corsica* to *Lentulus*, *Marcellinus*, and *P. Attilius*. Of the Coast of *Italy*, *L. Gellius* and *Cn. Lentulus* had Charge; and *Plotius* and *Ter. Varro* had the Command of the *Sicilian* and *Ionian* Seas as far as *Acarnania*. *L. Cinna* was stationed on the Seas of *Peloponnesus*, *Attica*, *Eubœa*, *Thessaly*, and *Macedonia*; and to *L. Cullius* his Care was committed the rest of the *Ægean*, with the Islands therein, together with the *Hellespont*. *Bithynia*, *Thrace*, the ᵐ *Propontis*, and the ⁿ *Bosphorus* were given in Charge to *P. Piso*; and *Lycia*, *Pamphylia*, *Cyprus*, and *Phœnicia* to *Metellus Nepos*. Each of these Officers had under his Command a sufficient Number of Ships; and *Pompey* having with sixty Sail scoured all the West part of the Mediterranean in forty Days, crossed the *Ionian*, and put in at *Athens*, from whence he proceeded to ᵒ *Coracesium* in *Cilicia*, which he took, with several other strong Holds in those Parts, the Receptacles of the Pirates; who now, unable to make head against a Force wherewith they were attacked in all Parts, and having no Place of Retreat, placed all their Hopes in the *Roman* Clemency, and

CHAP. XV. *Dissolution of the* Rom. *Empire.* 151

and surrendered themselves Prisoners at Discretion to *Pompey,* who extended Mercy to most of them, and planted a considerable Number in *Soli,* a City of *Cilicia,* which had been lately depopulated by *Tigranes,* King of *Armenia,* whence it was called *Pompeiopolis.* In the Space of four Months this War was entirely brought to a Conclusion, in which were taken five hundred large Ships, besides great Numbers of Frigates, and a vast Quantity of Materials for building others was set on fire. For some signal Service which *Ter. Varro,* one of the beforemention'd Officers, performed in this War, *Pompey* honoured him with a Naval Crown, which was of Gold, set round with Figures, resembling the Beaks of Ships, and was the first of this kind, as *Pliny* tells us, that was ever bestowed.

Upon *Pompey*'s happy Conclusion of this Business, the *Mithridatick* War was committed to him by Decree of the People, with a Commission to be Captain-General of all the Forces in *Asia*; and he, in pursuance thereof, repaired to *Galatia,* and took upon him the Command of the Army late under *Lucullus,* who, upon his Return to *Rome,* had, in the Triumph he celebrated, amongst the other usual Ornaments of such a Procession, a hundred Pageants resembling beaked Gallies, in Signification of his Successes at Sea: But while *Lucullus,* in his splendid Retirement from publick Affairs, abandoned himself to his Pleasures, *Pompey* drove the Enemy out of *Cappadocia,* entirely routed them in a Battel upon the Banks of the *Euphrates,* forced *Tigranes* to sue for a Peace, and *Mithridates* to dispatch himself, and added *Syria* and *Cilicia* to the *Roman* Empire. In Consideration of *Pharnaces,* Son to *Mithridates,* his Adherence to the *Roman* Interest, he appointed him King of *Pontus,* restored *Cappadocia* to *Ariobarzanes,* and left *Tigranes* in Enjoyment of *Armenia*; which done, he returned to *Rome,* and was received with the joint Acclamations and Applause both of Senate and People; having sent before him to the Mouth of the *Tiber* seven hundred Ships taken from the Enemy. In the Celebration of his Triumph there were a prodigious Number of Wains loaden with Beaks of Ships, before which marched Troops of the captive Pirates, who appeared only to adorn the Procession, being without Chains, and in their own Habits; and these were followed by Representations in Pieces of Painting, exposed to view also in Wains, of the Ships which were taken. *Pliny* has preserved to us the Inscription carried along in this Ceremony, signifying for what Victories it was celebrated; which was this:

The Mithridatick War committed to Pompey.

He adds Syria and Cilicia to the Roman Empire.

Year of the World 3886. Of Rome 689.

The manner of Pompey's Triumph.

Orâ maritimâ à prædonibus liberatâ & imperio maris Pop. Romano restituto; ex Asiâ, Ponto, Armeniâ, Paphlagoniâ, Cappadociâ, Ciliciâ, Syriâ, Scythis, Judæis, Albanis, Iberiâ, insulâ Cretâ, Basternis, & super hæc de regibus Mithridate atque Tigrane.

For

For the maritime Coasts being cleared of Pirates,
And
The Dominion of the Sea restored to the *Roman* People;
For the Reduction of *Asia, Pontus, Armenia,*
Paphlagonia, Cappadocia, Cilicia, Syria,
The *Scythians, Jews,* p *Albanians,*
q *Iberia,* the Island *Crete,* the r *Basterni,*
And
Of the Kings *Mithridates* and *Tigranes,*
This Triumph is celebrated.

p Scirwan, *a Province of* Persia *upon the* Caspian *Sea.*
q Georgia.
r Tartars *of* Oczakow, *and about the Mouth of the River* Nieper.

Pompey, out of his Share of the Spoils gotten in these Wars, built a Temple to *Minerva,* the Words of the Dedication whereof, the same *Pliny* has transmitted to us as they are here set down.

Cn. Pompeius Magnus Imper. bello XXX. *annorum confecto; fusis, fugatis, occisis, in deditionem acceptis, hominum vicies semel centenis* LXXXIII. M.; *depressis aut captis navibus* DCCCLXVI.; *oppidis, castellis* MDXXXVIII. *in fidem receptis; terris à Mæoti lacu ad Rubrum Mare subactis; votum meritò Minervæ.*

Cneius Pompey the Great, Captain-General,
Having ended a thirty Year's War,
Routed, put to flight, killed, or taken Prisoners
Two Millions a hundred and eighty three thousand Men,
Sunk or taken eight hundred threescore and six Ships,
Received by Surrender fifteen hundred and thirty eight Towns and Fortresses,
And reduced to Obedience
All the Nations from the Lake of *Mæotis* to the Red Sea,
In bounden Duty dedicates this to *Minerva.*

Chap. XVI.

Of the Naval Wars of the Romans, *from the Beginning of the first* Triumvirate, *to the Death of* Julius Cæsar.

Combination between Pompey, Crassus, *and* Julius Cæsar.

POmpey, soon after his Return to *Rome,* entered into a Combination with *Crassus* and *Julius Cæsar,* to let nothing pass in the Common-wealth without their joint Approbation. Pursuant to which Agreement they divided between themselves the best Provinces of the Empire, in consequence whereof, *Gaul* fell to the Share of *Cæsar,* who, to bind *Pompey* the more strongly in his Interests, gave him his Daughter in Marriage. *Julius Cæsar* had not long entered upon his Government, than by taking Advantage of the

CHAP. XVI. *Dissolution of the* Rom. *Empire.* 153

the Divisions of the *Gauls*, and, by espousing one Faction against another, making himself Master of both, together with the defeating those who resisted him in several Battles, he had reduced all that Country to his Obedience as far as the Ocean; where the *Veneti*, relying on their considerable Naval Force, and being supported by several other confederated People in those Parts of *Gaul*, opposed themselves to his Conquests, and even with such Success, that it was with much difficulty they were subdued, in the manner we have related in the first Book.

Cæsar reduces the Gauls.

People of Vannes and Parts adjacent in Bretagne.

The People of *Britain* having assisted the *Veneti* in this War, *Cæsar* had no sooner settled that Part of *Gaul*, but he resolved on an Expedition against that Island; of which the *Britains* having notice, they were under great Uneasiness, and dispatched Ambassadors to him, desiring the Friendship of the *Romans*, and offering Hostages for their good Behaviour. He gave them a favourable Audience, and advising them to persist in their good Intentions, amicably dismissed them: Mean while the *Morini*, a People inhabiting the Sea Coasts opposite to the nearest Parts of *Britain*, submitted to him of their own accord, excusing themselves for what they had hitherto done from their Ignorance of the *Roman* People. *Cæsar* having dispatched C. *Volusenus* with a light Frigate to view the opposite Coasts of the Island, (who, upon his Return, in five Days, gave him an account of what he had observed) got ready a sufficient Number of Ships for the Transportation of two Legions, which he put on board, and having issued the necessary Orders, sailed from [b] *Portus Iccius* about one in the Morning, and by ten arrived with his Squadron on the *British* Coast, where he saw all the Cliffs (supposed to be those about *Dover*) covered with the Enemy in Arms. Such was the Nature of the Place, that the *Britains* might cast their Darts with great Advantage from the impending Hills; wherefore, not thinking it convenient to land there, he cast Anchor, and waited for the coming up of part of his Fleet. Upon their Arrival, about three in the Afternoon, he called a Council of War, and communicating the Intelligences *Volusenus* had given him, he, when the Wind and Tide served, made the Signal for weighing, and having sailed about eight Miles further, arrived at a plain and open Shore, somewhere about *Deal*. The *Britains* being apprized of his Design, sent their Cavalry and Chariots before, and speedily advanced with the rest of the Army, in order to oppose his landing, a thing which he found very difficult, for the Ships drawing a considerable Depth of Water, they could not come within a great Distance of the Shore; so that the Soldiers were forced to leap into the Sea, loaden as they were with heavy Armour, and at the same time to encounter the Waves and the Enemy in a Place they were not acquainted with; whereas the *Britains*, either standing upon the Shore, or wading a little way in the Water where they knew it to be shallow, having the free Use of all their Limbs, could boldly cast their Darts, and spur their Horses forward. *Cæsar* observing that his Men abated of their usual Ardour, ordered the lightest Gallies to advance (a sort of Shipping the Enemy had not seen before) and attack

Cæsar resolves on an Expedition against Britain.

They send Ambassadors to him.

[b] *Calais, or rather Boulogne.*

Year of the World 3895. Of Rome 698. Before Christ 53.

Cæsar arrives on the Coast of Britain.

The Britains oppose his landing.

X

tack them in Flank with their Slings, Engines, and Arrows, which was performed with good Success; for the *Britains*, surprized at those Gallies, the Motion of the Oars, and the Engines, began to give Ground; when the Eagle Bearer of the tenth Legion observing the Backwardness of the Soldiers to venture into the Sea, first invoked the Gods for Success, and then cried out, *Follow me, Fellow-Soldiers, unless you will abandon your Eagle to the Enemy; for, for my part, I am resolved to perform my Duty to my Country and my General.* With this, he immediately leaped over-board, and advanced the Eagle against the *Britains*; whereupon the Soldiers, encouraging each other to prevent so signal a Disgrace, followed his Example. The Conflict was sharply maintained on both *A sharp Conflict, but the Britains are put to flight.* sides for some time, till the foremost Ranks of the *Romans* got footing on dry Ground, when they put the Enemy to flight, who, as soon as they were out of reach of danger, sent Ambassadors to *Cæsar* to desire Peace, promising to deliver Hostages for their entire Submission, which were accordingly received, and a Peace concluded in four Days after his Arrival. Eighteen Transports appointed for his Cavalry, which were not ready to embark with the rest of his Troops, having put to Sea after him, with an easy Gale of Wind, were already arrived within Sight of the *Roman* Camp, when *The Ships with the Roman Cavalry separated.* of a sudden there came up such a violent Storm, that they were all dispersed, some endeavouring, in the best manner they could, to reach the Port whence they came, while others driving down the Chanel, let fall their Anchors and attempted to ride it out, but finding their Endeavours ineffectual, bore away also for *Gaul*. The same Night the Moon being at the full, and causing a Spring-Tide, a Circumstance the *Romans* were ignorant of, the Gallies they had hauled up on the Sands were soon filled with Water, and the Ships of Burthen, *Many of Cæsar's Ships destroyed by a high Tide.* which rode at Anchor, were so violently agitated with the Storm, that several of them founder'd, drove from their Anchors, or lost their Masts and Rigging, all of them being render'd useless; and the *Romans* had no Materials to refit them, or other Vessels to transport themselves to the opposite Shore: nor had they made any Provision for wintering in *Britain*, insomuch that the whole Army was under a terrible Consternation. The Princes of *Britain*, who were assembled to perform their Agreement with *Cæsar*, knowing that he had neither Cavalry, Ships, nor Provisions, and thinking they should be more than an equal Match for the *Romans*, came to a Resolution to break with them again, which they accordingly did, and attacked them with their whole Force. After two or three Skirmishes, with doubtful Success, they came to a decisive Battel, *The Britains receive a total Defeat.* wherein the *Britains* received a total Defeat, and immediately thereupon had Recourse to their old Custom of sending Ambassadors to beg Peace; whereupon *Cæsar* commanded them to send him into *Gaul* double the Number of Hostages he had before required, and not thinking it safe to take a Winter's Voyage in his crazy Vessels, the Autumnal Equinox being near, he took the first Advantage of a Wind, and weighing Anchor about one in the Morning, in few *Cæsar returns to Gaul.* Hours arrived safe in *Gaul* with his whole Fleet.

Having

CHAP. XVI. *Dissolution of the* Rom. *Empire.* 155

Having settled the Winter-Quarters of his Troops in [e] *Gallia* [e] *The Netherlands.*
Belgica, (where two of the Communities of *Britain* sent their Hostages, all the rest neglecting it) he repaired to *Illyricum*, leaving Orders with the Commanding Officers of the Legions to clean and refit all the old Ships, and to build a Number of new ones, lower than usual, that so they might be the easier hauled ashore, and more expeditiously loaden; for he had observ'd that, by reason of the frequent changing of the Tide in these Parts, there did not run so great Seas as in the Mediterranean. He also ordered them to be built broader, that so they might carry the greater Number of Horses and Carriages, and to be contrived both for rowing and sailing, for which their low built would render them the more fit: And as for Rigging, and Naval Stores, he gave Orders for their being sent from *Spain*.

On his Return to *Gaul* the next Spring, he found the Fleet in Readiness; and the *Britains* having not sent the rest of their Hostages, according to Agreement, he left *Labienus* with three Legions, and two thousand Horse, to secure the *Portus Iccius*, and watch the Motions of the *Gauls*, and embarking with the like Number of Horse, and five Legions, about Sunset he weighed Anchor, *Cæsar returns* with an easy Gale at S.W, which dying away about Midnight, he *to Britain.* found, by break of Day, that the Currents had carried him too far to the Eastward; but the Tide then returning, and all Hands labouring hard at the Oars, (wherein was not enough to be commended the Diligence of the Soldiers, who made the Ships of Burthen keep up with the light Gallies) about Noon he gained the Land, and put in at the same Place he came to before; where he found no *Britains*, for they had retired at the first Sight of so numerous a Fleet, which, including Vessels of all sorts, consisted of eight hundred Sail. *Cæsar*, having landed his Army, marked out a Camp, and learning from some Prisoners which fell into his Hands where the Enemy were encamped, he left twelve Cohorts, and three hundred Horse for the Security of his Fleet, which he thought was in no danger from the Weather on such a smooth open Shore, and having appointed *Q. Atrius* to command, advanced himself by Night in *Advances against the Britains.* quest of the Natives. He had not marched above twelve Miles e'er he saw them, who having posted their Horses and Chariots on the Banks of the [d] River, endeavoured to oppose his Passage, but being [d] *The Stower.* repulsed by the *Roman* Cavalry, fled to the Woods, notwithstanding the Advantage they had of Ground. *Cæsar* would not permit his Men to follow them, because the Day was far spent, he intending to employ the Remainder of it in intrenching his Camp; and next Day News came from *Atrius* that the Fleet had suffer'd ex- *His Fleet suffers much in a* tremely by a Storm, most of the Ships having broken from their *Storm.* Anchors, and fallen foul of one another, or ran ashore; whereupon he immediately sent to call in the Parties he had detached out to scour the Country, and returned with his Army to the Sea-side, where he found about forty of his Ships lost, and the rest so much disabled, that they could not without difficulty be repaired. However, he set all the Carpenters he had to work upon them, and sent
X 2 for

for others from *Gaul*, ordering at the same time *Labienus* to dispatch to him as many more Ships as possibly he could. Considering then that tho' it were a Work of great Labour and Difficulty, yet it would be of singular Importance to haul the Ships up, and include them within the same Retrenchment as the Camp, he resolved to set about it, and it was performed in ten Days, his Men labouring both Day and Night.

He includes his Ships within a Retrenchment.

This done, he left the same Number of Troops for the Protection of the Ships as before, and advanced to the Place he had lately removed from, where he found the Enemy's Forces greatly encreased under the Command of *Cassivellaunus*, one of the Kings of the Island (whose Territories lay beyond the ᵉ *Tamesis*) whom they had now chosen for their Generalissimo. With him *Cæsar* had several Skirmishes with various Success; but at length forced him to retire into his own Dominions, whither he resolved to march after him. Arriving at the Banks of the *Tamesis*, he saw the Enemy's Forces drawn up in a considerable Body on the opposite side, which was fortified with sharp Stakes, and many Piles of the like kind were driven into the bottom of the River, the tops whereof were under Water. *Cæsar*, notwithstanding, crossed the River at this Place, (supposed to be *Coway-Stakes* near *Chertsey*) and put the *Britains* to flight; so that *Cassivellaunus* lost all hopes of Success by Battel, and retaining with him not above four thousand Chariots, could only observe the Motions of the *Romans*, and prevent their making such Excursions as otherwise they would have done. In the mean time the ᶠ *Trinobantes*, ᵍ *Cenimagni*, ʰ *Segontiaci*, ⁱ *Ancalites*, ᵏ *Bibroci*, and ˡ *Cassii* submitting to him, and the Kings of ᵐ *Cantium* having miscarried in their Design upon the Naval Camp, *Cassivellaunus* sent Ambassadors to treat of a Surrender. *Cæsar*, designing to Winter in *Gaul*, accepted his Submission, demanded Hostages, and appointed the yearly Tribute which the *Britains* should pay to the People of *Rome*, which Hostages having received, he marched his Army back to the Sea-shore; where finding his Fleet refitted, he ordered them to be launched, and had Thoughts of transporting the Troops at twice, because his Ships were not sufficient to receive them and the great Number of Prisoners; for of those sixty which *Labienus* had built, very few were arrived. *Cæsar* having in vain expected them for some time, and doubting the Navigation might be hazardous, since the Equinox was approaching, he made a shift to croud all his Troops on board those Ships he had, and setting sail about ten at Night, arrived the next Morning on the opposite Coast.

ᵉ The Thames.

Beats Cassivellaunus, the British General.

Crosses the River of Thames, and Cassivellaunus treats of a Surrender.

ᶠ *Middlesex and* Essex.
ᵍ *Suffolk, Norfolk, Cambridgshire, and Huntingtonshire.*
ʰ *The Hundred of* Holeshot *in* Hampshire.
ⁱ *The Hundred of* Henley *in* Oxfordshire.
ᵏ *The Hundred of* Bray *in* Berkshire.
ˡ *Caishow-Hundred in* Hertfordshire.
ᵐ Kent.

Cæsar returns to Gaul.

The *Gauls*, during his Absence, had been concerting a general Revolt, which this Winter they put in Execution, but he in a short time reduced them to Obedience, killing *Indutiomarus*, one of the principal Authors of the Rebellion. Having passed the *Rhine*, and overcome the ⁿ *Sicambri* on the other side that River, he quelled another Rebellion in *Gaul*, and taking *Vercingentorix* Prisoner, settled the Country in Peace; about which time *Crassus* being slain in the East, the Triumvirate was dissolved, and *Cæsar's* Daughter
Julia,

ⁿ *The People inhabiting* Zutphen.

CHAP. XVI. *Dissolution of the* Rom. *Empire.* 157

Julia, the Wife of *Pompey,* dying, the mutual Grudgings that had long been between them two broke out into an open War. The immense Riches of *Cæsar,* and his Favour with the People, rendered him suspected to *Pompey,* as *Pompey*'s great Power, and Interest with the Senate, were very much laid to Heart by *Cæsar,* the one not being able to bear an Equal, nor the other a Superior. The Senate, influenced by *Pompey,* ordered *Cæsar,* when he petitioned for a second Consulship, to disband his Army, and appear as a private Person at the Election; which he refusing, unless *Pompey* were obliged to do the like, they looked upon it as a Denunciation of War, and appointed *Domitius,* with five Legions, to succeed him in the Government of *Gaul.* *Cæsar* having Advice of what passed at *Rome,* marched his Army with wonderful Expedition into *Italy,* and crossed the °*Rubicon, Pompey*'s Troops not daring to oppose him: He placed Garrisons in all the strong Places of *Italy,* defeated *Petreius* and *Afranius, Pompey*'s Lieutenants in *Spain,* and took *Brundusium;* where causing all the Ships to be brought together, that could be got from the several Parts of the Mediterranean in his Interest, he sent *Q. Valerius,* his Lieutenant, to *Sardinia* with one Legion, and *Asinius Pollio* with three to *Sicily* against *Cato,* who kept that Island for *Pompey,* and had not only ordered all the Ships belonging thereunto to be refitted, but that each City should build a Number of new ones; who yet, notwithstanding these Preparations, immediately abandoned the Island upon the Arrival of *Pollio,* and leaving all the Ships behind him, fled to *Pompey* at *Corcyra.*

Cæsar and Pompey break into open War.

Domitius appointed to succeed Cæsar in Gaul.

° *Pisatello.*

Cæsar beats Pompey's Lieutenants.

Cato abandons Sicily.

When *Cæsar* was in *Spain,* he dispatched *Curio* over to *Africa* with five Legions, and twelve Ships, against *Attilius Varus,* and *Juba,* King of *Mauritania;* who soon after coming to an Engagement with them at the River *Bagrada,* not only lost his own Life, but most of his Men were cut in pieces. *Cæsar* himself marching against *Petreius,* the Inhabitants of ᵖ *Massilia* were the only People who shut their Gates against him, having received *Domitius* into their Port, with seven light Frigates he had hired in *Sicily* and *Sardinia* of private Persons, which he had manned with his own Slaves, and such Country Fellows as he could get. To him the *Massilians* committed the Defence of their City, and sending out their Gallies to cruize, they brought in all the Merchant Ships they could meet with, which they made use of against the Enemy; whereupon *Cæsar* advanced with three Legions, and encamping before the Place, raised Towers, erected Penthouses to cover his Men in carrying on the Approaches, and ordered twelve Gallies to be built at ᑫ *Arelate,* which were completely finished, rigged, and fit for Service within thirty Days after the Timber was cut down; and having brought them before the Place, he gave the Command of them to *Brutus,* leaving *Trebonius* to carry on the Siege by Land. The *Massilians,* by Advice of *Domitius,* fitted out seventeen large Gallies, besides a great Number of Barks, designing by such a numerous Appearance to strike a Terrour among the *Romans* under *Brutus.* They manned them with Archers, and the People of the Mountains about *Massilia,* whom they had called in to their Assistance, and having encouraged

Curio beaten in Africa.

ᵖ *Marseilles.*

Cæsar encamps before Massilia.

ᑫ *Arles.*

S

raged them by large Promises to behave themselves gallantly, *Domitius* embarking with the Men he had brought, they all advanced against the *Romans*, who were at Anchor among the [†] Islands which lie before the Town. *Brutus* was much inferior to them, both in Number of Ships and Men, but those he had were all chosen Troops, and their Officers such as voluntarily offered themselves for this Service. The Fight was very obstinate on both sides, the Mountaineers, who had been disciplin'd a long while, behaving themselves with great Bravery, and *Domitius*'s Slaves performed Wonders, in hopes of procuring their Liberty. Their Ships being light and nimble, eluded, with great Dexterity, the Shock of *Brutus*'s Gallies, and, spreading themselves out to a good Distance, endeavoured to encompass the *Romans*; but failing in that Design, they attempted, in passing swiftly by, to brush off their Oars. The *Romans* had neither experienced Pilots, nor good Rowers, being all raw Seamen, and scarce acquainted with the Terms of Navigation; besides, their Gallies were heavy and unwieldy, having been run up in haste of green Timber, so that their whole Dependance was on the Goodness of the Troops they had on board; and in order to the making this advantagious to them, they used all Endeavours to come to a close Fight, which they at length effected. Being well provided with Javelins, Darts, Arrows, and other missive Weapons, together with large Hooks, and grappling Irons, they frequently attack'd two Ships of the Enemy's at once, which, seizing with those Instruments, they boarded, fighting from both sides of their own with much Resolution. Having made a great Slaughter among the Mountaineers, and *Domitius*'s People, and sunk or taken nine Gallies, with all their Men, they forced the rest to retire with the utmost Precipitation into the Harbour; which ill Success, however, did not diminish the Courage of the Besieged, who bravely sustain'd all the Efforts of the Enemy by Land; and in a short time after ventured upon another Engagement at Sea, encouraged thereunto by the Arrival of *Nasidius* with sixteen Sail from *Pompey*. *Brutus* having by this time also found means to encrease his Strength, the two Fleets came to a Battel, in view both of the Town and *Roman* Camp, when the *Massilians* charged with much greater Fury than those did which *Nasidius* had brought with him, and held the Victory in suspense for some time, who at length perceiving two of their Gallies, which attacked the Ship *Brutus* had hoisted his Flag in, accidentally rush against each other, and sink with the Violence of the Shock, he retired with his Division from out of the Line, whereas had he had the Courage to continue the Fight, he might have procured the Victory to the *Massilians*, who being thus basely deserted, were no longer able to make head against *Brutus*, by whom five of their Ships were sunk, four taken, and the rest forced to retire in Confusion; however, the Besieged held out for some time, and were, with great difficulty, obliged at length to surrender.

While this Siege was carrying on, and *Cæsar* was reducing *Spain* to his Obedience, *C. Antonius* and *Dolabella*, who had it in charge from him to secure the *Adriatick*, were encamped the first in the Island

[†] Les Pomegues.

A Battel between the Roman and Massilian Fleets.

A second Fight between the Roman and Massilian Fleets.

Cæsar takes Massilia.

CHAP. XVI. *Dissolution of the Rom. Empire.* 159

Island *Corcyra Melæna*, and the other over against him upon the Continent of *Illyricum*; but *Pompey* being now considerably more potent at Sea, *Octavius Libo*, his Lieutenant, arrived with a good Number of Ships, and landed his Troops both on the Island and the Main; thus hemming in *Dolabella*, as well as *Anthony*, the latter of whom being hard pressed in the Island for want of Provisions, he, in order to escape to the Continent, having no Ships with him, caused several Floats to be made, composed of Timbers laid a-cross small Boats which were chained together, and was in hopes that the Numbers of Men he proposed to put upon each Float might deter the Enemy from attacking them. *Libo*, on the other hand, by Advice of some of the old *Cilician* Pirates, ordered Cables to be laid under Water from his Ships, a-cross the Place where the Enemy's Floats must necessarily pass, which were fastened to the opposite Rocks. Two of the Floats he suffered to pass unmolested, but when the third came, on which were six or seven hundred Soldiers of *Opitergium*, it was, by means of these Cables, forced ashore to a Place covered with his own Troops. The *Opitergians* sustain'd the joint Efforts of the Enemy's whole Land and Sea-Force for some time, but at length finding no means to escape from such unequal Numbers, *Vulterius*, who commanded, worked them up to a Resolution of dispatching themselves, which they (following the Example of *Vulterius* himself) desperately performed, by falling on each others Swords.

Cæsar returning to *Rome*, after the Reduction of *Spain*, he, by his own Power, assumed the Consulship, and having joined to himself *P. Servilius* in the Execution of that Office, he proceeded first to *Brundusium*, then to *Epirus*, and from thence advanced to *Pharsalia* in *Macedonia*. *Pompey* having had a Year's Time to provide for his Defence, had gotten together from *Asia*, the Islands *Cyclades*, *Athens*, *Corcyra*, and *Ægypt*, a Fleet of six hundred Sail, with some of which he secured the Sea-Ports, and ordered the rest to cruise about the *Ionian* and the Mouth of the *Adriatick*, to prevent *Cæsar*'s passing over to *Macedonia*. He appointed *Lælius* to command the Ships of the Provincial *Asia*; to *Triarius*'s Care he committed those of *Syria*, to *Cassius* the Rhodian, to *Marcellus* and young *Pompey* the *Liburnian*, and to *Tribonius* and *Octavius Libo* those of *Achaia*. The Night after *Cæsar* had landed in *Epirus*, he sent back his Ships to *Brundusium*, thirty of which fell into the Hands of *Bibulus*, who commanded in Chief for *Pompey* in the *Ionian* Sea, by whom they were set on fire, and all the Men on board them burnt.

After *Pompey*'s Defeat in the Battel of *Pharsalia*, (from whence he escaped to *Cyprus*, and thence to *Ægypt*, where he was slain) *Lælius*, ignorant of what had happened, came with his Squadron to *Brundusium*, and possess'd himself of the Island which lies before that Port, when *Vatinius*, who commanded there for *Cæsar*, manning out a great Number of Longboats, took one of *Lælius*'s Gallies of five Tire of Oars, together with two small Frigates, but could not dislodge him from the Island; and at the same time *Cassius*,
with

with the *Rhodian*, *Phœnician*, and *Cilician* Ships repaired to *Sicily*. The Fleet which *Cæsar* had in those Parts was then divided into two Squadrons, one under the Command of *Sulpitius* at ʸ *Vibo*, without the streight of *Sicily*, and the other with *Pomponius* at *Messana*, which Port *Cassius* reached before *Pomponius* had any Intelligence of him, and finding the Enemy lay careless, and in Disorder, he filled several Vessels of Burthen with Pitch, Hemp, and other combustible things, which, with a strong Wind, that blew directly into the Port, he sent toward *Pomponius*'s Ships, and burnt them all, being in Number thirty six, and would at the same time have made himself Master of the Town, had not the News of *Pompey*'s Defeat at *Pharsalia*, which just then arrived, confirmed the People in the Interest of *Cæsar*. *Cassius* from hence proceeded towards *Vibo*, where lay *Sulpitius*; and, with the like Advantage of a favourable Wind, sent against him no less than forty Fire-Ships, which set on Fire the Gallies at each End of his Line, five whereof were presently consumed with the Flames. Some veteran Troops of *Cæsar*'s that were posted ashore for the Protection of this Squadron, immediately went on board, bore down against the Enemy's Fleet, and charged them with such Violence that they soon made themselves Masters of two Gallies of three Tire of Oars, and as many of five, one of which was *Cassius*'s own Gally, who leaped into a Boat, and escaped with the rest of his Fleet. Notwithstanding this, he continued in those Parts, till he received Advice of *Pompey*'s Defeat, and then made the best of his Way toward *Asia*; but, in his Passage thither, fell in with the little Barks which were transporting *Cæsar*'s Troops from *Greece* to *Asia*; and though he might have easily taken them all, with *Cæsar* himself, yet he was so much over-awed by that great Man's Presence and Behaviour, that he immmediately surrendered both himself and Ships.

Cæsar made but a short Stay in *Asia*; for hearing that *Pompey* had been at *Cyprus*, he guessed he would make for *Ægypt*, and therefore following him with his usual Diligence, he soon arrived with his Troops at *Alexandria*, on board ten *Rhodian* Gallies he had taken from *Cassius*, and some Ships of *Asia*. Upon his landing he received the News of *Pompey*'s Death, whose Head was presented to him, with the Ring which he used for his Signet, which mournful Spectacle drew Tears from his Eyes; and to shew the Respect he had for him, he caused a magnificent Sepulchre to be built near the Place where he was murdered, with an Edifice which he called the Temple of Wrath, and then he set himself towards making up the Differences between King *Ptolemy* and his Sister *Cleopatra*, relating to the Succession of the Kingdom, whom he summoned to appear before him for that Purpose. *Photinus* had then the Administration of Affairs, who refusing to adhere to *Cæsar*'s Proposals, procured *Achillas* to march to *Alexandria* at the Head of two and twenty thousand Men, which obliged *Cæsar* to take great Care, after he had secured the King's Person, to strengthen himself in the Town, not being able to meet the Enemy in the Field, and to cause his own Quarters to be strongly fortified; where, nevertheless, he was shortly after

CHAP. XVI. *Dissolution of the* Rom. *Empire.* 161

after attacked by *Achillas.* His Troops bravely repulsed the Enemy, whose chief Design was to get Possession of fifty Ships, and two and twenty Gallies that were in the Haven, which obliged *Cæsar,* after a long and doubtful Fight, to make himself Master of the Island *Pharos* (where was the celebrated Watch-Tower of that Name) lying before the Harbour, and to set fire to those Vessels, which Situation made him Master by Sea; but he was close shut up by Land, and the People of the Town were generally against him. *Photinus* being soon after slain, *Ganymedes* the Eunuch, under Pretence of assisting *Arsinoe,* King *Ptolemy*'s youngest Sister, and by declaring her Queen had caused *Achillas* to be murdered, and procured to himself the Command of the Army, pushed the Siege with much Vigour, and reduced *Cæsar* to great Extremities by spoiling all his fresh Water, which he remedied by his extraordinary Diligence, and by digging Abundance of Wells.

This was the Posture of *Cæsar*'s Affairs, when he had Advice that the twenty fourth Legion was arrived at a *Peninsula,* two or three Leagues short of *Alexandria,* but could not reach that Port, the Wind blowing fresh at S. E, in which Quarter it continued for some Days, so that they began to be in Want of Water; Advice whereof being sent to *Cæsar,* he embarked on board his Ships with the Mariners only, and repaired to the aforesaid *Peninsula.* The Enemy knowing he was without Soldiers, attacked him, but he soon overcame them, joined his Legion, and returned to *Alexandria*: And though this first Action astonished the *Ægyptians,* they nevertheless refitted their Ships, and came against him with a stronger Fleet than before, but were again routed, and forced to retire under the Peer of *Pharos,* which joined the Island to the City. *Cæsar* was only Master of the Island and Tower, who making an Attack upon the Peer with some little Success, was, notwithstanding, at length repulsed, and his Soldiers put in so much Disorder, that not being able to hinder their throwing themselves on board his Ship in Crowds she sunk, and they all perished, he saving himself by swimming, wherein he shew'd so much Presence of Mind as to preserve his Papers, by holding them out of the Water with one Hand, while he secured his military Robe in his Teeth. Having some Days after enlarged *Ptolemy,* at the Request of the *Alexandrians,* in order to facilitate a Peace, he received Advice of the Arrival of *Mithridates* of *Pergamus,* with an Army from *Lycia* to his Assistance, who had taken *Pelusium,* and attempted to pass the River *Nile* at *Delta. Ptolemy* being informed thereof, advanced in Person to oppose, as *Cæsar* did to assist him, who, before the Arrival of either, had beaten some of *Ptolemy*'s Troops. *Cæsar* also defeated others before he could join *Mithridates,* and having assaulted and taken a small Fort which was between him and *Ptolemy,* he the next Day, attacked, and forced his Camp, when the King endeavouring to save himself by Water, was drowned. Hereupon he returned to *Alexandria,* which immediately submitting to him, together with the rest of the Kingdom, he established *Cleopatra* therein.

attack'd in Alexandria by Ganymedes.

Reduced to Extremities by Ganymedes.

Cæsar attack'd at Sea, but is successfull.

He again beats the Ægyptians at Sea.

Cæsar saves himself by swimming.

Mithridates of Pergamus comes to assist Cæsar.

King Ptolemy drowned, and Ægypt submits to Cæsar.

Y While

M. Octavius ranges over the Adriatick.

While these things were transacting in *Ægypt*, *M. Octavius*, one of *Pompey*'s Commanders at Sea, ranged over the *Adriatick* with a considerable Fleet, and having taken several Places in *Illyricum*, was not without Hopes utterly to have driven out *Cornificius*, who commanded in that Province for *Cæsar*; but by the Vigilance of that Officer, and the Bravery of *Vatinius*, his Designs were frustrated. *Cornificius* having sent *Vatinius* Advice of the Posture of Affairs, and that the Enemy had not only made a League with the *Barbarians* of the Country, but attacked several of his Garrisons, both maritime and inland, he resolved, notwithstanding the Rigour of the Season, and his Indisposition, for he lay ill at *Brundusium*, to repair to his Relief, and tho' he had not any thing in readiness for such an Expedition, his Valour and Industry surmounted all Difficulties. He wrote to *Kalenus* in *Achaia* immediately to send over to him the Ships he had there, but they not arriving with that Expedition so pressing an Occasion required, he got together all the Barks and small Frigates that could be found, and armed their Prows with Beaks, tho' scarce one of them was of a proper Size for Battel. With these, and the few Gallies he had, he set Sail for *Illyricum*, with a considerable Number of veteran Troops *Cæsar* had left behind him sick at *Brundusium*, and, immediately upon his Arrival, recovered several maritime Towns, confirming others with his Presence which were wavering, but made it his chief Care by all possible means to come up with *M. Octavius*, and hearing he was before [x] *Epidaurus*, where *Cæsar* had a Garrison, thither he hastened, but upon his Approach he raised the Siege and retired. *Vatinius*, with the Garrison of that Place, sailed again in quest of *Octavius*, who relying on the Goodness of his own Ships, and the Account he had of the Craziness of those with his Enemy, lay in wait for him at the Island [y] *Thauris*, by which he knew he would pass. As *Vatinius* was advancing towards that Island, without thinking the Enemy was so near, he perceived of a sudden a Ship, full of Soldiers, crowding down to him with all the Sail she could make, which was soon followed by several others, whereupon he put himself in a Posture to receive them, and hoisted his Flag as a Signal for Battel. The Enemy came on well prepared and in good Order, while the other was surprized and in Confusion; so that *Octavius* fought most regularly, but *Vatinius* with the greatest Resolution: For, tho' he was much inferior both in the Number and Quality of his Ships, yet he first charged *Octavius* with such Fury, that by the first Shock he tore off the Beak of his Gally. The Fight was at the same time maintained with great Obstinacy in all Quarters, but more especially near the two Generals, to whose Aid many crouded on both sides; but as soon as they came to a close Fight, *Vatinius*'s Men, by their superior Courage and Bravery, abundantly made amends for the Weakness of their Ships. *Octavius*'s own Gally was sunk, with diverse others, being transfix'd with the Beaks of *Vatinius*'s Vessels, and several being taken, the Troops on board them were kill'd, or thrown into the Sea. *Octavius* leaped into a Boat, which presently sinking with the great Numbers that crouded into her, he swam aboard one of his *Brigantines*, and,

Vatinius goes to aid Cornificius.

[x] Old Ragusa.

[y] La Brazza, on the Coast of Dalmatia.

Vatinius overcomes Octavius's Fleet.

with

with the shatter'd Remains of his Fleet, escaped by favour of the Night and bad Weather. *Vatinius* made a Signal to forbear chasing, and sailed victoriously, without the Loss of one Ship into the Port, from whence the Enemy came to engage him, where he stayed the next Day to refit his own Ships, and those he had taken from *Octavius*, (which were one Gally of five Tire of Oars, two of three Tire, and eight of two,) and then made the best of his way to the Island ᵖ *Issa*, to which Place he believed *Octavius* was fled. On his Arrival there he had the Town surrendered to him, which as it was one of the richest in those Parts, so was it the most devoted to the Enemy's Interest, and there he received Advice that *Octavius* was gone with a few small Ships for *Greece*, with Design to sail for *Sicily*, and thence to *Africk*: So that having thus, in so short a time, settled the Province in Peace in *Cornificius*'s Hands, and entirely cleared the *Adriatick* of the Enemy's Ships, he returned triumphantly to *Brundusium*.

ᵖ Ile Grande

Cæsar repaired from *Alexandria*, where we left him, into *Asia* against *Pharnaces* King of *Pontus*, who being soon defeated and slain, he appointed the aforementioned *Mithridates* of *Pergamus* to succeed him in that Kingdom, and then returning to *Italy*, he passed from thence over to *Africk*, where in a short time he overcame *Scipio* and *Juba*, and going back to *Rome* celebrated four Triumphs, on four successive Days, for the Wars he had so prosperously concluded, the first and second of which were for the Reduction of *Gaul* and *Ægypt*, the third for the Defeat of *Pharnaces*, and the fourth of *Juba*. The two Sons of *Pompey* having now rallied the scatter'd Forces of that Party in *Spain*, *Cæsar* repaired thither, and overcame them in a bloody Battel near ᑫ *Munda*, where they lost thirty thousand Men, and *Cneius*, the youngest of them, soon after, his Life; when returning from this Expedition, he was received with extravagant Applause, and the Senate decreed him the most unusual Honours; for they gave him the Title of Father of his Country, coined Money with his Image, ordered publick Sacrifices on his Birth-day, and his Statue to be set up in all Cities, and in the Temples at *Rome*. Which invidious Honours, and his Subversion of the Liberties of his Country, by retaining the supreme Power in his Hands, after the Settlement of Affairs, soon brought upon him the Conspiracy of *Brutus*, *Cassius*, and other Noblemen of *Rome*, by whose Hands he was slain in the Senate House.

Cæsar defeats Pharnaces King of Pontus. overcomes Scipio and Juba.

and Pompey's Sons in Spain.
ᑫ Ronda Veja, near Malaga.

The Honours done to Cæsar, and his Death. Year of the World, 3906. Of Rome 709. Before Christ, 42.

Chap. XVII.

Of the Naval Wars of the Romans *from the Death of* Julius Cæsar *to the Battel of* Actium, *and the Establishment of the Empire by* Augustus.

Octavius arms himself against M. Anthony.

OCtavius, Nephew of this great Man, being by the last Will of his Uncle adopted into the *Julian* Family, and made his Heir, he, by Authority of the Senate, in Conjunction with the Consuls *Hirtius* and *Pansa*, raised an Army against *Marc Anthony*, who, under Pretence of revenging the Death of *Cæsar*, exercised all manner of Tyranny, and had no other Design but to secure the Government of Affairs to himself. In the first Engagement they had, *Hirtius* was killed, and *Pansa* dying soon after, the sole Command of the Army came into the Hands of *Octavius*, who being now neglected by the Senate, closed with *Anthony*, and entering into a Treaty with him and *Lepidus*, formed that Association called the second Triumvirate.

An Association between Octavius, Anthony *and* Lepidus.

Octavius's first Care now was to cause all those who had been concerned in the Death of his Uncle to be proclaimed Enemies to the State, and marching against *Brutus* and *Cassius*, defeated them at *Philippi*, and put to Death several noble *Romans* of both Sexes by Proscription, but *Sextus Pompey*, after the Death of his Brother in *Spain*, made a shift to escape thence, and being neglected by *Julius Cæsar*, as not worthy of his Notice, for some time exercised Piracy in an obscure manner; till at length gathering together the scattered Remains of his broken Troops, and arming a great Number of Slaves, he possessed himself of *Sicily* and *Sardinia*, became very formidable, and routed the Fleet *Cæsar* sent against him under *Carina*, whom he put to Flight, as he did afterwards *Asinius Pollio*, who was employed on the same Service. Being upon the Assassination of *Cæsar*, recalled from Banishment, he retired to *Massilia*, and there for some time waited the Event of the War that was begun between *Anthony* and *Brutus*: But when the Senate gave the Provinces of *Macedonia* and *Syria* to *Brutus* and *Cassius*, and decreed War against *Dolabella*, *Pompey* was, by their Authority, commissioned to command the Fleet and the Sea Coasts, and to have the whole Administration of their Naval Affairs. Hereupon assembling his old Fleet from *Spain*, and the Parts adjacent, and having considerably increased it with a Number of new Ships, he ravaged the Seas for some time, and then repaired to *Messana*, which, together with all the rest of *Sicily*, he reduced to his Obedience, defeating *Salvidienus*, Admiral of *Octavius Cæsar*'s Fleet, in an Engagement between *Rhegium* and *Sicily*.

Sextus Pompey takes Sicily, and beats Cæsar's Fleet.

Obtains the sole Charge of Naval Affairs, reduces Sicily, *and beats* Octavius's *Fleet.*

Whilst *Salvidienus* was refitting his shatter'd Gallies, *Octavius*, who was then busy about *Rhegium* in raising Troops, and making all Preparations for War, received an Express from *Anthony* to come to him at *Brundusium*: In the Neighbourhood of which Place *Statius*

Anthony sends for Octavius to Brundusium.

CHAP. XVII. *Dissolution of the Rom. Empire.* 165

tius Murcus, of the Faction of *Brutus* and *Cassius*, had been with a strong Squadron, for some time, to prevent the Transportation of the Army to *Macedonia*. *Murcus*, upon Advice of *Octavius*'s Approach, retired from before *Brundusium*, yet kept hovering at a distance to observe the Enemy's Motions: But notwithstanding all his Precautions, *Octavius* and *Anthony* transported all their Troops in Safety to *Macedonia*. Soon after *Domitius Ænobarbus* joined *Murcus* with a considerable Squadron, so that their united Fleet consisted of a hundred and thirty Sail, with which they scoured the *Ionian* and *Adriatick* Seas, and let nothing escape their Hands, *Pompey* at the same time doing the like through the rest of the Mediterranean. While the two Armies were marching and countermarching in *Macedonia* (where after the Battel at *Philippi Brutus* and *Cassius* fell by their own Hands) a Fleet of Transports, going with two Legions to *Octavius*, under Convoy of a few Gallies, fell in with *Murcus* and *Ænobarbus*, who took some, burnt others, dispersed several, and forced the rest ashore, where they besieged them for five Days, when the Troops having spent all their Provisions, they desperately forced their way and escaped.

Domitius Ænobarbus joins Murcus with a Squadron.

Murcus and Ænobarbus rout Octavius's Transports.

Cleopatra, in her Conduct with Respect to the contending Parties, endeavour'd to trim between both; for tho' she had assisted *Dolabella*, yet *Serapion*, her Lieutenant in *Cyprus*, fought for *Cassius*; and after the Defeat of him and *Brutus*, she fearing the Resentments of the Conquerors, resolved in Person to meet *Anthony*, and, conscious of her own Charms, try how efficacious her Wit and Beauty would be in her Cause, he having summoned her to render an Account of her Behaviour. Crossing the Mediterranean to *Cilicia*, where *Anthony* then was, she came up the River *Cydnus* in a Vessel, the Stern whereof was of Gold, the Sails of purple Silk, and the Oars of Silver, which gently kept Time to the Sound of soft Musick. She placed her self under a rich Canopy of Cloth of Gold, habited like *Venus* rising out of the Sea, with beautiful Boys about her, like *Cupids*, fanning her; and her Women, representing the *Nereids* and *Graces*, leaned negligently on the Sides and Shrowds of the Vessel, while Troops of Virgins, richly drest, marched on the Banks of the River, burning Incense and rich Perfumes, which were covered with an infinite Number of People, gazing on with Wonder and Admiration. The Queen's Success with *Anthony* was answerable to her Expectations, for, far from shewing any Resentments, he from that Moment entertained a Passion for her which was the Source of all his future Misfortunes; and abandoning himself entirely to Love he accompanied her to *Ægypt*, where he spent the following Winter, dissolved in Luxury and Pleasure. There he received Letters that *Fulvia* his Wife, and his Brother *Lucius*, then Consul, disagreeing with *Octavius* had been obliged to retire from *Italy*; and at the same time News coming that the *Parthians*, assisted by *Labienus*, had made an Irruption into *Syria*, he began to rouse from his Lethargy and advanced with his Legions to *Phœnicia*. Proceeding thence, he, on the Coast of *Ionia*, received Intelligence that his Brother *Lucius*, having seized and fortified *Perusia*, had

Cleopatra determines to go to Anthony.

Anthony falls in Love with her.

Anthony goes from Ægypt to Phœnicia.

had afterwards surrendered that Place to *Octavius*, and been reconciled to him again; and coming soon after to *Athens*, he was met there by his Mother *Julia*, with some Gallies which *Pompey* had assisted her with in her Escape from *Italy*; who also brought *Pompey*'s Offers of an Alliance with him, if he intended to break with *Octavius*. *Anthony* returned *Pompey* his Thanks, letting him know he should gladly accept of his Proposal in case of a Breach, and that if they accommodated Matters, he might be included in the Treaty.

He comes to Athens, and there meets Pompey's Offer of an Alliance.

While *Octavius* and *Anthony* were making new Levies, and preparing for War, News came that *Fulvia*, *Anthony*'s Wife, was deceased at *Sicyon*; which proved of no small Consequence towards extinguishing the Flames of War which were just breaking out, the Friends of both these great Men never ceasing in their Sollicitations till they had brought them to lay down their Arms, and be reconciled to each other by means of a Match between *Anthony* and *Octavia*, the Sister of *Cæsar*. Hereupon ensued a Treaty, wherein was made another Partition of the Empire, allotting to *Octavius Italy*, *Gaul*, *Spain*, *Sicily*, *Sardinia*, and *Dalmatia*; and to *Anthony* all the other Provinces beyond the *Ionian* Sea. At the same time *Pompey* was declared a publick Enemy; who, upon Advice of these Proceedings, sent out his Officers to ravage the Seas of *Italy*, and plunder the Coasts, while himself, securing *Sicily*, *Sardinia*, and *Corsica*, kept *Rome*, and all the rest of *Italy*, from receiving any Supplies of Corn, which used to be carried thither, in great Quantities, from those Countries; and if he had landed there, and pushed his Fortune, he might, in all Probability, have come off Conqueror, being in Reality Master of a greater Force than *Octavius*, and abundantly more acceptable to the Senate and People of *Rome*: But being young, and unskilful in Affairs, he thought it enough to act upon the Defensive, when he should have boldly attacked the Enemy. This he had Encouragement enough to do, especially after the Accession of *Murcus*'s Force, who joined him with a Fleet of eighty Sail; and *Ænobarbus*, who commanded a strong Squadron in the *Ionian*, was very inclinable to do the like. The pressing Necessities, and frequent Mutinies of the People, on account of the Scarcity of Corn, at length obliged *Octavius* and *Anthony* to come to a Treaty with *Pompey*, wherein, among other things, it was agreed, that *Pompey* should retain the Islands he possessed, and have *Peloponnesus* besides; that he should restore the Freedom of Navigation, by leaving the Sea open, and supply *Italy* from time to time with certain Quantities of Corn. Matters being thus settled, he entertain'd *Octavius* and *Anthony* on board his Fleet, then lying off the Promontory *Misenum*, when *Menodorus*, his Vice-Admiral, calling him aside, putting him in mind, that he had it now in his Power to cut off the two Rivals for the Empire of the World, and seize it himself; and if he would but speak the word, it should be performed. *It cannot be done*, replied *Pompey*, *now you have acquainted me with it, for I have given them my Word and Honour, which I would not forfeit for that World*. After this Interview, *Pompey*

An Agreement between Octavius and Anthony.

The Empire divided.

Pompey declared a Traitor, secures Sicily, Sardinia, &c.

Octavius and Anthony come to a Treaty with Pompey.

CHAP. XVII. *Dissolution of the Rom. Empire.* 167

pey made the best of his way for *Sicily*, and *Octavius* and *Anthony* returned to *Rome*, from whence the latter, in a short time after, set out for *Asia*, where his Lieutenant *Ventidius* had defeated the *Parthians*.

Pompey seemed for a while to be satisfied, but as the Treaty between him and *Octavius* only regulated their Pretensions, not their Ambition, a Breach was soon made again; for which the Pretence on *Pompey*'s side was, that *Peloponnesus* being yielded to him by that Treaty, *Anthony* refused to quit it till he was satisfied for such Monies as were due to him from the Inhabitants. *Pompey* would by no means hear of this, but immediately fitting out a new Fleet, and providing himself of Forces, put to Sea, and renewed his former Piracies: But *Menodorus*, his Vice-Admiral beforementioned, in a short time revolted to *Octavius*, bringing in with him *Sardinia* and *Corsica*, with three Legions, which *Menodorus* was *Pompey*'s Freed-man, whom *Octavius*, in Requital of this Service, ranked among the *Ingenui*, promoted him to the Equestrian Order, and made him the next Commanding Officer to *Calvisius*, then Admiral of his Fleet. Against these *Pompey* sent *Menecrates*, another of his Freed-men, with a strong Squadron, with whom they came to an Engagement between the Island [a] *Ænaria* and *Cumæ*. The two Admiral-Ships charging each other with great Violence, immediately grappled, and *Menecrates*, by receiving a dangerous Wound, being no longer able to execute his Charge, and finding the Enemy like to make themselves Masters of his Ship, threw himself into the Sea and perished. Thus it fared with the Left Wing; and in the Right *Calvisius* breaking the Enemy's Line, forced several Ships to fly, which he chased with great Eagerness. *Democharies*, the next Commanding-Officer on *Pompey*'s side, laid hold of this Occasion to attack the rest of the Enemy's Ships their Admiral had left behind, of which he forced a considerable Number against the Rocks, where their Men deserting them, he set them on fire, and had destroyed them all, but that by the Return of *Calvisius* he was obliged to retire. About the same time *Cornificius* going with a Squadron to *Tarentum*, met with a furious Storm off [b] *Scyllæum*, wherein they suffered extremely, but more from the Loss he sustained by *Apollophanes*, one of *Pompey*'s Officers, who came out from *Messana*, and took several of his Ships. Upon these Advantages, *Pompey* was so swell'd with Vanity, that he styled himself *Neptune*'s Son, coined Money with that Inscription, whereon he was represented by a Trident and a Dolphin, and put on Robes of a Sea-green Colour, instead of Purple, which was usually worn; nor failed he to renew his Incursions with greater Fury, cruelly ravaging the Coasts of *Italy*, and sending *Apollophanes* into *Africk*, whom *Menodorus* followed, and gave him a signal Defeat on that Coast.

Octavius having received from *Anthony*, in pursuance of a new Treaty between them, a Reinforcement of a hundred and thirty Ships, bent his whole Thoughts upon the Reduction of *Pompey*, and the Island *Sicily*; and having appointed *Agrippa* his Admiral for that Expedition, and made a Lustration of the Fleet, with great

Pompey, Octavius, and Anthony fall out again.

Pompey's Vice-Admiral revolts to Octavius.

[a] *Ischia.*

Pompey is victorious at Sea.

[b] *Sciglio.*

Cornificius his Ships suffer in a Storm, &c.

The Vanity of Pompey on his Successes.

His Lieutenant beaten in Africk.

Cere-

Ceremony, he erected Altars at the Water's Edge, whereon he sacrificed to appease *Neptune*, and to procure a favourable Passage for the Fleet, when weighing Anchor from [c] *Puteoli*, he sailed toward *Sicily*, which Island was at the same time to be attacked by *Lepidus* from *Africa*, with eighty Gallies, a thousand Ships of Burthen, and twelve Legions, and by *Taurus* from *Tarentum* with the two hundred and thirty Sail which *Anthony* had sent. For the Reception of *Lepidus*, *Pompey* left *Plinius* with a good Force at *Lilybæum*, and placing strong Garrisons in all the Sea-Port Towns thereabouts, assembled the best part of his Fleet at *Messana*. *Taurus*, in his Passage from *Tarentum* to join *Octavius*, was forced back by bad Weather, with the Wind at South; and *Lepidus* sailing with the same Wind from *Africk* for *Lilybæum*, lost several of his Ships: so that in this Storm *Octavius* had two and thirty large Gallies, with some *Liburnian* Frigates, sunk or split against the Rocks. This unlucky Accident made him once resolve to defer the Prosecution of his Design till next Year, but the Clamours of the People for want of Corn obliged him to set about refitting his Ships, and go on with the Invasion. *Menodorus*, thinking he was not enough regarded, being only Lieutenant to *Calvisius*, and having procured an Assurance of a favourable Reception from *Pompey*, now deserted *Octavius* with the same Levity as he had before joined him, and going over with seven Gallies, burnt or sunk a considerable Number of *Octavius*'s Ships, which lay under the [d] Promontory *Palinurus*. Upon Advice that all the Shore of *Sicily* between [e] *Tyndaris* and [f] *Mylæ* was covered with *Pompey*'s Fleet and Troops, *Octavius*, concluding *Pompey* was there in Person, ordered *Agrippa*, with great part of his Fleet, which was now refitted, to proceed thither, and endeavour to bring the Enemy to a Battel; while himself sailing from [g] *Strongyle* to *Vibo*, there disembarked, and went overland with three Legions to the Fleet at *Tarentum* under the Command of *Taurus*. Off *Mylæ Agrippa* fell in with *Pompey*'s Fleet under *Demochares*, and they presently joined Battel with great Courage and Resolution; but *Pompey*'s Ships were by much the lightest and nimblest, and his Men by long Service the more experienced Sailors, *Agrippa*'s being of a much stronger Built, and consequently the most serviceable in a close Fight, so that several of *Pompey*'s were sunk at their sides; and *Agrippa* having greatly the Advantage, the others made a Signal to retreat: However, the Victor did not think fit to chase, but returned to *Strongyle*, content with the Damage he had already done them, having sunk or taken thirty of their Ships.

About this time *Octavius* sailed from [h] *Leucopetra*, with the Fleet under *Taurus*, and his Land-Forces, and came before [i] *Tauromenia*, where being refused Entrance, he passed on to the Mouth of the River *Onobola*, and landing his Troops, formed a Camp. *Pompey* coming thither with unexpected Celerity, *Octavius* left three Legions, five hundred Horse, a thousand light-armed Soldiers, and two thousand Auxiliaries under the Command of *Cornificius*, and went himself on board the Fleet to fight the Enemy. The Right Wing he

CHAP. XVII. *Dissolution of the* Rom. *Empire.* 169

he committed to *Titinius*, the Left to *Corcinus*; and sailing about *Octavius bea-*
the Fleet in a Yacht, he exhorted the Officers to do their Duty, *ten at Sea by*
when going on board his own Ship, he ordered the Flag to be struck, *Pompey.*
that so the Enemy might not know where he was. In this Battel
he received a total Defeat, and, with difficulty, made his Escape,
with only one Servant: Mean while *Papias*, one of *Pompey's* Lieutenants, falling in with some Transports, which were bringing from
Africk a Reinforcement of four Legions for *Lepidus*, he sunk or *Transports go-*
took the greatest Number, with the Troops on board; and those *ing with*
which escaped him fell into the Hands of *Tisienus Gallus*, one of *Troops to Le-*
Pompey's Governours of the Sea-Coasts. *Octavius*, re-assembling *pidus taken.*
his scattered Forces, joined *Lepidus*, and both advanced to besiege
Messana; but *Lepidus* being not well affected to him, for that he
was rather treated as a Lieutenant than his Partner in the Triumvirate, made an underhand Treaty with *Pompey*. It was not a pro- *Lepidus*
per time for *Cæsar* to take notice of this, wherefore he dissembled *makes a Trea-*
ty under-hand
his Resentments, not but that he had Spies who narrowly watched *with Pompey.*
his Conduct, that so he might not attempt any thing against him:
And, in order to his getting the sooner rid of so precarious and deceitful an Ally, he willingly accepted of *Pompey's* Offer of another
Battel at Sea. Off [k] *Naulochus* both the Fleets were drawn up, con- [k] *Cibaruso,*
sisting each of them of about three hundred Sail; and in this Acti- *between Tin-*
daro and
on the Courage and good Conduct of *Agrippa* were very conspicuous, *Messina.*
who, by help of the Turrets which he caused to be erected on his
Ships, his Engines, and his grappling Irons, (Inventions improved
by him to render them more serviceable) contributed very much to
obtaining the Victory. The Army beheld the Engagement from
the Shore with great Impatience, and Anxiety for the Event; and
when *Agrippa* perceived the Enemy began to give way, he renewed his Attacks with redoubled Fury, insomuch that at length he
entirely defeated them; for though seventeen of *Pompey's* Ships *Agrippa en-*
which first began to fly escaped with much difficulty, yet all the rest *tirely van-*
quishes Pom-
being encompass'd by *Agrippa*, were either burnt, sunk, or taken. *pey's Fleet.*
Upon this *Octavius's* People, and the Army ashore, paid their Vows
to the Sea-Gods, and sung Hymns in their Praise, while aboard
Pompey's Fleet there was nothing but Weeping and Despair, he himself flying, in the utmost Confusion, to *Messana*, and abandoning
his Land Army, which thereupon surrendered to *Octavius*; which
signal Victory was obtained on his side with the Loss only of three
Ships; and for the good Services of *Agrippa* therein, he, besides
other Princely Rewards, honoured him with a Naval-beaked Crown,
the second which was given of that kind.

The unhappy *Pompey*, who, before this great Overthrow, was
Master of a numerous and potent Fleet, fled but with six or seven
to *Asia*, hoping to find a favourable Reception from *Anthony*, in
Requital of past Favours; but, instead of that, he met with Disho- *Pompey ill*
nour, Chains, and at last an ignominious Death: Providence, by a *treated, and*
put to Death
remarkable Dispensation, making the three different Parts of the *by Anthony.*
then known World the Scene of the last Moments of the three fa-
Z mous

mous *Pompeys*; the Father being slain in *Africk*, the youngest Son in *Europe*, and this at *Miletus* in *Asia*. The same Year *Cæsar* came to an open Rupture with *Lepidus*, who aimed at keeping *Sicily* in his own Hands; but his Troops deserting him, he was soon reduced to Obedience; however *Cæsar* pardoned him, and suffered him to live a private Life at *Rome* with the Office of *Pontifex Maximus*.

Octavius had now got rid of one Competitor for the supreme Power, and, being desirous to have it all in his own Hands, *Anthony* was next to be subdued, whose Conduct, indeed, was of late very unworthy of his Character, and furnished *Octavius* with very reasonable Pretences for a War; for, besides the Injuries done to his Sister by *Anthony*'s Disregard to her, and giving himself up to the Love of *Cleopatra*, his Crimes of a publick Nature were, that he declared that Princess Queen of *Ægypt*, *Lybia*, *Cyprus*, and the lower *Syria*, associating with her *Cæsario*, the Son she had by *Julius Cæsar*; and as to the Children he had by her himself, he caused *Alexander*, the eldest, to be proclaimed King of *Armenia*, *Media*, and *Parthia*, and *Ptolemy*, the other Son, of *Phœnicia*, *Upper Syria*, and *Cilicia*. After several Reproaches by Letters on both sides, *Octavius* declared War against *Cleopatra*, and, by Decree of the Senate, divested *Anthony* of his Authority; who thereupon ordered *Canidius*, his General, to pass with all Expedition with sixteen Legions over to *Europe*, himself, with *Cleopatra*, coming to *Ephesus*, where his Lieutenants had assembled eight hundred Sail of Ships, of which *Cleopatra* furnished two hundred, with [l] twenty thousand Talents, and Provision for all his Forces. Early the next Spring *Octavius* seized upon the Island *Corcyra*, which was contained in *Anthony*'s Partition of the Empire, and crossed over with his Army into *Epirus*. *Anthony* had passed the Winter at *Patræ* in *Peloponnesus*, but the greatest part of his Fleet lay near *Actium*, at the Entrance of the [m] Gulph of *Ambracia*, where also was his Army encamped ashore. *Octavius* having landed his Troops in *Epirus*, ordered them to march towards *Actium*, and himself repairing with the Fleet to that Place, offered *Anthony* Battel, whose Gallies were not then ready for an Engagement, having but very few Men; however, he put them in a fighting Posture, with their Oars a-peek, as if he intended to bear down upon *Octavius*; who thereupon stood off to Sea without shewing any Intentions to engage. *Anthony* being perfectly well acquainted with the Country thereabouts, cut off the Water from *Octavius*'s Camp on every side, which very much distressed his Army; but the Success of *Agrippa* in taking *Corinth*, *Patræ*, and *Leucadia* about this time, much revived the Soldiers of *Octavius*, and occasioned the coming over to him of some of the principal Persons about *Anthony*; who, after several Deliberations whether he should trust his Empire and Life to the Decision of a Battel by Land or Sea, at last determined on the latter. He was, indeed, greatly superior to his Enemy; for *Octavius*'s Fleet consisted but of two hundred and fifty Sail, whereas he had

CHAP. XVII. *Dissolution of the Rom. Empire.* 171

had five hundred, and those of a much greater Magnitude than the other's, there being great Numbers of six, and some of nine Tire of Oars, with Towers erected on them, so that they appeared like floating Castles; the Water seeming to groan under their Weight, and the Winds to labour in driving them along. In *Anthony*'s Army were a hundred thousand Foot, and twelve thousand Horse; in *Octa-* *vius*'s, which was opposite to it, on the other side of the Gulph, were the like Number of Horse, and ninety two thousand Foot; and the former put on board his Fleet two and twenty thousand fighting Men, with two thousand Archers. The Battel was deferred by both Parties for some Days on account of the Badness of the Weather, but when it proved fair, the two Fleets bore up to each other, *Anthony* taking upon himself the Command of his Right Wing, assisted by *Publicola*; *Cælius* had the Left, and *Marcus Octavius*, with *Marcus Justeius* were in the Centre. *Agrippa* commanded in the Left of the Enemy, and *Octavius* in the Right. *Anthony* in a Yacht went about his Fleet, and encouraged his Officers to behave with their accustomed Bravery and Resolution, directing the Pilots to keep the Ships constantly in their Stations during the Battel; and telling the Soldiers that the Largeness of their Vessels gave them Opportunity of fighting as firmly, and with as much Assurance as on Land. *Octavius*, in like manner, exhorted his Soldiers to do their Duty, and, among other things, told them, that *the Enemy's Ships were laden indeed, but not manned; and that if they exceeded in Multitude of Men, he surpassed them in Number of Soldiers.*

Both sides prepare for Fight.

All things being thus in Readiness on both sides, and the greatest Appearance that could be of an approaching Battel, *Octavius* had Intelligence sent him, that what Countenance soever *Anthony* put upon the Matter, *Cleopatra*, who was absolute Mistress of his Resolutions, being frighted by some ill Presages which had lately happened, and the Scarcity of Provisions which already began to be in the Army, had persuaded him to determine on returning to *Ægypt*, so that they were only intent on making their Retreat in the handsomest manner they could. *Octavius*, taking his Measures according to these Advices, resolved not to interrupt their Design of retiring, but when they should be under Sail to charge them in their Rear, for his Ships being of a light Built, and consequently much the best Sailors, he thought he might easily come up with them, and by the Terror such a Proceeding would produce, oblige most of them to surrender. But *Agrippa* being apprehensive that the Enemy might be too quick for them, and, by the help of their Oars and Sails, (of both which they were well provided) make their Escape; and observing that *Octavius* his Ships and Men had suffered very much by the late bad Weather, which had happened to be more violent in the Gulph than in the Road, he prevailed with him to change his Design, and immediately attack them; so that having directed some of his principal Officers to go about the Fleet in Pinnaces, and not only give the necessary Orders to those who fought the Ships, but advise him from time to time of the Posture

Agrippa prevails with Octavius to attack Anthony's Fleet.

Z 2 of

of Affairs, he advanced ahead of his Fleet (which followed at some Diſtance) to take a nearer View of the Enemy; who being drawn up before the Entrance of the Gulph, made no other Motion upon his Approach than increaſing the Number of their head-moſt Ships, which was contrary to *Octavius*'s Expectation, who thought they would have bore away; ſo that he, in ſome Confuſion, cauſed his Gallies to lie on their Oars, and then changed his Order of Battel, diſpoſing the Fleet in form of a Half-Moon. Now *Anthony*, who had hitherto immoveably kept his Station, fearing to be ſurrounded, advanced againſt *Octavius*, and the Battel began, wherein the Ships of the latter, as the Fight was managed, had greatly the Advantage; for being incomparably more light and nimble than the others, they bore up againſt them with incredible Swiftneſs, and having damaged them with their Beaks, retired with the ſame Celerity. *Anthony*'s People, by reaſon of the Bulk and Unwieldineſs of his Ships, were unable to purſue, but endeavoured to remedy that Defect by pouring down Showers of Stones and Darts upon their Enemies as they approach'd, attempting at the ſame time to grapple them with their Irons, wherein, if they ſucceeded, they preſently ſunk them at their ſides, the Certainty of which Deſtruction made the Enemy rely wholly on their Swiftneſs, and Dexterity to avoid a cloſe Fight; ſo that the Fleet of *Anthony* might juſtly be compared to a ſtrong Body of Infantry, which keeping its Ground, ſuſtains the Enemy's Attacks; and that of *Octavius* to Squadrons of light Horſe which briskly charge and retreat.

Cleopatra flies with ſixty Sail.

The Victory hung long in ſuſpenſe, being bravely and obſtinately diſputed on both ſides, when at length *Cleopatra*, who lay at Anchor with ſixty Sail in the Port, ſeeing ſo bloody a Conteſt, and being doubtful which way Fortune would incline, could no longer bear the Uncertainty of the Event, but, in no ſmall Terror, cauſed the Signal to be made for weighing, and with full Sails paſſing through *Anthony*'s Fleet, put them in great Diſorder; who no ſooner ſaw them got clear, and ſteering Southward, as if they made for *Ægypt*, but, unable to ſupport the Thoughts of *Cleopatra*'s Abſence, he im-

Anthony follows Cleopatra.

mediately went into his Barge, and, accompanied with only two of his Domeſticks, made all the haſte he could after her: Thus, abandoning all Thoughts of Honour and Safety, and playing the Part of a cowardly Soldier, while each of his Men performed the Office of a couragious General. For tho' this baſe Deſertion of his could not but ſomewhat diſhearten them, yet the Battel continued for ſeveral Hours after; nor could *Octavius* at laſt have won the Day, had he not made ſeveral unuſual and extraordinary Efforts of Courage and Bravery. He would very gladly have made himſelf Maſter of the Fleet, if poſſible, without doing any great Execution among the Ships, becauſe of the immenſe Riches they had on board; but finding the obſtinate Defence *Anthony*'s People made, he at length gave

Octavius orders Anthony's Ships to be ſet on fire.

Orders for ſetting them on fire, whereupon his Men hurled flaming Darts, Torches, and Pots filled with Pitch, and burning Coals, into them, and plied them with ſuch Quantities of theſe Combuſtibles, that they were ſoon in Flames. *Anthony*'s Soldiers had now ſo much

Work

CHAP. XVII. *Dissolution of the* Rom. *Empire.* 173

Work on their Hands, some in endeavouring to extinguish the Flames, some in attempting to secure the valuable Effects, and others to repulse the Enemy, that *Octavius*'s People made a very great Slaughter. Some, upon their being attacked in this Distraction, leaped into the Sea, others were smothered in the Smoak, and many were burnt alive, the Wind spreading the Fire with great Violence. *Octavius* at last obtained the Victory, and finding no more Resistance, gave order for extinguishing the Flames, from which three hundred Ships were rescued, and with them, and the rest of his Fleet, he intended to pursue *Anthony* and *Cleopatra*, but found they were gone too far for him to come up with them. The Army which *Anthony* left ashore having been seven Days without receiving any Advices from him, at length surrendered themselves; and the same Day that *Octavius* made himself Master of the Ships, he consecrated to *Apollo* (who had a celebrated Temple at *Actium*) a Gally of each rate from three Tire of Oars to ten; causing not long after to be built a City on the opposite side of the Gulph, which he called ⁿ *Nicopolis*, as an eternal Monument of so signal a Victory. *Anthony's Army surrenders to Octavius.* A. M. 3919. Of Rome, 722. ⁿ *Now Prevesa.*

Agrippa was shortly after sent back to *Italy* with a Body of Troops, to prevent any Commotions which might happen there, *Octavius* himself repairing to *Athens*, and from thence to *Samos*; mean while *Anthony* parted with *Cleopatra* off the º Promontory *Tænarium*, whom he advised to proceed to *Ægypt*, there to appease any Disorders which might arise upon the News of this Defeat; and he following her soon after, was informed that his Troops in *Lybia* had revolted, and that his Army in *Syria* was ready to do the like. Arriving at *Alexandria*, he found *Cleopatra* attempting a stupendous Piece of Work, which was the carrying her Gallies over-land from the Mediterranean to the Red Sea, that so, if the Necessity of her Affairs should require it, she might escape, with her immense Riches, to some Country in the East, and avoid the Dishonour of submitting to *Octavius*. But several of these Gallies, with the Carriages, being burnt by the People of *Arabia Petræa*, who united against her, she laid aside that Design, and set about securing her Ports and Harbours toward the Mediterranean, resolving to conquer, or die in her own Dominions. º *Cape Matapan.* *Anthony follows Cleopatra to Ægypt.* *Cleopatra attempts to carry her Gallies by Land to the Red Sea.*

Octavius was by this time arrived in *Ægypt*, where *Cornelius Gallus* had seized *Parætonium* for him; and *Anthony*, with his Troops, and a considerable Number of Ships, resolving to dislodge them, came before the Place. *Gallus* made a successful Sally, wherein the Besiegers received some Loss both in their Army and Fleet, and then bethought himself of this Stratagem: He, in the Mouth of the Port of *Parætonium*, caused Chains to be laid in the Night under Water, and the next Day kept no Guards about the Harbour, as if he had feared nothing from the Enemy on that side, who thereupon tumultuously entered the Port with their Ships; which they had no sooner done, but by certain Engines the Chains were hawled up, and their Retreat cut off; and *Gallus* at the same time assailing them from all Parts, burnt or sunk much the greatest Number of them. *Anthony comes before Parætonium.* *His Ships burnt or sunk.*

The

174   *Naval Transactions before the*   Book II.

<small>p Damiata.

Anthony takes Pharos, &c. but is beaten, and his Fleet goes over to Octavius.

Anthony and Cleopatra kill themselves.</small>

The next Day *Anthony* receiving Advice that *Octavius* had made himself Master of p *Pelusium*, he raised the Siege, and with the Remains of his Fleet advanced to *Alexandria*, where he hoped to make an easy Conquest of *Octavius*'s Troops, since they were fatigued and spent with a long Voyage at Sea. He presently, by means of his Fleet, possessed himself of the Island *Pharos*, and engaging with the Enemy ashore, put them to Flight, with which little Success being encouraged, he again gave the Enemy Battel, but his Troops being defeated, and his Fleet going over to *Octavius*, he, in this desperate Posture of Affairs, soon after stabbed himself; and his Death was presently followed by that of *Cleopatra*, who to avoid the Shame of making Part of *Octavius*'s Triumph, poisoned her self, as hath been generally believed, by the Application of Asps to her Arms. *Octavius* having reduced *Ægypt* into the Form of a Province, appointed *Gallus* to govern it, and making a Progress through *Syria*, and the *Lesser Asia*, returned to *Rome*, where he was received with an universal Joy and Satisfaction, as a Person who had put an End to the Miseries and Calamities which had so long reigned in the greatest Part of the World. He triumphed three Days for *Illyricum*, for the Battel of *Actium*, and the Conquest of *Ægypt*, with extraordinary Splendor and Magnificence; after which he made a Disposition of his Naval Forces in the most convenient Places of the Empire, in the manner we have related in the first Book, that they might be ready upon any Emergency.

Chap. XVIII.

Of the Naval Wars of the Romans, *from the Establishment of the Empire by* Augustus *to the Dissolution thereof by the Irruptions of the barbarous Nations.*

<small>Little maritime Affairs till Constantine the Great.

Year of the World 3941. Before Christ, 7.

a Danube.
b Nieper.</small>

THE *Roman* Empire being thus settled by *Octavius*, (who now assumed the Name of *Augustus*,) its Dominions brought almost to their utmost Extent, and the whole established in Peace; there happened from this Time till the Days of *Constantine* the Great, very few Naval Wars, so that the maritime Affairs of three Centuries will come within a narrow Compass. Not that it is to be supposed that the World was in Peace all this while; for scarce in any Period of Time have there been more violent Wars, but their Fury raged mostly in inland Countries. There it was that *Varus* and his Legions were cut to pieces by the *Germans*. There it was that *Drusus* fell, after having slain infinite Multitudes of those People: And thither it was that *Tiberius* was sent nine times by *Augustus* to harrass and subdue the then barbarous Inhabitants of *Germany*. These Wars were followed by those with the *Getæ*, beyond the a *Ister*, and the *Sarmati*, on the other side of the *Vistula*, and the b *Borysthenes*:

till

CHAP. XVIII. *Dissolution of the* Rom. *Empire.* 175

till at length the *Goths* of several Denominations, the *Alans, Hunns, Vandals, Francs, Saxons,* and other immense Swarms of *Barbarians,* without Number or Name, broke in upon the Empire, some of them passing over the *Danube* into *Greece* and *Italy,* some over the *Rhine* into *Gaul* and *Spain,* and others crossing the Ocean into *Britain.* All this while there seemed to be a general Tranquillity at Sea, by the few Accounts we have of Transactions there, and that they made no other Use of Shipping than for Trade, or the bare Transportation of Forces.

The first Naval Occurrence we meet with after *Augustus* is in the time of his Successor *Tiberius,* when *Germanicus* took the ᶜ Island of the *Batavi,* subdued the *Sicambri,* and defeated the ᵈ *Brusteri* in a Sea Fight at the Mouth of the River ᵉ *Amisius.* The Fleet he made use of in this Expedition consisted of a thousand Sail, which he caused to be built on purpose of a peculiar Structure, for they were between Ships of War and those of Burthen, being not so long as the first, and longer than the latter, bellying out in the Waste for the greater Convenience of Stowage; and they were yet more particularly remarkable for having no Poop, one End being equally sharp and pointed with the other, with a Rudder at both, the Reason of which Singularity was because of the many Turnings and Windings of the Chanels in those Parts, and the extreme Difficulty of Navigation. After the Defeat of the Enemy, he, sailing into the Ocean, lost the greatest Part of his Fleet in a Storm, several of them being swallowed up in Whirlpools, and others driven away to the ᶠ *Orcades* Islands. Some Ships were sent, when the Tempest was appeased, in quest of those that were dispersed, and after they were re-assembled, the People on board related the most dreadful Stories of strange Kinds of Birds, frightful Sea Monsters, Men of unusual Form, and other such Fancies which their Fear suggested to them.

ᶜ *Province of Holland.*
ᵈ *Groeningen and Embden.*
ᵉ *Embs. After the Birth of Christ,* 18. *Germanicus defeats the Brusteri at Sea.*

Several of the Ships with Germanicus lost in bad Weather.
ᶠ *Orkney Isles.*

During the Reigns of *Caligula, Claudius, Nero,* and *Galba,* there happened little remarkable at Sea, the latter of whom was succeeded by *Otho,* and he by *Vitellius;* but between *Otho*'s and *Vitellius*'s Forces there was a Naval Rencounter in the Mouth of the ᵍ *Padus,* and *Otho* with the stationary Fleet at *Misenum* possessed himself of ʰ *Gallia Narbonensis.* About this time sprung up an Impostor, who pretending to be the Emperor *Nero,* made some Disturbance, but his mock Reign was of a very short Date; for *Calpurnius Asprenas* being then Governor of *Galatia* and *Pamphylia,* he, among the Islands of the *Ægean,* hearing some of his Lieutenants had been sollicited by this *Nero* to a Revolt, sent out a small Squadron of Ships, with which the Impostor engaging, he lost his Life in the Conflict, not but that he defended himself with greater Bravery than was suitable to the Character of the Emperor he personated.

A Rencounter at Sea between the Ships of Otho and Vitellius.
ᵍ *Po.*
ʰ *Languedoc and Provence.*

A Counterfeit Nero overcome at Sea.

Upon the News of *Otho*'s Death, (who slew himself after the Overthrow of his Forces by *Vitellius,*) *Vespasian,* being then in *Judæa* with a great Army, aspired to the Empire, and sent *Mucianus* before him to carry on that Design, who assembling a small Fleet in the *Euxine,* repaired to *Byzantium,* and there increasing them, made the best of his Way for *Italy,* where he seized *Brundusium*

Vespasian, on the Death of Otho, aspires to the Empire.

dusium and ⁱ *Tarentum*, and made himself Master of ᵏ *Calabria* and ˡ *Lucania*. The opposite Party were unable to make any Resistance at Sea, the Fleet at *Misenum* having but one Legion aboard; and that at *Ravenna*, wavering in its Fidelity to *Vitellius*, did not act at all in his behalf: But while *Mucianus* with the Fleet of *Pontus*, now without a Guard, was thus successful in *Italy*, a War broke out in that Kingdom under the Conduct of *Anicetus*, who took up Arms for *Vitellius*. He invented a new Kind of Ships something resembling the Description we have of *Noah*'s Ark, and having got together a considerable Number of Vessels of that Built, seized on ᵐ *Trapezus*, and other Cities of *Asia*, and by his great Successes began to acquire a considerable Reputation. *Vespasian*, upon Advice of these Proceedings, dispatched *Virbius Geminus* against him, an able and experienced Officer, who, when he set out on this Service had not so much as one Ship with him, but with great Dispatch caused Timber to be cut down, and built a Fleet, with which he, in the very first Rencounter, forced *Anicetus* to betake himself to Land, and setting fire to his Ships, soon after constrained him to surrender, and put him to Death. In another Part of the World the *Batavi* took the Part of *Vespasian*, who, under the Conduct of *Civilis* and *Cannefas*, their Generals, surprized *Vitellius*'s Fleet of twenty four Sail in the Mouth of the *Rhine*; soon after which *Lucilius Bassus*, Admiral of the Fleet at *Ravenna*, declared for *Vespasian*: And *Fabius Valens*, an Officer of *Vitellius*'s, being drove by bad Weather from before *Pisa* to the Port of ⁿ *Hercules Monæcus*, and thence to the ᵒ Islands *Stœchades*, *Valerius Paulinus*, who commanded in those Parts for *Vespasian*, sent some light Frigates against him, which defeated and took him Prisoner, whereupon all submitted to the Conquerour, the Fleet at *Misenum* revolted, and *Spain*, *Gaul*, and *Germany* declared for him: Which was soon followed by the Murder of *Vitellius*.

After a long Series of succeeding Emperors, during whose Time we meet with nothing remarkable at Sea, *Gallienus* came to the Imperial Purple, who commissioned *Cleodamus* and *Athenæus*, two Citizens of *Byzantium*, to inspect the Condition of the maritime Towns, and rebuild such as were gone to decay: And in his Time the *Scythians*, crossing the *Euxine*, entered the Mouth of the ᵖ *Ister*, and committing terrible Devastations in the *Roman* Provinces on that side, *Venerianus*, Admiral of *Gallienus*'s Fleet lying at *Byzantium*, engaged them, and gave them a signal Defeat; notwithstanding which, these *Scythians* (united and intermixed with the *Goths*, so much celebrated in after Times) in a short time repaired their Loss, and with immense Multitudes, and a Fleet of two thousand Sail, renewed the War. Off ᑫ *Marcianopolis* in *Mœsia*, the Emperor *Claudius*, who succeeded *Gallienus*, came to an Engagement with them, who, by his extraordinary Valour and Conduct, overthrew those barbarous Nations, and made an incredible Slaughter of them, killing and making Prisoners three hundred thousand Men, nor took he less than two thousand Ships; so that whole Houses were filled with their Targets, Shields, Swords, Lances, and other Habiliments

CHAP. XVIII. *Dissolution of the* Rom. *Empire.* 177

biliments of War; of all which the Emperor gave an Account in writing to the Senate. *Claudius* was succeeded by *Aurelian*; he by *Tacitus*, and *Tacitus* by *Probus*, which Prince having reduced all *Germany* to his Obedience, planted a prodigious Multitude of the *Francs* (then inhabiting in and about that Circle of the Empire now called *Franconia*) that he had taken Prisoners in the War, along the Coasts of the *Euxine* Sea, with Design to curb the *Scythians* by a People of the like Rudeness and Ferocity with themselves: But it was followed by an Event very different from what he proposed. *The Emperor Probus plants the Francs along the Euxine, to curb the Scythians.*

He was succeeded by his Son *Carus*, and his Successor, after *Numerius* and *Carinus*, was *Dioclesian*, about which time happened a memorable Naval Event, whereby, if the greatest Courage, Dexterity and Dispatch had not been used to prevent it, the *Roman* Empire had then gone near to have been rent in pieces by the formidable Power of *Barbarians* at Sea. There was one *Carausius*, a Native of the Country of the ʳ *Menapii*, who had acquired a singular Reputation for his Courage and Bravery in several military Exploits, but especially at Sea; and the *Cimbri*, *Saxons*, and other maritime People of *Germany*, very much infesting the *British* Seas at this time, *Carausius* was thought considerable enough to have committed to him the Defence of the Provinces against these Barbarians: Which Power he employed only to serve his own Interest and Profit, with little or no Detriment to the Enemy. For these Pirates ravaging the Coasts as cruelly as ever, he took no Care to attack them but at a time when he knew they were very richly laden with Booty; when, using them like Sponges, he seized their Wealth, and set them at liberty, never executing any of them, nor restoring the Effects to their Owners, nor laying them apart for the publick Treasury, but applied all to his own Use. *Dioclesian*, upon Notice of this Behaviour of his, gave Orders to *Constantius* and *Maximin* to cut him off, the readiest Way to do which *Maximin* thought was by the Hands of a Ruffian, and therefore employed one for that Purpose. *Carausius*, finding what was in Agitation against him, began to think his only Security lay in his Boldness, and therefore since he might no longer have the Command of the *British* Fleet, (as that under his Direction was called) he resolved to set up for the Dominion, not only of the Province of *Britain*, but of the World it self, and try his Chance for the Empire. This he did with such a full Consent of his Army, which was very considerable, that never was the Imperial Purple assumed with greater Applause of the Soldiery; for in these Days every little Army thought themselves invested with a Power of disposing of the Empire. *ʳ Flanders and Brabant. Carausius appointed to guard the British Seas from Pirates. Dioclesian gives Orders to cut off Carausius. Carausius sets up for the Imperial Dignity. A. D. 287.*

To support these Pretensions, he, besides the whole *Roman* Fleet in the Ocean, which he had under his Command by virtue of his Office, caused a prodigious Number of Ships of the like Force to be built, assembling People from all Parts for the carrying on of this Armament; and this he did with the more Confidence, for that having perfectly secured the *Roman* Fleet in his Interest, he knew *Constantius* and *Maximin* must be at the Disadvantage of building *Builds a great Fleet.*

A a one,

one, and employing none but raw Men both at the Oar and Sail. They, on the other hand, being sensible of the Importance of the Business they were engaged in, divided the Work between them; so that *Maximin* from the Naval Arsenals on the *Rhine* fitted out a Fleet of a thousand Sail; and *Constantius* took upon himself to deal with the Enemy by Land. Hearing that *Carausius* was at *Portus Gessoriacus*, and continued there not only to sound the Minds of the *Gauls*, but to excite them to a Revolt, he advanced thither with his Army, it being a well fortified Town, and the most considerable in those Parts; but *Carausius* having the Sea open, so as that he might supply the Place from time to time both with Men and Provisions, very little regarded *Constantius*'s Attempts by Land, who being as sensible as they of this Advantage, resolved to deprive them of it, and therefore caused a prodigious Number of large Trees to be cut down which were fixed like Piles in the Mouth of the Harbour; when throwing in immense Quantities of Earth and Sand, he in a short time blocked it up, notwithstanding the Violence of the Waves, and all the Efforts *Carausius* made to interrupt the Workmen; who amazed at this stupendous Work, thought it not safe to trust to the Walls any longer, now his Communication by Sea was cut off, and, under Favour of a tempestuous Night, escaping with a few Followers through the *Roman* Camp, went on board a Frigate, wherein he got over to his Fleet and Army in *Britain*; but he soon repented his hasty Resolution, when it was known by him that the Day after he had left the Place, the Sea had carried away all *Constantius*'s Work.

We took Notice but now of the Emperor *Probus*'s transplanting a great Number of the *Francs* to the Coasts of the *Euxine* Sea, with a view of making them Enemies to the *Scythians* and *Barbarians* in those Parts; but their Similitude of Manners, and Enmity to the *Roman* Name, soon made them good Friends; so that uniting their Forces together, they embarked aboard an incredible Number of Ships, and passing through the *Thracian Bosphorus*, came down into the Mediterranean, which they filled from East to West with their Depredations. They seized and burnt *Syracuse*, whence proceeding Westward, they passed through the Streights of *Gades*; and having committed terrible Devastations on the Sea along the Coasts of *Spain* and *Africk*, they returned laden with Spoils, and, without any Opposition, arrived at their Habitations in *Pontus*. *Carausius*, tho' divided by so many Countries from these People, made a League with them, in pursuance whereof they equipped another Fleet as numerous as the former, and came down again to the Streights of *Gades*, with intent to proceed round and join his Fleet in the *British* Ocean. Never was a greater Terrour spread throughout the *Roman* Empire, for there was no Safety in any Place where these Pirates could have Access with their Ships: So that Trade and Merchandise lay dead; for if in Summer, the Season for Navigation, they adventured to Sea, they could go no where without falling into the Hands of the *Barbarians*, and if in Winter, they became a Sacrifice to the Winds and Storms, tho' of the two the latter

CHAP. XVIII. *Dissolution of the* Rom. *Empire.* 179

ter were the gentler Enemies: nor is it to be doubted that if a Junction of the two Fleets had happen'd, pursuant to the Project between *Carausius* and the *Franks*, it would have given a terrible Shock to the *Roman* Power. In this Situation of Affairs Dispatch was of the last Importance; wherefore *Constantius*, taking under his Command the thousand Sail of Ships which *Maximin* had got ready in the Mouth of the *Rhine*, assembling several others, and causing more new ones to be run up with the greatest Expedition, he disposed several Squadrons in convenient Stations along the Coasts of *Britain*, *Gaul*, and *Spain*, as far as *Gades*, to prevent *Carausius* his bringing his Naval Forces together, and attempting to join the *Franks*. Then, with the main Body of the Fleet, he proceeded to meet those People who had by this time passed the Streights of *Gades*, and in few Days came up with them. He first by several slight Skirmishes tried their Strength, and the manner of their fighting, when attacking them with his whole Fleet, they came to a general Engagement, wherein he gave them so absolute and entire a Defeat, that there was not a Man left to return to *Pontus*, nor was there in that Country so much as the Name of a *Frank* ever after heard of. A brave and successful Captain he was, that by so prudent a Distribution of his Forces, and by one well-timed Battel, could restore Peace and Security to the World.

Constantius goes with a Fleet against Carausius and his Allies.

The Franks and Scythians entirely defeated at Sea.

After this Victory, *Constantius* returned to *Gaul*, in order to pass with his Land-Forces over to *Britain* against *Carausius*, who had taken up his Residence in that Island; but while he was preparing for this Expedition, *Carausius* was murdered by one *Allectus* his familiar Friend, who thereupon assumed the Purple, tho' not Master of one of *Carausius*'s good Qualities to countenance his Presumption. Having Advice that *Constantius* lay in the Mouth of the ʳ *Sequana*, he rendezvous'd his Fleet at the ˢ Island *Vectis*, with a full Resolution to fight the Enemy, if Opportunity should offer. *Constantius* weighed Anchor from the *Sequana* with the same Design, but a thick Fog coming up, the two Fleets missed each other, and he landed in *Britain* before *Allectus* had any certain Intelligence of his being put to Sea. When all his Troops were disembarked, he ordered the Ships to be burnt, that they might be sensible there was no returning, unless they came off Conquerors. *Allectus*, as soon as he had Advice of the Enemy's Landing, came also on shore, but declining a Battel with *Constantius*, fell in with *Asclepiodatus*, his Lieutenant; and finding in the first Charge his Troops give way, he threw of his Imperial Robes with the same Rashness he had put them on, and rushing among the thickest of the Enemy, was slain without Distinction. *Constantius*, upon this Victory, behaved himself with great Moderation, nor permitted he any of the Islanders to suffer either in their Lives or Fortunes.

Carausius is murdered in Britain. and Allectus assumes the Purple.

ʳ *Seine.*
ˢ *Isle of Wight.*

Allectus overcome by Constantius, and slain.

Upon the Resignation of *Dioclesian* and *Maximian*, *Constantius* and *Galerius* became Emperors, and divided the *Roman* World between them. The first had *Italy*, *Africk*, *Spain*, *Gaul*, *Britain*, and that part of *Germany* next the *Rhine*; and the latter *Greece*, *Illyricum*, *Asia*, and *Ægypt*, with the Countries on the other side

A. D. 291.

The Roman Empire divided between Constantius and Galerius.

A a 2
the

the *Danube*. But *Constantius*, like a prudent Husbandman, would keep no more in his Hands than he could well cultivate, and therefore resigned his Pretensions to *Italy* and *Africk*, which were thereupon committed by *Galerius* to his eldest Son *Severus*, as at the same time *Asia* was to his youngest Son *Maximin*; himself, as Arbiter on the World, taking up his Residence in *Illyricum*, that so he might on one hand be in the Neighbourhood of *Italy* and the West, and of the other of *Asia* and the East. In the mean time *Maxentius*, the Son of *Maximian*, was saluted Emperor at *Rome* by the Prætorian Cohorts, against whom *Severus* advanced with an Army; but his Troops deserting him, he fled to *Ravenna*, and was there slain. *Maximian* began now to entertain Thoughts of resuming the Empire, and endeavoured to cut off his Son *Maxentius*, but failing in that Design, he fled into *Gaul* to *Constantine*, (the Son of *Constantius* lately deceased) who had married his Daughter. He tampered with that Lady to procure the Death of her Husband, but she rightly preferring the Duty of a Wife to that of a Daughter, discovered the Matter to *Constantine*, who, in his own Defence, having caused *Maximian* to be slain, he marched into *Italy* against *Maxentius*, and coming to a Battel with him under the Walls of *Rome*, gave him an entire Defeat, wherein *Maxentius* attempting to get over the Bridge of *Milvius*, fell into the River, and was drowned.

Licinius had married the Sister of *Constantine*, and being assumed by him his Partner in the Empire, was to have the East for his Division. *Maximin*, the Son of *Galerius*, beforementioned, being in Possession of those Countries, marched with a great Army against *Licinius*, but by the way died of a sudden Distemper, or, as others say, by the Sword; so that now *Constantine* and *Licinius* were only remaining (for by this time *Galerius* also was dead) to divide the Empire between them, of which one possessed the West, and the other the East; and the *Hellespont* being the common Boundary to both, gave occasion to a Naval War between them. *Licinius*, not contented with *Asia*, would also have some footing in *Europe*, and seized on part of *Thrace*, with the Cities ᵗ *Adrianopolis* and ᵘ *Byzantium*; whereupon *Constantine* repaired with a great Army to ʷ *Thessalonica*, and reflecting of how great Importance to his Affairs it would be, if he could first make himself Master of the Streights between *Europe* and *Asia*, he gave Orders for assembling all the Ships of *Greece*, *Dalmatia*, and *Illyricum* at the *Portus Piræus* in *Attica*, where accordingly rendezvoused two hundred Gallies of thirty Oars each, and two thousand Ships of Burthen which might, by fixing on of Beaks, be made fit for War. *Licinius*, at the same time, being apprehensive lest the Enemy should seize the *Bosphorus*, *Propontis*, and *Hellespont*, and thereby cut off his Communication with his great Armies in *Asia*, also set about getting ready a Fleet, and issued out Orders to all his maritime Provinces for that purpose. In a short time *Phœnicia* provided thirty Gallies of three Tire of Oars, *Ægypt* as many, the People of *Doris* and *Ionia* sixty, the *Cypriots* thirty, the People of *Caria* twenty, the *Bithynians* thirty, and the *Africans* fifty. And now *Rausimodus*, King of

CHAP XVIII. *Dissolution of the Rom. Empire.* 181

of the *Sauromati*, crossing the *Ister* with a great Army, diverted *Constantine* for a while from his Naval Affairs, who proceeding against him, forced him to repass the River, and closely pursuing, gave him an entire Defeat, taking a great Number of Prisoners.   *Rausimodus, King of the Sauromati, overcome by Constantine.*

On his Return to *Thessalonica*, he gave Orders for the Fleet to proceed from *Piræus* to the *Hellespont*, where the Enemy's Fleet were by this time assembled under the Command of *Abantus*. *Constantine*'s Officers having particular Regard to the Narrowness of the Place they were to fight in, drew out only eighty of their small Gallies for their Line of Battel against the numerous Fleet of *Licinius*, consisting of Gallies all of three Tire of Oars. The Enemy relied wholly on this Advantage of their Superiority of Force, and thought of nothing more than driving *Constantine*'s People before them, while they, on the other hand, sustained the Enemy's Attack in a firm and compact Order, fearing nothing if they could but support the first Charge. This Behaviour of theirs so broke the Enemy's Measures, that *Constantine*'s People now became the Assailants, and the Enemy began to retire out of the *Hellespont* in Disorder, whom they vigorously charged in that Confusion, some on their Broad side, some a-stern, and others a-head, without fear now of being surrounded by so scattered a Fleet, tho' so much more numerous. *Abantus* behaved the whole Day with singular Courage and Bravery, and frequently rallying his flying Ships, renewed the Battel for a while, but at length Night coming on, the two Fleets were separated. *Constantine*'s Gallies retired to *Eleus*, just without the Streight, where lay the rest of the Fleet; and *Licinius*'s to *Æantium* in the *Hellespont* up towards *Byzantium*. The next Day *Abantus* sailing out with his Ships as if he would come to another Engagement, found the Coast clear, and no Appearance of the Enemy; but soon receiving Advice that they lay at *Eleus*, where they were increased with thirty Sail more, he began to consider whether he had best to proceed and attack them there, or wait their Motions in the Place where they had fought the Day before. While he was deliberating hereupon, the Wind came up at N.W, and with such Violence, that his whole Fleet was cast away upon the *Asiatick* Shore near *Lampsacus*, where perished a hundred and thirty Ships with all the Seamen and Soldiers on board; *Abantus* himself with great Difficulty escaping with only four small Vessels into *Asia*. Thither *Licinius* also made a shift to escape from *Byzantium*, where he was besieged by *Constantine*, who, upon Advice of his Arrival there, put his Troops on board, and sailed over to *Chalcedon*, from whence he sent part of the Fleet to block up *Byzantium* by Sea, and prepared to fight *Licinius* ashore, who, having a very great Army, soon gave *Constantine* an Opportunity of coming to a Battel. Between *Chalcedon* and an ancient Temple of *Juno*, just at the Mouth of the *Thracian Bosphorus*, the two Armies met, and *Licinius* was totally defeated, losing very great Numbers on the spot; and tho' he himself escaped thence, yet was he soon after taken Prisoner, sent to *Thessalonica*, and suffered to live a few Days; but it was dangerous for a Man to be in Being who had once been at the Head of Affairs, in-
Constantine's Fleet overcomes that of Licinius.

Licinius his Ships lost in a Storm.

and his Army totally defeated by Constantine. A.D. 323.

forasmuch

182 *Naval Transactions before the*, &c. Book II.

Licinius put to Death. — somuch that *Constantine* soon sent Orders for putting him to Death. Having settled the Affairs of *Asia*, he returned to *Byzantium*, the Inhabitants whereof then opening their Gates to him, he not only received their Submission, but forgave them; and attentively considering the Situation of the Place, began to think it worthy of being the Seat of the Empire; wherefore, resolving so to make it, *Constantine makes Byzantium the Seat of the Empire.* — he inclosed a very large Space of Ground to add to the City, erected a vast Number of fine Edifices, both publick and private, made *Forums, Circus*'s, Temples, Portico's, and Arches, in like manner as was at *Rome*, and gave it the Name of *New Rome*; but Posterity has ever since continued to it his own.

Constantine, by this fatal Mistake of removing the Seat of the Empire, leaving *Italy* and the Western Provinces exposed to the barbarous Nations which lay ready to seize on so rich a Prey, the Empire so far declined in its Strength, that, in less than a hundred Years after, those Provinces were torn in pieces and destroyed by the Barbarians, and not only all other Parts of *Italy*, but *Rome* itself was pillaged, and entirely possessed by the *Goths*. Those Nations which made their Irruptions into the Empire about these Times having founded many different Kingdoms and States, several of which subsist to this Day, I shall go on to treat of the Naval Transactions of all such among them, as well as the other Nations of *Europe*, as have been considerable at Sea. Of these the *Goths* beforemention'd were the first who became celebrated, with an Account of whose Naval Wars I shall begin the next Book.

A COM-

A COMPLEAT HISTORY

Of the moſt Remarkable

TRANSACTIONS at SEA.

BOOK III.

Containing an Account of the moſt remarkable Naval Tranſactions of all Nations that, ſince the Ruin of the *Roman* Empire, have been conſiderable at Sea; and, among them, of the *Engliſh* down to the Revolution in the Year 1688.

CHAP. I.

Of the Naval Wars of the Goths.

THE *Goths* are generally ſuppoſed to have been originally a People of *Scandinavia*, where to this Day the moſt conſiderable Province of *Sweden* is called *Gothland*, and an adjacent Iſland in the *Baltick* Sea goes by the ſame Name. Here growing too populous for ſuch narrow Bounds, they croſſed the *Baltick* into *Germany*, where ſubduing the *Ulmerugi* and *Vandali*, they mixed among them, and part of them received thoſe Names: Thence proceeding Southward,

The Successes and Settlements of the Goths.
ᵃ *Danubius.*

ward, they settled in *Dacia*, where Dissensions arising among them, some marched into *Scythia*, and sat down about the *Palus Mæotis*, and others crossing the ᵃ *Ister* seated themselves in *Thrace*, and on the Coast of the *Euxine*, all which were from thenceforward called the *Ostrogoths*, or Eastern *Goths*; those which remained in *Dacia* being distinguished by the Name of *Visigoths*, or the *Goths* of the West. From the time of *Constantine* to that of *Valens* they remained somewhat quiet, but then taking up Arms, that Emperor marching against them, was cut off, with the greatest Part of his Army. In the Reign of *Arcadius* and *Honorius*, the *Visigoths* proceeding from the Banks of the *Ister*, under the Conduct of *Alaric*, took *Rome*, setting up *Attalus*, a *Roman* Citizen, for Emperor; and after this they marched into *Gaul* under the Command of *Adaulphus*.

They cut off the Army of Valens.

Alaric takes Rome.

A. D. 408.

The Vandals and Alans do great Mischief to the Romans.

and make Carthage the Seat of their Kingdom.

Genseric takes and pillages Rome, and does other Mischiefs.

About the same time the *Vandals*, that Nation of the *Goths* who had their Seats about the *Palus Mæotis*, joining themselves with the *Alans*, a neighbouring People, and headed by *Gogidiscus*, fell down into *Spain*, who having over-ran that Country, covered the Sea with their numerous Fleets; and every where turning out the *Roman* Garrisons, seized *Gades*, the Islands of *Sardinia*, *Majorca*, and *Minorca*, together with *Corsica*, and invading *Sicily*, possessed themselves of all the Country about *Panormus*. From hence they were invited into *Africa*, under their King *Genseric*, by *Bonifacius*, Governor of that Country for the Emperor *Valentinian* the third; where carrying every thing before them, and entirely dispossessing the *Romans*, they made *Carthage* the Seat of their Kingdom. *Genseric*, elated with this Success, passed with a great Fleet over to *Italy*, where taking *Rome*, and lading himself with the Spoils of that City, he returned to *Africk*. Hearing soon of the Death of *Valentinian*, he renewed his Excursions on the Coasts of *Sicily* and *Italy*, where he took several Cities, and levelled them with the Ground; whence proceeding Eastward, he did the like on the Coasts of *Greece* and *Illyricum*, and among the adjacent Islands; when returning back to *Sicily* and *Italy*, he burnt and destroyed whatsoever had escaped him in his former Expeditions.

Basiliscus and two others sent against him.

Heraclius beats his Fleet.

To repress these Insolences, the Emperor *Leo* sent out *Basiliscus*, his Wife's Brother, with a strong Squadron, and another under *Marcellianus* to *Sardinia*: A third Squadron he committed to *Heraclius*, who, off of *Tripolis*, gave the Enemy a notable Defeat, at which time if *Basiliscus* had attacked *Carthage*, there might have been an end put to the Power of the *Vandals* in *Africk*, and all would have reverted to the *Romans*. But *Leo* dying about this time, and both the Eastern and Western Empires being filled with intestine Disturbances, *Genseric* reigned quietly long after in *Africk*, and having extended his Dominions as far as *Ægypt* and *Æthiopia*, at length died, and transmitted them in Peace to his Successors, who maintained the same without Interruption till the Time of *Justinian*.

Justinian sends a Fleet against the Vandals.

That Emperor fitted out a Fleet of five hundred Sail against *Gilimer*, then King of the *Vandals*, under the Command of *Calonymus*

CHAP. I. *Ruin of the* Rom. *Empire.* 185

of *Alexandria*, who had with him besides ninety two Gallies, with a sort of Covering to protect the Rowers from the Enemy, which they called *Dromones*, or Runners. There was also a considerable Body of Land-Forces got ready to be put on board, and a Commission was given to *Belisarius* to command the whole. *Gilimer*, upon Notice of these Preparations, likewise equipped a Fleet of a hundred and twenty Sail, giving the Charge thereof to his Brother *Tzazon*. *Epiphanius*, the Patriarch of *Constantinople*, having, with great Solemnity, bestowed his Benediction on the Emperor's Fleet, they weighed Anchor from *Constantinople*, and fell down the *Hellespont* to *Abydus*, from whence they proceeded to [b] *Methone* to join *Valerian* and *Martian*, who had the Government of *Greece*. Then they set sail for *Sicily*, whence they passed over to *Africk*, where the Troops refusing to fight by Sea, they were put ashore, and *Belizarius* in a short time reduced *Carthage*, and took *Gilimer* and his Brother *Tzazon* Prisoners, whom he carried in Triumph to *Constantinople*; soon after which his Lieutenant *Cyrillus* recovered *Sardinia* and *Corsica*, as another did *Mauritania*, with the Cities of [c] *Septa* and *Gades*. *Apolliciarius* also, another of the General's Officers, reduced [d] *Ebusus*, *Majorca*, and *Minorca*; which great Successes of *Belisarius* sufficiently increased the Number of his Prince's high Titles, who thereupon assumed those of *Gothicus*, *Alanicus*, *Vandalicus*, and *Africanus*.

[b] Modon.

[c] Ceuta.
A. D. 533
[d] Yviça.

Belisarius overcomes the Vandals in Africk.

Thus was *Africa* again united to the Empire after it had been a hundred Years dismember'd from it; but *Italy* was yet remaining to be subdued, of which the *Goths* were now entirely Masters, together with most part of the Island *Sicily*: both which *Belisarius* in a short time reduced to Obedience. He being recalled to *Constantinople*, the Emperor dispatched another Fleet, with a considerable Army, under *Maximinus*, with the Title and Character of *Præfectus-Prætoria* of *Italy*, the better to govern the Officers, and supply the Army; but he being a Man altogether unpractised in War, and, besides that, a Coward, loitered upon the Coasts of *Epirus*. *Justinian* after him sent *Demetrius* as his Lieutenant, who had formerly commanded under *Belisarius*; mean while the *Goths*, under their King *Totilas*, had recovered almost all *Italy*, and were now besieging [e] *Neapolis*, which began to be sorely distressed. *Demetrius* hearing of this, had a great Desire to relieve it, but not having with him a sufficient Number of Troops, he caused several Ships to be laden with Corn, and other Provisions in *Sicily*, hoping to fright the Enemy, who hearing of an huge Navy, expected a great Army would accompany it. Had he directly made for *Neapolis*, he had undoubtedly driven away the Besiegers, and done his Work; but being afraid to put in there, he failed on for [f] *Portus* to gather up Soldiers, who being lately beaten by the *Goths*, refused to follow him against *Totilas*, so that he was constrained either to stay where he was, or undertake the Relief of *Neapolis* with those few he had brought along with him. Chusing the latter Course, *Totilas*, when he had notice of his coming, manned out a considerable Number of nimble Frigates, which falling on him on a sudden,

Africa again united to the Roman Empire, as also Italy and Sicily.

The Goths recover great part of Italy.
[e] Naples.

[f] Porto, at the Mouth of the Tiber.

Totilas beats the Roman Fleet on the Coast of Neapolis.

B b

as he lay on the Coast near *Neapolis*, surprized and defeated him, and took all his Ships, with the Men aboard them, except such as at the first Alarm leap'd into their Boats, amongst whom was *Demetrius* himself. *Maximinus* being fairly advanced as far as *Sicily*, sat still at *Syracuse*, afraid of the War; for though the Commanders in *Italy*, especially the Governor of *Neapolis*, importuned him to come to their Succour, he still wore out the Time, till fearing the Emperor's high Displeasure, and wearied with the Sollicitations he had from all Parts, he resolved, by staying behind, to save one, and to send the Army to *Neapolis* under the Command of others.

The Roman Fleet forced on shore among the Goths.

Now was it the Depth of Winter, and the Fleet coming off that City, met with a violent Storm, which, maugre all the Efforts the Seamen could make, drove them ashore at the Place where the Enemy lay encamped, who had so easy a Game of it, that they sunk Ships and killed Men as they pleased, without any Resistance, insomuch that but few escaped, the rest being taken, together with *Demetrius*. Him did *Totilas* lead with a Rope about his Neck to the Town Wall, where he compelled him to persuade the Citizens to yield, by telling them that they were to expect no farther Succours, and that all their Hopes had perished with the Navy; of which Truth being too sensible, they soon after surrendered the Place.

Neapolis is given up to the Goths.

Totilas invests Rome, and Belisarius is sent to its Relief.

In this manner did the *Roman* Affairs in *Italy* again decline, and *Totilas* shortly after invested *Rome*, which had endured the Siege a long time, and began to be hard pressed with Famine, when the Emperor thought it necessary to send *Belisarius* again into *Italy*, to retrieve his Losses. Upon his Arrival he found the City would be inevitably taken, unless he could immediately throw in a Supply of Provisions; to prevent which *Totilas* had upon the *Tiber*, about eleven Miles below *Rome*, where the Chanel is narrowest, laid a Bridge of Planks, at each side whereof he built wooden Towers, and put good Garrisons in them. *Belisarius*, to effect his Purpose, fixed two Barks together, upon which he raised a Tower of Wood higher than those the Enemy had made at the Bridge, and launched into the *Tiber* two hundred Pinnaces, the sides whereof were full of Port-holes, out of which they might shoot at them. Aboard these Pinnaces he caused to be put Corn and other Provisions, and in Posts of Advantage, down the River, placed on either side thereof Horse and Foot, to hinder any Designs upon [g] *Portus*, at the Mouth of the *Tiber*, the only Place in those Parts which he had in his Hands, the Defence whereof he committed to *Isaac*, with strict Orders not to stir from thence on any account whatsoever, while he himself conducted the Pinnaces, and caused the two Barks with the Turret to be towed after, on the top of which he put a little Boat full of Pitch, Rosin, Brimstone, and other combustible Matters: And that these his Devices might the better succeed, he sent Orders to *Bessas*, the Officer who commanded in *Rome*, to make a general Sally, and alarm the Enemy's Camp: But he, intent on making Advantage of the Corn which had been laid up for the Soldiers, and therefore unwilling the Siege should yet be raised, neg-

Porto

lected

CHAP. I. *Ruin of the* Rom. *Empire.* 187

lected to put these Orders in Execution. *Belisarius* making the best of his way up the River, found an Iron Chain laid a-cross near the Bridge, which after he had killed some and driven away the rest who made Opposition, he easily removed, and passing on to the Bridge, fell presently to work. The *Goths* from their Towers valiantly defending themselves, he caused the Barks with the Turret to be rowed near that Tower, which stood in the Water by the way from *Portus*. Then was the Boat full of combustible Stuff set on fire, and shoved down just upon the said Tower of the Enemy, which was instantly in Flames, and within it were burnt two hundred *Goths*, together with their Officer, one of the most valiant of their Nation, the *Roman* Soldiers in the mean time plying such as came from the *Gothick* Camp to the Relief of their Fellows so warmly, that being amazed at the Accident, they ran all away. They laid Hands on the Bridge, and had suddenly pulled it down and gotten into *Rome* without Opposition, if *Isaac*, the Governor of *Portus*, had not unluckily heard of their Success; who, desirous to have a Share in the Honour, marching out, contrary to his General's Orders, with a hundred Horse, and charging a Body of the Enemy which lay on the other side of the River near *Ostia*, was taken Prisoner, with all his Men. Upon the first Notice of whose Defeat, *Belisarius*, thinking *Portus* and all was lost, drew back his Forces in order to recover that Place; which false Steps in both these Officers render'd fruitless all which had hitherto been done for the Relief of *Rome*, so that the City in few Days fell into the Enemy's Hands.

Belisarius advances up the Tiber.

A Tower of the Goths burnt.

The intended Relief of Rome frustrated.

After this they had several Engagements with various Success, sometimes *Belisarius*, and sometimes the *Goths* getting the better; and the latter with a considerable Number of Ships made Descents in *Corcyra* and the adjacent Islands, as also on the Costs of *Epirus*, *Acarnania*, and *Ætolia*, which they ravaged with Fire and Sword. Then was the War committed to *Narses*, under whom *John*, Admiral of the Fleet of *Illyricum*, consisting of forty Sail, and *Valerian* from before *Ravenna* with twelve, came to a Battel off *Ancona* with the *Gothick* Fleet commanded by *Alidas* and *Gothildus*, who presently engaging hand to hand with Swords and Spears, fought for some time with various Success, till at length the *Goths* pressing too close together, fell foul of each other, and being in great Disorder, used their best Endeavours to sheer off. Ten of their lightest Frigates retiring towards the Shore, ran themselves aground, where the *Goths* set fire to them, to prevent their falling into the Enemy's Hands; and as for the rest, they were all either taken or sunk. The victorious Fleet then enter'd the Port of *Ancona*, to the great Joy of that City, which the *Goths* had closely besieged for some time, but were now obliged to rise from before it with such Precipitation, that they left their Camp and Baggage behind, *Valerian* returning to *Ravenna* with his Squadron, and *John* with the rest of the Fleet to *Salonæ*. Much about this time was *Artabanes* sent with a strong Squadron to *Sicily*, where meeting with the *Goths* dispersed about that Island, he easily overcame them; and *Narses* entering *Italy* from *Dalmatia* through *Istria*, sate down about *Aquileia*,

A. D. 547.

The Goths make Descents in Corcyra, &c.

They are beaten at Sea.

Ancona relieved.

The Goths overcome at Sicily.

Bb 2

quileia, which City, lately laid waste and deserted by *Attilianus*, he caused to be rebuilt. Thence he proceeded to *Ravenna*, where he was joined by *Valerian* and *Justin*; and after this several strong Places were in a short time taken from the *Goths*, amongst which was the City of *Rome*. *Totilas* was also slain in a Battel, nor was it long e'er *Teias*, his Successor, had the same Fate; and the immense Treasure heaped up by the former at *Cumæ* fell into *Narses's* Hands. Thus were the *Goths* at length expelled out of the best Part of *Italy*, and forced to take up their Habitations on the other side of the *Po*, in the seventy first Year after their Settlement in that Country under *Theodoric*. But in *Spain*, after this Expulsion of them out of *Italy*, reigned a long Series of *Gothick* Kings from *Athanagild* to *Roderic*, in whose Time an end was put to their Power by the *Saracens*, under the Conduct of *Abderames*, who over ran the greatest Part of that Country.

A. D. 552.

Rome, *and other Places taken from the* Goths.

A. D. 554.

The Saracens *expel the* Goths *from* Spain.
A. D. 713.

Chap. II.

Of the Naval Wars of the Saracens.

ABOUT a Century before the Ruin of the *Gothick* Power in *Spain*, those People, the *Saracens*, began to be formidable in *Africk*, whose Name is thought to be derived from that of *Sarah*, the Wife of *Abraham*, being esteemed the Posterity of *Agar*, her Handmaid. They inhabited *Arabia* for many Ages before, but were taken very little Notice of, till the Impostor *Mahomet*, their Countryman, broach'd his new Religion, by which having acquired a great Number of Followers, and being favoured by the unactive indolent Government of the Emperor *Heraclius*, he first took several Castles on the *Persian* Frontiers, and then, assisted by the *Persians*, who greedily followed his monstrous Superstitions, reduced all *Arabia* to his Obedience, with great part of *Syria*; and assuming the double Office of King and Priest, became the first *Caliph* of the *Saracens*. There were four principal Officers called *Emirs*, who, under him, had the Direction of Affairs both by Land and Sea, from which Word many of the Learned have derived Amiral or Admiral, the Term by which, in most of the modern Languages, is signified the Commander in Chief at Sea; though there are not wanting several other Derivations of that Name. *Mahomet* was succeeded by *Ebu-beker*, and he by *Haumar*; and the first maritime Expedition of the *Saracens* was very unsuccessful; for passing down to the Streights of *Gades*, with a Fleet of two hundred and seventy Sail, *Wamba*, King of the *Goths* in *Spain*, engaging with them, burnt or sunk all their Ships; but soon after, when *Osman*, or *Otmen*, the Successor of *Haumar*, came to the Throne, their Affairs wonderfully prospered at Sea.

The Rise of the Saracens.

The Success of the Impostor Mahomet.
A. D. 622.

The supposed Derivation of Admiral.

At

CHAP. II. *Ruin of the* Rom. *Empire.*

At this time the *Constantinopolitan* Emperors had some part of *Africa* remaining in their Hands, but the Majesty of the Empire was now so much diminished, that the Governours they sent thither looked on themselves more as Kings than Subjects. *Gregorius* the *Patrician* was he who now ruled the Province of *Carthage* for the Emperor *Constans*, against whom *Osman* sent his *Emir Hucba*, who defeating *Gregory*, took and destroyed *Carthage*, and seized *Tunis*, which afterwards became the Head of a particular Government, as it continues to this Day. About the same time *Muhavias*, another *Emir* of *Osman*'s, proceeded from *Ægypt* with a Fleet of seventeen hundred Sail for *Cyprus*, and having laid waste that Island, landing in *Syria*, he took up his Quarters at *Damascus*. The next Spring he repaired again to *Cyprus*, and having wholly reduced the Island to Obedience, sailed over to *Phœnix*, a Port of *Caria*, where lay the Emperor *Constans* with a Fleet, which *Muhavias* attacking, gained an entire Victory, with such a prodigious Destruction of the *Greeks*, that the Sea was said to be dyed, to a considerable Distance, with the Blood of the slain: and the Emperor, in Disguise, escaped with Difficulty, in a small Boat to *Constantinople*. The Conqueror hereupon invaded *Rhodes*, where he demolished the celebrated *Colossus*, and thence proceeding towards *Sicily*, wasted that Island with Fire and Sword, as he had done several of the *Cyclades* in his Way. Hither *Olympius* the Exarch of *Italy* repaired against him, and coming to an Engagement at Sea, at length gained the Victory, but so bloody a one, and so dearly bought, that he landed in the Island more like the Vanquished than the Conquerour.

Osman sends his Troops against Carthage.

Cyprus laid waste by the Saracens,

they overcome the Emperor's Fleet in Caria.

A. D. 654. *Waste Rhodes and Sicily,*

but their Fleet is beaten by the Exarch of Italy.

Muhavias by the Death of *Osman*, and his Successor *Aly*, becoming Caliph, so considerably encreased his Power that he rendered the Emperor *Constantine Pogonatus* his Tributary; in the fifth Year of which Prince's Reign, the *Saracens* coming up with a great Fleet and Army to *Constantinople*, they seized on all that lay between the *Hebdomum* and *Cyclobium*, two Suburbs of that City; whereupon *Constantine* brought out his Fleet, and they fought every Day from Morning till Night in the Port there. From the Month of *April* till *September* they continued their Siege, when despairing of Success, they departed to, and wintered at *Cyzicum*, and in Spring renewed the War. This they continued to do for four Years successively; but at length their Courage being quite spent, they in great grief retired, having lost a very great Number of their Men, after which followed the Destruction of their whole Fleet, which was in the Winter Season cast away off the [a] Promontory of *Scyllæum*, where perished thirty thousand Men. There was a new Invention of Sea-Fire, as they called it, which would burn under Water, and was of great Service to the Defendants in the Siege; with which Secret *Callinicus*, an *Heliopolitan* of *Ægypt*, the Author of it, fled to the *Romans*. While one Party of the *Saracens* thus employed themselves against *Constantinople*, another Captain of theirs, *Suphianus*, the Son of *Aphus*, engaged with the *Roman* Forces commanded by *Florus*, *Petronas*, and *Cyprianus*, but to no other Effect than that he lost thirty thousand of his Followers: And now would

A. D. 673.

The Saracens and Greeks fight off of Constantinople.

[a] *Cape* Schill.

The Saracens Fleet destroyed by Tempest.

Are again beaten, but the Emperor grants them Peace.

190   *Naval Transactions since the*   Book III.

A. D. 676.

would the Majesty of the *Roman* Empire have revived and flourished, if the Emperor had not ingloriously granted Peace to *Muhavias*, and thereby saved the *Saracens*, whose Power (if he had prosecuted his Successes) might have been then easily crushed in its Cradle, the Remains of which is to this Day so formidable in their Successors the *Turks*. Presently after the Conclusion of this Peace, *Muhavias* died at *Damascus*, then the Seat of his Empire, having increased the *Saracen* Dominions on the West with *Ægypt* and *Africk*, Eastward with *Mesopotamia*, and to the North with great Part of *Asia Minor*.

Justinian II. beaten by the Saracens. A. D. 688. Leontius assumes the Purple.

After *Gizid* and *Marvan*, who next succeeded, *Abdelmelich* became *Caliph*, in whose time the Emperor *Justinian* the second broke the Peace with the *Saracens*, with whom coming to a Battel, he received a great Defeat, and soon after was dispossessed of his Dignity by *Leontius*, who banishing him to *Cherſona*, in the *Taurican Cherſoneſus*, assumed the Purple himself. *Abdelmelich* encouraged by his late Successes, sent an Army to *Thrace* under the Conduct of *Moamed*, and at the same time gave Orders for a Fleet to be got ready to scour the Sea, and defend the Coasts of *Africa*, with which *John*, *Leontius*'s Officer, who was sent with a Squadron against them, durst never come to an Engagement. *Abdelmelich* dying, he was succeeded by *Ulit*, who sent *Muza*, then Emir, or Governor of *Mauritania*, against *Roderic*, King of the *Goths* in *Spain*, at the Instigation of Count *Julian*, a Man of great Power and Authority in that Country, whose Daughter *Roderic* had ravished. The Success of this Expedition was the Reduction of all *Spain*, from whence they penetrated into *Gaul*, and possessed themselves of the greatest Part of [b] *Gallia Narbonenſis*.

The Saracens invade Spain.

A. D. 713.
[b] Provence and Languedoc.
Reduce Spain, and Part of Gaul.

Under *Zullimin*, or *Soliman*, the Successor of *Ulit*, the *Saracens* again besieged *Conſtantinople* both by Sea and Land, with an Army commanded by *Maſſalnias*, and a Fleet by *Haumar*. Their Insolence was a little repressed by *Leo*, then Prætor of *Armenia*, but *Zullimin* himself repairing to the Siege with a Fleet of three thousand Sail, had gone near to have taken the City, but that he dyed before the Place, leaving his Son *Haumar* his Successor; and the Siege having continued two Years, the greatest Part of the Ships were sunk by Tempests, or burnt by artificial Fires, most of the Men perishing with their Vessels; to repair which Loss *Gizid* advanced with a new Fleet of three hundred and sixty Sail to *Bithynia*, where he was entirely defeated and put to Flight.

But are overthrown before Conſtantinople, A. D. 721.
and in diverſe other Places.

A. D. 800.

We purposely omit the great Overthrows the *Saracens* received some time after in the West from *Charles Martel*, *Pipin*, and *Charles* the Great, before *Avignon*, *Narbonne*, and other Places in *France*, where *Abderames*, *Atinus*, and others of their Leaders were cut off, together with their vast Armies: The *Turks* at the same time rushing down from *Scythia* through the Pass of *Caucaſus*, and attacking them in the East. But the *Saracens* did not fall unrevenged, though vanquished in so many Places, nor could they soon be rooted out who had acquired so extensive a Dominion; the Diſſenſions that reigned in the eastern Empire yielding them too good

an
4

CHAP. II. *Ruin of the* Rom. *Empire.* 191

an Opportunity to retrieve their Affairs. Being called to the Af sistance of *Thomas*, who endeavoured to gain the Empire from *Michael Balbus*, they gave a signal Overthrow to that Emperor's Fleet off *Abydus*, and soon after defeated his Army commanded by *Albianus* and *Catacella*, as also another considerable Fleet that was fitted out against them. About the same time a great Body of them sailing over from *Mauritania* to *Corsica* and *Sardinia*, in order to settle in those Islands, they were beaten in a Sea Fight by *Boniface*, Admiral to *Pipin* (Son of *Charles* the Great) King of *Italy*, and forced to retire from thence. They soon after made another Attempt on *Sardinia*, but were again defeated, off of that Island, by *Charles, Pipin*'s Brother, assisted by Count *Ruchard*; but about the same time a numerous Body of them putting to Sea, over-ran *Crete*, where they built the City *Candia*, which now gives Name to the whole Island. There *Craterus*, the Emperor *Michael*'s Admiral, after an obstinate and bloody Dispute, gave them a great Overthrow, killing and taking Prisoners a vast Multitude of them. Those that escaped, retired into the Town of *Candia*, who finding *Craterus* careless after the Victory, and his People taken up in drinking and revelling, made a general Sally the ensuing Night, and cut him off with his whole Army; to retrieve which Misfortune *Oryphas* was sent out with a Fleet, who harassed them in several Engagements and Skirmishes by Sea.

They overcome the Fleet of the Emperor Michael Balbus.

A. D. 807.

Pipin's Admiral overcomes them.

Are beaten off of Sardinia, but over-run Crete, and build Candia

Michael the Emperor's Admiral, and the Saracens alternately beaten.

About this time *Euphenius*, a *Sicilian*, fearing the Emperor's Resentments for some Crimes by him committed, went over to the *Saracens*, and offered to make them Masters of *Sicily*, provided they would let him enjoy the Sovereignty there, who accordingly, under his Conduct, possessed themselves of that Island; and as *Ambulacus*, one of their Leaders, who had ravaged the Coasts of *Calabria*, and *Corsica*, was returning to *Africa* laden with Spoils, *Ermengarius*, Governor of the *Baleares* Islands for *Bernard* King of *Italy*, fell in with, and defeated him, setting at liberty a great Number of Christian Slaves. The *Saracens*, however, did not yet desist from their Depredations, but shortly after surprized ᶜ *Centumcellæ*, which they burnt and destroyed, when ravaging the Coast of *Gallia Narbonensis*, they made another Attempt on *Sardinia*, where *Ermengarius* falling unexpectedly upon them, gave them so great a Defeat that very few of their Ships returned to *Africk*; and *Boniface*, Count of *Corsica*, giving them chace, but not being able to come up with them, landed a Body of Troops between *Utica* and *Carthage*, with which he so harrass'd and fatigued them, that they were forced to withdraw their People from *Sicily* to their Relief. *Bonifacius* then returning home with his victorious Fleet, the *Saracens* resolved to revenge their late Disgraces, and putting to Sea, again seized and plundered *Centumcellæ*, and laid Siege to *Rome* it self, where they burnt the *Vatican*, with all the Churches thereabouts, and having laid waste the Suburbs and neighbouring Towns, repaired on board their Ships.

A. D. 818.

The Saracens master Sicily, but are beaten by the Italian Fleet.

ᶜ Civita Vecchia.

They take Civita Vecchia, but are beaten off of Sardinia.

A. D. 830.

They plunder Centumcellæ, and besiege Rome.

After this, under the Conduct of one *Saba*, they came over to *Tarentum*, and laid Siege to that Place, which being somewhat distressed, the *Greek* and *Venetian* Fleets were sent to its Relief;

A. D. 843.

I whereupon

whereupon *Saba* making a Shew of Fear, withdrew from before the Place into the Bay of ᵈ *Crotona*, where falling upon the Enemy's Fleet, he presently forced the *Greeks* to fly, and the *Venetians*, bravely fighting on board their Ships, were all slain to a Man. The same *Saba* soon after, cruising with a Squadron in the *Adriatick*, fell in, off ᵉ *Tergeste*, with a rich Fleet of *Venetian* Merchant Ships bound home from *Syria*, all which he took, putting to Death the Merchants and Sailers; and in his Way down the *Gulph* seized and plundered *Ancona*. After this *Basilius Macedo*, Emperor of the East, making War on the *Saracens* in *Candia*, received a great Defeat in a Sea Fight, and narrowly missed being taken Prisoner: But not long after the Emperor's Fleet, in another Engagement in the Ægæan, burnt or sunk almost all their Ships. Those few who escaped from this Battel, in Rage and Despair ravaged the Coasts of *Peloponnesus*, and the neighbouring Islands, till at length they were all cut off by the Emperor's Admiral in three other Skirmishes off ᶠ *Methone*, ᵍ *Pylus* and *Patræ*. The *Saracens* in *Mauritania* hearing of these Losses, and *Manuel* the Patrician being sent into *Sicily* with a strong Squadron, they there attacked and entirely routed him, with great Slaughter of his Men, whence they proceeded up the *Adriatick* to *Dalmatia* and *Istria*, where, as they were besieging *Grado*, they were attacked and defeated by *Ursus Particiatus*, then *Doge* of *Venice*. They soon after received another Overthrow from *Narsanes*, the Emperor *Basilius*'s Admiral, who prosecuting his Victory, took in several Towns of *Calabria* and *Apulia* that were garisonned by the Enemy.

Romanus, coming to be Emperor, made a Peace with the *Saracens*, on whose Side Fortune had long continued, but now, inconstant as she is, began to declare against them, for a vast Multitude of them perished as they were crossing out of *Italy* from *Rhegium* to *Messana*, which Misfortune was soon after followed by another as signal; for *Hugh* King of *Italy* burnt a great Fleet of theirs on the Coast of *Provence*; and, in the East, the Provinces of *Natolia* and *Cilicia*, with the City of *Antioch*, were taken from them. After this they received a great Defeat among the *Cyclades* from *Nicephorus Carantenus*, the *Constantinopolitan* Emperor's Admiral; a considerable time before which they had lost the Island *Crete*, and been stript of almost all they had in *Italy* by *Otho* the first, Emperor of *Germany*. The Source of these Misfortunes were the Divisions amongst themselves, with which weakening one another, they at length became an easy Prey to their Enemies. In *Persia*, *Syria*, *Ægypt* and *Africk* they were forced to give way to the *Turks*; and in *Calabria* and *Apulia* to the *Norman* Princes. They held out longest in *Spain*, where they flourished after this for several Centuries, till the time of *Ferdinand* V. King of *Castile*, who conquered *Muley Boabdelin*, King of *Granada*, the only Kingdom they had remaining, and put an End to their Power in that Country.

CHAP.

CHAP. III.
Of the Naval Wars of the Normans.

TOward the Decline of the *Saracen* Power, the *Normans* began to grow confiderable, who were a People of *Norway*, that had for many Ages before been ufed to Piratical Depredations in the Northern Seas, which they chiefly made ufe of againft their Neighbours of *Denmark* and *Sweden*, wherein fometimes the one, and fometimes the other got the better. It was in the Times of the Emperors *Charlemagne*, *Louis* the Pious, and *Lotharius*, that thefe People began to make their Excurfions to the Southward; when mixing with the *Danes*, they came down in Swarms, under the Conduct of a Son of *Regnerus*, one of their Kings, and ravaged the Coafts of *Saxony*, *Friefland*, *Holland*, and *Flanders*, whence coafting along, they entered the *Seine*, the *Loire*, and the *Garonne*, feizing and plundering the Towns upon thofe Rivers.   *The Normans invade Saxony, Flanders, &c.*

After this, *Addingus*, one of their Leaders, fatiated with the Spoils of *Gaul*, began to caft his Eyes on *Italy*, (poffefs'd by the *Longobardi* or *Lombards*, originally their Neighbours, having come from *Schonen* in *Sweden*) who putting to Sea, failed round to the Mediterranean, and coming on the Coaft of *Tufcany*, took the City of [a] *Luna*, ignorantly fuppofing it to be *Rome*. Hence proceeding Weftward to the Iflands on the Coaft of *Provence* and the Mouth of the *Rhofne*, *Charles* the Bald, King of *France*, thought fit to offer a Place of Habitation for himfelf and his Followers, which was the City of *Chartres*, and the adjacent Country. There he lived quietly till the time of *Rollo*, who coming from *Norway* with a great Fleet to *Neuftria* (fo all the North Part of *France* was then called) landed his People, and fettled himfelf there, giving the Name of *Normandy* to Part of the Country, and affuming the Title of Duke. About thefe times there reigned in *Norway Harold Graafield*, of whom it is related that the Emperor *Otho* fending a Naval Force againft him, either to reprefs his Piracies, or attempt the Converfion of his Country to Chriftianity, he advanced with his Fleet to fight them, but before the Battel, facrificed his two Sons to the Winds and Tempefts, and the Gods of the Sea, whereupon (fay the *Norwegian* Hiftorians) the Dæmons of the Air, pleafed with the impious Offering, raifed fuch a Storm as entirely deftroyed the Emperor's Fleet.   [a] *Sarzana, near Porto Spezza.* A. D. 857. *Settle at Chartres, and the adjacent Country.* A. D. 895. *Rollo from Norway fettles in Normandy.* *The Emperor Otho's Fleet deftroyed by Tempeft.*

From this *Rollo* beforementioned fprang a double Race of *Normans*, of which one, in the Mediterranean, poffeffed *Apulia* and *Calabria*; and the other, in the Ocean, the Kingdom of *England*. *Rollo* was fucceeded in the Duchy of *Normandy* by his Son *William*, firnamed *Longfword*, who interpofing in the Affairs of the North, overcame *Sueno* King of *Denmark*, and fettled *Harold* in that Kingdom. *William* was fucceeded by *Richard*, who being affifted by a great Body of *Danes* againft *Lotharius* King of *France*, he,   *William Longfword overcomes the King of Denmark.*

C c

he, when he had no further Occasion for them, perſuaded them to an Expedition into *Spain*, to which Purpoſe he ſupplied them with Ships, Arms, and Proviſions, and they accordingly ſailing thither, defeated the *Saracens* in two or three Skirmiſhes, and poſſeſſed themſelves of ſeveral Towns.

The Normans beat the Saracens.

After this *Richard*, there reigned in *Normandy* two others of the ſame Name, the latter of which was ſucceeded by *Robert*; and *Tancred*, Lord of *Hauteville*, being by ſome reckoned a Son of his, had himſelf twelve, of whom the moſt conſiderable were *William Fierabras*, *Drogo*, *Humfrey*, *Godfrey*, *Robert Guiſcard*, and *Roger Boſſu*. *Tancred*, going in queſt of new Adventures, carried theſe his Sons with him into *Italy*, where after having ſucceſsfully waged War for ſome time, he dyed at *Salerno*, his Sons being entertained by *George Maniaces*, General of the *Greek* Emperor *Michael*'s Forces in *Apulia* and *Sicily* againſt the *Saracens*. They paſſing over into *Sicily*, forced *Meſſina* and *Syracuſe* to ſurrender, and overthrowing *Apoloſarus* and *Apocapſes*, the *Saracen* Leaders, in a pitcht Battel, ſoon reduced the greateſt Part of the Iſland to Obedience. Though *Maniaces* thus gloried in his Succeſſes, yet was he as unfortunate in diſtributing the Spoils of the War, for, indulging his avaricious Temper in retaining the greater part to himſelf, he ſoon diſobliged the brave *Normans*, whoſe Swords had acquired them; whereupon *William Fierabras* returned to *Apulia*, and ſeizing ſeveral Towns, maintained them. Having ſtrongly fortified *Melfi*, to which *Maniaces* laid Siege, he ſally'd out, defeated him, and forced him to fly into *Sicily*; and reducing the reſt of the Country to Obedience, he, with the Conſent of his Brothers, took upon himſelf the Title of Count of *Apulia*, but dying without Iſſue, left his Brother *Drogo* to ſucceed him, who overcoming the Emperor's Forces that were ſent againſt him, left his Dominions in Peace to his Brother *Godfrey*. He beſieged and took *Benevento*, and in a Battel near *Civita di Chieti* took Pope *Leo* IX, with ſeveral Cardinals, but uſed his Victory with ſuch Moderation, and ſo handſomely treated his Priſoners, that he received from the Pope his Apoſtolical Benediction, and a Confirmation of his Poſſeſſions in *Apulia*. *Godfrey* was ſucceeded by *Robert Guiſcard*, who reduced all *Calabria*, and annexed it to his Dominions; at which time *Nicholas* II. was Pope, who being engaged in a Quarrel with his Nobles, was aſſiſted by *Robert*, whom for that Service he honoured with the Title of Duke of *Apulia*, and appointed him to command in an Expedition for expelling the *Saracens* out of *Italy*, where they had yet ſome footing. *Bivona*, *Sciglio* and the neighbouring Towns his Brother *Roger* took in, while himſelf reduced *Biſignano*, *Coſenza*, *Martirano*, *Nicaſtro*, *Maja* and *Canne*.

Take Meſſina and Syracuſe, and beat the Saracens.

Fierabras, one of Tancred's Sons, beats the Greek General.
Taking the Title of Duke of Apulia, dies. Drogo, and after him Godfrey ſucceeds.
1049.
Godfrey takes Pope Leo IX, and ſeveral Cardinals.
Robert Guiſcard ſucceeds, and conquers Calabria, is by the Pope made Duke of Apulia.
The Succeſſes of Robert and his Brothers.

At this time Fortune paved the Way for the *Norman* Power in *Sicily*; for the People of *Meſſina*, being hard preſſed by the *Saracens*, begged Aid of *Robert Guiſcard* and *Roger Boſſu*, to whom they offered to ſubmit, if they delivered them from their inſulting Enemies. *Roger*, ſending *Bettumenus*, one of his Officers, to view the Coaſt and Country about *Meſſina*, ſailed from *Regio*, and coming to

CHAP. III. *Ruin of the* Rom. *Empire.* 195

an Anchor near *Melazzo*, landing his Troops he joined Battel with *the Saracens*, whom having totally defeated, and killed their General, he returned triumphantly, laden with Spoils, to *Regio*. After this with another Fleet he overcame those People, and plundered *Messina*, forcing *Baleanes* to retire with his Ships out of the Port of that City; besides which, he took *Rametta*, and several other Towns in the Plain of *Melazzo*, together with *Maniacium* on the Skirts of Mount *Ætna*, a Place lately built by *Maniaces*. *Robert Guiscard* hastening over to the Assistance of his Brother, came to a Battel with the *Saracens*, wherein he gained a complete Victory, killing ten thousand of them; which was followed by the Surrender of several strong Places. But now Dissensions arose between the two Brothers, because *Robert* having promised to the other one half of *Calabria*, and all *Sicily*, had not equally divided the former, but retained the greatest part to himself, so that letting alone the *Saracens*, they warred against each other, but at length came to an Agreement, for *Robert* being taken Prisoner, and generously set at liberty, he, to recompense that Civility, equally shared *Calabria* with his Brother.

Roger beats the Saracens in Sicily. A. D. 1060. *He beats them again, and plunders Messina.*

Robert assisting his Brother, takes many Places in Sicily.

The two Brothers quarrel, but are reconciled. A. D. 1063.

Now was *Roger* again at leisure to pursue his Designs in *Sicily*, where he was attended with constant Success, the *Saracens* flying every where before him, and herein he was assisted by the *Pisans*, who with seven Gallies attempted to seize the Port of *Palermo*, while he was to besiege it by Land: But at the same time the People of *Bari* and *Trani*, two Towns the *Greek* Emperors yet possessed in *Apulia*, making great Disturbances in that Country, the Siege of *Palermo* was put off to another Opportunity, and both the Brothers repaired to invest those Places, which they took in a short time, when returning to *Palermo*, it soon after underwent the same Fate. Of all the Acquisitions in *Sicily Robert* retained only this City to himself, from which afterwards he took the Title of Count; and repairing to *Apulia*, he seized *Brindisi, Otranto, Taranto* and *Salerno*, and overcoming *Goselinus*, Admiral of the *Greek* Emperor's Fleet, before *Bari*, took him Prisoner.

Roger again successful in Sicily.

They reduce Bari and Trani, as also Palermo.

Robert takes Brindisi, Otranto, and other Places.

The *Greeks* were assisted by the *Venetians*, whose Admiral *Contarini* used his utmost Endeavours, at the Request of the Emperor *Nicephorus*, to prevent the taking of *Brindisi*, but without effect, being defeated in a Sea Fight off that Place. *Robert* also overthrew *Mabrica*, the Emperor *Alexius*'s Admiral, in an Engagement near *Corifus*; after which he espousing the Cause of the Emperor *Michael*, whom *Nicephorus* had dethroned, committed the Affairs of *Italy* to his Son *Roger*, gave the Command of his Fleet to his youngest Son *Boëmond*, and himself setting Sail, accompanied with *Michael*, soon arrived at *la Valona*, where landing the Troops, they proceeded to *Durazzo*, so that siege was laid to that Place by Sea and Land, which, maugre all the Efforts the Townsmen could make, though assisted by a Squadron of *Venetians* in the Port, and countenanced by a considerable Naval Force on the Coast, was in a short time forced to surrender; and the *Venetian* Fleet, commanded by *Dominicus Sylvius*, then Doge, received so great a Defeat, that he was deprived of his Dignity,

Beats the Fleets of the Emperor Alexius.

Takes Durazzo, and beats the Venetian Fleet.

C c 2

A. D. 1083. nity, after he had governed that Republick thirteen Years. Soon after which, Count *Roberts*'s Fleet obtained another Victory over the *Venetians* upon the Coast of *Dalmatia*, which was shortly follow'd by a third Engagement between them, off the Island *Saseno*, wherein the *Venetians* were also again defeated. At length, after the Reduction of most of the maritime Places in *Epirus*, *Livadia* and *Albania*, with several of the Islands of *Greece* and *Dalmatia*, *Robert Guiscard* deceased at *Santi Quaranta* in *Epirus*, leaving part of *Apulia*, with *Dalmatia* and his foreign Acquisitions, to *Boëmond*, and the rest of his Dominions to *Roger*; which *Boëmond*, after several signal Successes against the *Saracens*, was created Duke of *Antioch*. *Roger*, the Uncle of these, Count of *Sicily*, resolving to revenge the Destruction of *Nicotera*, a Sea-Port of *Calabria*, lately burnt by *Benavirus* the *Saracen* General, set upon their Fleet in the Port of *Syracuse*, which he utterly destroyed, killing *Benavirus* with his own Hand, and those of the City driving out the *Saracens*, opened their Gates to the Conqueror, soon after which the rest of *Sicily* followed their Example. Not satisfied with this Success, he proceeded to *Malta*, then possessed by the *Saracens*, which he presently made himself Master of, together with the adjacent Island *Gozo*.

Robert, after other Successes, dies, and divides his Dominions.
Boëmond created Duke of Antioch.
Roger the Uncle destroys the Saracens Fleet at Syracuse, A. D. 1086. reduces Sicily,
and takes Malta and Gozo.

Roger was succeeded by his Son of like Name, as the Duke of *Apulia* was about the same time by his Son *William*, between whom there happened a bloody War; for *William* being to marry one of the Daughters of the *Greek* Emperor, and sailing to *Constantinople* for that purpose, *Roger* immediately invaded his Dominions, which, when *William* died, he kept Possession of, as the sole Heir left of the chief Family of the *Normans*; and not content with the Appellation of Count, or Duke, took upon himself the Title of King of *Italy* and *Sicily*. But the *Roman* Pontiffs by no means approving his Title of King of *Italy*, he discontinued it, and assumed those of King of *Sicily*, Duke of *Apulia*, and Prince of *Capua*. He now turned his Thoughts to the enlarging his Dominions, and, to that purpose, with a considerable Fleet, invaded those Parts of *Barbary* opposite to *Sicily*, where meeting with great Success, *Tripoli*, and *Africa* (a Town so called) together with *Sfax* and *Capes*, were in a short time surrendered to him, and the King of *Tunis* became his Tributary. When he had also reduced the Island *Corfu*, and taken the Cities of *Thebes* and *Corinth*, with the Island of *Negroponte*, he assisted *Louis* VII. of *France*, engaged in the Holy War, and rescued him out of the Hands of the *Saracens*, giving the Infidels a great Overthrow at Sea, as well as the *Greeks*, who were also at ill Terms with the *French*. Leaving *Louis* at *Joppa*, he sailed to *Constantinople*, and ravaged the Suburbs of that City in Sight of the Emperor *Emanuel*, but at length coming to a Battel with the *Venetian* Fleet employed in the Assistance of the Emperor, they were found to be so good a Match for him, that he thought fit to withdraw, and return to *Sicily*, where dying, he left his Son *William* King of that Island and *Naples*, who getting together a numerous Fleet, proceeded to *Ægypt* against the *Saracens*, and took several Towns on that and the neighbouring Coasts, particularly

A bloody War between the Successors of Roger, and the Duke of Apulia.
Roger, the Son of Roger, takes on him the Style of King of Italy and Sicily.
A. D. 1129.

He takes several Places in Barbary, and the Islands Corfu, Negropont, Thebes and Corinth.

Effectually assists Lewis the VIIth of France.

He dies, and William his Son succeeds.
William takes Ptolemais, and beats the Grecian Fleet.

CHAP. IV.   *Ruin of the* Rom. *Empire.*   197

ticularly the ſtrong City of *Acre*, or *Ptolemais*, which he plundered. As he was returning from thence, he fell in with the *Greek* Emperor's Fleet, which he engaged, and, tho' very much inferior in Numbers, took a hundred and fifty of their Ships, and then ſailed triumphantly to *Sicily*.

He was ſucceeded by his Son *William*, ſurnamed the Good, after whom reigned *Tancred*, and another *Roger*, and then the Emperor *Henry* VI, who, by the Procurement of Pope *Celeſtin* III, married the Princeſs *Conſtantia*, the Heireſs of the *Norman* Family; in whoſe Line the Kingdom continued till the Year 1266, when *Charles*, Count of *Anjou* and *Provence*, having received the Inveſtiture of it from the Pope, diſpoſſeſs'd them.   *William the Good ſucceeds, and after him Tancred and Roger, and then the Emperor Henry VI. Charles Count of Anjou King of Sicily.*

But the other Race of *Normans*, which, as we have obſerved, reigned in *England*, was of much longer Duration. *Robert* Duke of *Normandy* left *William* his natural Son to ſucceed in that Dukedom, who aſpiring at greater things, (no leſs than the Kingdom of *England*) embarked his Army on board a numerous Fleet, with which ſailing to *Pevenſey* in *Suſſex*, he there landed, and giving Battel to *Harold* near *Haſtings*, gained an entire Victory, and with it the Crown; ſo that the Affairs of this Branch being now become the ſame as thoſe of *England*, they may be more properly treated in another Place.   *William ſucceeds Robert Duke of Normandy, and conquers England.*

CHAP. IV.

Of the Naval Wars of the Venetians, *from the Foundation of their Republick, to the Time of the League of* Cambray; *and of their Dominion of the* Adriatick *Sea*.

WE have already, in the firſt Book of this Work, mentioned the Building of *Venice* to have been upon occaſion of the Devaſtations *Attila*, King of the *Huns*, made in *Italy*, though we are not ignorant that ſome eſteem its Foundation to have been ſome Years before, upon the more early Irruptions of the barbarous People into that Country. However that Matter may be, we find the firſt Naval Effort of the *Venetians*, after their Settlement, was againſt the People of *Iſtria* and *Dalmatia*, whom having worſted in ſeveral Skirmiſhes at Sea, they forced to quit that Element, and betake themſelves wholly to the Land. They defeated the People of *Trieſte*, in the Waters of *Caorle*, and put to flight *Pipin* Son of *Charles* the Great, with a ſort of light and nimble Veſſels they built on purpoſe for the Shoals at the bottom of the *Adriatick*. Soon after which the People of *Narenza*, in *Dalmatia*, very much infeſted the *Venetians* at Sea, and extended their piratical Depredations as far as *Caorle*; inſomuch that *Urſus Particiacus*, upon his Acceſſion to the Ducal Dignity, thought fit to come to a Treaty with them, that he might be more at leiſure to make head againſt the   *The Venetians reduce the Iſtrians and Dalmatians, put to flight Pipin's Fleet,*   A. D. 864.

the Saracens; who sailing with their Fleet up the *Adriatick* to *Grado*, he forced them to retire from thence, and pursuing them as far as the Gulph of *Taranto*, there came to an Engagement with them, wherein he gave them a signal Overthrow. The *Narenzans*, being used to a piratical Life, could not long continue quiet, but attacked the People of *Istria*, in Alliance with the Republick, who thereupon sent a Squadron of thirty Gallies to their Assistance; with which the Doge engaging the *Narenzans*, he entirely defeated them. It was not long however e'er they put to Sea again, and with a strong Squadron ranging about the *Adriatick*, *Peter Candianus*, who was then Doge, sailed in quest of them with twelve Gallies, and engaging them on the Coasts of *Dalmatia*, obtained the Advantage in the beginning of the Fight; but they being on their own Coasts, and receiving continual Supplies from thence, he was obliged to yield to superior Numbers, and at length lost the Battel, with his Life. This Victory so encouraged the Enemy, that they advanced to the City itself, and threaten'd the *Venetians* to fire it about their Ears; but the Doge, *Tron*, besides all other necessary Care to prevent their Approach, secured the Entrance of the Port with a strong Boom.

Scarce were there ever any People at one time involved in so many Difficulties as were now the *Venetians*, being on one side infested by the *Narenzans*, on another by the *Saracens*, both of *Ægypt* and *Barbary*, who were every now and then attacking them with their powerful Fleets. But a more formidable Enemy than any of these were the *Hunns* and *Avarians*, who, uniting themselves into one Body, were now first called *Hungarians*, and marching down, through the *Valteline*, into *Lombardy*, laid waste the Country; and having defeated an Army of fifteen thousand Men, under King *Berengarius*, took their way toward *Venice*, with design to enrich themselves with the Spoils of that City. To this purpose they provided themselves of a vast Number of Boats, which they made of Wicker covered with Hides, and putting off from the Shore, seized upon several of the Islands among the Shoals, reduced *Citta Nuova* in *Istria*, with *Chiozza*, and other Towns; and having greatly increased their Strength by the Addition of abundance of Vessels they took at those Places, resolved next to attack *Rialto* itself. The Doge, with incredible Diligence and Industry, manned all the Ships and Boats which could be got together, to resist these numerous Invaders, whose Fleet covered the whole Space between the City and the Shore, and vigorously attacking them, gave them so total a Defeat, that the few Remains which escaped being killed or drowned, fled with the utmost Precipitation.

This War being ended, the *Narenzans*, who had come to another Treaty, soon took occasion to break it, and seizing on all the Merchant Ships they could meet with, forced the *Venetians* to declare War against them, the Conduct of which being committed to the Doge, *Ursus Bodoaro*, who succeeded *Tron*, the *Narenzans* again sued for Peace, which they obtained upon Condition of making good all the Damages the *Venetians* had sustained by their Depredations.

CHAP. IV. *Ruin of the* Rom. *Empire.* 199

predations. Soon after this, the People of *Istria* having committed some Violences upon them, the *Venetians* attacked and defeated them also; and now becoming sensible of their own Strength, seized the City of *Capo d'Istria*; and, on the other side of them, laid siege to *Comacchio*, whose Inhabitants at length surrendering, they received their Submission, upon promise they would continue in peaceable Subjection to them: And these were the first Steps the *Venetians* made toward extending their Conquests ashore. *The* Venetians *reduce Capo d'Istria and* Comacchio.

Some time after this *Peter Urseolus* coming to the Ducal Chair, the *Venetian* Affairs received great Advantages from his prudent Government. The first thing he began his Administration with, was the sending an Embassy to *Basilius*, and his Brother *Alexius*, (by others called *Constantine*) who were joint Emperors of *Constantinople*, to desire that the *Venetian* Merchants throughout their Dominions might be exempted from paying any Duties or Customs by Sea or Land. This it would have been a shame to have denied to that People to whom all Christendom had so many Obligations, and therefore it was accordingly granted; which not only proved very beneficial to the *Venetians* in their private Capacity, as a trading People, but also mightily increased their Credit and Reputation among foreign Nations. There was one thing which the Doge thought lay very hard upon the Republick. The *Venetians*, as we have already seen, had had several Disputes with the *Narenzans* about the Mastership of the *Adriatick*; for the *Narenzans*, upon account of their long Possession of it, pleaded an hereditary Right, and, in support of their Pretensions, had sometimes made the *Venetians* their Tributaries. *Urseolus* thinking this Dishonour no longer sufferable, resolved to break with the *Narenzans*, and entirely rid his Country of that Enemy. While he was making Preparations for this purpose, frequent Complaints came from *Dalmatia* of the Injuries the *Narenzans* did to the People in those Parts; whose Agents residing with the Republick, made Remonstrances, setting forth, that, if they would but send a good Fleet against the *Narenzans*, and deliver the Coasts from the Robberies and Oppressions of that People, all *Istria*, *Morlachia*, and *Dalmatia*, and the whole Country from one end of the *Adriatick* to the other, would willingly submit to their Obedience. *Urseolus*, highly pleased with these Offers, and so glorious an Opportunity of enlarging the *Venetian* Territories, got ready a numerous Fleet, and setting sail from *Malamocco*, proceeded to *Aquileia*, where having received a consecrated Banner from the Patriarch of that Place, he proceeded over to the Coast of *Istria*, and coming before *Parenzo*, made Preparations for besieging it; but was soon prevented by the Bishop of that Place his coming out, and, in the Name of the Inhabitants, making a formal Surrender of it. From thence he proceeded to *Pola*, on the same Coast, whose Inhabitants following the Example of *Parenzo*, the People of all the neighbouring Cities sent Deputies thither to the Doge, with Offers of their Lives and Fortunes to the Service of the Republick. Some Days being spent at this Place in giving Audience to the several

A. D. 990.

War with the Narenzans.

Urseolus *reduces* Parenzo *and* Pola.

veral Deputies, and receiving the Ships, Soldiers, and Seamen which they voluntarily sent to join the Fleet, the Doge made sail to the Southward, and soon came upon the Coasts of the *Narenzans*; who were all so surprized with this great Turn of Affairs, and by the Presence of the Doge, that Deputations presently came to him from their respective Towns with Proposals of Peace. Peace he did not refuse to grant them, but the Conditions were the Matter which admitted of Dispute. At length he concluded a Treaty with them upon these Terms, "That they should observe the Exercise of the "Christian Religion with greater Strictness than they had used to "do, compensate to the *Venetians* all the Damages they had done "them, and pay the Charges of the War; that they should not "exact any Tribute for the future from the Ships sailing in the *A-* "*driatick*, nor any longer continue to practise Piracy." To all which the *Narenzans*, tho' with much Reluctance, were forced to agree. There were now only remaining to be reduced the two Islands *Curzola* and *Lesina*, whose Inhabitants would gladly have accepted Peace upon the same Terms, but were told by the Doge that their Case was different from that of the other People, and that their Fate should be decided by the Sword. For these two Islands lying about the mid-way down the *Adriatick*, no Ships could well go in or out, or navigate any where in that Sea, without being exposed to the Depredations of their Inhabitants: So that the Doge had resolved, for the Security of Trade and Navigation, and of the neighbouring People, to destroy the Cities of both those Islands. *Lesina* he attacked first, and immediately made himself Master of the Port; as for the City, it being well fortified both by Art and Nature, the Townsmen resolved to make a vigorous Defence; but the Walls being soon cleared of the Defendants by the continual Showers of Arrows both from the Ships and the Troops on shore, the *Venetians* scaled the Walls of the Citadel, which the Enemy chiefly trusted to, and presently entered the Place; the Doge giving Orders to spare such as threw down their Arms, but to kill all who made Resistance. Then having levelled the Town and Citadel with the Ground, he went over to *Curzola*, and having done the like there, proceeded to attack *Ragusa*. But the Bishop of that Place coming out to the Doge, presented him with the Keys of the City, and beseeching him, by the Crosier he bore in his Hand, and the Mitre on his Head, to spare the Lives and Fortunes of the Citizens, who by him made their humble Submission, they were pardoned, and received into the Protection of the Republick. *Urseolus* having thus happily succeeded in this Expedition, returned to *Venice*, where, in a full Senate, having made an Oration, setting forth his Services, and that he had reduced to their Obedience all the Coasts of *Istria* and *Dalmatia*, as far as the Frontiers of *Albania*, he was unanimously saluted Duke of *Dalmatia*, and from that time the Doges of *Venice* have always assumed that Title. At the same time came Ambassadors from all the Princes and States of the neighbouring Countries, to give the Republick their Thanks for freeing the Sea from the Piracies

CHAP. IV. *Ruin of the* Rom. *Empire.* 201

racies and Robberies with which it had, for some Ages past, been infested, and restoring the Safety and Security of Commerce

And thus ended the War with the *Narenzans,* after it had held, with various Success, for about a hundred and seventy Years; for so long, according to *Sabellicus,* did the *Venetians* and that People contend for the Dominion of the *Adriatick.* Their City was of very ancient Original, and they themselves the true Descendants of the old *Illyrians,* who, under their Queen *Teuta,* for some time asserted their Rights on that Sea against the Power of the *Romans:* and they are reckon'd up by *Ptolemy* among the People of *Dalmatia,* and placed above the *Sinus Rhizonicus,* upon the River *Naron,* at the Mouth of which stands the City *Narenza,* or *Narona,* as it was anciently called. Taking Advantage of the favourable Situation of their City, they used, from very ancient Times, to exact a Duty or Tax from all Ships which navigated the *Adriatick* Sea; which if any refused to pay, they were presently treated as Enemies. This all the neighbouring People looked upon as a downright Robbery, and joined in a Complaint against them to the Senate and People of *Rome,* as we have before related. And when the *Romans* sent their Ambassadors to *Teuta* concerning this Affair, she defended this Right of her People's by ancient Custom. It must be confessed, indeed, that, whilst the *Roman* Power prevailed, the Exercise of this Right was interrupted for several Ages: For it seemed to be beneath the Dignity of the *Romans,* amidst a Series of such glorious Victories, to stoop to the exacting Toll-Money from Merchant Ships. But at the Dissolution of that Empire, the Inhabitants resumed the old Trade of their Ancestors, and revived their Pretensions to those Rights. After which, when the *Venetian* Republick began to flourish, the *Narenzans* and they, becoming Rivals to each other at Sea, entered into frequent Disputes about this Duty, which sometimes the *Narenzans* forced the *Venetians* to agree to the Payment of, and at other times consented to remit it to them; and the *Venetians* one while would please to pay it, and at another absolutely refuse it, till at length becoming more powerful, they entirely crushed the *Narenzans,* and reduced them to their Obedience. For some time after which, there was no mention made of the Exercise of any Dominion in that Sea: But when the Affairs of the *Venetians* began to be more confirmed, they assumed to themselves that Right of which they had stripped their Enemies, without any Opposition being made to them on that behalf. For being not only arrived to a very considerable Power, but being also very high in the Favour of all the People bordering on the *Adriatick,* upon account of their great Successes against the *Saracens,* that Right they had acquired by force of Arms received a Confirmation from the general Consent and Authority of the neighbouring Nations: And so that Custom being continued, which was supported by such just Pretensions, in process of Time it obtained the Validity and Force of a full and ample Right. Tho, at length, when People began to be rid of their Fears of the *Saracens,* there were not wanting some

The Origine of the Narenzans, and their Pretensions to the Dominion of the Adriatick.

The Venetians *pretend to the Dominion of the* Adriatick.

D d who

who pretended to make Exceptions against this Jurisdiction: And then the Affair began to be canvassed not only among the Vulgar, but it also became a Dispute among the Learned, and particularly the Civilians, who argued the Case in several Treatises written thereupon. But that side always got the better which asserted to the *Venetians* the Dominion and Possession of the *Adriatick* Sea, and the Right of exercising Sovereignty therein: so that the *Venetians*, now a days, support their Pretensions, not only by pleading their Title derived by Right of War from the *Narenzans*, and by Custom, founded upon most equitable Reasons, and confirmed by the Consent of Christendom; but also by the declared Opinions of the Learned in the Laws, and the Authority of Cases adjudged.

In this manner it is that the learned Dr. *Ryves* deduces the Right of the *Venetians* to the Dominion of the Gulph of *Venice*, which having thus made good, he takes occasion to discuss that Question so much controverted in his Time, Whether the Sea be capable of Dominion, or not? In which Discourse having fully proved the Affirmative by several curious Arguments, most of them unthought of by any but himself, I judged it might be inexcusable in me should I not afford Place in this History to so great an Ornament.

Dr. Ryves his Arguments to prove that the Sea may be held in Dominion.

As for those, says he, who assert that the Sea is uncapable of Dominion, and having particular Proprietors, they forget that Law given by God himself, at the Creation of the World, *Have Dominion over the Fish of the Sea*. It will not be denied then, I suppose, but that we may have Dominion over the Fish; but why not also over the Sea which contains them? For if these Words do not impart to us a Right to the Sea, neither do those which follow give us any to the Air we breathe in, or the Earth we walk upon. *Have Dominion*, says the Creator, *over the Fish of the Sea, and over the Fowl of the Air, and over every living thing that moveth upon the Earth*. Now no body can doubt but that God, by the the Delivery of these things to us, did, as it were by putting the Keys into our Hands, give us the Possession of this earthly Habitation. That the Land is subject to private Dominion, and capable of having particular Proprietors, we all very well know: Now the Land and Water make but one Globe, and one and the same Point of the Universe; therefore if the Land be capable of Dominion, so also is the Sea; for that which is one and the same thing cannot be imagined to be subject to different Rights. Nor is it any thing to the purpose what *Grotius* says of the fluid Nature of the Sea; for *Flumen* [a River, or, as we often express it in Poetry, a Flood] is derived *à fluendo*, from flowing, or being fluid, and yet whoever pretended to deny that Rivers were capable of Dominion, both publick and private?

But *Grotius* pretends that, *by reason of this flowing Condition of the Sea, it cannot admit of having Boundaries and Partitions in it.* Must we then pronounce *Procopius* a Fool for telling us, in his History of the *Goths*, that a Line drawn from the [a] Promontory *Pachinus*, in *Sicily*, to the Island of [b] *Melita* parts the *Tyrrhene* from the

[a] Cape *Passaro*.
[b] Malta.

the *Adriatick* Sea? Muſt we call *Ptolemy*, and the whole Tribe of Geographers Blockheads, for demonſtrating to us, as they have done, that by means of Lines drawn from the Centre of the Earth to the Orb of the fix'd Stars, the Sea as well as Land may be accurately parted and divided? For thoſe Lines perform the ſame Office to the Learned in dividing and marking out the different Quarters and Situations of the Earth and Water, as Pales, Fences, Ditches and Land-marks do to the illiterate Farmer in ſetting out the Limits of his Grounds. Pope *Alexander* VI, when he was made Arbitrator of the Difference between the *Spaniards* and *Portugueſe*, about the new Diſcoveries in *India* and *America*, did not divide thoſe Countries between them by any Boundaries on the Land, but by a Line drawn croſs the Sea: I do not ſay what Right he had ſo to do, (for 'tis plain he had none) but inſtance it only as a Mark of his Ingenuity, which, every body muſt own, was very conſpicuous in this Particular. And, in former times, until it came otherwiſe to be provided for in Treaties, by particularizing the Limits within which, and Time when ſuch Treaties ſhould take effect, tho' there were ever ſuch a firm Peace ſubſiſting between the Crowns of *England* and *Spain*, yet the Moment either of their Subjects came beyond the Æquinoctial Line they were in a State of War, and as if, by paſſing that Boundary, they had immediately changed their Natures, attacked one another with all the Violence and Fury imaginable. Seeing therefore that notwithſtanding the Fluidity of the Sea, it may have Bounds deſigned, and Limits laid out in it, the Partiſans of *Grotius*, according to his Argument, cannot refrain granting that it may alſo be acquired and poſſeſſed. But if they ſhould ſtill perſiſt to be troubleſome, and alledge that, becauſe of its moveable and unſtable Nature, the Sea cannot have Boundaries and Partitions, and is therefore not acquirable; they may as well, by the ſame Argument, pretend to prove that great part of *Barbary* and *Ægypt*, and ſeveral other vaſt Tracts of Land in *Africa*, are *Res nullius*, and belong to no body, and may not be acquired or poſſeſſed. For the Sands there are as unſtable as the Surges of the Sea, and the Winds toſs them about, and raiſe Mountains, and ſink Vallies in them as they do in the Waters of the Ocean; and as whole Fleets have been ſwallowed up by one, ſo have Armies of Men been overwhelmed in the other, as *Cambyſes*, one of the Kings of *Perſia*, in an Expedition againſt the *Ammonii*, a People of the Country now called *Barca*, dearly experienced. And yet theſe Countries do not want Owners, but are the Propriety and Poſſeſſion of ſeveral Princes. What then ſhould hinder but that the Sea ſhould have its Princes and Proprietors alſo? Why truly, as *Grotius* will have it, *becauſe thoſe who pretend to Dominion and Propriety in the Sea, divide it not by Boundaries, or Limits made by Nature, or*

---

* *The Ancients often included under the Name of the* Adriatick *not only what we now call the Gulph of* Venice, *but alſo all that Sea which is between* Italy, Sicily, *and* Greece; *as they called the* Tyrrhene Sea *all that part of the* Mediterranean *which is to the Weſt of* Italy, Sicily, *and* Malta, *even to the Streights of* Gibraltar.

the Hand of Man, but only by a fantaſtick imaginary Line: (meaning the forementionʼd Boundary made by Pope *Alexander*, which was a Meridian Line five Degrees Weſt of the Cape *Verde* Iſlands;) yet theſe Lines *Grotius* ſo contemptibly calls *imaginary*, are thoſe for the Invention, or, at leaſt, Perfection of which *Ptolemy* ſo deſervedly values himſelf, and proves, beyond contradiction, that this way of aſcertaining the Extent of Dominions and Countries, and meaſuring the whole Surface of the Land and Water, by Parallels of Latitude and Meridians of Longitude, is infinitely better and more certain than any other. Nor need we be under any Apprehenſion, as *Grotius* pretends to be, that *if we admit of ſuch Inventions, the Geometricians may ſteal away the Earth from us*: For, far from that, ʼtis well known that, by the Invention of their Art, every Manʼs Property in *Ægypt* was firſt ſecured to him; for the Overflowing of the *Nile* laying the Country under Water, and leaving it covered with Mud, it was only by the help of Geometry that each Perſon knew the Extent of his own Lands. And as little occaſion have we to fear, what he feigns to do, *that the Aſtronomers ſhould rob us of the Heavens*; ſince even that Axis itſelf by which they are ſuſtained, and round which they turn, is nothing elſe but an imaginary Line drawn through the Centre to both the Poles of the World, and the pure Contrivance of the Aſtronomers for ſolving to us the Phænomena of Nature. What Obſtinacy is it then to ſlight thoſe Boundaries which have been ſo nobly and uſefully invented, and pretend, in the Depths of the Sea, to look for Limits placed by the Hand of Man; and by ſuch ſophiſtical Quirks to pave a Way for War and Deſtruction throughout the World!

But *Grotius* will have it that *the Sea is* Res communis, *a thing common to all, and therefore cannot be challenged by any one as his Property or Poſſeſſion*. And is not the Earth the common Parent of us all; and yet do we not dig it, and plow it, and contend about every Foot of it, and call it *Meum* and *Tuum*, and that, as I hope, without Offence? Why then ſhould we not do the ſame by the Sea? For, how common ſoever they would have it, it was not, ſurely, at firſt more ſo than the Earth and Air; for the Earth, Air, and Water were ever reckoned, in the State of Nature, to be equally common. And ſeeing our Antagoniſts, who have entered into this Diſpute, have not ſcrupled to bring for Authorities Paſſages out of the Poets, there is no reaſon why I ſhould not be allowed the ſame Liberty. That at firſt the Land was common to all, I ſhall produce the Teſtimony of the divine *Virgil*, who, in his *Georgics*, ſays,

Ante Jovem nulli ſubigebant arva coloni:
Nec ſignare quidem, aut partiri limite campum
Fas erat. ⸺

Eʼer this no Peaſant vexʼd the peaceful Ground,
Which only Turfs and Greens for Altars found:

CHAP. IV.   *Ruin of the* Rom. *Empire.*   205

No Fences parted Fields; nor Marks, nor Bounds
Distinguish'd Acres of litigious Grounds:
But all was common.──────
Mr. Dryden.

And to the same purpose, *Ovid*, in his *Metamorphoses*, tells us, that after *Saturn* was dethroned, and *Jupiter* came to reign, then first began the Claims of Right, and particular Possession of Things,

Communemque prius, seu lumina solis & auræ,
Cautus humum longo signavit limite mensor.

Then Land-marks limited to each his Right,
For all before was common as the Light.
Mr. Dryden.

And *Horace*, yet more expressly, says,

Nam propriæ telluris herum natura neque illum,
Nec me, nec quemquam statuit.──────

For Nature doth not him, or me, create
The proper Lord of such and such Estate.
Mr. Creech.

From all which it is plain that the Earth's being capable of distinct Property, and Possession, does not proceed from Nature, but is of human Institution. If therefore the Land, which was at first free and common to all, and divided by no Limits or Boundaries, might be taken Possession of and acquired, both by Numbers of People, and particular Persons for their Use, and be set out, distributed, and distinguished into different Parts and Parcels, without any Injury to Mankind, or Violence to the Law of Nations, why may not the Sea be liable to the same Rights? Or what has it in its Nature to make it less capable of being acquired and possessed than the Land? If you answer, its *Community*; I have shewn that the Land and Sea are just one as common as the other, and yet the Land is capable of all kind of Dominion and Possession; so that the Sea is consequently subject to the same Rights.

Nor does it signify any thing, what *Grotius* urges, that *Placentinus*, an ancient Author, has said, *the Sea is so much a thing Common, that only God himself is Lord of it*. For, first, whether *Placentinus* has so said or not, is altogether uncertain to me; for where he has said it, I have not been able, with all the Search I could make, to find. But, grant he has said so, what does it make to the purpose? Are we not told by a much more ancient and greater Author than *Placentinus*, even the Psalmist *David*, that *the Earth is also the Lord's, and the Fulness thereof*? If we would think and speak rightly, we are but Tenants, and Inhabitants at will upon this Earth, or rather only Guests and Strangers in it; and yet,
never-

nevertheless, if we possess ever so small a spot of it, we are called Lords of our Lands; why may we not, therefore, as well be called Lords of the Sea, if any part of it be in our Possession?

But *Grotius* alledges that *Joannes Faber*, a learned Commentator upon the Civil Law, asserts, that *the Sea is left in its first and primitive Right and State, wherein all things were common.* The Princes and Potentates of the World have taken mighty care of that indeed! But let us suppose, with him, that when, of old time, the Land was seized and occupied to the use of particular Persons, the Sea was left in common, and exempted from private Possession; I would fain know by what Law? by what Decree of Mankind? Or, (since we must have recourse to the Equity of the Law of Nations) by the Edict of what universal Judge was it so ordained? For if none of all these can be produced for support of that Assertion, what does it signify that one learned Man has taken it into his Head to say so? *Very much, Grotius* will say: *For how, in the Sea* (he will ask) *can there be that* corporis ad corpus adjunctio, *that joining of Body to Body, which is necessary to make Entry on, or take Seisin of any thing, and without which no Dominion can commence?* I am no Conjurer at Riddles, but, as I take it, *Grotius* (having a View to the Etymology of the word *Possessio*, which some derive *à pedis positione*, from treading with the Foot) means to ask us how we can tread with our Feet upon the Sea, to take Possession, and commence our Dominion of it. If that be his Meaning, that learned Man might have found what he looks for in the Lake of *Gennesareth*, where, we know, that, of old, both our Saviour Christ, and St. *Peter* did tread with their Feet, and walk upon it. But, not to insist upon that, have not the *Euxine*, or Black Sea, the Sea of *Marmora*, the Streights of *Caffa*, and *Constantinople*, and the *Dardanelles*, been very often so frozen, that they might be trod, walked, and trampled upon as well as the Land? You will say they are all within the *Mediterranean*: I own it. But what will you say of the great Northern Ocean, which the Ancients called *Mare Cronium* and *Glaciale*, the frozen Sea, and we Moderns know very often to be so? Now if the Ocean may be frozen up, it may also be trampled upon, and bear the Tread, not only of the Foot of Man, but of the Hoofs of Horses, and sustain the Weight of Carriages, as well as those Streights and inland Seas; from whence it follows that it is also capable of being possessed: For, I suppose, it will not be pretended that the Ocean, when it freezes, ceases to be the Ocean. But now, to come to the liquid unfrozen Ocean; why, I pray, will not that also bear the *pedis positio*, and the *corporis ad corpus adjunctio*, the treading of the Foot, and the joining Body to Body, that is to say, the being taken Possession of? For if I am upon the Deck of a Ship sailing in the Sea, it cannot be denied but that I am upon the Sea; if it were, you might as well say that, when I am on Horseback, I am not upon the Earth. And if you would alledge that, then you might, by the same Rule, affirm, that, if I go with my Shoes on and tread on my Land, I shall have done nothing towards taking Possession, nor ever be reckoned to have joined Body to Body, unless I walk bare-foot upon it, when I make Entry thereon: And how ridiculous an Assertion that would be, every body is a Judge. But the Poet *Ovid* says even of the Sea-Monster which was sent by *Ammon* to devour *Andromeda*, that he *possessed* the Sea which was under him.

    ——— *Venienfque immenso bellua ponto*
   Imminet, & latum fub pectore possidet æquor.

    ———*Flouncing o'er the Main*
   The Monster comes, and with his ample Train
   A spacious Sea beneath him does possess.

And I don't see why a Ship itself, or the Master, who is as it were, an animating Form to it, may not be said to possess the Sea which is under it. But if that should seem a little forced, and too far fetched, yet nothing can be plainer than what is said by *Dædalus*, in the same Poet,

    ———*Terras licet, inquit, & undas*
   Obstruat: at cœlum certè patet: ibimus illac:
   Omnia possideat: non possidet aëra Minos

   The Land and Sea tho' Minos does possess;
   The Air is free; and thence I'll seek redress.

So that if *Minos*, of old, could possess the Sea as well as Land, what should hinder but that the Princes and States of our Times may use the same Right, and possess their Seas also? Or what, after all, is that way of arguing *à notatione nominis*, from the Etymology of Words, which some People so much boast of? To me it appears not only to be very often deceitful, but always very weak, and most commonly very ridiculous; and is nothing but a mere trifling with Words and Syllables. For if there be no Possession without the *pedis positio*, the treading with the Foot, pray how comes it to pass that the *Greek* Language, which is so rich and fruitful in the Derivation and Composition of Words, has found no Term answerable to that Etymology of *possessio*? Certainly *Theophilus*, that learned Lawyer, who translated *Justinian's* Institutes into *Greek*, never once renders *possessio* by ποδὸς θέσις, treading with the Foot, but always by νομή, a Word which, in its first Signification, means Distribution, Division, and acquiring by Partition, and has no manner of relation to treading with the Foot. Thus, *longi temporis possessio*, he translates ἡ χρονία νομή; *res quæ possidetur*, τὸ πρᾶγμα ὁ νέμεται; *rei possessor*, ὁ νεμόμενος; and lastly, *bonæ fidei possessio*, βονεφίδει νομή. The *Greeks* also use another Word for *possidere*, to possess, to wit κτήσασθαι, but neither has that any relation to treading with the Foot. And who does not know that both νέμειν and κτήσασθαι, in their strictest and properest Sense, signify to acquire any thing? But because what we acquire we do most commonly also possess, they are applied to express both those Acts of acquiring and possessing. Seeing therefore that *Minos*, and other Princes could acquire the Dominion of the Sea, they may, with great Propriety of Speech, be said also to have possessed the Sea itself.

But, as I take it, the main Stress of the Dispute does not lie here, but rather upon this Point, whether there be any such *Commercium* of the Sea, that is, whether it is capable of being so exchanged or transferred, that a Right, or Title, that is to say, a Cause of possessing, may, by any Colour or Pretence, be pleaded and made out to it. Which, why we should make any doubt of, I see no Reason; especially if we have any manner of Regard for the Poets. Let us hear therefore, if you please, from *Virgil*, how *Neptune*, one of the Sons of *Saturn*, King of *Crete*, defends his Right against *Æolus*, and in a mighty Heat affirms,

Non illi imperium pelagi, sævumque tridentem,
Sed mihi sorte *datum.*————

The Realms of Ocean and the Fields of Air
Are mine, not his; by fatal Lot to me
The liquid Empire fell, and Trident of the Sea.
Mr. Dryden.

So that, we find, the Dominion of the Sea (that of *Crete* for example, or any other) could be given by *Lot*; why may it not therefore as well be made over by Donation, bequeathed by Testament, or transferr'd by any other Title from one to another? But these, you'll say, are Fables: I don't deny it. Yet they sufficiently shew that it is not absurd, nor contrary to Reason, to say that the Sea is capable of the *Commercium*, and that it may be possessed, or made over, by virtue of a Title. For Commerce is said to be of all those things which can be applied to the Use of Man, be subjected to Dominion, be brought into Obligation, or be acquired and alienated, all things of that Nature being liable to be transferred. And the Sea, as appears by the foregoing Example, being of that kind, no body can deny but it is capable of *Commerce* also.

Grotius further says, that, *by the Law of Nations, any one People has a Right to trade with any other which they can come at by the help of Shipping.* This I can by no means agree to: For suppose any People at this time (as we know several did of old, and that for very just Causes) should prohibit all foreign Merchants from coming among them, may they, by the Law of Nations, be compelled, against their Will, to admit them? So far from that, that among the *Romans* (who were certainly not ignorant of the Law of Nations) if any Person came from a foreign Country, between which and them there was no Friendship nor Treaty subsisting, and with which they had no Intercourse, such Person immediately became a Slave, and if any *Roman* fell into the Hands of the People of any such other Country as beforementioned, he was by the *Roman* Law looked upon as their Slave, and excluded from the Rights of a Citizen,

tizen, as is expressly said by *Pomponius* in the *Digest, l. 5. §. In pace. Tit. De captivis, & postliminio*. It is not lawful therefore for Strangers to go and visit any Country they please, without the Consent of the Prince or Possessors of such Country, neither for the sake of Trading, nor on any other account whatsoever. Now if it be not lawful, without our Consent, to set foot upon our Land, neither is it so to sail in our Sea, nor even to breathe in our Air, without our Consent. For all those things, tho' they are free and open to our Friends, Allies, and those with whom we have Intercourse; they are not so to our Enemies and to Strangers, except our Leave and Consent be first obtained: much less is it allowable for them to occupy our Coasts, to dry Nets, to take Fish in our Sea, or being taken, to salt or dry them upon our Shores, unless it be so stipulated by some Article of Peace, or Treaty of Agreement. Who is there that does not see, therefore, how much these kind of Speeches, *The Sea is free to sail upon*; *It is common to all*; *It cannot be comprized within Boundaries*; *It is incapable of Dominion or Commerce*; *It cannot be possessed*, and the like; Who is there, I say, that does not see how much they resemble the Sayings of the Levellers, who are for a Community in all things, if they were not coined in the same Mint? As if, by such Jesting, rather than Argument, the *Venetians* would suffer themselves to be dispossessed of the *Adriatick* Gulph, the King of *Denmark* of his Streight of the *Sound*, or our most gracious Sovereign of the *British* Seas, which they have so long been in Possession of: Or, as if these were the first who claimed Dominion of certain Seas, and there were not Precedents of the like in all Ages. For the *Cretans, Lydians, Thracians, Athenians, Lacedæmonians, Rhodians, Phœnicians, Ægyptians, Carthaginians*, and very many others have in their Turns (as we have already seen) one while held the Dominion of the Sea, and another lost it again. And whosoever is possessed of the Dominion of a Sea does possess every thing therein, in such manner as that it is not lawful for another, without his Consent, to meddle with any thing in such Sea, nor come upon it, any more than it would be to do so on the Land; as is plain from the Behaviour of all those People in their Turns, and from many other Instances in this History. So the *Romans*, upon the Conclusion of the second *Punic* War, obliged the *Carthaginians* to keep no more than such a certain Number of Ships of War; in which Circumstance they no sooner found the *Carthaginians* had once transgressed, but they immediately began a third War against them, which ended not but with the Destruction of *Carthage*. In like manner they obliged *Antiochus*, King of *Syria*, not to come on this side the Promontory *Calycadnus* with more than one Ship of War, and that only in case of sending Tribute or Ambassadors to *Rome*: By complying with which Terms, that great Monarch of the East owned his Conquerors, the *Romans*, to be no less Lords of the Sea than of the Land. But these things, you will say, might perhaps be done in the *Mediterranean*, whereas in the Ocean the Case is different. And yet the Emperor *Claudius* subdued the Ocean itself, as *Seneca* tells us in his *Apocolocynthosis*, whose Words I shall set down;

>   ——*Ille Britannos*
> *Ultra noti littora ponti, & cæruleos*
> *Cute Brigantes, dare Romuleis colla catenis*
> *Jussit, & ipsum nova Romanæ jura securis*
> *Tremere Oceanum.*——

> *The* Britains *seated on the distant Main,*
> *And the* Brigantes *with their painted Skins,*
> *He forc'd to yield to* Rome*'s Imperial Pow'r;*
> *Nor could the Ocean's self escape his Yoak,*
> *But trembles still at its new Laws and Masters.*

This is so full and plain, that it will be almost needless for me to mention *Constantius Chlorus*, the Father of *Constantine* the Great, who, after his Victory at Sea over the *Francks*, and his defeating of *Carausius*, is said by *Eudemus*, in his Panegyrick upon him, to have *added to the Empire another Element greater than the Earth*, thereby meaning the Ocean. Not that it is to be supposed that, by this Success, the universal Mass of Waters, or the whole *Atlantick*, or the great Southern, and Eastern Oceans, were subjected to the *Romans*, (for much the greater part of them they knew nothing of) but only that *Constantius*, by such a signal Victory, had subdued and made their own all that part of the Ocean bordering upon the Empire: For such Expressions as these in Authors are to be taken, as we say, with Grains of Allowance. Nor if, even in the Gospel itself, you read that *there went out a Decree from* Cæsar Augustus, *that all the World should be taxed*; are you to understand it of the *Bactrians*, the *Sogdians*, or *Parthians*, or any other People without the Pale of the Empire, but only of the *Roman* World. With what Right therefore *Constantius* subjected to the *Roman* Empire all that part of the Ocean on the Coasts of *Africk*, *Spain*, *Gaul*, *Germany*, and *Britain*, by the same Right do the Kings of *England*, with respect to the *British* Seas and the Kings of *Denmark*, with respect to the *Sound*, assert the Dominion of them to belong to them and their Crowns. And that, in so doing, they may not be accused of acting by Force rather than Right, pray hear what that most profound Lawyer *Baldus* says upon the whole Matter. *In mari jurisdictio est sicut in terrá. Nam mare in terrá, i. e. in alveo suo fundatum est, quum terra sit inferior sphæra.* That is, "There is a Jurisdiction upon the Sea, "as well as on the Land. For the Sea is placed in the Land as in "its Bed, the Earth being the lowermost Element." And farther he says, *Videmus de jure gentium in mari esse Regna distincta sicut in aridá terrá: ergo & jus civile, i. e. præscriptio, illud idem potest operari. Et hæc præscriptio quandoque aufertur alteri: sed quum applicatur alteri, ita quod alii non aufertur ista est consuetudo; & sic Venetiarum & Januensium Respublicæ sua maria distincta ex inveteratissimá consuetudine habent. Sed num quid hoc*

Bald. ad l. 2. Tit. de Rerum divisione

CHAP. IV. *Ruin of the* Rom. *Empire.* 211

hoc prætextu navigantibus per ipsorum mare, possunt imponere gabellas, & confiscare merces, inconsulto Principe? That is, "We "see that by the Law of Nations there are distinct Kingdoms on "the Sea, as well as the Land, and therefore by the Civil Law, "that is, by Prescription, there may be so too. And this Prescrip-"tion is sometimes taken from another: but when it is applied to "one without having been taken from another, it is then Custom: "And thus the *Venetians* and *Genoese*, by most ancient Custom, "have each their distinct Seas. But whether or no may they up-"on this Account impose Taxes on those who sail therein, and "confiscate their Merchandizes, without consulting the Emperor?" Which Question of his own he answers in the Affirmative, and for this Reason, *Quia totus mundus hoc jure utitur;* "Because all the "World uses this Right." And after this, he says, *Minimè mutanda videntur quæ consuetudinem certam semper habuerunt.* That is, "Those things by no means ought to be changed which have "been established by certain Custom." Thus you see, Reader, how this great Oracle of the Law gives a full Answer to all the Cavils of our Gainsayers: and that Jurisdiction, Dominion, Commerce, (that is, a Right of transferring Dominion, either by Prescription, Custom, or any other Title) and distinct Limits and Boundaries, may be had and held, not only by the Emperors, but by other Kings and Commonwealths, upon the Sea as well as the Land, and that not by Force, but by Right, and by the Civil Law, as well as the Law of Nations.

But some of our Adversaries will alledge, that the Law itself disclaims all Dominion upon the Sea, as well the Mediterranean as the Ocean. And if I ask, What Law? They will answer, That given by the Emperor *Antoninus Pius*, as it stands in the Digest: *Ego quidem mundi dominus, lex autem maris. Lege id Rhodiâ quæ de rebus nauticis præscripta est, judicetur.* That is, "I am, indeed, "Lord of the World, but the Law is of the Sea. Let that Matter "be judged by the *Rhodian* Law concerning Sea Affairs." But I reply that that Rescript, which was made in *Greek*, and is also set down in the same Place in that Language, is falsified by the foregoing *Latin* Translation of it. The *Greek* Words are, Ἐγὼ μὲν ξ κόσμου κύριος, ὁ ἢ νόμος τ͂ θαλάσσης τῷ νόμῳ τ Ῥοδίων κρινέσθω τῷ ναυτικῷ. Now here, pray, what Word is there answerable to the *id* (that matter) in the *Latin* Translation? Certainly none. Therefore if we will leave that Word out, it will plainly appear that Mr. *Selden*'s Opinion about the false Pointing in the *Greek* Text, may pass for an Oracle; for instead of a full Stop after θαλάσσης, as most of the printed Books have it, he reads it as I have set it down above. And then, agreeable thereto, the *Latin* will stand thus. *Ego quidem mundi dominus: Lex autem maris lege Rhodiâ quæ de nauticis præscripta est, judicetur.* That is, "I am, indeed, Lord of "the World: but let the Rights of the Sea be judged by the *Rho-*"*dian* Law concerning Sea Affairs." And this the learned *Dionysius Gothofredus*, in his excellent Annotations upon that Place, seems first to have perceived, when he tells us, that the Sense of this Law

L. Ἀξιῶσις Dig. de Lege Rhodiâ.

E e 2   is

is no other than as if it had been said, *The Prince himself is indeed Lord of the World, or Earth; but the Rights of the Sea shall be determined from the* Rhodian *Law*. And *James Gothofredus*, the worthy Successor to his Father's great Reputation in the Law, in his *Hypomnema de Dominio Maris*, plainly shews the Falsity of the vulgar Pointing of this Place, and that his Father was the first who observed it. It is ridiculous therefore to say the Emperor disclaims the Dominion of the Sea by this Rescript: and it is most certain that the *Rhodian* Law never did, nor possibly could, enact that he should. Thus far the learned Dr. *Ryves*. From which ingenious Dissertation of his, and what has been said in the first Book upon this Subject, I don't doubt but my Reader is fully convinced that the Sea is capable of Dominion, and he will, perhaps, wonder that any one should ever have been so hardy as to deny it. And now, from this long Digression, to return to the *Venetian* Story.

From the time of the Doge *Peter Urseolus* there fell out nothing remarkable (except the quelling a Rebellion in *Dalmatia* by his Son and Successor *Otho*, and some Civil Dissensions which happened under the three following Doges) till *Dominicus Sylvius* came to the Chair, who at the Sollicitation of *Nicephorus*, Emperor of the East, whose Daughter he had married, made War on *Robert* Count of *Apulia*, whom he defeated in a great Sea Fight off *Durazzo*, but being worsted by him in a second Battel, he lost his Reputation, and was deposed.

The Doge Sylvius beats the Count of Apulia, but is afterwards defeated by him, and deposed.

And now the *Venetians* turning their Arms towards *Asia*, defeated the *Pisans* off *Rhodes*, took the City of *Smirna*, laid waste the Coasts of *Phœnicia*, seized *Faramida* on the Coast of *Ægypt*, and made themselves Masters of *Sidon, Tyre,* and *Ptolemais*, sinking and destroying great Numbers of the Ships of the Infidels: For which good Services *Baldwin*, King of *Jerusalem*, granted large Priviledges to the *Venetians* for their Trade in those Countries. After this the *Dalmatians* rising in Rebellion, were reduced to Obedience, and *Croatia* annexed to the Republick, at which time the Dukes of *Venice* added to their other Titles that of Prince of *Croatia*. These Successes were followed by a memorable Expedition into *Syria* under *Dominicus Michael*, then Doge, who, with a Fleet of two hundred Sail, undertook to remove the *Saracens* from the Siege of *Joppa*, which he bravely effected, with the entire Destruction of their Fleet which lay before the Place. In his way home, laden with the Spoils of the Infidels, he took from the Emperor *Emanuel*, who had declared War against him, the Islands of *Scio, Samo, Metelin, Andri,* and others, in the *Archipelago*, and after ravaging the Coasts of *Greece*, returned triumphantly to *Venice*.

The Venetians beat the Pisans, and take Tyre, Sidon, &c.

Dalmatia reduced and Croatia annexed to Venice.

A. D. 1120.

The Doge destroys the Saracen Fleet at Joppa, takes from Emanuel Scio, Samo, Metelin, &c.

A. D. 1131.

Peter Polani succeeding him in the Government, put his Brother and one of his Sons at the Head of the Fleet, who not only defeated *Roger* King of *Sicily*, but subdued the Island of *Corfu*; and War being now declared against *Emanuel*, Emperor of *Constantinople*, for taking some Towns from them in *Dalmatia*, they soon recovered *Traw* and *Ragusa*, and suddenly invading *Scio* again, totally

The Venetians defeat Roger King of Sicily at Sea, and take Corfu.

reduced

CHAP. IV. *Ruin of the* Rom. *Empire.* 213

reduced that Island, from whence they proceeded to *Metelin,* thence *Their great* to *Stalimene,* and *Scyro,* all which they subdued. *Vitalis Michael* *Success against* becoming Doge, in three Months time there were fitted for the Sea *the Greeks.* a hundred Gallies, and twenty Ships of War against the Emperor *Emanuel,* in which Expedition most of the Seamen being poisoned *Venetian Sea-* by the Fraud of the Enemy, the People unjustly ascribed it to their *men poisoned* Doge, and killed him in a Tumult. *by the Greeks.*

Sebastian Ziani succeeding, he took part with Pope *Alexander* 1173. III. against the Emperor *Frederick Barbarossa,* whose Son *Otho,* at the Head of a Fleet of seventy five Sail, he defeated off the *Punta* *The Venetians* *di Salvori* in *Istria,* taking forty eight of the Ships, among which *beat the Fleet* was the Admiral-Gally, wherein *Otho* himself was. *Ziani* return- *Barbarossa,* ing into the City, was met by the Pope, who congratulating him *and take his* upon his Success, presented him with a Gold Ring, saying, *Take this* *Son Otho.* *Ring, and with it bind the Sea to thee in Wedlock: This you and* *the Sea to the* *your Successors shall do every Year, that latest Posterity may know* *Venetians.* *that you have acquired the Dominion of this Sea by Right of Conquest, and that as the Wife is subject to her Husband, so is that to the Republick of* Venice. And accordingly the Ceremony of marrying the Sea, by throwing in of a Gold Ring, is performed every Year, with great Solemnity, on Ascension Day.

Some time after this the People of *Zara* rebelled against the *Venetians,* who no sooner approached the neighbouring Islands, which had done the same, than they submitted again; but that Place being well fortified, and supported by the Pirates of the *Adriatick,* maintained the War against them some Years, until a Fleet of forty five *Zara is forced* Sail being built to reduce them to Obedience, of which twenty five *to submit to* were Gallies, the rest Ships of Burthen, *Renier Zeno,* who was appointed to command them, repaired to *Dalmatia,* and at length forced *Zara* to surrender. About the same time the People of *Pisa* being come to an open Rupture with the *Venetians,* suddenly surprized *Pola,* a City of *Istria,* Tributary to them; whereupon they fitting out a Fleet of ten Gallies, and six Ships of Burthen, soon made themselves Masters of the Place, and burnt all the *Pisan* Ships which *They beat the* lay there. The Town being dismantled also, that so it might not *Pisans, and* any more prove a Receptacle for the Enemy, the *Venetians* pro- *Pola.* ceeded to *Modon,* in order to meet with a Fleet of *Pisan* Merchant Ships there, those which could escape from *Pola* having repaired thither to protect them; and off that Place coming to an Engagement, they worsted the *Pisans,* and took two of the Merchant Ships.

Now was the Reputation of the *Venetians* arrived to a great height, and as on the one hand the *French* and *Germans* sollicited Ships *The Aid of* of them to transport their Troops to *Syria,* so on the other *Alexius* *Venice desir-* *Junior* begged their Aid against his Uncle *Alexius,* who had trea- *French and* cherously usurped the Empire of the East. They undertaking his *Germans, and* Support, seized *Constantinople,* and burnt the Enemy's Ships *young Alexi-* in the Harbour; but finding themselves nevertheless perfidi- 1195. ously treated by *Alexius,* they and the *French* divided the Empire

The Venetians and French divide the Greek Empire.

pire between them, the latter having allotted to them *Constantinople*, *Romania*, *Macedonia*, and *Greece*, and the others *Candia*, with all the Islands of the *Archipelago* and *Ionian* Sea. These Acquisitions were so numerous, that the Publick was at a Loss not only how to maintain, but even to get Possession of some of them; wherefore a Law was made that whatever private Persons, either Citizens or Allies, would repair to any of those Islands, late belonging to the *Greek* Emperors, they should for ever enjoy such Shares of them as each Person could acquire; whereupon numerous Adventurers undertaking this Service, turned out the present Possessors, and settled themselves and Families in their room, whereby the Islands were secured to the Republick, which was no less engaged in providing for the Settlement and Security of those of greater Consequence. A Fleet of thirty Sail was fitted out under the Command of *Renier Dandolo*, and *Roger Permarino*, who had no sooner got out of the Gulph, than they were met by *Leo Vetrani*, a famous *Genoese* Captain, with nine Gallies, whom they defeated, took him Prisoner, and presently reducing *Corfu*, that had rebelled, hanged him in that Island; from whence proceeding they seized *Modon* and *Coron*, then two Nests of Pirates; so that having the Sea thus open, they advanced to take Possession of the Islands. M. *Dandolo* and *James Viadri* jointly attacked and made themselves Masters of *Gallipoli*, on the *Hellespont*. M. *Sanutus*, and others, reduced *Nicsia*, *Pario*, *Milo*, and *Andri*; as *Rabanus Carcerius* did the Island and Gulph of *Negroponte*. *Andrew* and *Henry Glassi* subdued *Tina*, *Micone*, *Scyro*, *Policandro*, and *Stalimene*. In the mean time *Henry Piscator*, Governor of the South Parts of the *Morea*, assisted by a Fleet of *Genoese*, made an attempt to drive the *Venetians* out of *Candia*, but *Renier*, the *Venetian* Admiral, repulsing him, sunk four of the *Genoese* Ships; and soon after a strong Reinforcement was sent to *Candia* to keep the *Greeks* in order.

The Venetians beat the Genoese at Sea,

and take many Places.

Four Genoese Ships sunk by the Venetians.

The Genoese beaten, sue for Peace.

The *Genoese* now scouring the Seas, *John Trevisano* was sent against them with a Squadron of nine Gallies, who off *Trapani*, on the Coast of *Sicily*, took twelve of their Ships; which so humbled them, that they sued for a Peace, which was granted. A strong Reinforcement was sent to *Corfu*, the better to secure that Island, but under the Notion of defending the Inhabitants against the Enemy: And there being reason to apprehend some Disturbances in *Candia*, a considerable Body of Troops was also sent thither. Hence the War was removed toward the Streights of *Constantinople*, in the Port of which City *Leo Cavala*, Admiral of the *Greek* Fleet, was beaten and put to flight, having four and twenty Gallies either sunk or taken. After this *John Michael*, a *Venetian*, Prætor of *Constantinople*, went out with sixteen Gallies, which lay in the Port for the Defence of that Place, against *John Vatazi*, who came to besiege it with twenty five Gallies; and they coming to an Engagement, the *Venetians* taking ten, forced the rest to retire, and leave the Sea open to the Citizens.

The Greeks Fleet beaten at Constantinople.

Not

Not long after, the Quarrel with the *Genoese* broke out again on this occasion. All the Nations of Christendom which were engaged in the Holy War, after the taking of *Ptolemais*, or *Acre*, from the Infidels, shared that City amongst them, each having a separate Division; and those of the *Venetians* and *Genoese* lying contiguous, they had but one Church between them, the Use of which gave occasion for a mutual Emulation and Hatred, which at length came to a War. The *Genoese* took their Opportunity to seize the Church, and fortified it like a Castle, which the *Venetians* highly resenting, they brought out thirteen Gallies from *Tyre*, and under the Command of *Laurence Tiepolo*, coming before *Acre*, forced the Chain which lay a-cross the Harbour, broke in, and seized three and twenty Merchant Ships, with two Gallies of *Genoa* which lay there; and having plundered them of their Merchandize, and taken out the Naval Stores, they set fire to them; and then recovering the Church, rifled the very Sepulchres of the *Genoese*; who, provoked with this Loss, manned out forty Gallies, and ten *Saetia*'s, with which they engaged the *Venetians* off *Acre*; but they, being assisted by the *Pisans*, came off Conquerors, and the *Genoese* having lost five and twenty Gallies, with great Numbers of Men, ignominiously retreated to *Tyre*. The following Year a *Venetian* Ship, called the *Lion*, manned with two hundred Seamen, and a hundred Soldiers, accompanied with two small Gallies, was attacked near *Tenedos* by twenty Vessels belonging to *Genoa*, which the *Venetians* dealt with so well, that they forced them all to retire towards *Constantinople*: and this same Year it was that *Michael Palæologus* defeating *Baldwin* II, and the *French*, recovered the Empire of the East into the Hands of the *Greeks*.

The War rekindled between Venice and Genoa.

The Genoese suffer at Ptolemais,

A. D. 1258.

and lose several Gallies.

Michael Palæologus recovers the Greek Empire of the East.

After this the Senate committed a Number of Gallies to *James Dandolo*, for the Defence of *Dalmatia*, with Orders, if he found it for the Service of the Republick, to increase them, as he saw occasion, with others which were to attend the Islands. He accordingly taking from *Zara* three, and being joined by as many from *Candia*, four from *Negroponte*, and ten from *Ragusa*, commanded by *Gradenigo*, sailed toward *Sicily*, where, off *Marsala*, he sunk three *Genoese* Gallies commanded by *Lanfranc de Bourbon*. Thence proceeding to *Trapani*, he fell in with twenty eight Sail more, with which he came to a Battel, which was fought with great Obstinacy on both sides, the *Genoese* chusing rather to die than yield; but two thousand five hundred of them were saved by the Mercy of the Conqueror, after no less than twelve hundred had been slain, and as many drowned. Four Ships were sunk in the Engagement, and twenty four taken, which the *Venetians* sent to *Modon* for the Security of the Coast thereabouts; and soon after they fitted out another Fleet of sixty six Sail under the Command of *Roger Morosini*, to infest the *Genoese* in the Black Sea, where they managed a great Trade, and had several Colonies. *Pera*, one of the Suburbs of *Constantinople*, was then possessed by them, together with *Fochia-Vecchia* in *Natolia*, both which Places, then very rich, the *Venetians*

The Genoese worsted at Sea

A. D. 1266.

The Venetians take Pera and Fochia-Vecchia from the Genoese,

netians burnt and destroyed; to revenge which, the *Genoese* fitted out a considerable Fleet, and defeated the *Venetians* in two Engagements, first off *Corfu*, and afterwards in the Entrance of the *Dardanels*. After these Victories the *Genoese* scouring the Gulph of *Venice* without Controul, the Senate was in a Consternation, and began to be afraid of their City; insomuch that they set about repairing and enlarging their old Arsenal, causing it to be inclosed with a Wall, and, setting all Hands at work on building Ships and Gallies, filled the Magazines with Naval Stores.

but are defeated at Sea,

and in fear for their City.

About this time was made a noble Discovery of great Importance to Navigation, and the Service of Mankind, I mean that of the Mariner's Compass, which was now invented at *Amalfi*, a Sea-Port in the Kingdom of *Naples*; which (tho' the *Venetians* had no Hand therein) I mention here, because it happened in *Italy*, and their Affairs are the first which bring us so forward as the Time when it did. But the Person to whom the World is obliged for this fine Invention is involved in such Obscurity, that we know not under what Name to record his Memory, and pay him the Tribute of our Thanks; some calling him *Flavio* of *Amalfi*, others *John Goja*, or *Gioia*, and others *Flavio Gira*. Whatsoever his Name was, he was a Citizen of *Amalfi*, who first found out, whether by Chance or Study, is uncertain, that the Load-stone, like another little World, had its Poles and Axis; its Poles converted to the Poles, and its Axis parallel to the Axis of the World: and that (besides drawing Iron and Steel to it, and communicating to them the Power of doing the like, which the Ancients knew) it could also, by its Touch, cause those Metals to partake of that Quality, so that a Needle being touched therewith, and duly poised on a perpendicular Pin, would always lie in a Meridian Line, and point to the Poles of the World. And to this curious Contrivance it is that we owe the Navigation to *India*, and the Discovery of *America*, (both which happened in the succeeding Age) and all the other numerous Advantages which attend the Safety and Certainty of sailing.

The Mariner's Compass invented by a Citizen of Amalfi. A. D. 1301.

The *Venetians* had now a declared War not only with the *Genoese* but the *Turks*, so that a Fleet was set out under the Command of *Peter Zeno*, who sailing to *Syria*, sunk several of the Enemy's Ships, secured the Coasts from the Infidels, and advancing to *Smyrna*, not only took that Place, but put to Death most of the Inhabitants, and placed a strong Garrison in it. A Squadron at the same time was committed to *M. Rucinius* against the *Genoese*, with which repairing to *Caristo* in *Negroponte*, where lay the Enemy with fourteen Sail, he attacked them, and took ten, with the Admiral who commanded them, as also seventy *Genoese* Noblemen, and great Numbers of Prisoners of less Note, which Victory the Senate looked upon to be of so great Importance, that they ordered the Day on which it was obtained to be kept for an annual Festival. They were aided in this War by the *Greeks*, *Pisans*, and the King of *Arragon*, whose united Fleet was beaten by the *Genoese* in the Streights of *Constantinople*, but they soon revenged that Disgrace in a Battel with

They take Smyrna,

and ten Genoese Gallies. with their Admiral, &c.

The Genoese have the Advantage at Sea, but soon after are overcome.

CHAP. IV. *Ruin of the* Rom. *Empire.*

with them off *Cagliari* in *Sardinia*, where, after a bloody and obstinate Dispute, wherein they fought hand to hand as if they had been ashore, *Grimaldi*, the *Genoese* Admiral, betook himself to flight with two or three Ships, having lost no less than one and forty Sail, either sunk or taken. The Spirits of the *Genoese* were so broken with this Defeat, that they submitted themselves to *John* Duke of *Milan*, upon Condition he would defend them against the *Venetians* and *Arragonese*; so much dearer to them was their Revenge than their Liberty: But having soon after gained some Advantages over the *Venetians*, and being weary of their Subjection, they struck up a Peace with them, and threw off the Government of the Duke of *Milan*. *They submit to the Duke of Milan, but are soon weary of his Government*

When *Laurence Celsi* was Doge, *Candia* revolted, on occasion of a Tax imposed upon the Inhabitants, the Insurrection being begun by some of the *Venetians* themselves which were there settled; but the Island was soon reduced to Obedience by *Buchinus Verimius* of *Verona*. Then was the War renewed with the *Genoese* for the Island of *Tenedo*, which the *Venetians* had lately seized, and this Affair brought the Republick to the Brink of Destruction; for being beaten in an Engagement off *Pola*; *Humago*, *Grado*, *Caorle*, and *Chiozza* were seized by the Enemy, and they fought almost in the Streets of the City; which, if *Victor Pisani* (whom they brought out of Prison, and made General of the Gulph) had not strenuously defended, would certainly have fallen into the Enemy's Hands, being just ready to surrender. But resuming Courage, they defeated *Louis Fiesque*, the *Genoese* Admiral, off Cape *d'Anzo*, whom they took Prisoner; and securing the Avenues to their City by sinking Ships, laying Chains a-cross, and placing strong Garrisons in the adjacent Islands, they began to retrieve their Affairs. Forty Gallies were fitted out under the Command of *Andrew Contarini*, then Doge; and that the Men might be used to the Sea, and exercised before they went against the Enemy, the Fleet was rowed every Day from the *Jews* Quarter to St. *Nicholas* Church. It was of great Service to the Republick at this time that the Senate made a Law, that out of the Number of such Families as should contribute to supplying the Fleet or Army, either with Men, Money, or Provisions, thirty should be chosen into the Nobility, and that such of them on whom the Lot happened not to fall should have the yearly Income of five thousand Crowns; for above sixty Families subscribed great Sums of Money toward the publick Service. While these things were doing, *Charles Zeno* was expected home with the Fleet which was on foreign Service, in which Expedition he took a Fleet of *Genoese* Corn-Vessels in *Sicily*, and on the Coast of *Italy* sunk several Merchant Ships, seized three *Saetia*'s richly laden, and laid waste all the Country from *Porto-Spezza* to *Genoa*. Off *Tenedo* he took a *Neapolitan Saetia* trading on the Enemy's Account; in sight of *Rhodes* made himself Master of two *Genoese* Ships, and as many off *Cyprus*, where he received Orders to repair home to the Relief of his Country. While he was on his way, *Victor Pisani*, with another *A. D. 1361. Candia revolts from Venice, but is reduced. The Venetians beaten off of Pola by the Genoese. They beat the Genoese, and begin to retrieve their Affairs. Encourage their Subjects to supply the State with Men and Money. The Genoese suffer at Sea.*

other Fleet, fell down to the Port of *Brondolo*, who maintained his Station there as well as the *Genoese*; and *Zeno*, on his Arrival, being sent to support him, broke the Chain the Enemy had laid a-cross a Streight to defend themselves, and sunk two Ships of Burthen there, to hinder their coming out; all the rest of the Avenues having so shallow Water that a Ship could not pass. The rest of the Fleet engaged and defeated the *Genoese* near *Loredo*, in which Dispute fell *Peter Doria*, their Admiral, being slain by a Cannon Ball, with six hundred others; and in this War it was, according to some, that Ordnance were first used, though others alledge that *Edward* III, King of *England*, had great Guns at the Siege of *Calais* in 1347.

<small>*The Genoese beaten, and* Doria *their Admiral slain.*
A. D. 1379.
Great Ordnance supposed to be first used.</small>

The Communication of the City of *Venice* being now opened, which had suffered very much for want of Provisions, they were plentifully supplied from all Parts; whereas, on the other hand, the Enemy were close blocked up, and apprehending nothing less than Famine, used their utmost Endeavours to enlarge themselves; to which purpose they attempted to dig a Canal for twenty Gallies to pass through, but while they were employed in that Work, the *Venetians* attacked the Fort of *Brondolo*, and carried it, set fire to the Gallies, killed most of the Garrison, and forced them to retreat to *Chiozza*. *Victor Pisani* having possessed himself of the Town and Port, carried ten of the *Genoese* Ships which were appointed to protect *Molone*, to *Venice*, setting adrift the small Vessels, after he had first secured the People on board them, and *Chiozza* and *Grado* were soon after taken; but, in the Recovery of the first,. the *Venetians* met with the most difficulty, a new Fleet being sent to the Support of the *Genoese* there, which however they overcame, sinking and destroying fifty of them, and taking four thousand Prisoners. Such as escaped this Overthrow, fled towards the Coast of *Friuli*, where, in the Port of *Marano*, they refitted their shatter'd Vessels: Mean while *Le Bebe*, and the other Towns in and about the Shoals round *Venice*, were surrender'd; and some of the *Genoese* having thrown themselves into *Capo d'Istria*, that Place was besieged by *Pisani*, and in a short time reduced. As he was following the Enemy he died, and *Aloise Loredano* took upon him the Command of the Fleet till the Senate should appoint a Successor to *Pisani*, which Honour they soon conferred on *Charles Zeno*. He cruising on the Coast of *Dalmatia*, took and set fire to twelve Vessels belonging to the Pirates, and others on those Coasts, having first secured the Goods on board them; and soon after on the Coast of the *Morea* he seized a *Genoese* Merchant Ship very richly laden: However they bore up against all these Losses so vigorously, that the *Venetians* being apprehensive of another Siege, a Treaty of Peace was begun, and in a short time concluded; whereby it was agreed, that the Island of *Tenedo*, which had occasioned the War, should be sequester'd in the Hands of *Amedée* Duke of *Savoy*, the Mediator of the Peace, for the Space of two Years, and the Garrison was to be withdrawn from the Castle, (where they were allowed to keep one till that time) which was then to be demolished, and the *Venetians*

<small>*Genoese Gallies burnt at* Brondolo.

The Venetians *take* Chiozza, *and* Grado.

Destroy the Genoese *Fleet.*

Take Capo d'Istria.

Destroy the Pirates Vessels.

A. D. 1381.
A Peace concluded between Venice *and* Genoa.</small>

tians to be wholly excluded from the Island. Upon the Conclusion of the War, which lasted six Years, the Senate, pursuant to their Agreement, assumed into the Body of the Nobility thirty of those Families which had contributed to the Necessities of the Publick, and paid to the others the promised Pension beforementioned; however, the Restitution of *Tenedo* occasioned some Disturbance; for *John Mutatio*, who commanded there, refused to surrender it; but the publick Faith was not to be violated for the Obstinacy of one Citizen; wherefore *Fantinus George* was sent out at the Head of a Fleet, with Instructions to see the Castle demolished, and the Conditions of Peace put in Execution, which he accordingly performed, *The Castle of Tenedo demolished.*

The City was now flourishing in Peace, and only intent on cultivating Trade, when the Proceedings of the *Genoese* forced them to a new War, who had built about this time one and twenty Gallies, and sixteen *Saétia*'s. This Fleet was reported to be fitted out against the King of *Cyprus*, as in reality it was, being commanded by *Boncicaut*, a Marshal of *France*, (the Republick having submitted to the *French* King) and manned with Soldiers of that Nation and *Genoese* Seamen. *Charles Zeno*, who was then General of the Gulph, being apprehensive lest they should fall on some Place belonging to the *Venetians*, as soon as he had Advice they were passed the Height of the *Morea*, followed them; and *Boucicaut*, after he had settled Affairs in *Cyprus*, repaired to *Rhodes*, where *Zeno* arrived presently after him with the *Venetian* Fleet. *Boucicaut*, being indispos'd, sent to desire an Interview with *Zeno* on board his Ship, under Pretence of concerting Measures with him for acting against the Turk; but *Zeno* excusing himself, let him know that he had not received any Instructions in that Matter from the Republick, but when he did, would with Pleasure join in any such Service; acquainting him withal, that by the fundamental Laws of his Republick, it was Death for an Admiral to leave his Ship on any pretence whatsoever. *Boucicaut*, provoked with this Answer, resolved to be revenged, and with that view steered his Course to *Baruth* in *Syria*, where the *Venetians* had a great Trade for Spices; and being joined by three Ships of *Rhodes*, he landed within a League of the Town, and easily made himself Master of the Castle, the Garrison being in no Apprehension, because of the Peace which was between the two Nations; when entering the Town, he gave the Plunder of it to the Soldiers, the Inhabitants, on the Castle's being seized, having all fled to save their Lives. *Zeno*, afraid of the very Appearance of being the first Aggressor, sent one of his Officers to *Boucicaut* to complain of this Proceeding, and desire him to cause Restitution to be made of the Effects taken from the Merchants of his Nation; but he returned for answer, that the Plunder being already divided among his Soldiers, it was impossible to recover it, and endeavoured to excuse what he had done, under Pretence that the Inhabitants denied him Entrance into their Port. *The Venetians and Genoese quarrel again. Baruth taken and plundered by the Genoese.*

Ff 2 *Zeno,*

Zeno, not being able to obtain any Satisfaction, returned towards the *Archipelago*, to cover the Islands belonging to the *Venetians*, and especially *Candia*, whither he was soon followed by the Enemy, who suddenly surprized and entered the Port of *Sapienza*. *Zeno*, who was at *Modon* with eleven Gallies, and two Galeasses, thought himself strong enough to fight the *Genoese* Fleet, and gave them Defiance; so that both of them sailed out by Break of Day, one from *Modon*, the other from *Sapienza*, and met half way between those Places. *Zeno* having ranged his Gallies in Order, bore down on the Enemy with all the Sail he could make, while *Boucicaut*, who was also prepared for the Battel, and well knew that the Victory depended chiefly on the Behaviour of the General, detached three of his Gallies to attack the *Venetian* Admiral, which was performed with great Dexterity and Resolution; for two of these Gallies separating, received *Zeno*'s between them, and the third charged her a-head. After the *Genoese* and *French* had poured great Numbers of Darts and Arrows on the *Venetians*, they grappled *Zeno*'s Gally, and boarded her in three several Places, making diligent Search for the Admiral, but not knowing his Person, miss'd of him, who being thus hard pressed, delivered himself from the Danger by a new and extraordinary Stratagem. He caused his whole Ship's Company, with a great deal of heavy Lumber, to be placed on the Starboard side of his Gally, in order to bring the upper Part thereof down to the Water, by which means he not only prevented any more from boarding on the Larboard Side, but struck such a Terrour amongst those that had already entered, who thought he was going to sink the Ship, that many of them leaped into the Sea, and the rest threw themselves over into their own Vessels: The Confusion this caused among the Enemy afforded Time for other Gallies to come to the Relief of their Admiral, which they performed with such Success, that the three *Genoese* Ships beforementioned were all taken, and *Zeno* was no sooner disengaged, than he bore down to *Boucicaut*, who would fain have retreated, but was so closely followed that he was forced to save himself in his Boat. All the rest of the Gallies betaking themselves to Flight, *Zeno* towed the three he had taken in to *Modon*, whither he also conducted his Prisoners, among whom were *Chateau-Morant*, the *Genoese* Vice-Admiral, and *Paul Sanudo*, one of their Captains: However their Gallies that escaped revenged this Disgrace upon several *Venetian* Merchant Ships they met with in their way home, which they plundered: But notwithstanding these Proceedings on both sides, the matter did not come to a declared War between them, for their Losses in the whole being pretty near equal, the Name of the Peace yet continued.

After this the Republick purchased *Zara*, with its Dependences, of *Ladislaus* King of *Hungary*: And if *Philip*, Duke of *Milan*, had not molested them, would have enjoyed another Interval of Repose. *Piccinini*, the Enemy's General, having taken, by Treachery, the Town of *Bresello* on the *Po*, attempted likewise to seize the Castle; and the *Milanese* Fleet on that River being commanded by

CHAP. IV. *Ruin of the* Rom. *Empire.* 221

by *Eustachius* of *Tesino*, the *Venetians* detached *Francis Bembo* a- *Overcome the* gainst him. The Fleets on both sides consisted of flat bottom'd Vef- *Fleet of Mi-* fels; and *Bembo* placed eight of these in a Line in Front, which to *lan.* render firm and indissoluble, he secured together with Cables. In this Order he advanced toward *Eustachius*, whom he drove before him up to *Cremona*, where the Enemy quitting their Vessels, they all fell A. D. 1431. into *Bembo*'s Hands; but here he was stopt from proceeding farther by a new Contrivance of the Enemy, who had caused to be built on the River several floating Castles, which however he bravely attacked, and set on fire. Landing his Troops he came to a Battel on shore, but was defeated, and thereupon retiring to his Ships, fell down the *Are beaten be-* River: And soon after *Nicholas Trevisano*, another Admiral of the *fore Cremo-* *Venetians*, was beaten before *Cremona*. The Senate highly resenting the Behaviour of the *Genoese*, who had manned the Enemy's Fleet with their Seamen, (having now put themselves under the Protection of the Duke of *Milan*) fitted out eighteen Gallies against them, under the Command of *Peter Loredano*, who with unexpected Celerity, sailing round to *Leghorn*, was there joined by five Gallies of the *Florentines*, together with *Adorni* and *Fiesque*, two *Genoese* Noblemen then in Exile, Enemies to the *Milanese* Faction, with several others of that Party; at the Appearance of whom off *Genoa*, it was thought their Friends in the City would expel the opposite Party, and receive them to recover their Liberties; but the *Milanese* proving the strongest, five and twenty Gallies were sent out under the Command of *Francis Spinola*. The *Venetian* Fleet was by this time arrived in the Gulph of *Rapallo*, within five Leagues of the City, whither the *Genoese* advanced toward them with great Resolution, being flushed with the Remembrance of their late Victory on the *Po*. Off *Cape di Monte* (the Head-land that makes the Gulph of *Rapallo*) they came to an Engagement, but *Loredano They over-* finding the Enemy had the Wind of him, retreated, as if afraid, in- *come the Ge-* to the Gulph, whither the *Genoese* following him, he got to Wind- *Gulph of Ra-* ward, and bore down upon them. *Spinola* received him with great *pallo.* Gallantry, but the *Venetians* fought with such Resolution, that they soon took him Prisoner with his own Gally and eight others, the rest, in the utmost Disorder, retreating into *Porto Fino*, or making the best of their Way to *Genoa*, while the victorious Fleet repaired to *Reco*, which voluntarily surrendering to *Fiesque*, they returned to *Leghorn*; and in this Battel were slain on both sides eight hundred Persons, and four thousand wounded. At the Request of Pope *Eugene* IV, *Loredano* sailed to *Civita Vecchia*, in order to reduce the Castle of that Place, which was held out against him, and having in *And reduces* a short time forced it to surrender, he repaired to *Corfu*, expecting *for the Pope* to meet with a Reinforcement, with which he intended to proceed *Civita Vec-* against *Peter Spinola*, whom the *Genoese* had sent out with a new *chia.* Fleet; but they were prevented from coming to an Engagement, because the *Genoese* had thrown off the Government of the Duke of *Milan*, and a Peace thereupon ensued between the two Republicks. *A Peace be-*
At the same time the Quarrel being renewed with that Prince, *and Genoa.* and the Duke of *Mantua*, his Ally, the Seat of Naval War was now

to

The Naval War remov'd to the Lake di Garda. to be removed from the Sea to the Lake *di Garda*, in order to prevent the Enemies poffeffing themfelves of *Brefcia*. The *Venetian* Senate were debating by what means they might provide a Fleet in that Lake, there being neither Woods thereabouts for Timber, nor any Communication of Rivers (except the *Menzo*, entirely poffeffed by the Enemy) to carry Ships from *Venice*; When one *Sorbilus*, who was well acquainted with the Country, affured them, if they would furnifh him with what was neceffary, he would engage to convey Gallies thither from the City. They approving his Scheme, fupplied him with what he demanded, and he fetting about the Work, caufed two large Gallies, three fmall ones, and twenty five Boats to be rowed up the *Adige* to *Verona*, from whence they were towed by feveral Yoke of Oxen to *Mori* near *Roveredo*, where being placed on Rowlers, by the help of great Multitudes of Peafants, who levelled the Country, and cut through Rocks to make way for them, they were, in three Months time, conveyed to *Torbole*, at the Head of the Lake, and being launched into it, lay at the Mouth of the *Sarca*, which difembogues it felf near that Town. There, by a triple Row of Piles, in form of a Semicircle, and a Fort which the *Venetians* built afhore, they were defended from the Incurfions of the Enemy, who had one Gally and feveral fmall Veffels upon the Lake, which were brought up the *Menzo*, by which it communicates with the *Po*. Thefe the *Venetians*, confiding in their own Strength, defpifed, but coming to an Engagement, *Zeno* their Admiral, was taken Prifoner, and if a timely Retreat had not been made by the reft into *Torbole*, all the Fleet muft have fallen into the Enemies Hands. The Lofs the *Venetians* fuftained was fo great, that the Remainder of the Fleet was not able to do any thing without a new Supply, which the Senate refolved to fend, but in another manner than the former. Materials for eight Gallies, as many Galleons, and four Boats, were laden in fix hundred Waggons, and fent to *Torbole*, where being foon put together, they were launched into the Lake; and *Stephen Contarini* was appointed to command them. In the middle of the Lake, he engag'd the Enemy's Fleet, and obtained an entire Victory, which was followed by the Surrender of *Garda* and *Riva*, two confiderable Towns on the Banks, and the raifing of the Siege of *Brefcia*, whereupon a Peace enfuing with the Dukes of *Milan* and *Mantua*, the Republick turned her Arms againft the Pirates who now very much infefted the Seas.

An undertaking to carry Gallies to the Lake.

The Venetians are beaten on the Lake.

But reinforce their Squadron,

and get an entire Victory.

A Peace concluded, and the Venetians go againft the Pirates.

On this Service three Ships of War and one Gally were fitted out to cruife in the Mediterranean, and four to fcour the Gulph, the latter under the Command of *Anthony Dieda* who attacked *Antivari* in *Albania*, and being favoured by a Party in the Town, foon reduced it to the Obedience of the Republick. After this he was by a violent Storm, driven to *Viefte* in *Capitanate*, a Province of *Naples*, the chief Rendezvous of the Pirates, who feized his Ships and his Perfon: But having obtained his Liberty, and the Reftitution of his Naval Force, by Direction of *Alphonfus*, King of *Naples* and *Sicily*, he went out again in queft of the Pirates, and having taken feveral of their Ships richly laden, returned triumphantly to *Venice*.

The Venetian Admiral feiz'd by the Pirates, but being releafed overcomes.

At

CHAP. IV. *Ruin of the* Rom. *Empire.* 223

At that time *Aloise Loredano* was sent out against the *Turk* with ten Gallies, the Charge of six whereof was defrayed by Pope *Eugene* IV. *Amurath* II. was then Emperor of that Nation, of whose Fleet *Loredano* took several Ships, and having secured the Colonies of the Republick from their Depredations, returned to *Venice*. Soon after he was dispatched with a Fleet of thirty five Gallies, and ten Ships of Burthen, against King *Alphonsus*, who had expelled the *Venetians* out of his Dominions, where they had for some time been possessed of several Towns on the Coast of *Naples* in the *Adriatick*. With this Force proceeding to *Messina*, he there burnt a Vessel of the King's on the Stocks, besides several Ships in the Port, from whence he advanced to *Syracuse*, and seized two Merchant Ships of great Burthen. To prevent any farther Mischief, the *Genoese*, to whom one of those belonged, and others who fled from the *Venetians* at Sea, sunk two Merchant Ships in the Port, and laid a Boom across it of an immense Thickness: And from the Walls of the Town to the Ships in the Port they erected Scaffolds, that so if the Enemy should break in, they might, as Occasion should serve, either defend the Ships, or retreat into the Town. *Loredano*, at his first Approach, made an Attack upon the Boom, but it was so well defended by the *Genoese* and *Syracusans*, that after a long and obstinate Dispute he was obliged to retreat. Having failed in Force, he resolved next to have recourse to Artifice; and filling a Ship with Gunpowder and Faggots, put thirty stout Men on board, and sent her before a brisk Gale of Wind to the Mouth of the Harbour, where she came against the Boom with such Violence that it presently gave way, and opened her a free Passage to the Ships in the Port, the Enemy all the while looking on with Surprize and Amazement. When she was approached near enough to the Enemies Ships for the Execution of the Design, the Persons on board set fire to her, and leaping into the Boat, rowed off to the Fleet, and the Fire presently bursting out seized the next adjacent Ships, which communicated it to the rest, so that they were all presently in Flames, and great Numbers of the Enemy were burnt, many drowned, a few only being saved by swimming; after which *Loredano*, dividing his Fleet, sent Part of it to *Venice*, and with the rest cruised about the *Adriatick*.

Alphonsus growing weary of the War, concluded a Peace with the Republick; which would have been very glad to have enjoy'd a long Interval of Repose; but three Years were scarce expired, e'er a great Battel was fought with the *Turks* with considerable Loss on the Christians side, the *Venetian* Fleet little availing against so potent an Enemy; not but that some time before the Republick had possessed her self of several Towns, as *Misistra*, *Aulis*, *Larsus*, *Lembro*, *Setines*, (the ancient *Athens*) *Fochia Nova*, and other Places of less Note. While the *Turks* were engaged in a War with the *Persians*, *Mocenigo*, Admiral of the *Venetian* Fleet, took *Smyrna*, and *Passagio*, a Town in *Natolia* opposite to the Island *Scio*, with *Satalia*, *Curco*, and *Selechia* in *Carmania*.

This *Mocenigo* was the first *Venetian* who had the Affairs of *Cyprus* committed to him, and it was thus occasioned. *James de Lusignan*, the last King of the Island, married *Katherine* the Daughter
of

of *Marc Cornaro*, a noble *Venetian*, which Prince dying, he left his Confort great with Child, which Child by his laſt Will he declared ſhould ſucceed him in the Throne under the Guardianſhip of the Republick. The Infant dying within a Year after his Father, *Charlotte*, the Siſter of *James*, laid claim to the Crown, and created great Diſturbances in the Iſland, which were at length entirely quelled by the Prudence and good Conduct of *Mocenigo*, who expelled the factious Party, and ſettled the Kingdom in Peace. *James Marcelli* being then appointed to ſucceed him in the Adminiſtration of this new Province, *Mocenigo* was ordered by the Senate to look to the Defence of *Scutari*, and guard the Coaſt of *Albania*, againſt the Attempts of the Turks; purſuant whereto he repaired thither, and placed ſtrong Garriſons in *Durazzo*, *Budoa*, *Antivari*, and *Dulcigno*, appointing a Gally to attend the Service of each.

Quarrels about Cyprus.

About this time deceaſed in *Nixia John Criſpus*, Lord of that Iſland, and of *Phermene*, *Scyro*, and *Melo*, three other of the ancient *Cyclades*, the Inhabitants of which Iſlands having been very weary of his Government, and *Nicolas Capello* happening accidentally to be at that time in the Port of *Nixia*, with ſix *Venetian* Ships, which he commanded againſt the Pirates, they made their Application to him to receive their Submiſſion to the Republick, which he readily accepted, and left with them a Citizen of *Venice* to adminiſter their Government.

A Peace between the Turks and Venetians.

The Turks now preſſing the *Venetians* very hard, they were obliged to come to a Peace, whereby they gave up *Scutari*, the Caſtle of *Maina*, near Cape *Matapan*, and the Iſland of *Stalimine*, and agreed to pay eight thouſand Ducats a Year for Freedom of Trade in their Seas: However there were after this ſeveral ſlight Skirmiſhes between them, the Iſlanders under the *Venetian* Government creating ſome Diſturbances, as did alſo the Pirates who were ſecretly countenanced by the Turks. *Aloiſe Giorgi* came to an Engagement with the Pirate *Arige* off Cape *Matapan*, where, after an obſtinate Diſpute, they both ſeparated with equal Loſs. On the Coaſt of *Africa Bernard Cicogna*, the *Venetian* Admiral, fought *Peruca*, another Pirate, defeated and took him Priſoner: And off *Cotrone Andrew Loredano* killed *Peter de Biſcay*, with ſeveral of his Aſſociates.

The Venetians overcome the Pirates.

And now the War breaking out again with the *Turks*, a Fleet was ſent againſt them under the Command of *Anthony Grimani*, who obſerving with how much Difficulty the People contributed toward the late War they had in *Italy* by Land with the *French* and *Florentines*, lent the Republick eighty Pounds of Gold to pay the Wages of the Seamen, engaging to raiſe ſo many in *Corfu* and other Places as would man the Fleet. Off *Modon* he came to a Battel with the Turks, but was defeated, and forced to retreat to *Prodeno*, a neighbouring Iſland; where hearing the *French* Fleet was at *Zante*, he ſailed thither to join them, after which he had ſeveral ſlight Skirmiſhes with the Enemy, but meeting with little or no Succeſs, he again ſeparated from the *French*. The Troops on board the Fleet having entertained a Notion, that if he had attacked the Enemy

A War rekindled between the Turks and Venetians.

The Venetians beaten by the Turks.

CHAP. V. *Ruin of the* Rom. *Empire.* 225

Enemy with his whole Force, he might have entirely destroyed them, drew up and sent their Opinion to *Venice*, where a Resolution was taken to remove *Grimani* from his Command, which was accordingly done: And because *Thomas Zeni*, whom they pitched upon to succeed him, was indebted to the Exchequer, and that, by an ancient Law, none who were so, could enjoy any Place of Trust, they made an Act that this Law should not take place with respect to him, whom they put at the head of the Fleet. But he met with no better Success than his Predecessor, the Turks taking *Navarino*, *Modon*, and *Coron*, with the Islands of *Engia* and *Metelino*. However, after the Departure of the Turkish Fleet, *Engia* was presently recovered by *Benedict Pesaro*, who having also ravaged *Metelino* and *Tenedo*, fell on the Rear of the Turkish Fleet, then entering the Gulph of *Negroponte*, and took several Ships, the Companies whereof he nailed to Crosses along the Sea-shore. After this he reduced the Island *Samandrachi*, plundered *Carista*, recovered *Cephalonia*, and in the Gulph of *Larta* seized twelve of the Enemy's Ships loaden with Stores of War, carrying them all to *Corfu*.

Are again beaten, and several Places taken; but soon after have Success.

CHAP. V.

Of the Naval Wars of the Venetians, *from the Conclusion of the League of* Cambray, *to the present Times.*

ABOUT this time it was that almost all *Europe* united, at the Instigation of Pope *Julius* II, to procure the Destruction of the Republick of *Venice*, the Design whereof was concluded at *Cambray*, by a Treaty between that Pontiff, the Emperor *Maximilian* I, the *French* King *Louis* XII, *Ferdinand* King of *Spain*, and other Princes of less Consideration: Which Treaty was carried on with such Secrecy, that the Republick never had the least notice of it till they were attacked. The Blow was so sudden, that they immediately lost all they had on the *Terra Firma*, and were confined to their City, against which the Emperor levelled his great Guns from the Continent, and were it not for his want of Shipping, had crossed over thither, and possessed himself of that likewise. Thus was the *Venetian* Lion forced to couch to the *German* Eagle, and that State, which had remained unconquered for above a thousand Years, to become an humble Suppliant to the Emperor. They quitted all their Pretensions on the Continent, and agreed to pay an annual Tribute; but at length their Artifices prevailed so far as to break the Confederacy, and then having to deal with those Princes singly, they recovered all which had been taken from them, and pretty well secured themselves against any such Disaster for the future.

A. D. 1508.
The Princes of Europe unite against Venice.

They are confined to their City, and submit to the Emperor.

The Alliance broken, and the Venetians recover themselves.

G g It

It was the same Pope *Julius* II. who, being unwilling to allow the Republick any thing, demanded of them, by his Nuncio, by what Right, or whose Donation, they pretended to the Dominion of the *Adriatick*; to which they answered, that they much wondered his Holiness should act in a manner so disagreeable to his usual Justice, by asking them for those very Writings which he had at *Rome* among his own Records; for that if he would please to look for the Donation of *Constantine*, he would find on the back of that what he desired: By which facetious Answer they wisely gave the Pope to know, that as he did not enjoy so many Cities and Provinces on shore, so they did not hold their Dominion of the Sea, by virtue of any Grant or Donation from any Emperor, either *Greek* or *Roman*, nor ground it on the beforemention'd Compliment to them of Pope *Alexander* III; but on the long Exercise of that Dominion, confirmed by the continued Knowledge and Sufferance (that is the Consent and Authority in this Case) of the Parties concerned to oppose it; and that they would defend by Arms a Right so lawfully acquired, and secured by so long Prescription, against all who should pretend to attack it.

A subtle Answer made by the Venetians to the Pope.

The next great War the Republick was engaged in was with *Selim* II, Emperor of the Turks, for the Island of *Cyprus*, who pretended it was become a Shelter for Pirates, which disturbed the Commerce of the Mediterranean, and that he being Master of the Countries which lay about it, (to one of which, viz. *Ægypt*, he said, it did of Right belong) it was incumbent on him to secure the Navigation to those Parts, and therefore demanded they would yield it up to him. The Senate's Answer was, that they were so far from entertaining or encouraging Pirates, that they kept constantly a Number of Gallies at *Cyprus* to cruise against them; and that if he made these Pretences to break with them, they were resolved to defend themselves; whereupon the Turks repaired with a numerous Fleet to the Island, and there landing an Army of a hundred thousand Men, laid Siege to *Nicosia*, the capital City, which in a short time was taken by Storm, and *Mustapha*, who commanded on this Expedition, after he was Master of the Town, caused above twenty thousand Persons to be put to the Sword, and as many were made Slaves, cutting off the Head of *Dandolo*, the Governour, which he sent as a Present to the Officer who commanded in *Famagusta*; the Place he was going next to besiege. Then having selected the richest of the Spoils, consisting of Plate, and other valuable Effects, with several fine Women and beautiful Children of Quality, of both Sexes, gathered from all Parts of the Island, he put them on board three of the largest Ships of the Fleet, and committed them to the Charge of four hundred Janizaries, to be conveyed as a Present to the Grand Signior, either in token of his Success, or to conciliate to himself the doubtful Favour of his Prince. The Slaves were all put together in one Ship, where a young Lady, reflecting on the Calamity which had already happened to her Country and her Friends, and what farther she was to expect when she should be in the Power of *Selim*,

War betwixt Selim II and the Venetians about Cyprus.

The Turks take Nicosia.

A hardy Deed of a Cyprian Lady.

CHAP. V. *Ruin of the* Rom. *Empire.*

Selim, began to revolve some uncommon Thoughts in her Mind. They had now weighed Anchor, and were just got under Sail, when there being occasion to fetch up Powder to charge the Guns, this Woman found means to get down with a Light to the Powder-Room, where having an Opportunity of executing her dreadful Purpose, she looks alternately towards her Country and Heaven, and, grown bold by having resolved to die, desperately applies the Fire to the Powder, so that in a Moment all were in Flames, and with a dreadful Blast the Ship was thrown in pieces into the Air: Nor did the Destruction thus end; for the burning Fragments falling into the two other Ships, set them also on fire, and in few Minutes Space, all the Spoil which had been so carefully collected through the whole Island, with every Soul on board the Ships, except four Seamen, who by great Accident escaped, and swam to Land, where consumed, within Sight of the Shore, *Mustapha* himself looking on at the dismal Spectacle.

Mustapha advancing to *Famagusta*, invested that Place, where *Bragadini*, a brave and experienced Officer, was Governor, who with a handful of Men made a most gallant Defence against the Enemy's numerous Army, but at length was obliged to surrender, which he did upon honourable Terms, the Garrison being not only permitted to march out with flying Colours, Arms and Baggage, but were to be supplied with Vessels to transport them to *Candia*, and a Squadron of Gallies for their Convoy: Notwithstanding which, the perfidious *Barbarian* treacherously broke the Treaty, seized the principal Officers, and put them to Death in cold Blood, and made Slaves of all the rest of the Garrison. *Bragadini* himself was saved from this Slaughter, to be yet more inhumanly treated for having so bravely done his Duty; for they first cut off his Nose and Ears, and then threw him, with Irons on his Legs, into a Dungeon, from whence the Executioners drew him out once a Day, to carry Earth in a Basket for repairing the Fortifications, making him bow down with his Burthen, and kiss the Ground every time he past before *Mustapha*, who came to oversee the Work. He was afterwards put on board the Fleet, where, among other Indignities, they fixed him in a Chair, and hoisted him up to the Yard-Arm of a Ship, that so the Deformity of his mangled Visage might be more conspicuous, and be seen by the Christians which were yet in the Port. Then bringing him ashore, they carried him to the Market-Place, where after he had been tied up by the Heels and flay'd alive, his Skin was stuffed with Straw, and hung up at the Yard-Arm of *Mustapha's* Gally, in which manner it was carried about in Triumph on the Coasts of *Syria* and *Ægypt*. It was afterwards put into the Arsenal of *Constantinople*, from whence it was redeemed by the Posterity of the deceased Hero at a great Price, and is to this Day kept as the most glorious Trophy of their Family.

The Cruelty of the Turks upon taking Famagusta.

They cruelly massacre Bragadini.

At the Beginning of the War, the *Venetians* had set on foot a Treaty of Alliance with Pope *Pius* V, and *Philip* II, King of *Spain*, which was at length concluded, and both those Princes aided them with

An Alliance between the Pope, King of Spain, and Venice.

G g 2

with Naval Forces. Those of the first were commanded by *Marc Anthony Colonna*, and of the latter by Don *John* of *Austria*, natural Son to the Emperor *Charles* V, the Navy of the Republick being conducted by *Sebastian Venier*. At length, after tedious Delays on the part of the *Spaniards*, the confederate Fleet rendezvous'd at *Messina*, where a Council of War was called to consider of the Operations of the Campaign; and, after several Debates, it was resolved, through the earnest Entreaties of *Colonna* and *Venier*, to make the best of their way towards the *Morea*. Every thing being in readiness for sailing, the Generals, Officers, and Soldiers repaired on board, and the Wind presenting fair, they weighed Anchor amidst the Prayers and Blessings of the neighbouring People of *Sicily* and *Italy*, who came down to the Coasts, in infinite Multitudes, to see the most numerous Navy the Christians ever fitted out.

A. D. 1571.
The confederate Fleet come to Messina.

Their strength, and how disposed.

It consisted of twelve Gallies of the Pope's, eighty one Gallies, and twenty Ships of Burthen of the King of *Spain's*, and a hundred and eight Gallies, six large Galeasses, and two Ships of Burthen of the *Venetians*, the whole under the Command of Don *John* of *Austria*, who divided his Fleet into four Squadrons, three of which made up the main Body and two Wings, and the fourth what was judged necessary for a Reserve. The Right consisted of fifty three Gallies, commanded by *John Andrew Doria*, who hoisted a green Flag on the Main-top-mast Head: The Left, of the like Number, was put under the Command of *Augustine Barbarigo*, who carried a yellow Flag, fixed on the Starboard side of his Main-top; and Don *John* himself, displaying a blue Flag, conducted the main Body, consisting of sixty one Gallies; the Reserve being led by *Alvarez Basano*, Marquis of *Santa Cruz*, who carried a white Flag in the Poop, which Squadron consisted of thirty eight Gallies, and from it eight were detached, under the Command of *John de Cardona*, to sail about six Leagues ahead of the Fleet, with Orders to send Advice by Boats, from time to time, of what he could discover, and as soon as he descry'd the Enemy, to retreat to the Fleet, and divide his Ships between the two Wings. The six great Galeasses were placed about half a Mile ahead of the Line, two before each Division, and distant from one another about a Mile, but they being unwieldy and heavy Sailers, the General gave Orders that, as there might be occasion, they should be towed by others.

The Disposition of the confederate Fleet.

He took his Post in the Centre of the main Body, having *Marc Anthony Colonna*, admiral of the Pope's Gallies, on his Right, and *Sebastian Venier*, the *Venetian* Admiral, on his Left. Next to *Colonna* was the Admiral Gally of *Genoa*, commanded by *Hector Spinola*, on board of which was the Prince of *Parma*; and next to *Venier* was the chief Gally of *Savoy*, commanded by *Leynius*, having on board her the Prince of *Urbin*; and astern of Don *John*, *Colonna*, and *Venier*, were placed the Patronne Gally of *Spain*, with that of the great Commander of *Castile*. In the right Point of this main Body was the principal Gally of *Malta*, commanded by

the

CHAP. V.   *Ruin of the* Rom. *Empire.*   229

the Prior of *Messina*, and in the Left another of the largest size, on board of which was *Paul Jordano*. As for the two Wings, *John de Cardona* was to take Post in the left Point of the Right, and on the other Point *Andrew Doria*, who commanded that Division. In the Left Wing *Marc Anthony Quirini* was stationed in the Right Point, together with *Anthony Canali*; and *Augustine Barbarigo*, who commanded that Wing, in the Left Point. The Gallies of each Nation were separated, and intermixed amongst others, that so in the Day of Battel they might not have Opportunity of taking particular Resolutions, and this the *Venetians* prevailed to have done, because they were jealous, as they had good reason to be, of the *Spaniards*, but insinuated that their Intentions were no other, than that all might equally share the Honour and Danger, and mutually animate each other to behave well.

In this Order the Fleet crossed the *Ionian* Sea, and passing the Islands *Pachsu*, and *Antipachsu*, came off the Gulph of *Larta*; but not being able to reach *Cephalonia*, they slacken'd sail, and making but little way all Night, arrived the next Day at that Island, where they received Letters from *Paul Contareni*, Governor of *Zante*, that the Enemy's Fleet lay but in an ill Condition in the Gulph of *Lepanto*, and that *Oluz-Aly*, with forty Ships, being separated from the rest, was sailed towards *Modon*: And soon after they heard from the Governor of *Candia*, that *Famagusta* had surrendered; upon which Intelligences it was unanimously agreed to advance and attack the Enemy. *The confederate Fleet comes to Cephalonia.*

The *Turks* in the mean time did not remain idle, for *Aly Pasha*, being arrived at *Lepanto* with the Fleet, detached *Mehemet Bey* with sixty Gallies up to *Aspropiti*, to receive on board ten thousand Janizaries, and the like Number of Volunteers, with a large Supply of Provisions, that so they might be in a Readiness for all Events. While this was doing *Caracozza*, one of his Officers who had been sent out for Intelligence, brought Advice that the Christian Fleet was arrived at *Cephalonia*, and that having counted the Gallies, they were not above a hundred and twenty; whereupon *Aly* determined to give them Battel; but for his Justification, in case of need, he summoned the principal Officers to a Council of War, wherein, tho' some of the most able and experienced declared themselves against fighting, it was nevertheless resolved, after several Debates, to engage, and accordingly they made sail, with intent to surprize the Christian Fleet at *Cephalonia*, hoping to find the Officers and People ashore. The Fleet of the Infidels consisted of two hundred and seventy five Sail, disposed in a main Body, two Wings, and a Body of Reserve. In the Right Wing, commanded by *Mehemet Siroch*, Governor of *Alexandria*, were fifty six Gallies, in the Right Point of which was *Mehemet Bey*, Sangiac of *Negroponte*, and in the Left the said *Mehemet Siroch*. In the Centre of the main Body, consisting of ninety six Gallies, was *Aly Pasha*, the Admiral and Commander in Chief, supported on each Hand by *Pertaub Pasha*, and the Treasurer of the Fleet; and in the Right and Left Points of *The Strength of the Turkish Fleet.* *They resolve to fight the Christians.* *The Disposition of their Fleet.*

that

that Division were *Dardaganus*, Governor of the Arsenal of *Constantinople*, and *Haſſan Bey*, Governor of *Rhodes*. The Left Wing was compoſed of ninety three Sail, led by *Oluz-Aly*, *Dey* of *Algier*, who had his Poſt in the Right Point of that Diviſion, in the Left of which was *Caraus Hozias*, a famous Pirate; and the Body of Reſerve was commanded by *Amurath Dragut Rays*, conſiſting of thirty Gallies.

In this order the *Turks* ſailing from *Lepanto* the ſeventh of *October*, arrived that Evening off *Galanga*, and about the ſame time the confederate Fleet weighed Anchor from *Cephalonia*, in order to go in queſt of the Enemy, it being intended, if they happened not ſuddenly to fall in with them, to repair to the Entrance of the Gulph of *Lepanto*, attack the Caſtles there, and lay waſte the Country in order to provoke them to a Battel. Both Fleets being thus in Motion, with the ſame Deſign of engaging each other, they arrived off *Peſchera*, having only one of the *Curzolaires* Iſlands between them, *The Turks diſcover the Chriſtian Fleet.* when at Break of Day the *Turks* deſcryed the Confederates coming about a Point of the Iſland, and were, when the whole appeared in view, greatly ſurprized at the Number and Strength of the Gallies, ſo contrary to the Intelligence they had received.

When they were advanced within a Mile of each other, *Aly* fired a Gun, as a Signal for engaging, which was anſwered in like manner from the Gally of Don *John*, and then the *Turks*, with great Shouts, advanced towards the ſix Galeaſſes diſpoſed in a Line ahead *The Battel of Lepanto begins.* of the confederate Fleet; but were received by ſo terrible a Fire from thoſe floating Caſtles, that, at the firſt Diſcharge, ſeveral of the *Turkiſh* Gallies quitted the Line; nevertheleſs they kept on their way, but in paſſing between the Galeaſſes, were ſo cruelly battered from their Broad-ſides, that not only many Maſts came by the Board, but they were alſo much diſabled in their Yards and Rigging. Some Ships were ſhot through and through, others had their Rudders ſtruck off, ſeveral were ſeen in Flames, and ſome deſerted by their Companies, who in Deſpair leap'd into the Sea, which was covered with floating Oars, Maſts, Yards, Casks, and Men. Such great Execution did theſe Galeaſſes do among the Enemy, which was a Contrivance as ſucceſsful as it was new.

In the midſt of this Diſorder, *Siroch*, who commanded the Enemy's Right Wing, ſeparating from the reſt of the Fleet, bore down under the Shore towards the Chriſtians Left, but *Auguſtine Barbarigo*, who commanded there, perceiving his Motion, advanced in good Order to meet him, and diſpoſed that Diviſion ſo advantageouſly near a Headland called *Mahangulo*, that the Infidels were pent up, and could not proceed in the manner they deſigned, ſo that in this Poſture they began a terrible Fire, which did great Execution on both ſides. *Oluz-Aly* in the Left of the Enemy, and *Doria* in the Confederates Right Wing, approached each other ſeveral times, in order to engage, but both, being excellent Seamen, ſtill expected an Opportunity of ſome particular Advantage. *Oluz-Aly*, prepared for all Events, waited to ſee how the Battel went in the other Diviſions;

visions; but *Doria* being greatly inferior to the Enemy, who had ninety Sail, and he but fifty, endeavoured only to keep *Aly* in suspense, that so he might not interpose in assisting the other Squadrons.

In the main Body Don *John*, *Colonna*, and *Venier*, met the *Turks* in excellent Order, and, as they advanced, discharged their Broadsides twice or thrice, and some five times, which did great Execution, and terribly dismayed them, who having very few skilful Gunners, and their Gallies being high-built, many of their Shot flew over those of the Christians: But notwithstanding all these Disadvantages, they obstinately advanced, and on both sides were discharged such Showers of Arrows and Bullets as seemed to darken the Sky. Here were four Gallies engaged with three, there six with four, and in some Places one sustained the Attacks of several, the Men boarding each other's Vessels, and with Swords, Cutlasses, Pistols, and Weapons of all sorts committing a dreadful Slaughter, so that in a short time the Sea was dyed with the Blood of the Slain.

In the mean time *Siroch* and *Barbarigo* having been smartly engaged, the former found the other's Division impenetrable, and that he could not advance a Ship's length farther, so that many of his Gallies being much shattered, their Masts brought by the Board, and Rigging shot to pieces, he only endeavoured to keep his Men to their Duty, and act upon the Defensive; but notwithstanding all his Precautions, several Commanders of his Gallies found the Work so very hot, that they quitted the Line, and ran them ashore, where their Companies leaped over-board in order to swim to Land, except such as were wounded, whom they left to the Mercy of the Assailers. In boarding the Enemy's Gallies, the Christians gave no Quarter, so that, after *Siroch* was slain, as he was bravely fighting and encouraging his Men, the rest of the Infidels followed the Example of the others, and swam ashore, save what fell by the Hands of the Slaves, who, when they found their Fellow-Christians like to prevail, broke their Chains, seized the Arms of those which had been killed, or whatever came next to Hand, and being more animated by Thoughts of revenging their cruel Usage, than hopes of Liberty, massacred their Patrons and Officers, insomuch that several *Turkish* Gallies were lost by the Fury and Rage of these desperate People *Quirini* and *Canali*, who were in the other Point of this Left Wing, could not advance to that opposite to them, until most of the *Turks* had quitted their Vessels, and swam ashore, but the Gallies were every one taken or sunk, and all the Men found on board them slain.

In the Centre Don *John* singled out and engaged the Gally of *Aly*; nor wanted *Colonna* and *Venier*, on each side of him, their Antagonists, whom they fought with great Valour; and as each of the Admirals were attended with some small Gallies, so did they from time to time supply them with Men in room of those who fell, insomuch that here the Battel raged in all its Fury. They had been long engaged

gaged without any apparent Advantage on either side, till News coming to Don *John* of *Barbarigo*'s Success in the Left Wing, he, jealous of being robbed by the *Venetians* of the Glory of this Victory, redoubled his Attacks, and fired with incredible Fury upon the Enemy. *Aly*, as he was encouraging his People by his own Example to bear up against this vigorous Charge, was slain by a Musket-shot, upon which the *Spaniards* immediately boarding his Gally, struck his Standard, and the Christians cried out *Victory, Victory*, to encourage one another, and terrify the Barbarians, so that there was now an exceeding Slaughter of the *Turks*, who suffered themselves to be killed without Resistance.

Doria and *Oluz-Aly* were yet observing each other's Division, till at length the former, fearing he should be forced against his Will to engage, got farther out to Sea, whereby he still gained his End of keeping his Enemy in suspence. But eight of the *Venetian* Commanders mistrusting *Doria*'s Intentions, and imagining he was shifting for himself, separated from that Wing, and lay still with their Oars apeek between it and the main Body, whose Example was presently followed by five others. *Oluz-Aly* immediately took the Advantage of surrounding these Gallies, but the *Venetians*, though so very much unequal in Number, defended themselves with great Valour, till at length being overcome, they were all put to the Sword. He then made the best of his way towards the main Body of the *Turkish* Fleet, and *Doria* perceiving Don *John*'s Success, struck in with his whole Right Wing against the Barbarians, who began to fly. The Marquis of *Santa Cruz*, as soon as the Smoak would permit him to see what was to be done, also came in with his Body of Reserve to join in Pursuit of the Enemy; and *Oluz-Aly* finding that not only *Aly*'s Standard was struck, but that the Body of the Fleet was entirely broken, crouded all the Sail he could, and escaped with thirty Gallies, all the rest of his Division being either sunk or taken; and hereupon the *Turks* ceased from making farther Resistance. In the midst of the Confusion and Disorder occasioned by the Flight of the Vanquished, and Pursuit of the Conquerors, *Pertauh* escaped in Disguise in a small Boat, his Gally having been taken by *Paul Ursin*.

The Turks are overcome, and great Numbers killed and taken.

The *Turks* lost thirty thousand Men in this Engagement, the bloodiest they ever knew since the Establishment of their Empire, and five thousand being taken Prisoners, there were amongst them the two Sons of *Aly*, with several other Persons of Distinction. The Christians took no less than a hundred and thirty Gallies, with a very great Booty; ninety more were either ran ashore, sunk or burnt, twenty thousand Christian Captives set at liberty, and besides the Pillage of the Islands, there were many rich Effects the Enemy had taken out of Merchant Ships, all which was divided among the Seamen and Soldiers, except the Prisoners, Gallies, and Artillery, which were shared by the three confederate Powers engaged in the War. This Battel was fought very near the same Place where *Augustus* defeated *Marc Anthony*, and howsoever that Fight has been celebrated

CHAP. V.   *Ruin of the* Rom. *Empire.*   233

brated by the Ancients, 'tis hard to judge which was the moſt conſiderable; for as the firſt exceeded in the Number of Veſſels, the Fame and Magnificence of the Preparations, and the great Concourſe of ſeveral Nations; ſo this ſurpaſſed in the good Condition and Strength of the Gallies, the Length of the Action, and the Courage and Obſtinacy of the Combatants. *Marc Anthony*'s Flight immediately crowned his Enemy with Victory, but here the Chriſtians diſputed a long time before they could obtain it, and loſt many more Men, tho' they did not draw near ſo great Advantages from it. *Compariſon between this Action, and that of Auguſtus and Marc Anthony.*

Eight thouſand of the braveſt in the Fleet loſt their Lives, of which Number were twenty *Venetian* Captains, of the moſt ancient Families of the Republick; and *Auguſtine Barbarigo*, who commanded the Left Wing, was ſingly regretted almoſt as much as all the reſt. He had broke the Enemy's Right Wing, and as he was animating his Men to proſecute their Advantage, expoſing himſelf too much, was ſtruck in the Eye with an Arrow, which render'd him ſpeechleſs, but he lived long enough to underſtand a compleat Victory was gained, and then expired in the Arms of his Friends, with Marks of the higheſt Satisfaction. *Many Chriſtians ſlain in the Battel.*

Night drawing on, and the Sea beginning to grow tempeſtuous, the Conquerors were obliged to repair to the neareſt Harbours, from whence they diſpatched Couriers to the Pope, the Republick, and all the Chriſtian Princes, with the News of their Succeſs. *Colonna* ſet out for *Rome*, Don *John* repaired to *Palermo*, in *Sicily*, there to ſpend the Winter, and *Onuphrius Juſtiniani* was ſent to *Venice* by *Venier* with an Account of the Battel. *The Chriſtians retire to the neareſt Harbours.*

That Officer committed a fatal Miſtake in neglecting to improve this Victory, ſince, if he had taken Advantage of the Confuſion and Diſorder the Enemy were in, and landed in the *Morea*, or any of their Dominions thereabouts, he could not have failed of Succeſs, the *Greeks* only waiting their Appearance on the Coaſt to throw off the *Turkiſh* Yoak, and declare for them. *Venier commits a fatal Error by not landing in the Morea.*

When the News came to *Conſtantinople*, the Inhabitants were as much alarmed as if the Enemy had been at the Gates; and *Selim*, who was then at *Adrianople*, building a *Moſque* and Hoſpital with the Spoils of *Cyprus*, immediately repaired to his capital City, to calm the Minds of the People, and by his Preſence ſomewhat appeaſed the Diſorders there. *Great Confuſion at Conſtantinople.*

Among the Priſoners which were taken in the Fight, and fell to the Pope's Share, was *Mehemet Bey*, Sangiac of *Negroponte*, a Perſon of Wit and good Senſe, who was acquainted with the Manners, as well as Cuſtoms of the Chriſtians; and ſome *Romans* who had been in the Action, took great delight in diſcourſing with him about it. He told them two things principally gained the Chriſtians the Day; the firſt, their great Numbers of Muſketeers, whoſe Arms were of much more Advantage in Fight than the *Turks* Darts and Arrows; and the ſecond, the Boards ſet up Breaſt-high on the ſides of their Gallies, in manner of Parapets, with which their Soldiers being ſheltered, they fired on their Enemies with far greater Aſſurance. *Mehemet Bey his Sentiments of the Battel.*

H h

rance. One of these Gentlemen saying that the Grand Signior's Loss in the Battel of *Lepanto* was much greater than the Advantage he reaped by the Conquest of *Cyprus*, *Mehemet* answered with a Smile, That they had only shaved his Master's Beard, which would soon grow again; but that the taking of *Cyprus* was lopping off a a Limb from the Body of the *Venetian* State, which would never be rejoined. And indeed what he said was soon verified, by the *Turks* fitting out, with incredible Dispatch, a numerous Fleet under the Command of *Oluz-Aly*, with which he came down to the Coasts of the *Morea*, and some slight Skirmishes happened between him and the *Venetians*: Who at length, being not duly supported by the King of *Spain*, became weary of the War, and struck up a Peace with the *Turk*, by which they relinquished all further Pretensions to the Isle of *Cyprus*.

The Turks fit out a numerous Fleet,

but

Venice soon after makes Peace with them.

About this time it was that *Henry* III. of *France*, going from *Poland* to *Paris*, to succeed in the Throne then become vacant by the Decease of his Brother *Charles* IX, took the City of *Venice* in his way; and the Senate, who thought themselves highly honoured with his Presence, being willing to shew at once both their Power and Magnificence, among other Honours and splendid Entertainments, they invited him one Day to dine at their Arsenal. As he sate down to Table they shewed him a Launch so entirely clear, that there was not so much as a Stick of Timber on it; but they immediately went to work on a Ship, and run her up in his Sight with such Expedition, that she was compleated, and all her Guns put on board time enough to be fired at the first Health the King began, after Dinner, to the Prosperity of the Republick.

The Venetians build a Galley in few Hours.

The next Naval War the *Venetians* were engaged in was with the *Uscoques*, a vagabond sort of People, consisting of *Hungarians*, *Servians*, *Croatians*, and *Dalmatians*, who committed Piracy in the Gulph of *Venice*, and were Enemies both to Turks and Christians; but more particularly to the *Venetians*, who had the greatest Trade in that Sea. They received some Protection from the Emperor, as Archduke of *Austria*, and made *Zegna*, a Sea Port of *Croatia*, within that Prince's hereditary Dominions, their chief Place of Residence; for which Reason it the more concerned the Republick to extirpate them: they gave the *Venetians* a great deal of trouble for above twenty Years, during which the War was carried on with little or no Interruption, and most barbarous Hostilities were practised on both sides; but at length they were obliged to transport their Families from *Zegna*, and deliver up the Vessels they used to commit Piracy with, which were all burnt.

Naval Wars between Venice and the Uscoques.

The Venetians very much molested by Pirates.

A. D. 1618.

Amurath IV, Emperor of the *Turks*, being engaged in a War with *Persia* (where he undertook the Siege of *Babylon*) he, to secure himself on the Side of *Christendom*, called together all the Corsairs of *Tunis*, *Tripoli* and *Algier*, and committed to them the Guard of the *Archipelago*; which Pirates, under Colour of that Business assigned them, committed terrible Depredations in the Gulph of *Venice*, plundered all Ships they met with, and ravaged the Coasts

both

both of *Naples* and *Dalmatia*. To reprefs thefe Infolences, *Marinus Capello*, the *Venetian* General, went againft them with a Number of Gallies well equipped, and engaging them off *La Valona*, gave them a fignal Defeat, wherein they had fifteen hundred Men killed, four Gallies funk, and twelve taken, with above fixteen hundred Chriftian Captives on board, who were reftored to their Liberty. *The* Venetians *overcome other Pirates of* Algier, *&c.*

In 1645, a War broke out between the Republick and the *Turks*, upon occafion of the taking a Galeon, wherein was an old Officer of the *Seraglio*, who was going to *Ægypt* in his way to *Mecca*, with feveral other *Turks* of Quality of both Sexes. The Knights of *Malta* had feized this Veffel the Year before, and to make it appear the more confiderable in the World, gave out, that they had taken a Son of the Grand Signior's, whom his Mother was fending to *Mecca* to be circumcifed. The Sultan then reigning was *Ibrahim*, one of the moft brutal of Mankind, who hearing of this Lofs, fell into the moft furious Paffion, and making a thoufand Vows that he would root out the Chriftian Name, he immediately fet about the greateft Preparations for War which had ever been known in the *Ottoman* Empire, efpecially by Sea. Upon this the Pope, the King of *Spain*, and all the Princes of *Italy* were mightily alarmed, and waited with Anxiety to fee where the Storm would break out: But the Republick had moft occafion to fear, as being much more expofed, wherefore they omitted nothing which was neceffary for her Defence. The Sultan, indeed, gave them the moft pofitive and exprefs Affurances that his Preparations were only levell'd againft the Ifland of *Malta*, and that he had not the leaft Thoughts of molefting them; notwithftanding which, on the twenty fourth of *June* 1645, the *Turkifh* Fleet confifting of three hundred and fixty eight Ships and Gallies, on board which were embarked fifty thoufand Men, having made a Shew of failing towards *Malta*, fuddenly came to *Candia*; where the Captain *Pafha* landing his Troops, immediately invefted *Canea*, the fecond City of the Ifland, which, after two Months fiege, he made himfelf Mafter of, but not without the Lofs of a prodigious Multitude of Men. The *Turks* had fpent two or three Years in reducing *Retimo*, and feveral other Places of lefs Note in the Ifland; when *Morofini*, who commanded the *Venetian* Fleet, hoping to make them abandon the Ifland, failed up the *Archipelago*, and lay before the *Dardanelles*, blocking up the *Turkifh* Fleet almoft in fight of *Conftantinople*. Immediately hereupon the Sultan iffued his Orders for affembling all the Ships from *Barbary*, and the Places about the *Archipelago*, making great Levies of Men in *Greece* and *Macedonia*; and *Muffa Pafha* having got together three hundred Sail, broke through the *Dardanelles* with little Lofs, and having landed forty thoufand Men on the Continent, bore away again with his Fleet: But *Morofini*, accompanied with the Pope's Gallies, and thofe of *Malta*, following him in the Rear, brought him to a Skirmifh, wherein they both loft their Lives. *Grimani*, another of the *Venetian* Admirals, was drowned in a great Storm; 1645. *A new War between the Turks and Venetians. The* Turkifh *Fleet comes to* Candia. *They take* Canea. *The* Venetians *proceed up the* Dardanelles *The* Turkifh *Fleet breaks through the* Dardanelles.

H h 2

Storm; and the same Year the *Turks* opened the Siege of the City of *Candia*.

James de Riva being next Year General at Sea, and receiving Advice that the *Turkish* Fleet was at *Fochia* in *Natolia*, he repaired thither, and attacked them with such Success, that he took, sunk, or otherwise destroyed the whole Fleet, on board which was an immense Sum of Money, great part of which was taken; and not long after, at the Entrance of the *Dardanelles*, the *Turks* were twice put to flight by the *Venetian* Fleet under the Command of *Mocenigo*. Their Losses this Campaign were so great, that they durst not once put to Sea the next Summer; but in 1654, *Foscolo*, the *Venetian* Admiral, was obliged to retire before the *Turkish* Fleet; yet *Mocenigo* rallying against them, committed great Slaughter, but unfortunately died in the Close of the Campaign. *Morosini*, the *Proveditore* General, blocked up the Entrance of the *Dardanelles*, which the *Turks* endeavoured to break through; but, after an obstinate Dispute of eight Hours, they were repulsed and defeated; when *Morosini* proceeding to *Volo*, in *Thessaly*, took that Place, with all the Stores of War and Provisions which were laid up there for the *Turkish* Fleet, and this in Sight of the *Beglerbey* of *Greece*.

The next Year *Laurence Marcello* repaired to the *Dardanelles*, where, in the Month of *June*, he came to a Battel with the Enemy, wherein he fell one of the first; but the next Officers *Barbaro*, *Contarini*, and *Morosini*, concealing his Death, continued the Fight, and at length, after a whole Day's Engagement, obtained the Victory, with great Loss of the Infidels. In this Battel were released no less than five thousand Christian Slaves, and this Success was followed by the Reduction of *Tenedo* and *Stalimine*, though the Enemy indeed soon after regained those Islands.

In 1662 the *Venetian* Fleet, having wintered at the Island *Pario*, repaired very early to its old Station before the *Dardanelles*, where a Squadron lay ready to proceed to the Relief of *Canea*, then hard pressed by the *Venetians*, and about the same time the Fleet from *Ægypt* was expected at *Constantinople*; wherefore the *Venetian* Admiral, leaving a Squadron to block up the *Dardanelles*, repaired in quest of the *Ægyptian* Fleet, and happily falling in with it, took most of the Ships.

The two following Campaigns were disputed mostly ashore: *Barbarigo* was then General at Sea, to whom one *Paulini* was Secretary, who, writing somewhat freely to one of his Friends at *Venice* concerning the State of the Fleet, the Vessel by which he sent his Letter, with other's of the General's, happen'd to be ran ashore; so that the Dispatches were taken out and brought back to the General, who, finding this Letter inclosed in one of his Packets, opened and read it, and immediately in a most violent Rage sent for *Paulini*, gave him but two Hours to prepare himself for Death, and, when the Time was expired, threw him into the Sea. An Instance of a most barbarous and unreasonable Severity, to punish a Fault of Indiscretion with the same Rigour as if the Offender had been

been guilty of Treason, and corresponded with the Republick's Enemies. Nor will it excuse him if we suppose the Person was placed in his Service to be a Spy on his Conduct, (a thing frequently practised by the *Venetians* with respect to their Officers) since he was his Fellow-Subject, and a Member of the same Community with himself.

The next Year the Republick was embroiled in a Dispute with Pope *Alexander* VII. That Prince, well known for being engaged in several Designs little suitable with the Sanctity of his pretended Character, took it into his Head to dispute the *Venetians* Right to the Dominion of the *Adriatick*, in pursuance of which the Republick makes the Ships that sail there pay something of a Duty for the Liberty and Security of the Navigation, with the Protection whereof the *Venetians* charge themselves. The Pope pretended his Subjects ought to be exempted from paying this Duty, and issued general Orders, forbidding them to make any such Acknowledgment. He carried the Matter so far as to seize some Ships of the *Venetians* in his Harbours upon this Occasion: But the Senate issuing out Letters of Reprizals, and having much greater Opportunities of procuring Satisfaction to themselves that way, than the Pope, the Trade of the Subjects of the Ecclesiastical State was presently at a stand, and the Seas shut up from them; which coming, with loud Complaints of the People who had suffered, to the Ears of the Pope, he was forced to revoke his Orders, and be glad to let that Affair stand upon its old footing.

A. D. 1665.
The Pope disputes the Venetians Right to the Adriatick;
but is humbled by them.

In 1667 the *Venetians* fitted out a considerable Fleet, which they divided into three Squadrons, one to take its Station at the *Dardanelles*, another to cruise about the *Archipelago*, and the third off *Sapienza* against the *Corsaires*. In 1669 the City of *Candia* was surrendered, after a Siege of one and twenty Years, wherein died before it above sixty thousand *Mahometans*, the *Venetians* having spent in the Defence thereof four Millions two hundred and fifty five thousand Ducats, besides the Charge of Stores and Provisions, and had sacrificed the Lives of above twenty nine thousand Men, when they delivered up the Town, reduced to a heap of Rubbish, upon honourable Terms. Being now exhausted with this War of five and twenty Years Continuance, they were forced to incline to Peace, and quit all Pretensions to *Candia*, retaining only some few Places in the Nighbourhood of that Island.

1667.
1669.
Candia surrendered.
Peace between the Venetians and Turks. 1684.

In 1684 they entered into an Alliance with the Emperor, and the Crown of *Poland* against the *Turks*; in which War, under the Conduct of their General *Morosini*, they reduced all the *Morea* to their Obedience, and had several other signal Successes both by Land and Sea. The ducal Dignity was in 1688 conferr'd on *Morosini*, who still continuing General, took the Castles of *Patras* and *Romelia*, which guard the Entrance of the Gulph of *Lepanto*, together with the City of that Name, and several other considerable Towns; and the Republick's General, *Cornaro*, also took *Castel Novo* in *Dalmatia*; but *Morosini* failing in his Design of surprizing *Negroponte*,

The War renewed, and the Venetians reduce the Morea, &c. 1688. and take several other Places.

took

took however *Napoli di Romania*. Under *Sebaſtian Valier*, *Morofini*'s Succeſſor in the Government, the *Turks* retook the Iſle of *Scio*, which obliged the Republick to increaſe her Forces both by Sea and Land. In 1697 the *Venetian* General ſailed to the *Iſthmus* of the *Morea*, where he defeated ſeven thouſand *Turkiſh* Foot, and three thouſand Horſe, ſupported by the Fleet, which alſo ſuffered; and in a Naval Engagement near *Andri*, the Enemy loſt five thouſand Men.

The Turks retake Scio.
1684.

At length a Peace was concluded with the Infidels, in the Beginning of the Year 1699, at *Carlowitz*, in *Sclavonia*, by which the *Venetians* continued in Poſſeſſion of all their Acquiſitions, to wit, the *Morea*, or *Peloponneſus*, with the Iſlands, and Places of *Albania* which were taken in the Beginning of the War: But they thought fit to abandon their Conqueſts in *Livadia*, becauſe, having no ſtrong Fortreſſes on that ſide, their Subjects would be continually expos'd to the Inſults of the *Turks*, and might afford endleſs Matter for Broils between the State and that Nation. Since that time they enjoyed a profound Peace till the Year 1713, which, by the great Preparations making through the *Ottoman* Emprire, threatned them with a new War.

A Peace again concluded at Carlowitz.
1699.

1713.

Having ſaid thus much relating to that fam'd Republick of *Venice*, we come next, according to the Order obſerved in the firſt Book, to the *Piſans*; but their Affairs are ſo much involved with thoſe of the *Genoeſe*, who next follow, that it would be ſuperfluous to treat of them in particular; wherefore we ſhall paſs on to the Naval Wars between the *Genoeſe*, and thoſe they had to contend with.

Chap. VI.

Of the Naval Wars of the Genoeſe, *containing thoſe they were engaged in with the* Piſans, *and with the* Venetians.

THE City and Coaſt of *Genoa* being ſubdued by the *Romans* about the Year of the City 599, was poſſeſſed and governed by them in form of a Province, 'till the Irruption of the barbarous Nations into the Weſtern Empire, when the *Lombards* became Maſters of it, who being reduced by *Charlemagne*, it continued under his Succeſſors 'till the Year 1099, at which time the *Genoeſe* threw off all foreign Dominion, and the Capital City choſe Conſuls for the Government of the whole. It continued a Scene of great Revolutions and Changes of Government 'till the Time of the Emperor *Charles* V, when it was ſettled in that Form of Government by which it is now ruled.

How the Genoeſe were at firſt governed.

They throw off the Yoak, and chuſe Conſuls.

The

CHAP. VI. *Ruin of the* Rom. *Empire.* 239

The Naval Wars of the *Genoese* were chiefly with these three Nations, the *Saracens*, the *Pisans*, and the *Venetians*; and their most ancient Expeditions, after the Reduction of *Corsica* and *Sardinia*, were those to *Syria*. In the first Holy War after the taking of *Antioch*, *Hugh Embriachi*, Admiral of the *Genoese* Fleet in the *Levant*, reduced *Seleucia*, *Antipatris* and *Cæsarea*, together with *Acre*, *Gibel*, *Tripoli*, *Baruth*, and several other Cities of *Syria* and *Phœnicia*: And so vigilant were they, that wheresoever the *Saracens* appeared, there presently were the *Genoese* ready with a Fleet to oppose them. They recovered from out of their Hands the Island of *Minorca*, and took *Almeria* in *Granada*, and *Tortosa*, in *Catalonia*, with prodigious Slaughter of the Infidels, who defended them: Long before which, they dispossessed them of the Islands of *Corsica* and *Sardinia*, in which Conquests they were assisted by *Pipin* (the Son of *Charlemagne*) then King of *Italy*: And so powerful were they at Sea, that in the Mediterranean none were able to oppose them, if the *Pisans* and *Venetians* had not undertaken to war against them. We shall first discuss their Broils with the *Pisans*, then those with the *Venetians*, and lastly those with other Nations in general.

They take several Cities in Syria and Phœnicia.

Also Minorca, and several Places from the Saracens.

They war with the Pisans.

The Coasts of *Sardinia* and *Corsica* were for a long time the constant Seat of War, the *Saracens*, *Genoese*, and *Pisans*, as it were taking their Turns in the Possession of those Islands, and driving out one another. In 1115, the *Saracens*, under their Leader *Musactus*, burnt the City of *Pisa*, and repairing to *Sardinia*, expelled the *Pisans* from thence; and reduced the Island; whereupon the *Genoese* were invited into an Alliance with the *Pisans*, and undertook an Expedition with them to *Sardinia*, wherein they were so successful, as not only to recover all that the *Pisans* had lost, but, in a Sea Fight, took *Musactus* Prisoner, and sent him to *Genoa*; however Disputes arising between the two Allies, about the Division of the Spoil, they had two or three successive Wars and Reconciliations, 'till at length the *Pisans* were forced to yield to the *Genoese*. Their Sea Fights, in which sometimes one and sometimes the other were Conquerors, are so numerous that it will be necessary to pass by very many of them, and take Notice only of the most remarkable.

1155
The Saracens burn Pisa, and recover Sardinia.

The Pisans assisted by the Genoese recover all they had lost.

The *Genoese*, in a sharp and bloody Engagement, having given the *Pisans* a great Overthrow, reduced *Corsica*, and possessed themselves of *Piombino* and the adjacent Country, and laying siege to *Pisa*, would not rise from before it, till they had obliged the Inhabitants (who were reduced to great Extremities) to agree that all the Houses of the City should be pulled down to the first Story, and that there should not be any built higher. The *Pisans*, stung with this Disgrace, suddenly attacked the *Genoese* in the *Levant*, in *Sicily*, and upon their own Coast, and gained several Advantages over them, defeating *Baldwin Guiercio*, the *Genoese* Admiral in a Sea Fight, and routing other of their Fleets on the Coasts of *Tuscany* and of *France*. After this the *Pisans* received a great Defeat off *Syracuse*, wherein they lost their whole Fleet, except five Gallies,

A. D. 1127.
The Pisans and Genoese quarrelling, the former are reduced to great Extremities.

The Pisans have success against the Genoese, and beat them at Sea.

The Pisans are beaten, but recover themselves. lies, but soon retrieved their Affairs so well, that they attacked *Sardinia*, reduced *Algueri* (or *Larghes*) a Sea Port there, and took *Trapani* in *Sicily*; and, had it not been for the Valour of the *Dorias* and *Spinolas*, had gone near to have accomplished the Ruin of the Republick. In three Days time a Fleet of seventy Gallies was fitted out under the Command of *Aubert Doria*, nine under *Henry Mari*, and twenty under *Caccianimico de la Volta*. The *Pisans* at the same time committed the Management of their Naval Preparations to Count *Ugolin* and *Andrew Saraceni*, who soon fitted out a Fleet of forty four Sail under the Command of *John Cavalca*, which Officer repaired with twenty of the best Gallies to *Sardinia*, in quest of *Mari*, and off that Island came to an Engagement with him, which lasted from Morning till Night, wherein at length he *They are again beaten.* lost fifteen Sail, and had much ado to escape with the remaining five to *Pisa*.

It was now the time for chusing a new Podestat at that Place, the annual chief Magistrate of that Republick, and they elected *Peter Morosini* a *Venetian*, hoping by such a Choice to engage that State on their side, which ever since the Beginning of the War had continued Neuter. They sent out their new Podestat with seventy two Gallies against the *Genoese*, who on their Part detached a Fleet of eighty Gallies and eight Frigates under the Command of *Aubert Doria*, *Conrade Spinola* being his Vice-Admiral. Between the *A notable Fight between the Fleets of Pisa and Genoa, and the former routed.* *Mallora* and *Leghorn* the two Fleets met, where *Doria*, to prevent the Enemy's escaping, placed one Squadron between them and the Shore; and another Division, under *Benedict Giacaria*, was disposed at a convenient Distance, to come in, upon occasion, to the Relief of such Gallies as should be distressed, with a Tender for each Gally. The *Pisans* were much inferior in Number, but notwithstanding *Doria*'s Precautions, they got near enough to the Shore to fight under the Protection of the Castles of *Leghorn*. *Morosini* had the Command of their Right Wing, and the Son of Count *Ugolin* was in the Left, in the Admiral Gally of *Pisa*, displaying the chief Flag of the Republick. The Dispute was long and obstinate, till at length the *Genoese* made themselves Masters of the Admiral Gally, and struck the Flag; whereupon ensued a general Terror amongst the *Pisans*, insomuch that the *Genoese* gained a compleat Victory, possessing themselves of thirty Gallies, having already sunk seven in the Heat of the Engagement, the rest with difficulty, under Covert of the Night, getting safe to *Pisa*. The Number of the Slain on the Side of the *Pisans* amounted to above five thousand, and very many were taken Prisoners, among whom was the Podestat himself, and the Son of Count *Ugolin*, who were sent, with the rest to *Genoa*, where they were found to be no less than nine thousand; which gave Rise to a Saying in *Italy* that, *If one would see* Pisa, *he must go to* Genoa. This Victory was so considerable that the A. D. 1284. *Genoese* Senate caused the 6th of *August*, the Day on which it was obtained, to be kept as a solemn Anniversary, and the Flag that was taken from the Enemy was hung up in the great Church of St. *Matthew* as a Trophy of their Success. After this they reduced the Island

Island of *Elba*, plundered *Leghorn*, destroyed the Tower at the Entrance of the Port of *Pisa*, and carried away the Chain which was laid across for its Security. This Blow was so fatal to the *Pisans*, that they could never recover it, and at once there was an end put to that Power which had formerly quelled the *Saracens*, and drove them out of *Sardinia*, that had reduced *Tunis*, and sent its King Captive to the *Roman* Pontiff, taken *Palermo*, the Capital of *Sicily*, from the *Saracens*, with prodigious Slaughter of the *Barbarians*; had opened the way to *Syria* for the Christian Princes, and had been greatly assistant both to the Kings of *Arragon*, and the Emperors of *Germany*: But there opens next a Scene of War to the *Genoese* with a more formidable Enemy, the *Venetians*.

The Genoese take the Island Elba, and do great Mischief to the Pisans.

An end put to the Pisan Power.

The Venetians and Genoese quarrel, and why.

Henry *Piscator*, Governor of the South Parts of the *Morea*, with a Number of *Genoese* Ships which were sent as Auxiliaries to him, took the City of *Candia*, and several other Places of that Island from the *Venetians*: And soon after a great Dispute happened between the two Nations at *Acre* in *Syria*, as we have before mentioned. *Palæologus*, Emperor of the *Greeks*, having given to the *Genoese* the City of *Smyrna*, and the Island of *Scio*, it created a great Animosity in the *Venetians*, and administer'd frequent Occasions of Disputes between them. The *Genoese* were then Masters of the City of *Tyre*, in *Syria*, as the *Venetians* were of *Acre*, so that there was no navigating in the *Levant* without the utmost Hazard from one or other of the two Nations. In the beginning of the War, ten *Venetian* Merchant Ships, richly laden, were taken by *Stephen Grilli*, the *Genoese* Admiral, under the Walls of *Durazzo*; the *Venetian* Fleet was also forced to retreat from before *Tyre*, to which they had laid Siege; and *Aubert Doria* took and plundered the City of *Canea*, and levelled great part of it with the Ground. Soon after the *Genoese* fitted out a Fleet of five and twenty Gallies, under the Command of *Luke Grimaldi*, assisted by two Persons of Senatorian Rank in the Nature of Collegues, which *Grimaldi*, in his way to *Syria*, took three *Venetian* Ships, and attacking the Citadel of *Acre*, in a short time forced it to surrender; to revenge which Loss, the *Venetians* surprized and plundered *Pera* and *Fochia*, two wealthy Settlements of the *Genoese*, and carried off a Booty of immense Riches. As they were returning home, under the Command of *Roger Morosini*, they were attacked by *Nicholas Spinola*, the *Genoese* Admiral, who recovered the Booty, and entirely defeated them, taking five and twenty of their Gallies.

The Genoese take Candia, &c.

several Merchant Ships,

and the City Canea from the Venetians.

Alternate Successes of the Venetians and Genoese.

Having got ready a Fleet of seventy three Sail, they put *Lambo Doria* at the Head of it, who sailing into the *Adriatick* in quest of the *Venetians*, fell in, off *Curzola*, with their Fleet commanded by *Andrew Dandolo*, consisting of double the Number of the *Genoese*. Notwithstanding this great Superiority, he bravely engaged them, and with so good Success, that he took or destroyed the whole Fleet, except twelve Gallies which got off, very much shattered. The *Venetian* Admiral was taken Prisoner, with above seven thousand others; with which Misfortune he was so much afflicted, that he

A. D. 1298.

They beat the Venetian Fleet.

he beat out his Brains on the Poop of the Ship on board which he was carried. Nor did the *Venetians*, under *Mark Baffo*, engage the *Genoese* with more Success near the *Dardanelles*, where they lost sixteen Gallies: and after this *Philip Doria* laid waste the Island of *Negroponte*, and took the chief Town of the same Name.

Beat them again near the Dardanelles,

Then the *Greek* Emperor and the King of *Arragon* entering into an Alliance with the *Venetians*, the *Genoese* yet more increased their Reputation, by defeating the united Force of so many Enemies confederated against them. The *Venetians* fitted out forty Gallies under the Command of *Nicholas Pisani*, and *Pancratius Justiniani*, Captain of the Gulph; and the King of *Arragon* eighty, under the Command of Don *Pontius de Leon*, who sailing up the *Archipelago*, joined the Fleet of *John Catacuzenus* the *Greek* Emperor. The *Genoese* Fleet consisted of sixty Sail, under the Orders of *Pagan Doria*, a Captain of great Reputation, who near *Pera*, in the Streights of *Constantinople*, fell in with the Fleet of the Confederates, and upon their approaching him, he disposed his Fleet in two Divisions, and made the Signal for engaging. The *Venetians* received the *Genoese* with great Courage, but being too near the Shore, they could not sufficiently extend their Front, so that several of their Gallies were rendered useless, which gave the *Genoese* a great Advantage; and having fought very bravely all Day, they were at length forced to betake themselves to flight, and leave the *Genoese* Masters of the Sea, having lost near four thousand Men, among whom were two hundred *Catalan* Knights; and Don *Pontius de Leon*, *Stephen Contarini*, Procurator of St. *Mark*, *John Strevo*, and *Pancratius Justiniani* were of the Number of the slain; whereas the Loss of the *Genoese* did not amount to above seven hundred. Thirty of the *Venetian* Gallies were taken, with eighteen of the *Arragonese*; but the *Greeks* being in the Rear, they had no Share in the Engagement, so that they retreated without any Loss. The shattered Remains of the *Venetian* Fleet made the best of their way to *Candia*, while *Doria* came with his victorious Gallies before *Constantinople*, whereby he so dismayed the *Greek* Emperor, that he was glad to consent to a Peace with the Republick. This *Pagan Doria* defeated two Years after, off the Isle of *Sapienza*, another Fleet of the *Venetians* commanded by the same *Nicholas Pisani*, in which Engagement the *Venetians* had five thousand Men taken Prisoners, among whom was the Admiral himself, and near as many more slain; and *Doria*, having sent the Prisoners to *Genoa*, sailed up the *Adriatick*, where he burnt and plundered the Town of *Parenzo* in *Istria*.

and afterward, beat the united Forces of the Greek Emperor, Arragon, and Venice,

and again beat the Venetians and their Confederates.

A. D. 1352.

The Greek Emperor forced to make Peace with Genoa.

The Genoese again overcome the Venetians.

This War was followed by another with *Cyprus*, which was set on foot and supported by the *Venetians*, who instigated *Peter de Lusignan*, King of the Island, against the *Genoese*. *Peter Fulgose* was thereupon detached to *Cyprus* with a Fleet of forty three Gallies, where he laid siege to *Famagusta*, and having made himself Master of the Place, soon reduced the King of *Cyprus* to such Extremities, that he was obliged to accept of a Peace at the Discre-

Take Famagusta, and oblige the King of Cyprus to ask Peace.

CHAP. VI. *Ruin of the* Rom. *Empire.*

Discretion of the Conquerors, granting them the Possession of *Famagusta*, and agreeing to pay them an annual Pension of forty thousand Crowns. So high at this time ran the Reputation of the Republick, that her Friendship was earnestly courted by several States, and by some purchased with Mony. *Andronicus Junior*, undertaking to dispossess his Uncle of the same Name, who sate on the the Throne of the *Greek* Empire, he, in order to engage the *Genoese* in his Interest, gave them the Island of *Tenedo* in the *Archipelago*, which *Emanuel*, the Son of *Calo Johannes*, about the same time promised to the *Venetians*, if they would assist him in obtaining the Empire.

The Friendship of the Genoese courted.

Hereupon a new War broke out between the *Genoese* and *Venetians*, with the former of whom sided *Lewis* King of *Hungary*, *Francis Carraro*, Prince of *Padua*, the Archduke of *Austria*, and the Patriarch of *Aquileia*; and with the latter *Barnaby Visconti*, Duke of *Milan*, with *Peter de Lusignan*, King of *Cyprus*, who took this Opportunity of breaking his late Treaty. The *Genoese* Fleet under *Lucian Doria*, entring the *Adriatick*, fell in with that of *Venice*, commanded by *Victor Pisani*, and immediately engaging each other, they fought with great Bravery on both sides; in which Dispute the *Genoese* Admiral was slain with an Arrow. But that which usually occasions the Loss of a Battel, (which often follows the Fate of the General) here greatly contributed to the obtaining the Victory; for those who were near him, seeing him fall, vowed Revenge to his *Manes*, while those who were at a greater Distance, (deceived by another Person who took his Post, appeared with the same Arms, and fought with the like Resolution) thought it a Dishonour not to imitate the Example of their supposed Admiral: So that at length they gained a compleat Victory, the Enemy retiring with the Loss of fifteen Gallies. Hereupon the *Genoese* sailed up the *Adriatick* after them, and seized *Humago*, on the Coast of *Istria*, which Success was followed soon after by the Reduction of *Grado* and *Caorle*. Proceeding thence, they attacked *Palestrina* and *Chiozza*, both in the Neighbourhood of *Venice*, and carried the first with little or no Resistance, but the latter cost them a Siege. This was undertaken by *Peter Doria*, whom the *Genoese* had sent out with a Reinforcement of fifteen Gallies to succeed *Lucian*, slain in the late Fight. He forced *Chiozza* to surrender, and reduced the *Venetians* to such Extremities, that they would gladly have accepted a Peace on any Conditions, and sent Ministers to implore it at his Hands; but he fatally resolving to continue the War, well nigh compleated the Ruin of his Country. However, after this, he reduced the Town and Island of *Malamocco*, but in a short time was slain in an Engagement near *Loredo*, as is beforementioned, and left the *Genoese* Affairs in an ill Condition to his Successor *Gaspar Spinola*. After this the *Venetians* had such signal Successes, that they dispossessed them of all their Acquisitions in those Parts, and forced them to retire out of the *Adriatick*; so that the *Genoese* becoming weary of the War, were glad now to accept of a Peace they had of late so haughtily refused.

A new War breaks out between Genoa and Venice with the reason thereof.

The Venetians beaten at Sea, and several Places taken by the Genoese.

They take Chiozza, and reduce Venice to great Extremities.

Venice dispossesses Genoa of all her Acquisitions, and they accept of Peace. A. D. 1381.

A War breaks out between the Genoese and Florentines.

A War soon after breaking out between the *Genoese* and *Florentines*, the *Venetians*, taking part with the latter, entered the Territories of *Philip* Duke of *Milan*, who was in Alliance with *Genoa*, and in their Engagements ashore had good Success, but were worsted when they came to fight with their Gallies on the *Po*. *Nicholas Trevisano* commanded those of the *Venetians*, as *John Grimaldi*, an expert *Genoese* Captain, did those of the Duke of *Milan*; who falling down from *Pavia* with his Fleet, near *Cremona*, engaged that of the *Venetians* (which was greatly superior) with such Success, that he obtained a signal Victory, and took twenty eight of the Enemy's Vessels.

The Venetians who sided with the Florentines beaten near Cremona.

1431. Are again beaten near Scio.

In 1431, *Andrew Mocenigo*, Admiral of the *Venetian* Fleet, making an Attempt upon the Island of *Scio*, was defeated by *Raphael Montaldo*, who sunk several of his Ships there, the rest being destroyed by Tempests in his Return home. He had scarce made his Retreat from thence, when *Peter Spinola* arrived with a Fleet of twenty four Sail from *Genoa*, who finding the Enemy retired, attacked, and reduced the Islands of *Nacsia* and *Andri*. In this manner was the War carried on between them with various Success, till the Year 1432, when a Peace was concluded between them by the Mediation of the Marquis of *Ferrara*, upon Terms the most advantagious to the *Venetians*; since which time the *Genoese* have not been in any Capacity to cope with that Republick.

The Genoese take the Islands Nacsia and Andri.

A. D. 1432. A Peace made between Venice and Genoa, and the Power of the latter eclipsed.

Chap. VII.

Of the Naval Wars of the Genoese, *containing those they have been engaged in with other Nations besides the* Pisans *and* Venetians.

HAVING thus related their Wars with the *Pisans*, we come now to treat of those they were engaged in with other People in general. In the Year 1206, *John Strozza* being Podestat of *Genoa*, (for so their chief Magistrate was then called) there were appointed (besides the Consuls, who executed the Office of Judges) four of the principal Citizens to assist him in the Care and Cognizance of maritime Affairs, who were called the Consuls of the Sea. The Republick was then in a very flourishing Condition; for the Cities of *Nice* and *Vintimiglia* had, of their own accord, submitted to her Obedience; and she possessed *Ceuta* in *Barbary*, the City of *Tyre* in *Syria*, and the Islands of *Corsica* and *Sardinia*.

The Wars of the Genoese in general. 1206.

What Places the Genoese possessed.

The City and Port were greatly enlarged when the Families of *Doria* and *Spinola* bore the chief Sway, sometimes ruling alternately, and sometimes jointly, till at length they became divided in the Factions of the *Guelphs* and *Gibellines*. The *Doria*'s, who took part with the *Gibellines*, being expelled the City, laid waste

A. D. 1300. The Factions of the Guelphs and Gibellines.

all

CHAP. VII. *Ruin of the* Rom. *Empire.*

all the Coasts of the Republick, with their Depredations; whereupon *Frederick Marabota* was sent out against them with a Fleet, who coming up with the Ships of the *Doria*'s, found them greatly superior; so that not thinking it proper to hazard an Engagement, if it could be possibly avoided, he used his best Endeavours to get clear of them, and Night coming on, by help of the following Stratagem, favoured his Escape. He took a Number of wooden Shields, and placing Lamps in the Hollow of them, set them afloat, which the *Doria*'s imagining were the Lights of the Gallies, went in quest of the Shields, while he, steering another Course, got out of the reach of his Enemies.

Frederick Marabota sent with a Fleet against the Doria's; but avoids them by a Stratagem.

At length, the Subjects of *Arragon* very much infesting the Coasts of the Republick, and of *Sardinia*, the two contending Factions united for their common Defence, and fitted out a Fleet of forty five Gallies, the Command whereof was given to *Anthony Grimaldi*, who repairing to the Coasts of *Catalonia*, surprized a considerable Number of Ships belonging to *Tarragona*, which lay at Anchor under the Shore, and set them all on fire. From thence stretching over to *Majorca*, he there made a Descent, and formally declared War in the Name of the Republick against the King of *Arragon*, to whom that Island, with *Minorca*, then belonged; and departing thence, he, off Port *Mahon*, fell in with the Enemy's Fleet of forty two Gallies, which he engaged and put to flight.

The two Factions join against those of Arragon, and beat them at Sea.

A. D. 1333.

The next Year, *Salagro Nigri* cruising off *Minorca* with ten of the Republick's Gallies, fell in with four stout Ships of War of the Enemies, in their Passage from *Cagliari* to *Barcelona*, with several noble *Catalans* and their Families. He was resolved not to let so rich a Booty escape him, and therefore, though the Enemy were going right afore the Wind with a fresh Gale, he would not leave any thing unattempted which might contribute to his coming up with them, insomuch that he lightened his Gallies of every thing which could retard their way, and threw over all his Provisions, telling the Seamen there was enough on board the Ships before them, and that they must overtake them, or starve. This succeeded so well, that he soon came up with the Ships, and, after a smart Dispute, made himself Master of them, killing a considerable Number of Men, and taking seven hundred Prisoners. Thence making the best of his way for *Sardinia*, he on that Coast met with ten Sail of the Enemy's Ships, which he also engaged, and taking them all, returned in Triumph to *Genoa*: And now the Quarrel between the *Guelphs* and *Gibellines* reviving, there was nothing more done against the *Arragonese*; but the Divisions in the City were so great, that it caused an Alteration in the Form of Government, *Simon Boccanigra* being made the first Doge.

The Genoese meet with, and take several Ships of Arragon.

The Quarrel between the Guelphs and Gibellines revives.

Under his Administration, *Simon Quarto* was sent up the *Archipelago* with a Squadron of nine Gallies, who arriving at *Pera*, had great Complaints made to him of the Depredations committed on the *Genoese* Ships by *Zarabis*, a *Mahometan* Prince, who then possessed *Sinopoli*; whereupon he made sail towards that Place, in order to lay siege to it; but on his Arrival there, *Zarabis* engaging

A. D. 1340. *Simon Boccanigra the first Doge.*

*gaging by Treaty not to moleſt the *Genoeſe* in their Trade any more, he repaired to *Capha*, in *Little Tartary*, then a flouriſhing Settle-

The Treachery of a Mahometan Prince.

ment of the Republick's. Upon his Departure, the Infidel, without any regard to his Treaty, reſolved to ſeize on ſome *Genoeſe* Merchant Ships richly laden, in their way to the *Helleſpont*, and went out with a Squadron of ten Gallies for that purpoſe; but *Quarto* receiving Intelligence of his Deſign, reinforced his Squadron

The Genoeſe entirely defeat his Fleet.

with ſome Gallies which were at *Capha*, and ſailed in queſt of *Zarabis*, with whom engaging, he entirely defeated him.

About the ſame time a Fleet of twenty Sail was ſent under the Command of *Giles Boccanigra*, the Doge's Brother, to the Aſſiſtance

They aſſiſt the King of Caſtile againſt the King of Morocco.

of *Alphonſus*, King of *Caſtile*, then engaged in a War with *Ben-Jacob*, King of *Morocco*, who rendered great Service to that Prince againſt his Enemies; and ſoon after *Buſſenus Ægubius* was ſent out with another Fleet on the ſame Service, who took or deſtroyed twelve of the Enemy's Gallies.

A. D. 1345.

In 1345, a Fleet of twenty nine Sail was fitted out under the Command of *Simon Vignoſo*, on board each of the Ships whereof were put two hundred Archers; and before the Admiral ſet ſail, the Standard of St. *George*, Patron of *Genoa*, was with great Ceremony put into his Hands by the Doge, in the Place of St. *Laurence*.

Overcome the Count of Fundi, and recover the Iſland Scio.

With this Fleet *Vignoſo* repaired firſt to *Terracina*, againſt *Nicholas*, Count of *Fundi*, who had declared againſt the Republick, and by ſeizing that Place, with ſome of his Caſtles about *Gaeta*, ſoon brought him to Reaſon; and proceeding thence to the *Archipelago*, recovered the Iſland *Scio*, on whoſe Inhabitants he conferred the Privileges of Citizens of *Genoa*, and reduced both *Fochia Nova* and *Fochia Veja* to the Obedience of the Republick.

The *Genoeſe* could not long continue without a Change of Go-

A. D. 1353. *Genoa ſubmits to the Government of the Duke of Milan. They beat the Pirates of Tripoli, and the Doge is reſtored.*

vernment, and now in 1353, the prevailing Faction ſubmitted to *John Viſconti*, Duke of *Milan*, under whoſe Adminiſtration *Philip Doria* went out with a Fleet of twenty Sail to the Coaſt of *Barbary*, where having defeated a conſiderable Force of the Pirates, he ſeized and plundered *Tripoli*, their Place of Habitation, and laid waſte all the adjacent Country. *Viſconti*'s Government was ſoon at an end, and *Simon Boccanigra*, the late Doge, was again reſtored to that Dignity, who dying, was ſucceeded by *Gabriel Adorni*, and

A. D. 1371. *The Genoeſe reduce Malta.*

he by *Dominick Campoſulgoſo*; in whoſe Time the Iſland of *Malta* was reduced to the Obedience of *Genoa* by *Thomas Marchi*.

A. D. 1387.

In 1387, *Anthony Adorni* being Doge, the *Genoeſe* made a famous Expedition to *Tunis*, towards which they received great Aſſiſtance both from the *French* and *Engliſh*, of which latter there was ſent to them a Regiment, conſiſting moſtly of Gentlemen Volunteers, under the Command of the Earl of *Derby*. But the Succeſs of this Undertaking was not anſwerable to the great Preparations made for it, or the Strength of the Fleet and Army; which

and with their Allies go againſt Tunis, but take only the Iſle of Zerbi.

after having ſuffered very much, returned without having gained any other Advantage than the Reduction of the Iſle of *Zerbi*, a Place of ſmall Conſequence on the Coaſt of *Tripoli*.

Ten

CHAP. VII. *Ruin of the* Rom. *Empire.*

Ten Years after they submitted to the *French* King, *Charles* VI, and received for Governour from him *Valerand de Luxembourg*, Count of St. *Paul*, but in a short time growing weary of him, they massacred all the *French* in the City, and invited the Marquis of *Montferat* to accept of their Obedience. In his time the *Genoese* renewed their old Quarrel with the *Catalans*, and under the Command of *Baptist Lisardo*, and *Paul Lercaro*, defeated their Fleet off of *Alexandria* in *Ægypt*; while *Andrew Doria* repairing with another Squadron to *Barcelona*, burnt some of the Enemy' Ships in the Road there.

They submit to the French *King, but soon after kill the* French, *and put themselves under the Marquis of* Montferat.

They beat the Fleet of the Catalans.

The *Genoese* not long after threw off the Government of the Marquis of *Montferat*; and in 1417, *Thomas Fregose* being Doge, made a Peace with the *French*, who 'till that time only waited an Opportunity to recover the Government of the Republick into their Hands; but now the *English*, under *Henry* V, being Masters of the greatest Part of the Kingdom, the Regent willingly came into an Accommodation that might be of use to him against his Enemy. By this Treaty *Fregose* engaged to furnish the *French* with eight great Carracks, as many Gallies, and six hundred Cross-bow Men, commanded by *John Grimaldi*, who did great Service against the *English*. The two Fleets, each consisting of above a hundred Sail, came to an Engagement in the Mouth of the *Seine*, where the *Genoese* for a long time sustained the most vigorous Attacks of the Enemy, and the Ship commanded by *Laurence Foglietta* defended it self against seven *English* Ships, 'till she was at length disengaged by the Dexterity of a Sailor, who cut the Cordage which held the Stage the *English* had thrown over to her Deck from one of their Ships. But notwithstanding all the Efforts the *Genoese* could make, the *French* lost the Battel, wherein *John de Franquimont*, the Son of the Vice-Admiral was slain, and the Bastard of *Bourbon*, who commanded the Fleet, remained a Prisoner to the *English*, who also took four of the *Genoese* Carracks, on board which was a Sum of Money for the Payment of three Months Wages for the whole Fleet.

A. D. 1417.

Throw off the Government of Montferat, *and make Peace with* France.

They aid the French *against the* English.

A Sea Fight between the French, Genoese *and* English.

The French *and* Genoese *beaten.*

In 1420, *Alphonsus* King of *Arragon* invading the Island of *Corsica*, had *Calvi* presently surrendered to him, and proceeding thence to *Bonifacio* laid siege to that Place, carrying on the same with such Vigour that the Inhabitants being soon reduced to great Distress, dispatched a Messenger to *Genoa* to desire speedy Relief, whereupon *John Baptist Fregose* was sent with a Squadron of seven great Ships to their Assistance. King *Alphonsus*, to prevent the City's receiving any Relief by Sea, shut up the Entrance of the Harbour with a floating Boom, consisting of great Planks chained together, which was defended within by five large Ships ranged in a Line, from the two outermost whereof were Stages laid across to the Shore, as there were also from one Ship to the other; and on each side of the Harbour's Mouth were raised Batteries of Cannon. On the Arrival of *Fregose* off of *Bonifacio*, the Garrison sent him Advice, by a dextrous Swimmer, of the State of their Affairs, by whom he signified his Directions to them to keep a good look out on their Walls, and

A. D. 1420.

The Genoese *help those of* Corsica *against the* King *of* Arragon.

and to be very vigilant, that so they might prevent a Surprize, which the Enemy would probably now attempt; and when they should observe he was attacking the Boom and Ships, to sally out with a Body of stout Fellows, each with an Ax in his Hand, and cut the Cables by which the Ships were held. The first Ship that began the Attack was one of considerable Force, commanded by *James Benicia*, which going afore the Wind with a brisk Gale, forced her way through the Boom, and opened a Passage to the Enemy's five Ships. Being immediately followed by others, there began a warm Dispute, which was maintained for a long time with considerable Loss on both sides. At length a skilful Diver, armed with a Helmet on his Head, and a Scymitar hung to his Side, threw himself into the Sea, and swimming under-Water to the Enemy's Ships, cut their Cables; which being thus loosed soon fell foul of one another with great Destruction. The Harbour being thus opened, *Fregose* put into the Town his Reinforcement for the Garrison, with a Supply of Provisions, and passing through the midst of the Enemy's Fleet, which waited for him off the Harbour's Mouth, returned safely to *Genoa*.

And breaking the Boom in Bonifacio Harbour.

They relieve Corsica.

Now fresh Disturbances arising in the City, several who had been busie in sowing Sedition, were sentenced to Banishment, who repairing to *Philip* Duke of *Milan*, so effectually pleaded their Cause with him, that he resolved to attack the Republick, and for that purpose hired eight Gallies of the *Arragonese*, which he added to a number of his own, to attempt them by Sea. This Fleet he put under the Command of *Raymond Corvariani*, who, in the Mouth of the *Arno*, engaged the *Genoese* Fleet, and with such Success that he took five Gallies, together with *Baptist Fulgose*, the Admiral who commanded them; upon the News of which Defeat the City submitted it self to *Philip*. Under his Government their Affairs very much declined, the *Turks* taking from them all that they possessed in the *Black* Sea, and infested them with a Squadron of Gallies even in their very Port, where the Infidels landed, and carried off a great Booty. *Philip* being engaged in a War with *Alphonsus* King of *Arragon* (who was also King of both *Sicilies*, to wit, the Island of that Name and the Kingdom of *Naples*) he sent out *Biugio Assereto* at the Head of the *Genoese* Fleet, who entirely defeated the Enemy off *Gaeta*, and took *Alphonsus* himself Prisoner, together with several other Persons of great Quality.

The Duke of Milan resolves to attack them.

He beats them at Sea, and they submit to him.

The Turks do much Mischief to them.

They beat the Fleet of Arragon.

Soon after this, the *Genoese*, upon occasion of the Duke of *Milan*'s ill Treatment of them, resolved to throw off his Yoke, and, under the Conduct of *Francis Spinola*, executed their Design, driving all the *Milanese* out of the City, and killing *Opizini Alzate*, the Person whom the Duke had made their Governour. Then settling the Administration of the Government in the Hands of six Officers, with the Title of Defenders of the publick Liberty, (in opposition to *Philip* and *Alphonsus*, who were now reconciled) they espoused the Cause of *René* Duke of *Anjou*, *Alphonsus*'s Competitor for the Crown of *Naples*, and, notwithstanding all the Efforts of their Enemies, established him in that Kingdom.

Shake off the Duke of Milan, and settle their Government on six.

They establish René Duke of Anjou in Naples.

Not

CHAP. VII. *Ruin of the* Rom. *Empire.*

Not long after happened another Change of Government among them, and *Raphael Adorni* was made Doge, who was succeeded by several others in that Dignity, 'till at length the Republick came again into the Hands of the Dukes of *Milan*; and under *Lewis Sforza*, one of those Princes, they became engaged in a War with *Charles* VIII. the *French* King. The *Genoese* Fleet was commanded by *Spinola*, and that of the *French* by *Miolani*, who fought before *Rapallo*, when the latter received a total Defeat, *Miolani* being taken Prisoner, with all the rest of the Officers and Seamen who were not slain in the Fight; and the Recovery of *Rapallo*, then held by the Enemy, was the Reward of the Victory. But *Francis* I. in 1515, revenged this Disgrace, and outed *Maximilian Sforza* of his Dominions; so that not only the Dutchy of *Milan*, but the State of *Genoa*, came into the Hands of the *French*, who administer'd the Government of the latter by *Octavian Fulgose*.

The Government of the Doge re-established, but soon after they submit to the Duke of Milan.

The French Fleet beaten by that of Genoa.

A. D. 1515. *The French make themselves Masters of Milan and Genoa.*

In his time the Seas about *Genoa* were mightily infested by the Depredations of *Cortologi*, a Pirate of *Barbary*, in quest of whom a Squadron was detached under the Command of *Frederick Fulgose*, the Brother of the Governour; who sailing over to *Barbary*, where they little expected such a Guest, enter'd the Port of *Biserta*, and surprized fifteen Gallies and seven *Saetia*'s lying there, with a great Number of Christian Slaves on board, all which he safely brought off with him, after having first fired the Suburbs of the Town. The *Genoese* did not long continue in Subjection to the *French*, the Emperor *Charles* V. laying siege to the City and reducing it to his Obedience; from whom nevertheless the *French* soon after re-took it, and their Faction, under the Command of *Philip Doria*, defeated, in an Engagement at Sea, the Emperor's Fleet commanded by *Hugh de Moncada*. That Officer was slain in the Fight, and several Persons of Quality remained Prisoners to the *Genoese* only two Gallies of the Enemy's whole Fleet making their Escape. The Prisoners were sent to *Andrew Doria* then the *French* King's Admiral in the Mediterranean, who soon after quitting the *French* Interest, and entering into the Emperor's Service, obtained of him, as a Reward for his Defection, (which was attended with that of *Genoa*) the Power of restoring his Country to its Liberty, at which time he settled the Government of it in the manner it continues at this time.

The Genoese take several Barbary Pirates.

Genoa reduced by the Emperor, but recovered by the French, and the Emperor's Fleet is beaten.

A. D. 1528. *Doria quits the French and serves the Emperor.*

Under the Conduct of this *Doria*, who was at the same time at the Head of the Emperor's Fleet, they took *Coron* in the *Morea* from the *Turks*, and burnt several of the Enemy's Ships there, but *Doria* put a *Spanish* Garrison into the Place. The next Year he repaired again to the Relief of *Coron*, being then besieged by *Lasi Bey*, *Sangiac* of *Gallipoli*: And though his Fleet consisted of no more than thirty Ships, and twenty seven Gallies, a Force very much inferior to the Enemy's, yet he relieved the Town with a great Supply of Men and Provisions, which obliged the *Turks* to raise the siege. But in his return home three *Genoese* Gallies commanded by *Adorni*, parting Company with the rest of the Fleet, were taken on the Coast of *Calabria* by *Sinan Pasha*.

1532 *He burns several Turkish Ships and takes Coron.*

In

K k

1535
He goes with the Emperor to Africa, *who restores Muley Hassan in* Tunis.
A. D. 1537.
Barbarussa *makes* Doria *retreat.*

In 1535, *Doria* accompanied the Emperor to *Africa*, where that Prince having reduced the Castle of *Goletta*, with the Cities of *Tunis* and *Bona*, re-established *Muley Hassan* in the Kingdom of *Tunis*, who had been dispossessed of it by *Haradin Barbarussa*, the famous Pirate. In 1537, *Doria* defeated a Squadron of twelve *Turkish* Gallies off *Corfu*, and the following Year he gave Battel to the forementioned *Barbarussa*, then Admiral of the *Turkish* Fleet near the Island of St. *Maure*; but Fortune was not so favourable to him in this Engagement as she was wont; however he did not shew less Courage or Conduct in the Retreat he made, than in his former Victories; and toward the End of the Campaign found means to reduce *Castel Nuovo* in *Dalmatia*. The same Year *Barbarussa* came with his Fleet before the Port of *Genoa*, and sent in to demand of the Senate the Person of *Hameth Reys Saleth*, a Son of *Sinan Pasha's*, who had been taken Prisoner, which was at first refused him, but in revenge he so ravaged the Coasts of the Republick, that they were at length forced to comply with his Demand.

Barbarussa *obliges the* Genoese *to deliver a Son of* SinanPasha's.

A. D. 1553.

In 1553, the *French* having possessed themselves of the Island of *Corsica*, *Doria* went against them with a Fleet, having on board a Body of seven thousand Land Men, where he so effectually dealt with the Enemy, that he soon recovered the greatest Part of the Island, and at length forced the *French* entirely to abandon it. This great Man, during his Life-time, kept the Republick in a peaceable Condition at home, but after his Death, which happened in 1560, the State was miserably rent with Divisions between the ancient and new Nobles, which at length, in the Year 1575, were composed by the Mediation of the Pope.

Doria *forces the* French *to abandon* Corsica.
A. D. 1560.
Genoa *distressed by Factions.*
A. D. 1575.

A. D. 1624.

Their History affords not any thing material from that time 'till the Year 1624, when, being under the Protection of *Spain*, they became engaged in a War with the *French* King and the Duke of *Savoy*, then at War with that Crown about the *Valtoline*: But they concluding a Peace two Years after, the *Genoese* were of course included therein; but not long after they were embroiled with the *Spaniards*, and in 1636, the Duke of *Ferandina*, Admiral of the *Neapolitan* Gallies, came before *Genoa* with a Design of surprizing it, to facilitate the Execution whereof a Body of Troops was marched from out of the *Milanese* to *Novi*; but the Senate having Intelligence of the intended Project, refused him Entrance into the Port, and putting themselves into a Posture of Defence, frustrated the Design.

The Neapolitan *Admiral endeavours to surprize* Genoa.

A. D. 1645.
The Pope presses the Genoese, *with others to relieve* Candia.

The *Turks* in 1645, attacking the Island of *Candia* with a vast Fleet and Army, the then Pope *Innocent* X. was very pressing with all the Princes of *Italy* to join with the *Venetians* against the common Enemy; and particularly he sollicited the *Genoese* to send their Gallies to their Assistance; but the Republick resolved, e'er they embarked in that Business, to get terminated in their Favour the Difference they had long had about Salutes with the Gallies of the Great Duke of *Tuscany*, and those of *Malta*. Upon their making that Demand, the Pope proposed that, to avoid Disputes, there should be no other Flag than his own, under which all the maritime Forces

of

CHAP. VII. *Ruin of the* Rom. *Empire.*

of other Princes or States of *Italy* might fight, as Auxiliaries or Volunteers, without drawing any thing into Precedent as to Posts or Salutes. This Expedient the *Genoese* did not approve of, and resolving to take Advantage of the great Want there was of their Assistance, they not only demanded the Preference in this matter of the Gallies of the great Duke, who equall'd them in Power, and was superior to them in Dignity, and of those of the *Maltese*, who had on their Side long Prescription, and a Declaration of *Charles* V, but they went so far as to require that their Ministers at *Rome* should be treated with the same Honours as the Ambassadors of Crowned Heads. It not being possible to grant them these Privileges, without disobliging all the rest of *Italy*, the Pope declined any farther Sollicitations with them, and made a vigorous Effort to send the *Venetians* himself the Assistance that was wanted.

High Demands of the Genoese, which the Pope refuses.

In 1656 the Republick was much afflicted with the Plague, and at the same time the *Corsaires* of *Barbary*, with a great Force, scoured the adjacent Seas, and interrupted all Commerce; whereupon a Fleet was fitted out against the Infidels, under the Command of *Hippolytus Centurioni*, who falling in with the Enemy's Fleet, consisting of forty Gallies, (a Number greatly superior to his own,) defended himself with signal Valour against them, and, after an obstinate Dispute, got clear of them, without the Loss of one Ship, or any other Damage, save the Misfortune of having one of his Hands shot off by a Cannon Ball in the Heat of the Engagement; and in *September*, the same Year, he went over to the Coast of *Barbary*, where, off of *Algier*, he took several Ships of the Enemy's. In 1658, the *Rovers* of *Barbary* took a *Genoese* Gally called the St. *Bernard*; but attacking the *Diamond*, a very rich Ship, bound home from *Lisbon*, her Captain, finding himself not able to defend her against so great odds as three of the Enemy's Ships, resolved to blow her up, and laying Match to the Powder, jumped into his Long boat, where he had the Satisfaction of seeing his Enemies thrown up in the Air, with the Fragments of his Ship, as soon as ever they had boarded her.

A. D. 1656. *Genoa is afflicted with the Plague.*

The Genoese go against the Rovers of Barbary.

A. D. 1658.

The Master of a Genoese Ship blows her up.

The Republick in 1672 was attacked by the Duke of *Savoy*, with whom the following Year they came to a Peace, which was mediated by the *French* King; since when, the most remarkable Circumstance in their Affairs is the Bombardment of their City in 1684, by the Fleet of that Prince who was their late Mediator, which was occasioned by their Attachment at that time to the Interests of *Spain*, in pursuance whereof they had entered into some secret Negotiations with the Governor of *Milan*, which the *French* King apprehended to be against him. He therefore laid hold of the first Opportunity to quarrel with them, and in 1683, gave Orders to his Envoy at *Genoa*, to signify to the Senate, that if they launched the four new Gallies they had built, he should look upon it as a Declaration of Hostilities, and would issue Orders to his Subjects to seize them, or whatever else belonged to the Republick, wheresoever they should be met with on the Sea. Upon this Declaration of the *French* Envoy's,

A. D. 1672. *The Genoese are attack'd by the Duke of Savoy, but Peace made.*

France quarrels with Genoa, and why.

K k 2

voy's, the *Spanish* Resident demanded Audience of the Senate, and assured them of his Master's Protection and Support, who, he said, had already given Directions to the Governor of *Milan*, and the Admiral of his Fleet, to assist them, in case they should be attacked.

The Spaniards *declare War against* France. *A. D.* 1684.

The *Spaniards* declared War with *France* in the beginning of the next Year, when the *Genoese*, having refused all the Demands of the *French* Envoy, and sent to Sea their Gallies, notwithstanding the positive Declaration he had made against it, were well assured the *French* King would not fail to express his Resentments, and therefore sent to demand Succours of the Governor of *Milan*, who marched down several Companies of *Spanish* Foot into their Territories. The *French* Envoy sending Advice of these Proceedings, was immediately recalled, and the King his Master took a Resolution to be revenged of the *Genoese*, to which purpose having provided a sufficient Force at *Toulon*, he sent the Marquis *de Seignelay*, then Secretary of State, down to that Place to take upon him the Command of the Fleet, consisting of fourteen Ships of War, twenty Gallies, ten Bomb-Vessels, two Fireships, eight *Flutes*, and seventeen *Tartanes*, with which he was to proceed to *Genoa*, and procure Satisfaction of the Republick.

The French *send a Fleet with Bomb-Vessels against* Genoa.

Accordingly setting sail, he arrived the seventeenth of *May* before the City, and the same Day the ten Bomb-Vessels, having each of them two Mortars on board, came to an Anchor within Cannon-shot of the Walls, disposing themselves in a Line from the Light-House, on their Left, to the Suburb of *Bisagno*, on the Right, the Ships of War being disposed in another Line astern of the Bomb-Vessels, at the Distance of about a quarter of a Mile; in the two Points of which Line were placed the Gallies in two Divisions. The *Flutes* and *Tartanes*, on board which were the Bombs and Powder for the Mortars, were ranged at a small Distance astern of the Gallies, but so near, as that they could easily supply the Bomb Vessels with what they should have occasion for.

The Appearance of the Fleet in this Posture, soon brought out a Deputation from the Senate to the Marquis *de Seignelay*, to know what was his Master's Pleasure: Who having acquainted them with the Grounds of the *French* King's Resentments, (wherein, amongst other things, he accused them of concerting with the *Spaniards* a Design of burning his Ships and Gallies in the Ports of *Toulon* and *Marseilles*) made his Demands of Satisfaction, and gave them to understand, if they were not complied with, he had Orders to make them sensible of the King his Master's Indignation. The Deputies acquainted him they would make a Report of his Demands to the Senate, and then return him an Answer, which they did the same Evening, by a general Discharge of all their Artillery next the Sea, on the Ships of the Fleet.

The City of Genoa *bombarded by the* French.

Thereupon the Signal was made for the Bombardiers to play on the City, which they did with such Success, that in two Hours time several of the Palaces and publick Buildings were seen to be on fire. The Mortars having continued playing, with great Execution, for three

CHAP. VIII. *Ruin of the* Rom. *Empire.* 253

three Days, in which time they threw in ten thousand Bombs, it was resolved to take Advantage of the Confusion the City was in, and make a Descent, which they did in the Suburb of St. *Pietro d'Arena*, where was a great Number of stately Palaces, which they entirely ruined in revenge to the Nobility, who obstructed the Republick's Submission to the Terms proposed, which the Commonalty would gladly have agreed to. The *French* having performed this, but not without some Loss, retreated to their Boats; and when the Troops were all got on board, the Mortars began to play again, which having thrown in above thirteen hundred Bombs more, the Fleet weighed Anchor, and made sail to the Westward.

At length, by Mediation of the Pope, an Accommodation was brought about between the *French* King and the *Genoese*, who were forced to comply with most of his Demands, and to send their Doge in Person, accompanied with four Senators, to make their Submission at *Versailles*; and since the Affairs of *Genoa* from the Conclusion of this Difference, afford not any thing material to our purpose, we proceed next to the Naval Transactions of the *Portuguese*. *The* Genoese *send their Doge with their Submission to the French.* A. D. 1685.

CHAP. VIII.

Of the Naval Wars of the Portuguese.

PORTUGAL (containing the greatest part of that Country the *Romans* called *Lusitania*) coming, together with the rest of *Spain*, under *Rederick* the last King of the *Goths*, into the Hands of the *Saracens*, or *Moors*, continued for a long time in their Possession. But *Alphonsus* VI, King of *Castile* and *Leon*, about the Year 1093, making great Preparations of War against that People, procured Aid from several Nations of Christendom, and amongst others who came to his Assistance was *Henry* of *Besançon*, a *Burgundian*, who performed such considerable Services against the Infidels, that King *Alphonsus* gave him a natural Daughter of his in Marriage, with so much of *Portugal* as was then in the Hands of the Christians for her Dowry, which he erected into a County upon that Occasion. A. D. 1093. *The* Portuguese *War against the* Saracens.

This Count was succeeded by his Son *Alphonsus Henry*, who aspiring at a greater Title, easily paved his way to it by his signal Valour and Successes against the *Moors*, from whom he recovered several Provinces, and having greatly increased his Dominions, was the first who assumed the Style of King of *Portugal*. Amongst the many Places he took from the *Moors*, were *Lisbon*, (now the Capital of the Kingdom) *Atmada*, and *Villamuerda*, in the Reduction whereof he was assisted by a Fleet of *English*, *French*, and *Dutch*, who put into one of his Ports in their way to *Syria*, then the Seat of the Holy War. *Sancho*, the Son and Successor of *Alphonsus*, imitating the Example of his Father, hospitably received into his Lisbon *and other Places taken from the* Moors.

Port

Port of *Lisbon* another Fleet of *English* and *French* Ships, which were going on the like Service as the former; and by their Aid, together with eight Ships of *Philip* Count of *Flanders*, he reduced *Lagos* and *Silves* in the *Algarve*; and on the Conclusion of these Expeditions, he employed his Time in building, adorning, or fortifying several of those which are now the most considerable Cities of the Kingdom, from whence he had the Surname of the Builder.

The Portuguese assisted by the English and French

After that Prince's Reign, *Portugal* for a long time kept itself disengaged from any Wars of Consequence, except those with the *Moors*, with whom they had several fierce Disputes, and in 1409, their King, *John* I, took from them the Town of *Ceuta* in *Barbary*. The following Year his Son *Henry*, Infante of *Portugal*, discovered the Islands of *Madera*; and in these Times it was that the *Portuguese*, first among the Moderns, sailed round *Africa* to the *East Indies*. For after *Alphonsus* V, who succeeded to the Crown in 1438, had taken *Tangier*, *Arzille*, and *Alcazar*, the *Portuguese* Power grew so formidable in *Africk*, that all the Coasts of that part of the World as far as *Æthiopia*, fell almost at once under their Obedience; and under *John* II, *Æthiopia* itself was discovered, even to the extremest parts of it, which the Ancients thought inaccessible, and uninhabited. Then were the Stars about the South-Pole first seen by *Europeans*, and that great Promontory of *Africa* discovered, which stretches itself beyond the Tropick of *Capricorn*: to which was then given the Name of the *Tempestuous* Cape, because of the Storms and bad Weather the Discoverers met with thereabouts; but the same *John* II. afterwards named it the Cape of *Good-Hope*, because when that was once gained, the way was supposed to lie open to the *Indies*.

A. D. 1409.
Ceuta, in Barbary, taken from the Moors; as also Tangier, and other Places.
A. D. 1438.
The Portuguese powerful in Africk.

The Cape of Good-Hope discovered.

That Prince, a little before his Death, adopting *Emanuel* for his Son and Successor, put at the same time a Globe into his Hands, as it were denoting that he gave him Possession of the Earth; nor did the Omen prove unsuccessful, for in *Emanuel*'s Reign, not only all the East was discovered, but the Sea-Coasts of *India* were for the most part subdued to the Obedience of *Portugal*. Under the Auspices of this Prince, *Vasquez de Gama* was the first of the *Portuguese* who doubled the Cape of *Good-Hope*, which having passed, he called the Country on the Eastward of it St. *Raphael*, now better known by the Name of the Coast of *Caffres*. He there heard the good Tidings that there lay an easy Way from that Place to *India*, whence Spices might be fetched at a very cheap rate, whereupon he named one of the Rivers in the Country *Rio de Bueña Señas*, and erected on the Banks of it a Stone Cross with the Arms of *Portugal*. *Gama* proceeding thence, passed by *Sofala*, remarkable for its great Plenty of Gold, and advancing to *Mozambique*, went on to *Monbaze* and *Melinde*, from whence it was but a short Cut over to *Malabar*, the so much desired Region of Spices. Thither the *Portuguese* steering the Course, were not content with the Advantage of Traffick, but desirous of having the Country under their Obedience, which necessarily occasioned a War with the Inhabitants, to whom finding themselves inferior in Strength, they thought fit

A. D. 1497.
The Indian Sea-Coast subdued by the Portuguese.

New Discoveries made.

The Portuguese baffled by those of Malabar.

to

CHAP. VIII. *Ruin of the* Rom. *Empire.* 255

to make the best of their way back to *Portugal*. In their Return, passing by the Gulph of *Persia* and the *Red Sea*, (from entring which they were only prevented by fear) they came down to *Magadoxo*, on the Coast of *Ajan*, where finding a Fleet of *Arabian* Vessels in the Port, they set fire to them, and passing by *Melinda*, the Island *Zanzibar*, *Quiloa*, and *Mozambique*, they again doubled the Cape of *Good Hope*, and proceeded homewards, sailing between the Continent of *Africk*, and the Cape *Verde*, *Canaries*, and *Madera* Islands, in the same Route as *Cadamustus* had before taken. *They burn several Arabian Ships.*

This *Cadamustus* having navigated to *Madera*, the *Canaries*, the Isle of *Argin*, *Senega*, Cape *Verde*, *Gambra*, the Islands of *Bonavista*, St. *Jago*, and *Palma*, and made Discoveries as far as Cape *Roxo*, giving to the respective Places such Names as he thought fit, had returned to *Lisbon* in the Year 1455, where communicating to *Peter Sinzia* an Account of his Voyage, and the Observations he had made therein, it inspired him with a Desire of penetrating farther. *Sinzia* being furnished with two Ships for that purpose by the foremention'd Prince *Henry*, (the Son of *John* I.) discovered as far as Cape *Palmas*. *Other Discoveries.*

A. D. 1455.

He was succeeded in these Undertakings by the aforesaid *Gama*; and he by *Peter Alvarez Capral*, to whose Conduct was committed a Squadron of thirteen Ships for another Expedition to *Malabar*. In his way thither he was driven by Tempests on the Coast of *Brasil*, (before that time unknown) of which he took Possession in his Master's Name, and raised a Pillar with the Arms of *Portugal* thereon: Which done, he pursued his Voyage, and touching at *Quiloa*, proceeded thence to *Calecut*, where engaging some of the *Malabarians* at Sea with good Success, he struck up a League with the Kings of *Cochin* and *Cananor*, and returned to *Portugal*. Then *Gama* was again thought fit to be sent out in quest of new Lands, or to subdue those already discovered, and a Squadron of ten Sail was put under his Command, with which arriving at the Port of *Mozambique*, he there ran up a Carvel, (which sort of Ship he thought would be particularly useful to him when he should arrive in *India*) and thence proceeded to *Quiloa*, where having imposed a Tribute on the King of the neighbouring Country, he crossed over to *Malabar*, and declared War against the King of *Calecut*, took the People of *Cranganor* into the Protection of *Portugal*, renewed the Treaties with the Kings of *Cochin* and *Cananor*, and taking in a rich Lading of Spices, made the best of his way home. *Brasil accidentally discovered.*

The Portuguese declare War against the King of Calecut

About the time of his Return, the Kingdom of *Congo* (which was discovered by *James Canuso* in 1484) was supplied with a new Colony from *Portugal:* Mean while, the King of *Calecut*, taking Advantage of the Absence of the *Portuguese*, attacked *Trimumpara*, King of *Cochin*, their Ally, and dispossessed him of his Kingdom; the News whereof coming to *Francis Albuquerque*, one of the *Portuguese* Admirals, then in the East, he made the best of his way to that Country, where he left his Ships under the Command of *Edward Pacheco*, and went ashore with a Body of Troops, with whom *The King of Calecut dispossesses the King of Cochin.*

whom he forced the People of *Calecut* to retire out of the Territories of *Cochin*. The King being restored to his Dominions, gave Permission to *Albuquerque* to build a Fort, for defending the Country against the Incursions of the Enemy, of which he immediately laid the Foundation, and finished it with extraordinary Expedition, for fear the King should repent him of his Grant: mean while *Anthony Saldanha*, who had set out from *Portugal* soon after *Albuquerque*, arrived at the Island *Zocotora*, near the Entrance of the Red Sea, where he spent the Winter, and cruized against the trading Ships of the Infidels in those Parts. He also attacked *Zanzibar*, and imposed an annual Tribute on the King of the Island; and soon after destroying the King of *Monbaze*'s Fleet in the Port of that Name, he proceeded to *Brava* on the same Coast, and reduced it to the Obedience of *Portugal*. *Pacheco*, who continued at *Malabar*, was kept there well employed against the People of *Calecut*, who attacked him with a great Number of Ships, but they fought with ill Success, tho' of infinitely superior Force, against so expert a Seaman, for he gave them an entire Defeat; and having established the Kingdom of *Cochin* in Peace, received as a Reward for his good Services one of the richest Governments in *Africa*.

He was succeeded by *Lovanius Suarez*, whose most remarkable Act was the burning of the City of *Cranganor*; about which time *Francis de Almeyda* was sent out by King *Emanuel* with a Commission to be Viceroy of the East, (being the first who had that Character) who arriving with his Fleet in the Port of *Quiloa*, subdued the King of the neighbouring Country, and appointed another, named *Mahomet*, in his room. He thence proceeded to *Monbaze*, and destroying that Town, went on to *Melinda*, from whence he made the best of his way to *Malabar*, where, in the Kingdom of *Cananor*, he erected a Fort to keep the fickle Inhabitants to their Duty; when entring into an Alliance with the King of *Narsinga*, he appointed *Nambeadara* King of *Cochin* in the room of *Trimumpara*, who voluntarily resigned the Government

About this time another Squadron of eight Ships was sent out to seek for new Lands, by which was discovered the Island of *Madagascar*, otherwise called St. *Laurence*, because it was first seen on the Day dedicated by the Church of *Rome* to that Saint. *Almeyda* also detached a Squadron under his Son *Laurence de Almeyda* on the same Service, who first repaired to the *Maldives* Islands, from whence he was driven by a violent Tempest to the Isle of *Ceylon*, (by most thought the *Taprobana* of the Ancients) where landing, he took the Inhabitants into the Protection of *Portugal*, and imposed a Tribute on their King; nor was the Viceroy in the mean time less employed, but defeated the *Calecutians* in a great Battel at Sea. Then dividing his victorious Fleet, he committed one part of it to *Emanuel Pazagno*, and the other to his Son, upon his Return from *Ceylon*, appointing the first to accompany the trading Ships of *Cochin* to Cape *Comorin*, for their Security against the Rovers in those Seas, and the other to cruise at large about the Coasts, for

CHAP. VIII. *Ruin of the* Rom. *Empire.* 257

for the Defence of the Islands and Ports. It became now an established Rule among these new Inhabitants of the *Indies*, that whosoever came into those Parts without a Pass from some *Portuguese* Admiral, or Governor of a Fort, should be esteemed as Enemies, and lose both Ships and Goods; whereby they engross'd all the Wealth of the East to themselves; and, the better to maintain their Authority, King *Emanuel* sent out yearly new Reinforcements and Supplies.

None permitted to come in to the Indies, *without a* Portuguese *Pass.*

In the Year 1508, fifteen Ships were fitted out under the Command of *Tristan de Cunha*, with which repairing to the Coast of *Zanguebar*, he assisted the King of *Melinda* against his rebellious Subjects, and burning the Cities of *Hoia* and *Brava*, failed to *Zocotora*, where reducing the chief Town of the Island, he left a Garrison in it, and made the best of his way to *Malabar*, where joining the Fleet of *Almeyda*, they repaired against the People of *Calecut*, who were now assisted by a Fleet from *Arabia*, and before *Panana*, one of their Towns, gave them a signal Defeat. Not long after they engaged, off of *Chaul*, near *Bombay*, the Fleet of *Campson*, Sultan of *Ægypt*, coming to the Assistance of the Enemy, which they entirely ruined, and every where came off Conquerors, excepting that the forementioned Son of *Almeyda*, falling in with a Squadron of *Cambayan* and *Ægyptian* Ships was unfortunately slain with an Arrow, as he bravely defended himself against them.

A. D. 1508.

The Portuguese assist the King of Melinda.

They beat the Calecut *and* Arabian *Fleets.*

They ruin the Fleet of the Sultan of Ægypt.

Alphonsus Albuquerque was now arrived in the East with a strong Squadron from *Portugal*, with which designing to subdue the Isle of *Ormus*, at the Mouth of the *Persian* Gulph, he first reduced the Cities of *Curiate*, *Mascate*, *Sohar*, and *Orfacan*, lying along the Coasts of *Arabia*, then subject to the King of *Ormus*: after which defeating the Enemy in an Engagement in the Port of that City, he landed in the Island, and prepared to invest the Place; when the King (called *Zerfadin* II.) gave leave that the *Portuguese* should build a Fort on the Sea-Coast, and engaged not only to pay them an annual Tribute, but to defray the Charges of the War. The Time of *Almeyda*'s Viceroyship being now near at an end, he resolved to revenge the Death of his Son, and going out with a Squadron of nineteen Sail, attack'd off *Diu*, a great Fleet of *Cambayans*, *Ægyptians*, *Calecutians*, and other of the Enemies of the *Portuguese*, by whose Hands his Son fell, and entirely routing them, with great Slaughter, subdued all the Coast from *Diu* to *Cochin*, forcing the several Princes to yield themselves tributary to *Portugal*. His Commission being now expired, he delivered the Government, with great Reluctance, to *Albuquerque*, and having passed the Cape of Good Hope, in his way homewards, was, with his Companions, unfortunately slain by some *Barbarians* on the Coast of *Africk*.

The Island of Ormus *made Tributary to* Portugal.

Another Fleet of the Ægyptians, &c. *routed, and several Princes made Tributary to* Portugal.

The first Business the new Viceroy undertook was the Reduction of *Goa*, a flourishing City in an Island of the same Name, of which one *Zabaim* was King; who being become odious to his Subjects for his intolerable Exactions, the People voluntarily surrendered the Place to *Albuquerque*, he promising to remit a third part of their Taxes.

A. D. 1510.

Goa *reduced by the Portuguese.*

L l

Taxes. *Zabaim* was then absent from the Island, but upon the News of its Surrender, embarking, with great Celerity, a numerous Body of Troops, he repaired thither, and landing his Men, presently recovered the Place, but not without a very considerable Slaughter among them by the *Portuguese*. *Albuquerque* having engaged the Enemy's Ships, defeated them, and being reinforced with a new Squadron from *Portugal*, opened his way, Sword in Hand, to the City, and again expelling the Enemy, placed a strong Garrison in the Citadel, and, the better to secure the Place in its Obedience, caused his Soldiers to intermarry with the Women of the Island. Having settled Matters at *Goa*, he set sail with a Fleet of twenty three Ships for *Malacca*, and in his way thither fell in with a large *Indian* Ship which he caused to be attacked; the *Portuguese* had no sooner boarded her, than from all Quarters of the Vessel there burst forth violent Flames, whereupon they precipitately retreated to their Ships, but repented their Haste soon after, when they understood it was only a harmless lambent Flame which gave Light, but did not burn, and could be extinguished at pleasure. Pursuing his Voyage, he arrived soon after in the Port of *Malacca*, and laying siege to the City, took it by Storm, being forced to burn great part of it through the obstinate Resistance of the Inhabitants, the King having first secured himself by flight. An immense Booty was found in this Place, to secure which in its Obedience, *Albuquerque* raised a strong Fortress with the Stones taken from the Sepulchres of the Kings of *Malacca*. Here he applied himself to make farther Discoveries, and to that purpose fitted out several Ships to sail to different Quarters; one of which Squadrons he committed to *Anthony Abrei*, who repairing to *Amboina*, and *Banda*, two of the *Molucca* Islands, returned richly laden with Spices to *Malacca*.

Some new Commotions at *Goa* requiring his Presence, he repaired thither, and having appeased the Disorders, and given Audience to the Ambassadors of the Kings of *Persia* and *Æthiopia*, who now courted the Friendship of the *Portuguese*, he made Preparations for an Expedition to *Arabia*; mean while *Andrade*, whom he left Commander in Chief of *Malacca*, coming to a Rupture with the King of *Java*, engaged his Fleet, many Ships whereof he burnt, and putting the rest to flight, returned victoriously to *Malacca*. *Albuquerque* prosecuting his Designs on *Arabia*, repaired to *Aden* near the Entrance of the Red Sea, to which he laid siege, but was forced to rise from before it. Having soon after erected a Fortress in the Port of *Calecut*, he defeated a great Fleet of the King of *Linga*'s, fortified the Town and Island of *Ormus*, (which he had now entirely master'd) with several Works, and having very much increased the *Portuguese* Power in those Parts, he deceased, and was succeeded in the Government by *Lopez Suarez*. *Albuquerque* is said to have had once a Design of attacking *Mecca* in *Arabia*, in order to make himself Master of *Mahomet*'s Tomb, and disperse those Ashes to which such an impious Adoration is paid; and that the Infidels, for fear of some such Accident, removed the Impostor's Remains higher up in the Country to *Medina*. He is also said, upon

Promise

CHAP. VIII. *Ruin of the* Rom. *Empire.*

Promise of Assistance from the *Abyssines*, to have had another Project, to wit, of cutting a Canal from the *Nile* into the *Red Sea*, as well to hinder the Trade of the *Ægyptians* in the *Indian* Commodities, as to put an end to the Fertility of their Country, by preventing the Overflowing of that River by such a Diversion of its Waters. *and to cut a Canal from the* Nile *into the Red Sea.*

Suarez was no sooner enter'd upon his Administration, but the People of *Aden* sent Ambassadors to him, to let him know they were ready to comply with his Demands, but he took no notice of their Submission; and having a Design on the *Ægyptian* Fleet, which he heard was coming down the *Red Sea*, he, to keep his People employed till their Arrival near the Streights of *Babel-mandel*, attacked *Zeila*, a Town on the Coast of *Africk*, opposite to *Aden*, and gave the Plunder to his Soldiers and Seamen. But *Suarez* too late repented him of his Neglect of the People of *Aden*'s Offers, for the expected Fleet of *Ægyptians* never appeared, and that City changed soon after its Resolution of submitting to *Portugal*. To the Loss of this happy Opportunity succeeded another Misfortune, for *Campson* the Sultan of *Ægypt*, being overcome by the Emperor *Selim*, and his Dominions becoming part of the *Turkish* Empire, the Coasts of *Ægypt* and the *Red Sea* were much better guarded than before, several new Forts being erected there, and supplied with good Garrisons. In the mean time *Andrade*, who commanded in Chief at *Malacca*, made an Expedition for settling Trade to the Coast of *China*, where he was hospitably entertained for some Months; but, growing insolent upon his kind Reception, he committed several Violences, and was forced to quit the Country with the Loss of a great Number of his Followers. Zeila, *opposite to* Aden, *taken by the Portuguese. The Portuguese forced to quit China.*

The *Portuguese* Affairs in *India* were now but in an indifferent State, and the new Forts lately finished in *Ceylon*, and the Kingdom of *Coulan*, were scarce sufficient to keep the Inhabitants in their Duty, so that *Suarez* being looked upon as unequal to so great a Charge as the Government of those Acquisitions, was recalled, and *James Lopez* appointed his Successor. He, on his Arrival in *India*, having quell'd some Insurrections there, and overcome the King of *Bintam*, whom he forced to accept a Peace on his Terms, repaired to *Ormus*, and defeating *Mocri*, King of *Baharem*, an Island in the *Persian* Gulph, reduced it to the Obedience of *Portugal*. *Lopez* was succeeded by *Edward de Meneses*, who restored the King of *Pacem*, in the Island *Sumatra*, to his Dominions, on Condition of his paying a Tribute, and giving leave for the erecting a Fort upon his Coasts. In the first Year of this Viceroy's Administration died *Emanuel* King of *Portugal*, the greatest Prince which ever sate on the Throne of that Kingdom, who having reduced to his Obedience not only the Coasts of all *India*, both within and without the *Ganges*, but of the Gulph of *Persia*, and most of those of the *Red Sea*, and, covering with his Fleets the *Æthiopian* and *Atlantick* Oceans, shut up the Navigation to those Countries from all others, thereby totally excluding the *Venetians* from the Commerce of the East, whose Merchants had ever since the Year 1269, *Their Affairs in* India *in an ill State.* A. D. 1518. *The King of* Bintam, &c. *overcome.* 1521. Emanuel, *King of Portugal, dies. His great Conquests.*

to that time, wholly engrossed that Trade. He also subdued great part of the Coast of *Barbary*, making himself Master of *Asafia*, *Tita*, and *Azamor*, near Cape *Cantin*, and defeated the Forces of the Emperor of *Morocco* in several Rencounters.

John III. succeeds Emanuel.

He was succeeded by his Son *John* III, about which time the Viceroy of *India* appointed *Lewis de Meneses*, with a strong Squadron, to keep the People of *Ormus* in Obedience, and sent *Garcias Henriquez* with another to the Eastward, to make farther Acquisitions; which latter sailed round the Islands *Banda*, *Mira*, and *Gumanapy*, and proceeding thence to *Tidore*, there fell in with one of the Ships which had been sent out under *Magellan*, by the Emperor *Charles* V, to make new Discoveries, which *Henriquez* attacked, and made himself Master of, putting to Death, or making Slaves of all the *Spaniards* on board: This done, he erected a Fort in the neighbouring Island *Ternate*, and strictly enjoined the Inhabitants not to vend their Spices to any other than the *Portuguese*. The next Year *Hector Sylveira* being appointed Admiral of the *Indies*, was joyfully received by the Viceroy of *Goa*, from whence he proceeded to *Malacca*, then besieged by *Laqueximenes*, the King of *Bintam*'s Admiral, and having happily raised the Siege, detached *Alonzo de Souse* to the Coast of *Bintam*, which having ravaged, he gained a great Victory over the Ships of *Pahang*, *Patane*, and *Java*, killing great Numbers of the Enemy, and taking several Prisoners; after which proceeding to *Machian*, and *Bachian*, two of the *Molucca* Islands near *Tidore*, he plundered them, and carried off a great Booty.

A. D. 1522.

The Portuguese take one of the Ships of Magellan's Squadron.

Relieve Malacca, and beat the Fleets of the Pagans.

Some of the Molucca Islands plundered.

The next Year *Vasquez de Gama* was appointed Viceroy of the *Indies*, but as he was in a very advanced Age, it being improbable he should live long, a Commission was made out for *Henry de Meneses* to succeed, in case of his Decease before the three Years of his Viceroyalty should be expired. There was a third Commission to *Peter Mascarenhas*, appointing him Viceroy, if *Meneses* should die; and a fourth to *Lopez de Sampayo*, to succeed in case of the Death of *Mascarenhas*; the *Portuguese* by this means almost securely providing that their Acquisitions in *India* should not remain without a Head. And the Event shew'd the good Effects of their Care; for *Gama* did not long enjoy his new Honour, but having first defeated the People of *Calecut* in an Engagement at Sea, died within few Months after his Arrival at *Goa*, so that the Viceroyalty devolved upon *Henry de Meneses*. The Commission by which he was appointed to succeed was seal'd up, with this Superscription, *Not to be opened till (which God forbid) Vasquez de Gama, Viceroy and High Admiral of the Indies, shall be departed this Life.* This being now opened by the next Commanding Officers, in the Great Church at *Cochin*, *Meneses*, who was then absent from the Place, was proclaimed Viceroy; whose Administration was likewise but of a short Date, and diversifyed with both good and bad Fortune; for after several Engagements with the *Calecutians*, with various Success, he defeated their Fleet in the Port of *Culeta*, and made himself Master of most of their Ships; soon after which he destroyed

Those of Calecut defeated at Sea.

CHAP. VIII. *Ruin of the* Rom. *Empire.* 261

destroyed a Fleet of *Turkish* Ships off *Dabul*, another of *Moors* off *Zeila*, worsted that of the Prince of *Patane*, and *Laqueximenes*, the Admiral of *Bintam*, and then advancing to relieve the *Portuguese*, besieged by the Enemy in the Fortress of *Calecut*, he performed the same, but died of a Wound he had received in his Leg by an Arrow. *Ships of the Turks and Moors destroyed by the Portuguese. A. D. 1526.*

Mascarenhas, the next succeeding Officer, being then at *Malacca*, *Lopez de Sampayo*, the fourth substituted Viceroy, took upon himself that Charge, and gave the *Malaburians* a signal Defeat in an Engagement at the Mouth of the *Bacanor*: But *Mascarenhas* highly resenting it that *Sampayo* should usurp the Viceroyalty out of his Turn, would by no means acquiesce with that Proceeding, but assumed to himself the Title and Office of Viceroy, and being forced to wait the proper Season for coming down to *Goa*, took that Opportunity to repair with a Fleet of nineteen Sail to the Coast of *Bintam*, where he defeated *Laqueximenes* the Enemy's Admiral, together with the Fleet of *Pahang*, which came to their Assistance, and when taking the City of *Bintam* by Storm, he burnt it; and the King dying with Grief at his ill Success, *Mascarenhas* appointed another in his room, on condition that he should maintain no Army nor Fleet without leave from the *Portuguese*, but commit himself wholly to their Protection. This done, he went down with his Fleet to *Goa*, where he desired a Number of Arbitrators might be appointed to judge whether he or *Sampayo* was the proper Viceroy, but the latter at first refused to submit to any Arbitration, till at length he was prevailed upon by the Entreaties of his Friends to do it, but bribed the Judges so high that they declaring him Viceroy, *Mascarenhas* returned to *Portugal*. *The Fleet of Malabar defeated. The Fleet of the Pagans beaten, and Bintam burnt.*

The *Portuguese* Affairs were also now much prejudiced by another Contention; for they having, without any just Provocation, destroyed the chief Town of *Tidore*, it caused among the People of that Island, and of most of the rest of the *Molucca*'s, an implacable Hatred against them; soon after which a Squadron of the Emperor *Charles* V. arriving there, was welcomed by the People of *Tidore* with all the Marks of Kindness, on account of the *Spaniards* equal Enmity with them to the *Portuguese*, and being received into their Port, they raised Works for the Defence of it, in case of an Attack from the Enemy. The *Spaniards*, who were under the Command of *Ignigueza*, alledged that the *Molucca*'s belonged of right to them, as being first discovered by *Magellan*, with a Commission from the King of *Spain*, and that the Dispute having been submitted to Arbitration, was determined in their Favour. On the other hand, the *Portuguese*, under the Command of *Henriquez*, said that the unjust Sentence of the *Castilian* Arbitrators had been reversed by the Judges in *Portugal*, and that those Islands were discovered ten years before the Voyage of *Magellan* in the *Spanish* Service, by *Anthony Abrei*, who was sent out to make Discoveries by *Alphonsus Albuquerque*, in whose Company was *Magellan* himself before he had deserted his Country. Thus they disputed with Words for a while, but soon after came to Blows, the People of *Ternate* *A Dispute between the Emperor and Portuguese about the Moluccas.*

Ternate taking part with the *Portuguese*, and those of *Tidore* and *Gilolo* with the *Spaniards*. The latter struck the first Stroke by besieging the *Portuguese* Fortress in *Ternate*, where, at the first Attack, they took one of the Enemy's Ships. And now the *Spaniards* and *Portuguese* had gone near to have atoned for the Mischiefs they had done to the *Indians*, by the Destruction of each other, but that the Emperor being engaged in other Wars in *Europe*, neglected so remote an Acquisition, and for a certain Sum of Money yielded up all his Right in the *Molucca*'s to the King of *Portugal*.

The Emperor yields the Moluccas to the Portuguese. A. D. 1528.

Matters being settled in those Islands, the Viceroy, *Sampayo*, sent out *John Deza* with a Squadron to cruise off *Cananor*; and at the same time dispatched *Alphonsus Melia* to the *Sunda* Islands, who, just as he was turned the Cape of *Comorin*, met with some Deputies coming to *Goa* from the Prince of *Calecura* on the Pearl-fishing Coast, with Offers of Tribute and Submission, upon Promise of Assistance against his Enemies the *Calecutians*. In the mean time *Deza*, upon his Station, intercepted all Ships passing between *Calecut* and *Cambaya*, to the incredible Loss of the People of both those Places; and landing at *Mangalor*, the Inhabitants deserted the Town, which he plundered and set on fire; after which falling in with *Cutial*, the Admiral of *Calecut*, he engaged and defeated him, and carried him Prisoner to *Cananor*; and about the same time *Anthony Miranda* sailing to the Red Sea, took great Numbers of the *Arabian* Ships, and burnt several along the Shore. *Sampayo* himself, off *Cananor*, destroyed the greatest Part of a Fleet of a hundred and thirty Sail of *Moorish* Ships, bound to *Mecca* with Spices; and then repairing to *Porca*, (the Prince whereof was a formidable Sea-Rover) he landed there, and took the Town, forcing the Prince to betake himself to Flight, who left such a vast Booty to the *Portuguese*, that the Share of the meanest Sailor came to a thousand Dollars. From thence he sailed to the Northward, and, near the Island of *Bombay*, fell in with a Fleet of the Enemy's under the Command of *Halissa*, Admiral of *Cambaya*, whereupon proffering a Reward of a hundred Dollars to the first Man who boarded one of the Enemy's Ships, he immediately engaged, and having entirely routed them, committed the Fleet to the Command of *Miranda*, who, soon after the Viceroy's Departure, came to another Engagement with the *Malabarians*, before the Town of *Chaul*, and gave them a signal Defeat, killing great Numbers, and carrying off a rich Booty of Spices to *Cochin*: Soon after which the *Portuguese* reduced the Town of *Tanor*, made the Prince of the Neighbouring Country their Tributary, and again routed *Halissa*, the *Cambayan* Admiral.

The Portuguese are successfull, and particularly on the Red-Sea.

The Portuguese take Porca.

The Infidels beaten near the Island of Bombay.

Those of Malabar beaten at Sea.

In the mean time *Nunho de Cunha* set out from *Portugal*, with a Commission to be Governor, accompanied by his Brother *Simon de Cunha*, who was constituted Admiral of the *Indies*, and, in his way thither, attempting to put in at *Monbaze*, in order to pass the Winter Season there, was refused Entrance by the King, but forced a Passage into the Port, and making himself Master of the Town, gave the Plunder to the Mariners, and set it on fire. Departing thence early

The Portuguese plunder Monbaze.

early in the Spring, he made the best of his way to *India*, where he resolved to make himself Master of the Town and Fortress of *Diu*, situate in an Island of the same Name, near the Entrance of the Gulph of *Cambaya*; to which purpose repairing thither with the Fleet, upon his Appearance off the Place, he received an Envoy from *Badur*, King of *Cambaya*, with Offers of yielding the Fortress into his Hands; which being accordingly performed, it was committed to the Custody of *Anthony Sylveira*, Not long after the King of *Cambaya*, at the Instigation of the *Turks*, who were very desirous of getting *Diu* into their Hands, made an Attempt to dispossess the *Portuguese*, and recover the Place, but with an unfortunate Event, he, with his *Turkish* Auxiliaries, being entirely routed, most of his Fleet sunk, and himself receiving his Death's Wound in the Engagement. Soon after this, *Solyman*, the *Turkish* Emperor, sent the *Pasha* of *Cairo* to besiege it, with a Fleet of sixty two Gallies, six Galleons, and other smaller Vessels, having on board four thousand Janizaries, sixteen thousand other Soldiers, besides Gunners, Seamen, and Pilots, which on their Arrival before the Town, were joined by eighty Sail of Ships of *Cambaya*. The *Turkish* Pasha, landing his Forces, batter'd the Fortress with fifty Pieces of Cannon, but the Governor, with great Bravery sustained his Attacks 'till the Arrival of *Garcias de Noronha* (the new Viceroy) from *Goa* to his Assistance; who, by a Stratagem, passing thro' the midst of the Enemy's Fleet with Drums beating and Trumpets sounding, as if they had been some of their *Indian* Allies, the *Turks*, upon the Discovery of their Mistake, raised the Siege in the utmost Confusion, leaving behind them their Tents, Ammunition, Artillery, and above a thousand wounded Men, besides the like Number that were out on foraging, all which fell into the Hands of the *Portuguese*. After the Death of *Badur* beforementioned, *Mamud* became King of the *Cambayans*, and *John de Castro* succeeded *Noronha* as the *Portuguese* Viceroy, in whose time the *Cambayans* and *Turks* made another Attempt on *Diu*, but with the like ill Success as before, *De Castro* entirely routing them both by Sea and Land, with a very great Slaughter; after which he added several Works to the Place, and raised a new Citadel in a more advantageous Situation, and of much better materials than the former.

Diu surrendered to the Portuguese.

The Turks, and King of Cambaya routed by the Portuguese at Diu.

The Turks attempt Diu again, but were forced to raise the Siege.

In this prosperous Manner did the *Portuguese* carry all before them in *India* during the Reign of *John* III, who deceasing in 1557, was succeeded by *Sebastian*, then an Infant. That Prince, growing up, was so intent on his *Indian* Acquisitions, that he resolved on a Voyage thither himself, and 'twas with difficulty his Council found means to dissuade him from it. They did at length prevail in that point, but could not prevent his undertaking a Design more hazardous than the former, to wit, an Expedition against the Emperor of *Morocco*, and he embarking for that purpose with a great Army, and the Flower of the *Portuguese* Nobility, on board a numerous Fleet, landed at *Tangier*, and unadvisedly marching up into the Country, gave the *Moors* Battel near *Alcaçer*, where he was cut off with his whole Army. He was succeeded by *Henry* his Uncle,

The Success of the Portuguese in India.

The Portuguese routed near Alcaçer.

<small>1578
1580</small>

Uncle, then in an advanced Age, whose Reign is remarkable for nothing but the Disputes about a Successor to him. He dying in 1580, *Philip* II, King of *Spain*, who had Pretensions to the Crown, thought it most expedient to end all Disputes by the Point of the Sword, and understanding the great Inclination the *Portuguese* had (through hatred of a *Castilian* Government) to set *Anthony*, a natural Son of *John* III, upon the Throne, he ordered the Duke of *Alva* to march at the Head of a powerful Army into the Kingdom, who soon reduced it to his Obedience, forcing *Anthony* to withdraw to *England*, from whence, after some unsuccessful Attempts to recover his lost Dominion, he retired to *Paris*, and died there in 1595. The rest of the Territories of that Crown fell at the same time into the Hands of the Conqueror, except the *Azores*, or Western Islands, which were at length subdued to *Spain* by a great Victory obtain'd over a Fleet of *French* Ships, sent thither to maintain them in the Obedience of *Anthony*.

<small>Portugal reduced by Philip II. of Spain.</small>

As this Subjection of the *Portuguese* to the *Castilians* was very irksome and odious to them, so was it attended with Consequences very fatal to their Interests; for upon the first Commotions in the *Low-Countries*, *Philip* judging that one of the best Expedients to quell them, would be to deprive the Inhabitants of the Advantages they received by the Trade with *Portugal* and *Spain*, he prohibited all Commerce between them; for, in those times, the *Dutch* Ships made no longer Voyages than to these Countries for the Commodities of *India*, with which they afterwards supply'd the Northern Nations of *Europe*. But *Philip*'s Designs met with an Event very contrary to his Expectations; for the *Dutch* being thus excluded *Spain* and *Portugal*, they about 1595, boldly ventured to *India* themselves, and having, after many difficulties, got footing there, possessed themselves of several Places of great Importance, either for their Strength, or advantageous Situation, and did incredible Damage to the *Portuguese*, who had hitherto solely carried on all the Trade to those Parts. And in the Year 1622, the City of *Ormus*, the most wealthy of the *Portuguese* Acquisitions in the East, was taken from them by *Sha Abas* King of *Persia*, assisted by the *English* Merchant Ships in the Service of the *India* Company. Nor was this the end of their Misfortunes; for in 1630, the *Dutch* dispossessed them of great part of *Brasil*, and reduced several of their Settlements on the Coast of *Africa*: Nothing of which would the *Dutch* have had Occasion, or Opportunity to do, if *Portugal* had remain'd separate from the Crown of *Spain*. But in 1640 throwing off the *Spanish* Yoke, they set the Duke of *Braganza* upon the Throne, by the Name of *John* IV, and then clapped up a Peace with the *Dutch*, upon Condition that each Nation should retain what they were then possessed of; but it was not of long Continuance, because the Places the *Dutch* had made themselves Masters of in *Brasil*, revolted to the *Portuguese*, their former Masters, which the *Dutch* alledging was owing to the Fraud of the *Portuguese*, declared War against them. However, being forced to leave them in Possession of *Brasil*, they attacked them in *India*, took *Malacca*, entirely

<small>Philip prohibits Trade between the Low-Countries and Portugal.</small>

<small>A. D. 1595.
The Success of the Dutch in the Indies, and Africa.</small>

<small>A. D. 1622.
And the Portuguese dispossess'd of Ormus.</small>

<small>1630
And Part of Brazil.</small>

<small>A. D. 1640.</small>

<small>The Duke of Braganza made King of Portugal.
Brazil revolts to him.</small>

<small>The Dutch take several Places in India.</small>

60 Degrees West from London
Pag. 265.

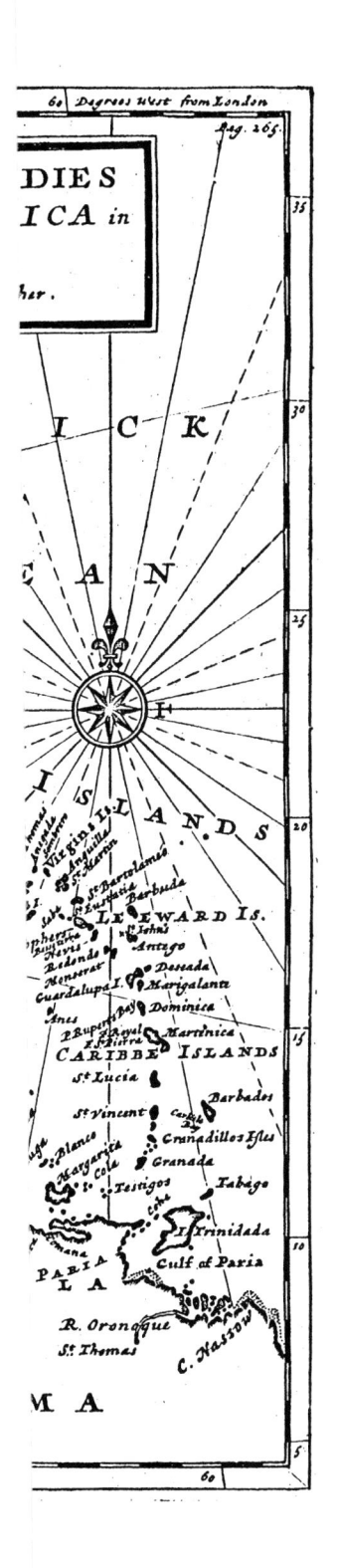

DIES
ICA in
her.

I C K
A N
I S L A N D S

Virgin Is.
St Bartolameo
St Eustatia Barbuda
LEWARD IS.
St Johns
Nevis Antego
Redondo Desada
Monserat
Guardalupa I. Marigalante
Anes Dominica
P. Rupert Bay
P. Royal Martinica
St Pierre
CARIBBE ISLANDS
St Lucia
St Vincent Barbados
Carlisle
Blanco Granadillos Isles
Margarita
Cola Granada
Testigos Tabago
I. Trinidada
PARIA Gulf of Paria
LA
R. Oronoque
St Thomas C. Nassow

M A

35
30
25
20
15
10
5
60

CHAP. IX. *Ruin of the* Rom. *Empire.* 265

entirely outed them of the Island *Ceylon* and Coast of *Cormandel*, reduced *Cochin*, *Cananor*, *Cranganor*, and other Places in *Malabar*, and had gone near to have taken *Goa* it self, their Capital City in *India*, if they had not come to a Peace with them in 1661; about which time *John* IV. dying, was succeeded by his Son *Alphonsus* VI, who being guilty of Mal Administration, and indeed incapable of Government, his Brother was substituted Regent of the Kingdom, and on the Decease of *Alphonsus* in 1683, took the Crown by the Name of *Peter* II. He dying in 1706, was succeeded A. D. 1706. by his Son *John*, the Fifth of that Name, who is now King of *Portugal*. During the War between *France* and the confederated Powers of *Europe*, which began in 1689, *Portugal* observed an exact Neutrality, yet in the last War they enter'd into the Grand Alliance in the Year 1703; but there not having happened any thing, during the Reign of the last or present Prince, remarkable to our purpose, we proceed next to the Naval Wars of the *Spaniards*.

CHAP. IX.
Of the Naval Wars of the Spaniards.

WHEN the *Roman* Empire was drawing towards its Dissolution, and became unable to defend its Provinces from the Irruptions of barbarous Neighbours, *Spain*, as we have elsewhere observed, fell a Prey to the *Goths*, who maintained themselves there, *The Goths overrun Spain.* under a Series of thirty Kings, from the Time of their first Settlement, *Anno* 418. to the Year 714; when the *Moors* or *Saracens*, A. D. 714. passing over from *Africa*, by the Treachery of Count *Julian*, in about nine Month's time reduced the greatest part of the Country to their Obedience. Nevertheless there arose up amongst the Remains of the *Gothick* Race, some great Men, who, by little and little, taking Advantage of the Dissensions amongst the *Moors*, made head against them and laid the Foundation of those Kingdoms, which in the end proved too mighty for the Infidels.

The first great Stand that was made against them was by the People of *Asturias* and *Biscay*, who being impatient of a foreign Yoke, and strengthened by great Numbers of other Christians who fled from the Fury of the *Moors* to those mountainous Countries, chose *Pelagius* for their King: Which Example was soon followed by those of *Navarre*, who about the same time set up *Garcias Ximenes*, the Founder of the Kingdom of *Navarre*, as *Pelagius* was of the Kingdom of *Leon*.

In the Reign of one of his Successors called *Ramir* I, who came to the Crown in 824, a numerous Fleet of *Normans* arrived on the 824. Coast of *Gallicia*, where committing great Devastations, *Ramir* *The Norman Fleet beaten by the Spaniards.* went against them, and forced them to retire with the Loss of seventy of their Ships, which he burnt. Those that escaped from 817. hence

M m

hence repaired to *Seville*, and plundering that City and the Country adjacent, went off with a prodigious Booty. In the time of *Ramir*'s Successor, *Ordogno* I, a Fleet of a hundred Sail of *Normans* came down to the same Coast of *Gallicia*, and after they had been out three Years returned home with great Spoil.

The Normans ravage Gallicia.

The Sea in these Times was very little the Element of the *Spaniards*, so that we hear nothing more of Naval Transactions till the Reign of *Alphonsus* VIII. King of *Castile*, who being engaged in a bloody War with the *Moors*, was aided by the other Christian Princes of *Spain* against them. The King of *Castile*'s Strength consisted in a Land Force, but *Raimond*, Count of *Barcelona* (by which Title he held the Sovereignty of *Catalonia*) sent his Fleet to his Assistance, under the Command of *Galceranus*, Admiral of *Catalonia*, and the Count of *Urgel*, who being joined by the *Genoese* Fleet, under *Ansaldi Doria*, repaired to *Almeria*, which they besieged and took by Storm; from whence they proceeded to *Tortosa*, and reduced that City likewise, taking an immense Booty therein, which the *Moors* had been laying up there for many Years: And for the Service which the *Genoese* performed in this Expedition, *Raimond* granted them an Immunity from all Customs or Duties in the Ports of *Catalonia*.

1146.

The Christians take several Places from the Moors.

The *Moors* in *Spain* were now all subordinate to the *Miramamolin* Princes, who had their Residence in *Africa*, and while they kept themselves so united under one Head, they maintained their Affairs very well in *Spain*, but when they afterwards split themselves into various Divisions, and set up different Kingdoms, throwing off all Submission to the *African Moors*, it became a much easier Work to the Christian Princes to subdue them. In 1236, they lost *Cordoua*, the Capital of their first Kingdom in *Andalusia*; after which fell *Valencia*, the Head of another Kingdom; and at length, after the Loss of all the rest, the Kings of *Murcia* and *Granada*, submitted to hold their Kingdoms of the Kings of *Castile*. In this manner was the Power of the *Moors* by Degrees brought low in *Spain*, and in 1248, only the Kingdom of *Granada* remained, which might also have been then easily reduced, but that the Christian Princes of *Spain*, being at variance among themselves, turned their Arms on each other.

The Moors lose several Places in Spain.
A. D. 1236.

A. D. 1248.

The Christian Princes at variance.
A. D. 1270.

About the Year 1270, the Kingdom of *Sicily* fell to *Peter* III. King of *Arragon*, in right of his Wife the Daughter of *Manfred*, King of that Island; but *Charles de Valois*, Brother to the *French* King *Lewis* IX, laying Claim thereto, *Peter* at first dissembled his Resentments, but afterwards fitted out a Fleet of forty Gallies, with several Ships of Burthen, under pretence of an Expedition to *Africa* against the *Moors*, but in reality designed for *Sicily*, to destroy the Remainder of the *French* there, who had survived the Massacre, known by the Name of the *Sicilian Vespers*. And having, accordingly, entirely cleared the Island of the *French*, he left a Squadron there of five and twenty Gallies, under the Command of *Roger Doria*, Admiral of *Arragon*, and repaired with the rest to *Sardinia*, there to be at hand in case of an Attack from the *French*.

The French driven out of Sicily.

1281.

Roger

Roger *Doria* having settled Affairs in *Sicily*, went out with his Squadron, and ravaging the Coasts of *Calabria*, endeavoured to bring the Enemy, (who then possessed the Kingdom of *Naples*,) to a Battel, which he effected, for *Charles de Valois* sent out his Son the Prince of *Salerno* against him, with whom *Doria* engaging in the Gulph of *Naples*, entirely defeated him, taking him Prisoner, with nine of his Gallies, and sinking all the rest of the Fleet. The French did not let this Loss go long unrevenged, for landing on the Coast of *Catalonia*, they committed great Devastations there, and took several Towns, but the Plague destroying great Numbers of their Men, they were forced to retire, and sent home the Ships they had borrowed of the *Genoese* and *Pisans*. In their way thither, off the Coast of *Genoa*, they fell in with *Roger Doria* the *Arragonese* Admiral, then coming from *Sicily* to his Master's Assistance, who thereupon hired them into his Service, and repaired with them to *Narbonne*, where he had Advice the Enemy's Ships lay, which he attacked and made himself Master of, but not being able to bring them off, set them on fire. *The French defeated at Sea by the King of Sicily. The French harrass the Coast of Catalonia. The King of Arragon's Admiral burns the French Ships.*

Peter King of *Arragon* dying, he was succeeded therein by his Son *Alphonsus* III, as he was in *Sicily* by his second Son *James*. The Islands of *Majorca* and *Yviça* having been conquered from the *Moors* by *James* I. of *Arragon*, were given by him, with the Title of King, to his Son *James*, (the Brother of King *Peter* beforementioned) who having took part with the *French* against his said Brother, *Alphonsus* now King of *Arragon* dispossessed him of his Dominions, which having done he also reduced the Island of *Minorca*, then held by the *Saracens*, and added it to his Dominions. About this time *Sancho* IV, King of *Castile*, made a successful Expedition against the *Moors*, from whom he took *Tariffa* and destroyed a great Fleet the King of *Fez* sent to the Enemy's Assistance. In the mean time *Mary*, the Wife of *Charles de Valois*, who governed the Realm of *Naples* during the Imprisonment of her Husband, sent *Renald à Balso* with a strong Force to *Sicily*, where having reduced *Catana*, he sent back his Gallies to *Naples* for a Reinforcement of Soldiers, to whom *Guy de Monfort* was at the same time proceeding from the Coast of *Tuscany* with a Body of chosen Troops levied in that Country; but *Roger Doria* being then at Sea with the Fleet, fell in with and destroyed both these Squadrons, the first off *Naples*, and the latter on the *Tuscan* Shore: Upon the News of which Loss the *French* presently quitted *Sicily*, and made the best of their way for *Naples*. About the same time *Alphonsus* dying, he was succeeded in the Throne of *Arragon* by *James*, King of *Sicily*, who thereupon gave that Island to his Brother *Frederick*, and on his Arrival in *Spain* entered into a League with *Ferdinand* IV. of *Castile* against the *Moors*, from whom the first recovered *Almeria*, and the latter took *Gibraltar*. *1285. Majorca, Yviça, and Minorca added to Arragon. The King of Castile beats the Moors. The Admiral of Arragon destroys the Ships of Naples, &c. Almeria and Gibraltar taken from the Moors. 1309.*

The Conclusion of this War was soon followed by the opening of another; for the Pope beginning now to stand in fear of the great Power of the *Genoese* and *Pisans*, thought fit, according to the ample Authority they pretend to be invested with, to bestow the Island

Island of *Corsica*, belonging to the former, and that of *Sardinia*, belonging to the latter, on the Kings of *Arragon*, under pretence that it was the only means to put an end to the long Discord which had been between those two Republicks. But neither of them abiding by so unjust a Donation, it was necessary for the *Arragonese* to have recourse to Arms to get Possession of those Islands. The *Pisans* were the least able to maintain their Right, and therefore *Sardinia* was first attacked, whither *Francis Carroso* repairing at the Head of a Fleet, besieged *Cagliari*, which he soon forced to surrender, and defeated Count *Manfred*, whom the *Pisans* had sent with a Squadron of twenty five Gallies to the Relief of the Besieged: Upon which Victory a Treaty of Peace ensued, whereby the *Pisans* agreed to hold the Island of *Sardinia* as a Fief of the Kingdom of *Arragon*. *Beringer Carroso*, the Son of the Admiral, was left with a Squadron at *Sardinia*, under pretence of defending it against any Attacks of the *Moors*, but in reality to prevent the *Sardinians* from rising in Rebellion; which nevertheless soon after happened, and a Fleet of twenty two Gallies were sent by the *Pisans*, and the *Genoese* of the *Gibelline* Faction, to their Assistance, under the Command of *Gaspar Doria*. Between him and the *Arragonese* were several sharp Disputes at Sea, but one more especially remarkable in the Bay of *Cagliari*, wherein *Francis Carroso*, the Admiral of *Arragon*, obtained a compleat Victory, and the *Pisans* were thereupon forced entirely to abandon the Island, which hath ever since remained to the Crown of *Arragon*. However, at first it proved no great Prize, the Possession of it being clogged by the Articles of Donation with such extravagant Taxes and Tribute to the Popes, who take care never to bestow Gifts but to great Advantage, that what with the Charge of Ships and Garrisons to maintain it in its Obedience, and other necessary Expences, it consumed not only its own remaining Revenues, but great part of those of *Arragon* and *Catalonia*; wherefore a Diminution of the Taxes was first sollicited and obtained, and not long after, upon pretence of its frequent Rebellions, and the vast Charge of maintaining it, a total Remission of them.

Aiton Doria cruizing about this time with a Squadron belonging to the *Genoese* of the *Gibelline* Faction, fell in, off *Torra*, a Port of *Sardinia*, with nine *Catalan* Ships, and took or destroyed them all, which struck a great Terror amongst the *Arragonese*, and inspired the *Sardinians* with Courage to take Arms, and make another Attempt for their Liberty: Whereupon the War was renewed, and a Fleet was fitted out from *Catalonia* consisting of forty Gallies, and thirty Ships and *Saétias*, which sailing over to *Italy*, ravaged the Coasts of *Genoa* from one end to the other, without Distinction of Friend or Foe, (for only the *Gibelline* Faction were their Enemies) which so exasperated both Parties, that they united against them, and resolved to be revenged. To that purpose they fitted out a Fleet of sixty Sail, with which first scouring the Coast of *Catalonia*, they then crossed over to *Sardinia*, where the *Arragonese* kept themselves close in Port, not daring to venture out to oppose

CHAP. IX. *Ruin of the* Rom. *Empire.* 269

pose them. But a new War breaking out, about *Majorca,* it hindered for a while the farther Prosecution of this Quarrel. *Peter* IV. was now King of *Arragon,* who not being contented with the Island of *Sardinia,* cast his Eye also on *Majorca* and *Minorca,* then possessed by *James* II, his Cousin-German and Brother-in-law: and, in order to reduce them, sent *Peter de Moncada* with a Fleet of a hundred Sail over to *Palma,* the chief City of *Majorca,* whereupon the King betaking himself to flight, that Island, with *Minorca,* peaceably submitted to his Obedience. *Majorca and Minorca conquer'd by Peter IV. of Arragon.*

In the mean time the *Moors,* with a great Fleet from *Africa,* attacked *Alphonsus* XII, who being aided by the other Christian Princes of *Spain,* the King of *Arragon's* Auxiliary Ships were commanded by *Godfrey Giralbert,* to whom being committed the Defence of the Streights Mouth, he was defeated and slain by the Enemy before *Algezira,* in the Bay of *Gibraltar.* The *Arragonese* not being able to maintain this Post, they were succeeded on the same Station by a *Castilian* Squadron, consisting of thirty three Gallies, and some Frigates, but with no better Success than the former, for the Enemy engaged and overcame them likewise, and slew the Admiral in the same Place they had so lately killed his Predecessor; which done, they landed their Troops in *Spain* without Opposition. After this *Alphonsus Ortiz Carderon* was appointed to command the Fleet, consisting of fifteen Sail which escaped from the late Fight, and twelve new Ships, with several others belonging to *Arragon* and *Portugal,* who repaired to the Relief of *Tariffa,* then besieged by a numerous Army of *Moors* under the Command of *Albohacen,* and cutting off their Communication with the *African* Shore, from whence they received all their Provisions, a Famine soon ensued, which forced them to raise the Siege, when making the best of their way to their Ships without any Order or Discipline, the *Castilian* Army ashore attacked them in the midst of that Confusion, and committed a prodigious Slaughter among them. *The Moors overcome the Christian Fleet at Gibraltar, and that of Castile. Land in Spain. Are forced to raise the Siege of Tariffa.*

After this Victory *Giles Boccanigra,* a *Genoese,* was appointed Admiral of the Fleet and Sea-Coasts, who in one of the Ports of *Granada,* seized twelve of the Enemy's Gallies, six whereof he burnt, and added the rest to his Fleet, which was soon after increased by ten Ships from *Portugal,* under the Command of *Charles Pesano.* In the mean time a numerous Fleet of the Enemy's sailed out from *Ceuta,* and entered the Mouth of the *Guadamecil;* whereupon *Boccanigra* repaired thither and blocked them up, and thirteen Gallies of *Algezira* arriving to the Relief of their *Moorish* Allies, he engaged them, and after an obstinate Dispute, took or sunk them all. Then attacking the *Moors* with his whole Force, he took thirty five Gallies, putting all the Men to Death, the rest of the Enemy's Ships making a hard shift to escape. Immediately hereupon, *Algezira* was besieged by Sea and Land, and notwithstanding the obstinate Resistance of the Inhabitants, forced to surrender; in the Reduction whereof *James Seriva,* and *Matthew Mercero,* who commanded twenty auxiliary Gallies of *Arragon,* having performed very signal Service, were suitably rewarded by the King of *Castile.* *And are overcome at Sea. 1342. Algezira taken by the Castilians.*

About

1346.

The Pope gives the Canary Islands to Lewis de Cerda.

About this time were strange Relations told concerning the *Canaries*, (the *Insulæ Fortunatæ* of the Ancients) which were now very liberally bestow'd by Pope *Clement* VI. on *Lewis de Cerda*, with the same Right of Donation as one of his Predecessors had before given away *Sardinia* and *Corsica:* But as what had been so kindly disposed of, could not be as easily acquired, we do not find that *de Cerda* ever got Possession of his Dominions.

1353.

The Genoese Fleet defeated by the Catalans and Venetians.

Sardinia reduced by the King of Arragon.

Not long after, the *Genoese* having instigated the *Sardinians* to a Rebellion, a Fleet of forty five Sail was fitted out from *Catalonia* under the Command of *Bernard Caprara*, who being soon after joined by twenty *Venetian* Gallies, commanded by *Nicholas Pisani*, proceeded to *Sardinia*, where, off *Algeri*, (otherwise called *Larguero*) he fell in with the *Genoese* Fleet, commanded by *Anthony Grimaldi*, which he engaged and entirely defeated, taking thirty five Gallies, and three thousand Prisoners. However *Sardinia* was not yet quiet, wherefore another Fleet was got ready at *Barcelona* to settle Affairs there, on board which embarked the King of *Arragon* himself, who proceeding to the Bay of *Algeri*, there landed his Troops, and expelling his Enemies, reduced the Island to Obedience.

The English Fleet beaten by the Spaniards.

A. D. 1393.

The Canary Islands discovered.

Some time after this *Ambrose Boccanigra* was sent by *Henry* II, King of *Castile*, with a strong Squadron to the Assistance of the *French* against the *English*, whose Fleet, commanded by the Earl of *Pembroke*, he engaged off *Rochel*, and entirely defeated, taking the Earl Prisoner, with most of his Ships, which was followed by the Surrender of the Town, then held by the *English*, into the Hands of the *French* who besieged it. In 1393, some private Ships belonging to *Biscay* and *Guipuscoa* sailed to *Lancerota*, one of the *Canary* Islands, where the *Biscayens* defeated a Company of *Barbarians* which opposed their landing, and sailing thence to the other Islands included under that Name, fully discovered them all. Upon their Return home, they made a Report of their Proceedings to King *Henry* of *Castile*, who thereupon gave leave to *John de Bethencourt*, a Native of *France*, to go and take Possession of those Islands, but reserved to himself and Successors the Right of Sovereignty therein.

The Castilian Squadron beat the Gallies of Portugal.

A Peace between the Kings of Castile and Portugal.

The *Castilians* under their King *Henry* III, then a Child, were now fitting out Ships to go on new Discoveries, when *John* King of *Portugal* attacking them, forced them to desist from such Enterprizes, and turn their Thoughts to their own Defence. A *Castilian* Squadron of five Sail, falling in with seven *Portuguese* Gallies, bound home from *Genoa*, with Troops and Arms on board, the *Spaniards* bravely engaged them, and with such Success, that they took three of the Enemy's Gallies, sunk one, and forced the rest to betake themselves to Flight. Soon after which Action, a Peace ensued between the two Crowns, during the long Continuance whereof, *viz.* till the Time of *Philip* II, the *Portuguese* discovered and carried on their famous Navigations to the East, as the *Spaniards* did to the new World they found out, within that Century, in the West. Then *Bethencourt* again renewed his Attempts for the Reduction of the

Canary

CHAP. IX. *Ruin of the* Rom. *Empire.* 271

Canary Iſlands, which had been interrupted during the late War, and having ſubdued *Ferro*, *Palma*, and *Teneriffe*, had the Title given him of King of thoſe Iſlands, together with *Lancerota*, before conquered by the *Biſcayans*, where he built a Fortreſs, and made a Port for the Security and Advantage of Commerce. After *Bethencourt*, one *Menault*, likewiſe a *Frenchman*, reigned in thoſe Iſlands, but with ſuch a tyrannical Conduct, that he was obliged to ſell his Government to *Ferdinand Perez*, a Knight of *Seville*, whoſe Poſterity continued in Poſſeſſion thereof till the Time of *Ferdinand* and *Iſabella*, King and Queen of *Caſtile*. <small>Bethencourt King of the Canary Iſlands.</small>

The *Arragoneſe*, in the mean while, were more intent on Arms than Trade, or the Deſire of new Diſcoveries, and engaged in a War in Defence of *Joan* II, Queen of *Naples*. Pope *Martin* V. had lately, by a Bull for that purpoſe, been pleaſed to diveſt Queen *Joan* of the Kingdom of *Naples*, and to confer it on *Lewis* Duke of *Anjou*, whoſe Cauſe was alſo favoured by the *Genoeſe*, and other Powers of *Italy*. *Alphonſus* V. was then King of *Arragon*, who fearing that if the *French* ſhould poſſeſs *Naples*, they would ſoon carry the War into his Iſland of *Sicily*, reſolved to divide his Enemy's Forces, and attack the *Genoeſe* in Alliance with them. Accordingly he made an Expedition to the Iſle of *Corſica*, belonging to them, where the War was carried on with great Deſtruction on both ſides, the *Genoeſe* making a very ſtrenuous Defence. At which time, to compenſate his good Services, Queen *Joan* adopted King *Alphonſus* for her Son, and conſtituted him Heir to her Crown; whereupon he ſent to her Aſſiſtance *Raimond de Perillos* with a Fleet of eighteen Gallies and fourteen other Ships of War. But at length a Quarrel ariſing betwixt the Queen and her new adopted Son, ſhe diſinherited him, and adopted the Duke of *Anjou* to be her Son and Heir in his room. By this means was *Alphonſus* at once cut off from all his fair Hopes of enjoying the Kingdoms of *Naples* and *Corſica*, and obliged to repair to *Spain*, to defend his Dominions there from the King of *Caſtile:* but in his way thither, reſolving to commit ſome Act of Revenge upon his Enemies, he enter'd the Port of *Marſeilles*, belonging to the Duke of *Anjou*, (who was alſo Earl of *Provence)* and having plundered that City, proceeded on his Voyage to *Spain*. <small>The King of Arragon arms in Defence of Joan Queen of Naples.</small> <small>Hot Diſputes between thoſe of Arragon and the Genoeſe about Corſica.</small> <small>The King of Arragon plunders Marſeilles.</small>

On his Arrival there, joining his Forces with thoſe of *Navarre*, he carried on the War with great Vigour againſt the King of *Caſtile:* During the Heat whereof, receiving News that Queen *Joan* and *Lewis* Duke of *Anjou* were both dead, and that *René*, the Brother of that Duke, was appointed by the Queen's laſt Will to ſucceed to the Throne of *Naples*, but that many of the Nobles of that Kingdom, being weary of a *French* Government, were inclined to eſpouſe his Cauſe, he fitted out a new Fleet, whereon embarking with his Army, he paſſed over into *Sicily*, from whence ſailing to the Coaſt of *Naples*, he formed the Siege of *Gaeta*, then garriſoned by the *Genoeſe* for the Duke of *Anjou*. To the Relief of that Place the Duke of *Milan* (to whom the Republick of *Genoa* had lately ſubmitted) ſent a conſiderable Fleet under the Command of *Biugio Aſſireto*, *fereto*, which falling in with that of *Arragon*, near the Isle of *Ponza*, off *Gaeta*, they came to an Engagement, wherein, after an obstinate Dispute, the Victory fell to the *Genoese*, and the Gally on board which King *Alphonsus* himself was, being stript of her Oars, and otherwise much disabled, the King surrendered himself Prisoner to *James Justiniani*, one of the Enemy's Captains; with whom at the same time were taken his Brother *John* King of *Navarre*, Henry the Prince *Infante*, and many other Persons of the first Quality, with thirteen Ships of War and several Gallies. The Prisoners of the common sort were more in Number than the whole Force of the *Genoese*, wherefore they set most of them ashore and dismissed them; and upon the News of this Loss, those of the *Arragonese*, who were before *Gaeta*, raised the Siege in the utmost Confusion. However *Alphonsus* being soon admitted to an Interview with the Duke of *Milan*, performed more by his Address than he was able to do by his Arms, and so wrought upon him, that he brought him over to engage in his Interests, and enter into a Treaty for that purpose; which so exasperated the *Genoese*, that they immediately threw off their Obedience to the Duke of *Milan*, and bound themselves by stricter Engagements to prosecute the Cause of the *French*. *Alphonsus*, now set at liberty and aided by the Duke of *Milan*, carried on the War for *Naples* with great Vigour, and laid siege to the capital City of that Kingdom, which he at length possess'd himself of, notwithstanding the utmost Efforts of the *French* to maintain it. The rest of *Naples* soon followed the Example of the chief City, so that after a twenty Year's War, (for so long it was since he was first adopted by Queen *Joan*) *Alphonsus* became entirely Master of the Kingdom.

In the mean time the Kings of *Castile* were endeavouring to encrease their Dominions by new Acquisitions, and to extend their Empire beyond the *Æquator*, sending out several Squadrons on such Enterprizes; one of which, commanded by *Peter à Vera*, spent three Years in reducing those of the *Canary* Islands which had not been already subdued. Another, under the Command of *Peter de Cobides*, made a Voyage to the Coast of *Guinea*, with very great Success, gaining a prodigious Booty, all which was shared between the Commander in Chief, the Soldiers and Seamen, except only a fifth part reserved for the King. The Nephew of the foremention'd *Alphonsus*, having married *Isabella*, the Heiress of *Castile*, became King thereof in 1474, by the Name of *Ferdinand* V, and by the Decease of his Father in 1478, succeeded also to the Dominions of *Arragon*; and having at length taken the Kingdom of *Granada* from the *Moors*, became Master of all *Spain*, except *Portugal*. For fear the *Moors*, tho' subdued, should yet, because of their great Numbers in the Kingdom, again gather Strength, and make head against him, he forced seventeen thousand Families of them to retire into *Africa*, where still he would not suffer them to rest, but with a considerable Fleet ravaging the Coasts of *Barbary*, took from them the Towns of *Marsalquivir*, *Oran*, *Peñon de Velez*, and *Melilla*.

About

About this time it was that *Christopher Columbus*, a *Genoese* Pilot, first addressed himself to *Henry* VII. of *England*, and offered to go and make Discoveries, in his Name, of great Tracts of Land, which he was assured lay to the Westward of our Continent, but being rejected by him, and his Council, as a whimsical Projector, he proposed the same thing to *John* II, King of *Portugal*, where meeting with the like Treatment as in *England*, he applied himself to the Court of *Spain*, and was favourably heard by the Dukes of *Medina Sidonia*, and *Medina Celi*, who introduced him to the King and Queen; and having the good Fortune to have his Project relished by Cardinal *Gonzales de Mendoza*, then Chancellor of *Spain*, was thereupon furnished with Ships and Men pursuant to his Proposals.

Christopher Columbus goes on foreign Discoveries.

In *August* 1492, he set sail from St. *Lucar* for the Westward, and having touched at the *Canary* Islands, in thirty Days sail from thence, he fell in with the Island of *Guanahani*, otherwise called St. *Salvador*, and by the *English Catt*-Island, being one of those now known by the Name of the *Bahama*'s. Which finding to be uninhabited, he proceeded thence to *Cuba*, from whence he took some of the Natives on board, who conducted him to *Cibao*, which he named *Hispaniola*, where he discovered several rich Gold Mines; and finding the Inhabitants of that Island to be of a more sociable and civiliz'd Temper than the former, he resolved to leave some of his People among them, while he returned to *Spain* to give an Account of his Expedition: And accordingly erecting a kind of a Fort with the Timber of one of his Ships, which he broke up for that purpose, he left some *Spaniards* to defend it, and setting sail for *Spain*, arrived in fifty Days at St. *Lucar*, bringing with him a Quantity of Gold, and twelve of the Natives of *Hispaniola* as Witnesses of his Discovery. The News of his Arrival was received with great Joy by the Court of *Spain*; but when *John* King of *Portugal* heard of the Discoveries which had been made, he, by his Ambassador at *Madrid*, complained to that Court, that they encroached upon his Dominions, for that the Countries they had found out did of Right belong to him, as possessing the Cape *Verde* Islands, and the Sovereignty of the Ocean, which his Ancestors first caused to be navigated. To which the *Spanish* Ministers made Answer, that what was not in any body's Possession before lay open to all Men, and that it could be no Injury to any one if they, by their Industry, made themselves Masters of what was till then unknown to the rest of the World. Hereupon ensued very high Words between the two Courts; but at length, to prevent these Disputes from breaking out into a War, they appealed to Pope *Alexander* VI. for his Determination of the Matter, who decided it in favour of the *Spaniards*, in this manner. By an imaginary Line drawn from North to South through both the Poles, in the Longitude of five Degrees West from the Islands of Cape *Verde*, he divided the World into two Parts, all Lands discovered, or to be discovered, to the Westward of which he assigned to the King of *Spain*, and those to the Eastward were to belong to the King of *Portugal*.

A. D. 1492.

The Pope's Division of all new discovered Countries in the World, between the Spaniards and Portuguese.

1493. Hereupon *Columbus* was, the next Year, ordered to return to these new-found Countries, with a Commission, styling him Admiral of the Indies; in which Voyage he discovered the Islands of the *Canibals*, the same which are now called the *Caribbees*, on each of which he imposed such a Name as he thought fit, naming one *Dominica*, because it was discovered on a Sunday; another *Santa Cruz*, from a Cross which he erected there; a third *Guadelupa*, because the Land appeared like a Mountain of that Name in *Spain*; a fourth, inhabited by only Women, like the *Amazons* of the Ancients, he named *Matanina*, being the same which is now called *Martinique*; a fifth he called *Monserat*, from its high Lands appearing indented in several Places like a Saw; a sixth *Rotonda*, (now *Redondo*) from its circular Form; and so the rest. At *Santa Cruz* he had a Skirmish at Sea with the Natives, who were led by a Woman, and shot poisoned Arrows, which killed many of his Men. Several of these *Barbarians* sinking their Boats, managed themselves upon the Water with such Dexterity, that they threw their Darts as if they had been on firm Ground, and retired fighting till they came to a neighbouring Rock, where being surrounded, and many of them hurt or killed, the rest surrendered themselves Prisoners to the *Spaniards*. *Columbus* proceeding hence, sailed to *Bahama*, and from thence repaired to *Hispaniola*, where he found his Fort destroyed, and the Men he had left cut to pieces by the Natives, of whom having put several to Death, in Revenge of their Barbarity, he went up into the inland Parts of the Island, (where one *Canoba* was *Cacique*, or King) which he found very fertile in Gold Mines, and there laid the Foundations of a City; which done, he went back to his Landing place, which he had before named Port *Royal*, and also built a Town there; and having made several other Discoveries in those Parts, he returned to *Spain*, but met there with a very ill Reception, altogether unsuitable to his glorious Services: both himself and his Brother, being accused by *Roland Ximenes* of High Crimes and Misdemeanours, and committed to Prison; where, however, he did not long continue, for his Innocence being made appear, he was restored to his Sovereign's Favour.

During his Disgrace, some of the Companions of his former Voyages undertook to make farther Discoveries in other Parts of this new World, which they were permitted to do, on condition none of them attempted it within fifty Leagues of any of the Places already discovered. Of these, *Pedro Alonzo Nigro* sailed to that now called the Province of *Paria*, in the *Terra Firma*, the Coasts whereof were very rich in Pearls; but *Columbus* having been there before, he only took in Provisions, and proceeding Southward, discovered part of the Coast of *Guiana*, where he had a Skirmish at Sea with the *Canibals*, who inhabited the Country. Mean while, *Vincent* and *Aries Pinsone*, who went out at the same time, but in a different Route, came on the same Coast, and discovered the rest of *Guiana* as far as *Brazil*.

Other foreign Discoveries.

A few

CHAP. IX.   *Ruin of the* Rom. *Empire.*

A few Years after, *Americus Vespucci,* an *Italian* in the *Spanish* Service, and afterwards in that of *Portugal,* making several Discoveries along the Coasts of the South Parts of this Continent, was, in this respect, more fortunate than any of his Predecessors, that the whole was from him called *America.* In the mean time *Vasco Nugnez* having got footing in the Province of *Darien,* from a high Mountain there, discovered the Pacifick Ocean, or South Sea, which he surveyed with greedy Eyes, as if it were already become the Propriety of his Master.

And now it was that *Ferdinand Cortez,* by his stupendous Conquests in *Mexico,* gained to himself immortal Honour, who passing over, in 1509, from *Cuba* to *Jucatan,* with a Body only of six hundred Men, there took *Pontochan,* a City of the *Indians,* to which he gave the Name of *Vittoria,* because before the taking of it he had defeated the Prince of the Country in several Battels. This done, he embarked his Troops, and sailed to the River *Alvaredo,* and thence to the *Zempoallan,* near which he built the Town of *Vera-Cruz,* and there sinking his Ships, cut off all Thoughts of a Retreat from his Soldiers, and gave them to understand they must either conquer or die: Leaving that Place with a small Garrison for the Defence of it, under the Command of *Peter Hircio,* he attacked the Town of *Zempoallan,* and presently reducing it, changed its Name to that of *Seville.* Thence opening his way, Sword in Hand, to *Mexico,* situate in a great Lake, he laid siege to that City, which he reduced to his Obedience, and, by a Stratagem, took Prisoner *Montezuma,* the King of the Country, and put him to Death; after which he was forced out of the City by an Insurrection, but rallying all his Forces, together with those *Indians* which were his Friends, he again attempted it by Land and Water, and after a long and tedious Siege, wherein infinite Multitudes of the Enemy were slain, again made himself Master of the Place, together with *Quahutimoca* the new King, whom he sent Prisoner to the Emperor *Charles* V, with his Share, the fifth part of the Spoil, which was of inestimable Value. Having repaired the Damages the City had suffered in the Siege, he proceeded thence to *Chila* on the Sea-Coast, which he rebuilt, and called St. *Stephen.* After which he carried his Arms through all the other Parts of that Province, and, having with a handful of Men subdued numberless Hosts of Enemies, and reduced the Country wholly to his Obedience, he peopled it with Colonies from *Europe;* and having settled it in Peace, being worn out with Years, and the Toils of War, he left his Conquests, and returned to lay his Ashes in *Spain.*

In the mean time *John Diaz* sailing Southward, along the Coast of *Brazil,* came to an Anchor in the Mouth of a great River called by the Natives of the Country the *Paraguay,* to which the *Spaniards* have since given the Name of *Rio de la Plata,* because the first Silver they received from *Peru* came down that River. Now also was *Peru* discovered, by Land, and an immense Extent of Country reduced, by the Slaughter of Millions of the Inhabitants, to the Obedience of the *Spaniards;* among whom however, at length,

Ferdinand Cortez his Conquests. A. D. 1509.

Mexico reduced by the Spaniards.

1521.

Peru reduced by the Spaniards.

length, there arose such Dissensions about the Division of the Spoil, that they had gone near to have destroyed one another themselves, and given the *Americans* an Opportunity of recovering their Losses, if the Emperor *Charles* V. had not timely sent over some Judges to *Nombre de Dios* to determine their Disputes, and put an end to those Dissensions, by some wholsome Severities upon the chief of the Offenders.

Magellan's Discoveries.

The Ambition and Avarice of the *Spaniards* was not yet so satisfied by the Discovery of all these Islands, and this vast Continent, but that they envied the *Portuguese* their Possessions in the East; and a shorter Passage must now be found out to them (as they hoped there might) by the West of *America*. For this purpose *Ferdinand Magellan*, a *Portuguese* Navigator, who had been disobliged at home, offered his Service to the Emperor, from whom receiving the Command of five Ships, he set sail from St. *Lucar* the tenth of *August* 1519, and, touching at the *Canaries*, proceeded to the Southermost Parts of *America*, beyond the foremention'd *Rio de la Plata*, (all which is from him since named *Terra Magellanica*) where the first Place he anchored in he called the Bay of St. *Julian*, and the Country the Land of *Giants*, because of the great Stature of the Inhabitants; the next River he came to he named *Santa Cruz*, whence proceeding farther Southward, he arrived at a great Promontory, to which, because he first saw it on St. *Ursula*'s Day, he gave the Name of the *Eleven thousand Virgins*, in allusion to a ridiculous Legend of the Church of *Rome* concerning that Saint. Having doubled this Cape, he enter'd into those Streights which have ever since bore his Name, and passing through the same, came into the South-Sea, where leaving *Chili* and *Peru* behind him, he sailed for many Weeks, and then passing the Æquinoctial, proceeded to the Islands he named the *Ladrones*, and from thence to those since called the *Philippines*, when he had with him only three of his five Ships, one of them having left him and returned to *Spain*, and the other being cast away. *Magellan* having sailed round several of these Islands, came at length to *Matan*, one of the Number, where, in a Battel with the Islanders, he was unfortunately slain by an Arrow. Hereupon the *Spaniards* chose *John Serrano* for their Leader, but he, with five and twenty of his Companions, being soon after treacherously killed at a Banquet by the King of *Cebu*, and the rest not being able to manage their three Ships, they burnt one of them at *Behol*, and thence came down to the *Moluccas*, where, at *Tidore*, having purchased a Quantity of Spices of the King of the Island, the two Ships departed thence for *Spain*, each a different way. That called the *Trinity* sailed Eastward, in order to touch at *Panama*, and return by the Rout she came, but being forced back by contrary Winds to *Tidore*, she there fell into the Hands of the *Portuguese*, and was taken, as we have before mentioned. The other, named the *Victory*, was the only one now left of *Magellan's* five Ships, which sailing through the *Indian* and *Æthiopick* Oceans, doubled the Cape of *Good Hope*, and then traversing the *Atlantick*, after a three Year's Voyage, happily arrived, under the

Command

Command of *Sebastian Cano*, at the Port of St. *Lucar*, and was the first Ship that navigated round the Globe.

Not long after Occasion offered for employing the *Spaniards* at Sea, much nearer home; for *Haradin Barbaruffa*, a notable Pirate in the Mediterranean, having taken the Castle of *Goletta* near *Tunis*, and dispossessed *Muley Haffan* of that Kingdom, as we have elsewhere observed, the outed Prince implored Aid of the Emperor *Charles* V; whereupon a great Fleet was fitted out to re-instate him, and appointed to rendezvous at *Cagliari* in *Sardinia*, whither repaired also, as Auxiliaries, several Ships of *Genoa*, a Squadron of *Portuguese* commanded by *Lewis*, the Brother of *John* King of *Portugal*, one of the Pope's, under the Command of *Paul Justiniani*, and *Virginius Urfini*, and another of the Knights of *Malta*. The Fleet being here all assembled, crossed over to *Porto Farina*, where landing the Troops, they put to flight those who opposed them, cut off a Body of Men that sallied out from *Goletta*, which they soon made themselves Masters of, as they did presently after of *Tunis* it self; and driving *Barbaruffa* out of the Kingdom, set *Muley Haffan* again on the Throne, he first agreeing to pay a Tribute to the Emperor, and yield him a Possession of the Towns of *Africa*, *Biferta*, and *Bona*, (with the neighbouring Islands,) and the Castle of *Goletta*.

1535. *The Fleet of Charles V. beats Barbaruffa.*

In the Winter of the Year 1541, the Emperor undertook another Expedition to *Africa*, in order to reduce *Algier*, contrary to the Advice of the Pope and others, who would have had him deferr'd it till the following Spring. His Fleet consisted of a hundred Ships, and eighteen Gallies, having on board two and twenty thousand Men, which he landed safely near Cape *Metafuz*, a point of Land a little to the Eastward of the City, of which he presently formed the Siege; but in a few Days there arose such a fierce Storm of Wind and Rain, as demolished all his Works, drove his Ships and Gallies from their Anchors, and made such universal Destruction, that he was forced to rise from before the place in the utmost Confusion, and embarking on board the Remainder of his Ships, he returned to *Spain* with the Loss of half his Fleet and Army.

A. D. 1541. *The Emperor forced to raise the Siege of Argiers.*

The famous Pirate *Dragut Raiz* having in 1551 taken *Tripoli* from the *Spaniards*, after they had been forty Years in Possession of it, *Philip* II who succeeded his Father *Charles* V. in the Kingdom of *Spain*, fitted out a considerable Fleet in 1560, for the Recovery of that Place; which sailing to the Coasts of *Tripoli*, reduced the Island of *Zerbi*, but was soon after attacked there by the *Turkish* Fleet, and utterly defeated, the Enemy making themselves Masters of the Island, killing eighteen thousand Men, and taking or destroying forty two of the Ships. However in 1564, he had better Success in his Attempts on *Peñon de Velez*, and recovered that Place from the *Moors*. Two Years after a strong Fleet was sent from *Spain* to the Relief of *Malta*, then besieged by the *Turks*, whom the *Spaniards* engaging, forced them to raise the Siege, and retire with a prodigious Loss. This Success was followed in 1571, by the signal Victory which *Don John* of *Austria*, with the *Spanish*

A. D. 1551.
1560. *The Fleet of Philip II. beaten by the Turks.*
1564. *The Emperor takes Peñon de Velez.*
1566.
1571. *The Turks beaten at Malta, and Lepanto.*

nish Fleet, in concert with that of *Venice*, the Pope, and the *Genoese*, obtained over the *Turks* near *Lepanto*, which gave such a Blow to the *Turkish* Naval Affairs, as they have never since been able to recover. In 1573, the aforesaid *Don John* made an Expedition to *Africa* to reduce *Tunis*, (which had revolted,) to its Obedience, and having made himself Master of that City, raised a strong Citadel for its Security; but the next Year the *Turks* repairing thither with a powerful Army, took the Citadel, not yet finished, and possessing themselves of *Goletta*, which was very ill provided for a Defence, entirely outed the *Spaniards* of that Kingdom.

1573.
Don John reduces Tunis, which is re-taken by the Turks. and also Goletta.

After King *Philip*'s Accession to the Crown of *Portugal*, in the manner we have elsewhere mentioned, a strong Squadron was sent under the Command of *Alvarez Bassano*, Marquis of *Santa Cruz*, to recover the *Azores* Islands, which held out for *Anthony* who pretended to that Kingdom; which, at the Isle of St. *Michael*, meeting with the *French* Fleet, commanded by *Philip Strozzi*, a Marshal of *France*, they both came to an Engagement, wherein the *French* received a total Defeat, losing most of their Ships, besides great Numbers of Men, among whom was the Marshal himself; who falling into the Hands of the Marquis of *Santa Cruz*, is said to have been barbarously slain in cold Blood, contrary to all the Laws of War and Honour, and his Body thrown into the Sea. The Monarchy of *Spain* being now raised to its highest Pitch of Glory, having united to the large Dominions it was before possessed of, all those of *Portugal*, and its Dependencies in the East; *Philip* formed his Design against *England*, and fitted out his invincible Armada, as 'twas termed, an Account whereof, and its Success will be better deferr'd till we come to the Part it had among our own Affairs.

1583.
The Portuguese beat the French at Sea near the Azores,

1588.
The Spanish Armada.

At length *Philip* dying in 1598, left his vast Territories in Peace (save the *Netherlands* which were still embroil'd) to his Son of the same Name; who, in *India*, by his Admiral *Peter Acunha*, defeated the *Dutch* in an Engagement at Sea, and repulsed them from the Islands *Ternate* and *Tidore*; and in the Mediterranean Sea, his Gallies routed the *Turks* before *Goletta*, and burnt thirty three of their Ships. Then entering into a Truce with the *Dutch* for ten Years, he made War on the Emperor of *Morocco*, and transported an Army into *Fez*, which, in conjunction with the Fleet, reduced *Larache* and *Mahmora*, two considerable Towns upon the Ocean. Soon after this, *Octavius Arrigon*, in the Mediterranean, sailed up the *Archipelago* at the head of the *Sicilian* Gallies, where, near *Scio*, he defeated a *Turkish* Squadron of ten Gallies, and took *Sinan*, who commanded them, Prisoner. In 1619 the Duke of *Ossuna*, Viceroy of *Naples*, took the same Route with the *Neapolitan* Gallies, and putting out *Turkish* Colours, and placing several Persons in *Turkish* Habits on the Decks, he entered the Port of *Tenedo*, where he surprized the *Pasha* of *Cairo*, then going to his Government, and brought him off.

The Spaniards beat the Dutch Fleet in India.
1608.
Turks Ships burnt by the Spaniards.

The Spaniards take Larache and Mahmora.
1610.
The Gallies of Sicily beat the Turks.
1619.

The *Spaniards*, upon their taking of *Mahmora* beforementioned, had erected a strong Fortress there, which being in the Neighbourhood of *Sallé*, was a great Curb to the Rovers of that Place, and therefore

CHAP. IX. *Ruin of the* Rom. *Empire.* 279

therefore a violent Eye-fore to the Emperor of *Morocco*, who in 1621 laid siege to it, wherein he was assisted by a Squadron of *Dutch* Ships, their Truce with *Spain* being now expired: But *Alphonsus Contrera* being sent to its Relief with the *Spanish* Fleet, happily effected it, and raised the siege with a great Slaughter of the Enemy. The same Year *Frederick de Toledo*, Admiral of *Spain*, being at Sea with the Gallies, fell in with a *Dutch* Fleet in the Streights Mouth, which he worsted, and took three of their Ships and sunk one: Some time after which, he was sent with a Fleet of thirty nine sail to *Brasil*, where in conjunction with six and thirty *Portuguese* Ships, under *Manuel de Meneses*, he attacked the Town of St. *Salvador*, which the *Dutch* had lately taken from the *Portuguese*; and defeating the Enemy's Fleet, forced the Besieged to surrender, on condition of being transported to *Holland*. But the *Spaniards* in a short time after dearly paid for this trifling Advantage; for *Peter Heyns* repairing with a Squadron of *Dutch* Ships to the Gulph of *Florida*, fell in, near the *Havana*, with the Plate-Fleet, and took most of the Galleons, which plundering of their Cargoes, he ran them ashore, and brought off with him near a Million, Sterling, of Silver, besides Jewels, Gold Chains, Amber-greece, Cochinil, and great Quantities of other rich Commodities.

1621. *The* Spaniards *beat the* Moors *and* Dutch.

The Dutch *Fleet beaten by the* Spaniards *and* Portuguese *at St.* Salvador.

1688. *The* Dutch *take the* Spanish *Plate-Fleet.*

In 1639 the *Spaniards* fitted out a considerable Fleet under the Command of *Antonio de Oquendo*, consisting of sixty seven large Ships and Galleons, manned with five and twenty thousand Seamen, and having on board twelve thousand Land-men, with what Design was not then known, but supposed to be to dislodge the *Dutch* Ships from before *Dunkirk*, and land the Troops there for the Relief of *Flanders* and the rest of the *Spanish* Provinces; tho' Monsieur *Puffendorf* says, it was afterwards found out to be intended against the *Swedes*, in favour of the *Danes*, who, against the Arrival of that Fleet at *Gottenburg*, had got ready an Army of twenty thousand Men to penetrate *Sweden* on one side, while the *Spanish* Troops should land and enter it on the other. However the *Dutch* having two or three Squadrons at Sea, the *Spanish* Fleet coming up the Chanel, was met, near the Streights of *Dover*, by one of them, consisting of seventeen Sail, under the Command of *Herpert van Tromp*; who, notwithstanding the Enemy's great Superiority, ventured to attack them, but finding himself too weak, got to Windward, sailing along towards *Dunkirk*, and continually firing Guns as a Signal to the *Dutch* Vice-Admiral, who lay off that Place, to come to his Assistance, who accordingly joined him the next Morning between *Dover* and *Calais*, where engaging the *Spaniards*, a very sharp Fight ensued between them, which lasted several Hours, wherein the *Dutch* had greatly the Advantage, and having taken one Galleon, sunk another and much shatter'd the rest, at length forced them upon the *English* Coast near *Dover*. This done, *Tromp*, being in want of Powder and Ball, stood away for *Calais* to borrow some of the Governour of that Place, who presently supplying him with what he demanded, he returned again to *Dover*; upon whose Approach the *Spaniards* got within the South Foreland

1639.

The Dutch *meet with a* Spanish *Fleet in the* British *Chanel.*

Foreland, and put themselves under the Protection of the neighbouring Castles.

The two Fleets continuing in this Posture for many Days observing each other, the Ministers of both Nations were not less employed in watching each other's Motions at *Whitehall*, and encountering one another with Memorials. The *Spanish* Resident importuned the King that he would keep the *Hollander* in Subjection two Tides, that so in the interim the others might have the Opportunity of making away for *Spain*, but the King being in Amity with them both, was resolved to stand Neuter, and whereas the *Spaniards* had hired some *English* Ships to transport their Soldiers to *Dunkirk*, upon Complaint made thereof by the *Dutch* Embassador, strict Orders were given that no Ships or Vessels belonging to His Majesty's Subjects should take any *Spaniards* on board, or pass below *Gravesend* without Licence: However after great plotting and counter-plotting on both Sides, the *Spaniard* at length somewhat outwitted his Enemy, and found means, by a Stratagem, in the Night, to convey away through the *Downs*, round by the *North-Sand Head* and the back of the *Goodwin*, twelve large Ships to *Dunkirk*, and in them four thousand Men; in Excuse of which gross Neglect of the *Dutch* Admirals in leaving that Avenue from the *Downs* unguarded, the *Dutch* Accounts say they were assured by the *English*, that no Ships of any considerable Burthen could venture by Night to sail that Way.

Several of the Spanish Ships escape to Dunkirk.

The two Fleets had now continued in their Station near three Weeks, when King *Charles* sent the Earl of *Arundel* to the Admiral of *Spain*, to desire him to retreat upon the first fair Wind; but by this time the *Dutch* Fleet was, by continual Reinforcements from *Zealand* and *Holland*, increased to a hundred Sail, and seeming disposed to attack their Enemies, Sir *John Pennington*, Admiral of His Majesty's Fleet, who lay in the *Downs* with four and thirty Men of War, acquainted the *Dutch* Admiral that he had received Orders to act in Defence of either of the two Parties who should be first attacked. The *Spaniards* however growing too presumptuous on the Protection, they enjoyed, a Day or two after fired some Shot at *Van Tromp*'s Barge, when he was himself in her, and killed a Man with a Cannon-Ball on board one of the *Dutch* Ships, whose dead Body was presently sent on board Sir *John Pennington*, as a Proof that the *Spaniards* were the first Aggressors, and had violated the Neutrality of the King of *England*'s Harbour. Soon after which the *Dutch* Admiral came to a Resolution of attacking the *Spaniards*; but before he put it in Execution, he thought fit to write to Admiral *Pennington*, telling him that the *Spaniards* having, in the Instances beforementioned, infringed the Liberties of the King's Harbour, and become the Aggressors, he found himself obliged to retaliate Force with Force, and attack them, in which, pursuant to the Declaration he had made to him, he not only hoped for, but depended on his Assistance; which, however if he should not be pleased to grant, he prayed the favour that he would at least give him

The English Fleet interposes between the Dutch and Spaniards in the Downs.

leave

CHAP. IX. *Ruin of the* Rom. *Empire.* 281

leave to engage the Enemy, otherwise he should have just Cause of Complaint to all the World of so manifest an Injury.

This Letter being delivered to the *English* Admiral, *Van Tromp* bore up to the *Spaniards*, in six Divisions, and charged them so furiously with his Broad-sides, and his Fireships, as forced them all to cut their Cables; and being three and fifty in Number, twenty three ran ashore and stranded in the *Downs*, whereof three were burnt, two sunk, and two perished on the Shore; one of which was a great Galleon, (the Vice-Admiral of *Gallicia*) commanded by *Antonio de Castro*, and mounted with fifty two Brass Guns: The Remainder of the twenty three stranded, and deserted by the *Spaniards*, were manned by the *English*, to save them from the *Dutch*. The other thirty *Spanish* Ships, with *Don Antonio de Oquendo*, the Commander in Chief, and *Lopez* Admiral of *Portugal*, got out to Sea, and kept in good Order, till a thick Fog arising, the *Dutch* took Advantage thereof, interposed between the Admirals and their Fleet, and fought them valiantly till the Fog cleared up, when the Admiral of *Portugal* began to flame, being fired by two *Dutch* Ships fitted for that Purpose, which *D'Oquendo* perceiving presently stood away for *Dunkirk* with the Admiral of that Place, and some few Ships more; for of these thirty, five were sunk in the Fight, eleven taken and sent into *Holland*, three perished upon the Coast of *France*, one near *Dover*, and only ten escaped.

Van Tromp forces the Spanish Ships on shore in the Downs.

Spanish Ships sunk and taken.

I have been the more particular in the Account of this Engagement because of the Relation it hath to our own Affairs, and have reported it in all its Circumstances, (the most material of which have been omitted even in that said to be Sir *John Pennington*'s own Account of it,) for that otherwise the *English* Government would appear to have departed from the common Rights of all Nations, in suffering one Friend to destroy another within its Chambers, and not animadverting upon the *Dutch* for that Proceeding, did it not appear that the *Spaniards* committed the first Hostility, which was the Plea the others made in their Justification: For though, by the Law of Nations, I am not to attack my Enemy in the Dominions of a Friend common to that Enemy and my self, yet no Laws Natural, Divine, or Human, forbid me to repel Force with Force, and act in my Defence when or wheresoever I am attacked. But, however, it must be confessed the *Dutch* well knew their Time, and had the like Circumstances happened twelve or fourteen Years after, when the Usurper ruled, they would probably have waited for farther Hostilities from their Enemy, (one or two Random Shot only, being liable to Exception, and to be excused as accidental) before they had ventured upon such an Action.

This was a Loss very fatal to the Naval Affairs of *Spain*, that Kingdom having used its utmost Efforts in this Armament, by much the greatest that had ever been made since the destructive Blow of 1588. And as one Misfortune generally falls on the Neck of another, this was followed by several successive Defeats at Sea from the *French*, both in the Ocean and Mediterranean Sea, particularly in the last, where the Archbishop of *Bourdeaux*, at the Head of the French

The French beat the Spaniards at Sea.

O o

French Gallies, engaged the *Spaniards* before *Tarragona*, and taking one, funk or burnt eleven others: At which time also happened the Revolt both of *Catalonia* and *Portugal*, the first of which cost the Crown of *Spain* eleven Years to recover, and the latter, after several fruitless Attempts, they were forced entirely to quit all Pretensions to by Treaty (in which our King *Charles* II. was Mediator,) and acknowledge it as an independent Kingdom.

<small>Catalonia and Portugal revolt from Spain.</small>

Since which time the most remarkable Incidents in the History of the *Spanish* Monarchy, are its three successive Wars, under *Charles* II. with the *French* King, the first terminated by the Peace of *Aix la Chapelle*, the second by that of *Nimeguen*, and the third by that of *Ryswick*; and lastly its War, under *Philip* II. the present King, in Conjunction with *France*, against the confederated Powers of *Europe*, which ended by the Peace of *Utrecht*; but not finding in all these any thing remarkable to our purpose, except in the two last Wars, (the principal Occurrences whereof at Sea, as they bear a Relation to our own Affairs, will be found in the fourth and fifth Books of this Work) I come in the next Place to the Naval Transactions of the *Dutch*.

Chap. X.

Of the Naval Wars of the Dutch.

THE People of *Holland* have from very remote Times been observable for their Application to the Sea, insomuch that we find, in the Reign of *Tiberius* the *Roman* Emperor, *Germanicus*, who was at the Head of the Legions in those Parts, designing an Expedition against the *Germans* between the [a] *Visurgis* and the [b] *Amisius*, and resolving to go up the latter of those Rivers, and attack them by Water as well as by Land, he, to that purpose, by the Assistance of the People of the *Insula Batavorum* (now the Province of *Holland*) built a Fleet of a thousand Ships, both for the Sail and the Oar; some of a round Form to sustain the Violence of the Waves; others with flat Bottoms, for the more convenient landing the Troops; many with two Rudders, one at each End, for the more expeditious turning them; and several with Decks laid over them, to carry the Warlike Machines, without incommoding the Horses or Provisions: With which Fleet *Germanicus* proceeded on his Design, and executed it with good Success, but the Ships in their Return home, meeting with a violent Storm, were most of them unfortunately lost.

<small>[a] Weser. [b] Embs
The Romans build a great Fleet, assisted by the Dutch.</small>

The next News we hear of these People at Sea is on their Revolt from the *Romans* under the Emperor *Vitellius*, whose stationary Fleet they attacked in the Mouth of the *Rhine*, and entirely destroyed, killing all the Troops on board, and utterly extirpating the

<small>The Dutch revolt from the Romans, and beat their Fleet.</small>

Roman

CHAP. X. *Ruin of the* Rom. *Empire.* 283

Roman Name in their Country. Their Affairs for several subsequent Ages are involved in such Obscurity, that we meet with nothing more of their Naval Exploits till the Time of the Counts of *Holland*, under whom the *Dutch* made several Expeditions, in conjunction with the neighbouring Nations, for recovering the Holy Land from the *Saracens*; where they gave many signal Proofs of their Valour, particularly at the Siege of *Damiata* in *Ægypt*; for to some Ships of *Harlem* was chiefly owing the Reduction of that Place, by means of a kind of Saw fixed to them, wherewith they cut the Chains which were placed under Water for the Security of that City. <small>*The* Dutch *under the Counts of* Holland, *to the Holy Land, assist in reducing* Damiata.</small>

Under *John* II, one of these Counts, his Son (who succeeded by the Name of *William* III.) gained a great Naval Victory, off of *Zirickzee* in *Zeeland*, over *Guido* of *Dampier*, Count of *Flanders*, wherein ten thousand of the *Flemings* were slain, and great Numbers of Prisoners taken, with most of the Ships; soon after which they gave the *Flemings* another signal Defeat off the Isle of *Cadsant*. But at length Count *William*, in his turn, was worsted several times upon the Coasts of *Zeeland*, particularly in an Engagement of *Duyvelant*, wherein one of his best Officers, *Guido* Bishop of *Utrecht*, was taken Prisoner, with many others, three thousand *Hollanders* slain, and himself narrowly escaped falling into the Enemy's Hands; but soon after fitting out a new Fleet, he sent for *Reyner Grimbaltz* from *Genoa*, (the same who was afterwards the *French* King's Admiral, and had that Complaint exhibited against him to our *Edward* I, which is at large cited in the first Book of this History) who having the Reputation of the most expert Seaman in that Age, he committed to him the Command of his Ships, came to an Engagement with the *Flemings* off *Zirickzee*, which continued till Night, when a violent Swell of the Sea parted them; in which Circumstance the Count of *Holland*, to keep his Ships together and in the same Order they had engaged, linked them to each other with large Grappling-Irons, which, in case of an Attack, would be Proof against any Force of the Enemy, who on the other Hand fasten'd theirs only with Ropes and Cables, which the *Hollanders* taknig an Opportunity to cut in the Night, thereby put the whole Fleet in the utmost Disorder, insomuch that the greatest part of the Ships fell into their Hands, together with Count *Guido* himself, who commanded them. Which Misfortune was soon after followed by another no less fatal; for both the hostile Fleets being disposed ready for Battel, the *Flemings* sent a Fireship against the *Dutch*, which, by a sudden Change of Wind, being forced back among their own Ships, caused great Destruction among them, at which time the *Dutch* briskly charging them, thereupon ensued the Loss of the whole Fleet, consisting of a thousand Ships, which were all either burnt or taken. <small>*Overcome the Fleet of the Count of* Flanders. 1304.</small> <small>*The* Dutch *are beaten on the Coast of* Flanders.</small> <small>*The* Dutch *overcome at Sea those of* Flanders.</small>

We hear nothing more of their Naval Wars for many Years; but about 1416, *William Bouckeld* is said to have first found out the Way of curing *Herrings*, which celebrated Fisherman dying in 1447, he was buried at *Biervliet*, a Sea Port of *Flanders*, at which Place the <small>A. D. 1416. *The curing of* Herrings *found out.*</small>

O o 2

the Emperor *Charles* V. happening to land, about a hundred Years after, paid so great a Respect to his Memory for that valuable Invention, as to go and visit his Tomb, accompanied with his Sister, *Mary* Queen of *Hungary*, and pray for the Peace of his Soul. In 1441, the *Dutch* managed so great a Trade and were so powerful at Sea for that Age, that they drew upon them the Envy of the People of the Trading Towns in the *Baltick* (called *Osterlings* or *Easterlings* in the Annals of those Times) who enter'd into a League against them, and waged War for three Years, but in the End the *Hollanders* proving too strong for them, they dissolved their League, and the *Swedes* came to a Truce with them for two Years, and the *Danes* and *Prussians* to a perpetual Peace.

1441. The Dutch improve in Trade, and a Naval Force, and War with the Easterlings.

In 1471, the *Dutch* had another Naval War on account of our *Edward* IV, whose Sister was the Wife of the *Duke* of *Burgundy*, then possessing all the *Low-Countries*; which Duke, espousing the Cause of his said Brother in Law after his Quarrel with the great Earl of *Warwick*, that Earl, being supported by the *French* King, scoured the Coasts of *Holland* with a strong Squadron, where in one Day he took thirty Sail of *Dutch* Ships, and soon after twenty more; whereupon *Henry Borsale*, Lord of *Veer* was sent out against him with a Fleet of thirty six Sail, who coming up with him on the Coast of *Normandy*, recovered ten of those Ships, and found means to set the rest on fire: Soon after which the Earl of *Warwick* quitted the Sea, that he might prosecute his Quarrel more vigorously ashore in *England*.

A. D. 1471. Assist King Edward IV.

The Earl of Warwick takes many Dutch Ships.

About the Middle of the following Century the Emperor *Charles* V. (who amongst his many other Dominions, was also Sovereign of the *Low Countries*) being at War with *France*, and they having Intelligence of a Fleet of *Dutch* Merchant Ships coming up the Chanel from the Southward, lay in wait for them off *Dover*, near which Place they engaged, when the *Dutch* being much more skilful in the Management of their great Guns, used their best Endeavours to avoid a close Fight, which would deprive them of the Advantage of their Experience; for which same Reason the whole Aim of the *French* was, if possible, to grapple their Ships together with those of the *Dutch*, and found means so to do with fifteen of them, whereupon ensued a bloody and obstinate Fight, which continued for some time, till the *French*, grown weary of so hot Work, set the Sails of one of their own Ships on fire, in hopes it would oblige the *Dutch* to sheer off from the Danger, but the Ships were so closely linked together that there was no disengaging them; so that the Flames spreading from one Vessel to another, raged with equal Violence among them all, and put an End to the Dispute, in which the *Dutch* say their Enemy lost a thousand Men, and themselves but three hundred.

French Ships destroyed by the Dutch.

In few Years after this ensued those Troubles in the *Low Countries* which lost the King of *Spain* seven of the Seventeen Provinces, and gave Rise to the flourishing Republick of the United Provinces, whose Naval Actions, if very particularly related, would of themselves require a just Volume. As if by a Sort of Fatality it were

The Rise of the United Provinces.

CHAP. X. *Ruin of the* Rom. *Empire.* 285

were a Fore-token of the maritime Power they should one Day arrive at, the great Blow to the *Spanish* Affairs, to which that Republick chiefly owes its Rise, was struck by Sea, and the Effects of a Naval Expedition. For, as Sir *William Temple* tells us, upon the Duke of *Alva*'s being appointed to the Government of the *Low-Countries*, and exercising that Charge with great Cruelty, many of the poorer, and more desperate sort of People fled to the Woods of the *Upper-Countries*, where they lived upon Spoil, and in the first Descent of the Prince of *Orange*'s Forces from *Germany*, did great Mischiefs to all scatter'd Parties of the Duke of *Alva*'s Troops in their March through those Parts. But after that Attempt of the Prince ended without Success, and he was forced back into *Germany*, the Count of *Marck*, a violent and implacable Enemy to the Duke of *Alva*, and his Government, with many others of the broken Troops, whom the same Fortune and Disposition had left together in *Friesland*, manned out some Ships of small Force, and betook themselves to Sea, beginning, with Commissions from the Prince of *Orange*, to prey upon all they could master which belonged to the *Spaniards*, scouring all the Coasts from the Mouth of the *Embs* to the Streights of *Dover*: And if at any time they happened to meet with bad Weather, or too considerable a Force of the Enemy's, they sheltered themselves in the Ports of *England*, till at length, at the Request of the Duke of *Alva*, they were forbidden by Queen *Elizabeth*, who was then at Peace with *Spain*. But now having gained considerable Riches by these Adventures; whether to sell or to refresh, whether driven by Storm, or led by Design, upon Knowledge of the ill Blood which the new Taxes had bred in all the Provinces, they landed in the Island of *Voorne*, assaulted and carried the Town of *Briel*, pulled down the Images in the Churches, professed openly their Religion, declared against the Taxes and Tyranny of the *Spanish* Government; and were immediately followed by the Revolt of most of the Towns of *Holland*, *Zeeland*, and *West-Friesland*, who threw out the *Spanish* Garrisons, renounced their Obedience to the King of *Spain*, and swore Fidelity to the Prince of *Orange*.

The Count of Marck *molests the Spaniards at Sea.*

Fidelity sworn to the Prince of Orange.

During the long Prosecution of this War there followed many Naval Skirmishes between the contending Parties, but none of them, in my Opinion, more remarkable than that at the Siege of *Antwerp* in 1585. That City having in 1579, with *Ghent*, *Bruges*, and others, enter'd into the Union with the Seven Provinces; the Duke of *Parma*, who commanded in the *Low-Countries* for the King of *Spain*, well knowing the vast Importance the Recovery of *Antwerp* would be to his Master's Affairs, formed, in *August* 1584, the Siege of that City; and having possessed himself of the Forts, and advantagious Posts in its Neighbourhood, at length resolved to lay a Bridge cross the *Scheld*, two Leagues below the Town, to prevent the Besieged from receiving any Succours from *Zeeland* that way, which was the only Avenue they had open. Being Master of the Country on both sides the River, he raised two strong Forts opposite

A. D. 1585.

The Duke of Parma *lays siege to Antwerp, with what happened thereupon.*

site to each other, one called St. *Mary*'s on the *Flanders*, and the other St. *Philip*'s on the *Brabant* side, to cover the intended Work; which done, he drove into the River large Piles of thirty, forty, fifty, and at length seventy Feet long, which were well secured together with cross Planks, to sustain a Bridge of Wood, (which he called a Palissado) whereon eight Men might march abreast. The River being in this Place four hundred and eighty Paces broad, and so deep that no Trees could be found tall enough for carrying the Work farther than eleven hundred Feet into it, *viz.* nine hundred from the side of *Brabant*, and two hundred from that of *Flanders*, there was a Space of thirteen hundred Feet left between the two Works, which was filled up with two and thirty Ships, placed at the Distance of twenty two Feet from one another; each secured against the Tide with an Anchor at Head and Stern, and held together by four Iron Chains, and as many Cables, passed from one Ship to the other; each Vessel having two Guns in the Forecastle, and two in the Poop, and thirty Soldiers on board for its Defence: Over all which Vessels there being Masts and Planks laid to join a Floor to the rest of the Work, the *Scheld* was compleatly shut up with a Bridge of near half a Mile long. For the Defence whereof, besides ninety seven Pieces of Ordnance, which (including the two in each Ship) were disposed through the whole length of the Work, there were placed on each side thirty three large Floats, composed of Ships Masts, Planks, and other Pieces of Timber, laid three in a Row, covering the River beyond the Breadth of the Ships on each side; and in each Row of them were raised forty round upright Pieces of Timber, headed with Iron, in the Nature of Spikes, all the Spaces between which were covered with empty Hogsheads, fastened to the Floats, the better to keep them above Water; and to maintain them in this order, from each Float were thrown out two Anchors, held by Cables of a proper Length, that so they might rise and fall with the Tide. Besides all which, forty Vessels, with Soldiers on board, were disposed, twenty on each side of the River, for its farther Security against any Attacks of the Enemy. It was above seven Months before the whole Work was compleated; and till the middle Space of it was filled up with the Ships, Vessels frequently passed to and from *Antwerp*, notwithstanding the continual Fire made from the Forts on each side.

The Besieged, and their Confederates, the States of the United Provinces, well knowing that if this Communication to the City could not be again opened, it would be inevitably lost, nothing was left unattempted for compassing that End. The Fleet of *Zeeland*, under the Command of *Justin* of *Nassau*, a natural Son of the Prince of *Orange*'s, set sail from *Middleburg*, and came up the *Scheld*, where attacking the Fort of *Liefkenshoeck*, the *Dutch* soon carried it, and made themselves Masters of all the Country on both sides the River as high as the Bridge: Which great Success hastened the Execution of a Design lately entered into, whereby it was agreed, that when the Besieged, with the Works they were preparing, should

attack

attack the Bridge, and open a Passage through it, the auxiliary Ships of *Zeeland* should immediately make their way through the Breach, and throw their intended Supply into the City. And lest the Floats beforementioned, which lay before the Bridge, should hinder the Performance of the *Antwerpians* Project, some of the *Dutch* Seamen went up in Boats in the Night, and some swam under Water, and with Hatchets, Scythes, and such like Instruments, cut the Cables which held the Floats at Anchor: Which, however, being soon discovered, the Duke of *Parma* caused Chains to be plac'd in the room of all the Cables, to prevent the like Damage for the future. The time appointed for the Execution of the Project against the Bridge was the fourth of *April* in the Evening, of which the Besieged gave notice to the *Zeeland* Squadron, assuring the Commander that they could not fail of ruining the Bridge, and therefore desiring that he would be ready with his Ships, well stored with Provisions, to sail through, without fear of the Enemy, to their Relief.

The Projector of this Design was one *Frederick Jambel*, an *Italian* Engineer, (sent over to them by Queen *Elizabeth*) who, by a new, and unexampled Contrivance, found means to make and spring Mines in the Water, which he performed in this manner. Having caused to be built four large Hulks with flat Bottoms, and very deep, as well as of an unusual Thickness and Strength, he first laid in the bottom of each Hulk a Floor of Brick from one end to the other, one Foot in Thickness, and five in Breadth, which having inclosed with Walls, and a Covering of a proportionable Strength, it formed a Mine of five Feet broad, and as many deep, which he filled with Gunpowder of a most exquisite Preparation, known only to himself. The Covering of this Mine consisted of large Tombstones and Mill-stones, over which he raised a Roof with Stones of the like Bulk sloped together so as to form a Ridge at top, to the end that when it blew up, it might deal its Destruction not only upwards, but sideways, and on all Quarters; the Cavity of which Roof he filled with Cannon Balls of Iron and Marble, together with Chains, Hooks, Nails, and Knives, and whatever other Instruments of Ruin a Genius so fruitful in Mischief could devise. The void Spaces between the Mine, with its Roof, and the sides of the Hulk, he built up with large square Stones, and Beams of Timber joined together with Iron, and then covering the whole with thick Planks, and a Brick Floor, he raised thereupon a large Pile of Wood, to be set on fire as a Blind to his Design, and to make the Enemy think that was all which was intended for the Destruction of the Bridge, which Wood having under it Pitch, Tar, and other combustible Matter, was not to cease burning till the Mine should take Fire, to the Mouth whereof was laid Match of a proper Length to continue burning till the Hulk should reach the Bridge: And to these four Hulks, prepared in this manner, the said Engineer added thirteen smaller Vessels, having their Decks covered with Piles of Wood and Fire-works.

The Duke of *Parma* was very well apprized of the great Preparations making for the Attack of the Bridge, but was totally ignorant of the manner wherein it was to be done; only supposing that the Besieged, with the Ships they were getting ready, were to assault it above, while the *Zeeland* Fleet should do the same below. All things being ripe for the Execution of this Design, as soon as it was Night the small Vessels were seen coming down the Stream all in Flames, whereupon the Alarm being presently taken in the Duke of *Parma*'s Camp, the Banks of the River and the Bridge were immediately covered with Troops. By this time the fatal Squadron being come within two Miles of the Bridge, the Persons who had the Management thereof, fixing in the middle of the Stream the Rudders of the four Hulks, in such manner as they might be carried directly against that part of the Bridge which consisted of the Ships, they set fire to the Piles of Wood and the Matches, and retired into their Boats; taking little or no care of the smaller Vessels, as being designed more to amuse and confound the Enemy, than to do any great Execution, so that most of them stuck on the Floats at a distance from the Bridge, or ran ashore upon the Banks: Nor did the Hulks, now destitute of Pilots, keep the Course as was designed, one of which springing a Leake, sunk in the midst of the River, the second and third were forced by the Wind upon the *Flanders* Shore, and no better Success seemed to attend the fourth, which fell foul of the Floats. Upon this the Enemy recovering their Surprize, began to deride so fruitless a Project as they supposed this would prove; but that last Hulk, which was the largest and strongest of them all, forcing its way, at length, through the Floats, and bearing directly upon the Bridge, their Fears began to revive, and immediately all Hands were set to work, some to fend it off from the Bridge with Poles and Staves, others to pull down the Pile of Wood, and endeavour to extinguish the Fire, the Duke of *Parma* himself appearing on the Bridge where the Ships joined to the Palissado, to encourage the Men with his Presence; from whence however being at length prevailed upon to withdraw to Fort St. *Mary*'s at the Foot of the Bridge, he was scarcely arrived there, when, the lighted Match having now burnt to the Powder, the Hulk blew up with such a dreadful Violence, that it seemed as if Heaven and Earth were coming together, and the World was shaken to its Centre: And amidst the horrid Blaze there flew such Tempests of Stones, Chains, and Cannon-shot, which caused so vast a Destruction as can only be believed because it happened. Great part of the Bridge next Fort St. *Mary*'s, and six of the Ships, with the Soldiers, Seamen, Pieces of Cannon, Planks, Guns, and various kinds of Arms, were all torn up together with one fatal Blast, and toss'd about like Chaff before the Wind; the same impetuous Violence forcing the River from its Chanel, and spreading it upon the adjacent Fields, where the Soldiers waded to their Knees, and the very Forts were filled a Foot deep. The Earth shook for nine Miles about, and many of the largest Stones, which were found a thousand Paces from the River, stuck a Foot deep in the Ground. The Duke of *Parma*, and

A dreadful Blast at the blowing up a Hulk at the Duke of Parma's Bridge.

several

several Officers about him in Fort St. *Mary's*, were beaten to the Earth with the violent Motion of the Air, and some of them hurt with the Fall of Pieces of Timber. Death appeared in variety of Shapes, and no less than eight hundred Men, with many Officers, were slain outright, besides great Numbers which were hurt and died afterwards of their Wounds, and many more were destroyed by the blowing up of one of the other Hulks upon the *Flanders* Shore, where the third that was near it (taking in so much Water as damaged the Powder) remained without effect.

The Darkness of the Night added to the Horror of this dreadful Blow, which struck a most terrible and universal Amazement amongst the Besiegers; notwithstanding all which, the Duke of *Parma*, as soon as he was recovered from his first Surprize, used such extraordinary Diligence to fill up the Breach made in the Bridge, partly with other Ships, and partly by slightly laying together again many of the Planks and Timbers which floated upon the Water, that before Day the Floor was entire, whereon he disposed a Body of Troops, with Colours flying, Drums beating, and Trumpets sounding, to make an Appearance of Opposition, and disguise as much as possible the Destruction: Which Artifice succeeded so well, that the *Zeeland* Fleet made no Attempt to come up the River, though they might without difficulty have broken through the slight hasty Work, and, by relieving *Antwerp*, have forced the Duke of *Parma* to raise the Siege. This he neglecting to do, in a short time fully repaired his Bridge, defeated another Attempt against it, and prosecuting the Siege with extraordinary Vigour, in few Months after made himself Master of the City, to the great Advancement of the King of *Spain*'s Affairs in the *Low-Countries*. *The Duke of Parma fully repairs his Bridge, and takes Antwerp.* This great Captain's Conduct before *Antwerp*, as well in building the Bridge, as in his dextrous repairing of it when ruined, the ingenious Historian, *Famian Strada*, has thought reasonable to compare with that of *Alexander* the Great at the Siege of *Tyre*, where he raised a like stupendous Work, as we have in its proper Place described: Nor, in my Opinion, is the Comparison unjust; but we must at the same time let the *Antwerpians* have the Honour of compleating the Parallel, by acknowleding the Bravery of their Defence to be equal to that of the Citizens of *Tyre*.

The *Zeelanders* we before mentioned to have come up the *Scheld* with their Fleet, finding nothing farther to be done towards the Relief of *Antwerp*, returned to *Middleburg*; but had not long after an Opportunity of revenging themselves by the Share they had with Us in the Destruction of the *Spanish Armada* in 1588, of whose Service therein I shall be more particular when I come to treat of that Action among our own Affairs; as I shall, in the same Place, of the part the *Dutch* bore in our Expedition to *Cadiz* under the Earl of *Essex*, in 1596.

About this time it was that the *Dutch*, being prohibited all farther Commerce with *Spain* and *Portugal*, to which they had hitherto traded, with great Advantage, under other Names, took a Resolution of visiting *India* themselves, and trafficking, at the first hand,

P p

The Dutch attempt a way to India by the North-East. hand, with the rich Commodities of that Country. To which purpose they endeavoured to find out a Passage thither by the North-East, which they proposed should be two thousand Miles shorter than that by the Cape of *Good-Hope*; and, in the Prosecution of this Design, some Ships of *Amsterdam*, and of the Town of *Veer* in *Zeeland*, penetrated a considerable way to the Eastward, and discovered *Nova Zembla*, and the Streights of *Weygatz*; but not being able to reach any farther, by reason of the Cold and Ice, they returned home; and that Project being laid aside, some Merchants

A. D. 1595. of *Amsterdam*, in the Year 1595, set out four Ships to proceed to *India* by the Cape of *Good-Hope*, which having traded in *Sumatra*, *Java*, and the Isle of *Baly*, safely returned home.

Dutch East-India-Company settled. Not long after this they were sent out again, in conjunction with several others under the Direction of the same Merchants, who were now incorporated into a Publick Society by the Name of the *East-India-Company*; whose Profits, in these early Voyages, were so great, that for every Venture of five or six Florins, they gained a hundred. These Ships were commanded by *Jacob Nek*; at the time of whose sailing from the *Texel*, two Ships of *Balthasar Moucheron*'s, and three of *Adrian Hendrickson*'s, proceeded on the same Voyage from *Zeeland*; as did also five from *Rotterdam*, under the Command of *James Mahu*; but the latter steered a different Course, and sailing through the Streights of *Magellan* to the *Molucca*'s, and thence home, navigated round the Globe. So good Success the *Dutch* met with in these Expeditions, that in 1598, eighty Ships sailed from *Holland* to the *East-Indies*, and returned home richly laden with *Indian* Commodities;

The Dutch settle a Trade in Turkey and Guiana. at which time some Ships were sent up the Mediterranean to settle a Trade in *Turkey*, and others to *Guiana* in *America*, to traffick upon that Coast. This Year also *Oliver de Noort*, sailing with four Ships from the *Maese*, made a Voyage round the Globe, in which he took a *Spanish* Ship richly laden at the Isle of St. *Mary*, and in an Engagement with two great Galleons at the *Philippines*, sunk one of them.

Other Discoveries made by the Dutch. The next Year a Fleet of seventy Sail repaired to the *Canary* Islands, under the Command of *Peter Dousa*, who landing in *Teneriffe*, took and burnt the Town of *Laguna*, and proceeding thence to *Gomer*, destroyed that Place likewise, from whence he made the best of his way for the Isle of St. *Thomas*, under the Æquinoctial Line, which he ravaged, and brought off a rich Booty from thence; but the great Heats of that Climate causing a Mortality amongst the Seamen, which proved fatal also to *Dousa* himself, the Fleet returned to *Holland* with the Loss of great Numbers of them. In another Expedition *Laurence Bicker*, with two Ships under his Command, after an obstinate Dispute at the Island of St. *Helena*, took a great *Spanish* Galleon called the St. *James*, having a very rich Cargo on board of Pearls, Gems, Gold, *Bezoar*-Stone, Amber, and other Goods of inestimable Value, which, with four hundred Prisoners, and seventeen Brass Guns, the *Dutch* put on board their Ships, and brought safe to *Zeeland*.

CHAP. X. *Ruin of the* Rom. *Empire.* 291

In 1602, *Frederick Spinola*, the Brother of *Ambrose*, a famous Captain of the *Spaniards* in *Flanders*, coming from *Spain* with eight Gallies thither, in order to cruise from thence upon the *Zeelanders*, was met off the *Goodwin* Sands by four *Dutch* Ships under the Command of the Vice-Admiral of *Zeeland*, who, by the help of Sir *Robert Mansel*, then cruising thereabouts with two of the Queen's Ships, destroyed all of them but one, which with great difficulty escaped to *Dunkirk*. The same Year a Fleet of thirteen Ships were sent to the *East-Indies* under the Command of the *Sieur Haghen*; from whence about the same time another Squadron returned under the *Sieur Hermansen*, after three Year's Voyage, wherein before *Bantam*, in the Isle of *Java*, they had taken, sunk, or otherwise destroyed a *Portuguese* Fleet consisting of eight Galleons, and twenty two Gallies, under Admiral *Mendoza*, whom they forced to retire to *Amboina*, and entirely expelling the *Portuguese* from *Bantam*, settled a *Dutch* Factory there in their room. *The Dutch and Sir Robert Mansel overcome some Spanish Ships.* *The Dutch destroy several Portuguese Ships at the Island Java.*

Not long after this the States made themselves Masters of the Town of *Sluys* in *Flanders*, and in the Port of that Place took ten Gallies, with fourteen hundred Men on board: And in *East-India* the *Dutch* outed the *Portuguese* from the Isle of *Amboina*, which they had possessed ever since the Year 1546; where continuing successful in all their Attemps, and in their Negotiations with the Princes in those Parts, they possessed themselves of *Tidore*, and most of the rest of the *Molucca*'s, and in a manner wholly engrossed the Spice Trade. The *Portuguese* suffering most sensibly in these Expeditions, besought the King of *Spain* to make Peace with the *Dutch*; and *Spinola*, his General in *Flanders*, advising the same thing, Deputies were accordingly dispatched to the *Hague*, but without Success. After this they sent their Admiral *Hemskirk* with a Fleet against *Spain*, who having Advice the *Spanish* Fleet was in the Harbour of *Gibraltar*, tho' they were very strong, and had a numerous Artillery, with some Regiments of their best Land-Forces on board, he bravely attacked them, and obtained a compleat Victory, but was himself slain in the Battel: Not long after which the *Dutch* came to a Truce with *Spain* for twelve Years, the Articles whereof were signed the ninth of *April* 1609. *The Dutch take Sluys, &c. and drive the Portuguese from Amboina.* *The Dutch almost wholly engross the Spice Trade.* *The Spaniards overcome by the Dutch at Gibraltar, and a Truce for twelve Years. A. D. 1609.*

The great Successes of the *Dutch* in *India* had now made their Name so famous in all Parts, that one Embassy came to them from *Japan* with Invitations of Friendship and mutual Commerce, and another from the Emperor of *Morocco*, with the like Offers of Liberty of Trade in that Country: And soon after they received Ambassadors from the Grand *Signior*, and King of *Persia*, with Proposals of Freedom of Commerce also through their respective Dominions. About this time one *Hudson*, an *Englishman*, was sent out by the *Dutch East-India* Company, to find a way to *India* by the North-West, but being stop'd by Ice in one Route, he steered another Course, and discovered those Streights, and that Bay since called by his Name, but could meet with no Passage open to *India*. *The Dutch courted by foreign Princes.* *Hudson's Bay discovered.*

P p 2   In

In 1612, the *Spaniards* and *Portuguese* envying the vast Advantages the *Dutch* received from their Trade, opposed their Commerce, and pretended that none but themselves had any Right to pass beyond the Æquinoctial Line; whereupon the States fitted out a Fleet to protect their Navigation. So soon did those People revive the Pretensions they had so strenuously asserted, and at length with so much Reluctance departed from in the late Treaty, on which occasion *Hugo Grotius* wrote his celebrated Treatise *de Mari Libero*, wherein, amongst his other Reasonings against the *Portuguese*, he endeavoured to prove the Sea to be wholly free and common, and uncapable of private Dominion, it produced our learned *Selden*'s *Mare Clausum*, which has so excellently refuted that part of his Argument.

Grotius writes de Mari Libero, and Selden Mare Clausum.

The Truce with *Spain* expiring in 1621, the *Dutch* shortly after made an Expedition against the Enemy's Settlements in *Brasil*, where their Admiral *Vilikens* took St. *Salvador*, and, in his Return home, falling in with some *Spanish* Ships, made himself Master of them, and brought them in with him to *Holland*; about which time also they struck up a League against the *Spaniards* with the Governments of *Tunis* and *Algier*, and some of their Ships, under *Leonard Frantz*, ravaged the Coasts of *Gallicia*, and carried off a rich Booty; while, in *India*, their People at *Amboina*, envying all Participation of Gain, contrived false Accusations against the *English* upon that Island, and exercised unheard of Cruelties upon them. In 1628 the *East-India* Company sent out a Fleet under the *Sieur Carpenter*, who discovered those Coasts of *New Holland* (part of the *Terra Australis*) since called from him *Carpentaria*; while, in *America*, *Peter Adrian*, with twelve Ships, attacked the Isle of *Cuba*, where he drove several Ships ashore, and plundering the Coasts, went home with a considerable Booty: And the same Year *Peter Heyns* took the Plate-Fleet on the Coasts of that Island, as we have before related, to whom, upon his Return to *Holland*, the States gave the Honour of Knighthood, made him an Admiral, and presented him with a Crown of Gold in form of a Laurel.

A. D. 1621. The Dutch successful in Brasil, and ravage the Coast of Gallicia.

The Dutch cruel to the English at Amboina. 1628. New Holland discovered, and Cuba attack'd by the Dutch.

The Spanish Plate Fleet taken.

In 1630 the *Dutch* being attacked in *Batavia* by the Emperor of *Java*'s Fleet, and an Army of two hundred thousand Men, they forced him to raise the Siege; and in *America* they were so successful, that they reduced all the Coast of *Brasil* to their Obedience. The next Year the *Spaniards*, with a great Fleet of Gallies, and other Ships, endeavouring to cut off the Communication betwixt *Holland* and *Zeeland*, were utterly defeated by Admiral *Hollar*, who took the whole Fleet, with near five thousand Men, only Count *John* of *Nassau*, who commanded it, escaping with a few Followers. In 1639 happened the Engagement between the *Spanish* Fleet under Don *Antonio de Oquendo*, and the *Dutch* Fleet under *Herpert Van Tromp* in the *Downs*, which we have already at large described; and the same Year their *India* Company possessed themselves of the Streights of *Malacca*, to the great Advancement of their Affairs in those Parts.

1630. The Dutch beat the King of Java, and master all Brasil.

1631. A Spanish Fleet taken by the Dutch.

1639.

Dutch East-India Company take the Streights of Malacca.

The

CHAP. X. *Ruin of the* Rom. *Empire.* 293

The *Portuguese* throwing off the *Spanish* Yoak in 1643, the *Dutch* made an Alliance with them, on condition each should retain their present Possessions: but the *Portuguese*, upon some old Pretences, in 1645, dispossessed them of *Brasil*. In 1648 was concluded the general Peace of *Munster*, wherein the King of *Spain* owned the *Dutch* as a Free and Sovereign People, and renounced for himself, and his Successors, all Pretences to Dominion over them: Which same Year they gained some Advantages in *Brasil*; but the Admiral who commanded there being obliged to return to *Europe*, for want of Soldiers and Ammunition, all was lost again, which almost ruined their *West-India* Company, but proved of great Benefit to them in the *East-Indies*, where, a War ensuing, which lasted till 1661, they took from the *Portuguese* almost all the Places they were possessed of in those Parts. *1645 Portuguese dispossess the Dutch of Brasil. The Portuguese dispossess'd of almost all they had in the East-Indies.*

In 1651 the new Republick of *England*, tho' keeping up the Forms of Peace, could not help betraying some Signs of Resentment, and that they only waited the Conclusion of the War in *Scotland* to let them feel the Effects of them. Their principal Allegations against the *Dutch* were, their foremention'd Cruelties exercised on the *English* in *Amboina* in the Year 1622; their neglecting to punish the Persons concerned in the Assassination of Dr. *Dorislaus*, their late Minister at the *Hague*; the Correspondence the *Dutch* Ambassadors in *England* had held with the King against the Parliament; and lastly, the great Losses and Injuries they had caused to the Subjects of *England* since the Year 1618, throughout the *East-Indies*, and in *Muscovy* and *Greenland*, the Reparation demanded for all which amounted to an immense Sum of Money. The *Dutch* dispatched an extraordinary Embassy into *England*, to endeavour to avert the Storm, but at the same time fitted out a Fleet of a hundred and fifty Sail. To take away all Umbrage on which account, their Ambassadors protested that Armament was made with no other View than to secure the Peace between the two Nations, by protecting their Trade, and keeping them from the Necessity of making Reprisals: For, indeed, the *English* had some Months before taken all the *Dutch* Ships they could meet with, the Number of which (say the *Dutch* Writers) amounted to near two hundred. The Parliament could not be perswaded but these Preparations were designed with hostile Views against them, since the States had no Enemy at Sea, and therefore resolved to humble a Power which seemed ready to dispute with them our ancient and rightful Sovereignty of the Seas, and immediately gave Orders for fitting out a powerful Fleet, and the next Year the War began between them; the principal Circumstances whereof, (as well as of the subsequent *Dutch* Wars) I find already so succinctly put together by a late Writer, from the *Atlas Historique*, and *De la Neuville*'s History of *Holland*, that I shall set most of them down from thence, only premising that they are related chiefly according to the Accounts the *Dutch* themselves have given of them. *A. D. 1651. Grounds of the Wars between England and the Dutch. The Parliament of England fit out a great Fleet. 1652.*

This Year 1652, the *Dutch* Admiral *Van Tromp* put to Sea with the Fleet to convoy home some Merchant Ships, but had Orders to avoid *A. D. 1652.*

avoid engaging with the *English*, if possible, and to pay the usual Respect to their Flag, if he chanced to meet them in the Narrow Seas. He was forced by a Tempest upon the *English* Coast, but quitted it again as soon as possible, and made towards *Calais*; but being informed that the *English* were pursuing some Merchant Ships, he advanced to their Relief, and met *Blake* with the *English* Fleet, who had Orders (the *Dutch* say) to attack them. *Tromp* prepared to give the usual Honours to the *English* Flag, and ordered one of his Captains to go on board with a Complement to the *English* Admiral; but *Blake* having no Regard to these Marks of Submission, fired twice at *Tromp*'s Ship, who made no Return till he received a third Shot, and then the Fight began, which lasted till Night parted them; and both Admirals sent an Account of the Action to their Principals, each excusing himself from being the Aggressor.

A Sea Fight between the English and Dutch.

The *Dutch* Ambassadors, (who continued still in *England*,) had Audience, upon this Occasion, of the Parliament, to whom they made a Speech, and did what they could to renew a good Understanding between *England* and *Holland*, but in vain. They sent another Ambassador, who made Application to the Parliament and Council of State, but without Success; so that they all returned home, and an Engagement happened betwixt *De Ruyter*, and the *English* Admiral *Ascough*, who had the worst. The *English* had also the Disadvantage in an Engagement near *Leghorn*, betwixt Commadore *Badiley* and the *Dutch* Commander *Van Galen*; but the *Dutch* were worsted in the Fight betwixt *Calais* and *Dover* under *De Ruyter* and *De Wit*, the *English* Fleet under *Blake* being much superior in Force. Another Engagement happened between *Tromp* and *Blake*, wherein the *English* were obliged to retire into the River *Thames*: But afterwards in another Fight betwixt the same Admirals, which lasted three Days, the *Dutch* were worsted; and *Van Galen* obtained an Advantage over the *English* in the Streights, but lost his Life in it.

The English have the disadvantage at Sea, but are afterwards successful. The Dutch and English alternately beaten.

A. D. 1653.

The *English* in 1653 inclined to a Peace, but were prevented by *Cromwell*, who dissolved the Parliament. That Year a bloody Battel was fought betwixt *Van Tromp* and the *English* Admirals *Dean* and *Monk*, wherein the *Dutch* were worsted, which occasioned Tumults in *Holland*: And the same Year in *August*, there was another bloody Engagement, wherein the *Dutch* were again defeated, and *Van Tromp* slain in the Action; who was buried with great State in *Holland*, and had a sumptuous Monument erected to his Honour at the publick Charge. This Victory was so great on the Side of the *English*, that the *Dutch* were glad next Year to accept of Peace, whereby they engaged to the Protector entirely to abandon the Interests of King *Charles* II, then in Exile, and to make a Declaration thereof in Form to the Kings of *Sweden* and *Denmark*, obliging themselves not to receive into their Dominions, or give Protection to any of the Enemies of the Commonwealth of *England*. They also renounced all Pretensions to Equality with the *English* at Sea, and agreed that all Ships of the United Provinces, as well those of War as Merchant Ships, meeting with any Ships,

A bloody Fight between Van Tromp and Dean and Monk.

Van Tromp slain.

The Dutch make Peace with Oliver, and agree to strike to the English, &c.

CHAP. X. *Ruin of the* Rom. *Empire.* 295

of War of the Commonwealth of *England*, within the *British* Seas, should strike their Flags, if they bore any, and lower their Top-Sails, in the same manner as had been practised in any former times, or under any former Government; engaging also to make Satisfaction for the Injuries done at *Amboyna*, and to do Justice on the Offenders, if any were yet living; and to make Restitution of several *English* Ships and Merchandizes seized by them in the Dominions of the King of *Denmark*, or pay the full Value thereof, on condition that Prince should be also comprehended in the Treaty: Besides which *Cromwell* imposed a yet harder Condition on them, whereby they were obliged to exclude the young Prince of *Orange*, because of his Relation to the Royal Family of *England*, from all publick Offices in the Commonwealth. *The Dutch obliged to exclude the young Prince of Orange.*

In 1656, the States, on account of their Trade, interposed in the Quarrel between *Charles Gustavus* King of *Sweden*, and *John Casimir* King of *Poland*, whom they brought to a Peace by the Treaty of *Elbing*, their Admiral *Obdam* overawing them both with his Fleet. The next Year Differences happened between the *French* and the *Dutch*, on account of some *French* Privateers which took their Ships, and disturbed their Commerce, of which the Dutch having long complain'd in vain, they took the Privateers, whereupon their Ships were seized in *France*, and the *Dutch* made Reprisals; but Monseur *de Thou* being sent into *Holland* by the Court of *France*, made up the Difference, and the Ships were released on both Sides. *1656. The Dutch oblige the Kings of Sweden and Poland to make Peace.*

In 1658 the States concerned themselves in the War betwixt the *Danes* and *Swedes*, and deliver'd the King of *Denmark*, who was much streighten'd in *Copenhagen*, Admiral *Obdam*, by the Defeat of the *Swedish* Fleet, relieving that Capital, and entring it in a triumphant manner. And the following Year de *Ruyter*, sailing to the *Baltick*, and joining the *Danes*, again defeated the *Swedes* at the Battel of *Nyborg:* Soon after which a Peace was concluded in the North by the Mediation of *England* and *France*. In the mean time the *Dutch* were very successful in *India* against the *Portuguese*, but by their Negligence gave the *Chinese* an Opportunity to seize the Isle of *Formosa*, to the great Loss of their *East-India* Company. *A. D. 1658. The Dutch beat the Swedish Fleet and relieve the King of Denmark. The Chinese take Formosa from the Dutch.*

In 1664 an *English* Squadron, under Commadore *Holmes*, unexpectedly surprized several of the *Dutch* Forts on the Coasts of *Guinea*; but *De Ruyter* soon after retook them. They did all they could nevertheless to avoid a War with *England*, but in vain, so that they came to an open Rupture the next Year, the Duke of *York* and his prevailing Faction at Court refusing all the advantagious Offers made by them; whereupon they sent a Fleet to Sea under Admiral *Obdam*, and gave him positive, but imprudent Orders, to fight the *English*, let the Wind be how it would; which he being forced to obey, contrary to the Opinion of his Officers, it had a fatal Effect; for the *English* Fleet, commanded by the Duke of *York*, Prince *Rupert*, and the Earl of *Sandwich*, defeated them, burnt and sunk nineteen of their Ships of War, and killed them six thousand *A. D. 1664. A Rupture between England and Holland. The English take and burn several Dutch Ships.*

thousand Men, with the Loss only of four Ships, and fifteen hundred Men on our Side, but among them were Rear Admiral *Sampson*, the Earls of *Marlborough* and *Falmouth*, the Lords *Portland* and *Fitzharding*, with fourteen other Persons of Note. Admiral *Obdam*, in the Beginning of the Action, attacked the Duke of *York*, sunk the three Yachts that attended him, and had almost disabled the Ship where he bore his Flag as High Admiral, but he was seasonably rescued by Vice-Admiral *Lawson* and Captain *Smith*, and *Obdam* being engaged with several other *English* Ships that had the Wind of him, he was blown up, either by an accidental Shot that enter'd his Powder-Room, or, as the *Dutch* say, by the Treachery of an *English* Gunner that served on board him. He was one of the ancient Nobility of *Holland*, and had a noble Monument erected by the States to his Memory.

Admiral Obdam blown up.

A. D. 1666.

De Ruyter succeeding him next Year in the Command at Sea, fought the *English* Fleet, under Prince *Rupert* and the Duke of *Albemarle*, for four Days; and though the *English* behaved themselves with their usual Gallantry, they lost (says the History of *Holland*) three and twenty great Ships and had six thousand Men killed (of which Number were Sir *William Berkely*, Vice-Admiral of the White, and Sir *Christopher Myngs*) besides two thousand six hundred taken; the *Dutch* losing six Capital Ships, two thousand eight hundred Soldiers and about fourscore Seamen, together with *Evertzen*, Admiral of *Zeeland*, *Vander Hulst* Vice-Admiral of *Amsterdam*, *Stackhover* Rear Admiral of *West Friesland*, and some other Officers, who were reckoned among the slain. However both sides attributing the Victory to themselves, publick Rejoicings were made for it as well at *London* as *Amsterdam*. In *August* the same Year another Engagement happened, wherein the *English* had the Advantage, for which *De Ruyter* blamed the Conduct of *Van Tromp*, who was thereupon discharged from his Employment, while *De Ruyter* himself acquired as much Glory by his Gallantry in the Fight, and brave Retreat, as if he had obtained the Victory: And, besides the Honours he received from the States, the *French* King, who was then their Ally, sent him the Collar of the Order of St. *Michael*, with a Gold Chain, and his Majesty's Picture set with Diamonds. Soon after this Engagement the States sent a Squadron to join thirty six *French* Ships in the Mediterranean, in order to destroy our Commerce there: And now a Treaty was set on foot by the Mediation of the Queen-Mother of *England*, which having no Effect, the *French* and Dutch made a Junction of their Fleets near *Dunkirk*, before whom our Fleet retired, with the Loss of one Ship of 50 Guns. Not long after this, twenty Men of War under Commadore *Holmes* made a Descent on the *Dutch* Coast near the *Vlie* and the *Texel*, where he burnt two Frigates, miss'd narrowly of destroying their *Russia* Fleet, and committed some other Hostilities, to countenance a Rebellion against the States raised by one *Hemskirk*, who revolted with some of their Ships under his Command, burnt about a hundred of their Merchant Men, and some Ships of War on the Stocks, but being pursued by a *Dutch* Squadron, he was killed in the

The English *have the worst of it in a Sea Fight.*

The English *beat* De Ruyter *and* Van Tromp.

The English *retire from the* French *and* Dutch *Fleets.*

Commadore Holmes *does mischief to the* Dutch.

A. D. 1667.

CHAP. X. *Ruin of the* Rom. *Empire.* 297

the Engagement, several of his Ships taken, and the Men on board them executed in *Holland*, while the rest made their Escape to *England*.

In 1667 the *Dutch* made Proposals of Peace which were treated of at *Breda*: But while the *English* protracted the Negotiation, *De Ruyter* put to Sea, and anchoring in the *Thames* Mouth, sent seventeen of his lightest Ships, with four Barks, and four Fireships up to *Sheerness*, where they took the Fort, demolished the Fortifications, and burnt or carried off the Naval Stores laid up there. After this they went up the *Medway* to *Chatham*, where they met with little Resistance, except from a few *Scots* Men under Captain *Douglas*, who was burnt on board one of the Ships of War as he bravely defended her; And before their Retreat they burnt six of our largest Ships, and took the Royal *Charles*, with a Frigate of forty four Guns; which hasten'd the Conclusion of the Peace to the Advantage of the *Dutch*; who presented their Commanders *De Ruyter*, *De Wit*, and *Van Ghent*, with a Gold Cup each, on which was engraven the Action of *Chatham* to perpetuate in their Families the Memory of this Enterprize.

A. D. 1667.
De Ruyter burns and takes some English Ships in the River Medway.

This Dishonour to *England* is chiefly to be ascribed to the underhand dealing of the *French*, who incited the *Dutch* to it during the Treaty, as being their Interest to foment Divisions betwixt the two Protestant maritime Powers, in order to destroy them both. However it did not interrupt the Negotiations at *Breda*, where a Peace was concluded between the *English* and *Dutch* Ministers in *July* 1667; two Years after which the States sollicited the Triple Alliance betwixt *England*, *Sweden*, and themselves, against the formidable Power of *France*, which ruined the *French* King's Measures at that time, but so highly provoked him, that he found means to break the said Alliance, and to engage *England* with him in a War against *Holland*. This the *Dutch* used all Endeavours to prevent, but in vain; for the *French* King, by the Interview at *Dover* betwixt King *Charles* II, and his Sister the Duchess of *Orleans*, had firmly riveted that Prince in his Interest: So that tho' he endeavoured to persuade the *Dutch*, by his Ambassador Sir *George Downing*, that he would faithfully adhere to the Triple Alliance, he at the same time prepared his Fleet to attack them by Sea, and sent Forces into *France*, under the Conduct of the Duke of *Monmouth*, and soon after, without any Declaration of War, ordered Commadore *Holmes* to attack their *Smyrna* Fleet in their Return home, off of the Isle of *Wight*; which he did, and took some of them after two Days Fight, wherein the *Dutch* made a brave Defence. Soon after which the King caused four of their *East-India* Ships to be seized in their Return from *Batavia*, and all their other Vessels in his Harbours: And in *April* following published his Declaration of War against them, grounded on their Infractions of the Treaty of *Breda*, their Disturbance of our Commerce in the *Indies*, the Injuries done to our Colony at *Surinam*, and there affronting the King's Person by infamous Medals and Pictures, and burning his Effigies in *Persia*, as they had indeed done in the most insolent manner.

Treachery of the French.

1667.
The Peace of Breda.

England and France war against Holland.

1671.
Dutch Ships seized.

The English declare War against the Dutch.

The

Q q

May 28 1672. De Ruyter attacks the English and French in Southwold Bay.	The ensuing Summer *De Ruyter* attacked the *English* and *French* Fleets in *Southwold* Bay under the Command of the Duke of *York*, and as the Battel was fierce, and maintain'd with great Bravery on both Sides, so was it almost with equal Advantage; tho' each attributed the Victory to themselves, and made publick Rejoycings accordingly. The Loss of Men was computed to be near the same, but the *English*, besides their Vice-Admiral the Earl of *Sandwich*, lost four Ships and the *French* two, whereas the *Dutch* lost but
1673. Tromp fights the English and French. Another Engagement.	three. The next Year the *Dutch* under *Van Tromp* had another Engagement with the *English*, commanded by Prince *Rupert*, near *Dengeness*, in which both pretended to the Victory; but the two latter losing most Ships, the *Dutch* made Rejoycings in *Holland*, and ordered a Day of Thanksgiving for their Advantage. In *July* after there was another bloody Engagement betwixt the Fleets, while the *English* prepared for a new Descent upon *Holland*, but after a sharp Engagement they both retired, without claiming Victory, and the Descent miscarried. And now the Parliament and People of *England* growing weary of the War with the *Dutch*, and uneasy at the
1674. Peace between England and Holland.	Progress of the *French* in the *Netherlands*, King *Charles* was put under a Necessity of coming to a Peace, than which the *Dutch* at the same time desiring nothing more, it was accordingly concluded in *February* 1674.
1675.	The next Year the States, upon Hopes of a Revolt on the Coasts of *Normandy*, set out a Fleet under *De Ruyter* and *Van Tromp*; but their Design was discovered, and that, as some supposed, by the King of *Great Britain*, for which the *Chevalier de Roan* was beheaded, and some others executed in *France*; but *Tromp* returning
Tromp defeats the Swedish Fleet.	from the Coasts of *France*, defeated the *Swedish* Fleet, and forced them to retire into their own Harbours, which was done in pursuance of the League the States had made with some Princes of the Empire against the *Swedes*, who had invaded the Elector of *Brandenburg*'s Dominions. In 1676 the Treaty of *Nimeguen* was set on
A. D. 1676. Treaty at Nimeguen without Success.	foot for a Peace between the *French* and *Dutch*, and the other Parties then at War, by the Mediation of King *Charles*, but then without effect; which same Year *De Ruyter* being sent to Sea against his Will, because he judged their Fleet was not of sufficient Strength,
De Ruyter fights the French, and is slain.	he had two Engagements on the Coast of *Sicily* with the *French*, and lost his Life by a Wound.
1679. Dutch make Peace with the Algerines. A. D. 1681.	In 1679, the States came to a Peace with the *Algerines*, who had for some time molested their Trade in the Mediterranean; but they were forced, as a Preliminary to their Treaty, to make the *Barbarians* a Present of eight Pieces of Brass Ordnance, with a considerable Quantity of Powder and Ball. In 1681, the *Dutch East-India* Company reduced their Tributary the King of *Ternate*, in the *East Indies*, for taking Part with the King of *Bantam*, whom they brought to their own Terms.
1685. King Charles dies.	King *Charles* II. dying in 1685, was succeeded by his Brother the late King *James*, who (says the History of *Holland*) tho' he had the greatest Reason to be satisfied with the States General, yet from the Moment he ascended the Throne, he betrayed Signs of his

Disaf-

Pag. 299.

of the
CK or
GULF of
&c.

Geographer.

ND

LIA
Wyborg
Richards I.
Peterburg
Shuulburg
Ladoga Lake
Slavnca
Lubia
D
Leysert
Crownflot
Coperio
INGRIA
Rus Nerva
PART OF
RUSSIA

A

A

T OF

ND

Disaffection to them, of which the next Year he gave manifest Proofs, by countenancing the *Algerines*, who were now again at War with the *Dutch*; for permitting them for some time to make use of his Ports, and sell their Prizes in *England*, they thereby had Opportunities, as they pleased, to go out and cruise against the *Dutch*, and in six Months Time took, in or near the Chanel, above thirty rich Merchant Ships from them. The same Year a Squadron of *French* Ships under the Duke de *Mortemar* took a *Dutch* Man of War upon the Coast of *Portugal*, but that matter was presently compromised and the Ship restored.

King James *permits the* Algerines *to make use of his Ports.*

Soon after this King *James* making those open Attempts upon the Constitution of this Kingdom, which at length occasioned an Invitation from the Principal Nobility and Gentry to the Prince of *Orange* to concern himself for the Preservation of their Religion and Liberties, his Highness communicated the same to the States General, who came to a Resolution of supporting him in that Undertaking with a Fleet and Army, soon after which ensued that happy Revolution in *England*, which set his late Majesty (of Glorious Memory) upon the Throne: Since which time the principal Naval Transactions of the *Dutch* having been in Conjunction with those of our own Nation, in the two last Wars with *France*, they will be accounted for in the fourth and fifth Books of this History; and therefore we proceed, according to our proposed Method, to the Naval Wars of the *Swedes*.

The Prince of Orange *invited to England, and The Dutch determine to support him.*

CHAP. XI.

Of the Naval Wars of the Swedes.

TACITUS in his Account of *Germany*, speaking of the *Swedes*, by the Name of *Suiones*, says they were potent not only in Men, but also in Shipping, and that the Form of their Vessels differed from those of the *Romans*, in that each End of them was shaped as a Prow, to avoid the Inconvenience of turning, and were navigated without Sails; nor were the Oars placed in Order in their Sides, like those of the *Romans*, but so as that they might be changed, as Occasion should serve, from one Part of the Vessel to another. *Wolfgang Lazius*, a good Collector of Antiquities, takes notice of several Migrations of these People, and tells us that a Number of them served in the Wars under *Alexander* the Great, that many were in the *Prætorian* Guards to the *Roman* Emperors, and that several Bodies of them settled on the Rivers *Weiffel* and *Elbe*, on the *Rhine* and the *Danube*, and in *Bohemia*, *Hungary*, *Suabia*, and other Parts of *Germany*. But these *Swedes* (if we may so call them) who made such distant Excursions, are better known under the Name of *Goths*, of whose Naval Affairs, when they came to make a Figure in the World, we have already given an Account. In

The ancient Form of the Swedish Vessels.

In the mean time the great Stock from whence these numerous Branches sprang, flourished within the Confines of the present *Sweden*, where, about the Time of Christ, reigned *Sigtrugus*, the third from *Woden*, from whom descended a long Race of Kings of *Sweden* and *Norway*; after which, with various Change of Fortune, the *Danes* were reduced to submit to them, and sometimes the *Swedes* to the *Danes*. In these Times we rarely meet with any Naval Wars of theirs, and those they had were only with Pirates who infested the Seas; against a Body of whom King *Haldanus* II. going out with a Fleet, he slew their Leader, and cleared the Seas of them for some time. He was succeeded by *Ungrinus*, and he by *Regnaldus*, in whose Time a Lady of the Royal Family, changing the Habit of her Sex for that of Men, put to Sea, and practised Piracy, with a Resolution and Courage more than Masculine. Nor in these Times was that Trade looked upon as dishonourable, for the Kings themselves, and the Princes their Sons, would frequently attempt to possess themselves of what they met with on the Sea, reckoning all fair Prize on that doubtful Element, whether belonging to Friend or Enemy.

The Danes and Swedes alternately submit to each other.

A Swedish Lady commits Piracies.

A. D. 387. *A fierce War between the Kings of Sweden and Denmark.*

About the Year 387 was waged a fierce Naval War between *Haquin Ringo*, King of *Sweden*, and *Harold*, King of *Denmark*, for which they were seven Years making Preparations of Ships, Arms, and Auxiliaries on either side. The *Dane* was assisted by the *Vandals*, *Angles*, *Frisons*, and *Saxons*; as was the *Swede* by the *Norwegians*, *Livonians*, *Carelians*, and *Ingrians*: And on both sides were many Women trained to War, who not only served among the common Seamen and Soldiers, but were also many of them at the Head of Squadrons. The two Fleets were so numerous that they covered the whole Length of the Streight between *Zeeland* and *Schonen*: where engaging, a long and bloody Battel was fought, with various Success, sometimes one giving way, and sometimes the other, till at length the Death of the *Danish* King confirmed the Victory to the *Swedes*; who because of the signal Service performed in the Engagement by *Hetha*, one of the warlike Ladies, appointed her, in reward thereof, and at the same time to disgrace the *Danes*, to rule them as Queen; but they refused to submit to her Authority, and yielded themselves to *Olo*, Son of the King of *Norway*, to whom *Ringo* had lately given *Schonen*. After a Succession of several Princes, *Regnerus*, King of *Denmark*, having killed *Charles* King of *Sweden* in a single Combat, and possessed himself of that Kingdom, he bestowed it on his Son *Biorne*, as he did *Norway* on his Son *Eric*, which latter (say the *Swedish* Historians) reduced the *Orkney* Islands, and defeated the King of *Scotland* in an Engagement on the Coast of that Kingdom.

The Swedes overcome the Danish Fleet.

The Danes possess themselves of Sweden.

Sweden descends to the Duke of Mecklenbergh. 1363.

After various Revolutions during a considerable Length of Time, the Crown of *Sweden* came to *Albert* Duke of *Mecklenbergh*, who, by several Acts of Tyranny, having drawn upon himself the Hatred of his Subjects, they applied to *Margaret*, Queen of *Denmark* and *Norway*, for Assistance, and offered her the Crown, on condition she would expel *Albert*: And she accordingly entering *Sweden*

with

CHAP. XI. *Ruin of the* Rom. *Empire.*

with an Army, gave him Battel, and entirely defeated him, taking the King and his Son Prisoners. Notwithstanding which great Victory, there ensued the Calamities of a Naval War; for the Duke of *Mecklenbergh*, the Earl of *Holstein*, and the *Hans* Towns, engaging in the Quarrel of *Albert*, sent continual Supplies by Sea to *Stockholm*, *Calmar*, and other Ports of *Sweden* yet held by *Albert*, whose Party being also furnished with a Fleet from the same Powers, ravaged all the Sea-Coasts, and so infested the *Baltick*, that they put an end to all Trade and Commerce in those Parts. After this destructive War had continued seven Years, a Treaty was set on foot between the contending Parties, and at length concluded, whereby it was agreed that *Albert*, with his Son, should be set at liberty, and within three Years make a formal Renunciation of all Right or Title to the Crown of *Sweden*, or else surrender himself Prisoner again; and that, in case of Failure of Performance, the Cities of *Lubeck*, *Hamburgh*, and the other *Hans* Towns should pay the Queen sixty thousand Marks of Silver.

Margaret, Queen of Denmark dispossesses the Duke of Mecklenbergh.

Matters being thus settled, *Margaret* appointed her Nephew, *Henry* Duke of *Pomerania*, her Successor, causing him to change his Name to that of *Eric*, that so he might be the more acceptable to the *Swedish* Nation. He was succeeded by his Nephew *Christopher* Duke of *Bavaria*, and Count *Palatine* of the *Rhine*; and he by *Charles Cnutesone*, Marshal of *Sweden*, whose Successor was *John*, the Son of *Christian* I, King of *Denmark*, after whom reigned his Son *Christian* II, surnamed the Tyrant. His Behaviour being suitable to that Title, *Gustavus Ericson*, descended from the ancient Kings of *Sweden*, was set up by the People against him, who every where forcing the *Danes* to fly before him, at length possessed himself of the City of *Stockholm*, by help of a Fleet which the *Lubeckers* sent to his Assistance, and soon after was solemnly crowned at *Upsal*.

Eric appointed by Margaret to the Crown of Sweden. 1396.

1441.

The Successors of Eric.

1520.

Gustavus Ericson crowned King of Sweden.

After quelling several Commotions in East and West *Gothland*, a new War was raised against him by the *Lubeckers*, who, in consideration of their former Services, having desired a Monopoly of the Trade to the Northern Coasts of his Kingdoms, and being denied so unreasonable a Request, demanded the Payment of some Monies due to them on an old Account, received into their Protection several Exiles which favoured *Christian*'s Party, and putting a strong Fleet and Army under the Conduct of *John* Earl of *Hoya*, (*Gustavus*'s Brother-in-law, but his mortal Enemy) designed nothing less than the Conquest of the Northern Kingdoms: To which purpose also they fomented a Sedition in the City of *Stockholm*, and endeavoured to prevail with a Body of the Citizens to cut off their King, promising to make that Place one of the *Hans* Towns And after *Frederick* the King of *Denmark*'s Death, and the Confusion which ensued thereupon, they persuaded also many of the Citizens of *Copenhagen* and *Malmoe* to join in their League, so that their Party being now very numerous, they obtained several very considerable Advantages at Sea, but the *Danes* having chosen *Christian* III. for their King, and *Gustavus* supplying them with Mony, and joining

joining his Ships and Forces with them, they came to an Engagement with the Enemy in the *Sound*, and utterly deſtroyed their whole Fleet. It was this *Guſtavus*, who, *Olaus Magnus* tells us, had, about the Year 1540, Gallies built in the *Baltick* by ſome *Venetian* Shipwrights, with deſign to reduce the Pirates of *Eſtland*, and *Muſcovy*, who infeſted the Trade on the Gulph of *Finland*. He alſo built a Ship of ſuch Force (ſays the ſame Author) as to carry a thouſand fighting Men, and three hundred Sailors. He was ſucceeded by his eldeſt Son *Eric*, who had a Naval War with the *Danes* and *Lubeckers*, which was long waged with various Succeſs on both ſides, but at length concluded with Diſadvantage to the *Swedes*. This Prince being depoſed for his Male-Adminiſtration, his Brother *John* was appointed his Succeſſor, who was ſucceeded by his Son *Sigiſmund*, King of *Poland*, and he by his Uncle *Charles* IX, the Father of *Guſtaphus Adolphus*.

The Fleet of the Lubeckers and their Adherents deſtroyed.
A. D. 1540.

Eric the Son of Guſtavus depoſed.

On *Guſtavus*'s Acceſſion to the Throne, in 1611, he became engaged in War with the *Poles*, *Ruſſians*, and *Danes*. The latter he attempted firſt, and with good Succeſs by Land, but at Sea the *Danes* had the better, becauſe the *Swediſh* Fleet was ill provided, and they took *Calmar*, a Sea-Port Town of great Importance: So that *Guſtavus* was forced to clap up a Peace with them on diſadvantageous Terms, to be the more at liberty to proſecute the War with *Poland*, whither he ſailed with a Fleet of eighty Ships, and ſix and twenty thouſand Land-Forces, and landing at *Pillaw*, marched into *Poliſh Pruſſia*, where he took *Braunsberg*, and *Frawenberg*, with *Elbing*, *Marienburg*, and moſt of the other Cities of that Province, and then laid ſiege to *Dantzick*; which Succeſſes ſo alarmed *Sigiſmund*, King of *Poland*, that a Treaty of Peace was preſently ſet on foot, and near concluded, when the Emperor engaging to aſſiſt the *Poles* with four and twenty Ships, and twelve thouſand Men, the Negotiation was broke off; and the *Swedes* and *Danes* join'd in ruining the *Poliſh* Fleet, as unwilling to ſuffer a third Naval Strength to riſe in the *Baltick*; and well would it have been for them had they purſued the ſame Politicks in theſe latter Times, and united to cruſh in its Infancy that maritime Power there, which ſeems in a fair way, in time, to ſwallow them both up.

A. D. 1611. Guſtavus Adolphus in War with the Poles, Ruſſians, and Danes.
The Danes beat the Swediſh Fleet.
The Swedes take Places from the King of Poland.
The Emperor engages to aſſiſt the Poles.
The Swedes and Danes ruin the Poliſh Fleet.

Guſtavus continuing before *Dantzick*, took three Ships belonging to that Place, and ſunk one; but being repulſed in an Attack he made upon the Fort, he blocked up the Harbour with a Squadron of eight Ships, which the *Poles* attacked with another of ten, and with ſuch Succeſs, that they killed the *Swediſh* Admiral, took his Ship, and obliged the Vice-Admiral to blow up his; but the *Poles* alſo loſt their Admiral, and four hundred Men in the Engagement. Not long after this, *Guſtavus* being called into *Germany* by the Proteſtants, to aid them againſt the formidable Power of the Emperor, he over-ran the greateſt part of that Country, and having obtained ſeveral glorious Victories, was at length ſlain in the Battel of *Lutzen*. He was ſucceeded by his Daughter *Chriſtina*, then but ſix Years of Age, and the Management of the War was committed to Count *Oxenſtiern*, Chancellor of *Sweden*, who maintained

The Danes and Swedes fight before Dantzick.

Guſtavus Adolphus ſlain in Germany.

tained their Affairs very well in *Germany*; but while they were wholly taken up in that Country, the *Danes* attacked them at home, against whom *Leonard Torstensohn* was sent, who took great part of *Holstein* from them, and beat their Troops in *Jutland* and *Schonen*: And in an Engagement at Sea the *Danish* Fleet was defeated, the greatest part whereof was either taken or sunk. The *Swedes* also made themselves Masters of the Bishoprick of *Bremen* and Island of *Bornholm*, insomuch that the *Danes* were obliged to agree to a disadvantageous Peace at *Bromesbro*, by the Mediation of *France* and *Holland*, whereby they gave up several Places of *Norway* to the *Swedes* for ever, together with the Isles of *Gothland* and *Oesel*: Nay the *Swedes* might have had yet better Terms, but that there was a *Dutch* Fleet in the *Sound* of eight and forty Ships of War, on whose Friendship they could not entirely depend. After this *Torstensohn* carried his victorious Arms again into the Heart of *Germany*, and penetrated into *Moravia*, and *Austria*, and had gone yet farther, but that he was deserted by Prince *Ragotzki*, who made a separate Peace with the Emperor. In 1648 the Peace of *Westphalia* was concluded, whereby the *Swedes* had yielded to them the Bishopricks of *Bremen* and *Ferden*, which were erected into Duchies, together with *Upper Pomerania*, and part of the *Lower*, with the Isle of *Rugen*, and the City of *Wismar*.

The Danes accepts of a disadvantageous Peace.

A. D. 1648. *The Peace of Westphalia concluded.*

Queen *Christina*, in 1654, surrendered the Crown to her Kinsman *Charles Gustavus*, who, in 1656, being recalled from the Prosecution of a War in *Poland*, to defend the Territories of *Sweden*, then attacked by the *Danes*, not only recovered all the Places they had taken in *Bremen* and *Holstein*, but marched over the Ice to the Island *Fuhnen*, thence to other Islands, and at last to *Zeeland*, and brought the King of *Denmark* to such Straits, that he was obliged to clap up a Peace at *Roschild*, by which he resigned to King *Charles* the Provinces of *Halland*, *Schonen*, and *Bleking*, with the Island *Bornholm*, and the Governments of *Bahus* and *Drontheim* in *Norway*. But this Peace proved of no long Duration, for the *Swedes* embarking a Body of Troops, which they gave out were designed for *Dantzick*, landed again in *Zeeland*, and King *Charles* besieged *Copenhagen*, while his Admiral *Wrangel* reduced the Castle of *Cronenburg*. The States of *Holland* interesting themselves in this Quarrel, espoused the Cause of the *Danes* against the *Swedes*, which latter were favoured by *England* and *France*. The King of *Denmark* made a brave Defence in *Copenhagen* against the Attacks of the *Swedes*, when at length the *Dutch* Fleet designed for his Relief, (which consisted of thirty seven Ships of War, with some Frigates, and six Fireships, with five thousand Seamen, and four thousand Landmen on board) setting sail from the *Texel*, arrived in a short time at the Entrance of the *Sound*. Thither the King of *Sweden* had before sent his Fleet, under the Command of Admiral *Wrangel*, who lay ready to receive the Enemy with eighteen great Ships from eighty to a hundred Guns, sixteen of a smaller Force, and fourteen Frigates, which were well manned, and had on board a considerable Number of *English* Seamen. The *Dutch*, on their near Approach,

A. D. 1654. *Queen Christina surrenders the Crown of Sweden.*

King of Denmark forced again to make Peace.

The Dutch assist the Danes.

A Battel at Sea between the Swedes and the Dutch, and the former beaten.

proach, put themselves in order of Battel, *Witte Witzen*, the first Vice Admiral, being in the Van, Admiral *Opdam* in the Centre, and *Peter Floris*, the second Vice-Admiral, in the Rear. *Witte* was first received with the whole Fire of the *Swedish* Admiral, who attempting to clap him on board, and grapple him to his own Ship, met with so warm a Reception, that he sheer'd off to undertake *Opdam*, who fired with such Fury upon him, that he was forced to retire under the Protection of the Castle of *Cronenburg*. In the mean time Vice-Admiral *Witte* having been forced to quit the Line of Battel in the Heat of his Engagement with *Wrangel*, was attacked by two large *Swedish* Ships, against which he defended himself with great Bravery for two Hours, without receiving any Assistance from his own Squadron, and at length sunk them both by his side, but his own Ship had the same Fate soon after, and he himself was carried ashore to *Elsinore* mortally wounded with two Musket-Balls. Admiral *Opdam* was surrounded with seven *Swedish* Ships, and bravely defended himself singly against them for some time, till he was at length disengag'd by two *Dutch* Captains, who came in to his Assistance, when he had just sunk the *Swedish* Vice-Admiral *Wrangel*, the Son of the Admiral, who chose rather to perish in the Sea, than owe his Life to the *Dutch*. The King of *Sweden* had ordered his Officers to make their principal Efforts against the Flag-Ships of the Enemies; so that after *Witte*, it fell to *Floris*, the other Vice-Admiral's Share to sustain the most vigorous Attacks of the *Swedes*, which he did with great Bravery, and made a prodigious Slaughter among them before he received his Death's Wound. The Engagement lasted four Hours amidst the Fire of three thousand Pieces of Cannon, when at length the Loss of so many Ships and Men made the Courage and Firmness of the *Swedes* begin to give way, and the Victory, which had continued long doubtful, appeared in favour of the *Dutch*, who lost in this bloody Action only one Ship, which was that of Vice Admiral *Witte*, but the *Swedes*, according to their Enemy's Account, lost fourteen, ten of which were burnt or sunk, and the other four carried into *Copenhagen*, whither

The Swedes forced from before Copenhagen.

the *Dutch* sailed triumphantly with their Succours for his *Danish* Majesty, who was then hard press'd with the Siege. This obliged the King of *Sweden* to turn it into a Blockade, which he continued for many Months, but was at length forced by the *Dutch* to rise from before it, and abandon all his Conquests in *Denmark*, who landing the Troops they had on board in the Isle of *Fuhnen*, gave the *Swedes* a total Overthrow there.

This Loss was so afflicting to King *Charles*, that it threw him into a Distemper, of which he died in the Flower of his Age, leaving his Son, an Infant of the same Name, to succeed him in the Throne. Hereupon a Peace was concluded with the *Danes* near *Copenhagen*; but another War ensued shortly after, wherein the greatest part of the *Swedish* Fleet was shipwrecked on the Coast of *Bornholm*, and they had many other Losses at Sea. To this War the Peace of *Nimeguen* put an end, and restored the *Swedes* to the Possession of their Dominions in *Germany*, and of all the Places the

A Peace between the Swedes and Danes, but soon after the Swedes suffer at Sea and Land. The Peace of Nimeguen.

Danes

Danes had taken from them; after which the King of *Sweden* applied himself to repair the Damage his Country had sustained during the Wars, and procured that great Revolution there in favour of the Kingly Prerogative, which, of a limited Monarch, made him a very absolute one; and at length dying in 1697, he was succeeded by his Son *Charles* XII, the present King. An Alliance being enter'd into against him by *Denmark*, *Muscovy*, and *Poland*, he sided with the Duke of *Holstein* against the *Danes*, and next Year the *English* and *Dutch* Fleets coming into the *Sound*, declared in his Favour, and, joining the *Swedish* Fleet, assisted in a Descent upon *Zeeland*, where the *Swedes* landing an Army, obliged the King of *Denmark* to come to an Accommodation by the Peace of *Travendahl*. Since which there having happened nothing remarkable to our purpose, I go on to the Naval Wars of *Denmark*.

A. D. 1697.

A. D. 1700.

The Peace of Travendahl.

CHAP. XII.

Of the Naval Wars of the Danes.

THE *Danish* Historians pretend to give very particular Accounts of the Affairs of their own Nation, for many Ages before the Birth of Christ; but those Narrations are looked upon by all the Learned as fabulous; nor is more Credit, perhaps, to be given to their History for some Centuries after that Period of Time. Cotemporary with our Saviour, according to them, was their King *Frotho* III, who enjoyed a long and peaceable Reign over his large Dominions, consisting (say they) not only of *Denmark*, *Sweden*, and *Norway*, but also great part of *Germany*, together with *England* and *Ireland*, and all the neighbouring Islands, which they pretend to have been conquered by their Kings many Ages before this Prince. After his Death *England* and *Norway* made Attempts to recover their Liberty, and their Pirates infesting the Coasts of *Denmark*, *Frotho* IV sent out one *Stercather* against them with a considerable Fleet, who entirely cleared the Sea of them, and restored the Freedom of Navigation, not claiming it (says *Meursius*, with a Glance at our Sea-Dominion) as the Propriety of his Master, but making it common to all peaceable Navigators and Traders. After this *Haldan* II, another of their Kings, is said to have repressed the Piracies of *Amund*, the Son of the King of *Norway*, who scoured the Sea with a strong Force. *Harold* III. appointing *Ubbo Frisius* Commander in Chief of his Fleet, he is said to have defeated a King of *Britain* in a Sea-Fight, to have ravaged the Coasts of *Aquitaine*, and commanded all at Sea from the River *Garonne* to the Coasts of *Denmark*.

About the Antiquity of the Danes.

About the Year 800, *Sigefrid* then reigning in *Denmark*, the *Danes* made an Expedition to *England*, which, more agreeably to the Truth of History than what is before related from their Writers, was

800.
The Danes make an Expedition to England.

was the first of their Attempts upon our Nation, in which they committed great Spoil in *Devonshire*, and the Parts adjacent: After which, invited by the fertile Soil, and temperate Climate, they made frequent Visits to it, and at length King *Sueno*, or *Swane*, as our Historians call him, reduced great part of the Country to his Obedience, and under *Canutus*, or *Knute*, his Son, the whole Kingdom was subdued, who leaving it to his eldest Son *Harold*, he was succeeded by *Hardiknute*, the last of the *Danish* Kings in *England*.

Swain reduces great part of England, and Knute conquers it.

The beforementioned *Sueno* appointed one *Wetheman* his supreme Officer at Sea against the Piracies of the *Vandals*, (by which Name in those Times were known all the People of *Germany* North of the *Elbe*, as well on the Ocean, as along the Coasts of the *Baltick* Sea) which Officer had Orders to take all Ships whatsoever which he could meet with, upon that Service, whether the Owners consented or not, only engaging each should have their Share of the Booty which might be taken. By this means a numerous Fleet being gotten together, he cleared the Sea of the Pirates, taking eighty seven of their Ships, and dispersing the rest to distant Countries. The *Vandals*, enraged at these Proceedings, made Inroads into *Denmark*, but *Sueno* well provided to give them a warm Reception, strengthening his Towns and Sea-Ports with Garrisons, and ordered Beacons to be fired by Night, and Smoak to be made by Day to give Notice of their Approach, and alarm the Country against them. He also threw up a Trench from *Slefwick* to the Sea, to prevent their Incursions, which *Waldemar* afterwards fortified with a strong Wall.

The Danes overcome the Vandals at Sea.

This *Waldemar* putting to Sea with a strong Fleet, having on board a Body of Troops, sailed over to the River *Warna*, where disembarking his Troops, he besieged *Rostock* by Sea and Land, and soon carried it; after which, in a Sea-Fight near *Stralsund*, he defeated the People of *Rugen*, and made himself Master of that Island, and at length annexed the whole Country of *Vandalia* to his Dominions; while his Fleet, in the mean time, under the Command of one *Esberne*, ruining the Pirates of *Esthonia* and *Courland*, restored the Freedom of Navigation throughout the *Baltick*. Which extraordinary Success of his Arms acquired him the Title of *Waldemar* the Great. His Son *Canute*, refusing to pay Homage to the Emperor of *Germany*, who pretended a Right of Sovereignty to his Dominions, he was by him dispossessed of the Isle of *Rugen*; but *Christopher* II. some time after recovered it again.

The Danes take the Island of Rugen, &c.

1180.
The Danes dispossessed of Rugen, but recover it.

Under *Eric* VI. the *Danes* defeated at Sea two great Fleets of the *Vandals*, taking thirty Sail of Ships, with a great Booty on board them. About which time *Gerard*, Duke of *Holstein*, (a part of *Vandalia*) fitted out a considerable Fleet against the *Danes*, which he caused to rendezvous in the Port of *Wismar*, from whence he set sail for *Copenhagen*, with design to attack the Citadel of that Place, and arriving before it, he laid Stages from one Ship to another, that so his Men might fight as on firm Ground, and sunk some Ships in the Entrance of the Port to block up the Passage; but the *Danes* cutting their Cables, the Stages were presently torn asunder, which

The Vandals and Holsteiners beaten by the Danes.

which produced such a Confusion and Disorder among the *Holsteiners*, that most of them were cut off, or fell into the Hands of the *Danes*.

Under *Waldemar* III, who came to the Crown in 1340, the *Danes* had a War at Sea with the *Hans* Towns, which was carried on for a considerable Time with various Success on both sides, but at length ended to the Advantage of the *Danes*: Since which what Naval Wars they have been engaged in having been with the *Swedes*, for whom we have already accounted, our proposed Method next brings us to those of *Muscovy*.

1340. The Danes have the better of the Hans Towns at Sea.

CHAP. XIII.

Of the Naval Wars of the Muscovites, and of the Turks.

THE maritime Power of the *Muscovites* is of so late a Date, that it may be rather said to be likely to be very fruitful in Events, that it may be the Subject of some future Naval History, than to furnish any for this; so that we can add little more to what we have said of them in the first Book, than that the *Czar* seems no less intent on procuring to himself a Naval Force upon the Black Sea, than in the *Baltick*; having, after the taking of *Asoph* from the *Turks*, ordered a good Harbour to be made there, and a Fleet to be built of eighty Gallies, and a hundred and fifty Brigantines; and, to open a new Course of Trade in those Parts, he has caused a Canal to be cut from the *Volga* (which disembogues itself in the *Caspian* Sea) to the River *Don*, which falls into the *Palus Mæotis* at *Asoph*. Indeed the taking of that important Place from the *Turks* was the Consequence of a Naval Victory; for, being maintained by a Garrison of ten thousand Men, the *Czar* had for some time besieged it with a hundred thousand Foot, and twenty thousand Horse; but having then no Shipping, the *Turks* threw in Supplies as they pleased, so that he was at length obliged to raise the Siege; but resolving to repair that Disgrace, he made greater Preparations of Artillery and Bombs than before, and provided a Number of large Gallies, some of them a hundred Feet in Length, with which engaging the *Turks* in Person, he took or sunk all the *Saiques* laden with Supplies and Provisions, and utterly defeated their whole Fleet; whereupon the Garrison in the Town immediately came to a Capitulation. Having thus briefly dismiss'd the *Muscovites*, the *Turkish* Naval Wars are what next claim our Consideration.

The Muscovites take Asoph, and build a Fleet.

Of the Naval Wars of the Turks.

THOSE People having continued for many Ages among their native Mountains of *Scythia*, and after their leaving those Habitations, and raising themselves to a considerable Power, their Seat of Empire having been for a long time chiefly in the Inland Parts of *Asia*, their History affords few or no Materials for our purpose, till *Mahomet* I. took the City of *Constantinople*, in 1453; after which time they became Masters of numerous and potent Fleets. The taking of that Place was soon follow'd by the Destruction of the Empire of *Trebizonde*, which City, after several Naval Skirmishes before it upon the *Euxine* Sea, was reduced to their Obedience. After which, with their Fleet, they took the Isle of *Metelino*, in the *Archipelago*, and transplanted the Inhabitants to *Constantinople*. Then having reduced *Negroponte*, *Mahomet* made a great Progress by Land, and enter'd *Stiria* and *Carinthia*, two Frontier Provinces of *Germany*, where carrying all before him, he thence penetrated into *Italy*, and gave the *Venetians* a signal Defeat at the River *Soutius*, which, not without Reason, struck a universal Terror through the rest of *Italy*; for his Fleet having already reduced *Otranto*, he had certainly marched to *Rome*, had not his Death shortly after prevented.

He was succeeded by his eldest Son *Bajazet* II, who took *Lepanto* and *Durazzo* from the *Venetians*, and defeated them in a Sea-Fight before *Modon*, which Place, with *Coron* and *Navarino*, fell at the same time into his Hands. His Son, *Selim* I, having defeated the *Persians*, carried his Arms into *Ægypt*, where having broke the Power of the *Mamalukes* in several Battels, the whole Country submitted to his Obedience. His Son and Successor *Solyman*, surnamed *the Magnificent*, with a great Fleet, and a numerous Army, attacked the Island and City of *Rhodes*, which, after a brave Defence by the Knights of St. *John* of *Jerusalem*, who then had their Residence there, was surrendered to him, and they removed thence to *Malta*. After which *Solyman* had *Tunis* reduced to his Obedience by the Pirate *Barbarossa*: and then assembling from the Black Sea, and other parts of his Dominions, a Fleet of a hundred and fifty great Gallies, with eighty of a lesser Rank, and two hundred and fifty other Vessels of divers sorts, he ordered an Attempt to be made on the Isle of *Corfu*, from whence the *Turks* having ravaged the Coasts, and killed and carried off great Numbers of the Inhabitants, again retired, and plundering *Zante* and *Cerigo*, laid waste the Island of *Engia*; after which they reduced *Nacsia* and *Pario*, while, in the mean time, other of *Solyman's* Squadrons scoured the Coasts of *Naples*, and the *Tuscan* Sea, and dispersed the united Fleet of the Emperor, the Pope, and the *Venetians*. Receiving into his Protection the Pirates *Barbarossa*, *Haidin*, *Sinan* the *Jew*, *Gallicola*, and others, he ordered them to infest the *Spaniards*, then preparing for the Reduction of *Barbary*, which

which they very effectually performed with a Fleet of sixty Sail; part of which, however, falling in with *Andrew Doria*, the Emperor's Admiral, were routed, but the *Spaniards* and *Italians* being overladen with their Booty, the *Turks* rallied, and attacking them again, entirely destroyed their whole Squadron. The *Portuguese* now commanding the *Indian* Ocean with their Fleets, and interrupting the Navigation between *Ægypt* and *India*, *Solyman* ordered the *Beglerbey* of that Province to infest them by all the means he was able; to which purpose he entered into an Alliance with the *Cambayans*, and repaired with a great Fleet to their Assistance in the Siege of *Diu*, as we have already shewn in treating of the Affairs of the *Portuguese*. In the mean time the *Turkish* Fleets reduced *Tripoli* in *Barbary*, and the Town of *Africa*, with the Isles of *Zerbi*, and *Gozo*, and ravaged the Coasts of *Sicily*, where *Guimerani*, the Admiral of that Island, was defeated and taken Prisoner, with all his Ships, by the Pirate *Dragut Raiz*. *The Turkish Fleet reduces Tripoli, &c.*

Solyman dying, he was succeeded by his Son *Selim* II, who with a numerous Fleet and Army took the Island *Cyprus* from the *Venetians* as he did also *Tunis* and *Algier* from the *Moors*; but his grand Fleet received a most signal Overthrow from the *Venetians* near *Lepanto*; which, with the rest of the most remarkable Naval Actions of the *Turks* to this Time, having been already taken notice of among the Affairs of the *Venetians*, *Genoese*, or *Spaniards*, with whom they happened to be engaged, I shall not trouble the Reader with a Repetition of them, but proceed to the Naval Wars, of the *French*, which are those the Order I have before observed next brings me to. *Selim II. takes Cyprus, with Tunis and Algier. 1571.*

Chap. XIV.

Of the Naval Wars of the French.

HOW considerable some of the ancient Inhabitants of *Gaul* were at Sea, will have been already seen by the Account which hath been given of the People of *Marseilles* and *Vannes*, in the first Book of this History; but from the Time that the *Franci*, or *Franks*, a People of *Germany*, crossed the *Rhine* into *Gaul*, and settling there, gave their Name to the whole Country and People, we hear of no Naval Exploits of the *French* till the Government of *Charles Martel*; who we find, about the Year 728, made an Expedition against the People of *Friesland*, whom he overcame in a Sea Fight, and burnt and laid waste the Islands of *Amistrache* and *Austrache*, as they are called by the Writers of those Times, which I suppose to be the Isle of *Ameland*, and *Oostergoe*, a Part of present *Friesland*. His Grandson *Charlemagne*, seeing the great Advantage a Naval Strength would be to the Defence of his Empire, made several convenient Harbours in different Parts of the Kingdom, and built *728. The French beat the Frieslanders at Sea. Charlemagne prepares a Fleet, and makes Harbours.*

built a Number of Ships of War, which he put under the Command of the Constable *Buchard*; who off of *Genoa* engaged the *Saracens*, then mightily infesting *Corsica* and *Sardinia*, and entirely routed them, taking thirteen of their Ships, and putting the rest to Flight. And at the same time, in the *Adriatick*, with twenty Ships borrowed from the *Venetians*, *Charlemagne* defeated *Desiderius* King of *Lombardy*, and forced him to quit the Sea: While on the Coasts of the Ocean, one *Rutland* bore the chief Naval Command, under whom were maintain'd several Fleets in the Mouths of the *Loire*, the *Seine*, the *Rhine*, and the *Elbe*, against the Depredations of the *Danes* and *Saxons*: On which Coasts were also disposed several Bodies of Troops for their Defence against those *Barbarians*.

The French beat the Saracens at Sea, and the Lombards. A. D. 807.

Charlemagne having thus provided for the Security of his Empire, called in his Sons to be Sharers with him therein, placing *Charles* in *Germany*; appointing *Pepin* King of *Italy* to defend his Acquisitions there against the *Greeks*, and the *Duke* of *Benevento*; and to *Lewis* he committed *Aquitaine* to make head against the *Saracens* of *Spain*. *Pepin*, having ended the War with the Duke of *Benevento*, turned his Arms against *Paul*, who commanded the Fleet of *Nicephorus*, Emperor of the East, whom he engaged off *Comacchio*, in the *Adriatick*, and obtained the Victory, the *Grecian* Fleet being so disabled that it had much ado to make its Retreat over to *Dalmatia*. The *Venetians* having espoused the Part of *Nicephorus*, he next attacked them, and having defeated their Doge, sailed over to *Dalmatia*, and ravaged the Coasts, whither the forementioned *Paul*, with the Eastern Emperor's Fleet, now reinforced, repairing against him, he returned to *Ravenna*, with a considerable Booty. After which *Pepin* seized the Port of *Broudolo*, with *Chiozza*, *Palestrina*, and other Places in the Neighbourhood of *Venice*, and then taking *Malamocco* it self, where in those times was the Ducal Palace, forced the Doge *Obelerius* to remove to *Rialto*, where has ever since been their Residence. There were three Naval Commanders appointed by *Charlemagne* for the Service of his Son *Pepin*, whose Names are recorded in History; one was *Emardus*, with the Title of Admiral, who was afterwards slain in a Sea Fight by the *Saracens* then possessing *Corsica*; another was *Archambot*, Chancellor to *Charlemagne*, who had the Command of the Fleet of *Genoa*; and the third was the forementioned *Buchard*, who killed five thousand *Saracens* in an Engagement off *Sardinia*, and expelled all their Garrisons from that Island and *Corsica*.

Charlemagne shares the Empire with his Sons.

Pepin beats the Greek Fleet.

Pepin takes several Places from the Venetians.

Pepin was succeeded in the Kingdom of *Italy* by his Son *Bernard*, in whose time the *Saracens* again invading *Corsica*, plundered the Island, and carried off a great Booty; but *Ermengarius*, who was *Bernard*'s Viceroy in *Majorca*, falling in with the Enemy at Sea, routed them, and took several of their Ships, releasing a considerable Number of Christian Slaves that were found therein. The *Saracens*, nevertheless, still continuing their Depredations, surprized and plundered *Civita Vecchia*, and proceeding thence ravaged the Coasts of *Languedoc*, whence they repaired to *Sardinia*, and laid waste that Island; but *Ermengarius* happening to be there, while they

Bernard King of Italy overcomes the Saracens.

The Saracens lay waste several Places.

CHAP. XIV. *Ruin of the* Rom. *Empire.* 311

they carelessly straggled about the Country, he cut off great Numbers of them, intercepted some of their Ships, which he burnt, and forced the rest to retire in Confusion to *Africa*. *The* Saracens *Ships burnt.*

Charlemagne dying, he was succeeded by his Son *Lewis*, surnamed *the Pious*, in whose time *Abderames*, King of the *Saracens* in *Spain*, sent a numerous Fleet, under the Command of *Aburmau*, to the Coasts of *Aquitaine*, which he cruelly ravaged from one End to the other. But we don't meet with any Naval Battel fought in this Prince's Reign, though he is said to have provided a considerable Fleet at *Boulogne* in *Picardy*, and to have had another stationary one in the Mouth of the *Scheld*, where he erected a Light-House for the Benefit of Navigation. *Charles* II. his Successor, fortified the Mouth of the *Seine* against the Depredations of the *Saxons*, and to the same Purpose erected several Castles along the Coasts on each Side of that River. *Charles* IV. following the Example of *Lewis*, caused a Light-House to be built at *Sluys* in *Flanders*, erected another at *Rochelle*, and a third between *Bourdeaux* and *Xaintonge*, I suppose in the same Place where now is the *Tour de Cordouan*. *The* Saracens *ravage the Coast of* Aquitaine.

Charles II. *prepares for the Defence of his Coasts.*

Under *Lewis* II. the *Saracens* were beaten by the *French* in an Engagement before *Bari*, and again in the Golf of *Gaeta*, soon after which *Calabria* came into the Hands of that Prince. But from that time we meet with no more Naval Expeditions till *Philip* I, in whose Reign the *French*, out of a Desire to recover the Holy Land from the Infidels (as was the Humour of those Times) made an Expedition into *Asia*, *Alexius Comnenus* being then Emperor of *Constantinople*. Crossing the *Hellespont* they entered *Bithynia* under the Command of *Hugh* the Brother of King *Philip*, and proceeding thence, reduced *Lycia*, *Pamphylia*, *Cilicia*, *Armenia*, and *Syria*, with the Cities of *Tripoli*, *Tortosa* and *Baruth*. Lewis II. *beats the* Saracens, *and takes* Calabria.

Philip *makes an Expedition to* Asia, *and takes several Places.* A. D. 1097.

After this, a great Fleet setting Sail from *Provence* for *Constantinople*, there took on board King *Lewis* VII, who had engaged in a like Undertaking, and having landed him in *Asia*, in order to prosecute the War against the Infidels on Shore, in the Mouth of the River *Mæander* they engaged a Fleet of the Enemy's and defeated them. *Lewis* having performed great Exploits against them by Land, and received the Palm, as was the Custom, in token of the Expedition's being at an End, he went on board his Fleet at *Joppa*, in order to come for *Europe*, when, in his way, the perfidious *Greeks* envying his Successes, tho' against their own mortal Enemies, attacked him with their whole Naval Strength, and had gone near to have utterly destroyed the whole Fleet, had not the Viceroy of *Sicily* timely arrived to their Assistance, and forced the *Greeks* to retire. *The French beat the Fleet of the* Saracens.

The Greeks *treacherously attack the* French Fleet A. D. 1147.

After this, *Lewis* having, nevertheless, betrothed his Daughter, the Princess *Agnes*, to *Alexius*, the Son of the Emperor of *Constantinople*, she was arrived there with a very numerous Company of *Frenchmen*, when *Andronicus* seizing the Empire, threw *Alexius* into the Sea, and forced all the *French*, of whom there were some thousands, out of the City. These, getting together five and twenty Andronicus *forces the* French *from* Constantinople.

ty Gallies, to revenge this Treatment cruised about the Streights of *Constantinople*, the *Mer di Marmora*, the *Dardanelles*, and the *Archipelago*, and ravaged all the Coasts and Islands with Fire and Sword; against whom the *Greeks* sending out a Fleet of fifty Sail under the Command of *Philantropenus*, they came to an Engagement in the Golf of *Armiro*, wherein the *French* defeated them, and took several of their Ships; and by the Reputation of their Victory retained *Negroponte* and *Candia* in their Obedience.

The French beat the Fleet of the Greeks.

Philip II. now reigning in *France*, he sent a Fleet to *Africa* against *Saladin*, Sultan of *Ægypt*, under the Command of *James d'Avesnes*, who reduced several Places on the Coast of *Barbary*. About which time *Lewis*, the Son of King *Philip*, sailing with another Fleet from *Marseilles*, was shipwrack'd in a Storm, on the Coast of *Sicily*, but at length repairing his shatter'd Navy, proceeded therewith to *Syria*, where, in an Engagement off of *Tyre*, he destroyed the Fleet of *Saladin*. After which putting *Boniface*, Marquis of *Montferat*, at the Head of another Expedition, he join'd with the *Venetians* in aiding *Alexius Angelus*, Son of *Isaac* Emperor of *Constantinople*, against his Uncle *Alexius Comnenus*, who had treacherously usurped the Empire from his Brother; and the *French* and *Venetian* Fleets attacking *Constantinople* in Conjunction, broke the Chain which was laid across the Entrance of the Port, for its Security, and there took twenty *Grecian* Ships; which done, they landed their Men, who bearing down all Opposition, forced the Tyrant *Alexius Comnenus* to fly, and set *Alexius Angelus* their Ally on the Throne. But he being soon after deposed in a Tumult, one *Murzuphlus* assumed the Empire, and attacked the *French* and *Venetians*, and in order to destroy them sent out sixteen Fireships before the Wind against their Fleet, but they getting out to Sea separated, and made a Passage for the Fireships to sail through them, so that that Device was render'd ineffectual: And the Confederates re-assembling their dispersed Fleet, attacked *Constantinople*, the *French* by Land, and the *Venetians* by Sea, who joined the Hulls of two Gallies with a Floor laid across, and thereon erecting Towers higher than the Ramparts of the City, threw in lighted Torches, and other combustible Matter, which presently setting that Quarter in Flames, they poured in Showers of Arrows upon the Soldiers and Citizens that went about to extinguish the Fire; while the *French* in another Place made a Breach in the Walls, and forced their Entrance into the City. *Constantinople* being thus taken, *Murzuphlus* saved himself by Flight, and with the universal Consent of all Parties (*Alexius* having been before slain by the Usurper) *Baldwin* Count of *Flanders* was saluted Emperor, the Marquis of *Montferat* being at the same time made King of *Thessaly*, and the *Venetians* having the Island *Candia* yielded to them.

The French beat the Fleet of Saladine.

The French and Venetians attack Constantinople.

Constantinople taken by the French and Venetians.

A. D. 1204.

1250.

Some time after this *Lewis* IX, hiring a Fleet of *Genoese* Ships and Sailors, put an Army of *French* Soldiers on board, and embarking at *Marseilles* proceeded to *Cyprus*, where rendezvousing at the same time *William* Prince of *Achaia*, with the Fleet of the *Morea*, and *Robert* Duke of *Burgundy*, with many Transports, having on board

CHAP. XIV. *Ruin of the* Rom. *Empire.* 313

board a confiderable Number of Horfe, they repaired in Conjunction to *Ægypt*, and befieged *Damiata* by Land and Water, which in few Days they forced to furrender, but foon after they received a great Overthrow in a Battel on fhore, wherein the King himfelf was taken Prifoner by the Infidels; who having purchafed his Ranfom with a great Sum of Money, and the Reftitution of *Damiata*, embarked at *Acre* with the fmall Remains of his Army, and returned to *France*. This ill Succefs in *Afia* was not fufficient however to deter him from another Expedition againft the Enemies of the Chriftian Name; for fome Years afterwards he enter'd into another Croifade (as they called thefe Expeditions) and fitting out a confiderable Fleet, embarked at *Aiguefmortes* in *Languedoc*, and fet Sail for *Cagliari*, the Rendezvous appointed for the Companions of the War, where holding a Council, it was refolved therein to attempt the City of *Tunis*. Setting Sail they foon came before Cape *Carthage*, where they attacked the Caftle that defends the Entrance of the Port of *Tunis*, which after a long Siege being furrendered to them, they proceeded to *Tunis* itfelf, and invefted that Place, but the Plague reigning in the Camp, King *Lewis* was feized with that Diftemper and there died. After which the King of *Sicily* arriving with another Fleet, they brought the Enemy to a Compofition, but could not take the Place; fo that the Confederate Army being confiderably diminifhed by Sicknefs, they broke up, and returned to their refpective Countries.

The French and their Allies take Damiata, but are beaten on Shore.

Lewis IX. lays Siege to Tunis, but dies of the Plague.

After this *France* being greatly divided with Civil Diffenfions, and alfo embroil'd with its Neighbours, kept it felf fufficiently employed at home, and abandoned all Projects againft *Syria*, *Ægypt*, or *Barbary*. *Edward* I. King of *England* having fent out fix Sail of Ships for *Bourdeaux*, as they coafted along *Normandy*, they were attacked and taken by fome People of that Province, which he highly refenting, ordered his Admiral, *Robert Tiptot* to fail with a Squadron to *Normandy*, who entering the *Seine* funk all the Ships he found in that River; after which he took feveral Ships laden with Wine that were coming round from the Weftern Coafts of *France*. Hereupon the *French* fitted out a Number of Ships under the Command of *Charles* Count *de Valois*, who engaging the *Englifh* received a total Defeat: But the *French* foon after repairing their Fleet failed to *Dover*, and furprizing that Town, plundered and fet it on fire.

France divided by Civil Diffenfions.

A. D. 1294.

The Fleet of Edward I. fink feveral French Ships.

The French Fleet beaten, but they burn Dover.

Some time after this there broke out a more bloody War between *Edward* III. King of *England*, and *Philip* VI. the *French* King, for no lefs Caufe than the Crown of *France*, which *Edward* laid Claim to in Right of his Mother the Daughter of *Philip* IV, and Sifter of *Charles* IV, the laft King, who died without Iffue. The *Englifh* and People of *Flanders* their Allies, having received a Repulfe before *Lifle*, then in the Hands of the *French*, King *Edward* was croffing from *England* to *Sluys* with a confiderable Fleet, having a Body of Troops on board for the Profecution of the War, when the *French* Fleet confifting of four hundred Sail, endeavoured to intercept him in his Paffage, and prevent his Landing, whereupon

S f

A. D. 1340. *A bloody Fight at Sea between the English and French.*

upon enfued one of the moſt bloody Engagements that any Age hath produced; wherein, according to the Account of the *French* themſelves, they loſt thirty thouſand Men, and both their Admirals; but with the Loſs to the *Engliſh* (ſay the ſame Accounts) of ten thouſand Men, beſides many Perſons of Quality; and King *Edward* himſelf received a Wound in his Thigh. However the Victory was entirely on the *Engliſh* Side, and the King landing his Men, marched, in Conjunction with thoſe of *Flanders*, his Allies, and laid Siege to *Tournay:* After which he gained thoſe great Victories in *France* which make ſo bright a Figure in the *Engliſh* Hiſtory.

The Engliſh *take* Tournay, *&c.*

1371.

The French take and ſink Engliſh *Ships.*

In 1371, the *French* King, *Charles* V, having built a Fleet at *Roan,* and being aſſiſted alſo with the Ships of *Henry* King of *Caſtile,* had a ſucceſsful Engagement off of *Rochelle,* with an *Engliſh* Squadron of thirty five Sail, which were all either ſunk or taken, and moſt of the Men ſlain in the Fight. This Squadron was intended for the Relief of *Rochelle,* then cloſely beſieged by the *French* Army, commanded by the Conſtable *du Gueſclin* and the Duke of *Berry,* by whoſe Direction all the Ships taken from the *Engliſh,* with ſome of their own that were unfit for Service, were ſunk in the Entrance of the Harbour of *Rochelle,* to prevent the Town's receiving any Supply by Sea, and at the ſame time the Siege being vigorouſly carried on by Land, the Place was ſhortly after ſurrendered to the *French.*

The French ſink ſeveral Ships at the Entrance of Rochelle.

A. D. 1385.

The French aid the Scots againſt the Engliſh

Under this Prince's Succeſſor, *Charles* VI, a Fleet was ſent out, with a Land Army on board, commanded by *John de Vienne,* to the Aſſiſtance of the *Scots,* then at War with *England,* but Diſſenſions ariſing between the *French* and *Scots* about the manner of carrying on the War, he returned without doing any thing remarkable. Next Year the *French* King deſigning to make an Expedition in Perſon againſt *England,* cauſed a Fleet of twelve hundred and eighty Sail to be got ready in the Port of *Sluys,* but the Rubs the Duke of *Berry,* who was no Friend to this Project, threw in the Way, render'd all theſe Preparations ineffectual. The Admiral of *France* had, for the ſame Purpoſe, made an Armament of ſeventy two Ships on the Coaſt of *Bretagne,* which, having on board many Engines and Machines of a new Invention, with other Utenſils for Sieges, put to Sea from *Treguier,* in order to ſail for *Sluys,* but in their way meeting with a violent Tempeſt were all diſperſed, and many of them being drove into the *Thames* fell into the Hands of the *Engliſh,* ſeveral were caſt away on the Coaſt of *Zealand,* others periſhed amidſt the Waves, and but very few eſcaped to *Sluys* with the Tidings of their Diſaſter.

The French *diſperſed by Tempeſt*

A. D. 1389.

The French *aid the* Genoeſe *againſt the Pirates of* Barbary.

Shortly after this the *Genoeſe* imploring Aid againſt the Pirates of *Barbary,* who cruelly ravaged their Coaſts, the Remains of the two Fleets beforementioned were diſpatch'd to their Aſſiſtance, under the Command of *Henry* Duke of *Bourbon,* who ſailing into the Mediterranean, joined the *Genoeſe* Fleet, and proceeded to the Coaſt of *Barbary,* where he reduced the Town of *Africa,* and ſate down before the City of *Tunis;* but after a long Siege, not being able to make himſelf Maſter of the Place, he conſented to a Treaty with the Enemy

CHAP. XIV. *Ruin of the* Rom. *Empire.* 315

Enemy, by which they engaged never in time to come to infest the Coasts of *France* or *Genoa*, to pay ten thousand Ducats for the Charge of the War, and set at liberty all the Christian Slaves in their Power. Under *Charles* VII. the next succeeding Prince, *John le Bourfier* is said to have defeated the *English* in an Engagement before the Town of *Blaye*, upon the *Garonne*, wherein he sunk five large Ships of *Bourdeaux* which came to their Assistance, and besieging *Blaye* by Land and Water, at length forced it to surrender. *The English defeated at Sea.* A. D. 1450.

During the long Reign of *Lewis* XI. there happened nothing remarkable at Sea; but his Successor *Charles* VIII. carrying his Arms into *Italy*, in order to reduce the Kingdom of *Naples*, a Naval Force was found very necessary for the Furtherance of that Design, and accordingly a Fleet was fitted out under the Command of the Duke of *Orleans*, who in a Sea Fight, off of *Porto Venere*, on the Coast of *Genoa*, worsted the Enemy's Gallies commanded by *Frederick*, Brother of *Alphonsus* King of *Naples* and *Sicily*, and keeping in awe all the Coasts of *Italy* from *Genoa* to *Naples*, struck such a Terror into *Alphonsus* himself, that he fled into *Sicily*, and left the Defence of his Realm of *Naples* to his Son. Soon after which that Kingdom wholly submitting itself to the *French*, the Reputation of their Arms was so great, that the Inhabitants of the *Morea*, and the rest of *Greece*, only waited the Appearance of their Fleet on their Coast, to revolt and throw off the *Turkish* Yoak; but the Prosecution of these Matters was hindered by the Intrigues of the *Venetians*, who grew jealous of the Encrease of the *French* Power, and had rather have the *Turk* their Neighbour on one side, than the Most Christian King on both. *The French Fleet overcome that of Naples. Naples subjected to France.*

Under *Lewis* XII. one *Pregent* was put at the Head of a Fleet in the Mediterranean, with the Title of Vice-Admiral of the *Levant*, with which encountering a *Venetian* Squadron off of *Genoa*, he sunk fifteen of their Gallies, and forced the rest to retire. After this he was ordered to conduct his Gallies round into the Ocean, to defend the Coasts of *Bretagne* and *Normandy* against the *English*; and falling in off *Conquêt* with their Fleet, under the Command of Sir *Edward Howard*, they both came to an Engagement, wherein that Admiral losing his Life in the first Charge, the *English* thought fit to retire to their own Coasts. *The French beat the Venetians at Sea. The English Fleet retire from the French.*

Francis I. next succeeded to the Crown, in whose time *Andrew Doria* of *Genoa* was appointed General of the *French* Gallies, with which he reduced *Salerno*, and other Places on the Coast of *Naples*, while *Philip Doria*, his Nephew, ravaged the Island of *Sardinia*, and engaging the Emperor's Fleet in the Gulph of *Naples*, entirely destroyed it. But some of the great Men at Court envying the Favour and Protection the *Genoese* enjoyed, and their great Successes, put some Indignities upon *Doria*, whereupon he quitted the *French* Service, and entering into that of the *Spaniards*, under *Charles* V, carried over with him to that side the good Fortune which had hitherto attended the *French* in this War, and thereupon ensued their utter Expulsion out of the Kingdom of *Naples*, and Republick of *Genoa*. He was succeeded in the Command of the *The French take Salerno, and other Places. A. D. 1528. and destroy the Emperor's Fleet. The French driven from Naples and Genoa.*

S s 2

the *French* Gallies by *Anthony de la Rochefoucauld*, and he by *Francis* of *Bourbon*, Count of *Anguien*, who, *Claude d'Annebault* being then Admiral of *France* and besieging *Boulogne*, sent round from *Marseilles* to his Assistance a Squadron of Gallies under the Command of *Paulin*, Baron *de la Garde*. He joining the Admiral off *Boulogne*, they repaired in conjunction to the Coasts of *England*, where, arriving at St. *Helen*'s, they had a slight Skirmish with the *English* Fleet, which came out of *Portsmouth* to engage them, and then landing in the Isle of *Wight*, they plundered some Villages, and retreated, though they had once a Design of erecting Forts there, and maintaining the Island, which had they done, (say the *French*) they had soon forced us to abandon *Boulogne*, (lately taken by *Henry* VIII.) and cut off our *Navigation* to *France* and *Spain:* But *Annebault*, with his fifty Men of War, sixty Ships of Burthen, and fifteen Gallies, being content to have only alarmed the Coasts, returned ingloriously home. About this time was built by the *French* King's Direction, at *Havre de Grace*, a Ship of War of a very considerable Burthen, the largest *France* had ever been Mistress of before: And at *Vannes*, in *Bretagne*, were ordered to be set up a Number of large Galleons.

The French land in the Isle of Wight.
A. D. 1544.

Annebault was succeeded by *Gaspard de Coligny*, as Admiral of *France*, and several Years after, the foresaid Baron *de la Garde* was made General of the Gallies, but the Civil Wars now reigning in *France*, for a considerable time, there happened little or nothing memorable at Sea, in regard they were so warmly engaged by Land. However, the Protestants, having got several strong Towns into their Possession, and greatly encreased their Power, at length began to take to the Sea; and having assembled a Squadron of nine Ships of War in the Port of *Rochelle*, under the Command of Monsieur *de la Tour*, they added several other small Vessels to them, which cruising in the Bay of *Biscay*, intercepted all the Ships they met with, whether *French* or *Spanish*, forcing the Men they found on board to take on in their Service. *De la Tour* being killed in the Battel of *Bassac*, the Protestant Navy was committed to Monsieur *Sora*, who at *Palma*, one of the *Canary* Islands, sunk the greatest Part of the *Brasil* Fleet, under the Command of *Lewis* the Governor of that Colony. The forementioned *Gaspard de Coligny* being barbarously murder'd in the Massacre of *Paris*, was succeeded as Admiral of *France* by *Honorat de Savoye*, who deputed the *Sieur de Lonsac* to command the Fleet. Against him the *Rochellers* sent out a Squadron of twelve Sail, commanded by Monsieur *de Claremont*, but most of those Ships being cast away, or taken by the Enemy, the Duke of *Mayenne*, who commanded the King's Land Army, recovered the Isle of *Oleron*, and Town of *Brouage* from the Protestants.

A. D. 1569.

The Protestants of France *arm several Ships, and sink great part of the* Brasil *Fleet*
A. D. 1572.

The Ships of the Protestants lost in a Storm.

Whilst *Andrew de Brancas* and *Charles de Montmorency* were successively Admirals of *France* under *Henry* IV, the *French* planted their Colony of *Canada*, or *New France*, which they discovered first in the Reign of *Francis* I, under the Conduct of *John Verezano*, a *Florentine*, commission'd by that Prince. But in the mean time new Troubles beginning in *France*, the Sieurs *Blanquet, Gaillard,*

The French plant their Colony of Canada.

Gaillard, *Trelebois*, and *Pontenille*, Gentlemen of the Proteſtant Party, putting to Sea with a Squadron, greatly infeſted the Mouth of the *Garonne*, where taking their Station off *Royan*, they cruiſed on their Enemies, and took ſeveral Prizes. There being a Fleet of a hundred and fifty Merchant Ships ready to ſail from *Bourdeaux*, the Sieur *de Barrault*, Vice-Admiral of *Guienne*, was ordered with nine Men of War to convoy them out to Sea, upon whoſe Approach *Blanquet*, with his Party, retired to a Place of Security; but *De Barrault* in his return falling in with them, they came to an Engagement, wherein *Blanquet* received a total Defeat, loſt all his Ships, and himſelf, with *Gaillard*, were taken Priſoners, the reſt flinging themſelves into the Sea, and eſcaping to Land. Mean while, in the Mediterranean, the Pirates of *Barbary* ſcouring the Coaſts of *Provence*, Monſieur *de Beaulieu* was ſent out againſt them with a Fleet of fifty Sail of Ships and Gallies, who, off St. *Tropez*, took one of their Veſſels, and going out to Sea in queſt of their main Force, met another of their Ships, commanded by a Renegado of *Rochelle*, who having obſtinately defended himſelf for ſome time, at length in deſpair ſunk his Ship, and was drowned with his whole Company. Another Renegado of *Arles* he forced to make his Eſcape on Shore; and having ſunk a fourth of their Ships, not being able to come up with the reſt, he returned to *Marſeilles*.

A. D. 1617.

The French Proteſtants ſuffer at Sea.

The French go againſt the Pirates of Barbary.

All things were now tending in *France* to a fierce Civil War, and the Duke of *Eſpernon*, with an Army, blocked up the Avenues to *Rochelle* on the Land ſide; but the Sea remaining open to the Beſieged, they ſent out a Squadron of ſix Ships, and one Gally, beſides ſeveral ſmall Veſſels, againſt Monſieur *Chalard*, Admiral of *Guienne*, whom they engaged in the Port of *Brouage*, and after an obſtinate and bloody Diſpute, wherein many Men were ſlain on both ſides, they ſeparated, and left the Victory uncertain; but ſoon after a Squadron of the King's, under the Sieurs *de St. Luc* and *Razilly*, defeated thirty Ships of the *Rochellers* near the Iſle of *Ré*; while, in the mean time, the Duke of *Soubize*, at the Head of the *Rochellers* Forces, took *Royan* upon the *Garonne*, ravaged the Iſlands of *Oleron* and *Argentan*, landed in *Medoc*, and laid waſte the Country; whence retreating, he penetrated into *Xaintonge*, and thence retiring to the Iſlands of *Rié* and *Mont*, ſituate amongſt Marſhes and Canals on the Coaſt of *Lower Poictou*, there fortified himſelf, and became ſo formidable, that the King himſelf marched in Perſon againſt him; upon whoſe Approach, and Preparations to attack him, he thought fit to retire, and got ſafe into *Rochelle*; but fifteen of his Ships which were left aſhore at low Water fell into the King's Hands, with the People on board, who were all condemn'd to the Gallies. Upon this Succeſs the *French* King ordered *Rochelle* to be again inveſted, the Blockade whereof had been for ſome time diſcontinued, and to cut off its Communication with the Sea, directed the Duke of *Guiſe* to come before it with forty Men of War, and twelve Gallies, who accordingly putting to Sea, made the beſt of his way for that Place. The *Rochellers*, with their Fleet, lay ready at the *Foſſe de l'Oye*, in the Iſle of *Ré*, to give the King's Ships Battel,

The French King's Fleet, and the Rochellers engage.

The Rochellers defeated at Sea, but take ſome Places.

The French King goes againſt the Duke of Soubize, and takes ſeveral of his Ships.

Rochelle inveſted by Sea and Land.

and

A. D. 1622. and on their Approach bravely engaged them, and fought with such Resolution, that they held the Victory long doubtful, but were at length forced to yield to superior Numbers, and retire with the Loss of ten Ships, and fifteen hundred Men.

The Rochellers are overcome at Sea.

Soon after this ensued a Peace between the contending Parties, but it proved but of short Duration, and the Duke of *Soubize* putting to Sea from *Rochelle*, repaired to *Blavet*, or Port St. *Louis*, in *Bretagne*, and seizing the Ships the Duke of *Guise* had laid up there, made himself also Master of the Town; but failing in his Enterprize on the Citadel, and the Duke of *Vendosme*, Governor of the Province, marching towards that Place, he quitted it, and retiring to his Ships, proceeded thence to the *Païs de Medoc*, on the Coast of *Guienne*, where he possessed himself of *Chastillon*, and other Places on the *Garonne*. Being at length obliged to quit those Parts, he retreated to the Isle of *Ré*, and there fortified himself. To dislodge him from thence, the *French* Fleet was fitted out, under the Command of the Duke of *Montmorency*, Admiral of *France*; and an auxiliary Fleet was procured from *Holland*, under the Command of the Sieur *Halstein*, and some Ships from *England*, which being all joined, mounted to fifty Sail; but the Duke of *Soubize*, at the Head of nine and thirty Ships, found means to burn the *Dutch* Vice-Admiral. Upon the Arrival of the *French* Admiral on board the Fleet, a Body of Troops was landed on the Island, where they met with a very warm Reception from the *Rochellers*, who; however, after the Loss of a considerable Number of Men, were worsted, and the Duke of *Soubize* made his Escape to the Isle of *Oleron*, whither he was followed by the Remains of his Fleet, which having been engaged at the same time, was lessened by nine Snips, and two which were stranded, whereof one was with great difficulty taken by the Enemy, and the other blew up, and destroyed four of the King's Ships.

1625.

Soubize fortifies himself in the Isle of Re.

Soon after this the Sollicitations of the Protestants with the *English* Court, added to the Misunderstandings then arisen between them and *France*, procured to be sent to the Aid of the *Rochellers* a Fleet and Army under the Conduct of the Duke of *Buckingham*, of which unsuccessful Expedition intending to give an ample Account among our own Affairs, I shall not anticipate the Reader in this Place; more than to tell him, that our Defeat there was followed not long after by the Surrender of *Rochelle*, and the Ruin of the Protestant Arms in *France*. For, as their principal Strength consisted in that Town, it being of the utmost Importance to the *French* King to reduce it, he left no Stone unturned for the compassing that End, and carried on the Siege in the most vigorous manner against it: But the Cardinal *de Richelieu*, then his chief Minister, considering that all Efforts by Land were in vain, so long as the Besieged kept open their Communication with the Sea, bent his whole Thoughts to block them up also that way. To this purpose he first employed a celebrated Engineer to lay a strong Barricade of Masts, and other Pieces of Timber chained together, across the Entrance of the Harbour; but the first heavy Sea which came in carrying all that away,

The Duke of Buckingham sent to the Isle of Re.

The Protestant Interest ruined in France by the taking of Rochelle.

CHAP. XIV. *Ruin of the* Rom *Empire.* 319

away, he began a Causway of large square Stones from each side of the Harbour, which he at length happily perfected, leaving a Space in the middle for the Passage of the Tide, where, to prevent any Succours from going in that way to the Relief of the Town, he filled up several Vessels with Mason's Work, and sunk them in that Space, which was besides defended by a Barricade of forty Ships linked together, and three Squadrons, one between the Causway and the Town, and two without it, which had on board several Regiments; so that tho' the Relief of the Place was thrice attempted by the *English*, there was no effecting it, and Famine beginning to rage among the Besieged, they were compelled to surrender.

Some time after this the Office of Admiral of *France* was suppressed, in favour of Cardinal *Richelieu*, who had the Charge of that Employment given him, with the Title of Great-Master, Chief, and Superintendant General of the Navigation and Commerce of *France*. Which Minister, after the Reduction of *Rochelle*, kept three Fleets constantly at Sea, one for the Security of all the Coasts of *France* in general which lie on the Ocean, a second to defend the Coasts of *Languedoc* and *Provence* on the Mediterranean, and a third upon the Coasts of *Guienne* and *Gascogne*, to accompany to Sea, and give Convoy to the Fleets bound to *Canada*. *Cardinal Richelieu made Chief of Naval Affairs.*

Some time after this, in the Year 1636, the *Spanish* Fleet, consisting of five large Ships of War, twenty two Gallies, and eighteen small Vessels, under the Command of the Duke of *Ferrandina*, and the Marquis of *Santa Cruz*, repairing to the Coasts of *Provence*, landed some Troops in the Islands of St. *Marguerite* and St. *Honorat*, who presently becoming Masters of the Forts built for their Defence, maintained themselves there till the ensuing Spring; when the Cardinal sent round from *Rochelle*, to join the Count *de Pontcourlay*, General of the Gallies in the Mediterranean, a Fleet of forty two Sail, under the Command of the Count *d'Harcourt*, assisted by the Archbishop of *Bourdeaux*, as President of the Council for Sea Affairs, who accordingly repairing to the Coast of *Provence*, the Ships and Gallies proceeded thence in conjunction against the Enemy. The *Spaniards* had by this time encreased their Fleet with the whole Strength of *Sicily*, *Naples*, and *Tuscany*, with which the *French* falling in off of *Monaco*, there ensued a sharp Engagement between them, wherein the *Spaniards* were at length forced to give way, and retired under Covert of the Night; when the Count *d'Harcourt* not thinking fit to chace them far, repaired to *Sardinia*, to annoy the Enemy in that Island, and landing there, ravaged the Country, and made himself Master of *Oristagni*. This done, he returned to the Coasts of *Provence*, and attacking the *Spaniards* in the Islands of St. *Marguerite* and St. *Honorat*, presently recovered those Places out of their Hands, and leaving sufficient Garrisons in them, repaired to the Isles of *Hyeres* to clean and refit. After which the Count *d'Harcourt* remaining with the Ships upon the Coasts, the Count *de Pontcourlay* went out to Sea with the Gallies, where, upon receiving Intelligence of a considerable Number of Transports bound from *Spain* to *Italy* with Recruits for 1636.

The Spaniards beaten by the French at Sea.

The French ravage Sardinia, &c.

the

The French attack Spanish Ships in Sight of Genoa.

the Enemy's Forces in that Country, he lay in wait to intercept them, and, within Sight of *Genoa*, came to an Engagement with their Convoy, wherein, after a long and obstinate Dispute, he utterly disabled the Admiral of *Sicily*, killed near four hundred of the Men on board her, together with the Commander, and having taken six other Gallies, the rest escaped into the Port of *Genoa*, but not without the Loss of two thousand Men slain, and nine hundred taken Prisoners, of which Number were twelve Captains; while, on the side of the *French*, there were lost only three Gallies, but among their slain a hundred Men of Note.

The French overcome the Sicilians.

Not long after the Prince of *Conde* and Duke of *Valette* penetrated with an Army into *Biscay*, as far as Port *Passage*, and seizing that Place, made themselves Masters of a Fleet of Galleons, and many other Ships in the Port; mean while the Archbishop of *Bourdeaux*, being returned from the Mediterranean, scoured the Sea-Coasts with the Fleet under his Command, and in the Port of *Guetaria*, near St. *Sebastian's*, burnt fourteen Galleons and three Frigates, besides several other Vessels. But the two Generals before-mentioned differing about carrying on of the Siege of *Fontarabia*, which they had invested, the *Spaniards* resuming new Courage, vigorously repulsed them, and forced them to retire within their Frontiers with a very considerable Loss.

The French do considerable Damage to the Spaniards, but are forced to retire.

The Marquis *de Breze* had, some time after, better Fortune with the Fleet then under his Command, who cruising with one and twenty Sail off the Streights Mouth, and having understood by an *English* Merchant Ship, which he had rescued from a Pirate of *Sally*, that the *Spanish Flota*, designed for the *West-Indies*, consisting of six and thirty Sail of Ships, besides twelve Galleons, lay in the Bay of *Cadiz*, ready to sail with the first fair Wind, he continued in the Offing of that Place, and engaged them on their coming out with such Success, that he sunk the Admiral Galleon, destroyed four others with his Fireships, and so disabled the whole Fleet, that many of the Ships sunk before they could get back into the Bay of *Cadiz*, but the Marquis following them, generously took up the Men, and set them on shore. In 1642, the same Officer being at the Head of the Fleet in the Mediterranean, where he was to act on the Coasts of *Spain* in concert with the Army under the Marshal *de la Mothe*, for the Reduction of *Catalonia*, burnt several of the *Spanish* Gallies in the Gulph of *Valencia*, and engaging the rest of their Fleet before *Barcelona*, he, after a long and fierce Dispute, which lasted two Days, obtained the Victory, with the Loss of only four hundred Men on his side; but to the *Spaniards* of near two thousand.

1640.
The French beat and disable the Spanish Fleet.
1642.

The Spaniards beaten by the French off of Barcelona.

Upon the Death of the Cardinal *Richelieu* the following Year, the said Marquis *de Breze*, who was his Nephew, succeeded him in the Office of Great Master, Chief, and Superintendant General of the Navigation and Commerce of *France*. Some time after which an Army being marched into *Italy* against the *Spaniards*, a Fleet was sent to the Coasts of that Country, under the Command of the same Marquis, who engaging the Enemy's Gallies before *Orbitello*,

CHAP. XIV. *Ruin of the* Rom. *Empire.* 321

bitello, on the Coast of *Tuscany*, his Fleet obtained the Victory, but he was himself slain in the Action by a Cannon-Ball. *The Spaniards again beaten, but the Marquis de Brezé slain.* 1646.

The Civil Dissensions which ensued shortly after in *France* continuing for some Years, wholly employed those People by Land, so that we hear nothing more of their Naval Transactions till the Year 1666, when, in the War between the *English* and *Dutch*, the *French* King, who espoused the Cause of the latter, ordered the Duke *de Beaufort* to join them with his Fleet. But in the next *Dutch* War the Scene was greatly changed, and the *French* King sent the Count *d'Estrées*, Vice-Admiral of *France*, with eight and forty Men of War, manned with eleven thousand Men, and mounted with nineteen hundred and twenty Guns, to join the *English* Fleet under the Duke of *York*; in conjunction with whom they engaged the *Dutch* at *Solebay*, but, in the Heat of the Engagement, quitted the Line of Battel, and left the Duke exposed to the *Dutch*, tho' not without the Loss of two of their best Ships, one of eighty Guns, which was burnt, and the other of seventy, which was sunk. However the *French* Fleet, under the same Admiral, bore a part in the next Naval Engagement, which happen'd in 1673, between the *English* under Prince *Rupert*, and the *Dutch* under *De Ruyter*, as also in the other ensuing Actions which happen'd the same Year, as will be more particularly related in the Account of our own Naval Transactions. In 1676, the *Dutch* sending a Squadron under the Command of *De Ruyter*, to the Assistance of the *Spaniards* in the Mediterranean, the *French* Fleet under Monsieur *du Quesne*, Lieutenant General of the Naval Armies of *France*, had two Engagements with the *Dutch* Admirals on the Coast of *Sicily*, wherein neither side could well claim the Victory; but in the last of them *De Ruyter* received those Wounds of which he died in few Days. *1666. The French espouse the Dutch against England. The French join the English, but leave them exposed. 1673. The French join the English again. 1676. The French engage the Dutch in the Mediterranean.*

Some time after this the *Corsairs* of *Tripoli* interrupting the Trade of the *French* in the Mediterranean, Monsieur *du Quesne* was sent out with a Fleet against them, who having Intelligence that eight of their Cruisers were in the Port of *Scio*, in the *Archipelago*, where they hoped to be secure under the Protection of the Grand *Signior*, *du Quesne* nevertheless attacked them, and destroyed them all in that Port: Whereupon the Government of *Tripoli* were glad to accept of a Peace, which *Du Quesne* shortly after agreed upon with them. The next Year, upon account of the like Piratical Depredations committed by those of *Algier*, *Du Quesne* went before that Place, and threw in such a Number of Bombs as ruined most part of the Town; and the following Year renewed the Bombardment, which brought the *Algerines* also to his Terms. *1681. Du Quesne destroys the Ships of Tripoli at Scio. 1682. The French bombard Algier. 1683.*

In 1684 happened the Bombardment of *Genoa*, by the *French* Fleet, under the Directions of the Marquis *de Seignelay*, of which we have already given Account among the Affairs of that Republick: And next Year, upon new Differences with the Government of *Tripoli*, the Marshal *d'Estrées* repaired before that Place, and threw in eleven hundred Bombs, which forced that People again to accept of a Peace, whereby they gave up all the *French* Slaves they had, and engaged to pay five hundred thousand *1684. 1685. The Tripolines again forced to a Peace.*

T t sand

1687.

The Algerines worsted by the French.

sand Crowns for the Prizes they had taken. In 1687 the *Algerines* having broken their late Peace, the *French* Ships cruised against them, and, near *Ceuta*, after a sharp Dispute, sunk their Vice-Admiral, having killed thirty of the Men on board, and taken ninety Prisoners: And in the Close of the same Year the Marquis *d'Amfreville*, commanding a *French* Squadron, ran one of their Ships of thirty six Guns ashore in *Sardinia*, and took most of her Company Prisoners.

1688.

The French take two Dutch Ships in the Mediterranean.

France declares War against England.

Soon after this happened the Revolution in *England*, which, for the part the *Dutch* had in it, bringing on the *French* King's Declaration of War against *Holland* in 1688, before the Close of that Year, two of his Ships of War in the Mediterranean, after an obstinate Fight, took two *Dutch* Ships coming from *Messina* to *Leghorn*, the one a Man of War, and the other a *Turkey* Merchant Ship of a very considerable Value. Shortly after which he declaring War also against *England*, the Naval Actions of the *French* since that time have been chiefly with our own Countrymen in the two last Wars, and are at large accounted for in the fourth and fifth Books of this History.

Chap. XV.

Of the Naval Wars of the English, *from the first known Times of* Britain, *to the* Norman *Conquest*.

AFTER having thus taken a View of the Naval Transactions of the rest of the World, 'tis time we now come to those of our own Nation, which appeared very early at Sea, and has been one of the most fruitful in Naval Events.

Observations on the early Naval Force of the Britains.

Altho', in my Opinion, all particular Accounts of *Britain*, and its Affairs, before the Time of *Julius Cæsar*, are deservedly exploded as fabulous, yet (as Mr. *Selden* has ingeniously observed) from the Memoirs that great Man has left us of his Wars in *Gaul*, it may be very fairly concluded that the *Britains* were, long before *Cæsar*'s Time, Masters of a considerable Sea Force: For upon occasion of that sharp Naval War, (taken Notice of in the first Book of this History) which the *Veneti*, or People of *Vannes*, waged against him, he observes that they not only received Aid therein from *Britain*, but also (speaking of the great Power of those People above the rest of the *Gauls* in those Parts) says they were Masters of great Numbers of Ships, with which they used to navigate to that Island. And speaking in another Place of his Motives for making an Expedition to *Britain*, and the Steps he took preparatory thereto, to gain proper Intelligences of the Country, he says he was at a great Loss in his Enquiries therein of the *Gauls*, because the *Britains* permitted none but Merchants to visit their Country, and they

only

ENGLISH CHANNEL
PART of FRANCE
Dunkirk
Calais
Boulogne
Dieppe
C. Barfleur
C. Hague
Garnsey
S. Forsland
Dover
Straits of Dover
Beachy Head
New Haven
Rye
KENT
SUSSEX
Arundel
Chichester
Portsmouth
Southampton
Wight I.
St. Hellens
Pool
Portland
Bridport
Lime
Exmouth
Exeter
Tor Bay
Dartmouth
Start Pt.
Plimouth
Fowy
Falmouth
Eddistone
Lizard Pt.
Pensance
Mounts Bay
St. Ives
Padstow
Beddiford
Barnstable
C. Cornwal
The Lands End
Scilly I.
Cape Clear
Missen Head
51
50

only those Parts of their Coasts which lay over against *Gaul*. This being so, as Mr. *Selden* argues, it is not to be doubted but that, besides the Boats made of Wicker and Hides, elsewhere taken notice of by *Cæsar*, the *Britains* had also a potent Navy which might, at pleasure, if they so thought fit, dislodge from their Coasts those Ships of the *Veneti* beforementioned, though so well equipped as *Cæsar* has described them. How otherwise could it be (says Mr. *Selden*) that the *Britains* should have it in their Power to admit none but Merchants, or whom they pleased, to their Coasts? Besides, after the Defeat the *Veneti* had received from *Brutus*, and that *Cæsar*, in punishment of their Revolt, had put to Death their whole Senate, (in which were included all the People of any Rank or Consideration among them, so that their Merchants were consequently of the Number) though there were Multitudes of that People still remaining, who were made Slaves, yet was there not one to be found among them who was acquainted with any Port of *Britain*, as is plain from the same *Cæsar*; but how that could possibly be true, (continues Mr. *Selden*) can by no means be comprehended, if the Naval Power of the *Veneti*, which used to sail thither, was more considerable than that of the *Britains*, nor unless the *British* Sea Force was greatly superior to that of the *Veneti*. Nor need it appear strange, that in *Cæsar*'s Expedition to *Britain*, soon after the Reduction of that People, there were no Ships found on our Coasts to oppose him, or that the *Roman* Writers make mention of no other than Vessels made of Wicker; for the *Veneti*, in their Naval Battel with *Brutus*, had assembled together all the Ships which could any where be found amongst themselves, or their Allies. Now if the *British* Fleet which was sent for to their Aid was amongst that Number, (as certainly it was) it was all lost before the Arrival of *Cæsar*; for the whole Strength of the *Veneti* perished in the foresaid Naval Engagement, as he expressly says. And after the *Romans* had reduced the Island to their Obedience, it is not to be imagined they would have suffered the Natives to be Masters of any Ships of Force; whence it is that the *Roman* Writers, after the Time of *Cæsar*, take notice of no other but those Vessels made of Wicker and Hides. Agreeable to these Reasonings of Mr. *Selden*'s are the Sentiments of the learned Monsieur *Huet* upon this Point, who says, in his Treatise of the Commerce and Navigation of the Ancients, that when the *Britains* aided the *Gauls* against the *Romans*, which they often did, as *Cæsar* himself affirms, and in particular when they assisted the People of *Vannes*, it is not to be supposed that they fought against the *Romans* in Leathern Boats, or that they sent their Men thither without furnishing them with Ships fit for Naval Engagements, it being rational to believe that, seeing their Enemies had strong Ships of War, they would endeavour to imitate them, for their own Preservation and Advantage.

Although *Cæsar* met with all the Success he could reasonably expect in his two Expeditions to *Britain*, (the Particulars whereof are before related among the *Roman* Affairs) yet the *Romans* made no Account of purſuing their Conqueſts therein till the Time of *Claudius*, which Emperor undertook an Expedition thither in Perſon, and having reduced great part of the Iſland to the Form of a *Roman* Province, returned to *Rome*, where celebrating a Triumph for the ſame, he cauſed a Naval Crown to be hung up in the Imperial Palace, in token that he had ſubdued the *Britiſh* Ocean. *Plautius*, who was one of his principal Officers in this Expedition, he left to rule the Province in quality of *Proprætor*, who was ſucceeded, in Order, by *Oſtorius*, *Didius*, *Veranius*, *Paulinus*, and others, who fought ſeveral Battels with the *Britains* with various Succeſs.

A. D. 44.

At length, in the Reign of *Veſpaſian*, *Julius Agricola*, a Perſon of great Skill and Experience, as well in Civil as Military Affairs, was ſent to govern the Province, who arriving in *Britain* about the end of Summer, (a Time when other Generals begin to look out for Winter-Quarters) immediately proceeding with his Troops towards the Iſle of ᵃ *Mona*, ſeparated from the main Land by an Arm of the Sea, at once marched them through the Shallows, and penetrated into the Iſland; which the Inhabitants looking upon as a kind of Miracle, were preſently terrified into Obedience, as thinking it vain to reſiſt him to whom the Sea itſelf ſeemed to give way, and afford a ſafe Paſſage through its Waves. The Reduction of this ſmall Iſland was looked upon to be of ſuch Importance, that *Agricola* is praiſed for his great Moderation, in not adorning with Laurel his Letters to the Senate, giving an Account of his Succeſs; for ſo did their Generals Letters uſe to be decked which brought Advice of any extraordinary Advantage. The *Romans* were however yet unacquainted with the more Northern parts of *Britain*, and *Agricola* being very deſirous to know its utmoſt Boundaries, and whether it were an Iſland, or joined to the Continent, he aſſembled a Fleet at the Iſle of *Mona*, which he ordered to coaſt along to the Northward, but conſtantly to keep ſo near the Land, as that every Night it might be in ſight of the Body of Troops which marched along the Coaſts on the ſame Deſign. Purſuing this Route, the Fleet and Army in a ſhort time came to the Gulph of *Glota*, (now the Firth of *Clyd*) where *Agricola* being arrived, and underſtanding that oppoſite thereunto, on the Eaſtern ſide of the Iſland, there was another great Inlet of the Sea, called *Bodotria*, (now the Firth of *Forth*) he fortified the Space between with Caſtles and Garriſons. After which having ſeveral bloody Engagements with the Inhabitants of thoſe Parts, wherein they were at length totally defeated, he became abſolute Maſter of all the Country on this ſide of the Firths, and, by his Fortifications between them, ſhut the Natives out, as it were, into another Iſland; and now reſolving entirely to ſatisfy his Curioſity, as to the Extent of the Country, and to penetrate to the uttermoſt Ends of the Earth, (as the Ancients ſuppoſed the extreme Parts of *Britain* muſt be) he again ſent out the Fleet, which proceeding Northward from the Firth of *Clyd*, went about the *Orkneys*, and coming round thence to the ᵇ *Portus Trutulenſis*, from whence it firſt departed, diſcovered to the *Romans* that *Britain* was an Iſland. *Agricola*'s Reduction, and Settlement of ſo much of this Iſland in a peaceable

Julius Agricola comes againſt Britain.
A. D. 79.

ᵃ Angleſey.

He reduces the Iſle of Angleſey.

Agricola diſcovers Britain to be an Iſland.

ᵇ Richborow near Sandwich.

CHAP. XV. *Ruin of the* Rom. *Empire.* 325

peaceable Submission to the *Roman* Name, was esteemed so considerable an Atchievement, that it drew upon him the Hatred of the Emperor *Domitian*, (a Prince with whom great Virtues were more punishable than open Crimes) who, under pretence of doing him farther Honour, by conferring upon him the Proconsulship of *Asia*, recalled him to *Rome*, and there took him off by Poison. *Domitian poisons Agricola.*

Under several succeeding Emperors we meet but with little mention of *Britain*, and of its Naval Affairs nothing, save that in the Reign of *Antoninus Pius*, it appears, from the *Digest*, that one *Seius Saturninus* was Commander in Chief of the *Roman* Fleet here. Under *Dioclesian*, *Carausius*, a Native of *Gallia Belgica*, was possessed of that Command, who became so considerable, that he set himself up for Emperor, and being absolute Master of *Britain*, maintained his Authority there for several Years, as we have already shewn among the *Roman* Affairs, where his Naval Exploits are particularly related. *A. D. 285. Carausius makes himself Master of Britain.*

In the Time of the Emperor *Gratian*, *Theodosius* (whom he afterwards assumed into a Partnership of the Empire) performed several great Atchievements in *Britain* against the *Picts* and *Scots*, who ravaged the Inland Provinces of the Island, while the *Saxons*, with frequent Descents, harrassed the Southern Coasts. The former he forced to retire to their native Mountains in the North, and the *Saxons* he overthrew in several Engagements at Sea. *Theodosius beats the Saxons at Sea.*

That People were now, and had been for some time very considerable on float, and remarkable for their Robberies and Cruelties exercised upon all their Neighbours, both by Sea and Land. Yet before another Century came about, near the time when *Attila* King of the *Huns* penetrated with his *Barbarians* into *Italy*, the *Britains*, harrassed by the frequent Inroads of the *Picts*, and deserted by the *Romans*, (who had now enough to do to defend themselves) invited these *Saxons* over to their Assistance: A small Number of whom, under the Conduct of *Hengist* and *Horsa*, two Brothers, arriving in *Britain*, render'd considerable Service against the *Picts*, and had the Isle of *Thanet*, where they first landed, assigned them as a Reward, and Place of Habitation. The Richness and Fertility of the Country was so agreeable to these *Saxons*, that they soon invited more of their Nation to share in their good Success, and were at length followed by such Droves of them, that, turning their Arms against their Entertainers, they defeated them in several Battels, and at length driving them out of the best part of the Island into that mountainous Country now called *Wales*, possess'd themselves of all that part of *Britain*, which from the *Angles*, one of the most considerable of the *Saxon* Tribes, has derived the Name of *England* which it now bears. Therein having by degrees established seven Kingdoms, they were at length all united into one Monarchy in the Person of *Egbert*. *The Saxons invited to Britain. A. D. 450. The Saxons master the greatest part of Britain.*

That Prince began his Reign over the *West-Saxons*, in the Year 800, at which time the *Danes*, brought down by the just Dispensations of Heaven, to retaliate, in great part, upon the *Saxons* what they had caused the *Britains* to suffer, made their first Expedition *800. The Danes come to Britain.*

o

to this Island. Twice in this Year they landed in different Parts of the Kingdom, one Body of them in the Isle of *Portland*, and another in the Mouth of the *Humber*, where plundering the adjacent Country, they got together some Booty; but behaving themselves more like Piratical Robbers than a declared Enemy, they were soon forced to their Ships, and carried off little with them at that time but a slight Knowledge of the Country. But the next Year landing in *Lindisfarne*, or *Holy Island*, they there gave the *Saxons* a great Overthrow, when imbarking aboard their Ships, they sailed round to the Coast of *Wales*, where the *Britains* (or *Welch*, as the *Saxons* called them) entring into Confederacy with them, they jointly proceeded against King *Egbert*, and gave him Battel, but received a total Defeat. Nevertheless the following Year, with a considerable Reinforcement of Shipping, they enter'd the *Thames* Mouth, and seized the Isle of *Shepey*, from whence they made Excursions throughout the whole County of *Kent*, and even to the very Gates of *London*, but were at length dislodged from thence by King *Egbert*, and forced to retire. However it was not long e'er they returned again, and their Attempts upon one Part or other of the Coast were so numerous, that there would be no End should we recount them all, there being hardly a Port in *England*, which more or less of them had not visited.

Egbert beats the Danes and the Welch. The Danes come up the Thames, and harrass Britain.

838.

About the Year 838, (*Ethelwolf* the Son of *Egbert* then reigning) they sailed up the *Thames* with a Fleet of three hundred and fifty Vessels, and burning all the Towns they came by, landed their Men, and marching up into the Country laid it waste with Fire and Sword; but *Ethelwolf* at length giving them a great Overthrow, they retired to their Ships, and returned home, not without Design of coming back with a more considerable Force. This they accordingly did in 866, arriving on the Eastern Coasts with a numerous Fleet under the Conduct of *Hinguar* and *Hubba*, two Brothers; and were followed shortly after by a Force no less considerable, under *Bascai* and *Halfden*, who landed in the West. These joining their Forces, and aiming at no less than the Reduction of the whole Kingdom, marched against King *Ethelred*, then reigning, with whom they fought several Battels with various Success, in one of which that Prince, with *Halfden*, one of the *Danish* Leaders, lost their Lives.

The Danes do great Mischief, but are forced to retreat.
866.
The Danes come again to England.

Ethelred slain.

Ethelred was succeeded by his younger Brother *Alfred*, who wisely reflecting that his Predecessors Neglect of their Naval Affairs for some time past had exposed the Country to the Attempts of the *Danes*, fitted out a Fleet, and obtained several signal Advantages over the Enemy, which, with the Loss of a hundred and twenty of their Ships, partly by Storm, and partly destroyed by the *English*, on the Coasts of *Devonshire*, repressed their Insolencies for some time. But at length those of them who were settled in *Northumberland*, and among the East *Angles*, equipping a Number of Gallies, sent them round into the Chanel, to cruise on the Coasts of the West *Saxons*. Whereupon King *Alfred* built a Number of Gallies, twice as long as those usual in these times, some whereof had

Alfred beats the Danes at Sea.

5

sixty

CHAP. XV. *Ruin of the* Rom. *Empire.* 327

sixty Oars, and some more, and were of a peculiar Built, of the King's own Invention, being both higher, swifter, and steadier, says my Author, than those of either the *Danes* or *Frisons*. These meeting with the Enemy off the Isle of *Wight*, a sharp Engagement ensued betwixt them, wherein at length, not without a considerable Loss on the *English* Side, the *Danes* were defeated, all their Ships being either taken or sunk, and the Men that escaped the Slaughter were taken Prisoners, and executed by the *English* as Pirates. In this Prince's Time also *Rollo* the *Norman* coming with a numerous Fleet from the North, landed on the *English* Coasts, but met with so warm a Reception, that he thought fit immediately to retire to his Ships, and go to seek Adventures in other Parts. *The Danish Fleet overcome by the English.* *Rollo the Norman lands in England, but forced back.*

Edward and *Athelstan*, who next succeeded in Order, had several successful Rencounters at Sea with the *Danes*; but *Edgar* who came to the Crown in 959, far surpassed all his Predecessors in Naval Glory, and provided himself a Navy of no less than three thousand and six hundred Sail, and those for that Age all stout Ships. This Force was divided into three Fleets, each of twelve hundred Sail, which he kept in constant Readiness for Service, one on the Eastern Coast, another on the Western, and the third on the Northern Coasts of the Kingdom, to defend them against the Depredations of the *Danish* and *Norman* Pirates, and secure the Navigation of the adjacent Seas: Which that he might the more effectually do, he every Year, after the Festival of *Easter*, went on board the Fleet on the Eastern Coast, and sailing Westward with it, scoured the Chanel of Pirates, and having looked into all the Ports, Bays, and Creeks between the *Thames* Mouth and the Land's End, quitted this Fleet and sent it back; and going on board the Western Fleet did the like in those Parts, as also on the Coasts of *Ireland*, and among the *Hebrides*, or Western Islands; where being met by the Northern Fleet, he went on board the same, and came round to the *Thames* Mouth, thus encompassing all his Dominions, and providing for the Security of their Coasts. This he did for the whole sixteen Years of his Reign; and as a more signal Declaration of his Power at Sea, going once to keep his Court at *Chester*, he summoned thither all the Kings who held of him, to wit, *Kenneth* King of *Scotland*, *Malcolm* of *Cumberland*, *Maccuse* of the *Isles*, and five Kings of *Wales*, and going on board his Barge caused each of them to take an Oar, and to row him down the River *Dee*, while he himself sate in the Stern, and held the Rudder; thus, in a sort of solemn Triumph, asserting his Right to that Sea-Dominion, derived from his Ancestors, which has been from him so happily transmitted down (with the Consent of all the Neighbouring Nations) to his latest Successors, and shall, I trust, continue with them so long as the Sea it self shall endure. *959. King Edgar's Naval Strength.*

The *Danes*, who in the Reign of this valiant Prince had remained more quiet, when he was deceased, and his Son *Ethelred* came to the Throne, renewed their Hostilities, and coming over in Swarms committed great Spoil on the Coasts: Against whom *Ethelred*, after the Example of his Father, prepared a powerful Navy, causing of every three hundred and ten Hides of Land in the Kingdom a Ship *The Danes renew their Hostilities in the Reign of Ethelred.*

Ship to be built; which however met with but ill Success, being for the most part either destroyed by Tempests, or, through Neglect, render'd unserviceable against the Enemy. So powerful were they now grown here, and so odious to the People, that nothing less than a general Massacre of them could satisfy, and accordingly the Design was put in Execution, without Regard to Age or Sex. To revenge this Treatment of his Countrymen, *Swaine*, King of *Denmark*, comes over with a numerous Fleet, and met with such good Success, that forcing *Ethelred* to retire into *Normandy*, he made himself Master of the greatest Part of the Kingdom; but dying soon after, *Ethelred* returned, and being presently furnished with a considerable Force, repaired to *Lindsey*, where he set upon *Knute* the Son of *Swaine*, with his Father's Shipping and Hostages, and forced him to betake himself to the Sea, and retire to his own Country; but *Knute* did not long continue there, for, within the Year, he came back with a more powerful Fleet and Army to *Sandwich*, where *Edric*, who had the Command of *Ethelred*'s Fleet, revolted to him with forty Ships; and landing at that Place, he met with so good Success, that in a short time he made himself Master of the whole Kingdom, and after a long and happy Reign, left it to *Harold* his eldest Son; who was succeeded by *Hardiknute*, *Harold*'s half Brother, the last of the *Danish* Kings in *England*.

Upon that Prince's Death in 1042, *Edward*, the Son of the late King *Ethelred*, was chosen King by joint Consent of the People, who were not a little influenced in their Choice by *Godwin* Earl of *Kent*, a Person of great Sway in those Times, who some while after disagreeing with the King, retired from Court, and betaking himself to Sea, got together a considerable Fleet, with which he committed great Spoil on the Coasts, took several Ships, and at length coming up to *London*, forced the King to grant him his Pardon on his own Terms. The Earl's Son *Harold*, upon the Decease of King *Edward*, succeeded to the Crown, who was hardly seated on the Throne, when his own Brother *Tosti* joining with *Harfager*, King of *Norway*, against him, invaded *England* with a great Navy, and landing at *Tinmouth*, marched their Army into the Heart of the Kingdom; but *Harold* soon repairing against them, they came to a Battel, wherein their Forces were utterly defeated, and *Tosti* and *Harfager* both slain.

William, surnamed *the Bastard*, Duke of *Normandy*, having Pretensions to the Crown of *England*, founded on the Last Will of the late King *Edward*, had just before this Invasion sent to demand of *Harold* the Surrender of the Kingdom to him, and to support that Demand in Case of Refusal, which he was sure to meet with, got ready a considerable Fleet and Army. To provide for his Security against this Force, *Harold* repaired to *Sandwich*, where he went on board his Fleet, and sailing thence to the Isle of *Wight*, disposed several Bodies of Men, as he went along the Coasts, in the Places where 'twas likely the Enemy would attempt to land. While he was employed in this manner, he received Advice of the Descent of his Brother in the North, whereupon thinking no time should be lost

loſt in laying that Tempeſt that firſt broke out upon him, he marched with a great Army Northwards, where he met with the Succeſs I have before mention'd. Winter approaching, and Proviſions beginning to grow ſcarce in the Fleet he had left in the Chanel, the Ships being no longer able to keep the Sea, returned into Port, which they had no ſooner done, but Duke *William*, lying ready at St. *Valery*, ſet ſail from thence with a Fleet of nine hundred Sail, with which in few Hours arriving at *Haſtings*, he there landed, and ſhortly after giving Battel to *Harold* near that Place, gained an entire Victory over the *Engliſh*, of whom ſixty thouſand with *Harold* himſelf were ſlain on the Spot; which was immediately followed by the Submiſſion of the whole Kingdom to his Authority.

Duke William ſets ſail for England, and gains the Crown. 1066.

Chap. XVI.

Of the Naval Tranſactions of the Engliſh *from the Norman Conqueſt to the End of Queen* Mary I.

THE Reign of the Conqueror paſſed without any conſiderable Diſturbance till the eleventh Year, when a formidable Conſpiracy was enter'd into againſt him by ſeveral *Engliſh* Lords, who being countenanced by divers of the neighbouring Princes, *Swaine* King of *Denmark* ſent a Fleet of two hundred Sail to their Aſſiſtance, under the Command of his Son *Knute*, and *Drone* King of *Ireland* furniſhed the Sons of the late King *Harold* with ſixty five Ships; but King *William* having ſeized the Conſpirators at home, made ſo good Preparations for the Reception of theſe foreign Enemies, that the *Iriſh* Ships returned without attempting any thing, and the *Danes* after having committed ſome Depredations on the Coaſts of *England* and *Flanders*, returned home alſo. But the latter, a few Years after, intending to repair this Diſhonour, and to aſſert their pretended Right to *England*, fitted out a Fleet of a thouſand Sail, to which were added ſix hundred by the Earl of *Flanders*, their Ally; but the Winds hanging out of the Way for two Years together (as our Hiſtorians ſay) or, what is more probable, through Deſpair of Succeſs, the Expedition was laid aſide, and *England* ever after freed from all Moleſtation from that Quarter.

Swain aſſiſts the rebellious Lords, but they and the Iriſh forced to return.

The Danes intend a great Fleet for England, but are prevented.

King *William* dying in 1087, was ſucceed by his Son *William* II, and he by his Brother *Henry* I, who was followed by *Stephen*, the Grandſon of *William* I, during all which Time there happened nothing remarkable at Sea. *Henry* II, Son of *Maud* the Empreſs, next ſucceeded in the Throne, who, in the Year 1172, reſolving to attempt the Reduction of *Ireland*, aſſembled a Fleet of four hundred Ships at *Milford* Haven, and there embarking with a great Body of Troops, croſſed over to *Waterford*, and landing his Army, in a ſhort time brought the whole Kingdom to his Obedience, which having

1087. The Succeſſors of King William.

1172. Henry II. ſails to and reduces Ireland.

having settled in Peace, and left a Deputy there to administer the Government, he returned triumphantly to *England*.

Richard I goes with a Fleet to the Holy Land. His Son and Successor *Richard* I. entring into the Holy War, in Conjunction with *Philip* II. of *France*, fitted out from his Realm of *England*, and his Dominions in *France*, a Fleet of a hundred and thirty Ships, and fifty Gallies, under the Command of the Archbishop of *Auxerre*, the Bishop of *Bayonne*, *Robert de Sabul*, and *Richard de Canvile*, which having ordered to sail to the Mediterranean, he himself went over-land to *Marseilles*, and proceeding thence to *Sicily*, there embarked, and made the best of his Way thence for *Syria*. Arriving off of *Cyprus*, he was forced by bad Weather to put in to that Island, where being refused the Freedom *Richard I. reduces Cyprus.* of landing, he forcibly attacked it, and in few Days reducing the whole Country to his Obedience, appointed *Richard de Canvile*, and *Robert de Turnham*, Governors thereof; when going over to *Syria* he landed there, and joining the *French* King, already arrived, laid Siege to *Acre*, then held by the Sultan of *Ægypt*, ordering his Fleet to lie before it, to prevent its receiving any Succours by Sea. Notwithstanding which, the Enemy endeavouring with their Naval *The English entirely defeat the Fleet of Ægypt.* Force to throw some Relief into it, the *English* engaged and entirely defeated them, taking most of their Ships, and in them two hundred and fifty Grappling Irons, a great Number of Vessels full of *Ignis Græcus* (a Composition of Pitch, Sulphur, Tartar, and other combustible Matters that would burn even in the Water) together with several Pots full of live Serpents, all which they had provided for the Destruction of the *English*, but by the Suddenness of the Victory were deprived of the Opportunity of using them. Immediately *Acre surrendered to Richard King of England.* upon this, no Hopes of Succours appearing, *Acre* was surrender'd to King *Richard*, soon after which he was, by universal Consent, chosen Captain-General of all the Christian Forces in *Asia*; where having obtained several glorious Successes against the Infidels, he was at length called home by the intestine Divisions in *England*, occa- 1199. sioned by his Brother *John*, who in 1199 succeeded him in the Throne.

The Pope gives England to the King of France. Upon Occasion of the Disputes between this King and his Clergy, the Pope having by his Bull deprived him of his Dominions, and transferred all Right and Title to them from him to the King of *France*, that Prince got together a great Fleet and Army, in order to take Possession of the Pope's Donative. Whereupon King *John* providing for his Defence against this Storm, assembled an Army of sixty thousand Men, with a Fleet greatly superior to that of the *The Pope restores King John.* *French*; but upon his Submission soon after to the Pope, he was restored to all his Rights; and the *French* King, being forbid by his Holiness to proceed on this Expedition, turned his Arms against the Earl of *Flanders*, for having refused to accompany him in the Prosecution of his Design against *England*, and taking part with King *John*, who thereupon sent over to the Assistance of the said Earl his Fleet, consisting of five hundred Sail, under the Command of the Earls of *Salisbury* and *Boulogne*; and they attacking the
French

CHAP. XVI. *Ruin of the* Rom. *Empire.* 331

French Fleet on the Coast of *Flanders,* near *Damme,* entirely defeated the same, and then landing their Troops, forced the King of *France* to retire with great Loss into his Dominions. *King* John *beats the French Fleet.*

King *John* was succeeded by his Son *Henry,* the Third of that Name, whose long Reign passed without any remarkable Occurrence at Sea: But his Successor *Edward* I, upon the *French* King's attacking his Dominions in *France,* fitted out a Fleet of three hundred and sixty Sail, which, with a considerable Land Force, he sent over to *Guienne,* under the Command of the Earls of *Lancaster, Lincoln,* and *Richmond.* Arriving in the *Garonne,* they in a short time reduced the Towns of *Bourg* and *Blaye,* upon that River, and raising the Siege of *Bourdeaux,* at length forced the Enemy entirely to quit the King's Territories. At the same time were employed at home, three Squadrons for the Defence of the Coasts against any Attempts that the *French* might make there, one on the Eastern Coast, called the *Yarmouth* Squadron, under *John de Botetort*; another on the Southern Coast, called the *Portsmouth* Squadron, commanded by *William de Leyburne*; and the third on the Western Coasts, and those of *Ireland,* under the Conduct of an *Irish* Knight, not named. Under *Edward* II, who next came to the Crown, *John Oturwin, Nicholas Kyriel,* and *John de Felton,* were employed in those Commands, and, on occasion of another War with *France,* took a hundred Sail of *Norman* Ships. This Prince having married *Isabel* the Daughter of *Philip the Fair,* and after her Father's Death, her three Brothers, *Lewis, Philip,* and *Charles,* who were successively Kings of *France,* dying without Issue, the Right of succeeding to that Crown, did of Consequence devolve to Queen *Isabel,* and in Right of her to her Son *Edward* III, who, upon the Resignation of his Father, in 1327, had been crowned King of *England.* But the *French,* under Colour of their pretended *Salique Law* passing him by, set up King *Philip* VI, surnamed *de Valois.* *Edward I. successful against France.*

Three Squadrons kept to defend the English Coasts.

The English Admirals take many Norman Ships.

1327.

King *Edward,* in Prosecution of his just Cause, declared War against *Philip,* and passing over to *France* with a great Army, obtained several Advantages, and having drawn the People of *Flanders* into an Alliance with him, returned to *England* to provide a strong Reinforcement for the more effectual carrying on the War. The *French* in the mean time having fitted out several Ships, committed great Depredations on the Coast of *England,* and having Advice that the King was ready to proceed with his Forces to *Flanders,* they assembled their whole Navy in the Port of *Sluys,* in order to oppose his Landing in those Parts. The *English* Fleet, nevertheless, consisting of two hundred and sixty Sail, having received the King with the Troops on board, set Sail from the *Downs,* and arriving near *Sluys,* found the *French* Ships in three Divisions, dispos'd in Order of Battel. When they were come up within a convenient Distance of each other, the King having the Advantage of the Wind, made the Signal to engage, whereupon the *English,* setting up loud Huzzas, poured out from their Long-Bows such Showers of Arrows upon the Enemy as immediately covered their Decks with dead Bodies; and then boarding the *French* Ships, pursued *Edward III. declares War against France.*

The English overcome the French Fleet.

U u 2 their

their Advantage with such Vigour, that in few Hours they gained a complete Victory, though not without the Loss of four thousand Men on their side. But the *French* lost two hundred and thirty Ships, and thirty thousand Men, most of whom were drowned; for not being able to abide the numerous Vollies of the *English* Arrows, great Multitudes of them desperately leaped into the Sea, and perished. The News of which great Loss the *French* King's Courtiers being perplexed how to communicate to him, his Jester took it upon him to do it, and going into the Presence, breaks out into the most violent Exclamations of, *Oh the cowardly* English! *paultry* English! *faint-hearted* English! Whereupon the King enquiring, *Why such Cowards? What had they done? Why*, replied he, *for not daring to jump into the Sea as your Majesty's brave* Frenchmen *have done*.

Edward lays siege to Tournay.

King *Edward* having entirely ruined the Enemy's Fleet, landed his Army, and marching to *Tournay*, laid siege to that Place, where after he had lain three Months, he was at length prevailed upon to grant the *French* a Truce for one Year. This was scarce expired, e'er King *Edward*, at the earnest Solicitation of *John de Monfort*, Duke of *Bretagne*, (then not annexed to the Crown of *France*)

Edward assists the Duke of Bretagne.

sent over a considerable Force to assist him against *Charles de Blois*, who pretended to that Duchy, and was supported in his said Pretensions by the *French* King. The Fleet which transported these Forces to *Bretagne* was commanded by *Robert d'Artois*, lately revolted from the *French*, and created Earl of *Richmond*, who being mortally wounded before *Vannes*, the King went over thither in Person with so numerous a Fleet and Army, that at one and the same time he laid siege to *Rennes*, *Vannes*, and *Nantes*, the three most considerable Cities of *Bretagne*, as also to the Town of *Dinant*, which he took by Storm; and at length, after several other Advantages, he concluded a Truce with the Enemy for three Years, and returned to *England*. This Truce was no sooner at an end, than King *Edward*, resolving to pursue his Right to the Crown of *France* with the utmost Vigour, made all suitable Preparations, and having assembled at *Portsmouth* a Fleet of a thousand Sail, embarked with his Army, and crossing over to *Normandy*, landed at *La Hogue*, from whence marching up into *Picardy*, he gained the signal Victory at *Creßy*, wherein thirty thousand of the Enemy were slain, and among them the Flower of the Nobility of *France*.

1343.

Edward prepares to invade France,

and

obtains a great Victory at Creßy. 1346.

Some Spanish *Ships sink others of* England.

Shortly after this, upon occasion of some Variance between *England* and *Spain*, a Fleet of that Nation, going to *Sluys* in *Flanders*, meeting in their way thither with some *English* Ships, bound home from *Gascogne*, seized ten of them, which they sunk, after they had plundered them of their Cargoes. The King, upon Advice of this, fitted out a Squadron of fifty Ships, and receiving Intelligence when the *Spanish* Ships were returning home from *Sluys*, went on board the Fleet, accompanied with the Prince of *Wales*, the Earls of *Lancaster*, *Northampton*, *Warwick*, *Salisbury*, *Arundel*, *Huntington*, and *Glocester*, with many other Persons of Quality,

CHAP. XVI. *Ruin of the* Rom. *Empire.* 333

lity, in order to intercept them in their Paffage. Off of *Winchelfey* they fell in with the *Spanifh* Fleet, confifting of four and forty Sail of large *Carracks*, which, compared with thofe of the *Englifh*, were like floating Caftles. Approaching each other, there enfued a bloody Engagement, wherein, after a long and obftinate Difpute, the *Englifh* Archers proving too hard for the *Spanifh* Crofs-bow Men, the King obtained a compleat Victory, taking feventeen of the Enemy's Ships, the reft with difficulty efcaping under covert of the Night. But fome time after this the Earl of *Pembroke* repairing with a ftrong Squadron to the Relief of *Rochelle*, then befieged by the *French*, received a great Overthrow before that Place from the united Fleet of the *French* and *Spaniards*, who took the faid Earl Prifoner, and poffeffed themfelves of all his Ships, as we have in another Place obferved. *Edward defeats the Spaniards at Sea.*

The Earl of Pembroke overcome at Rochelle by the French and Spanifh Fleets.

King *Edward* dying, he was fucceeded by his Grandfon *Richard* II, Son of the famous Black Prince, who coming to the Crown at eleven Years of Age, the *French* and *Scots*, thinking to take Advantage of his Minority, very much infefted the Coafts. Of the latter one *Mercer* appeared at the Head of a confiderable Number of Ships, and committed great Spoil on the Eaftern Coafts, plundering or taking all the Ships he met with: Which Infolences of his the weak Adminiftration of that time taking no care to reprefs, a wealthy Citizen of *London*, one *John Philpot*, fitted out at his own Charge a Number of Frigates, and going with them himfelf in queft of this Rover, he in a fhort time came up with him, and took him Prifoner, and recovered all the Prizes which had been taken from the *Englifh*, together with feveral *Spanifh* and *French* Ships richly laden; notwithftanding which confiderable Service, the Citizen was, upon his Return home, taken into Cuftody, as having levied a Force without Authority; but gave fo handfome an Account of his Intentions therein at the Council-Table, that he was difmiffed with Thanks. Some time after, upon the Apprehenfions the Nation was in of an Invafion from the *French* King, *Charles* VI, greater Care was taken to provide for its Defence, and a confiderable Fleet was fitted out under the Command of the Earls of *Arundel* and *Nottingham*, who putting to Sea, went over to the Weftern Coafts of *France*, and there cruifing againft the Enemy, took a hundred Sail of Ships, fome of them Men of War, and the reft trading Veffels laden with Wine. *The French and Scots moleft England.*

John Philpot fuccefsful at Sea.

Richard II. fits out a Fleet.

A hundred French Ships taken.

Henry IV. next fucceeded to the Crown, in the fourth Year of whofe Reign a Squadron of Ships belonging to *Bretagne* arriving at *Plimouth*, burnt that Town; to revenge which Proceeding the Weftern Ships were fent over to *Bretagne*, under the Command of *William Wilford*, who took forty Ships, and burnt as many; and landing at *Penmarc*, marched up into the Country, which having plundered and laid wafte, he retreated with a confiderable Booty to his Ships, and returned home. This however did not deter the Admiral of *Bretagne*, for he made another Attempt with his Fleet the next Year upon the Town of *Dartmouth*, where landing his Men, he vigoroufly attacked the Place, but was fo warmly received by the

Other French Ships taken and burnt.

The French in vain attempt Dartmouth.

the Townsmen, and those of the neighbouring Country, that he was forced to retire with the Loss of four hundred Men, and two hundred taken Prisoners. Shortly after this, upon occasion of a War with *Scotland*, Sir *Robert Umfrevile*, Vice-Admiral of *England*, repairing with a Squadron of ten Ships of War to the Firth of *Forth*, ravaged the Coasts on both sides for fourteen Days, and having burnt the largest Ship of that Kingdom, called the *Great Galliot*, and taken several Prizes, returned to the *English* Coasts.

The English ravage the Coasts of Scotland.
1437.

King *Henry* V, who succeeded his Father in 1437, reviving the just Pretensions of his House to the Crown of *France*, resolved on an Expedition to that Kingdom, and having got ready at *Southampton* sixteen hundred Sail of Ships, Hulks, and other Vessels, part whereof were hired from *Holland* and *Zeeland*, there embarked with his Army, and landing at *Caudebec* in *Normandy*, presently took in the Town of *Harfleur*, and soon after fought the famous Battel of *Agincourt*, to the eternal Honour of the *English* Nation. The next Campaign the *French* resolving by all means possible to attempt the Recovery of *Harfleur*, the Constable of *France* with a great Army invested it on the Land side, while the Vice-Admiral besieged it at Sea, with the whole Navy of that Kingdom. The Duke of *Exeter* commanding in the Place began to be hard pressed by the Besiegers, when the *English* Fleet, under the Command of the Duke of *Bedford*, accompanied with several other Persons of the first Quality, was ordered to repair to his Relief. Arriving in the Mouth of the *Seine*, they found the Enemy's Fleet, great part whereof consisted of *Genoese* Carracks, drawn up before the Port of *Harfleur*, and vigorously attacking them, after a Dispute of several Hours, entirely defeated them, and having sunk or taken five hundred Vessels, with three *Genoese* Carracks, went triumphantly into the Port, and relieved the Town, whereupon the Enemy's Land-Army immediately raised the Siege and retired.

Henry V. *lands in* France, *and fights the Battel at Agincourt.*

Harfleur *invested by Sea and Land by the* French.

The French *Fleet beaten, and* Harfleur *relieved.*

During the rest of this great Prince's Reign there happened nothing remarkable at Sea; where we hear of no more Exploits of the *English* till the thirty fourth Year of his Son and Successor *Henry* VI, at which time the great Earl of *Warwick* being Lord High Admiral, and then lately entered into the Interests of the House of *York*, he, to secure the Fleet to that side, assembling all such Ships as were in a Readiness for Service, suddenly repaired on board the same, and went out to Sea, where he fell in with five great Carracks, three of them *Genoese*, and two *Spanish*, which, after a most resolute Defence on their side, he made himself Master of, and carry'd them into *Calais*, of which Place he was Governor. King *Henry* having appointed the Duke of *Somerset* to succeed him in that Post, the Citizens of *Calais* were so devoted to their old Governor, that they refused him Admittance; whereupon the King ordered such of his Ships as the Earl of *Warwick* had left behind, to be got together at *Sandwich*, under the Command of the Lord *Rivers*, who was to carry over the Duke of *Somerset* to *Calais*, and instate him by force in that Government: But while they were preparing to execute these Orders, *John Dinham*, an expert Sea-Captain of the opposite Party, repairing to *Sandwich* with a Number of Ships, attack'd the

The Earl of Warwick *takes some* Spanish *and* Genoese *Ships.*

CHAP. XVI. *Ruin of the* Rom. *Empire.* 335

the King's Squadron, took all the Ships, and with them the Lord *Ri-* *Dinham takes*
vers, whom he carried Prisoner to *Calais*. Hereupon the King fit- *King Henry*
ted out another Squadron, which he put under the Command of Sir *at Sandwich.*
Simon Monford, Lord-Warden of the Cinque-Ports, with Orders to
look to the Defence thereof, and prevent the Earl of *Warwick*'s
landing in those Parts. But he suddenly crossing over from *Calais*,
surprized Sir *Simon Monford* with all his Ships at *Sandwich*, and *Warwick*
having plundered the Town, retired with his Prisoners and Booty *from Calais*
back to his Government; from whence returning in few Days af- *King's Ships*
ter to the *English* Coasts, he landed at *Sandwich*, where being met
by the Lord *Cobham*, and several others of his Party, with a great
Force, he prosecuted his Quarrel ashore against the *Lancastrians*
with such Success, that in few Months after the Duke of *York* was *Edward IV.*
crowned King of *England* by the Name of *Edward* IV. *crowned.*

The *French* supporting the Interests, as much as in them lay, of 1461.
the *Lancastrian* Family, King *Edward* fitted out a considerable
Fleet, on board of which were embarked ten thousand Soldiers, under the Command of the Earls of *Essex* and *Kent*, and the Lords
Audley and *Clinton*, who scouring the Seas for some time, landed
at *Conquet* in *Bretagne*, and having plundered the adjacent Country, repaired thence to the Isle of *Ré*, where they did the like;
and having cleared the Seas of the *French*, returned home with a *The English*
great Number of Prizes. Some time after this the Earl of *Warwick* *ravage the*
disagreeing also with King *Edward*, revolted to the House of *Lan-* *FrenchCoasts.*
caster, and set King *Henry* again on the Throne; but was at length *Henry again*
slain fighting in his Defence at the Battel of St. *Alban*'s; whereup- *set on the*
on King *Edward* was again re-established. While *Warwick* him- *Throne, and*
self was prosecuting this Quarrel by Land, the beforementioned Earl *ward.*
of *Kent*, who was his natural Son, did the like by Sea, and having
got together a considerable Number of Ships, and received on board
them part of the Garrison of *Calais*, entirely devoted to the Earl
of *Warwick*'s Service, he caused his Ships to come up the Ri- *The Earl of*
ver to *London*, and marching thither himself, with seventeen thou- *Kent endea-*
sand Men, attempted to make himself Master of the City, but met *ster London.*
with so vigorous a Resistance from the Citizens, that he was forced
to retire with the Loss of a great Number of Men, and retreating
to *Sandwich*, was pursued thither by King *Edward*, where his Ad- *The Rebels*
herents, upon Promise of Pardon, surrendered themselves, with all *surrender to*
their Ships. *Edward.*

The two following short Reigns of *Edward* V, and his unnatural
Uncle, *Richard* III, produce nothing memorable at Sea. *Henry*
VII. next succeeding to the Throne, he, by marrying the Lady *E-*
lizabeth, Daughter to *Edward* IV, united the so long divided Houses 1485.
of *Lancaster* and *York*; in the seventh Year of whose Reign, the
Lord *Ravenstein*, a Subject of the Arch-Duke *Maximilian*, then
also Duke of *Burgundy*, having raised a Rebellion against his Prince, *Ravenstein*
and, by the Assistance of the Citizens of *Ghent* and *Bruges*, seized *commits Pi-*
the Town of *Sluys*, he there got together a great Number of Ships *racies.*
and Barks, with which he cruised in a Piratical manner against the 1492.
Ships of all Nations that he met with, without distinction. The
English

English Merchants having suffer'd amongst others by these Rovers, and the King being willing to support *Maximilian* against *France*, with whom he was at Variance, fitted out a Squadron under the Command of Sir *Edward Poynings*, to assist the Arch-Duke in the Reduction of them, and of the Town of *Sluys* their Receptacle. Sir *Edward Poynings* accordingly setting sail with his Squadron, cruised some Days at Sea, and then repaired before the Town of *Sluys*, and upon Notice that the Duke of *Saxony*, who was also come to *Maximilian*'s Assistance, had invested it on the Land side, he laid close Siege to it by Sea, and attacking one of the two Castles wherein the Strength of the Place consisted, for twenty Days successively, was as often repulsed, though not without great Slaughter of the Enemy; but at length finding means to set fire to a Bridge of Boats by which the two Castles held Communication, the Enemy surrendered the Castles to the *English*, and the Town to the Duke of *Saxony*.

About this time it was that *Christopher Columbus*, a *Genoese* Mariner, whether from his Consideration of the spherical Body of the Earth and Water, conjecturing that there must necessarily be some other great Track of Land between the Western Coasts of *Europe* and *Africk*, and the Eastern Coasts of *Asia*, as it were to balance and counterpoise the vast Continent we live upon; or, as some alledge, being possessed of the Memoirs of an old Navigator, who had been driven by Tempests on the Coasts of *Hispaniola*, and on his Return from thence died at *Columbus*'s House at *Madera*, was from thence assured of the Being of some unknown Countries to the Westward. However that was, *Columbus*, full of his new Project, made Proposals to King *Henry* of going to discover these Countries, in his Name, and to his Use; but meeting with no Encouragement from him, and having made the like Proposals, and met with the like Neglect in *Portugal*, applied himself to *Ferdinand* and *Isabella*, King and Queen of *Castile*, and was by them furnished with Ships for the Prosecution of his Enterprize, and happily discovering the *West-Indies*, began the Conquest thereof for that Crown, as we have already related among the *Spanish* Affairs.

About six Years after this Discovery, *John Cabot*, a *Venetian*, who was settled at *Bristol*, conjecturing from *Columbus*'s Success that there might be also Lands to be found out to the North-West, presented a Memorial to the King, setting forth, that he made no doubt, if his Majesty would please to employ him, but that he could make some useful Discoveries in his Name, and find out Islands or Countries abounding with rich Commodities, as the *Genoese* Enterprizer had lately done; to which Proposal the King now lent a willing Ear, and fitting out a Ship from *Bristol*, gave *Cabot* the Command of her, with a Commission for the Discovery of Lands then unknown, and annexing them to the Crown of *England*. To this Ship some Merchants of *London* joining three more, laden with such slight Commodities as were thought proper for Commerce with barbarous People, *Cabot* departed with them from *Bristol*, and (as Sir *Henry Gilbert* relates it, who was employed afterwards by Queen *Elizabeth*

Chap. XVI. *Ruin of the* Rom. *Empire.*

beth on the like Services) sailed very far Westward with a Quarter of the North, on the North side of *Terre de Labrador*, till he came into the Latitude of 67½ Degrees, and finding the Seas still open, might and would, as he affirmed, have gone to *Cathay*, if he had not been prevented by the Dissensions between the Master and the Mariners. But this we find, by the Discoveries made in those Parts since that time, was more than he could have performed. However after this, he and his Son *Sebastian*, during the rest of this King's Reign, made several Voyages that way, and discovered the Island of *Baccalaos*, now much better known by the Name of *Newfoundland*, together with the rest of the North-East Parts of *America*, (where now we have so many flourishing Colonies) as far as the Cape of *Florida*; and landing in several Places, took Possession thereof in the Name of the King of *England*. *Newfoundland, &c. discovered.*

King *Henry* dying in 1509, was succeeded by his Son *Henry* VIII; in the beginning of whose Reign one *Andrew Briton*, a *Scots* Man, who had obtained Letters of Marque from his Prince against the *Flemings*, and other the Subjects of the King of *Spain*, under Colour of that Power practised Piracy upon our Coasts, where he seized and plundered several Ships, on pretence of their carrying *Spanish* Goods. To repress this Insolence, Sir *Edward Howard*, Lord High Admiral, and his Brother Sir *Thomas*, were sent out with two Ships, who meeting with *Briton*, off the *Goodwin* Sands, with the like Number, engaged him, and after a long and obstinate Fight, wherein the *Scotsman* was slain, took both the Ships, and brought them to *London*, where the Men, upon their Submission to the King's Mercy, were discharged and sent home. *1509. Andrew Briton, a Scots Man, turns Pirate. Briton reduced, and his Ships taken.*

Shortly after this King *Henry* declaring War against *France*, Sir *Edward Howard* repaired with a Squadron to the Coasts of *Bretagne*, where landing at *Conquet*, and other Places, he burned several Towns, and destroyed the Country for many Miles from the Sea. Whereupon the *French* using all Diligence to get together a great Fleet, the King reinforced his Admiral with five and twenty stout Men of War, which he put under the Command of the principal Persons about him. The largest Ship, called the *Regent*, of a thousand Tuns, was commanded by Sir *Thomas Knevet*, Master of the Horse; as the next Ship, called the *Sovereign*, was by Sir *Charles Brandon*, assisted by Sir *Henry Guilford* with sixty Yeomen of the Guard. This Fleet going over to the Coasts of *Bretagne* to watch the Motions of the *French*, arrived before *Brest* just as their Fleet, consisting of thirty nine Sail, was coming out from that Harbour, which they immediately attacking, a sharp Engagement ensued, wherein, at the first Charge, the two capital Ships on each side, to wit, the *English Regent*, and the *French Cordeliere*, being close grappled together, were accidentally set on fire and consumed, together with all the Officers and Seamen on board; the Sight whereof so dismayed the *French*, that they made the best of their way, without striking another Stroke, into *Brest*, and other Places adjacent. *Henry VIII. declares War against France. The French Fleet forced to fly by the English.*

X x The

The King intending the following Campaign to make an Expedition to *France* in Perſon, thought it proper beforehand to have the Sea cleared, if poſſible, by the Deſtruction of the *French* Fleet, and therefore early the next Spring the Lord High Admiral was ſent out with forty two Ships of War, beſides ſeveral ſmall Veſſels, who repairing to the Coaſts of *Bretagne*, received Intelligence that the *French* Fleet, which lay ready to ſail in *Breſt*, being in daily Expectation of being joined by ſix Gallies from the Mediterranean, under the Command of Monſieur *Pregent*, had determined to continue in that Port till their Arrival. Whereupon the Lord-Admiral thinking it moſt adviſable to attack the Enemy before their Junction with the Gallies, entered the Harbour of *Breſt* with his Fleet, where the *French* had ſecured themſelves with ſeveral Batteries raiſed on both ſides the Harbour, together with a Range of twenty four

The Engliſh *deſtroy the Country about* Breſt.

Hulks, linked together, to defend their Ships from our Fire. The Lord-Admiral immediately on his entering the Mouth of the Harbour, ſending out ſeveral Boats as if he intended to land there, drew all the *French*, to the Number of above ten thouſand, down to the Shore, while he going up higher, landed over againſt *Breſt*, and burnt the Country, in ſight of the Caſtle: But being in want of Proviſions, which were daily expected, he deſiſted from making any farther Attempts till he ſhould receive that Supply. In the mean time Monſieur *Pregent*, with ſix Gallies and four Foiſts, arrived in the Bay of *Conquet*, the Place neareſt to *Breſt* which he could put into, where fearing he ſhould be attacked by the *Engliſh*, who he underſtood were in *Breſt* Harbour, he ſecured himſelf between two Rocks, which had Bulwarks on them well furniſhed with Ordnance. Notwithſtanding this advantageous Poſture, Sir *Edward Howard* reſolved to attack him, and having two Gallies with him in the Fleet, went on board one of them himſelf, and committed the other to the Lord *Ferrers*, with which, accompanied with only two Barges, and two other Boats, he went into the Bay of *Conquet*, and coming along ſide of Monſieur *Pregent*, ordered his own Gally to be laſhed to the Enemy's, which he immediately enter'd with Sword in Hand, attended with ſeventeen Men; but his Gally, by ſome Accident, ſwinging off, he was left in the Hands of his Enemies,

The Lord High Admiral Howard loſes his Life.

who bore him over with their Pikes into the Sea, undiſtinguiſh'd from the reſt of his Followers. The Lord *Ferrers* ſeeing the Admiral's Gally fall off, and having ſpent all his Shot, retired with the other Veſſels, not knowing but that the Admiral was ſafe; but he being at length miſſed, the *Engliſh* ſent a Flag of Truce to the Enemy to know what Priſoners were taken, who made anſwer none but one Mariner, who ſaid that a Perſon they had puſhed over-board with their Pikes was their Admiral: Whereupon the Fleet, now with-

The French *do ſome Miſchief in* Suſſex.

out a Commander, returned to the *Engliſh* Coaſts. Thither Monſieur *Pregent*, encourag'd by this little Succeſs, ſoon followed, and landing in *Suſſex*, ſpoiled the Country, but was preſently repulſed; and Sir *Thomas Howard*, who ſucceeded his Brother as High Admiral, putting to Sea with a Squadron of clean Ships, ſoon forced him to retire, and clearing the Seas of the *French*, aſſiſted in tranſporting the

CHAP. XVI. *Ruin of the* Rom. *Empire.* 339

the King and his Army to *Calais*, who marching into the *French* Henry VIII. Territories, invested *Terouenne*, and having defeated the Enemy *lands at Calais, and de-* who attempted to relieve it, soon forced it to surrender, and then *feats the* in a short time reducing *Tournay*, returned to *England*. *French.*

Presently after this a Treaty of Peace was set on foot, but not concluded till some Years were expired, and then it proving but of short Duration, the King enter'd into an Alliance with the Emperor *The Emperor* *Charles* V. against *France*, who, pursuant to an Agreement made *joins the English Fleet a-* with King *Henry*, joined his Navy, consisting of a hundred and *gainst France.* eighty Sail, to the *English* Fleet, under the Command of Sir *Thomas Howard*, High Admiral, now made Earl of *Surrey*; who, with the King's leave, receiving a Commission from the Emperor to be his High Admiral also, repaired with the united Fleets over to the Coast of *Normandy*, and landing at *Cherbourg*, destroyed the adjacent Country, and returned to *Portland*. Thence proceeding *The united* in a few Days to *Morlaix* in *Bretagne*, he landed there, and taking *Powers do* the Town by Storm, sacked it, and having burnt seventeen Sail of *France.* *French* Ships on the Coast, detached a Squadron to continue cruising at Sea under the Command of Vice-Admiral *Fitz-Williams*, and repaired himself with the rest of the Fleet to *Southampton*, where the Emperor lay ready to embark for *Spain*, whom receiving on board, he in few Days landed him at St. *Andrew*'s in *Biscay*.

The next Summer a Squadron of six and thirty Sail was put under the Command of Sir *William Fitz-Williams*, to cruise on the Coasts of *France*, in order to intercept the Duke of *Albany* in his Passage from that Kingdom to *Scotland*, whereof he was Regent; who, meeting with twelve *French* Ships, which had on board several of the *Scotish* Nobility, forced them back into the Ports of *Dieppe* and *Boulogne*, where leaving some Ships to block them up, he proceeded with the rest along the *French* Coast, and landing in several Places, wasted the Country, and at length coming to *Tre-* *The English* *port*, he attacked that Town, and having burnt the Suburbs, and *Ships waste* destroyed all the Ships in the Haven, returned to the *English* Coasts *King's Coun-* with a considerable Booty. Of this Sir *William Fitz-Williams* it *try.* hath been observed, that there was not a serviceable Man under *Character of* him whose Name he knew not, not a Week passed but he paid his *Sir William* Ships, not a Prize but his Seamen shared in as well as himself, it *Fitz-Williams.* being his Rule that none fought well but those which did it for a Fortune.

After this Expedition we meet with no more at Sea till the 36th Year of this King's Reign, when his Majesty entering into a War against *Scotland*, the Lord *Lisle*, who succeeded the Earl of *Surrey* as Lord High Admiral, was ordered with the Fleet to invade that Kingdom, *The English* and having received on board at *Newcastle* the Earl of *Hertford*, *invade Scot-* Lieutenant-General of the North, and other Persons of Quality, *land.* with a considerable Body of Troops, proceeded thence to *Leith*, and there landing his Men, the *English* soon made themselves Masters of that Place, as also of the City of *Edinburgh*, which they Edinburgh burnt for three Days together, and were there joined by the Lord *Leith.* *Evers,*

X x 2

Evers, Warden of the East Marches, at the Head of a Land-Army. But not being able to take the Citadel, the Lord Admiral and the Lord-General retreated to *Leith*, to which setting fire, they reimbarked, and having scoured the Coasts of *Scotland*, and taken out of the Havens and Creeks all such Vessels as they found there, made the best of their way home; while the Land Army burnt *Seton*, *Hadington*, and *Dunbar*, and having destroyed all the Country in its March, retreated in Safety to *Berwick*.

<small>Other Places burnt in Scotland.</small>

At this time the King was also engaged in a War with *France*, whither having shortly after sent over an Army of thirty thousand Men, he followed himself in a Ship which had Sails of Cloth of Gold, and landing at *Calais*, proceeded thence to *Boulogne*, and formed the Siege of that Town by Land, while the Lord High Admiral attacked it with a Fleet by Sea; which being performed with great Vigour on both sides, the Town was in a few Days surrendered to the King upon Terms. For the Recovery of this important Place out of the Hands of the *English*, the *French* King assembles all his Navy on the Coast of *Normandy*, under the Command of Monsieur *d'Annebault*, Admiral of France, which having also reinforced with a Squadron of five and twenty Gallies from the Mediterranean, commanded by *Paulin*, Baron *de la Garde*, he ordered them to continue in a Readiness to repair before *Boulogne*, and prevent its being relieved by Sea, while he should besiege it by Land. But all things being not yet ready for forming that Siege, he gave Directions that the Fleet should make some Attemps on the *English* Coasts; which accordingly standing over to St. *Helen*'s for that purpose, King *Henry*, who, upon Advice of the Enemy's Preparations, was gone down to *Portsmouth* to hasten the fitting out of the Fleet, ordered his Ships to sail out to *Spithead*, and oppose the Enemy; but in their Passage thither, the *Mary-Rose*, one of the largest of them, commanded by Sir *George Carew*, by a little Sway of the Ship, (her Ports being made within sixteen Inches of the Water) was overset and lost, with her whole Company. The rest, to the Number of sixty, exchanged some Shot with the *French* till Night parted them, and then they returned. The next Morning the Enemy landed several Men in the Isle of *Wight*, but were presently repulsed; nevertheless they soon landed again, and began to deliberate about reducing and keeping the Island; but as that could not be done without erecting Forts, for which Men and Time were wanting, they reimbarked, and their Fleet made Sail for *Portet*, near *Boulogne*, in their way to which Place they landed some Men in *Sussex*, which were repulsed with considerable Loss. Having put ashore four thousand Men at *Portet*, and the Wind coming up Easterly, they again came over to our Coasts; upon Advice whereof, the King gave Orders that his Fleet should offer the Enemy Battel, which they at length accepted, and a sharp Engagement ensued for two Hours, till Night parted the two Fleets, when the *French* retired to *Havre de Grace*, and appeared no more. The Lord High Admiral followed them soon after to the Coasts, and landed six thousand Men at *Treport*, and having burnt that Town and Abby, together

<small>Henry VIII. besieges Boulogne by Sea and Land.</small>

<small>The French endeavour to recover Boulogne.</small>

<small>The French land in the Isle of Wight.</small>

<small>The English and French Fleets engage.</small>

<small>Treport, and some French Ships burnt.</small>

CHAP. XVI. *Ruin of the* Rom. *Empire.* 341

together with thirty Ships which lay in the Haven retreated with the Loss of only fourteen Men.

The next Campaign the *French* renewed their Attempts against *Boulogne*, and, in order to cut off its Communication with *Calais*, endeavoured to seize *Ambleteuse*, where they intended to fortify; but were prevented therein by the Diligence of the Lord-Admiral, and Earl of *Hertford*, who transporting an Army of nine thousand Men to that Place, encamped in the Neighbourhood; mean while, the Fleet had several Skirmishes with that of the Enemy's on those Coasts; where, particularly before *Ambleteuse*, eight of the King's Ships engaged an equal Number of the *French* Gallies, and, after a warm Dispute, took one of them, and forced the rest to retire. *Skirmishes at Sea off of Boulogne, &c. 1546.*

King *Henry* dying the next Year, he was succeeded by his Son *Edward* VI, in the Beginning of whose Reign a War breaking out with *Scotland*, a Fleet and Army were got ready for the Invasion of that Kingdom, the latter under the Command of the Duke of *Somerset*, and the former of the Lord *Clinton*; who, whilst the Land Army marched into *Scotland*, and gained the Victory at *Muselburgh*, with four and twenty Men of War, one Gally, and thirty other Vessels, scoured the Coasts, and landing in several Places, destroyed the Country. Shortly after this a War ensuing with *France*, the *French* King intending to reduce the Islands of *Guernsey* and *Jersey*, the only Remains we had now left of the Duchy of *Normandy*, fitted out a strong Squadron, which conducted thither a Body of two thousand Men: But Captain *William Winter* being immediately sent over with some Ships, and eight hundred Soldiers, he, notwithstanding the Enemy's great Superiority, attacked them with such Vigour, that they were forced to retire with the Loss of a thousand Men, and the Destruction of their Gallies. *Edward VI. invades Scotland by Sea and Land. The French attempt Guernsey and Jersey without Success.*

Some time after this, upon Proposals laid before the King by *Sebastian Cabot*, (who for his great Skill in Cosmography and Navigation, was retained in his Service with an honourable Pension) three Ships were fitted out at the Publick Charge for the Discovery of the North-East Passage to *China* and the *Indies*. They were put under the Command of Sir *Hugh Willoughby*, who departing from the *Thames*, sailed to the North Cape, (where one of his Ships left him and returned home) and proceeding farther Northwards, discovered that part of *Greenland*, since called by the *Dutch Spitzberg*; but the Severity of the Cold obliging him to return to the Southward, he was forced by bad Weather into the River *Arzina*, in *Muscovite Lapland*, from whence being not able to come out, he was found there the next Spring frozen to Death, with all his Ship's Company, having the Notes of his Voyage, and his last Will lying before him, whereby it appeared that he lived till *January*. But *Richard Chancellour*, in the third Ship, with better Success, after many Difficulties and Dangers, penetrated to *Archangel* in *Muscovy*, being the first Person who discovered the Passage to that Place; from whence, in the fourth Year of Queen *Mary*, after having made another Voyage thither, he brought over an Ambassador of the Czar of *Muscovy*'s, with Presents to the Queen, and an Invitation *1553. Willoughby sent to discover the N. E. Passage to China. Greenland discovered. Chancellour penetrates to Archangel. 1557.*

to

to settle a Trade to those Parts; but the Ship was cast away on the Coast of *Scotland*, where *Chancellour* in saving the Ambassador was himself unfortunately drowned.

Queen *Mary* about this Time engaging in a War with *France*, on Account of her Husband King *Philip* of *Spain*, the Earl of *Pembroke* was sent over into *Picardy* with seven thousand Men, to the Assistance of the *Spanish* Troops then besieging St. *Quintin*, whither the King presently after repairing, they greatly contributed to the signal Victory he obtained over the *French* that came to its Relief, as also to the Reduction of the Town, which was taken by Storm a few Days after, wherein the *English* were the foremost on the Attack. This Loss the *French* shortly after severely revenged on the *English*; for the Duke of *Guise*, in the midst of Winter setting down with a great Army before *Calais*, which was very ill provided for Defence, carried on his Attacks with such Vigour, that in a Week's Time he had the Town surrendered to him, after it had been in our Hands above two hundred Years. The Queen was inconsolably grieved for the Loss of this Place; but to be revenged in some measure on the *French* King, she sent out the Lord *Clinton*, her High Admiral, with a Fleet of a hundred and ten Sail, who being joined also by King *Philip*'s Admiral of the *Netherlands*, with thirty *Flemish* Ships, was ordered, if he judged it feasible, to attempt the Reduction of *Brest*. Sailing to the Coasts of *Bretagne*, he found that Design impracticable, but landing at *Conquet*, presently possessed himself of that Town, which he sacked and burnt, together with the Abby, and several other Places in the Neighbourhood, and then returned on board the Fleet with a very considerable Booty; but the *Flemings* straggling farther up into the Country were most of them cut off in their Retreat.

Chap. XVII.

Of the Naval Transactions of the English *during the Reign of* Queen Elizabeth.

QUEEN *Mary* dying in few Months after this Expedition, she was, happily for the Protestant Religion and the Liberties of *England*, succeeded by that glorious Princess Queen *Elizabeth*, who, in the Beginning of her Reign, coming to a Resolution of supporting the Protestant Party in *Scotland* against the Encroachments of the *French* (who, on Occasion of *Francis* II. his Marriage with *Mary* Queen of *Scots*, had usurped the whole Government, and committed great Disorders in that Kingdom) fitted out a Squadron under the Command of *William Winter*, Master of the Naval Ordnance, to act in Concert with the Land Forces which she intended to send into that Kingdom. Captain *Winter* proceeding with his Ships to the *Firth of Forth*, sailed up to *Leith* Road,

CHAP. XVII. *Ruin of the* Rom. *Empire.* 343

where several of the *French* Ships riding at Anchor, he attacked and took them, and then blocking up the Island of *Inch-Keith*, which was defended by a *French* Garrison, reduced the Enemy to great Streights for want of Provisions; and, by this time the Army under the Lord *Grey* being advanced to *Leith*, formed the Siege of that Town, wherein Captain *Winter* render'd considerable Service with his Ships. Within the Place was a numerous Body of *French* Troops, who defended themselves with great Courage and Bravery for several Weeks; but at length the *French* King, who was sensible 'twas impossible otherwise to prevent their falling into our Hands, made Proposals of Peace, wherein every thing being offered that the Queen could desire, the same was in few Days concluded, and the Fleet and Army returned to *England*. *Siege laid to Leith.*

The French King makes Proposals of Peace.

The King of *Spain*, and other *Roman* Catholick Potentates, perceiving the Queen inflexible in her Resolutions for the Support and Maintenance of the Protestant Religion, began to shew several Marks of their Indignation; wherefore the Queen, wisely providing for her Security against a future Storm, took Care to furnish her Magazines with Stores of War, cast several Pieces of Brass, and Iron Ordnance, and caused great Quantities of Gunpowder to be wrought up at home, which was the first that was made in *England*, and building a considerable Number of Ships, got together the most formidable Fleet that ever *Britain* had been Mistress of; for Defence whereof she raised a Fortress upon the Banks of the River *Medway*, where the Ships had their ordinary Station, which from a neighbouring Village was called *Upnore* Castle; and also greatly increased the Wages of the Naval Officers, and the Seamen: So that, says Mr. *Cambden*, she was justly styled by Foreigners the Restorer of Naval Glory, and the Queen of the Northern Seas. In Imitation of this laudable Example of the Queen's, many of her wealthy Subjects who lived near the Sea-Coasts, set themselves to building of Ships, so that in a short time those of the Crown, and of private Persons, were become so numerous as, on Occasion of any Naval War, might employ twenty thousand Men. The good Effects of these Preparations were shortly after seen in the War the Queen undertook in Behalf of the Protestants of *France*, wherein, besides the Land Forces she sent over into *Normandy* to their Assistance, her Ships scouring the Seas, sorely distressed their Enemies by taking great Numbers of Prizes from them, and at length totally interrupting their Trade.

1560.

The Queen supplies her Magazines,

and provides a potent Fleet.

1561.
The English take many Prizes.

Some time after this, *John Hawkins*, a Person of singular Skill in Navigation, making a Voyage with five Ships to *Guinea*, and thence with Slaves to the *Spanish West-Indies*, as he was going into the Port of St. *Juan de Ulloa*, fell in with the *Spanish* Flota, which he could easily, if he so pleased, have prevented from entring that Place, but resolving to do nothing in Violation of the Peace, he only required of them Security for him and his, and Liberty of Trade, to which the *Spaniards* willingly agreed, but watching their Opportunity, they a few Days after perfidiously fell on the *English*, and killing several of them, seized and plundered three of their Ships

1567.
Hawkins goes to the Spanish West-Indies.

The Spaniards perfidious to the English.

z

Ships. The News of this no sooner arrived in *England* but all the Seafaring People were in a Flame, and impatient to be revenged on the *Spaniards* for their Treachery. Soon after which King *Philip* prohibiting Commerce with *England*, and endeavouring to debauch the Duke of *Norfolk* and Earl of *Ormonde* from their Allegiance, who discovered his Intrigues, it is incredible with what Alacrity the *English* put to Sea, and cruised against the *Spaniards*, insomuch that the Queen was forced to put a stop to their Depredations, by a Proclamation forbidding the buying any Goods or Merchandize of those Cruizers.

The English do great harm to the Spanish Trade.

In the Year 1573, the *French* Protestants, who had taken to the Sea, grew so numerous and powerful, that they committed Spoil without Distinction on all they met, and plundered several *English* Ships, whereupon a Squadron was sent out under the Command of *William Holstock*, Comptroller of the Navy, who retook several of the *English* Ships, and seizing some of those Cruisers, dispersed the rest, and cleared the Seas of them for some time.

1573. The French Protestants powerful at Sea.

but are dispersed.

In 1576 the Privateers of *Zealand* and *Holland* committing the like Depredations on the *English* Merchant Ships, under pretence that they supplied their Enemies, the *Dunkirkers*, with Provisions, and carried on a collusive Trade with *Spain* for the *Antwerpians* and others, the same Officer was also sent with some Ships against them, who took above two hundred of their Mariners, and threw them into several Prisons on the Coasts. The same Year some Citizens of *London*, in Hopes of discovering the North-West Passage to *Tartary* and *China*, fitted out three Ships to attempt the same, under *Martin Forbisher*, who sailing to *North-America*, entered a Streight in the Latitude of 63 Degrees, but being prevented from proceeding farther by the Ice, tho' it were so early as the Month of *August*, he returned to *England*; and notwithstanding this ill Success prosecuted the same Design two Years after, but it proved to no better Purpose.

1576.

The English reduce the Privateers of Zealand and Holland. Forbisher goes to discover the North-West Passage.

About this time began Captain *Francis Drake* to acquire a great Reputation for his Exploits at Sea. He had been one of the Adventurers with the beforemention'd Mr. *Hawkins*, and in that Expedition lost all his Fortune, which he had, with great Industry, been long acquiring; but about five Years after having, in the Service of the Merchants, and in cruising against the *Spaniards* in the Narrow Seas, muster'd up a little more Money, he provided himself with a good Ship, well equipped for War, and two small Vessels, with which he resolved to make good his Losses from the *Spaniards* in the *West-Indies*; and tho' he was not furnished with Letters of Marque to justify his Proceedings, yet as *England* and *Spain* were then at very ill Terms, he boldly made use of the general Licence of the Times, and with these Ships proceeding to the *Isthmus* of *Darien*, he there made himself Master of the Town of *Nombre de Dios*, which he soon after lost; but meeting with Intelligence from some fugitive *Blacks*, that there was a great Quantity of Gold and Silver coming from *Panama*, he seized it by the Way, and carried all the Gold on Shipboard, but the Silver being not so portable

Capt. Francis Drake goes against the Spaniards.

CHAP. XVII. *Ruin of the* Rom. *Empire.* 345

table over the Mountains, he left Part of it, and buried the rest in the Ground. He then burnt a rich Storehouse of *Merchandizes* upon the River *Chagre,* called *Venta de Cruz,* and while he was ranging about the Country, discovering the South Sea from the Mountains, he was immediately inflamed with a Desire to navigate thither, and falling on his Knees implored the Divine Assistance therein, and binding himself by a Vow to attempt that Voyage, could never be at Peace in his Mind till he undertook it. *Drake discovers the South-Sea.*

But before he was in a Readiness to proceed, one *John Oxenham,* who had served under him in this last Voyage, and several others, having observed how defenceless the *Spaniards* were in those Parts, and with what Ease he might make a Fortune to himself, instead of sharing a small Proportion under another, he, with the little Money he had scraped together, provided himself of a Ship, and sailed to the same Place; where understanding the Convoy from *Panama* to *Porto Bello* was guarded by Soldiers, he drew up his Vessel into a woody Place, and covering it with Boughs, to prevent any Notice of his Arrival, marched with his Company over the Mountains, to a River that discharges itself into the Bay of *Panama,* where building a Galliot, he fell down with her into the said Bay, and went over to the *Pearl* Islands, a convenient Station for intercepting the Plate Ships coming from *Lima* to *Panama,* of which he in a short time took two, with sixty pounds Weight of Gold, and an hundred of Silver. An Account of this being soon dispersed by the *Spaniards* whom he set on shore from those Ships, a Body of a hundred Men were presently sent out in Quest of these new Invaders, and after some Search, they met with *Oxenham* and his Men as they were quarrelling about dividing the Spoil, who, on the *Spaniards* Approach, however made head against them tho' they were not half the Enemy's Number, but being at length overpowered, they were all either killed, or taken Prisoners, of which latter *Oxenham* being one, was carried to *Lima,* where he was examined whether he had any Authority from his Queen for such Proceedings, and not being able to produce any Commission, he was put to Death with his Companions, as a Pirate. *Oxenham goes against the Spaniards.*

Drake, in the mean time, altogether ignorant of *Oxenham*'s Adventure, set Sail, in *December* 1577, from *Plimouth* on his intended Voyage for the *South-Sea,* with five Ships and a hundred sixty three Seamen, and in five and twenty Days came off of Cape *Cantin* in *Barbary,* from whence proceeding to the Cape *Verde* Islands, he took in Refreshments at the Isle of *May,* and thence went over to St. *Jago,* the principal of those Islands, where he seized a *Portuguese* Ship laden with Wine, which he brought off with him, and dismissing her Company retained the Master of her, in order to make use of him for a Pilot on the Coasts of *Brasil,* with which he found him to be well acquainted. Thence setting Sail on his Voyage, he passed by *Fuego* and *Brava,* the two Southermost of those Islands, and crossing the Æquinoctial Line, he, after having been fifty five Days without seeing Land, arrived in Sight of *Brasil.* Coasting along that Country he came to the Mouth of *Rio de la Plata,* and thence *1577. Drake proceeds on his Voyage to the South-Sea.*

Y y

thence proceeding Southward arrived at the Port of St. *Julian*, where he found a Gibbet erected, as was supposed by *Magellan* for the Punishment of Mutineers; at which Place having occasion to animadvert upon *John Doughty*, a stout Seaman, but mutinous and turbulent, (who was the next in Command to himself) he brought him to his Trial, and being by a Jury of twelve Persons condemned to Death, he was there beheaded.

John Doughty beheaded

Prosecuting his Voyage from hence he arrived some time after with three Ships (for the two least he had before turned adrift in the Streights of *Magellan*, which having passed, after a difficult Navigation of sixteen Days, he came out into the great *South-Sea*, where meeting with very tempestuous Weather, he was forced back to the Westward near a hundred Leagues, and his Ships separated, one whereof, commanded by *John Winter*, returned through the Streight, and arrived safe in *England*, being the first Ship that ever came back that Way. *Drake*, with his single Ship was driven into 55 Degrees of South Latitude, from whence, with great Difficulty, he got up again into the Heighth of the Streight, and proceeded thence along the Coast of *Chili* to the Island *Moucha*, where he had Intelligence from an *Indian*, who took our Men for *Spaniards*, that a large *Spanish* Ship lay loaden at *Val Paraiso*, and sailing thither in search thereof, the *Spaniards* on board, supposing the *English* coming toward them to be some of their own Countrymen, beat their Drums, and drinking full Cups to them, received them with all Testimonies of Joy; but the *English*, clapping them on board, immediately thrust them under the Hatches, and possessed themselves of the Ship; which done they plundered the neighbouring Town of St. *Jago*, together with the Chapel, the Spoil of which latter, with a generous Justice, was bestowed on the Chaplain of *Drake*'s Ship. The *Spaniards* he put on shore, but carried away the Master with the Ship, wherein was four hundred Pounds Weight of *Baldivian* Gold.

Drake comes into the South-Sea.

St. Jago taken by Drake.

After this he landed at *Tarapasa*, where finding a *Spaniard* asleep upon the shore, with thirteen Bars of Silver by him, to the Value of four hundred thousand Ducats, he caused them to be carried off without so much as waking the Man. Then entering the Port of *Arica*, he found there three Ships with not a Man on board them, in which were, besides other Merchandizes, fifty seven Wedges of Silver, each weighing twenty Pounds. Hence he proceeded to *Lima*, the Capital of *Peru*, where he seized twelve Ships, and in them great Quantities of Silk, with a Chest full of coined Money, but they had not so much as a Boy on board any one of them, so great was the Security on those Coasts, where, by reason of their great Distance and Remoteness from *Europe*, they feared no Enemies; nor indeed had ever any one but *Magellan*, before *Drake*, navigated those Seas, except the *Spaniards* themselves, who built there all the Ships they had in those Parts.

Spanish Ships seized at Lima.

Having set these Ships adrift, he, with all the Sail he could make, gave Chace to the *Cacofogo*, a very rich Ship, which he understood had lately sailed from thence for *Panama*, and by the Way met with a *Brigantine*, out of which he took eighty Pound Weight of Gold,

Gold, a Crucifix of the same Metal, some Emeralds of a Finger's *A Spanish Carrack taken by Drake.*
Length, and some Munition. In few Days after he came up with
the *Cacofogo*, and shooting her Foremast by the Board, presently
made himself Master of her, wherein, besides Pearls and precious
Stones, he took eighty Pounds Weight of Gold, thirteen Chests full
of Silver coined, and so great a Quantity of other Silver as would
almost serve to ballast a Ship. Having removed all this into his own
Ship, he let the *Cacofogo* go, the Master whereof, at parting, is reported to have thus merrily bidden him farewel; "We resign the
"Name of our Ship to yours: Let that for the future be called the
"*Cacofogo*, that is, (if the Interpretation offend not) the *Shite-*
"*fire*; and ours the *Cacoplata*, that is, the *Shite-plate.*

Captain *Drake*, continuing his Course to the Northward, sailed
along the Coast of *Mexico*, and landing at *Aguatulco* sacked that
Town; and having now made more than sufficient Reprisals on the
Spaniards for his former Losses, resolved to make the best of his Way to
England, to which he boldly attempted to find a Passage by *North*
America, sailing to the Latitude of 42 Degrees on that Coast, but
then meeting with nothing but Severity of Cold, and open Shores
covered with Snow, he came back into the Latitude of 38, and there
putting into a convenient Harbour in the North Parts of *California*, met with a very kind Reception from the *Indians* inhabiting
the same, who by many significant Tokens offered to make him their
King. To this Country he thought fit to give the Name of *New*
Albion, and raising a Pillar put an Inscription thereon, containing
the Date of the Year, the Name of Queen *Elizabeth*, and their Arrival there, and under it some of the Queen's Coin.

Leaving this Coast, he made Sail to the Westward, and at length
arriving at the *Moluccas*, he was kindly entertained by the King of *Drake comes to the Moluccas, and other Places.*
Ternate, one of those Islands; from whence departing, he prosecuted his Voyage through those dangerous Seas so bespread with Islands
and Rocks, where his Ship striking upon a blind Rock, stuck fast
for twenty seven Hours, which put all the Company in Despair, but
when they had lighten'd her, by throwing over board eight of her
Guns, and some Merchandise, a bearing Gale of Wind fortunately
took her in the Quarter, and heaved her off. Then touching at *Java*, where he received great Civility from one of the Kings of the
Island, he continued his Course for the Cape of *Good Hope*, and
thence to *Rio Grande* in *Negroland*, where taking in Water he
made the best of his Way for *England*, and at length happily arrived
at *Plimouth*, from whence he first set out, having in three Years 1580.
sailed round the Globe, to the great Admiration of all Men. The *Drake returns to England.*
Queen received Captain *Drake* very graciously, and the Ship being
brought round to *Deptford*, was laid up in a Dock there, and consecrated, with great Ceremony, as a Monument of so successful a
Navigation about the World, at which time the Queen honoured
the Captain with her Presence on board at Dinner, and conferr'd upon him the Dignity of Knighthood. *Jackman and Pett sent to find a North-East Passage to China.*

Whilst *Drake* was thus prosperously sailing round the Globe,
Jackman and *Pett*, two noted Pilots, were sent out by some Merchants

chants of *London*, in search of a Passage by the North East, through the Northern Ocean, to *China* and the *Indies*, in pursuit whereof they sailed a few Leagues beyond the Streights of *Weygatz*, where they met with such uncertain Tides, so many Shelves, and such Mountains of Ice, that they were prevented from proceeding any farther, and had very much to do to get back again into the main Sea. About this time also Sir *Humphrey Gilbert*, a Gentleman of great Reputation, and a very enterprizing Genius, set himself about planting a Colony in *Newfoundland*, which we before mentioned to have been discovered by the *Cabots*. He sold his Estate for the more effectual carrying on that Design, but suffered so much by Shipwrecks, and Want of Provisions, that the Project became frustrate, and he was himself, in his Return from that Place to *England*, unfortunately drowned.

Gilbert goes to settle at Newfoundland. 1583.

Queen *Elizabeth* resolving at length to take the States of the United Provinces into her Protection, thought fit to make a publick Declaration thereof in the Year 1585; but well knowing the King of *Spain* would keep no Measures with her for the future, that she might find him Employment abroad, she sent out Sir *Francis Drake*, now made an Admiral, to the *West-Indies*, with a Fleet of one and twenty Sail, having above two thousand Land-men on board, under the Command of *Christopher Carlisle*: Who taking the Cape *Verde* Islands in their Way, landed in St. *Jago*, and surprizing the chief Town of the same Name, sacked the Place, and carried off a considerable Booty: And thence proceeding to *Hispaniola*, they made themselves Masters of the Town of St. *Domingo*, the Inhabitants whereof having redeemed it from being burnt, with five and twenty thousand Ducats, the Fleet sailed over to *Carthagena*, which, after a short Defence, was also taken by Storm, and ransomed for a hundred and ten thousand Ducats, which were shared among the Seamen and Soldiers. The Calenture that raged amongst the Men taking off many of them, the Admiral laid aside his Design of attacking *Nombre de Dios*, and setting Sail for *England*, passed between *Cuba* and *Jucatan*, and going along the Coast of *Florida*, seized and burnt St. *Anthony*'s and St. *Helen*'s, two small Towns the *Spaniards* had abandoned; whence continuing his Course along the shore, he came to a Colony, settled by Sir *Walter Raleigh*, in a Country, by him called *Virginia*, in Honour of his Virgin Mistress Queen *Elizabeth*. But the Planters being reduced to a small Number, and distressed for Want of Provisions, the Admiral at their earnest Request, took them on board, with their Governor, *Ralph Lane*, and brought them Home. Thus concluded this Expedition, the Booty taken from the Enemy being valued at threescore thousand Pound, besides two hundred Pieces of Brass and Iron Cannon, but with the Loss of seven hundred Men, who all, or most of them, died of the Calenture.

1585.

Queen Elizabeth sends Drake to the West-Indies.

St. Domingo and Carthagena taken by Drake.

Other Places taken by Drake.

1585. *Davis sent to discover a new Passage to India.*

Whilst these things were doing in the torrid Zone, *John Davis*, with two Ships fitted out at the Charge of *William Saunderson*, attempted to discover a Passage through the North West Parts of *America* to the *East-Indies*, and penetrating as far as to the Latitude

of

CHAP. XVII. *Ruin of the* Rom. *Empire.* 349

of 66 Degrees, discovered the Streight which still bears his Name; when returning home full of hopes of perfecting the Discovery, he went again the next Year, and obtained some farther Knowledge of the Seas in those Parts; which encouraged him to undertake a third Voyage, wherein he reached as far as 83 Degrees of North Latitude; but not being able to proceed any farther for the Ice, he returned to *England*.

Some time after this, when, upon the putting to Death of *Mary* Queen of *Scots*, Queen *Elizabeth* understood the King of *Spain* was making a great Naval Armament against her, she sent out Sir *Francis Drake* with a Squadron of Ships to interrupt his Preparations, and destroy his Shipping in his Ports, who accordingly sailed to the Bay of *Cadiz*, and presently forcing under the Castles six Gallies which made shew of opposing him, took, sunk, or burnt about a hundred Ships which lay in the Bay, in which were great Quantities of Stores of War and Provisions, and among them a great Galleon of the Marquis of *Santa Cruz*, and a rich Merchant Ship of *Ragusa*. Returning from hence to Cape St. *Vincent*, he surprized three Castles in the Neighbourhood of that Place, and burning all the Fisher-boats and their Nets in his way, proceeded to *Cascais*, at the Mouth of the *Tayo*, where he challenged the Marquis of *Santa Cruz* to an Engagement, who could by no means be brought out, but suffered him to spoil the Coasts without Controul. From thence steering his Course towards the *Azores* Islands, he fell in with a large *Spanish* Carrack richly laden, bound home from the *East Indies*, and soon possessed himself of her.

1587.

Drake does great Mischief to the Spaniards at Cadiz.

Other Damage done to the Spaniards by Drake.

About this time, in another part of the World, the *Spaniards* were distressed by Captain *Thomas Cavendish*, a Gentleman of *Suffolk*, who having departed from *England* about two Years since with three Ships, had passed through the Streights of *Magellan*, and sailing along the Coasts of *Chili*, *Peru*, and *New Spain*, burnt several of the *Spanish* Towns there, and near *California* took and pillaged nineteen *Spanish* Ships, among which was a very rich one of the King's. Proceeding to the *Philippine* Islands, the *Molucca*'s, the Cape of *Good Hope*, and the Isle of St. *Helena*, he returned home the next Year with great Wealth and Glory, being the third from *Magellan* who sailed round the World.

The Spaniards suffer much from Cavendish.

Altho' Sir *Francis Drake*, in his late Expedition, had done the King of *Spain* very great Damage, yet so universal and vast a Preparation as he was making against *England*, was not so easily to be defeated. He had now been employed about it three Years, and had at length got together a Fleet, called by the arrogant Name of the *Invincible Armada*, which consisted of a hundred and thirty large Ships, wherein were nineteen thousand two hundred and ninety Soldiers, eight thousand three hundred and fifty Seamen, two thousand and eighty Gally-Slaves, and two thousand six hundred and thirty Pieces of Brass and Iron Ordnance. It was commanded in Chief by Don *Alphonzo Perez de Gusman*, Duke of *Medina Sidonia*, (the Marquis of *Santa Cruz*, famous for his Behaviour in the

1588.

The Spaniards fit out a great Fleet against England.

the Battel of *Lepanto*, who was defigned for that Poſt, dying whilſt the Fleet was fitting out) and under him was placed Don *Martinez de Recalde*, an old experienced Sea Officer of *Biſcay*.

Queen Elizabeth prepares againſt the Spaniards.

Queen *Elizabeth* having early Intelligence of the great Deſign againſt her, made a ſuitable Preparation for her Defence, and fitting out her Fleet under the Command of *Charles* Lord *Howard* of *Effingham*, Lord High Admiral of *England*, ordered him to repair to the Weſtward in conjunction with Sir *Francis Drake*, whom ſhe made his Vice-Admiral. And the Lord *Henry Seymour* ſhe commanded to lie on the Coaſt of *Flanders* with forty *Engliſh* and *Dutch* Ships, (the latter under the Command of *Juſtin* of *Naſſau*, Admiral of *Zealand*) to prevent the Duke of *Parma*'s coming out of the Ports there with the Force he was providing to join the *Spaniſh Armada* on its Arrival. There were alſo diſpoſed along the Southern Coaſts of *England* twenty thouſand Land Men, beſides an Army of two and twenty thouſand Foot, and a thouſand Horſe, encamped at *Tilbury*, under the Command of the Earl of *Leiceſter*, and another of four and thirty thouſand Foot, and two thouſand Horſe, under the Leading of the Lord *Hunſdon*, for the Guard of the Queen's Perſon.

The Spaniſh *Fleet ſeparated by Storm.*

The *Spaniſh* Fleet ſet ſail on the firſt of *June* from the River of *Lisbon*, and ſteer'd for the *Groyne*, but were by a violent Tempeſt ſeparated, and three of the Gallies, by the Stratagem of an *Engliſh* Slave, in conjunction with ſome of the *Mooriſh* ones, being run into a Port of *France*, the reſt of the Ships arrived ſoon after in a diſabled Condition at the *Groyne* and the neighbouring Ports. This Circumſtance had like to have proved more fatal to the *Engliſh* than the *Spaniards* themſelves; for the Miniſters in *England* thinking the Damages to the Fleet had been ſo great as that it could not proceed till the next Year, Secretary *Walſingham* ſignified the Queen's Pleaſure to the Lord High Admiral to ſend back four of his largeſt Ships into Port; but he, with more Diſcretion, retained them, alledging how dangerous it was to be too credulous in a Matter of ſo great Importance, and that he would rather keep the Ships out at his own Charge; ſo that making ſail towards the Coaſt of *Spain*, in order utterly to deſtroy the Enemy's Fleet if it were already ſo diſabled, or to gain certain Intelligence concerning it, if otherwiſe; he was not far from that Kingdom, when the Wind coming about to the Southward, he thought fit (his Inſtructions being to guard the *Engliſh* Coaſts) to return to *Plimouth*, leſt the ſame Wind ſhould carry the Enemy by him unſeen. And indeed, with the very ſame Wind, the Duke of *Medina Sidonia* ſet ſail with the whole *Armada* the twelfth Day of *July*, and in two or three Days detached a Veſſel to the Duke of *Parma*, with Notice of his proceeding ſo far, and his Advices to him to be ready with the Troops and Ships he was directed to provide, in order to be wafted over to *England* under his Protection, immediately on his Arrival in the Streights of *Dover*.

The Spaniſh *Fleet ſails from the* Groyne.

At length the Fleet, after an indifferent Paſſage over the Bay of *Biſcay*, arrived, on the nineteenth, in Sight of *England*; on which

CHAP. XVII. *Ruin of the* Rom. *Empire.*

which same Day the Lord-Admiral being informed by Captain *Flemming* that the Enemy had entered the Chanel and got the Heighth of the *Lizard*, he, though the Wind blew hard into *Plimouth* Sound, got his Ships out to Sea, but not without great Difficulty, and no less Diligence and Industry, he encouraging the Seamen to labour by his Presence among them, and setting his own Hands to their Work. The next Day the *English* discover'd the *Spanish* Fleet in form of a Half-Moon, (the Points whereof were about seven Miles asunder) coming slowly up the Chanel, tho' with full Sails, the Ships appearing like so many floating Castles, and the Ocean seeming to groan under the Weight of them. The Lord-Admiral willingly suffered them to pass by him, that so he might chace them in the Rear, with all the Advantage of the Wind. The twenty first of *July*, he sent a Pinnace before him, called the *Defiance*, to denounce War against the Enemy by the Discharge of all her Guns, which he immediately seconded from his own Ship the *Ark-Royal*, by thundring furiously on one of the Enemy's, commanded by *Alphonso de Leva*, which he took to be the Admiral's Ship; *Drake*, *Hawkins*, and *Forbisher* at the same time vigorously engaged the Enemy's sternmost Ships under the Conduct of *Recalde*, who used all the Endeavours which a gallant Officer could do to keep his Ships together, but, in spight of all his Efforts, they retreated to the main Body of the Fleet, and at length, his own Ship being very much damaged, he was forced to retire thither himself. Although the *Spaniards* were so briskly charged by the *English*, they made a running Fight of it; for our Ships were so light and nimble, that they found it would be in vain to act otherwise, and so held on their Course with all the Speed they could make. The Lord-Admiral continued to ply them briskly for two Hours together, and then thought fit to desist, because forty of his Ships were absent, being hardly yet got out of Port.

The Spaniards discovered off Plimouth.

The English attack the Spaniards.

The following Night, a Ship of the *Spaniards*, called the St. *Katherine*, being very much disabled in this Fight, was received into the midst of the Fleet in order to be repaired, and a large *Biscayan* Ship, commanded by *Oquendo*, on board which was the Treasurer of the Fleet, was purposely set on fire by a *Dutch* Gunner who had been ill used; but the Flame was happily extinguished by some Ships which came to her Relief; among which a Galleon, commanded by Don *Pedro de Valdez*, having lost her Foremast, by falling foul of another, and the Night being so dark and stormy that they could not repair that Damage, she fell into the Hands of Sir *Francis Drake*, who sent her Captain Prisoner to *Dartmouth*, and left the Money on board her to be plunder'd by his Men. He had been ordered to carry Lights that Night, but being in full Chace of some *German* Merchant Ships, which he supposed to be Enemies, happened to neglect it; which occasioned most of the Fleet to lie by all Night, because they could not see the Lights. Nor did he, or the rest of the Fleet, get up with the Lord-Admiral till the next Evening, who, with only the *Bear* and the *Mary-Rose*, had closely followed the Enemy all the preceding Night. This whole

whole Day the *Spanish* Admiral spent in the Disposition of his Fleet, and, assigning each Ship its Station in Battel, enjoined their respective Commanders to keep the same on pain of Death; and dispatched another Messenger to hasten the Duke of *Parma*, and to advise him of his near Approach. The foremention'd Ship of *Oquendo*'s being much damaged with the Fire, he removed the Officers, Men and Mony into another, and set her adrift, soon after which she was taken by the *English*, and carried into *Weymouth*.

On the twenty third, by break of Day, the *Spaniards* tacked about, with the Wind at North, towards the *English*, who presently tacked likewise, and stood to the Westward, and after several Attempts on both sides to get the Weather-gage, they came to another Engagement, which was managed with Confusion enough and Variety of Success. While in one Place the *English* with undaunted Bravery rescued some Ships of *London* which were encompassed by the *Spaniards*, the *Spaniards*, with no less Courage in another, delivered their Vice-Admiral *Recalde* from the Hands of the *English*. The great Guns on both sides thundered with extraordinary Fury, but the Shot from the high-built *Spanish* Ships flew over the Heads of the *English* without doing any Execution, one Mr. *Cock* being the only *Englishman* who fell, while he was bravely fighting against the Enemy in a small Vessel of his own. Besides, the *English* Ships being so much less than the *Spanish*, and infinitely more nimble and better Sailors, attacked and retreated as they pleased, while those of the Enemy lay as certain Butts for the *English*, against which they could not well miss their Aim.

The twenty fourth of *July* there was a Cessation on both sides, and the Lord High Admiral having received a Supply of Powder and Ball, divided his Fleet into four Squadrons, one whereof he commanded himself, the second he committed to Sir *Francis Drake*, the third to Captain *John Hawkins*, and the fourth to Captain *Martin Forbisher*, intending to attack the Enemy's Fleet in the Dead of the ensuing Night; but was prevented by a Calm. The twenty fifth, one of the *Spanish* Ships, which could not keep up with the rest, fell into the Hands of the *English*, who had a sharp Dispute with some of the *Spanish* Galeasses which attempted to rescue her, but treated them so roughly, that none of those Vessels ever after ventured to engage them. The next Day the Lord Admiral knighted the Lord *Thomas Howard*, the Lord *Sheffield*, *Roger Townsend*, Captain *Hawkins*, and Captain *Forbisher*, for their good Behaviour; and at a Council of War it was determined not to make any farther Attempts upon the Enemy till they should be arrived in the Streights of *Dover*, where the Lord *Henry Seymour* and Sir *William Winter* lay in wait for them.

The *Spanish* Fleet, in the mean time, continued its Course up the Chanel, with an easy Gale at S. W. b. S, the *English* following close at their Heels: And so far was the Appearance thereof from alarming the Coasts with any terrible Apprehensions, that very many of the young Nobility and Gentry hired Ships at their own Charge, and repaired on board, in great Numbers, to join the Lord High Admiral,

CHAP. XVII. *Ruin of the* Rom. *Empire.* 353

Admiral, and share in the Honour of destroying it. The twenty seventh of *July* the *Spanish* Fleet came to an Anchor before *Calais*, and not far from them anchored the *English* Admiral, who by the Accession of the Ships under the Lord *Seymour* and Sir *William Winter*, had now a hundred and forty Sail, all stout Ships, tho' the main stress of the Engagement lay not upon more than fifteen of them. The *Spaniards* were now very importunate with the Duke of *Parma* to send out forty Flyboats to their Assistance, for that otherwise, by the Unwieldiness of their Ships, they could not engage the light and active Vessels of the *English*. They also desired him to use all speed in embarking his Army, and be ready to take the first Opportunity, under their Protection, of landing in *England*. But, besides that his flat bottom'd Boats were become leaky, and that he was not in other respects in that Readiness which had been concerted, he was prevented from complying with these Demands by the Ships of *Holland* and *Zealand*, which, under the Command of Count *Justin* of *Nassau*, continued to block up the Harbours of *Dunkirk* and *Newport*, the only Ports from whence he could put to Sea.

The Day after the two Fleets came to an Anchor, the Lord-Admiral, by the Queen's Command, singled out eight of the worst Ships, and having bestowed upon them good Plenty of Pitch, Tar, and Rosin, and well lined them with *Brimstone*, and other combustible Matter, he sent them before the Wind, in the Dead of the Night, under the Conduct of *Young* and *Prowse*, into the midst of the *Spanish* Fleet. Their Approach was no sooner discovered by the *Spaniards*, and the prodigious Blaze they made, but suspecting they were filled with Engines of Slaughter, (for many of them having been at the Siege of *Antwerp*, had seen the destructive Machines made use of there) they set up a most hideous Clamour, and immediately cutting their Cables, in a panick Fright put to Sea, with all the Confusion and Precipitancy imaginable. One of the Fleet, a large Galeasse, having lost her Rudder, was toss'd up and down for some time, and the next Day being flung upon the Sands before *Calais*, was taken by *Amias Preston, Thomas Gerrard*, and *Harvey*, after a sharp and doubtful Dispute, wherein Don *Hugo de Moncada*, the Captain of her, was slain, and the Soldiers and Rowers either drowned, or put to the Sword; and the Ship and Guns, after the *English* had plundered her of a considerable Quantity of Gold, fell to the Governor of *Calais*. The *Spaniards* reported, however, that their Admiral, upon the Approach of the Fireships, made the Signal for weighing Anchor, and ordered that each Ship, after the Danger was over, should return to her Post; and he himself did indeed return, and fired a Gun, as a Signal to the rest for doing the like; but the Report thereof was not heard by many, for their Fears had so dispersed them, that some had got a considerable way out to Sea, and others among the Shoals on the Coast of *Flanders*; yet those who heard the Signal endeavoured to come to their Rendezvous off of *Graveling*, where they were very warmly plied with Shot by *Drake* and *Fenner*, who were soon supported by the

Fireships sent against the Spaniards.

Z z Lord

Lord High Admiral with the rest of the Fleet; at which time the *Spanish* Captains *Leva, Oquendo, Recalde,* and some others, having, with much ado, got clear of the Shallows, stood the Brunt of the *English* Fire, as well as they could, till they were very much shatter'd. The Galleon St. *Matthew,* commanded by Don *Diego de Piementello,* coming to the Assistance of Don *Francisco de Toledo* in the St. *Philip,* which had received great Damage from *Seymour* and *Winter*'s Shot, was taken by *Peter Dousa,* one of the *Dutch* Commanders; and the St. *Philip,* after having been driven almost as far as *Ostend,* was seized by some Ships of *Flushing.* The *English* Commanders, in general, shewed, on all occasions, great Resolution and Bravery, and in this last Action the Lord *Henry Seymour,* the Lord *Thomas Howard,* the Lord *Sheffield,* the Earl of *Cumberland,* Sir *William Winter,* Sir *Robert Southwell,* Sir *George Beeston,* Sir *John Hawkins,* Captain *Edward Fenton,* Captain *Richard Hawkins,* Captain *George Ryman,* and Captain *Robert Crosse,* signalized themselves in a very particular manner.

The *Spaniards* having been closely plied all this Day, would fain have retreated early next Morning through the Streights of *Dover*; but the Wind coming up, with hard Gales, at North-West, forced them toward the Coast of *Zealand,* whither the *English* seeing them hasten fast enough to their own Destruction, did not continue to pursue them; for with that Wind they could not fail being driven among the Shallows and Sands of that Coast. But the Wind soon coming about to the South-West, the *Spaniards* tacked, and got out of that Danger, and in the Evening a Council of War considered what was to be done, when it was unanimously resolved, *The* Spaniards *determine to return home.* that, seeing they were in want of many Necessaries, especially of Cannon-Ball, that the Ships were very much shattered, and that they had no hopes of the Duke of *Parma*'s coming out to join them, they should return to *Spain,* North about the *British* Islands; pursuant to which Resolution they made all the Sail they could. The Lord High Admiral, leaving the Lord *Henry Seymour* with a Squadron to assist the *Dutch* in blocking up the Duke of *Parma* in the Ports of *Dunkirk* and *Newport,* pursued the *Spanish* Fleet, and kept them in a continual Chace as far as the *Firth* of *Forth,* from whence they kept on their Course round by the *Orkneys,* the Western Islands, and *Ireland,* and the poor Remains of the Fleet arrived at length in a miserable Condition on the Coasts of *Spain,* several of the Ships having foundered at Sea, and no less than ten being cast away on the Coast of *Ireland.*

Thus, in one Month's Time, was brought to Destruction that formidable *Armada,* which had been three whole Years in fitting out; the Loss of the Nobility and Gentry on board whereof was so great, that there was hardly a Family in *Spain* but was in Mourning on this occasion, insomuch that King *Philip* was forced by Proclamation to shorten the usual Time for the same; as the *Romans* of old, upon their great Defeat at *Cannæ,* found it necessary to limit the publick Grief to thirty Days. Mean while, *England* resounded with Acclamations of Joy, and all the Protestant Nations of *Europe* participated

CHAP. XVII. *Ruin of the* Rom. *Empire.* 355

ticipated therein: And the Queen having made a publick Thanksgiving, with great Solemnity, at St. *Paul*'s, applied her self to distribute Rewards to the Lord Admiral, and the Officers and Seamen of the Fleet, for their gallant Behaviour.

The next Year the Queen thinking it both more safe and more honourable to attack the Enemy than expect another Assault from them, gave leave for fitting out a Fleet, which Sir *John Norris*, Sir *Francis Drake*, and some others, with exemplary Generosity and Readiness, undertook to defray the Expence of, with very little Charge to her Majesty, except the keeping at Sea a few of her own Ships. The States of *Holland* willingly embarking in the same Design, sent some Ships to proceed in conjunction with these, and Don *Antonio*, the abdicated King of *Portugal*, who had retired into *England*, also joined them with some others, well hoping, by the help of this Force, to be reinstated in his Kingdom. Setting sail from *Plimouth* they arrived in few Days at the *Groyne*, where they assaulted the Lower Town, and carrying it by Storm, burnt a great Quantity of Ammunition and Provision which was laid up there for a new Expedition to *England*. Then they attacked the Upper Town, very difficult of Access, and sprung a Mine or two which did considerable Damage thereto, but a strong Body of *Spaniards* approaching to the Relief of the Place, Sir *John Norris* advanced against them, and having received their first Assault, charged them with such Fury, that they fled with the utmost Precipitation, and were slain for three Miles together. Having plundered and burnt all the adjacent Villages, it was thought fit to reimbark the Troops; and thence the Fleet proceeding to the Coast of *Portugal*, they were joined in their Passage by the Earl of *Essex*. On their Arrival before *Peniche*, near the *Burlings*, the Land-Forces were put ashore, and the Castle of that Place was presently surrendered to King *Antonio*; and, upon the Encouragement they received from that Prince, the Troops marched on to *Lisbon*, but perceiving no Disposition in the People to declare for him, and being grown sickly, they made the best of their way to *Cascais*, where the Fleet was already arrived, and had reduced that Place. The Admiral having blown up part of the Castle of *Cascais*, and seized sixty Sail of Ships belonging to the *Hans* Towns, which were just arrived there with Corn and Naval Stores, received the Troops on board, and set sail homewards; and having by the way burnt the Town of *Vigo*, and plundered the adjacent Country, the Fleet soon arrived in *England*, with a hundred and fifty Pieces of Cannon taken from the Enemy, and a very rich Booty besides.

1589.
A Fleet fitted out against the Spaniards.

The Groyne attempted.

The Earl of Essex joins the Fleet on the Coast of Portugal.

Cascais reduced, and many Ships taken

Vigo burnt, and the Country plundered.

Queen *Elizabeth* having now a happy Experience of the good Effects of a potent Navy, was pleased to put the same on a better and more regular footing than it had ever yet been, assigning the constant Sum yearly of eight thousand nine hundred and seventy Pounds for the Repairs thereof. About this time the private Adventurers in the Nation were grown very numerous, and being encouraged by having so rich an Enemy as the *Spaniards* to deal with, they went out in Swarms to cruise upon their Shipping. The Earl

1590.
The Queen regulates her Navy.

Z z 2

Earl of *Cumberland* was a noble Adventurer among them, who failing to the *Azores* Islands, seized the Town of *Fayal*, demolished the Castle, and brought off fifty eight Pieces of Cannon.

1591

The English *ruffled by the* Spaniards *at the* Flores.

In 1591 the Lord *Thomas Howard*, second Son to the Duke of *Norfolk*, was sent out with a Squadron to intercept the *Spanish* Plate Fleet in its Return from *America*, who repairing for that purpose to the *Azores*, had continued for six Months at *Flores*, one of those Islands, when Don *Alphonso Bassano*, who was sent out from *Spain* with fifty three Ships to convoy the Fleet home, came upon the *English* so unexpectedly, that the Admiral had much ado to get out to Sea, and Sir *Richard Greenvil* in the Vice-Admiral Ship, called the *Revenge*, staying for his Men, which were straggling ashore, was hemm'd in by the *Spanish* Fleet; with several of which he maintain'd a gallant Fight for fifteen Hours, till being himself mortally wounded, and his Ship much disabled, he ordered her to be sunk; but the rest of the Officers, not consenting thereto, yielded her up to the Enemy, on promise of their Lives and Liberties, and Sir *Richard* was carried on board the *Spanish* Admiral, where he died within two Days, with great Commendations from the very Enemy of his extraordinary Courage and Bravery: But the Ship founder'd shortly after at Sea, with two hundred *Spaniards* on board her. The Lord *Howard*, who had now with him but five Ships, would have engaged the Enemy, notwithstanding their vast Superiority, had he not been dissuaded by the other Officers from so rash an Undertaking; so that he returned homewards, and in his Passage made amends for the Loss of the *Revenge*, by taking several rich *Spanish* Ships.

Rich Spanish *Ships taken.*

Riman *and* Lancaster *set out for the* East-Indies.

About the same time *George Riman* and *James Lancaster* undertook a Voyage to the *East-Indies*, and doubling the Cape of *Good Hope*, proceeded to Cape *Corientes*, where *Riman* being lost in a Storm, *Lancaster* went on to the *Comorro* Islands, and thence to *Zanzibar*, where having winter'd, he continued his Voyage to *India*, and by the way taking some Vessels belonging to *Pegu*, and some *Portuguese* Ships laden with Pepper and Rice, he proceeded to *Ceylon*, and thence to the Isle of *Nicubar*, near *Sumatra*, where taking into Consideration that he had but thirty three of his Crew alive, and that his Provisions were grown very short, he made the best of his way homewards; and having touched at St. *Helena* for Refreshments, was, after leaving that Island, carried away by the Trade Winds to the Isle of *Trinidada*, in *America*, from whence he proceeded to *Mona*, near *Porto Rico*, where going ashore with some of his Men for Refreshments, their Ship was in the mean time forced away by Stress of Weather with only seven Persons on board her, but nevertheless got safe to *England* with her rich Lading; and at length *Lancaster* himself, with the rest of his Men, being taken on board by a *French* Ship, were also brought home; and by the Experience they had learned in this Voyage, first taught their Countrymen the Method of Commerce in the *East-Indies*, and laid the Foundation of that since most flourishing Trade. This same Year Captain *Thomas Cavendish*, already remarkable for his late Voyage round

CHAP. XVII. *Ruin of the* Rom. *Empire.* 357

round the World, went out with five Ships on another Expedition to the Streights of *Magellan*, but being prevented by contrary Winds and bad Weather from passing the same, was driven back to the Coasts of *Brasil*, and there died, charging *John Davis* with his last Breath with having treacherously deserted him.

Cavendish sets out for Streights of Magellan.

The next Year the Queen fitted out a Squadron of fifteen Ships under the Command of Sir *Walter Raleigh*, ordering him, as occasion should best serve, either to proceed to *America*, and seize on *Panama*, whither the Gold is brought in order to be exported to *Europe*, or to intercept the *Spanish Flota* after it had taken the same on board. But he being detained in Port by contrary Winds for three Months together, and the *Spaniards* having gained some Notice of the Design, order was taken that no Ships should sail from *America* that Year. Sir *Walter* had got the Heighth of Cape *Finisterre* before he received that Intelligence, and then resolving to return to *England* himself, divided his Ships into two Squadrons, one whereof he committed to Sir *Martin Forbisher*, with Orders to cruise on the Coast of *Spain*, and the other to Captain *John Burroughs*, second Son of the Lord *Burroughs*, directing him to proceed to the *Azores*, and there lie in wait for the *Portuguese East-India* Carracks, which also used to touch at those Islands in their way home. Thither Captain *Burroughs* sailing accordingly, found the Earl of *Cumberland* at *Flores* with three Ships on the same Design, and in a short time the expected Carracks arriving, they had so good Success, that they forced the *Portuguese* to set fire to one of them, to prevent her falling into the Hands of the *English*, and after a sharp Engagement, they took another called the *Mother of God*, a seven decked Ship, manned with six hundred Men, with a very rich Lading on board, valued at a hundred and fifty thousand Pounds on its Arrival in *England*, over and above what the Officers and Seamen had plundered her of when taken.

1592.
Sir Walter Raleigh sent against the Spaniards.

The Portuguese fire one of their Ships, and another rich one is taken.

In 1593 *Richard Hawkins*, the Son of Sir *John Hawkins*, the famous Seaman we have before mentioned, went out with three Ships, with a Commission from the Queen to infest the *Spaniards* in *South-America*, and sailing first to the Isle of St. *Anne*, where the least of his Ships was accidentally burnt, proceeded thence to the Mouth of *Rio de la Plata*, where he took a *Portuguese* Ship, and from thence repairing to the Streights of *Magellan*, was by the way deserted by another of his Ships. Having past the Streights with great Difficulty, he sailed along the Coasts of *Chili*, where, at *Val Paraiso*, he took five laden Merchant Ships, one of which he carried off, and ransomed the rest: Thence proceeding to the Gulph of *Atacama*, he was encounter'd by the *Spaniards* with eight Ships, with which having maintained an obstinate Fight for three Days, he was at length forced to accept of the Enemy's Offers of Life and Liberty for himself and his Men, and surrender'd upon those Terms.

1593.

Hawkins takes a Portuguese Ship.

The Spaniards overcome Hawkins.

The next Year *John Lancaster*, who had been sent out with three Ships and a Pinnace on a private Account, had better Success against the *Spaniards* on the Coast of *Brasil*, where he took thirty nine of their Ships, and then joining Company with some other *English*, *Dutch*

1594.
Lancaster takes many Spanish Ships on the Coast of Brasil.

Dutch and *French* Ships that were cruising in those Seas, resolved to attempt *Pernambuca* a Town upon that Coast, where he understood a considerable Treasure was lodged that had been saved from an *East-India* Carrack, cast away near that Place. Accordingly making a Descent there, he took the lower Town and the Port by Storm, and having maintained it for a Month, in which time he loaded fifteen Ships with the Cargo of the foresaid Carrack, and other rich Commodities, then quitted the same, and returned in Safety to *England*.

Pernambuca taken by Lancaster.

And now, upon the universal Rumour spread throughout *Europe*, that the *Spaniards* were about to invade *England* with a more formidable Fleet than the former, the Queen fitted out two Squadrons, the one to remain in the *British* Seas, to withstand the Enemy there, and the other designed for a Diversion to them in *America*, under the Command of Sir *Francis Drake* and Sir *John Hawkins*. The former of these Squadrons did not keep so good a look-out, but that *Don Diego Brocher*, with four *Spanish* Gallies, arriving at Break of Day in *Mount*'s Bay in *Cornwall*, landed some Men, and burnt *Mouse-hole*, *Newlin*, and *Penzance*, with a neighbouring Church, but without so much as taking or killing a Man; and they were the last *Spaniards* that ever landed in *England* as Enemies. The Fleet in the mean time, under *Drake* and *Hawkins*, who were joint Admirals, setting Sail from *England*, with a Body of Land Forces on board, commanded by Sir *Thomas Baskerville*, repaired first to *Grand Canary*, the Chief of the Islands of that Name, and after a fruitless Attempt to reduce the same, with Intent to have kept it, proceeded to the Island *Dominica*; where making too long a Stay to build some Pinnaces, the *Spaniards* had Notice of their Arrival, and put themselves every where in a Posture of Defence: so that upon their coming before St. *Juan de Porto Rico*, the Place their chief Design was against, they found it so well secured, that, after an Assault or two, wherein they were repuls'd with considerable Loss, they sailed over to *Terra Firma*, and burnt *Rio de la Hacha*, and *Sta. Martha*, two considerable Towns in those Parts; and thence proceeding to *Nombre de Dios*, destroyed that Place likewise with the Shipping there, but met not with a Penny of Money in the Town. From thence a Body of seven hundred and fifty Land Men marched over-land towards *Panama*, but as they were on their Way through some Defiles they were to pass, they were so gauled with Shot from the Woods, and finding besides the Pass defended by a new erected Fort, that they made the best of their Way back to the Fleet; where Sir *Francis Drake* being seized with a bloody Flux, what with that Distemper, and Discontent at the ill Success of this Expedition, died in few Days, and Sir *John Hawkins* being already deceased at *Porto Rico*, the Fleet was left deprived of both its Admirals, and made the best of its Way to *England*. Near the Isle of *Pines*, off of *Cuba*, they were attack'd by the *Spanish* Fleet, which had lain in wait for them some time, but gave them so warm a Reception that the Enemy soon sheer'd off; and the Fleet, at length, after

1595. Two strong Squadrons fitted out against the Spaniards.

The Spaniards burn Penzance, and other Places in Cornwall.

Drake and Hawkins repulsed at Porto Rico.

The English burn Rio de la Hacha and Sta. Martha, &c.

Hawkins and Sir Francis Drake die.

CHAP. XVII. *Ruin of the* Rom. *Empire.* 359

after having been eight Months out on this unsuccessful Expedition, returned to *England*.

In the Beginning of the same Year, Sir *Walter Raleigh*, who had fallen into some Disgrace with the Queen, on account of an amorous Intrigue he had entertain'd too near her Majesty's Person, in order to recover her Favour by some worthy Exploit, undertook a Voyage at his own Expence, to *Guiana* in *America*, where, misguided by the Reports of some *Spaniards*, he was in Hopes to have found great Store of Gold. Repairing first to *Trinidada*, he took the chief Town of that Island, and there leaving his Ship, went over with a hundred Men in a few Pinnaces to *Guiana*, and sailed up the great River *Oronoque*, four hundred Miles into the Country, encountering with infinite Difficulties in his Passage, so that he was at length forced to return to *Trinidada*, without any other Advantage than having gained some Knowledge of the Country. From thence repairing to *Comana*, he burnt that Town, upon the Inhabitants refusing to ransom it on his Terms, after which setting fire to several Cottages at *Rio de la Hacha* and *Sta. Martha*, he made the best of his Way to *England*; and notwithstanding his Disappointment in this Expedition, made one or two more on the same Design, tho' the *Spaniards* had planted a numerous Colony at *Trinidada* to oppose his Attempts. About the same time the Captains *Preston* and *Sommers* pillaged the Isle of *Porto Santo* near *Madera*, and thence repairing to *America*, plundered the Isle of *Cobe*, near *Margarita*, with the Towns of St. *Jago de Leon* and *Coro* in *Terra Firma*. And a few Months before, three Ships, fitted out by the Earl of *Cumberland*, under the Command of Captain *Cave*, sailing to the *Azores*, attacked a large *Portuguese* Carrack, called the *Five Wounds of Christ*, which being set on fire in the Engagement, was burnt with all her Cargo, and had like to have involved the *English* that engaged her in the same Fate.

A sharp Dispute between the English and Spaniards. Raleigh undertakes a Voyage to Guiana.

Comana and other Places burnt by Raleigh.

Several Places in America plundered by Preston, Sommers, &c.

The Reports of the King of *Spain*'s great Preparations still continuing, and he having by the Accession of *Calais*, lately taken from the *French*, and the late unsuccessful Expedition of *Drake* and *Hawkins*, received some Encouragement to renew his Attempts against *England* and *Ireland*, the Queen, in order to divert the Storm, thought it proper to attack the Enemy in his own Ports, and to that purpose fitted out a Fleet of a hundred and twenty six Men of War, seventeen whereof were her Majesty's own Ships, and the rest hired, with seven thousand three hundred and sixty Land Men on board, the whole under the joint Command of the Earl of *Essex* and the Lord High Admiral *Howard*, assisted by a Council of War consisting of the Lord *Thomas Howard*, Sir *Walter Raleigh*, Sir *Francis Vere*, Sir *George Carew*, and Sir *Coniers Clifford*. To this Armament the States General added a Squadron of twenty four Ships, under the Command of the Sieur *Van Duvenvoord*, and the Fleet set Sail from *Plimouth*, with a seal'd Rendezvous (appointed to be at *Cadiz*) delivered out to each of the Commanders not to be open'd till they were past Cape St. *Vincent*.

1596.
A great Fleet fitted out against the Spaniards, under Essex and Howard.

The Fleet comes to Cadiz.

In few Days arriving at *Cadiz* the Fleet came to an Anchor before St. *Sebastian*'s; whereupon, as soon as the Tide came in, the *Spanish* Ships of War ran up to the *Puntal*, and the Merchant Ships over to *Port-Real*. A Council of War being held on board the *English* Fleet, it was resolved to attack the Enemy with the lightest and nimblest Ships, and that the Lord *Thomas Howard*, Sir *Walter Raleigh*, Sir *Thomas Southwell*, Sir *Francis Vere*, Sir *George Carew*, and Sir *Robert Cross*, with some others should execute this Service, who couragiously passing by the Fire of the Town, bore up towards the *Spanish* Ships, several of which endeavoured to preserve themselves by Flight, and making the best of their Way to to the Bottom of the Bay, where the Island of *Cadiz* is join'd to the Continent by the Bridge of *Suaco*, were conveyed by a Machine through a narrow Chanel into the Sea on the South Side of the Island, except only two or three of them that were prevented from escaping by Sir *John Wingfield* in the *Vanguard*. However many of the Galleons and Gallies kept their Station at the *Puntal*, and received the Broadsides of the *English*, which they returned for some time with equal Fury; but were at length so shatter'd and disabled, and had so many Men killed, that the *Spaniards* thinking them no longer tenable set them on fire, with such Precipitation, that great Multitudes of Men were forced to throw themselves into the Sea, where they must have miserably perished, had they not been generously relieved and taken up by the *English*. At the same time the *Spanish* Admiral called the St. *Philip*, a Ship of 1500 Tuns, was blown up by a *Moorish* Slave's setting fire to the Gunpowder, which destroyed two or three other Ships that lay near. The *Dutch* bravely attacked and carried the Fort of *Puntal*, where the Earl of *Essex* presently landed with a Body of Troops to attempt the City on the Land Side, while the Ships should do the like from the Sea, by whose joint Efforts the Town was taken in few Hours, and the Castle surrender'd next Day upon Terms.

Spanish Galleons and Gallies burnt.

Puntal taken by the Dutch, and Cadiz by the English.

Sir *Walter Raleigh*, the mean while, was ordered to go over with some of the lightest Frigats to *Port-Real*, to destroy the Fleet of Merchant Ships which had retreated thither, to whom was offered a Ransom for them of two Millions of Ducats, but while the Lord Admiral was consulted about it, who refused to save them on any Terms, the Duke of *Medina Sidonia*, who commanded in those Parts, saved the *English* the Labour, and set them on fire himself, by which the King of *Spain* lost in Shipping, Money, and Provisions to the Value of above twenty Millions of Ducats. The *English* being now in full Possession of the Town and Castle of *Cadiz*, the Earl of *Essex* was for maintaining the same, which he offered to do with only four hundred Men and three Months Provisions, and with him concurred Sir *Francis Vere*, and the *Dutch* Admiral *Duvenvoord*; but the Lord High Admiral, with all the other Commanders, being utterly averse thereto, after they had plundered the Island, demolished the Forts, and burnt down several Houses in the City, the Fleet set Sail from thence, and repaired to *Faro* in the *Algarve*, which Place they found deserted by the Inhabitants. After

The Spaniards set fire to their Merchant Ships.

ter which the Earl of *Essex* proposed they should repair to the *Azores*, and there wait for the *East-India* Carracks, but not any shewed their Consent thereto save the Lord *Thomas Howard*, and the *Dutch* Admiral, so that laying that aside, he prevailed with them to repair to the *Groyne*, where there was not so much as a single Ship, nor in the neighbouring Port of *Ferrol*. He was very earnest to have made an Attack nevertheless on the *Groyne*, or to have attempted the *Spanish* Ships in the Port of St. *Andrew*, or St. *Sebastian*'s, wherein the *Dutch* agreed with him, but was over-ruled in all these Points by the Lord Admiral and the other Officers, so that the Fleet making the best of its Way home, arrived in Safety, bringing with them two Galleons, and a hundred Brass Guns, with a very rich and valuable Booty besides, having destroyed eleven of the King of *Spain*'s most serviceable Ships of War, forty *Indian* Merchant Men, and four others, besides a vast Quantity of Provisions and Stores both for Sea and Land Service. The Earl of *Essex* believing that at his Return several Objections might be made to the Conduct of the Expedition, his Lordship drew up a Paper, in which he stated the same, together with his Answers thereunto, the Substance whereof is as follows, and very much agrees with the foregoing Account. *The Fleet returns home.*

Objection. That the first and principal Thing omitted in the Voyage was, that they did not endeavour to possess themselves of the Fleet which was bound to the *Indies*, since the Loading thereof would not only have defrayed all the Charges of the Expedition, but have enabled the Crown for a long while to have continued the War with *Spain*.

Answer. If I had been followed the first Morning when we came before the Harbour of *Cadiz*; or if we had entered the same on Sunday in the Afternoon, when we were under Sail, and within Cannon-shot of the Enemy's Fleet, or after the Ships of War were taken and burnt the next Day: I say if any Number of our Ships had gone up, as I my self urged by Message to Sir *Arthur Asheley* (who, being Secretary at War, was to record every Man's Services or Omissions) that Fleet might have been seized without any great Difficulty, for the first Morning their Men were not on board, (as hath been confessed by our Prisoners) nor could they have had time to consult what was fitting to be done for their Preservation.

In the Afternoon of the same Day we should have found the Men of War, and the Merchant Ships together, so that we might have engaged them at the same time, and defeating the one have possessed ourselves of the other. And even the next Day, presently after our Success against the King's Ships, the others would have been so confounded, that we might not only have taken them, with their valuable Loading, but the Gallies also, as our Prisoners, and Captives redeemed out of the said Gallies, have assured us.

But the first Morning when I was entering into the Harbour, almost all the Fleet came to an Anchor by the Point of St. *Sebastian*'s, a League wide of me, and thereby gave the Enemy an Opportunity of sending Men and all Necessaries on board their Ships.

A a a   When,

When, in the Afternoon, I was going in, I could not get many Ships to weigh their Anchors, nor would those that did so go in with me; and the next Day I had much ado to make our Ships fight at all. Nay even when it had pleased God to give us Victory, neither my Persuasions, nor Protestations could prevail with those who were Sea-Commanders to attempt the *Indian* Fleet, while we assailed the Town, so that the Enemy had almost forty eight Hours time to burn their own Ships.

Objection. That we abandoned *Cadiz* when we were possessed of it, whereas the holding that Place would have been a Nail in the Foot of the *Spanish* Monarchy, and been of great use to us in our Wars in those Parts.

Answer. Some of the Sea-Commanders, and especially my Collegue, did not only oppose that Design, (whose concurrent Advice my Instructions obliged me to follow) but when we came to consider what Force was necessary to be left there, I was assured that every Ship complained of Wants, insomuch that there was a general Discourse of the Necessity of returning home; and I found I could not have one Ship to remain at *Cadiz*, and that there was not so much Victuals for the Garrison as might suffice them two Months; wherefore Necessity, and not Choice, induced me to abandon it.

Objection. That we did not continue to lie in the Way of the Carracks and Ships from the *Indies*, when we were on the Coast at the time when it was thought they would return, and consequently the most proper for intercepting them.

Answer. I must, in the first Place, refer to the Testimony of all our Commanders by Sea and Land, whether I did not, in our Return from *Cadiz*, when we had doubled Cape St. *Vincent*, urge the proceeding to the *Azores*; and my Reasons for so doing were these. First, that we might be more certain of meeting the *Spanish* Fleet upon their making the Land, where we were assured they must touch, than by seeking them in the wide Sea. Secondly, that the Intelligence sent from *Spain*, and *Portugal*, since our being on the Coast, might meet them amongst the Islands, and make them alter their usual Course from thence, but could hardly find them beyond, and divert them from coming thither: Besides, the *Spaniards*, after our Action at *Cadiz*, could not so much as suspect we would proceed from thence to the Islands.

This Counsel being rejected, I, when we came within Sight of *Lisbon*, pressed again the lying in wait for them, with a Squadron of Ships to be particularly appointed, and offered, on that condition, to send home the Land Forces, and all such Ships as, either by Want of Provisions, or by other Ailments, were reduced unfit to continue longer abroad. But the Lord Admiral, and then Sir *Walter Raleigh*, protested under their Hands against the first Proposal I made: And when we came to the second, *viz.* what Ships were fit, and which of their Captains content to continue abroad, there was not besides the Squadron of the *Low Countries*, any more found than the Lord *Thomas Howard* and my self: Insomuch that by the whole Council of War it was determined, that not only what I had proposed,

posed, but that my Opinion also, together with that of each other Person, should be attested under his Hand, and that we should not stay to await the Fleet from the *Indies*, except the Lord Admiral would consent to leave, besides some of the Queen's Ships, eight or ten of those of the Merchants, which he refusing to do, that Design was frustrated.

Objection. That since the chief of our Service consisted in the taking or destroying the *Spanish* Shipping, and Naval Stores, why did we not look into their principal Ports, and do them all the Mischief we were able?

Answer. That my End in going to *Cadiz* was, not only because it was a principal Port, but the most likely to be held by us, in Regard not only to the Situation and natural Strength thereof, but that also from thence we might (if some greater Service did not divert us) go to all the Ports betwixt that and the nethermost Parts of *Biscay*, which seemed better to me than to have alarmed the Enemy first in the midst of his Country, or the nearest Part thereof to ours, in Regard that by acting in that manner our Attemps would have been more difficult, and our Retreat at last from those farthest Parts less safe, considering the Wants, Sickness, and other Inconveniencies which generally attend Fleets and Armies in long Voyages. But after we had done what we could at *Cadiz*, it was by all our Sea Officers thought a capital Offence so much as to mention the passing over the Bar of St. *Lucar*.

Between St. *Lucar* and *Lisbon* there is not any good Port, and from the latter I was restrained by my Instructions: Nay though we had been permitted to have gone thither, yet I found our Seamen of the same Cast, that Sir *Francis Drake* and his Company were, when they lost the Opportunity of taking that Place, not caring to pass by the Castle of St. *Julian*.

From *Lisbon* to the *Groyn* there is not any Port capable of containing either the King of *Spain*'s, or other large Shipping; but to the latter Place I, at length, prevailed with them, not without great Difficulty, to go, having both vowed and protested against their Refusal, and even parted Company with them when they offered to hold on their Course; but when we came to the Mouth of the Harbour, and sent in some small Vessels, we could not discover any thing there, nor at *Ferrol*, for in that Port we also looked.

After this we held our last Council, and then I urged going to St. *Andrew*'s *Passage*, St. *Sebastian*'s, and all the principal Ports along the Coast, but the Lord Admiral absolutely refused going farther, complaining of Wants, and representing the Danger of being embayed, with many other Inconveniencies, in which opinion Sir *Walter Raleigh* confirmed him, so that both of them seemed desirous to have the Honour of frustrating the Design; and as to our landing at the *Groyn*, and attempting the Town, they would by no means hear of it, but every one presently cry'd out, let us make Sail homewards, since which time they have used such Speed, that by my endeavouring to bring with me the St. *Andrew* taken at *Cadiz*, and the Flyboat with our Artillery, I have lost Company with them all, except

cept Monsieur *Duvenvoord* and his Squadron, and some small Ships.

The King of Spain assembles his Fleet at Lisbon, but many destroyed by Tempest at Sea.

To revenge these Losses sustained in the foremention'd Expedition, and recover his ruined Credit, the King of *Spain* assembling his Ships from all Parts to *Lisbon*, there he prepared his Fleet, and taking up all the foreign Ships in his Kingdom, embarked a Body of new raised Forces, with a great Number of *Irish* Fugitives, at the Port of *Ferrol*, in order to transport them to *Ireland* and *England*; but in their way they were surprized with so violent a Tempest as destroyed the greatest part of the Ships, and put an end for the present to the Design.

1597.

A Fleet of English and Dutch Ships fitted out under Essex, &c.

The next Year the Queen, upon fresh Advices of the Continuance of the King of *Spain*'s Preparations against *Ireland*, had recourse to her usual Practice of finding him Employment at home, and to that purpose fitted out a Fleet of forty Ships of War, with seventy victualling Ships and Tenders to accompany them, and a considerable Body of Land-Forces on board, to which the States adding ten Men of War under the Sieur *Van Duvenvoord*, the whole was divided into three Squadrons, the first under the Command of the Earl of *Essex*, who was General and Commander in Chief in this Expedition, the second under the Lord *Thomas Howard*, and the third under Sir *Walter Raleigh*.

Impracticable to attempt the Ships at the Groyne and Ferrol.

The Design in View was first to surprize the *Spanish* Ships in the Harbours of the *Groyne* and *Ferrol*, and then to intercept the *Indian* Fleet at the *Azores*. And accordingly the Fleet, after having suffered one or two Repulses by bad Weather, repaired to the *Spanish* Coasts, but by their hovering near the Shore of *Asturias*, instead of running in directly to *Ferrol* and the *Groyne*, the Enemy were forewarned of their Approach, and had so much time to prepare for their Defence, that, in a Council of War, the Execution of the first Design was thought impracticable, and they came to a Resolution to proceed to the *Azores*, at the same time making the Disposition of each Squadron to the Station it should take at those Islands, allotting to the Lord *Essex*, Admiral and Commander in Chief, the Isle of *Fayal*, that of *Gratiosa* to the Lord *Howard*, and the Island *Pico* to Sir *Walter Raleigh*; which latter having broke his Main-Yard off of Cape *Finisterre*, was not come up with the Fleet when this Resolution was taken; but, upon a right Judgment of what would be determined, when he had repaired his Damage, continued his Course to the *Azores*, where, at the Island *Flores*, he recovered the rest of the Fleet.

The Fleet comes to the Azores.

Raleigh being in want of Water, landed some Men without leave from *Essex*, in order to furnish himself therewith, and had scarce began to fill his Casks, when immediately the General sent him Orders to follow him to *Fayal*, which he did accordingly; but not meeting with him there, and upon taking a View of the Harbour, finding the Inhabitants were securing their Goods, and the Garrison throwing up Retrenchments, he, with the other Commanders in his Company, unanimously agreed to attack the Place if the Lord *Essex* should not arrive in four Days, which he not doing, they accordingly

CHAP. XVII. *Ruin of the* Rom. *Empire.* 365

cordingly landed, and presently putting the Enemy to flight, pos- *Fayal taken*
sessed themselves of the Town: This Action, performed in *Essex by Raleigh.*
his Absence, and without his Orders, bred ill Blood between him
and *Raleigh*; but for the present laying aside their Resentments,
they sailed, in conjunction, with the rest of the Fleet to *Gratiosa*,
another of the *Azores*, the Inhabitants whereof submitted them- *Gratiosa ta-*
selves to the Mercy of the *English*; and there the Lord-General de- *ken.*
signed to have waited the Arrival of the *American* Fleet, till being
unluckily dissuaded from it by one of his Pilots, on pretence it was
not a commodious Harbour for Shipping, he sailed thence with the
best part of the Fleet to St. *Michael's*, leaving Sir *Francis Vere* and
Sir *Nicholas Parker* to cruise between *Gratiosa* and St. *George's*
Island, and the Earl of *Southampton*, and Sir *William Monson*, to
do the like to the Westward of *Gratiosa*.

Essex had no sooner left that Island, but the *Flota* from *America The* American
arrived there, consisting of forty Sail, which immediately upon no- *Flota come to*
tice that the *English* were in those Parts, bore away thence to *Ter- the Absence of*
cera, and arriving all there in Safety, (except three straggling Ships *Essex.*
which were taken by Sir *William Monson*) ran into the Port of *Angra*, the chief Place of the Island, which was defended with several
Forts, well garrisoned, and mounted with Guns. *Southampton*, *Vere*
and *Monson* immediately dispatched a Frigate to St. *Michael's* to
give the Lord General Advice thereof, who in a Day or two after
joining them off of *Tercera*, took a View of the Enemy, and finding them in a very advantageous Situation, with their Ships drawn
up close under the Forts, came to a Resolution not to make any
Attempt on them, and returned with the Fleet to St. *Michael's*; *Impracticable*
where intending to make a Descent, and attack *Ciudad*, the chief *to attempt the*
Town of the Island, he went out himself in a Boat to discover a *Tercera.*
convenient Landing Place, but found all things there also so well
prepared for his Reception, that that Design was likewise judged impracticable. However, leaving *Raleigh* with some Ships to amuse
the Enemy at that Place, he went himself with the rest to *Villa
Franca*, a Town about six Miles distant, which he surprized and *Essex takes*
plundered. *Villa Franca.*

In the mean while *Raleigh* discovered at Sea an *East-India* Carrack, the Commander whereof perceiving, by the firing of Guns on
board one of the *Dutch* Ships, that an Enemy was near, and presently after discovering the Ships which lay in wait for her, vio- *The* Spaniards
lently ran her ashore just under the Town, where her Cargo being *run a rich*
with all Expedition thrown out, she was set on fire, and burnt for *Ship on shore.*
two Days together. So that Fortune seeming to declare herself a-
gainst the *English* by so many Disappointments in this Expedition,
they resolved to make the best of their way home, and setting sail
accordingly from St. *Michael's*, they three Days after met with a
violent Storm, which dispersed the Fleet for several Days. About
the same time the *Spanish* Fleet which lay at *Ferrol*, having put
from thence for the Coast of *England*, was encountred by the same
Storm, which handled them very roughly, so that they lost several *Spanish Ships*
of their Ships, and one of them was forced by Stress of Weather *lost in a Storm.*
into

into *Dartmouth*, with her Men almost famished, who reported that the Enemy's Design was to have seized some Port in *Cornwall*, and maintained the same, to find the *English* Diversion at home, and facilitate their Conveyance of Succours from *Spain* to *Ireland*, by having an Harbour to retreat to in case of bad Weather. Our Fleet, however, about the End of *October* arrived in *England* in a much better Condition, without having lost so much as one of its Number, tho' somewhat shattered and disabled by having been out so late in the Year.

The Fleet arrives in England.

1598.

The following Year the Earl of *Cumberland*, having fitted out eleven Ships at his own Expence, sailed with them to the Coasts of *Portugal*, with design to intercept the *East-India* Carracks bound out from *Lisbon*; but the Enemy, upon notice of his lying off the Coast, determined to lose their Voyage, and not go out till next Season; of which he having Intelligence, thought it would be to no purpose to wait for them, and therefore made the best of his way to the *Canaries*, where he took and plundered the Island and Town of *Lancerota*; from whence he made sail for *America*, and arriving at the Island *Porto Rico*, landed some Men, and attacking the Town, soon made himself Master of it, with the Loss of not above thirty of his Men, tho' there were in the Place a Garrison of four hundred Soldiers, besides the Inhabitants. Being possessed of this Town and Port, he intended, on account of its convenient Situation, to have made it his Seat of War, and from thence to have cruised against the Enemy, and with that View turned out all the Inhabitants, notwithstanding the vast Offers of Gold and Silver Plate they made for their Continuance. But, after about forty Days Stay there, the bloody Flux and other Distempers carried off such great Numbers of his Men, that he was forced to quit the same, and returned to *England* with more Glory than Wealth, bringing with him above sixty Pieces of Brass Cannon.

Earl of Cumberland takes Lancerota, and proceeds to America. He takes Porto Rico.

Sickness of his Men obliges the Earl of Cumberland to return.

1600.
Queen Elizabeth erects an East-India Company.

Soon after this Queen *Elizabeth*, for the Increase of Trade and Improvement of Navigation, erecting an *East-India* Company, they in the Year 1600 sent out three Ships to that Country, under the Conduct of *James Lancaster*, whom we have already mentioned as the first *Englishman* who made a Trading Voyage to those Parts. Thither the Company continued to send Ships every Year, and in a short time established several Factories in the *Mogul*'s Empire, in both the *Peninsula*'s of *India*, and in *Sumatra*, *Java*, *China*, and *Japan*.

1601.

The *Spaniards* having about this time brought some Gallies to *Sluys*, in order to cruise from thence chiefly against the *Zealand* Privateers, they did also take their Opportunities sometimes to infest the Coasts of *Kent*; whereupon the Queen thought fit to build likewise some Gallies, to the Charge whereof the City of *London* very liberally contributed, and they were furnished with Men for the Oar from the several Jails; but this Project proved in the end to little purpose.

The English build Gallies.

1602.

The next Year was fitted out a Squadron of eight of her Majesty's Men of War, to which being added some hired Ships, they were put under

under the Command of Sir *Richard Levifon*, and Sir *William Mon-* *A Squadron under Levifon and Monfon.*
fon, for an Expedition to the Coasts of *Spain*. The former setting
Sail with part of the Squadron, left *Monfon* to wait for the Arrival
of some *Dutch* Ships which were to join in this Service, but having expected them several Days in vain, he made the best of his
way after Sir *Richard Levifon*, who in the mean time having fallen in with the *Spanish Flota*, from *America*, consisting of thirty *Levifon engages the Spanish Flota.*
eight Sail, had bravely engaged them with his few Ships, though as
it happened without Effect. Upon Sir *William Monfon's* joining
him, they continued for seven Days cruising on the Coast of *Portugal*, and there receiving Intelligence that a large Carrack was just
arrived at *Cezimbra*, near St. *Ube's*, and that there were eleven
Gallies in the same Harbour, (three of them *Portuguese*, and the
rest bound for *Flanders*, under the Command of *Frederick Spinola*,
to cruise against the *Dutch*) Sir *Richard Levifon* took a Resolution
of attacking them, and entering the Harbour, came to an Anchor
before the Gallies, which having cannonaded very furiously for seven Hours together, they, unable to hold it out any longer, used *The Enemy's Gallies attack'd at Cezimbra.*
all their Endeavours to escape, but two of them were taken and
burnt, with a great Quantity of Gunpowder on board, and the rest,
much disabled, made a shift to get round to *Lisbon*. Hereupon
the Admiral sent a Message to the Commander of the Carrack, willing him immediately to surrender the Ship, Guns, and Cargo, if he *The English take a rich Carrack.*
expected any Mercy, which, after two or three Parleys, he consented to do, and the *English* triumphantly sailed home with their
Prize, valued at a Million of Ducats.

Sir *William Monfon* was presently sent out again to remain on
the *Spanish* Coasts till the middle of the Winter, for preventing any
Attempts from thence on *Ireland*, about which time *Spinola*, with
his eight Gallies which had escaped from *Cezimbra*, making the best
of his way for *Flanders*, arrived near the Streights of *Dover*, where
Sir *Robert Manfel*, with some of her Majesty's Ships, was cruising
off the *South Foreland* to intercept him, as were also some *Dutch*
Ships on the *French* and *Flemish* Coasts with the like Design, who
falling in with the Enemy near the *Goodwin*, attacked them with
such Success, that, out of the eight Gallies, only that commanded *The Spanish Gallies taken near Dover.*
by *Spinola* himself escaped to *Dunkirk*, the rest being all either
sunk in the Engagement, or lost on the Coast of *Flanders*.

Shortly after, Death put an end to this long and happy Reign of 1603.
Queen *Elizabeth*, who, by these many great Exploits performed *Queen Elizabeth dies.*
under her Influence, raised the Nation's Glory to the highest Pitch
it ever before reached, and fully made good the Titles bestowed on
her in the Beginning of her Reign, that she was the Restorer of Naval Glory, and the Mistress of the Ocean.

CHAP.

Chap. XVIII.

Of the Naval Transactions of the English, from the Beginning of the Reign of King James I. to the breaking out of the first Dutch War in 1652.

English foreign Plantations settled by King James.

During the pacifick Government of King *James* I. there happened but little remarkable at Sea. The Tranquillity of the Times, however, afforded Leisure and Opportunity for settling the Plantations in *Virginia, New England,* and the Isle of *Bermudas,* which, tho' some Planters had been transported thither in the late Reign, were never thoroughly settled and established till now. And the King, tho' such a Lover of Peace, did not omit to provide against a War, by taking the prudent Care to build so many Ships as increased the Royal Navy, (then indeed a small one) to almost double the Number it was on his Accession to the Crown, as we have elsewhere observed.

Several Ships added to the Royal Navy by him. 1617.

Raleigh proceeds with a Squadron to Guiana.

In 1617 Sir *Walter Raleigh*, who had lain long in the Tower, on account of a Conspiracy in the Beginning of this Reign, got some Proposals laid before the King concerning the Discovery of Gold Mines in *Guiana,* whereupon he obtained his Enlargement to go in search thereof, and several private Gentlemen embarking in the Design, a Fleet of twelve Ships was fitted out at their joint Charge, with which *Raleigh* arriving at *Trinidada* Island, after a long and troublesome Passage, found the *Spaniards* in those Parts fully apprized of his coming, and provided for their Defence; King *James* having at the same time he granted him his Commission, communicated the Project to the *Spanish* Ambassador Count *Gondamore,* who, doubtless, did not fail to dispatch Advice thereof to his Master. Nevertheless Sir *Walter Raleigh,* being himself ill of a dangerous Sickness, and therefore remaining at *Trinidada,* sent the five lightest of his Ships up the River *Oronoque* in search of the Mines, under the Conduct of Captain *Keymish,* who arriving at the Town of St. *Thomas,* near which the Mines lay, found the Passages thereto so difficult, and so well lined with *Spaniards* and *Indians,* who fired thick upon him, that he was forced to give over the Enterprize, and return without performing any thing but plundering and burning the Town of St. *Thomas,* which the *Spaniards* (not being numerous enough to defend both that and the Mines) had deserted: And upon his Arrival at *Trinidada,* Sir *Walter Raleigh* made the best of his way home from this unsuccessful Expedition; which the *Spanish* Ambassador so aggravated to the King, as an Infringement of the Peace and Amity between the two Crowns, (tho' certainly the King's granting the Commission was every whit as much so) that the unfortunate Gentleman was called up to the former Sentence of Death passed upon him for the aforesaid Conspiracy, (altho' the Commission, granted after, it could not but most effectually invalidate the same)

King James discovers Raleigh's Design.

The Town of St. Thomas plundered.

CHAP XVIII. *Ruin of the* Rom. *Empire.* 369

same) and was sacrificed upon the Scaffold to the Resentments of the Raleigh *executed* King of *Spain*.

Count *Gondomar*, that Prince's Ambassador in *England*, had now gained so great an Ascendant at our Court, that, at his Sollicitations, there was fitted out a Fleet for the Mediterranean, under the Command of Sir *Robert Mansel*, to humble the *Algerines*, who much infested the *Spaniards*. Which Fleet did accordingly sail to *Algier*, but meeting with little or no Success there, soon returned home, and the *Algerines* took the next Year about five and thirty *English* and *Scotch* Ships. 1620.
Sir Robert Mansel *sent against the* Algerines.

Shortly after this the *English* suffered a worse Treatment from the *Dutch* at *Amboina*, in the *East-Indies*, where, under pretence of a Plot formed by the *English* Factory, to expel them the Island, (though we had but twenty Men upon it, and they above two hundred Garrison Soldiers in the Castle, and eight Ships riding in the Road) they put them to the most exquisite Tortures, thereby to force them to a Confession of this pretended Conspiracy, which yet they were not able to do. Ten of them having expired on the Rack with Protestations of their Innocency, the rest, who survived their Torments, had the favour to be transported to other of the *English* Plantations in those Parts, and the *Dutch* obtaining their End, engrossed into their Hands the whole Trade of the Island, which they have ever since enjoyed. 1622.
The Dutch *use the* English *barbarously at* Amboina.

King *James* a little before his Death (which happened in 1625) in a Treaty which he made with *France*, engaged to send the *French* King some Ships to be employed against the King of *Spain*, or his Allies in *Italy*. To comply with this Agreement, King *Charles*, on his Accession to the Throne, sent Captain *John Pennington* with his Majesty's Ship the *Vanguard*, and six hired Merchant Ships over to the Coast of *France*, to be employed in the *French* Service. But the *French* King being hotly engaged in a War with his Protestant Subjects, now intended to make use of them for the Reduction of *Rochelle*; which *Pennington* becoming sensible of, immediately wrote Advice thereof to the Duke of *Buckingham*, then Lord High Admiral, and desired to decline so odious a Service, and that he might have leave to return to *England*; whereupon his Orders were more strongly enforced, and lest the Lord High Admiral's should not be thought sufficient, the King himself signed an Order to him to employ the Ships on such Service as his Most Christian Majesty should direct; from whom at the same time he received a Letter, requiring him to take on board a Number of *French* Soldiers, with his Admiral the Duke *de Montmorency*, and repair before *Rochelle*. This Captain *Pennington*, with a true *English* Heart, bravely refused to do; whereupon the *French* Officer who had conveyed the Orders to him, came on board the *Vanguard* to protest against him as a Rebel to his King and Country; and not contented with having once done it, returned a second time to enforce his Protestation with Threats and Menaces, at which the Seamen were so enraged, that, in a violent Fury and Tumult, they weighed Anchor, and set sail, crying, *They would rather be hanged at home*, 1625.
Pennington *sent with a* Squadron *to* France.

Pennington, *and those with him, refuse to serve against the* Rochellers.

B b b *than*

than be Slaves to the French, and fight against their own Religion; and accordingly returned to the Downs. The Captain sending an Express to Court with Advice of his Proceedings, immediately received a positive Order under the King's Sign Manual to return and deliver up the Ships into the Hands of a French Officer at Dieppe, which he was at length forced to comply with, but quitted the Command himself, as all the Englishmen, both Officers and Seamen except one, did their Ships, and returned to England. So hard is it for the honest English Sailor to be made subservient to Popish Interests.

The scandalous Treatment the late King had receiv'd from the Spaniards, relating to the Match and the Palatinate, had, notwithstanding all his Inclinations to Peace, enforced him, a little before his Death, to resolve on a War with Spain. In prosecution whereof, King *Charles*, upon his coming to the Crown, fitted out a Fleet for an Expedition against that Kingdom. The Command thereof, instead of being bestowed on Sir *Robert Mansel*, an old and experienced Seaman, and Vice-Admiral of *England*, was given to Sir *Edward Cecil*, a Soldier trained in the *Low-Country* Wars, who, for the Honour of the Enterprize, was created Viscount *Wimbledon*; and agreeable to the Choice of the General was the Success of this Expedition. His Fleet consisted of eighty Sail, of which Number some were Ships of the States-General; and the Earls of *Essex* and *Denbigh* were his Vice and Rear-Admirals; with which setting sail from *Plimouth*, when he was got some few Leagues at Sea, he was encounter'd with a violent Storm, which dispersed the Fleet, so that they were many Days before they got together at their appointed Rendezvouz off Cape St. *Vincent*. From thence proceeding to the Bay of *Cadiz*, they found there, near the *Puntal*, fourteen great Ships, and twelve Gallies, which, through Neglect and Mismanagement, they suffered to escape; for though the Earl of *Essex*, pursuant to the General's Orders, did very resolutely and bravely attack them, yet the rest of the Fleet not coming up timely to his Assistance, the *Spanish* Ships, after having given the Earl a warm Salute or two, retired over to Port *Real*: To which Place it was not thought fit to follow them, whether through the Ignorance of the Pilots, or Unskilfulness of the General, is hard to determine. So that failing in this Enterprize, they attacked the Castle of *Puntal*, and, with the Loss of a great many Men, made a shift to atchieve the Reduction of that Place: After which having made some ineffectual Efforts against the Town of *Cadiz*, the Troops were reimbarked, and the Fleet set sail for Cape St. *Vincent*, to cruise in the Offing of that Place for the *Flota* from *America*, where having waited for some time in vain, the Men began to grow very sickly; when, to compleat the Miscarriages of this Expedition, the sick Men were distributed through the whole Fleet, two to each Ship, by which means the Sickness was increased to such a degree, that there were scarce Hands enough left to carry the Fleet home, which in the Month of *December* returned ingloriously to *England*.

King Charles *fits out a Fleet against the* Spaniards, *under the Lord* Wimbledon.

The English *and* Dutch *arrive at Cadiz.*

Puntal *Castle taken.*

The Fleet ingloriously returns.

The

CHAP. XVIII. *Ruin of the* Rom. *Empire.* 371

The forementioned delivering up of the Ships under Captain *Pennington* to the *French*, was so highly distasteful to the People of *England*, and made them so jealous of the Court, that it was thought fit, when it was publickly known they had been employed against the *Rochellers*, to exclaim against that Proceeding as a Collusion of the Treaty whereby they were lent, and to demand the immediate Restitution of them; which the *French* King excusing himself from complying with at present, on pretence that his Subjects by whom they were manned would not now quit them, when they were on immediate Service, the Lord High Admiral issued out Commissions of Reprizal, whereby the St. *Peter* of *Havre de Grace* was taken with other *French* Merchant Ships: Whereupon the *French* King not only absolutely refused to restore the seven Ships, but seized on all the *English* Merchants Effects throughout his Dominions. However, for some Reasons of State, these Breaches were patched up for a while, and mutual Restitution made on both sides, till soon after, upon the Dismission of the Queen's *French* Servants, an open Rupture ensued, by the *French* King's seizing a hundred and twenty *English* Merchant Ships in the several Ports and Rivers of his Kingdom, which was immediately followed by a Declaration of War on our side. The Grounds thereof, among others, were the *French* King's Breach of his Articles with his Protestant Subjects, and his blocking up their Towns, Garrisons and Forts. In order therefore to relieve them, a Fleet of thirty Ships was immediately fitted out under the Earl of *Denbigh*, with Orders to proceed to *Rochelle*; but the Ships, when they were gotten a few Leagues into the Sea, suffered so much by bad Weather, that they were forced to return into Harbour, and the Season was so late, (being the latter end of *October*) that they could not be sent out again till next Year.

The English resent the lending Ships to France.

The French refuse to return our Ships, and seize the English Effects.

English Merchant Ships seized by the French.

England declares War against France. 1626.

A Squadron sent to relieve the Rochellers to no purpose.

Against that time was prepared a more considerable Fleet for this Service, consisting of above a hundred Sail of Ships, ten of them the King's Men of War, and the rest pressed or hired from the Merchants, with a Body of six or seven thousand Land-Soldiers, the whole to be commanded by the Duke of *Buckingham*, both as Admiral and General, but the Success was very unworthy the Greatness of the Preparations.

The Duke of Buckingham sent to relieve the Rochellers.

There are various Accounts of this inglorious Expedition, though all of them agree as to the ill Conduct throughout the whole; but that it may appear in as clear a Light as I am able to set it, from some Papers which I have had the Perusal of, (having unfortunately lost an original Journal kept by Sir *William Beecher*, who was Secretary to the Duke of *Buckingham*) I refer the Reader to the following Narrative.

After the Fleet had been a Fortnight at Sea, they arrived off of the Isle of *Rhe*, on the eleventh of *July*, when a Council of War being called, the General gave Orders for putting the Troops on shore. There was not any thing more done that Night, than the firing some Shot from the Ships of War against the Fort *de la Prée*, by which the Enemy received little or no Damage; but next Day the Duke of *Soubize* was sent to *Rochelle*, in Company of Sir *William*

The English arrive off of the Isle of Rhe. 1627.

Duke of Soubize sent to Rochelle.

Bbb 2

liam Beecher, Secretary to the General, to inform themselves of the Intentions of those People, whom (though they had very much pressed for our Assistance) they found not inclinable to declare for us, until they had consulted the Heads of the League. The same Day about four in the Afternoon the Soldiers began to disembark, and no sooner were there landed between twelve and fifteen hundred Men, with three or four small Field-Pieces, than the Enemy from the Citadel of St. *Martin*'s, (the chief Place of the Island) to the Number of about two hundred Horse, and a thousand Foot, attacked them, and the Cavalry charging with great Fierceness before the *English* were formed, put them in no small Disorder, insomuch that many in the Rear were drowned; but at length, by the gallant Behaviour of our Officers, they rallied, and killed about a hundred of the Enemy's Horse. Their Foot seeing the Cavalry had suffered, came on very unwillingly, and after they had stood two or three Vollies of Shot, and received some Damage from our Pike-Men, they betook themselves to flight, and left our Troops Masters of the Ground, but with the Loss of some of our bravest Commanders.

Some of the English landing, were attacked.

That Night the Horse began to disembark, and the Foot were busied in making Retrenchments, that so they might be the better able to maintain the Ground they had gotten; but had the Enemy been as discreet as they at first shewed themselves valiant, we should not so easily have made good our landing; for had they began to charge with their Foot, and received our first Fire, and then have flanked us with their Horse, they would doubtless have done much more Damage; but, to our great good Fortune, it happened otherwise, occasioned, as it was said, by a Dissension among themselves; for Monsieur *Toiras*, Governor of the Island, having promised the Baron St. *Andrew* the Honour of the first Charge, he afterwards gave it to his own Brother, whereat, it is said, the Baron being much discontented, would not charge at all, nor suffer his Troops to second the Van; but a much greater Miscarriage happened on our side; for had our Troops, while the Enemy were in this Confusion, followed them immediately, there was good reason to believe they might have soon made themselves Masters of St. *Martin*'s, which was very indifferently provided for Defence; but instead of that, five Days were spent to no purpose e'er they marched from their Camp, during which time the Enemy had Opportunities of getting in Provisions and strengthening themselves.

The English Horse disembark.

The Enemy did not attack as they ought.

The English give the Enemy time to provide for their Defence.

Two Days after the Baron *Ambellent* came to bury their Dead, of whom the better sort were carry'd to St. *Martin*'s; as for the rest, our Soldiers had Money from him to put them under Ground; and in the Afternoon, about three a Clock, the Duke of *Soubize* came from *Rochelle* with some few Gentlemen, and about five hundred Soldiers, whereupon our Troops marched out of their Trenches, at the Distance of about three or four Bows Shot, where, it being late, both Horse and Foot quartered that Night.

Duke of Soubize returns from Rochelle.

The fifteenth in the Morning our Troops, to avoid the Fort *de la Prée*, which was situated in their direct way, marched five or six Miles about on sandy Ground, by which they were very much fatigued,

The English neglect taking a Fort.

CHAP. XVIII. *Ruin of the* Rom. *Empire.* 373

fatigued, and thereby an Opportunity was not only loft of taking the faid Fort, which the Enemy had then abandoned, but the Advantage of fecuring a Retreat, and they thereby gaining time, repoffeffed themfelves of it, and put it into fuch a Condition, as enabled them to annoy us very much afterwards.

As our Troops paffed along, all the Villages fubmitted to them; and they received no Interruption in their March that Day, tho' towards the Evening fome of the Enemy's Horfe appeared upon a diftant Hill, but did not think fit to approach. When it was near Night our Troops came before a little Town called *la Flotte*, into which Place they entered the next Morning early, and ftayed there the beft Part of the Day, when Monfieur *Toiras* fent a Challenge to fight forty of his Horfe againft the fame Number of ours; but this being done on purpofe to gain time, it was therefore not accepted, for the Enemy had been very remifs in furnifhing the Citadel with fufficient Provifions, although they had been advertized of our intended Expedition, not only from *England*, but by a *Dutchman*, who fet Sail from *Portfmouth* at the fame time our Fleet did, loaden with Powder, Shot, Pikes, and other warlike Implements, and when our Ships were difperfed by chafing feveral *Dunkirkers*, took that Opportunity of getting into St. *Martin*'s five or fix Days before the General arrived.

Villages fubmit to the Englifh.

A Challenge fent by Toiras.

The Enemy had notice of our Defign.

On the Approach of the Army to St. *Martin*'s, Monfieur *Toiras* quitted the Town, and retired into the Citadel, when fome of the Chief of the Place coming with a white Flag to the Duke, and defiring him to take the Town into his Protection, our Troops marched in, upon whom the Enemy fired all Day, but did little or no Harm.

The Englifh *enter St. Martin's.*

A Council of War being called, Sir *John Burroughs*, who had well viewed the Citadel, affured the Duke that it was impoffible to take it by Affault, and that now to ftarve them was equally difficult; for they had Opportunities of conveying confiderable Quantities of Provifions thereinto, between Wednefday the time of our coming to the Ifland, and Tuefday following, when we arrived at St. *Martin*'s: wherefore he advifed his Grace to pillage the Ifland, and to go to *Oleron*, or fome other Place where they might have a better Profpect of Succefs; but his Advice was not adhered to, for the Duke, befides the Engagement of his Honour, as he pretended, rely'd too much on thofe who flattered him, and promifed effectually to prevent the Enemy's conveying any Succours into the Fort.

The 18th Sir *William Beecher* and Mr. *Grahme* were difpatched to *England*, to haften the *Irifh* Troops which were defigned for this Service, together with Money and Provifions; and on the 21ft Sir *Peregrine Bertie*'s Regiment was fent to *la Flotte*, to join with Sir *Henry Sprye*'s, which, together with the Horfe, were to maintain that Place; and our People having landed fome Ordnance, and erected a Battery, there was almoft a continual Fire between the Army and the Citadel, for two or three Days, wherein we had the worft;

Sir William Beecher fent to England to haften Irifh Forces.

Englifh and the French fire at each other.

worst; for as our Men lay much exposed, so was it not in our Power to do the Enemy any considerable Damage.

The 24th there was little more done than the burning some Windmills, in one of which were 30 Musqueteers, who surrender'd; and on the 27th, notwithstanding all our Precautions, three or four Barks loaden with Provisions got in to the Relief of the Citadel, from whence there came a Person three Days after, who pretended to be a Deserter, and desired to be admitted to the Duke. His confident Behaviour render'd him suspected, and being search'd by some of the Duke's Favourites, there was found about him, as they said, a poisoned Dagger, whereupon being threatened with the Torture, he confessed that he was sent by the Governor to kill the *English* General; but however the Fact itself was, Monsieur *Toiras* sent to his Grace, and assured him that he was altogether ignorant of any such Design.

A pretended Deserter came to the Camp.

Notwithstanding it had been concluded at a Council of War that it was impossible to take the Citadel, otherwise than by starving the Garrison in it, yet in all the time our Troops lay before it, there were not any measures taken to block them up by a Line of Circumvallation, but, instead thereof, Batteries were raised before we made our Approaches, so that the Passage was open for carrying what Provisions they had into the Fort, and to give Intelligence of the Circumstances of our Army.

Remissness of the English.

At length, when Necessity compelled thereunto, our Troops began to entrench the 3d of *August*, and two Days after some of the Pioneers and Soldiers being at Work, between thirty and forty of the Enemy's Horse sally'd out of the Fort upon them, but were repulsed with little Loss on our Side.

English entrench.

On the 9th the Duke caused five hundred Seamen to be brought on shore, and gave the Command of them to Captain *Weedal*, with a Commission to be Colonel, but they having but little Experience in Land Affairs, and being but ill provided for annoying the Enemy, or even to defend themselves, it was no marvel they did but little Service. On the 12th the *French* which came with Monsieur *Soubize*, together with Captain *Shugborow*, and Captain *Padon*, following the Directions of the Duke, contrary to the Advice of Sir *John Burroughs*, fell upon the Enemy's Works, but were repulsed with considerable Loss.

A Body of Seamen landed.

The 2d of *September* the *Irish* Supplies arrived under the Command of Sir *Ralph Bingly*, and Sir *Peter Crosby*, and this Day those in the Citadel desired a Parley. The Gentleman who came with the Message said that those in the Fort knew of the Arrival of the additional Troops as soon as we did in the Camp, but the Subject of his Errand was not known to any one besides the Duke himself. It was pretended, indeed, that he came to see a Brother of his who had been taken Prisoner; and, besides this, there were divers other Messages past between the Governor and his Grace, with Presents of Mellons and other Things, insomuch that the Duke grew very distasteful to the Officers of the Army, since he did not think fit to impart

Irish Supplies arrive.

Citadel desires a Parly.

The Duke distasteful to the Army.

CHAP. XVIII. *Ruin of the* Rom. *Empire.* 375

part any thing to them, or to permit them to the Speech of any of the Meſſengers. However, the Governor being alarmed at the Arrival of our Supplies, ſent an account thereof to the *French* King his Maſter, who drew his Army towards *Rochelle*, and by forming, as it were, a Blockade, made a Shew as if he deſigned to take the Town, though his real Intentions were to land Men on the Iſland, which was ſoon after effected. *French King draws towards Rochelle.*

At laſt the *Rochellers* declared for the *Engliſh*, and the Duke of *Rohan* gave Commiſſions to raiſe Forces for Preſervation of the Edict of Peace lately granted, but violated by the *French* King, who on the other hand declared he would obſerve the ſaid Edict, and proclaiming the Dukes of *Rohan* and *Soubize* Traitors, offered Rewards for killing them. *Rochellers at laſt declare for the Engliſh. Duke of Rohan, &c. declared Traytor.*

By this time the *French* had got a conſiderable Supply of Shipping from the *Spaniards*, which with their own Navy made up above a hundred, a Force ſuperior to that of ours, for although the *Engliſh* Fleet at firſt ſetting out conſiſted of more then a hundred Sail, yet were there not above ten of the King's own Ships among them. But though the Enemy were thus ſuperior in Naval Strength they declined engaging, and propoſed nothing more to themſelves than the getting neceſſary Supplies into the Citadel, and to tire out the Beſiegers; to carry on which Deſign the Governor pretended to enter into a Treaty to ſurrender on honourable Terms, and prevailed with the Duke to give ſafe Conduct for a Meſſenger he was ſending to the *French* King, on condition that an *Engliſh* Gentleman ſhould accompany him, and be ſuffered to paſs through *France* into *England*, but on their Arrival in the *French* Camp, the *Engliſh* Gentleman, contrary to Faith given, was detain'd in Cuſtody, while the *Frenchman* effectually performed his Errand, and returned to St. *Martin's*, upon whoſe Arrival Monſieur *Toiras* put an end to the ſham Treaty. Some Days after Preparations were making for the Aſſault of the Fort *de la Prée* (which by our Neglect, as hath been already obſerved, the Enemy had re-poſſeſſed and ſtrengthened) and in order thereto ſeveral Pieces of Ordnance were landed at *la Flotte*. Sir *Alexander Brett* had undertaken this Service, but it was afterwards thought not convenient to divide the Forces for a matter judged of ſo ſmall Conſequence, though in effect it proved otherwiſe, for what was thus ſo much ſet at nought, proved a ſevere Thorn in our Sides e'er the Troops left the Iſland. *French Navy encreaſed by the Spaniards. An Engliſh and French Gentleman ſent to the French King. The French detain the Engliſh Gentleman.*

On the 11th a Bark of forty or fifty Tuns arrived at the Citadel with Proviſions, at which Veſſel about five hundred Shot were to no Purpoſe fired from the Ships, and ſoon after Sir *John Burroughs* (a valiant and experienced Commander) was ſlain, while he was viewing our Works, with whom ended all reaſonable Hopes of Succeſs. *Proviſions got into the Citadel. Sir John Burroughs ſlain.*

The 17th Mr. *Aſhburnham* who had been ſent in Company with *Toiras*'s Meſſenger to the *French* King, (as aforeſaid) returning to the Camp, was preſently diſpatched for *England*, and two Days after Monſieur *St. Serin* came to the Army, with whom the Duke at firſt deny'd to ſpeak, and ſent him a Priſoner on board of the Ship commanded *Monſieur St. Serin comes to the Engliſh Camp.*

commanded by Captain *Porter*, but there he did not long remain, for returning to the Army again, he was entertained by his Grace with great Respect.

The 20th about Break of Day a great Number of Boats were discovered making towards the Citadel, but the Alarm being given they put back again, and our smallest Ships chasing them, took five loaden with Victuals and warlike Stores. On the 24th Sir *Henry Palmer* arrived from *England*, with thirteen Ships loaden with Provisions, and Necessaries for the Army, and two or three Days after that there came to the Citadel fifteen or sixteen Boats from the Main, with at least two Months Provisions, Powder and Shot, which they stood in great need of, for they had not for fifteen Days before fired so much as one Shot; and our Soldiers marched to their Guards in open View of them, without running the Hazard even of a Musket Ball; insomuch that had not this Supply arrived as it did, they would have been obliged to surrender. And now, to add to our Misfortunes, the Soldiers began to fall sick, and the Provisions which came from *England* were quickly spent, or render'd unfit for Men to eat, not but that the *Rochellers* assisted them with what they were able.

Provisions, &c. arrive from England. and Supplies are gotten into the Fort.

On the 13th great Preparations were made for an Assault, after the Enemy had had but too many Opportunities of strengthening themselves; nor would the Duke have been persuaded from it, if foul Weather had not happened, and this although the Generals, and Field Officers had given it under their Hands that it was a thing altogether impracticable, and withal persuaded him to depart before the Enemy had landed too many Men on the Island; but this their wholsom Advice was answered with Contempt.

Provision made for an Assault.

The 21st his Grace, upon Advice that a Reinforcement for the Enemy was landed near the Fort *de la Prée*, ordered the Troops to quit the Trenches, and march to oppose them, which was no sooner done but those in the Citadel sallied out, and possessed themselves of them, so that after our People had had tolerable Success, and forced the *French* Recruits to retire under the Cover of the Guns of the Fort *de la Prée*, when they returned to the Camp they were obliged to dispute for the Recovery of the Trenches, and many Men were lost before they could gain them. About the middle of *October* the Duke held a Council of War, and had Thoughts of returning to *England*, which the Officers also advised; but *Soubize* dissuaded him from it, alledging that the Enemy's Recruits were not considerable, that the Earl of *Holland* was coming from *England* with a Reinforcement; that a Retreat would occasion the Loss of *Rochelle*, and bring great Dishonour to the King, by undertaking such an Enterprize to so little purpose; whereupon the Duke resolved to continue the Siege, and to storm the Citadel and Works, which was accordingly done in few Days, wherein after we had lost a considerable Number of Men, it was found inaccessible.

The English ordered to quit the Trenches, which the French possess themselves of.

Soubize prevails with the Duke not to retreat.

The Citadel stormed to no purpose.

Although the Enemy were daily reinforced, yet would not the Duke be persuaded to be gone, even though Sir *Edward Hawley*, and Major *Brett* came to him, in the Name of the Council of War, to entreat him to march away; but some of Sir *William Cunningham*'s Horse coming to his Grace, and informing him that they heard great firing on the Main, he commanded the Troops to march, which they did, but left several sick Men behind, whose Throats were inhumanly cut by the Enemy, and their Bodies sent off in a Bark from the shore two or three Days after.

The Duke orders the Troops to march off.

The great Oversight of not having taken Possession of the Fort *de la Prée*, to cover and secure the Embarcation of the Troops in Case of a Retreat, now too visibly appeared; for the Enemy being by this time grown so strong in that Place, and the adjacent Parts of the Island where the Duke had landed, that he durst not venture thither, to have an Enemy both before and behind him, there was now no Place left where the Troops could embark, but the Isle *de l'Oye*, separated from the rest of the Island by Salt-Pits and a small Chanel, the Passage to which lay over a long and narrow Causeway. Thither the Duke taking his March, was immediately followed at the Heels by the Enemy, that were equal in Foot, but much superior in Horse, who well knowing the Advantage they should soon have of the *English* when they came to the Causway, forbore to attack them, though they faced about several times, and offered them Battel. But no sooner had the Troops entered the Causway than they charged them in the Rear with great Fury, when the Horse giving way pressed in upon the Foot, and made the Croud so tumultuous that great Numbers fell into the Salt-Pits, or perished in the Chanel, besides those whom the Enemy killed, which were very many. When they had passed the Causway they drew up, and made a brave Stand against the pursuing Enemy, who, after a short Dispute, thought fit to repass it, and the *English* having guarded it with some chosen Troops all Day, burnt it down at Night, and without any farther Attempts from the Enemy, were the next Day put on board the Fleet; with which the Duke having just appeared before *Rochelle* to send in a Message, made the best of his Way to *England*, having lost since his first landing on the Island about fifty Officers, near two thousand common Soldiers, five and thirty Prisoners of Note, and forty four Colours, which were carried to *Paris*, and hung up as Trophies in the Cathedral there. And thus ended this Expedition with great Dishonour to the *English*, and equal Glory to the *French*, but in particular to Monsieur *Toiras*, who for having so bravely, with a handful of Men, defended a small Fort (for no other is it, tho' our Journals and Accounts dignify it with the Title of a Citadel) against a numerous Fleet and Army, was not long after advanced to the high Dignity of a Mareschal of *France*. Nothing but a Concurrence of several Miscarriages could have render'd this Attempt in all Points so ineffectual on our Side; and one who was employ'd in the Expedition sums them up in the following Particulars.

Oversight in not taking the Fort de la Prée.

The French attack the English in their Retreat.

The Losses of the English at the Isle of Rhe.

1. The Want of timely Supplies of Money.
2. The not adhering to the Resolutions at first taken; for although all the Ships had their sealed Rendezvous for St. *Martin*'s, yet was it determined, when the Fleet was at Sea, to go to *Bourdeaux*; and although the chiefest Hopes of Success depended on Expedition, yet were

Principal Causes of our ill Success as the Isle of Rhe.

were many Ships ordered to chase some which belong'd to *Dunkirk*, until it was within an Hour of Night, insomuch that the Fleet was thereby divided, and those which gave chase wandered to and fro at least eight Days, not daring to go either to St. *Martin*'s or *Bourdeaux*, lest they should be discovered, nay even those forty which remained in a Body were upon the Point of returning, for Want of sufficient Provisions for the Soldiers.

3. That before *Soubize* was sent to *Rochelle*, the Duke acquainted him with his Thoughts of landing the Troops on the Isle of *Oleron*, which he well approved of, the Forces there being but few, and the Forts weakly mann'd and victual'd, dissuading him at the same time from going to the Isle of *Rhe*, because there was on that Island a considerable Force of Horse and Foot, and a Citadel well fortified; but the Duke not staying for the Return of *Soubize*, altered his Resolution, and shaped his Course for the Isle of *Rhe*.

4. When the Troops were landed, and had, by the Assistance of Providence, put to flight the Enemy's Troops that oppos'd them, the taking Advantage of the Fear and Confusion they were in was wholly neglected; for four Days time was given them to gather into the Citadel most of the Provisions of the Town and Country.

5. The leaving the Fort *de la Prée* behind them near the Place where they landed, without so much as summoning it, which gave the Enemy an Opportunity of landing three or four thousand Men, and two hundred Horse in the Month of *October*, by which our Troops were defeated, as hath been related.

6. That although our Fleet was of sufficient Strength to engage all they might have met with, yet for Want of small, and proper Vessels, the Enemy's Barks very often carried Supplies to the Citadel which lay open to the Sea.

7. The General's not being governed by the Opinion of the Officers at a Council of War, who were (as hath been already observed) not only against attacking the Citadel, but gave their Reasons for the same under their Hands, notwithstanding which the Duke ordered an Assault to be given to it, wherein we lost near five hundred Men, without doing the Enemy any considerable Damage.

The French King blocks up the Rochellers and the Earl of Denbigh sent to their Assistance. 1628.

Our Fleet and Troops being gone, the *French* King closely blocked up the *Rochellers*, who yet had some Dependence on the Duke of *Buckingham*, for he promised them to return to their Assistance; and tho' he did not go in Person, a Fleet of about fifty Sail were fitted out, under Command of the Earl of *Denbigh*, who set Sail therewith from *Plimouth*, the seventeenth of *April*, and came to an Anchor in the Road of *Rochelle* the first of *May*. Before the Harbour's Mouth he found twenty of the *French* King's Ships, to which he was superior in Strength, and sent word into the Town that he would sink them as soon as the Winds and Tide would permit; but being on the eighth of *May*, favoured both by one and the other, and the *Rochellers* expecting he would do what he had promised, he, without attempting it, returned to *Plimouth* the twenty sixth, which caused no small Murmurings and Jealousies in *England*.

He returns without attempting any thing.

A third

CHAP. XVIII. *Ruin of the* Rom. *Empire.* 379

A third Fleet was prepared for the Relief of *Rohelle*, to be commanded by the Duke himself, the Town being then reduced to the last Extremities, but he being, on the twenty third of *August*, stabbed at *Portsmouth* by one *Felton*, a discontented Officer, the Earl of *Lindsey* was appointed to command it, and set Sail the eighth of September. The Ships were but ill supplied with Stores and Provisions, and coming before *Rochelle*, they found no *French* Navy to oppose them, but a very strong Barricado across the Entry of the Port, to force which many brave Attempts were made, but in vain, so that the *Rochellers* being thus distressed, and in Despair, implored the *French* King's Mercy, and surrender'd on the eighteenth of *October*; soon after which a Peace ensued between the two Crowns, and the Protestants were glad to submit to any Terms, with the bare Toleration of their Religion. But very remarkable it is that our Fleet was no sooner departed from before *Rochelle*, than so great a Part of the Barricado fell down, as to make an Opening sufficient for a large Ship to pass through. *Duke of Buckingham stabbed at Portsmouth. A Fleet sails to Rochelle with the Earl of Lindsey. Rochellers submit to the French King.*

Our Reputation at Sea had suffered so much by these late Miscarriages, that Pirates of all the neighbouring Nations took the Liberty to infest the narrow Seas; and the *Dutch*, upon Pretence of some Arguments for the Freedom of Navigation, and Community of the Sea, which the learned *Hugo Grotius*, their Countryman, had made use of in a Treatise beforementioned, styled *Mare Liberum*, began to challenge a Right to the Fishery on our Coasts, which, by the Connivance of our Princes, they had been tolerated in the Use of. To refute those Arguments of theirs, and defend that Claim of ours, the famous Mr. *Selden* was employed by the King, (as we have before observ'd) to write his excellent *Mare Clausum*, wherein he having with great Industry, Learning, and Judgment, asserted the Right of the Crown of *England* to the Dominion of the *British* Seas, the King paid such Honour to the Performance, that, shortly after the Publication, he made an Order in Council that one of those Books should be kept in the Council Chest, another in the Court of Exchequer, and a third in the Court of Admiralty, as a faithful and strong Evidence to the Dominion of the *British* Sea. But more effectually to assert the same, a Fleet of sixty stout Ships of War was, the same Year, fitted out under the Command of *Algernoon* Earl of *Northumberland*, now made Lord High Admiral, who sailing to the Northward, where the *Dutch* Busses were fishing on our Coasts, required them to desist, which they not readily doing, he fired at them, took and sunk some, and dispersed the rest; whereupon the *Dutch* sollicited the Admiral to mediate with the King that they might have Leave go on with their fishing this Summer, for which they would pay to his Majesty thirty thousand Pound; and they accordingly did so, and signified their Inclination to have a Grant from the King to do the like for the future, upon paying a yearly Tribute. *Pirates of all Nations infest the English Seas. Grotius writes his Mare Liberum, and Selden his Mare Clausum.*

1636.

Dutch fishing Busses attacked by the Earl of Northumberland. The Dutch pay a Tribute to fish.

In 1639 the *Spanish* Fleet under *Don Antonio de Oquendo*, appeared on the *English* Coasts, and had that Engagement with the *Dutch*

1639.

Ccc2

Dutch in the *Downs*, which I have already given an Account of among the Affairs of *Spain*.

CHAP. XIX.

Of the Naval Transactions of the English, *from the Breaking out of the first* Dutch *War in* 1652, *to the Revolution in* 1688.

<small>Civil Wars in England.</small>
NOT long after this broke out our unhappy Civil Wars, during which, from the time the King, upon the first open Rupture with the Parliament, failed in his Design of seizing the Fleet, we find nothing memorable at Sea, (except the Reduction of the Isles of *Scilly* to the Obedience of the Parliament by Admiral *Blake*, and of *Barbadoes*, *Nevis*, and St. *Christopher*'s by Sir *George Ascough*) till the Beginning of the first War with the *Dutch* <small>1652.</small> in 1652. The Occasion thereof, as we have elsewhere related, was <small>Occasions of the first War with the Dutch.</small> the Neglect of the *Dutch* in punishing the Assassinators of Dr. *Dorislaus*, the Parliament's Agent, and the Slight put upon their Ambassadors soon after; the not giving Satisfaction on the old Affair of *Amboina*, and other Injuries done to the *English* in their Trade in the *Indies*, and elsewhere. The *Dutch*, however, seemed willing to come to any reasonable Terms, and a Treaty was in Agitation when *Van Tromp*, their Admiral, with a Fleet of forty four Sail (said by the *Dutch* to be fitted out only for the Protection of their Trade) came, on the seventeenth of *May*, into *Dover* Road, which the *English* interpreting as a Challenge to a Battel, Admiral *Blake*, who lay in the *Downs* with about fifteen Ships of War, plied up to him; whereupon *Tromp* stood away to the Eastward, but two Hours after tacking about, he bore down to the <small>Blake fights the Dutch Fleet.</small> *English* Fleet, which drew up in a Line of Battel; and the Admiral, on the Approach of *Van Tromp*'s Ship with his Flag hoisted, fired three Shot, at some distance from each other, at the Flag, to make him strike. At the third Shot, *Van Tromp* discharged a Broadside on the *English* Admiral, who answer'd it in like manner, and after the Exchange of two or three more Broadsides, Captain *Bourne* coming in to *Blake*'s Assistance with eight stout Ships, it came to a general Engagement, which lasted from four in the Afternoon till Night, when they both separated; the *English* having not so much as one Ship disabled, and but very few Men killed, but the *Dutch* lost two Ships, the one sunk, and the other taken, and had about a hundred and fifty Men slain. The *Dutch* Ministers then at *London*, being very desirous the Treaty should go on, disowned this <small>The Dutch disown the Proceedings of Tromp.</small> Proceeding of their Admiral's, and the States sent another Ambassador on purpose to excuse it; but the Parliament would now hear

of

CHAP. XIX. *Ruin of the* Rom. *Empire.* 381

of no Propositions, without being first paid and satisfied for the Charge they had been at this Summer, on account of the States Preparations: Whereupon the Ambassadors were recalled, and Resolutions taken on both sides for vigorously prosecuting the War. Very soon after this *Van Tromp* came to Sea again with a Fleet of a hundred and twenty Sail, but was not early enough to prevent Admiral *Blake*'s sailing to the Northward with seventy Men of War, to disperse the *Dutch* Herring Busses, (several of which he took, with twelve Ships of War which attended them) and to look out for five *East-India* Ships of that Nation, then expected home by the North of *Scotland*. Blake *attacks the* Dutch Busses.

In the mean time Sir *George Ascough* arriving in the *Downs* from *Barbadoes* with a Squadron of fifteen Men of War, and several *Dutch* Prizes he had taken by the way, received Orders to remain there till he should be reinforced by some Ships fitting out from the River; of which *Van Tromp* receiving Intelligence, came with the main Body of the Fleet, and lay between the North Foreland and the North-Sand Head, in order both to prevent Sir *George*'s Retreat that way, and intercept the Ships coming from the River to his Assistance, and detached a strong Squadron to continue off the South Foreland and hinder his escaping that way. But upon Notice of this Posture of the Enemy's, the Ships in the River were countermanded, and *Tromp*, tired with expecting them, resolved to attack Sir *George Ascough* in the *Downs*, but he found so good Preparation made for his Reception by the Militia's being drawn down to the Coasts, and a Platform suddenly raised between *Deal* and *Sandown* Castles, that he thought fit to abandon that Design, and returned to *Holland*.

Their *Baltick* Trade being now ready to sail, *Tromp* was ordered to see them in Safety towards the *Sound*, which having done, he sailed in search of *Blake*, concerning whom he received Advice that having dispersed the Herring Busses, and taken their Convoy, he was gone to the *Orkney* Islands. Steering his Course thither, he luckily fell in with the five *East-India* Ships, but off those Islands met with so furious a Storm as forced him to get out to Sea, and dispersed his Fleet so, as that he returned to *Holland* with two of the *East-India* Men and half his own Ships missing; which at length came all in, except six Frigates, which fell into the Hands of Admiral *Blake*, who soon after arrived in *Yarmouth-Roads*. Tromp *proceeds Northward in search of* Blake. *The* Dutch *Fleet dispersed by a Storm.*

In the mean while Sir *George Ascough* cruising off of *Plimouth* with about forty Sail, for the Protection of our homeward bound Trades, was met by the *Dutch* Admiral *De Ruyter*, with about fifty Men of War, with which he was convoying a Fleet of Merchant Ships bound outward. Both Admirals immediately prepared to engage, and Sir *George*, with nine of his head-most Ships, charging through the *Dutch* Fleet, got the Weather-gage, and vigorously attacking them again, continued warmly so to do for some Hours; but the rest of his Ships not duly seconding him, and the Night coming on, he thought fit to retire to *Plimouth*, and the *Dutch* having also enough of it, made the best of their way up the Chanel, Ascough *and* De Ruyter *engage off of* Plimouth.

nel, having had two Captains killed in the Engagement, with a confiderable Number of Men; and the Lofs on our fide was pretty equal with theirs.

Shortly after this, *Witte Wittens* and *De Ruyter* being appointed joint Admirals for the *Dutch*, in the room of *Van Tromp*, who, on account of fome Reflections on his Conduct in the late Expedition, had defired to remain afhore, they put to Sea in *October* with a numerous Fleet, and repaired off of the North Foreland. Thereupon Admiral *Blake*, being juft arrived in the *Downs* from the Weftward with his Fleet, made the beft of his way out to engage them. He had with him Vice-Admiral *Penne*, and Rear-Admiral *Bourne*, which latter began the Engagement, and was immediately fupported by the whole Fleet, who fought the Enemy with great Courage and Refolution for feveral Hours, and were received by them with equal Bravery, till at length the *Dutch* Rear-Admiral being boarded and taken, two of their Ships funk, and another blown up, the *Dutch* Admirals fheered off with the reft of their Fleet very much fhattered to the Coafts of *Zealand*, within twelve Leagues of which they were purfued by the victorious *Englifh*.

The Englifh *and* Dutch *Fleets engage near the North Foreland.*

Whilft the War was profecuted in this manner at home, Captain *Badily*, who commanded four or five *Englifh* Frigates in the Mediterranean, was attacked by fixteen Men of War under the Command of *Van Galen*, the *Dutch* Admiral in that Sea, with whom he bravely engaged, but was forced to give way to fo unequal an Enemy, and having loft the *Phœnix*, one of his Ships, retired with the reft under the Protection of the Duke of *Tufcany*'s Caftle of *Porto Longone*: But *Van Galen* loft his Life in the Engagement, and the *Phœnix* was fhortly after retaken.

Badily *attack'd by the* Dutch *in the* Mediterranean.

Van Tromp being foon reftored to the Office of Admiral, and refolving on fome great Enterprize to wipe off the late Reflections caft on him, he in a fhort time got together a Fleet of eighty Ships of War, with ten Firefhips, with which he repaired off of the Goodwin Sands, near the Place where the late Battel was fought. *Blake* being then in the *Downs* with forty Sail, refolved, tho' fo much inferior, to give him Battel, and got under fail accordingly, fending out feven Ships ahead to difcover the Enemy; which being met on the twenty ninth of *November* by nine of theirs on the like Service, they began the Engagement, and were foon fupported by their refpective Admirals, with the reft of their Fleets, who fought with great Fury from two in the Morning till fix at Night, when the fuperior Numbers of the *Dutch* prevailed, and *Blake* retired to the *Downs*, with the Lofs of the *Bonadventure* and *Garland* taken by the Enemy, of another Ship which was burnt, and three funk; and had not the Night favoured his Retreat, the whole Fleet had gone near to have been deftroyed. As for the *Dutch*, they purchafed the Victory at a dear rate, having loft a great Number of Men, and had one of their Flag-Ships blown up, and the other two much damaged. *Van Tromp* proceeding thence to the Ifle of *Rhe* for the *Dutch* homeward-bound Trade, which were to rendezvous at that Ifland, is faid to have paffed down the Chanel with a Broom at his

Blake *fights the* Dutch *Fleet near the* Goodwin Sands.

CHAP. XIX. *Ruin of the* Rom. *Empire.* 383

his Main-top-maſt Head, as it were to ſweep the Seas of the *Engliſh*.

In the mean time the Parliament were very induſtrious to repair the late Diſhonour, and with great Expedition fitted out a numerous Fleet to intercept the *Dutch* in their Return, which was put under the joint Command of *Blake, Monk,* and *Deane.* Upon Advice of theſe Preparations, the States ſent an Expreſs to *Tromp,* at the Iſle of *Rhe,* to return with all ſpeed, and prevent the *Engliſh* from coming out by blocking up the River; but *Tromp,* to his great Amazement, when he was got the Heighth of *Portland,* fell in with the *Engliſh* Fleet, conſiſting of eighty Sail, he having with him ſeventy ſix Men of War, with three hundred Merchant Ships under his Convoy. The eighteenth of *February,* about eight in the Morning, the *Triumph,* wherein were the Admirals *Blake* and *Deane,* with twelve Ships more, for the reſt could not yet come up, engaged board and board with the Groſs of the *Dutch* Fleet, and the *Triumph* having received many Shot in her Hull, began to be hard preſſed by the Enemy, when ſhe was bravely relieved by Captain *Lawſon* in the *Fairfax.* Thoſe two being incloſed by a Number of the Enemy's largeſt Ships, ſuffered much from them, and had each about a hundred Men killed and wounded: *Blake* himſelf received a Hurt in his Thigh, and his Captain and Secretary were both ſlain by his ſide. The *Proſperous,* of forty four Guns, was boarded by the *Dutch,* but preſently recovered again. The Captain of the *Vanguard* was killed, and ſeveral of the Ships much diſabled, but not one taken. As for the Enemy, they had ſix Men of War either ſunk or taken, one of which carried a Flag, and great Deſtruction was made among the Officers and Seamen on board *Tromp*'s own Ship; who having been thus roughly handled, made the beſt of his way up the Chanel. The *Engliſh* Admirals having ſent into *Portſmouth* the Ships which had ſuffered moſt in the Fight, followed the Enemy, and coming up with them off of *Dungeneſs,* began another Engagement. *Tromp* putting his Merchant Ships before him, bravely ſtood the firſt Charge, but then made a running Fight of it, retreating toward the *French* Coaſt; in which Retreat Captain *Lawſon* boarded one of the *Dutch* Men of War, and brought her off, and other of our Ships took ſeveral of their Merchant-men. The next Morning the Fight was renewed, and laſted with great Fury till four in the Afternoon, when the *Dutch* retreated to the Sands before *Calais,* and from thence tided it into the *Wielings,* having loſt in theſe three Days Actions eleven Ships of War, and thirty Merchant Ships, fifteen hundred Men killed, and a great Number of Priſoners. On our ſide there was but one Ship ſunk, though the Number of our Slain was not much inferior to the Enemy's.

margin: 1653. Blake and Deane fight the Dutch near Portland.

margin: Another Fight near Dungeneſs.

margin: A third Engagement.

Soon after this the Parliament ſetting out a Fleet of a hundred Sail under the Command of the Generals *Monk* and *Deane,* aſſiſted by Vice-Admiral *Penne* and Mr. *Lawſon,* now made a Rear-Admiral, they went over to look for the Enemy on their own Coaſts, who were come out on the ſame Errand with a hundred and four

Sail,

Sail, commanded by *Van Tromp, De Ruyter, Witte Wittens,* and *Evertz.* Off of *Newport* the two Fleets came to an Engagement, which lasted, with very little Intermission, from eleven in the Morning till Night, wherein at the first Charge General *Deane* was shot off in the middle by a Cannon Bullet. *Lawson* performed great Exploits during the whole time, and pressed so hard upon *De Ruyter*, that he had like to have carried him, had he not been seasonably relieved by *Van Tromp*; but he nevertheless sunk one of the Enemy's Ships of forty two Guns. The next Day, about Noon, the Fight was renewed with greater Fury, and continued till ten at Night, wherein six of the Enemy's best Ships were sunk, two blown up, and eleven Ships and two Hoys taken, with thirteen hundred and fifty Prisoners, six of them Captains of Note; with which Loss the *Dutch* retired among the Flats on the *Flanders* Coast, whither it was not thought safe to follow them, though *Blake* was come in, toward the Conclusion of the Battel, with eighteen fresh Ships.

Monk and Deane fight the Dutch near Newport.

Upon this Defeat the States made private Overtures of Peace to *Cromwell*, who had now got rid of his Parliament, and managed all Affairs himself; but at the same time they used the utmost Diligence in fitting out a strong Fleet, to recover, if possible, their lost Reputation by another Battel: And by the latter end of *July*, *Tromp* put to Sea with ninety five Ships from *Zealand*, being soon after joined by *Witte Wittens* with twenty five from the *Texel*.

The Dutch make Overtures of Peace to Cromwell.

At the head of this Force he was met, on the twenty ninth of *July*, by the *English* Fleet of about a hundred and six Ships, under the Command of *Monk, Penne,* and *Lawson*; and presently there began the most fierce and bloody Battel which had been yet fought; for *Monk* having observed that the War was very tedious and burthensome to the Nation, and that the taking of Ships in a Fight always weakened the Fleet by sending off other Ships with them, he, to make short work of it, gave Orders that his Captains should neither give nor take Quarter: So that in few Hours the Air was filled with the Fragments of Ships blown up, and human Bodies, and the Sea dyed with the Blood of the Slain and Wounded.

Monk, Penne and Lawson fight the Dutch.

At length, after a Fight of about six Hours, *Van Tromp*, as he was bravely performing his Duty, encouraging his Men, and dispensing his Orders, was shot with a Musket Bullet into the Heart, of which he presently fell dead; and the rest of his Fleet being by this time cruelly broken and shattered, discouraged by this Loss, made the best of their way to the *Texel*. The *English* having sunk thirty three of the Enemy's Ships in this Battel, and taken about twelve hundred Prisoners, (which, notwithstanding the forbidding of Quarter, they compassionately took up as they were swimming about) did not think fit to pursue far, but retired to *Solebay*, having purchased the Victory with considerable Loss; for they had four hundred Men and eight Captains slain or drowned in the Fight, and about seven thousand wounded. The *Dutch* had suffered so extremely, that they presently sued for a Peace, and were glad to accept

Van Tromp killed.

cept it on *Cromwell*'s own Terms, which we have mentioned in another Place.

Not long after this, the Protector resolving to break with *Spain*, fitted out a strong Squadron under the Command of Vice-Admiral *Penne*, with a considerable Body of Land Forces on board, commanded by General *Venables*, to make some profitable Attempt in the *Spanish West-Indies*. And since this Expedition was what the Protector had very much at Heart, being induced to hope, from the Encouragement given him by a Person who had long resided in those Parts, that with the Fleet and Army he should be able not only to make himself Master of the Islands, but of great part of the Continent also, with the Riches thereof; and that the Miscarriage in a Design which put the Nation to so great an Expence, and ended so much to his own Dishonour, gave him more Disquiet than any one thing of the like Nature which had happened during his usurped Government, I have thought it necessary to set down the best Account I am able to come at, from the beginning to the end of this fruitless Expedition, which was so, in all its Circumstances untill the Land-Forces were taken on board from *Hispaniola*, and, with the Fleet, proceeded to *Jamaica*, and took that Island.

1654. Penne *and* Venables *sent to the West-Indies.*

In the first Place, therefore, it is proper that I acquaint you what Instructions *Oliver* thought fit to give to General *Venables* for his Government in this Affair, it having not been in my Power to procure a Copy of those which General *Penne* received; nor is the want of them of any great Consequence, since their Contents could be no better than the requiring him to protect the Troops in their Passage; to add some of the Seamen to them when there should be occasion, and otherwise assist them when put on shore; to conduct them from one Place to another, and to seize or destroy any Shipping of the Enemy which he might meet with, or find at those Places, the said *Penne*, as well as *Venables*, (besides the Power given them as Generals at Sea and Land) being joined in Commission with other Persons, without whose Advice, and Concurrence, or that of some of them at least, they were not to undertake any thing of Moment, in the whole Course of an Expedition from which so much Advantage was expected by *Oliver* and his Council.

Instructions to General Robert Venables. *Given by his Highness, by Advice of his Council, upon the Expedition to the* West-Indies.

WHereas we have, by our Commission, constituted and appointed you Commander in Chief of the Land-Army and Troops raised, and to be raised, as well in *England*, as in the Parts of *America*, for the Ends and Purposes in the said Commission; you shall therefore,

I. Immediately upon the Receipt of these Instructions repair with the Forces aforesaid unto *Portsmouth*, where we have appointed the Fleet

Fleet defigned for the aforefaid Service, under the Command of General *William Penne*, to take you, with the faid Army and Land-Forces, on board, and to tranfport you unto the Parts aforefaid.

II. Whereas fome additional Forces, as the Service fhall require, are to be raifed in the Ifland of *Barbadoes*, and other the *Englifh* Iflands and Plantations, you fhall, upon your Arrival there, and upon Confideration had with the Commiffioners appointed to attend this Service, or any two of them, (wherein alfo, if you think fit, you may advife with fome of the moft experienced Men in thofe Parts) concerning the prefent Defign, and the Nature thereof, to ufe your beft Endeavours by fuch Means and Meafures as you, with the Advice of the faid Commiffioners, or any two of them, fhall judge moft convenient and expeditious, to levy and raife fuch Numbers of Soldiers as fhall be found neceffary for the better carrying on of this Defign, the faid Soldiers to be either taken with you upon your firft Attempt, or to follow you, as fhall be, by the Advice aforefaid, agreed and directed. And we have thought fit to leave unto your Difcretion, by the Advice aforefaid, what Numbers of Men fhall be raifed, as alfo the manner and means of doing thereof, becaufe you may not, at that diftance, be tied up by any Inftruction which may not fuit with, and be agreeable to fuch Accidents as may happen and fall out upon the Place, but may be at liberty to proceed upon the Defign either without any Addition of Forces in the Iflands and Plantations aforefaid, or with a lefs or greater Addition, as you fhall find the Nature of the Service to require. And you have alfo Power and Authority, from time to time, by your Warrant, to caufe fuch farther Supplies of Men to be levied in any of the faid Iflands for the aforefaid Service as you, with the Advice aforefaid, fhall find neceffary.

III. The Defign in general is to gain an Intereft in that part of the *Weft-Indies* in the Poffeffion of the *Spaniard*, for the effecting whereof we fhall not tie you up to a Method by any particular Inftructions, but only communicate what hath been under our Confideration. Two or three ways have been thought of to that purpofe.

1. The firft is to land on fome of the Iflands, and particularly *Hifpaniola*, and St. *John*'s Ifland, one or both; but the firft, if that hath no confiderable Place in the South part thereof but the City of St. *Domingo*, and that not being confiderably fortified, may probably be poffeffed without much difficulty, which being done and fortified, that whole Ifland will be brought under Obedience. The chief Place of St. *John*'s Ifland is *Porto Rico*, and the gaining of thefe Iflands, or either of them, will, as we conceive, amongft many others, have thefe Advantages.

(1.) Many *Englifh* will come thither from other Parts, and fo thofe Places become Magazines of Men and Provifions for carrying on the Defign upon the main Land.

(2.) They will be fure Retreats upon all occafions.

(3.) They lie much to Windward of the reft of the King of *Spain*'s Dominions, and being in the Hands of the *Spaniards*, will enable

enable him to supply any part which is distressed on the Main, and being in our Hands, will be of the same use to us.

(4.) From thence you may possibly, after your landing there, send Force for the taking of the *Havana*, on the Island of *Cuba*, which is the Back-door of the *West-Indies*, and will obstruct the passing of the *Spaniards* Plate-Fleet into *Europe*; and the taking of the *Havana* is so considerable, that we have had Thoughts of beginning the first Attempt upon that Fort, and the Island of *Cuba*, and do still judge it worthy of Consideration.

2. Another way we have had Consideration of, is, for the present, to leave the Islands, and to make the first Attempt upon the main Land, in one or more Places between the River *Oronoque* and *Porto Bello*, aiming therein chiefly at *Carthagena*, which we would make the Seat of the intended Design, securing some Places by the way thereto, that the *Spaniard* might not be to the Windward of us upon the main Land, wherein, if you have Success, you will probably,

(1.) Be Masters of all the *Spanish* Treasure which comes from *Peru* by the way of *Panama* in the *South Sea*, to *Porto Bello* or *Nombre de Dios* in the *North Sea*.

(2.) You will have Houses ready built, a Country ready planted, and most of the People *Indians*, who will submit to you, there being but few *Spaniards* there, as is informed.

(3.) You will be able to put the Country round about under Contribution for the Maintenance of the Army, and therewith by the Spoil, and otherwise, probably, make a great present Return of Profit to the Commonwealth.

3. There is a Third Consideration, and that is mixed, relating both to the Islands, and also to the main Land, which is, to make the first Attempt upon St. *Domingo*, or *Porto Rico*, one or both, and having secured them, to go immediately to *Carthagena*, leaving that which is to the Windward of it to a farther Opportunity, after you have secured and settled that City, with what does relate thereto, if God doth please to give that Place into your Hands.

These are the Things which have been in Debate here, and having let you know them, we leave it to you, and the Commissioners appointed, to be weighed upon the Place, that after due Consideration had among your selves, and such others as you shall think fit to advise with who have a particular Knowledge of those Parts, you may take such Resolutions concerning the making the Attempts, in the managing and carrying on the whole Design, as to you, and the said Commissioners, or any two of them, shall seem most effectual, either by the ways aforesaid, or such others as shall be judged more reasonable. And for the better enabling you to execute such Resolutions as shall be taken in the Premises, you are hereby authorized and required to use your best Endeavours, wherein General *Penne*, Commander in Chief of the Fleet, is by us required to join with, and assist you with the Fleet and Sea-Forces, as often as there shall be occasion, to land your Men upon any of the Territories, Dominions, and Places belonging unto, or in the Possession of the *Spa-niards*

niards in *America*, and to surprize their Forts, take, or beat down their Castles, and Places of Strength, and to pursue, kill, and destroy, by all means whatsoever, all those who shall oppose or resist you therein, and also to seize upon all Ships and Vessels which you find in any of their Harbours, and also upon all such Goods as you shall find upon the Land.

IV. Such Resolutions as shall be taken by you and the other Commissioners, concerning the way and manner of making your first Attempt, and what you do design thereupon, you shall certify unto us by Express, and as many other ways as you can, to the end we may know whither to send unto you upon all Occasions which may fall out.

V. In case it shall please God to give you Success, such Places as you shall take, and shall judge fit to keep, you shall keep for the use of us, and this Commonwealth, and shall also cause such Goods and Prizes as may be taken to be delivered into the Hands of the said Commissioners, that so they may be brought to a just and true Account for the publick Advantage.

VI. You have hereby Power, with the Advice of the said Commissioners, or any two of them, to place Garrisons in any such Places as shall be taken in, and to appoint fit Governors thereof, and to give them Commissions under your Hand and Seal accordingly, and to slight the said Garrisons, and remove the said Governors, as you, by Advice aforesaid, shall think necessary, and for our Service.

VII. You have hereby Power and Authority, by the Advice aforesaid, to give reasonable Conditions to such Persons as will submit to our Government, and willingly come under our Obedience, and also to treat and conclude for the surrendering of any Fort, Castle, or Place into our Hands, having in all your Transactions care of preserving the Interest of this Commonwealth. And you are to use your best Endeavours, as far as it is practicable, that no dangerous Persons be suffered to abide long in any Place possessed by you, unless they be in Custody; and such as shall be taken as Prisoners, you shall use your best Endeavours, either by sending them into *Europe*, or otherwise, as you shall find most expedient, that they may not be again serviceable to the Enemy in those Parts.

VIII. You shall have Power, by the Advice aforesaid, to raise such Forces as shall be judged necessary, in any of the Parts which you shall gain the Possession of, as aforesaid, and to appoint Commanders and Officers over them, and to arm, lead, conduct, and dispose of them for the Purposes aforesaid.

IX. You shall give unto us as frequent Accounts as may be of all your Proceedings, that so you may receive our farther Directions thereupon, as shall be necessary.

X. Whereas all Particulars cannot be foreseen, nor positive Instructions for such Emergences so, beforehand, given, but most things must be left to your prudent and discreet Management, as Occurrences may arise upon the Place, or from time to time fall out; you are therefore, upon all such Accidents relating to your Charge, to

use

use your best Circumspection, and by Advice either with the said Commissioners, or your Council of War, as occasion may be, to order and dispose of the Forces under your Command, as may be most advantageous for the Publick, and for obtaining the Ends for which those Forces were raised, making it your especial Care, in discharge of that great Trust committed to you, that the Commonwealth may receive no Detriment.

When General *Venables* (who had been very serviceable to the Protector in the Reduction of *Ireland*) was first pitched upon to command the Troops designed on the aforementioned Expedition, he made it his Request that he might be furnished with Arms, Ammunition, and all things necessary for a Design of this Nature, for that otherwise very great Disappointments might happen, should he not carry them with him from hence, since they could not possibly be found abroad. He also made it his Request that he might not be cramp'd by Commissions, or Instructions to other Persons, for he then knew that *Oliver* intended to send Commissioners, with large Power to inspect into, advise, and controul the Actions of those who were to be principally employed in this Expedition; but how little regard was had to what he thus desired, will appear in the ensuing Relation, as also how he was contradicted and slighted by those in chief Authority. *Demands of Arms, Ammunition, &c. made by Venables.*

The Squadron, commanded by General *Penne*, being ordered to rendezvous at *Portsmouth*, where the Land-Forces were to embark, Complaints were made to *Venables* of Disorders and Discontents among the People, and more particularly about the Badness of the Provisions, which, by his means, being made known to General *Desborow*, he, by very harsh Expressions, signified his Discontent thereat, and particularly charged *Venables* with design of frustrating the intended Expedition, by being the Author of Reports which were false, while he, on the other hand, endeavoured to justify himself, and to shew that he intended no otherwise than for the publick Good: And there was a shrewd Suspicion that *Desborow*'s Dissatisfaction herein arose from his being concerned with those who had the Management of victualling the Navy. *Complaints made of the Provisions.*

After *Venables* had attended near four Months, without any positive Assurance whether the Government was determined to go on with the Design or not, although it was publickly discoursed of, and the *Spaniards* had thereby not only the Knowledge thereof, but Opportunities of providing for their Defence, he was some time after sent to, and directed to hold himself in a Readiness to proceed; and though he then requested that the Draughts which were to be made out of the Regiments might be Men in all respects fitting for the intended Service, yet the Colonels were permitted to pick and cull them as they pleased, insomuch that most of them were raw, and altogether undisciplined, and amongst them many *Irish* Papists, nor had the half of them Arms in any degree serviceable. And so far were the Council from permitting him to stay till better could be furnished in their room, that they sent him positive *Venables at length hastened to his Charge.*

Neither Arms or Men fit for the Service

tive Orders to leave the Town next Day upon Pain of Imprisonment.

The Troops shipped off before the General could view them.

Before he came to *Portsmouth* many of the Troops were embarked, and the rest shipping off with utmost haste, so that he had no Opportunity of viewing, much less of exercising them on shore, and thereby informing himself of their Condition, with Respect to their Abilities, or otherwise. And although he was promised that the Storeship with Arms and other Necessaries should join him at *Spithead*, he was at last told that no Delay must be made in staying for her, but that he might expect her coming to him at *Barbadoes*.

Greatest Part of the Provisions left behind.

He was likewise assured that he should carry out with him ten Months Provisions for ten thousand Men, but the most Part thereof was sent back to *London*, to be shipped off there, under Pretence that there was not sufficient Room for the same in the Ships at *Portsmouth*, although the Officers of the Fleet found Passage in them for no inconsiderable Quantities of Goods, which they designed to traffick with when they arrived at the aforesaid Island.

The Squadron arrives at Barbadoes. 1654.

The Forces being embarked, and the Wind presenting fair, the Squadron sailed, and arrived at *Barbadoes* the twenty ninth Day of *January* 1654, soon after which General *Venables* wrote to the Protector, the Lord President of the Council, *Lawrence*, the Lord *Lambert*, and several others, letting them know in what a miserable Condition the Army was, and how destitute they were not only of Provisions, but of Arms and other Necessaries proper for carrying on the intended Design, insomuch that they were constrained to make the hardest Shifts to supply themselves with the small Quantities, either of one or the other, that could be had in those Parts.

The bad Condition of the Army.

Some Dutch Vessels seized at Barbadoes.

The first thing which was done after the Fleet's Arrival at *Barbadoes* was the seizing such *Dutch* Ships and Vessels as were found there, and General *Penne* appointed a Nephew of his to take an Account of their Cargoes, and all Things belonging to them, without admitting any Checque on him, as General *Venables* desired and insisted on, that so no Embezzlements might be made.

A Council of War of Land Officers.

The eighteenth of *March Venables* thought it necessary to hold a Council of War of the Land Officers, to consider of the State of the Army, and it was resolved to make these Propositions to *Penne* among several others, *viz.*

1. That as the Officers of the Army had resolved not to desert the Fleet, he with his Officers would reciprocally resolve not to leave the Army, at least not till such time as their expected Supplies arrived from *England.*

2. That it should be proposed to the Commissioners that a fitting Quantity of Shipping might be taken up for transporting the Forces.

3. That they might not proceed on Service with less than twenty Tuns of Ball, and that they might likewise be furnished from the Fleet with two hundred Fire Arms, six hundred Pikes, besides Pistols, Carabines, and two hundred Half-Pikes.

To this *Venables* received no satisfactory Answer from *Penne*, and the Stores not arriving from *England*, he again desired to know

from

CHAP. XIX. *Ruin of the* Rom. *Empire.* 391

from him what Arms, Shot, Match, and other Necessaries he could furnish from the Fleet, General *Desborow* having assured him, when in *England*, that the Commissioners had Power to dispose of what might be on board the Ships to the necessary Use of the Army; but to this *Penne* returned him an Answer, that fifteen Shot a Man, and a few Tuns of Match, was all he could spare; besides which he, at length, prevailed with him to add thereunto a few half and quarter Pikes, which gave occasion to one of the Commissioners to let fall some Words, as if he doubted they were betrayed. *But small Supplies of Arms, &c. from the Fleet.*

Besides all these Disappointments, and the Badness of the Provisions sent from *England*, yet even of that the Soldiers were put to short Allowance, while the Seamen were at whole, which occasioned no little Discontent, and rendered them very sickly and weak. And as the Commissioners were empowered and required to dispose of all Prizes and Booty taken, towards defraying the Charge of the Expedition, and only a Fortnight's Pay was offered to the Officers and Soldiers, in lieu of whatever Booty should be taken at St. *Domingo* (whither they were first designed from *Barbadoes)* it very much increased the Dissatisfaction of the Army, for most of the Officers, when they set forward on the Expedition, were in Hopes of bettering their Fortunes very considerably. *The Soldiers at short Allowance of Provisions.* *The Soldiers restrained from Booty.*

At length General *Venables* prevailed with the Officers and Men to accept of six Week's Pay instead of their Plunder, and thereupon himself and *Penne* issued out Orders restraining all Persons from pillaging without Licence, or from concealing the same on Pain of Death, and Forfeiture of their Pay; but although the Officers were willing to submit to this, yet the Commissioners refused to sign to it, insomuch that the Soldiers publickly declared they would return to *England*, and never more strike Stroke where there were Commissioners who should have Power to controul the Army.

The Fleet being now in a Readiness to sail, General *Venables*, with some of the Commissioners, and the Officers of the Army, proposed that they might proceed directly into the Harbour of St. *Domingo* but (for what Reasons it doth not appear, unless it was for Want of experienced Pilots) that was refused, and a Resolution taken to land the Troops at the River *Hine*, that so they might endeavour to force the Fort and Trench. *Venables proposes to go into the Harbour of St. Domingo.*

It was also resolved among the Land Officers. *Determinations how to land the Troops.*

1. That the Regiments should cast Lots which of them should go on shore first.

2. That two or three Regiments should be landed at once.

3. That the Seconds to each Regiment should be appointed.

4. That the Ships wherein the Regiments were should keep near each other for their more regular Landing.

And it was farther determined that if the Surge of the Sea ran high, and that the Enemy were prepared to defend the Fort and Trench, the Army should be landed behind the second Point to Leeward, and that, when on shore, one Regiment should be ordered to march Eastward of the City, provided General *Penne* would engage to furnish the Army with all Necessaries.

Lots

Lots having been cast as aforesaid, it fell to Collonel *Buller*'s Regiment to land first; and there was one *Cox*, who had lived in those Parts many Years, was to have been their Guide, but he had been sent on some Errand by *Penne*, so that he was at this time absent; and Vice-Admiral *Goodson* declaring that he neither had Orders to go into *Hine* River, nor Pilots to conduct the Ships thereinto, the Army were constrained to land at the West Point (which *Venables* protested against) and by that means were exposed to a tedious March of forty Miles through a thick woody Country, without any Guide, insomuch that both Horse and Men by the Fatigue, and Extremity of Heat, fell down with Thirst, and were miserably afflicted with the Flux by their eating Oranges, and other green Fruit, having no Water to moisten their Mouths with.

The Troops much exposed for Want of Provisions, &c.

After four Days March the Army came to the Place where they might have been first put on shore, but by that time the Enemy had summoned in the whole Country to their Assistance, and even now many of the Soldiers had no more than one Day's bare Provisions of the three that had been promised them from the Ships.

Colonel *Buller* being sent with his Regiment to a particular Station near *Hine* River, and ordered not to stir from thence until the rest of the Army joined him, he was so far from complying with those Commands from the General, that he marched away under the Guidance of *Cox*, who was now arrived from the Fleet, insomuch that for Want of the said Guide, the General mistaking the Way marched ten or twelve Miles about, and *Buller* having suffered his Men to straggle, they fell into, and suffered much by Ambuscades laid by the Enemy.

Col. Buller leaves the Station assigned him.

The Hardships the Forces had undergone for Want of Provisions, and their being deny'd what Plunder they might happen to take at St. *Domingo*, so exasperated them, that the Seamen first, who had been set on shore, and soon after those of the Land, were in a general Mutiny. However, in this Condition, they forded the River *Hine*, with a Resolution to march to the Harbour, that so they might be furnished with Provisions and Ammunition from the Ships, but they were altogether Strangers to the Way, neither had they any Water to drink.

A Mutiny.

At length Colonel *Buller*, and *Cox* the Guide joined them, and promised to conduct them to a Place where they might be supplied with Water; but some of the said Colonel's Men having rambled about for Pillage, encouraged the Enemy to lay Ambuscades for them in their March, who falling upon the Forlorn routed them, and killed several Officers, but they were soon after beaten back with Loss, and pursued within Cannon shot of the Town, not but that when the Action was over, many Men, as well as Horses, perished with Thirst.

The Spaniards attack our Forlorn.

A Council of War being called to consider the Condition of the Army, it was found that many of the Men had eat nothing for four Days together, unless it were some Fruits they gathered in the Woods, and that they were without Water, the *Spaniards* having stopt up all their Wells within several Miles of the Town, neither knew they

the

CHAP. XIX. *Ruin of the* Rom. *Empire.* 393

the Country, or how to get to their Ships, for *Cox* their Guide was slain in the late Skirmish. However, after mature Consideration, it was resolved to march to the Harbour in the best manner they could, and at length arriving there, they stay'd three or four Days to furnish themselves with Provisions and other Necessaries, and then advanced with a Mortar Piece, in order to reduce the Fort; but the Enemy having laid an Ambuscade, they charged the Van, which was to have been led by Adjutant General *Jackson*, very vigorously, and were answered in like Manner, whereas *Jackson*'s Parry running away, and the Passage through the Woods being very narrow, they fell upon the General's own Regiment, who, to no purpose, endeavoured to stop them with their Pikes, for they first disordered that Regiment, and soon after Major General *Haynes*'s; mean while the Enemy followed very eagerly, and giving no Quarter, the said Major General, and the best of the Officers, who preferred Death before Flight, fell in the Action. *The Army marches to the Ships for Provisions, &c. and Are attack'd by the Spaniards.*

At length the General's own Regiment making Head against them, as also that of the Seamen, commanded by Vice-Admiral *Goodson*, they with their Swords forced the Runaways into the Woods, rather chusing to kill them than they should disorder the rest, which the Enemy perceiving, they retreated, and our Men kept their Ground, though the Shot from the Fort killed many of them. *The Spaniards retreat.*

The Troops nevertheless were so very weak and disheartened, that not any of them could be brought to play the Mortar against the Fort; and though the General was reduced to a very low Condition, by Reason of the Flux, he caused himself to be led from Place to Place to encourage them, but fainting at last, was forced to leave the Care to Major General *Fortescue*, who soon found that he could prevail no more than the General himself. *The English Troops disharten'd.*

It was resolved soon after at a Council of War, that since the Enemy had guarded every Pass, and that the Army were under very great Necessities for Want of Water, they should march to a Place where they had been informed a Supply thereof, and of other Necessaries, had been put on shore for them from the Ships; but in that March the Soldiers accompanied their Officers no farther than till they found them in Danger, and then left them; insomuch that the Commissioners owned, by a Letter they wrote to the Governor of *Barbadoes*, that had not the Enemy been as fearful as our own Men were, they might in a few Days have destroyed the whole Army; and withall they let him know that those who had occasioned the greatest Disorder were those of *Barbadoes* and St. *Christopher*'s, insomuch that they the said Commissioners, who were *Penne*, *Winslaw* and *Butler*, had resolved to leave the Place, and try what could be done against the Island of *Jamaica*. *The Soldiers desert their Officers when in Danger. Resolved to proceed to Jamaica.*

The Army was accordingly in little time embarked, but the sick and wounded Men were kept on the bare Decks for forty eight Hours, without either Meat, Drink, or Dressing, insomuch that Worms bred in their Sores; and even while they were on shore the Provisions sent to them were not watered, but candied with Salt, notwithstanding they had not Water sufficient to quench their Thirst; *The Army under great Hardships.*

E e e Nay

Nay after their Misfortunes on shore, *Venables* averred that *Penne* gave Rear-Admiral *Blagge* Orders not to furnish them with any more Provision of what kind soever, so that they eat up all the Dogs, Horses and Asses in the Camp, and some of them such things as were in themselves poisonous, of which about forty died; and before the Forces were embarked, Adjutant-General *Jackson* was try'd at a Court Martial, and not only sentenced to be cashier'd, and his Sword broken over his Head, but to do the Duty of a Swabber, in keeping clean the Hospital-Ship; a Punishment suitable to his notorious Cowardise.

Adjutant General Jackson cashier'd.

The Fleet and Troops arriving at *Jamaica*, Orders were issued by General *Venables* that where it should be found any Man attempted to run away, the next Man to him should put him to Death, or that if he failed so to do, he should be liable to be try'd for his Life; and now all the Troops being ready for Service, they advanced towards the Fort, which they made themselves Masters of with little Loss; and next Morning, when the Sun arose, they began to march to the *Savana*, which was near the Town, when some *Spaniards* came towards them, and desired to treat, but the General refused so to do, unless they would send them a constant Supply of Provisions, then much wanted, which they punctually did according to the Promise they had made. Soon after this the following Articles were agreed on, *viz.*

The Fleet and Army arrive at Jamaica.

The Fort taken.

Articles upon the Surrender of Jamaica.

1. That all Forts, Arms, Ammunition, and Necessaries for War, and all Kinds of Shipping in any Harbour in the Island, with their Furniture, &c. as also all Goods, Wares, Merchandizes, &c. should be delivered up to General *Venables*, or whom he should appoint for the Use of the Protector, and the Commonwealth of *England*.

2. That all and every of the Inhabitants of the Island (except some that were particularly named) should have their Lives granted, and as those who inclined to stay had leave so to do, so was it agreed to transport the others to *New Spain*, or some of the Dominions belonging to the King of *Spain* in *America*, together with their Apparel, Books, and Papers, they providing themselves with Victuals and Necessaries.

3. That all Commission Officers, and none others should be permitted to wear their Rapiers and Poniards.

4. All Artificers, and meaner Sort of People were permitted to remain on the Island, and to enjoy their Goods, provided they conformed themselves to the Laws which should be established.

Thus was the Island of *Jamaica* reduced, which the Crown of *England* hath ever since been possessed of; but General *Venables* being at length so much weakened by the Flux as that the Physicians despaired of his Life, and the Officers of the Army having unanimously pitched upon him, in case he recovered, as the only fitting Person to repair to *England*, and acquaint the Protector with their miserable Condition, being in great Want of all things, as well for Support of Life, as otherwise, he desired General *Penne*, and Colonel *Butler*, one of the Commissioners, to come to him, in order to the opening the sealed and ultimate Instructions, which two Days

CHAP. XIX. *Ruin of the* Rom. *Empire.* 395

Days afterwards they confented to do, when, with their Concurrence, he refigned his Command to Major-General *Fortefcue*, as he had Power from the Protector by the aforefaid fealed Orders to do, in cafe of any Inability; and *Penne* foon after thought it convenient, either upon the Score of Sicknefs, or otherwife, to refign, in like manner, the Command of the Fleet to Vice-Admiral *Goodfon*, fo that both of them came Home, where when they arrived they were committed to the Tower; but before that Commitment they were called before *Oliver* and his Council, where both of them, efpecially *Venables*, were feverely reprimanded for leaving the Services committed to their Charge without Authority fo to do, as was then alledged. *Venables*, notwithftanding his very bad State of Health, was not permitted to abide for fome time in his own Lodgings, but was very feverely dealt with; for as the Protector infifted on it that he fhould own his Fault in leaving the Army, and throw himfelf on his Clemency, fo he judging he had committed no Crime, but that being render'd incapable by Sicknefs, to continue in thofe Parts longer, without an inevitable Hazard of his Life, and the Protector having, in fuch Cafe, empowered the Commiffioners to commit his Charge to fome other fitting Perfon, was not willing to be his own Accufer; and though even *Penne* himfelf affured him that he would not, in the manner that was expected, own himfelf guilty of a Fault, yet (for Reafons beft known to himfelf, and the Perfuafions of others near the Protector's Perfon) he made his Submiffion before *Venables* could be prevailed with to do it, and thereupon was difcharged from his Imprifonment fome time before the other was; that Part of the Fleet which remained abroad, together with fuch of the Land Forces as were not thought neceffary to remain at *Jamaica*, being brought Home by Vice-Admiral *Goodfon*.

Penne and Venables refign their Commands, and come home, and are committed to the Tower.

While thefe things were doing in the *Weft-Indies*, Admiral *Blake*, commanding the Protector's Fleet in the Mediterranean, repaired before *Tunis*, to demand Satisfaction of that Government for their Depredations committed on the *Englifh*, amd the Reftitution of the Captives, where meeting with an infolent Reply, that he might addrefs to their Caftles of *Goletta* and *Porto Farina*, which would anfwer him with their Ordnance, he entered the Bay of *Porto Farina*, and coming within Mufquet fhot of the Caftle, under the Fire of fixty great Guns that were planted there, and in a Line the Enemy had thrown up along fhore, play'd fo furioufly upon it, that in two Hours it was made defencelefs, the Guns all difmounted, and great Part of it beaten down. Then fetting fire to nine of their Ships that lay in the Bay, he proceeded thence to *Tripoli* and *Algier*, and having made advantageous Treaties with thofe Governments, came again before *Tunis*, and found the Inhabitants now glad to fubmit to his Terms. Shortly after this, cruifing, in conjunction with General *Mountague*, off of *Cadiz*, to intercept the *Spanifh* Flota, Captain *Stayner*, with three Ships of the Fleet, fell in with eight Galleons, with which he dealt fo effectually in two or three Hours Engagement, that one was funk, another fet on fire, two were forced afhore, and two he took, having on board in Money

Blake burns the Ships at Tunis.

1656.

Capt. Stayner burns and takes fome Spanifh Galleons.

E e e 2 and

and Plate, to the Value of six hundred thousand Pounds, and only two escaped into *Cadiz*.

1657.

Early the next Spring Admiral *Blake* went out with a strong Squadron on the same Design of intercepting the *Spanish West-India* Fleet, and took his Station off of *Cadiz*, where receiving Intelligence that those Ships were arrived at *Teneriffe*, he made the best of his way to that Island. The *Flota* lay in the Bay of *Santa Cruz*, drawn up in form of a Half-Moon, with a strong Barricado before them; the Bay itself defended by seven Forts disposed round the same, with two Castles at the Entrance, which were well furnished with Ordnance: In which Posture the *Spanish* Admiral thought himself so secure, that he sent out word by a *Dutch* Merchant, *Blake might come if he durst*.

The Admiral having taken a View of the Enemy's Situation, sent in Captain *Stayner* with a Squadron to attack them, who soon forcing his Passage into the Bay, was presently supported by *Blake* with the whole Fleet. Placing some of his Ships so as that they might fire their Broadsides into the Castles and Forts, himself and *Stayner* engaged the *Spanish* Fleet, and in few Hours obtaining a complete Victory, possessed himself of all the Ships; but being not able to bring them off, he set them on fire, and they were every one burnt.

Blake *burns* Spanish Ships *at Santa Cruz.*

After this glorious Atchievement he returned to the Coasts of *Spain*, and having cruised there some time, was coming home with the Fleet to *England*, when he fell ill of a Scorbutick Fever, of which he died just as he was entering *Plimouth* Sound. *Cromwell*'s Parliament, upon the News of his Exploit at *Santa Cruz*, had ordered him a Jewel of five hundred Pound, and now upon his Death bestowed on him a solemn and sumptuous Funeral, interring him in *Henry* VII's Chapel.

Blake *dies.*

Observations *on General* Blake.

It is remarkable that this great Seaman was bred a Scholar in the University of *Oxford*, where he had taken the Degree of a Master of Arts; and it is an Observation very pertinent to Sea-Affairs which the Noble Historian, who hath written of those Times, hath left us concerning him. " He was, says he, the first Man that declined
" the old Track, and made it manifest that the Science might be at-
" tained in less time than was imagined; and despised those Rules
" which had been long in practice, to keep his Ship and his Men
" out of Danger; which had been held in former Times a Point of
" great Ability and Circumspection; as if the principal Art requi-
" site in the Captain of a Ship had been to come home safe again.
" He was the first Man that brought the Ships to contemn Castles
" on shore, which had been ever thought very formidable, and were
" discovered by him to make a Noise only, and to fright those who
" could rarely be hurt by them. He was the first that infused that
" Proportion of Courage into the Seamen, by making them see by
" Experience what mighty things they could do if they were re-
" ceiv'd; and taught them to fight in Fire as well as upon the Wa-
" ter: and though he hath been very well imitated and followed,
" he

CHAP. XIX. *Ruin of the* Rom. *Empire.* 397

"he was the first that gave the Example of that kind of Naval Courage, and bold and resolute Atchievements."

In the latter end of the Year 1658, upon occasion of the War between *Sweden* and *Denmark*, the Powers which ruled in *England* taking part with the former, sent out a strong Squadron to their Assistance under the Command of Sir *George Ascough*, but it proving a very severe Winter, he was prevented by Ice from getting farther than the *Scaw*, and returned home; and the next Year another Fleet was sent out for the same purpose under the Command of General *Mountague*; who not long after employed the same Ships in a much more honourable Service, that of bringing over from *Holland* his Sovereign King *Charles* II, who now, in the Beginning of the Year 1660, was invited by his People to come and sit on the Throne of his Ancestors.

1658. England assists the Swedes against the Danes.
1659.
General Mountague brings over King Charles II. 1660.

In 1662, the same Officer, now created Earl of *Sandwich*, was sent at the Head of a numerous Fleet, to conduct from *Lisbon* the Queen-Consort, whom receiving on board, he landed in Safety at *Portsmouth*, having off of *Lisbon* detached Sir *John Lawson* with a strong Squadron to the *Mediterranean*. That Admiral appearing before *Algier*, *Tunis*, and *Tripoli*, induced those Governments to renew their Treaties with *England*; and, in pursuance of his Negotiation at the former of those Places, above a hundred and fifty *English*, *Scotch*, and *Irish* Slaves were redeemed from Captivity by a generous Contribution of the dignified Clergy of *England*. About the same time Possession was taken of *Tangier* in *Africa*, and the Island *Bombay* in the *East-Indies*, which were part of the Queen's Portion; the former of which Places King *Charles* made a free Port, granting it all Privileges which might make it a trading City; and indeed its Situation was very advantageous for that purpose, as well as for the Security of our Commerce, and enlarging our Command in those Seas; but these Advantages were at length found not to countervail the vast Expence of fortifying and defending it against the continual Assaults of the *Moors*; so that some Years after it was found necessary to demolish it, as we shall see in its Place.

1662. The Earl of Sandwich brings the Queen from Portugal.
Sir John Lawson renews the Treaties with Algier, Tunis and Tripoli.
The English take Possession of Tangier and Bombay.

The *Dutch* having for some time continued to make great Encroachments on the *English* Trade in all Parts, and not only neglected to give any Satisfaction to the King's Minister at the *Hague* for the same, but committed open Hostilities upon the *English* on the Coast of *Guinea*, the Nation was impatient for a War with them; and they having suffered very much in the *Mediterranean* from the Pirates of *Algier*, *Tunis*, and *Tripoli*, had sent their Admiral *De Ruyter* with some Ships to accompany Vice-Admiral *Lawson* in his foremention'd Expedition thither; where *De Ruyter*, under the Countenance of the *English* Fleet, having obtained good Terms of those People, he, in Gratitude for that Act of Friendship, parting with Sir *John Lawson*, made the best of his way for *Guinea*; and having attacked our Ships on that Coast, under Rear-Admiral *Holmes*, and destroyed some of our Factories there, sailed away thence to *Barbadoes*, where he attempted to land, but being repulsed

1665. De Ruyter attacks our Ships at Guinea, &c.

fed with Loss, proceeded to *New York* and *Newfoundland*, and committed great Depredations in those Parts. The King soon receiving Advice of the treacherous Action in *Guinea*, with all Expedition fitted out a Fleet under the Command of the Duke of *York*, Prince *Rupert*, and the Earl of *Sandwich*, which sailing over to the Coasts of *Holland*, struck a universal Terror amongst the *Dutch*, who, though they had also assembled a great Fleet, under the Command of *Opdam*, durst not venture out with it from *Goree*. And while their Ships were thus pent up, their *Bourdeaux* Fleet, in its way home, fell most of them into the Hands of the *English*, who in few Weeks took above a hundred and thirty of their Merchant Ships. About this time also Vice-Admiral *Allen* cruising with a Squadron off the Streights Mouth, fell in with the *Dutch Smirna* Fleet, which he attacked and routed, sinking some of the Ships, killing *Brachel* the Commander in Chief, and possessing himself of four of the richest Ships, one of which had suffered so much in the Engagement, that she foundered at Sea in her way to *England*. The Duke of *York* not being able to draw the Enemy out, returned to the *English* Coasts, which he had no sooner done, but the *Dutch* Fleet, under *Opdam*, put to Sea from *Goree*, and came over to the *Dogger-Bank*, from whence they detached a Squadron to their own Coasts to lie in wait for the *English Hamburgh* Fleet; which, with their Convoy, supposing the Duke to have been still on the Coast, fell into the Enemy's Hands.

The English *take many Dutch Merchant Ships.*

Allen *routs the* Dutch Smirna *Fleet.*

The Dutch *take the* English Hamburgh *Fleet.*

The Duke of *York* highly incensed at this Loss, resolved to revenge it on the Enemy, and, in order to come to an Engagement with them, weighed Anchor from *Solebay* the first of *June*, and on the third coming up with the *Dutch* Fleet, did accordingly engage them, and obtained an entire Victory, taking eighteen of their largest Ships, sinking or burning about fourteen more, blowing up their Admiral *Opdam* in his own Ship, and taking two thousand sixty three Prisoners, whereof sixteen were Captains. But the Victory was purchased dear on our side by the Loss of many brave Men, though we had but one Ship missing; there being slain in the Battel the Earl of *Portland*, the Earl of *Marlborough*, and Rear-Admiral *Sampson*; Sir *John Lawson* died of his Wounds; and the Earl of *Falmouth*, the Lord *Muskerry*, and Mr. *Boyle*, were all three taken off by one Cannon-shot, so near the Duke's Person, that he was sprinkled with their Blood and Brains.

The Duke of York *beats the* Dutch *Fleet, and* Opdam *is blown up.*

The victorious Fleet having been refitted with wonderful Dispatch, was, in few Weeks, gotten out again to *Solebay*, to the Number of about sixty Sail, now under the Command of the Earl of *Sandwich*, who carried the Standard, having under him in the Red Squadron Sir *George Ascough* and Sir *Thomas Tyddeman*, with their subordinate Flags. In the White Squadron were Sir *William Penne*, Sir *William Berkeley*, and Sir *Joseph Jordan*; and the Blue Flag was carried by Sir *Thomas Allen*, having Sir *Christopher Myngs* and Sir *John Harman* for his Vice and Rear-Admirals. The Earl of *Sandwich*, upon Advice that the *Dutch* were not yet ready for the Sea, set sail with his Fleet for the North Seas, where, he had Intelligence,

ligence, their *Turkey* Fleet, with some of their *East-India* Ships, were got North about into *Bergen* in *Norway*. Appearing off of that Place, he sent in Sir *Thomas Tyddeman* with two and twenty Men of War to attack them, which he did with great Resolution, and notwithstanding the utmost Efforts of the *Dutch*, and the *Danes*, who had raised a strong Battery for their Defence, burnt some of their Ships, and did considerable Damage to the rest. This Service performed, the Fleet made sail for the Coasts of *Holland*, whence being again forced to the Northward, they met with the *Dutch East-India* Men, under a good Convoy, and several other of their Merchant Ships, and took eight Men of War, two of the best *India* Ships, and twenty of the other Merchant Men; with which, and some other Prizes, with four Men of War which they took afterwards, they returned to the *English* Coasts.

Tyddeman attacks Dutch Ships at Bergen.

The Earl of Sandwich takes Dutch East-India Ships, and their Convoy.

The *French* King at this time pursuing his Interest to keep up the Divisions between the two maritime Potentates, he, in order to weaken both, and that the *Dutch* might be induced to continue the War they found themselves unequal to, became a Party with them in it, and declaring War against *England*, fitted out a Fleet under the Command of the Duke *de Beaufort*. The *Dutch*, in hopes of this Assistance, used their utmost Diligence to get early to Sea the next Spring; and on our side all Preparations were made for doing the like. The Fleet was put under the Command of Prince *Rupert* and the Duke of *Albemarle*, who arriving in the *Downs* the twenty ninth of *May*, received Advice that the *French* Fleet was come out to Sea in order to join the *Dutch*. Upon this News Prince *Rupert*, with the White Squadron, made the best of his way to the Isle of *Wight*, in order to intercept them as they came up the Chanel. With the same Wind which carried the Prince to St. *Helen*'s, the *Dutch* put to Sea, and finding the *English* Fleet divided, resolved not to lose so favourable an Opportunity, and therefore engaged the Duke of *Albemarle* with a vast Superiority. The Duke, far from declining the Battel, encounter'd them with singular Bravery, tho' so much inferior in Strength; and although the Wind, blowing hard at South-West, made his Ships stoop so, that they could not use their lower Tire of Guns, they fought three Days successively; and in the first Day's Engagement the *Dutch* had two of their great Ships fired; in the second, they lost three Sail more; and on the last, when Prince *Rupert* came in with his Squadron, the *English* charged through the *Dutch* Fleet five several times with good Advantage, and so broke them, that they had not above five and twenty Ships remaining in a Body, which only maintained a running Fight, and retreated to their own Coasts, having lost above fifteen Ships, with one and twenty Captains, and above five thousand common Men.

The French join with the Dutch.

1666.

The Dutch attack Albemarle in the Absence of Prince Rupert.

Prince Rupert joins Albemarle, and the Dutch are routed.

This Engagement was on the third of *June*, and by the nineteenth of next Month the Fleet was at Sea again, under the same Commanders in Chief, accompanied by Sir *Joseph Jordan*, Sir *Robert Holmes*, Sir *Thomas Allen*, Sir *Thomas Tyddeman*, Captain *Utburt*, Sir *Jeremy Smith*, Sir *Edward Spragge*, and Captain *Kempthorne*, who carried the Flags; and coming soon after to another

A compleat Victory over the Dutch.

other Engagement with the Enemy, obtained a compleat Victory, sinking or burning above twenty of their Ships, killing *Evertz*, Admiral of *Zealand*, *Tirrick Hiddes*, Admiral of *Friesland*, and Rear-Admiral *Van Saen*, with above four thousand common Seamen, and wounding near three thousand. The Enemy's Fleet retired in Confusion to the *Wielings*, over the Flats and Banks, whither our great Ships could not follow them; and our Fleet sailed triumphantly along the Coasts of *Holland* to the *Ulie*, where the Generals

Dutch Ships at the Ulie destroyed by Sir Robert Holmes.

sending in a Squadron under Sir *Robert Holmes*, he burnt and destroyed a hundred and sixty rich *Dutch* Merchant Ships which lay there, and landing a Body of Men on the *Schelling*, also fired the Town of *Brandaris* upon that Island, and brought off a considerable Booty, which was all performed without any other Loss on our side, than of six Men killed, and as many wounded.

The *Dutch*, under all these Misfortunes, put their Fleet to Sea again before a Month was at an end, which, in hopes of being joined by the *French* Fleet under the Duke *de Beaufort*, (who lay at *Rochelle* with forty Sail) passed by *Dover* the first of *September*.

Prince Rupert goes after the Dutch to Boulogne.

Prince *Rupert* with the *English* Fleet stood after them to the Road of *Boulogne*, where, to avoid fighting, they haul'd close in with the Shore, and had been there burnt, or run aground by the Prince, if a violent Storm suddenly coming on had not forced him to retire to St. *Helen's*. In the mean while the *French* Fleet put to Sea from the Westward, but three or four of their Ships, which separated from the rest, falling in with Sir *Thomas Allen*'s Squadron in the *Soundings*, he took one of them, called the *Ruby*, of a thousand Tons and five hundred Men, with which Loss the Duke *de Beaufort* was (or pretended to be) so discouraged, that he immediately returned into Port, as the *Dutch* did to their own Coasts.

Beaufort comes out, but soon returns to France.

1667.
A Treaty of Peace on foot.

In the beginning of the next Year a Treaty of Peace between *England* and *Holland* was set on foot by the Mediation of *Sweden*; in confidence of the Success whereof, the King forbearing to set out a Fleet, whilst his Ministers were negotiating at *Breda*, the *Dutch*, with seventy Sail of Ships, under *De Ruyter*, appeared in the *Thames* Mouth, and sending in a Squadron, possessed themselves of the Fort at *Sheerness*, though bravely defended by Sir *Edward Spragge*. The Duke of *Albemarle*, who was Lord-General, with all Expedition hastened down thither with some Land Forces, and, to oppose the Enemy's Progress, sunk some Vessels in the Entrance of the *Medway*, and laid a strong Chain across it: But the *Dutch*, with a high Tide, and a strong Easterly Wind, broke their way through, and burnt the three Ships which lay to defend the Chain, and going up as far as *Upnore-Castle*, burnt also the *Royal Oak*, and having much damaged the *Loyal London* and the *Great James*, fell down the River again, carrying off with them the Hull of the *Royal Charles*, which the *English* had twice fired, to prevent that Dishonour, but the Enemy as often quenched again. In this Action

The Dutch do mischief in the River Medway.

Captain Dowglass his noble Resolution.

one Captain *Dowglass*, (who was ordered to defend one of those Ships which were burnt) when the Enemy had set fire to it, receiving no Commands to retire, said, *it should never be told that a Dow-*

CHAP. XIX. *Ruin of the* Rom. *Empire.*

a Dowglass *quitted his Post without Order*, and resolutely continued aboard and burnt with the Ship; falling a glorious Sacrifice to Discipline and Obedience to Command, and an Example of so uncommon a Bravery as, had it happened among the ancient *Greeks* or *Romans*, had been transmitted down to Immortality with the illustrious Names of *Codrus, Cynægyrus, Curtius,* and the *Decii.*

The *Dutch* getting out to Sea with the Loss of only two Ships, which ran aground in the *Medway,* and were burnt by themselves, proceeded next to *Portsmouth,* with a Design on the Shipping of that Harbour; but the Earl of *Macclesfield,* and Captain *Elliot,* had so well provided for their Reception, that they thought fit to desist from any Attempt, and sailing to the Westward, entered *Torbay*, with intent to land there, but being repulsed, returned to the *Thames* Mouth; and tho' they knew the Peace was now actually concluded, came up with five and twenty Sail as far as the *Hope,* where lay all the Ships of Force we had then fitted out, which were about eighteen, under the Command of Sir *Edward Spragge,* who happening not to be on board, the Enemy did considerable Damage with their Fireships; but he immediately repairing to his Post, and being presently joined with some small Vessels under Sir *Joseph Jordan,* the *Dutch* were forced to retire with some Loss. But, having first appeared off *Harwich,* and alarmed those Parts, they returned a third time and attacked Sir *Edward Spragge* again in the same Station, who was obliged to withdraw to *Gravesend,* and leave the Enemy at Anchor in the *Hope*; from whence they soon after retreated, and sailed down the Chanel to the Western Coasts, and having alarmed the Country with several Offers of Landing, at length, when they could dissemble their Knowledge of the Peace no longer, they made sail to their own Coasts.

The Dutch do farther mischief in the Hope.

The Dutch attack Sir Edward Spragge in the Hope.

The next Summer a Squadron was fitted out, under the Command of Sir *Thomas Allen,* to repress the Insolences of the Pirates of *Algier,* who, in the Month of *September,* coming before that Place, obliged the Government there to offer a Release of all their *English* Captives, and to renew their former Treaties, with the Addition of some new Articles to our Advantage. The same Year was concluded the Triple Alliance between *England, Sweden,* and *Holland,* for the Defence of the *Spanish* Provinces, against the *French* King; who nevertheless, in a short time, dealt so effectually with King *Charles,* that, what with the *French* Intrigues, and the Insults the *Dutch* had used towards his Person, by burning his Effigies in *Persia,* and publishing abusive Pictures and Medals of him in *Holland,* he came to a Resolution in the Year 1671, of breaking with them, and joining with *France* in their Destruction. And to begin the War with Advantage, though with Dishonour, before any Declaration of War, Sir *Robert Holmes* was ordered to lie off the Isle of *Wight* to intercept the *Dutch Smyrna* Fleet, in their Passage homewards.

1668.

Sir Thomas Allen sent against the Algerines.

Triple Alliance between England, Sweden, and Holland.

1671.

King Charles joins with France against the Dutch.

Sir *Robert* having shot at them to make them strike their Flags and lower their Topsails, and they neglecting to do the same, he again fired upon them, when they lowered their Topsails, but still refused

F f f

Holmes attacks the Dutch Smyrna Ships. refused to strike their Flags; upon which he immediately engaged them, and, after an obstinate Fight, which lasted till the Evening of that Day, and all the next, took five of their richest Merchant Men, with their Rear-Admiral, which was so disabled in the Engagement, that she sunk in a few Hours, in our Possession.

In the mean time Sir *Edward Spragge* being at the Head of a Squadron in the *Mediterranean* to repress the Piracies of the *Algerines*, who had violated their late Treaty, he repaired to *Bugia*, the most considerable of their Towns next *Algier*, where forcing the Boom which lay across the Entrance of the Harbour, he went in and burnt nine of their best Ships as they lay under the Cannon of the Castle; which Action so terrified the *Barbarians*, and put them in such Confusion and Disorder, that they struck off their Dey's Head, and set up another, whom they forced to come to Terms of Agreement with that Admiral.

Declaration of War against the Dutch. In few Days after Sir *Robert Holmes*'s Exploit against the *Dutch* Fleet, the King issued out his Declaration of War, and Preparations were made on both sides for vigorously carrying on the same. The Naval Force of the *French* King being to act in conjunction with ours, the Count *d'Estrées*, Vice-Admiral of *France*, arrived the third of *May* at *Portsmouth*, with a Squadron of Ships of that Nation; and our Fleet soon after repairing thither from the *Downs*, they both put to Sea, the Duke of *York* being Commander in Chief, Monsieur *d'Estrées* acting as Admiral of the White, and the Earl of *Sandwich* being Admiral of the Blue.

1672. *Count d'Estrées joins the English Fleet.*

On the nineteenth of *May* they discover'd the *Dutch*, about eight Leagues E. S. E. of the *Gunfleet*, and prepared to engage the next Day; but thick Weather coming up, they lost sight of each other, and the *English* and *French* Fleets put into *Solebay*, where continuing till the twenty eighth, the *Dutch* appeared unexpectedly in the *Offing*, bearing up to them, and had like to have surprized them in the Bay.

The Enemy's Fleet was commanded by *Banckert*, who led the Van, and attacked the White Squadron under Monsieur *d'Estrées*; by *De Ruyter*, the Commander in Chief in the Centre, who engaged the Red Squadron under the Duke; and by *Van Ghent*, in the Rear, who fought with the Blue Squadron under the Lord *Sandwich*. The *Dutch* began the Engagement with the White Squadron, as hath been observed, and the *French* received them at first with great Courage and Bravery, but were soon tired, and sheered off from the Battel. In the mean time the Duke and *De Ruyter* were warmly engaged for some Hours, so that his Royal Highness was forced to change his Ship the St. *Michael*, and go on board the *Loyal London*. The Earl of *Sandwich*, in the *Royal James*, maintained a bloody Fight with the Enemy's Rear-Admiral, who was soon taken off with a Cannon-shot; but one of *De Ruyter*'s Squadron coming up to that Ship's Assistance, with four Fireships, laid his Lordship on board, who after a Fight of five Hours, having bravely repulsed him with three of the Fireships, was

The Duke of York and the French engage the Dutch.

De Ruyter is slain.

CHAP. XIX. *Ruin of the* Rom. *Empire.* 403

at length fired by the fourth, and perished in the Ship with several *The Earl of* gallant Men. *Sandwich his Ship burnt.*

The Battel lasted with great Fury till nine at Night, when Sir *Joseph Jordan* getting the Wind of the *Dutch*, they stood away to the Eastward, and afforded the Duke the Honour of pursuing them. However they laid claim to the Victory, as well as the *English*, and indeed the Loss of Men was near an Equality, but of Ships the most were missing on our side, there being two burnt, three sunk, and one taken of the *English*; of the *French* one was burnt and another sunk; and among the Slain were many brave Men of Quality, as the noble Earl of *Sandwich*, Captain *Digby* of the *Henry*, Sir *Fretcheville Holles* of the *Cambridge*, Sir *John Fox* of the *Prince*, Monsieur *de la Rabeniere* the *French* Rear-Admiral, the Lord *Maidston*, Mr. *Mountague*, Mr. *Nicholas*, and Mr. *Vaughan*, the two last of the Bed-chamber to the Duke, and many other Persons of Consideration. The Body of the Earl of *Sandwich* was taken up floating at Sea, and afterwards interred with great Solemnity, at the King's Charge, in *Westminster* Abby.

The rest of this Campaign passed without any thing remarkable; but great Preparations were made for setting out a strong Fleet, against the next. And in the beginning of *May* the Fleet put to Sea, 1673. under the Conduct of Prince *Rupert*, who being joined off of *Rye* *The French* by the *French* Fleet under the Count *d'Estrées*, sailed in quest of *join Prince Rupert off of* the Enemy to the Coasts of *Holland*. *De Ruyter*, who had been *Rye.* first at Sea, having failed in a Design of intercepting our *Canary*, *Bourdeaux*, and *Newcastle* Fleets, in their Passage into the River, was returned to the *Schonevelt*, where the Confederate Fleet fell in *The English* with him, and soon began a sharp Engagement. The *French* Ad- *and French fight the* miral carried the White Flag, as he had done before; but now, to *Dutch near* prevent his deserting us, as he had done in the late Fight, his Ships *Schonevelt.* were intermixed with the *English*. Their united Force consisted of about a hundred and ten Ships, and the Enemy were near a hundred.

The Fight was began between Sir *Edward Spragge*, Admiral of the Blue, and the *Dutch* Vice-Admiral *Van Tromp*, and continued with great Fury till it was dark; when, after a considerable Loss on both sides, the two Fleets separated. This Battel was fought the twenty eighth of *May*, and on the fourth of next Month they came to another Engagement near the same Place, which was also *Another Battel near Scho-* began again by *Spragge* and *Tromp*, and lasted with equal Fury till *nevelt.* Night parted them, when both sides challenged the Victory, which, by their gallant Behaviour, they both deserved; the *Dutch* got within their Banks, and the *English* Fleet returned to their own Coasts.

By the middle of *July* Prince *Rupert* got out to Sea again, and *Prince* Rupert fought another Battel with the Enemy off of the *Texel*, wherein *fights the Dutch off of* *Banckert*, with the *Zealand* Squadron, meeting with very little *the* Texel. Resistance from the Count *d'Estrées*, join'd with *De Ruyter* in attacking the Red Squadron, and distressed Prince *Rupert* very much; while Sir *Edward Spragge* in the Blue Squadron was hotly engaged with Admiral *Tromp*, whom he forced once out of his Ship, and

F f f 2 was

was compelled by *Tromp* to change his twice; but as he was going into a third, his Barge was funk with a Cannon-fhot, and he
was unfortunately drowned; who, with Sir *William Reeves*, and
Captain *Heyman*, were the only Perfons of Note which were loft
on our fide. The *Dutch* had two Flag-Officers killed, and two of
their largeft Ships funk, with four or five Firefhips deftroyed; whereas on our part the only Lofs was that of the *Henrietta* Yacht,
which was funk by the fide of the Lord *Offory*, Rear-Admiral of
the Blue. It is very remarkable that, notwithftanding all the Precautions Prince *Rupert* could ufe, the *French* could not be brought
to take any great fhare either in this or the two former Engagements, Monfieur *d'Eftrées*, by one means or other, eluding his Orders, and keeping aloof from the Fury of the Battel.

In the mean time Sir *Tobias Bridges* failing with a Squadron of
fix Ships from *Barbadoes* to *Tabago*, a neighbouring Plantation belonging to the *Dutch*, poffeffed himfelf of that Ifland, with a Booty
of about four hundred Prifoners, and as many Negros; and foon after was alfo taken from them St. *Euftace*, another of the *Caribbee*
Iflands, in their Poffeffion. About which time four of their *Eaft-
India* Ships having reduced the Ifland of St. *Helena*, Captain *Richard Munden* was ordered thither with four Ships of
War, and immediately recovered the fame, with a Lofs more fatal to the *Dutch*, of three rich *Eaft-India* Ships, which there fell
into his Hands. But in revenge of thefe Proceedings, the *Dutch*
Vice-Admiral *Evertz* failing, with fifteen Men of War, to our Plantations on the Continent, took feveral Ships, and did other confiderable Mifchief, and thence going down to the *Caribbees*, recovered the Ifle of St. *Euftace*, which we had lately taken.

By this time the People of *England* being alarmed at the vaft
Progrefs of the *French* King's Arms in the *Netherlands*, grew very
uneafy at the Continuance of the War with the *Dutch*, and induced the King to come to a Peace with them, which was concluded
in the beginning of the next Year; by which Treaty they agreed,
among other things, to the Right of the Flag, to fettle the Affairs
of Commerce in the *Eaft-Indies*, and to pay his Majefty eight hundred thoufand Petacoons.

In the latter end of the Year 1675, Sir *John Narbrough* was fent
with a Squadron to the *Mediterranean*, to chaftife the Pirates of
Tripoli, who had interrupted our Trade in that Sea, and coming before that Place, in the Dead of the Night, manned out his Boats,
and fent them into the Port, under the Conduct of his Lieutenant,
Mr. *Cloudfley Shovell*, who firft feizing the Enemy's Guard-Boat,
went on undifcovered, and furprized four of the *Tripoline* Ships
(which were all they had in Port) as they lay under the Caftle and
Walls of the Town, and having burnt them, returned triumphantly
to the Ships without the Lofs of one Man; foon after which Sir
John Narbrough concluded a Treaty with the Government of *Tripoli*, upon advantageous Terms.

Some time after this the *Algerines* breaking with us, and cruifing
on our Ships trading in their way, Admiral *Herbert* failed, in the
beginning

CHAP. XIX. *Ruin of the* Rom. *Empire.*

beginning of the Year 1682, with a Squadron to the *Mediterranean*, and forced that People to come to a Peace, by a Treaty which still subsists with their Government.

Admiral Herbert *sent against the* Algerines. 1682.

The King being now weary of the vast Charge of maintaining the Garrison and Fortifications of *Tangier*, his Majesty came to a Resolution of demolishing the same, and making choice of the Lord *Dartmouth* for the Performance of that Service, sent him thither in *August* 1683, at the Head of a considerable Squadron, with a Commission to be General of his Forces in *Barbary*. His Lordship, on his Arrival there, immediately set about that Work, and tho' all possible Diligence was used in ruining the Place, it was many Months before its Destruction was compleated. It had a very fine Mole, on which vast Sums of Money had been expended since it came into the Hands of the *English*, which cost the Workmen the most trouble of any thing else, the Stones being cemented together to the same Hardness as the natural Rock, so that they were forced to drill it in several Places, and blow it up by Piece-meal. The Mole, together with the Rubbish of the Town, was thrown into the Harbour, to fill it up, and did so effectually spoil the same, as it can never again be made a Port. By the King's Direction there were buried among the Ruins a considerable Number of mill'd Crown-Pieces of his Majesty's Coin, which haply, many Centuries hence, when other Memory of it shall be lost, may declare to succeeding Ages that that Place was once a Member of the *British* Empire.

1683.
The Lord Dartmouth *sent to destroy* Tangier.

The Town, Mole and Harbour destroy'd.

Soon after this King *Charles* dying, there happened nothing remarkable at Sea during the short unhappy Reign which followed, till near the Conclusion of it by the Glorious Revolution, which placed the Prince of *Orange* and his Illustrious Consort on the Throne, the Naval Incidents whereof, and of the long War which ensued thereupon with *France*, will be related in the next Book.

King Charles II's *Death.*

A COM-

A COMPLEAT HISTORY

Of the moſt Remarkable

TRANSACTIONS at SEA.

BOOK IV.

Containing an Account of the Naval Tranſactions of the *Engliſh*, from the Revolution in 1688, to the Peace of *Ryſwick*, in the Year 1697.

CHAP. I.

The Proceedings of the Engliſh *Fleet, upon the Preparations made in* Holland, *till the Prince of* Orange's *landing in* England.

AS the Invitations which the Prince of *Orange* received in the Year 1688, induced him to make Preparation in *Holland* for an Expedition to this Kingdom, that thereby he might ſecure to us our Religion, Laws, and Liberties, ſo had King *James* Advice from time to time of the Progreſs his Highneſs made; and although his Majeſty was not at firſt thoroughly convinced that his Deſign was to waft his Forces hither, (notwithſtanding he had then an Ambaſſador

1688. King James has notice of the Preparations in Holland.

bassador at the *Hague*) yet being afterwards well assured thereof, and having a small Squadron of Ships in Pay, commanded by Sir *Roger Strickland*, then Rear Admiral of *England*, he thought it convenient to appoint them a Place of Rendezvous, and about the middle of *June* sent out some Scouts to observe the Motions of the *Dutch* Fleet. Not long after that the Squadron was ordered to Sea, and made two short Trips to and from *Southwold* Bay, the last whereof was after King *James* had visited them at the *Buoy of the Nore*, and consulted with his Flag Officers, and Captains, what was most adviseable to be done for intercepting the Prince in his Passage; for at that time it was altogether unknown at the *English* Court to what Part of the Kingdom he was designed.

Scouts sent out.
A Squadron sent with Sir Roger Strickland.

The Preparations in *Holland* advancing apace, King *James* deemed it necessary to send Instructions to Sir *Roger Strickland* how to govern himself in so important an Affair; of which Instructions it may not be improper to insert the following Copy.

James R.

King James's Instructions to Sir Roger Strickland.

WHereas We have been lately given to understand, that great Preparations are at this Day making by the States of the United Provinces, for increasing their Naval Force now at Sea, by the Addition of a considerable Number of their greater Ships; and forasmuch as We think it behoving, that, for preventing, as much as may be, the Evil that may be intended towards Us, Our Government, or the Trade of Our Subjects, you, with the Commanders of Our Ships under your Charge, be, without Delay, advertised thereof, We have, to that Purpose, caused this, by Express, to be dispatched to you, to the end that, upon Receipt hereof, you may immediately apply your self to the considering, and putting in Execution, whatever you, with the Advice of such of Our Commanders as you shall call to your Assistance, shall judge expedient, for the putting, and keeping Our Ships in a Condition of attending the Motion of those of the States, as you shall from time to time conceive most for Our Service. To which end, though such is Our Reliance upon your approved Diligence, Integrity, Valour, and Experience in maritime Affairs, that We do hereby entirely commit the whole Conduct thereof, in all Emergencies, to your sole Direction, yet We conceive it not unuseful (without Constraint) to recommend to you, in your Proceedings therein, the following Considerations, *viz.*

1. That two of Our Ships (to be changed once a Week) may be always kept cruising off of *Orfordness*, in order to as early discovering as may be the Approach, or Motion of those of the States, with Instructions not to fail, so soon as any such Discovery shall be made, to repair with Advice thereof your self to the *Downs*, or where else you shall appoint for their meeting you.

2. That so soon as the Wind shall come Easterly, and while it so continues, the like be done by Ships to be by you employed between

tween the *Goodwin Sands* and *Calais*, for preventing the States Ships paſſing by undiſcovered to the Weſtward.

And here you are to take notice, that for the more effectual ſecuring of timely Advice to you of the Proceedings of the Ships of the States, and eaſing you in the Ships to be ſpared for this uſe, We have determined to cauſe ſome *Barking* Smacks, or other ſmall Craft, proper for that Work, to be without Delay taken up, and ſent forth to that Purpoſe, with like Inſtructions to repair from time to time to you, with Advice, as before; of the Readineſs of which Veſſels to proceed on this Service, you ſhall be farther informed from the Secretary of Our Admiralty.

3. That upon your being advertiſed of the *Dutch* Ships being come to Sea, and of their Motion there, it may be adviſeable (which Way ſoever they bend, whether to the Northward, down the Chanel, into the River, or towards the *Downs*) that you with Our Squadron do get under Sail, and (quitting the *Downs* either by the North, or South *Foreland*, according to your Diſcretion) endeavour to follow them, ſo as always, if poſſible, to keep between them and their Home. And in Caſe of their attempting to make any Deſcent, by landing of Men upon any of Our Coaſts, you are to proceed hoſtilely upon them, for the preventing, or interrupting them as much as may be in their ſaid Attempt.

4. That Care be timely taken, by Orders to be given in that behalf, that effectual Proviſion be always made for our Ships reſorting to ſome known Places of Rendezvous, in Caſes of Separation; and that as frequent Accounts of the Proceedings of the *Dutch* be by you diſpatched, as conveniently may be, to the Secretary of Our Admiralty, for Our Information. And whereas, for the better inforcing the preſent Squadron of our Ships under your Command, We have determined upon converting thoſe of the fifth Rate into Fireſhips, and fitting out others of the third and fourth Rates in their room, in the doing whereof all Endeavours of Diſpatch will be made, Our Will and Pleaſure is, that you do forthwith iſſue out your Orders to the Lord *Berkeley*, to take the firſt Opportunity of Wind and Weather for bringing the *Charles* Gally to *Sheerneſs*, that her Company may be removed into ſuch other Ship as we ſhall by Our Commiſſion appoint for him. But We are pleaſed to direct, that in caſe the *Reſerve* be ſtill with you, and that you conceive her to be in any Condition of being kept abroad a little while longer, for anſwering the preſent Exigence, till theſe Recruits, or Part of them, can come to you, you do reſpite the ſending her to *Portſmouth* till farther Order. For which this ſhall be your Warrant. Given at Our Court at *Windſor*, the twenty ſecond Day of *Auguſt*, 1688.

By Command of his Majeſty,

S. PEPYS.

Sir *Roger Strickland* being thus inſtructed, I refer you to the following Account of the Strength of the Squadron, and of what Ships were ordered to be got in a Readineſs to join him, *viz.*

Ships defigned to intercept the Dutch Fleet.

Number and Rates of Ships which were with Sir Roger Strickland.

Rates	Number
3	1
4	16
5	3 } 26
6	2
Firefhips	4

Ordered to be fitted out to join him.

3	10
4	11
6	1 } 35
Firefhips	13

in all 61

Befides fix Tenders, which were to be employed as Scouts.

Sir *Roger* found that thofe Ships he had with him were very ill manned, and fince there was but little Profpect of a fpeedy Supply of Seamen, he defired that fome Soldiers might be fent on board to make up that Deficiency, which was done, but not with that Speed the Nature of the Service required. He advifed with thofe Officers in the Squadron whom he judged the moft experienced, and communicating to them the Contents of his Inftructions, both he and they were of Opinion, that they ought, when victualled, to fail to the *Buoy of the Gunfleet*, on this Side *Harwich*, fince they might fooner get Intelligence there of the Motion of the *Dutch*, than by ftaying in the *Downs*, for that with Wefterly Winds it would be five or fix Days before the Scouts off of *Orfordnefs* could ply it up; whereas the Squadron might fooner put to Sea from the *Gunfleet*, upon Notice that the *Dutch* were come out. But if when this fhould be confidered by his Majefty, it met not with his Approbation, he propofed that one or two of the Scouts might fail directly to the Coaft of *Holland*, to make Difcoveries, whilft he, at the fame time fent two of his cleaneft Ships off of *Orfordnefs* for that purpofe.

Sir Roger's Opinion to fail to the Gunfleet.

Soon after King *James* received this Propofition, he fignified his Pleafure thereupon, and that in fuch a manner, as made it apparent the Opinions of the Flag Officer, and Captains under him, were not fo much adher'd to as might have been expected from the Contents of his Majefty's firft Inftructions; for he let Sir *Roger Strickland* know, that having confidered well of what he had propofed, and debated the fame with feveral of the moft experienced Commanders, and Mafters, he was fully convinced, that it could not in any wife be convenient for his Service to put the fame in Execution; for that the *Gunfleet*, at fuch a Seafon of the Year was a very ill Road, and that, if the Wind fhould hang Eafterly, he would be liable to be driven up the River by the *Dutch*, which ought above all things to be avoided. Wherefore he directed him to go out of the *Downs* with the firft Eafterly Wind, and to place himfelf between the *North-Sand* Head,

King James's Directions to him thereupon.

and

CHAP. I. *from the Year* 1688, *to* 1697. 411

and the *Kentish Knock*, there to continue under Sail in the Day time, and at Anchor in the Night, if fair Weather; but if it happened to blow hard, and that the *Dutch* Fleet did not appear, to proceed by the back of the *Goodwin Sand* to *Bologne* Bay, and there remain until he was satisfied they were either passed down the Chanel, or gone up the River; in the former of which Cases it was recommended to him to follow them as near as he judged convenient, until they were between the *Lizard* and *Scilly*, and finding them proceeding farther, to return to St. *Hellen*'s Road, or *Spithead*; but if they bent their Course into the River, he was to endeavour to return by the back of the *Goodwin*, and to get the Wind of them. For the rest it was left to him to proceed as he should judge most proper, with this only Caution, that as soon as the Wind came up Westerly, and that not any of the forementioned Cases happened, he was to repair to the *Downs*. These Directions, rather to proceed to *Bologne* Bay than the *Gunfleet*, were determined upon a solemn Debate the Day before they bore Date, (*viz.* the 26th of *August*) in King *James*'s Closet, at *Windsor*, the following Persons being present, who were particularly summoned from *London*, namely, the Lord *Dartmouth*, Mr. *Pepys*, Secretary of the Admiralty, Sir *John Berry*, and three elder Brothers of the *Trinity* House of *Deptford Strond*, Capt. *Atkinson*, Capt. *Mudd*, and Captain *Rutter*, together with Captain *John Clements*.

The second of *September* Sir *Roger Strickland* had Advice from one of the Scouts, that twenty five Sail of the *Dutch* Fleet, sixteen of them great Ships, were off of *Gorée*, on the Coast of *Holland*, some of them under Sail, with three Flags, *viz.* Admiral, Vice, and Rear, and that they all lay with their Topsails loose upon the Windward Tide. *Advice of the Readiness of the Dutch Fleet.*

King *James* thinking his Squadron (which though but very weakly manned, were, for what Reason I know not, forbid to press Men even out of homeward bound Merchant Ships) not of sufficient Strength to intercept the *Dutch*, ordered them to retire to the *Buoy of the Nore*; but commanded that two of the cleanest Frigates should ply off of *Orfordness*, and that upon the first Approach of a foreign Fleet, one of them should immediately repair to the *Nore*, with Advice thereof, and the other remain in her Station, to observe whether the said Fleet made up towards *Harwich*, or the River, and then also come to the *Nore*, and give notice thereof by the usual Signals. And that the Motions of the *Dutch* Fleet might be the better known, it was recommended to Sir *Roger Strickland*, as a Matter of greatest Importance, so to employ all the Scout Vessels, as that he might have from them, and King *James* himself from him, the most frequent and exact Accounts of their Proceedings on their own Coast, and of their Departure thence. *The Squadron ordered to the Nore.*

The Beginning of *October* King *James* appointed the Lord *Dartmouth*, Admiral of the Fleet, who diligently apply'd himself towards the hastening to the *Buoy of the Nore* all Ships and Vessels which were fitting out in the Rivers of *Thames* and *Medway*, and received the following Instructions for his Government. *Lord Dartmouth appointed Admiral of the Fleet.*

Ggg 2 *James*

James R.

Instructions to the Lord Dartmouth.

WHereas We have received undoubted Advice, that a great and sudden Invasion from *Holland*, with an armed Force of Foreigners, and Strangers, will be made speedily, in an hostile manner, upon this Our Kingdom; Our Will and Pleasure is, that all necessary Orders being by you issued for the hastening Our Ships and Vessels, now fitting forth out of the Rivers of *Thames* and *Medway*, and from *Portsmouth*, together with those already at Sea under the Command of Sir *Roger Strickland* Knight, Vice-Admiral of our said Fleet, to their intended Rendezvous at the *Buoy of the Nore*, (a perfect List of which Ships, Fireships, and other Vessels, is hereunto annexed) you do, with all possible Diligence, repair on board our Ship *Resolution*, Captain *William Davis* Commander, or such other of Our Ships as you shall now, and at any times hereafter, think fit to bear Our Flag, as Admiral, upon taking upon you the Charge and Conduct of Our said Fleet, and what other Ships shall at any time hereafter be by Us set forth for reinforcing the same. Which Fleet, and every Part thereof, We (out of Our entire Reliance upon your approved Loyalty, Valour, Circumspection, and Experience) do hereby authorize and empower you to lead, and by Our Orders, to direct and dispose of, at all Times, and in all Emergencies, as you in your Discretion shall judge most conducing to Our Honour, and the Safety of Our Dominions, and particularly in the preventing the Approach of any Fleet, or Number of Ships of War from *Holland*, upon any of Our Coasts, or their making any Descent upon the same. Towards your more effectual Execution whereof, We do hereby empower and require you, to endeavour, by all hostile means, to sink, burn, take, or otherwise destroy and disable the said Fleet, and the Ships thereof, when and wheresoever you shall meet with, or otherwise think fit to look out for and attack them, giving a perfect Account of your Proceedings therein to the Secretary of Our Admiralty for Our Information. And for so doing this shall be your Warrant. Given at Our Court at *Whitehall* this first Day of *October* 1688.

By his Majesty's Command,

S. PEPYS.

The following List of the Fleet was annexed to the foregoing Instructions.

Ships for the main Fleet.

Rate.	Ships Names.	Where they were.
3	*Mary*	
	Mountague	
4	*Assurance*	
	Jerzey	Coming to the *Nore* with Sir *Roger Strickland*.
	Constant Warwick	
	Bristol	
	Nonsuch	

CHAP. I. *from the Year* 1688, *to* 1697. 413

Rate.		Ships Names.	Where they were
4		*Crown*	
		Dover	
		Mordaunt	
		Greenwich	
		Tyger	Coming to the *Nore* with
		Bonadventure	Sir *Roger Strickland*.
6		*Larke*	
	Fireships	*Sally Rose*	
		Half Moon	
		St. Paul	
	Yachts 3		In the River.
4		*Foresight*	At the *Nore*.
		Deptford	Off of *Orfordness*.
	Fireship	*Dartmouth*	
4		*Faulcon*	Coming to the *Nore* from
	Fireship	*Sampson*	*Yarmouth*.
6		*Saudadoes*	In the *Downs*.

Ships fitting out.

3		*Defiance.*	At *Blackstakes* near *Sheer-*
		Resolution	*ness.*
		Henrietta	
		Cambridge	
		Elizabeth	
		Pendennis	At *Chatham.*
4		*Newcastle*	
		Woolwich	
3		*Rupert*	In the *Hope.*
		York	
		Dreadnought	
		Plimouth.	
		Pearl	At *Portsmouth.*
		Richmond	
	Fireships	*Charles & Henry*	
		Unity	
4		*Advice*	At *Spithead.*
		Diamond	
		Ruby	
		St. David	
		Centurion	
		Portsmouth	In *Longreach.*
6		*Firedrake*	
		Guardland	
	Fireships	*Guernsey.*	
		Swan.	

Rate

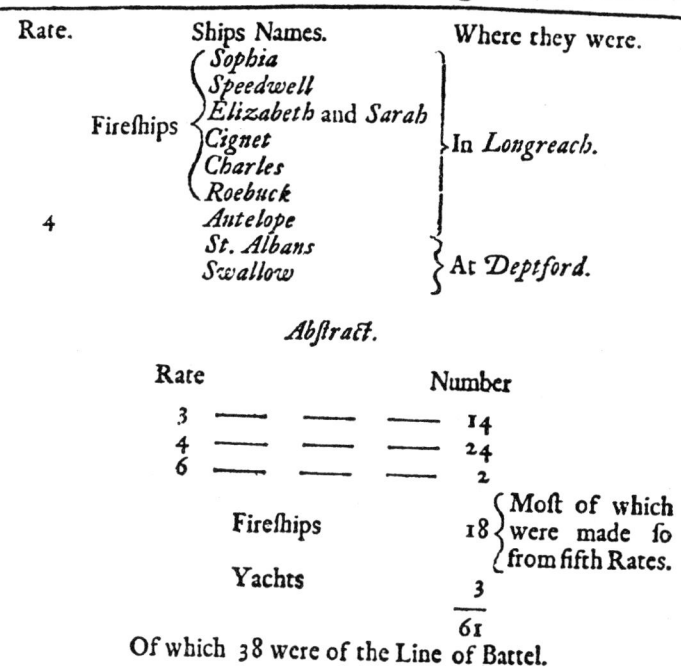

Rate.	Ships Names.	Where they were.
	Fireships { Sophia, Speedwell, Elizabeth and Sarah, Cignet, Charles, Roebuck	In *Longreach*.
4	Antelope, St. Albans, Swallow	At *Deptford*.

Abstract.

Rate	Number	
3	14	
4	24	
6	2	
Fireships	18	Most of which were made so from fifth Rates.
Yachts	3	
	61	

Of which 38 were of the Line of Battel.

A Council of War at the Gunfleet.

The Fleet being at the *Gunfleet*, and ready in all respects to proceed to Sea, his Lordship called a Council of War, and by a great Majority it was resolved to continue there: not but that some, and particularly Sir *William Jennings*, (who commanded a Ship of the third Rate) thought it much more adviseable to proceed over to the Coast of *Holland*, and there attend the coming forth of the *Dutch* Fleet. This last Proposal did certainly carry the greatest Weight with it, had there been a real Design of obstructing the Prince of *Orange* in his Passage to *England*; but, instead of that, Matters were so concerted, and agreed among the Commanders (who had frequently private Meetings to consider the Circumstances of Affairs) that had the Admiral come fairly up with the *Dutch*, it would not have been in his Power to have done them much Damage, although I have reason to believe his Lordship and some of the Captains would have exerted themselves to the utmost.

The Dutch Fleet passes by the Gunfleet.

Things being at this pass, the Ships of the States-General, commanded by Admiral *Herbert*, passed by the *Gunfleet* in a very foggy Day, and some of the Transports with Soldiers were even within sight; while the *English* Fleet rid with their Yards and Topmasts down, and could not, by reason of the Violence of the Wind, purchase their Anchors.

The Dutch Forces land at Torbay.

The same Wind which thus detained the *English* Fleet, was very fair to carry the Prince down the Chanel, and continued so until he arrived in *Torbay*, where his Forces landed the fourth of *November*, which were about fourteen thousand Men; but

but since (as I have been informed) his Highness was rather expected in the North, it was some time before the Gentlemen of the Country could conveniently put themselves into a Condition of joining him; insomuch that calling a Council of War, to consider what was most advisable to be done, his Return to *Holland* (as it hath been reported) had like to have been determined. However the Country came in by degrees, and King *James*'s Army thereupon deserting, even by whole Regiments, and the best of his Officers also leaving him, while others shewed no greater Inclination than the common Men to engage in his Quarrel, the Prince marched with little Blood-shed to *London*, and the unfortunate King, with his Queen, retired to *France* not long after.

But since this Matter hath been more amply related by others, I shall return to the *English* Fleet, which put to Sea as soon as they could purchase their Anchors, and taking their Course Westward, came in few Days off of *Torbay*, where the *Dutch* Ships lay. The Lord *Dartmouth* had not viewed them long, e'er a Storm arose, which forced him out of the Chanel; but returning in little time, and being again off of the aforesaid Bay, his Lordship gave them an Opportunity of seeing what his Strength might have enabled him to have done, had our Inclinations been to treat them as Enemies. The Prince being landed, as aforesaid, and all things favouring his Designs, his Lordship sailed to the *Downs*, where several Officers, known, or at least suspected, to be *Roman* Catholicks, were dismissed from their Employments, which was followed by an humble Address to his Highness; and not long after the Ships were dispersed, some to the Dock Yards to be dismantled and laid up, others to be clean'd and refitted, while those in the best Condition for the Sea were appointed to necessary Services.

The English Fleet sail in quest of the Dutch.

The English retire to the Downs.

CHAP. II.

Admiral Herbert's *engaging a* French *Squadron on the Coast of* Ireland, *with an Account of what happened in that Kingdom; and of Admiral* Russel's *carrying the Queen of* Spain *to the* Groyne.

ALL possible Diligence being used in preparing for an early Campaign the next Year, and particularly to prevent the *French* King's sending King *James*, with a Body of his own Troops, into *Ireland*, Mr. *Herbert* (soon after created Earl of *Torrington*) was appointed Admiral of the Fleet the fourteenth of *March*, who coming to *Portsmouth* the twentieth of that Month, found that the Ships which were ordered to join him from the East lay Wind-bound in the *Downs*. The twentieth of *April* all those designed for the *Mediterranean* were added to him; and he having had notice some Days before

King William appoints Admiral Herbert Admiral of the Fleet. 1689.

before that King *James* was landed in *Ireland*, he haftened to that Coaft with all the Strength which could poffibly be gotten together, hoping he might intercept the Ships of War which were his Convoy; the reft he ordered to follow him, and to do it rather fingly, than lofe time by ftaying for another; and the Places appointed for Rendezvous were the Coaft of *Ireland*, or ten Leagues Weft of *Scilly*.

His Proceedings to the Coaft of Ireland, and engaging in Bantry Bay.

Coming before *Cork* the feventeenth of *April*, with only twelve Ships of War, one Firefhip, two Yachts, and two Smacks, he was informed that King *James* (who was conducted over by twenty two Ships from *France*) landed at *Kinfale* about two Months before. This led him to proceed firft off of *Breft*, and then to range to and fro in the *Soundings*, in hopes of meeting thofe Ships; but failing thereof, and returning to the *Irifh* Coaft the twenty ninth of *April*, he difcovered in the Evening, off of *Kinfale*, a Fleet of forty four Sail, of which he loft fight the next Day; but judging them to be to the Weftward of him, he bore away, with the Wind Eafterly, for Cape *Clear*, and in the Evening faw them ftanding into *Bantry* Bay. He lay in the Offing until Morning, and then ftood towards them, having encreafed his Strength to nineteen Ships of War, but the *Dartmouth*, a fmall Frigate, was one of the Number. The *French* were at Anchor, being twenty eight, moft of them from fixty to upwards of feventy Guns, and fome bigger, with five Firefhips; and the Tranfport Ships (which carried to *Ireland* about five thoufand Men) were at fome Diftance plying to Windward.

Upon fight of our Ships, thofe of the Enemy got under fail, and when the Admiral had, not without difficulty, worked up within two Miles of them, they bore down on him in a very orderly Line, and one of their Ships being within Musket-fhot of the *Defiance*, which led our Van, they two began the Fight, as did the others after as foon as 'twas poffible. His Lordfhip made feveral Boards, intending thereby to gain the Wind of the Enemy, or at leaft to engage clofer than they feem'd willing to do; but finding he could not do either, and that it was not advifeable to maintain in fuch a manner fo unequal a Fight, he ftretched off to Sea, not only to get his Ships into a regular Line, but to gain the Wind, if poffible; but fo very cautious were the *French* in bearing down, that he could not meet with any Opportunity of doing it, fo that continuing the Fight upon a Stretch, until about five in the Afternoon, the *French* Admiral tack'd and ftood in towards the Shore; and as our Ships had fuffered fo much in their Mafts and Rigging, that not the one half of them were in a Condition for farther Action, fo doubtlefs the *French* received confiderable Damage. How far their Admiral was reftrained by Orders I cannot learn, but certain it is that he made very little ufe of the greateft Advantage; for as he had the Wind, fo had he double the Force, befides Firefhips. Confidering therefore all Circumftances, and that moft of our Ships were very ill manned, they came off more fortunately than could reafonably have been expected; for there were no more than ninety Men killed, and two hundred

CHAP. II. *from the Year* 1688, *to* 1697.   417

dred and seventy wounded, Captain *George Aylmer* being the only Captain slain in the Action.

After this Dispute was over the Admiral repaired to his Rendezvous, which was ten Leagues West from the Islands of *Scilly*, where he was in hopes of meeting with such an additional Strength, as might have enabled him to proceed in search of the *French*; but being disappointed therein, he returned to *Spithead*, where Orders were lodg'd for the immediate fitting the Ships, and all such as had not before join'd the Fleet, but were so far advanced as *Plimouth*, or *Scilly*, were remanded to *Spithead*, at which Place those coming from the East were also directed to rendezvous till farther Orders. *The Admiral returns to Spithead.*

Such Dispatch was made, that the Admiral arrived with the Fleet off of *Torbay* about the middle of *June*, and not many Days after several Ships of the States-General reached *Spithead*, with their Admiral, a Vice, and Rear Flag; and they, together with Mr. *Russel**, then Admiral of the Blue, sailed the second of *July* to join the Body, as did several others, as they came in, and received Orders so to do. *Admiral Russel and*

Vice-Admiral *Killegrew* had been for some time with a Squadron off of *Dunkirk*, to keep the *French* Ships in that Port; but he finding no more than four in *Flemish* Road, and three of them small ones, was also ordered to join the Fleet. This little Squadron were Merchant Ships hired into the Service, except the *Kent*, a third Rate, two small Frigates, and two Fireships, so that they were disposed of to several necessary Stations, being in no wise proper for the Line of Battel. *Vice-Admiral Killegrew join the Fleet.*

The Admiral cruised on the *French* Coast, and to and fro in the Soundings, without meeting any thing remarkable; and being the latter end of *August* in very great want of Beer, was obliged to come to *Torbay*, a Place very convenient for the Refreshment of the Fleet though it does not altogether please some People on shore, who (without reason) think it a Loadstone which does too much attract. And now the Winter Season being so far advanced as not to admit of keeping the Fleet at Sea in a Body, those Ships which wanted greatest Repairs, especially of the biggest Rates, were ordered into Port, and the Remainder divided into Squadrons; of which Squadrons, as I come now to give some Account, so will I first mention that detached with Sir *George Rooke* † in the Month of *May*. *The Admiral arrives again off the French Coast. The great Ships sent in, and others divided on several Services.*

The Admiral thought it for the Advantage of the King's Service to send him with several Ships to the Coast of *Ireland*, that he might assist the Generals of the Land-Forces in the Reduction of that Kingdom. With part of them he arrived off of *Greenock* about the tenth of *May*, and then sent Orders to *Chester* for the *Bonadventure*, and other Ships, to join him off of *Cantire*. That which first required his Assistance was the Relief of *Londonderry*, to which Place he determined to proceed as soon as the rest of the Ships could join him, for he had yet no more than the *Deptford*, *Antelope*, *Greyhound*, *Kingsfisher* Ketch, and *Henrietta* Yacht. Being off of Cape *Sir George Rooke sent with a Squadron to Ireland, and his Proceedings there. 1689.*

* *Now Earl of* Orford.
† *Afterwards Admiral of the Fleet, and Vice-Admiral of* England.

H h h   *Cantire*

Cantire the twenty second, he received Advice from Captain *Young*, who commanded the King's Forces thereabouts, that a Body of *Scotch* were got together in the Iflands *Gega* and *Kara*, lying on the Weft fide of *Cantire*, whither he proceeded, and, not without great Difficulty and *Hazard*, got his Ships in, and laid them to pafs; but the Enemy feeing Captain *Young* difembarking his Forces, haftened to their Boats in great Confufion, and fo made their Efcape.

The eighth of *June* he fell in with the *Bonadventure*, *Swallow*, and *Dartmouth*, and a Fleet of Tranfport Ships with Major General *Kirk*, with whom he proceeded towards *Derry*, but was forced to *Rathlin*'s Bay, and detained there till the twelfth. When he arrived with the Forces off of *Lough Foyle*, he ordered the *Dartmouth*, *Greyhound*, and *Kingsfifher* Ketch to follow the Major-General's Orders, for they, being the fmalleft, were the moft proper to go up the River, and the King had before put the *Swallow*, a fourth Rate, under the Major General's Command; fo that the *Deptford*, *Bonadventure*, *Portland*, and *Antelope* lay off of the Harbour's Mouth, to affift upon any occafion, and protect the Forces from Attempts by Sea.

A Confultation about relieving Londonderry. 1689.

The Major-General being advanced near the Place, called a Council of War on board the *Swallow* the nineteenth of *June*, at which there were prefent Colonel *Stuart*, Sir *John Hanmer*, Lieutenant Colonel *St. John*, Lieutenant Colonel *Woolfeley*, Lieutenant Colonel *Dampier*, Lieutenant Colonel *de la Barte*, Lieutenant Colonel *Lundini*, Major *Rowe*, Major *Tiffin*, Major *Carville*, Major *Richards*, Engineer, Captain *Wolfran Cornwall* of the *Swallow*, Captain *John Leak* of the *Dartmouth*, Captain *Gillain* of the *Greyhound*, Captain *Sanderfon* of the *Henrietta* Yacht, and Captain *Boys* of the *Kingsfifher* Ketch. They were almoft affured that there was a Boom laid athwart the River, a little above *Brook-Hall*, at a Place called *Charles-Fort*; that the faid Boom was framed of a Chain and Cables, and floated with Timbers; and that at each end thereof there were Redoubts with heavy Cannon. They were informed that the fides of that narrow River were intrenched, and lined with Musqueteers, as alfo that feveral Boats were funk, and Stockades drove in with great Spikes of Iron: Nor was there any room to doubt of that part which related to the Cannon, for the *Greyhound* received confiderable Damage from them in going up the Day before: Wherefore it was refolved to ftay until their Force was augmented, and then, by making a Defcent, endeavour to oblige the Enemy to raife the Siege.

In the mean time the Major-General defigning to poffefs himfelf of the Ifland *Inch*, the Commadore took on board the Ships of War a Detachment with Colonel *Stuart*, with whom arriving the ninth of *July* in *Lough Swilly*, he came to an Anchor near the Ifland, and the next Morning the Men were landed. The Pafs from the Ifland to the Main was fecured the fixteenth by two Redoubts, and a Battery of Cannon, on each fide whereof the *Greyhound* and *Kingsfifher* Ketch were moored; and then the Commadore failing with the *Deptford*, *Bonadventure*, and *Portland*, towards *Lough Foyle*,

CHAP. II. *from the Year* 1688, *to* 1697. 419

Foyle, met the Major-General coming down with his Transports from *Kilmore*, in order to land the Forces on the Island of *Inch*; and being informed by him that some *French* Ships of War had been on the Coast, and taken two small *Scotch* Frigats off of *Carrickfergus*, and two *English* Vessels near *Cantire*, and that they were gone from thence with some Forces to the Isle of *Mull*, he immediately sailed, and arrived at the said Island the next Day; but the *French* Ships had left it four Days before, and shaped their Course for the South Coast of *Ireland*. The very Morning he arrived a Battalion of about four hundred Men were transported from the Island to the Main, and their Officers were following in two small Vessels; but seeing our Ships doubling the Land, the *Irish* got on shore, and ran up to the Mountains. After the Commodore had batter'd the Castle on the Island belonging to Commissary *Macklaine*, he sailed, and the next Morning, off of the Island *Ila*, met a small Boat with an Express from Duke *Hamilton*, giving him an Account that the *Irish* designed to transport more Forces from *Carrickfergus*, for which reason his Grace desired him to continue to cruize in that Station to prevent them.

The twenty second of *June* the *Portland* brought him a Letter from the Major-General, advising him that our Forces in *Londonderry* were reduced to so great Extremities for want of Provisions, that they had lived for some time on Hides, Dogs, and Cats: That he was returned from *Inch* with the *Swallow*, and three victualling Ships, and was resolved to attempt getting up to the Town, but believed the Countenance of some other of the Ships might be very serviceable. Upon this the Commodore left the *Bonadventure* and *Portland* in his Station, and with the *Deptford* and *Dartmouth* proceeded towards the Major-General, the last of which Ships he sent up to *Kilmore* to receive his Orders, and then returned to the *Bonadventure* and *Portland*, with Intention to continue there until the Arrival of the three Ships he expected from the Earl of *Torrington*, Admiral of the Fleet. By this Assistance the Supplies were safely convey'd to *Derry*, the Siege of which Place was soon after raised: And about this time the King's Forces, commanded by Colonel *Berry*, near *Linaskea*, had a signal Victory over the Enemy, insomuch that, with the Number killed by the Army, and those which were knocked on the Head by the Country People, they lost not less than four thousand Men; and their Cannon, with most of their surviving Officers, were taken, among whom was Major-General *Mackartie*, who was shot through the Thigh, and run into the Back.

The Hardships the People of Derry suffered for want of Provisions.

Supplies sent into Londonderry, and the Siege raised.

A Victory obtained by the King's Forces near Linaskea.

Soon after the Commodore met the Duke of *Schonberg*, with the Transport Ships coming into *Bangor* Bay, in *Carrickfergus* Lough, where he landed part of his Army the same Night; but many of the Transports were wanting, and with them several small Frigates, the *Charles* Gally, *Supply*, *Saudadoes*, *Dartmouth*, and *Pearl*, in quest of which the *Portland* was sent to the Isle of *Man*.

Duke Sconberg arrives in Ireland with Forces.

Hhh 2 The

The twenty fifth of *August* the Ships in the *Irish* Seas were disposed of as follows:

Ships	Station
Deptford, *Bonadventure,* *Mary* Gally, *Antelope,* *Supply,* *Fanfan* Sloop, *Anne* Ketch, *Charity* Ketch, *Kingsfisher* Ketch, *Edward* and *Susan* Hoy,	At *Carrickfergus,* before which Place the Army encamped the twentieth, and it surrendered the twenty eighth.
Dartmouth, *Princess Anne,*	At *Hylake.*
Charles Gally, *Greyhound,* *Unity* Ketch,	Cruising off of the Isle of *Man.*
Pearl, *Henrietta* Yacht, *Monmouth* Yacht,	Cruising between *Dublin* and *Man.*
Portland, *Saudadoes,* *Welcome* Ketch,	Off of Cape *Cantire,*
Swallow,	With Major-General *Kirke.*

The Squadron having continued at *Carrickfergus* some time, the Commadore was desired by the General to take with him the *Deptford, Bonadventure, Mary* Gally, *Swallow, Portland, Antelope, Dartmouth, Archangel, Sampson, Scepter, Princess Anne, Hannibal, Smyrna Merchant, Supply, Greyhound,* and *Henrietta* Yacht, together with several Ketches, and to cruise with them off of *Kinsale* and *Corke,* or where he should judge he might so do with most Advantage, the General keeping with him at *Carrickfergus* the *Charles* Gally, *Pearl, Saudadoes, Fanfan, St. Malo Merchant,* and several smaller Vessels, which were put under the Command of Captain *Roach* of the *Charles* Gally.

Sir George Rooke ordered to cruise with part of the Squadron off of Kinsale and Corke.

The Commadore putting to Sea, endeavoured all that possibly he could to get Southward, but was forced by bad Weather into *Bangor* Bay, where he received Orders from the Lords of the Admiralty to lend all the hired Ships of War to *Hylake.* In his Passage from *Carrickfergus* he was obliged by a strong Southerly Wind to bear up and Anchor at the *Skerrys,* about twelve Miles from *Dublin,* where sending the Yacht in to gain Intelligence of the Army, several Shot were fired at her from the Shore, upon which he ordered the Ketches in, and manning all the Boats, landed about two hundred Men, who beat out of the Town those which pretended to defend it: But the Hills being covered with Horse and Foot, he ordered the Seamen off, lest they should be too much exposed;

He is directed to send all the hired Men of War to Hylake.

for

CHAP. III. *from the Year* 1688, *to* 1697. 421

for they are far from being the most orderly in a Retreat: However, before they embarked they either staved, or brought off all the small Vessels and Fisherboats.

The sixteenth of *September* the Commadore came into *Dublin* Bay, where he had Thoughts of Anchoring, and to send the Yacht and Ketches into the Harbour to attempt the taking or burning the Enemy's Ships and Vessels; but the Wind veering out, and blowing hard, he was forced away, so that arriving off of *Corke* the eighteenth, he ordered the Yacht and the four Ketches into the Harbour for Intelligence, and to assure the People of their Majesties Protection upon Submission; but the obstinate *Irish* having planted fourteen or fifteen Guns on both sides the Harbour's Mouth, plied upon the Vessels both with great and small Shot; notwithstanding which, they proceeded, landed their Men, and took Possession of the *Great Island:* But the Ships being very foul, and in want of all Species of Provisions, the Commadore was constrain'd to leave his Station, and repair to the *Downs,* where he arriv'd the thirteenth of *October.* *The People of Corke oppose the Vessels sent into that Harbour by Sir George Rooke. Sir George Rooke arrives in the Downs.*

Vice-Admiral *Killegrew* was on the twenty eighth of *December* 1689 appointed Admiral and Commander in Chief of a Squadron designed for the *Mediterranean,* which was composed of one Second Rate, four Thirds, seven Fourths, one Fifth, and two Fireships, with which (upon Admiral *Russel*'s Arrival at *Spithead,* or so many of them as should then be with him) he was to put himself under his Command, and to follow his Orders for proceeding to the Streights; but several Accidents happened which prevented his joining the said Admiral. *Vice-Admiral Killegrew appointed to command a Squadron bound to the Streights. 1689.*

Admiral *Russel* being appointed to conduct the Queen of *Spain* from *Holland* to the *Groyne,* and for that Expedition, as is already said, to have had some of the Ships of the *Mediterranean* Squadron, namely, the *Duke, Berwick,* and *Mountague*; that I may make my Account as methodical as possible, I shall first relate his Proceedings to the *Groyne,* and then those of Vice-Admiral *Killegrew* to and from the Streights. *Admiral Russel ordered to carry the Queen of Spain to the Groyne.*

The twenty fourth of *November* the Admiral was ordered to proceed to *Ulishing,* in *Zealand,* with the Ship *Duke* beforementioned, of the Second Rate, four Third Rates, two Fourths, and two Yachts, there to receive on board the Queen of *Spain,* and her Majesty's Retinue, and from thence to repair to *Spithead* for farther Orders; and upon her Majesty's coming on board, as well as during the Time of her Stay, he was ordered to bear the Union Flag at the Maintopmast Head. *1689. His Proceedings on that Expedition*

He arrived at *Ulishing* the twelfth of *December,* having been obliged to continue about twenty four Hours on that Coast, in such hazey Weather, that it was impossible to make the Land, from whence her Majesty was brought to the *Downs,* where both her self and her Retinue were removed into more proper Ships, and the twenty fourth of *January* she arrived at St. *Hellen*'s, whence the Admiral proceeded into the Sea as soon as the Winds would permit, but was forced back to *Torbay* the twenty third of the next Month,

as

as he was the second of *March*, after another Attempt to fail: But at length getting clear, he had Sight of the *Groyne* the sixteenth; where having put the Queen, and her Attendance on Shore, and dispatched what was otherwise necessary to be done, he set Sail, but by contrary Winds was forced into the Harbour of *Ferrol*, very near the *Groyne*, where, in a violent Storm, the Ship *Duke* drove on Shore, but with great Care and Pains was luckily got off again with little or no Damage. The Ships which were appointed for Part of the Mediterranean Squadron the Admiral timely dispatched to *Cadiz*, and then taking the first Opportunity of a Wind, he reached *Plimouth* the twenty fifth of *April* with the Remainder, and arriving at *Portsmouth* the twenty eighth, landed there the Ladies, and other Persons of Quality that attended the Queen of *Spain* in her Passage, who, if I guess right, did not meet with that entire Content in the *Spanish* Court, which a Princess of her Birth and incomparable Perfections ought to have enjoyed.

1690.

Chap. III.

Vice-Admiral Killegrew's *Proceedings from the time of his sailing to the* Mediterranean *to that of his Return to* England.

I Come now to give some Account of Mr. *Killegrew*'s Proceedings to, and in the *Mediterranean*, before I mention any thing of the Transactions of the Body of the Fleet at Home the next Year: And in the first Place, it may not be improper to let you know that he had the following Instructions for his Government in that Expedition, *viz.*

Instructions to Vice-Admiral Killegrew.

1. When he arrived at *Cadiz* he was to send the *Happy Return* and *Oxford* (two fourth Rate Ships) with the Trade to *Malaga* and *Alicant*, and to give them Orders for their Return to *England* with the Merchant Ships from those Ports.

2. At such time as he should judge it most convenient he was to order the *Portland*, *Faulcon*, *Tyger*, and *Sapphire*, to proceed with the Trade to *Genoa*, *Livorne*, *Naples*, and *Messina*, and to see those bound for *Gallipoly* and *Zant* as near to those Places as they could conveniently. These Ships of War were to keep Company with the *Turky* Trade to the Height of *Candia*, where parting, the *Tyger* and *Faulcon* were to conduct those bound to *Smyrna* first, and then the others within the *Dardanelles*, after which they were to return to, and remain at *Smyrna* sixty Days. The other two Ships, the *Portland* and *Sapphire*, were to convoy the Trade bound to *Scanderoon*, and to continue in that Port sixty Days, at the Expiration whereof they were respectively to sail, with all the Trade that should be ready, to *Messina*, the Place desired by the *Turky* Company

CHAP. III. *from the Year* 1688, *to* 1697. 423

Company for their Rendezvous. But it was neverthelefs left to the Admiral to give them other Directions, in cafe he judged it more advifeable, and to fend them Home, with the other Trade for *England*, in fuch Manner as (according to Intelligence) he fhould think moft proper.

3. Having difpatched away thefe Convoys, he was, with the *Duke, Berwick, Refolution, Mountague, Burford, Newcaftle* and *Greenwich*, together with the *Dutch* Ships appointed to join him, and the *Half Moon*, and *Cadiz Merchant*, Firefhips, to attend the Motion of the *French*, either in a Body, or in fuch Manner as might moft conduce to the intercepting them, and to the Safety of the Trade, and to attack them if he found himfelf of Strength fufficient; but if they happened to pafs the Streights, he was, upon the firft Notice thereof, to follow them.

The feventh of *March* he failed from *Torbay*, but arrived not at *Cadiz* till the eighth of the next Month; for he met with extreme bad Weather, infomuch that feveral Ships of the Squadron were much fhatter'd, and two *Dutch* Men of War unhappily founder'd, one of feventy two, and the other of fixty Guns, having before but one Maft ftanding between them, and that but a Mizen. In repairing thofe Damages he met with no little Difcouragement and Interruption from the the then Governor of *Cadiz*, who on this, and all other Occafions, demonftrated how much he inclined to an Intereft which was entirely oppofite to that of the Allies. *His failing from Torbay; and Arrival at Cadiz.*

Mr. *Killegrew* received on the ninth of *May* three feveral Expreffes, one from the Conful at *Alicant*, another from him who refided at *Malaga*, and the third from Captain *Skelton*, who was with Part of the Squadron at *Gibraltar*, all of them letting him know that the *Thoulon* Squadron commanded by Monfienr *Chateau Renault*, was feen from thofe Places, and that it confifted of ten Sail, three of them Ships of eighty Guns each. A Council of War was hereupon called, where it was refolved to fail with as many Ships as were in a Condition, and to join the fix *Englifh* and *Dutch* which Captain *Skelton* had with him at *Gibraltar*, who was ordered not to attempt any thing untill fo joined, but to take an efpecial Care for his Safety. Accordingly the Admiral failed the tenth, at four in the Morning, with the *Englifh* Ships following, *viz.* the *Duke, Mountague, Eagle, Tyger, Portland, Faulcon, Happy Return, Richmond,* and *Sapphire*, being one fecond Rate, two thirds, four fourths, and two fifths, as alfo two Ships of the Line of Battel of the States General, called the *Guelderlandt* and *Zurickzee*, with which was Lieutenant-Admiral *Almonde*, but there were left behind a third Rate, the *Refolution*, and a fourth Rate, named the *Newcaftle*, as alfo a Prize taken by Captain *Bokenham* of the *Happy Return*, called the *Virgin's Grace*, which were found not to be in a fit Condition for the Sea. *The Advices he received of the Thoulon Squadron. Refolution of a Council of War.*

The tenth, at eleven at Night, the Wind was at W. N. W. and the Squadron had then Cape *Trafalgar* E. and by N. about four Leagues off. At four a Clock the next Morning they fteer'd away for the Streight's Mouth, and had Cape *Spartell* S. W. diftant about *His Proceedings in Search of the French Squadron.*

bout six Leagues, at which time the Admiral detached the *Portland* to *Gibraltar*, with Directions to Captain *Skelton* to get ready and join him. About one in the Afternoon he got into the Bay, when there came on board him three *Spanish* Gentlemen from the Governor of the Town, with Advice from the Commander in chief at *Ceuta*, a *Spanish* Garrison on the *Barbary* Coast, that there had been seen the Night before fourteen Ships at Anchor in the Bay of *Tetuan*, a Town about seven Miles from *Ceuta*; and the whole Squadron being now under Sail, consisting of one second Rate, three thirds, six fourths, two fifths, and two Fireships of the *English*, and five Ships of the States General, they stood over for *Ceuta* Point, with a fair Gale at West, where they lay by all Night. Early the next Morning Mr. *Killegrew* steered away for the Bay of *Tetuan*, where he found only two Ships, one at Anchor in the West Part of the Bay, the other under Sail about two Leagues Eastward of her. The latter escaping put abroad the Colours of *Algier*, but the other being imbayed, she was taken by Vice-Admiral *Almonde*, and proved to be a *French* Ship bound to *Antegoa*.

The Thoulon Squadron discover'd. The Wind shifting to the E.S.E. a small Gale, our Squadron stood over for the *Spanish* Shore, and having *Ceuta* Point W.N.W. distant about two Leagues, the Men at the Mast-head saw ten Ships to the North, lying with their Heads Eastward. Notice was given of this to Monsieur *Almonde*, who could not so soon discern them, because he was about two Leagues Southward of our Ships, and in a very little time after the whole Squadron stretch'd over for *Gibraltar* Hill, the *Mountague* being sent ahead to observe and give Notice of the Enemy's Motions. At eleven a Clock she fell astern, her Captain having discovered that four Ships were under his Lee, so that all Endeavours were used to get up with them, and about one a Clock they were not above two Miles off, when it being discerned that they ran, our Ships set their Top-gallant Sails, and crowded after them as much as possibly they could; but the *French* had the better Heels, for they were just cleaned, whereas some of ours had been seventeen Months off of the Ground.

The Thoulon Squadron escapes. The Chase was continued till ten the next Day, and as then the Enemy were about four Leagues ahead, so were the *Dutch*, with several of the *English* Ships, near hull to astern; nor had the Admiral more than the *Duke, Mountague, Eagle,* and *Portland* near him. Notwithstanding this, Monsieur *Chateau Renault* kept on his Way, who had thirteen Ships, *viz.* six Men of War, three Fireships, a Tartane, and three Merchant Ships; and there being no Prospect of coming up with them, the Chase was given over; but between nine and ten in the Morning, the *Richmond* and *Tyger* forced one of the Merchant Ships on Shore Westward of *Tariffa*, opposite to *Tangier*, which with great Labour was got off. The Admiral lay by until it was three a Clock, and then the rest of his Squadron coming up, he bore away for *Cadiz*, but, by Reason of contrary Winds, could not reach that Place until the twenty first. From thence he dispatched away the several Convoys, namely, the *Tyger, Newcastle,* and *Oxford*, for *Smyrna*, commanded by Captain *Coal*; the *Portland,*

Our Ships repair to Cadiz, from whence the Vice-Admiral sends away the Trade up the Streights.

land, *Greenwich*, and *Faulcon*, to *Scanderoon*, under the Conduct of Captain *Ley*, and the *Sapphire* and *Richmond* were appointed for *Malaga* and *Alicant*, under the Command of Capt. *Bokenham*.

This being done, and all things put in order for the Squadron's Return for *England*, since the *French* Ships had passed the Streights, the Admiral set Sail, and in thirty five Days arrived at *Plimouth*, with one second Rate, and four thirds of ours, together with the *Virgin Prize*, and *Half-Moon*, and six *Dutch* Men of War. At *Plimouth* he received Letters from the Lords of the Admiralty, by which he was informed that the *French* Fleet, after an Engagement, had obliged ours to retire, and that they hover'd about *Rye*, *Dover*, and those Parts; for which Reason he was advised to take care for the Security of his Squadron. This occasion'd his calling a Council of War, where it was determined to proceed with the Ships into *Hamoze* within *Plimouth Sound*, for it was judged they could not be otherwise safe should the *French* attempt them; for, being great Ships, they could not run in at any time of the Tide, nor were they in a Condition to put forth to Sea, until such time as they had taken in Water, Stores, and Provisions. At this Consultation there were Vice-Admiral *Killegrew*, Vice-Admiral *Almonde*, and Rear-Admiral *Evertson*, as also Sir *Cloudesly Shovell*, Rear-Admiral of the Red, who was arrived at *Plimouth* from the Coast of *Ireland*.

Vice-Admiral Killegrew arrives at Plimouth.

He is advised to remain there, the French Fleet being in the Chanel.

Chap. IV.

An Account of the Earl of Torrington's engaging the French Fleet off of Beachy.

THE Engagement off of *Beachy*, in *Sussex*, (which happened the thirtieth of *June*) between the two Fleets commanded by the Earl of *Torrington*, and Monsieur *Tourville* being some Days before Mr. *Killegrew*'s Arrival at *Plimonth*, it naturally leads me to the giving the following Account of that Action.

1690.

The Earl of *Torrington* being with the Fleet at St. *Helen's*, was not a little surprized at the Advice he received from *Weymouth*, that the *French* were entered into our Chanel; for so far was he (by all the Intelligence he had received) from believing they were in that forwardness, that there were not at that time any Scouts Westward to observe and bring an Account of their Motion: But as this News was soon confirmed from many other Places, it was judged high time to muster up all the Ships within Reach, both *English* and *Dutch*, and to put them into the best Condition that might be of Defence; which being done, his Lordship sailed the twenty fourth, early in the Morning, with the Wind at E. N. E. and stood to the S. E. the *French* having been seen the Day before, by the Scouts lately sent out, on the Back of the Isle of *Wight*; and the next Day our Fleet being

The Earl of Torrington receives Advice of the French Fleet's being in the Chanel.

His Proceedings thereupon.

I i i

being reinforced by the *Lion*, a third Rate, and several *Dutch* Ships of War, were with a N. E. Wind in Sight of the Enemy.

About four a Clock next Morning the Admiral edged towards the *French*, who were about three Leagues from him, and tho' when the Wind shifted to the S. E. and S. E. by S. he tacked and stood Eastward, yet at three in the Afternoon the whole Fleet went about, and stood Westward again. The *French* took several People from the Shore, and when they had punished them for magnifying our Strength, they were pleased to dismiss them, with a Letter to the Admiral (as I am informed) from Sir *William Jennings*, (who commanded an *English* Ship of War at the Revolution, and now served in no better a Post than that of third Captain to the *French* Admiral) by which he presumed to promise Pardon to all Captains who would adhere to the Interest of King *James*.

A farther Reinforcement arrived of seven *Dutch* Ships; with Admiral *Evertson*, and another Flag-Officer; but the two Fleets continued looking on each other, without Action, until the thirtieth; for the Admiral was not willing to engage before the Ships he expected from the East had join'd him. But notwithstanding the Enemy were so much superior in Strength, as seventy odd Sail to fifty, and that their Ships were generally larger, positive Orders were sent to him from Court to give them Battel: Whereupon the Signal was put abroad, as soon as it was light, for drawing into a Line, which being done, the whole Fleet bore down on them, while they were under Sail, by a Wind, with their Heads Northward.

Receives Orders to engage the Enemy.

An Account of the Engagement off of Beachy.

At eight in the Morning the Signal was made for Battel, when the *French* bracing their Head-Sails to the Mast, lay by; and about an Hour after the *Dutch* Squadron, which led the Van, began to engage Part of the Van of the *French*; half an Hour after which our Blue Squadron encounter'd their Rear; but the greatest Part of the Red, which were in the Center, could not engage until it was near ten; and as they were then at a considerable Distance from the Enemy, so was there a great opening between them and the *Dutch*.

It was observed that as our Ships bore down on the *French*, they lasked away, tho' probably that might be only to close their Line; and afterwards several of their Ships towed round with their Boats until they were out of Shot, insomuch that it was hoped the Advantage would have fallen on our Side; but it was not long e'er it appeared the *Dutch* had suffered very much, and chiefly by their being (for Want of a necessary Precaution) weathered and surrounded by those *French* Ships which they left ahead of them when they began to engage.

No sooner did the Admiral perceive their Condition, than he sent them Orders to come to an Anchor, and with his own Ship, and several others, driving between them and the Enemy, anchored about five in the Afternoon, at which time it was calm; but judging it not safe to renew the Fight at so great a Disadvantage, he weighed at nine at Night, and retired Eastward with the Tide of Flood.

The

The first of *July* in the Afternoon, he called a Council of War, where it was resolved to endeavour to preserve the Fleet by retreating, and rather to destroy the disabled Ships, if they should be prest by the Enemy, than hazard another Engagement by protecting them.

Our Fleet retires Eastward, and the French pursue.

The *French* very indiscreetly pursu'd in a formal Line of Battel, whereas had they left every Ship at Liberty to do her utmost, ours would undoubtedly have been more roughly handled, especially those which were cripled in Fight; but each one shifting for her self, (as 'tis natural to do in such Cases) and Caution being had in anchoring most advantageously, with regard to the Tides, which the *French* took little or no notice of, we thereby got Ground considerably of them. However they pursued as far as *Rye* Bay, and one of the *English* Ships, called the *Anne*, of seventy Guns, was run on Shore near *Winchelsea*, having lost all her Masts, where two *French* Ships attempting to burn her, the Captain saved them that Labour, by precipitately setting fire to her himself.

The Body of the *French* Fleet stood in and out off of *Bourne* and *Pemsey* in *Sussex*, while about fourteen more lay at Anchor near the Shore, some of which attempted to destroy a *Dutch* Ship of about sixty four Guns, that lay dry at low Water in *Pemsey* Bay; but her Commander so well defended her every high Water, when they made their Attacks, that they at last thought it convenient to desist, so that this Ship was got off, and safely carried to *Holland*; but it fared not so well with three others of that Nation, which were on Shore on the said Coast, for their Officers and Men not being able to defend them, they set them on fire; so that with the three Ships destroyed by the *French* in the Action, the States General lost six of the Line of Battel.

On the eighth the *French* Fleet stood towards their own Coast, but were seen the twenty seventh following off of the *Berry* Head, a little to the Eastward of *Dartmouth*, and then, the Wind taking them short, they put into *Torbay*. There they lay not long, for they were discover'd the twenty ninth near *Plimouth*, at which Place very good Preparations were made, by Platforms and other Works, to give them a warm Reception. The fifth of *August* they appeared again off of the *Ram* Head, in number between sixty and seventy, when standing Westward, they were no more seen in the Chanel this Year.

The French repair to their own Coast.

Our Fleet retreated towards the River of *Thames*, and the Admiral going on Shore, left the chief Command to Sir *John Ashby*; but first gave Orders to Captain *Monck* of the *Phœnix*, together with four more fifth Rates, and four Fireships, to anchor above the Narrow of the *Middle Grounds*, and to appoint two of the Frigates to ride one at the *Buoy of the Spits*, the other at the lower End of the *Middle*, and to take away the *Buoys*, and immediately retreat, if the Enemy approached: Or if they press'd yet farther on him, he was ordered, in like manner, to take away the *Buoys* near him, and to do what Service he could against them with the Fireships; but still to retire, and make the proper Signals in such Case.

Care taken to preserve our Ships, had the Enemy come towards the River.

This

This Apprehension was soon over by the Enemy's drawing off, as is beforementioned, so that the chief thing to be done, was to put the Fleet into a Condition to go to Sea again: Not but that this unlucky Accident occasioned various Reports and Conjectures, and the *Dutch* were very uneasy upon account of the Damage they had sustain'd, insomuch that several Persons of Quality were sent to *Sheerness* to examine thoroughly into the whole Matter upon Oath; and after the Earl of *Torrington* had continued Prisoner in the Tower for several Months, he was at last try'd, and unanimously acquitted by a Court-Martial, held at *Sheerness* the tenth of *December*, where Sir *Ralph Delavall* presided, who had acted as Vice-Admiral of the Blue in the Engagement: And, if I mistake not very much, this was the first time that ever an *English* Admiral was called to an Account in such a manner.

Several Noblemen and others appointed to examine into the Action upon Oath. The Earl of Torrington try'd at a Court-Martial, and acquitted.

CHAP. V.

An Account of the joint Admirals, Sir Richard Haddock, *Mr.* Killegrew, *and Sir* John Ashby, *their proceeding with the Fleet to* Ireland, *and Return from thence.*

THE Fleet being in a good Forwardness, it was put under the joint Command of Sir *Richard Haddock*, Mr. *Killegrew*, and Sir *John Ashby*. Two of those Admirals arrived in the *Downs* the twenty first of *August*, and sailing from thence the twenty fifth, were join'd by Mr. *Killegrew* off of *Dover* with the Ships he brought from the Streights, which had been confined at *Plimouth* by reason the *French* were in the Chanel, as has been before observed; and the Fleet arriving at *Spithead* the twenty eighth, the Admirals received Instructions in what manner to proceed, and to take the Ships hereafter mentioned under their Command, which were then dispersed at the several Places express'd against their Names, *viz.*

The Fleet put under the Command of Sir Richard Haddock, Admiral Killegrew, and Sir John Ashby.

The Strength of the designed Fleet.

Rates.	Ships.	Where.
1	Sovereign	
2	Sandwich	
	Coronation	
	Duchess	
	Royal Katharine	
	Neptune	At *Spithead*.
	Duke	
	Ossory	
3	Captain	
	Grafton	
	Defiance	

5 Rate.

CHAP. V. *from the Year* 1688, *to* 1697   429

Rates.	Ships.	Where.
3	Elizabeth Berwick Hope Breda Edgar Hampton-Court Expedition Suffolk Sterling-Castle Restauration Lenox Warspight Cambridge Exeter Kent Northumberland Monmouth Essex Swiftsure Resolution Eagle Burford Montague	At *Spithead*.
2	St. Michael	At *Blackstakes*.
3	Harwich	At the *Nore*.
	Modena hir'd	In *Longreach*.
4	Sampson hir'd	At the *Nore*.
	Wolf hir'd	In *Longreach*.
	Charles Gally	Gone to *Holland*.
	Dragon	In *Longreach*.
Fireship	Hopewell	At *Deptford*.
6	Saudadoes. Salamander Fubs Yacht.	
Fireships	Griffin Cadiz Merchant Charles Hunter Owner's Love Wolf Vulture Hound Pelican	At *Spithead*.

So that the whole Fleet, besides *Dutch*, were forty three, great and small, *viz.* one First Rate, eight Seconds, twenty eight Thirds, four Fourths, three Sixths, and ten Fireships, of which all but eight were joined, and they were all ordered to be victualled at *Portsmouth* as follows; the First and Second Rates to the twelfth of *October*,

tober, and the Third Rates, and under, to the twenty sixth of that Month, having at this time on board them the Earl of *Marlborough*, General of his Majesty's Forces, with upwards of five thousand Soldiers, bound to *Ireland*.

The great Ships sent about to Chatham.

But the Winter Season advancing, the Admirals were directed to send the great Ships to *Chatham*, which were the *Sovereign*, *Duke*, *Coronation*, *Duchess*, *Sandwich*, *Neptune*, *Ossory*, and *Royal Catharine*; so that they hoisted the Union Flag on board the *Kent*, a Ship of the Third Rate.

A Scarcity of Seamen and Provisions. The Admirals proceed and arrive in Ireland.

Provisions fell very short, and there was a great want of good Seamen to navigate the Ships; however the Admirals put to Sea, pursuant to the Commands they had received from the King, and arrived before *Cork* Harbour the twenty first of *September*, where they anchor'd; for the Tide of Flood being done, the Pilots would not venture in. Next Day they weighed, and in a Calm towed in towards the Harbour's Mouth, from the Larboard side, whereof several Shot were fired at them from a small Battery of eight Guns, but some of the Boats being sent on shore to attack them, the Enemy were soon forced from their Guns, which being dismounted, their Carriages were thrown into the Sea, and the Ships got in without farther Interruption.

Proceedings against Cork.

Next Day, between two and three in the Morning, the greatest part of the Soldiers were put into proper Vessels, which carried them up to a Place called *Passage*, and in the Afternoon the rest, together with the Marines, were landed.

The Day following, about five or six hundred Seamen, Gunners, and Carpenters were put on shore, who proved very useful in drawing up the Cannon to batter the Town; and the Powder and Shot taken out of the great Ships at *Portsmouth*, was made use of by the Army.

The City of Cork taken.

The twenty fifth, before Day, ten Pinnaces, were sent up with armed Men to assist in attacking the Town; and the Admirals were put in hopes by the Earl of *Marlborough*, that it would be in the Possession of the King's Troops in three or four Days, as indeed it happened, for they took it the twenty ninth.

The Fleet ordered by the King to return to the Downs, but some Ships left at Cork under Command of the Duke of Grafton. Prisoners sent from Ireland by the Earl of Marlborough.

The King now commanded the Admirals to return to the *Downs* with the Fleet, and to leave behind them such Ships only as were needful, who accordingly appointed seven Third Rates, one Fifth, one Sixth, the *Owner's Love* Fireship, and a Tender to each, to be under the Command of the Duke of *Grafton*, then in a Ship called by his own Title, and with the rest of the Fleet they arrived in the *Downs* the eighth of *October*, bringing with them, by the Earl of *Marlborough*'s Desire, Colonel *Macullicot*, who was Governor of *Cork*, the Earls of *Tyrone* and *Clancarty*, Lord *Carr*, Colonel *Owen Macartny*, Lieutenant Colonel *Rycot*, Major *Macartny*, and Captain *Muffy*; and having disposed of the Fleet, according to the Lords of the Admiralty's Orders, by sending some to the *Nore* with Sir *Ralph Delavall*, and others to *Portsmouth* and *Plimouth*, the rest were left with Sir *Cloudesly Shovell* in the *Downs*.

His

His Grace the Duke of *Grafton* was unfortunately wounded at *Cork* with a Musket Ball from the Walls, when he was shewing his wonted Bravery and Zeal, by encouraging the Seamen on shore, and labouring as much as any of them at the great Guns, of which Wound after having languished some Days, he died, leaving the chief Command to Captain *Matthew Tenant*, who being blown up in the *Breda*, in *Cork* Harbour, the Conduct of the Squadron regularly fell to Captain *John Crofts* of the *Charles* Gally; and as soon as they had taken on board the General, with the Soldiers, Marines, and Prisoners, they left *Ireland*, and arrived in the *Downs* the twenty seventh of *October*.

The Duke of Grafton killed at Cork.

Chap VI.

Sir Cloudesly Shovell's *Proceedings on the Coast of* Ireland *with a Squadron under his Command.*

THE Expedition with that part of the Fleet which was commanded by the joint Admirals, ending, as hath been before related, it may not be improper to say something concerning the Squadron with Sir *Cloudesley Shovell*, who had been cruising in the *Soundings*, and on the Coast of *Ireland*, between the Months of *December* and *July*; and having convoy'd his Majesty from *Hylake*, was honoured (and not undeservedly) with a Commission appointing him Rear-Admiral of the Blue.

I have already said that he arrived from the Coast of *Ireland* the beginning of *July* 1690, and that he was prevented in joining the Fleet by reason the *French* were to the Eastward of him; wherefore it now remains I inform you, that his Majesty receiving Intelligence the Enemy intended to send upwards of twenty small Frigates, the biggest mounting not above thirty six Guns, into St. *George*'s Chanel, to burn the Transport-Ships, commanded Sir *Cloudesly Shovell* to cruise off of *Scilly*, or in such Station as he should judge most proper, for preventing them in that Design, and to send Frigates to ply Eastward and Westward, to gain Intelligence of the Body of the *French* Fleet, that so he might be the better able to provide for his own Safety: And if he met with Vice-Admiral *Killegrew* in his Return from the Streights, he was to apprize him of all Circumstances, that so he might likewise take care not to be intercepted.

Sir Cloudesly Shovell's Proceedings with a Squadron in the Soundings.

Pursuant to these Orders he cruised up and down in the aforesaid Station till the twenty first of *July*, without meeting any thing remarkable; when the *Dover* and *Experiment* join'd him from the Coast of *Ireland*, with a Ketch from *Kinsale*, on board of which Vessel was Colonel *Hacket*, Captain *John Hamilton*, *Archibald Cockburne*, Esq; *Anthony Thompson*, Esq; Captain *Thomas Power*, Mr. *Wil-*

Mr. *William Sutton*, and six Servants, who were following King *James* to *France*, in order to their accompanying him in his intended Expedition to *England*. They gave an Account that he took Shipping at *Duncannon*, and sailed to *Kinsale*, but that not staying there above two Hours, he proceeded to *France*, with two *French* Frigates, which had lain ready for that purpose a considerable time, and that his Majesty carried with him the Lord *Powis*, Sir *Roger Strickland*, and Captain *Richard Trevanion*.

King James his embarking from Ireland for France.

The twenty first of *July* Sir *Cloudesly Shovell* received Orders to sail to *Kinsale* with the Ships under his Command, and to endeavour to intercept several *French* Frigates said to be there; but in the Execution of those Orders, when he was near the River of *Waterford*, he had notice from the Shore, that although the Town of *Kinsale* had surrender'd two or three Days before, yet upon summoning *Duncannon* Castle, they refused all Conditions offer'd to them; whereupon he let Major-General *Kirke* know that he was ready to assist him with some Frigates in attacking that Place, and the manner of doing it being agreed on, he went in with the *Experiment* and *Greyhound*, and all the Boats of the Squadron; but after the Castle had made some fire on them, they declar'd that they were ready to surrender on Terms; so that next Day, being the twenty eighth of *July*, Governor *Bourk* marched out with about two hundred and fifty Men, with their Arms and Baggage, leaving forty two Guns mounted in the Castle. Here the Rear-Admiral had Advice, that all the *French* Ships which had been on the Coast of *Ireland* were sailed to *Limerick*, as also the Privateers, and Merchant Ships, in order to secure the Retreat of their Army, if they should attempt another Battel and be routed: And the Lords of the Admiralty being informed that they were gone from *Limerick* to *Gallway*, there to embark for *France*, upon a Squadron of Ships which sailed from the former Port, and were reinforced by Monsieur *d'Amfreville*, they ordered the Admirals to send to Sir *Cloudesly Shovell* at *Plimouth* (where he was arrived with part of his Squadron) four Third Rates, four Fourths, three Fifths, and four Fireships, which joined to those with him, would compose a Squadron of five Third Rates, ten Fourths, eight Fifths, and six Fireships; and with these he was ordered in quest of the Enemy: But other pressing Services suddenly calling for the Ships, Directions were sent to him, pursuant to the King's Commands, the eighteenth of *September*, to detach ten of them into the *Soundings* for Security of the Trade, and to repair to the *Downs* with the Remainder.

Sir Cloudesly Shovell ordered to proceed to Kinsale.

Duncannon Castle surrender'd.

Pursuant hereunto, he left under the Command of Captain *Carter* (who had joined him with several Ships) three Third Rates, four Fourths, and three Fifths; and being himself off of the *Blasket* Islands, lying at the North side of the Entrance into *Dingle* Bay, he got Advice that the *French* Fleet had been gone from *Gallway* about a Week, but that there still remained five Sail at that Place; whereupon he sent two Frigates thither, not thinking it proper to go in with the whole Squadron, since it is a deep Bay, and that a Number of Ships could not well get out but with an Easterly Wind.

Those

CHAP. VII. *from the Year* 1688, *to* 1697.

Those two Frigates returned to him the twenty sixth, and brought the following Account; That on the thirteenth of *September* Monsieur *d'Amfreville* sailed from *Gallway* with about sixty Ships and Vessels, whereof eighteen were Men of War: That they took with them only a few sick Men, besides the Earl of *Tyrconnel*, Mr. *Fitz James*, (natural Son to King *James*) *Busslo*, late Governor of *Lmerick*, and about three or four hundred *Irish*: That on the fifteenth they were joined by the *Grand Monarch*, and eleven more Capital Ships, which had been in the *Shannon* near a Week, and could not get to *Gallway*, and that having notice of our Squadron's coming, they steered away right into the Sea, and came not near the Coast of *Ireland*, although they had not any reason to apprehend Danger, considering their superior Strength. *Monsieur d'Amfreville's sailing from Gallway, and carrying Lord Tyrconnel, and others with him to France.*

The tenth of *October* Sir *Cloudesly Shovell* arrived in the *Downs* with part of his Squadron, having appointed the Remainder to attend on necessary Services; and there he met with Orders from the Lords of the Admiralty to proceed to *Plimouth* with all the Ships which were in a Condition for the Sea, and from that Port to take others, with which he was to cruise in the *Soundings* for Security of the Trade. Having gotten together what Ships he could, he proceeded with them to the aforesaid Port of *Plimouth*, and sailing thence the third of *December*, chased several Sail in the *Soundings*, but could not come up with them, for most of those he had with him were foul. At length the *Deptford* and *Crown* took a small *French* Man of War, of eighteen Guns and ten Patereroes, called the *Frippon*, which Ship had before fought four *Dutch* Privateers, wherein she received considerable Damage, and had thirty of her Men killed and wounded: Her Captain's Name was *St. Marca*, who, with the Lieutenant, were wounded, and her Master was killed, and fighting very obstinately, she yielded not till the *Crown* shot away her Main-mast, and boarded her. *Sir Cloudesly Shovell arrives in the Downs. He is sent out again; and cruises for some time in the Soundings.*

The Rear-Admiral having ended his Cruise, he sent some of the Ships to the Coast of *Ireland*, left others in the *Soundings*, and arrived himself in the *Downs* the middle of *January*, from whence he attended his Majesty to *Holland* in the Squadron commanded by Sir *George Rooke*. *He arrives in the Downs.*

CHAP. VII.

Admiral Russell's *Proceedings to and from the* Soundings *in Search of the* French *Fleet; with what happened till the Reduction of* Ireland.

THE twenty third of *December* Mr. *Russel* was appointed Admiral of the Fleet, and the greatest Diligence being used in order to an early Campaign, he had Instructions to sail to such Station

1690.

tion in the *Soundings*, or on the *French* Coast, as might be most proper, for annoying the Enemy, and protecting our Trade; but it was particularly recommended to him not to leave the *Downs* until he should be joined by twenty *Dutch* Ships of War, or at least eighteen, and that he had appointed a Squadron to look after the *French* Ships at *Dunkirk*, with the Commander in Chief of which Squadron he was to leave Instructions how to join the Fleet, should there be occasion for it. But here it may be observed, that although he was thus empowered to proceed, from time to time, in such manner as might best enable him to destroy the Enemy, either by Sea or Land, without expecting particular Orders, yet was it expressly provided, that if bad Weather rendered it unsafe for him to keep the Sea, he should repair to, and remain at *Torbay* till farther Order; the Consequences of which Restraint was not, I am apt to think, so thoroughly consider'd as it ought to have been.

With these Instructions he received a List of the Ships and Vessels appointed for the main Fleet, the Rates and Numbers whereof were as follows, *viz.*

Strength of the Fleet.

Rates	Number
1	5
2	11
3	32
4	9
5	4
6	3
Fireships	20
Hospital Ships	4
Sloop	1
Brigantine	1
Yacht	1
	91

Of which fifty seven were of the Line of Battel, besides the *Dutch*, whose Quota was generally five to eight.

1691.
The Fleet ordered into the Soundings. The Admiral ordered to send a Squadron to Gallway to intercept the French Succours.

The Fleet being victualled, and indifferently well mann'd, the Admiral had Orders from the Queen, dated the seventh of *May*, to proceed into the *Soundings*, provided the *Dutch* had joined him, and that he thought it proper to venture the great Ships there at such a Season of the Year. From the *Soundings* he was to detach a considerable Number of Ships and Fireships to *Gallway*, in *Ireland*, either to prevent the *French* landing Succours there, or to destroy them, if in that Harbour; and it was left to his Discretion to lie with the Body of the Fleet in such Station, as that this Detachment might most readily join him, to prevent the ill Consequences of his being attack'd by the *French* when separated.

Altho' the Admiral thought it not adviseable to venture the Fleet so early to Sea, but more especially the great Ships, yet he declar'd his Readiness to proceed, if it was her Majesty's positive Commands he

CHAP. VII. *from the Year* 1688, *to* 1697.   435

he should. He did not approve of sending any considerable Squa- *His Reasons*
dron to *Gallway*, because many Accidents might have hinder'd their *for not sending a Squa-*
joining the Fleet, the Consequence whereof, should the *French* get *dron to Gall-*
between them, he judg'd of the last Importance, and that it carried *way.*
greater Weight with it than the Reduction of *Ireland* that Summer;
but yet he had no Objection to the sending some Ships thither, if
her Majesty was satisfied that the *French* were so backward in their
Naval Preparations as that our Fleet might with Safety be thus separated.

He was likewise unwilling (and that with good reason too) that *As also for*
Dunkirk should be left unregarded, until the uncertain Arrival of *Dunkirk un-*
other *Dutch* Ships, "since the River's Mouth would be left open *regarded.*
" to the *French*; that the Trade and Fishery on all the Coast would
" be thereby exposed, and *Newcastle* not only be liable to be block'd
" up, but an Opportunity would be given to the Enemy of sinking
" Vessels at the Bar of that Harbour, so as that no Ships of Burthen
" would be able to float over it.

Nothing was wanting but a fair Wind to enable him to sail from
the *Nore*; and before he received these Orders from the Queen, he
had thoughts of rendezvousing in *Torbay* until the Summer Season
was somewhat more advanced: But being now commanded to repair
forthwith into the Soundings, he judged Cape *Clear* the most pro- *Cape Clear*
per Place to rendezvous at, since Frigates might be more conveni- *Rendezvous,*
ently sent from thence to *Kinsale*, for Intelligence from the Lords *and the Reason thereof.*
Justices of *Ireland*.

Before I proceed, let us consider what were the Reasons which
induced her Majesty to send the Admiral these Instructions. They
were these; The Intelligence received from *Holland*, dated the
twenty first of *April*, that the *French* King designed to send a Body *Intelligence of*
of Troops from *France* to *Ireland* in near two hundred Ships, and *Recruits going from France*
that about a hundred and fifty of them were at *Belle* Isle, on the *to Ireland.*
South Coast of the Province of *Bretagne*, the Place appointed for
all of them to rendezvous at, as well as the twenty five Men of
War designed their Convoy, of which five were said to be at the Isle
of *Daix* from fifty to sixty Guns: And it was farther reported,
that those Transports were loaden with all things necessary for the
Subsistence and Cloathing of Men, with a considerable Sum of Money to pay the Army commanded by Monsieur *St. Ruth*.

Most part of the Fleet being got together, the Admiral composed *The Line of*
a Line of Battel, an Abstract whereof follows. *Battel.*

Squadron.	Division.	Rate of Ships.	Small Craft.
		1ˢᵗ, 2ᵈ, 3ᵈ, 4ᵗʰ.	
Blue.	Vice-Admiral	1, 2, 5, 2.	One sixth Rate, four Frigates.
	Admiral ——	0, 3, 5, 1.	Two sixth Rates, three Fireships, two Hospital Ships, one Bomb Squadron.
	Rear-Admiral	1, 1, 6, 1,	Three Fire Ships.

K k k 2

Squadron.	Division.	Rate of Ships.	Small Craft.
		1ˢᵗ, 2ᵈ, 3ᵈ, 4ᵗʰ.	
Red.	Rear-Admiral	0, 2, 6, 1.	Three Fireships.
	Admiral	2, 1, 5, 2.	One fifth Rate, one sixth Rate, three Fireships, two Hospitals, one Yacht.
	Vice-Admiral	1, 2, 5, 2.	Three Fireships, and small Frigates.

		Nº.	
Dutch.	Of 92 Guns	3.	
	84	1.	
	76	2.	One of forty four Guns, one of sixteen, two Fireships.
	72	2.	
	70	1.	
	64	5.	
	50	3.	

So that of *English* and *Dutch* there were seventy four Ships of the Line, besides others which the *Dutch* Admiral expected, and there was some Probability, at least, would join the Fleet.

Interruptions in the timely manning the Fleet.

It cannot be said that the Ships were so well mann'd as could have been wish'd, tho' great care had been taken, and the Nation put to an extraordinary Expence in Tenders, and other Methods, for impressing and entertaining Men. One thing, among others, which gave no little Obstruction was, the Proclamation forbidding pressing Men from Colliers, which encouraged sick Men, as soon as they could crawl from their Quarters, to scramble up to *London*, and, for the sake of greater Wages, enter themselves on a *Newcastle* Voyage, and many of them without any regard to their being made Run, and thereby losing all they had earn'd in the publick Service. Besides, there were many Letters, even at this time, scatter'd by ill meaning Persons among the Ships, advising the Sailers to desert; so that no Remedy remain'd to cure this Disease, but recalling the aforesaid Proclamation, or keeping the Men on board, when sick, and suffering them to die miserably. Many more Obstructions there were to the timely manning the Fleet, but the chiefest was the extravagant Wages given to Seamen by the Merchants, who, for lucre thereof, sculked up and down, and hid themselves, until the Ships whereto they belonged were ready to proceed to Sea, insomuch that very great Numbers, even of the best Seamen, were by this means useless to the Crown.

The Admiral was acquainted on the tenth of *May* by a Principal Secretary of State, that there was reason to apprehend the *French* intended not only to send Ammunition and other Instruments of War to *Ireland*, but to transport also a considerable Number of *Irish* from thence to *Scotland*; and that therefore it was the Queen's Pleasure he should endeavour to intercept them in their Passage to *Gallway*, or to destroy them in that Harbour; for which reason her Majesty commanded him to send the Fleet to St. *Helen's*,

or

CHAP. VII. *from the Year* 1688, *to* 1697. 437

or *Spithead*, and to repair himself immediately to Town and attend her, that so this, and all other Affairs relating to the Expedition, might be maturely considered of: And her Majesty concurring with him that *Dunkirk* ought not to be neglected, ordered him to take care, before the Fleet sailed, for blocking up that Port, if the *Dutch* Ships expected there did not timely arrive. *The Admiral ordered to send the Fleet to St. Helen's, and to come to Town to be advised with.*

When he returned to the Fleet he had Orders to send some Ships into the *Irish* Chanel (as he himself had propos'd) to cruise upon the Coast of *Scotland*, without *Cantire*, that so they might prevent the *French* in transporting any Forces from *Ireland* to that Kingdom; and he was inform'd that Letters from *Dublin* gave an Account the Enemy were not then arrived, but that if a late Report from a *Dane* might be depended on, it was very probable they would soon be there; so that it was earnestly recommended to him to hasten to *Gallway*, and endeavour to destroy the Ships before they could unlade, and receive those Soldiers which were to embarque. *He ordered to send some Ships to intercept Forces from Ireland to Scotland.*

This Order would have been immediately complied with, but that the Fleet could not well stir from the *Downs* until join'd by the Ships off of *Dunkirk*, for several of them were of the Line of Battel; but since the falling of the Tides would prevent the *French* getting out of that Port, ours were soon expected thence, and when they were arrived, the Admiral proposed sending thither a Squadron of ten Ships, *English* and *Dutch*, such a Number being all he could well spare, so as to have the Fleet of any considerable Strength. It was his Opinion, indeed, that they would not be sufficient; and therefore he desired the Lords of the Admiralty to join others to them; and when he discoursed the *Dutch* Admiral about this Affair, he found him not willing to part with any of his Ships, for he alledged that he had positive Orders from the King not to do it until his Number was thirty six, of which no more than twenty eight (even at this time of the Year) were arrived. This put Matters under some Difficulty; and as the leaving so many Ships from the *English* Fleet would very much weaken it, so was it therefore desired that Admiral *Allemonde*'s Orders might be thus far dispensed with, as to allow of his sparing a proportionable Number of *Dutch* Ships to join with ours; which might have been the rather granted, since they would have had Opportunity of returning to the Fleet as soon as Mynheer *Toll* arrived with the Squadron designed for *Dunkirk*. *The Fleet could not sail till join'd by the Ships off of Dunkirk.* *The Reasons why the Dutch Admiral did not spare Ships for Dunkirk.*

To this the Admiral received for answer, that the Queen had not any Advice from the King that the *Dutch* Admiral was ordered not to part with any of his Ships until he had thirty six, but that she had written to his Majesty that he would be pleased to send Orders to the said *Allemonde* to follow his Directions. And now the Queen commanded that the Fleet should proceed as soon as it was possible, according to her former Instructions, without staying for the Return of the *Dunkirk* Squadron; directing withal, that if the *Dutch* Admiral would appoint four or five Ships to join ours off of that Port, Orders should be left for those that were to return from thence to make the best of their way to the Fleet; but that if the said Admiral could not consent to leave such a Number of Ships, a fitting Squadron *The Queen orders him to sail as soon as possible, without staying for the Dunkirk Ships.*

Squadron of ours should be detached, and Orders left that when any *Dutch* Ships arrived there so many *English* should repair to the Fleet: And that there might not be a want of Ships for this Service, Orders were lodg'd in the *Downs* for such *Dutch* Men of War as should arrive there, after the Fleet's sailing thence, to proceed and join ours off of *Dunkirk*; of which Admiral *Allemonde* was acquainted, that so he might leave the like Orders, least the *Dutch* Captains should scruple to obey before they had actually join'd the Fleet.

A Proposal made for destroying Dunkirk, but not attempted.

Much about this time a Proposal was made for destroying the Port of *Dunkirk*, which the Admiral was directed to communicate to the Commander in chief of the Squadron appointed to lie off of that Place, and to leave behind him two Fireships to be employ'd on that Service; but it was not thought advisable to put the Project in Practice this Summer.

The twentieth of *May* the Fleet was ready, and the Admiral intended to sail next Morning from the *Downs* to *Torbay*, and to leave Orders for Mr. *Churchill* to follow him thither, with the Squadron under his Command off of *Dunkirk*: To supply the Place of which Ships he appointed three Third Rates, two of the best sailing Fourths, and a Fireship, to join with those three the *Dutch* Admiral was at length prevailed with to leave; by which Detachment, and the three sent to *Ireland*, eight Ships of Force were taken from the *English*.

A South-West Wind prevented the Fleet's sailing as was intended; and now the Vice-Admiral of *Zealand*, and three *Dutch* Ships arrived; for which Reason, and that if the Wind continued as it was but one Day longer, those off of *Dunkirk*, that were relieved by others more proper, might also join the Fleet, the Admiral alter'd his Resolution of calling at *Torbay*; and the twenty second of *May* received the Queen's Orders for proceeding before *Brest*.

The Fleet ordered off of Brest, which alter'd the Admiral's Measures.

This broke the Measures he had proposed to take; for he intended to have gone first ten Leagues off of *Brest*, from thence sixty Leagues right into the Sea, and so to have fallen in with Cape *Clear* in his Return; it being generally believed that the *French* would first come to *Belle* Isle to get Intelligence, so that in their traverse Home, our Fleet might luckily have gain'd Sight of them: Besides, the Admiral was in doubt, that if the Fleet continued off of *Brest* till Mr. *Aylmer*'s Arrival with the Homeward bound *Smyrna* Ships, (a Matter which was very uncertain) the Men, by their long continuance at Sea, would fall sick; but notwithstanding these reasonable Objections, he assured Her Majesty that he would punctually obey Her Commands, and that tho' he wish'd for nothing so much, as the meeting with the whole *French* Force with the Ships he then had, yet he earnestly desired that no Intelligence, or Motive whatever, might prevail with Her Majesty to take any considerable Number from him.

The Fleet sails but is forced back to the Downs.

He sailed the twenty third of *May* in the Morning, but being got as far Westward as *Dengey Nesse*, was forced back to the *Downs* with a hard Gale at S. W. and soon after there came News from *Dublin*, that the *French* were arrived in the River *Shannon* with an hundred

CHAP. VII. *from the Year* 1688, *to* 1697. 439

dred Sail of Transports, and that the Men of War which convoyed them cruised between that River and *Gallway*; whereupon Her Majesty signify'd Her Pleasure to the Admiral, that as soon as he had left a Squadron for *Dunkirk*, agreeable to what he proposed, he should proceed with the Fleet off of *Brest*, and send a Frigate to *Kinsale*, to learn from the Lords Justices whether the *French* were gone to *Scotland*, or where they might be found: And if, upon upon such Intelligence, he judged they might be destroy'd in *Ireland*, or prevented in going to *Scotland*, he was to send a Squadron either to the West of *Ireland*, or through St. *George*'s Chanel to *Scotland*, with Orders to them to return to the Fleet when they should have done their utmost in the Performance of that Service. *Farther Orders from the Queen for the Fleet's sailing off of Brest. The Admiral ordered to send a Detachment to Ireland to destroy French Ships.*

It was likewise recommended to him to get the best Information he could of the Body of the *French* Fleet, and to have a particular Regard to the Safety of the Trade expected from *Smyrna*, as also to order the Ships on the *Irish* Coast to return to the Fleet as soon as the Services they were employed on would admit thereof; and when he should think it convenient to come from before *Brest*, he was to repair to Cape *Clear*, and to send Notice by the Way of *Kinsale* of his Arrival: But it was again recommended to him to remain before *Brest*, or thereabouts, if Wind and Weather would permit, until the *Smyrna* Fleet arrived, and as long time after that as he should judge necessary. And although it was represented to him what Advantages might be taken against *Gallway* by Sea, yet Her Majesty let him know that she was not willing to have it attempted, untill such time as the Army had made those Advances which might enable them to attack it also by Land. *The Care of the Smyrna Fleet recommended to him.*

There was at this time Advice that the *French* intended to come out of *Dunkirk* the next Spring-Tide, which the Admiral was desired to communicate to Captain *Bokenham*, who commanded the Squadron off of that Port, and, withal, to consider with the Flag-Officers the Project for burning the said Place, and to give Instructions accordingly. But how little Effect it would have had, was sufficiently shewn some Years after, when the Crown was, to little or no purpose, put to a very considerable Expence in making such an Attempt, of which I shall give a more particular Account in it's proper Place.

The first of *June* the Admiral was acquainted, that it was hoped there would be no Occasion for sending Ships to *Scotland*, since the News of the Duke of *Berwick*'s being gone thither was contradicted, the Report having been occasioned by the Sight of several Ships off of *Slego*: He was also informed that Mr. *De Cardonnell*, of *Southampton*, had been assured by the Master and Seamen of a *French* Prize, that all their Fleet fitted out at *Brest* (except four not ready) were gone to *Belle* Isle, and that the Ships of *Rochefort* and *Thoulon* had join'd them there, as it was supposed fifteen Gallies from *Rochfort*, and as many more from *Havre de Grace*, had also done. *The News of the Duke of Berwick's being gone to Scotland contradicted. Advice that the French Fleet rendezvous'd at Belle Isle.*

This News of the *French* Fleet's being gone to *Belle* Isle gave the Admiral no little Satisfaction, for he was in hopes it might luckily occasion

occasion his meeting them; and he was of Opinion that they would naturally chuse to hazard a Battel, rather than remain at *Brest*, and expose themselves to be attempted in that Harbour; a Jealousie whereof was probably given them not only by Monsieur *du Quesne*, but by Monsieur *Gennes* also, who were not long before in *England*, and one, or both, consulted about this Affair, the latter of whom some time after found an Opportunity of conveying himself to *France*, that so he might be able to communicate what he had heard at the *English* Court. There were other Reasons also to suspect that our Designs had taken Air, for several things contain'd even in the Queen's Instructions were hinted in the *Paris* Gazette.

The Admiral is informed that the French Squadron was gone back from Ireland; *and therefore is advised to sail as soon as possible off of* Brest.

Not many Days after the Admiral received Advice from Court that the *French* Squadron was certainly gone back from *Ireland*, and that, in all Probability, the Transports would get clear of that Kingdom before our Fleet could arrive; and therefore it was recommended to him to sail to *Brest*, *Belle* Isle, or some Station thereabouts; and the rather, for that the *French* Fleet's attempting our *Smyrna* Ships might prove of very ill Consequence to *England* and *Holland*. To this were added these following Reasons; that should the *French* Fleet be in *Brest* they might be block'd up there; their Trade be interrupted, and ours secured; and that if Intelligence could be gain'd they had set out any number of Ships, with Intention to interrupt our aforesaid Trade from *Smyrna*, a Squadron might be the better sent from thence in Quest of them.

Captain *Toll* was now arrived off of *Dunkirk* with the *Dutch* Ships, but it was judg'd the Squadron would be too weak to awe the *French* in that Port; so that a Council of War being called, it was resolved that they should be strengthened by four Ships, in regard Admiral *Allemonde* had now his number of thirty six, and that he was therefore willing to make a Detachment for this Service. But notwithstanding Captain *Toll* was ordered to join the *English* Ships, he lay before *Newport*, and writ to his Admiral for Directions how he should proceed, who thereupon sent a Frigate with positive Orders to him to act in conjunction with them.

The Admiral takes notice that the Queen's Orders obliged him to lie off of Brest *till the Smyrna Fleet arriv'd.*

The Weather continued so very tempestuous that the Fleet could not stir from the *Downs* with any manner of Safety; but that they might be the better able to do Service when at Sea, the Admiral thought it necessary to take notice a second time, that he was tied up by the Queen's Instructions to lie off of *Brest* until the *Smyrna* Fleet arrived, and desired that that Matter might be explain'd; because if the *French* Fleet were out, it was his Opinion they ought to be followed to *Belle* Isle, or any other Place. In Answer to this he was acquainted, that it was not intended he should be tied up by those Instructions so much as he imagined, though several Lords of the Privy Council had made the very same Objections, but were satisfy'd upon the Orders being read and explain'd to them.

The Weather began now to be fair, so that he determined to tide it away Westward, and to leave for the *Dunkirk* Squadron two *English* Ships of sixty Guns each, three of fifty, and one of fifty six, with a Fireship, and a Sloop; and of the *Dutch* five of fifty Guns,

one

CHAP. VII. *from the Year* 1688, *to* 1697.   441

one of fifty four, one of fifty two, one of forty, one of thirty six, one of thirty four, one of twenty six, one of twenty four, and another of twenty, making in all twenty one. Accordingly he sailed, and being on the fourteenth of *June*, six Leagues S. E. from the Isle of *Wight*, it was by a Council of War of the Flag-Officers agreed, that the Station should be eight Leagues West from *Ushant*, and that from thence some Ships should be detached to look into *Brest* for Intelligence. The nineteenth of *June*, tho' the Wind had been continually contrary, (as it was all along from the time the Fleet first arrived in the *Downs*) he got off of *Plimouth*, but by bad Weather was forced back to *Torbay*; and now he received a Letter from Mr. *Aylmer*, (dated off of Cape St. *Vincent*) by which he judged the *Smyrna* Fleet was in *Ireland*, or at least very near the Soundings. *The Fleet sails a second time from the Downs.* *The Admiral receives Advice of the Smyrna Fleet,*

The Weather being fair, the Admiral got under Sail the twenty second of *June*, and when he was off of *Dartmouth*, an Express came from Mr. *Greenhill*, then Naval-Agent at *Plimouth*, with Advice that the Enemy were at Sea with eighty Ships, whereupon all possible Diligence was used to get over to the *French* Coast, and on the twenty eighth (*Ushant* bearing E. S. E. nine Leagues distance) some Fishermen were taken from the Shore, who confirmed the News, and said the *French* Fleet had lain becalmed four Days off of that Island. Upon this the Flag-Officers being consulted, it was resolved to stretch over to Cape *Clear* for the Preservation of the *Turky* Fleet, and not meeting with News there, immediately to return off of *Brest*; and the Place of Rendezvous was appointed to be six Leagues West from *Scilly* with a Westerly Wind. *and, of the French being at Sea with eighty Sail.* *A Council of War unanimously resolve to stand over to Cape Clear.*

There was at this time a Project on foot to join some Ships to the *Spanish Armada* (as they called their insignificant Fleet) in the Streights, his Catholick Majesty having offered not only to fit out ten, (such as they were) but condescended also not to expect or give Salutes, or to have the Command in chief in those Seas; so that all things were to be concerted at a Council of War, and each Nation to do the best they could for the publick Good; but tho' the King did not think fit to determine any thing in this Matter, until such time as it could be seen what Success might be had against the *French* in these Parts, yet afterwards a very considerable Part of the Naval Force of *England* and *Holland* was sent thither under the Command of Mr. *Russel*, at which time the *French*, with many Ships from *Brest*, and their whole *Thoulon* Squadron, were endeavouring to make their utmost Efforts in the *Mediterranean*, and had entered with their Land Forces on the Confines of *Catalonia*; which Expedition shall be particularly treated of in its proper Place. *A Project for joining some of our Ships to act with the Spanish Armada in the Streights.*

The Fleet being now at Sea, such Care was taken to preserve the *Smyrna* Trade, that single Ships were appointed to cruise for them on every proper Point of the Compass, while the main Body pass'd over to Cape *Clear*; and when the Admiral came off of *Kinsale* he found they were safely arrived there. Mr. *Aylmer*, who commanded the Squadron, was ordered to come out and join him, it being resolv'd to conduct them as far as the Islands of *Scilly*, and there to leave them *The Fleet joins the Smyrna Convoy off of Kinsale.*

L l l   if

if they had a fair Wind to proceed up the Chanel: But that they might not run the least Hazard, a Frigate was sent before to *Plimouth*, to bring the Admiral Advice, eight Leagues S. W. from *Scilly*, whether any of the Enemy's Ships were on the Coast.

He had determined upon his parting with this Trade to go off of *Ushant*, and if the *French* were gone from thence to follow them to *Belle Isle*; but being afterwards of Opinion that they lay in the Sea, purposely to avoid our Fleet, he altered his Resolutions, and resolved to go into a more proper Station in Search of them; so that parting with the *Smyrna* Ships off of *Scilly* the thirteenth of *July*, he first shaped his Course towards the *French* Coast, from whence he sent a Letter to the Secretary of State, desiring that it might be considered whether the Fleet, before its Return, could be serviceable towards the Reduction of *Ireland*, for that the Provisions would last no longer than the latter End of *August*, and after that Month was expired, he thought it not safe for the great Ships to be out of Harbour; but desired that a Supply of Provisions might be ready at *Plimouth*, that so the Want thereof might not obstruct any necessary Service.

The Smyrna Convoy parted with, and the Fleet proceeds off of the French Coast.

No sooner was *Ushant* discovered from the Mast-head, than Sir *Cloudesly Shovell* was sent with a Squadron to look into *Brest*, and the Admiral himself followed at a convenient Distance. When he was about a League from St. *Matthew*'s Point, he saw about forty Sail coming out of *Brest* Harbour, which proved to be small Coasting Vessels of *Bretagne*, with three Men of War, of about thirty six or forty Guns each; and one of them standing to the Leeward of him, he shot down her Main-Yard, but she putting before the Wind escaped through the Rocks called the *Chickens*, where the *French* Pilots on board our Ships did not think fit to venture. He got Intelligence that the *French* Fleet had been at Sea near forty Days; that not above a Week before a Ship of eighty Guns sailed from *Brest* to join them, and that a Water-Ship had not been long come in, which left them about forty Leagues Westward of *Ushant*, where, and up and down in the *Soundings*, it was reported they had been ever since they put forth to Sea.

Sir Cloudesly Shovell ordered with a Squadron to look into Brest.

And gets Intelligence of the French Fleet.

Sir *Cloudesly*, to decoy the aforemention'd Ships, stood in with Part of his Squadron under *French* Colours, the others having none at all; and the *French* in those Parts being informed that their Fleet had taken several *English* Ships, believed their Admiral had sent them home, so that they were coming out to meet them, imagining that our Ships which shewed *French* Colours were their own Men of War, and that those without Colours were their Prizes; but finding their Mistake, every one shifted for himself in the best manner he could. At this time the Marquess of *Carmarthen*, since Duke of *Leeds*, took with his Sloop two Men out of a Boat, who were going off, as they thought, to visit their Friends. These Men reported the *French* Fleet to be eighty four Ships of the Line of Battel, which though the Admiral thought to be almost impossible, yet, the Wind being fair, he made the best of his Way to be an Eye-Witness thereof, having ordered the Rendezvous, in case of Separation, to be ten

Sir Cloudesly Shovell decoys several French Ships by putting abroad White Colours.

CHAP. VII. *from the Year* 1688, *to* 1697. 443

ten Leagues S. W. from *Scilly*, and for any Ships in Distress, by bad Weather, or otherwise, *Torbay*, or *Plimouth*.

The twenty seventh of this Month of *July*, the Fleet being about thirty Leagues from *Ushant*, several Vessels were seen under Convoy of a Man of War, and two Ships supposed to be Fireships; and it was reasonable to believe by their working that they took ours for the *French* Fleet, which we endeavoured to confirm them in, by shewing White Flags and Colours; but one of our Captains being too forward in chasing, gave the Alarm, so that only three of the small Vessels fell into our Hands. *Several French Ships and Vessels seen thirty Leagues from Ushant, and some of them taken, who gave an Account of their Fleet.*

This Convoy was going with fresh Provisions to their Fleet, which the Prisoners reported consisted of seventy six Sail, from an hundred to fifty Guns, and thirty Fireships; that they lay sixty Leagues West, or W. S. W. from *Ushant*, the very Place where our Fleet was at this time, though none of our Scouts had yet gotten Sight of them, which created a Belief of what the Prisoners said, that Monsieur *Tourville*, their Admiral, had Directions from the King his Master to avoid us; in order whereunto they kept their Scouts at a considerable Distance from their Fleet, on all Points of the Compass by which they could be approached, and being chased by ours, ran away and made Signals to others within them; so that it was impossible to come up with their Body, although the *English* and *Dutch* Fleets sailed in such a Posture, as that the Scouts on each Wing, and those ahead and astern, could, in clear Weather, see twenty Leagues round: So difficult a Thing it is for the chief Commander of one Fleet to bring his Rival at the Head of another to an Engagement, if he seeks to avoid it, especially when, by his being in the open Sea, he hath Opportunities of so doing, and of discovering by his Scouts all the Movements he makes, or knowing what Approaches he either can, or cannot make towards him, according as the Winds may be. *No Probability of coming up with theEmy, who industriously avoided us.*

The Admiral finding that all Methods for coming up with the Enemy proved ineffectual, he desired to know how he should proceed with the Fleet; for though he thought it not adviseable, while the *French* were out, to anchor in any Bay, yet he feared the continuing so long at Sea might very much endanger the Health of the Men, it having not been customary to furnish them with such Refreshments at Sea as the *French* constantly had; nor was it indeed equally in our Power so to do, by Reason of the Remoteness of our Ports.

The twenty ninth of *July* her Majesty sent Directions to the Admiral, that if the *French* Fleet, was not at Sea, or in such a Station where prudently he could attack them, he should forthwith repair to the Coast of *Ireland*, for Security of our Merchant Ships; but left him at liberty to go to *Kinsale* to refresh his Men, or to remain in such Station near that Place, where he should judge the Fleet might be most safe, and in the greatest Readiness to execute Orders. *The Fleet ordered to the Coast of Ireland, and the Reason thereof.*

The chief Occasion of this Order for proceeding on the *Irish* Coast was the King's Success in that Kingdom which was so great, that His Majesty thought he might employ a considerable Part of his Army this Year on a Descent in *France*; but it was to be given out

L ll 2 that

that the Preparations were for *Flanders*. It was judg'd that this would not only give a Diversion to the Enemy, but probably induce them to venture a Battel at Sea to prevent it; so that it was thought necessary the Fleet should be on the *Irish* Coast, not only to protect such a Transport, but to assist in it too, by taking on board Soldiers which could not otherwise be embarked. But in regard the Troops could not be ready in less than three Weeks, the Admiral was advised not to leave the *French* Coast so as to neglect an Opportunity of fighting, which probably he would either soon have, or not at all this Summer.

Several Privateers get out of Dunkirk and do mischief Northward.

About this time fifteen or sixteen Privateers got out of *Dunkirk*, and ranging along the Northern Coast, under Command of Monsieur *Du Bart*, landed in *Northumberland*, where they burnt a House of the Lord *Widdrington*'s, and did some other Mischief.

The Fleet having continued in the Station, sixty Leagues W. S. W. from *Ushant*, three Days longer than was determined by the Council of War, in hopes the *French* might come thither, the Admiral left the said Station the thirty first of *July*, and once more stood for *Ushant*: And that he might be the better enabled to keep the Sea, he ordered the Vessels with Beer at *Plimouth* to come to him eight Leagues West from the said Island, there being a great want thereof in the *English* Ships, and the *Dutch* had no more Provisions than what would last them to the twentieth of *August*.

Three Days after the Admiral left the Station he ordered some Ships to chase off of *Ushant*, of which Number that commanded by the Marquis of *Carmarthen* was one, and his Lordship's Sloop being also in Company, saw upwards of a hundred Sail in *Broad Sound*, which were judged, and that rightly too, to be the *French* Fleet going to *Brest*. This being made known to the Admiral, a Council of War was called on the fifth of *August*, where it was resolved, that since the Winds hung Westerly, and that both *English* and *Dutch* wanted Water and Beer, it was absolutely necessary to sail to *Torbay* to recruit, and refresh the Men, who had been two Months at Sea, When he arrived there, the necessary Orders were given for putting every Ship into a speedy Condition for Service; but there was a great want of Men occasioned by Sickness; nor did the Supplies of Provisions answer Expectation; for the *Dutch*, with what they met there, had no more than would last them to the latter end of *September*.

The French Fleet get into Brest.

Our Fleet comes to Torbay for Provisions.

The Admiral having represented to the Queen some Difficulties that arose to him, with respect to the several Services required by her Majesty's Orders, the same were explain'd; As first, that the going with the Fleet upon the *French* Coast was repeated to him, left the Appointment of the other Services might look like a Revocation of that, and consequently an Opportunity of fighting should be thereby prevented. But that, secondly, in regard such an Opportunity might not, at that Season of the Year, be met with, the next Concern was for the Trade coming from the *West-Indies*: And that, thirdly, it was necessary some care should be taken of the Transports with the Troops from *Ireland*; which latter depending

Her Majesty's Orders explain'd.

on

CHAP. VII. *from the Year* 1688, *to* 1697.

on the hop'd-for Success at *Limerick*, it would consequently be the last Service in order of Time: But that, however, her Majesty left it to his Choice to place himself in such a Station as might most effectually answer these Ends, because, as a Seaman, he could best judge of it, and that it greatly depended upon the Intelligence he might have from *Brest*, with relation to the *French* Fleet, or from the Sea off of the Coast of *Ireland*, which probably the *West-India* Ships would first make; or from *Kinsale*, whence he might have the earliest Notice of the Transports intended for that Kingdom. But since he thought it necessary that the three-deck'd Ships should be sent home at the Expiration of this Month, her Majesty was pleas'd to approve thereof, and directed that they should be accordingly ordered to *Spithead*.

Soon after this he received a Letter from the Lords of the Admiralty, by which not only his own, but the Opinion of the Flag-Officers was desired, How long it might be convenient to keep the Fleet at Sea in a Body? How long they might be ventured at Sea, in case the *French* did not disarm their Ships, or the publick Service should require so great a Fleet? And when the great Ships could no longer keep the Sea, where they might with most Safety remain for some time before they were laid up, so as to be ready to join the rest of the Fleet in case the *French* should come upon our Coast? Hereupon a Council of War was call'd the nineteenth of *August*, where were present the Flag-Officers following; *viz.*

The Lords of the Admiralty demand how long it may be advisable to keep the Fleet out in a Body, &c.

A Council of War called.

English.

Admiral *Russell*,
Admiral *Killegrew*,
Vice-Admiral *Ashby*,
Vice-Admiral *Delavall*,
Rear-Admiral *Rooke*,
Rear-Admiral *Shovell*.

Dutch.

Admiral *Allemonde*,
Vice-Admiral *Vandeputte*,
Vice-Admiral *Callemberg*,
Rear-Admiral *Evertson*.

Who taking the several Particulars into Consideration, determined that the following Answers should be made thereunto, *viz*

1. That it was not convenient for her Majesty's Service the Fleet should continue at Sea longer than the last of *August*.
2. But if the Service did absolutely require their staying out longer, the utmost time ought to be the tenth of *September*.
3. That when the great Ships could not longer keep the Sea, the most convenient Place for them to remain at for farther Orders was *Spithead*.

And

And it was also agreed that between ten and twenty Leagues W. S.W. from *Scilly* was the most proper Station for the Fleet to cruise in, so as to enable them to do Service.

Her Majesty's Pleasure signify'd upon the Result of a Council of War.

This Resolution of the Flag-Officers being communicated to the Queen in Council, her Majesty was pleas'd to let the Admiral know, that altho' she had, by former Orders, sufficiently informed him what Services she expected from the Fleet; yet since the *French* were now in *Camaret* Bay, and that probably he might have an Opportunity of attacking them there, she thought it ought not to be neglected; for that it was reasonable to believe the Attempt might be made before the Expiration of the Time the Council of War had limited for sending home the great Ships. However, her Majesty considering the Season of the Year, which was far advanced, and other Accidents at Sea, (not to be foreseen or judged of at Land) did not think fit positively to command the Fleet's returning before *Brest*, but declar'd she would be satisfied with the Resolution of a Council of War in that Matter; altho' she thought there was not any thing so desirable, or so much for the publick Interest as a Battel, could it be attempted without too great Hazard on the *French* Coast.

The Admiral takes notice that he is ordered by the Admiralty to remain in Torbay till farther Order.

The Admiral returning an Answer the twenty fourth, observed, that he had no Orders from the Lords of the Admiralty to obey either the King's or her Majesty's Commands, as the Earl of *Torrington* formerly had when he commanded the Fleet; nor any Orders from their Lordships contradictory to their first Instructions, (altho' he had several times writ to them on that Subject) which directed him, on his Return to *Torbay*, to remain there till farther Orders; and that though, upon considering the Contents of the foregoing Letter from the Secretary of State, he had once resolved to sail, yet in regard of the Hazard, as well as the Inconveniences he might himself be exposed to, he did not think it safe for him to carry the Fleet to Sea without particular Orders; and the Day after he dispatch'd away this Answer, he called a Council of War, where the Flag Officers came to the following Resolutions, in relation to the attacking the *French* Fleet in *Camaret* Bay.

A Council of War debate about attacking the French in Camaret Bay.

" That although the Enemy were there, yet considering the
" Scarcity of Provisions, and the bad Weather which might be ex-
" pected at such a Season of the Year, it was in no wise adviseable
" to make any Attempt upon them.

They also adhered to their former Opinions, " That the most
" proper Station for the Fleet to lie in was ten or twenty Leagues
" W. S. W. from *Scilly*; and that the Ships ought not to continue
" in a Body longer than the last of this Month, unless there should
" be an absolute Necessity; and if so, not beyond the tenth of *Sep-
" tember*. But it was thought necessary (if Wind and Weather
" would permit) to go before *Ushant*, (and not *Brest*) that so the
" *French* might know we were at Sea, and then forthwith to re-
" turn to the aforesaid Station off of *Scilly*.

" That they were sensible a Battel might be of great Advantage
" to the Publick, but wished the Enemy would give an Opportu-
" nity

CHAP. VII. *from the Year 1688, to 1697.* 447

" nity for it, without putting the Fleet under a hazard of Destruc-
" tion by attempting them in their Harbours, especially at the Ap-
" proach of the Winter Season.

"And upon considering what Squadron of Ships ought to be kept
" at Sea, after those with three Decks should be sent in, it was found,
" That none of those of the States General could continue out, for
" that their Provisions would last no longer than the twentieth of
" *September*, and his Majesty's Orders required their returning by
" that time to *Holland*: So that if the Queen expected their longer
" stay, there wanted Orders from his Majesty for the same, as well
" as for their Re-victualling; for the King being Stadtholder of that
" Republick, their Admirals received all their Instructions imme-
" diately from him.

" But altho' it was the Opinion of the Council of War, that
" there was an absolute Necessity for a Squadron to be kept abroad,
" and that if a sufficient Quantity of Victuals could be provided, a
" Detachment of proper Ships might be made for a Month; yet
" they were cautious in advising the Number, not knowing what
" Strength the *French* would have at Sea.

The twenty fifth of *August* the Admiral received Orders from *The Admiral-*
the Lords of the Admiralty, prepared in Obedience to her Majesty's *ty order the*
Pleasure signified at the Cabinet Council, whereby he was directed *and to lie in a*
forthwith to proceed to Sea, and to lie in such a Station as he judg- *proper Station*
ed most proper, as well for meeting the *French* Fleet, should they *French Fleet,*
come out again, as for the Security of the homeward-bound Trade, *and secure the*
the Ships in the River *Shannon*, and the intercepting Succours from *Trade.*
France to *Ireland*: But when the first and second Rates could be
no longer continued abroad with Safety, he was to order them to
Spithead, there to remain till farther Directions, and to appoint the
Ships of smaller Rates, (both *English* and *Dutch*) which were in a
Condition for it, to cruise until the thirtieth of *September* (if their
Provisions would last so long) in the most proper Station for answering the three last Services beforementioned; which Station their
Lordships were of opinion ought to be between twenty and thirty
Leagues S.W. off of Cape *Clear*, though they thought fit to leave
that Matter to his Determination. He was also farther directed
when he came in with the great Ships, to appoint three of the *Eng-*
lish Flag-Officers to remain with the cruising Squadron, and to order the Senior of them, at the Expiration of his Cruise, to bring
home with him the Ships of War in the *Shannon*.

Pursuant to these Orders the Admiral put to Sea with the very *The Fleet sails.*
first Opportunity of a Wind, and on the thirty first of *August*, about
ten in the Morning, made the Land of *Ushant*. The Fleet stood in
until six that Night, and then, being but four Leagues from the
Shore, tack'd, and laid it off with an easy Sail till break of Day, at
which time they stood in again; and at twelve at Noon, when they
were about three Leagues from the Land, there was not any thing
seen like a Sail, so that the Admiral steered away for the *Lizard*, ten
Leagues W.S.W. from which Place was the appointed Station.

Had

Had the *French* inclined to a Battel, a fairer Opportunity than this could not have been given them; for they might have had the Advantage of the Weather-Gage on their own Coast, but they contented themselves with lying safe in Port.

The Fleet was now in great want of Beer, which obliged the Admiral to desire that some Vessels might be sent to *Kinsale* with a Supply, that so a stop might be put to the Inconveniences and Clamour which would unavoidably attend the Men's drinking Water in the Winter; and he represented that, without a present Prospect of doing Service, the hazard so many unwieldy Ships would run in long Nights, attended with so uncertain Weather, was too great, since the Nation did not stand in need of any thing more at that time, than a Squadron strong enough to protect the homeward-bound Trade, to resist what Force the *French* would probably set forth, and to give Countenance to our Affairs in *Ireland:* All which Services were but too much interrupted by the whole Fleet's going out again; for had the three Deck'd Ships been furnished with Provisions sufficient only to have carried them to their Ports, the others might have been much sooner supply'd, and dispatched to their intended Station: Nor were his Apprehensions groundless, that the dividing our Strength at Sea might have very much exposed the whole; for had the *French* got notice that it was so intended, it was reasonable to think they would not have slip'd so promising an Opportunity of intercepting so many of the best Ships of *England* and *Holland*; for with an Easterly Wind they might have reached the *Lizard*, near to which Place those Ships would have been obliged to pass as they stood up the Chanel.

The Admiral of opinion the great Ships ought not to be hazarded without a present Prospect of Service.

He also objected against the great Ships going to *Spithead*, since by coming to an Anchor there, an Opportunity of Wind might thereby have been lost, for their getting timely about to *Chatham*, which would not only have encreased the Charge, by keeping the Men longer in Pay, but have occasioned Delay in their refitting; a Work which called for all possible Diligence and Application, since so great a Number of Capital Ships were to be docked and repaired for the next Summer's Service.

The Admiral's Objections against the great Ships staying at Spithead when ordered in.

And that I may in some measure shew what hazard such great, and consequently laborious, Ships do run at such a Season of the Year, I desire you will be referred to the following Instance thereof, *viz.*

The Fleet being in the *Soundings* the second of *September*, a violent Storm arose, insomuch that all which could possibly be done for their Preservation was to bear up for so dangerous a Port as *Plimouth*; and what from the Continuance of the Wind, and Haziness of the Weather, the Ships were so confusedly scattered, that the greatest part of them were not seen when the Admiral himself came to an Anchor in the *Sound:* But when it grew somewhat clearer, one of the second Rates (which prov'd to be the *Coronation*) was discovered at an Anchor off of the *Ram-Head*, without any thing standing but the Ensign-staff, and foundering soon after, her Commander, Captain *Skelton*, together with her Company, except

The Hazard the whole Fleet ran by a Storm in the Soundings, which forced them to bear up for Plimouth.

cept a very inconsiderable Number, were lost. Many of the biggest Ships not being able to weather the Eastermost Point of Land at the Entrance into *Plimouth* Sound, were constrain'd to take Sanctuary there, in that Confusion which a Lee Shore, thick Weather, and a very hard Gale of Wind must unavoidably occasion; insomuch that the *Harwich*, a third Rate, ran on shore and was bulged; the *Royal Oak* and *Northumberland*, Ships also of the third Rate, tailed on the Ground, though afterwards they were happily gotten off; a great *Dutch* Ship was seen at an Anchor above five Leagues in the Offing, with all her Masts gone, and several others very narrowly escaped the Danger of the Rock called the *Edistone*.

The Ships which were to Windward had indeed the good Fortune to carry it clear; but although it pleased God to terminate this Matter with no other Loss than is already mentioned, unless in Masts, Sails, and Rigging, which were miserably shatter'd, yet, in the Eye of common Reason, it might have proved of very fatal Consequence.

Many Objections were made, at the beginning of the War, against the Fleet's returning so late into the Sea, though at that time it consisted of no more than sixty Sail, and but one of them superior to a third Rate; and consequently a greater Hazard was now run with a Fleet of eighty Ships, twenty six whereof were of the greatest Magnitude. Nor could the *French* themselves have desired a better Game, than thus to know the Strength of *England* and *Holland* were contending with Winds and Waves while they secured themselves in Harbour.

The Admiral having given Orders for refitting such Ships within his reach as had received damage, and left Sir *Cloudesly Shovell* at *Plimouth* to see the same perform'd, put forth to Sea, and arriv'd at St. *Helen*'s the eighth of *September*, but before he sailed he ordered Sir *Cloudesly* to send five Fourth, three Fifth, and two Sixth Rates to cruise in the *Soundings*, in such Numbers together, and in such Stations, as might most effectually conduce to the Security of the homeward-bound Merchant Ships, and then, with the rest of the Ships fit for the Sea, to repair to *Spithead*. *The Admiral arrives at St. Helen's, having left Sir Cloudesly Shovell to fit the Ships at Plimouth.*

Soon after the Admiral received Orders from the Lords of the Admiralty to send the three-deck'd Ships about to *Chatham*, grounded (as I suppose) upon the Inconveniences he had represented might attend their continuing at *Spithead*: And his Majesty signify'd his Pleasure to the *Dutch* Admiral, that he should likewise repair home with the great Ships of the States-General. But since her Majesty, during the King's Absence in *Flanders*, had ordered to Sea a Squadron of thirty Ships, and as many more as were in a Condition, to intercept Succours from *France* to *Limerick* in *Ireland*, Admiral *Allemonde* was forbid to send home any of his Squadron, under the First and Second Rate, fitting to be continued on Service, but to employ them, on this occasion, in conjunction with our Ships, without insisting on the exact Proportion. *The three-deck'd Ships ordered up to Chatham, and the great Dutch Ships sent home.*

The Squadron of *English* and *Dutch* Ships being formed, the Admiral transmitted a List of their Names to the Secretary of State, and acquainted him that they should be sent away with all possible Dispatch; but observed withal, that if the *French* arrived at *Limerick* before this Force could possibly get thither, the small Squadron which was on the Coast of that Kingdom would run the greatest hazard of being destroy'd.

Sir Ralph Delavall ordered with a Squadron into the Soundings. His Instructions.

Sir *Ralph Delavall*, (then Vice-Admiral of the Blue) who was appointed to command on this Service, was ordered to govern himself according to the following Instructions.

In the first Place he was to take under his Command the *English* and *Dutch* Ships, and to send such of them as were first ready to the appointed Station, between twenty and thirty Leagues S. W. of Cape *Clear*, to which Place he was to follow with the rest as soon as possibly he could.

There, or thereabouts, he was to cruise in such manner as he should think proper, for protecting the Trade, and to prevent the Town of *Limerick*'s being succoured by the *French*, which it was reported they intended to attempt with twenty Ships of War under the Command of Monsieur *Chateau Renault*.

He was cautioned to have a particular regard to the Safety of those Ships which had for some time been employed under the Command of Captain *Thomas Coal* in the *Shannon*, and ordered to bring them thence at his Return home, if not otherwise disposed of by the Lords of the Admiralty.

But notwithstanding these Orders pointed at a particular Station, yet, if (from any Intelligence of the Enemy's Proceedings) he should judge it for the Service to alter the same, it was entirely left to his Discretion; and the time limited for his Cruise was the thirtieth of *September*, when he was to return to *Spithead*, and to send the several Ships to the respective Places assigned for their being refitted at, if he received not Orders to the contrary before.

To these Instructions her Majesty in Council was pleased to direct the following Particulars should be added, *viz.*

1. That he should continue on the Station until the fifteenth of *October*, unless he received contradictory Orders, or heard sooner of the Surrender of *Limerick*.

2. That he should not recal the Ships from the *Shannon* without the Consent of the Lieutenant-General.

The Reasons why Sir Ralph Delavall was forbid calling the Ships home from the Shannon.

That which occasioned the forbidding his calling off the aforesaid Ships in the River *Shannon*, was a Letter from Lieutenant-General *Ginkle*, signifying his Doubts, that if those Ships were recall'd, *Limerick* could not be taken this Year; but that otherwise, he was in hopes of being Master of it in a Month. The Reasons he gave were these, That he could stay longer before the Town, having Ships to carry off the Cannon; and that, for want of such a Convenience, if he succeeded not, he should be oblig'd to leave them behind him. He was also of opinion, that the Ships would be very useful in preventing the landing Succours from *France*, and that since they were so near the Town, he did not foresee any great Danger would attend them, for that the Enemy would be cautious how they ventured with their Squadron fifty Miles up the *Shannon*,

non, at a time when we had a confiderable Strength at Sea.

Sir *Ralph Delavall* was thrice beaten back by contrary Winds, and having attempted a fourth time to get out, he was on the fixteenth of *October* obliged to bear up for *Torbay*, where he received Orders the eighteenth to proceed fifteen Leagues S.W. from *Scilly*, with fuch part of the Squadron as remained; for the King had ordered five of the *Dutch* Ships from him, two of them to *Holland*, and the other three to the *Mediterranean*. At this time Sir *Ralph* was inform'd by the Mafter of a *French* Ship, taken by the *Dutch*, that he was ten Days before in Company of thirty *French* Ships of War, and twenty Merchant Ships, near *Belle* Ifle, the latter loaden with Corn and Provifions, and that it was reported by the Mafter of one of thefe Merchant Ships, they did intend, when the Squadron got out to Sea, to divide in the manner following, *viz*. ten of the Men of War, with fome of the Ships with Corn, for the *Weft-Indies*, other ten Men of War, and the remaining Provifion Ships for *Limerick*, and the reft for the *Mediterranean*. *Sir Ralph forced back to Torbay, after he had four times attempted to fail, and then ordered into the Soundings, with part of the Squadron. He had advice of thirty French Men of War, and twenty Ships with Provifions, and where they were bound.*

The Squadron put to Sea again, but the want of Provifions, (a thing which too frequently happen'd, and very much obftructed Service) and the bad Condition of the Ships foon oblig'd them to return to *Spithead*; nor were the *Dutch* willing to go to *Ireland*, as was defigned: But the *French* not attempting to relieve *Limerick*, (as it was reported, and believed they would have done) that Town foon furrender'd; which Succefs was follow'd by a total Reduction of a Kingdom that had proved fo long troublefome to his Majefty's Affairs. *The Squadron came to Spithead for want of Provifions. Limerick furrender'd, and a total Reduction of Ireland foon followed.*

CHAP. VIII.

Captain Lawrence Wright *fent with a Squadron of Ships to the* Weft-Indies; *with an Account of what happen'd in thofe Parts during the Time of his Command, and that of Captain* Ralph Wren, *who fucceeded him.*

HAVING in the foregoing Chapter attended the Motions of the Grand Fleet, and the detached Squadrons, from the time of their leaving to that of their returning to their refpective Harbours; and there being nothing more of this Year's Expedition at home to treat of than what relates to the Winter-Guard, which affords little of Moment, befides what pafs'd between fingle Ships of ours, and thofe of the *French*, when they happened to meet and encounter with each other, I fhall not trouble you with thofe Matters here, but proceed to fuch remarkable Tranfactions as happened in the *Weft-Indies*; and I do the rather choofe to mention the fame in this Place, altho' the Squadron commanded by Captain *Lawrence Wright* was fent thither towards the clofe of the Year 1689, for that

M m m 2 this

this Year compleated the said Expedition, and that the whole will better appear together, than if I had given a distinct Account of each Year's Transactions in those Parts.

Captain Lawrence Wright appointed to command a Squadron going to the West-Indies. 1689.

The twenty first of *December* the aforesaid Captain *Wright* was appointed Commander in Chief of the Squadron designed for the *West-Indies*, being one Third Rate, seven Fourths, two Fifths, two Fireships, and one Ketch. He was ordered to rendezvous with them at *Plimouth*, there to take on board a Regiment of Foot of his Grace the Duke of *Bolton*'s, and that being done, to proceed to *Barbadoes*, where he was to consult with the Governor and Council how he might best secure the *English* Plantations, and recover those which might be fallen into the Hands of the *French*;

His Instructions.

but he was not to stay longer there than was absolutely necessary for refreshing the Regiment, and to take in such Men, and Provisions, as the said Governor and Council should think proper. Then he was to repair to such of the *Leeward Caribbee* Islands, as (by Intelligence of the Enemy's Proceedings, and his advising with the aforesaid Governor and Council) should be thought most for the Service: And if he saw a good Opportunity of attacking the Enemy, or their Ships, at *Martinica*, or elsewhere, in his Passage to the aforesaid Islands, it was recommended to him to make the best use thereof that possibly he could.

At the *Leeward* Islands he was to apply himself to General *Codrington*, and in all things relating to the Land-Service to act according to his Directions, and the Opinion of a Council of War, either for landing the Regiment, and attacking the *French* Colonies, recovering any of our Islands, or annoying the Enemy in any other manner. In Enterprizes at Sea, he was to act as should be advised by the Governor and Councils of War, when he had Opportunity of consulting them, and, when it was necessary, to spare as many Seamen as he could with regard to the Safety of the Ships. And that the Islands might not be exposed to Insults, he was forbid to send any Ships from the Squadron until the Governor and Council were informed thereof, and satisfied that the Service did not require their immediate Attendance.

If when he arrived among the *Leeward* Islands he found them all in the Possession of the *French*, and that it should not be judged necessary to remain there, or to attempt the Enemy in those Parts, he was, without delay, to repair to *Barbadoes*, there to consult with the Governor and Council, whether it might not be most for the Service to stay with all, or any of the Ships, or to go to other of the Plantations for their Defence; and, pursuant to what should be so agreed on, he was to proceed, and to do the best Service in his Power, till he received Orders to return to *England*. And lest the *French* should attempt any of the *Dutch* Plantations, and prevail upon them for want of timely Assistance, it was recommended to him to give them what help the Circumstances of our own Affairs, both by Sea and Land, would conveniently admit of.

CHAP. VIII. *from the Year* 1688, *to* 1697.   453

Captain *Wright* sailed from *Plimouth* the eighth of *March*, with a considerable Number of Merchant Ships under his Convoy; but such was the Extremity of the Weather, not long after he parted from the Land, that most of the Ships received very considerable Damage, especially in their Masts, Sails, and Rigging; and after he had beat it up and down the Sea several Days without seeing any of his Squadron, or of the Merchant Ships, he reached *Madera* the second of *April*, where he found all the Men of War, except the *Jersey, Guernsey, Quaker* Ketch, and *Richard and John* Fireship, and about twenty Sail of the Merchant Ships. Here he stayed to recruit, and to take in Wine for the Men, and then proceeded towards *Barbadoes*, where he came to an Anchor in *Carlisle* Bay the eleventh of *May* following, but in so sickly a Condition, that it was difficult to find a sufficient Number of healthy Men to get up his Anchors; not but that the Sick soon recovered, by the care which was taken to put them on shore, and to provide them Necessaries when there. *After much bad Weather he arrives at the Madera's. 1690. Arrives at Barbadoes.*

The twenty seventh of the same Month he sailed towards the *Leeward* Islands, and arriving the thirtieth at *Antigoa*, enter'd into Consultation with General *Codrington* and the Council there (of which he was sworn a Member) what Place in the Possession of the *French* they should first attack, but could come to no Resolution therein till they had first muster'd up their Strength in the other Islands; in order whereto the Commadore sailed with his Squadron the third of *June* down to *Monserrat*, where he was joined in few Days by the General from *Antigoa* with some Ships and Sloops having Troops on board, from whence they repair'd in Conjunction to *Nevis*, where having made the proper Disposition of the Forces, and put all things in a Readiness for proceeding against the Enemy, they came to a Resolution in a General Council of War, held the seventeenth, to attack St. *Christopher's*, of which the *French* had since the breaking out of the War entirely dispossessed us. Among other means agreed on for the Execution of this Design, it was resolved, That the Commadore should with five of his Squadron, and three light Sloops, first sail along Shore, not only to alarm the Enemy, but to draw them after him, which he accordingly endeavoured to do, but Day-light appear'd before they could reach *Friggot's* Bay, the Place appointed to land at; so that being discovered, they durst not then attempt it, because the Enemy were very strongly intrenched. The following Afternoon it was agreed that Sir *Timothy Thornhill*, with about five hundred Men, should land at a Place Eastward of *Friggot's* Bay, and accordingly some part of the Men were put on shore about One in the Morning, who began their March up the Hills by the Assistance of a Black Guide. Somewhat before Day they met on the West-side of the top of the Hill a Party of *French*, who were soon put to flight, and followed so closely, that our People entered with them into their Trenches, where, indeed, they made a stout Resistance for almost two Hours: But such Bravery was shewn on our side, especially by the Officer who commanded, that the *French* were beaten out of their Trenches, *Sails to the Leeward Islands; Where General Codrington and he agree to attack St. Christopher's. Sir Timothy Thornhill with three hundred Men landed at St. Christopher's,*

3   and

and put a second time to the Run. In the Heat of this Action the rest of the Army landed, and about seven in the Morning pitched their Colours in the Enemy's Works; and being soon after drawn out, they began their March for *Basse Terre*, but having several Hills to pass over, the routed *French* posted themselves between two of them, in order to a second Encounter.

They march to, and attack Basse Terre, defeating several Parties of the Enemy.

As soon as our Forces came up the Enemy fired vigorously on them, but were answered so warmly that after an Hour's Dispute they ran, nor did they appear again to impede General *Codrington* (who was now at the Head of our Men) in his March to *Basse Terre*.

At eleven in the Morning the Squadron weighed, and sailed to *Basse Terre* Road, with Intent to batter the Town and Forts, but the *French* eased them of that Trouble, for no sooner did our Ships appear than they struck their Colours, and abandoned the Place, part whereof they set on fire, and betook themselves to the Mountains. The Army consisting of about three thousand Men, (Seamen included) marched on, burning all before them, and in the Evening lodged themselves in a Plain about a Mile from the Town, near the Jesuits College.

The Town and Forts abandoned.

I may not here omit taking notice of the Zeal and Bravery of the Officers and Men, but more particularly of Sir *Timothy Thornhill*, who, though very much wounded at his first Entrance into the *French* Trenches, did nevertheless go on till they were routed, and suffered not his Wound to be dressed before he came on board the Squadron.

In this Action we had killed and wounded about one hundred and thirty Men, and Captain *Keigwin*, a Sea-Commander, who was appointed Colonel of the Marine Regiment (which consisted of about two hundred and thirty Seamen) was shot through the Thigh, of which Wound he died before he could be carried on board, and Captain *Brisbane*, who acted as first Captain to the Marines, receiving a Shot through the Body, expired the next Night on board the *Bristol*.

The General began his March the twenty fourth towards Fort *Charles*, or the *English* Fort, and it was thought necessary that the Squadron should sail to the *Old Road*, and anchor there, until such time as the Army appeared, which they did in the Evening, where encamping, they rested that Night and the next Day.

General Codrington marches with his Army to Phrips Bay.

The twenty sixth, early in the Morning, they marched to *Phrips* Bay, and part of them encamped about three Quarters of a Mile from the Fort, some about half a Mile's Distance, and others marched up *Brimstone* Hill, an Eminence that looked into it.

The thirtieth two chase Guns were mounted, of about nine Feet long, carrying somewhat above a five Pound Shot, and the General sending the Commadore word that he should be ready next Morning to fire into the Fort, he weighed with his seven Ships, and passing by it within half Shot, fired his upper Tire of Guns, being not able to do Service with those on the lower Deck. After the Ships were all passed they plyed to Windward, and being got a second time into their

CHAP. VIII. *from the Year* 1688, *to* 1697.

their firſt Order, they again ſailed by the Fort; but not being capable of doing any conſiderable Damage, they plyed again to Windward, and anchored in the Road; and in this Action the Gunner of the *Aſſiſtance* was loſt, and five Men were wounded. *Fort Charles attack'd.*

The chief Officers being met in Council the ſecond of *July*, it was their Opinion that it was neceſſary to put nine good Guns on Shore, in order to batter the Fort, and that the Army ſhould intrench, and endeavour to gain Ground on the Enemy. Immediately nine Twelve-Pounders were landed, and with the Help of the Seamen mounted in their Carriages, ſo that now all was ready but the Platform and Trenches; mean while our Guns from the Hill gauled the Fort, and battered down the Houſes; nor were the Enemy behind hand in their Endeavours to do us Miſchief with their great Guns and ſmall Arms. *A Council of War called.*

Some Days after the General began his March with eight hundred Men round the Iſland, to bring in all the Stragglers he could meet with, and to fight any Body of *French* that ſhould attempt to face him, the reſt of the Army daily approaching nearer the Enemy by the Help of Retrenchments.

It was not long e'er the General returned, bringing with him many Negroes, and ſeveral *Frenchmen* that had quitted their Arms and ſurrender'd; and the twelfth in the Afternon the Enemy ſent a Flag of Truce from the Fort, deſiring three Days Ceſſation, which being followed the next Morning with Articles of Surrender, the Fort was given up, the *French* marching out with all the Baggage they could carry, and about forty Gentlemen were allowed their Arms. *The Enemy ſend a Flag of Truce, and the next Day ſurrender.*

When our People came into the Fort, they were not a little ſurprized to ſee the Houſes ſo miſerably ſhattered, by the Shot only from the Guns on the Hill, which the Enemy themſelves confeſſed conſtrained them to ſurrender much ſooner than otherwiſe they would have done.

The ſeventeenth a Council of War was called, and it was reſolved that Sir *Timothy Thornhill* ſhould with his Regiment be tranſported, in the General's Sloops to St. *Euſtatia*, a neighbouring Iſland which the Enemy had taken from the *Dutch*, where he landed on the nineteenth without any Reſiſtance, and the Squadron anchored there the ſame Evening. The twentieth the Fort deſired a Parley, but no Agreement enſued, and the next Day three of the Ships of War, anchored within Shot thereof, which ſtill held out, although very warmly ply'd from the Sea, and the four Guns on Shore. The People who defended this Fort (ſaid to be about fourſcore) behaved themſelves with great Bravery, firing only towards the Land, and wholly neglecting what was done againſt them from the Sea; but the other Battery of two Guns being fixed the twenty third, and ſeveral Shot fired from thence, a Flag of Truce was ſent from the Fort in the Afternoon, and next Morning our People marched in upon the Enemy's Surrender: Which being the only ſtrong Place there, the reſt of the Iſland fell of Courſe into our Hands. *Sir Timothy Thornhill with his Regiment ſent to St. Euſtatia. The Fort of St. Euſtatia ſurrender'd.*

The twenty ſixth at Night the Squadron ſailed from St. *Euſtatia*, and anchored next Day at St. *Chriſtopher's*, in a ſandy Bay Weſtward

The Squadron returns to St. Christopher's, and a Council of War agreed to make no more Attempts till the Men were recover'd.

Westward of *Charles* Fort, where they took on board the Guns that were mounted on Shore: But the Army being now very sickly of the Flux, a general Council was held on the third, where it was agreed not to attempt any other Place until the Men were in better Health, and that the expected Hurricanes were over; so that on the second of *August* the Squadron sail'd to the *Old Road*, and water'd, and the next Morning to *Nevis*; but the Winds shifting to the W. N. W. obliged them to depart from thence, and on the fifth they came to an Anchor off of the *Five Islands* at *Antigoa*, where they put the Soldiers on Shore, and having supplied themselves with Wood, proceeded from thence the seventh, and arrived at *Barbadoes* the thirteenth. The Commadore was fearful the Hurricanes might take him in this Road, and therefore sailed the next Day about thirty Leagues Southward, the better to avoid those boisterous Winds, it being intended as soon as they were over, to attack *Guadalupe*, if all things should be found in a Condition for such an Undertaking.

The Squadron arrived at Antigoa after the Hurricanes were over.

The Hurricanes were no sooner over than the Squadron sailed for the Leeward Islands, and on the sixth of *October* anchored in *Five Islands* Bay at *Antigoa*; but not finding General *Codrington* there, they proceeded to *Nevis*, and from thence to St. *Christopher's*, where they met with him.

A Resolution taken to attack Guadalupe.

On the eleventh a Council of War being called, it was determined to attack *Guadalupe*; in order whereunto the General went forthwith to *Nevis*, *Montserrat*, and *Antigoa*, to get the Army in Readiness that so no time might be lost in shipping them when the Squadron should come to each of those Islands; but, by Reason of the great Mortality, the whole Force would not have exceeded fifteen hundred Men, if three hundred and fifty designed for St. *Christopher's* were left there: Nevertheless they intended to carry on the Expedition, when in the midst of their Preparations, the Commadore received Orders to return to *England* with Part of his Squadron, which put an end for the present to the Design on *Guadalupe*.

The Squadron arrives in Carlisle Bay, but wanted Provisions.

The fifteenth of *December* the Squadron sailed from St. *Christopher's*, and anchored the thirtieth in *Carlisle* Bay in *Barbadoes*, where they were in Hopes of finding Provisions from *England*, for there was so great a Want, that, with an equal Dividend, it would not last longer than the End of *January*; nor was there less Scarcity of Stores: And the Commadore being obliged to send the *Guernsey* and *Quaker* Ketch to *Jamaica*, the *Success* to convoy the Ships from thence to *England*, and another Ship to do the like from *Barbadoes* and the *Leeward* Islands, there remained but seven, and those were in the following Condition, *viz.*

Mary	Her Fore-mast sprung.
Tiger	Had a Jury Main-mast.
Assistance	The Head of her Main-mast shot with a 24 Pounder, and the Ship leaky

Bristol

CHAP. VIII. *from the Year* 1688, *to* 1697.

Briſtol	{ Her Fore-maſt ſprung, and the Ship leaky.
Antelope	Her Main-maſt was ſprung.
Hampſhire	In like Condition.
St. Paul	A Fireſhip.

In few Days after Captain *Wright*'s Arrival in *Carliſle* Bay, he received other Orders from the Lords of the Admiralty, directing his Continuance abroad in the *Weſt-Indies*; and on the twentieth of *January* the Victuallers arrived under Convoy of the *Jerſey*, when greateſt Diligence was uſed in the diſtributing to each Ship her Proportion; and the *Briſtol* returning the thirty firſt from her Cruiſe off of *Martinica*, the Captain of her reported, that fifteen Days before he ſaw fourteen Sail of *French* Men of War enter into that Port. Upon this Captain *Wright* called a Council of the Captains, before whom Captain *Haughton* declared what he had ſeen, and it was inſtantly agreed that ſix of the beſt Merchant ſhips ſhould be taken up to ſerve as Men of War, *viz.* one of forty Guns, two of thirty two, and three of thirty Guns each, together with a Fireſhip; but there was not time ſufficient for fitting her. For the more expeditious victualling theſe Ships three Commiſſioners were appointed out of the Council, namely, Col. *Lillingſton*, *George Andrews*, and *John Bromley* Eſquires, the Governor himſelf disburſing what Money was neceſſary for purchaſing the ſame.

The victualling Ships arrive from England.

A Council of War called upon notice that 14 French Men of War were at Martinica.

And now the Commadore reſuming the Deſign againſt *Guadalupe*, he ſet Sail the twelfth of *February* for the *Leeward* Iſlands, where he arrived in few Days; but there being no good Underſtanding between him and General *Codrington*, there were ſuch tedious Delays in the furniſhing the Aſſiſtance neceſſary from thence for the intended Expedition, that it was the twenty firſt of *March* before they proceeded thereon; when (it having been reſolved at a Council of War that *Marigalante*, another of the *French* Iſlands, in the Neighbourhood of *Guadalupe*, ſhould be firſt attacked) the Squadron and ſeveral Sloops with Soldiers on board ſteered their Courſe for that Iſland, where they arriv'd the twenty ſeventh, and the next Day landed about nine hundred Men under the Command of Col. *Nott*, who immediately poſſeſſed themſelves of the Town and Fort without any Oppoſition, the Enemy having abandoned them and retired into the Country; whither the Troops marching after them, in few Days they brought in the Governor and Lieutenant-Governor of the Iſland, with ſome other Priſoners. By this time General *Codrington* was arrived there with the reſt of the Troops under his Command, and our Men having ruined all the Plantations, and utterly deſtroyed the Country, it was agreed in a Council of War, held the tenth of *April*, to re-imbark the Troops, and proceed to the Attack of *Guadalupe*. Sailing over to that Iſland, they landed the Army the twenty firſt, in a Bay on the Weſt Side thereof, from whence (having firſt defeated a Body of *French*, after a warm Diſpute, wherein ſeveral were killed on both Sides,) they took their March towards *Baſſe Terre*, where they arrived the twenty third,

Marigalante attack'd. 1691.

Guadalupe attack'd.

and burnt that Town; but there were two strong Forts in the Neighbourhood thereof, which would require some time to reduce.

The twenty sixth the Squadron proceeding according to the Motion of the Troops, came to an Anchor off of *Basse Terre*, and put ashore several Barrels of Powder, with Cartridges and Utensils for a Siege; and the next Day upon a Proposal of the Commadore, approved by the General and Officers ashore, it was resolved, at a Consultation of the Captains of the Squadron, that the Ships should weigh and ply to Windward, and come down thence in a Line and batter the Forts. To this Purpose they accordingly weighed about two Hours before Midnight, and ply'd to Windward all Night; but the next Morning found the Current so strong against them, setting to the Northward, that they could not fetch the Place from whence they came, but in spight of all their Efforts were forced to come to an Anchor, some nine Miles, and some much farther, to Leeward.

The next Day they towed up again, and put ashore some Guns and a Mortar-Piece, with which the Troops having played on the Forts from two Batteries for several Days, but with no great Success, at length on the fourteenth of *May*, one of the Scout Ships that had been sent out to cruise in the Offing, came in with Intelligence that she had seen eleven Sail of *French* Ships, which were supposed to be Monsieur *du Casse*'s Squadron (of whose Arrival in those Parts they had heard some Days before) coming from *Martinica* to the Relief of *Guadalupe*. This Advice the Commadore communicating to General *Codrington*, it was thereupon resolved in a Council of Officers, to quit the Island, and the same Night all the Troops were embarked, but with such Precipitation that they left their Mortar-Piece behind them, with all their Utensils for breaking Ground: And the next Morning the Squadron set Sail, and ply'd to the Eastward, with very blowing Weather. Two Days after which they saw the *French* Squadron to Windward, which they supposed had landed a Reinforcement on *Guadalupe*, and Captain *Wright* gave Chase to six Sail, among whom was a Rear-Admiral; but they being clean Ships, and his very foul, it proved to little Purpose, so that, after some Hours Chase, he bore up to the rest of his Squadron, and the next Day came to an Anchor under the Island *Marigalante*. There holding a Consultation with the Captains, they came to a Resolution that, in Consideration of a sudden malignant Distemper which began to rage among the Ships Companies and Soldiers, that the hired Ships were very weak, that a *French* Squadron was abroad, and that they were themselves in want of all manner of Stores, they should all proceed to *Barbadoes*, except the *Antelope* and *Jersey*; which were ordered to take on board the Blue Regiment, and carry them down with General *Codrington* to *Antigoa*, or where else he should direct. Thither they accordingly set Sail, as the Commadore did with the rest of the Ships for *Barbadoes*; but falling sick a Day or two after, as soon as he arrived in *Carlisle* Bay, he left the Squadron, by the Advice of the Physicians, (how justifiably I shall not say) and coming to *England*, the Ships were divided,

some

CHAP. VIII. *from the Year* 1688, *to* 1697. 459

some to particular Services in the *West-Indies*, while the Remainder came Home, and brought with them such Trade as were ready to sail, as will be more particularly related in the following Account of *Captain Wren*'s Proceedings in those Parts.

The latter End of *October* the said *Captain Ralph Wren*, who was then in the *Norwich*, had Orders to take also under his Command two other Ships of the Fourth Rate, the *Diamond* and *Mordaunt*, and upon arriving with them at St. *Helens*, he was to receive on board there one hundred and fifty Soldiers, Recruits for the Duke of *Bolton*'s Regiment then in the *Leeward* Islands. *Capt. Wren commands the Ships in the West-Indies.*

There were also other Land Forces to be carried in Transport Ships, which, with Victuallers, and the Trade, he was to convoy to *Barbadoes*, where he was to stay no longer than might be absolutely necessary for the Refreshment of the Men, but to proceed to the *Leeward* Islands. On his Arrival in the *West-Indies*, he was to take under his Command the Ships following, viz. the *Mary*, *Antelope*, *Assistance*, *Hampshire*, and *Jersey*, (the first being a Third, and the rest Fourth Rates) as also the *St. Paul* Fireship, one whereof he was to send to *Jamaica*, in order to her convoying the Trade from thence to *England*. *Instructions to Capt. Wren.*

It was particularly recommended to him so to employ the Ships under his Command as that they might best secure our Plantations, and annoy the Enemy; and in the Spring of the Year he was ordered to return with them home.

When there might be Occasion for any Enterprize at Land, he was to govern himself as should be agreed by Colonel *Codrington*, General of the *Leeward* Islands, and a Council of War; and in Enterprizes at Sea, he was to advise with them; as he was also to do during his Stay at *Barbadoes* with the Governor and Council there; and at all such Councils of War wherein the Service of the Squadron was requir'd, he was to preside next to the Governor, and three of the eldest Captains of the Squadron were to have Votes at those Consultations.

Thus was Captain *Wren* instructed, and sailing from *Plimouth* the twelfth of *December*, he arrived the sixteenth of the next Month at *Barbadoes*; but before he came to an Anchor, received Advice by a Sloop from the Governor, that nine *French* Ships of War were seen to Leeward of the Island, and that there was among them the *Jersey*, a Fourth Rate of ours, which had been taken some time before off of *Dominica*. *Capt. Wren comes to Barbadoes.*

At *Barbadoes* the Commadore was join'd by the *Antelope*, and *Mary*, and there he learn'd that the *Assistance, Hampshire*, and *St. Paul* Fireship, part of the Ships that were to compose his Squadron, were at the *Leeward* Islands.

The twenty third the Governor called a Council of War, where it was agreed, that as soon as the *Antelope* could be got ready all the Ships should proceed directly for *Antigoa*; but presently after this a Sloop arrives, which had been sent to *Martinica* with Prisoners, and gave an Account that the *French* had eighteen Ships of War in those Parts, eight of them actually cruising off of *Barbadoes*, and the *A Council of War.*

Nnn 2

the rest fitting out with all Expedition; so that on the twenty fifth, another Council was assembled, and then it was resolved that two Merchant Ships should be fitted, in a warlike manner, and that, with their Assistance, the Squadron should attempt the Enemy.

All things being ready, and the Soldiers put on board, the Commadore sailed the thirtieth of *January*, and plied to Windward, having with him five Ships of War, besides the two Merchant Ships, and two Privateer Sloops.

He continued to cruise five Days, but not finding any of the Enemy's Ships, returned to *Barbadoes*, and there another Council of War was held the fifth of *February*, where it was determined, that since the *French* were gone off the Coast all possible Dispatch should be made in following them; so that the Squadron sailed from *Barbadoes* the seventeenth of *February*, the Commadore having before sent two Sloops to *Martinica*, to make what Discovery they could, and then to join him at *Antigoa*.

Capt. Wren meets with the French Ships.

But when he came off of *Deseada*, near *Guadalupe*, he espied a considerable Number of *French* Ships, which proved to be eighteen Men of War, two Fireships, and about five or six small Vessels; among which there were three of our Ships which they had taken, namely the *Jersey* beforementioned, the *Constant Warwick*, and *Mary Rose*; and this Squadron was commanded by the Count *de Blanac*.

Captain *Wren* was obliged to bear down about six Leagues to Leeward, in order to join some of his Squadron, and to tow the Merchant Ships out of Danger, mean while the Enemy followed him all Night in a Line of Battel, within Gun-shot. At eight the next Morning some of our Ships had not a Breath of Wind, though at the same time the Enemy had a fresh Gale, and by that Advantage four

They engage.

of them bore down upon the *Mary*, which Ship defended her self very well until the Commadore himself could come to her Assistance; and at the same time the *Mordaunt*, with one of the hired Ships, namely the *England* Frigate, were warmly engaged.

The Commadore finding the great Disproportion, as to Strength, and that the Merchant Ships which were under his Care had taken the proper and usual Methods for their own Security, he wisely provided for the Safety of the Ships of War under his Command, by bearing away, but did it with so little Sail, that he secured the three Ships which the Enemy gave chase to, and anchored in *Carlisle* Bay at *Barbadoes* the twenty fifth.

By what has been said, the Reader may perceive what little Use the Enemy made of this Advantage, and that they contented themselves with trying an Experiment whether three of their Ships could beat one of ours, without exposing themselves to what might have attended a general Engagement between both Squadrons; for had they acted as they ought to have done our Ships could not possibly have escaped as they did.

Captain *Wren* dying some time after, the Command of the Squadron fell, by Seniority, on Captain *Boteler*, who with part thereof sailed from *Barbadoes* the fourteenth of *June*, according to Instructions

CHAP. IX. *from the Year* 1688, *to* 1697.   461

strictions from the Admiralty, and arrived in *England* the eleventh of *August* following, the rest being left to attend the Plantations.

CHAP. IX.

An Account of Admiral Russell's *engaging the* French *Fleet off of* La Hogue, *and of what happened till the time of his coming on shore.*

HAVING thus given an Account of Transactions abroad, I return to the Body of the Fleet, of which Mr. *Russel* was again appointed Admiral, by Commission bearing Date the third of *December* 1691. The greatest care imaginable was taken to give the quickest Dispatch to the Ships, so as that they might be early out; and on the twenty second of *April* he sent from the *Buoy of the Nore* to the *Flats of the Foreland* all Ships of the third and fourth Rate, and Fireships, as were ready, and ordered the rest to follow as soon as they should be in a Condition so to do: mean while Advice-Boats were employed to gain Intelligence of the Enemy's Preparations at *Brest*, and the Ports thereabouts. *Admiral Russel appointed a second time to command the Fleet.* 1691.

Sir *Ralph Delavall* was suddenly expected from *Cadiz* with the Squadron he commanded, and it was reported that the *French* designed to endeavour to intercept him, and the *Dutch* Ships in their Passage: To prevent which, Orders were sent to him the twenty ninth of *February*, by the *Groyne* Packet-Boat, to avoid coming near Cape *St. Vincent*, and to keep so far out to Sea as not to make Cape *Clear*; but rather to sail to *Dingle* Bay, the Mouth of the *Shannon*, or some other Port in *Ireland* thereabouts, the better to shun the Danger which not only the Ships, but the Effects of the Merchants might be exposed to by meeting the *French* Squadron. Lest these Orders should not timely meet with him at *Cadiz*, there was the like Caution given by a small Vessel, which was ordered to cruise off of Cape *Clear*, or thereabouts, to look out for him, and her Commander directed to endeavour to gain Advice, and communicate to him what he should be able to learn of the Enemy's Proceedings. And if neither he, nor Sir *Ralph* himself, could get any Intelligence, he was ordered to repair with his Squadron to *Cork* or *Kinsale*; but both these Orders missing him, he had the good Fortune to arrive safe in the *Downs* the beginning of *March* following. *Notice sent to Sir Ralph Delavall to take care of the Enemy in his Passage from the Streights.*

He arrives in the Downs, without meeting the said Advice.

There was likewise at Sea, under the Command of Rear-Admiral *Carter*, a Squadron of five Third Rates, six Fourths, six Fifths, one Sixth, three Fireships, and other small Vessels, with which he was ordered the fourteenth of *April* to sail to the Islands of *Jersey* and *Guernsey*, and there taking on board Pilots, to proceed to and cruise on the Coast of *France*, near St. *Malo*, for the Space of forty eight Hours, *Rear-Admiral Carter on the French Coast with a Squadron.* 1692.

The Instructions given him. Hours, longer than which time it was not thought convenient he should stay, unless he found an Opportunity of doing Service. From thence he was to stretch away to Cape *de la Hague*, and to stand as near in towards *Havre de Grace* as he could with Safety to the Ships; and if no Service could be done there, to return to *Spithead*, if it should not be found for the Security of the Islands to continue longer on the *French* Coast, in which Case the earliest Advice that possibly might be was to be sent of his Intentions. These Orders were followed by others of the twentieth and twenty third of *April*, the former directing him to repair with all speed to the *Flats of the Foreland*, (for there was now Advice received that the *French* were preparing to come to Sea) and the other requiring him, in his Return, to keep the Enemy's Coast on board, and to endeavour to join the Squadron going forth with Sir *Ralph Delavall*, but upon missing him to return to the *Downs*.

Notwithstanding the aforemention'd Orders, he was, on the fifth of *May* directed to cruise between Cape *de la Hague* and the Isle of *Wight*, and to endeavour to join the Body of the Fleet when it should arrive thereabouts; which Orders were sent to him by Sir *Ralph Delavall*, who on the twenty fourth of *April* received Directions from the Admiral to proceed to the *South Foreland*, with all the third, fourth, fifth, and sixth Rates, and Fireships, which were ready, together with the Bomb-Vessels, and then passing in sight of *Calais*, to stretch away Westward along the *French* Coast as far as Cape *de la Hague*, and there to send the smaller Ships as near in with the Shore as with Safety they might, to discover what the Enemy were doing at St. *Valery*, *Diepe*, and *Havre de Grace*, at which Places he was ordered to attempt any thing on their Shipping he should think practicable. When he arrived as far Westward as Cape *de la Hague*, he was to cross over to the Isle of *Wight*, and finding no Orders there, to return to, and range along the *French* Coast until he came off of *Dover*, where he was to call for Orders, but if he met not with any there, to repair to the *Flats of the Foreland*. The Admiral caution'd him to keep Scouts out, to prevent the Enemy's surprizing, or passing to the Eastward of him; and if they came in sight, and he judged them them too strong, he was not to engage, but to retreat to the *Flats of the Foreland*, and send immediate Advice to the Flag-Officer there; and upon meeting Rear-Admiral *Carter*, he was to take him under his Command. But notwithstanding he was thus directed to return to the *Flats of Foreland*, when he had stood over from Cape *de la Hague* to the Isle of *Wight*, other Orders were, upon farther Consideration, sent him the same Day by the Lords of the Admiralty, to cruise between that Cape and the Isle of *Wight*, until he should be joined by Admiral *Russel*, unless the Enemy came to Sea with a superior Strength.

The Admiral ordered to Sea with a Fleet, and to join the aforesaid Squadrons. At this very time the Admiral himself had Instructions to sail with the Body of the Fleet, both *Dutch* and *English*, and to place himself between Cape *de la Hague* and the Isle of *Wight*, in order to join the Squadrons with Sir *Ralph Delavall* and Rear-Admiral *Carter*;

CHAP. IX. *from the Year* 1688, *to* 1697.

ter; which Station was particularly appointed, upon Confideration of a Letter from him, wherein he defired that a certain Place might be fixed for the faid Junction, and Orders accordingly given to all Perfons concerned; though it appears by another Letter, that the Admiral was of Opinion it might have been more proper for him to anchor off of *Dengy Neffe*, or *Beachy Head*, and when joined there by the Squadrons, to have proceeded from thence on Service. However, being fenfible of what Importance it was to the Nation that the great Ships fhould join the others as foon as it was poffible, he plied it down through the Sands with a very fcanty Wind, contrary to the Opinion of many of the Officers, and all the Pilots, who were againft venturing fo many of the largeft Ships of *England*, without a more favourable Opportunity. *He plies down through the Sands with the great Ships, contrary to the Advice of the*

On the eighth the Admiral arrived off of *Rye*, paffing through the *Downs* without making any Stay; and in the Evening he fent to the *Dutch* Flag-Officer (who was at an Anchor in the *Downs*) to weigh, and make fail after him: And now Captain *Merfe* was difpatched with a Squadron of fmall Ships in fearch of Sir *Ralph Delavall*, carrying Orders to him to join the Fleet off of *Beachy*, or to fend a Frigate with Advice where he was, that fo there might be no Uncertainty of their meeting. *Pilots, and arrives in Rye Bay. A Squadron fent in fearch of the two Squadrons.*

The ninth of *May*, about feven in the Afternoon, the *Dutch* Ships joined the Fleet from the *Downs*, and one of their Rear-Admirals, with the reft of their Ships under three Decks, was at Anchor off of *Dengy Neffe*; fo that a Council of War being called, both of *Englifh* and *Dutch* Flag-Officers, they came to the following Refolution. *A Council of War called.*

That confidering the Orders which had been given to Sir *Ralph Delavall*, it would be moft proper to remain with the Fleet in *Rye* Bay forty eight Hours, for the more fure and fpeedy joining him; that a Ship fhould be forthwith fent off of *Beachy* in fearch of him, which upon difcovering his Flag, fhould make a Signal to another Frigate ftationed between *Beachy* and *Rye*, that fo fhe might give the like Notice thereof to the Fleet. But it was farther determined, That if the Wind blew hard Wefterly, or Eafterly, it was in the firft cafe moft convenient for the Fleet to anchor off of the *Neffe*, and in the latter, to proceed to St. *Helen's*.

Three Days the Wind continued Eafterly, but no more of the *Dutch* Ships arrived which were expected; and on the eleventh of *May* the Admiral failing from *Rye* Bay, he was join'd at St. *Helen's* on the thirteenth by the Squadrons with Sir *Ralph Delavall* and Rear-Admiral *Carter*, who had met each other four Days before, when the former was ftanding over to the Ifle of *Wight* from Cape *de la Hague*, and the other from St. *Helen's* in fearch of him. But that all Delays might be prevented, the Admiral had before difpatched a Frigate to the *French* Coaft, with Orders to Rear-Admiral *Carter* to join him, and left Inftructions for all *Englifh* and *Dutch* Ships which fhould come into *Rye* Bay to follow him to St. *Helen's*, that fo the Fleet might be entire. *The Fleet fails and is joined by Sir Ralph Delavall and Rear-Admiral Carter at St. Helen's.*

The

A Council of War agrees to sail to the French Coast near Cape de la Hague.

The fifteenth of *May* a Council of War was call'd of the Flag-Officers, as her Majesty had commanded, and though it was unanimously agreed that the Fleet ought not to proceed Westward of St. *Helen's*, until there should be certain Advice of the Enemy; yet it was thought reasonable to sail the first fair Weather to the Coast of *France*, near the Capes *de la Hague* and *Barfleur*, and to continue there four Days, if it might conveniently be done, and then to return to St. *Helen's*, for that was judged to be, for the present, the most proper Place of Rendezvous.

I cannot omit taking notice, that much about this time Reports were spread, as if several Captains in the Fleet had given Assurance to the Disaffected Persons on shore of their Readiness to adhere to to them; but her Majesty was graciously pleased to let the Admiral know, she could not believe that any of them were capable of such ill Designs; and that the Queen might be thoroughly satisfied with their Integrity, they unanimously sign'd to a Paper, declaring thereby their steady Zeal and Loyalty, which the Admiral, at their Request, convey'd to her Majesty: And since it is a Justice due to the Gentlemen of the Sea to publish the Contents of the said Paper, I shall here insert the same. *viz.*

The Flag Officers and Captains address her Majesty, upon account of some malicious Aspersions.

"We your Majesty's most Dutiful and Loyal Subjects and Servants, Flag-Officers and Captains in your Majesty's Fleet, out of a deep and grateful Sense of your Majesty's good and just Opinion of our Loyalty and Fidelity, imparted to us by the Right Honourable Admiral *Russel*, in a Letter to him from the Earl of *Nottingham*, Principal Secretary of State, do, in behalf of our selves, and all the other Officers and Seamen, humbly presume to address our selves to your Majesty at this juncture, to undeceive the World, as to those false and malicious Reports which have been lately spread in Prejudice of your Majesty's Service, by People disaffected to the Government, and who have an Aversion to the Quiet and Good of their Country, that there are some among us who are not truly zealous for, and entirely devoted to the present happy Establishment. We do therefore most humbly beg leave to add to our repeated Oaths this Assurance of our Fidelity, That we will, with all imaginable Alacrity and Resolution, venture our Lives in the Defence of the Government, and of the Religion and Liberty of our Country, against all Popish Invaders whatsoever. And that God Almighty may preserve your Majesty's most sacred Person, direct your Councils, and prosper your Arms, by Sea and Land, against your Enemies, may all People say *Amen* with your Majesty's most Dutiful and Loyal Subjects. Dated on board the *Britannia* at St. *Helen's* the fifteenth Day of *May* 1692."

Having made this short Digression, let us return to the more immediate Business of the Fleet. When all the Ships, both *English* and *Dutch*, were together, the Admiral proposed that six or eight Frigates might hover about the Coast of *Normandy*, and that at the same time the Forces intended for a Descent on *France* should embark, and be landed at St. *Malo*, while the Body of the Fleet lay Westward

CHAP. IX. *from the Year* 1688, *to* 1697. 465

Westward of that Place to protect them from the *French*: which he thought would not only contribute to our Success on shore, but oblige the Enemy to come to a Battel at Sea, rather than be bare Spectators of the Invasion of their Country.

One part of this Proposition was immediately approved of at Court; and that Intelligence might be had of the Enemy's Proceedings, the Admiral sent six light Frigates for forty eight Hours off of *Havre de Grace*, and the *French* Coast thereabouts: And since it was entirely left to him to proceed in such manner as should be agreed at a Council of War, he sailed on the eighteenth of *May* towards the Coast of *France*, and the Day after, about three in the Morning, Cape *Barfleur* bearing S.W. by S. distant about seven Leagues, the Scouts Westward of the Fleet (which were the *Chester* and *Charles* Gallies) fired several Guns, which Ships in a short time after coming within sight, made the Signal of discovering the Enemy, and lay with their Heads Northward; whereupon the Fleet was drawn into a Line of Battel, and notice given for the Rear thereof to tack, that so if the *French* stood Northward, we might the sooner come up and engage; but the Sun having dispersed the Fog soon after Four, they were seen standing Southward, forming their Line with the same Tack which our Ships had on board; upon which the Admiral caused the Signal for the Rear to Tack to be taken in, and bore away with his own Ship so far to *Leeward*, as that every one in the Fleet might fetch his Wake, or Grain, and then bringing to, he lay by with his Fore-Topsail to the Mast, that so others might have the better Opportunity of placing themselves, according as they had been before directed.

A small Squadron ordered off of Havre de Grace.

The Enemy's Fleet discovered.

About Eight our Line was indifferently well formed, which stretched from S.S.W. to N.N.E. the *Dutch* in the Van, the Admiral in the Centre, and the Blue in the Rear; and by Nine the Enemy's Van had almost stretched as far Southward as ours, their Admiral and Rear-Admiral of the Blue (who were in the Rear) closing the Line, and their Vice-Admiral of the same Division standing towards the Rear of our Fleet. About Ten they bore down upon us with little Wind, and the Admiral (who still lay by with his Fore-Topsail to the Mast) observing that Monsieur *Tourville* had put out his Signal for Battel, commanded that his should not be spread until the *French* (who had the Weather-Gage) were come as near as they thought convenient.

A particular Account of the Engagement.

At this time Admiral *Allemonde*, who commanded the *Dutch* Squadron, was sent to to tack, and get Westward of the *French* as soon as any of his Ships could weather them, and those in the Blue (then at some distance astern) were order'd to close the Line; but the Fleets had not been long engaged e'er it became quite calm, so that these Directions could not possibly be complied with.

About half an Hour after Eleven Monsieur *Tourville*, in the *Royal Sun*, (a Ship of one hundred and ten Guns) brought to, and began the Fight with our Admiral, at the distance of about three quarters Musket-shot; in which Posture he lay about an hour and half, plying his Guns very warmly, but then began to tow off in great Disorder,

O o o

order, his Rigging, Sails, and Topsail-Yards being very much wounded; nor could it be discerned that any great Endeavours were used to repair the same.

Near Two a Clock the Wind shifted to the N.W. by W. and in a little time five Ships of the Enemy's posted themselves three ahead and two astern of their Admiral, and fired very smartly until it was past three; so that Mr. *Russel* and his two Seconds (Mr. *Churchill* and Mr. *Aylmer*) had six or seven Ships to deal with. About Four a Clock there was a thick Fog, insomuch that not a Ship of the Enemy's could be seen, whereupon all firing ceas'd; but it clearing up in a little time, the *French* Admiral was discovered towing away Northward, and our Chief, that he might the better come up with him, ordered all the Ships of his Division to do the like; and there happening a small Breeze of Wind Easterly, about half an Hour after Five, the Signal was made for chasing, and Notice sent to every Ship within reach that the Eemy were standing away.

At this time many Guns were heard to the Westward, and tho' the Ships which fired could not be seen by reason of the Fog, it was concluded they were our Blue Squadron, which had, by a shift of Wind, weather'd the *French*; but it proved to be the Rear-Admiral of the Red (Sir *Cloudesly Shovell*) who was gotten to Windward of Monsieur *Tourville*'s own Squadron, and between him and their Admiral of the Blue. After they had fired some time, the Ships of both sides came to Anchor, but could not discover each other by reason of the Thickness of the Weather; and in this Scuffle Captain *Hastings*, who commanded the *Sandwich*, a second Rate, was killed, who could not avoid driving amidst these Ships of the Enemy, by reason his Anchors were not clear.

Things being now in great Confusion, the Admiral thought it most adviseable to order the Ships which were nearest him to chase Westward all Night, and let them know he intended to follow the *French* to *Brest*, believing it more proper so to do than to Anchor; and so indeed it proved; for next Morning he found himself nearer the Enemy than those Ships which had dropp'd their Anchors.

About Eight at Night there was Firing heard Westward, which lasted about half an Hour, part of our Blue Squadron having fallen in with some of the Enemy's Ships in the Fog; and in that Dispute Rear-Admiral *Carter* was killed, whose last Words to his Captain (Captain *William Wright*) sufficiently shewed that there was no reason to suspect his Zeal to the Service, for he recommended it to him to fight the Ship as long as she could swim.

Our Fleet chases the French.

It continued foggy, with very little Wind, all Night, and so hazey was it in the Morning, that not any Ships of the Enemy's, and but very few of ours, could be seen; but the Weather clearing up about Eight, the *Dutch*, who were to the Southward, made the Signal of seeing the *French* Fleet, and soon after about thirty four Sail were discovered between two and three Leagues off, the Wind being then at E.N.E. and they bearing W.S.W. our Ships chased them with all the Sail which could be made, but not in the Line of Battel, as they did after the *Beachy* Fight; for the Signal for a Line was taken

in,

CHAP. IX. *from the Year* 1688, *to* 1697.

in, that so every Ship might make the best of her way. Between Eleven and Twelve the Wind veer'd to the S.W. when the *French* crouded away Westward, and we after them; but near Four in the Afternoon the Tide of Ebb being done, both Fleets anchor'd, Cape *Barfleur* then bearing S. by W. but they weighed about Ten at Night, and both plying Westward, our Admiral's Fore-Topmast came by the Board near Twelve, it having been shot in several Places.

He continued chasing until Four next Morning, and then, the Tide of Ebb being done, anchor'd in forty six Fathom, Cape *de la Hague* bearing S. by W. and the Island of *Alderney* S. S. W. but by reason of his wanting a Topmast, the *Dutch* Squadron, and the Admiral of the Blue, with several of his Ships, got considerably to Windward of him.

About seven in the Morning part of the *French* Ships, which had advanced far towards the *Race* of *Alderney*, were perceived driving Eastward with the Tide of Flood, without Ground-Tackle to ride by, for they had in the Engagement, and the Morning after, cut away all their heavy Anchors. When they were driven so far, as that our Admiral judged he could reach them, he made the Signal for the Ships nearest to him to cut and chase, which accordingly himself and they did; but Sir *John Ashby*, with his Division of the Blue Squadron, and several *Dutch* Ships who were Weathermost, rid fast (as Mr. *Russel* had made the Sign for them to do) to observe the Motion of the rest of the *French* Ships which continued at an Anchor in the *Race*. *Several French Ships near the Race are pursued.*

The Dutch Admiral and Sir John Ash by ordered to look after them which rid fast.

Three of their great Ships being under the Shore, tacked about eleven a Clock and stood Westward, but after making two or three short Boards, the biggest of them (being the *Royal Sun*) ran on Ground, and presently her Masts were cut away; mean while the other two to Leeward (which were the *French* Admiral's Seconds) ply'd up to her. This it was judged they did because they could not get to Windward of the Weathermost Ships, nor stretch out a head Eastward. The Admiral observing that many Ships of our Fleet hover'd about them, sent Orders to Sir *Ralph Delavall*, Vice-Admiral of the Red, who was in the Rear, to keep a Strength with him sufficient to destroy them, and to order the rest to follow the Body of the Fleet; which Service was effectually performed. *The Royal Sun, and two more of their biggest Ships burnt at Cherbourg.*

About Four in the Afternoon eighteen of the *French* Ships which were gotten Eastward of Cape *Barfleur*, haled in for *La Hogue*, where our Ships anchor'd about Ten at Night, and lay until near Four the next Morning, at which time the Admiral weighed and stood in near to the Land. The Flood coming on, he anchor'd again; but at Two in the Afternoon got under sail, and plied close in with *La Hogue*, where he found thirteen of the Enemy's Ships very near the Shore.

On *Monday* the twenty third of *May* he sent in Sir *George Rooke*, then Vice Admiral of the Blue, with a Squadron, Fireships, and the Boats of the Fleet, to destroy those Ships; but they had got them so far in, that not any but the small Frigates could advance near enough for Service: However the Boats burnt six of them that Night,

O o o 2

Many more of the French Ships of War burnt at La Hogue. Night, and about Eight the next Morning the other seven were set on fire, together with several Transport Ships, and some small Vessels with Ammunition, wherein not only all the Officers, (among whom the then Lord *Carmarthen* signalized himself) but the Men behaved themselves with great Resolution and Gallantry. Thus at *La Hogue* and *Cherbourg* were burnt two Ships of one hundred and four Guns each, one of ninety, two of eighty, four of seventy six, four of sixty, and two of fifty six Guns, from which time, to that when Peace was concluded, in the Year 1697, the *French* did not attempt to fight us at Sea, but contented themselves to prejudice our Trade by their smaller Ships of War and Privateers.

The French Ships escape the Dutch Admiral and Sir John Ashby, who join the Fleet. This Service being over, the Admiral sailed out of *La Hogue* Bay the twenty fifth, and ordered Sir *John Ashby* (who was returned without doing any Execution on the other part of the Enemy's Fleet) to run with a Squadron of *English* and *Dutch* along the *French* Coast as far as *Havre de Grace*, and to look out for those five Ships which he said he had seen standing Eastward; but even in this he had no better Success than before.

Remarks upon the Resolution of the French in bearing down to engage. The Resolution with which the *French* bore down upon our Fleet was not a little surprising; for they were not above fifty Ships, from one hundred and four to fifty six Guns; and I am apt to think it occasioned at first some Jealousy among us: But, if so, it was soon blown over, for every one endeavoured to do what he was able. As for Monsieur *Tourville*'s running this Hazard, I can attribute it to no other Reason than the positive Orders he had from his Master to fight the *English* Fleet, which, had he thought fit, he might have avoided, even after we saw each other, for he was several Leagues to Windward: And, as I am credibly informed, when he called his Flag-Officers together, they did unanimously give their Opinions not to engage, but that he at last produced an Order under the *French* King's own Hand, which shewed them the Necessity there was for their so doing.

Doubtless these Orders were given him upon a Presumption that our great Ships, and the *Dutch*, could not possibly join Sir *Ralph Delavall* and Rear-Admiral *Carter*'s Squadrons (then cruising on their Coast) before he might have had an Opportunity of coming up with them: And, in truth, had not Mr. *Russel* sailed from the River even at the very time he did, contrary to the Opinion of the Pilots, (as I have already observed) the Winds which afterwards happened would have prevented his coming timely to their Assistance; so that the Enemy might, in all Probability, have had equal, if not greater Success than we had over them: Not but that the *French* Court (by what means I know not) had such early Notice of the Junction of our Fleet, or at least of the sailing of our great Ships, that I could almost venture to affirm the Vessel which Captain *Wivell* took off of Cape *Barfleur*, had Orders from the King for Monsieur *Tourville*, contradicting those positive Directions he had received for Fighting; but the Master of the Vessel threw the Packet into the Sea when he found himself in danger of being taken.

To

CHAP. IX. *from the Year* 1688, *to* 1697.

To this may be added, that Providence concern'd itself for the Safety of the two Squadrons beforementioned; for several Days before the great Ships join'd them, the *French* Fleet was got as far into the Chanel as off of *Plimouth*, but were forced into the Sea by a strong Easterly Wind; so that as they were thus prevented in their well-laid Design, they were a second time interrupted therein by the Conjunction of our Fleet: And had they met with Success, the Forces which lay ready at *La Hogue*, and the adjacent Places, would not have been long out of our Country; though if, when there, they had behaved themselves no better than in the Defence of their Ships when burnt, there would not have been much Mischief done; for notwithstanding their Numbers, and the Opportunity they had of making Resistance, the whole Service was performed with the Loss of no more than ten Men, besides those who were accidentally blown up in one of our Long-Boats. *The beating the French Fleet prevented their Descent on England.*

And here it may be observed, without Vanity, that although the Confederate Fleet was considerably stronger than theirs, yet were they beaten by an inferior Number: For, by reason of the Calm, and the Thickness of the Weather, it was not possible for many of the *Dutch* Ships, or of the Blue Squadron to engage; whereas had we been favoured with clear Weather, and a Gale of Wind, it is very probable that not so much as one of the *French* Ships would have escaped. *The Enemy beaten by a less Number of Ships.*

Possibly they, foreseeing this, might in some measure be daunted, and that it occasioned their Retreat sooner than otherwise they would have done; but considering with what Deliberation they bore down, and how warmly they ply'd our Ships, there was little Reason to believe the Strength they discovered baulk'd their Resolution, since they had their Master's positive Commands to engage.

Having thus given an Account of the Battel, and of what Success the Admiral himself had against the Ships he chased, I cannot proceed without lamenting the Escape of those which the *Dutch*, and our Admiral of the Blue were left to look after. I shall not lay the Want of Judgment, Diligence, or ought else to any one's Charge; but since so fair an Opportunity offered itself for destroying the most considerable Part of the *French* King's Navy, such ill Success in that Affair was the greatest Misfortune to us; for had a happy Push been made, the maritime Power of *France* could not in this Age, whatever it might in the next, have given *England* any great Disturbance. *Observations upon the Enemy's escaping, the Dutch Admiral and Sir John Ashby.*

But since all Hopes of meeting them were groundless, the Admiral resolved to repair with the Fleet to St. *Helen's*, and that Determination was happily put in Execution; for such was the sudden Extremity of Weather, that had the Fleet kept out at Sea they must have been exposed to very great Danger, especially those Ships which in the Battel had received Damage in their Masts. But before he left the *French* Coast, he ordered Sir *John Ashby* with twelve *English* Ships of War, and three Fireships, in Conjunction with as many *Dutch*, commanded by Vice-Admiral *Callemberg*, to proceed off of *Havre de Grace*, and endeavour to destroy several *French* Ships said *The Fleet comes to St. Helen's, and thereby escape very bad Weather. Sir John Ashby sent to destroy some Ships off of Havre, but they were harboured.*

said to be in those Parts, which it was found had harboured themselves before they arrived.

The Admiral proposed to make the intended Descent at this time.
The Court of *France* being now in no little Consternation, the Admiral thought it the most proper time for making the intended Descent on their Coast; for although not only King *James* himself, but the *French* also had great Numbers of Men encamped at *la Hogue* and the adjacent Places, yet the little or no Interruption they gave us in destroying their Ships, would incline any one to believe that a Body of Regular Troops might have made a very considerable Progress into their Country. Mean while all possible Diligence was used in the re-fitting the Fleet, and although the *French*, had they at first been joined, would have been near ninety Ships, from one hundred and four to fifty Guns, yet considering what part of them were destroy'd, seventy *English* and *Dutch* of the Line of Battel were now thought sufficient for any Service the remaining Part of this Year; for although it was probable that the Enemy might come out again, and make a Flourish, yet was there no great Reason to believe they would expose themselves to a second Danger in one Summer.

Orders sent for embarking the French Forces as soon as their Fleet came into the Chanel.
Very fortunate it was for *England* that our Fleet did so happily join; for no sooner had Monsieur *Tourville* sent an Express of his being on the *French* Coast, than Orders were dispatched for the Army's embarking, which might have been done, and the Troops safely wafted over to *England*; for as their Strength was much superior to the Squadrons with Sir *Ralph Delavall* and Rear-Admiral *Carter*, so could they have run no great Hazard from our Capital Ships, in regard they must unavoidably have remain'd Wind-bound in the River, had they not sailed from thence the very Moment they did; or at least the Enemy might have hindered their joining the others. But the valuable Service of this great Man who effectually defeated the Enemy's Designs (for which he was most graciously, and in the most obliging Manner, thanked both by the King and Queen) was so far from screening him from Envy, that it occasioned several Articles of Accusation against him, but the Enquiry thereinto ended very much to his Honour and Reputation.

The Admiral gets Advice of the Enemy's Ships got into St. Malo.
The twelfth of *June* in the Afternoon there came into the Fleet a Ketch from *Dartmouth*, which met with a Privateer called the *Cloudesly* Gally, and had three Men put on board her taken by the said Gally out of a *French* Snow. This Vessel was sent out to gain Intelligence, and then immediately to return to such Port in *France* as she could first reach, and send an Account thereof by Express to St. *Malo*, her Master said that there were at that Port the Vice-Admiral of the Blue, and twenty five Ships of War more, great and small, including Fireships; that they had pretty well repair'd the Damages received in Fight, and watched an Opportunity to get from thence to *Brest*.

The Fleet sails to prevent their getting into Brest.
Hereupon the Admiral sailed from St. *Helen's* the fourteenth of *June* with such Part of the Fleet as were in the best Condition, and ordered Sir *Cloudesly Shovell* to follow with the Remainder. His Design being to keep to the Westward of St. *Malo*, and, if possible, to intercept those Ships in their Passage from thence to *Brest*, or, when he came to a proper Station, to consult with

the

CHAP. IX. *from the Year* 1688, *to* 1697.   471

the Flag-Officers what might be attempted againſt them at the former Place; and on the twenty firſt he received Advice that all the Tranſport Ships were ordered to *Portſmouth*, where it was intended our Forces ſhould embark.

He was of Opinion that the *French* Ships might get out of St. *Malo* and go North about, if they would venture on ſo dangerous a Navigation, unleſs he could anchor, and ride in Safety before that Port, which he determined to inform himſelf of from the Pilots: But even if this could be done, he was apprehenſive it might occaſion their drawing all their Forces to the Succour of the Place, and of their Ships, and that thereby our Attempt, both by Sea and Land, would be rendered more uncertain.

The twenty fifth of *June* a Council of War was called in *Torbay* of all the *Engliſh* and *Dutch* Flags, occaſioned by the Advice the Admiral had received that all our Troops were ordered to *Portſmouth*, and that her Majeſty would not give any Directions for the Diſpoſal of them, until the Flags, and General Officers of the Army had conſulted, and tranſmitted to Her their Opinion. This Council of War took into Conſideration how the Fleet could ſooneſt, and with moſt Certainty join the Tranſport Ships, that ſo it might be then debated how to attempt the Enemy at St. *Malo*; and it was thought moſt adviſeable that a conſiderable Part of the Fleet ſhould be appointed to lie about fifteen or twenty Leagues North from the Iſle of *Bas* for intercepting the *French* Ships ſhould they attempt to puſh towards *Breſt* from that Port, and that the Remainder ſhould forthwith proceed to *Spithead*, and join the Tranſports: But it was farther reſolved, that if the Winds happened to hang Weſterly, the whole Fleet ſhould repair to *Spithead*, or if Eaſterly, continue in *Torbay* in Expectation of the ſaid Tranſport Ships.

A Council of War called, in relation to the Land Forces.

The Eaſtern Parts of *France* were at this time in great want of Neceſſaries for Life, as Salt, Wine, Brandy, and other Commodities, which our Cruiſers prevented their tranſporting from one Place to another; for ſome Ships ſent to cruiſe off of the *Fourn* Head burnt a great Flyboat of about four hundred Tuns, loaden with Proviſions, nor could they have miſs'd of taking or deſtroying many more, under Convoy of two Men of War, had they not precipitately harboured themſelves in ſome little Places where they could not be attempted.

The Fleet being now at Sea, the Wind came up at N. N. W. and blew for a conſiderable time ſo very hard, that it drove them near twenty Leagues Weſt of *Uſhant*, inſomuch that ſeveral of the Ships received Damage in their Maſts and Rigging. This Accident ſerved as another Argument that the great Ships, and ſuch Numbers of them too, ſhould not be ventured at Sea but where they might have Room to drive 48 Hours any Way, or let go an Anchor and ride; for ſix Hours with a Shift of Wind makes either Side of the Chanel a Lee Shore; and had not the Admiral luckily brought-to early in the Morning, it is likely a melancholy Account would have been given of the Fleet. However, this ſtorm being over, he ſafely arrived in the Road of the Iſland of *Guernſey* the third of *July*, where

The Fleet expoſed in a Storm near Uſhant.

The Admiral arrives in Guernſey Road.

he was conftrain'd to anchor, for the Weather being thick, the Pilots, (whofe Judgment there was Reafon to fufpect) would not venture over to St. *Malo*; but that which gave the Admiral the greateft Uneafinefs was the Account he received from two Captains, who had long ufed that Trade, that there was not good Ground for more than forty Ships to ride; fo that calling a Council of War, to confider whether it might be moft proper for the whole Fleet to go over or to fend a Detachment to view the Place, they came to the following Resolution, *viz.* "That part of the Fleet fhould proceed "off of St. *Malo*, to inform themfelves whether the whole, or what "Number of Ships might ride there;" and accordingly Vice-Admiral *Rooke* was fent, in Company of Vice-Admiral *Callemberg*, who commanded the *Dutch* Detachment.

Part of the Fleet fent to obferve how many Ships might ride off of St. Malo.

Our Court was at this time under great Uneafinefs left the *French* Ships fhould get from St. *Malo* to *Breft*, and therefore her Majefty was very intent upon having them attack'd; but although eight Days were advanced in *July*, the Transport Ships were not arrived at *Portfmouth* from the River; and fince the *French* might meet with many Opportunities of getting out, the Admiral was of Opinion that the moft probable way to intercept them was by the Fleet's riding in *Camaret* Bay, at the Entrance of *Breft*, if it could certainly be depended on that they were defigned to that Port.

Delay made in the Tranfports coming to Portfmouth.

The Fleet was forced by bad Weather to *Torbay*, where the Admiral impatiently expected the Return of Sir *George Rooke*; and the rather, for that the late Winds gave him fome Apprehenfions of him, efpecially when he confidered how dangerous that Coaft was to which he was gone. Nor did he think himfelf under a little Streight, fince when the Fleet and Army were joined, a Refolution was then to be taken what fhould be done; whereas it would have been much more for the Service, had fomewhat been determined in that Matter before the Junction; fince if the Forces were obliged to keep the Sea until the Place for Action was refolved upon, bad Weather might have expofed them to Hardfhips, and confequently render'd them of but little Service on fhore: And as for St. *Malo*, it was reafonable to believe that half the Number of Men a Month before would have performed more than the whole Body which was now intended; for as the Enemy's Fears were greater, fo, doubtlefs, were their Preparations for Safety carried on with all poffible Induftry.

The Fleet forced to Torbay.

The Admiral was under fome Uneafinefs that it was not determined what to attempt with the Forces.

The thirteenth of *July* Sir *George Rooke* return'd from St. *Malo*, who (befides the Report he made of the feveral Soundings near that Place) gave the Admiral his Opinion, and Obfervations of the Coaft thereabouts, which may not be improper to infert in his own Words, *viz.*

Sir George Rooke returns from St. Malo, and gives an Account of the adjacent Coaft.

1. "The Ground is flat and even from *Guernfey* to Cape *Fre-*
"*helle*, fhoaling a Fathom or two every two or three Miles all the
"Way over to the Cape: And it is alfo generally very rough, and
"in fome Places rocky, efpecially near *Sefembre*.

2. "The Tides run very quick in the Offing on the Coaft of
"St. *Malo*'s; but to the Eaftward of Cape *Frehelle*, within three

or

CHAP. IX. *from the Year* 1688, *to* 1697.   473

" or four Miles of the Shore, not above two and a half, or three
" Knots, at spring Tides.

3. " There are some sandy Bays between Cape *Frehelle* and St.
" *Malo*'s, but not very commodious for putting Men on Shore, be-
" cause the Land rises in most Places quick from the Strand; be-
" sides the River of *Dinant* (or the *Rance*) must be passed before
" they can come to St. *Malo*.

4. " There are about thirty five or thirty six Sail of Ships rigg'd,
" of which twelve lay in the *Rance*, and of them four or five great
" Ships, the rest being up at *Salidore*.

5. " Not one of the Pilots would undertake to carry in any Ship
" of War, or Fireship, to make any Attempt on the *French* Ships
" at St. *Malo*, though I offered an hundred Pound Encouragement
" to each Man.

G. Rooke.

July 13. 1692.

Upon this a Council of War was called, and, as it was agreed, *The Fleet sails from Torbay, but a considerable Part of it is placed to intercept the St. Malo Ships.* the Fleet sailed from *Torbay* the fifteenth, but Care was taken the Day before to place Ships on the Coast of *France* in the manner following. Captain *Nevil*, in the *Kent*, was sent with thirty *English* and *Dutch*, ten Leagues North from the West End of the Isle of *Bas*: The *Adventure* and *Saudadoes* were ordered to lie between *Brehac* and the *Seven Islands*; the *James* Galley and *Greyhound* between the *Seven Islands* and *le Bas*; two *Dutch* Frigates between that and the *Fourne*; and all these small Frigates, as well as those with Captain *Nevil* were ordered to lie close in with the Shore. This the Admiral judged would more effectually impede the Passage of any thing Eastward or Westward from St. *Malo*; and the remaining Part of the Fleet either lay in a proper Station, or cruised to and fro, as Wind and Weather would permit.

From the fourteenth to the eighteenth no Advice came from Captain *Nevil*, so that it was concluded the *French* had not attempted to push Westward from St. *Malo* with the Easterly Wind, and it was generally believed that they would not stir till towards Winter, when we could not be so well able to keep the Sea to intercept them.

About this time the *James* Galley brought into the Fleet a Privateer of St. *Malo*, which she took off of the Land's End, the Captain whereof reported, that Orders had been several times sent for disarming the Ships at *Brest*, but that they were commonly contradicted in two Days after. This Privateer came from St. *Malo* the Day before Sir *George Rooke* was off of that Port, and said it was then intended that eight of their Men of War should winter there.

The eighteenth and nineteenth the Wind was Westerly, with a *The Fleet returns to Torbay, and takes in Provisions.* continual Fog, and the Admiral fearing it might put him to the Eastward of *Torbay*, thought it most adviseable to repair thither, where he took in the Provisions, and thereby prevented the Inconvenience which might have attended the victualling Ships not timely joining the Fleet, had they put out to Sea in Search of him. His Intentions

A Consultation how the Fleet might best join the Transports.

tentions were to get under Sail again as soon as possibly he could, that so he might relieve the Squadron on the *French* Coast, which was both in want of Provisions and Water; but before he was able to sail, he received Orders from the Queen relating to the Descent, and on the twenty fifth of *July* consulted with the *English* and *Dutch* Flag Officers thereupon, by whom it was agreed in what manner the Fleet might best join the Transports; and that no time might be lost in improving this Affair to the best Advantage, the Admiral sent an Express to the Duke of *Leinster* (afterwards Duke *Schonberg*) letting him know, that if the Wind continued Westerly he would come with the Fleet to the Transports at *Spithead*, but if Easterly, he had determined to remain for them in *Torbay*.

He was not a little uneasie at the Delay that had been made, for when this Matter had been under Consideration in the Winter, it was resolved that all things should be ready in the Month of *May* at farthest; and had that been complied with, there might have been much more Probability of Success. But even at this time, late as it was, the General Officers had no Account of the Posture of Affairs at St. *Malo*; nor was there indeed any Resolution taken at Court what the Forces should do when embarked, otherwise than that it was recommended to a Council of War (as I have said before) to consider what might be done at *Brest*. However the Transport Ships being join'd, a general Council was called the twenty eighth of *July*, on board of the *Breda*, where were present the Admiral himself, and the several Persons following, *viz.*

A Council of War of Sea and Land Officers upon joining the Transport Ships.

Flag-Officers.

English.

Sir *Ralph Delavall*, Vice-Admiral of the Red.
George Rooke, Esq; Vice-Admiral of the Blue.
Sir *Cloudesly Shovell*, Rear-Admiral of the Red.
David Mitchel, Esq; first Captain to the Admiral.

Dutch.

Admiral *Allemonde*,
Vice-Admiral *Callemberg*,
Rear-Admiral *Vandergoes*,
Rear-Admiral *Evertsen*.
Rear-Admiral *Muys*.

General and Field-Officers.

His Grace the Duke of *Leinster*, Lieutenant-General of all the Forces,
Earl of *Gallway*,
Sir *Henry Bellasise*,
Monsieur *de la Meloniere*,

Sir

CHAP. IX. *from the Year* 1688, *to* 1697. 475

    Sir *David Collier*,
    Colonel *Beveridge*,
    Monsieur *du Cambon*,
    Colonel *Selwin*,
    Earl of *Argyll*.

And since I cannot better explain the Sense of those Gentlemen, than by inserting a Copy of the Paper which was signed by them, I have done the same as follows, *viz.*

"The Matter of burning the Ships at St. *Malo* being maturely considered, Vice-Admiral *Rooke* and Vice-Admiral *Callemberg* (who were lately sent with a Squadron of Ships before that Port) representing the great Difficulty of carrying the Ships in there, by reason of the Multitude of Rocks, and the Rapidity of the Tides; and the Pilots refusing to conduct any Frigates or Fireships into the Harbour, because the Marks might be removed, it was the Opinion of the Flag-Officers, that it was not practicable to attempt any thing against the Enemy's Ships at St. *Malo*'s with any Part of the Fleet, until the Town it self could be so far reduced by the Land Forces as that the Ships might not receive any great Annoyance from the Enemy's Guns in the Attempt. And the General and Field-Officers of the Army were of Opinion that the Troops could not do any Service at that Place without the Assistance of the Fleet. *Agreed to be impracticable to attempt the Enemy's Ships at St. Malo with the Fleet.*

"It was then considered whether it was feasible to make any Attempt on the Enemy's Ships at *Brest*; and although the Flag-Officers were of Opinion that an Attempt might be made there with some Hopes of Success, if the Summer had not been so far spent, yet considering the Winter was approaching, they did not think it proper to attack the Enemy's Ships in that Port, since the Fleet might be exposed to very great Inconveniencies should they be Wind-bound near that Place: And it was the Opinion of the General and Field-Officers of the Army, that they should not be able to do any Service there against the Enemy, unless they could be protected by the Fleet. The Flag-Officers likewise thought it not safe for the Fleet to attempt any thing against the Enemy at *Rochefort*, the Season of the Year being so far spent, and the Place it self lying so deep in *the Bay*. *They think it not fit to attempt them at Brest, the Winter Season being advanced. Nor at Rochefort.*

"It was in the next Place considered whether the Fleet might lie with Safety on the Coast of *Normandy*, to protect the Army in an Attempt either at *Havre de Grace*, *la Hogue*, or any Place thereabouts: And the Flag-Officers judged that it might lie with Safety on that Coast until towards the latter End of the next Month, in case their Majesty's Service should require it. *Determined to lie on the Coast of Normandy to protect the Army in any Attempts there.*

Besides these Resolutions of a General Council of War of Sea and Land-Officers, the Flags themselves came to the following Determination.

"That since the Transport Ships with the Land-Forces were come to the Fleet, in order to try what might be done against the Enemy either at St. *Malo*, *Brest*, or *Rochefort*, it was their Opinion that something might have been attempted, with probability *The Sea-Officers of Opinion 'twas too late in the Year for the Fleet to go to Brest, or of Rochfort.*

P p p 2

" of Succefs, were not the Seafon of the Year fo far fpent as not to
" admit of the Fleet's going with Safety thither.

Sir John Afh-
by *fent with
a Squadron
towards the
Ifle of* Ba.s

Purfuant to what was determined the following Orders were given to Sir *John Afhby*. That he fhould fail with one Firft Rate, Six Seconds, Seventeeen Thirds, One Fourth, and Four Firefhips, together with feveral *Dutch* Ships, over to the Coaft of *France*, and place himfelf about fifteen Leagues North from the Weft End of the Ifle of *Bas*, and by ftationing fome of the Ships nearer to the Shore, endeavour to intercept the *French*, fhould they attempt to pafs from St. *Malo* to *Breft*; befides which, he was cautioned to look out carefully for any of the Enemy's Ships which might be coming from the Weft of *France*. Thus was he to employ himfelf until he received farther Orders, for which he was directed to fend to *Dartmouth* by all convenient Opportunities: And if he met the Squadron with Captain *Nevil*, he was from them to encreafe the *Englifh* Ships to thirty, fending the Remainder to St. *Helen's*, with a Wefterly Wind, or, if Eafterly, to *Torbay*, that fo they might join the Body of the Fleet.

On this Service he remained as long as the Weather would permit, when coming in, without meeting any of the Enemy's Ships, and being at *Spithead* the fourteenth of *September*, the Collecter of the Cuftoms at *Cowes* fent to him the Mafter of a *French Tartane*, which had been taken fome Days before off of *Portland*.

This Man faid that he failed from St. *Malo* the feventh Day of this very Month, in Company of a Vice-Admiral, and fixteen Ships of War, from fixty to eighty Guns, together with fix Firefhips, which, by reafon of little Wind, anchored under Cape *Frehelle*, and remained there till the tenth, and then, at fix in the Morning, failed with the Wind at E. by S. for *Breft*.

In fine, although upon the Admiral his parting with Sir *John Afhby*, it was agreed at a Council of War, that the reft of the Fleet fhould proceed to the *French* Coaft off of *La Hogue*, and thereabouts; yet, in his Paffage from *Torbay*, he received Orders from the Queen, whereupon he with the Tranfport-Ships came to St. *Helen's*, and there lay a confiderable time Wind-bound, infomuch that the Winter-feafon being very far advanced, the great Ships were ordered about to *Chatham*, the Land-Forces put on fhore, and the Fleet divided into Squadrons, according as it was judged moft for the Advantage of the Service.

CHAP.

C H A P. X.

Sir Francis Wheler's *Proceedings with a Squadron, and Land-Forces to and from the* West-Indies.

IN the Month of *November* a Squadron was ordered to be got ready for Service in the *West-Indies*, which was composed of two Third Rates, six Fourths, three Fifths, one Sixth, three Fire-ships, a Store-Ship, an Hospital, and a Bomb-Vessel; about fifteen hundred Soldiers being put on board of them, and such Transports as were particularly appointed for their Reception. Sir *Francis Wheler* was the Person made choice of to command this Squadron, who received Instructions from the Lords of the Admiralty, dated the twenty fifth Day of the aforesaid Month of *November*, how to govern himself not only in proceeding to, but also when he should be in the *West-Indies*, where he was at liberty to take under his Command three other fourth Rates, namely, the *Norwich*, *Diamond*, and *Mordaunt*; but besides these Instructions, he received Orders from his Majesty, directing what Places belonging to the Enemy he should attempt, and in what manner he should act in Conjunction with the Land-Forces commanded by Colonel *Foulkes*.

1692.

It was the beginning of *January* before this Squadron could be got ready, and then the Commadore sailing, he arrived off of *Dartmouth* the ninth, having received Power (for the greater Grace of an Expedition from which so much was expected) to put abroad the Union Flag at the Main-top-mast-head, as soon as he should be out of the *Soundings*.

The twenty sixth of *January* he reached the Island of *Maderas*, and having taken in Wine there for the Ships Companies, arrived in *Carlisle* Bay at *Barbadoes* the first of *March* following, where he was joined by several Ships which had separated from him in his Passage.

The Squadron arrives at Maderas.

A Council of War determined to make an Attempt first on *Martinica*, and two Regiments were joined to about eight hundred Land-Men provided at *Barbadoes*, commanded by the Captains *Salter*, and *Butler*, Advice whereof was sent to Colonel *Codrington*, General of the *Leeward* Islands, who was desired to cause the Forces in those Parts to meet the rest with all the speed that might be at *Martinica*; and yet farther to strengthen these Forces, upon occasions of Service, there was formed a Battalion of Seamen, of which the Commadore was himself Colonel.

Resolution to attack Martinica.

The Squadron arriving at *Cul de Sac Royal* in *Martinica* the fifteenth of *April*, a general Council of War was called of Sea and Land-Officers, and the Question being put, Whether the Soldiers should land first, and destroy Fort St. *Pierre*, and the Plantations thereabouts, or begin with attacking Fort *Royal*, it was agreed

A Council of War called.

to

to land at or near Fort St. *Pierre*, and that the Fleet should sail the next Morning to countenance this Attempt.

Another Council of War.

Being before the Town of St. *Pierre* the twentieth of *April*, another Council of War was called, and a Debate arising, Whether a close Siege should be laid, and Attack made on the Town and Fort of St. *Pierre*, or whether the Forces should be taken on board, and that then it should be considered what was fit to be done; it was moved by the President, (Sir *Francis Wheler*) that every Man should give his Opinion in Writing.

Reasons for not attacking Fort St. Pierre.

Thus each Officer, both by Sea and Land, took the Matter into Consideration, and having drawn up their Reasons, and signed to them, they were delivered in: But few there were among them, if any, except Sir *Francis Wheler* himself, and, I think, Lieutenant-Colonel *Colt*, who were for making an Attempt, but rather to retire, and land the Men in some other Place, in order to despoil the Enemy.

Most of the Officers alledged that the *French* were superior to our Forces, and that since at least one third of our Men were *Irish* Papists, there could be but very little Confidence put in them; and another Objection was made, That the greatest Number of the Men they were to trust to had not born Arms before this very Expedition.

Other Scruples were raised, such as these; That the Roads were almost impassable, and the Hills inaccessible; That the Attempt would not only too much expose the Men to the Enemy, but to Sickness also, by reason of the Fatigue, eight hundred of the three thousand (including the *Irish*) being either found killed, wounded, or sick, within three Days after Landing.

Others, and particularly General *Codrington*, were of Opinion, that should our Army be beaten, it would be almost impossible to retreat on board the Ships, so that not only *Barbadoes*, but the *Leeward* Islands also, would be in a very great measure expos'd to the Enemy, most of the Forces having been drawn from those Places for this Service.

Resolv'd to sail to Dominica. 1693.

In fine, it was resolved at a Council of War, held the twenty second of *April* 1693, that the Army should embark, and the Squadron sail to *Dominica*, that there they might take in Water, and refresh the Men, who at this time were in but very indifferent Circumstances of Health.

Resolved not to attack Guadalupe.

At *Dominica* another Council of War was called the twenty fifth of *April*, and the Question being put, whether they should attack *Guadalupe*, it was carried by great Majority in the Negative; whereupon it was resolved to send home all the Forces belonging *Barbadoes* and the *Leeward* Islands, with proper Convoys, and that the Squadron should proceed to and rendezvous at St. *Christopher's*.

Sir *Francis Wheler* considering the great Charge the Crown had been at on this Expedition, was of Opinion that *Dominica* ought immediately to be attack'd, and General *Codrington* was also of the same

CHAP. X. *from the Year* 1688, *to* 1697. 479

same mind, as was Colonel *Foulkes*, provided the Squadron and Army could remain there six Weeks, or two Months; for in less than that time it was believed it could not be effected, because here the Enemy were as strong, or rather stronger, than at St. *Pierre*. But Sir *Francis* informing them that the King had positively ordered the Fleet should not continue in those Parts longer than the last of *May*, and the Forces belonging to *Barbadoes* pressing very earnestly to be gone, he having refreshed the Officers and Men, bent his Course to *New England*, and arrived at *Boston* the twelfth of *June*. *The Squadron arrives at New England.*

Sir *Francis Wheler*, according to the Commands he had received from his Majesty, proposed to Sir *William Phips*, Governor of *New England*, the going to, and attempting *Quebeck*. But he having not had any previous Advice thereof, which he said he ought to have had four Months before, so as to have gotten all things ready; and that Expedition requiring the Squadron's sailing by the first of *July*, and a Strength of four thousand Men, at least, which very much exceeded the present Numbers, that Affair was no longer thought of; so that on the first of *July* the recovered Men began to embark, and the third of *August* the Squadron sailed from *Boston*. *Reasons for not attempting Quebeck.*

The Commadore being desirous to do something, though in so weak a Condition, before he made sail for *England*, proceeded to *Newfoundland*, and arriving at *Placentia* the eighteenth of *August*, he was informed that the *French* were very strong there, not only in large Privateers, (for during the whole Expedition there was not any Account received of a Squadron of Ships of War) but that they had at least two thousand Men, reckoning both Soldiers and Inhabitants. That the Mouth of the Harbour (which was not above a Ship's length in breadth) was guarded by three Cables athwart, and a strong Fort, whereon were mounted more than thirty large Cannon, and pallisado'd to the Land; and that the neighbouring Hills were also fortified. *The Squadron arrives at Newfoundland.*

Upon this he called a Council of War of the Sea and Land-Officers, and earnestly press'd that the Land-Forces might make an Attempt on shore, while the Fleet did the same by Sea, and that some Soldiers might be taken from the Transport Ships to assist in the Ships of War, which had not more Men than were sufficient to ply one Tire of their Guns. This was rejected by the Land-Officers, there being eleven of them to six of the Sea against going in with the Ships to batter the *Great Fort*: However, he sent some of the Frigates, and part of the Soldiers, under Command of Major *Rabifiner*, to destroy the *French* at St. *Peter*'s, which was effectually done. *A Council of War called, and resolved not to attempt Placentia.*

The twenty eighth of *August* the Squadron arrived in the Bay of *Bulls* on the East side of the Island, and took in Water and Wood, where being detained by bad Weather until the twenty second of *September*, the Commadore then sailed for *England*, and arriving on the eighteenth *Sir Francis Wheler arrives in England.*

teenth of *October*, he received a Commission at *Portsmouth*, appointing him Rear-Admiral of the Red.

Thus ended this Expedition, from which *England* gained no manner of Reputation, although it was attended with the unfortunate Loss of many good Officers and Men; and it had like to have happen'd much worse from the want of Hands sufficient to bring the Ships home, which were in a very bad Condition, both as to their Hulls, and other Particulars.

Chap. XI.

The Proceedings of Mr. Killegrew, *Sir* Cloudesly Shovell, *and Sir* Ralph Delavall, *joint Admirals of the Fleet, in the* Chanel *and* Soundings; *and of Sir* George Rooke *his falling in with the* French *Fleet in* Lagos Bay.

$169\frac{2}{3}$.

THE eighteenth of *March* Mr. *Killegrew*, Sir *Ralph Delavall*, and Sir *Cloudesly Shovell* (who were jointly appointed Admirals of the Fleet) received Instructions from the Lords of the Admiralty to proceed to Sea, and (without expecting particular Orders, by which Opportunities of Service might be lost) to use their utmost Endeavours to annoy the Enemy, and protect the Trade. The Number of Ships (besides *Dutch*) appointed for the Body of the Fleet, were six First Rates, ten Seconds, twenty eight Thirds, six Fourths, four Fifths, and five of the Sixth Rate, together with Fireships, a Bomb Vessel, and four Hospitals.

There was at this time a great want of Men, and for the more speedy raising them, general Orders were issued (but soon after contradicted) for taking half the Seamen from all the Privateers. However, that the Fleet might be put into as early a Condition for Service as it was possible, five Regiments of Foot were ordered to be embark'd at *Portsmouth*; and that the Provisions might last the longer, the Ships Companies were to put Six to Four Men's Allowance of all Species, except Beer; for there was not yet such a Quantity provided as would enable them to keep out at Sea as long as the Service might require.

Five Regiments of Foot put on board.

The Fleet arrived at St. *Helen*'s the seventh of *May*, where the Admirals formed their Line of Battel; and since it is not altogether necessary to insert the same in the exact Form, with every Ship's Name, and that of her Commander, as they were appointed to follow each other, I shall explain the Strength of each Division in the manner following, *viz.*

The Admirals arrive at St. Helen's, and form their Line of Battel. 1693.

English.

CHAP. XI. *from the Year* 1688, *to* 1697.   481

English.	Rates.						Fireships.
	1ft,	2d,	3d,	4th,	5th,	6th,	
In the Division of the Vice-Admiral of the Blue,	0,	3,	5,	1,	0,	0,	3.
Admiral of the Blue, ——	2,	1,	5,	1,	0,	1,	3.
Rear-Admiral of the Blue, ——	0,	2,	6,	1,	0,	0,	2.
Rear-Admiral of the Red, ——	1,	2,	5,	1,	0,	0,	2.
Admiral of the Red, ——	3,	1,	5,	1,	2,	2,	3.
Dutch.							
Vice-Admiral, —— ——	1,	2,	4,	2,	0,	0,	2.
Admiral, —— ——	2,	1,	6,	1,	0,	2,	3.
Another Vice-Admiral, ——	3,	0,	4,	3,	0,	1,	1.
	12,	12,	40,	11,	2,	6,	19.

Thus the Fleet, *English* and *Dutch*, would, when join'd, have consisted of one hundred and two Sail, besides Brigantines, Bomb-Vessels, and Hospital Ships, whereof seventy were Ships of the Line of Battel; and although those of the *Dutch*, which I reckon according to Rates, (a Method not used by that Nation) are more or less inferior to those of the *English*, yet have I taken great care to marshal them together as near as those Differences would admit of it.

The Day after the Fleet arrived at *Spithead*, the Flag-Officers took into Consideration, pursuant to her Majesty's Commands, what Number of Ships might be proper for them to carry off of *Brest*, as also what might be attempted when there; and it was agreed, that if the Fleet could be made up to Seventy, they would proceed to the said Port, and endeavour to attempt the *French* Ships; their Reason for insisting on such a Number being the Uncertainty whether or not the Ships from *Thoulon* had joined them. *A Consultation about attempting the Ships at Brest.*

Another Council of War was called the fifteenth of *May*, to consider how the Streights Fleet, with the Trade bound to *Turkey*, might most safely proceed under the Conduct of Sir *George Rooke*. Having debated this Matter, they were of Opinion that if the *Thoulon* Squadron was come out of the Streights, and join'd to those of *Brest*, ten Men of War, a small Frigate, and a Fireship, would be sufficient for the aforesaid Convoy, and that the separate Convoy for *Spain* ought to proceed with them, while the Body of the Fleet accompanied both out of the Chanel; but that if the *French* were not joined, it was proper the whole Squadron should forthwith proceed with their Convoys. On the other hand, if the *French* Ships were joined, and at Sea, it was judged adviseable for the main Fleet to proceed with the *Mediterranean* Squadron as far as a Council of War might think proper when they should be in the *Soundings*; but that if no certain Advice could be got of the *Thoulon* Squadron's *Another Consultation about sending forward the Turky Convoy.*

Q q q   being

being come out of the Streights, or where they were, before the Fleet sailed from St. *Helen's*, the *Mediterranean* Squadron (that is to say, ten Ships of War, a Frigate, and a Fireship) should remain at St. *Helen's* until Intelligence could be gained.

The Admirals ordered by the Lords of the Admiralty to sail with the Fleet and the Turky Convoy.

The nineteenth of *May* the Lords of the Admiralty (in Obedience to her Majesty's Commands) sent Orders to the Admirals to sail in Company of the Squadron bound to the *Mediterranean*, and of the *Virginia* and *Bilboa* Convoys, and that after they had proceeded with them as far as might be judged requisite, they should order those bound to the Streights to steer such a Course to *Cadiz* as might be thought most safe by a Council of War, with respect as well to the *Brest* Fleet, if gone out, as to the *Thoulon* Squadron, and then with the Body of the Fleet to put in Execution the Instructions they had received.

Determination where to part with the Turky Convoy.

A Council of War being hereupon called, it was determined that the Fleet and *Mediterranean* Squadron should proceed together thirty Leagues W. S. W. from *Ushant*, and that when the Admirals spread a blue Flag at the Main-top-mast-head, and fired three Guns, Sir *George Rooke*, as well as the other Convoys, should go forward, according to the Orders they had received from the Lords of the Admiralty.

Agreed to accompany the said Convoy twenty Leagues farther.

The Fleet being on the fourth of *June* thirty Leagues W. S. W. from *Ushant*, a Council of War of *English* and *Dutch* Flag-Officers determined, That since they had no Intelligence of the Enemy, they would accompany the *Mediterranean* Squadron twenty Leagues farther, and then return to the former Station to take up the Cruisers, from whence it was judged adviseable to proceed to the Rendezvous ten Leagues N. W. of *Ushant*; so that leaving the Streights Squadron on the sixth in the Evening, they arrived at the said Rendezvous two Days after.

Advice from Sir Lambert Blackwell *of the* Thoulon *Squadron.*

During this time they met not with any Intelligence of the Enemy's Fleet; but the Lords of the Admiralty received Advice on the thirteenth from Sir *Lambert Blackwell*, (who was then Consul at *Leghorn*) which he had from the Master of a *Maltese* Bark, that the *Thoulon* Squadron, with thirty five Gallies, were ready to proceed from *Marseilles*; and some time before this the Country was alarm'd with a Number of Ships seen off of *Scilly*, which were thought to be the *French* Fleet, but they proved to be only *Danes* and *Swedes*, under Convoy of a Man of War of about forty four Guns.

None of the Enemy's Ships could be seen at Brest.

Some Ships being sent to gain Intelligence on the *French* Coast, one of them, the *Warspight*, returned to the Admirals the seventeenth of *June*, with an Account that she had stood in as near with St. *Matthew's* Point as to bring *Brest* Bay open, and that neither Ship, nor other Vessel, could be discovered there, except two or three small Fishing Boats; whereupon it was determined to sail off of *Scilly* in quest of the Enemy, (having not yet been informed that the Ships which gave the Alarm were only *Danes* or *Swedes*) and from thence to repair to *Torbay* with the sixty nine Ships of the Line of Battel which were then in Company, forty five whereof

were

CHAP. XI. *from the Year* 1688, *to* 1697.   483

were *English*, and twenty four *Dutch*. There they arrived the twenty first of *June* in great want of several Species of Provisions, but more especially Beer, Butter, and Cheese, and a Council of War was called the twenty third, upon Commands from her Majesty, concerning Sir *George Rooke*, it being apprehended that he might be in danger from the *French* Fleet, as indeed it happened. *The Fleet arrives in Torbay.*

It was by this Council determined to proceed to *Lisbon*, in order to join him; but it was found, upon strict Enquiry, they had not Provisions to enable them so to do. Nevertheless, since it was judged that the *Mediterranean* Squadron did greatly require the Assistance of the Fleet, it was resolved to proceed in search of the Enemy, if the Provisions could in fourteen Days be compleated to ten Weeks at whole Allowance. *Resolution of a Council of War, upon Apprehensions of the Turky Convoy's being in danger.*

Much about this time Advice came from the Consul of *Oporto*, dated the ninth of *June*, that on the first of that Month an Express arrived at *Lisbon* from the *Algarve*, with an Account that Monsieur *Tourville* with the *French* Fleet, consisting of seventy five Ships of War, and several other Ships and Vessels, in all to the Number of one hundred and fourteen, were come into the Bay of *Lagos*, between Cape St. *Vincent* and *Faro*. It was said that at first they shew'd *English* Colours, and some of them *Dutch*, and that by *English* Men sent on shore, they pretended to be of those Nations; but that next Day the Governor sending on board of the Admiral, he insinuated as if he had been forced in there by bad Weather, and that he intended to sail the following Morning; though doubtless his real design was to intercept our Ships of War and their Convoys. *Advice received of the French Fleet's being in Lagos Bay.*

Besides this Intelligence, an Express was sent to the Bishop of *Algarve*, with an Account that the Count *d'Estrées* was join'd with Monsieur *Tourville*, and that the whole Body of the *French* Fleet seem'd to stand off to Sea, in order first to double Cape St. *Vincent*, and then to proceed Northward: Besides which, there was Advice at *Cadiz*, that they had been discover'd in *Lagos* Bay the sixth of *June*, in all about one hundred and twenty Sail, of which seventy great Ships, together with sixteen Fireships, and six Bomb-Vessels, and that twenty of them were cruising Westward.

These Advices reaching the *English* Court, the Lords of the Admiralty sent Orders to the Admirals on the twenty third of *June* to distribute the expected Provisions equally as soon as it arrived, and to cause each Captain to take on board what Water he could, inasmuch as it was probable the Service might require the Fleet's continuing at Sea a considerable time; and Directions were given to the Commissioners for Victualling to provide as fast as possibly they could, and hasten to the Fleet, what Provisions was then shipped off; for at that time what they had on board would not suffice longer than is hereafter mention'd, according to the Computation made thereof by the Agent to the said Commissioners. *The Admirals ordered to distribute Provisions equally to the Ships.*

The Bread would end by *August* 16.
Beer — — — *July* 21.

The Beef would end by *September* 13.
Pork ——— ——— *August* 16.
Peafe ——— ——— *September* 13.
Oatmeal ——— ——— *August* 16.
Butter ——— ——— *September* 13.
Cheefe ——— ——— *September* 13.

Their Reasons for not going with the Fleet to the Affiftance of Sir George Rooke.

The first of *July* the Flag-Officers submitted it to her Majesty whether it might be adviseable for the Fleet to proceed to *Lisbon*, for that if the *French* were join'd, and fail'd Northward, the Coast of *England* would be expos'd to Insults. That which had before induced them to propose going thither, was for the Security of Sir *George Rooke* and the Merchant Ships, and proceeding with him farther, or accompanying him home, as it should be thought most proper: But since Orders were sent to him to return, it would be very uncertain where to meet him; besides, they were of Opinion that her Majesty's Orders to him being very full, there was no occasion for the making any Additions thereunto, since he was by those Orders directed, if he found himself obliged to go into the River of *Lisbon*, and that he received certain Intelligence during his Stay there the *Thoulon* Squadron had join'd the rest of their Fleet, and were gone together Northward from off the Coast of *Portugal*, to leave a proper Number of Ships, both *English* and *Dutch*, to proceed up the Streights with the *Turky* Trade, and return himself with the rest, and join the Body of our Fleet in these Seas, but not meeting them in his Passage, to repair to the Port of *Plimouth*, and there expect farther Directions. These Orders being not sent away before the third of *June*, they could not possibly timely arrive; for he being the seventeenth of that Month about sixty Leagues short of Cape St. *Vincent*, he thence ordered the *Lark*, a nimble sixth Rate, to stretch ahead of his Scouts in *Lagos* Bay, and get what Intelligence could be had there of the Enemy; which Ship hawling the Shore on board in the Night more than the rest of the Fleet did, she lay becalmed.

The French Fleet first discovered in Lagos Bay by Sir George Rooke.

Next Day the Scouts discovered two of the Enemy's Ships, and giving chase until somewhat after Noon, the *Chatham*, of fifty Guns, came up with one of them mounted with seventy, and engaged her a small time; but seeing eight or ten Sail under the Cape, she left her, and repaired to the Admiral with an Account of what had been discovered. Hereupon a Council of War being called, where were the other two Flag-Officers, namely, Rear-Admiral *Hopson*, and Vice-Admiral *Vandergoes*, the Admiral proposed keeping the Wind, or laying by all Night, that so a Discovery of the Enemy's Strength might be made the next Morning: But in this he was overruled, it being urg'd, that as the Wind was fresh Northerly, it gave a fair Opportunity of pushing for *Cadiz*. The Admiral being apprehensive that such an Attempt might prove of ill Consequence, by drawing the Fleet into a greater Force of the Enemy than he could be able to disengage himself from, thought it requisite, before the Result of this Council of War was signed, to call to him five or six of the

CHAP. XI. *from the Year* 1688, *to* 1697.   485

the Captains who happened to be then on board, whose Opinions being asked, they all concurred in what had been before resolved; so that making sail, he ran along Shore all Night with a press'd Sail, and forced several of the Enemy's Ships to cut from their Anchors in *Lagos* Bay.

Next Morning, by break of Day, being off of *Villa Nova*, it fell calm, when about ten Sail of the Enemy's Ships of War, and some other small ones with them, were seen in the Offing. Those Ships stood away with their Boats ahead, setting fire to several, and abandoning others of the smaller Vessels, some of which fell into our Hands, and in one of them there was a Train laid which blew up twenty Men. A Fireship of theirs was also taken, by falling into the Fleet in the Night, and the Men belonging to her informed the Admiral, that the Squadron consisted of no more than fifteen Ships of the Line of Battel, but that there were three Flags, namely, Monsieur *Tourville*, Monsieur *Villet*, and Monsieur *Lemon*; and that they had with them forty odd Sail of Store-ships and Merchant Men bound to *Thoulon*, or to meet Monsieur *d'Estrées*. They said also that the Squadron had been becalmed off the Cape, and that having watered in the Bay, they were bound directly into the Streights, without any Intention of seeing our Fleet. This, with the hasty Retreat of their Men of War in the Morning, and the deserting and burning their small Vessels, caused a perfect Belief in the Admiral, and the rest of the Flag-Officers and Captains; but afterwards it was judged (and with Reason too) that the precipitate Retreat of this little part of the Fleet (unless they were at first surprized, and judged our whole Strength might be together, from the Number of Merchant Ships) was on purpose to amuse us, and thereby draw our Squadron insensibly into the Body thereof.

Some Ships of the French hastily retire to draw our Squadron into their Body.

About Noon the Sea Breeze sprang up at W. N. W, and North-West, when the Admiral bore away along shore upon the Enemy, discovering their Strength the more the nearer he came to them, and at last counted about eighty Sail, but the Number they ply'd up to him with was not above sixteen, with three Flags, *viz.* the Admiral, Vice-Admiral of the Blue, and Rear-Admiral of the White; for the Vice-Admiral of the White stood off to Sea, that so he might weather our Squadron, and fall in with the Merchant Ships, whilst the Body of their Fleet lay promiscuously to Leeward of one another, as far as they could be seen, especially their biggest Ships.

The Enemy's whole Strength discovered, and sixteen bear up towards our Squadron.

At Three in the Afternoon our Squadron being within four Miles of the Enemy, Vice-Admiral *Vandergoes* brought to, and sent to Sir *George Rooke*, letting him know that he was then sensible of the Deceit, for that their whole Fleet might be discovered, for which reason he was for avoiding Fighting, if possible, being fearful that not only many of the Merchant Ships would be lost, but that an Engagement there might certainly occasion the Ruin of the whole. The Admiral judged he was advanced too near to think of a Retreat, and therefore, before the Receipt of this Message, he had resolved to push for it; but reflecting afterwards upon the Inconveniences he might expose himself to by engaging, and thereby hazarding the

The Dutch Vice-Admiral against fighting them.

Loss

Sir George Rooke thereupon stands off.

Loss of the Squadron, contrary to the Opinion and Advice of the *Dutch* Flag-Officer, he brought to, and stood off with an easie Sail, that so the *Dutch*, and the heavy Ships might work up to Windward, sending at the same time the *Sheerness* with Orders to the small Ships which were near the Land, and could not (as he judged) keep up with the Fleet, to endeavour to get along Shore in the Night, and save themselves in *Faro*, St. *Lucar*, or *Cadiz*.

The Opportunity our Ships had to escape, by the Enemy's following some Dutch Ships into the Shore.

The Admiral and Vice-Admiral of the Blue, with eight or ten of the Enemy's Ships fetched very fast upon our Squadron, which obliged them to make Sail; notwithstanding which they came up with the Leewardmost about six a Clock, which being two or three *Dutch* Men of War, and some of their Merchant Ships, they (soon after they were engaged) tack'd and stood in for the Shore, as the Enemy did after them, thereby giving a fair Opportunity to our Ships which were to Windward, and ahead, to make their Escape. The Admiral stood off all Night with a prest Sail, having a fresh Gale at N. N. W. and on Sunday Morning fifty four of the Merchant Ships, with several Men of War were about him, but of the latter no more than two of those belonging to the *Dutch*, and one *Hamburgher*, five Sail of the Enemy's Ships being to Leeward, and two to Windward, which last kept Sight of him until it was Night.

Next Day the Admiral called the Officers of the Men of War and Merchant Ships on board him, to inform himself from them what Account they could give of the rest of the Fleet, and to advise what was best to be done for their Security. Some of them said they saw forty or fifty Ships bear away to the Southward, about Ten on Saturday Night, and that among them were the *Monk*, and a *Dutch* Man of War of fifty Guns, and there was great Hopes that the *Chandos*, *Asia*, and several other large Ships bound to *Turky* were safe, because the Admiral's own Ship was the Leewardmost of the Fleet on Sunday Morning, and that now there could be discerned no more to Leeward than five *French* Ships which were standing away towards *Cadiz*. But one of the Masters of the Merchant Ships was for looking towards the Streights Mouth; the rest were positively against it: Some inclin'd for *Lisbon*, others for the *Groyne*, but most for *Ireland*; so that the Admiral determined to steer away either for *Cork* or *Kinsale*, the two principal Ports in that Kingdom.

With great Art the Enemy drew our Squadron and the Trade into this Misfortune; but had they pursued the Advantage with as much Conduct and Resolution, not a Ship could well have escaped; for the Admiral and Vice-Admiral of the Blue were within Shot of Sir *George Rooke* when they tacked and stood in to the Shore after the *Dutch*; which tacking (as I have said before) saved the rest of the Fleet.

In what manner the Squadron and Merchant Ships were separated.

Having given this Account, it may not be improper to inform you how the Fleet, both Ships of War, and those of the Merchants, were by this unlucky Accident separated, *viz.*

CHAP. XI. *from the Year* 1688, *to* 1697.   487

English Ships of War.

Royal Oak,
Breda,
Monmouth,
Lion,
Woolwich,
Newcastle,
Chatham,
Tyger Prize,   } All these were with the Fleet
Lumley Castle,   when the *French* stood in
Princess Anne,   towards the Shore.
Loyal Merchant,
Lark,
Salamander,
Dispatch Brigantine,
Speedwell, } Fireships.
Vulture,
Muscovia Merchant,
   Storeship.
Susannah, Bomb Storeship.

Monk,   { Bore up with the *Chandos*,
                   { *Asia*, &c.

Sheerness,   { Tack'd and stood in for the
Smyrna Factor,   { Shore with the Merchant
                   { Ships.

Dutch Ships of War.

Captain General,   } These were also in the Fleet.
Guelderland,

Oosterstellingwerfe, { Were already gone Convoy to
Dé Bescermer,   { *Oporto* and St. *Ube's*, and so
                     { forward for *Cadiz*.

Nimmegen,   { Bore up with the *Chandos*,
                   { *Asia*, &c.

Zeelandt,   { Tack'd and stood in for the
De Hadt Medezel,   { Shore, soon after the Enemy
Schiedam,   { had reach'd and engag'd them.

Merchant Ships in the Fleet.

George,
Concord,   } Bound to *Smyrna*.
Crown,

Aleppo Factor,   } Bound to *Scanderoon*.
Reward,

Phœnix,   Bound to *Messina*.
Merchants Goodwill, Bound to *Gallipoli*.
Lambeth,
Poplar Frigate,   } Bound to *Alicant*.
Terra Nova Merchant,

Hunter,

Hunter,
Andalusia,
Relief, } Bound to *Cadiz.*
Sarah,
George,
Fidelity, Bound to St. *Lucar.*

English Merchant Ships missing.

Chandos,
Asia,
Italian Merchant, } Bound to *Smyrna.*
Mary,

Joseph, { Bound to *Leghorn*, *Smyrna*, and *Scanderoon.*

Loyalty, Bound to *Scanderoon,*
Jacob,
Prosperous Africa,
Ruby, } Bound to *Venice.*
Golden Frigate,
Great Tunifeen, Bound to *Tunis.*
Three Brothers,
Susanna, } Bound to *Alicant.*
Oxenden, Bound to *Messina.*
Merchants Goodwill, Bound to *Barcelona.*
Friendship, Bound to *Malaga.*
Success,
Malaga Factor,
Benjamin, } Bound to *Cadiz.*
Frog Doggar,
Sarah,
John and Samuel,
John and Thomas, Bound to St. *Lucar.*

All the *Dutch Turky* Ships were missing.
All the *Hamburgher* Convoys were missing, except one Man of War and one Merchant Man, the other Ship of War sailed to St. *Ubes.*

Sir George Rooke proceeds to Madera to water.
After the Admiral had dispatched the *Lark* to *England* with an Account of the Disaster, he bore away with the Fleet to *Madera* for Water, where he had Hopes of meeting some of the scattered Ships, but found only the *Monk*, commanded by Captain *Fairborne*; wherefore putting himself into the best Condition he could, he sailed from *Madera* the twenty seventh of *June*, and arrived at *Cork* in *Ireland* the third of *August*, where *He arrives at Cork in Ireland.* he received Orders from the joint Admirals to send the *Royal Oak*, *Breda*, *Monmouth*, *Lion*, *Woolwich*, and *Lumley Castle* to the main Fleet: But since all the Ships with him were in great Want of several Species of Provisions, and that no sudden Service could be expected

CHAP. XI. *from the Year* 1688, *to* 1697.

pected from those that were to remain at *Kinsale*, he sent them thither under Command of Captain *Fairborne*, and came himself with the beforementioned Detachment to the Fleet.

After our Squadron had thus fortunately escaped (for indeed as hath been already observed, the Enemy made not much of the offered Advantage) the *French* Admiral proceeded up the Streights, and came to an Anchor before the Town of *Malaga* the twentieth of *July* in the Morning, to the Governor of which Place he gave Assurance that he had no Design against either it or the Inhabitants, but that his Intentions were to burn all the *English* and *Dutch* Ships in the Port; adding withall, that if the City endeavoured to defend them, (which indeed it was in no good Condition of doing) he was resolved to bombard it. The Governor returned Answer, that he would do his utmost to protect the Ships according to the King his Master's Orders, and next Day the *French* placing their Broadsides against them in the Mold, being four *Dutch*, and one *English*, attempted to burn the *Union* Frigate, but were twice repulsed; nevertheless they continued to fire very hotly, and all having been done that possible could be to defend the said Merchant Ships, their Masters at last sunk them. *The French Fleet proceeds up the Streights.*

The French attack our Merchant Ships at Malaga, whose Masters sink them.

The Dispute between the City and the *French* lasted about six Hours, but they did no great Damage one to the other, nor were there above eight or ten Men killed and wounded on Shore. After this the Enemy returned down the Streights and anchored in the Bay of *Cadiz*, where they were so far from doing Mischief, that at the Desire of the *French* Admiral (for there was no need of Compulsion) the Governor of the Place gave him a handsome Present of Refreshments. The same Afternoon they sent away all their Prizes to *Thoulon* (being about eighteen) under the Convoy of two Men of War, and detached about fourteen Ships, and two Bomb-Vessels toward *Gibraltar*, in which Bay they arrived the eighth in the Morning, within Gun-shot of the Fortifications, which together with the Mold and Ships fired on them all Day, but they made no Return. *They then repair to Cadiz Bay, and receive Refreshments from the Governor.*

They detach a Squadron to Gibraltar.

The eleventh in the Morning Captain *James Littleton* of the *Smyrna Factor*, sent from her, and several of the Merchant Ships, about ninety Seamen, to enable the Masters of those four which were bound for *Turky* to defend themselves, on whom the *French* fired, and sent in one of their Frigates to attack them; but the warm Reception she received soon obliged them to rescue her with their Boats; not but that when the *French* began to fling Bombs into the Mold, those Masters (as the others had done at *Malaga*) boring Holes in their Ships sunk them, and thereupon the *French* retired to *Lagos* Bay. *Our Merchant Ships sunk by their Masters, and then the Enemy repair to Lagos Bay.*

It is needless to spend more time in attending the Motion of the *French* Fleet, or in relating the mighty Feats they did, by throwing away some Bombs on other Ports in the Streights in their Passage to *Thoulon*; and therefore I shall again return to the Body of our Fleet at Home, which could by no means have arrived time enough to the Assistance of Sir *George Rooke*, had they had sufficient Provisions,

ons, and all other things necessary. But since there was an absolute Necessity for their going to Sea, a Council of the Flag-Officers
was called the ninth of *July*, by whom it was resolved to proceed
forty Leagues S. W. from *Ushant*, and then to consider whether it
might be most proper to remain there, or to remove to some other Station, for intercepting the Enemy. To put this in Execution they attempted to sail the eleventh, but were forced back by extreme bad
Weather, which did considerable Damage, and many of the Ships
lost their Topmasts and Anchors.

A Council of War called to consider how to dispose of our Fleet.

The Misfortunes of the Merchant Ships with Sir *George Rooke*,
had not long been known at our Court, e'er several Questions were
sent to the Admirals by the Lords of the Admiralty, with Respect
to the Time and Place of their parting from the Squadron, and
their not endeavouring to gain Intelligence at *Brest*, &c. but they
adhering to the several Councils of War which were held upon that
Subject, the whole Matter ended with some Examinations before
the House of Commons.

The *Victory*, *Dutchess*, *Suffolk*, *Ossory*, and *Elizabeth*, which
wanted the greatest Repairs, were sent from the Fleet to *Chatham*,
towards the latter End of *August*, but it was ordered that if any other
damaged Ships could be made fit for the Sea in *Torbay*, they should
be immediately gone in hand with; and at this time all the *Dutch*
Ships were in a tolerable good Condition, except that wherein Vice-
Admiral *Callemberg* bore his Flag; but the Winter Season being some
what advanced, the Admirals received Orders the twenty fifth to
come with the Fleet to St. *Helen*'s; where being arrived, the four
Regiments which were put on board, for the better manning them,
were landed at *Portsmouth*, and the Ships with three Decks sent to
Blackstakes, except four of them, the St. *Andrew*, St. *Michael*,
Neptune, and *Vanguard*, which were appointed to be fitted at the
said Port of *Portsmouth*; and on the nineteenth of *September* fifteen
Dutch Ships of the Line of Battel, with two Frigates of thirty
six Guns each, were ordered by his Majesty to *Holland*, so that
the Body being now separated, it was determined that one Second
Rate, seventeen Thirds, seven Fourths, one Fifth, seven Fireships,
and two Hospital Ships should be the Winter Guard.

The Admirals come with the Fleet to St. Helen's, and the great Ships sent to Chatham.

CHAP. XII.

An Account of Sir Francis Wheler's *Proceedings to the*
Mediterranean, *to the Time of his unfortunate Loss, and
what happened afterwards*

SIR *Francis Wheler* being appointed Admiral and Commander
in Chief of the Squadron designed for the *Mediterranean*, I
shall now give an Account of what passed in those Parts during his
time, and after his unfortunate Loss, under the Conduct of Rear-
Admiral

CHAP. XII. *from the Year* 1688, *to* 1697.

Admiral *Nevil*, until such time as he was joined at *Cadiz* by Admiral *Ruffel* with the *English* and *Dutch* Fleets.

He was directed by the Lords of the Admiralty, by their Orders bearing Date the twentieth of *November*, to proceed to *Cadiz* with sixteen Third Rates, seven Fourths, one Fifth, one Sixth, six Fireships, two Bomb-Vessels, an Hospital Ship, and a Storeship, in Company of several *Dutch* Ships of War appointed to join him, and to take under his Convoy all Merchant Ships bound to *Turky*, or any Port in *Spain* or *Italy*. Sir Francis Wheler's Instructions.

If he arrived at *Cadiz* before the *Spanish* Plate Fleet, he was to cruise in such Station as should be agreed on at a Council of War, not exceeding thirty Days, to secure them in their Passage; and when the said Fleet came into Port, or if they did not so do within the aforesaid time, he was to proceed into the *Mediterranean* with seven Third Rates, as many Fourths, one Fifth, one Sixth, four Fireships, two Bomb-Vessels, and the Hospital Ship, and Storeship, together with the *Dutch*. The rest of the Squadron he was to leave at *Cadiz*, with Orders to the senior Officer to remain one and twenty Days there, and then to return to *England* with all the Trade that should be ready to accompany him; and if the *Spanish* Ships of War arrived at *Cadiz* before Sir *Francis Wheler*'s Departure thence, he was to concert with their Admiral where to join him at his Return from convoying the *Turky* Trade.

He had particular Instructions what Convoys to send to *Turky*, and to other Ports up the Streights, which he was to accompany as high as the Chanel of *Malta*; but was cautioned (as usual) not to block up any of the *Grand Signior*'s Ports, and if he took any Ships wherein were the Persons or Effects of that Prince, or his Subjects, he was ordered to set both one and the other on Shore at the first convenient Place.

When he had thus sent forward the several Convoys, he was to return with the *English* and *Dutch* Ships of War, and join the *Spanish* Squadron, and with their Assistance to endeavour to annoy the Enemy, and protect the Trade; and when he judged the *Turky* Convoys might be on their Return, he was to repair to the appointed Rendezvous for joining them, and accompany them to *England*, bringing with him the several Trades from the Ports in the Streights, and *Cadiz*.

He was also farther directed, when he should be in the *Mediterranean*, to send two or three Ships before *Algier, Tunis*, and *Tripoli*, to confirm the Peace with those Governments, and to deliver his Majesty's Presents to them.

From the twentieth of *November* to the twenty seventh of the following Month he lay at St. *Helen*'s, before which time all things necessary for his Voyage could not be, or at least were not, in a Readiness, and then he sailed, leaving behind him two or three of of the smaller Ships at *Portsmouth* and *Plimouth*, to convoy the Storeships and Victuallers after him. 1693.
He sails and sends in his Convoys to Portugal.

The twenty ninth in the Evening he took his Departure from the Land, being joined by most of the Ships he had left behind, and also

also the Victuallers from *Portsmouth* and *Plimouth,* and the fourth of the next Month, near the length of the Northward Cape, he appointed a Convoy to the Ships bound to *Oporto,* and other Places thereabouts. Two Days after he sent in with the *Lisbon* and St. *Ube*'s Ships three Third Rates, two Fourth Rates, and a Fireship, being informed that there were five Sail of the Enemy either off of the Rock of *Lisbon,* or Cape St. *Vincent.*

The thirteenth at Night, as he was standing E. by S. the Wind N. by E. about ten Leagues from Cape St. *Vincent,* he saw four big Ships, and immediately made the Signal for some of his Squadron to endeavour to speak with them; but they bearing away, and it being dirty Weather, ours were called off, to prevent losing Company. Next Morning he discovered six Sail astern of him, about seven Leagues N. of Cape St. *Vincent,* for which he lay by with little Wind, that so, if they were some of his own Number, they might come up, or if Enemies, give an Opportunity to his Ships to get together.

The Wind was contrary the fifteenth at Night, but it veering about in the Morning to the N. N. W. he made sail, and presently saw four *French* Ships of War, one of them larger than the others, about three Leagues to Windward of the Fleet, near *Lagos,* and two more at a distance under the Shore. This induced him to command all the Merchant Ships to bear down to Leeward of him, for their better Security, and he ordered Vice-Admiral *Hopson,* and five Sail more, to chase to Windward; but the Enemy's Ships being clean, and at a considerable Distance, there was no coming up with them.

Rear-Admiral Nevil *sent in quest of some French Ships off Cape St.* Vincent.

A Council of War determined that Rear-Admiral *Nevil,* with the *Warspight, York, Chatham,* and two *Dutch* Men of War of seventy Guns each, with two Fireships, should stand away towards Cape St. *Vincent* in quest of them, and having cruised there six Days to join the *Lisbon,* St. *Ube*'s, and *Oporto* Convoy, and bring them to *Cadiz,* where Sir *Francis Wheler* himself arrived the nineteenth of *January,* having lost Company in his Passage with no more than one of the one hundred sixty five Ships he carried with him from *England,* for the *Canary* Convoy separated before at a convenient Station.

Sir Francis Wheler *arrives at Cadiz.*

An Account of the Spanish Armada.

In *Cadiz* Bay he found the *Spanish Armada,* being about sixteen Sail, but all unrigg'd. Their Admiral assured him they should be ready about the latter end of *March,* though, according to the Dispatch they usually made, some Months more might reasonably have been allowed them. Of the *Dutch* seven accompany'd him from *England,* two more he found at *Cadiz,* and four others were suddenly expected as Convoy to their Trade, but in the room of them the like Number were to return home; so that considering the Convoys he was to appoint, the Smallness of the Squadron, and the Uncertainty of timely Assistance from the *Spaniards,* he was not a little doubtful of the Success of the Expedition.

The Flota *arrived safe in Cadiz Bay.*

The *Flota* he found safely arrived in *Cadiz* Bay, so that his Care for them was at an end; and the twenty fifth of *January* Rear-Admiral *Nevil* returned with the Ships ordered to cruise off of Cape St. *Vin-*

CHAP. XII. *from the Year* 1688, *to* 1697. 493

St. *Vincent*, having there luckily joined the beforemention'd Convoys, when in sight of the *French* Squadron.

After he had appointed two Third Rates, two Fourths, and a Fireship, with four *Dutch* Men of War, two whereof were Ships of seventy Guns, to convoy the homeward-bound Trade, and given Vice-Admiral *Hopson* the necessary Instructions for the Performance of that Service, he put to Sea, having not had a Westerly Wind, after he was ready to sail, before the tenth of *February*; but when he had gotten the Entrance of the Streights open, he was forced to bear up again for the Bay of *Bulls*, where he anchored the next Day. *Vice-Admiral Hopson ordered home with the Trade, and Sir Francis Wheler sails, but is forced back.*

The seventeenth in the Afternoon he sailed from thence, and being off of the Bay of *Gibraltar*, he lay by with an easy Gale at West; but the next Morning about two a Clock made sail again, with little Wind Northerly. At seven the Wind came up at S. E. then to the E. N. E. with Thunder, Lightning, and Rain; so that the Fleet laid their Heads to the South, but at One in the Afternoon they wore, and lay Northward under a main Course, it blowing a hard Gale at E. S. E. the Hill of *Gibraltar* bearing W. S. W. distant about six Leagues. At four a Clock the Land Westward of *Fuengirola* (which is about two Leagues from *Malaga*) was seen N. E. by E. and between Four and Five the Squadron went about, but Rear-Admiral *Nevil* getting his Tacks on board, stood Southward, lying up S. E. under his Courses. At Six the Admiral himself hauled up his Fore, and tried with his Mainsail, with his Head Southward; but at Twelve at Night the *Dutch* Vice-Admiral *Callemberg*, made the Signal for coming to sail, and Rear-Admiral *Nevil* doing the like, got his Foretack aboard. About one it blew very hard, and his Foresail being lost, he was forced to lie under a Mainsail and Mizen all Night. Next Day, about Five in the Morning, the Rear-Admiral's Mainsail also gave way, and seeing about an Hour after the Southward part of the Hill of *Gibraltar* W. S. W. of him, at the Distance of about three Leagues, and at the same time fourteen Sail of the Fleet to Windward, some under their Mainsails, others under their Mizen only, and some without Masts, he immediately brought a new Foresail to the Yard, and hoisted his Ensign, thereby to give Notice to the other Ships of the Fleet, which were in sight, of his seeing the Land; and himself discerning the Mouth of the Streights, he stood away for it, as did Vice-Admiral *Callemberg*; but other Ships having the Bay of *Gibraltar* open, and mistaking it, in all Probability, for the Entrance into the Streights, put in there, not being able to see the Land Westward by reason of the Haziness of the Weather, with much Rain, which occasioned their running into that unhappy Misfortune; for it being a Lee Shore, foul Ground, and their Sails flying in pieces into the Air, they were forced to let go their Anchors, of which many were lost, most of their Cables spoiled, and some of the Ships forced on shore. *A violent Storm. The Ships receive Damage in their Sails, &c. Several Ships mistake the Bay of Gibraltar for the Streights Mouth, and run ashore.*

The Rear-Admiral foreseeing the Danger, was not able timely to give them notice of it, but stood away directly through the Streights, *Rear-Admiral Nevil and others bear away through the Gut.*

as hath been before observed, and at Night got into St. *Jeremy's* Bay, on the Coast of *Barbary*, where he plied to and fro (it being then a Weather-shore, and smooth Water) until the twenty third, at which time a small Gale coming up Westerly, he made the best of his way for *Gibraltar*, and had there the melancholly News of the Loss of Sir *Francis Wheler*, whose Ship, the *Sussex*, founder'd in the Storm, and only two *Turks*, of five hundred and fifty Men, were saved, the Admiral's Body being not long after taken up on the Shore very much mangled.

The Sussex founder'd, and Sir Francis Wheler drowned.

Besides this Loss, there were many others, both as to Ships and Men, a particular Account whereof (as near as it can be collected) is hereafter mentioned, *viz.*

Other Losses.

	Men.
The *Cambridge*, a Ship of seventy Guns, was forced on shore about Four in the Morning, and lost	100.
The *Lumley Castle* had the like Misfortune near Ten at Night, and lost	130.
The *Serpent* Bomb-Vessel founder'd, and lost	15.
The *William* Ketch ran on shore, and lost	15.
The *Mary* Ketch founder'd, and lost	16.
The *Great George*, a *Turky* Ship, ran on shore, and lost	90.
The *Aleppo Factor* ran on shore, and lost	3.
The *Golden Frigate* of *Venice* ran on shore, and lost	23.
The *Berkshire*, a *Turky* Ship, ran on shore, and lost	15.
The *Indian Merchant*, another *Turky* Ship, ran on shore, and lost	1.
The *William*, bound for *Leghorn*, ran on shore in the Evening, and lost	1.
	409.
Lost in the *Sussex*	448.
In all	857.

The *Hollandia*, a *Dutch* Ship of seventy Guns, ran on shore in *Gibraltar* Bay, but got off again, with the Loss of all her Masts.

Several other Ships, both *English* and *Dutch*, were on the Ground, and few or none of the whole Squadron escaped without considerable Damage.

The Squadron re-unites at Gibraltar.

But the greatest part of them being got together at *Gibraltar*, it was thought adviseable by a Council of War, to repair to the Bay of *Cadiz* with all such Ships as were in a Condition, since it was judged they might be there most safe from the *French*; but in doing that they were prevented by contrary Winds until the beginning of *May*.

I lately mentioned the Orders which were given by Sir *Francis Wheler* to Vice-Admiral *Hopson*, for returning from *Cadiz* to *England* with the Trade, after he had staid a certain time there; but before he could leave that Place, the Governor thereof received an

Order

CHAP. XIII. *from the Year* 1688, *to* 1697.   495

Order from his Catholick Majesty, directing him to give an Account to the Captains of the *English* and *Dutch* Ships of the Motion of the Enemy, to prevent any Surprize should they leave that Port: However, the Vice-Admiral having a fair Opportunity, sailed with his Convoys, and arrived off of the Land's End of *England* the fifth of *April* 1694.

Vice-Anmiral Hopson arrives in England with his Convoys.

Rear-Admiral *Nevil* had also Advice at *Cadiz*, that on the fourth of *May* there passed by *Gibraltar*, to the Eastward, a Fleet of fifty three Sail, thirty five of which appear'd to be large Ships, but that not any of them shewed their Colours; and this was the Squadron ordered from *Brest* to join that at *Thoulon*, which had been some time before within the Streights, and burnt four *Spanish* Men of War in their Passage to *Barcelona* with Soldiers.

The Brest Squadron get into the Streights. 1694.

The *Spaniards* about this time had a Defeat in *Catalonia*; and in the beginning of *June* the Duke of *Ossuna* was ordered from Court, with Power to fit out the Galleons at *Cadiz*, that so they might join our Forces; but he died on the Road, and, as some thought, not of a natural Distemper.

The Duke of Ossuna, coming to Cadiz to fit out the Galleons, dies.

Thus stood Affairs in that part of *Europe*; but soon after, Admiral *Russel*, with the most considerable part of the Fleets, both *English* and *Dutch*, then in Pay, arrived at *Cadiz*, after he had left the Lord *Berkeley*, Admiral of the Blue, with the Remainder for the Expedition against *Brest*; an Account of whose Proceedings, from the time he sailed from St. *Helen*'s, as also of the ill Success our Forces had in the Attempt they made on that considerable Port of the Enemy's, I shall now proceed to give you.

C H A P. XIII.

Admiral Russel's *Proceedings with the Fleet in the Chanel, with an Account of the Attempt made on* Brest, *and other* French *Towns*.

THE whole Fleet being at St. *Helen*'s, and the Forces design'd on Service against *Brest* on their March towards *Portsmouth*, where they were to embark, Mr. *Russel* gave Order to Sir *Cloudesly Shovell*, on the third of *May*, to remain there with three First Rates, nine Seconds, thirteen Thirds, seven Fourths, four Fifths, and three of the Sixth, until the Men belonging to them were paid, and to consider during that time how many of the Land Forces (supposed to be about six thousand) each Ship could conveniently take on board, and what Numbers might embark in the Tenders left there for that purpose, wherein he was ordered to advise with Lieutenant-General *Talmarsh*.

Mr. Russel leaves Sir Cloudesly Shovell to take in the Forces at Portsmouth design'd against Brest.

With

He sails into the Soundings with the rest of the Fleet.

With the rest of the Fleet the Admiral sailed, and reached the appointed Station, which was fifteen Leagues S.S.W. from the *Lizard*, the nineteenth of *May*, where he was informed by the Master of a *Swedish* Ship, who came from *Brest* but three Days before, that the Ships which had for some time been ready to sail from that Port, departed thence the twenty fifth of *April* O. S. with a strong Easterly Wind, and that forty or fifty Merchant Ships lay in *Bertheaume* Bay, bound Eastward under Protection of a Man of War or two.

Has Advice when the French sailed from Brest.

Upon this he ordered the *Monmouth* and *Resolution*, with a Fireship, to go between the Trade-way and the Main, and endeavour to take or destroy them. Captain *Pickard*, who commanded them, brought with him into the Fleet two of the Vessels, a large Flyboat, and a Pink, loaden with Salt, having, as he reported, forced on shore thirty five Sail.

Some French Merchant Ships destroyed in Bertheaume Bay.

When the Fleet had been some Days in the aforesaid Station, it was judged necessary to repair to *Torbay*, that so the other part thereof, with the Soldiers, might be the sooner joined: In order whereunto, the Admiral wrote to Sir *Cloudesly Shovell*, letting him know, that if the Wind continued Westerly he had thoughts of coming to *Spithead*, but if Easterly, to remain in *Torbay* for him. Sailing according to this Resolution, he arrived at St. *Helen*'s the twenty third, and applied himself with the greatest Diligence towards the Distribution of the Land-Forces, and compleating the Provisions, that so an Opportunity of the first fair Wind might not be lost; and Cruisers were ordered on proper Stations to gain Intelligence.

The Admiral arrives at St. Helen's.

All things being dispatched, he sailed, and by stopping of Tides, got off the *Berry-Head* the second of *June*, being confirmed in his former Opinion by other Advices he had received, that the *French* Ships were gone from *Brest* to *Thoulon*.

Sails again from thence.

It was agreed that when the Fleet was in a proper Station, the Squadron appointed to act with the Land-Forces should separate upon making the appointed Signal, and steer away for *Brest*, and that then the Admiral himself should take his Course towards the *Mediterranean* with the Remainder: And, that no time might be lost, he prepared Orders, before he sailed from St. *Helen*'s, by which *John* Lord *Berkeley* was directed how to govern himself, the Contents whereof follows, *viz.*

Lord Berkeley's Instructions for attempting Brest.

1. He was informed what Ships, both *English* and *Dutch*, were to be under his Command, and directed to proceed with them to *Brest*, and when there, to land the Officers and Soldiers in such manner, and at such Place, or Places, as should be agreed on by a Council of War of the General-Officers, both at Sea and Land, who were to consider, before they arrived at *Brest*, how the Forces might be best assisted by the Ships, either in going on shore, or otherwise, as also when it might be most proper for the Squadron to go into *Brest* Water, to assist in the carrying on the Design against the Town, and the Ships there.

2. When they had done all they were able against *Brest*, it was to be considered what Service might be performed on any other of
the

the *French* King's Ports, and how the same might be most effectually put in Execution.

3. And when a Council of War should judge that no farther Service could be done, either by Sea or Land, and think it adviseable to have the Forces taken on board again, he was to cause the same to be performed, and then repair to, and remain in *Torbay*, or at *Spithead*, until he received Orders from the King, or the Lords of the Admiralty.

4. His Lordship was also directed to use his best Endeavours to protect the Forces, at all times when it should be thought proper to land them, and to embark them again: And if the General Officers should at any time judge it necessary to have part of the Seamen put on shore, to strengthen the Troops, and that the Ships might conveniently spare them, he was to appoint such a Number as the said General Officers should desire, or at least so many as he could without hazard of the Ships.

Having now given you the Contents of the Instructions to the Lord *Berkeley*, it will appear by the following Account what Naval Strength was sent with him on this Service, *viz.*

The Naval Strength with Lord Berkeley.

Rates.	Number.
1	3
2	4
3	12
4	1
5	2
Fireships	10
Hospitals	3
Brigantines	3

Besides Bomb-Vessels, Advice-Boats, &c.

Dutch.

Ships of the Line of Battel	19
Fireships	4

For the more regular carrying on this Design, his Lordship was ordered to cause the Ships and Vessels beforementioned, as well as the Tenders and Well-Boats, (which latter were particularly built for putting Men on shore) to keep near the Flags whereto they were respectively appointed, and to shift their Pendants accordingly, that so when the Signal should be made for parting, each might follow his proper Flag without Confusion; for at this time there were not many of the Officers who knew the Fleet was to be thus divided.

Care being taken as to that part of the Fleet bound to *Brest*, and *Camaret* Bay appointed the Rendezvous in case of Separation, the Admiral considered what was necessary to be done with respect to the Ships which were to proceed with him in the *Mediterranean*; and knowing what ill Consequences might attend Separation, in case the

the Ships so separated knew not certainly where to join again, he gave to each Captain the following Rendezvous, *viz.*

The Rendezvous given by the Admiral of the Ships designed for the Streights. That if they happened to lose sight of the Fleet when fifty Leagues S.W. from the *Lizard*, and that the Winds blew so strong Westerly as to oblige him to bear up, they should repair to *Torbay:* But that if they happened to lose Company in a Fog, or by any other Accident, when to the Eastward of the aforesaid Station, they should make the best of their way fifteen Leagues West from Cape *Spartell*, and remain there until joined by the Fleet, or that they were otherwise ordered; and they were strictly forbid to chase out of their way, on any Pretence whatever, or to discover where they were bound to any Ship or Vessel they should meet with. But since they might probably join him before he reach'd the Rendezvous near Cape *Spartell*, he let them know, that, as the Winds proved, he designed to haul in within twenty five Leagues West of Cape *Finisterre*, and within twenty of Cape St. *Vincent*, and that from thence he would proceed directly to the aforesaid Rendezvous: And all the Captains were expressly directed not to break open the Rendezvous which was delivered to them sealed, unless they should happen to be separated with the Wind Easterly, and then informing themselves of the Contents thereof, they were, pursuant thereunto, to repair to the Fleet fifteen Leagues S.W. from the Land's End of *England*.

All things being now adjusted for the Fleet's Separation, a Council of War was called the thirty first of *May* of the Flag and General Officers, who taking into Consideration the several Particulars relating to the Squadron appointed for *Brest*, came to the following Resolutions, *viz.*

Result of a Council of War about attacking Brest. 1. That the Lord *Berkeley* should with the said Squadron make the best of his way to, and anchor in *Camaret* Bay, and the Land-Forces be immediately set on shore; and that the Ships should continue at an Anchor, until they received Advice from General *Talmarsh* of the Condition of the Fort on the Star-board-side going in, and of what Forces he found there.

2. That it was not proper to come to any positive Resolution at what time the Fleet should go into *Brest-Water*, and therefore that Matter was left to be considered when they arrived in *Camaret* Bay.

3. That a red Ensign at the Fore-top-mast-head on board the Lord *Berkeley*'s Ship, with the firing of a Gun, should be the Signal for the Soldiers to embark on board the small Craft and Boats; and the taking down that Signal, with the firing of two Guns, for their going on shore.

There were present at this Council

Admiral *Russel*,
John Lord *Berkeley*,
Sir *Cloudesly Shovell*,
Vice-Admiral *Aylmer*,
Rear-Admiral *Mitchel*,

The Marquis of *Carmarthen*,
George *Byng*, Esq; first Captain to the Admiral

Lieutenant-General *Talmarsh*,
Earl of *Macclesfield*,
Lord *Cutts*,
Sir *Martin Beckman*.

Dutch.

Admiral *Allemonde*,
Vice-Admiral *Vanderputt*,
Vice-Admiral *Schey*,
Rear-Admiral *Vandergoes*,
Rear-Admiral *Evertson*,
Captain *Vander Duſſen*.
} *Dutch* Flag-Officers.

The sixth Day of *June* in the Afternoon the two Fleets parted, *The Fleet separates.* and since that commanded by the Lord *Berkeley* came soonest to their appointed Service, it may be proper to give an Account first of what was done by them, and then follow the Admiral himself to the Streights.

My Lord *Berkeley* being arrived in *Camaret* Bay, a Council of War was called on board the Ship *Queen* the eighth of *June*, where was present his Lordship, Lieutenant-General *Talmarsh*, and all the Flag and General-Officers, by whom it was resolved that the Lieutenant-General should go on shore with the Troops as soon as it was possible, and endeavour to make himself Master of the Fort at *Camaret*, and that four or five Frigates should cover him in landing. *Resolution taken about landing near Breſt.*

Accordingly a considerable Number of the Forces were put on shore, but the *French* Coast being fortified, and intrenched almost in every Place, our Men received so warm a Reception, that they were soon obliged to return to the Boats, and that too in no little Disorder. *Some of the Forces are put on ſhore, but repulſed.*

In this Action we lost about six hundred Men; and the Lieutenant-General himself being wounded in the Thigh, died soon after at *Plimouth*. The *Monk*, *Charles* Gally, and *Shoreham*, some of the Ships which were sent in to protect the Landing, and to batter the *French* Forts, were very much shatter'd, and in them, and the others, about a hundred and twelve Men were killed and wounded; a *Dutch* Frigate was sunk, and her Captain killed; besides which, we received many other Damages. *Lieutenant-General Talmarſh dies of his Wound.*

The whole Extent of the Bays of *Camaret* and *Bertheaume* (which lie on each side of the Entrance into *Breſt-water*) was in a manner a continu'd Fortification; for where there was any Place to put Forces on shore, there had the *French* Batteries and Retrenchments, and they threw Bombs at our Ships from five or six Places.

As soon as the Land-Forces were embarked, a General Council of War was held, and since they found it impracticable to attempt any thing farther at *Breſt*, it was considered what might be done with *A Council of War called to conſider what might be farther done.*

with the Fleet and Army. The Lieutenant-General informed them that he had not sufficient Authority to attempt any other Place, and therefore proposed that a Squadron of small Frigates, with the Bomb-Vessels, might be sent into that Harbour, to try if they could bomb the Town. This was thought by no means advisable, for the Ships could not go in without a Westerly, nor come out without an Easterly Wind; and since it was not known what Strength the *French* had in that Port, they might run the hazard of falling into their Hands: Besides, one of them was sunk in battering the Forts, and most of the others render'd unfit for Service; so that it was agreed to repair to *Spithead*, as the most proper Place to land the Troops at, and to refit the Ships.

Thus ended this unlucky Expedition; but I cannot leave it without making this Observation, That the *French* would not in all Probability have been in such a Posture to receive our Troops, had not early Advice been given of the Debates and Resolutions concerning this Affair, by *French* Men who were consulted and advised with therein, as hath been before observed.

The Fleet arrives at St. Helen's.

The Fleet sailing from *Camaret* Bay, arrived at St. *Helen's* the fifteenth of *June*, and there Orders were received from the Queen, that a Council of War of the Flag and General-Officers should consider how the Ships and Troops might be best employed, who were of Opinion, that the Fleet should sail to the Coast of *France*, and annoy the Enemy not only with the Bomb-Vessels, but by landing in the Country; and that the same might be better effected, it was desired that some more small Frigates might be sent to the Fleet to sustain the said Bomb-Vessels, which the greater Ships could not do.

A Council of War resolve to annoy the Enemy by bombing, and landing Men.

The eighteenth of *June* another Council was call'd, when it was judged that some Place on the Coast of *Normandy* might with most Success be bombarded, and that four Regiments would be sufficient to secure the Bomb-Vessels against the Attempts of the *French*, as well as for other necessary Services.

The Fleet being refitted, and the Seamen and Land-Forces refreshed, the Queen's Orders were received the twenty seventh of *June*, and thereupon another Council was called, where it was agreed, that since the Wind was fresh Westerly, the Fleet should first proceed and bombard *Dieppe*, and then do what other Prejudice they could along the *French* Coast. Being arrived there, they were prevented in making any Attempt by bad Weather, which not only dispersed the Ships, but damaged some of them in their Masts and Rigging, so that they were constrain'd to return to the Coast of *England*, and anchor off of *Denge Nesse*, where the scatter'd Ships and Vessels join'd the fifth of *July*, and sailing thence again to *Dieppe* Road, it was intended to bombard that Town the ninth in the Morning; in order whereunto several of the Bomb-Vessels advanced near in with the Shore, but it blowing hard at Night, they were prevented by the great Sea which then ran.

Dieppe bombarded.

The thirteenth the Town of *Dieppe* was bombarded, and so effectually too, that it appeared all in Flames; and the Night before a Machine Vessel was blown up at the Pier-Head, but with little or no Success, occasioned, as was supposed, by the Head's lying so low. Captain *Dunbar*

CHAP. XIII. *from the Year* 1688, *to* 1697. 501

Dunbar, who commanded this Vessel, behaved himself with great Bravery, for the *Fusee* going out, he went on board again, and set fire to it, for which, both himself and the Men he took with him, were deservedly rewarded.

The Fleet sailed from *Dieppe* the fourteenth in the Afternoon, most of the few Houses which were standing being on fire, and on the sixteenth the Bombardment of *Havre de Grace* began, which had so good an Effect, that the Town was in Flames in several Places, and burnt all that Night and the next Day; nor was the Fire extinguished the eighteenth, insomuch that it might be reasonably conjectured at least a third part thereof was consumed. The nineteenth the Weather was very bad, so that all the Bomb-Vessels were ordered off, not above five of them being serviceable, for the Mortars were either melted, or the Vessels themselves so shattered, that no present use could be made of them, and one of them, called the *Granadoe*, was entirely blown to pieces by a Bomb which fell into her. *Havre de Grace bombarded.*

A Council of War agreed it would be losing of Time to stay longer before *Havre de Grace*, and therefore determined to proceed to St. *Helen's*, and endeavour to repair the Damages received; but it was thought adviseable, if Wind and Weather would admit of it, to proceed first to *La Hogue*, or *Cherbourg*, or both, thereby to alarm the *French*, and draw their Land-Forces farther Westward. Accordingly the Fleet sailed, and appeared off of those Places, tho' they met with ruffling Weather. This alarm'd the *French* so much, that they fired several Guns, and made many Fires on shore; but our People being not able to do any Service on them, stretched it over to St. *Helen's*, where they arrived the twenty sixth in the Afternoon, and then all the Bomb-Vessels and Well-Boats were sent into the Harbour to be refitted, and six of the Regiments were put on shore by the Queen's Order. Some time was spent in getting all things ready, so that the Fleet could not reach the *Downs* (as ordered) before the ninth of *August*, and there a Council of War was called on the seventeenth, upon a Signification of her Majesty's Pleasure, that an Attempt should be made on *Dunkirk*, if it should be thought practicable, and that it might not too much expose the Ships of War at such a Season of the Year on so dangerous a Coast. This Matter was debated, and all the *English* Pilots, with one of the *Dutch*, (the only one in the Squadron) were consulted, who would not undertake to carry a Squadron of Frigates and Fireships into *Flemish* Road; for that the Distance between the Brake and the Wooden Forts was not above Pistol-shot, and that there was not Water enough for the Ships to ride Eastward; nor could they (as they said) come out again with the same Wind which would carry them in. Upon Consideration whereof, and that the Season of the Year was too far advanced, as also that there were no more than five Frigates (not a fourth part of what was necessary to sustain the Bomb-Vessels, and bring off their Men, because of the Number of small Ships and Vessels the *French* might make use of to intercept them) it was agreed by a Council of War, as it was by Sir *Martin Beckman*, Colonel *The Fleet proceeds off La Hogue, Cherbourg, &c. and then repairs to St. Helen's.*

The Fleet arrives in the Downs.

A Council of War judge it impracticable to attempt Dunkirk this Year.

lonel of the Artillery, and Mr. *Meesters*, the Inventer of the Machine Vessels prepared for this intended Exploit against *Dunkirk*, that it was impracticable to attempt any thing at this time on that important Place.

But the Plan of *Calais* having been sent to the Fleet from *Flanders*, by the King's particular Command, it was the Opinion of a Council of War that some Service might be done there, and determined to sail thither with the Bomb-Vessels; but before the Weather would let them stir, the Lord *Berkeley* received Orders from the Lords of the Admiralty, who thereupon called the Sea-Officers together, and consulted with them only, what Attempts might be made, with Prospect of Success, upon the *French* Ships of War in *Dunkirk* Road: And although the Pilots, who were discoursed thereupon, absolutely refused to carry in so much as a Fourth Rate Frigate, yet it was agreed, that if able Pilots could be procured, well acquainted with the Eastern and Western Chanels, the Ships in the Road might be destroy'd upon a Spring Tide (the only proper time for doing it) with double the Number of Frigates to those of the *French*, some Fireships, Brigantines, and other Tenders.

The Three-Deck Ships ordered to the Nore.

But now the Winter Season being advanced, the Three-Deck Ships were ordered to the *Nore*, and the Lord *Berkeley* coming to Town, the rest of the Fleet was put under the Command of Sir *Cloudesly Shovell*, who was in daily Expectation of proper Pilots for making the Attempt on the Ships at *Dunkirk*; but soon after Rear-Admiral *Hopson* (who, with several *Dutch* Ships, was off of that Port to watch the Motions of *Monsieur du Bart)* informed him that all the Pilots with them were very averse to carry in our Ships, not but that it was his Opinion, as it was of the Captains of each Nation, that with twelve Frigates, and eight Fireships, with the Sloops and Brigantines, as Sir *Cloudesly* had proposed, Service might be done on the Enemy's Ships.

Mr. Meesters proposes the destroying the Forts at Dunkirk.

About this time Mr. *Meesters* (who I have before mentioned) made a Proposal for the destroying the Forts before *Dunkirk* with his Machines; but whatever Success might have been hoped for from those Vessels in the midst of Summer, there was but little Probability of their doing much Service at this Season of the Year, so that it was not particularly insisted upon that Sir *Cloudesly Shovell* should attempt the Forts, but Orders were sent him to proceed to the Coast of *France*, and not only endeavour to keep in the Ships, but to attempt them if practicable; if not, to send the Bombs, Machines, and other Vessels to the *Nore*.

Pursuant to these Orders he sailed, but was obliged to anchor off of the South *Foreland* the fifth of *September*, to stay for the small Craft, which ran no little Hazard at this time of the Year, some of them being no bigger than Long-Boats. Here he received a Letter from Mr. *Meesters* at *Ostend*, by which he seem'd confident of doing considerable Service with his Machines at *Dunkirk*, and let him know, that, in Order thereunto, he was coming to the Squadron with all the Haste he could. This made Sir *Cloudesly Shovell* repair to the *Downs*, because there Mr. *Meesters* might much more

conve-

CHAP. XIII. *from the Year* 1688, *to* 1697. 503

conveniently have put his Veffels into a Condition for his Enterprize.

Mr. *Meefters* arrived in the *Downs* the feventh with about twenty fix *Dutch* Pilots, and (among other things propofed by him for the better effecting his Defign) he defired that a Captain might be appointed to command the fmall Ships, with Inftructions to follow his Advice in failing and anchoring. That he might be gratified in this Particular, Captain *Benbow* (afterwards a Flag-Officer) was appointed to that Command, and on the eighth of *September* Orders were fent to Sir *Cloudefly*, that in cafe thofe Pilots Mr. *Meefters* had brought with him from *Flanders*, would undertake to carry in fuch Ships as fhould be thought neceffary, he fhould proceed and attempt the Pier, Harbour, and Town, or the Ships in the Road. *Mr. Meefters comes to Sir Cloudefly Shovell in the Downs with Dutch Pilots.*

The Squadron being on the Coaft of *Flanders* with a Northerly Wind, Mr. *Meefters* acquainted Sir *Cloudefly Shovell* that his Pilots were of Opinion the *French* could not carry out their Ships at the Eaft Chanel of *Dunkirk*, wherefore he anchored in *Graveline Pits*, and the Boats and Brigantines went before *Dunkirk* under the Protection of the *Sally-Rofe*, and founded to make themfelves the better acquainted with the Weftern Chanel between the Brake and the Main; for all the Pilots, unlefs it were two or three, declared themfelves ignorant of that Paffage. Captain *Benbow* found the Narrow to be above three Cables length in Breadth, and in Depth from $3\frac{1}{2}$ to feven Fathom, at low Water; and the Brigantines and Sloops, which lay to and fro on the Back of the Brake, difcovered a large Chanel of feven, eight, nine, and ten Fathom at low Water, about a Mile and a half broad, and fomewhat more, that is, fo far as they went into it, which was until they had *Dunkirk* South of them. *Captain Benbow founds the Paffage into Dunkirk, and gives an Account.*

The Sight of our Veffels, put the *French* into a great Confternation, and a Frigate of about twenty Guns that lay in the Road fired very fmartly at our Boats which were got within the Brake. Many Guns, and fome Bombs were alfo fired from the Citadel, the *Ris-Bank*, and the Forts at the Pier-heads, and as five of their Frigates, from forty to fifty Guns each, were hawled out of the Bafin, and rigged, fo were there three or four fmall Ships placed in the Chanel between the Pier-heads and the Town; but notwithftanding all this, our little Fleet of Boats, &c. came off in the Night without any Damage. *The French at Dunkirk in a Confternation.*

Next Day the Wind fhifting from the North to the North-Eaft, and it being fair Weather, all the Boats and fmall Veffels were fent in again, as was the *Charles* Gally, two Bomb-Veffels, and fome of the Machines, which Mr. *Meefters* had appointed; and when the Veffels came near the Brake, the *French* Frigate which lay without got up her Anchor, fired her Broadfide, and ran into the Pier. *The Boats and fome of Mr. Meefters Machines fent in.*

In the Afternoon two of the Machines were blown up at a little Diftance from the Pier heads, but without Succefs; nor was there any great Hopes of better Service from the reft, for the *French* had driven Piles without thofe Heads, and funk four Ships on the Back of the Weftermoft Pier very advantageoufly. *Two of the Machines blown up without Succefs.*

s   Mr.

Mr. *Meesters* now informed Sir *Cloudesly* that, since the Spring-Tide was past, his Pilots would not undertake to carry the Ships through the Sands to the Eastward of *Dunkirk*, and that therefore he thought it not proper to continue longer with his Vessels on the *French* Coast, so that they were sent to the *Downs*, and at the same time a small Frigate was ordered thither with Sir *Martin Beckman*, to bring the Vessels which were designed to bombard *Calais*, who arriving with them the sixteenth, the Squadron forthwith proceeded off of that Place, but the Weather proved so very bad several Days that little Service was done, for both the Ships of War and others were constrained to come into the *Downs*, from whence the Bombs and Machines were sent into the River of *Thames*.

Mr. Meesters returns to the Downs, and the Bomb-Vessels are sent for, but bad Weather prevented any Service.

Thus ended our Attempts on the *French* at Home this Year; and although I will not pretend to make an exact Computation of the Expence these Bombardments put the Nation to, yet I do verily believe it was more than equivalent to the Damage the Enemy sustain'd from them.

Chap. XIV.

An Account of Admiral Russel*'s Proceedings with the Fleet in the* Mediterranean *to the Time of his Return to* England.

MR. *Russel*, as I have said before, parted with the Lord *Berkeley* on the sixth of *June* 1694, and on the twenty fifth of that Month he got into the Latitude of thirty nine Degrees, off of the Rock of *Lisbon*, at which time the *Mary* and *Adventure*, under Command of Captain *John Jennings*, were sent to Cape *St. Vincent*, where, or at some Place thereabouts, he was ordered to send his Boat on Shore for Intelligence whether the Enemy were, or had been on that Coast; and if he gained certain Advice of their being there, but that they were not so placed as to prevent the *Adventure*'s passing them, he was to send her to the Bay of *Cadiz*, with a Packet to Rear-Admiral *Nevill*, (a Duplicate whereof he was also ordered to dispatch to him by Land) by which he was required to sail with all the Ships under his Command, except the *Turky* Convoy, and join the Fleet; and for his better Government therein, the Admiral let him know that he designed to come South fifteen or twenty Leagues from Cape *St. Vincent*, and (if the Wind continued fair) the same Distance from Cape *St. Mary*'s, and then fifteen Leagues from Cape *Spartell*. These Orders he was directed to communicate to Vice-Admiral *Callemberg*, who commanded several *Dutch* Ships, that so he might accompany him, but not to discover the Reason of his Sailing to any but those who necessarily ought to be acquainted with it.

Admiral Russel arrives off of the Rock of Lisbon.

Rear-Admiral Nevill ordered to join him from Cadiz.

The Fleet being got thus far, the Admiral settled the proper Places for Rendezvous in case of Separation in his Passage up the Streights; and the thirtieth of *June* the *Portsmouth* was dispatched off of Cape *Spartell*, to call the *Mary*, *Adventure*, and *Lark*, to the Fleet, and to inform the *Spanish* Admiral, if he met with his Squadron at Sea, of our Approach.

Rear-Admiral *Nevil*, and the two *Dutch* Vice-Admirals, *Callemberg* and *Evertson*, joining the Fleet from *Cadiz*, with eight *English*, and as many of the Ships of the States General (which made the whole Number sixty three of the Line) a Council of War was called of all the Flag-Officers, by whom it was thought most adviseable that the Merchant Ships bound up to the *Levant* should repair to *Carthagena*, and remain there until Care could be taken for their proceeding farther on their Voyage with Safety; and those Gentlemen taking also into their Consideration the Intelligence of the *French* Fleet's being off of *Barcelona*, and the adjacent Coasts, came to a Resolution forthwith to proceed thither. *A Council of War called of English and Dutch Flags. Agreed the Fleet should sail to Barcelona.*

Notwithstanding there happened bad Weather and contrary Winds, the Fleet got off of Cape *Spartell* the first of *July*, having received no other Damage than the Loss of two small Vessels which attended on the Admiral's own Ship.

The *Spaniards* sailed from *Cadiz* with nine Ships of War at the same time that Rear-Admiral *Nevil* did, but had not yet join'd the Fleet, and there was now Advice received that the Enemy were with seventy Sail between *Alfaques* and *Barcelona*; so that our Force (when join'd by the *Spaniards*) would have been almost equal to theirs. *Advice of the French Fleet.*

The Admiral acquainted Mr. *Stanhope*, our Envoy at *Madrid*, that he hoped to be so timely at *Barcelona* as to prevent farther Mischief from the *French* in those Parts: And for the greater Safety of the Fleet, two Frigates were ordered to sail on the Starboard, and two others on the Larboard Bow, but not at so great a Distance as to hinder their Sails being seen above Water: Nor were they upon meeting any *French* Ships to chase beyond Cape *de Gates*; and if they fell in with any Ships or Vessels, of what Nation soever, they were ordered to bring them into the Fleet to be examined. There were also three Frigates sent on the Coast of *Barbary*, with Directions to stretch from Cape *Tres Forcas* over to the *Spanish* Shore, for intercepting any thing the others might meet with, and chase Eastward. *Cruizers sent out for Intelligence.*

During the Fleets being under Sail all possible Care was taken to put every Ship in a Condition of doing Service, by taking Stores and other Necessaries from such as could best spare for those that wanted; and the strictest Orders were given that all possible good Husbandry should be used in expending their Provisions.

The Admiral being informed that several of the Ships of War belonging to the Government of *Algier* did intend to come into the Fleet, he desired both the *Dutch* and *Spaniards* that not only they, but the Ships of *Tunis* and *Tripoli* (with whom we were likewise at Peace) might have that Liberty, without any Acts of Hostility being offered to them in Sight of his Flag, provided they came immediately *The Algerine Men of War permitted to come into the Fleet, but one of them seized by the Dutch.*

mediately to him with their Colours flying; but notwithstanding his Hopes that this would be complied with, one of the Ships of *Algier* was soon after seized in his Sight by a *Dutch* Man of War, though such Measures were soon after taken for her Release, as that neither his Majesty's Honour, nor the Government of *Algier* suffered thereby: Nor were those People a little satisfied as well at the generous Usage they received in this particular, as in the seeing a Fleet in these Parts superior to what had ever been known there before, or probably ever may be hereafter.

The Fleet arrives at Carthagena.

The thirteenth of *July* the Confederate Fleet got as far as *Carthagena*, the Passage thither having been very tedious, for the Wind had been Easterly from the time they entered the Mouth of the Streights. This Impediment was very unlucky, for the Season of the Year was far advanced, and so much of their Provisions expended, that soon after they could possibly get as high as *Barcelona*, there would be a Necessity of returning again. The *French* having Notice of our Approach retired to the Isles of *Hyeres*, off of *Thoulon*, and it was thought that they would either disarm their great Ships, and send Squadrons up the *Levant*, or go with their whole Fleet as high as *Malta*, where they knew very well ours could not pursue them. I must here observe that the principal Reason of our Fleets coming so late into those Parts, was the Delay made at home in the Dispatch of the Troops designed against *Brest*, and shipping them off when at *Portsmouth*; for had that Service been performed a Month sooner, there would have been a fairer Prospect of doing something this Summer within the Streights.

The French retire to the Isles of Hyeres.

The Marquess of *Camarassa*, General of the *Spanish* Gallies, upon the Admiral's approaching *Carthagena*, sent a Letter to him desiring to know where the Fleet and the Gallies should join; to which he returned a Compliment, and acquainted him that he intended for *Barcelona* with all Speed.

The Fleet stops at Altea to water.

The seventeenth of *July* it was determined at a Council of War to stop at *Altea* Bay for a Supply of Water, and that the *Turky* Convoy should remain at *Carthagena* until farther Intelligence could be had of the Enemy; to obtain which three Frigates were sent to cruise between Cape *Martin* and *Yviça* for twenty four Hours, and the *Adventure* was ordered eight Leagues, the *Lark* five, and another two Leagues E. S. E. from the Eastermost Part of *Altea* for thirty six Hours. But notwithstanding what was thus agreed, it was, upon farther Thoughts, judged necessary to order the *Turky* Fleet to *Alicant*, and to reinforce them there by two *English*, and one *Dutch* Man of War; and left they should want Provisions, or other Necessaries, the Consul at *Carthagena* was written to to furnish them therewith.

An Account of the Spanish Ships that joined us.

The twenty fifth of this Month the Admiral writ to Monsieur *Schonenberg*, Envoy from the States General at the *Spanish* Court, concerning the Circumstances of that King's Affairs; and first as to his Ships which had joined the Fleet, he acquainted them they were in Number ten, four whereof might indeed (for want of better) have been admitted into the Line of Battel, but that the rest were

of

3

CHAP. XIV. *from the Year* 1688, *to* 1697. 507

of but little Force, and withal so rotten that they would hardly bear the firing of their own Guns. He farther observed to him, that the Sea-Port Towns were unprovided both as to Men and all other warlike Preparations, so that it was much to be feared if a small Number of the Enemy's Ships should appear before *Malaga*, or *Alicant*, and attempt to cannonade those Places, they would instantly be abandoned. He also let him know his Doubts that *Catalonia* would not be able to resist the Enemy when the Fleet retired, since the *French* Army (as it was reported) consisted of near twenty five thousand well disciplined Men, with all things necessary, and that the *Spaniards* did not exceed nine thousand, and even they without Tents, or other Materials proper for an Encampment; as also that there was Reason to apprehend if the *French* could make themselves Masters of *Barcelona*, they would soon attempt the Island of *Minorca*, which could not well resist two thousand Men forty Hours, under its present ill Circumstances. In fine, it was his Opinion, and a well grounded one too, that unless the Vice-Roy of *Catalonia* could make some brisk Effort on the *French* soon after the Fleets coming there, that Principality would be in greatest Danger, since he should be obliged to return in very little time, the Ships of the States General having not Provisions for more than all the next Month. Indeed had the *French* proceeded with Vigour, that Country would long before have fallen into their Hands; for there was not an Army capable to resist them, and even most of those that were in Arms seem'd to be more fit for an Hospital than a Camp; nor was there Money to pay them, notwithstanding the large Contributions of the *Catalonians*, the exacting whereof by the General Officers to the utmost Extent, render'd those People so miserable, that in Expectation of better Usage from *France*, a little Matter would have inclined them to a Revolt.

The Admiral acquaints Monsieur Schonenberg with the bad Circumstances of the King of Spain's Sea-Affairs.

At this time a noble Lord * proposed the Fleet's wintering in the *Mediterranean*; but the Admiral acquainted him he could by no means think it adviseable, since there was not any Place fit to receive and protect them but *Mahon*, in the Island of *Minorca*, where there was a total Want of Provisions; nor could any Stores be timely got thither to refit the Ships against the Spring. That as for *Naples*, there was no Defence, and *Messina* was not large enough. But there remained yet another material Objection, which was this; that should such a Strength have been detained from *England* and *Holland* all the Winter, the *French* might have made themselves too strong in the Spring for what could possibly have been fitted out in these Seas.

The Admiral's Reasons against wintering in the Streights.

The first of *August* the Admiral received a Letter from the Marquess *Villena*, Vice-Roy of *Catalonia*, desiring his Opinion in several Particulars, whereupon a Council of War was called, and each Article being considered, the following Resolutions were taken thereupon.

* *Earl of* Gallway.

T t t 2

Article

Article I. That the better to reinforce the *Spanish* Army, ten thousand, or at least eight thousand Soldiers might be put ashore from the Fleet, to join those they had, and such as should be ordered from the *Spanish* Ships and Gallies.

Answer. That not any of the Ships of his Majesty of *Great-Britain*, or those of the States General had Soldiers on board them.

Article II. That if the first Proposal could not be complied with, the Fleet might go in Pursuit of the Enemy, and endeavour to destroy them.

Answer. That formerly there was not only Hopes of meeting the *French* Fleet off of *Barcelona*, or at Sea, but that they would have given an Opportunity of engaging them, but finding them retired to *Thoulon*, within Fortifications too strong to be forced, the going thither could have no other Effect than losing time; however, if certain Advice could be had that they were at Sea, or in any Port where they might be attacked with Probability of Success, the Fleet would immediately proceed in quest of them.

Article III. How long the Fleet could continue in those Seas?

Answer. That if any Enterprize should be undertaken on the Sea-Coast with his Forces, in order to the regaining any Places from the *French*, in which the Fleet might be assisting, it would be readily embraced, provided it could be done without Delay, for that they had no more Provisions than were absolutely necessary for them in their Passage to *England*.

The Vice-Roy of Catalonia his Answer to the Results of a Council of War.

The Vice-Roy replied that the only Enterprize which could be made on that Coast was the regaining of *Palamos*, wherein the Sea-Forces might be very useful; but that, in such Case, the *Spanish* Army ought to be reinforced from the Fleet; and if that could not be done, he proposed that the Naval Force might make some Invasion on the Coast of *France*, and what Infantry should be wanted for such a Service, he promised to supply from his Army.

The Admiral lets him know the Assistance he could give him.

To this the Admiral said, that the Fleet was provided for an Engagement at Sea, but not to invade the Enemy on Shore, insomuch that it was not possible for him to furnish any Men to reinforce the *Spanish* Army; but that if he thought it convenient to send a Body of Soldiers in the Fleet and Gallies to attempt *Palamos*, (which is between twenty and thirty Leagues to the Eastward of *Barcelona*) all possible Assistance should be given therein, by arming the Boats and small Vessels on any sudden Assault; to which his speedy Answer was desired, for that it was convenient to proceed in Search of the Enemy's Fleet.

The Spanish Forces not of Strength to attack Palamos.

The Vice-Roy having considered this, acquainted the Admiral that the Forces of his Catholick Majesty were much inferior to those of the *French*, and that having not any Prospect of augmenting them, he did not think it adviseable to attempt *Palamos*, or any other Place in which the Fleet could be assisting to him; but desired to know how long he could conveniently stay on that Coast. The Admiral informed him, that, upon his first Representation of the State of *Catalonia*, Care was taken to furnish the Ships of the

States-

CHAP. XIV. *from the Year* 1688, *to* 1697. 509

States-General with fourteen Days Provisions from the *English*, that so the Fleet might stay there as long as possible; but that since there was at this time a general want, and that many Inconveniences might thereby happen by the setting in of Westerly Winds, it was absolutely necessary to retire towards the Streights Mouth in five or six Days.

The Vice-Roy had represented, indeed, that there were Provisions for three hundred and fifty thousand Men for a Day at *Carthagena*, but it plainly appeared he was very much misinformed in that Particular; for a single Ship which demanded at that Port enough only for seven Days, could not be furnished therewith; nor was there more than two thousand Quintals of Bread; no other Provision having been made, besides what the Admiral himself had given Orders for to the Consul, as he passed up the Streights. *The Vice-Roy misinformed about the Provisions made for the Fleet.*

The Vice-Roy was under great Apprehensions, that if the Fleet left the Coast of *Catalonia* while the Season of fair Weather lasted, the *French* would appear by Sea before *Barcelona*; but if they really had such an Intention, it could not have been prevented, since our Ships were not in a Condition to stay longer without running the greatest Hazard; for Provisions could not be supplied from *Spain*, especially in that part thereof, but from Day to Day, which would not only have render'd it impossible for them to return to *England*, but to have proceeded on any pressing Service whatever. But that the *French* might be as long Strangers to our Fleet's retiring as possible, the Vice-Roy was desired to keep it secret, or at least to give it out that we were going Eastward; for by this means the Admiral was in hopes they would not have had any certain Advice until he got as low as *Malaga*, when the Month of *September* would have been well advanced, and in all Probability produce bad Weather. The Vice-Roy was also desired not to let it be known that there was not a Number of Ships to be left in the Streights; because if the Enemy wanted Information in these two Points, they could not easily conclude what Measures to take, until it might be too late for them to attempt any thing considerable. *He is in fear for Barcelona when the Fleet retires.*

The ninth of *August* the Admiral wrote to the King of *Spain*, and acquainted his Majesty how much it troubled him that the Fleet could do no other Service than the keeping the *French* from farther Attempts in *Catalonia* during his remaining on the Coast; that he had hopes his Majesty's Troops might have made some considerable Effort, at least have endeavoured to regain *Palamos*, and other Towns, with the Assistance of the Naval Power: And he likewise represented to his Majesty, that unless care was immediately taken to put *Catalonia* into a better Posture of Defence, it would be next to an Impossibility to preserve it many Weeks under his Subjection; and that the Kingdom of *Valencia*, as well as the Sea-Port Towns, were in no better a Condition. That as for the Fleet, since there was no hopes of bringing the *French* to a Battel, or forcing them, with any Probability of Success, at *Thoulon*, nor of employing it so as to do any considerable Service, he designed to return therewith to *England*, but that he could not leave *Barcelona* without inform- *The Admiral writes to the King of Spain, and acquaints him of the ill Posture of his Affairs in Catalonia, &c.*

ing

ing his Majesty that the Vice-Roy had not only treated him with all imaginable Civility, but zealously promoted all things that were represented to be necessary.

The fifteenth of *August* two Third Rate Ships, and one of the Sixth Rate were ordered to *Cadiz*, there to refit and victual, and then to convoy the Trade to *England*; and now the Fleet being ready to leave *Barcelona*, a Council of War was called to consider in what manner the same might be done, so as to keep it most private. It was agreed that when they sailed an Appearance should be made the first Day as if they were going Eastward, but that in the Night an Opportunity should be taken of getting out to Sea, and proceeding Westward; and the Places necessary for Rendezvous were settled in case of Separation.

An Amusement for the French when the Fleet sailed down the Streights.

Before the Admiral sailed, he wrote to the Dey of *Algier*, letting him know that the King his Master had sent his Fleet into the Streights to put a stop to the Proceedings of *France* against *Spain*, and that, notwithstanding their Insinuations that *England* could not spare Ships for those Parts, they thought it convenient to retire from him, and secure themselves at *Thoulon*. He also acquainted that Government that the Summer was too far spent to admit of his coming to their Port, as he had designed, and that therefore he took the present Occasion to assure them of the great Esteem the King his Master had of their Friendship and Amity.

Contents of a Letter from the Admiral to the Government of Algier.

This Letter was sent to *Algier*, and recommended to Consul *Baker*, who was then upon coming from thence, after he had resided there many Years in that Capacity, and that by his discreet and zealous Negotiations, and the particular Friendship the Dey had for him, he had contributed very much to the settling a good and firm Understanding between his Majesty and that Government.

When the Fleet was got down the Streights as far as *Malaga*, the Admiral (contrary to his Expectations) received Orders from his Majesty, under his Royal Signet and Sign-Manual, dated *August* the seventh, requiring him to continue in those Seas, and to winter at *Cadiz*, for the more effectual preventing the Designs of the *French* in *Catalonia*. Thus a full stop was put to all those Methods which had been determined for proceeding with the Fleet to *England*, and a Council of War being called, it was resolved forthwith to repair up the *Mediterranean* again, as high as *Alicant*, that so the Ships of the States-General might take in the Provisions said to be there ready for them; and several Victuallers being arrived from *England*, Orders were dispatched to *Cadiz* for their going within the *Puntal*, for the Admiral had already taken care to procure as much as might be necessary until his Return thither, which he intended not before some time in *October*, unless he had certain Information that the *French* had disarmed their Ships.

The Admiral, when off of Malaga, does, contrary to Expectation, receive Orders to winter at Cadiz.

Resolved to proceed as high as Alicant.

He acquainted the Vice-Roy of *Catalonia* that he had Commands to remain in the *Mediterranean*, and desired to hear from him at *Alicant*, and particularly whether he had any Account of the *French*, or that the Fleet might be of Service to that Principality. He also desired Mr. *Stanhope*, our Envoy at *Madrid*, to procure Orders from

He writes to the Vice-Roy of Catalonia.

CHAP. XIV. *from the Year* 1688, *to* 1697.

from that Court that the *Puntal* might be made clear for the Ships against their Arrival at *Cadiz*, for the more convenient refitting them; and writ very pressingly to the Lords of the Admiralty for a timely Supply of Men and Provisions, and that one of the Commissioners for Victualling might be sent out to take care of that Affair, since it had already given him more trouble than he was any longer able to undergo: And it may be truly said that such care was taken by him therein, that never were Men furnished with better Provisions and Wine, and even that with so good Husbandry to the Publick, that the Crown was not put to more Charge, altho' the Fleet was great, and consequently required very considerable Quantities, than for single Ships formerly: Nay in many Circumstances the Men were victualled considerably cheaper; nor did he boggle at the engaging his own personal Estate to give this so necessary Credit to his Country. *Writes to England for a Supply of Men and Provisions. Observations about victualling the Fleet in the Mediterranean.*

The Fleet being at *Alicant*, the Admiral sent from thence two light Frigates to *Majorca*, and directed the chief Commander of them to apply himself not only to the Vice-Roy, but the Consul also for News; but more particularly for the latter to inform himself from all the *Saetias*, and other small Vessels lately arrived there, whether they had met with any Account of the Enemy. At this time Rear-Admiral *Nevil* was also sent from the Fleet with ten Ships Southward of the Island of *Formentera*, with Orders to cruise between those Parts and the *Barbary* Shore, for intercepting the Enemy's Ships, and protecting ours, which were ordered to cut Wood for the use of the Fleet, and then to return Northward to *Alicant*, between the Islands and Cape *Martin*, if Wind and Weather would permit. *The Admiral sends to Majorca for News. Rear-Admiral Nevil sent with a Squadron off of Formentera.*

During the Fleet's riding before *Alicant* the Admiral was taken dangerously ill of a Fever, and a Bloody Flux, which in few Days obliged him to go on shore, and my self at that time falling under the same Distemper, attended him: But that the Fleet might not lie idle in his Absence, he gave Orders to Vice-Admiral *Aylmer* to take upon him the Command thereof, and to proceed and join the Ships with Rear-Admiral *Nevil* as soon as possibly he could. It was particularly recommended to him to endeavour to gain Intelligence of the Proceedings of the *French*, and to prevent their getting out of the *Mediterranean*, in order whereunto he was to place himself in such Stations, and to employ the Ships of the Fleet in such manner, as should from time to time be judged most adviseable by a Council of War; and upon meeting the Enemy's Fleet, or any part thereof, he was directed to use his best Endeavours to come up with and destroy them, and to chase them with the whole Fleet, or such a Number of Ships as should be thought most proper, without having any regard to his being on shore, or expecting farther Orders from him for his Proceedings. It was also recommended to him to take care upon his discovering any *French* Squadron standing Westward, and endeavouring to pass the Streights, that such a Number of Ships as might at least be equal to their Force were sent after them as far as they should go, or until such time as they could come up with and attack *The Admiral taken dangerously ill, and the Fleet committed by him to Vice-Admiral Aylmer. Instructions to Vice-Admiral Aylmer.*

attack them, and to proceed himself with the Remainder to *Cadiz*, where he was to remain for farther Order. But if he did not see the *French* in six Days after his being at Sea, or gain Information that they were come from *Thoulon*, he was to repair with the whole Fleet to *Alicant*; for by that time the Admiral had hopes he might be in a Condition to return on board.

Pursuant to these Orders Mr. *Aylmer* put to Sea with the Fleet, but meeting with nothing remarkable, returned the tenth of *September*; however the Admiral being not then recovered of his Sickness, he sent him Orders to call a Council of War, and maturely to consider of the several Particulars following, that so no time might be lost when he himself could be able to return, and take upon him the Command,

Mr. Aylmer ordered to consider of several Particulars at a Council of War.

1. Whether it was necessary for the Fleet to continue within the Streights?

2. Whether it might be convenient, when they return'd to *Cadiz*, to leave some Ships either within or without the Streights, for intercepting any of the Enemy's Ships that might attempt to proceed into the Northern Seas: And if so, what Number of each Rate, and on what Station they might most properly lie to effect the same?

3. And since it was reported that the *French* kept their Ships at *Thoulon* in a constant Readiness to proceed to Sea, by which it was reasonable to believe they intended to proceed either with the whole, or part of them to *Brest*, as soon as an Opportunity should offer for their passing the Streights, he was therefore to consider what Ships in the Fleet were in the best Condition, and most proper to follow them, that so the latter part of his Majesty's Orders might be complied with, in case they should make such an Attempt?

This was the care the Admiral took, notwithstanding his Indisposition had brought him very low; for the *French* kept themselves in a constant Readiness at *Thoulon*, both as to Provisions and Men, so that if they had endeavour'd to pass the Streights, and our Fleet had been at the same time at *Cadiz*, they might have had many Advantages of us; for, in the first Place, most or all of their Ships were kept clean, whereas ours were foul, and consequently little Benefit could have attended their chasing them. Next, there was an Impossibility of doing it, for we had Provisions but from Hand to Mouth, much less for a Squadron for a Voyage to *England*: Besides, whatever the *French* might attempt, upon the score of their being so well appointed, yet considering the ill Circumstances of most of our Ships, the Hazard would not have been inconsiderable, in sending them home at a Season of the Year wherein they must have been exposed to the worst of Weather, especially the nearer they drew towards our Chanel; nor indeed were they sufficiently mann'd for such a Voyage.

Advantages the Enemy had for passing the Streights, and our ill Condition to follow them.

The Admiral received Intelligence from the Vice-Roy of *Catalonia* of the *French* Fleet's being at Sea, and the Consul of *Majorca* acquainted him that he had met with the like Information; but he had other Advices, more to be depended upon, that they were harboured

CHAP. XIV. *from the Year* 1688, *to* 1697.   513

boured at *Thoulon*. However, that he might not want a constant *Methods taken for getting Intelligence.* and true Account of their Motion, he desired the said Consul to hire some proper Vessel, and to send her from time to time to *Thoulon*, loaden with Goods that might most conveniently, and with least Suspicion, be vended there, under the care of some trusty and discreet Person, who might inform himself, and give frequent Accounts of the Circumstances of the Enemy's Fleet. And lest they should attempt to pass thro' the Streights along the *Barbary* Shore, a Frigate was sent to *Oran*, whose Commander was directed to inform himself whether they had been seen off of that Coast, and then to join the Fleet, another being sent on the like Errand along the said Coast as low as *Tetuan*.

The Court of *Spain* was now informed that his Majesty had ordered the Fleet to remain in the *Mediterranean*, and thereupon a Memorial was sent to the Admiral, by order of his Catholick Majesty, from Don *Alonso Carnero*, Secretary of the Universal Dispatch, proposing, among other things, that the Fleet might winter at Port *The Spaniards propose the Fleet may Winter at Port Mahon. The Admirals objections thereto.* *Mahon*. The Admiral returned him for Answer, "That he was "not a little surprized at such a Proposition, for that not any thing "could be had from the Island of *Minorca*, should the Fleet be un- "der never so pressing Necessities. Besides, all the Stores and Pro- "visions to be sent from *England* must, in such case, have been "brought to Port *Mahon*, so that the *French* would have had a "large Sea to range in search of them; and should there have hap- "pened .want but of the least thing for enabling a Ship to pro- "ceed on Service, there she must have lain, until such time as it "could have been conveyed to her from *Cadiz*, or *Naples*: Where- "as if the Fleet wintered at *Cadiz*, as the King had ordered, it "would then be in his Power to send Ships from thence to protect "any Supplies coming from *England*, or to furnish himself there "upon any emergent Occasion.

The Admiral being now in a better State of Health, he repaired on board the Fleet in the Road of *Alicant*, and having given the necessary Orders, and appointed the Rendezvous in case of Separation, both within and out of the Streights, he sailed and arrived at *The Fleet arrives at Cadiz.* *Cadiz* the eighth of *October*, but first sent thither some light Frigates, that so they might be timely clean'd in order to their being employ'd as Cruisers.

His Catholick Majesty having received Advice that the *French* *The French being at Palamos, the King of Spain desires the Admiral to sail that way.* were come to *Palamos*, with a Design to carry on the Siege of *Barcelona*, he desired the Admiral to repair with the Fleet that way, whereupon it was determined, that as soon as the *Dutch* Ships could be furnished with Provisions, the whole Fleet should proceed up the Streights. But the Admiral acquainted his Majesty, "That "he much doubted the Truth of the Intelligence, and observed "withal, that if some considerable Strength was not put into *Bar- "celona*, there would be no great occasion for the *French* to draw "their Naval Forces thither, for that, under its then Circumstances, "he was of opinion it could not hold out against a Siege of four "Days.

U u u   The

All Vessels stop'd in Cadiz Bay to prevent Intelligence.

The Admiral endeavoured by all ways to gain Intelligence of the Motion of the Enemy's Fleet, and that they might not have Accounts of his Proceedings at *Cadiz,* he ordered the Ships which rid farthest out in the Bay, to speak with all Embarcations, either coming in, or going thence, and to detain those bound Eastward, until such time as it should be considered whether it might be proper to let them proceed.

Resolution where the Fleet might best lie to prevent the Enemy coming through the Streights.

The twenty second a Council of War was called, in order to consider how the Fleet might be best posted to prevent the *French* passing the Streights, and it was agreed to repair off of Cape *Spartell* as soon as the Wind came up Easterly, but up the Streights with a Westerly Wind, and anchor off of *Malaga;* nevertheless to return to the Station off of Cape *Spartell* when the Wind should come up Easterly: And several Ships were some Days after sent to cruise off of the said Cape, and along the *Barbary* Shore, Cape St. *Vincent,* and the Rock of *Lisbon,* with strict Orders that upon gaining any Intelligence of the *French* Fleet, they should repair to *Cadiz* Bay with an Account thereof.

A great want of Men, and the Admiral writes home for a Supply, and two thousand Land Soldiers. Groundless Fear of the Spaniards, that the French would attack us in Cadiz Bay.

At this time there was but little Prospect of Service; nor indeed was the Fleet in any extraordinary Condition for it, the *English* and *Dutch* wanting very near three thousand Men of their allow'd Number; for which reason the Admiral writ to *England* very pressingly for a timely Supply, and withal desired that two thousand well-disciplined Soldiers might be sent out to him: And being informed by the *Spanish* Secretary of State that the People of *Catalonia* were freed from their Apprehensions of the *French* for that Season, but that it was much feared they would attack the Fleet in the Bay of *Cadiz,* he, to divert him from that melancholy and groundless Apprehension, assured him, " That as he would never " have above two or three Ships disarm'd at a time, the Enemy " would be very daring indeed, if they attempted to force him in " that Harbour, unless their Numbers did much exceed his; but " that he thought it necessary to put him in mind his Catholick " Majesty had not above four Ships which were able to swim, and " that if he intended to join any Force to the *English* and *Dutch* " the next Spring, some care ought to be taken for putting his *Armada* into a better Condition for Service.

The Repairs of the Fleet gone vigorously in hand with.

Notwithstanding it had been determined to put forth to Sea with the Fleet, yet since the Weather continued very violent the eighth of *November,* with Rain, Thunder, and Lightning, it was then judged not fit to stir, especially since there was not any News of the *French* Fleet, and that in all Probability they would not venture out when the Winter Season was so very far advanced: Wherefore it was thought necessary to make all possible Dispatch in putting each Ship into the best Condition that might be for Service; a Task not very inconsiderable, regard being had to the Number and Magnitude of the Ships, and the want of several necessary Materials: However the Work was very vigorously carried on, and care was not only taken to prevent a Surprize, but to be in a condition to follow the *French* upon any Intelligence the Cruisers should bring;

CHAP. XIV. *from the Year* 1688, *to* 1697. 515

bring; for all the Ships not sent within the *Puntals* to clean (which were but few at a time) remained in a constant Readiness for going to Sea, the First and Second Rates with not less than a Month's Water each, and those inferior to them with six Weeks.

The King of *Spain* being in want of Shipping to transport about seven thousand Men from *Italy* to *Barcelona*, desired the Admiral that he would make some Provision for that Service; but his Majesty was acquainted by him, "That tho' he would do his utmost "to comply with his Commands in this and all other things, yet "it was impossible for him to find Convenience for the Transpor-"tation of those Troops, because the Men of War were not able "to receive them, and that it would not be safe, even if they could "take them on board, considering the Sickness it might occasion, "as well to the Seamen as Soldiers, by their being so much pe-"stered: Besides, the sending a Squadron of Ships for transporting "such a Number of Men would have wholly obstructed the refit-"ting of the Fleet; and therefore he proposed to his Majesty that "a sufficient Number of Transport-Ships might be got ready at *Ge-*"*noa*, which if his Majesty approved of, he engaged to appoint a "proper Convoy for them, since none of the *Spanish* Ships of "War were fit for such Service: But even in this Case he desired "that he might know the certain time when they would be ready "to embark, and that the Design might be kept with all possible "Secrecy, for that otherwise he could not well answer for their "Security, since the *French* might send from their neighbouring "Ports a Squadron to intercept them.

The King of Spain desires the Admiral to transport seven thousand Men from Italy to Barcelona. His Objections thereunto.

The Admiral promises a Convoy to the Transports.

Notwithstanding this the Governor of *Cadiz* delivered him another Letter from the King, letting him know that his Majesty intended five thousand Men only should be transported from *Genoa* to *Savona*, and that care should be taken for Embarcations for those designed from *Naples*: But as for those five thousand his Majesty recommended it to him to cause them to be transported to *Barcelona* on board some of the Ships of the Fleet.

The Governor of Cadiz proposes the transporting five thousand Men only.

The Admiral had some Discourse with the Governor of *Cadiz* on this Subject, who thereupon seemed to be thoroughly convinced that these Troops could not be conveniently received on board the *English* Ships of War; but he was of opinion that *Genoa* would not be the most proper Place to hire Transports for them; whereupon the Admiral offered to assist in providing Vessels at *Cadiz*, and promised he would have a Convoy ready for them, altho' even that would greatly obstruct his Measures. He also assured them that he would write to *England* for the adding two thousand Land Soldiers to the Number already promised; and that his Catholick Majesty might have a true Account of what passed in relation to this Matter, he sent it to him through the Hands of his Secretary of State.

The Admiral discourses him thereupon.

The latter end of *December* several Ships arrived from *England*, and brought the Admiral a Commission by which he was appointed Admiral, Chief Commander, and Captain-General of their Majesty's Navy, and Ships employed, and to be employed in the *Narrow*

Uuu 2 *Seas,*

Some Officers and Stores arrive at Cadiz.

Seas, and in the *Mediterranean*; with which Convoy came some Officers and Artificers, as well as Stores, for refitting the Fleet; not but that the Work was in a great measure already performed.

Captain Killigrew sent up the Streights with a light Squadron. His Instructions.

The *Plimouth, Falmouth, Carlisle, Newcastle, Adventure,* and *Southampton,* were sent from the Fleet, under Command of Captain *James Killigrew,* who was directed to proceed as high as *Alicant* in search of some *French* Ships said to have been seen off of that Coast; but if he got not any Intelligence of them, to cruise six Days off of the South End of *Sardinia,* unless himself and the Captains with him should think it proper to run off of Cape *Corsica.* When the six Days were expired he was to sail to Cape *Passaro* the South-East Point of *Sicily,* and about that Island, or between that and *Malta,* to cruise until the twelfth of *February,* for protecting the Trade, and annoying the *French.* When he had so done, he was to call in at *Messina,* and if he found the *Turky* Convoy there, to accompany them to *Cadiz,* but if they were not arrived, to leave a Letter with the Consul for the Commander in Chief of the said Convoy, whereby he was directed (if Captain *Killigrew* should be come away) to remain at *Messina* for the Security of the Ships, and to give early Advice to the Admiral of his Arrival, unless he should be thoroughly satisfied that the *French* had not any Force to intercept him in his Passage to *Cadiz*; and Captain *Killigrew* was farther directed, if he came down the Streights without the said Convoy, to call at *Leghorn* and *Barcelona,* and to bring from thence what Advice he could get of the Proceedings of the Enemy.

This Squadron meets with two French Ships of War, and takes them.

In the Execution of these Orders he met with two *French* Ships of War between Cape *Bona,* upon the Coast of *Barbary,* and the Island of *Pantalarea,* with which he himself first engaged, and in a little time his Foremost was shot away by the *Content,* of seventy Guns, nor was it long e'er he was unfortunately killed. The *Falmouth* and *Adventure* fell to work with the other, called the *Trident,* of sixty Guns; but Captain *Norris,* of the *Carlisle,* the sternmost of our Ships, fetch'd just to Leeward of the *Falmouth,* and to Windward of the *Plimouth,* who having fired at the *Trident,* stood after the *Content* with all the Sail he could make, and took her after a Chase of fifty Leagues, her Main-mast, Mizen, and Mizen-top-mast being shot by the Board, and the other Ships took the *Trident*; so that this Action preventing their proceeding farther on the Service whereon they were appointed, they brought their Prizes to the Fleet.

The Dilatoriness of the Spaniards in fitting their Ships.

The Admiral finding that little or no Preparations were made for equipping those few Ships the King of *Spain* had, he thought it necessary to represent the same to that Court; as also, that if they could not get their Transports ready so timely as that the Convoy he designed to send with them might return by the latter end of *February,* it would not be safe for him to comply with what he had promised as to that Particular, in regard the Enemy would, in all Probability, have part of their Fleet at Sea, even near the Place where the Forces were to be transported, whereby the Ships of War, as well as the said Forces, might be exposed to the greatest Hazard.

The

CHAP. XIV. *from the Year* 1688, *to* 1697. 517

The fifth of *February* a Supply of Provisions arrived from *England*, and very seasonably too; for there was not only a great Want thereof in the Fleet, but such Victuals as was proper could not be had without great Difficulties in *Spain*. *A Supply of Provisions arrives from England.*

The Governor of *Cadiz* at length informed the Admiral that the Transport Ships he had been so long providing there were ready to proceed to *Final* for the Soldiers; but to that he was answered, that the time proposed for the Convoy's going with them was elapsed, and since it was not known what Forwardness the *French* were in at *Thoulon*, and that the whole Fleet would probably be ready to sail in fourteen Days, he thought it proper to consider well of it before he exposed so many of the King his Master's Ships on this Service. *The Governor of Cadiz presses sending the Convoy with Transports, and is told the Fleet would sail in fourteen Days,&c.*

The third of *March* the Governor writ him another Letter, earnestly desiring him to send away the Convoy; but the Admiral let him know, that since they were of Necessity to pass by the *French* Ports, it might be of worse Consequence to *Catalonia*, should the Convoy with the Forces be intercepted in their Passage from *Final* to *Barcelona*, than the detaining the Ships some few Days longer at *Cadiz* could possibly be, in order to their going under the Protection of the whole Fleet; and that he was the rather inclined to have a more than ordinary Regard to their Safety, since it was hinted at, both in the *French*, and *Spanish* Prints, that he had promised to detach a Convoy from the Fleet. *The Hazard a separate Squadron would be exposed to.*

It was reasonable to think that if the *French* did intend to pass the Streights with the whole, or part of their Naval Force, they would be now drawing down, and therefore the Admiral detached a strong Squadron off of Cape *Spartell*, under Command of Rear-Admiral *Nevil*, to intercept them, should they make such an Attempt; but he was nevertheless at Liberty, as Winds and Weather might happen, to anchor in *Tangier* Bay, or to station himself Eastward of the Streights Mouth, and if he received not Orders to the contrary in twelve Days, he was to return to the Fleet in the Bay of *Cadiz*. *Rear-Admiral Nevil detached with a strong Squadron to hinder the French going through the Streights.*

Soon after this the whole Fleet was ready to sail, staying only for the greatest Part of the Victuallers, which were not yet arrived from *England*: But as for the *Spanish Armada*, they were so far from being in a Condition for the Sea that not one of the Ships was careened, so that but little Service could be expected from them: However, the Admiral acquainted the *Spanish* Secretary that he had Hopes their Gallies would be ready at *Barcelona*, because if any thing could be done against the Enemy by landing Men, they would be of great Use, as they might likewise be if he met the *French* Fleet, who doubtless would have theirs in Company with them. *The ill Condition of the Spanish Armada. The Admiral desires their Gallies may be ready.*

The embarking the Soldiers at *Final* did greatly trouble the *Spanish* Court, insomuch that on the eighth of *April* the Governor of *Cadiz* pressed very earnestly that a Convoy might be forthwith sent with the Transport Ships, to prevent Desertion, and the ill Consequences which might attend their not being landed before the *French* opened the Campaign in *Catalonia*. The Admiral acquainted him that he was not without Thoughts of all the Inconveniences which might *The Governor of Cadiz presses again the sending a Convoy for the Forces. 1695. The Admiral's Answer.*

might attend a Disappointment of this Nature, and that it did not a little trouble him they would not follow his Advice in providing Transports for the Forces at the Ports in *Italy*; for that very much time had been lost by taking up at *Cadiz* such Ships for this Service as were by Agreement to be first freighted at that Port: However he assured him that as soon as the Weather was fair he would proceed with the whole up the Streights, although he was in great Want of Provisions, but more especially Bread.

Brigadier-General Stuart arrives with the Land-Forces from England.

Not many Days after the Land-Forces under Command of Brigadier General *Stewart* arrived, being his own Regiment, and those of the Marquess *Puizar*, Colonel *Brudenell*, and Colonel *Coote*, in all, about four thousand five hundred Men, Officers included; and with the same Convoy came the remaining Victuallers, and twelve Bomb-Vessels, so that it was not many Days before the Fleet sailed; but e'er the Admiral left *Cadiz*, he desired the Protection and Favour of the Governor towards the King his Master's Subjects trading thither; and although I do in some Measure know the Reason of this Request, yet I shall not say more of it here, than that there was Occasion to put him in mind of doing so good an Office.

The Fleet sails from Cadiz.

Cruisers sent out, and the Directions given them.

The Fleet being now at Sea, Cruisers were sent on several Stations for Intelligence, with Directions that if they met with any News from foreign Ships or Vessels, they should detain the chief Officer until such time as it could appear whether the same were true or false; for it had often been found that several of them were not overmuch sincere, particularly the *Genoese*, who in that, as well as many other Particulars, did not so behave themselves as might have been reasonably expected.

The Turky Convoy ordered to remain at Messina.

The Fleet comes to Barcelona.

The fifth of *May* Orders were sent to the Commander of the *Turky* Convoy at *Messina* to remain there in a constant posture of sailing, until an additional Strength could be sent to him; and the Fleet arriving at *Alicant*, but little Stay was made there, for they came to *Barcelona* the eighteenth. Before they anchored in the Bay the Admiral sent to the Marquess *Gastanaga*, and desired to know from him what Intelligence he had of the Enemy's Proceedings, that so he might the better govern himself in appointing a Convoy for the Transport Ships; but to this he received not a very satisfactory Answer.

Invitation to several English, &c. in the French Army to come in to us.

During the Fleet's being at *Barcelona*, the Admiral was well assured that several Subjects of *England*, who had been compelled to serve the *French* King in *Catalonia*, were desirous to return to their own Country, and therefore he issued out several Declarations, promising not only them, but those of other Nations, who would quit the *French* Service, and repair to the Consul at *Barcelona*, that they should be either entertain'd among our Land-Forces, in the marine Regiments, or in the Fleet, and that whenever any of them desired to return home, they should have a Passport so to do. Besides which, each Man, upon his appearing on board the Admiral's own Ship, was promised Clothes; and a Pistole in Money, and this Project had, in a great Measure, its desired Effect.

CHAP. XIV. *from the Year* 1688, *to* 1697.   519

The twentieth of *May* in the Morning the Admiral sailed, and the next Day directed Rear-Admiral *Nevil* that when he made a Signal, by an *English* Ensign at his Fore-topmast-head, and fired a Gun, he should make the best of his Way to *Final* with five Third Rates, one Sixth, two Fireships, a Brigantine, and an Advice-Boat of the *English*, and three Ships of War of the States-General, of seventy two Guns each. He was directed to take with him the Transport Ships, and to make all possible Dispatch in getting the Soldiers on board, and then to repair to the Rendezvous off of the Isle of *Hyeres*, but if he found not the Fleet there, to come to *Barcelona*; and a Frigate was sent off of the Cape of *Thoulon* for Intelligence of the Enemy's Proceedings. *The Fleet sails from Barcelona, and Rear-Admiral Nevil sent to Final with the Transports.*

By Rear-Admiral *Nevil* the Admiral sent a Letter to the Earl of *Gallway*, by which he desired his Lordship to let him know whether there was a Probability of doing any Service with the Fleet at the *French* Ports, and particularly if with our Troops, and such Strength as the Duke of *Savoy* could add to him, they, and the Fleet together, might not attempt even *Thoulon* itself with Hopes of Success. This Letter was communicated to his Royal Highness and the Marquess *Leganez*, whereupon a Council being called, it was determined that not any thing could be done therein, for that they thought it reasonable to adhere to their former Resolutions to attack *Casal*, of which Place they soon after made themselves Masters. *The Admiral proposes to the Court of Savoy the attempting Thoulon with their and our Forces. His Royal Highness's Determination thereupon.*

The first of *June* Sir *David Mitchell*, then Rear-Admiral of the Red, was ordered to proceed off of *Marseilles*, when the Admiral should make the appointed Signal for his so doing, and to take with him one Third Rate, Six Fourths, two Fireships, and two Brigantines of the *English*, and three *Dutch* Ships commanded by Vice-Admiral *Evertsen*. It was recommended to him carefully to observe the Fortifications said to be erected there, and to report his Opinion whether there might be any Probability of doing Service with the Bomb-Vessels: And Brigadier-General *Stewart*, with the Colonels of the Land-Forces, were appointed to accompany the Rear-Admiral, as also Sir *Martin Beckman*, an Engineer, who had the Command of those Vessels: But the next Day a violent Storm arose, which drove the Fleet fifty Leagues to the Southward, under their main Courses only, which made the Ships complain much of Leakiness, and the Rear-Admiral was thereby prevented in putting his Instructions in Execution. *Sir David Mitchell sent with a Squadron off of Marseilles. A violent Storm drives the Squadron fifty Leagues Southward.*

Orders were sent the seventh of *June* to the *Turky* Convoy to repair to *Cagliari*, in the Island of *Sardinia*, there to be joined by some more Ships for the greater Security of that Trade, for which purpose the *Newcastle* and *Adventure* were sent thither: And now the Transport Ships being come to the Fleet, they were dispatched with a Convoy to *Barcelona*, and a small Frigate was sent to *Thoulon* to get an Account of the Enemy's Ships in that Harbour. *The Turky Convoy ordered to Cagliari. The Transports arrive, and are sent to Barcelona.*

Soon after the *Greyhound* was dispatched with Advice to the *Conde de Attamia*, Vice-Roy of *Sardinia*, that the Fleet would suddenly touch there to take in Water; but the Admiral let him know it *The Admiral acquaints the Vice-Roy of Sardinia, that the Fleet will come there to water.*

it was of great Confequence to keep it a Secret, until fuch time as he returned again to the *French* Coaft, and therefore defired that a ftrict Embargo might not only be laid, but continued on all the Embarcations in every Part of the Ifland, untill he fhould be got to Sea again, that fo the Enemy might not have an Opportunity of flipping away Weftward; but yet that this Embargo might be laid in fuch manner as that it might give the leaft Ground of Sufpicion he was coming thither.

The Fleet being fupplied with Water, and the *Turky* Ships not yet arrived, the Admiral judged it not convenient to ftay longer for them, but left the *Greyhound* with an Order for the Commander of the Convoy, directing him to proceed immediately to *Majorca,* and if he met not with Intelligence of the Enemy or Orders to the contrary there, to repair to, and remain at *Carthagena.* But before the Fleet got clear of *Cagliari* this Convoy appeared, and inftead of their rendezvoufing at *Majorca,,* if feparated before they came to *Carthagena, Alfaques,* on the Coaft of *Catalonia,* was now appointed, and there they were to remain until fome farther Provifion could be made for conducting them fafely down the Streights.

The Turky Convoy ordered to Alfaques in Catalonia.

The nineteenth of *July* the Fleet arrived off of *Barcelona,* when the Admiral acquainted the Vice-Roy with his Defign of going to *Thoulon,* but that if he found there could not be any thing done there, or at *Marfeilles,* or that the Duke of *Savoy* propofed not any Service, now *Cafal* was taken, he would return to the faid Port of *Barcelona.* Soon after this he received a Letter from the Vice-Roy, defiring that the whole, or Part of the Fleet might go off of *Blanes*; whereupon (although a Council of War had before thought it moft proper to proceed to the Coaft of *Provence*) the Admiral prepared to repair forthwith to that Place, but e'er he failed he ordered the *Turky* Convoy to *Cadiz,* and from thence to *England,* with fome Ships appointed to ftrengthen them thither.

The Fleet arrives at Barcelona.

The Vice-Roy defires him to proceed to Blanes.

The Turky Convoy ordered to Cadiz.

That the Lords of the Admiralty might be particularly informed of the State of the Ships of the Fleet, with refpect to their Hulls, &c. he caufed a ftrict Survey to be taken of them, and thereupon reprefented that the greateft Part of the Firft, Second, and Third Rates, were in fuch a Condition as to require their going to *England* the firft Seafon of fair Weather; but that the *Sovereign, St. Andrew, Duke, St. Michael, Sandwich, Suffolk, Grafton, Edgar, Warfpight,* and fome other Ships, ought even at that very time to be fent home, for that fhould they be continued at *Cadiz* another Winter, it was his Opinion they would hardly be able to fwim; for which Reafon he affured them that he would rather take his Fortune with a fmall Strength, than hazard the Nations lofing fo many Ships; and without them there would remain with him but forty four *Englifh* and *Dutch* from the Fourth Rate upwards.

A Survey taken of the Condition of the Fleet, and the Admiralty acquainted therewith.

He directed Brigadier-General *Stuart* to acquaint the General of the *Spanifh* Forces that the Troops could not longer be on Shore than fix or feven Days, that fo the Vice-Roy might confider how they could be moft ferviceable to him in that time for the regaining of *Palamos:* And that no Mifunderftanding might arife about this Matter

The Spanifh General acquainted how long our Forces could continue on Shore.

CHAP. XIV. *from the Year* 1688, *to* 1697.   521

Matter, he defired that what paffed between them might be in Writing.

The Admiral was the more inclined to remain fome little time longer at *Barcelona*, becaufe he was not in a Condition to deal with the Enemy, now he had fent fo many Ships home under Command of Sir *John Munden*, fhould they, upon his Approach, come out of *Thoulon* with their whole Strength, at leaft not untill the *Dutch* Ships expected from *Cadiz*, which were Part of their Quota, had join'd him. Nor did he labour under fmall Difficulties from the various Importunities of the *Spaniards*, and the little Regard they had to the doing even what might have been of Service to themfelves, or in the enabling him to contribute towards it; infomuch that he thought himfelf obliged to reprefent the whole Matter to the Court of *Spain*, and to let them know how little they had complied with their Promife to him when at *Cadiz*, in affifting him with their Ships of War, and Gallies, according to the Treaty; and withall he told them that he thought the King his Mafter had been very ill ufed, and the Affairs committed to his Truft and Charge very much obftructed by their dilatory Proceedings. In fine, that he having promifed the Vice-Roy of *Catalonia* all the Affiftance he could be able to give him on any fudden Enterprize, if no fuch thing could be undertaken, he fhould be neceffitated to lay hold of proper Meafures for his Mafter's Intereft, and to leave the Management of Matters in *Spain* to their own Conduct.

The Reafons of the Admiral's ftaying fo long at Barcelona.

A reafonable Complaint made by the Admiral, of the little Affiftance given by the Spaniards.

The Admiral alfo acquainted the Vice-Roy that he could not, with Prudence, admit of our Troops marching far into the Country, fince their Return might be very uncertain, and that the Fleet would for Want of them be expofed to Hazard fhould the *French* appear; but that if any Place could be attempted without the Formality of a long Siege he would to his utmoft affift in it.

Hereupon the Vice-Roy determined to march towards *Palamos*, defigning to be fo near that Place on the feventh of this Month, as that when the *Englifh* and *Dutch* Forces were on Shore, an Hour's March might enable them to join him; and by their Affiftance he was in Hopes to oblige the Forces in that Place to a fpeedy Surrender. The Admiral communicated this to Brigadier-General *Stuart*, and it being agreed in what manner the Forces fhould land, Care was taken to furnifh them with Provifions, and all Things neceffary; and as a confiderable Number of Marine Soldiers were incorporated with them, fo was it determined between the Vice-Roy and the Brigadier-General that the Forces fhould be put on Shore the ninth in the Morning, and that he fhould follow the Orders of the faid Vice-Roy, or any other fuperior Officer, according to the Difcipline of War.

The Vice-Roy determines to march towards Palamos.

All the Long-Boats in the Fleet were got ready, with a Lieutenant, and two Gunners Mates to each, to attend Sir *Martin Beckman*, upon the firft Signal that fhould be made for bombarding *Palamos*; and the Admiral did not only recommend it to the Vice-Roy to give the Brigadier-General the Poft due to him on all Occafions, but defired alfo that the Soldiers might be in Readinefs to embark

It is agreed to put the Land-Forces on Shore from the Fleet.

X x x

embark upon a Signal of the Enemy's approaching with a Naval Force.

The Admiral's Opinion about attacking Palamos.

The Admiral receiving from the Brigadier-General frequent Accounts of his Movements, he let the Vice-King know his Opinion, that since the Enemy appeared in *Battalia*, it was to prevent his laying Siege to the Town, and that therefore if his Troops, with the Reinforcement from the Fleet, were not sufficient both to attack the Place, and face the Enemy, there was but small Hopes of carrying it, insomuch that it was most adviseable for the *Spanish* Forces to march off to their former Posts, while he with the Bomb-Vessels endeavoured to lay the Town in Ashes.

An Account of the Proceedings of our Forces in conjunction with the Spaniards.

Although the Business of the two Armies doth not so properly relate to the Design in hand, yet possibly it may be expected that I should give some farther Account of that Matter; and therefore please to take it as follows, *viz.*

On Friday the ninth of *August* there were landed near four thousand Men, *English* and *Dutch*, the first commanded by Brigadier-General *Stuart*, the latter by Count *Nassau*, and marching by nine in the Morning they encamped at Night half Way between the Landing-Place and *Palamos*. At this time there was no other Account of the Enemy, than that they were at a Place called *Lo Bisbal*, about three Leagues off, but the next Morning, when our Men, who had the Van of the Army, marched into a Defile, they appeared in great Numbers, especially Horse; notwithstanding which our People marching on possessed the Ground designed for them near the Town, and then the whole encamped, as well as any Body of Men could that had not any one Thing necessary for it.

Next Morning the Enemy appeared in *Battalia* upon the Hills, about a League off, and (as the Deserters said) were resolved to come to a Battel, so that all this Day, and the next Night too, the Army lay under their Arms, our Men being not only without Tents, but even the very Bread which the *Spaniards* had promised to provide for them: Nay so little Care had they taken of this, or indeed of any Thing to secure themselves, that had not our People carried on Shore some Pickaxes, Spades, and other Conveniencies, not any Intrenchments could have been made.

Early the next Day the *French* appeared drawn up within half an Hour's March, but after advancing about two hundred Yards they wheeled off; and this gave our Men the first Opportunity of Rest since their landing.

The Town and Castle of Palamos bombarded.

The Admiral now ordered the Town and Castle to be bombarded, which was done so effectually, notwithstanding the Sea ran high, that most part both of one and the other was beaten down, and the Remainder was on fire in several Places. Thus ended the Attempt on *Palamos*; for the Vessel sent to the Coast of *Provence* return'd to the Fleet next Day, and brought two of the Inhabitants of *Thoulon*, who positively affirmed that the *French* had sixty Ships of War there, ready in all respects to put to Sea; whereupon the Admiral sent to the Marquess *Gastanaga*, and desired the Troops might be returned, the better to enable him to go in Search of the Enemy, advising

CHAP. XIV. *from the Year* 1688, *to* 1697.   523

advising him not only to march away at the same time with the *Spanish* Army, but representing how improbable it was for him to take *Palamos*, since our Forces and theirs thus joined were but equal to the Enemy, and barely so too. The Vice-Roy was of the Admiral's Opinion, but all or most of his General Officers were for setting down before the Town; and such was their Uneasiness, that some of them could not refrain letting Words fall to the Prince of *Hesse*, who commanded the Emperor's Forces, which bespoke in them no ill liking to the Interest of the *French*: However, within two Days their Army decamped, and marched to St. *Feliu*, from whence they designed for *Ostalric*; and our Troops with those of the States-General, returned on board the Fleet, very little obliged by the *Spanish* Officers; for during the whole time they were on Shore, hardly one of them had an Invitation to partake of so much as an ordinary Repast.
The Admiral advises the Spanish General to retire with his Forces.

He accordingly retires.

The Forces were no sooner embarked than the Fleet proceeded to the Coast of *Provence*, where they met with such violent Storms, accompanied with Rain, Thunder, and Lightning, as render'd a Continuance there very hazardous, so that the Admiral judged it adviseable to retire down the Streights, and arriving in *Cadiz* Bay the latter End of *September*, he appointed Sir *David Mitchell*, then Rear-Admiral of the Red, to take upon him the Command of eight Third Rates, and as many Fourths, besides small Frigates, Bomb-Vessels, and others of the *English*, and seven *Dutch* Men of War, from seventy four to fifty Guns, and to employ all, or part of them, in such manner as he judged might be most for the Service, but to put himself under the Command of Sir *George Rooke*, when he should arrive, who was expected with a Squadron of Ships from *England*.
The Forces being embarked, the Fleet sails towards the Coast of Provence, but bad Weather obliges them to retire. The Fleet arrives at Cadiz. Sir David Mitchell left with a Squadron at Cadiz.

With the rest of the Fleet the Admiral himself sailed for *England*, being one First Rate, seven Seconds, one Third, three Fourths, one Fifth, and three Fireships, besides the *Dutch*, and arrived the Beginning of *November*.
The Admiral sails for England with the greatest Part of the Fleet.

I cannot but take notice here of the Unkindness of the *Spaniards* at *Cadiz*; for Rear-Admiral *Mitchell* applying to the Governor that the sick Men might be put on Shore into the Marine Hospitals, was answered that it could not be admitted without an Order from Court, in regard they had expended much Money the last Year upon that Account. A very gratefull Acknowledgment for the Charge the *English* Nation, as well as *Holland*, had been at on their Score: Not but that (as I am informed) they did, by several Subsidies, enable the *Dutch* to bear part at least of their Expence, but as for the *English*, they had not one Penny more than a certain Quantity of Wine and Provisions, and that of no extraordinary Value, which was equally distributed among the Ships as soon as they arrived in the Fleet.
Unkindness of the Spaniards as to our sick Men.

Xxx 2   CHAP.

CHAP. XV.

An Account of Sir George Rooke's proceeding with a Squadron of Ships as far as the Bay of Cadiz, and of his Return to England.

Sir George Rooke arrives at Cadiz. 1695. Contents of his Instructions.

THE sixteenth of *October* Sir *George Rooke* with the Ships from *England* arrived in the Bay of *Cadiz*, the Character given him by his Commission being Admiral of the White, and Admiral and Commander in Chief of his Majesty's Ships in the *Mediterranean*; and by his Instructions he was required to annoy the Enemy on all Occasions; to prevent their being furnished from these Seas with Naval Stores and Provisions; to take under his Command the Ships of War left at *Cadiz* by Admiral *Russel*; and if he received certain Advice that the *French* had passed the Streights with the whole, or part of their Fleet, to follow them, or detach after them such a Strength as might be proportionable to what they had.

A Council of War agree how to send up the Turky Convoy.

The twenty first of *November* he called a Council of War, where were present himself, Rear-Admiral *Mitchell*, Rear-Admiral *Nevil*, and his First Captain, Captain *Bokenham*. They considered how the Ships bound to *Turky* might be most safely convoy'd thither, and determined that their Guard should consist of four Ships of War, two for *Smyrna*, and two for *Scanderoon*, and that they should be accompanied with a Squadron of four or five more, and two Fireships, as far as Cape *Matapan*, the most Southern Promontory of the *Morea*, or higher, if it should be judged reasonable: That then the Squadron should return, and in their Way call at *Algier*, after that cross over to *Alicant*, and so along the Coast of *Spain*, unless they had Advice that the *French* had a stronger Force abroad.

The Fleet very sickly.

The Fleet at this time was very sickly, and with great Difficulty the *Spaniards* were prevailed with to permit one hundred and fifty Men to be lodged in the Hospitals at *Cadiz*; nor was that granted, but upon Condition that we should find Beds, Medicines, and Refreshments.

We had not Force to oppose the Enemy.

Our Force united was not sufficient to oppose the Enemy, and therefore all that could be done was to protect the Trade, until such time as the additional Strength expected from *England* were joined; and Sir *George Rooke* being convinced, by all Advices, that the *French* were making great Dispatch for an early Campaign, he called the Officers together, to consider what might best be done, who (both *English* and *Dutch*) agreed, that since there were but thirty Ships of the Line of Battel (not above half the Number it was believ'd the *French* would come out with) they could not be able to impede their Passage through the Streights, and that therefore it was not reasonable to put to Sea and lie in their Way, but nevertheless to keep out Cruizers for Intelligence.

A Council of War agree not to put to Sea.

This

CHAP. XV. *from the Year* 1688, *to* 1697.   525

This Council of War was held the nineteenth of *January*, and 169¾.
fresh Intelligence occasioned another the twenty third following, *Another*
when the Flag-Officers found no reason to alter their former Reso- *Council re-*
lutions: But lest the *French* Fleet should appear at *Cadiz* before *tire within*
the Reinforcement from *England* arrived, it was agreed that the *Puntal Castles*
Ships should be removed within *Puntal* Castles, and formed in *for their Se-*
three Lines as follows; the first (to consist of the largest *English* Ships) *curity.*
to lie from *Puntal* athwart the Chanel, to the Creek's Mouth called
Truccadero, next within the North Castle; the second (to be composed of the smallest *English* and *Dutch* Ships) along the Shoal on
the South side of the Harbour; and the third (to be of the biggest
Dutch Ships) to begin from the upper end of the second Line, and
to trench away athwart the Chanel to the Mouth of the upper
Creek which goes to Port *Real*; and the small Frigates, Bomb-
Vessels, and Fireships, were to be posted to the best Advantage, as
the Wind, and other Circumstances might permit. This indeed was
all which could be done, for the Ships, generally speaking, were
not above half mann'd, and those of the *Dutch* were so very foul,
that had they met a greater Strength of the Enemy at Sea, they
would in all Probability have been a Prey to them.

Things being at this pass, and our Squadron in a manner blocked up at *Cadiz*, an Account came from the Vice-Roy of *Andalusia*,
that he had notice, by an Express from *Portugal*, of five *French*
Ships in *Lagos* Bay, from seventy to eighty Guns, and thereupon *Rear-Admiral*
Rear-Admiral *Mitchell*, with eight clean Ships, and two Fireships, *Mitchel sent*
was sent in quest of them, but contrary Winds soon constrain'd him *in search of*
to bear up. *some French*
Ships.

The Admiral considering the Weakness of the Force with him,
and how strong the Enemy intended to come forth, he, about the
middle of *February*, sent home a Frigate for Instructions how he
should proceed: But before he returned to him, he received Orders
from his Majesty, dated the twenty seventh of *January*, to repair *The Admiral*
to *England*, unless he had good Intelligence that the *French* de- *receives Or-*
signed not to fit out their Fleet from *Thoulon* early in the Spring, *for England*
or that they did not intend to come to Sea with a greater Number *conditionally.*
than he could be able to oppose with the Strength he had with him,
in which case he was to remain in the Streights, and comply with
his former Instructions.

These Orders occasioned a Council of War, where it was deter- *A Council of*
mined to repair to *England* as soon as the Naval Stores could be ta- *War resolves*
ken on board: And in case the *French* should pass the Streights be- *come home,*
fore that could be effected, it was agreed to follow them immediately, *but to pretend*
and to leave a proper Convoy to bring home the Storeships, though, *ing to Port*
to amuse the Enemy, it was pretended that the Fleet, and the great- *Mahon.*
est part of the Stores, were to be removed to Port *Mahon*; but it
was impossible to keep his real Intentions long private; for there
were several Letters which gave an Account that the Ships designed
from *England* were stopp'd, and that it was expected our Fleet
would be called home: Nor was it indeed adviseable to continue
longer in those Parts, for if the intended Reinforcement had timely
arrived

arrived, the Strength would, even then, have been very much inferior to that of the Enemy.

The Fleet forced back to Cadiz.

About the middle of *March* Sir *George Rooke* put to Sea, but when he had beat it to and fro five Days, in very dirty Weather, wherein several of the Ships Masts were sprung, their Sails blown away, and the greatest Ships much shaken, he was constrain'd to return to *Cadiz*; and very lucky it was he did so, for had he kept the Sea, the tempestuous Weather which soon after happened might have put the Fleet into the greatest danger. It begun, and continued with such Extremity, that divers of the biggest *Dutch* Ships, and of our *English* Merchant Ships, were forced from their Anchors even in the Bay, and several were lost upon the Coast, among which three belonging to the States-General, one of them named the St. *Peter*, of forty four Guns, between *Cadiz* and Cape *Trafalgar*.

Damages suffered by the Storm.

The Fleet arrives in England. 1696.

The Weather was no sooner moderate than he sailed again from *Cadiz*, and arrived in the *English* Chanel the twenty second of *April*, where I shall leave him until I have given some Account of what passed at home, and in other Parts abroad, from the time that Sir *Cloudesly Shovell* had finished his Services against *Dieppe*, *Calais*, and other of the Enemy's Ports, to this of Sir *George Rooke*'s returning to *England*, believing that it would tend more to the Reader's Satisfaction to have the aforegoing Account of Affairs in the Streights entire, because its interfering with other things which happened elsewhere, within that time, might make a Confusion necessary to be avoided.

Chap. XVI.

Attempts made by John Lord Berkeley on several of the French King's Ports.

A Council of War agree to attempt St. Malo.

THERE being a considerable Number of Ships got together at *Spithead*, *John* Lord *Berkeley* was ordered to take the Command of them, and arriving there about the middle of *June*, his Lordship called a Council of War, where it was agreed to attempt St. *Malo*'s, if Pilots could be had to carry the Ships near the *Quince* Rock, and the Frigates and Bomb-Vessels within it. But to render this Undertaking the more successful, small Frigates were wanting to secure the Bomb-Vessels, and four or five hundred Soldiers to be put on board them and the Well-Boats; and if two Machine Vessels could be had, it was judged they might have been serviceable against the *Quince* Rock, if there was a Possibility of doing any good with them any where.

Although there was no extraordinary Prospect of Success against St. *Malo*, yet that Attempt was first intended, since the very Alarm might

CHAP. XVI. *from the Year* 1688, *to* 1697. 527

might oblige the Enemy to make such Preparations as would put them to no small Expence and Inconvenience: But yet the Flag-Officers were of opinion, that if the *French* should find them imbayed at St. *Malo* with a greater Force, it would infinitely expose our Ships; and therefore, since there were not together above six *English* Ships of the Line of Battel, they desired that other of the larger Rates might be forthwith sent to join them.

Admiral *Allemonde* soon after acquainted the Lord *Berkeley*, that tho' he had Orders to act under his Command, and to attempt what Places should be judged reasonable by a Council of War, yet the King had given him positive Commands to try what might be done at *Dunkirk* first. This was communicated to the Lords of the Admiralty, and by them to the Lords Justices, in his Majesty's Absence, by whose Directions another Council of War was called, to consider whether the separate Attempts designed to be made on St. *Malo* and *Dunkirk*, might not be undertaken at the same time, by means of such mutual Assistance as the *English* and *Dutch* could give each other: And according to what should be determined his Lordship was to act. It was thereupon resolved to attempt St. *Malo*'s; for as to *Dunkirk* it was not thought convenient to do any thing there, until the Machines, and other things preparing by Mr. *Meesters*, were ready, and the *Dutch* would not hear of acting separately. *The Dutch Admiral ordered by the King to attempt Dunkirk first.*

The separate Attempts of Dunkirk and St. Malo considered.

Agreed to attempt St. Malo.

Although his Lordship had but one small Frigate of the *English* with him, (which kind of Shipping was more necessary on such Occasions than bigger) he was unwilling to lose time, and therefore sailed, and got Westward of *Portland* the twenty third of *June*, but meeting with bad Weather, was obliged to return to St. *Helen's*, and the Well-Boats appointed for landing of Men were so very leaky, that it was with much difficulty they were brought in.

However, the Squadron arrived and anchored before St. *Malo* on the fourth of *July*, about Ten in the Morning, in twenty Fathom Water, the *Quince* Rock bearing S. E. by S. near five Miles distant, Cape *Frehelle* W. S. W. three Leagues and a half, and *Cancale* Point E. by S. three Leagues. At Noon the Signal was made for the Captains of the Bomb Vessels, and about two Hours after, they together with the Frigates and Well-Boats, under Command of Captain *Benbow*, and with some Frigates and Bomb-Vessels of the *Dutch*, standing close in, five of the said Bomb-Vessels played on the *Quince* Rock until near Eight, but with no great Success. *The Squadron arrived at St. Malo.*

About Four next Morning the Squadron weighing Anchor, stood near in, and a Signal was made for the Frigates and Bomb-Vessels to go as close in towards the Town as possibly they could, by doing whereof they soon obliged the Gallies and Guard-Boats to retreat. At half an Hour past Five the Squadron anchored in eighteen Fathom Water, the *Quince* Rock bearing S. by E. distant about a League, and at Eight the *Charles* Fireship, commanded by Captain *Durley*, and one of the *Dutch*, were ordered to run in against the aforesaid Rock, who placing themselves to Windward of it, so much annoyed the Enemy, that they forbore firing; and immediately upon blowing *The Attempts on, and bombing St. Malo.*

up

up of those Ships, the Fort taking fire burnt two Hours. About Nine a Clock the Squadron with the Bomb-Vessels got in somewhat nearer, and the latter play'd with that Success, that at Four in the Afternoon a great Fire broke out in the West part of the Town, which burnt very furiously until about Seven at Night; and as it may be modestly computed that nine hundred Bombs and Carcasses were thrown into it, so I will not trouble the Reader with the Expence not only of the Bombs themselves, but of the Vessels wherein the Mortars were plac'd, otherwise than by taking notice it was very considerable.

During the whole time, the *French* fired from *Quince* Rock, the Great and Little *Bee*, Fort *Royal*, and Point *D'Ambour*; and at last the Ammunition which the Bomb-Vessels carried in with them being spent, a Signal was made between Seven and Eight at Night to call them off, and one of them, which had received much damage, was sunk, to prevent her falling into the Enemy's Hands: But before I end this Account, suffer me to inform you in what manner the Council of War had determined the Place should be attacked; which was as follows:

1. That the six *Dutch* Bomb-Vessels, and three *English*, should batter the *Quince* Rock, and the Fort called *D'Ambour*, five whereof were to attack the former, and four the other.

2. The other nine Bomb-Vessels were at the same time to batter the Town, to be supported therein by several *English* and *Dutch* Frigates, and other small Vessels; and so many Boats as could be spared were to go in with small Anchors and Hawsers, to tow the Bomb-Vessels and Frigates, if there should be occasion.

3. Two *Dutch* Ships were to cruise W. N. W. of the Squadron, or off of Cape *Frehelle*, and all the rest to lie as near as conveniently they could.

The Town of Granville destroyed. A Feint made of going to Havre de Grace.

In the next Place it was resolved to proceed to *Granville*, on the neighbouring Coast of *Normandy*, with eight Frigates and as many Bomb-Vessels, but that the Squadron should stay at St. *Malo* a Day or two, and then repair to, and remain at the Island of *Guernsey*. They met not with much difficulty in destroying *Granville*, (which was a fair large Town) even without the Loss of a Man, and joining the Squadron on the ninth, a Feint was made of going to *Havre de Grace*, thereby to amuse the Enemy, but in the Evening they bore away for *Portsmouth* to refit the Bomb-Vessels, and to get all things ready for attacking *Dunkirk*.

His Lordship propos'd to the Lords of the Admiralty that the great Ships at *Spithead* might accompany him, because the Season of the Year was very proper, and that the Difference of the Draught of Water between them and the Ships he had with him was not much; besides their Countenance was necessary, and their Boats would have afforded considerable Assistance.

The Squadron arrives in the Downs

The Squadron being come to the *Downs*, his Lordship received Orders there to take on board four hundred Land-Soldiers; but neither Mr. *Meesters*, nor his Pilots were then to be found; who coming soon after, a Council of War was held, where he was present,

CHAP. XVI. *from the Year* 1688, *to* 1697.   529

sent, and it was resolved to attempt *Dunkirk* in the manner following, *viz.*

1. To begin with bombarding the *Ris-Bank* and wooden Forts *The manner*
with six or eight Bomb-Vessels, which were to cease firing as soon *agreed on to*
as the Frigates and Machines came near the Forts.   *attempt Dun-*
kirk.

2. Four *English* Frigates were first to go in with *Dutch* Pilots,
and to carry on two Fireships, with as many Machines, to be laid
against the wooden Forts. These were to be supported by four Ships
of the States-General, of about fifty Guns each, design'd to anchor
against, and batter the said Forts; and three small *Dutch* Frigates,
one *English* Brigantine, with an Advice-Boat, were to go near in
with the Fireships and Machines, in order to take up their Boats
when the Men had set them on fire.

3. At the same time two *English* Frigates, two Ketches, and two
Fireships were to be sent on the Back of *Brake*, to disperse the E-
nemy's small Craft; two Machines, with as many Fireships to burn
against the *Ris-Bank*, and a Brigantine and four Well-Boats were to
bring off their Boats.

4. Two Fireships and as many Machines were to be ready for a
second Attack upon the Western Wooden Fort, (if the first should
fail) to be supported by an *English* Frigate, two Men of War Pinks,
and a Ketch; and the rest of the *Dutch* Frigates were to be placed
at an Anchor, Westward of the *Brake*, ready for any Service.

5. All the great Ships were to be posted off of *Gravelin*; for it
was the Opinion of the Pilots that not any one which drew above
fifteen or sixteen Foot Water could go out of the Eastern Passage
with Safety.

And now Mr. *Meesters* informing the Council of War that he
had every thing ready, it was resolved to sail the next Morning, as
they did; but it blowing fresh, the small Craft were dispersed;
however the Squadron continued on the *French* Coast, and Orders
were sent to those which were absent to repair to the Rendezvous,
which was *Gravelin Pits*, Mr. *Meesters* being particularly summoned thither, who had thought fit to retire to the *Downs*; but
although he represented it to be dangerous on the *French* Coast with
a N. W. Wind, positive Orders being sent to him to join the Squadron, he took Courage, and did the same the twenty ninth of *July*,
when the Weather being fair, it was determined to make the Attack
the next Day, or as soon as it might possibly be done; so that on
the first of *August*, early in the Morning, the Bomb-Vessels got un- *The Attack*
der Sail, and stood in to bombard the wooden Forts, and the *Ris-* *begun at Dun-*
kirk.
Bank. About Nine they were all placed, and began to throw their
Bombs very briskly, the Frigates at the same time going in to protect them from the Enemy's small Craft, of which they had great
Numbers; and many of their half Gallies and Boats coming out of
the Pier-heads, lay under the Cannon of the *Ris-Bank*. About
One a Clock the Frigates, Brigantines, Well-Boats, &c. which were
appointed to go in with the Fireships and Machines to burn upon
the Pier-heads and *Ris-Bank*, and to take up their Boats, weighed
and went pretty near in, plying to and fro within shot of the E-
nemy's

Y y y

nemy's Forts and Gallies; and about two a Clock there was sent in four Smoak-ships, that by being burnt against the Forts, the People might be blinded who were in them; but they had no manner of Success; for one of them ran on ground, and the others were set on fire long before they came to the Forts: Besides, their Smoak was so inconsiderable, that had they been carried nearer, it could not have much incommoded the Enemy.

Mr. Meester's Smoak Ships unsuccessful, and indeed of no use.

The Bomb-Vessels fired until it was five a Clock, at which time both they, the Frigates, Brigantines, &c. were ordered off. Several of the Shells fell into the *Ris-bank*, and upon the Pier-heads, and three of the Enemy's half Gallies were sunk; but they had in all Places made such Preparations for their Defence, with Boats, Bombs, Chains, Piles, and Pontons with Guns upon them, as render'd this Attempt altogether impracticable.

In this manner ended an Expedition which for some Years past had been designed against this important Port; and considering the ill Success, and that the simple Machines (as Mr. *Meesters* himself acknowledged) would be of little use without Smoak-Ships, (as indeed none of them could have been, either single or together) a Council of War resolved to sail to *Calais*, where it was agreed at another Consultation, that since Mr. *Meesters* had thought fit to retire with all his Machines the Night before, not any thing should be attempted until he returned pursuant to the Orders which were sent to him, but that when they arrived, all the Boats, and the small Frigates, should be sent in to support them, which Boats were to be commanded by a Captain of each Nation, the *English* to go Westward, and the *Dutch* Eastward of the Vessels which were to be burnt, or blown up against the Fort: But Mr. *Meesters* declining this second Attempt, the whole Affair ended, though it afterwards occasioned some Examinations before the Council, upon Complaints exhibited against him by my Lord *Berkeley*, and by Mr. *Meesters* against the Conduct of the Sea-Officers.

A Council of War resolve to sail for Calais.

Mr. Meesters declined a second Attempt with his Machines, &c.

Not long after, according to what was agreed at a Council of War, an Attempt was made on *Calais* in the manner following. There was a new wooden Fort at the Entrance of the Pier-heads, whereon were mounted fourteen heavy Cannon, and the Enemy had several other Batteries to the West, which were great Obstacles to the Undertaking; wherefore it was resolved to attack, and endeavour to burn the said wooden Fort in the Night; for which purpose Colonel *Richards* was not only ordered to fill up two Well-Boats with the Materials of the *Blaze* Fireship, but a formal Attack was designed with the Boats, at which time Colonel *Richards* was to begin the Bombardment of the Town. Accidents prevented the putting this in Execution until the seventeenth in the Morning, when anchoring Eastward of the Town, the Bombardment began, and with such good Success, that it was on fire in several Places by one a Clock, at which time the Enemy's half Gallies came out, and stood Eastward under the Shore, thinking thereby to annoy the Line of Bomb-Vessels; but the small Ships of War and Brigantines standing in, put them in so great Confusion, that with much ado they

The manner of our attacking Calais.

they regained the Pier-heads; and after this they gave no other Disturbance than with their Cannon and Mortars from their several Works. The Bombardment continued till Five at Night, during which time there were fired from the *English* Vessels about six hundred Shells, and in the whole Action our Loss was very inconsiderable.

CHAP. XVII.

Captain Robert Wilmot *sent with a Squadron of Ships, and Land-Forces, to the* West-Indies, *with an Account of his Proceedings.*

IT now follows that I relate what pass'd in the *West-Indies* under Command of Captain *Robert Wilmot*, who was appointed Commander in Chief of a Squadron of Ships, composed of one Third Rate, three Fourths, one Fifth, and two Fireships, and received Orders the fourteenth of *January* to proceed from *Plimouth* towards *America* with twelve Vessels appointed to transport Soldiers, Stores, and Provisions, where he was to take under his Command two Fourth Rates, and a Fifth.

169¾.

It was thought necessary to keep the Service private on which he was designed, even to himself, until such time as he got out to Sea, and therefore the general Instructions by which he was to be governed in the *West-Indies*, were sealed up, with positive Orders to him not to open them before he came into the Latitude of forty Degrees, and then to do it in the Presence of the Commander in Chief of the Land-Forces.

The general Instructions not opened till the Squadron came to Sea.

By the said Instructions he was directed,

Contents of the said general Instructions.

1. To sail to *Jamaica*.

2. To consider with the Governor of that Island, at a Council of War, what might be done against the Enemy; and if he should think fit, he was ordered to proceed to *Petit Guavas*, (a Town and Harbour in that part of *Hispaniola* possessed by the *French*) according to such Informations as could be gained of the Posture of the Enemy, and to take with him so many of the Land-Soldiers, and of the Militia of *Jamaica*, as the Governor should appoint.

3. To order some of his Squadron to cruise off of *Petit Guavas*, and by all other ways to intercept Supplies going to the *French* from *Europe*, or any of the Windward Islands.

4. Upon landing the Troops at *Petit Guavas*, or on any other part of the Coast of *Hispaniola* in Possession of the *French*, (if it should be thought proper to do the same at a Council of War) he was to use his utmost Endeavours to reduce the Forts, &c. and to destroy the Sugar-works, Engines, and Plantations.

5. If *Petit Guavas* could be taken by our Forces, he was to difpose Matters fo, as that Poffeffion thereof might be kept.

6. To give notice to the Commander in Chief of the Ifland of *Hifpaniola*, or the City of St. *Domingo*, of his Arrival near that Coaft, and to defire his Affiftance by Shipping, and the Conjunction of the Forces, or Militia there, for deftroying the Enemy on that and the adjacent Iflands; to which End the faid Governor had received Inftructions from the King of *Spain* his Mafter.

7. But if by the Readinefs of the Preparations at *Hifpaniola*, or Advices from the Governor of *Jamaica*, it fhould be judged adviseable at a Council of War to attack the *French* before his going to *Jamaica*, he was to do the fame.

8. If he gain'd Intelligence at his coming to *Jamaica*, or before his Arrival there, that the *French* were poffeffed of that Ifland, he was to endeavour to recover it, either by a Diverfion, or otherwife, as a Council of War fhould judge moft proper.

9. To hold Councils of War as often as there fhould be occafion, to confift of the Lieutenant-Governor of *Jamaica*, himfelf, the reft of the Sea-Captains, and of the Colonel, Major, and Captains of the Regiment, when thofe Perfons fhould be on the Place, the Governor being to prefide, if prefent, otherwife himfelf; and in his Abfence, and that of the Lieutenant-Governor of *Jamaica*, the Colonel, or Commander in Chief of the Regiment.

10. If the Councils of War were held at *Jamaica*, there were to be added thereunto the chief Officers of the Militia, not exceeding fix; yet in no other cafe than when the Matters to be debated fhould relate to the Defence of the Ifland: But the Governor was not to meddle with the Difcipline of the Squadron; nor was the Commadore to fend any of the Ships to cruife remote from the Ifland without the Confent of the faid Governor and Council, if it might be conveniently had.

11. The Spoil his Majefty gave between himfelf, the Officers, Seamen, Soldiers, and Militia, except Guns, Ammunition, and Naval Stores, according to the Diftribution which will be hereafter expreffed.

12. After he had done his utmoft to annoy the Enemy, and for the Security of the Ifland, and remained thereabouts not longer than two or three Months, unlefs a Council of War judged it abfolutely neceffary for fome efpecial Service, he was to return to *England*, and to leave five Fourth Rates, and one of the Sixth for the Guard of *Jamaica*: But in his Paffage (if the Seafon of the Year fhould not be too far advanced) he was to call at the *French* Settlements in *Newfoundland*, and endeavour to deftroy their, and protect our, Fifhery; after which he was to do the like to their Veffels on the *Bank*.

Laftly; And fince the Succefs of this Expedition depended very much upon the good Agreement between him and the Commander in Chief of the Land-Forces, (which was, indeed, not only in this Cafe, but many others, found a very difficult thing) he was enjoined to take care to prevent any unneceffary Scruples or Difficulties on that Account.

The Distribution of the Prizes and Booty that should be taken in the West-Indies.

1. All Prizes taken at Sea were to be distributed according to an Act of Parliament in that behalf: And of all the Booty at Land, a third part was to be set aside for the Lieutenant-Governor of *Jamaica*, when Commander in Chief on any Expedition, or to the Commander in Chief for the time being; the other two Thirds to be distributed among the Officers and Soldiers, as will be hereafter more particularly expressed.

2. His Majesty's part of all Prizes at Sea was to be divided among the Seamen only, and the Booty at Land among the Land-men.

3. But when Land-men happened to be commanded on board upon any Expedition, or if in their Passage to the *West-Indies* the Transport Ships should be engaged, and a Prize taken, such Landmen were to be considered as Seamen, and their Officers on board to receive a Share according to their Pay; and in like manner the Seamen, and their Officers when on Shore, were to receive a Dividend according to their Pay.

4. That of all Booty taken in Service on shore, wherein the Commander in Chief of the Squadron for the time being should assist with four hundred Seamen, or more, the said Commander in Chief was to have the Share allotted to a Colonel, and the Officers appointed by him to command those Men to be considered as Land-Officers.

5. No Officer of the Militia was to be considered as a Colonel, who commanded less than five hundred Men; nor as a Captain, if he had less in his Company than fifty, unless such Regiment, or Company, should, after their proceeding on the Expedition, happen to be reduced by Sickness, or Accidents of War.

Two Thirds of the Booty taken at Land was to be thus divided.

To Field and Staff-Officers.

	Shares.
Colonel, as Colonel,	18
Lieutenant-Colonel, as Lieutenant-Colonel,	10½
Major, as Major,	7½
Captain,	10
Adjutant,	6
Chirurgeon,	6
Chirurgeon's Mates, — 2, 4 shares each,	8
Quarter-Master,	6
Total	72

One Company.

	Share
Captain,	12
Two Lieutenants, each 6 Shares,	12
Enfign,	4 ½
Six Serjeants,	12
Six Corporals,	9
Two Drummers,	3
Two hundred private Men,	200
Five Companies more, confifting of the like Number,	1262 ½
The Commiffary of Stores and Provifions, Paymafter of the Forces, Commiffary of the Mufters, and Judge-Advocate.	12
Total	1599

To the Officers of the Ordnance.

Enfign	15
Mafter Gunner	7 ½
Gunner's Mate,	4 ½
Twelve Gunners, each three Shares,	36
Firemafter	7 ½
Six Bombardiers, each 3 ¾ Shares,	22 ½
Mafter Carpenter	6
Three Mates, each 3 ⅔ Shares,	11
Chirurgeon,	6
	116
	1599
Total	1715

Two Thirds of the King's Part of the Prizes at Sea were to be divided after this manner, *viz.*

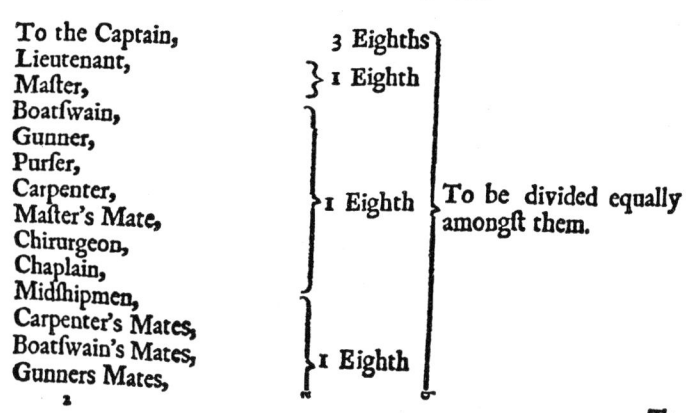

To the Captain,	3 Eighths	
Lieutenant, Mafter,	} 1 Eighth	
Boatfwain, Gunner, Purfer, Carpenter, Mafter's Mate, Chirurgeon, Chaplain, Midfhipmen,	} 1 Eighth	To be divided equally amongft them.
Carpenter's Mates, Boatfwain's Mates, Gunners Mates,	} 1 Eighth	

To

Chap. XVII. *from the Year* 1688, *to* 1697.

To the Corporals,
Yeomen of the Sheets,
Coxwain,
Quarter Masters,
Doctor's Mates,
Chirurgeons Mates,
Yeomen of the Powder-Room,
} 1 Eighth

Trumpeter,
Quarter-Gunner,
Carpenters Crew,
Steward,
Cook,
Armourer,
Steward's Mate,
Gunsmith,
Swabber,
Ordinary Trumpeter,
Barber,
Able Seamen,
} 2 Eighths

To be divided equally amongst them.

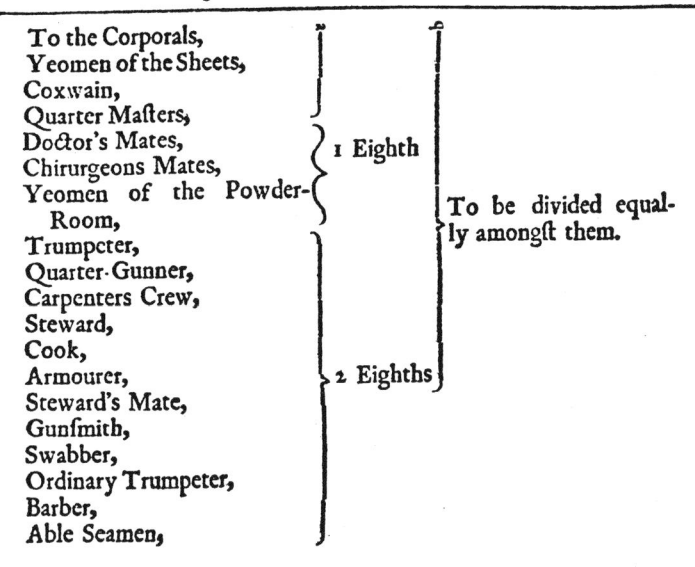

Lastly, such Officers, Soldiers, and Seamen as should happen to receive Wounds in any Action where Booty or a Prize should be taken, were to have a double Share, in Consideration of the said Wounds.

Pursuant to these Instructions Captain *Wilmot* sailed from *Plimouth*, and arriving in the *Old Road* at St. *Christopher's*, one of the *Leeward* Islands, departed from thence the twenty eighth of *March* for the Island of *Savona*, which lies at the Eastermost End of *Hispaniola*, intending if the Governor of St. *Domingo* was ready to march to Port *de Paix*, to sail on the West Side of the Island, and assault it by Sea, which he could not have done had he gone down to St. *Domingo*, or on the South Side, because it would have been a great Hindrance to the Transport Ships, which sailed very ill, and could not so well keep a Wind. *Captain Wilmot sails from Plimouth, and arrives at Hispaniola 1694.*

The *French* at this time had nineteen Privateers out of *Guadalupe* and *Martinica*, and three Ships of War, one of forty four Guns, another of forty, and the third a small *Dutch* Ship taken at *Camaret* Bay, which Privateers were chiefly supported by such Merchant Ships and Vessels of ours as they frequently took, loaden with Provisions for the Islands: Besides, the *French* General had notice of our coming, and daily expected the Squadron at *Hispaniola*, where they had muster'd up all their Strength together, and this notwithstanding the great Care which was taken at home for keeping the Expedition private. *The French had several Privateers from Guadalupe and Martinica.*

When the Squadron arrived at *Savona*, the Commadore met with a Letter from the Governor of St. *Domingo*, by which he assured him that if he would come there he should be assisted in attempting the Enemy on that Coast; whereupon he sailed with three Ships of War, *The Squadron proceeds to St. Domingo.*

War, and two Fireships, having sent the Transports with the Remainder of the Squadron to the Gulph of *Samana*, on the North Side of the Island.

When he landed he desired the Assistance of the President of St. *Domingo*, and delivered to him the King of *Spain*'s Letters; but although he made at first a Shew of Readiness to comply therewith, yet he soon raised insignificant Scruples, by which twelve Days time were lost, and then it was agreed that he should forthwith march with seventeen hundred of his Men, and one hundred and fifty *English*, to *Machaneel* Bay, on the North Side of the Island, where the Squadron was to meet him.

They arrive at Cape Francis, *and are fired upon from the French Fort.*

Accordingly the Commodore proceeded to Cape *Francis*, which was the very Windermost Settlement the *French* had, and when he had put on Shore the rest of the *English* Forces within three Leagues of the Cape, he moved forward until he came within Gun-shot of the Fort, from whence the *French* fired very warmly at our Ships, and in some Measure disabled one of them, called the *Swan*.

Resolution about attacking the Town and Fort.

It was concluded that as soon as the Soldiers could march to one End of the Town, the Ships should batter the Fort, whereon were mounted forty Guns, and that the Seamen should assault the Back of it, the Ground there being higher than the Fort itself; in order whereunto a convenient Place was sought for to land at, but they were repulsed: However, the next Evening they went with a greater Strength, and the Enemy imagining that we then intended to land, they blew up the Fort, and burnt the Town, laying Trains of Powder to the Houses where any Plunder was, which had like to have done much Mischief to our Men.

The French *destroy them both.*

Resolution of marching to Port de Paix *not executed.*

Next Day the Commodore sent to the *Spanish* General to know when he could be ready to go to Port *de Paix*, upon whose Answer it was agreed at a Consultation, that Major *Lillingston* should march thither with three hundred *English*, in Company of the *Spanish* Forces, it being (as they said) about fourteen Leagues off; but what was thus determined being not put in Execution, and the Men being unruly, they straggled up and down the Country for Plunder, by which Means several of them were lost.

The Commodore lands Seamen to sustain the Troops, and they fall into an Ambuscade.

The Commodore not hearing from the Forces since they moved from Cape *Francis*, he called a Council of War, and proposed to land four hundred Seamen, to see if they could join them, for he had Reason to doubt they were in Danger. Accordingly such a Number of Men were landed about five Miles Eastward of Port *de Paix*, though they received some Opposition, yet they burnt and destroyed the Enemy's Plantations to the Fort it self, to which the *French* retired; but not hearing any thing of the Land-Forces, they came on board the Ships at Night.

Some Cannon and Mortars put on Shore, but a great Delay in mounting them.

Soon after this Captain *Wilmot* had notice that several of the Soldiers had straggled near Port *de Paix*, whereupon he landed the like Number of Seamen again, in order to join them, and the next Day put on Shore the Cannon and Mortars, but there was not so much Dispatch made in mounting them as might have been expected.

It

CHAP. XVIII. *from the Year* 1688, *to* 1697. 537

It was now resolved that the Squadron should sail to the Westward of Port *de Paix*, where there was a commodious Hill to annoy the Enemy, much nearer than the first intended Battery, and there ten Pieces of Cannon were mounted, which so much galled them, that in few Days part of the inward Fort was beaten down, and many People who retired thither were killed. *The inward Fort of Port de Paix battered down.*

The third of *July*, between the Hours of Twelve and One, the French sallied out with about three hundred Whites, and two hundred Blacks, well armed, but the Commadore having notice thereof by a Negro, detached one hundred and fifty Men to receive them, being in a Readiness with the rest, both Seamen and Soldiers, to join them upon Occasion, by which means many were killed, especially their commanding Officers, and several taken Prisoners; and after this Defeat our Forces immediately took Possession of the Fort, wherein they found eighty Cannon mounted, with good Store of Powder and Shot. *The French sally out, but are beaten. 1695. The Fort taken.*

The Colonel of the Land-Forces was soon after desired to send his sick Men to *Jamaica*, and to keep those who were in Health to assist in the intended Service at *Leogane* and *Petit Guavas*; but neither he, nor the *Spanish* General thought it adviseable considering the Weakness of the Troops; so that the Fort was demolished, and the Guns and Stores carried off, which done, the Commadore sailed to *Jamaica*, where having refitted the Ships, and put all things into the best Order he could, he took his Departure for *England* the third of *September*, leaving behind him the *Reserve*, *Hampshire*, *Ruby*, and *Swan*, the last to bring Home some Merchant Ships when loaden, and the three first (being Fourth Rates) to guard *Jamaica* untill farther Order; but such Difficulties they met with in their Passage, not only by bad Weather, but the violent, and uncommon Distemper which seized the Men, that it was almost next to a Miracle the Ships got Home, Captain *Wilmot*, the Commadore, with a great Number of the Officers dying, and one of the Fourth Rates, for Want of Men to trim her Sails, running on Ground, was lost on the Sholes of Cape *Florida*. *The Fort demolished, and the Squadron sails from thence to Jamaica, and so to England.*

CHAP. XVIII.

An Account of the speedy getting together a Squadron of Ships, when the French *designed to make a Descent from* Dunkirk: *With Sir* George Rooke's *Proceedings in the* Chanel *and* Soundings.

THE Expeditions at Sea, both at home and abroad, the last Year, ending as hath been before related, and no more Ships being kept out than what were absolutely necessary for guarding the Coast and to convoy the Trade, the rest were ordered to the several

veral Ports, that so they might be timely fitted for the next Year's Service: But his Majesty receiving Advice that the *French* intended to take this Opportunity of embarking an Army from *Calais, Dunkirk*, and the Ports thereabouts, and therewith to make a Descent on *England*, signified his Pleasure by Admiral *Russell* to the Lords of the Admiralty the twenty first of *February*, that all the Ships in the Rivers of *Thames* and *Medway*, as well as those at the *Nore, Spithead, Plimouth*, and elsewhere, which could be got ready, should be ordered to repair immediately to the *Downs*; and for the greater Expedition, Orders were given to those at *Portsmouth* and *Plimouth* to take the Men out of Merchant Ships, and to bring as many more as they conveniently could to other Ships in Want. The Civil Magistrates of *Kent*, and about *Portsmouth*, were also ordered to secure all straggling Seamen, and to send them to the Naval Commissioners residing nearest to the Place where they should meet with them; and the Commander in Chief in the River *Medway* was likewise directed to hasten all the Ships from thence and the *Nore* to the *Downs*, as the Master-Attendant on Float was all Ships of War, Fireships, and other Vessels, fitting out in the River. All the Boats belonging to the Ships at the *Nore* and *Blackstakes* were ordered to impress Watermen, Bargemen, Lightermen, and others working on the River *Medway*: Besides which, general Orders were issued to impress all without Distinction, except such as were employ'd on necessary Services of the Navy, Ordnance, or Victualling; and there being an Embargo laid on all Merchant Ships, it was ordered that a third Part of the Men belonging to those which were outward bound should be taken from them, for the more speedy putting the Fleet into a Condition to prevent the Enemy's Design. Mr. *Russell* himself (after he had assisted as first Lord of the Admiralty in these Preparations) repaired, by the King's particular Command, to the *Downs*, to conduct this important Service, where he arrived the twenty fourth; and though he found no more Ships there than one First, two Thirds, six Fourths, and two Fifth Rates, with one Fireship, a Ketch, and a Brigantine, yet such speedy Orders were issued, and so diligently were they put in Execution, that he was joined within three Days after by Sir *Cloudesly Shovell* at the *South-Sand-Head* with thirteen more, besides eleven *English* and *Dutch* from *Spithead*, and the next Day his Number was increased by ten Ships from *Plimouth*, at which time he was standing Eastward along the *French* Coast.

The first of *March* there sailed from the *Downs* to join him ten more, great and small; and although there were not in the *Downs* on the twenty fourth of *February* above eleven Ships, and that all the rest in Pay were in Places distant one from the other, and most of them but very poorly manned, yet by the twenty eighth of that Month the Admiral had with him off of *Gravelin*, one First, twelve Thirds, twenty four Fourths, and three Fifth Rates, besides Fireships of the *English*; together with twelve Ships of War of the *Dutch*, and two of their Fireships, and in few Days after they were

CHAP. XVIII. *from the Year* 1688, *to* 1697. 539

were augmented to near fourscore Sail, reckoning into the Number of small Sixth Rates, Brigantines, &c. with which there were the several Flag-Officers following, *viz.* the Admiral himself, the Lord *Berkeley* Admiral of the Blue, Sir *Cloudesly Shovell* Vice-Admiral of the Red, Mr. *Aylmer* Vice-Admiral of the Blue, and two *Dutch* Rear-Admirals.

The Admiral came to an Anchor off of *Gravelin* the twenty eighth of *February* with Part of the Fleet, and the Lord *Berkeley* lay between him and *Dunkirk*.

As he sailed close in with *Calais* he perceived that Harbour so much crouded with all Sorts of Embarcations, that they were judged not to be less than between three and four hundred, all which had their Sails to the Yards. In *Flemish* Road there were about seventeen Ships of War, great and small, with which they would probably in few Days have come over with the Transports; for, as some Prisoners related, they were of Opinion that since our great Ships were gone in to refit, and those from the Streights not arrived, we had not any Force at Sea; and it is reasonable to believe they designed to strengthen this Convoy by other Ships from *Brest*, and the Ports of West *France*. Thirteen of these seventeen Ships retired as close into the Pier of *Dunkirk* as possibly they could, which, according to the best Judgment that could be made of them, were four of about seventy Guns, three between fifty and sixty, and the rest small Frigates. *Many Transport Ships seen at Calais.*

And what Ships of War they had at Dunkirk.

Sir *Cloudesly Shovell* with several Captains was sent to look on them, but found there could not be any thing attempted with Hopes of Success; and the *Dutch* Pilots sent by Mr. *Meesters* being examined, they declared that when the Tides were mended, if the Wind was from the S. to the W. S. W. and a fresh Gale, they would venture to carry such of our Ships as drew not more Water than fifteen or sixteen *Dutch* Feet through *Flemish* Road, and out of the East Chanel by *Newport*, provided they did not anchor: But if any Accidents happened, by the Ship's Masts coming by the Board, or other Interruption, they were apprehensive they might be exposed to imminent Danger. *Impracticable to attempt the Ships at Dunkirk.*

Those Pilots who came from *Newport* owned themselves ignorant of the Sands or Chanels about *Dunkirk*, so that it was concluded not safe to make any Attempt, and therefore the Admiral resolved to come with the Fleet to *Dover* Road, or the *Downs*, but first to leave a proper Squadron to attend the Motion of the Enemy's Ships, and Cruisers in other convenient Stations, which Squadron was put under the Command of Sir *Cloudesly Shovell*. *A Squadron left off of Dunkirk with Sir Cloudesly Shovell.*

The twenty third of *March* three Bomb-Vessels join'd Sir *Cloudesly Shovell*, who then called a Council of War, at which were present the Captains of all the Ships as also Colonel *Richards*, and Captain *Benbow*, who agreed that it was not adviseable to bombard *Calais* with the small Number of Mortars they had, but rather to stay until they could be augmented, and that more favourable Weather offered for such an Undertaking. *They staid for more Mortars to bomb Calais.*

The twenty eighth a *Swedish* Vessel came into the *Downs* which had

Zzz2

540 *Naval Transactions of the* English, Book IV.

The Master of a Swedish Vessel's Account of the intended Descent.

had been the Day before at *Calais*, the Master whereof said that about five Weeks before, when he was off of that Port, in his Way to *Nantes*, he went on Shore to get some Water, and being there seized, his Ship was carried in, as he believed, for transporting Part of their Forces to *England*. He added that King *James* had been at *Calais*, but went from thence soon after Admiral *Russel* came before that Place; that in the Parts thereabouts they had near twelve thousand Soldiers, and about three hundred Vessels for Transportation, which were dispersed before his coming away, so that there was no more left in *Calais* than the ordinary Garrison, and that one hundred and fifty of the small Vessels were also gone to the several Places whereunto they belonged, none of the Masters thereof, nor of other *Danes* and *Swedes* taken up for this Service, having had any Recompence for their Trouble and Loss of Time.

Admiral Allemonde, and several Ships come into the Downs.

The thirty first of this Month of *March* Admiral *Allemonde* came into the *Downs* from *Holland* with six Ships of the Line of Battel, and two Fireships, as did next Morning several of ours from *Spithead*, and the Day following Sir *Cloudesly Shovell* received Directions from the Lords of the Admiralty to return with all the Bomb-Vessels to the Coast of *France*, in order to attempt the burning of *Calais*, with the Transport Ships and Vessels there, being empowered to take with him such of the small Frigates in the *Downs* as he should think necessary for that Service.

Sir Cloudesly Shovell arrives off of Calais, and the Town bombarded.

He arrived off of *Calais* the third, and from that Day at Noon until Night, about three hundred Bombs, and Carcasses were thrown into the Town, where, and among the Embarcations in the Pier, many were seen to break, which undoubtedly did them considerable Damage; not that any thing could be distinctly seen, more than a small Vessel on fire in the Harbour, and the Town flaming in three or four Places, which was soon extinguished.

In this Action the Bomb-Vessels and Brigantines received much Injury in their Rigging, and all the Mortars but two were disabled: Several of the Frigates were also damaged, and the Wind coming about next Day from S. S. E. to the S. W. with hard Gales, it was thought convenient to return to the *Downs*, from whence Sir *Cloudesly* appointed a Squadron to endeavour to keep the *French* in at *Dunkirk*, and received Orders on the eleventh to proceed with the Fleet to *Spithead*, in Company of all the *Dutch* Ships, at which time there were with him two First Rates, five Seconds, nine Thirds, eleven Fourths, one Brigantine, and seven Fireships, those hereafter mentioned, which were designed to join him, being employed on particular Services by the Lords of the Admiralty.

Sir Cloudesly Shovell ordered to Spithead with the Fleet.

Ships not in the *Downs* when Sir *Cloudesly* sailed from thence.

Rates.	Ships Names.	
3	*Berwick,*	
	Captain,	
	Defiance,	Off of *Calais*.
	Edgar,	
	Kent,	
4	*Burlington,*	Rates.

CHAP. XVIII. *from the Year* 1688, *to* 1697.   541

Rates.	Ships Names.	
3	*Burford,* *Mountague,* *Resolution,* *Suffolk,*	Off of *Dunkirk.*
6 Fireship	*Lark,* *Firebrand,*	
3	*Royal Oak,*	Gone to *Sheerness* for a Foremast.
4	*Norwich,*	Gone to *Portsmouth* to refit.
	Severn,	Gone to the *Nore* to bring victualling Ships to the *Downs.*
6	*Greyhound.*	Ordered from *Shoreham* to the *Downs.*
1	*Britannia,* *St. Andrew,*	
2	*Royal Katharine,*	At several Places, under Orders to proceed to the *Downs.*
3	*Content,* *Restauration,*	
4	*Litchfield,* *Portland.*	

Here it may be observed, that the early fitting out of the Fleet, and the Untowardness of the Weather, occasioned great Sickness among the Men, insomuch that near five hundred were put on shore at *Deal,* and many who remained on board the Ships were in an ill Condition. *The Sickness of the Men occasioned by the early fitting out of the Fleet.*

A Line of Battel was now formed of all such Ships as either were with him, or that might reasonably be expected upon any pressing Occasion, which amounted in the whole to two First Rates, five Seconds, twenty two Thirds, and seventeen Fourths of the *English*; and of the *Dutch* four of ninety, or ninety four Guns, seven of seventy, and six from sixty six to sixty, besides eight *English,* and five *Dutch* Fireships, with five of our small Frigates, and seven Brigantines: Moreover there were two First Rates, the *Britannia* and *St. Andrew,* and a Second Rate, the *St. Michael,* which being under Orders to proceed to him to the *Buoy of the Nore,* join'd him the twenty third of *April.* *A Line of Battel formed.*

About this time there was Advice from *Ostend* that Monsieur *Du Bart* was fitting out at *Dunkirk* eight Ships of War and two Fireships. The Reports of his Design were various; some said, it was to join the whole Fleet; others, to protect the Vessels bound from St. *Malo* and *Havre de Grace* to *Dunkirk* and *Calais*; whereas some thought that he intended to cruise in the North Chanel; while others had a Jealousy that he intended to attack his Majesty in his Passage to *Holland,* though in my Opinion there was little reason to apprehend the latter; for at the beginning of the War he did not think fit to attempt it, although his Majesty had with him no other *Du Bart fitting out a Squadron at Dunkirk. Observations upon Du Bart's meeting the King in his Passage to Holland.*

other than foul Ships of any Strength, whereas *Du Bart* had several juſt come out of *Dunkirk* clean, with which he lay by for ſome time, not much beyond the Reach of Gun-ſhot, without daring to gain himſelf the Reputation of giving our Ships one Broadſide, although he might, at pleaſure, have run round them, without expoſing himſelf to any great Danger: But Blows being not his Buſineſs, he reſerved his Squadron for ſome better Opportunity of Advantage on Merchant Ships, or ſuch as could not make any conſiderable Reſiſtance.

Sir George Rooke arrives in the Downs from the Streights, and takes the Command of the Fleet. He arrives at Spithead. 1696.

Before Sir *Cloudeſly Shovell* could proceed to *Spithead* with the Fleet, Sir *George Rooke*, Admiral of the White, arrived in the *Downs* from the *Streights*, and took upon him the ſole Command; and after he had diſpatched ſuch Matters as were neceſſary, with reſpect not only to the Fleet, but thoſe Ships he was ordered to detach therefrom on particular Services, he ſailed and arrived at *Spithead* the thirtieth of *April*, having left ſome ſmall Ships and the Bomb-Veſſels behind, to bring after him near a thouſand Men in ſick Quarters at *Deal, Dover, Sandwich, Ramſgate*, and other Places thereabouts.

Orders ſent him to proceed into the Soundings.

A Council of War reſolve to ſail when the Ships could be furniſhed with what they wanted.

The ſecond of *May* he received preſſing Orders to proceed into the *Soundings*, but the Ships which came home with him from the *Streights* being not in a Condition for immediate Service, ſince, beſides other things, they more eſpecially wanted Beer and Stores, he thought it adviſeable to call a Council of War, where it was determined to ſail with the very firſt Opportunity, after they ſhould be ſupplied with what was abſolutely neceſſary to enable them to keep at Sea; but that in the Interim the State and Condition of the Fleet ſhould be repreſented to the Lords of the Admiralty, which conſiſted of ſix Firſt Rates, eight Seconds, twenty two Thirds, and three Fourths, of the *Engliſh*; and of the *Dutch* ſixteen, whereof there were three of ninety Guns, eight of ſeventy and ſeventy four, four of ſixty and ſixty four, and one of fifty, beſides the Fireſhips, Frigates, and ſmall Veſſels of both Nations, being in the whole of the Line of Battel but fifty five, and the *Engliſh* Ships, from the Firſt to the Third Rate, wanted upwards of three thouſand three hundred Men of nineteen thouſand five hundred their allowed Complement.

The reaſon of the Fleet's being reduced to a ſmaller Number than deſigned.

The reaſon of the Fleet's being reduced to ſo ſmall a Number, was the other Services hereafter mentioned, on which many of the Ships at home were employed, *viz.*

Rate.	Ships Names.	
3	*Reſolution,*	
	Monmouth,	
	Dunkirk,	Cruiſing in the *Soundings* to protect the Trades expected home.
	Content,	
	Defiance,	
4	*Severne,*	
	Fireſhips, Two,	

Rate.

CHAP. XVIII. *from the Year* 1688, *to* 1697. 543

Rate.	Ships Names.	
3	*Berwick,* *Edgar,* *Lion,*	} Appointed Convoys for *Bilboa, Portugal,* and the *Canaries.*
4	*Medway,* Firefhips, Three,	
3	*Cornwall,* Firefhips, Two,	} Ordered to the *Nore.*
4	*Pembroke,* Firefhips, Two,	} Off of *Dunkirk.*
3	*Humber,* *Sterling-Caftle,*	} In *Portfmouth* Harbour.
	Elizabeth,	{ Gone to *Holland* with the King.
	Breda.	{ Laid up at *Portfmouth.*

So that feventeen *Englifh* Ships (befides *Dutch)* were taken from the Number firft appointed for the Body of the Fleet, all which were of the Line of Battel.

Sir *George Rooke* was, foon after his Return from *Cadiz,* appointed Admiral and Commander in Chief of the Fleet, and directed to proceed therewith, and place himfelf in fuch a Station as he might judge moft proper for preventing the Squadron expected from *Thoulon,* with their Convoys, getting into any Port of *France;* and according to fuch Intelligence as he fhould get of their Proceedings, to remove to other Stations, for the more effectual Performance of that Service. Upon meeting them, or his being informed they were got into any Port where he might attack them, he was to endeavour to do it: But if he received certain Advice they were got into *Breft,* he was then to come with the Fleet to *Torbay,* and remain there until farther Order. *Sir George Rooke ordered to lie in a Station to prevent the Thoulon Ships getting to Breft.*

Thefe were the Contents of his Inftructions; but he was under no little Uneafinefs how to put them in Execution, by reafon of the great want of Men, as well as the fmall Strength of the Fleet, as to the Number of Ships, and therefore he called another Council of War, where it was neverthelefs refolved to proceed Weft fifteen Leagues from *Ufhant,* and that in their Paffage fome fmall Frigates and Brigantines fhould be fent for Intelligence, and particularly to difcover whether the *Thoulon* Squadron was got into *Breft:* But yet the Council of War thought it convenient to reprefent, That fince the Fleet was reduced to thirty feven *Englifh* Ships, and twenty *Dutch,* of the Line of Battel, they would be of lefs Strength than the *Thoulon* Squadron, and that of Monfieur *Nefmond's,* if join'd. However, to ftrengthen them all that poffibly could be, he was ordered to take with him three Third Rates, one Fourth, and three of the Firefhips which were appointed for foreign Convoys. *A Council of War refolve on the Station.*

Being off of *Dartmouth* the eighth of this Month, the *Oxford* join'd him, whofe Captain was in the Morning informed by the Mafter of a *Portuguefe* Ship bound to *Rotterdam,* that fix Days before *The Fleet off of Dartmouth.*

Sir George Rooke receives Advice of the French Ships.

before in the Latitude of forty five Degrees, Cape *Finisterre* then bearing South, distant about forty Leagues, he met with a Fleet of *French* Ships of War, being in all forty Sail, thirty four of them from fifty to eighty Guns, as nigh as he could judge, and that they were then steering away N. N. E. with the Wind W. N. W. four of them Flag-Ships, *viz.* the Vice and Rear-Admirals of the White, and Vice and Rear-Admirals of the Blue.

A great want of cruising Frigates.

The Admiral was in great want of cruising Frigates for Intelligence, insomuch that the *French* Scouts and Privateers made their Observations without Interruption; and by reason of small Gales Southerly, our Fleet was kept on the Coast of *England* until the twelfth.

The Lime brings an Account of the French Ships coming thro' the Streights.

The Night before the *Lime* came in, which Ship the Admiral had left to cruise about the *Streights*, her Captain having received Advice the second of *April* from the *English* Consul at *Malaga*, that the *French* Fleet were seen off of *Almeria* Bay the twenty eighth of the preceding Month; and the ninth of *April* he was farther informed that they were plying Westward off of Cape *de Gates*, and that eight of their best Sailers were got as low as *Motril*. Three Days after, by the help of a strong *Levant*, he got through the *Streights*, when lying off of Cape *Spartell* to observe their Motion, about Three in the Afternoon he made four of them coming down the *Barbary* Shore, which giving him chase, they forced him the next Day into the Bay of *Cadiz*, where he had Advice the sixteenth, by an Express from *Gibraltar*, that the Enemy were at an Anchor off of that Place. The twenty first he plied up to his Station off of Cape *Spartell*, and saw near fifty Sail coming down under the Land before the Wind, but five of them making towards him, he could not discover the Body of the Fleet again until next Morning about Ten, when they were between the Bay of *Lagos* and Cape St. *Vincent*, going away large with a prest Sail, the Wind at E. S. E.

The Fleet coming off of Ushant.

The fourteenth of *May*, in the Morning, our Fleet came on the Coast of *Ushant*, and then a Squadron of Ships, with small Vessels, were sent under the Command of Captain *Bazil Beaumont* between that and the Main for Intelligence. Without any Resistance he stood in to *Camaret* and *Bertheaume* Bays, and saw as much in *Broad Sound* as it was possible to do without passing their Forts, counting twenty two Sail, seventeen or eighteen of which he judged were Ships of the Line of Battel, and eight or nine of them with three Decks, with four Flags, *viz.* Admiral, and Vice, Rear-Admiral of White and Blue, and Rear-Admiral of the White, which, according to the Opinion of the Pilots, were all the Ships of Force they had

Advice received of the French Ships being got into Brest.

there: But by the Captain of a *French* Man of War, called the *Foudroyant*, taken by Captain *Norris*, the Admiral was informed the *Thoulon* Fleet got into *Brest* the fifth, Old Style, and that they were forty seven Ships of the Line, four others being obliged to return to *Thoulon*, by reason of the Damage they received before they passed the *Streights*. This Prize had not been at Sea, but was now going to join Monsieur *Chasteau Renault*'s Squadron, one of which he took Captain *Norris*'s Ship to be, their Station

being,

being, as he faid, about S. W. and by W. forty eight Leagues from *Scilly*, in Number two Ships with three Decks, two of feventy Guns, two of fixty, and two of about thirty; but by the Account given by Captain *Fitz Patrick*, it was judged that even this Squadron was feen going into *Breſt*, fome whereof he had certainly engaged with, had they not retired upon difcovering other of our Ships advancing towards them.

Upon the firſt Account given by Captain *Beaumont*, a Council of War of all the Flag Officers was called, and ſince it appeared uncertain whether or no the *Thoulon* Fleet was got into *Breſt*, it was reſolved to continue in the appointed Rendezvous as long as the Winds hung Eaſterly, in Expectation of the Ships ordered to reinforce the Fleet, and in the mean time to endeavour to gain farther Intelligence, by taking People from the Shore, and ſending a ſmall Frigate, with an Advice Boat to *Belle Iſle*, to diſcover whether any part of the *French* Fleet was there. But upon the aforemention'd Account, received afterwards from Captain *Fitz-Patrick*, and what was reported by fome Perſons taken from the Shore, it was judged there was no room to doubt of the *Thoulon* Fleet, and Monſieur *Neſmond*'s Squadrons being in *Breſt*; ſo that the Flag-Officers were called together again the eighteenth, when they reſolved to lie as near the Rendezvous as poſſible, while the Winds hung Northerly or Eaſterly; but upon the firſt ſhift Southerly, or Weſterly, to repair to *Torbay*, as the Lords of the Admiralty had directed by their Orders of the twenty ninth of the laſt Month.

A Council of War reſolve to continue in the Station.

It is afterwards determined to come to Torbay with the firſt Southerly or Weſterly Wind.

The next Day Vice Admiral *Evertſon*, with twelve *Dutch* Men of War, joined the Admiral, together with an *Engliſh* Fourth Rate, the *Sunderland*, and the *Fortune* Fireſhip, as Vice-Admiral *Aylmer* alſo did in the *Elizabeth*, with the *Newark* and *Mary*, and between thirty and forty Sail more, among which were the Bomb-Veſſels and Tenders: But, according to what was determined, the Fleet came to *Torbay* the twenty third, ſeveral Cruiſers being ſtationed between *Uſhant* and the Iſle of *Bas*, the *Start* and *Uſhant*, and off of the *Lizard*. At this time the whole Naval Strength was one hundred and fifteen Ships and Veſſels, ſixty ſeven of them *Engliſh*, and forty eight *Dutch*, whereof eighty five were of the Line of Battel, of which forty nine were *Engliſh*, viz. ſix Firſt Rates, eight Seconds, twenty eight Thirds, and ſeven Fourths. Of the *Dutch* there were thirty ſix, eight of which carried ninety Guns, fourteen between ſeventy and ſeventy four, eleven of ſixty four, and three of about fifty; but ſeveral of their Companies were very ſickly, eſpecially thoſe which came from the *Streights*, inſomuch that there wanted full four thouſand Men in ours; nor was there any great Proſpect of their ſudden Recovery, ſince the little Villages thereabouts were not capable of receiving many.

Several Dutch and Engliſh Ships join the Fleet.

The Fleet comes to Torbay.

Chap. XIX.

John *Lord* Berkeley's *Proceedings with the Fleet in and about the* Chanel, *and of several Attempts made on the French Coast,* &c.

Sir George Rooke order'd to his Duty at the Admiralty Board, and John Lord Berkeley to command the Fleet.

THE twenty seventh of *May* Sir *George Rooke* was ordered to return to his Duty at the Admiralty-Board, and to leave the Command of the Fleet to the Lord *Berkeley*, who was appointed Admiral thereof; but before he came on shore, he had Advice from Commissioner *St. Loe* at *Plimouth* that one of our Advice-Boats, the *Mercury*, had counted a little above *Camaret* Bay seventy Sail of *French* Men of War, all ready to come to Sea, with four Flags flying, three whereof Blue and one White, and in the Bay itself five small Ships more; which Account he communicated to the Lords of the Admiralty. Being come to Town, he made the following Proposal to the Duke of *Shrewsbury*, Principal Secretary of State;

A Proposal made by Sir George Rooke for attempting the French at Camaret.

" That the Body of the Fleet should lie in *Camaret* and *Bertheaume*
" Bays, and a Detachment be made to sustain the small Frigates and
" Bomb-Vessels, while they went in to do what Mischief they could.
" It was his Opinion that by thus blocking up the Enemy's Fleet in
" their principal Port, insulting their Coasts, and burning their Towns
" at the same time, it would expose them to the World, make them
" very uneasy at home, and give Reputation to his Majesty's Arms;
" and this he believed might be done, if speedily undertaken, with
" the Assistance of some small Frigates, which were much wanted.

The Lord *Berkeley* arriving in *Torbay* the third of *June*, he immediately betook himself to the Dispatch of all things necessary;

A Council of War think it not practicable to attempt the French in Brest Harbour.

and since a Council of War, both of *English* and *Dutch* Flag-Officers, thought it not practicable to attempt the *French* in the Harbour of *Brest*, he was ordered to consult with them how the Fleet might be best employed the remaining part of the Summer.

It was agreed, if the *French* disarmed not, to proceed to the Coast of *France* for the Space of fourteeen or fifteen Days, for that thereby if they had not an Opportunity of destroying some of their Shipping, yet it might very much alarm them, and occasion the weakening their Armies by keeping up their Militia, and standing Forces.

It was also determined, that upon notice of their sending any Squadrons to molest our Trade, an equal Strength should be detached to oppose them, and that when the *French* disarmed their Ships, it would be convenient to divide ours, some to bombard their Towns, and others on necessary Services: but yet that the whole should be so disposed of as that they might unite upon any emergent Occasion.

On the sixteenth a Council of War was called, upon the Receipt of Orders from the Lords of the Admiralty, touching the Fleet's lying

CHAP. XIX. *from the Year* 1688, *to* 1697. 547

ing in *Bertheaume* and *Camaret* Bays, and a Squadron's being sent with the Bomb-Veſſels to deſtroy ſome of the *French* Towns; and though it was judged that the Fleet could not ride in either of thoſe Bays out of Bomb-ſhot, yet was it reſolved to ſail, when Weather would permit, and look thereinto, and endeavour to deſtroy what Ships they might meet with there. Accordingly the Admiral turn'd it up as high as *Dartmouth*, but the Tide of Ebb being ſpent, and it blowing hard at W. S. W. he was conſtrained to repair to *Torbay*, and the next Day, being the nineteenth, the *Dutch* Admiral had Orders from his Majeſty to ſend to *Holland* eight Ships of the Line of Battel. *A Reſolution to ſail to Bertheaume and Camaret Bays.*

Eight Dutch Line of Battel-Ships ordered home.

The Weather being fair, and the Fleet ſailing the twenty fourth of *June*, with the Wind at N. N. W. they had the good Fortune to get out of the Chanel, and in *Broad Sound* one of our Ships took a *French* Privateer which came from *Breſt* fourteen Days before. The Priſoners ſaid all the great Ships were up in the River; that there were about thirty Sail in *Breſt-Water*, cleaned, and going out in two Squadrons, one under the Command of Monſieur *Chateau Renault*, and the other with Monſieur *Neſmond*; whereupon it was determined to ſail with the Fleet to *Belle* Iſle, and from thence to ſend ten Ships to protect the Bombardment of St. *Martin*'s and *Olonne*. *Advice received of the fitting out two Squadrons at Breſt for Monſieurs Chateau Renault and Neſmond.*

The fourth of *July* the Fleet anchored about two Leagues from *Belle* Iſle, ſome of our Men having been landed before at *Grouais*, where they burnt moſt part of the Villages, and killed and brought off many Cattel without any Reſiſtance, for the People had deſerted the Iſland. A little before the Fleet came to an Anchor, all the Barges and Pinnaces were ſent to *Houat*, one of the Iſlands called the *Cardinals*, where the Men landed, and brought off about three hundred Head of Cattel. Next Day the *Kent*, *Boyne*, and *Torbay*, with two *Dutch* Ships of War, and all the Long-Boats of the Admiral's Diviſion, were ſent to *Grouais*, and about ſeven hundred Soldiers and Marines landing there, they finiſhed what had been begun, by burning almoſt twenty Villages. The Boats employed againſt *Houat* were ordered on the like Service againſt *Heydic*; ſo that, upon a modeſt Computation, there were deſtroyed about twenty Veſſels, and thirteen hundred Houſes; and near ſixteen hundred Head of black Cattel and Horſes were killed. Upon the Iſland *Grouais* there were not any Fortifications, but on each of the *Cardinals* there was a Fort, with a deep Ditch and a double Wall, to which the Inhabitants, with ſome Soldiers, retired. Theſe Services being performed, the Admiral had thoughts of landing on *Belle* Iſle; but ſince there were but two hundred and forty of Colonel *Norcott*'s Men, (the reſt being gone with the Bomb-Veſſels) it was not judged adviſeable; for the Enemy had there twenty five Companies of the Regiment of *Picardy*, beſides three thouſand Iſlanders, who could carry Arms. *The Fleet anchors off of Belle Iſle, and did miſchief at Grouais and other Places.*

The reaſon why we landed not at Belle Iſle.

Thus ended theſe little Enterprizes, and a Council of War determined that the Fleet ſhould ſtay off *Belle* Iſle five Days longer, to cover the Ships at the Iſle of *Rhe*, and then proceed off of *Uſhant*, the

the said Ships, with the Bomb-Vessels, having very much damaged the Towns of St. *Martin*'s and *Olonne*; which leaving on fire, after having expended almost two thousand Bombs and Carcasses, they join'd the Fleet.

Damage done to St. Martin's and Olonne.

On the nineteenth Captain *Beaumont* met with a Ship from *Lisbon* bound to the *Downs*, whose Master informed him that four Days before he fell in with a Squadron of nine Sail, commanded by Monsieur *Nesmond*, in the Latitude of 46, about eighty Leagues from the Northward Cape; that he was on board the Commadore, and understood they had not been above four Days from *Brest*, being bound off of Cape St. *Vincent* to look for the *Spanish West-India* Ships.

Monsieur Nesmond seen at Sea by a Merchant Ship.

The Fleet being now in great want of most Species of Provisions, the Admiral judged it absolutely necessary to move Eastward, lest what they had yet remaining should spend faster than they could be supplied, but more especially if the victualling Ships expected from *Portsmouth* happen'd to be detained by Westerly Winds; and having made a hard shift to victual ten third Rates, two Fourths, and two Fireships, he put them under the Command of Vice-Admiral *Mitchell*, whom he ordered to cruise in the *Soundings* for protecting the several Trades expected home.

Vice-Admiral Mitchell ordered into the Soundings with a Squadron.

So many of the *Dutch* were withdrawn, that there remained but eleven, seven whereof were to be part of the Western Convoy; and by these Detachments the Body of the Fleet was so very inconsiderable, that when the Convoys of both Nations came to *Torbay*, Admiral *Allemonde* was forced to go with his own Ship, in Company of others particularly appointed, to secure them well into the Sea; and it was render'd yet weaker, by Sir *Cloudesly Shovell*'s being ordered by the Lords of the Admiralty with five Ships to *Spithead*; insomuch that the Admiral soon after received Orders to repair thither also, where he arrived the thirtieth, with six First Rates, as many Seconds, and four Thirds, together with four Fireships, and some small Vessels, from whence he came to Town; but before he left *Torbay* the *Portland* brought in a Sloop of the Enemy's, whose Commander gave his Lordship an Account that Monsieur *Chateau Renault* sailed from *Brest* about fifteen Days before (on what Design he knew not) with sixteen Men of War, and two Fireships, which were victualled for five Months.

The Body of the Fleet very inconsiderable by reason of Detachments.

Lord Berkeley arrives at Spithead.

Advice of Monsieur Chateau Renault's being at Sea.

And now the Service of the main Fleet in a Body being over for this Year, it remains that I give some Account of Vice-Admiral *Mitchell*'s Proceedings in the *Soundings*, who chasing on the sixteenth of *August* three Ships which stood Eastward, which he judged to be Privateers, there happened on a sudden a violent Storm of Wind and Rain which blew away every Ship's Mainsail that was set; the *Torbay*'s Fore-top-mast came by the Board, although there was not a Knot of Sail on it, and the *Restauration*, a Third Rate, was so disabled, that she was forced to go to *Spithead*, having sprung her Bowsprit, broke her Mainyard, and her Main and Mizentop-mast.

An Account of Vice-Admiral Mitchell's Proceedings in the Soundings.

The

CHAP. XX. *from the Year* 1688, *to* 1697.   549

The twenty ninth the Vice-Admiral was informed from the Lords of the Admiralty that the *East-India* Company defired the Squadron might cruife three hundred Leagues Weft from *Ireland*, between the Latitudes of 49 and 50, for the better Security of their Trade expected home; but it appearing that the Ships had not more than four Weeks Water, and not above three Weeks Butter, Cheefe, and other Neceffaries, it was not thought practicable for them to proceed fo far Weftward as the Company expected they fhould.

After this a Letter from Captain *Crow*, dated the tenth of *Auguft*, to the Lord *Berkeley*, was taken into Confideration, by which he gave an Account that our *Portugal* Fleet was daily expected home, whereupon a Council of War refolved to continue in the former Station, fixty Leagues S.W. from the *Lizard*, until the feventh of *September*, and then to rendezvous S.W.W. forty Leagues from the faid Place, until the fifteenth: And fince their Provifions would be then reduced to about ten or fifteen Days, it was determined to make the beft of their way to *Spithead*, where arriving, he, purfuant to Orders from the Lords of the Admiralty, took care forgetting the *Boyne*, *Sunderland*, *Expedition*, *Hampton-Court*, *Mary*, and *Severne*, ready to go into the *Soundings*, in Company of the *Newark*, *Chichefter*, and *Reftauration*; and having prepared the neceffary Inftructions for their fo doing, was conftrained to go on fhore for Recovery of his Health.

This Squadron Captain *George Meeze* being appointed to command, he was on the twenty ninth of *September* ordered to proceed therewith into the *Soundings*, and to cruife there and elfewhere between Cape *Clear* and Cape *Finifterre*, for Security of the Trade; and accordingly he continued in that Station as long as his Provifions would laft, and then returned to *Spithead* with three *French* Privateers, one of 38 Guns, another of 36, and the third of 14. *Capt. George Meeze appointed to command a Squadron, and fent into the Soundings.*

In his Cruife he met with a Veffel from *Newfoundland*, whofe Mafter informed him that eight Privateers, one of which had 50 Guns, three of 40 each, and another 36, the others fmaller, together with two Firefhips, came on that Coaft the beginning of *September*, and deftroyed the Plantations of *Ferryland*, *Agna Fort*, *Fermooze*, *Renooze*, *Loude's Cove*, *Breakhurft*, and the Bay of *Bulls*; in which Bay our own People burnt the *Sapphire*, a Fifth Rate, to prevent her falling into the Enemy's Hands. *Intelligence of the Mifchief the French had done us at Newfoundland.*

CHAP. XX.

Rear-Admiral Benbow's *Proceedings with a Squadron of Ships appointed to cruife againft thofe of* Dunkirk.

THE Beginning of *May* Rear-Admiral *Benbow* was ordered to command the Squadron which lay off of *Dunkirk*, to prevent Monfieur *Du Bart*'s getting thence, which Ships he found lying

ing North from that Port about five Leagues. He went with his Boat within a Mile of the Enemy's Ships in *Flemish* Road, which were nine, all ready to sail, and since the Wind was then out of the Western Quarter, with fair Weather, and that the Tides were coming on, he expected them out of the North *Chanel*; wherefore having not Ships sufficient to cover both, he spread those he had, *English* and *Dutch*, before that Passage, and it being hazey next Day, he sent a Ship into the West *Chanel*, where there was not any thing to be seen; and next Morning a Boat which was ordered close in with the Shore, brought an Account that there was not any Ships in *Flemish* Road; so that he found Monsieur *Du Bart* had given him the Slip out of the East *Chanel*.

The French Ships get cut from Dunkirk.

On the twentieth the Rear-Apmiral spoke with the Master of a Vessel from *Norway*, who had seen *du Bart*, on the West End of the *Doggar Bank*, with eleven Sail, laying his Head Eastward under his Low-Sails, the Wind at N. N. E. and being of Opinion that he would cruise some time between that Place and the *Texel*, he proceeded thither; but the *Dutch* having no Orders so to do, refused to accompany him,

The Rear-Admiral proceeds to the Doggar Bank in Search of them.

The twelfth of *June* he received Advice in *Yarmouth* Roads that Monsieur *Du Bart* had met with, near the South End of the *Doggar Bank*, five *Dutch* Men of War, and about seventy Merchant Ships bound to *Holland* from the East Country, the former of which he had taken, and about thirty of the others, but set fire to four of the Frigates upon the Approach of thirteen *Dutch* Ships which gave him chase.

Du Bart takes several Dutch Men of War and Merchant Ships.

The Rear-Admiral no sooner received this Advice than he ordered the Ships bound to the East Country to anchor, and getting under Sail with his Squadron he came up with the Trade from *Hull*, under Convoy of five *Dutch* Men of War, by whom he was informed that they saw eight Sail to the South-East that very Morning, whereupon they proceeded together in Search of them; but not meeting those *French* Ships, nor any farther Account of their Proceedings, he returned again to *Yarmouth* Roads, and sailing from thence arrived at *Gottenburgh* with the East Country Trade the thirtieth of *June*, having detached necessary Convoys to the Ships bound to the several Ports. At *Gottenburgh* he was informed by the Master of a *Danish* Ship who came from the *Cow* and *Calf* in *Norway*, that he had left Monsieur *Du Bart* there with ten Sail, cleaning and watering, who had, for his greater Security, placed a considerable Number of Guns on Shore.

Rear-Admiral Benbow and some Dutch Ships of War go in quest of du Bart.
He hears at Gottenburgh that he was at the Cow and Calf.

Our Ships were not in Condition to go in Search of him, otherwise they might very probably have done Service; but since there was a Want of Provisions, and many other Necessaries, the Rear-Admiral was constrained to return to *Yarmouth* Roads, and from thence to the *Downs*, where being supplied, he repaired to *Hamburgh*, in order to his securing from thence a rich Trade, which had only two Frigates for their Convoy.

The Rear-Admiral returns to Yarmouth Roads, and then proceeds to convoy the Trade from Hamburgh.

In his Passage towards that Place he was informed the said Trade was arrived off of *Orfordness*, so that his Care for them being over, he he proceeded off of the *Broad Fourteens* to look for Monſieur *Du Bart*, where on the fifteenth Day of *September* he met with ten *Dutch* Men of War, which came from the North, bound to the *Maes*; and on the eighteenth he ſpoke with the *Ruby*, together with three *Engliſh Eaſt-India* Ships, which had come North about, being deſigned with eleven *Dutch* for the *Texel*. *The Trade being arrived he goes off of the Broad Fourteens.*

Next Day he diſcovered ten Ships W. N. W. of him, and making all the Sail he could to ſpeak with them, found by their working that they were Monſieur *Du Bart*'s Squadron, who had miſſed the faireſt Opportunity imaginable of taking thoſe fourteen *Eaſt-India* Men: Two of our Ships got within an *Engliſh* League of him, but the reſt were near three aſtern; and when Mr. *Benbow* came to ſteer the ſame Courſe they did, it plainly appeared they wrong'd him very much; ſo that loſing Sight of them, when the Night came on, and they ſhewing no Lights, he gave over the Chaſe. *He ſets Du Bart, and chaſes him.*

About this time the King having Advice that the *French* were making great Preparations at *Breſt*, in order to a Deſcent on this Kingdom, Sir *Cloudeſly Shovell* was ſent off of that Port with a conſiderable Squadron of Ships; but ſoon after it was found that this Equipment was no other than a Squadron of Ships for Monſieur *Ponty*, with which he ſailed to *Carthagena*, as will be related in its proper Place. *Apprehenſion of a Deſcent from Breſt, and Sir Cloudeſly Shovell ſent out. Proved to be Monſieur Ponty's Squadron fitting out.*

CHAP. XXI.

Rear-Admiral Nevil's *Proceedings to and in the* Weſt-Indies, *with an Account of his engaging a* French *Squadron, and of Mr.* Meeze's *taking* Petit Guavas.

I Now come to the Squadron ſent abroad under the Command of Rear-Admiral *Nevil*; who arriving at *Cadiz* the ninth of *December*, apply'd himſelf to the Governor, but could get no certain Account of the *Spaniſh* Flota, nor did he find there was any Squadron of *French* Ships cruiſing for them. On the ſixteenth of *January* Vice-Admiral *Evertſon*, with three *Dutch* Men of War, and forty five Merchant Ships of ſeveral Nations, which had been ſeparated in a Storm, as alſo the *Turky* Convoy, joined him, and as ſoon as he had diſpatched the ſaid Trade home, he put to Sea with the Squadron, in Obedience to the Commands he had received from his Majeſty. When he had reached fifty Leagues S. W. by W. from *Cadiz*, he opened other Orders from the King, and purſuant thereunto, made all the Sail he could to the Iſland of *Madera*, where he was to be joined with ſome Ships under Command of Captain *George Meeze*, who was appointed Rear-Admiral in this Expedition. He ply'd about that Iſland fifty eight Days before any Part of this additional Strength from *England* arrived, and even then no more *1696. Rear-Admiral Nevil arrives with a Squadron at Cadiz. Is joined by ſome Dutch Men of War, and the Turky Convoy. Sailing from Cadiz he opens the King's private Orders, and proceeds to Maderas. He cruiſes there a long time for Rear-Admiral Meeze.*

more joined him than the Rear-Admiral with his own Ship, the *Bristol*, and *Lightning* Fireship; the others both *English* and *Dutch*, having been separated in a Fog just as he left the Isle of *Wight*; but the Place appointed for their Rendezvous being *Barbadoes*, the Vice-Admiral put out to Sea, and stretched it away Southward, that so he might fall into the Way of a Trade Wind. Being the first of *April* about four hundred Leagues S. W. of *Madera*, he sent the *Bristol*, a good Sailor, to *Barbadoes*, with a Letter to the Governor, desiring him to dispatch a Sloop, or some proper Vessel to *Martinica*, to gain Intelligence of Monsieur *Ponty*, or any other considerable Force the *French* might have in those Parts; and arriving himself at *Barbadoes* the seventeenth, he found there all the Ships except those of the States-General, the *Gosport* and *Blaze* Fireship; and the Sloop coming to him from *Martinica* brought an Account that there were but two small Ships at that Place, judged to be Privateers. Not long after this the *Dutch* together with the *Gosport* joined him; so that after staying a few Days to take in Water, and to settle some other necessary Matters, he got up his Anchors, and bore away for *Antegoa*, the Place of Rendezvous, but kept an easy Sail, that so the *Dutch* Ships might come up with him, which had hooked some Rocks, and therefore could not readily follow.

He proceeds towards Barbadoes.

Arrives at Barbadoes.

Sails for Antegoa.

1697.
Consults with General Codrington.

The third of *May* he went on Shore to advise with Colonel Codrington, Governor and Captain-General of the *Leeward* Islands, who had Intelligence from St. *Thomas*'s, *Curaçao*, and *Providence* Island, that the *French* designed to attack St. *Domingo*, in order whereunto they had for several Months past been cutting a Path through the Woods, that so they might march by Land thither from *Petit Guavas*.

A Council of War called, and agreed to sail in search of the Spanish Flota.

The Vice-Admiral hereupon consulted all the Officers, both *English* and *Dutch*, who agreed it was proper to sail to *Punta de la Guada*, on the N. W. Side of *Porto-Rico*, for the better Security of the *Spanish* Fleet, (for that was a principal thing recommended to him by his Majesty's Instructions) where it was usual with them to stop to refresh their Men; and there it was determined to remain until farther Intelligence could be got of the Enemy, for had the Squadron gone to *Jamaica*, they could not have beat it up to Windward time enough from thence to St. *Domingo*, or any other Place on *Hispaniola*. The same Day that this Resolution was taken he sailed, and the next sent one of the Frigates to St. *Thomas*'s for a Pilot to conduct her to *Porto-Rico* for Intelligence, from whence she was to return to *Punta de la Guada*, the Place of Rendezvous; but if the Squadron did not arrive there in seven Days time, to make the best of her Way to *Jamaica*.

This Frigate joined him on the eighth of *May*, and brought with her Mr. *Price*, who commanded an *English* Merchant Ship that had been seized by the *French*, and carried to *Petit Guavas*, as also two *Spanish* Gentlemen, one of them the Lieutenant of the *Margareta Patache*, taken on the Coast of *Curaçao*, and the other Lieutenant of the *Santo Christo*, Vice-Admiral of the *Barlovento*

CHAP. XXI. *from the Year* 1688, *to* 1697.   553

vento Fleet; who all declared, that Monsieur *Ponty* sailed from *Petit Guavas* the eleventh of *March*, Old Style, with twenty six Ships, small and great. This occasioned a Council of War, where it was resolved forthwith to proceed to *Jamaica*; and being off of the East End of that Island the fifteenth of *May*, the Vice-Admiral met with a Sloop, whose Master informed him there was a flying Report of the *French* Squadron's being before *Carthagena*; wherefore he stayed no longer than was absolutely necessary to take in Water, but sailed from *Port Royal*, and attempted to go out of the *Leeward* Chanel, wherein he was prevented by the dying away of the Land-Breeze; for, contrary to the Knowledge of all Persons acquainted in those Parts, the Wind out of the Sea blew six Days and Nights together. During this time an *English* Sloop came in, which left *Porto Bello* the eighteenth of this Month, in Company of the Galleons, (which were fifteen in Number) and two Days after parted with them, steering away N. N. E. for *Jamaica*, where they intended to take in Provisions, being so much streighten'd that they had not enough to carry them to the *Havana*. The Vice-Admiral sent out two Sloops to look out for them, one off of the Keys of *Point Pedro*, and the other those of *Porto Morant*, on the East End of *Jamaica*, with Orders to let their General know that he was going to *Carthagena*, to see what could be done against the *French*, but that he would return to *Jamaica* in a short time.

He receives Intelligence of Monsieur Ponty's Squadron.

He heard a flying Report of Ponty's being at Carthagena.

Had Advice of the Galleons.

The twenty fourth taking the Advantage of a small Gale off of Shore, he got clear of the *Keys*, steering away S. E. by S. and S. S. E. for *Carthagena*, and being the twenty seventh about half Seas over, that Part of his Squadron which was to Windward made the Signal of seeing Ships standing Westward, whereupon he immediately tacked and stood after them with a prest Sail, judging them to be either *French*, or the *Spanish* Galleons. Early next Day he discovered them to be ten Ships of War, and two Flyboats, to which giving chase, the *Warwick*, a Ship of 50 Guns, coming on the Broadside of one of them, fired at her; but the *French* Ship by wronging her very much in sailing got clear. Soon after this the aforesaid Ship the *Warwick* came up with a Flyboat loaden with Powder, Cannon-Ball, Shells, and one Mortar, which Vessel she took; and by this time our Squadron had gained considerably upon the Enemy; but the Wind coming to the N. E. they got to Windward.

In his Passage to Carthagena he meets with and chases Monsieur Ponty.

In the Afternoon the *Bristol*, *Trident*, *Gosport*, and *Newcastle*, being near them, they put themselves into Order of Battel, Monsieur *Ponty* himself firing several Shot at the *Bristol*; but soon after it was judged that Monsieur *de Labbé*, who acted as Vice-Admirla, with another of their Ships had a Design to leave them, as indeed it proved; for they being shot considerably a-head, did not endeavour to close the Line. Somewhat before eight at Night there happened a Squall of Wind, when our Ships which were nearest the Enemy made a Signal that they had tacked, whereupon our whole Squadron went about, and stood Southward all Night with a stout Sail.

B b b b   The

The next Morning, being the twenty ninth of *May*, it began to blow fresh, when Monsieur *Ponty*, with five Sail more, was about six or seven Miles a-head of the Vice Admiral, not but that some of our Ships were much nearer him, and the Chase being continued with a fresh Gale, which occcasioned a great Sea, the *Bristol*, *Southampton*, and *Trident*, lost their Top-masts, and the Vice-Admiral's own Ship, as well as that where Rear-Admiral *Meeze* bore his Flag, sprang also their Fore-top masts: However they chased all Day, and in the Evening the *Rupert*, *Gosport*, *Sunderland*, *Colchester*, and a *Dutch* Ship of War, were not far from the Enemy, who, without tacking again, stood on Southward.

The Damages which our Ships received in their Masts and Sails.

Next Morning, as soon as it was light, Monsieur *Ponty* was seen with five Ships about four Miles a-head, but all ours were out of Sight of the Flag except the *Sunderland*, *Pembroke*, and *Gosport*, and even they were considerably a-stern by reason of the Loss of their Top-masts; but as the Day came on others joined, and then it was found that the *Rupert*, *Colchester*, and a *Dutch* Ship had in the Night met with the like Misfortune.

The Vice-Admiral weathered and forereached upon Monsieur *Ponty*, insomuch that he made a Signal for those Ships, which kept a better Wind than he did, to bear down to him; nay he was once so near the sternmost of them that they had like to have come to Blows. As the Day came on the Gale freshen'd, and about nine it blew hard, at which time the *Pembroke*'s Top-mast came by the board, and about ten the Vice-Admiral's Main-Sail gave Way in two Places, which he was forced to repair as it lay on the Yard.

When the *French* saw these Misfortunes (of which they had themselves no Share) they all took in their Fore-top-Sails; for being sharp Ships they could not well endure the great Sea. The Vice-Admiral quickly set his Main-Sail again, but running up with the Enemy the Clew of his Fore-Sail gave Way, the Sail itself splitting from Clew to Ear-ring, and soon after his Fore-top-Sail flew in pieces; so that before other Sails could be brought to the Yards, the *French* were shot a great Way a-head; but he made the Signal for the *Sunderland* and *Gosport* to keep Sight of them. The Main-top-mast of the first of those Ships went by the board, and as the Weather-Clew of her Fore-top-Sail failed; so the *Gosport* also sprung her Fore-Mast. Through these Misfortunes, which so unaccountably followed one after the other, the *French* Ships gained so much of ours that they could not be seen in the Night, nor was it known whether they tack'd or bore up, or which Way they stood, wherefore the Vice-Admiral kept on his Course Southward, but not any more of his Squadron were in Sight the next Morning than the *Sunderland* and *Gosport*, and they a-stern. These unlucky Accidents prevented that rich Booty's falling into our Hands which Monsieur *Ponty* had gotten together at the taking of *Carthagena*, and indeed it is somewhat strange that our Ships only should thus suffer in their Top-masts and Sails.

The supposed Occasions of so great Loss of Masts and Sails.

I know it has been alledged that the Heat in those Parts eats out all, or greatest Part of the Tar, whereby the Sails are weakened, and apt

CHAP. XXI. *from the Year* 1688, *to* 1697.

apt to split even in the very Seams; but certain it is they as often rent in the Canvas too: And if our Sails were made of as good Stuff, and work'd up as well, I can see no Reason why they should not have proved as durable as those of the *French*, who being chafed were obliged to put theirs to as great a Trial, even after they had been longer exposed to the Heat of the Country. As for the Top-masts, it is probable that the Loss of them might chiefly proceed from the not letting them down far enough to the Head of the lower Masts; or rather, the not lengthening the Heads of those low Masts, that so one might have the greater Hold of the other; a thing that hath since been rectified.

The Weather at this time was very close, and the Vice-Admiral judging himself to be about eighteen Leagues short of *Carthagena*, the appointed Rendezvous, he stood in for that Place to pick up his shatter'd straggling Squadron, and in the Evening brought to within Sight of the Land, Rear-Admiral *Meeze*, with six Ships more, then joining him, which likewise had had all their Sails blown away. *The Vice-Admiral having lost the French fleers for Carthagena.*

Next Evening he anchored before *Boca Chiga* Castle, at the Entrance of *Carthagena* Harbour, about five Miles Northward of the Town, when seeing a great Breach, he concluded the *French* had dismantled and quitted it; but that he might be better informed, he sent in a Boat with a Lieutenant and a *Spanish* Pilot in the Night, who found in the Town not above forty *Spaniards*, three or four of whom being brought to him, they gave an Account that the *French* had taken and quitted the Place, and that all the People had deserted it for fear of the Privateers, who were gleaning Monsieur *Ponty*'s Leavings. Hereupon he weighed, and coming to an Anchor before the Town, offered to assist the Inhabitants with Men, Powder, Muskets, &c. but although they began to flock into the Place, with Intention to stay as long as the Squadron continued there, yet would not the Governor advance from the two Days Journey he had made into the Country; and the People were so terrify'd by the Privateers, who, after Monsieur *Ponty* sailed, put many of them to the Torture, that they declared they would not stay a Moment longer than the Squadron did. *The Condition he found the Town in.* *The Cruelty of the Privateers after Ponty sailed.*

At length the Governor took Courage, and coming into the Town next Day, sent his Lieutenant to inform the Vice-Admiral that he had not a Grain of Powder, no small Arms, or so much as a Musket-Ball; nor was it reasonable to believe (considering how the *Spanish* Garrisons in those Parts of the World, as well as in these, are generally provided for) that he was over-stocked when the Attempt was made; but notwithstanding his present Want, he neither condescended to ask for, or to purchase any; however the Vice-Admiral let him know that he was going that Night to Sea, being apprehensive the Galleons were in Danger, but that if the Winds should hang out of the Way he would spare him what Necessaries he was able. *The Want of Powder and Ammunition at Carthagena.*

I may not here omit observing, that had he proceeded directly to *Carthagena*, instead of *Jamaica*, when, as it is said, he first received Advice from the Island of St. *Thomas* that the Enemy, after

Bbbb 2 having

Observations on Vice-Admiral Nevil's not proceeding directly to Carthagena.

having plundered that Place, were carelesly lying with their Ships in Port, it is very reasonable to believe he might have made himself Master of all the Riches they had on board them. Whether he himself inclined to make this Attempt, or, if so, he was diverted therefrom by the Majority of the Officers in the Squadron; (among whom, if I am rightly informed, there was no great Harmony) or whether Credit was given to the Intelligence, I am not able to say, it not appearing that an Affair of this Consequence was, as hath been customary, debated at a Council of War; but, however it happened, this is certain, that by the *English* and *Dutch* Ships proceeding to *Jamaica* before they went in Search of the *French* Squadron, they lost an Opportunity not only of enriching themselves, but of performing a Service which would have been very prejudicial to the Enemy.

The Vice-Admiral sails from Carthagena.

Next Day at Noon the Wind came Westerly, when the Vice-Admiral not hearing any thing from the Governor, he weighed and stood Eastward, leaving Orders for the Ships which were missing to follow him; and on the sixth discovering eight Privateers under the Shore of *Sambay*, he sent the *Colchester, Gosport, Virgin-Prize,* and *Lightning* Fireship to destroy them, which were afterwards to stand over to Cape *Tubaron*, the Place of Rendezvous, where if they found not the Squadron, they, and the other Ships missing, were ordered to repair to *Petit-Guavas*; but the Vice-Admiral being not able to fetch in with either of those Places, proceeded to *Hispaniola*, and having taken a Privateer of 24 Guns off of the Island of *Navaza*, Westward of *Hispaniola*, which the *Colchester* had given chase to, and burnt another of 12 Guns, that ran on shore near Cape *Donna Maria*, he anchored the nineteenth of *June*, in order to Water and Wood; but four or five Days before he had sent a Frigate to St. *Jago*, on the South part of *Cuba*, with a Letter to the Governor of the *Havana*, another to the General of the Galleons, which floating Magazines of Silver were certainly in great want of Provisions, otherwise they would not have ventured out of *Porto Bello*, knowing that they should be obliged to come up as high as *Carthagena* before they could stretch over and weather the Shoals: And as they did not come out above two Days before Monsieur *Ponty* left *Carthagena*, or without Knowledge of his being there; so is it not unreasonable to believe that he had Advice of their Departure from *Porto Bello*, and that he was cruising for them at the very time our Squadron met him and gave him chase.

He writes to the Governor of Havana, *and General of the Galleons.*

The hazard the Galleons were in from Ponty's *Squadron.*

The twenty second of *June* the Vice-Admiral was informed by Sir *William Beeston*, Governor of *Jamaica*, that it would be of great Service if he could destroy *Petit-Guavas*, whereupon he ordered Rear-Admiral *Meeze* thither with nine Ships of the Squadron; of whose Proceedings therein it is now proper to give the following Account. Before he arrived at *Petit-Guavas* he made a Detachment of about nine hundred Men from the Ships, two hundred and fifty whereof he put into a Sloop, one hundred on board a Fifth Rate Frigate, and the rest into the Boats; and when he came within sixteen or seventeen Leagues of the Place, he left the two Ships,

Rear-Admiral Meeze *sent with a Squadron to destroy* Petit-Guavas.

with

CHAP. XXI. *from the Year* 1688, *to* 1697. 557

with Orders to their Commanders not to appear in fight, but to get in early the next Morning; but finding he could not reach the Port himself that Night, he directed them not to come in until the next Day.

On *Monday* the twenty eighth of *June*, at half an Hour after Three in the Morning, he landed, with Colonel *Kirkby*, Captain *Lytcot*, Captain *Holmes*, Captain *Julius*, Captain *Elliot*, and Captain *Moore*, and four hundred Men, a Mile Eastward of *Petit-Guavas*, and then marched directly to the Town; the Sloop, with some of the Boats, which had on board them about one hundred of the Men, not being able to keep up with him. He thought the Place might with much more ease be taken by Surprize, with those Men he had, than by discovering himself, which he must have done by staying for the rest, and therefore entering it just at the Dawn of Day, he marched directly to, and immediately took the Grand Guard. When this was done he sent one hundred Men to secure two Batteries of four Guns each; and while the same was doing most of the *French* quitted the Town. *Our People land at Petit-Guavas, and make themselves Masters of it.*

Soon after the Sun was up the Sailers began to be so unruly that they could not be diverted from Plundering, and in an Hour or two most of them were so drunk, that notwithstanding the well-laid Design of Mr. *Meeze* towards making himself and them Masters of the Plunder, by appointing a Captain, with some trusty Men, to begin at each end of the Town, and so to have met one another, he was constrain'd to set fire thereunto much sooner than he intended, otherwise he could not have depended on fifty sober and serviceable Men; so that not any thing was carried off except a few Negroes, and other inconsiderable Matters, although it was reported, (how truly I cannot say) that two Days before four Mules were brought into the Town loaden with Gold and Silver from the Isle of *Ash*, part of what the Privateers rifled at *Carthagena*. *The Disorders of the Sailers prevent the carrying off the Plunder.*

Our Officers and Men behaved with Bravery on this Occasion, the latter having chearfully rowed many Leagues in that hot Country, and it was great pity that their Ungovernableness deprived both themselves and their Officers of what would have sufficiently made them amends for their Fatigue.

Having thus taken up a little of your time concerning *Petit-Guavas*, I will yet farther intrude on your Patience, by giving a short Account of the manner of Monsieur *Ponty*'s attacking *Carthagena*.

The thirteenth of *April* he appear'd before the Place with twenty six Ships, great and small, and bombarded it until Ten in the Morning of the fifteenth. Then he attack'd the Castle of *Boca Chiga* with three Ships, two thousand Men, and two Mortars by Land, and about Five in the Afternoon made himself Master of it. Next Day the Fleet entering the Bay, he sent two thousand four hundred Men to the Castle of *Boca Grande*, which was found deserted; and landing the seventeenth at *Terra Firma*, he attacked and dispersed two hundred and forty *Mulatto*'s, who defended themselves very well: After which they marched to a Hill called *De la Poupe*, *The manner of Monsieur Ponty's attacking Carthagena. 1697.*

Poupe, and there planted their Colours. On the eighteenth they attack'd the Fort called St. *Lazar*'s, at the Foot of the said Hill, and after four vigorous Assaults the Defendants retired to the Town. The twentieth, twenty first, and twenty second, they batter'd the Suburb called *Gigimani*, by the Half-Moon at the Island-Gate, but on the twenty third and twenty fourth they ceased firing, the Men being employ'd in mounting five Mortars and twenty four great Guns, with which they batter'd the Fortifications the twenty fifth, twenty sixth, twenty seventh, and twenty eighth; and having opened a great Breach, they took in the Suburb the twenty ninth, after a handsome Defence; immediately after which they batter'd the Walls of the Town not only with the Guns from the Ships and on the Shore, but with Mortars also; whereupon the Alderman (the Civil Magistrate of the Place) finding the City so briskly attack'd, proposed its being delivered up, but the Governor refused, and began to make inward Works to resist the Assaults: Nevertheless coming soon after to a Parly, he was prevailed upon, and Monsieur *Ponty*, with Monsieur *Du Casse* concluded the Capitulations; which were, "That the Governor should march out on " Horseback, with two Field-Pieces, the Garrison with their Arms, " and the Men, Women, and Children with all the Cloaths they " could carry.

The twenty third of *May* the *French* took Possession of the City, and so civil were they to the Inhabitants, that they executed a Soldier for attempting to take a Ring from a *Mulatto* Woman. What Riches they met with is variously reported, but I am apt to think it fell short of the Ten Millions which it was said they carried away.

I return now to Vice-Admiral *Nevil*, who having wooded and watered the Ships, he got under sail the twenty ninth of *June* to meet Rear-Admiral *Meeze*, by whom being joined the next Day, he sailed for *Jamaica*, that so he might get the Ships from thence, and proceed directly for the *Havana* in Search of the Galleons, of which he had not yet any certain Account.

The eleventh of *July* he made the Isle of *Pines*, the thirteenth came up with St. *Anthony*'s, the West End of *Cuba*, and the sixteenth he got about a Range of Rocks called the *Colleradoes*; but the Men were at this time very sickly, and next Day Rear-Admiral *Meeze* died.

Rear-Admiral Meeze dies.

The Vice-Admiral comes to the Havana, and is denied Water and Refreshments by the Spaniards.

The Squadron arriving at the *Havana* the twenty second of *July*, the Vice-Admiral acquainted the Governor that he was in great want of Water and Refreshments, and therefore desired leave to come into the Port, that so he might make Provision for his Voyage to *Cadiz*, to which Place he designed (according to his Instructions) to see the Galleons in Safety. This he was not only refused, but almost every thing he requested, the Don alledging, that the King his Master's Instructions would not justify his permitting the Squadron to come into that Port, but that if he would repair to *Mutanses*, (a Place where there was not Depth of Water for his Ships) he would endeavour to supply his wants; not but that he

doubted

CHAP. XXII. *from the Year* 1688, *to* 1697.   559

doubted his Capacity of doing it effectually, since the Galleons had already dreined the Place of Provisions.

The Vice Admiral writ also to the General of the Galleons, letting him know that the Squadron he commanded was sent chiefly to secure those rich Imbarcations, and to conduct them safe to *Cadiz*; but he was pleased to answer, that he had received no Orders of that Nature from the King of *Spain*, and was therefore obliged to follow those he had, being sorry he could not have the Opportunity of accompanying him. *The Vice-Admiral acquaints the General of the Galleons that he had Orders to convoy them home. His Answer.*

It cannot be thought but that this Treatment was very surprising; nor, possibly, should I be much in the wrong in judging, that the natural Jealousy of the *Spaniards* gave them Apprehensions that our Ships would endeavour not only to make themselves Masters of the Place, but of the Galleons too. In fine, the Vice-Admiral finding that not any thing could be had there, he put the Ships into the best Condition that possibly he could, and sailed for *Virginia*, where he died the twenty seventh of *August*, occasion'd, as I am apt to believe, by Grief for the Misfortunes he had met with. By the Death of him, and the Rear-Admiral, the Command of the Squadron devolved on Captain *Thomas Dilkes*, who having done all that possibly he could towards refreshing the Men, and procuring Provisions, sailed from *Virginia*, and arrived in *England* the twenty fourth of *October* with part of the Squadron, the rest, which were separated in bad Weather, dropping in both before and after. *The Squadron sails for Virginia, and the Vice-Admiral dies. Captain Dilkes proceeds home with the Ships.*

CHAP. XXII.

An Account of Monsieur Ponty's *coming with a* French *Squadron to* Newfoundland *while Sir* John Norris *was with a Squadron of* English *Ships there.*

MOnsieur *Ponty* having narrowly escaped the Squadron with Vice-Admiral *Nevil*, got not to *Brest* without running the hazard of being twice more intercepted, first at *Newfoundland* by Captain *Norris*, and afterwards in the *Soundings*, by a Squadron commanded by Captain *Thomas Harlow*, with which he engaged; for coming to *Newfoundland* (the first Country he touched at after he left the *West-Indies*) Captain *Norris*, who commanded a Squadron of Ships there, had Intelligence that several *French* Men of War were seen off of *Cape-Land* Bay; which was confirmed the next Day by some fishing People; and the firing of Guns was heard both by Day and Night. But it being believed by some that this was Monsieur *Nesmond*'s Squadron, or part thereof, two Booms were laid cross the Harbour of St. *John*'s, and the Squadron put into the best Order of Defence that might be, which was composed of four Fourth Rates, two Fifth, two Sixth, two Fireships, and two Bomb- *Ponty's Ships thought to be Monsieur Nesmond's Squadron, we provide for the Safety of St. John's.*

Bomb-Veſſels, with a Hag-Boat. Colonel *Gibſon*'s Regiment, which were carried by the Squadron from *England*, embarked on board the Ships, ſeveral Guns were mounted on the Batteries aſhore, and five Ships were ſeen the twenty third, about four Leagues into the Sea, which in the Evening ſtood in for *Conception* Bay.

A Council of War agree to continue at St John's. A Council of War was called next Day of the Sea and Land Officers, by whom it was agreed to continue in the Harbour of St. *John*'s, and the *Mary* Gally being clean, ſhe was ſent out to diſ-

The French *ſeen off Carboniere; but reſolved ſtill to continue at St.* John's, *tho' Captain* Norris *was of a contrary Opinion.* cover the Enemy. About Noon Advice was received from *Carboniere* that five *French* Men of War were ſeen off of that Port, and another Conſultation being thereupon held, the Majority were ſtill for continuing at St. *John*'s; but Captain *Norris* gave his Opinion for going in ſearch of them, judging that if thoſe five Ships in *Conception* Bay had any Communication with others at Sea, it would have been diſcovered from Cape St. *Francis*, or *Baccalao*, if within fifteen Leagues one of the other; and that if they had any Deſign to attack St. *John*'s by Land, he muſt have had notice of their Forces being put on ſhore.

Mr. Cumberbatch *gives an Account of the* French *Squadron.* Next Day he received a Letter from Mr. *Alexander Cumberbatch*, Maſter of a Ship taken by the *French*, and ſent on ſhore to aſſiſt in getting them freſh Proviſions, by which he was informed that Monſieur *Ponty* was in *Conception* Bay, with five Ships from 50 to 60 Guns, very richly loaden with the Spoil of *Carthagena*. This Notice he ſent him in hopes it might be ſerviceable to his Country, and adviſed him, withal, to be very expeditious in attacking them, for that they were but weakly manned.

A Council of War ſuſpects Cumberbatch, *and again determine to remain at St.* John's. A general Council of War being hereupon held, it was voted that they had reaſon to believe Monſieur *Nesmond* was come to *Newfoundland* with a Squadron, and that *Cumberbatch* was ſent on ſhore by him to enſnare them, becauſe he ſaid in his Letter he was to return to the *French* Ships; ſo that it was again determined to continue at St. *John*'s, for that by attacking the Ships in *Conception* Bay, Monſieur *Nesmond* might thereby have had an Opportunity of making himſelf Maſter not only of St. *John*'s, but conſequently of the whole Country; yet the Commadore, Captain *Norris*, was ſtill for going to Sea, for his former Reaſons.

The twenty ſixth at Noon there was Intelligence that the aforeſaid five *French* Ships were ſeen the Night before at Anchor a little Eaſtward of *Belle* Iſle, by *Portugal* Cove; and the next Day, up-*Intelligence of the* French *Squadron, by Officers ſent on purpoſe.* on a Meſſage from Colonel *Gibſon*, another Conſultation was held, when this Intelligence was read; but it was again reſolved to remain at St. *John*'s until the two Captains arrived who were ſent to make Diſcoveries. Soon after one of them came with twenty *French* Men, taken in a Boat at *Carboniere*, who ſaid they were ſent by Monſieur *Ponty* to procure freſh Proviſions. The other Captain return'd alſo from *Portugal* Cove, who had ſeen the *French* Ships at Anchor, one of them of three Decks, two from 60 to 70 Guns, and two more of about 50. The Court adjourn'd until next Morning, when they called the Priſoners before them, who related all they knew, fearing that otherwiſe they ſhould be very ill treated.

CHAP. XXII. *from the Year* 1688, *to* 1697.   561

ed. They said the Squadron had not been at any other Port since *Account of* they left the *West-Indies*, and that Monsieur *Ponty* hearing of Vice- *the Squadron* Admiral *Nevil*'s being in those Parts, appointed the Rendezvous at *taken.* St. *Peter*'s, or *Placentia*, in *Newfoundland*; but not making the Island about *Placentia* plain, by reason of thick Weather, the first Place he drop'd Anchor at was *Conception* Bay. While the Council *Captain Des-* of War was sitting Captain *Desborow* arrived, and gave them an *borow's Ac-* Account that the *French* Ships lay under their Top-sails, plying up *count.* and down in the Bay, but that he being about five Miles off from them, could not well discover their Force. Notwithstanding all this, the Majority of the Council of War were still of Opinion that Mon- *A Council of* sieur *Nesmond* (who had sailed from *France* a considerable time be- *War believe* fore with eleven Ships of War and three Fireships) was on the Coast, *mond on the* and therefore, contrary to the Opinion of Captain *Norris*, deter- *Coast, and* mined not to attempt the *French*, for that, as they judged, the *solve not to* Port of St. *John*'s might thereby be exposed to imminent Danger by *stir.* separating the Ships and the Forces: And had not the Land-Officers been there, or at least not been empowered to sit at Councils of War, it is probable there might have been a better Account given of the Enemy; for several of them were unwilling to leave St. *John*'s, a Place which was particularly recommended to them to protect.

Captain *Desborow* was again sent out to observe the Enemy's *Captain Des-* Motion, with Orders to bring early Advice thereof, who returning *borow is a-* the thirty first at Noon, gave an Account that the twenty eighth at *and brings* Midnight he saw four Sail under his Lee-Bow, which he made to *Intelligence.* be *French*; that soon after the sternmost Ship fired a Gun, and then making several false Fires, the Lights were instantly put out, so that he lost sight of them. That at Two in the Morning he stood Northward, with little Wind at N. N. E. and not seeing any Ships when the Day appeared, made the best of his way to *Carboniere*; but the Wind veering at Noon to S. S. W. the Current had set him by the twenty ninth at Night between *Harbour Grace* Island and that Bay.

As soon as he had declared what he had thus discovered, he was sent out a third time, with Orders to sail right into the Sea until he came on the Bank of *Newfoundland*, and if he saw not the aforesaid Ships, or any other Squadron, to repair to Cape *Race*, and endeavour to gain Intelligence from *Placentia*. The ninth of *August* in the Morning he returned, and related, That about Twelve at Night, on the Saturday before, he saw several Lights to Windward; that at two a Clock four of the Ships he discovered fired three Guns each, and then tack'd and stood from the Shore, which induced him to make sail and keep his Wind, in order to get under Cape *Race*, but that as soon as it was light he stood within three times Gunshot of the headmost, and then laid by and looked on the Enemy's Ships, which he judged to be sixteen, the Admiral of them with three Decks, four of about 80 Guns, six from 70 to 60, two of 50, and the other three either Frigates or Fireships. When he had thus view'd them well, he wore his Ship, and brought to towards the Shore, but they tacking at six a Clock, and standing off, and per-
Cccc   ceiving

ceiving that he followed them, one of them stood in towards the Shore to cut him off from the Cape.

A Squadron of sixteen Ships appear off St. John's with three Swallow tail'd Flags.

The eighteenth in the Morning this Squadron came off the Harbour of St. *John's*, which was about thirty two Days after the first Notice of Monsieur *Ponty*'s being at *Newfoundland*. They were in all sixteen, with three Swallow-tail'd Flags, ten of them from 50 to 70 Guns, the others either Fireships or small Frigates, as Captain *Desborow* had reported, and having viewed our Ships, they stood off again; but at Noon approaching the Harbour, the Wind took them short, so that they laid their Heads off and brought to; from which time they were not seen until the twenty third, nor came they after that near the Port.

The Method taken to defend our Ships and the Harbour.

The Method taken to defend the Ships and Harbour was this; All the Men of War lay in the Shape of a Half Moon to the Harbour's Mouth, and the Broadside of each commanded the two Booms. Colonel *Gibson*'s Regiment was posted at the two Batteries, and other proper Places, while Captain *Richards* (who was the Engineer for fortifying the Harbour) threw up such Works as he judged necessary on this Occasion; and that the Squadron might be the better able to do Service, all the Men were taken from the Merchant Ships, and put on board them.

Chap. XXIII.

An Account of an Engagement in the Soundings *between a Squadron of* English *Ships, and that commanded by Monsieur* Ponty.

HAVING already informed you in what manner Monsieur *Ponty*, with his rich Squadron, escaped Vice-Admiral *Nevil* in the *West-Indies*, and Captain *Norris* at *Newfoundland*, it remains that I follow him to *Brest*, for before he reached that Port he fell in with the Ships commanded by Captain *Harlow* in the *Soundings*, as hath been lately mentioned.

Captain Harlow meets with Monsieur Ponty in the Soundings. 1697.

The fourteenth of *August* the said Captain *Harlow* being with a Squadron of five Ships and a Fireship, *viz.* two of 80 Guns, two of 70, and one of 30, about ninety Leagues W. S. W. from *Scilly*, one of them the *Defiance*, made the Signal of seeing Lights to Windward, and as the Day came on five Sail were plainly discover'd. They bore down on him about Eight in the Morning, and he plying up to them, endeavour'd to get into a Line of Battel.

Monsieur *Ponty* having viewed our Squadron, thought it convenient to make some Alterations in his Line, but nevertheless he bore down with all the Sail he could, and brought to about Two in the Afternoon out of Gun-shot. He continued not long in that Posture, but edged nearer, and worked his Ships so as if he intended

to

to press the Van of our Squadron, upon which Captain *Harlow* sent to the *Devonshire* to fill her Sails, and stand away upon a Wind, that so she might the better fall in with Monsieur *Ponty*'s Ship, who about Three in the Afternoon brought to directly against her within two thirds Gun-shot, and began the Fight.

After the Squadrons had been engaged about two Hours, the *French* Commadore made the Signal for Tacking, but as there was little Wind, not any of the Ships would stay, unless it was that which was opposite to the *Defiance*; and the Head of her Main-top-mast being disabled, which occasioned the Yard's falling down on the Slings, she wore not without great difficulty, when, keeping her Wind, she stood out of the Line, which put Monsieur *Ponty* himself in some Disorder; but although he was constrain'd to bear up for her, he soon closed the Line again. *They engage.*

About Six in the Evening the Gale freshened, and shifted from W. by S. to S.W. by S. and S. S.W. whereupon the Enemy tacking, our Commadore made the Signal for his Rear to do the same; and setting his Main sail, that he might be sure of staying, he was no sooner about than he spread all the Canvas he could after them, as they did from him. In the Night he lost sight of them, not but that he discovered some of their Lights between eight and nine a Clock, and by that means had an Opportunity of steering after them, they bearing then N. E. and N. E. by N. After Ten those Lights being no more seen, he stood away between the N. E. and E. with an easy Sail, that so some of the Ships which were very much astern might come up with him. *The French retire.*

Next Morning, between Four and Five, the Weather being very clear, the Enemy were seen between the S. E. by E. and E. S. E. at the distance of about three or four Leagues, and the Wind being then variable between the S. and S.W. but a gentle Gale, all Sails were set, and the Chase continued until it was Evening, when they were near the same distance as in the Morning; but so much did they wrong our Ships in sailing, that they could, at pleasure, lower a Yard or a Topmast, to prevent their coming by the Board; and this was occasioned by ours being fouler than theirs, even though they came from so remote Parts; for it is not to be doubted but they made a shift to heel and scrub them in the best manner they could when abroad. *The French wronged us very much in sailing.*

Early next Morning they had shot ahead about four or five Miles, and no sooner were our Ships discovered by them than they let out the Reefs of their great Sails, and set all their small ones; so that although when they first made from us, the Hulls of them could be seen down to the Water-Line, yet in six Hours time they ran so much out of sight that not above half their Top-sails could be discovered.

About eleven a Clock it blew fresh, and the Weather inclined to be thick and hazey, so that Captain *Harlow* seeing no Possibility of coming up with them, he brought to; and thus Monsieur *Ponty* had the good Fortune to escape the third time, who without farther Interruption, carried the Spoil of the *Spaniards* into *Brest*. What it

Observations about Monsieur Ponty his engaging our Squadron. it was that induced him to bear down and engage our Ships, is uncertain; for although the Strength of his Squadron, and ours, was almost equal, yet considering the Riches he had on board, I think he should in Prudence have declined a Battel, which doubtless he might have done, since (as it proved) his Ships had much the better Heels.

CHAP. XXIV.

Sir George Rooke, *Admiral of the Fleet, his Proceedings to and fro in the* Soundings; *with those of Vice-Admiral* Mitchell *in the same Place.*

1697.

LET us now return to the Body of the Fleet in the Year 1697, of which Sir *George Rooke* being appointed Admiral, he with the great Ships arrived off of the *South-Foreland* the second of *June*, and intended to stop Tides from thence to *Spithead*, and being the next Day at an Anchor off of *Dover*, a strong South-West Wind obliged him to return to the *Downs*.

Sir George Rooke arrives with the Fleet at St. Helen's.

Setting Sail again he arrived at St. *Helen*'s the tenth in the Evening, where he met Rear-Admiral *Nassau*, with ten *Dutch* Ships of War, which were first to convoy several Merchants to *Holland*, and then to return and join the Fleet.

A Council of War resolve to proceed to Sea, with as many Ships as could be manned and victualled.

The fourteenth a Council of War was called, where were besides the Admiral himself present, Sir *Cloudesly Shovell*, Admiral of the Blue, Vice-Admiral *Aylmer*, and Vice-Admiral *Mitchell*, and it was agreed that since there was a great Want of Men and Provisions, and but little Prospect of a sudden Supply, so many Ships should be sent to Sea as could be manned up to their middle Complements, while those from which the Men were taken, secured themselves in *Portsmouth* Harbour; and the next Day, at another Consultation, where were also present the *Dutch* Admiral, Vice-Admiral *Callemberg*, Rear-Admiral *Meuys*, and Mr. *Bokenham*, first Captain to the Admiral, it was resolved to proceed off of *Ushant* for Intelligence, and then to govern themselves as a Council of War should think most adviseable.

A great want of small Frigates.

There was a great Want of small Frigates, and other proper Vessels to prevent the Enemy's Snaws discovering the Weakness of our Squadron; for although the intended Fleet, when all together, would have made up forty seven *English*, and twenty three *Dutch* of the Line of Battel, besides seventeen Fireships, and other small Craft, yet were there at this time forty three of those seventy Ships absent on the following Services, *viz.*

Rates

CHAP XXIV. *from the Year* 1688, *to* 1697.

	Rates				Ships absent from the Fleet on other Services.
	1st	2d	3d	4th	
With Vice-Admiral *Mitchell* in the *Soundings*.	1	0	8	0	
With Captain *Beaumont* in the *North Sea*.	0	0	4	0	
With Rear-Admiral *Benbow* in the *Soundings*.	0	0	1	1	
Off of Cape *de la Hague*,	0	0	1	0	
Convoy between the *Downs* and *Falmouth*.	0	0	1	0	
At *Woolwich*.	0	0	0	1	
At *Hudson*'s Bay.	0	0	0	1	
On the Fishery.	0	0	0	1	
At *Hull*.	0	0	1	0	
Between the Isle of *Wight* and *Portland*.	0	0	0	1	
At the *Nore*.	0	0	1	0	
Unmanned at *Blackstakes*.	0	3	0	0	
Unmanned at *Portsmouth*.	0	3	3	0	
With Rear-Admiral *Nassau* on the Coast of *Holland*.	0	8	1	0	
Expected from *North-Holland*.	0	1	1	0	
In all, *Dutch* and *English*	1	15	22	5	

So that had not Rear-Admiral *Nassau* joined with the ten *Dutch* Ships before mentioned, there could not have gone to Sea more than thirty five, great and small; nor was the Fleet at this time victualled with more than a Month's Bread and Beer, a very little more Butter and Cheese, somewhat above two Month's Flesh, but not a Fortnight's Pease and Oatmeal. However, Orders were sent for the Ships which were ready to proceed to Sea, they being but thirty three, *Dutch* and *English*, and eight Fireships, besides the Ships in the *Soundings* with Vice-Admiral *Mitchell* and Rear-Admiral *Benbow*, which join'd the Fleet the twenty fifth of *June* off of *Plimouth*; so that now the Admiral had forty four Ships of the Line, and with them he got off of *Ushant* the twenty eighth, but for want of Wind he was prevented in laying hold of that Coast until the fourth of the next Month, at which time Rear-Admiral *Benbow*, who had been sent to discover the Posture of the Enemy at *Brest*, brought an Account that there were in that Port but ten Ships armed and ready for the Sea.

Rear-Admiral Nassau joined the Fleet.

Vice-Admiral Mitchell, and Rear-Admiral Benbow also come in to the Soundings.

But ten Ships at Brest ready for the Sea.

A Council of War being thereupon called, it was resolved to enlarge the former Station from ten to forty or fifty Leagues W. N. W. from *Ushant*, thereby to cover the Chanel, and secure the Trade; that nine *English*, and four *Dutch* Ships of War should cruise from eighty to a hundred Leagues West from *Scilly* fourteen or sixteen Days, and that after the Fleet had continued in the aforesaid Station near a Fortnight, the whole should rendezvous in *Torbay*. Vice-Admiral *Mitchell* commanded this Squadron, and it was made thus strong, lest he should happen to meet with Monsieur *Nesmond* in his Cruize, or Monsieur *Chateau Renault* in his Return to *Brest*, in case he was then at Sea.

The Station resolved on at a Council of War.

Vice-Admiral Mitchell detached with a Squadron.

The twenty first of *July* the Fleet was ten Leagues off of the *Lizard*, having not met with any thing in their Cruise but Privateers, and
there

The Fleet returns to Torbay.

there the Admiral received Orders to leave a sufficient Squadron off of *Brest* to keep in the *French* Ships designed from thence with Monsieur *Chateau Renault*, if not already sailed, or to intercept them should they attempt to come out; but this could not be complied with, because he had not together above eleven *English* Men of War, of which ten were Three-Deck Ships, and but ten *Dutch*, Flag-ships included; nor had they more than twenty one Days Provisions at short Allowance, and not any Pease or Oatmeal; so that the Admiral was obliged to return to *Torbay*, where, on the twenty third of *July*, he received a second Order to send Ships off of *Brest*, and others into the Bay; to comply with which he ordered eleven Third Rates and two Fireships to be victualled for a Month, but was constrained to draw the same from the great Ships; insomuch that had there been never so pressing an Occasion for Service, it would have inevitably have been prevented for Want of a timely Supply of Provisions.

Vice-Admiral Mitchell returns to Torbay.

Two Days after Vice-Admiral *Mitchell* was seen working into the Bay, having sent from his Squadron two Third Rates and a Fifth to convoy the Trade to *Ireland*, and the *Dorsetshire* and *Content* to see some others safe to *Plimouth*: And he being informed that a considerable Fleet of Merchant Ships were expected in the Chanel, sent four Third Rates, one Fifth, and a Fireship, under Command of Captain *Harlow* to cruise for their Security; who, during his Cruise, met with Monsieur *Ponty* in his Passage to *Brest*, of the Engagement between whom I have already given an Account, chusing so to do that the whole Proceeding of that *French* Squadron, in their Expedition to and from *Carthagena*, might be related without interfering with other Matters.

The Admiral found that by drawing Provisions, as aforesaid, from the great Ships for those designed off of *Brest*, it would so much reduce them, as that, without a speedy Supply, they might be brought to great Necessity, wherefore he contradicted the Orders he had given therein, and proposed to the Lords of the Admiralty, that the Ships might repair to, and victual at *Spithead*.

The Fleet comes to Spithead.

Nevertheless a Squadron was sent out, which cruised for some time in the *Soundings*, but were by bad Weather forced in; and, pursuant to Orders sent to the Admiral, he arrived at *Spithead* the twenty eighth of *August*, with five First Rates, four Seconds, two Thirds, two Fireships, two Hospital Ships, and two Yachts, together with twelve *Dutch* Ships of War, and as many Fireships.

Vice-Admiral Mitchell ordered with a Squadron as far as Cape St. Vincent to look out for Vice-Admiral Nevil. 1697.

Vice-Admiral *Mitchell* was again appointed to command a Squadron of eight Third Rates, six Fourths, and three Fifths, together with Count *Nassau*, who had under his Command six *Dutch* Ships of War and two Fireships, and received Orders in *Torbay* the ninth of *September* (the very Day he arrived there) to proceed with the said Squadron to Cape *St. Vincent*, on the Coast of *Portugal*, there being Advice that the *French* were gone or going to Sea. The Design of his being ordered thus far was to sustain Vice-Admiral *Nevil*, in case the Galleons should have come under his Protection, (for as yet there was not any Account received of his Squadron)

as

Chap. XXIV. *from the Year* 1688, *to* 1697. 567

as well as the Trade from *Cadiz*, and therefore he was directed, when he arrived off of that Cape, to send a Frigate to the said Port, with Orders to the Commander in Chief of the Ships there to put to Sea within three Days after his Receipt thereof, and join him; and when he should be so joined he was to make the best of his Way to *England*; but if he met with the *Cadiz* Fleet in his Passage, he was to return home with them, which he was to do without them, if he received Advice by the detached Frigate that they were sailed from *Cadiz*, and that he judged they were passed by him. But if, during his Stay off Cape *St. Vincent*, he met with Vice-Admiral *Nevil*, in his Passage from the *West-Indies* with the Galleons, he was to accompany them as far as *Cadiz*. A farther Provision was yet made, that if he met with the Galleons, while the *Cadiz* Squadron was in Company with him, he should so dispose of the Ships under his Command as might most contribute to the Security of both; but he was himself to return to *England* with the Trade.

These Orders the Vice-Admiral communicated to Rear-Admiral *Nassau*, who having not any at that time from the King, and being not victualled longer than to the last of the following Month, he could not proceed; nor had the *English* Ships more than for two Months, if all Species proved good; and indeed the Scarcity of Provisions did too often, throughout the whole Course of the War, obstruct many Services. But as I shall not take upon me to blame any particular Person, or Body of Men on this Account, yet sure I am, that unless effectual Care be hereafter taken, in time of Action, to have a sufficient Stock in a constant Readiness to answer all unforeseen Services, *England* will too soon find the great Inconveniences that will attend it. *The Squadron in great Want of Provisions especially the Dutch.*

This Scarcity of Provisions being represented to the Lords of the Admiralty, their Lordships sent him Orders to proceed with the *English* and *Dutch* Ships, so far towards Cape *St. Vincent*, in order to meet the Trade from *Cadiz*, as that he might have left sufficient to bring him back again; upon which it was agreed by himself and the *Dutch* Flag-Officer, (who had now supplied his Ships with some Provisions) to sail one hundred Leagues S. W. from *Scilly*, provided he could reach that Station by the first of *October*, for no longer would the Victuals on board the *Dutch* permit them to stay abroad: But if Westerly Winds prevented their doing the same by or before that time, it was thought most adviseable to proceed fifty Leagues S. W. from *Scilly*, there to continue until the eighth of *October*, otherwise to repair twenty eight Leagues W. S. W. from thence, and after lying in that Station until the fifteenth of *October*, to come to *Spithead*. *The Vice-Admiral is ordered to proceed so far towards Cape St. Vincent as to have Provisions to bring him back again. His own and the Dutch Flag's Resolution thereupon.*

The seventeenth the Vice-Admiral received Advice from the Captain of the *Shrewsbury* Gally, that Mr. *Nevil* had been at, and was returned from the *Havana*, without the Galleons, or being permitted by the *Spanish* Governor so much as to water his Ships there; but having already given a particular Account of that whole Matter, I proceed to inform you, that notwithstanding the aforesaid Orders *He receives Advice of Vice-Admiral Nevil.*

He is ordered to stay at Sea but twenty Days.

Orders from the Lords of the Admiralty to Vice-Admiral *Mitchell*, others were sent to him the eighteenth Day of the same Month of *August*, to remain no longer at Sea than twenty Days, in Expectation of the *Cadiz* Fleet, whereupon it was agreed between him and the *Dutch* Flag that the Squadron should proceed forty Leagues W. by S. from *Scilly*, and cruise there till the eighth of *October*.

Is obliged to come to Torbay, but ordered to Sea again.

The twenty fourth of *September* he sailed from *Torbay* with fair Weather, and the Wind at N. W. by N. but being off of the Start about ten at Night, it shifted to the S. and S. S. W. and blew very hard, with much Rain. He was at this time near the Shore, and consequently met with great Difficulty in getting into *Torbay*, most of the Ships having received considerable Damage in their Sails. The next Day after his coming to an Anchor he received Orders to remain there, but the ninth of *October* other Directions were sent him, by an Express, to proceed to Sea, either with or without the States-Generals Ships, for protecting the *Cadiz* Fleet, and to continue out as long as his Provisions would last, which it would not do above twenty eight Days, at two thirds of the usual Allowance; and these last Orders were sent him upon Intelligence that Monsieur *Chateau Renault* was at Sea with a Squadron, and that divers Privateers were lurking up and down the Chanel to pick up our Trade.

Vice-Admiral Mitchell proceeds into the Soundings.

The tenth of *October* the Squadron got under Sail, and the fifteenth at Night, about twenty five Leagues N. E. by E. from *Scilly*, the Vice-Admiral parted with the Ship *Captain*, a *Dutch East-India* Ship called the *Nassau*, and some small Vessels bound Southward. He continued cruising from twenty five to forty Leagues S. W. by W. from *Scilly* until the twenty third, but had not the good Fortune to meet with the *Cadiz* Fleet; so that then his Provisions growing short, he thought it necessary to repair to St. *Helen*'s, where he anchored the twenty seventh at Night, and there luckily met him at Sea, and came in Company with him thither, fifteen *Dutch East-India* Ships, which had spent almost all their Provisions, and lost most of their Anchors and Cables off of the Cape of *Good Hope*.

The Czar of Muscovy comes to England.

Soon after this the Vice-Admiral attended the Czar of *Muscovy* from *Holland* with a Squadron, and, by his Majesty's particular Command, he not only accompanied that Prince during the time he continued in this Kingdom, but afterwards carried him back to *Holland*.

CHAP.

CHAP. XXV.

Rear-Admiral Benbow's *Proceedings in the* Soundings, *and before* Dunkirk, *being the last Expedition of the War; with Observations on the whole, and a Comparison of the Losses* England *and* France *sustained in their Naval Force during this War.*

REar-Admiral *Benbow* sailing from *Spithead* the tenth of *April* with seven Third Rates and two Fireships, he cruised twenty seven Days between the Latitudes of 50^d and 48^d, 30^m, from ten to eighty Leagues from *Scilly*, but met not with any thing of Note until the third of *May*, when he gave chase to five *French* Men of War, but found himself not able to come up with them. Next Day he was joined by three Third Rates, one Fourth, and one Fifth, but not any thing remarkable happened until the ninth, and then he saw nine Ships Westward of him, one whereof separated from the others, to which he gave chase, the rest made *English* Signals, and some of them proved to be our Men of War bound with the Trade to the *West-Indies*, which, under the Command of Captain *Symonds* had been engaged with four of the *French* King's Ships in the manner following. He being on the fifth of *May* 1697, with the *Norwich, Chatham, Sheerness, Seaford,* and a Fireship, in the Latitude of 49^d and 13^m about forty eight Leagues from *Scilly*, met with the said *French* Ships about four in the Morning, with *English* Colours, the biggest of them mounting between 60 and 70 Guns, another of 50, the third 36, and the fourth about 24. They bore right down upon him, whereupon he fired a Gun for the *Seaford*, the Fireship, and his Convoys which were to Windward, to join him, and at seven the *French* Ships taking in their *English* Colours began to fire, the Fireship by reason of her ill sailing, was soon taken by the two smaller Frigates and their Boats, while the two bigger took the *Seaford*, after they had first shot down her Main-Yard, and then her Main-mast; but finding she was not able to swim, they burnt her. The Fight continued very smartly for two Hours, and then the *French* gave over, but followed our Ships until the eighth, though not within Gun-shot. That Morning they bore down again, and engaged about three Hours, when leaving off they chased the Merchant Ships, which at the Beginning of the Engagement were taking the usual Care for their own Security, and in this Action our Frigates were so much disabled that they were forced to bear up for *Plimouth* to refit.

An Engagement between a Squadron commanded by Captain Symonds and the French.

The Rear-Admiral endeavoured to intercept the Ships of the Enemy, but having not above twelve Days Provisions at short Allowance, was constrained to repair to *Portsmouth* for a Supply, not being able to reach *Plimouth*, by reason he chased a Number of Ships to the Eastward of that Port, which proved to be *Swedes*

The Rear-Admiral comes in for Want of Provisions.

from *Lisbon*. After he had furnished himself with Provisions, he received Orders from Vice-Admiral *Mitchell*, the twenty first of *May*, to proceed again into the *Soundings*, with four Third Rates and two Fireships, which were victualled for no longer than a Month at short Allowance, and from *Plimouth* he was to take the *Anglesey* and *Plimouth*, if ready, with three *East-India* Ships, which he was to see well into the Sea. The twenty fourth he sailed from St. *Helen's*, and the twenty sixth in the Morning arrived off of *Plimouth*, where he left Orders for the two Ships beforementioned to follow, taking the *Medway* with him. His cruising Station was from ten to one hundred Leagues West from *Scilly*, and the general Rendezvous forty Leagues W. S. W. from thence, so that he lay until the fifth of *June* between the Latitudes of 50^d and 49^d, about thirty Leagues West of those Islands; but being then driven far in, he sent the *Kent* to *Plimouth*, with the Fireship in her Company, the former having sprung her Fore-mast, and was so leaky that one Pump could hardly free her. However the Weather being more moderate, he proceeded with the three Third Rates one hundred and twenty Leagues Westward of *Scilly*, and then seeing no Ships of the Enemy, parted with those bound to *India* on the eighth of *June*, in the Latitude of fifty, the Wind at N. W. and believing (since three Days before the Wind had been Southerly) that the *Virginia* Fleet were gone for Cape *Clear*, or some Part of the Coast of *Ireland*, he stood over thither, but hearing soon after they were not arrived, stretched out to Sea again, and met with a Ship which had parted from them in the Latitude of 49^d 30^m the tenth of this Month, about two hundred and fifty Leagues from the Land.

Rear-Admiral Benbow returns into the Soundings.

This Intelligence, and the Shortness of his Provisions induced him to repair towards *Plimouth*, in his Way to which Port he had the good Fortune to join the *Virginia* and *West-India* Fleets, with their particular Convoys off of the *Lizard*; and meeting soon after with Vice-Admiral *Mitchell* near the *Start*, he was by him directed to repair to *Plimouth* in Company of the Merchant Ships, where he received Orders from Sir *George Rooke* to join the Fleet then passing Westward, and to take Care for sending Eastward a Convoy with the Trade; but these Orders were contradicted by others from the Lords of the Admiralty, dated the tenth of *July*, and he, in Obedience to them, proceeded to the Squadron before *Dunkirk*; which Captain *Beaumont* had commanded a considerable time before, consisting of six Third Rates, besides the *Newark*, two Fourths, one Fifth, and two Fireships; but three of those Third Rates were called off to the *Downs* by the Lords of the Admiralty.

Rear-Admiral Benbow brings in the Virginia and West-India Fleets.

No sooner had he joined the Squadron than he went in his Boat before the Pier-Heads of *Dunkirk*, but found not any Ships in the Road, fifteen or sixteen tall ones he saw within, one of them with a Flag at the Fore-top-mast-head; and Captain *Beaumont* delivered to him, for his government, two Orders which he had received from the Lords of the Admiralty, one to pursue Monsieur *Du Bart*, and to destroy his Ships, if possible, at any Place whatever, except under Command of the Forts in *Norway* or *Sweden*, and the other

Rear-Admiral Benbow arrives off of Dunkirk.

CHAP. XXV. *from the Year* 1688, *to* 1697. 571

to obey the King's Commands, which the Lords of the Admiralty directed him to do, in Obedience to the Orders they received from his Majesty to that Purpose.

The thirtieth of *July* Rear-Admiral *Vandergoes* joined him with eleven *Dutch* Ships, and then it was proposed that one of the Squadrons should be so placed as that *Dunkirk* might be South of them, and the other in, or near *Ostend* Road, that if Monsieur *Du Bart* should attempt to pass out either at the North or East Chanel, they might the better discover him; but no other Answer was made thereunto by the *Dutch* Flag, than that his Ships being foul, they were not in a Condition to pursue him. *Some* Dutch *Ships join ours off of* Dunkirk.

The *French* Ships at *Dunkirk* were eleven, from 52 to 26 Guns, and about the beginning of *August* they were all, except Monsieur *Du Bart*'s own Ship, hauled into the Basin to clean, so that it was judged they had a Design to come out the next Spring-Tide; but since our Ships, as well as the *Dutch*, were all foul, not any great Success could be expected from their chasing; and it was almost next to an Impossibility to block up clean Ships at *Dunkirk* with foul ones. Wherefore the Rear-Admiral propos'd that four of the best Sailers might be ordered to *Sheerness* to clean, and that the others might come to the *Downs*, not only to take in Water, which they very much wanted, but to heel and scrub, which he judged might have been done before the approaching Spring would give Opportunity to the *French* of getting over the Bar: But at this very time it was not thought adviseable, although he afterwards received Orders for it; so that at present he only sent the Ships to the *Downs* for Water, as they could best be spared. *The Force of the* French *Ships at* Dunkirk.

The seventeenth of *August* the Rear-Admiral observ'd five clean Ships ready to sail out of *Dunkirk*, and believing they would push through the East Chanel, he shifting his Station, lay between *Ostend* and *Newport*, giving notice thereof to the *Dutch*; but there was not any thing remarkable happened until the twenty third, when, at Five in the Morning, he discovered five Sail Eastward of him, *Newport* then bearing South, distant about four Leagues; upon which he immediately made the Signal for chasing, the Wind being at S.W. and the *French* steering away N.E. but finding they wronged him very much, he brought to at Four in the Afternoon. The smaller Ships, indeed, namely, the *Dragon*, *Falmouth*, *Romney*, and *Adventure*, continued the Chase until Six, and took a *Dunkirk* Privateer of ten Guns and sixty Men, which had been cruising in the North Seas two Months. *Some of the* French *Ships get out of* Dunkirk.

After this the Rear-Admiral endeavoured to regain his Station, but the twenty fifth at Night he was obliged to anchor about five Leagues West from the *Galloper*, the Wind blowing hard at S.W. There he continued until Eight the next Morning, when he saw eight Sail, at the distance of about five Leagues, standing Eastward, and two more Southward, the latter whereof proved to be the *Romney*, and a Flyboat she had taken; the others he pursued, but could get no Account of them.

Dddd 2 Thus

A short Observation upon the whole.

Thus ended this long and chargeable War, for little or nothing remarkable happen'd afterwards, Peace being proclaim'd the eighteenth Day of *October*; and the whole may be briefly summ'd up thus. That although the *French* at the beginning of the War got more early to Sea, and with greater Strength than we did, (I mean than we had in a Body) particularly in the Actions at *Bantry* and *Beachy*, when the Fleet was under the Command of the Earl of *Torrington*; yet when our Affairs came to be better settled, and that both we and the *Dutch* took the necessary and timely care to be early and strong at Sea, the Enemy did not, more than once afterwards during the whole War, dare to look us in the Face; and even that once was when the Court of *France* thought themselves secure of destroying two Squadrons of our Ships on their own Coast, commanded by Sir *Ralph Delavall* and Rear-Admiral *Carter*, before the bigger Ships could possibly join them. It was that which occasion'd positive Orders to Monsieur *Tourville* their Admiral, and it was these Orders which obliged him to engage, although he found our whole Force to be join'd. But from that very time they ever avoided meeting with us, as they did also the Year before the said Engagement, although they then had all the Strength in a Body which they could possibly equip. Finding therefore that they could not, with hopes of Success, attempt any thing on our Fleet, they suffered themselves to be insulted, their Towns to be bombarded, and the *Spaniard* to be relieved by our Forces in the *Mediterranean*, contenting themselves (as possibly they may do on other like occasions) with putting the Crown of *England*, and the States-General of the United Provinces, to a very great Expence in setting forth large Fleets, while they, with their cruising Frigates, and numerous Privateers, made their utmost Efforts towards seizing of our Trade, which being not only almost as great as in time of Peace, but very rich also, was a sufficient Invitation to them to equip great Numbers of private Ships for such an Enterprize; whereas their little Commerce, especially in these Parts of the World, was hardly worth while to look after. In this, though they were but too successful, yet I may venture to say, that had the Masters who were intrusted by the Merchants been more careful in sailing with the Convoys provided for them, or, when under the Protection of such Convoys, more diligent in keeping Company with them, (many Instances of whose Neglect herein I am able to give) the Enemy would, in a very great measure, have miss'd of their Aim even in this Particular.

As for the Losses which *England* and *France* sustain'd during this War in the Ships of their Royal Navies, it will have a much better Face on our side than that of the Trade; for having collected the same with as much Exactness as possibly I could, the Reader may find in the following Account both one and the other compared, by which it will appear, that the Enemy (considering the Magnitude of their Ships) were much the greater Sufferers.

CHAP. XXV. *from the Year* 1688, *to* 1697.

An Account of the English *Ships taken by the* French, *during the War, and what were burnt, or taken of theirs,* viz.

English.

Nº. of Ships.	Guns each.	Total of Guns.
1	of 70	70
1	of 54	54
2	of 48	96
1	of 46	46
3	of 42	126
3	of 36	108
6	of 32	192
2	of 30	60
4	of 24	96
2	of 18	36
2	of 16	32
2	of 12	24
11	of 10	110
5	of 8	40
1	of 6	6
4	of 4	16

Total 50.　　Total 1112.

French.

2	of 104	208
1	of 90	90
2	of 80	160
3	of 76	228
1	of 74	74
1	of 70	70
1	of 68	68
2	of 60	120
4	of 56	224
1	of 50	50
1	of 48	48
1	of 42	42
1	of 40	40
5	of 32	160
5	of 30	150
5	of 28	140
1	of 26	26
3	of 24	72
3	of 20	60

Nᵒ. of Ships.	Guns each.	Total of Guns.
6	of 18	108
1	of 16	16
2	of 12	24
6	of 10	60
1	of 6	6
Total 59.		Total 2244.

The Number of Guns on board the *French* Ships which were either taken or burnt, more than in the *English*, were 1132, and most of them much superior in their Nature.

A COMPLEAT HISTORY

Of the moſt Remarkable

TRANSACTIONS at SEA.

BOOK V.

Containing an Account of the Naval Tranſactions of the *Engliſh*, from the Year 1698, to the Year 1712.

CHAP. I.

Containing Rear-Admiral Benbow's *Proceedings to, in, and from the* Weſt-Indies.

THE Peace concluded at *Ryſwick* was no ſooner ratify'd, than Notice was given thereof as well abroad as to our Shipping at home, that ſo all farther Acts of Hoſtility might timely ceaſe; and ſince it was not then neceſſary to put the Nation to the Expence of maintaining at Sea ſo great a Part of the Navy as had been employed in time of Action, many Ships were brought into the Harbours, eſpecially thoſe of largeſt Dimenſions, that ſo their Hulls, very much worn by continual Service, might be ſearched into, and thoroughly repaired; and by the particular Care of that excellent Miniſter, the Earl of *Godolphin*, the then Lord High Treaſurer,

576 *Naval Transactions of the* English, Book V.

The Naval Expence retrenched upon the Peace.

surer, to furnish Mony for paying off the Seamen, our Naval Expence was gradually reduced to what was not more than absolutely necessary for the Honour of the Nation, and for answering those Services which required Shipping; one whereof, and that judged to be of as great Consequence as any, was the sending a Squadron to protect our Trade in the *West-Indies* from any Attempts which might be made thereon by Pirates, or otherwise; and of the Proceedings of that Squadron I will in the first Place give some Account.

1698. Rear-Admiral Benbow sent to the West-Indies.

His Instructions.

In the Month of *November* Mr. *Benbow*, Rear-Admiral of the Blue, was ordered to those Parts with the *Glocester*, *Falmouth*, and *Dunkirk*, all of them Ships of the Fourth Rate, to which there was added a small *French* Prize called the *Germoon*. He was directed first to call at the *Leeward* Islands, and there to dispose of Colonel *Collingwood*'s Regiment as the Council at *Nevis* should judge most proper, for by the Death of General *Codrington* the sole Management of the Affairs of those Islands devolved on them.

This being done, he was to bend his Course directly to *Jamaica*, and having remained there as long as it should be judged necessary for the publick Service, he was to visit *Barbadoes* and the *Caribbee* Islands, and so to employ the Ships under his Command, from time to time, as might be most proper for the Defence of the Plantations and Trade, as aforesaid.

To endeavour to seize on Kidd the Pirate.

And since the Government was informed that one *Kidd*, who sailed from *England* a considerable time before, on a private Account, in a Ship called the *Adventure* Gally, with a Commission under the Great Seal, and Power to seize on Pirates, and their Effects, had so far broke his Instructions, and indeed the real and only Design of his Voyage, as to commit several notorious Piracies himself, the Rear-Admiral was particularly charged to make diligent Enquiry after him, and to seize on, and secure his Person, together with his Men, Ship, and Effects, that so they might be brought to deserved Punishment.

He arrives at Maderas.

Pursuant to these Instructions he sailed from *Portsmouth* the twenty ninth of *November*, and was the eighteenth of the next Month in the Latitude of 36 Degrees North, and 12 Degrees West from the *Lizard*, in his way to the *Maderas*, where in few Days after he put in for Wine, and such other Refreshments as are absolutely necessary for the Preservation of Men on such Voyages.

1698/9. Comes to Barbadoes and the Leeward Islands.

Santa Martha.

He reached *Barbadoes* the twenty seventh of *February*, and having supplied the Ships with what was wanting, proceeded towards *Nevis*, one of the *Leeward* Islands, whence (having dispatched what Business he had there) he steered his Course for *Terra Firma*, and in a short time made the high Land of *Santa Martha*, at the Distance of about twenty Leagues, which lies in the Latitude of 12 Degrees, and as the upper Parts thereof are constantly cover'd with Snow, so is it (he says) esteemed as high, if not higher Land than hath been elsewhere seen. He stood not so near the Shore as to discover whether there was any commodious anchoring, but continued his Course for *Carthagena*, where he found the Bay to be large,

Arrives at Carthagena.

with

CHAP. I. *from the Year* 1698, *to* 1712.

with good Ground, and very gradual Soundings; for as there was five Fathom Water within a Mile of the Shore, so had he not more than eight at six times that Distance.

Before he dropped Anchor, he sent a Letter to the Governor, and was informed by the Messenger, that the *Spaniards* had often consulted, both there, and at *Porto Bello*, how they might most effectually raise Men to dislodge the *Scotch*, who were then endeavouring to settle themselves at *Darien*, but that they had not formed any Resolutions, being cautious of exposing themselves to a War with *Scotland*, at a time when they had an entire Friendship with *England*. But notwithstanding these specious Pretences, they had actually seized on two or three of our Merchant Ships, which they designed to equip in warlike manner, and to employ against the *Scotch*, in Conjunction with their *Armada* (as they termed them) at *Porto Bello*, which were no more than three Ships, and they in no better a Condition than commonly those of the *Spanish* Nation have been known to be, especially in these latter Times. *Spaniards endeavouring to dislodge the Scotch at Darien.*

The Rear-Admiral arrived soon after before *Bocca Chica*, at the Entrance of the Harbour of *Carthagena*, which he judged to be much the better Road, and was defended by a Castle, whereon were mounted about 16 Guns. There he endeavoured to furnish the Ships with Water, but meeting with Opposition from the Governor, he judged it incumbent on him to resent such uncivil Treatment, and let him know that he would enter the Harbour, and force from thence the *English* Ships, if he did not immediately send them out to him. The Governor made frivolous Delays, but yet promised that if he would get up his Anchors, and come before the Town, the Ships should be sent out that very Moment; for (as he alledged) the Inhabitants were jealous and uneasy at his blocking up the Harbour. *The Rear-Admiral refused to water at Carthagena.*

In Expectation that this would be complied with, the Rear-Admiral did as the Governor had desired, but finding the Ships were nevertheless detained, he taxed him with the Breach of his Word, and gave him to understand that he would assuredly endeavour to force them out of the Harbour, if they were not immediately dispatched to him, at which the Governor being somewhat startled, and not caring to abide the Extremity, suffered the Ships to be set at liberty.

The little Quantity of Water which the *Spaniards* would permit our Ships to take in at this Place, subjected the Men to the Belly-ake, to prevent the ill Consequences whereof the Rear-Admiral stood away for *Jamaica*, and in his Passage met with an unknown Shoal, about fourteen Leagues Eastward of the *Serrana*, which extends itself N. E. and S. W. about nine Miles. *An unknown Shoal Eastward of the Serrana.*

The Southermost part of this Shoal he represents to be a Hill of Sand about the length of two Cables, supposed to have been thrown up by the Sea, and that there were on it many Timbers of a Ship seen above Water: a Mile to the Southward whereof he discovered a Reef of Rocks, to the N. E. of which all the Ground was foul; nor was there any thing to be seen but a Rock which appeared like the *Other Shoals.*

Eeee

the bottom of a Long-boat, not far from which he espied another Wreck, and within two Miles of the aforesaid Shoal, there was not any Ground to be found with seventy Fathom of Line. This he observed to be distant about fifteen Leagues from a known Shoal called *Point Pedro*, and that it bore from it S. by W.

He comes to Jamaica.

When he arrived at *Jamaica*, the Governor and most of the trading People requested him to sail to *Porto Bello*, there to demand from the *Spaniards* their Ships, Goods, and Men, which they had wrongfully taken, and that chiefly at the Instance of the Admiral of the *Barlovento* Fleet, Ships which are employed in carrying Mony from the *Havana* to pay the Garrisons to Windward, and for the Defence of those Parts.

Proceeds to Porto Bello.

Sails give way.

To comply with this reasonable Request he sailed with the *Glocester*, *Falmouth*, *Lynn*, and *Saudadoes-Prize*, and arrived at *Porto Bello* the twenty second of *March*, having been much hindred in his Passage by the Badness of the Sails, which frequently gave way; a Misfortune of the last ill Consequence, and which hath, on other Occasions, too often happened, to the very great Prejudice of the Service.

Finding there the Admiral of the *Barlovento* Fleet, he acquainted him with the reason of his coming, but was answered roughly, that what he had done arose from the Attempt the *Scotch* had made at *Darien*, whose Interest and that of *England* he esteemed to be the same.

Several Messages passed between them, but at length he was assured that if he would retire from before the Port, the Ships, Men, and Goods should be sent out to him; but the Dispute continuing until the twentieth of *April*, and the Rear-Admiral then finding his own Ship very leaky, he sailed with her and the *Germoon-Prize*, leaving the others before the Place to see his Demands complied with.

Description of the Harbour of Porto Bello.

He represents the Harbour here to be very commodious, and that it was fortified with three Castles; one at the Entrance (which is about half a Mile wide) of 18 Guns, another over the Town, near Gun-shot from the first, whereon was twenty Cannon, and the third a small old Fort, on which were mounted 12, and in the Harbour was the *Spanish* Admiral beforementioned, with four Ships from 56 to 36 Guns.

1699.

The Rear-Admiral returning to *Jamaica* the fifteenth of *May*, sailed thence soon after in the *Saudadoes-Prize*, which Ship, in Company of the *Falmouth*, and *Lynn*, arrived the Night before from *Porto Bello*, without having been able to effect any thing there, notwithstanding the solemn Promises the *Spaniards* had made. The reason of his going to Sea with the aforesaid Prize only, was the Intelligence he had received that *Kidd* the Pirate was hovering about the Coast; but when he had for some time unsuccessfully sought him, he returned to *Jamaica*, and had there Advice that he was near St. *Domingo*.

Seeks Kidd without Success.

The former Experience he had of the Badness of the Sails, made him doubt they would not well endure the strong Gales which frequently

CHAP. I. *from the Year* 1698, *to* 1712. 579

quently happen at such a Season of the Year, and therefore he hired a Sloop, and with her, and the *Germoon-Prize*, endeavoured (tho' to no purpose) to gain a more certain Account of *Kidd*; but before he left *Jamaica* he gave Orders to the Captains of the other Ships to cruise between the Isle of *Ash*, on the Coast of *Hispaniola*, and the East End of *Jamaica*, the better to preserve the Health of the Men, who are not so much subject to Sickness at Sea, as when they are committing Irregularities on shore. *A second time.*

When, after his returning to *Jamaica*, the sick Men were recovered, he sailed with the *Glocester* and *Maidstone*, and being near the East End of *Hispaniola*, was informed of the Loss of a Sloop near Cape *Alta Vela*, on the said Island, which was the Vessel wherein Captain *Lloyd* of the *Falmouth* was sent in quest of *Kidd*, and with her both himself and all the Men unhappily perished. *Capt. Lloyd of the Falmouth drowned.*

At the Request of the President of the Council of *Nevis* he sailed to the Island St. *Thomas*, inhabited chiefly, if not altogether, by Subjects of *Denmark*, and demanded by what Authority they bore the Flag of that Nation on *Crabb* Island, since it appertained to the King of *England* his Master. He also let the Governor know, that it was not agreeable to the Law of Nations to trade with Pirates, (it being evident that he had suffered great part of *Kidd's* Effects to be landed at that Port) and demanded of him all Subjects of *England* who were Non-resident there. The Governor seemed surprized at his making any Objections to the Flag, and insisted that the Island whereon it flew was actually the King of *Denmark*'s. The Port he said was free, and since the *Brandenburgh* Factors had received part of *Kidd*'s Effects, he could by no means molest, but, on the contrary, was obliged to protect them. He averred that there were not any of the Subjects of *England* on the Island, Captain *Sharp*, a noted Pirate, only excepted, who was confined for Misdemeanours, and having sworn Allegiance to the King of *Denmark*, could not justifiably be delivered up; so that the Rear-Admiral was obliged to desist, for his Instructions did not empower him to act in an hostile manner. *The Rear-Admiral sails to the Isle of St. Thomas. Expostulates with the Governor about Kidd.*

This Island of St. *Thomas*, about twenty Miles in length, is one of the Westermost of those called the *Virgins*, lying at the East End of *Porto Rico*. Its Harbour (which is very commodious) is on the South side, being capable of receiving Ships of any Rank; and it is well known that the Island itself hath been, as it now is, a Receptacle for Free-Booters of all Nations. *Description of the Isle of St. Thomas.*

The latter end of *October* the Rear-Admiral sailed from thence, and cruised eleven Days between the West End of *Porto Rico*, and the East End of *Hispaniola*, when stretching into the Bay of *Samana*, he remained there until the eighteenth of *November*. Four Days after he came before St. *Domingo*, and sent in the *Maidstone* to demand an *English* Sloop which the *Spaniards* had taken some time before; but in this Case he got no more Satisfaction than in the former, wherefore returning to *Jamaica*, he had there an Account that the *South-Sea Castle*, and *Biddeford*, the one a Fifth, the other a Sixth Rate, were lost on *Point Bagne*, near the Isle of *Ash*. *Demands an English Ship at St. Domingo. South-Sea Castle and Biddeford Ash, lost.*

E e e e 2

Aſh, in their Paſſage from *England* to *Jamaica*, occaſioned, as it was generally believed, by their keeping that Shore too cloſe on board in the Night, which, in the Extremity of Weather they met with, they could not diſengage themſelves from; nor was the Place itſelf ſo deſcribed then in any of the Sea-Charts, (if at all) as to caution them of the danger.

Receives Orders to return home. At *Jamaica* he found a Supply of Proviſions from *England*, which he diſtributed amongſt the Ships, and ſoon after received Orders to return home; but firſt to conſult with the Governor what might be done for the publick Service with the Ships under his Command; and if he himſelf judged it practicable, he was to range along the Coaſt between the Gulph of *Florida* and *Newfoundland*, to free thoſe Parts from Pirates.

Coming to New England, he found Kidd was ſent home. Sailing from *Jamaica* with the *Gloceſter*, *Falmouth*, *Lynn*, *Shoreham*, *Maidſtone*, and *Rupert-Prize*, he left the *Saudadoes-Prize* and *Germoon* to attend the Iſland, inſtead of the *South-Sea Caſtle* and *Biddeford*; and being near the *Havana*, he ſent the *Falmouth* home from thence, for ſhe was too weak to be truſted in the Seas about *New England*, on which Coaſt arriving himſelf the twentieth of *April*, he found that *Kidd* had been ſent from thence towards *England* ſome time before; for being ſeized by the Earl of *Bellomont*, Governor of that Country, (who, with other Perſons of Quality, were concerned in the Ship) he was put on board one of our Frigates of the Fourth Rate, called the *Advice*, with conſiderable Riches, but not the Moiety of what he had actually gotten, the Remainder being lodged in the Hands of Perſons unknown, or at leaſt ſuch as could not be come at.

Kidd tried and executed. This Arch-Pirate had not been long in *England* e'er he was tried at a Seſſions of Admiralty, held at the *Old-Baily*, and he, with ſeveral of his Accomplices, being condemned, they were executed, and expoſed in Chains in proper Places on the Banks of the River of *Thames*, to deter others from committing the like Villanies. I *Kidd tampered with.* might here take notice of ſeveral Paſſages relating to this hardened Wretch, but more eſpecially as to the great Induſtry which was uſed to prevail with him to impeach ſome Noble Lords who were concerned in ſetting him out, with a Commiſſion under the Great Seal, as I have ſaid before; but ſince it is ſomewhat remote from the Buſineſs in hand, I will leave it with this Remark only, that although *Kidd* was in other things a notorious Villain, yet he was ſo juſt in this Particular as not wrongfully to accuſe the innocent.

CHAP.

CHAP. II.

Vice-Admiral Aylmer *sent with a Squadron to the* Mediterranean; *Captain* Andrew Leake, *and, after him, Captain* Stafford Fairborn *to* Newfoundland, *and Captain* Thomas Warren *to* Madagascar.

BEsides the Ships of War sent to the *West-Indies* with Rear-Admiral *Benbow*, (from which the Kingdom received no other Advantage than the Protection of our Trade from Pirates) there were other Squadrons employed abroad, *viz.* one under the Command of Vice-Admiral *Aylmer* * in the *Mediterranean*, for Security of the Trade to *Italy* and *Turky*, who also confirmed the Treaties with the Governments of *Algier, Tunis*, and *Tripoli*. Captain *Andrew Leake*, and after him Captain *Stafford Fairborn* † were sent to *Newfoundland* for the Security of our Fishery there, and for conducting them safe to the Ports in the *Mediterranean* and *Portugal*, and thence home. The latter, in his Passage up the *Levant*, put in at *Thoulon*, about the middle of *September*, where he was not only civilly entertain'd by the Marquis of *Nesmond*, but permitted to view their Magazines and Ships, which were thirty two of the Line of Battel, three Fireships, and as many Bomb-Vessels. In his return he visited the Prince of *Hesse Darmstat* at *Barcelona*, who was some time before removed from the Vice-Royship of *Catalonia* (wherein he had given great Satisfaction) to make room for the Count of *Palma*, Nephew of Cardinal *Portacarrero*, which Prelate had been very instrumental in setting the Crown of *Spain* on the Head of the then Duke of *Anjou*, Grandson to the *French* King, and was the principal occasion of the ensuing Rupture.

Other Squadrons sent abroad.

1700. *Sir Stafford Fairborn comes to Thoulon, and was civilly treated.*

Soon after Captain *Fairborn* arrived at *Cadiz*, but was obliged to hasten from thence, for the *Spaniards* had notice a War was declared between the *Dutch* and them.

Forced to hasten from Cadiz.

Another small Squadron was sent to the *East-Indies* under the Command of Captain *Thomas Warren*, for the greater Security of that rich Trade, and suppressing Pirates in those Parts. He, with others, jointly commission'd under the Great Seal, had Power to treat with that Nest of Sea-Robbers, who were strongly settled on the Island of *Madagascar*, his Majesty having issued his Royal Declaration of Pardon, if they would surrender themselves; but those hardened Villains were so wedded to their loose Life, that his Majesty's gracious Intentions towards them prevailed but on very few to lay hold thereof, nor was it in the Power of our Ships of War to force them thereunto; so that after they had continued a long time in those Parts, to the no little Expence of the publick Trea-

Capt. Warren sent to treat with Pirates at Madagascar.

---

* *Now Lord* Aylmer, *and Rear-Admiral of* England.
† *Since Knighted, and a Flag-Officer.*

sure,

sure, they returned home under the Command of Captain *James Littleton* *, (for Captain *Warren* died soon after the landing of Sir *William Norris*, his Majesty's Ambassador to the *Mogul*) who had the good Fortune to burn or destroy some of the Ships belonging to these Sea Robbers at those Places abroad where they lurked.

Another Course taken with Pirates.

And as for Pirates in general, his Majesty soon after issued his Royal Proclamation, (upon a Proposal humbly made by my self) promising not only Pardon, but a Reward to such who would discover their Ring-leaders, so as they might be apprehended and brought to Punishment; nay even such who would voluntarily surrender themselves were likewise assured of the King's Mercy; and this had in a great Measure the desired Effect; for although few, or none came in, yet they grew so jealous one of another, that rarely any of them attempted to disturb the Seas many Years.

Captain Munden sent with some Ships to Salley.

Another small Squadron was sent before *Salley*, in the Kingdom of *Fez*, under the Conduct of Captain *John Munden* † to cruise against the Pirates of *Barbary*, but more especially those of the aforesaid Port, the principal one they have. He was also empowered to negotiate a Truce with them, and Captain *George Delavall* ‡ was at the same time employed to treat for the Redemption of our Captives, wherein he had very good Success. There was a general Contribution throughout *England* for the Benefit of those miserable Christians, many of whom had suffered a long time under the intolerable Hardships of Slavery, insomuch that by what was so collected, and what the Government advanced towards this charitable Design, a great Number received their Liberty, who were brought in a decent Procession through the City of *London*, where a Sermon was preached to them at the Church of St. *Mary le Bow*, suitable to the Occasion.

A Contribution for the Redemption of Captives.

Chap. III.

Containing an Account of Sir George Rooke's *Proceedings in the* Baltick *for reconciling the Kings of* Denmark *and* Sweden.

IN the Month of *November* Sir *George Rooke*, Admiral of the Fleet was ordered to take upon him the Command of a Squadron of his Majesty's Ships, which were to be joined by several *Dutch* Men of War, and afterwards by the *Swedish* Fleet in the *Baltick* Sea, and to be employed towards composing the Difference between the two Northern Crowns, which, if not timely effected,

---

* *Since a Flag-Officer and Commissioner of the Navy.*
† *Afterwards Knighted, and a Flag-Officer.*
‡ *Since a Flag-Officer.*

CHAP. III. *from the Year* 1698, *to* 1712. 583

might have proved of very ill Consequence to the Affairs of *Europe*.

Sir *George* was not only to command our Ships of War, but those of the States-General, at the Head whereof was Lieutenant-Admiral *Allemonde*; and having received such Orders from his Majesty as were judged proper for the designed Expedition, he sailed towards the Coast of *Holland* to join the *Dutch* Squadron, which were one Ship of 94 Guns, four of 72, five of 64, one of 54, and two of 56, with two Fireships, and three Frigates; and ours were one of 80 Guns, two of 70, and seven of 50, with two Frigates, and one Fireship, besides Bomb-Vessels. *The Strength of the English and Dutch.*

About the middle of *May* he arrived at the *Hague*, where conferring with the Pensioner, and the *Swedish* Ambassador, as also with Admiral *Allemonde*, and our Envoy, Mr. *Stanhope*, it was determined that the Place for joining the *Dutch* Ships should be off of *Egmont op Zee*, about three Leagues Southward of the *Texel*, but that if they did not all arrive in eight Days he should proceed to *Gottenburgh*, and leave Orders for the rest to follow. From thence they were to steer their Course as a Council of War should think most advisable, upon Intelligence of the Readiness of the *Swedish* Fleet, and the Answer which the Ministers of the King of *Denmark* should make to the Declaration of his Majesty of *Great Britain*, and the rest of the Guarrantees, for adhering to the Treaty of *Altena*. 1701.

The twenty fourth of *May* Sir *George Rooke* was joined off of *Scheveling* by Admiral *Allemonde*, with five Ships of the Line, a Frigate, a Fireship, and two Bomb-Vessels, as he was some little time after by Rear-Admiral *Vanderduffen*, and the rest of the *Dutch* Ships, so that getting under Sail, he came off of *Gottenburgh* the eighth Day of *June*. *English and Dutch Ships join.*

Five Days after he called a Council of War, and (according to what was then resolved) advanced towards the *Sound*; but was informed the *Danish* Fleet were so stationed, as that they might be able to give him considerable Opposition. When he arrived at the Entrance of the *Sound*, he found them to be twenty eight Sail, proper for the Line of Battel, and that they were ranged athwart the narrow Passage, under the Guns of their Castle of *Cronenberg*, opposite to *Helsingberg*; and here he received Assurance from Count *Watchtmeister*, Admiral-General of *Sweden*, that he would take the very first Opportunity of joining him with the Squadron under his Command. *They arrive off of Gottenburgh. The Danish Squadron.*

Not long after a Signal was made, as had been agreed, from *Helsingberg*, that the *Danish* Fleet were under Sail, whereupon our Admiral weighed Anchor, and advanced into the *Sound*, to prevent any Mischief which might otherwise happen to the *Swedes*; but the *Danish* Ships anchored again on this Side of the *Grounds*, not only to guard the Passage, but to prevent our joining with the *Swedish* Squadron, which were now come down to the South Side of that Chanel. *English and Dutch advance into the Sound.*

In

Swedes slow in joining.

In this Posture the Fleets lay for some time, Sir *George Rooke* expecting that the *Swedes* would, according to what had been promised, have pushed thorough, which in all Probability they might have done in less than two Hours, for it had blown fresh at S.S.E. but the Opportunity being lost, he got under Sail, and came nearer to the Island *Huen*, mean while the *Danes* ply'd towards him in a Line of Battel, but anchored about Noon near three Leagues off in the Mouth of the Chanel leading up to *Copenhagen*, and the *Swedes* were much about the same Distance on the other Side of the *Grounds*.

Soon after Count *Guldenlieu*, High Admiral of *Denmark*, sent a Frigate to Sir *George Rooke*, with Admiral *Geddé*, and Monsieur *Hansen*, a Counsellor of State, assuring him that the King of *Denmark* had accepted the Mediation of *England* and *Holland*, with that of *France*, for reconciling the Difference between his Majesty and the Duke of *Holstein*; but Sir *George* being not fully satisfy'd therein, because he had not received any Notice thereof from Mr. *Cresset*, our Minister, and finding that the *Swedish* Fleet had passed the Chanel of *Flinterrena* the third of *July*, he got under Sail the next Day, and anchoring off of *Landscroon*, he joined them the

Danish Ships secure themselves in Harbour.

sixth, whereupon the *Danes* retreated into their Harbours, and the Winds being not only fresh, but contrary, the Admiral could not get into *Copenhagen* Road before Tuesday Noon, when viewing the *Danish* Fleet, he found they were secured not only by sunken Vessels, but by floating Stages, whereon they had placed many Guns, and by Booms athwart their Harbour. Besides, they had, for their greater Safety, got some of their Ships within the *Talboate*, and the rest into a Place called the *Reefs Hole*, insomuch that it was judged impracticable to attempt them with the Frigates and Fireships; but (as a Council of War had resolved) there were four

Danish Ships bombarded.

Bomb-Vessels sent as near in as the Bombardiers thought fit, and that Night they threw away about an hundred and forty Shells, for they did little or no Damage.

Soon after this there were sent to *Gottenburgh* a Fourth and a Fifth Rate of the *English*, and three Ships of the States-General, to cover the Forces which the King of *Sweden* intended to transport to *Tonningen*, on the River *Eyder*, and three *English*, with six *Swedish*, together with three *Dutch* Ships were ordered into the South Chanel, going into *Copenhagen*, with the Bomb-Vessels

Bmboarded a second time.

from whence they bombarded the *Danish* Fleet some Hours, but not with greater Success than before; nor did those on our Side receive any Damage from their Shells, or the Shot from the Town, Ships, and Puntoons.

Strength of the Swedish Ships, and of the whole.

Here it may be not improper to inform you, that the *Swedish* Ships which joined the *English* and *Dutch* were three of 80 Guns each, one of 76, one of 74, seven of 70, four of 64, one of 62, two of 56, three of 54, three of 52, and four of 50, with three Frigates, five Fireships, and one Bomb-Vessel, and with them there were three Admirals, two Vice-Admirals, and three Rear-Admirals;

so

so that the whole Strength consisted of fifty two Ships of the Line of Battel, from 94 to 52 Guns.

Preparations were now making for a vigorous Descent in *Koge* Bay, and between *Copenhagen* and *Elsinore* at the same time; but the Winds being contrary, those Troops which embarked at *Udstedt*, being chiefly Horse, could not get over to the aforesaid Bay, as was intended, so that they were put on Shore, and ordered to *Landscroon*, and *Helsenburg*, to be transported from thence; and the latter End of *July* the King of *Sweden* landed with about five thousand Foot near four Miles on this Side *Elsinore*, without any great Loss, although the *Danes* had brought down a Body of Horse and Foot, and three or four Field-Pieces to oppose them.

King of Sweden lands near Elsinore.

The young King remained intrenched in his Camp, until he was strengthened by several Squadrons of Horse, and then he purposed to besiege the City; but although Matters were at this Pass, it was agreed on all Sides that the Commerce should not be interrupted, so that Shipping passed and re-passed the *Sound* as usual; nor did any farther Acts of Hostility ensue, for all Differences were soon after happily accommodated, and the Squadrons thereupon returned home. Thus were these two Northern Monarchs reconciled, or at least the King of *Denmark*, who was the Aggressor, submitted to reasonable Terms, which King *William*, and his Allies the States-General had determined to constrain him to do: And had they not thus gone roundly to work with the *Danes*, by assisting the *Swedes* with so considerable a Part of their Naval Force, and letting them see that if they declined an amicable Accommodation, they had nothing else to expect but a vigorous Attack on their Country, the Quarrel between those two Princes, which must have drawn after it other ill Consequences, would not have been so soon brought to a happy Issue.

Differences accommodated.

Chap. IV.

Containing an Account of Sir George Rooke's *Proceedings with the Fleet in and about the Chanel, and of the Naval Preparations of the* French.

IN the Month of *February* the *English* Flag-Officers were dispatched to the several Ports, not only to hasten out the Ships, but to send them to the Rendezvous in the *Downs*, for there was at that time a Suspicion that the *French* (although it was not thought a War would immediately break out) had a Design to cover a Transport, some time in *March*, with a Squadron from *Dunkirk*, and that they would land Forces in this Kingdom, wherefore Orders were sent to Rear-Admiral *Benbow*, who commanded in the *Downs*, to use his best Endeavours to frustrate such a Design. And that as ma-

170⅔.

Suspicion of a Descent from France.

ny Ships might be got together, and as early too, as it was possible, those which had more than their middle Complements of Men were ordered to discharge them into such as wanted of that Number: But the *French*, if they really had any such Intentions, did not think it convenient at this time to put them in Execution.

Spithead the Rendezvous for the Fleet.

It was, upon farther Consideration, thought adviseable to appoint *Spithead* for the Rendezvous, and to that Place Sir *Cloudesly Shovell* (then Admiral of the Blue) was ordered to proceed with the Fleet from the *Downs*, but first to leave a proper Squadron to look after the *French* Ships at *Dunkirk*, which was put under the Command of Sir *John Munden*, who had for some time continued at *Sheerness*, and been very diligent in the Dispatch of the great Ships from *Chatham*. And that the Fleet might be got together as soon as it was possible, Vice-Admiral *Hopson*, whose Flag was flying at *Spithead*, was ordered to detain all such Ships as might touch there, either from the *Downs* or the Western Ports.

1701.

Captain Billingsly sent to discover the Enemy's Preparations.

In the Month of *April* a nimble Frigate called the *Lizard*, commanded by Captain *Rupert Billingsly*, was sent to discover what Naval Preparations the *French* were making at *Brest*, Port *Louis*, and *Rochefort*, who meeting with several of their Burses, he was assured by the Masters of them that the Ships at the latter of those Places were preparing for the Sea, and that seven Frigates lately arrived from *Spain*, rid under the Isle *Daix*.

Proceeding on, he ran up towards the *Pertuis d'Antioche*, until he had the aforesaid Isle S. E. about four Miles distant, and then anchored. There was in the Road *de Basque* a *French* Ship of 70 Guns, but that he might be the less suspected, he ordered his Lieutenant on board of her, with a Pretence that he was sent thither in Search of an *English* Ketch that had been ran away with from *Milford* by several prest Men, which Vessel he heard had been in the Bay of *Biscay*.

The Lieutenant was very civilly treated, and after some Discourse with the Captain of the *French* Ship, he sent him on Shore to the Governor of *Rochelle*, and Monsieur *Du Casse* (for he was then at that Place) ordered the *French* Officer who accompanied him to take care for his being supplied with what he wanted.

When the Lieutenant returned on board the *French* Ship, the second Captain of her discovered himself to him, said his Name was *Bennet*, and that he commanded the *Trident* when she and the *Content* were taken the last War in the *Mediterranean*, having made his Escape from *Messina*, where he had for some time been a Prisoner.

Monsieur *Du Casse* was designed to Sea in this Ship of 70 Guns, but under Orders to remain in the Road *de Basque* until the Remainder of his Squadron joined him there, some whereof were suddenly expected from *Brest*, and others from Port *Louis*, all equipped for foreign Service; and Part of this Squadron were the Ships which Vice-Admiral *Benbow* afterwards met with, and engaged in the *West-Indies*, of which unfortunate Action an Account shall be given in its proper Place.

On

CHAP. IV. *from the Year* 1698, *to* 1712.

On the fourth of *May* Captain *Billingsly* anchored at the Entrance of *Brest* Harbour, and sent his Lieutenant on Shore, under Pretence of enquiring for the straggling Ketch, and to bring off some Water. The Lieutenant had no sooner landed than he was conveyed to Monsieur *Cotlongon*, who then commanding there, let him know, that he was no Stranger to the real Business he came about. However, the Lieutenant requested Liberty to fill some Water, but was answered that *Brest* was not a Place for him to be furnished with it, and therefore he gave him a Letter to the Governor of *Camaret* Tower to suffer him to fill what Water he wanted, and to supply him with whatever else he should desire; but as he had no present Occasion, he returned without making any use of this Courtesy. In the Port of *Brest* the *French* were getting ready their great Ships, and there were four Frigates, sheathed and fitted for a foreign Voyage, bound, as it was judged, to *Rochefort*, where Monsieur *Du Casse* lay. *Preparations at Brest.*

The Lieutenant of the *Lizard* having given his Commander an Account of what passed on Shore, he sent him to the Governor of *Camaret* with the aforesaid Letter from Monsieur *Cotlongon*, who advised him to hasten to his Ship, for that if she did not suddenly depart the Road he would fire on her; whereupon Captain *Billingsly* got under Sail in the Evening, and made the best of his Way to *Spithead*, where, to his no little Mortification, he received Notice of the War, for he had met with a *French* Merchant Ship of about 16 Guns, which he judged came from the *West-Indies*, and probably would have been a very good Booty to him. *Captain Billingsly obliged to go out of Camaret Bay.*

Having made this little Digression, I return to the Body of our Fleet, which at the Beginning of the Year was in great Want of Men, and therefore it was ordered that all the Ships, except the Squadron designed for the *West-Indies*, should enter no more than their lowest Complements, for by this means it was judged that each of them might be the sooner put into a tolerable Condition for Service; and since many of the Men of that Squadron were raw, and unexperienced, the Ships were frequently sent out to cruise, that so they might be exercised, and inured, in some Degree, to the Service before they proceeded on the Voyage.

Sir *Cloudesly Shovell* arrived at *Spithead* the fifteenth of *April*, with forty six *English* Ships, and ten *Dutch*, including small Frigates and Fireships, from whence there were Squadrons sent to *Ireland*, for conducting Troops from thence to *Holland*, and Cruisers into the *Soundings*, and elsewhere, for Security of the Trade, while others were employed for Intelligence; for the *French*, according to the best Advices which could be gained, were at this time making all imaginable Dispatch in fitting out, and manning their Ships at *Brest*, and the Ports in the *Bay*. *Sir Cloudesly Shovell comes to Spithead, and Squadrons sent from the Fleet.*

Captain *John Leake*[*] being sent out in the Month of *August* with some Frigates for Intelligence, was informed, when off of *Brest*, that eight Ships of War were gone from that Port towards the Mediter- *Capt. John Leake sent for Intelligence.*

---

[*] *Afterwards knighted, and Admiral of the Fleet.*

Ffff 2 ranean.

ranean. One of his Lieutenants was on board a *French* Vice-Admiral in *Brest* Water, and found there were nineteen Ships in that Harbour, of which the *Hope*, of 70 Guns, taken from us the last War, was the least, as also four Fireships, and one Frigate, all lying with their Top-sails loose, unmoored, in order to sail the first fair Wind, and with them there were a Vice, and two Rear-Admirals.

A Squadron ready at Brest.

The Admiral of the Fleet, Sir *George Rooke*, went on board the *Triumph* in the *Downs* the second of *July*, (at which time his Majesty was convoyed to *Holland* by Vice-Admiral *Hopson*) and arriving at *Spithead* the fourth, received Directions to follow the King's Orders. In few Days he was joined by Rear Admiral *Munden*, with two Third Rates, six Fourths, and one Fifth, and then he formed his Line of Battel, which was composed of the Numbers and Rates of Ships following, *viz.*

Sir George Rooke *Admiral of the Fleet arrives at* Spithead.

Strength of the Fleets, English *and* Dutch.

English.

Number.	Guns each.
2	90
6	80
13	70
11	60
16	50

48 Besides small Frigates, Fireships, Bomb-Vessels, &c.

Dutch.

1	92
1	90
2	72
4	64
1	52
6	50

15 And they had also small Frigates, and other necessary Vessels.

With the *English* Fleet there were, besides the Admiral himself, the several Flag-Officers hereafter mentioned, *viz.*

Sir *Cloudesly Shovell*,	Admiral of the Blue.
Sir *Thomas Hopson*,	Vice Admiral of the Red.
John Benbow, Esq;	Vice-Admiral of the Blue.
Sir *John Munden*,	Rear-Admiral of the Red.

Of the *Dutch.*

Lt. Admiral *Allemonde.*
Vice-Admiral *Vandergoes.*
Rear-Admiral *Wassenaer.*

He

CHAP. IV. *from the Year* 1698, *to* 1712.

He was obliged to remain at St. *Helen*'s until the middle of *August* for want of Provisions, and many other Necessaries, to enable him to proceed to Sea; but sailing then, and stopping Tides, gained his Passage to *Torbay*, where he was forced to anchor the twenty first by a strong S. W. Wind. Some Days after he sailed, but was no sooner got clear of the Land, than he met the Wind fresh at S. W. again, which encreasing, and several Ships having lost their Top-masts, and split their Sails, he was obliged to return to *Torbay*, to prevent the Fleet's being driven as far Eastward as St. *Helen*'s.

The twenty ninth in the Morning weighing with the Wind at N. W. and fair Weather, he reached off of the *Fourn-head*, near the Isle of *Ushant*, the first of *September*, from whence (in pursuance of the Orders of the Lords-Justices of the Kingdom, in the Absence of his Majesty) he detached six Third Rates, nine Fourths, one Fifth, one Sixth, two Fireships, a Storeship, and an Hospital, of the *English*, under the Command of Sir *John Munden*, and ten *Dutch* Ships, besides Fireships, and small Frigates, commanded by Baron *Wassenaer*, to see the Squadron bound to the *West Indies* well into the Sea. *The Fleet comes off of Ushant, and sends forward the West-India Squadron.*

The Admiral was informed by the Master of a Hoy off of *Falmouth*, which came from *Brest* the twenty ninth of *August*, (where he had been detained a considerable time) that on the third Day of the said Month the *St. Esprit* of 78 Guns, and the *St. Francis* of 52, sailed to the *West Indies*, with a small Frigate, a Fireship, and four large Storeships, and that the very Day he came out Monsieur *Chateau Renault* put to Sea with three Ships of three Decks, five of 70 Guns each, two of 50, and four Frigates from 30 to 40 Guns, three Fireships, and four Storeships, all of them victualled for six Months. He added that the Count *D'Estrées* was arrived at *Brest* from *Cadiz*, to command in the Absence of Monsieur *Chateau Renault*, and that there were laid up in that Harbour eleven Three-Deck Ships, and four of 70 Guns, which they were stripping, and repairing against the next Summer; and about a Fortnight before this Master of the Hoy came from the said Port of *Brest*, there sailed from thence two Ships of the first Rank, and four others, bound (as it was reported) for *Lisbon*, to assist the King of *Portugal* in fitting out his Fleet, for then it was suspected that that Prince would have declared in favour of *France*. *Several French Ships sail from Brest. French Ships sent to assist the King of Portugal.*

Sir *George Rooke* being ordered, if he found Monsieur *Chateau Renault* was sailed from *Brest*, to cruise with the remaining part of the Fleet (after the Detachment was made with the *West-India* Squadron) in such Stations as might be most proper for the Security of the several Trades expected from foreign Parts, it was resolved by a Council of Flag-Officers to cruise in the Latitude of $49^d \cdot 30^m \cdot$ between twenty and fifty Leagues from the Islands of *Scilly*; but as they were of Opinion it was not safe to keep the great Ships at Sea after the tenth of *September*, so did they, for that reason, resolve to repair then towards St. *Helen*'s, or indeed sooner, if the Winds happened to set in, and to blow hard Westerly. *Station agreed for our Fleet to cruise in.*

Having

Having therefore cruised to the Extent of that time, the Admiral left the Station, and beat up several Days between the *Start* and *Plimouth*, to prevent his being forced into the *Sound*, a dangerous Place for Ships of that Magnitude; insomuch that he arrived not at St. *Helen*'s until the twentieth of *September*, and then received Orders to come with the great Ships to the *Downs*, the *Dutch* being already gone to *Spithead*, after they had paid the Complement of a Salute, a thing which is usual at the end of an Expedition.

The Fleet returns to St. Helen's.

This Year's Service at home ending thus, I return to the Squadron sent to the *West-Indies* under the Command of Vice-Admiral *Benbow*, and shall give a particular Account of Affairs in those Parts, before I enter on any thing which happened in the Chanel, or elsewhere, that so the same may appear at one View.

Chap. V.

Containing an Account of Vice-Admiral Benbow's *Proceedings in the* West-Indies *(and particularly his engaging a Squadron of* French *Ships in those Parts) till the time of his Death, when the Command devolved on Rear-Admiral* Whetstone.

1701.

Vice-Admiral *Benbow* parted with Sir *George Rooke* off of *Scilly* the second of *September*, and had then with him not only his own proper Squadron, but the other *English* and *Dutch* Ships before-mentioned, which were detached to see him part of his way; but from the third to the ninth it blew extreme hard, which occasioned the Loss of many Sails and Top-masts.

Arrives at the Isle of St. Mary's.

On the twenty eighth he made St. *Mary*'s, (one of the *Azores*, *Tercera*'s, or Western Islands) when calling the Flag-Officers and Captains on board, he communicated to them his Instructions, who thereupon came to a Resolution to cruise between the Latitudes of 36^d, 30^m, and 35^d, 30^m, about twenty Leagues Westward of the said Island, and not to go Eastward of it until they could get better Intelligence, for procuring whereof he sent a Frigate to St. *Michael*'s, and the *Dutch* detached two of theirs to St. *Mary*'s. Ours brought an Account that the *Portuguese* were under great Apprehensions of a War, and that they daily expected their *Brazil* Fleet at the *Tercera*'s. The Captains of the *Dutch* Frigates (which returned the fourth of *October)* related, that on the twenty eighth of *August*, O. S. there pass'd by St. *Mary*'s thirty two Ships, part of them the *Spanish Flota*, and the rest *French* Ships of War, with a Rear-Admiral, whereupon the Flag-Officers were consulted; but since they could not give entire Credit to the Report, it was agreed to stand as far Westward as

Measures taken for Intelligence.

Flores

CHAP. V. *from the Year* 1689, *to* 1712.

Flores and *Corvo*, with the first Opportunity of an Easterly Wind, and to cruise between the Latitudes of 37 and 35 Degrees.

On the fifth they made sail, and continued so until the tenth, when the Beer in those Ships which were with Sir *John Munden* being in a great measure expended, the Vice-Admiral gave him Orders to make the best of his way to *England*, and proceeded himself with his proper Squadron towards the *West-Indies*, which being composed of two Third Rates, and eight Fourths, he arrived with them at *Barbadoes* the third of *November*, having not met any thing remarkable in his Passage; and here he left a Fourth Rate to follow the Governor's Orders till another arrived from *England*.

Sir John Munden *parts with Vice-Admiral* Benbow, *who arrives at* Barbadoes, *and*

Coming to *Martinica* the eighth of the next Month, after he had ran down fairly in view of all the *French* Fortifications, and Ports, where were several Merchant Ships, but no Men of War, he found them under great Apprehensions of a Rupture, and that they were busying themselves in fortifying the Island, whereon (as was reported) they had three thousand Whites, and daily expected a Squadron from *France*.

Martinica.

The next Day he came to an Anchor in Prince *Rupert*'s Bay, where he supplied himself with Water, and other Refreshments. It is on the N. W. End of *Dominica*, which is inhabited chiefly by *Indians*, who (by reason of their Neighbourhood to and Intercourse with the *French* Islands on each side of them) generally speak that Language; and as they were very friendly to our People, so was the like Civility shewn to them.

The Vice-Admiral arriving at *Nevis*, found the *Leeward* Islands in so good a Condition as not to want any immediate Assistance from him; so that he left them, and proceeding to *Jamaica*, arrived there the fifth of *December*, and anchor'd in *Port Royal* Harbour, where he found two of our Ships, the one a Fifth, and the other a Sixth Rate. The Inhabitants of this Island expecting War, were providing the best they could for their Defence; and about twenty Days before Mr. *Benbow* arrived, there were seen off of Cape St. *Antony*, on the West End of *Cuba*, five *French* Ships; but there being no certain News of the *Flota* from the *Havana*, he hired a Sloop, and sent her to discover whether they were still there.

Mr. Benbow *comes to* Jamaica.

Within few Days he had notice from a *Spanish* Sloop that the *Flota* were at *La Vera Cruz*, the Mony ready to be put on board, and that twelve *French* Ships of War lay at the *Havana* ready to convoy them home; and in *January* he was informed that this Squadron was augmented to sixteen; that Monsieur *Cotlongon* was made Captain-General, and Commander in Chief of the *Spanish* Maritime Forces in those Parts, and that the *Flota* was daily expected at the *Havana*.

The Spanish Flota *at* La Vera Cruz.

Towards the latter end of *January* Brigadier-General *Selwyn* arrived at his Government of *Jamaica*, and with him one Fourth, one Fifth, and one Sixth Rate, a Bomb-Vessel, a Hulk, a Fireship, and three Vessels with Naval Ordnance Stores. By these Ships the Vice-Admiral had Advice that a *French* Squadron arrived at *Martinica*

170½. *Governor* Selwyn *arrives at* Jamaica.

French Squadron at Martinica. — *tinica* about two Months before, and that they were considerably stronger than ours, which put the Governor and Council of *Jamaica* under such Apprehensions, that they provided, at their own Expence, two Fireships for the better Safety of the Island.

The beginning of *March* the Vice-Admiral was informed that Monsieur *Cotlongon* (who commanded the *French* Squadron at the *Havana*) had joined Monsieur *Chateau Renault* at *Martinica*, and *Barbadoes alarmed.* — that they were put to Sea. This alarmed *Barbadoes*, (for there they had also notice of it) and the more so, because we had nothing in those Parts (especially of Sea-Force) which could oppose the *French*.

Not long after this there was Intelligence that the *French* Squadron had been seen off of the S.W. End of *Porto Rico*, the latter End of *February*, in Number forty Sail, with three Flags; but since it could not be entirely depended on, a Sloop was sent up the South, and down the North side of *Hispaniola*, to look into all the Bays and Harbours. This Vessel proceeded as high as *Porto Rico*, and round the Island of *Hispaniola*, and looked particularly in at *Samana*, but steering along the Shore off of *Logane*, a large Ship giving her chase, forced her to Leeward. The next Day, near *Petit-Guavas*, she met with a *French* Sloop, and learnt from her that *Monsieur Chateau Renault in the Gulph of Logane.* — Monsieur *Chateau Renault* was then in the Gulph of *Logane* with thirty Ships of War, and that he had some time before sent ten of the biggest Ships home: But though their Strength was indeed considerable in those Parts, yet did it not amount to what was reported of them.

Governor Selwyn dies, much lamented. — The beginning of *April* Governor *Selwyn* died, who was deservedly very much esteemed by the Inhabitants of *Jamaica*; for during the little time he had been there, he shew'd great Care and Zeal for the Good and Defence of the Island, insomuch that his Loss occasion'd a general Grief.

Although there was at this time a great want of Men in the Squadron, yet the Vice-Admiral determined (since he had no farther Account of the *French*) to sail the beginning of *May* between *Jamaica* and *Petit-Guavas*, not only for the Preservation of the Health of those he had, but to inform himself of Affairs in those Parts, having not yet received Advice from *England* whether there *Rear-Admiral Whetstone joins Mr. Benbow.* — was Peace or War. Accordingly he sailed from *Jamaica* the eighth of *May*, but before he got clear of the Island he met with Rear-Admiral *Whetstone*, with whom he returned, to communicate to the Government some Orders received from *England*, having first sent the *Falmouth*, *Ruby*, and *Experiment* to cruise off of *Petit-Guavas*.

1702. *Advice of a French Squadron.* — He had Advice about the middle of *May*, that on the seventeenth of the preceding Month there passed by *Comanagotta*, on *Terra Firma*, seventeen tall Ships, which steered towards the West-End of *Cuba*. These Ships he judged to be part of Monsieur *Chateau Renault's* Squadron, and that they were bound to the *Havana* to offer their Service for convoying home the *Flota*; but he had not Strength to follow them, without subjecting the Island

CHAP. V. *from the Year* 1698, *to* 1712.   593

Island to the Insults of those Ships which (by the best Intelligence he could gain) were at *Logane*.

Some little time after the Master of a *Spanish* Sloop from *Cuba* acquainted him that Monsieur *Chateau Renault* was at the *Havana*, with twenty six Ships of War, waiting for the *Flota* from *La Vera Cruz*, and this was confirmed by the Ships he had sent out, which in their Tour in those Parts had taken four Prizes, one of them a Ship mounted with 24 Guns, but capable of carrying 40. The Vice-Admiral being likewise informed by a Sloop from *Petit-Guavas* that four Ships with Provisions were bound from thence to the *Havana*, he sent three Frigates to intercept them between Cape *St. Nicholas* and Cape *Mayze*, the very Track leading thither, (for now he had Advice of the Rupture) but they had not the wished-for Success. The same Day he detached Rear-Admiral *Whetstone* (for Captain *Martin*, who was Vice-Admiral of the Squadron, died soon after his coming to *Jamaica*) with two Third Rates, three Fourths, and a Fireship, to intercept Monsieur *Du Cass*, who he heard was expected at *Port Louis*, at the West End of *Hispaniola*, a little within the Isle of *Ash*, with four Ships of War, to settle the *Assiento* at *Carthagena*, and to destroy the Trade of the *English* and *Dutch* for Negroes, resolving to sail himself in five or six Days with the Remainder of the Squadron in search of those *French*, lest the Rear-Admiral should miss them.

Other Advice.

Rear-Admiral Whetstone sent in quest of Monsieur Du Cass.

The eleventh Day of *July* he sailed from *Port Royal* with two Third Rates, six Fourths, one Fireship, a Bomb-Vessel, a Tender, and a Sloop, with design to join the Rear-Admiral; but three Days after meeting Intelligence by the *Colchester* and *Pendennis* that Monsieur *Du Cass* was expected at *Logane*, he plied up for that Port.

Vice-Admiral Benbow goes in quest of Monsieur Du Cass, at Logane.

Coming into the Gulf of *Logane* the twenty seventh, he saw several Ships at Anchor near the Town, one of which being under sail was taken by the Vice Admiral's own Boat. The Men informed him that there were five or six Merchant Ships at *Logane*, and that another Ship in view was a Man of War capable of carrying 50 Guns, but that she had then no more than 30 mounted. This Ship he pursued, and press'd her so close, that when there was no farther hopes of escaping, her Captain ran her on shore, where she blew up. He lay as near the Land as conveniently he could all Night, and coming before the Town in the Morning, found that all the Ships were sailed, except one of 18 Guns, in order to secure themselves in a Harbour called the *Cue*: However, some of our Frigates which were between them and home took three, and sunk another. That Ship with 18 Guns was hauled on shore under a Fortification whereon was mounted 12, but yet the Boats which were sent in burnt her on the Ground, and brought off some others with Wines, Brandy, &c.

A French Ship blown up.

French Ships taken.

The twenty ninth he came before *Petit-Guavas*, but there being no Ships at that Port, he went not in. There were indeed three or four in a Harbour which lies much within the Land, but since it was strongly fortified, as well by Nature as by Art, he thought it not

People at Petit-Guavas surprized.

Gggg

not convenient to run so great a Hazard for so small a Matter, but continuing in the Bay until the second of *August*, stretched from one end of the inhabited part thereof to the other, thereby fatiguing the People, who were apprehensive that he would land, which his Circumstances would by no means permit him to do.

Some little time after he arrived in a Bay at Cape *Donna Maria*, on the West End of *Hispaniola*, a very convenient Place for Water, from whence he sent the *Colchester* to cruise on the North, and the *Experiment* and *Pendennis* on the East End of *Jamaica:* And being informed that Monsieur *Du Cass* was gone to *Carthagena*, and bound from thence to *Porto Bello*, he resolved to sail to that Coast with two Thirds and four Fourth Rates, Rear-Admiral *Whetstone* (who had taken a *French* Ship of War of 18 Guns, and two Sloops in his Cruise) being now at *Jamaica*, with necessary Orders for the Security of that Island.

Mr. Benbow sails from Cape Donna Maria towards Santa Martha, and discovers several French Ships.

The tenth Day of *August* he sailed from Cape *Donna Maria*, and stretching over towards the Coast of *Santa Martha*, he, on the nineteenth in the Evening, discovered ten Sail near that Place. Standing towards them, he soon found the greatest part were *French* Ships of War, whereupon making the usual Signal for a Line of Battel, he went away with an easy Sail, that so his sternmost Ships might come up and join him, the *French* steering Westward along Shore, under their Top-sails.

They were four Ships from 60 to 70 Guns, with one great *Dutch* built Ship of about 30 or 40, and there was another full of Soldiers; the rest small ones, and a Sloop. Our Frigates astern were a long while coming up, and the Night advancing, the Admiral steer'd along side of the *French*, but although he endeavour'd to near them, yet he intended not to make any Attack until the *Defiance* was gotten abreast of the headmost. Before he could reach that Station the *Falmouth* (which was in the Rear) attempted the *Dutch* Ship, the *Windsor* the Ship abreast of her, as did also the *Defiance*; and soon after the Admiral himself was engaged, having first received the Fire of the Ship which was opposite to him; but the *Defiance* and *Windsor* stood no more than two or three Broadsides e'er they luft out of Gun-shot, insomuch that the two sternmost Ships of the Enemy lay upon the Admiral, and gauled him very much; nor did the Ships in the Rear come up to his Assistance with that Diligence which might have been expected. From four a Clock until Night the Fight continued, and though they then left off firing, yet the Admiral kept them Company; and being of opinion that it might be better for the Service if he made a new Line of Battel, and led himself on all Tacks, he did so, but all to little purpose, although the Enemy seemed rather to decline than renew the Engagement.

Our Ships engage the French, but some did not their Duty.

Mr. Benbow to little purpose alters his Disposition.

The twentieth, at break of Day, he found himself very near the *French* Ships, but that there were not any more of his Squadron up with him than the *Ruby*, the rest being three, four, and five Miles astern; and it was somewhat surprizing that the *French*, when they had the Flag himself within their Reach, were so good natur'd as not to fire one Gun on him. At Two in the Afternoon they drew

CHAP. V. *from the Year* 1698, *to* 1712.   595

drew into a Line, but yet made what Sail they could from our Squa- *Mr. Benbow* dron, however the Vice-Admiral's own Ship and the *Ruby* kept *with one Ship* them Company all Night, plying their chafe Guns. *more engages the French.*

Next Morning early he was on the Quarter of the second Ship of the Enemy's Line, within point-blank Shot, but the *Ruby* being ahead of him, she fired at her, as the other Ship also did which was ahead of the Flag, who engaging that Ship which first attack'd the *Ruby*, plied her so warmly, that she was forced to tow off, and he would have followed her with more speed, had he not been obliged to stay by the *Ruby*, for she was very much shatter'd in her Masts, Sails, and Rigging. This Action continued almost two Hours, during which time that Ship of the Enemy's which was in their Rear, happened to be abreast of the *Defiance* and *Windsor*, and even *Captain of* within Gun-shot, but (as it was credibly reported) their Captains *Defiance and Windsor's* did not think fit to spend so much as one Ounce of Powder *shameful Behaviour.* on her.

A Gale sprung up about eight a Clock, and then the *French* making what sail they could, the Vice-Admiral chased, with great Desire of coming up with them; for as his Ships were in very good order for Battel, so had he hopes that the Captains would, at last, have done their Duty. At length he got abreast of two of their sternmost Ships, and fired on them, as some of our Ships did which were a small Distance astern of him; but they pointing their Guns *The Enemy* wholly at the Vice Admiral's Ship, galled her Rigging, and dis- *fire chiefly at* mounted two or three of her lower Tire of Guns, though at the *the Vice-Admiral.* same time they edged away, and were within two Hours out of reach.

The twenty second in the Morning, at Day-light, the *Greenwich* was about three Leagues astern, though the Signal for a Line of Battel was never taken in; but all the other Ships, except the *Ruby*, were nearer, and the *French* almost a Mile and a half ahead. At Three in the Afternoon the Wind, which was before Easterly, changed to the S.W. and gave the Enemy the Advantage of the Weather-Gage; but the Vice-Admiral, by tacking, fetched within Gun-shot of the sternmost of their Ships, when each of them fired at the other. Our Line was now much out of order, some of the *The English* Ships being at least three Miles astern; notwithstanding which the *Disorder.* *French* appeared to be very uneasy, for they did often, and very confusedly too, alter their Course between the West and North.

Next Morning they were about six Miles ahead, and the great *Dutch* Ship stood away at a considerable Distance from them, when some of our Squadron (particularly the *Defiance* and *Windsor*) were four Miles astern of the Flag; but the *French* tacking about ten a Clock, with the Wind at E. N. E. the Vice-Admiral fetched within point blank Shot of two of them, and each gave the other, his Broadside.

The *Ruby*, by reason of her Defects, was sent to *Jamaica* to re- *The Ruby* fit, and the rest of the Ships now mending their pace, they were *sent to Jamaica.* all fairly up with the Vice Admiral about Eight at Night, the Enemy being then near two Miles off. There was now a Prospect of

Gggg 2   doing

doing some Service, and Mr. *Benbow* himself made the best of his way after them, but all the Ships of his Squadron, except the *Falmouth*, fell much astern again. At Twelve the *French* began to separate, and he steering after the sternmost, came so near her at Two in the Morning, that he fired his Broadside, and round and partridge Shot from his upper Tire of Guns, which the *French* Ship returned very briskly; and about three a Clock the Admiral's right Leg was unhappily broken by a Chain-shot. The Skirmish continued until it was Day-light, when there was discovered a Ship of about 70 Guns with her Main and Fore-top-sail Yard disabled, and her sides very much torn by our double-headed Shot. The *Falmouth* assisted well in this Action, but no other Ship, and no sooner was it Day than the *French* came towards our Squadron with a strong Squall of an Easterly Wind. At this time the *Pendennis, Windsor*, and *Greenwich* stood ahead of the Enemy towards the Vice-Admiral, and bore to Leeward of the disabled Ship beforementioned, but passed by her, after firing their Broadsides, and stood Southward, without any regard to the Line of Battel. The *Defiance* followed them, and running also to Leeward of the said disabled Ship, fired some of her Guns; but when there had been no more than twenty return'd, her Commander put her Helm a-weather, bore away before the Wind, lower'd both her Top-sails, and ran down towards the *Falmouth*, which was even then above Gun-shot to the Leeward of the Admiral.

The Enemy seeing these Ships stretch away Southward, expected that they would tack and stand with them, for which reason they brought to with their Heads Northward, at about two Miles distance, the Vice-Admiral being within Half-Gun-shot of the disabled Ship; but the *French* perceiving that those three Ships did not tack, as they had reason to think they would have done, they bore down upon our Flag, and running between him and their shattered Ship, gave him all the Fire they could; nor was there at this time any of his Ships near him, for they were in a hurry, and shewed as little regard to Discipline as they did to their own Honour. The Captain to the Admiral fired two Guns at those Ships ahead, to put them in mind of their Duty, but the *French* seeing the great Disorder they were in, brought to, and lay by their disabled Ship, remann'd her, and took her in a tow.

When the Vice-Admiral's tatter'd Rigging was repaired, Orders were given to chase the Enemy, who were at least three Miles to Leeward, steering N. E. the Wind at S. S. W. but our Ships continued to run to and fro very confusedly. The Flag being under great Uneasiness at such scandalous Proceedings, commanded the Captain of the *Defiance* on board of him, who, in a very odd manner, endeavoured to dissuade him from renewing the Engagement, since he had (as he alledged) tried the Enemy's Strength six Days together with so ill Success: And the other Captains being likewise called, most of them were of opinion that it was not adviseable to continue the Fight, although they were at this very time on the Enemy's Broadsides, with the fairest Opportunity of Success that had yet offer'd:

CHAP V. *from the Year* 1698, *to* 1712.   597

fer'd: Besides, our Strength was one Ship of 70 Guns, one of 64, one of 60, and three of 50, their Masts, Yards, and all things else, in as good a Condition as could be expected, and not above eight Men killed, except those in the Vice-Admiral's own Ship; nor was there any want of Ammunition; whereas the Enemy had no more than four Ships from 60 to 70 Guns, and one of them in a tow by reason of her being disabled in her Masts and Rigging. The Vice-Admiral finding himself under these Disappointments, thought it high time to return to *Jamaica*, where he soon after joined the rest of his Squadron with Rear-Admiral *Whetstone*.

Vice-Admiral Benbow returns to Jamaica.

These *French* Ships with Monsieur *Du Cass* carried from the *Groyne* the Duke of *Albuquerque*, with a considerable Number of Soldiers, who was sent from his Employment of Vice-Roy of *Andalusia* to reside in that Quality in *Mexico*, and part of them were the very same which got into the *Groyne*, when some of our Ships were cruising in those Parts under the Command of Sir *John Munden* to intercept them, of which I shall give a particular Account, when I can enter thereon without entangling it with this Transaction in the *West-Indies*.

An Account of the French Squadron.

This *French* Squadron, which at first was composed of eight Ships of War, and fourteen Transports, touching at *Porto Rico*, supplied themselves with Wood and Water, and after three Days stay proceeding Westward, they separated off of the East End of *Hispaniola*, which was about the tenth of *August*; the Vice-Roy running down the North side thereof for *La Vera Cruz* with two of the Men of War, one of 70, and the other of 60 Guns; Monsieur *Du Cass* with the other six, and three Transports, bent his Course along the South side, with five hundred *Spanish* Soldiers, and stopp'd at St. *Domingo*; but making little or no stay there, sailed for *Rio de la Hacha*, where he lay not above two Hours, but leaving two Ships of War, one of 50, and the other of 40 Guns, to settle the *Assiento* for Negroes, steered towards *Carthagena* and *Porto Bello* to land his Forces.

The twentieth of *September* the *York* and *Norwich* arrived at *Jamaica*, bringing a necessary Supply of Stores and Provisions; and as soon as the Vice-Admiral could have Matters got in Readiness for trying at a Court-Martial those Captains who had so scandalously failed in the Performance of their Duty, he ordered Rear-Admiral *Whetstone* to examine thoroughly thereinto, chusing rather so to do, (though he had not Authority to delegate his Power to another) than to sit as President of the Court himself; and after several Days were spent in examining Witnesses, and hearing what the Prisoners could alledge in their own Justification, the Captains of the *Defiance* and *Greenwich* received Sentence of Death, which was not put in Execution until they arrived in the *Bristol* at *Plimouth*, aboard which Ship they were shot; for the Orders sent from hence did not come timely to *Jamaica*. The Captain of the *Windsor* was cashiered, and sentenced to be imprisoned during her Majesty's Pleasure; he who commanded the *Pendennis* died before the Trial, otherwise he would, in all Probability, have received the same Sentence

Some of the English Captains sentenced to Death.

tence as those of the *Defiance* and *Greenwich*; and the Vice-Admiral's own Captain, with the Commander of the *Falmouth* were suspended, for signing to the Paper drawn up and delivered by the others, wherein they gave their Reasons for not renewing the Engagement; but he having represented that those two Gentlemen had behaved themselves very well in the Action, the Lord High-Admiral was pleased to send Orders for their being employed again.

Observation of Mr. Benbow's Conduct.

As I have forborn mentioning the Names of those two unhappy Gentlemen who suffered, (one of whom on other Occasions had distinguished himself) more for the Sake of their Relations than any other Consideration, so thus much may be observed as to Vice-Admiral *Benbow*'s Conduct; that although he was a good Seaman, and a gallant Man, and that he was qualified, in most respects, to command a Squadron, especially in the *West-Indies*, in which Parts of the World he had had long Experience, yet when he found his Captains so very remiss in the Performance of their Duty, I think he ought, in point of Discretion, to have summoned them, (and even that at first) on board his own Ship, and there confined them, and placed their first Lieutenants in their Rooms, who would have fought well, were it for no other Reason than the Hopes of being continued in those Commands had they survived.

Vice-Admiral Benbow dies, and Capt. Whetstone commands the Squadron.

The fourth of *November* the Vice-Admiral died, the Pain which he laboured under, and his Uneasiness for other Misfortunes, having for some time before thrown him into a deep Melancholy, so that the Command of the Squadron fell on Captain *Whetstone*, who had acted before as Rear-Admiral. He made what Dispatch he could in putting the Ships into a Condition for the Sea, and then leaving Part of them for Security of the Island, he cruised with the Remainder upon the North and South Sides of *Hispaniola*, but could not get any other News of the Enemy, than that Monsieur *du Cass* with eight Ships of War had been for some time at the *Havana*.

$170\frac{2}{7}$.
A Fire at Port Royal.

I cannot here pass over a melancholy Accident; which is this. On the ninth of *February* a Fire broke out in the Town of *Port-Royal*, on the Island of *Jamaica*, which between Noon, and twelve at Night, laid the whole Place in Ashes; for little or nothing escaped the Fury of the Flames but the two Fortifications. Several of the Inhabitants were burnt, the major Part of their Stores and Goods destroyed, and what was saved was by the Industry of the Seamen. The Rear-Admiral seeing them in this deplorable Condition, put forth a Declaration, and, as he thereby promised, entertained, and relieved many of them on board her Majesty's Ships, till such time as they could be otherwise provided for.

The Beginning of *February* the Ship *Gosport* arrived at *Jamaica* from *New-England* with a small Supply of Provisions, and when the Rear-Admiral had taken on board the Company of Soldiers which Governor *Dudley* had raised in that Colony, and sent by her, he dispatched her back to *Boston* to follow the said Governor's Orders.

CHAP.

CHAP. VI.

Containing an Account of Sir William Whetstone's, *Captain* Hovenden Walker's, *and Vice-Admiral* Graydon's *Proceedings in the* West-Indies.

I Should indeed, according to Course of Time, have given you an Accouut, e'er now, of what happened nearer Home, and of Sir *George Rooke*'s Expedition, with a Fleet of *English* and *Dutch* Ships to *Cadiz*; but, for my former Reasons, I will first bring this *West-India* Squadron to *England*, and those which were sent to join them. Let it therefore suffice, at present, that I acquaint you, Sir *George Rooke*, in his Return from *Cadiz*, did (pursuant to Orders he received from her Majesty, dated the seventh of *June* 1702) direct Captain *Hovenden Walker** of the *Burford*, to proceed with that Ship, and five more Third Rates, together with ten Transports, to *Barbadoes*, and there, or in some of the *Leeward-Islands*, to disembark the four Regiments, amounting to near four thousand Men, which were on board the said Transports and the Men of War. He was directed to continue in those Parts, and for the Defence of the Island of *Jamaica*, till farther Orders; and, for the better enabling him so to do, to advise from time to time with the respective Governours of those Islands and Plantations. *1702. Sir George Rooke detaches Captain Walker with a Squadron to the West-Indies.*

He lay off of Cape St. *Vincent* two Nights, and as many Days, taking in Provisions from the victualling Ships, and would have touched at *Maderas* for Water, had he not been prevented by hard Gales of Wind, which obliged him to bear away for the Cape *de Verde* Islands, where he arrived the twenty fourth of *October*, and furnished himself with Refreshments. Sailing from thence the fourteenth of the next Month, he first reached *Barbadoes*, and proceeded from thence the Beginning of *January* towards the *Leeward-Islands*, pursuant to Orders which he received from *England* by the *Edgar*, *Anglesey*, and *Sunderland*, which Ships brought with them Recruits of Land-Forces, as well as Stores and Provisions for the Ships in those Parts, and the two first were immediately dispatched by him to General *Codrington*, with such Instructions and Letters as they had carried for him from hence.

While he lay at *Barbadoes* there came into the Road a *French* Vessel with a Flag of Truce, which he caused to be seized, as were part of her Men also on Shore, who being tried at a Court Martial, one of them was condemned to die, for it plainly appeared that they came thither as Spies. The chief Occasion of this Resort of *French* Vessels to *Barbadoes*, was the Cartel that Island had made with *Martinica* for the Exchange of Prisoners, and by that means there were not only Opportunities found for carrying on a collu- *A French Spy condemned at Barbadoes.*

---

*Afterwards a Flag-Officer.

five

five Trade, but of giving the Enemy Intelligence of our Proceedings. Many Privateers were also fitted out from the Island, for which the Government took Men from the Merchant Ships, and sent many more from the Shore, insomuch that the Squadron wanted the Service of them; and indeed their Wants were very considerable, for the Distempers incident to those Parts had swept away great Numbers.

There arrived very luckily in *Barbadoes* Road six of our *East-India* Ships, very richly loaden, and Mr. *Walker* considering how necessary it was that they should be safely conducted Home as soon as it was possible, he, with the Advice of the Captains with him, agreed to send the *Expedition* as their Convoy, a Third Rate Ship commanded by Captain *Knapp*, with whom they safely came to *England*.

170½. The nineteenth of *January* Vice-Admiral *Graydon*, then of the White Squadron, was appointed Commander in Chief of the Ships in the *West-Indies*, and had the following Instructions for his Government in that Expedition, *viz*.

Vice-Admiral Graydon's Instructions for commanding in the West-Indies.

First, To sail to *Plimouth* in the *Sheerness*, a Fifth Rate, and from thence to *Barbadoes* with her, the *Resolution* and *Blackwall*, the former a Third and the other a Fourth Rate. There he was to take under his Command the aforementioned Ships with Captain *Walker*, and such others as he should find at that Place; but if they were sailed from thence, to repair to *Nevis*, or any other of the Plantations where they might be met with, and thence to proceed in such manner as should be found most for the Service, upon its being considered at a Council of War of the Sea Captains, and the Chief, and other proper Officers of the Land-Forces; and if he attempted any thing in the *Leeward-Islands* that might occasion his making any considerable Stay there, he was to send a Frigate to Rear-Admiral *Whetstone*, with Orders to get himself ready, in all respects, to sail against his Arrival at *Jamaica*.

Secondly, He was not to stay longer in attempting any of the *French* Plantations than the twentieth of *May*, and then (or before, if possible,) to proceed with all the Ships of War, and the Transport Ships with Soldiers, Ammunition, and Stores, and such Forces as the Commander in Chief of the Land Forces should appoint, to *Port-Royal* in *Jamaica*; and this he was forthwith to do, if he found that Captain *Walker*, with the Ships and Troops, had done what they were able against the said *French* Plantations, and gone to *Jamaica* before he arrived.

Thirdly, When he came to that Island he was to put the Ships of War, and other Ships and Vessels, into the best, and most speedy Condition for their return Home; to cause to be received on board them so many Land-Soldiers as the Commander in Chief should desire, and to bring also to *England* such Prisoners as should be taken during the Expedition.

Fourthly, He was to consider what two Ships of the Fourth Rate, one of the Fifth, and another of the Sixth, might be most properly

left

CHAP. VI. *from the Year* 1689, *to* 1712.   601

left at *Jamaica*, and accordingly to leave them there, with the Fire-ships provided by the Inhabitants for the Defence of the Island.

Fifthly, Three other Ships he was to send with the Trade bound from *Jamaica* to *England*, as soon, as they should be ready to sail; and he was ordered to leave two at the said Island, to bring Home the latter Trade the Beginning of *August*.

Sixthly, Besides these Detachments, he was to send two fourth Rates to *Virginia*, to joyn some others at that Place, and to accompany the Trade from thence to *England* at the Time prefixed for their Departure.

Seventhly, This being done, he was with the rest of the Squadron, and all the Transport Ships with Soldiers, Victuallers, Storeships, and others, to make the best of his way to *Newfoundland* but to leave at *Jamaica* the Hulk and Stores for the use of such Ships as might be sent thither.

Eighthly, when he came to *Newfoundland* he was to consider at a Council of War, of Sea and Land Officers, how the *French* might be best attempted and destroyed at *Placentia*, with the Assistance of the Land Forces, as well as at their other Settlements in those Parts, and to govern himself accordingly; and if he found that any of the Ships could be conveniently spared to attack the *French* Fishery on the *Bank*, he was to send them on that Service. But he was yet farther enjoined to repair to *Boston* in *New England*, if he judged, when he sailed from *Jamaica*, he should be too early at *Newfoundland*, and to take from that Government such Soldiers as it might be able to furnish, provided they could get Embarkations timely ready, not only to transport the said Soldiers to *Newfoundland*, but back again.

Ninthly, When he had done his utmost at *Newfoundland*, and on the *Bank*, he was to appoint two Ships to convoy the Fishing Vessels bound to *Portugal*, but to caution their Captains not to go into any Port, until they were thoroughly satisfied there was not a Rupture with that Crown; and having given these necessary Orders, he was to repair to *England* with the rest of the Squadron without Delay.

Notwithstanding Vice-Admiral *Graydon* was at first ordered to proceed from hence with only the *Resolution*, *Blackwall*, and *Sheerness*, (the latter whereof proved not fit for the Voyage) it was afterwards thought adviseable to appoint the *Mountague* and *Nonsuch*, of 60 and 50 Guns, then at *Plimouth*, to accompany him one hundred and fifty Leagues into the Sea, which they did accordingly, and parted not till the twenty sixth of *March*, in the Latitude of 43^d, about one hundred and seventy Leagues West from the *Lizard*, but on the eighteenth of that Month, in the Latitude of 47^d and 30^m, they saw four *French* Ships of War to Leeward, two of about 60 Guns each, one of 50, and the other 40, which latter being not only the smallest, but the sternmost, the *Mountague* commanded by Captain *William Cleaveland* [*], bore down to, and soon after engaged her. Hereupon the Vice-Admiral made the Signal for a Line of Battel, and consequently for the *Mountague*'s coming off, but her Fore-top-Sail being shot in pieces the second Broadside she received

The Mountague engaged with a French Ship.

---

[*] *Since a Commissioner of the Navy.*

Hhhh   from

from the Enemy, she could not tack so soon as otherwise might have been expected, insomuch that the other three *French* Ships wore and bearing down to the Ship that had been engaged, each of them fired her Broadside at the *Mountague*; but she being to Windward, and the Sea running high, as the *French* generally fire, in Hopes of wounding Masts, Yards, or Rigging, all their Shot flew over her, so that she received not any considerable Damage. The *French* Ships (which now made the best of their Way from ours) were four, for they were part of the Squadron under Command of Monsieur *du Casse*, with which Vice-Admiral *Benbow* engaged in the *West-Indies*; and (as 'twas reported) were very rich.

Considering what Strength Vice-Admiral *Graydon* had with him, it occasioned many Reflections, not only upon the Score of the *Mountague*'s bearing down singly, but his not endeavouring to engage the Enemy himself; wherefore I think it necessary to inform you, that when it was designed he should proceed with the *Resolution* and *Blackwall* only, he had positive Orders from his Royal Highness the Prince of *Denmark*, Lord High-Admiral, not to interrupt his Passage by chasing or speaking with any Ships whatever, nor even to hoist his Flag till such time as he joined the Squadron in the *West-Indies*, or a considerable part thereof; and these Orders were not contradicted when the other two Ships were appointed to accompany him into the Sea. It is likewise to be considered, that he carried with him the immediate Orders by which the whole *West-India* Squadron, and the Forces were to move, as also the necessary Supplies of Stores and Provisions, in Transport Ships taken up for that Purpose; wherefore although the Booty might have been very considerable had these *French* Ships been taken, yet, on the other hand, had he engaged, and been unluckily disabled, and, for that Reason, forced back to *England* to refit, the Service whereon he was going might have been very much hinder'd, if not wholly disappointed: Besides, had he taken these Ships of the Enemy's, he must have come to *England* with them, for otherwise he could not have secured the Prisoners, and have put them in a sailing Condition; and had he chased them any considerable time before he came up with them, (which in all Probability he must have done) his Convoys would have been exposed to the last Degree, for it was altogether impossible for them to have kept him Company.

Vice-Admiral Graydon ordered not to chase, and For what Reasons.

Before any farther Account came of him, or from Captain *Walker* of his Proceedings in the *Leeward Islands*, a Letter was received from Rear-Admiral *Whetstone*, who (as I have already said) was at the Head of the Ships in the *West-Indies*, which Letter was dated from *Jamaica* the fourteenth of *April*. He sailed from thence about the middle of *February*, and being informed, on the Coast of *Hispaniola*, that there was expected in those Parts from *France* a considerable Fleet of Merchant Ships, he cruised on both Sides of the Island in Hopes of meeting them. After he had unsuccessfully spent five Weeks time on this Service, he looked into Port *Louis*, but not finding any thing there, stood away for *Petit-Guavas* and *Logane*; and knowing in Vice-Admiral *Benbow*'s time, that when

1703. Rear-Admiral Whetstone goes out to cruise.

our

CHAP. VI. *from the Year* 1698, *to* 1712.   603

our Ships appeared on the one Side, the Enemy made their Escape from the other, he divided his Squadron, one part whereof he sent Southward, and proceeded himself Westward with the rest. When the first Part of the Squadron came in Sight, three Privateers which were in every respect ready for Service, stood away Northward, but the Rear-Admiral forcing two of them ashore, burnt them, and the other he took. Captain *Vincent*, who commanded to the Southward, rowed in the Night into a Place called the *Cue*, where he found four Ships, one of which he burnt, another he sunk, the third (which was a Consort of the Privateers aforementioned) he towed out, and boarding the fourth, she was blown up by the accidental firing of a Granadoe Shell. *Takes and destroys some of the Enemy's Ships.*

From this Place the Rear-Admiral sailed to *Port de Paix*, but found no Shipping there, for the beforementioned Privateers were all that the Enemy had in those Parts, with which, and five hundred Men, they designed to have made an Attempt on the North Side of *Jamaica*, and in these Ships were taken one hundred and twenty Prisoners.

Captain *Walker* was from the third to the eighteenth of *February* in his Passage from *Barbadoes* to *Antegoa*, and when he arrived there, he found the Land-Forces had no Ammunition, and that unless he stopt the Victualling Ships bound to *Jamaica*, there would not have been Provisions sufficient to have enabled them to make any Attempt. At the Desire of Colonel *Codrington*, General of the *Leeward-Islands*, he supplied the Forces with Powder, but it was not a little surprizing, that among the great Number of Flints they had on board, there were not, as he represented, fifty in a thousand fit for Muskets; nor was there any Provision made of Mortars, Bombs, Pick-axes, Spades, or any thing indeed, proper and convenient for a Siege. *Capt. Walker arrives at the Leeward-Islands.*

He sailed from *Antegoa* the latter End of *February*, and the Squadron, as well as the Forces, being got together the ninth of the following Month, in a Bay at the North End of *Guadalupe*, a small Party of Men were put on shore without any Opposition, but came on board again when they had burnt some Plantations and Houses. Next Day he anchored in another Bay nearer the Town, and on the the twelfth of *March*, in the Morning, a considerable Part of the Forces landed upon *Guadalupe*, under Command of the General, who were so warmly received by the *French*, that several of our Officers and Men were killed and wounded; but the Commadore ordering one of the Ships, named the *Chichester*, to fire upon some Batteries the Enemy had between our Forces and the Town, they soon after quitted them, which our Men after they had got Footing, possessed themselves of. *Our Troops are repulsed at Guadalupe.*

Next Day the rest of the Soldiers, and four hundred Seamen from the Ships were put on shore, and then the General made himself Master of the North Part of the Town, but the Enemy retired to a Castle and Fort, which commanded the most Part thereof. *They land again.*

Some Cannon and proper Ammunition were put on shore the fifteenth, in order to the raising Batteries against the Fort and Castle,

Hhhh 2   which

604   *Naval Transactions of the* English, Book V.

The French blow up the Castle and Fort.

which the Enemy kept Possession of until the second of *April*; but then two of the Frigates being ordered to ply their Guns upon them, and their Line of Communication and Trenches; and the Castle being already much shattered by our Batteries, they blew it up the next Morning, together with their Fort, and retired into the Woods and Mountains, where they looked on themselves to be in greatest Safety; for as they were inaccessible for an Army, so could not any thing oblige them to surrender but want of Provisions.

General Codrington returns to Nevis.

After this there was but very little done more than the sending out Parties to burn the Country, and to bring in Cattel, which were much wanted; for all the while the Army was on shore, which was two Months, they were supplied with Provisions from the Ships, so that the Men were at short Allowance from the latter end of *April*. It was then that General *Codrington* returned to *Nevis*, having been for some time very much indisposed; and soon after Colonel *Whetham* (who was dangerously ill) took his Passage in the *Burford* to *Antegoa*, which Ship carried also thither three Companies of Soldiers, and the Guns taken from the Enemy at *Guadalupe*.

Colonel Wills *commanded the Troops.*

Colonel *Wills* had now the Command of the Land-Forces on shore, and a Council of War being held of the Sea and Land-Officers, it was agreed that the Troops should embark the seventh of *May*, and accordingly they were all on board that Morning by three a Clock, the Retreat being made without the Loss of a Man.

The Town on Guadalupe burnt, and the Fortifications demolished.

The Enemy's Town was burnt to the Ground, all their Fortifications demolished, and their Guns either brought off or burst ashore: And considering the Circumstances our Troops were in, there was a Necessity for retreating, the *French* having, some Days before, conveyed about nine hundred Men from *Martinica* to *Dominica*, and from thence to *Guadalupe*.

In this Undertaking there was no Assistance to be got of Pilots, and the Road before *Guadalupe* was so exceeding bad, that several of the Ships lost their Anchors, for the Ground was foul, and the Water very deep, so that one or other was daily forced out to Sea: And never did any Troops enterprize a thing of this Nature with more Uncertainty, and under so many Difficulties, for they had neither Guides, or any thing else which was necessary.

The Forces being embarked, the Squadron pass'd by *Monserat* the eighth of *May*, and after lying by until the Soldiers allotted for that Island were put on shore, the Commadore arrived at *Nevis* that Night, and from thence sent other Soldiers to St. *Christopher's*. In this Action there were Officers killed on our side one Major, two Captains, six Lieutenants, and wounded two Colonels, seven Captains, and nine Lieutenants; and two Colonels, four Lieutenants, and three Ensigns died. One hundred and fifty four Soldiers were killed, two hundred and eleven wounded, seventy two died, fifty nine deserted, and twelve were taken Prisoners.

1703. Vice-Admiral Graydon arrives at Barbadoes.

Vice-Admiral *Graydon*, beforemention'd, arrived at the Island of *Madera* the tenth of *April*, where he took in Water, and sailing the fourteenth, at Five in the Afternoon, came to *Barbadoes* the twelfth of *May*. He found there a Brigantine which had lately left
Guada-

CHAP. VI. *from the Year* 1698, *to* 1712.

Guadalupe, and being informed by her Master that the Seamen and Soldiers, with Captain *Walker's* Squadron, were at half Allowance of Provisions, he applied himself to the Agent-Victualler, and being furnished with what Beef, Pork, Bread, and Pease could be procured, he sailed the seventeenth. The twentieth he ran in so close with the Fort and Town of *Guadalupe*, as that he had a plain sight of the Ruins, when stretching away for *Antegoa*, he met the Sloop which he had sent with Notice of his Arrival; and coming into *Nevis* Road the twenty third, there he found the Squadron and Army in very great want of Provisions, which he supplied in the best manner he could, to enable them to accompany him to *Jamaica*. *Comes to the Leeward-Islands.*

Leaving *Nevis* the twenty fifth of *May*, and arriving at *Jamaica* the fourth of next Month, he ordered a Survey to be immediately taken of the Condition of all the Ships with him, which (generally speaking) proved to be very defective, not only in their Hulls, but also in their Masts, Stores, and Rigging, nor were they in a better Condition as to Men. There were no more Stores than what had been sent thither in a Brigantine, and among them but five Suits of Sails, one for a Third Rate, two for a Fourth, one for a Fifth, and one for a Sixth; and this was the more unfortunate, because five of the Ships which Sir *George Rooke* sent with Captain *Walker* were not fitted for Service in the *West-Indies*, and consequently wanted much more than they could be furnished with there. *Vice-Admiral Graydon arrives at Jamaica. The Ships in a bad Condition.*

These Difficulties, as well as Misunderstandings between him and some of the chief Persons of *Jamaica*, induced him to make all possible Dispatch in putting the Squadron into a Condition of returning to *England*, pursuant to the Instructions he had received; and then leaving the *Norwich*, *Experiment*, *Seahorse*, and *Harman* and *Earl* Gally Fireships, together with the St. *Antonio*, and *Recovery* Sloops, to attend on the Island, and the *Colchester* and *Sunderland* to convoy home the latter Trade, he sailed the twenty first of *June* for *Blewfields*, the most convenient Place for watering the Ships, and proceeding from thence, fell in with Cape *Pine*, in *Newfoundland*, the second of *August*. *He comes to Newfoundland.*

When he had got through the Gulf, it was agreed by himself and the General-Officers to send away the *Tryal* Sloop for Intelligence to Captain *Richards*, who commanded at St. *John's* in *Newfoundland*, and for Pilots for *Placentia*, as also to desire that he would come himself, not only to advise, and assist, as an Engineer, but with some necessary Stores, which though he readily complied with, yet could he not get on board until the twenty second of *August* in St. *Mary's* Bay; for on the fourth of that Month there came on a very great Fogg, which, to Admiration, continued thirty Days, so that it was difficult to discern one Ship from another, insomuch that it was found necessary to lie by, since they judged themselves clear of the Land. Herein they were deceived by the Current, for they not only saw the Land about Ten at Night under their Lee, but found themselves embayed, and the Ships, which had lost many Sails were not able to get out that Night; besides, the *Defiance*, (a Ship of 70 Guns) was without a Main-maſt, and therefore they put for, and with Difficulty got ſafe into a Harbour to Leeward of them called St. *Mary*'s.

But by reaſon of the Fog the Squadron was ſo diſperſed that they joined not again until the third of *September*, and then a Council of War was called, where were preſent the Vice-Admiral himſelf, Rear-Admiral *Whetſtone*, and thirteen Sea-Captains; and of the Land Officers, Colonel *Rivers*, (who commanded in Chief) ſix Captains, and an Engineer. They took into Conſideration her Majeſty's Inſtructions to Brigadier-General *Collembine*, (who died ſome time before) and thoſe from the Admiralty to Mr. *Graydon*, and finding the Ships in a very ill Condition as to their Hulls, Maſts, Sails, ſtanding and running Rigging, and Ground-Tackle; that they wanted many Men, and that even thoſe they had were very ſickly and weak; that they were at ſhort Allowance of Proviſions; that the Soldiers, by drinking Water in ſo cold a Climate, were not only benumm'd in their Limbs, but ſubjected to Fluxes and Scurvies; that the five Regiments were reduced to one thouſand and thirty five Men; that the five hundred Soldiers they ſhould have had from *New-England* were at firſt but ſeventy, and now no more than twenty five, and all of them unfit for Service; and that by the beſt Accounts from *Placentia*, the Enemy were not only ſuperior in Number, and conſequently able to make a good Reſiſtance; but that the Avenues to the Place were extremely difficult, the Grounds ſpungy, and no Planks, or other Materials, for mounting the Guns on the Batteries. Theſe Difficulties and Obſtructions being maturely conſidered, together with the good Circumſtances the Enemy were in, and the Aſſiſtance they might have from the Privateers, and other Shipping then at *Placentia*, the Council of War were unanimouſly of opinion, that to make any Attempt on that Place with the Ships and Forces at ſuch a Seaſon of the Year, was altogether impracticable, and that inſtead of any Probability of Succeſs, it might tend to the Diſhonour of her Majeſty's Arms.

Agreed not to attempt Placentia.

Next Day the Vice-Admiral ſent five of his Ships to cruiſe off of Cape *Race*, and ſailed ſoon after to the Bay of *Bulls* to make up the Fleet; which being done, he took his Departure for *England* the twenty fourth of *September*.

The Vice-Admiral leaves Newfoundland.

He met with very bad Weather in his Paſſage, inſomuch that on the fourth of *October* ſix of the Ship's Main-ſhrouds broke, and her Main-maſt being ſprung, he was conſtrained to bear away to ſave it, which occaſioned his ſeparating from the reſt of the Fleet; but joining Rear-Admiral *Whetſtone*, and ſix Sail more, on the fourteenth, he found them all in a miſerable Condition; and the *Boyne*, where he was himſelf, not only made ſix Feet Water a Watch, but was much diſabled in her Rigging; however he and the Rear-Admiral got ſafe into the *Downs* the twenty ſecond of *October*, and with them only the *Stromboli* Fireſhip; for as he had, before he left *Newfoundland*, appointed the *Canterbury*, *Bonadventure*, and *Sorlings*, to convoy the Fiſh-Ships to *Portugal*, ſo did he, when he came near the Coaſt of *Ireland*, order the *Reſolution*, *Yarmouth*, *Edgar*,

Our Squadron much diſabled in their Paſſage home.

Edgar, and *Windsor*, to conduct the Transport-Ships to that Kingdom, with what Officers and Men remained of the four Regiments.

The other Ships of the Squadron put in some at one Port, and some at another, and indeed it was the greatest good Fortune, considering their Condition, the Season of the Year, and their Weakness, as to Men, that they all arrived safe in *England*. Thus ended an Expedition, wherein no inconsiderable part of the Navy of *England* was employed, and many of them from the time that Vice-Admiral *Benbow* proceeded to the *West-Indies*, which was in *November* 1698.

I wish I could, by summing up the whole, make any tolerable Comparison between the Service this Squadron did the Nation, and the Expence which attended it, and, which is far more valuable, the Lives of many good Officers, Seamen, and Soldiers: But since I have already given a full Account of all the Benefits which arose from this tedious Expedition, I shall leave the Reader to judge, whether it could, in any Degree, turn to Account, to suffer a strong Squadron of Ships to lie so long in the *West-Indies*, without a real Prospect of any considerable Service from them, especially when other necessary occasions very often required their being much nearer home, and too often suffered for want of them.

Observation on the Expedition to the West-Indies.

CHAP. VII.

The Earl of Pembroke, *Lord High-Admiral, sends a small Squadron to bring the Effects of the* English *Merchants from* Cadiz, *upon Suspicion of a War: With the then Naval Preparations of the* French.

BEfore I proceed farther, suffer me to inform you, that his Majesty revoking the Letters-Patents to the Lords Commissioners of the Admiralty, appointed *Thomas* Earl of *Pembroke* and *Montgomery*, Lord High-Admiral of *England* and *Ireland*, and of all his foreign Plantations; a Person who, besides the Honour which he derives from his noble Ancestors, is Master of many extraordinary Virtues. His Lordship at the beginning, and towards the end of the last War, presided at the Board of Admiralty, when it was in Commission, where, as well as in the Office of Privy-Seal, his Transactions as one of the Plenipotentiaries for the Treaty of Peace at *Ryswick*, and in that honourable Post of President of his Majesty's Council, (from which he was called to that of High-Admiral, and to which he returned) he gave remarkable Instances of his Zeal to the Publick Service.

Earl of Pembroke appointed Lord-High-Admiral.

No sooner did this noble Lord enter on his important Trust, than he diligently applied himself to the Execution of it, and in such a manner as might most conduce not only to the Good of the Nation in general, but to the Trade, both at home and abroad, in particular, wherein he had the good Fortune to give a general Satisfaction; but he continued not a full Year in this Employment, for King *William* dying, and Queen *Anne* succeeding to the Throne, her Majesty was pleased to constitute to that great and troublesome Office, her Royal Consort, Prince *George* of *Denmark*, to assist him wherein he was empower'd under the Great Seal to appoint such Persons as he judged most proper to be his Council; and on the Death of his Highness, the Earl of *Pembroke* (who had been some time before Lord Lieutenant of the Kingdom of *Ireland*) was recalled to the Office of Lord High-Admiral, which he held not altogether so long as he had done before; for in less than twelve Months time it was put into Commission, his Lordship desiring to resign, foreseeing insupportable Difficulties, by reason not only of the great Arrear of Wages then due to the Seamen, but in many other Particulars.

Prince George constituted Lord High-Admiral.

It being thought that a War would suddenly break out, his Lordship consider'd how the Effects of our Merchants at *Cadiz*, but more especially what should be brought thither by the Fleet from *New-Spain*, might be in the best manner secured, and thereupon appointed three Frigates, the beginning of *November*, to proceed under the Command of Captain *Edmund Loades*, to take those Effects on board, and bring them to *England*; but he was cautioned not to go in, but only to cruise between Cape St. *Mary*'s and Cape *Spartell*, until he should be certainly informed that the *Flota* were arrived in the Bay of *Cadiz*, nor even then to go in, if a Rupture happened, but rather to lie in a proper Station, if the Merchants found they could send their Money to him by *Barcalongos*, or other small Embarkations.

1701.

Some Ships sent to Cadiz to bring home the Merchants Effects.

If this could not be done, he was so to place the Ships under his Command, as that they might most probably meet with the Convoys coming with Mr. *Graydon* from *Newfoundland*; and if he had notice that any Number of *French* Ships were cruising about Cape St. *Vincent*, he was to endeavour to keep Westward of them, and not only to give Mr. *Graydon* notice thereof, but to deliver unto him Orders, whereby he was directed to consult with the Masters of the Ships under his Convoy, and then to see the Trade to some Port on this side the Mouth of the Streights, or home, if that should be judged most proper; and for their greater Security, Captain *Loades* was ordered to accompany them with the Ships under his Command, in case they came home, but if they put into any Port of *Portugal*, or proceeded up the Streights, he was then to make the best of his way to *England*.

Instructions to the Ships sent to Cadiz.

Nevertheless, if the Merchants judged they could send to him their Effects, and, for that reason, should desire him to lie in a convenient Station, or to come into the Bay of *Cadiz*, he was to do it with two of the Ships under his Command, and to send the third

CHAP. VII. *from the Year 1698, to 1712.* 609

to look out for, and give the beforementioned Notice to the Commander of the *Newfoundland* Convoy; and since it was uncertain whether War might be declared before he came home, he was ordered, if it so happened, to endeavour to take, sink, or destroy any of the Ships of *France* or *Spain* which he might happen to meet with.

At this time her Majesty had at *Cadiz* a considerable Quantity of Naval Stores, which Captain *Loades* was ordered to bring home, together with the Store-keeper at that Place, but not being able to take on board the whole, there was a Necessity of selling the rest to the *Spaniards* much under their real Value; and soon after this, a Ship was sent to take out of the Bay of *Cadiz* the two Hulks made use of the last War for careening our Ships, and left there upon concluding the Peace, that so neither the *French*, nor *Spaniards*, might have the Advantage of them. This Service was effectually performed, for they were put into a Condition to sail, in order, as it was given out, to be brought to *England*; but since it was not possible to bring them home, by reason they were cut down so very low, the Captain of the Frigate sunk them at a convenient Distance from the Port of *Cadiz*, as his Instructions required him to do.

The Hulks and Stores brought from Cadiz.

Captain *Loades* sailed with the Ships under his Command on the aforemention'd Service, and the nineteenth of *October* 1701 came to his intended Station six Leagues S. S. E. from Cape St. *Mary*'s, meeting Mr. *Graydon* some few Days after, with his Convoys from *Newfoundland*, to whom he deliver'd the Instructions which he carried out for him.

Capt. Loades, his proceeding to and from Cadiz.

Not many Days after, he was constrained, by a strong Westerly Wind, to anchor in the Bay of *Bulls*, the Road to the City of *Cadiz*, and though the *English* Merchants, both there and at Port St. *Mary*'s, were very well satisfied with the care that was taken of them, yet had they no considerable Effects to send home. While he lay here, three *French* Flag-ships in the Bay of *Cadiz* made the Signal for weighing, whereupon all our Frigates stood out to Sea, to prevent an Insult, and cruising until the seventh of *November*, they returned to the Bay of *Bulls*, the aforesaid Flags being still in the Port; but Captain *Loades* believing they would sail with the fresh Easterly Wind which then blew, stood out to Sea again.

Three Flag-Ships in the Bay of Cadiz.

These Flag Officers sailed four Days after, with about twenty six Ships more, and stood Westward, upon which our Frigates returned to the Bay of *Bulls* the next Day, and remaining there till the sixteenth of *December*, Captain *Loades* having first acquainted the Factory that his want of Provisions would oblige him to sail by the beginning of *January*, at farthest, he came for *England*, when each of the three Ships under his Command had taken in upwards of sixty thousand Pieces of Eight, most of which was upon account of the Old and New *East-India* Companies, but more especially the former, for Money was at that time so scarce at *Cadiz*, that the Merchants could spare but very little until such time as the *Flota* arrived.

Iiii The

The Number of French Ships at Cadiz.

  The Count *D'Estrées* had lain all the Summer above the *Puntals* with twenty three *French* Ships from 100 to 50 Guns, and the latter end of *October* he was joined by Monsieur *Chateau Renault* from *Lisbon*, with fourteen more, from 50 to 80; besides which there were eight Fireships, four Bomb-Vessels, and several Ships with Stores and Provisions, making in all about seventy Sail.

Count D'Estrées sailed for Thoulon.

  The first of *November* the said Count *D'Estrées* sailed for *Thoulon* with seven Men of War, all of them, except one, having three Decks, and she mounted about 50 Guns. He carried with him four Bomb-Vessels, and as many Fireships, besides Storeships, and Victuallers, and in this Squadron was transported from *Cadiz*, *Gibraltar*, and *Malaga*, one thousand five hundred *Spanish* Soldiers, designed (as was reported) from *Thoulon* to *Naples*.

Monsieur Chateau Renault commands at Cadiz.

  In the Absence of Count *D'Estrées*, Monsieur *Chateau Renault* commanded in Chief, with a Vice-Admiral's Flag, Monsieur *Nesmond* bore that of a Rear-Admiral, and there were two other Flags flying with Swallow Tails, one of which was Monsieur *De Relingue*. The Number of *French* Ships then in the Bay were about thirty, of which four had three Decks, the rest of 56, 60, and 76 Guns, and as five of them were preparing for a long Voyage, according to their manner of victualling, so it was judged they were designed for the *West-Indies*, not only to secure the *Havana*, but to bring from thence the Galleons.

The care taken by the French to get Advice of our Fleet.

  During Count *D'Estrées*'s stay at *Cadiz* he employed Advice-Boats almost every Week, and sometimes oftner, not only to bring him Intelligence from *France*, but of the Motions of our Fleet in the Chanel, and of the Number and Strength of the Ships going with Sir *George Rooke* from *Spithead*; nay such Industry was used in this Affair, that he had Advice by one of those Vessels of our Fleet's sailing, by another of their putting into *Torbay*; a third brought him an Account of their Departure from thence, and another of their being twenty Leagues out of the Chanel: By a fifth he knew when Sir *George Rooke* parted from Vice-Admiral *Benbow*, (of whose Proceedings I have already given an Account) nor did he want Intelligence by another, when he returned into the Chanel; nor took they less care to inform themselves how Vice-Admiral *Benbow* steer'd his Course, from time to time, towards the *West-Indies*. Besides, the aforementioned *French* Ships in the Bay of *Cadiz*, there were the *Spanish* Admiral and Vice-Admiral, and great Preparations were making to put all of them into a Condition for the Sea.

CHAP.

CHAP. VIII.

Sir John Munden's *Proceedings for intercepting a Squadron of* French *Ships bound to the* Groyne, *and thence to the* West-Indies.

THE Earl of *Nottingham*, Principal Secretary of State, receiving certain Advice that there were raised in the Kingdom of *Spain* about two thousand Men, and that they were designed for the *West-Indies* with the Duke of *Albuquerque*, who (as hath been already said) was going from *Andalusia*, where he had been Vice-Roy to reside in the same Quality in *Mexico*, and that it was determined he should be at the *Groyne* on or about the eighth Day of *May*, New Style, where the Soldiers were to embark when the Shipping arrived, which were either to take on board, or give Convoy to the Forces, and the intercepting of them being esteemed of very great Consequence to our Affairs, the Earl of *Pembroke* (according to what was debated and agreed at the Cabinet Council) sent Orders to Sir *John Munden*, Rear-Admiral of the Red, the fifth of *May*, to make choice of such eight Ships of the Third Rate at *Spithead*, as he judged most proper for this Service, together with two Fireships, and immediately to man them out of other Ships there, and in *Portsmouth* Harbour, so as to put them in a Condition for Service. When he had done this, he was with the very first Opportunity of a Wind to repair with them to such Station off of the *Groyne* where he might receive the most speedy Intelligence of the Enemy's Proceedings.

1702.

His Instructions.

If he gained certain Advice that they were at the *Groyne*, or in any Port thereabouts, he was ordered to use his best Endeavours to destroy them, and having done his utmost, to return without loss of time into the *Soundings*, for the Security of the Trade, until he received farther Orders. But if he found the *French* Ships were not arrived at the *Groyne*, he was to cruise off of Cape *Finisterre*, and between the aforesaid Port and that Cape (according to the Advices he might receive, and as Winds and Weather should happen) in such manner as might give him best Opportunities of intercepting them, either in their Passage to the *Groyne*, or from thence towards the *West-Indies*: But he was particularly caution'd so to dispose of the Ships under his Command, as might best prevent his being discovered from the Shore, lest any Umbrage might be taken of his Design.

In this manner he was to cruise so long as he had any Prospect of doing Service upon the Enemy, or until he received farther Orders; but if he found the Ships and Forces were gone from the *Groyne* towards the *West-Indies*, and that there was not any Probability of coming up with them, he was forthwith to return into the *Soundings*, and there cruise in a convenient Station, but to send a Frigate to *Plimouth* with an Account of his Proceedings, and of the

the Station he made choice of, that so Orders might be with more Certainty dispatched to him.

Sir *John Munden* coming to *Portsmouth*, he enquired into the Condition of the Ships, and found he could not sail with the eight Third Rates in less than a Week's time; wherefore, since the Service was of Importance, and that consequently all possible Diligence ought to be used therein, he was empower'd by the Lord High-Admiral to take some of the Second Rates at *Spithead*, instead of Thirds, provided they were in a greater Readiness, but the Strength was to be equal to what was at first ordered, in case all the Third Rates could not proceed with him; and although there was not above two Months Provisions on board them, he was not permitted to make any stay on that account, but required to proceed without a farther Supply, having liberty to add to the Squadron any Ship of the Fourth or Fifth Rate at *Spithead* that was not under immediate Orders.

But notwithstanding those Directions, it was recommended to him, if he found he could not immediately get ready a greater Strength than what might be equivalent to five Ships of the Third Rate, to proceed even with them, and leave Orders for the others to follow him.

1702.
Sir John Munden his Proceedings.

The twelfth Day of *May* he was clear of the Land, and had with him eight Ships of the Third Rate, a Fourth Rate, called the *Salisbury*, and two small Frigates, and then, and not before, he communicated to the several Captains the Service whereon he was going, which had indeed been kept more private than oftentimes Matters of this Importance are, for it was not known to any but the Lords of the Cabinet Council, the Lord High-Admiral, and my self, as I had the Honour to be his Lordship's Secretary.

The sixteenth he was got about four hundred Miles, South, 18^d. West, from the *Lizard*, and he had no sooner made the Land of *Gallicia*, than he sent the *Salisbury* and *Dolphin* into the Shore for Intelligence, himself coming next Day to the appointed Rendezvous, N. W. about fifteen Leagues from Cape *Prior*, where he consulted with the Captains, by whom it was agreed to stand so near in as that they might plainly make the *Groyne*, which he did about Four in the Afternoon, and then stood off again for the Rendezvous.

The *Dolphin* and *Salisbury* not returning so soon as was expected, a Council of War, held the eighteenth, determined to bear away for Cape *Finisterre*, in order to meet them; and they joining the Squadron on the twenty second, brought a Prize from *Martinica*, but having not gained any Intelligence, it was agreed to return off of the *Groyne*, and to get Advice of the Enemy, if possible.

The twenty fifth at Night he sent in a Smack, with the *Salisbury* and *Dolphin*, and the next Morning they brought off a *Spanish* Boat, and a *French* Bark with several Prisoners, who reported, that there were thirteen *French* Ships of War bound from *Rochelle* to the *Groyne*. Hereupon Sir *John* carried a press'd Sail, the better to enable him to get to Windward, in order to his intercepting them,

if

CHAP. VIII. *from the Year* 1698, *to* 1712. 613

if poſſible, before they could harbour themſelves; and on the twenty ſeventh he communicated his Deſign to all the Captains, that ſo they might get their Ships in an immediate Readineſs for Battel.

Early the next Morning he diſcovered fourteen Sail between Cape *Prior,* and Cape *Ortegal,* cloſe under the Shore, and inſtantly gave them chaſe, for he was well aſſured that they were the Enemy; but they outſailing him very much, got into the *Groyne* before he could poſſibly come up to attack them, wherefore he called the Captains together, who took into Conſideration,

Sir John Munden diſcovers the French Ships. They get into the Groyne.

1. The Intelligence from a Perſon who belonged to a *French* Merchant Ship, from *Rochelle,* and ſome *Spaniards* taken from the Shore, the former affirming, that when he came from *Rochelle,* he left there twelve Ships of War in the Road, ready to ſail to the *Groyne* with the firſt fair Wind, that one of them had 70 Guns, one 50, and all the reſt 60, and that the *Faulcon* (a Fourth Rate taken from us the laſt War) was going thither before them.

2. That the *Spaniards* were very poſitive the Duke of *Albuquerque* was at the *Groyne* with two thouſand Soldiers, and that there were already in that Port three *French* Ships of War of 50 Guns each, and twelve more expected from *Rochelle.*

And ſince both theſe Accounts ſo well agreed, and that it was judged there were ſeventeen Ships of War in the Port, that the Place was ſtrongly fortified, and the Paſſage thereinto very difficult, it was unanimouſly determined that they could not be attempted therewith any Probability of Succeſs, and that by remaining in the Station they could not have any Proſpect of doing Service; ſo that it was judged proper to repair into the *Soundings* for protecting the Trade, of which Sir *John Munden* ſent an Account to the Lord High-Admiral by the *Edgar,* and ordered her forthwith to return to him into the Latitude of 49^d, 30^m, thirty Leagues without *Scilly*; but ſince the Water in the Squadron was near ſpent, and that the Ships had received Damage by bad Weather, it was reſolved, the twentieth of *June,* to repair into Port to refit, and to ſupply themſelves with what Neceſſaries they ſtood in need of; nor was Water and thoſe Neceſſaries the only things wanting, for the nine Ships of the Line of Battel had at leaſt thirteen hundred Men leſs than their higheſt Complements, (which in the whole amounted but to three thouſand eight hundred and ſeventy) according to the Accounts taken thereof about the middle of *June* from each Ship when at Sea; ſo that by Calculation they had not above three parts of five of the Number allowed them according to the then Eſtabliſhment.

Agreed not to attempt the Ships in the Groyne.

The Squadron returns to England.

This was a very unlucky Accident, but the ſame Misfortune might have happen'd to any other good Officer as well as Sir *John Munden,* who (to do him Juſtice) had, during his long Service in the Fleet, behaved himſelf with Zeal, Courage, and Fidelity; and although himſelf, and all the Captains in his Squadron, did unanimouſly conclude, that at leaſt twelve of the fourteen Ships, which they chaſed into the *Groyne,* were Men of War, their Number agreeing exactly with the Intelligence from ſeveral Perſons taken from the Shore, yet even in that caſe, it is reaſonable to think that he would have

have given a very good Acccount of this Affair, could he possibly have come up with them; but it was afterwards known that there were no more than eight Ships of Force, the others being Transports for the Soldiers.

As things of this Nature occasion various Reports and Reflections, wherein many People do freely give their Opinions, without considering, or being able to judge of Circumstances; so was this attended with no little Clamour, insomuch that it was thought necessary to have it thoroughly enquired into at a Court Martial; and accordingly his Royal Highness (who had some time before enter'd on the Office of Lord High-Admiral) gave his Orders for that purpose to Sir *Cloudesly Shovell*, Admiral of the White, who summoning a Court at *Spithead* the thirteenth of *July* 1702, where were present nineteen Captains, they took the several Articles exhibited against Sir *John Munden* under Examination, and came to the following Resolutons, *viz.*

Sir John Munden try'd at a Court Martial, and honourably acquitted.

1. That having thoroughly inspected into the Journals of the Captains, and other Officers of the Squadron, it appeared to them that Sir *John Munden* was no more than three Leagues from the Shore off of Cape *Prior*, at nine at Night, when he tack'd and stood off, and about seven Leagues at three in the Morning, when he tack'd again and stood in; and considering it was hazy Weather, that there was no anchoring on the Coast, and that Cape *Ortegal* (the Station to which he was designed) was a proper Place for intercepting the *French* Ships; and that he ordered Scouts in a convenient Station for giving him Notice of their appearing; the Court were of Opinion, that there was no Mismanagement, or Failure of Duty in this particular.

2. Then they considered of the next Article, namely his not following the Ships into the *Groyne*, and endeavouring to destroy them when there; and having duly weighed the Motives that induced him, and the Captains, at their Consultation, to desist from atempting the Ships in that Harbour, they were of Opinion it was neither adviseable, nor practiceable, in regard of the Difficulties that must have been met with in coming in, and the Strength of the Place.

3. The next thing was his calling off the *Salisbury*, when engaged with a *French* Ship of War on the sixteenth of *May*, and not sending some other Ship or Ships to her Assistance. To this Sir *John* answered, that the Ship, which the *Salisbury* gave chase to, was standing right in with his Squadron; and that therefore he had Hopes of her falling among them, which induced him to make the Signal for discontinuing the Chase; but that when he perceived the *Salisbury* was engaged, he stood to her Assistance with the whole Squadron, and continued so to do until they had made the Land, but not being able to come up with the Enemy's Ship, he pursued his Instructions, by keeping himself as much undiscovered as he could; so that the Court judged him not blameable in this particular.

4. The next Article of Complaint was his setting on shore the Persons taken in the *Spanish* Boat, for that otherwise they might have been exchanged for such *English* as were under Confinement at the *Groyne*; but it appeared to the Court that those who were

thus

thus taken, were either Women, or indigent People, and no military Persons amongst them, and that therefore what he did herein was conformable to Practice in like Cases, and deserved no Reflection, or Blame.

In fine, the Court Martial, after they had maturely deliberated on all the Particulars of Complaint, were of Opinion that Sir *John Munden* had fully cleared himself of the whole Matters contained therein, and (as far as it appeared to them) not only comply'd with his Instructions, but behaved himself with great Zeal and Diligence.

CHAP. IX.

Containing the Establishment of six Marine Regiments, with some Observations thereupon.

HERE let me take up a little of your time, by acquainting you that her Majesty was pleased to establish six Marine Regiments; but they were put on a different Foot than those which were thought necessary at the Beginning, but discontinued before the Close of the last War; for as the Soldiers were formerly discharged from the Regiments, and enter'd on the Ships Books as Foremast Men, when they had qualified themselves to serve as such, and Money allowed to the Officers to procure others in their room; so now when any of the Marine Soldiers died, or were otherwise missing, the Companies were only made full by Levy-Money to the Officers, without any regard to their being a Nursery for Seamen, which was one of the principal Motives for the first raising such a Body of Men.

The Charge of these Regiments was defrayed by the Navy, (as being part of the Men voted by Parliament for Sea Service) and Money was issued out from time to time by the Treasurer thereof, by Warrants from the Lord High-Treasurer, to a Person particularly appointed to receive and pay the same, so that the Navy Board, who (as well as the Admiralty) were in the former War put to considerable Trouble on this Account, had no other now, than the ordering the Payment of Money from time to time in gross Sums; and that the Reader may be informed what the annual Charge of these Regiments was, I have hereafter inserted the Establishment, and in the next Place the Rules appointed by her Majesty for their Government, *viz.*

Establishment of one Marine Regiment.

Field and Staff-Officers.	per Diem.			per Annum.		
	l.	s.	d.	l.	s.	d.
Colonel, as Colonel.	0	12	0	219	0	0
Lieutenant-Colonel, as Lieutenant-Colonel.	0	7	0	127	15	0
Major, as Major.	0	5	0	91	5	0
Chaplain.	0	6	8	121	13	4
Adjutant.	0	4	0	73	0	0
Quarter Master.	0	4	0	73	0	0
Chirurgeon 4 s. and one Mate 2 s. 6 d.	0	6	6	118	12	6
	2	5	2	824	5	10

One Company.

Captain.	0	8	0	146	0	0
First Lieutenant.	0	4	0	73	0	0
Second Lieutenant.	0	3	0	54	15	0
Two Serjeants, each 18 d.	0	3	0	54	15	0
Three Corporals, each 12 d.	0	3	0	54	15	0
Two Drummers, each 12 d.	0	2	0	36	10	0
Fifty nine private Soldiers, each 8 d.	1	19	4	717	16	8
	3	2	4	1137	11	8
Ten Companies more.	31	3	4	11375	11	8

One Company of Grenadiers to compleat this Regiment.

Captain	0	8	0	146	0	0
First Lieutenant.	0	4	0	73	0	0
Second Lieutenant.	0	4	0	73	0	0
Three Serjeants each 18 d.	0	4	6	82	2	6
Three Corporals, each 12 d	0	3	0	54	15	0
Two Drummers, each 12 d.	0	2	0	36	10	0
Fifty nine Grenadiers, each 8 d.	1	19	4	717	17	8
	3	4	10	1183	4	2
Total of One Regiment	39	15	8	14520	18	4
Of Five more	198	18	4	72604	11	8
In all	238	14	0	87125	10	0

The aforegoing being the Establishment of Pay, that for their Subsistence is set down in the following Account, *viz.*

For

CHAP. IX. *from the Year* 1689, *to* 1712.

For One Regiment.	*per Diem.*		
	l.	*s.*	*d.*
Colonel, as Colonel and Captain.	0	10	0
Lieutenant-Colonel, as Lieutenant-Colonel and Captain.	0	7	6
Major, as Major and Captain.	0	6	6
Nine Captains, each 4 *s.*	1	16	0
Thirteen Lieutenants, each 2 *s.*	1	6	0
Eleven Ensigns, each 18 *d.*	0	16	6
Chaplain.	0	3	4
Adjutant.	0	2	0
Quarter Master.	0	2	0
Chirurgeon 2 *s.* and Mate 15 *d.*	0	3	3
Twenty five Serjeants, each 6 *s.* a Week.	7	10	0
Thirty six Corporals, each 4 *s.* 6 *d.*	8	2	0
Twenty four Drummers, each 4 *s.* 6 *d.*	5	8	0
Seven hundred and eight Men, each 3 *s.* 6 *d.*	123	18	0
Total for a Week	184	9	1
for a Year	9592	18	4
for five Regiments more a Year	47964	10	8
In all	57557	9	0

Experience hath shewn that these Regiments have been very useful, but more especially upon fitting out Squadrons of Ships for any immediate Expedition; for as they are constantly quartered, when not at Sea, as near the principal Ports as possible, namely *Plimouth*, *Portsmouth*, and *Chatham*, so were they with great Facility put on board such Ships as had most Occasion for them, for they were under the immediate Direction of the Admiralty; and the Rules and Instructions for the better Government of them, settled by Her Majesty in Council the first of *July*, 1702, were as follows; *viz.*

1. They were to be employed on board Her Majesty's Ships, as there should be occasion, and quartered (as I have already said) at, or near as might be to the Dock Yards, when on Shore, to guard them from Embezlements, or any Attempts of an Enemy. *Rules for the Government of the Marine Regiments.*

2. In all matters relating to their Subsistence and Clearings, when on board and on shore, they were to be paid in like manner as the Land Forces, and the same Deductions to be made from them for Cloathing, and one Day's Pay, once a Year, from each Officer and Soldier for the Hospital.

3. They were to be allow'd an equal Proportion of Provisions with the Seamen, without any Deductions from their Pay for the same.

4. And to have the same Allowance for short Provisions as the Seamen, to be paid to themselves, or their Assigns.

5. Such Part of the Regiments as should be on shore were to be muster'd by a Commissary, or Commissaries, in the same manner as the Land Forces, excepting in this Case, that they the said Commissaries

K k k k

saries were obliged to allow, at each Muster, on his or their Rolls, all such Officers and Soldiers as should appear to him, or them, by Authentick Vouchers, or Certificates, to be put on board any of Her Majesty's Ships or Vessels; and that such Part of the aforesaid Regiments as should be at Sea might be paid while they were so, it was directed, that the commanding Marine Officer with them, should every two Months return to the Commissary General of the Musters, a perfect List of all the Officers and Soldiers on board each Ship, signed by himself, and all the Marine Officers, expressing the times of Entry, Death, and Discharge of each Man, that so the Commissary might compare the said Lists with the monthly Books sent to the Navy Office, and allow such of the said Officers and Soldiers as should appear to him fit to be so allowed.

6. To prevent Confusion, not less than fifteen Marine Soldiers, and with them an Officer, were to be put on board a Ship at any one time, unless in Cases of Necessity.

7. And for the Ease of the whole, a particular Paymaster was appointed, with Power to solicit the Arrears of the Regiments, and to receive all Sums of Money from the Treasurer of the Navy, and immediately upon the Receipt thereof to issue the same to the respective Colonels, or their Agents; he was also required diligently and carefully to adjust all Accounts relating to the Regiments, according to such Muster Rolls as should be delivered to him by the Commissary, or Commissaries, and those Muster Rolls were to be allow'd of, as sufficient Vouchers for the Charges in the Accounts, and for making out Debentures and Warrants.

8. To enable the aforesaid Paymaster to keep an Office, and to defray the Charge thereof, and of Clerks and other Contingencies, he was allowed 6 d. in the Pound, pursuant to the Subscription of the respective Colonels, which he had Power to deduct out of all Monies issued to him, in the same Manner as the Poundage is deducted from the Land Forces.

9. For rendering such Part of the Regiments as should be on Shore the more useful, Her Majesty declared it should be left to herself, or the High-Admiral to dispose of them at such Places nearest to the several Dock Yards as might be judged most convenient: And since there might be occasion for Labourers to dispatch necessary Works, Her Majesty empowered Her High-Admiral, or Commissioners for executing that Office, to cause to be employed in the aforesaid Dock-Yards, so many of the Marine Soldiers as should be judged fitting, and to make them such daily Allowance for the same, besides their ordinary Pay, as to him or them should seem reasonable.

And for the better regulating of these Regiments, his Royal Highness, as Lord High-Admiral, empowered Colonel *William Seymour*, (Brigadier, and since Lieutenant-General of Her Majesty's Forces) to take upon him the Command of them, and not only to see that they were well quartered, but that the respective Officers diligently attended their Duty, and that, when ordered on board Her Majesty's Ships, the Soldiers were supply'd with proper Sea Cloaths, Chests, and other Necessaries.

CHAP.

CHAP. X.

Containing an Account of Sir George Rooke's *Expedition with the Fleet to* Cadiz, *and the Land Forces under the Duke of* Ormond, *and of the successful Attempt made on the* French *Ships and* Spanish *Galleons at* Vigo.

Having made the beforegoing short Digression, give me leave now to observe, that for a considerable time before, the Declaration of War with *France* and *Spain* (which was on the fourth of *May*, 1702,) the greatest Diligence was used in getting the Fleet ready for Service; for it was well known that the *French* were making Preparations for Acts of Hostility. There was more than ordinary Pains taken in equipping a very considerable Squadron of Ships for an Expedition to *Cadiz*, in Conjunction with the *Dutch*, which the Earl of *Pembroke* was (as High-Admiral) to have commanded in Person, had not his Royal Highness the Prince of *Denmark* (as I have already informed you) been appointed to that Office. *Diligence used in getting the Fleet ready, before War declared.*

There were some Doubts whether his Lordship should have born at the Main-top-mast head the Royal Standard of *England*, or the Union, or, more properly speaking in the maritime Phrase, the Jack Flag, commonly worn by those who have, under the Lord High-Admiral, been appointed Admirals of the Fleet. Most of those who pretended to judge best of this Affair inclined to the latter, but I luckily having then in my Possession an Original Journal, kept by the Secretary to the Duke of *Buckingham*, in his Expedition to the Isle of *Rhé*, it plainly appeared thereby that he bore the Standard, as several High-Admirals had done before, by particular Warrants, as it is presumed, from the Crown empowering them so to do. *Lord High Admiral bears the Royal Standard at Sea.*

The Conduct of this Expedition was committed to Sir *George Rooke*, who otherwise would have served in the second Post, as Admiral of the White, and the Duke of *Ormond* was General of the Land Forces, which were about twelve thousand Men, very well appointed. *Sir George Rooke and the Duke of Ormond sent to Cadiz.*

When the Land Forces were embarked, and all other things in a Readiness, the Admiral sailed from *Portsmouth*, but reached not the length of the *Start*, until the twenty first of *July*, and having then but very little Wind; he thought it convenient to anchor, that so, by stopping a Tide, he might prevent his being driven Eastward. The next Day he got off of the *Deadman*, from whence proceeding cross the Bay of *Biscay*, with little Wind Northerly, he reached the Station for joyning Rear-Admiral *Fairborn* the thirtieth of *July*, who had been sent before with a Squadron to cruise off of Cape *Finisterre*, 1702.

K k k k 2

Finisterre, but being driven from thence by bad Weather, was working up to it again.

Sir George Rooke joins Sir Stafford Fairborne.

The Admiral, when joined, continued his Course towards *Cadiz*, and coming near to it the twelfth Day of *August*, anchored in the Offing about four in the Afternoon, and much about that time the next Day he got into the Bay of *Bulls*. In the Evening there was a Council of War of the Flags and General Officers, and although it was then agreed that the Troops should be ready to go on Shore at an Hour's Warning, it so happened that they were not landed un-

The Troops landed.

til the fifteenth in the Morning, when it was done by the Boats belonging to the Fleet, the General himself being in his Barge with the *English* Flag, and Baron *Spar* in another with that of the Emperor, putting the Men in order; and in the mean while the several small Frigates were so posted, as that they might best cover the Forces, and annoy the Enemy who were placed on the Shore to oppose them.

There happened to be a very great Swell of the Sea, insomuch that when the Boats came near the Shore, many of them were almost filled with Water, which constrained the Soldiers to wade thorough; and as by this unlucky Accident some were drowned, so were great Part of their Arms render'd unfit for immediate Service.

Action between our Men and the Spanish Horse.

When about one hundred Grenadiers were landed (at the Head of whom was Colonel *Peirce*) they were briskly attack'd by a Body of *Spanish* Horse with Sword in Hand, under the Command of a Lieutenant-General. Our Men were instantly put in Order, and then advancing with great Bravery towards the *Spaniards*, the Lieutenant-General was killed, some of them taken Prisoners, and the rest put to Flight.

The Enemy fired very hotly, while our Troops were landing, from a Fort called *St. Catharine*'s, whereby the *Dutch* received some Damage; but the *Lenox*, one of our Third Rates, (commanded by Captain *Jumper*) advancing within Reach of the Fort, by firing her Broadside obliged them in a little time to retire. The small Frigates drove them also from their Batteries on the left, and the *Dutch*, soon after their Landing, possessed themselves of the Guns mounted thereon.

The Town of Rota surrenders.

Next Morning early (being the sixteenth of *August*) the Forces marched towards a small Village called *Rota*, being met by the Governour, and some others, who surrendering the Town, about one hundred Grenadiers took Possession of it; and the General taking up his Quarters in the Castle, the Army encamped before the Place.

The Troops go to Port St. Mary's.

Between the seventeenth and nineteenth, the Field Pieces, and four Mortars, with proper Ammunition, as also the Dragoons, and Train-Horses were put on Shore, and the next Morning they marched to Port *St. Mary*'s, which Place was about seven Miles from the Camp, and is in a manner a general Warehouse or Magazine for *Cadiz* itself. Our Men lay on their Arms all Night when they had marched about half of the Way, the *Spaniards* making a Shew (but that

CHAP. X. *from the Year 1698, to 1712.* 621

that was all) as if they would defend the Pass; and next Day several Squadrons of their Horse were seen on the Hills, but upon the Approach of our Men they retreated into the Country; and this Day the Forces enter'd into Port St. *Mary*'s without Opposition, for the Soldiers and Inhabitants had abandon'd it.

The Troops were quarter'd in this Place, which afforded Plenty of Wines; and as great Numbers of them did for several Days partake very liberally of it, (a thing too often practised, and very hard to be restrained) so were the Goods and Merchandizes of the Inhabitants seized, and hurried on board the Ships and Transports, which were of no inconsiderable Value, and this notwithstanding the Duke had (as I am informed) declared it Death to any Man who should presume to Plunder. *Port St. Mary's plundered.*

The twenty second a Party was sent back under Command of Colonel *Peirce*, from Port St. *Mary*'s to St. *Catharine*'s Fort, which surrendered after some Opposition; and two Days after the Army marching out of Port St. *Mary*'s, encamped in two Lines, not far from thence, and where they were not well secured by the Ditches, such Methods were taken as might best contribute towards the Defence of the Front from the Enemy, who being encamped on a rising Ground towards the Country, about a Mile and half off, did sometimes alarm our People by their Parties of Horse. *Colonel Peirce takes St. Catharine's Fort.*

The Duke called a Council of War of his General-Officers the second of *September*, where were present Lieutenant-General *Belasis*, Lord *Portmore*, Sir *Charles O Hara*, Brigadier *Paland*, Brigadier *Matthews*, Brigadier *Hamilton*, and Brigadier *Seymour*, and it was resolved to propose the following Question to the Admiral, *viz.* In case the Army should, when at Port *Real*, endeavour to pass into the Island between the Bridge at *Suaco* and St. *Pedro*, but find it impracticable, and therefore come to the Mouth of the River *Xerez*, where Baron *Spar* had debarked his Troops, whether the Men, Horse, Artillery, and all things necessary, could be embarked from thence on board the Fleet? *A Council of War of General-Officers.*

Hereupon the Admiral called a Council of such Officers as he thought convenient, namely, Vice-Admiral *Hopson*, his own first Captain, and Captain *Thomas Ley*; and of the *Dutch*, Admiral *Allemonde*, Admiral *Callemberg*, Vice-Admiral *Vandergoes*, and Vice-Admiral *Pieterson*. They were of Opinion, that if the Winds came out (as might reasonably be expected from the approaching Season of the Year, the Autumnal Equinox being nigh) neither the Horse or Artillery could be embarked from the Mouth of the River *Xerez*, without great Difficulty and Hazard, but that from the Conveniency of the Mole at *Rota*, they might be from thence more safely taken on board; and, in such case, it was determined that there should be a Flag-Officer, and Captains appointed, not only to advise, but to assist in the doing thereof. *A Council of War of Sea-Officers.*

And now, and not before, it being thought convenient to have the Entrance into the Harbour above the *Puntals* examined into, Sir *Stafford Fairborn* (as order'd) called to his Assistance the Flags, and other Officers of the Ships which were in the Bay of *Cadiz*, *The Entrance of the Harbour examin'd into, though late.*

who

who on the fifth of *September* reported, that they had endeavour'd to inform themselves of the Passage in the best manner they could, with respect as well to the Boom, as the sunken Vessels (which latter obliged even the Enemy's Gallies, when they passed or repassed, to make several Traverses) and that, in their Opinion, it was not practicable to attempt the Entrance, while those two Forts which commanded it, namely the *Puntal* and *Mattagorda*, remained in the Enemy's Possession; and they represented the Difficulty to be yet the greater, for that they could neither find the certain Position of the sunken Vessels, nor come to buoy them, until one of those Castles, at least was reduced. But it may not be altogether unreasonable to believe, that if the Officers who were met at a Council of War had approved of the Proposition, which was made (as I am informed) by one of them, for ordering a Squadron of Ships, e'er the Fleet came in Sight of *Cadiz*, to have pushed through the Entrance of the Harbour, without so much as coming to an Anchor, which it is said he offered to undertake, we might, during the Surprize the *Spaniards* would have been in, have destroyed at least their Shipping, (as the Earl of *Essex* did in the Reign of Queen *Elizabeth*) if not taken the Place itself; but it being not thought adviseable to make an Attempt in the manner before-mentioned, they had not only leisure, while the Body of our Fleet lay in view, of sinking Vessels in the very Entrance of the Harbour, whereby the Passage thereinto was render'd altogether impracticable, but to put themselves into a much better Condition of defending the City itself, than consequently they would otherwise have been.

Baron Spar attempts the Mattagorda.

An Attack was made by Baron *Spar* with about six thousand Men on the *Mattagorda*, a small inconsiderable Fort over against the *Puntal*, and a Battery was raised of four Cannon in such a Place as that not above three Guns could point on it from the Fort; but by reason of the Spunginess of the Ground, and it may be, also, from the want of a necessary Precaution to lay the Foundation of the Battery as it ought to have been, it did us little or no Service; besides, not only the Fort, but the Gallies, and *French* Ships of War which lay within the *Puntal*, made all the Fire they could at our Men, and put them into no small Disorder; so that Baron *Spar* thought it convenient to return to the Army, after he had set fire to the Magazines at *Port Real*.

Magazines at Port Real burnt.

Agreed not practicable to attempt Cadiz.

These Difficulties occasioned another Council of War of the Flags and General-Officers the fifth of *September*, and it being judged by them, that if the *Mattagorda* were taken, it could not facilitate the Fleet's Entrance into the Harbour, because of the *Puntal* (a much stronger Fort) and the sunken Ships, it was agreed by the Land-Officers, that it would be to no purpose to make any Attempt towards the reducing of *Cadiz*, with the Troops only, for that with a much greater Number of Men, it would require more time than they could spend on it; wherefore it was resolved that all the Magazines of Naval and Ordnance Stores at Port *St. Mary*'s, and *Rota*, should be burnt and destroyed; that the Army should re-embark from *Rota*, as soon as 'twas possible, after the Boats had water'd the
Fleet

Fleet for their Voyage home, and that then it should be considered what might be farther done, for putting in Execution the Remainder of Her Majesty's Instructions.

The tenth of *September* a Council was held of the Flag-Officers, and several Letters from the Prince of *Hesse* to the Duke of *Ormond* and the Admiral were read; but since not one *Spaniard* of Note had yet come in, or shewed any Inclination so to do, (whatever they might have done with more civil Treatment) it was agreed that the Forces should be immediately embarked; and although it had been resolved some time before to bombard *Cadiz*, that Design was laid aside, because it was judged it could not be done with any manner of Success, considering the Swell of the Sea; so that all the Ships and Transports were immediately ordered into the Bay of *Bulls*, there to be in Readiness to receive the Army.

Five Days after, the Duke of *Ormond* acquainted the Admiral by Letter, that he desired nothing more than to have the Forces set on shore, either in the Island of *Cadiz*, *Ayamonte*, *Vigo*, *Ponte Vedra*, or wheresoever it might be thought most reasonable. This the Flag-Officers taking into Consideration, they were of Opinion that it was not adviseable (with regard to the Safety of the Fleet) to attempt *Cadiz* at this Season of the Year, for that the Ships might be much exposed when the Rains and Out-winds set in; besides, the General-Officers had determined before, that it could not be done with those Forces which the General had under his Command. *Duke of Ormond proposes landing at some other Place.*

As for landing the Army at *Ayamonte*, the Flags agreed it might be done if the Weather happened to be favourable, but that since the great Ships could not come near the Shore, nor remain on the Coast, great Difficulties might arise in landing the Horse and Artillery, because it could not be done any otherwise than by the Boats in the Fleet; and although they judged it almost impossible for a small Squadron to lie on that Coast in the Winter, yet they were of Opinion that such a Squadron might be clean'd at *Lisbon*, and cruise from time to time in countenancing and protecting the Army. *The Opinion of the Flag-Officers thereupon.*

As to *Ponte Vedra*, and *Vigo*, they judged, that unless they could reach those Ports by the first of *October*, New Style, it would be to no purpose to attempt any thing there; for Provisions fell short in the *Dutch* Squadron, and it would be difficult for Ships to depart from that Coast in the Winter; but that if it should be resolved to struggle with these, and other unforeseen Difficulties, there was a Necessity to send home the great Ships, in order to their gaining a safe Passage.

They also considered what had been proposed, and that part of the Instructions to the Admiral which related to the *Groyne*, and concluded that before they could possibly reach that Port, the Season of the Year would be too far advanced to make any successful Attempt there.

Next Day, being the seventeenth, a Council of War was held of the Flags and General-Officers, and it was considered whether it was adviseable to make a second Attempt in *Spain*, in regard not only

only of the Oppofition, but the Obftinacy of the *Spaniards* in *Andalufia* againft the Houfe of *Auftria*, the Difficulties which might arife from the Seafon of the Year; the Averfion which they apprehended in the People in other Parts of *Spain*; the want of Intelligence; that the *Dutch* Troops could not be furnifhed with Provifions from their Ships longer than for a Month; that the Army would be greatly diminifhed by the Detachment to be fent to the *Weft-Indies* with Captain *Walker*, (of whofe Proceedings I have already given an Account) and other Inconveniences which might arife through Sicknefs. After this Matter had been thoroughly debated, the Queftion was put, and determined in the Negative, and therefore it was refolved to take the firft Opportunity of proceeding to *England*.

Determined not to make a fecond Attempt in Spain, but return to England.

The Perfons who figned to this Refolution were,

Sea-Officers.

Sir *George Rooke*,
Admiral *Allemonde*,
Vice-Admiral *Hopfon*,
Vice-Admiral *Vandergoes*,
Vice-Admiral *Pieterfon*,
Rear-Admiral *Fairborn*,
Rear-Admiral *Waffenaer*,
Rear-Admiral *Graydon*.

Land-Officers.

Sir *Henry Belafis*,
Lord *Portmore*,
Sir *Charles O Hara*,
Brigadier *Hamilton*,
Brigadier *Seymour*,

King of Portugal offers them Affiftance.

Some few Days after two Letters were received from Mr. *Methuen*, Her Majefty's Envoy at *Lisbon*, one to the Duke of *Ormond*, the other to Sir *George Rooke*, by which he affured them that the King of *Portugal* would willingly affift in any thing which fhould be defired, not only at that Port, but in any other Parts of his Dominions.

The Flags adhere to the firft Refolution.

A General Council was thereupon called the twenty fecond of *September*, but they did not frame any Refolutions thereupon. They confidered whether Mr. *Methuen* fhould be defired to explain fome Particulars contained in his Letter, and the Fleet ftay for his Anfwer in *Lagos* Bay, but it was refolved to adhere to the former Refolution of proceeding to *England*, as foon as the *Weft-India* Squadron and the Forces fhould be detached; for they were of Opinion that Mr. *Methuen*'s Letters gave no great Encouragement to the wintering our Forces either in *Spain* or *Portugal*; and here it may be obferved, that, by the then Articles between *England* and the latter Crown, we could not be admitted to have more than fix Ships

CHAP. X. *from the Year* 1698, *to* 1712. 625

of War in the Port of *Lisbon* at one and the same time. To this Resolution all those Gentlemen signed whose Hands were to the aforegoing, except Brigadier *Seymour*.

The nineteenth of *September* the Fleet sailed from *Cadiz*, and were off of Cape St. *Vincent* the twenty fourth, where the *English* Flag-Officers, (namely the Admiral, Vice-Admiral *Hopson*, and the Rear-Admirals *Fairborn* and *Graydon*) taking into Consideration several Clauses in her Majesty's Instructions, relating to some of the great Ships their wintering abroad, if it should be too late to bring them safely home, it was concluded not to be adviseable, for several reasons, to send six of our capital Ships to *Lisbon*; for as there were not any Stores proper for careening and fitting them for the next Summer's Service abroad, so did they judge the Hazard less, and the Convenience of fitting them much more certain, by bringing them to *England*. *The Fleet comes off of Cape St. Vincent.*

Mr. *Bowles* (who acted as Agent to the Commissioners for Victualling) was left off of Cape St. *Vincent*, to supply the Ships designed for the *West-Indies*, as aforesaid, out of four or five Transport-ships, and then to follow under Convoy of the *Lenox*, and join the *Eagle*, *Sterling-Castle*, and *Pembroke*, which Ships the Admiral was obliged to send to *Lagos* Bay, about five Leagues East from Cape St. *Vincent*, that they, and some of the Transports, might there supply themselves with Water, the chief Reason of the latter's being in want thereof, was their employing the greatest part of their time in picking up Plunder at Port St. *Mary's*, though it happened to prove very fortunate, as I am now going to relate.

The Gentleman who commanded the aforesaid three Ships, *Eagle*, *Sterling-Castle*, and *Pembroke*, was Captain *Wishart*, (since Sir *James*, and a Flag-Officer in the Fleet) and the Admiral being the twenty second of *December* off of *Lagos*, he sent him Orders to join the Ships off of Cape St. *Vincent*, when he had watered those Ships and the Transports. He made all possible Dispatch in doing it, and sailed the twenty fifth in the Morning; but Captain *Hardy*, (since Sir *Thomas*, and a Flag-Officer) who commanded the *Pembroke*, being obliged to stay some little time astern, for his Boat which was on shore, a Gentleman came on board of him, who was charged with Letters from the Imperial Minister, directed to the Prince of *Hesse*, and Mr. *Methuen*. Captain *Hardy* industriously sounded this Person, and found that the Letters gave an Account of the Arrival at *Vigo*, in *Gallicia*, of thirty *French* Ships of War, and twenty two *Spanish* Galleons, about ten Days before, and he communicating this to Captain *Wishart* as soon as he could come up with him, they all made the best of their way, and arrived off of Cape St. *Vincent* about half an Hour after Four in the Afternoon; but not finding the Fleet, and Captain *Wishart* considering the Consequence of the Intelligence, and finding by the sealed Rendezvous that the Admiral was on his Passage for *England*, he consulted the Captains with him, who were of his Opinion, that it was absolutely necessary to detach a Ship to Sir *George Rooke* with the aforementioned Intelligence, so that at Five a Clock, the *Pembroke*, commanded *Captain Hardy gets an Account of the Enemy at Vigo.*

Llll

The News communicated to Sir George Rooke, and resolved to proceed to Vigo.

manded by Captain *Hardy*, (which was the best Sailor) was sent on this Errand, and luckily joining the Fleet on the seventh, the Admiral called a Council of War of *English* and *Dutch* Flag-Officers, by whom it was resolved to sail forthwith to the Port of *Vigo*, and immediately to attack the Enemy with the whole Fleet, if there should be found room enough so to do, or, if not, by such Numbers as might render the Attempt most effectual.

The Enemy discovered at Redondela.

They discovered Monsieur *Chateau Renault*'s Squadron on the eleventh, as also the *Spanish* Galleons about the Entrance at *Redondela*, but finding the whole Fleet could not attempt them without great Hazard of being entangled, it was resolved to send in fifteen *English*, and ten *Dutch* Ships of the Line of Battel, with all the Fireships, and that the Bomb-Vessels should follow in the Rear, and the great Ships move after them, that so they might likewise go in if there should be found occasion for it; and it was also determined to land the Army next Morning, that they might attack the Fort on the South side of *Redondela*.

An Account of Vigo and Redondela.

Vigo (from whence several Shot were fired at our Ships without Damage) is an inconsiderable Town at the Mouth of the Harbour, whose Inhabitants chiefly employ themselves in Fishing; nor is *Redondela* a Place of any great Consequence. The Harbour's Mouth is about the Breadth of a Shot from a Musket, and on the Entrance was a small Fort with a Trench running about a quarter of a Mile, whereon was a Battery of sixteen Guns; and the Harbour itself is surrounded in such manner with Hills, that it is capable of being made very strong. On the left Hand was a Battery of about twenty Guns, and between that and the Fort, on the right, a Boom was placed athwart the Harbour, made of Masts, Cables, and other proper Materials, the *French* Ships of War lying almost in the Form of a Half-Moon, a considerable Distance within this Boom; whereas had they anchor'd close to it, and laid their Broadsides to bear upon our Ships as they approached, we should, in all probability, have found the Task much more difficult; but they had so great a Dependance on the Strength of the Boom, as to think themselves sufficiently secur'd by that, and the Batteries on both sides of the Harbour.

A Boom athwart the Harbour.

The Forces land, and take the French and Battery.

The General, according to Agreement, landed with the Forces, when marching directly to the Fort, he attacked the Trench and Battery, and became Master of them after a hot Dispute. They chased the *French* and *Spaniards* into the Fort, and afterwards beat them from thence to their Boats, although they were, in and about this Place (as 'twas credibly reported) near twenty thousand strong; and indeed had not this Fort, and the Battery at the end of the Trench been first taken, there would have been much more Difficulty found in breaking the Boom, and burning the *French* Ships; but that Service was no sooner performed, than the Ships advanced, and Vice-Admiral *Hopson*, in the *Torbay*, crouding all the Sail he could, when he came to the Boom the Force which the Ship had (considering its great Length, and consequently its Weakness) brake it, and several other Ships soon after made their way through. There was at this time a very great Fire between our Ships and the Enemy,

Vice-Admiral Hopson first breaks the Boom.

CHAP. X. *from the Year* 1698, *to* 1712.

my, and one of their Fireships laid the *Torbay* on board; but the former having a large Quantity of Snuff in her, and blowing up, the very Blast extinguished greatest part of the Flames, and thereby enabled those few Officers and Men who staid on board (for the most part of them betook themselves to the Water) to preserve the Ship; for which good Service they were, when they came home, deservedly rewarded, some with Medals and Chains of Gold, and the rest according to their respective Qualities.

While Vice-Admiral *Hopson* was thus employed about the Boom, Captain *William Bokenham* in the *Association*, a Ship of 90 Guns, laid her Broadside to the Battery on the left of the Harbour, which he soon disabled; and Captain *Francis Wivell* in the *Barfleur*, a Ship of the like Force, was sent to batter the Fort on the other side, from which several Shot were fired which penetrated thorough the Ship, but he was restrain'd from answering them in the same manner, because it might have done great damage to our Troops, who soon after beat the Enemy from their Guns, and took the Fort, as I have already related. They fired on our Ships at first from all Parts, and our People were so far from being behindhand with them, that in about half an Hour's time they, in great Confusion, set fire to several of their Ships, and betook themselves to their Boats, mean while the Inhabitants, and others, in *Redondela*, deserted it.

The Battery on the left side disabled by Captain Bokenham, and Captain Wivell attack'd that on the other side.

Several Ships burnt, and Redondela deserted.

Having thus informed you of the Action, by the following List it will appear what *French* Ships of War, and what Galleons were either taken or burnt, *viz.*

An Account of the Enemy's Ships taken and destroyed.

Ships of War.

Le Fort	76	Guns	burnt.
Le Prompt	76		taken.
L'Assuré	66		taken.
L'Esperance	70		taken, but bilged.
Le Bourbon	68		taken by the *Dutch*.
La Sirene	60		taken, but bilged.
Le Solide	56		burnt.
Le Firme	72		taken.
Le Prudent	62		burnt.
L'Enflammé	64		burnt.
Le Moderé	56		taken.
Le Superbe	70		taken, but bilged.
Le Dauphin	46		burnt.
Le Volontaire	46		taken, but bilged.
Le Triton	42		taken.

Frigates.

L'Entreprenant —— 22 ⎫
Le Choquant —— 8 ⎭ —— burnt.

Fireships.

Le Favour.

Curvets 3.

There

There were also seventeen Galleons, four of which were taken on float, and two on shore by the *English*, and five by the *Dutch*. The others were burnt.

The Duke of *Ormond* writ to the Admiral the fourteenth of *October* from the Camp at *Redondela*, and complemented him upon his good Success, wherein the Land-Forces had indeed been very serviceable, and shewed the greatest Bravery; but had the *French* and *Spaniards* behaved themselves as it might have been expected, in defending so many of their Ships of War, and such great Riches, our Troops would certainly have been more roughly handled.

Duke of Ormond proposed wintering abroad.

His Grace now put the Admiral in mind of what had been formerly mentioned, namely, the Forces wintering abroad, but more particularly at *Vigo*, and offered to march directly to that Place, if a fitting Number of Ships could be conveniently left to sustain and take off the Forces upon any Emergency: for he was of Opinion that this might not only put us in the greater Readiness the next Spring, but probably incline the King of *Portugal* (who was yet Neuter) to declare for us and our Allies.

Objections made by the Admiral.

The Admiral acquainted the General that he was ready to do every thing in his Power for the Good of the Publick Service, and that if he thought it might be so to winter in this part of *Spain*, he would venture to leave five or six Frigates, although he doubted they would not be safe, unless they kept out at Sea, instancing the Misfortune which the *French* had been so lately exposed to in the Harbour of *Redondela*.

He also acquainted his Grace that he should not be able to leave more than six Weeks, or two Months Provisions for the Forces, for that a great Quantity was sent to the *West-Indies* with the Ships and Soldiers detached thither; and since there were on shore a considerable Number of sick Men, he ordered Boats to *Redondela* the next Morning to bring them off, and submitted it to his Grace, if it might not then be a fit time to consider and determine, whether it was most proper to march to *Vigo*, or to the Place proposed for embarking the Forces; and that if the former was agreed to, he was of Opinion it might be necessary to send the Prisoners to some Place from whence they could not possibly be able to reinforce the Garrison.

The Troops are embarked. Sir Cloudesly Shovell arriving, is left at Vigo.

In fine, the Forces were, upon farther Consideration, embarked on board the Ships, and Sir *Cloudesly Shovell* arriving the sixteenth of *October*, the Admiral left him at *Vigo*, with Orders to see rigged, and supplied with Men, the *French* Ships of War, and the Galleons, that so such of them as were our Prizes might be brought to *England*, but to destroy those he should not have a Prospect of bringing home, first saving so much of their Loading, Guns, and Rigging, as possibly he could. And as it was particularly recommended to him to take the utmost care to prevent Embezilments, so was he directed to suspend those who should be found guilty thereof, and at his Return, to recommend to the Lord High-Admiral for Encouragement such who had behaved themselves honestly and diligently

CHAP. X. *from the Year* 1698, *to* 1712.

in this Affair; and there being a Report that several *French* Ships, richly loaden, were expected from *Martinica*, he was directed to send three or four of his best sailing Frigates to cruise twenty Days off of Cape *Finisterre*, in order to intercept them; but they missed of the wished-for Success.

The Admiral having given these necessary Orders, and appointed nineteen Third Rates, ten Fourths, one Fifth, a Pink, six Fireships, two Storeships, and a Victualler, to remain with Sir *Cloudesly Shovell*, he sailed himself from *Vigo* with one First Rate, four Seconds, three Thirds, one Fifth, four Fireships, three Bombs, and two Yachts, together with several *Dutch* Ships of War, and one of the Galleons which was rigged, and arrived in the *Downs* the seventh of *November*, from whence the great Ships were brought to *Chatham* about the middle of that Month.

Sir George Rooke arrives in the Downs.

Thus have I given you an Account of an Affair which, after the News of our unfortunate Success at *Cadiz*, occasioned no small Joy; a thing, indeed, that Providence did in a very great measure put into our Power; for had not the Intelligence met the Admiral as it did, both Fleet and Troops would have return'd to *England* without effecting any thing answerable to the extraordinary Charge of the Expedition; for although all possible care was taken, as soon as it was known that Monsieur *Chateau Renault* was coming from the *West-Indies* with his Squadron and the Galleons, (which was about the beginning of *August*) to send Sir *Cloudesly Shovell* to cruise in a proper Station for intercepting them, if bound to any Port in the *Bay*; and that (upon Intelligence from the Captain of one of our Ships, the *Scarborough*, of his meeting them the fourth of *August*, in the Latitude of $35\frac{1}{2}^{d}$, as far Eastward as *Bermudas*) it was very pressingly recommended to Sir *Cloudesly Shovell* to look out carefully for them: That the Earl of *Nottingham* also received an Account, the beginning of *October*, that the said Ships and Galleons were arrived at *Vigo*, and that, when unloaden, the Men of War were to repair to *Brest*, whereupon Orders were dispatched the fifth of the aforesaid Month, so as to meet Sir *George Rooke* in his Return from *Cadiz*, by which Orders he was directed to consult with Sir *Cloudesly Shovell*, (if he met him in his Station) and either to exchange some Ships with him, or to make an Addition to his Squadron, if he judged him not strong enough; I say that notwithstanding all these Precautions, and that Sir *Cloudesly Shovell* was, about the middle of *October*, ordered to join ten Ships of Sir *George Rooke*'s Fleet from 70 to 50 Guns, and all the Fireships in Condition for the Sea; and that Orders were lodged at *Plimouth* for Sir *George Rooke* to send such Ships to him in his cruising Station, from fifteen to thirty Leagues W. S. W. from Cape *Finisterre*; yet if the Fleet had come into the Chanel with the Land-Forces, all the Strength which Sir *Cloudesly Shovell* could have thus carried with him, would hardly have enabled him to have performed the Service which was done at *Redondela*.

Observations on the Action at Vigo.

Sir *Cloudesly Shovell* (as I have already observed) being left at *Vigo* by Sir *George Rooke*, put in Execution the Instructions he he received from him in the manner following, *viz.*

Sir Cloudesly Shovel's Proceedings at and from Vigo.

In a Week's time the *French* Men of War, and other Prizes were put into the best Condition for their Passage home that the Place would admit of, and all the Loading was taken out of a Galleon which was on Ground, seized by one of our Ships, the *Mary*, as also of another Ship of 50 Guns, called the *Dartmouth*, taken from us the last War, and now made Prize by Captain *Wivell*. This Ship he brought home, and she was named the *Vigo*, for there was already one in the Royal Navy called by her former Name the *Dartmouth*.

He also took out of some *French* Ships of War, which were on the Ground, 50 Brass Guns most of them from fifty to sixty Hundred Weight, which with those brought from the Shore amounted to about one hundred and ten; and the Day before he sailed he set fire to all the Ships and Vessels that he could not possibly bring away.

The twenty fifth of *October* he left *Vigo*, but it proving calm, he anchored in the Chanel between that Port and *Bayonne*, where, with a Flag of Truce, he sent several Prisoners ashore, and had ours returned in lieu of them. Next Day he got under Sail again, with Design to go through the North Chanel, but the Wind taking him short, he was obliged to stand through that which lies to the South, where the Galleon, which was the *Monmouth*'s Prize, struck upon a sunken Rock, and immediately foundered, notwithstanding several of the Frigates were on each Side of her, but all the Men, except two, were saved. He had at this time with him at least seventy Sail, of all Sorts, and the next Day, being the twenty sixth, the *Dragon*, a Ship of 50 Guns, joined him, having been engaged with a *French* Man of War of between 60 and 70 off of the Cape, in view of two of our Ships which could not come up with them, though it may reasonably be thought that the Sight of them made the Enemy retire. The *English* Captain, whose Name was *Holyman*, was killed, but both before, and afterwards, the Fight was very gallantly maintained.

The Dragon *engaged a* French *Ship.*

Sir *Cloudesly Shovell* met with very bad Weather in his Passage, which much shattered and separated the Fleet, and a rich Prize from *Morlaix*, taken by the *Nassau*, founder'd. The *Moderate*, one of the *French* Ships lost her Main-mast, but care was taken to secure her home, and many of the Squadron spent their Sails, particularly that Ship wherein Sir *Cloudesly* bore his Flag. In this Condition every one made the best of his Way into the Chanel, which they had open, about seventy Leagues S. W. by W. or W. S. W. from *Scilly*, with the Wind from the N. W. to the W. S. W. and the Flag himself with those in his Company, groped their Way into it, for the Start the first Land they made.

Sir Cloudesly Shovell arrives in the Chanel.

Thus ended this Expedition, the Beginning whereof was attended with very ill Success, either from the general Aversion of the *Spaniards* (whatever Foundations our Hopes were grounded on) to the Interest of the House of *Austria*, or the Apprehensions they were under of being ill treated by the *French* King, should they have

made

CHAP. XI. *from the Year* 1698, *to* 1712. 631

made any Motions that Way, without so much as a proper Place to retire to for Assistance or Protection. But it luckily fell out that the latter End of this very expensive Affair made some Amends at least for the unsuccessful Beginning; for the Enemy (if we reckon their Loss in Shipping and Money, which latter they so greatly built their Hopes upon, and designed, as it was said, to have brought to some Port in *France*,) had now the most sensible Blow they had ever received since that considerable Damage which was done them at *La Hogue* and *Cherbourg*, by the Earl of *Orford* in the last War; the Want of the Money especially very much embarrassing their Affairs. *Remarks.*

I shall conclude this matter with one short Observation; and it is this; that as the *Spaniards*, when our Forces were on Shore at Port St. *Mary*'s, and thereabouts, gave Us no considerable Opposition, although they had it in their Power, from the Number of Horse and Foot which they had drawn together; so were not they, or the *French*, over active in defending their Ships, and Treasure at *Vigo*, considering their Strength, and the Preparations they had made for their Security.

CHAP. XI.

Containing an Account of Captain John Leake's *Proceedings with a Squadron of Ships at* Newfoundland.

THE 24th of *June* 1701, Captain *John Leake* received Instructions from his Royal Highness to proceed to *Newfoundland*, with a small Squadron, and to convoy the Trade bound to *Virginia*, and *New England*, as far as his and their Way should lie together. He was required to use his utmost Endeavours to get an Account of the Strength of the Enemy's Forts, and not only to annoy them there, in their fishing Harbours, and at Sea, but to assist the Admirals, Vice-Admirals, and Rear-Admirals, at our Ports and Harbours in those Parts; for by these Titles the Masters of the Merchant Ships who first arrive distinguish themselves, and have Command over others at the respective Places when there are not any Ships of War present.

1701.

His Instructions.

He had also particular Instructions for convoying the Trade from thence, when they should have made their Voyages, and to inform himself as to the several Heads of Enquiry transmitted to the Lord High-Admiral, by the Lords of the Council for Trade and Plantations (a thing usual when any Ships are sent thither) in relation to the Circumstances of our Affairs in that Country, and particularly the Fishery.

Captain *Leake* sailed, in pursuance of these Instructions, and came into *Plimouth Sound* the twenty second of *July*, but leaving that Place the next Day, and having parted with the
Merchant

Merchant Ships about one hundred Leagues W. S. W. from the *Lizard*, under Convoy of the *Loo*, *Reserve*, and *Firebrand* Fireship, he arrived the twenty seventh of *August* off of the Bay of *Bulls*, where he was informed by the Admiral of that Harbour, that there were two *French* Ships of War at *Placentia*, and that most of their Fishing Vessels which had made their Voyages were gone thither for Convoy. Hereupon he proceeded the very same Evening to the Southward of *Placentia* Bay, and on the twenty eighth twenty ninth, and thirtieth, visited the Harbours of *Trapassy*, *St. Mary*'s, and the Bay of *Colonas*, where, and at Sea in those Parts, he took eleven Ships, one from *Martinica*, nine with Fish, and one with Salt, and destroyed their Boats, Stages, and other Necessaries. The *Assistance* and *Charles* Gally he left at *St. Mary*'s, with Orders to their Commanders to see the Prizes into *St. John*'s, and then to cruise off of Cape *Race*, and the *Bank*, for fourteen Days; while he himself with the rest of the Squadron proceeded towards *St. Lawrence*, and the Island of *St. Peter*'s, at the Entrance of *Fortune* Bay, the former of which Places he arrived at the last of *August*, and seeing there four Sail, which he ordered the *Mountague* and *Medway* to take or destroy, and then to follow him, he with the *Exeter* and *Litchfield* stood away for *St. Peter*'s, where he arrived the next Day; but having some Reason to suspect the Judgment of his Pilots, and being informed that the Harbour was not only very narrow, but that the Ground without it was broken, it was his Opinion as well as Captain *Swanton*'s, and the Lord *Dursly*'s, who commanded the *Litchfield*, that it was convenient to wait for better Weather before they adventured in. This he had the good Fortune to meet with the next Day, and then stretching towards the Harbour, he saw eight Ships and small Vessels off of the Eastermost End of the Island, to which giving Chase, he discovered that the Harbour was on that Side, and in it seven or eight Ships at Anchor, so that had he born away the Morning before for the Place, the Pilots took to be the Entrance of the Harbour, he would not only have run the Hazard of being driven to Leeward of the Island, but also of falling on a Ledge of Rocks which lie off of the Point.

At Noon he took one of the Ships loaden with Fish, and leaving the *Litchfield* in chase of another, ply'd in for the Harbour to secure the rest; but when he was within a Quarter of a Mile of the Entrance (the Wind being then right out) he discovered four Sail endeavouring to make their Escape from the South Chanel, which his Pilots had affirmed was not navigable for any Vessel that drew above five or six Feet Water; and observing that the rest loosed their Top-sails to go out the same Way, he thought it to no Purpose to chase them, for it was then about seven at Night, the Harbour not above half a Mile over, and a dangerous Rock in the middle of it, which appeared but a very little above Water; wherefore he drove under his Top-sails until it was dark, the better to amuse them, but his real Design was to stand for the South Chanel to intercept them, had not the Haziness of the Weather prevented him, by which means they all escaped, except one laden with Salt taken by the *Litchfield*.

ERRATA.

PREFACE.

Page.	Line.	
3.	3.	for *Lipanto* r. *Lepanto*.
		for *Contrarini* r. *Contarini*.
5.	34.	for *Aages* read *Ages*.
6.	16.	after *Days* r. *including also the Merchant Ships of the Kingdom*.
13.	39.	leave out *be*.
21.	32.	for 700 *l*. r. 7000 *l*.
23.	31.	leave out *so*.
25.	22.	for *about* r. *above*.
29.	3.	for *Countries* r. *Counties*.

CONTENTS of Book V.

Ch. xv. l. 24. for *Beaumont* r. *Beaumont's Proceedings*.
Ch. xx. l. 17. for *them* r. *there*.
Ch. xxxi. l. 33. for *Adge* r. *Agde*.

BOOK.

10.	16.	after *of* r. *his*.
	32.	leave out *as*
11.	31.	r. *Æquator*.
14.	Marg.	for *Provena* r. *Provente*.
15.	17.	after *Ports* make a ,
28.	34.	r. *Vergivian*.
	39.	for *callenged* r. *challenged*.
33.	26.	for *the* r. *his*.
35.	5.	after *extend* r. *to*.
36.	36.	for *a* r. *an*.
37.	15.	after *far* r. *from being*.
38.	Marg.	for *of Breda* r. *for a Suspension of Arms in 1712*.
42.	20.	*Naval* twice printed.
44.	12.	for *Flegonus* r. *Telegonus*.
46.	last.	r. *some have*.
64.	43.	for *at* r. *as*. and a , at *Continent*.
66.	Marg.	for *Conon's* r. *Cimon's*.
71.	14.	*of* is twice printed.
73.	2.	for *them* r. *then*.
83.	10.	r. *taken and killed great Numbers of Men*.
84.	39.	for *Barks* r. *Beaks*.
85.	37.	for *them* r. *him*.
103.	34.	for *Cedrosians* r. *Gedrosians*.
110.	39.	for *Friendships* r. *Friendship*.
112.	18.	after *he* make a ,
	last.	for *Doso* r. *Doson*.
113.	41.	leave out *that Princess*, and make a , before the Words.
122.	41.	for *Albia* r. *Olbia*.
124.	20.	for *come* r. *came*.
126.	45.	for *Drepanum* r. *Drepanum*.
	Marg.	for *Trepano* r. *Trapani*.
128.	last.	for the Catch-word *or* r. *hundred*.
130.	39.	after *commanded* r. *in Corcyra*.
132.	Marg.	for *Miletus* r. *Melita*.
134.	last.	for *an* r. *and the*.
139.	20.	for *drew* r. *drove*.
141.	30.	leave out the , after *Ambassador*.
	31.	leave out *and*.
161.	Marg.	firstNote, for *Ganymedes* r. *Achilles*.
	9.	after *Eunuch* r. *who*.
168.	34.	after *Resolution* make a . and leave out *but*.
	36.	after *Sailers* add *but*.
	37.	after *Fight* leave out *so that*.
170.	38.	for *a-peck* r. *apeek*.
180.	6.	for *on* r. *of*.
	8.	for *of* r. *on*.
185.	31.	for *Pratoria* r. *Pratoria*.

Page.	Line.	
186.	32.	for *fixed* r. *fastened*.
219.	18.	for *Boncicaut* r. *Boucicaut*.
297.	48.	for *there* r. *their*.
307.	14.	after *Events* leave out the , and leave out *it*.
336.	20.	for *Track* r. *Tract*.
346.	9.	after *adrift* make)
349.	18.	for *hence* r. *thence*.
360.	11.	leave out *to*.
363.	40.	after *St. Andrew's* make a ,
368.	last	place the , after *it*.
387.	40.	after *Attempts* r. *and*.
408.	44.	after *thereof* r. *to*.
416.	5.	after *for* r. *ons*.
	30.	leave out *after*.
426.	15.	leave out the ; after *Ships*.
430.	16.	leave out the , after *side*.
440.	22.	for *interrupts* r. *intercepts*.
443.	41.	leave out the , after *French Fleet*.
466.	5.	for *our* r. *Our*, and a . before.
478.	48.	for *Dominica* r. *Guadalupe*.
	42.	after *by* r. *a great majority*.
518.	29.	for *a-ilsing* r. *sailing*.
525.	31.	for *he* r. *she*.
528.	11.	r. *the Quince Rock*.
529.	15.	before *Brake* r. *the*.
536.	12.	for *Cape Francis* r. *Cape François*.
	41.	after *Paix* r. *and*.
549.	14.	for *S. W. W.* r. *S. S. W.*
	18.	for *forgetting* r. *so, getting*.
554.	37.	after *failed*, instead of ; make a ,
556.	31.	after *Havana* r. *and*.
564.	21.	after *were* make a , and after *himself* a ,
566.	15.	after *would* leave out *have*.
570.	44.	instead of *but* r. *where he*.
	45.	after *Road* r. *but*.
575.	last.	leave out *the*.
576.	28.	for *broke* r. *broken*.
577.	41.	for *ake* r. *ach*.
584.	39.	after *Bomb-Vessels* make a ,
593.	23.	after *those French* r. *Ships*.
	31.	leave out *at Anchor*.
600.	36.	for *Forces* r. *Troops*.
601.	4.	after *soon* leave out the ,
614.	34.	for *coming* r. *going*.
618.	21.	after *Agents* make . and he with a great H.
619.	7.	leave out the , after *before*.
	37.	after *Wind* make a , instead of a ;
630.	44.	after *Start* r. *was*.
632.	32.	after *Place* leave out the ,
633.	13.	for *Gall* r. *Gally*.
635.	13.	after *Gunfleet* make a ,
652.	19.	for *esides* r. *besides*.
658.	11.	for *Ships* r. *Ship*.
	29.	after *which* r. *time*.
670.	40.	after *go* r. *to*.
678.	13.	for *lay* r. *lie*.
684.	20.	for *unmooring* r. *unmoored*.
692.	17.	after *to* r. *their*.
697.	24.	for *with* r. *by*.
715.	42.	for *hence* r. *home*.
719.	1.	for *Dungenesse* r. *Dengenesse*.
724.	last.	for *hey* r. *they*.
747.	46.	before *Admiral* r. *the*.
750.	43.	for *Lampourdan* r. *Ampourdan*.
773.	16.	for *from* r. *for*.
774.	46.	for *in England from* r. *from England at*.
791.	8.	for *for* r. *from*.
793.	6.	for *are* r. *were*.

CHAP. XI. *from the Year* 1698, *to* 1712. 633

It continuing to blow hard, and all the Enemy's Ships being got out of the Harbour, he bore away for *St. Lawrence*, where he had left the *Mountague* and *Medway*, the former whereof joined him the fourth of *September*, having parted with the other the Night before, making the best of her Way for the Harbour of *St. John*'s with her four Prizes, two of which were part of those which escaped from *St. Peter*'s; and as the other two were taken at *Great St. Lawrence*, so had they burnt two more at *Little St. Lawrence*, and destroyed their Boats and Stages. Here it was agreed to bear away for *St. John*'s, and to proceed from thence to *Chapeau Rouge*, on the North Part of *Newfoundland*. At *St. John*'s they arrived the eighth of *September*, and found there the *Medway*, *Assistance*, *Charles* Gall, *Loo*, and *Firebrand* Fireship, the two latter having seen their Convoys to the several Places whereto they were bound, and the *Reserve* was gone to survey the Harbours of *Trinity* and *Carbonier*.

Next Day the Commadore sailed from *St. John*'s with the *Mountague*, *Litchfield*, *Assistance*, and *Loo*, in order to visit *Bona Vista*, the most Northern Plantation we had in those Parts, where he judged he might most probably be furnished with Pilots for *Chapeau Rouge*, but he left the *Medway*, *Charles*-Gally, and the Fireship to go to, and destroy at *St. Peter*'s what they could meet with in that Harbour, and then to cruise off of Cape *Race* and the *Banks* of *Newfoundland*, until the twenty fifth of the aforesaid Month of *September*.

He arrived at *Bona Vista* the twelfth, but could not furnish himself with Pilots there able to carry the Ships to *Chapeau Rouge*, so that he determined to return to *St. John*'s without attempting to go farther Northward so late in the Year, in dark Nights, and without the Assistance of experienced Pilots; besides all the Ships were in great Want of Water and Wood, which, had he proceeded, he was in Hopes of supplying them withal.

The fourteenth of *September* he arrived at *St. John*'s, where he was informed by a Pilot of the Country, that although he did not well know *Chapeau Rouge*, he was acquainted with several good Harbours the *French* had Northward, but nevertheless refused to carry the Ships thither, because the Winter Season was too far advanced. They had, as he said, no Forts there, nor other Defence than what the Merchant Ships made with their Guns, to secure them from the *Indians* while they were fishing, who treat the Christians barbarously when they fall into their Hands; nor was there to the Northward, as he said, any other Fortification but that at *St. Peter*'s, and even that but a small Fort of not more than 6 Guns.

The second of *October* the *Medway* and *Charles* Gally, with a small Banker the latter had taken, came in from *St. Peter*'s, the Fort whereof they had demolished, and burnt and spoiled the Enemy's Habitations, Boats, and Stages; and it was now agreed that the *Mountague* and *Loo* should convoy the Ships bound to *Portugal*, the *Reserve*, *Charles*-Gally, and *Firebrand* Fireship those for *England*; and that the rest of the Squadron should, when the Trade

M m m m was

was ready to sail, proceed off of Cape *Race*, thence into the Latitude of 45^d, and there cruise ten Days to intercept the Ships from *Placentia*; and one of the *French* Prizes was given to the greatest Part of the Prisoners to carry them to *France*, as well to lengthen out the Provisions, as to keep the Ships Companies from Distempers.

The Commadore sailed from *St. John's* the eleventh of *October*, with the *Exeter*, *Medway*, *Assistance*, and *Litchfield*, leaving the rest of the Squadron to convoy the Trade as beforementioned, and two Days after he got to the Rendezvous, which was S. by E. from Cape *Race*, between the Latitudes of 44 and 45^d.

The eighteenth the *Medway* took a *French* Banker, and the twentieth one of the *Placentia* Ships, whose Master acquainted Captain *Littleton* that he had been separated in a Storm from the rest of the Fleet, which were about forty Sail, under Convoy of one Man of War of 50 Guns; and the Commadore believing, by what he gathered from the said Master, that Part of the Fleet was Eastward of him, made the best of his Way in Quest of them.

The twenty first and twenty second four more Bankers were taken, with another Ship from *Placentia*, and two more in few Days after, whose Masters confirming what the other had reported, the Commadore intended to have kept his Course Southward, in order to intercept others of them, but meeting with hard Winds at S. E. and S. S. E. he was forced as far Northward as the Latitude of 48^d, and then, his Provisions growing short, he made the best of his Way to *England*.

The Number of Ships taken at, and about Newfoundland. There were taken in all twenty nine Sail, and two burnt, three with Salt, twenty five with Fish, and one from *Martinica* with Sugar and Molosses; eight of them the *Exeter* took, the *Medway* seized on nine, the *Mountague* and *Litchfield* took each of them four; three fell to the Share of the *Charles*-Gally, and one to the *Reserve*.

Had our Ships arrived upon the Coast of *Newfoundland* a fortnight sooner, they might have given a better Account of the Enemy, for many of them had made their Voyage, and were gone from their several Stations to *Placentia*; and even those that escaped from *St. Peter's* must have gone with little or none of their Cargo, for, running away, they left Part thereof behind, which the *Medway* and *Charles*-Gally destroyed.

CHAP.

CHAP. XII.

Containing an Account of Captain Bazil Beaumont's *Proceedings, while at the Head of a Squadron employed against the* French *Ships at* Dunkirk.

IN the next Place it is necessary to acquaint you, that a Squadron of Ships were put under the Command of Captain *Bazil Beaumont* *, and they being particularly designed to observe the Motion of the Enemy's Ships at *Dunkirk*, he was ordered the twenty fourth of *June* to proceed over to that Port; and if by the falling of the Tides he judged that their biggest Ships could not get out to Sea, to divide his Squadron, and appoint one Part to cruise Northward, and the other Westward between the Coasts of *England* and *France*, but yet so, as that they might timely join at the general Rendezvous, which was to be either at the *Gunfleet* in the *Downs*, *Ousley* Bay, or *Yarmouth* Roads, as Winds and Weather, and other Circumstances might make it most proper.

The next Day there was Advice that the two biggest Ships at *Dunkirk* were got down to the *Heads*, and that three more were preparing for the Sea, so that Captain *Beaumont* was ordered to proceed immediately thither, with four Fourth Rates, and a Sloop, and when there to govern himself according to the aforesaid Instructions; but he was directed to leave Orders for the other Ships under his Command to follow him from the *Downs* as soon as possible; and there being a Squadron of *Dutch* Ships off of *Schonevelt* at this time, it was recommended to him, if he found himself not strong enough to keep Monsieur *Ponty* in, to join himself thereunto.

Pursuant to these Orders he sailed, and being off of *Dunkirk* the twenty eighth of *June*, sent the Sloop with an Account to the Admiralty that he had plainly seen eight large Ships in *Flemish* Road, which he believed would put to Sea that very spring Tide; and judging himself much too weak to oppose them, (for he had then with him no more than three Fourths, and one Sixth Rate) he resolved to join the *Dutch* Ships at *Schonevelt*, and with them endeavour to keep the Enemy in, or pursue them if they got out of the Harbour.

By this Sloop Orders were sent to him to remain off of *Dunkirk*, if joined with the *Dutch* Ships, and that the *French* were still in that Port: But lest Accidents might have brought him into the *Downs*, Orders were at the same time sent thither, directing him to proceed first to *Yarmouth* Roads, and then to use his best Endeavours to protect the Trades from *Hamburgh*, the *East-Country* and *Holland*.

He joined Vice-Admiral *Evertsen* off of *Schonevelt* the twenty ninth of *June*, and acquainted him what he had observed in relation

Capt. Beaumont joins the Dutch Vice-Admiral.

1702.

---
* Afterwards a Flag-Officer.

to the *French* Ships, but that Flag-Officer had received a particular Account of their Motions before, by a Man purposely sent to him from the States-General. He desired him to join some of his Squadron to our Ships, since he had eighteen, from 72 to 40 Guns, the better to prevent the Enemy's coming out, or to enable him to attack them if they did; but could by no means prevail with him to do it, for he had Orders not to separate his Squadron, or to depart from the Service whereunto he was appointed, which was to prevent a Descent upon *Zeeland*, a thing the States-General his Masters apprehended from the Ships at *Dunkirk* and *Ostend*, the Gallies, Bomb-Vessels, and Pontoons, which they had prepared, and an Army of near eight thousand Men, said to be drawn together near *Ostend*, as it was believed, for that purpose. Nay the *Dutch* Vice-Admiral judging himself not strong enough effectually to prevent such an Attempt, had sent some Days before to Captain *Beaumont* in the *Downs*, and desired his Assistance; but at last he condescended to go a little farther Westward with part of his Squadron, the better to sustain our Ships if the *French* should come out, which it was believed they would do, for the first of *July* they lay ready with their Top-sails loose.

The Dutch would not add any Ships to him, being apprehensive of Zeeland.

I may not omit the mentioning here an Accident (which may seem somewhat strange) which happened two or three Days before Captain *Beaumont* came on the Coast; which was thus. Six *French* Gallies from *Ostend* took a *Dutch* Ship of 50 Guns, not above a Mile from their Vice-Admiral, and his whole Squadron, and carried her into that Port; but they made use of the Advantage of a Calm to perform this Exploit; for as the Gallies had an Opportunity of rowing to her, so were the Ships of War prevented in coming to her Assistance, or she from withdrawing herself from them, for want of Wind.

Six French Gallies take a Dutch Ship of War.

The tenth of *July* our Squadron was strengthened to seven Fourth Rates, and one Sixth, and by Orders from the States-General Vice-Admiral *Evertsen* sent three Ships to join them five Days after; who, in order to the more effectual Performance of the designed Service, acquainted Captain *Beaumont*, that, as soon as the Ships could be victualled, a Rear-Admiral and thirteen Sail would be appointed to observe the *French*, who were (as he said) making all possible Dispatch at *Dunkirk* and *Ostend*, not only with their Ships of War, but Fire-Vessels, Pontoons, and all other Matters, for the Attempt which the *Dutch* so much apprehended in *Zeeland*.

The English Squadron strengthened.

Two Days after this Account was received from Captain *Beaumont*, he was ordered to proceed to *Leith* in *Scotland*, in case Monsieur *Ponty* was gone to Sea with his Squadron, and that he had no Prospect of coming up with him, for there was a Suspicion (how well grounded I cannot say) that he was designed to that Kingdom; but if he found him not there, nor Intelligence where he might meet him, he was to come to the *Gunfleet*, calling in at *Newcastle*, and the several Northern Ports, for the Trade bound into the River: And by other Orders, dated the fourth of *August*, it was recommended to him to take particular care of the Merchant Ships from

Russia

CHAP. XII. *from the Year* 1698, *to* 1712. 637

Ruſſia and the *Baltick* Sea, loaden with Stores as well for the Navy as the Merchants Service.

The twenty firſt of *July* he propoſed to Vice-Admiral *Evertſen* the adding ſuch a Number of his Ships to him as ſhould be thought proper at a Conſultation, that ſo he might be the better able to oppoſe the Enemy, ſhould they get out from *Dunkirk* and *Oſtend*; and for the yet better effecting that Service, he farther deſired that the ſaid Ships might lie as near *Dunkirk* as poſſible, and that if the *French* ſhould yet get out, and go Northward, they might be chaſed as long as there ſhould be any Intelligence of them, and afterwards proceed to and bring from *Leith*, and other Northern Ports, the Trades of both Nations.

Upon this there was a Meeting of the *Engliſh* and *Dutch* Officers, and the Inſtructions both to one and the other being taken into Conſideration, it was agreed that Captain *Beaumont*, with ſeven of Her Majeſty's Ships, and five of the States-General, ſhould lie South, and South by Eaſt from *Dunkirk*, and ſtretch away S. W. and N. E. the better to keep the Enemy in, or to attack them if they got out. It was alſo reſolved that the *Dutch* Vice-Admiral ſhould lie in the ſame Station, or near thereunto, with the reſt of the Squadron: But here it may be obſerved, that if the Enemy's Ships had left the Port, thoſe of the States-General could not have follow'd farther than five or ſix Leagues, until they were ſupplied with Proviſions; but even when that ſhould be done, Rear-Admiral *Vanderduſſen* had Orders to chaſe no farther than the *Dogger-Bank*, where he was to cruiſe until he received farther Directions, and to make up the five Ships with Captain *Beaumont* thirteen.

Agreement how to place Engliſh and Dutch Ships off of Dunkirk.

The *French* Squadron continued in *Flemiſh* Road, being on the twenty third of *July* joined by two ſmall Ships from the Harbour, ſuppoſed to be Fireſhips, and it was believed that four Gallies were alſo come from the Weſt. There were two Ships of War at *Oſtend*, one of 66, and the other of 50 Guns, ready for the Sea, and on the twenty ſixth the Enemy ſeemed as if they were preparing to ſail, which had they done, it was not to be doubted but our Ships would have given a very good Account of them, for the Commadore had with him ſeven *Engliſh* of the Fourth Rate, and five of the States-General.

They were in Motion even that Day, and as four of them made a feint of going out Weſtward, ſo did three others ſtand Eaſtward, but anchored about two Leagues each way from *Dunkirk*, within the Sands; and there remained in the Road two great Ships, with as many ſmall ones. The next Day all theſe Ships weighed again, and kept under Sail for ſome time, but attempted not to come out, being governed by Signals with Flags from the biggeſt Ship in the Road, where, in all Probability, the Commanding Officer was; and undoubtedly their dodging thus to and fro was chiefly to amuſe us; for in the Afternoon they all returned into the Road again, though it is very probable they had hopes to have drawn our Ships Weſtward, and by that means have given thoſe at *Oſtend* the better Opportunity of joining them at *Dunkirk*.

The French Ships in Motion.

The

The States-General ordered three of their five Ships from Captain *Beaumont* to the *Texel* the beginning of *September*, and the Vice-Admiral could not appoint others in their room without Orders from his Masters; besides, their Apprehensions of a Descent on *Zeeland* led their Flag-Officer, with his Squadron, farther Eastward from our Ships. Some few Days before this the *French* sent two Gallies from *Dunkirk* to *Ostend*, and the twenty sixth of *August* there were no more than three Ships to be seen in *Flemish* Road, so that it was uncertain whether the others were gone to Sea, or into the Basin, although the Commadore was almost positive they were not at Sea, by reason he could see a much greater Number of Masts in the Basin than could be discovered a few Days before.

Our Ships were very much exposed from the bad Weather which happens at this Season of the Year, but more so from the Danger of the Coast; besides, they were in no little want of Provisions: And since we had then no more than five, and the *Dutch* but two, the Enemy gave it out as if they intended to attack them, for so the Masters of some Ships of *Hamburgh* reported who came from *Dunkirk*; though by People who were taken in a *French* Fishing Boat by Captain *Wyat*, the twenty ninth in the Morning, Captain *Beaumont* was informed that all their Ships, except two, were gone into the Harbour, with Intention not to come out again the remaining part of the Year; but other Intelligence being received at the Admiralty, before this Account from Captain *Beaumont* came to hand, that most of the *French* Ships were gone to Sea, (though it proved afterwards to be false) the *Worcester* was sent from the *Downs* with Orders to him; the *Dartmouth* and *Kingsfisher* were also sent to him from thence, the *Crown* from the *Buoy of the Nore*, and the *Rochester* was ordered to hasten to him as soon as she had convoyed the Earl of *Winchelsea* to *Holland*, who was going with a Compliment from Her Majesty to the Court of *Hanover*. It was recommended to Captain *Beaumont* to satisfy himself whether the Enemy were at Sea, or in Port, and as he was, in the former Case, to leave off of *Dunkirk* a fitting Strength, with the two *Dutch* Ships, and to proceed with the rest to a convenient Station for securing the *East-Country* Trade and their Convoys, which were ordered to come from the *Sound* the last of this Month; so, on the other hand, if Monsieur *Ponty* was gone in, that only three Ships were in *Flemish* Road, and that he judged the others would not come out again, he was to leave a Strength sufficient to keep in those three Ships, and repairing to the *Downs* with the Remainder, there take in a Supply of Provisions; but nevertheless to order the Commander in Chief of the Ships off of *Dunkirk* to send him immediate notice if the Enemy should prepare to go out, that so he might use his best Endeavours to intercept them.

Some Ships left off of Dunkirk. Pursuant to these Orders he left off of *Dunkirk* the *Worcester* and *Salisbury*, which were Fourth Rates, and two *Dutch* Men of War, to observe the Motions of the *French* Ships in the Road, and came into the *Downs* with the *Tilbury*, *Blackwall*, *Dartmouth*, and *Kingsfisher*. Those Ships being victualled, two of them were ordered

CHAP. XII. *from the Year* 1698, *to* 1712.

ordered to cruise in the *Soundings*, and the Commadore to repair with the rest to *Margate* Roads, from whence, with some other Ships which there joined him, he convoyed the Yachts to *Holland*; and having cruised four Days between the *Well*, a Shoal off of the Coast of *Lincolushire*, and the *Dogger Bank*, in search of some Ships said to be got out from *Dunkirk*, he proceeded to *Helvoet-Sluys*, and conducted from thence to *England* the Earl of *Marlborough*, General of Her Majesty's Forces.

There was a Report during Captain *Beaumont's* being in *Holland*, as if Monsieur *Ponty* was actually got out of *Dunkirk*, but he was positive that neither he, nor any of his Ships, were at Sea, knowing it to be almost impossible, as the Tides fell out; and it afterwards appeared that he judged very right in this Matter. But (as I have already acquainted you) the *Worcester* being one of the Ships he had left off of *Dunkirk*, her Commander sent the Lords of the Admiralty an Account, that on the thirteenth of *October*, in the Morning, he had seen all the *French* Squadron at Anchor in *Gravelin-Pits*, except two which were under Sail.

The Day after he had dispatched this Advice he sailed from the Flats of the *Foreland*, and standing over towards *Calais* and *Gravelin*, saw under the Cliffs of *Calais* ten Sail turning to Windward, and four small ones to Windward of himself, which he took to be their Scouts. This Alarm occasioned the ordering those few Ships of War, and the Trade which were in the *Downs* to the *Buoy of the Nore*, since there they might be more safe, and a Squadron was formed at the *Gunfleet* with all possible Dispatch, which in the Absence of Captain *Beaumont*, was put under the Command of Captain *Thomas Foulis*, and he, on the eighteenth of *October*, ordered off of *Calais*, *Gravelin*, and *Dunkirk*, in search of the aforesaid *French* Ships. If he met them not there, he was to stretch away Northward for the Security of the Trades expected from the *East-Country*, *Russia*, and *Hamburgh*, and was ordered to call in at some Place about the *Naez* of *Norway* for Intelligence: But if when he came off of *Dunkirk* he found the *French* Ships were gone in, he was to come to the *Downs* with all the Squadron, except the *Worcester*, and a Fifth Rate, which two Ships he was to leave off of the Port to observe and bring him Intelligence of their Motion.

Preparations upon a mistaken Account of the French.

One of our Captains was informed by the Master of a *Swedish* Ship, that he saw a *French* Vice-Admiral with several Men of War off of *Solebay*; but this Intelligence was no more to be depended on than the many Amusements we had from the Masters of Ships of that Country the last War.

Captain *Foulis* having with him eight Fourth Rates, and three Fifths of ours, and two Ships of the States-General, he proceeded Northward in search of the Enemy, according to his Instructions, and being in *Yarmouth*-Roads the twenty fourth of *October*, (where he called in for Pilots) he spoke with the Master of a Ship which was taken and came from *Dunkirk* the seventeenth, who said that there were then in that Port thirteen Ships ready to go to Sea, and nine of them Men of War.

He

He sailed the twenty fourth in the Afternoon from the back of *Yarmouth* Sands, with the Wind at N.W. and N.N.W. and plied Northward, but the twenty fifth at Night it began to blow very hard, and continued to do so all the next Day, insomuch that they could not purchase their Anchors. The twenty seventh the Wind, and consequently the Sea, encreased, insomuch that the *Crown* was forced to bear away, as was the *Content* at Night, and it blowing extreme violent the twenty eighth, between the N.N.W. and N.E. with Rain and Hail, the *Dover* and *Fowey*'s Cables gave way, so that they were forced out of the Squadron.

The twenty ninth the Weather was more moderate, when the Signal was made for weighing with the Wind at North, but from thence it came to the N.E. and the Commadore having then with him no more than three *English* Fourth Rates, and one *Dutch* Ship, he proceeded, according to the Opinion of the Captains, to the Flats of the *Foreland*, to look for the rest of his Squadron.

Thus ended this Search after the *French* Ships, which had not indeed been out of their Port; and of this Captain *Beaumont* was so well assured, that by Letters, during his stay in *Holland*, he positively affirm'd that not any of their great Ships had been at Sea; so that in all Probability those which the Captain of the *Worcester* saw were Coasters going from *Dunkirk*, or *Ostend*, to some Ports in the West of *France*; for by reason of the Haziness of the Weather, he could not so well discover them as otherwise he might have done; besides, he being alone, it was not safe for him to stand too near them.

Chap. XIII.

Containing an Account of Sir George Rooke's *Proceedings with the Fleet in and about the Chanel.*

1703.

THE fourth of *April* Sir *George Rooke*, Admiral of the Fleet, was ordered to take under his Command that part thereof which was designed for Service in the Chanel, *viz.* five Firsts, six Seconds, eighteen Thirds, nine Fourths, nine Fifths, and one Sixth Rate, together with three Bomb-Vessels, six Fireships, and three Hospital Ships, as also the Squadron intended for the *Mediterranean* under Command of Sir *Cloudesly Shovell*, in case it should be found for the Advantage of the Service to put a Stop to that Expedition.

A French Squadron take the Salisbury, and Adventure.

Arriving in the *Downs* the twelfth of *April*, he was there informed that Her Majesty's Ships the *Salisbury* and *Adventure* had met with a Squadron of *French* Ships from *Dunkirk*, and (as 'twas fear'd) had fallen into their Hands. Upon this Rear-Admiral *Byng*, with the *Ranelagh*, *Somerset*, *Torbay*, *Cambridge*, and *Winchester*, was ordered

CHAP. XIII. *from the Year 1698, to 1712.* 641

dered to lie in the fair way for intercepting the Enemy in their Passage to *Dunkirk*; and Rear-Admiral *Beaumont* was sent off of that Port with his Squadron; but notwithstanding this early Care, the *French* had the good Fortune to carry in their Prizes before either of the Squadrons could possibly come up with them.

The Action was thus. Captain *Cotton*, who commanded the *Salisbury*, came with that Ship and the *Adventure* from *Goree*, in *Holland*, the ninth of *April*, and next Day about one a Clock discovered seven Sail bearing down on him with *English* Colours. These Ships proved to be three *French* and one *Spanish* Man of War, the others Privateers. The *Salisbury* was constrained singly to engage with most of them, that the Trade and the Yachts might the better secure themselves, in one of which was the Earl of *Winchelsea*, who was returned from the Court of *Hanover*. The *Adventure* was astern, and the *Salisbury* endeavoured to edge down all that possibly she could, to assist the Tail of the Fleet, with which was a hired Storeship of considerable Force, named the *Muscovia Merchant*, but she, without any Resistance, struck to the Enemy, and the *Adventure*, to save herself, stood away with all the Sail she could carry, so that the *Salisbury* bore the brunt upwards of two Hours. She was boarded by two of the *French* Ships, which were bravely put off, but soon after Monsieur *St. Paul*, who commanded in Chief, lying on her Bow ready to clap her on board again, another on her Broadside, the *Milford* (taken from us the last War) on one Quarter, and the *Queen of Spain*, a Ship of *Ostend*, on the other, all of them making what fire they possibly could, they disabled her Masts, Sails, and Rigging, dismounted several of her Guns, and her Hull was very much torn. This, with the killing eighteen, and desperately wounding both her Lieutenants, and forty three Men, together with the throwing into her Hand-Granadoes so thick, that they were not able to continue on the Deck, constrained the Captain to yield the Ship to them, which they afterwards fitted out, and employed against us.

An Account of the Action.

The Admiral lay some time Wind-bound in the *Downs*, but arrived at St. *Helen*'s the 17th of *April*, having then with him two First Rates, thirteen Thirds, three Fourths, four Bombs, and three Hospital Ships. It was his Opinion; and accordingly he proposed it as such, that the Fleet should forthwith go to Sea, without staying for the *Dutch*, and surround the Bay of *Biscay* with a strong Detachment, that so if the Enemy had any Men of War, or Merchant Ships without the Entrance of Port *Louis*, or of *Rochefort*, an Attempt might be made to surprize and destroy them; or at least it was judged that we might thus interrupt their Commerce. He was the better able to put this in speedy Execution, from the liberty he had to remove the Men belonging to two First, and four Third Rates, ordered to be paid off, into other Ships that most wanted them. And now Vice-Admiral *Leake* of the Blue Squadron, being returned with several Ships to *Spithead* from the *French* Coast, where he had missed of those he was sent to intercept, the Admiral farther proposed to go into the *Bay* with two First Rates, four Seconds,

Sir George Rooke arrives at St. Helen's, and proposes to go into the Bay of Biscay to annoy the Enemy.

Vice-Admiral Leake returns from the French Coast.

N n n n

Seconds, twelve Thirds, and six Fourths, of the Chanel Squadron, and one Third, two Fourths, two Fifth, and two Sixth Rates of Sir *Cloudesly Shovell*'s, as also two Bomb-Vessels, which were all the Ships and Vessels at this time at *Spithead* ready for Service, being two First, four Seconds, twenty one Thirds, one Fourth, three Fifths, and one Sixth Rate, with five Bomb-Vessels, ten Fireships, and three Hospitals: But besides these, there were on the *French* Coast, under Command of Captain *Charles Wager* * one Third, three Fourths, one Fifth, and one Sixth, and by them a Ship of 14 Guns was taken, but most of the trading Vessels, as well as their small Convoys, escaped to *Havre de Grace, Cherbourg, La Hogue,* and the Ports along the Coast: And there were also one Ship of the Second Rate, four of the Third, and ten of the Fourth, designed for the Fleet, which had not then joined the Admiral.

Some Ships on the French Coast with Captain Wager.

That the intended Service might be the more effectually carried on, the Admiral proposed that, if there should be occasion for it, Sir *Cloudesly Shovell* might lie off of the Isle of *Ushant* with his Squadron, for that there the *Dutch* Ships designed to proceed with him to the *Mediterranean* might as well join him as on our Coast; but yet he was of opinion there would be no occasion for this additional Strength, if the Intelligence of the Enemy's Preparations could be depended on.

The Queen orders Sir George Rooke to proceed as he had proposed.

The Lord High-Admiral having considered these Proposals, directed him to obey Her Majesty's Commands; and the Queen was pleased to order him to proceed on the aforementioned Expedition.

The 1st of *May* he received Directions to send a Frigate with Dispatches to Mr. *Methuen*, Her Majesty's Envoy at *Lisbon*, (who was then treating the Alliance some time after concluded with the King of *Portugal*) and on the 4th in the Morning he was under Sail, but contrary Winds prevented his getting clear of the Isle of *Wight*, and being at this time indisposed, he desired leave to go on shore, yet offered to proceed rather than the Service should suffer.

Sir George Rooke had leave to come on shore, and Mr. Churchill appointed to Command. However Sir George proceeds

Her Majesty was pleased to gratify him in this Request, and thereupon Mr. *Churchill* (Admiral of the Blue, and one of the Council to his Royal Highness) was ordered to take upon him the Command of this part of the Fleet, and to proceed on the intended Service, but Sir *George* not timely receiving leave to come ashore, went on, and was off of *Portland* the 6th of *May*, although he was not then, nor some considerable time after, able to get out of his Bed.

On the 8th of *May* he arrived with the Fleet off of *Plimouth*, where being joined by Vice-Admiral *Leake*, he appointed a Rendezvous for the *Dutch* Ships, in case they timely arrived, which, with the Wind Westerly, was *Torbay*, and from fifteen to twenty Leagues West from *Ushant*, if it should happen to blow Easterly.

He was not far from *Plimouth* when he received the Lord High-Admiral's Consent for his leaving the Fleet, but resolving still to proceed, he sent the *Hampton-Court*, a Third Rate, towards *Spithead*, to advise Admiral *Churchill* that he was gone to Sea; the

---

* *Afterwards Knighted, and a Flag-Officer.*

Captain

Captain of which Ship not coming to him in time, he went on to *Plimouth*, in Expectation of meeting the Fleet there.

On the 9th of *May*, about fifteen Leagues from *Ushant*, the Admiral called a Council of the Flag-Officers, namely Vice-Admiral *Leake*, and Rear-Admiral *Dilkes*, and his first Captain, Captain *James Wishart*, who perusing the Instructions from Her Majesty, and the Intelligence received from *Brest* of the Enemy's Preparations, together with the Project for a Descent in the Bay of *Verdon*, at the Mouth of the River of *Bourdeaux*, determined to send some Frigates through the *Race*, to gain farther Intelligence from *Brest*, and to proceed with the gross of the Fleet to *Belle* Isle, (it being judged unsafe to go farther so early in the Year) and that from thence some Frigates should be detached as far as St. *Martin*'s, to discover what the Enemy were doing in those Parts.

The Admiral calls a Council of War.

Captain *Robert Fairfax* * was sent the next Day on the aforesaid Service with the *Kent*, *Monk*, *Medway*, and *Dragon*, who steering along shore, passed within a Mile of *Conquet* Road, where there was not any thing to be seen but small Craft; but the Coast was fortified with near thirty Guns, between *Conquet*, and St. *Matthew*'s Point. He stood into the *Sound* without *Brest*, and to the Eastward of *Camaret*, but saw not any thing there; nor could he discover in the Harbour more than six Sail ready for the Sea, three of them from 60 to 70 Guns, and the others from 30 to 40.

Captain Fairfax sent for Intelligence.

A Fisherman was taken, who belong'd to a small Village about five Leagues from *Brest*, and he affirm'd that there sailed from that Port, the Sunday before, four Ships of three Decks, under Command of Monsieur *Cotlongon*; that there were between twenty and thirty more in the Harbour disarmed, and in the Road four Ships of War, and two Privateers ready to sail with Monsieur *D'Arteloire*.

An Account of Ships sailed from Brest.

The Admiral was of Opinion that the Winds which carried Monsieur *Cotlongon* to Sea, had given Opportunity to the other *French* Ships to sail from the Ports in the *Bay*, so that he could have but little Prospect of doing any Service there; and since he was obliged by his Instructions, as well from the Queen as the Lord-High-Admiral, to proceed as a Council of Flag-Officers and Captains should judge most proper, he summoned them the 12th in the Afternoon, where were present besides the Flag-Officers and Captain *Wishart*, seventeen other Captains. They considering again the Queen's Instructions, as also the Intelligence, particularly that from Captain *Fairfax*, concluded to sail as far as *Belle* Isle, and that a Detachment should be sent from thence to St. *Martin*'s, or elsewhere, for farther Advice of the Enemy, *Belle* Isle being appointed the Rendezvous from the 16th to the 20th of *May*, and afterwards in the Latitude of 46 and 47^d, S. S. W. from *Ushant*.

Another Council of War called.

The Fleet was prevented from getting into the *Bay* by Southerly Winds, Foggs, and Calms, and on the 15th the *Medway* was ordered to chase a Sail at some Distance, which she took in the Afternoon. This Ship came from *Pondicheri* on the Coast of *Cor-*

---

* *Afterwards one of the Council to the Prince of* Denmark, *when Lord High-Admiral.*

mandel,

mandel, and was bound to Port *Louis* with her Loading of Muslins and Callicoes, being the same which was taken from us the last War, under the Name of the hired Ship *Success*.

The 17th of *May* the *Winchester*, *Dover*, and *Litchfield* joined the Fleet, which two Days after got as far into the *Bay* as the *Seames*; but the Wind flying out very fresh at S. S. W. and S. W. obliged them to stand out again; and the aforesaid Ship *Winchester*, which was sent with the *Ipswich* into the Station off of *Ushant*, retook the *Sarah* Gally of *London* loaden with Sugar, Tobacco and Logwood from *Virginia*.

The Fleet stands into the Bay of Biscay.

The Wind coming about Northerly the 20th, the Admiral stood into the *Bay* with the Fleet, and the *Litchfield* and *Dragon* speaking with a *Dutch* Galliot the 23d, they were informed by a *French* Lieutenant, who was on board, and had taken her, that he saw, the Tuesday before, twenty six *French* Ships of War standing Westward, the Land about *Bourdeaux* then bearing E. by S. near fifteen Leagues off. Upon this a Council of War judged it convenient to proceed to *Belle* Isle, and that the Detachment design'd to St. *Martin*'s should not be sent thither, until it could be certainly known whether the Enemy's Ships were in those Parts, or gone to Sea.

An Account of a French Squadron at Sea.

The Fleet comes to Belle Isle.

The 24th of *May* the Fleet arriv'd at *Belle* Isle, where there was not any thing to be seen but some Fishing-Boats. As the Admiral was going in, he sent the Rear-Admiral with five Ships to the S. E. End of the Island, to intercept any Vessels which might attempt to come out that way, as he did the *Berwick*, *Ipswich*, and *Litchfield* to the Island of *Groy*, or *Grouais*, lying off of Port *Louis*, to surprize any Shipping which should be found riding off that Port, which last brought into the Fleet two small Barks taken from amongst twenty that were bound Southward from *Brest*, but the Remainder, (except some which were stranded) with their Convoy of 14 Guns, got into Port *Louis*. Hereupon, and upon what the Prisoners related, a Council of War of the Flags and Captains was called in *Belle* Isle Road, who resolved it was not adviseable to divide the Fleet, by sending a Detachment farther into the *Bay*, since there were so few Frigates, and even but two of them clean, and that if the Enemy were weaker they might go into their Ports at pleasure, or if stronger, attempt us to Advantage; so that it was determined that the Detachment intended thither, and the Design of destroying the small Embarkations at the Isle *de Dieu* (the latter whereof would have been a fine Exploit indeed for a Fleet of Ships) should be deferred until there could be a better Opportunity of effecting it by a Squadron of clean Ships, with sixth Rates, and Brigantines, to sustain the Boats on that Service, for there was not Water, or room enough, for any Ships of Force to lie before the Fort.

Methods taken for intercepting the Enemy's Ships.

A Council of War in Belle Isle Road.

It was also resolved to put in Execution the Orders which the Admiral had received, by repairing to the Station S. S. W. from *Ushant*, in the Latitude of 46 and 47, the better to meet with any of the Enemy's Ships bound into or out of the *Bay*, and in case of Easterly Winds to stretch half a Degree more to the Southward, for that thereby

Resolved to repair to a Station off of Ushant.

CHAP. XIII. *from the Year* 1698, *to* 1712.   645

thereby they might have a Prospect of meeting the *French* Squadron beforementioned, if not gone from St. *Martin*'s; but if the Winds came Westerly, it was judged most adviseable to proceed North, so as to keep the Chanel open, and thereby be the better able to protect our Trade.

The 27th of *May* the *Dragon* took a Privateer of 16 Guns and 6 Patereroes, and ninety Men; at the South East end of the Island, loaden with six hundred and fifty Hogsheads of Sugar, and fifteen Barrels of *Indigo* from St. *Domingo*.

From the time that the Fleet came to an Anchor in *Belle* Isle Road, until the 1st of *June*, it blew very hard, but two Days after the Admiral weighed with an Easterly Wind, and stood towards the appointed Station; soon after which it came up Northerly, so that he was forced to ply thereinto; and receiving Orders the 5th by a Frigate called the *Lyme*, to detach two Ships for bringing our Trade from *Portugal*, he accordingly sent two Third Rates, the *Northumberland* and *Restauration*, on that Service, which they successfully performed. *A Convoy sent for our Trade from Portugal.*

About this time the Lord *Dursley**, who commanded the *Litchfield*, a Ship of 50 Guns, coming from the Body of the Fleet in the *Soundings*, met with a *French* Ship of War of thirty six Guns, and two hundred and sixty Men, which, after a stout Resistance, his Lordship took, as also a *French* Ship from *Martinica*, of 20 Guns, both which he brought with him to *Spithead*; and the Admiral having resolved to stay no longer on the Station than the 10th of *June* being desirous to be timely in *England* for any necessary Service, he shaped his Course homewards accordingly, and arrived at St. *Helen*'s after a tedious Passage, the 21st of the aforesaid Month, with two First Rates, three Seconds, five Thirds, four Fireships, the *William and Mary* Yacht, which attended on him, and an Hospital Ship, having ordered the *Medway* and *Dragon* to cruise between the *Lizard* and the *Ram-head*, and the *Monk*, *Lyme*, and *Lowestoff*, on the Station he came from, to give any Ships that might be sent to him an Account of his coming off. And thus ended an Expedition with a great part of the Fleet, from which very little Advantage accrued, whatever might have been expected; and in my poor Opinion a Squadron of small Ships might have had much better Success. *The Admiral returns to St. Helen's.*

After Sir *George Rooke* had been at *Spithead* some Days, the Prince sent him leave to go to the *Bath* for Recovery of his Health; but before he left the Place, he tried at a Court-Martial two Seamen that had deserted the Service, who were condemned and executed; and this was the first Instance in a long Series of Time that the Maritime Law was put in Execution on such Offenders.

When he came to Town again he was appointed to convoy the Arch-Duke *Charles* (soon after declared King of *Spain* by the Emperour his Father) from *Holland* to *Spithead*, and from thence to *Lisbon*; but before I enter on the Account of that Expedition, I

---

* *Now Earl of* Berkeley, *and Vice-Admiral of* England.

will

will acquaint you with Sir *Cloudesly Shovell's* Proceedings to and from the *Mediterranean,* and in the first Place set down the Instructions which he received for that Expedition.

CHAP. XIV.

Containing an Account of Sir Cloudesly Shovell's *Proceedings with a considerable Part of the Fleet in the* Mediterranean, *and of Damages done by the violent Storm which happened at his Return to* England.

Instructions to Sir Cloudesly Shovell *to proceed to the Mediterranean.*
1703.

ON the 4th of *May* 1703, Sir *Cloudesly Shovell* was directed by Her Majesty, to proceed (when in the *Mediterranean)* to the Coast of *France,* and lie off of *Peccais,* and Port *Cette* on the Coast of *Languedoc,* and if he saw any Persons on the Shore, to observe if they made Signals, if not to do the same to them, and finding them to be Friends, to send his Boat for such as should desire to come off to him, that so he might be informed of the Condition of the *Cevenois,* a People who had for some time taken up Arms against the Forces of the *French* King, in Defence of their Religion and Liberties. If he was satisfied that they could convey to their Companions any Powder, Bullets and Shoes (of the latter of which it is said he had a considerable Quantity in the Fleet, and they in extreme Want of them) he was to supply the same as might be proper, and likewise to furnish them with Money.

Relating to the Cevenois.

In the next Place he was to enquire whether it was feasible to destroy the Salt-Works at *Peccais,* and, in such Case, to land so many Marine Soldiers as might be necessary, to join such *French* as would willingly co-operate in the Attempt.

Salt-Works at Peccais.

2. This being done, or so much thereof as should be found practicable, he was to proceed to *Palermo* in *Sicily,* and there observe or make the Signals as aforesaid, and if any Persons were ready to receive him, to send for some of them, and concert the proper Methods of seizing on *Palermo,* and to assist in the Attempt with the Ships and Bomb-Vessels, together with such Marines as might be necessary, as well as by all other Ways that should be judged expedient.

To endeavour to seize Palermo.

and,

3. If he succeeded in this, and that he found it practicable to take *Messina,* he was in that, and in all other things, to do his utmost towards assisting those People in freeing themselves from their Subjection to *France,* and the then *Spanish* Government, and reducing the Island to the Dominion of the House of *Austria.*

Messina.

4. Then he was to proceed to the Coast of *Naples,* and, upon Signals made to him, to assist those People in like manner; and if he should find any Part of the Emperor's Army there, he was so far to assist the Officer commanding those Forces, in reducing *Naples,*

To assist the Emperor's Troops in Naples.

CHAP. XIV. *from the Year* 1698, *to* 1712. 647

or any Part of that Kingdom, as should be thought adviseable, and, in order thereunto, to land the Marines, supply them with Mortars and Cannon out of the Ships and Vessels, and in all respects to do his utmost to assist the Emperor's Army, or any others declaring for the House of *Austria*.

5. If in his Way to *Sicily* he judged it not proper to proceed himself to *Livorne*, he was to send a Ship thither; and if there should be found any Person there by the Appointment of Prince *Eugene* of *Savoy* to confer with him, the Captain of such Ship was to receive him, if he desired it, that so an Account might be had from him of the Designs of the said Prince, and the Admiral himself be thereby the better enabled to assist in the Attempts against the Enemy; in order whereunto he was directed to correspond with him, as he had Opportunities for it, and to comply with his Desires in all Things that might be fit and proper, regard being had to the Safety of the Fleet. *To go or send a Ship to Livorne. To correspond with Prince Eugene.*

6. By other Instructions, dated the 4th of *May*, he was ordered to go with the Fleet, or to detach some Ships to the Coast of *Barbary*, and (by virtue of the Power given him under the Great Seal) to authorize the Consuls of *Algier*, *Tunis*, and *Tripoli*, or some Persons belonging to the Fleet, or others, to treat with those Governments, for concluding a Peace, upon Terms and Conditions which were to be proposed, and thereupon to make the usual Presents. *To treat a Peace with Algier, Tunis, and Tripoly.*

7. If he could prevail with them to make War against *France*, and that some Act of Hostility was thereupon committed, he was, on that occasion, to give such farther Presents as should be judged proper: And in case of such a Rupture, and that the *Dutch* Admiral had Orders to treat a Peace with those Governments, he was to assist him in the Negotiation. *To endeavour to prevail with them to break with France.*

He was also ordered to detach two Ships, or more, to *Livorne*, some time before his Return, with Orders to the senior Captain to make use of all Opportunities of taking or destroying any of the Enemy's Ships going into, or coming out of that Port, and to declare the reason thereof to be, because the Grand Duke had not strictly kept the Neutrality with relation to the *French*, nor done Right to Her Majesty's Subjects; for which reason the aforesaid Commanding Officer was to require an immediate Punishment of the Governor of *Livorne*, by removing him from his Employment. *To seize Ships going into, or coming out of Livorne.*

9. Farthermore, he was to require a positive Declaration and Assurance from the Great Duke, that no Seaman, her Majesty's Subject, should for the future be detained by him against his Will, but permitted to embark freely on board the Queen's Ships, or those of her Subjects, or Allies: And if, upon those Demands, entire Satisfaction was not made, the Admiral was to return home by *Livorne*, and by all ways practicable to exact it. *To reclaim English Seamen from the Duke of Tuscany.*

10. If he detached any Ships into the *Adriatick* Seas, pursuant to other Instructions he had or should receive, he was to order their Captains to take all Opportunities of destroying any *French* Ships or Vessels in the *Venetian* Ports, and to require from that State a Release of Her Majesty's Subjects detained in their Ships, Gallies, *To endeavour to destroy French Ships in the Venetian Ports.*

or Dominions; and in case of Refusal, to endeavour to take their Subjects out of their Ships, and to detain them until ours were cleared, otherwise to bring them to *England*. And he was farther to require of them immediate Satisfaction, and Reparation, for the Ship and Loading they suffered to be burnt by the *French* at *Malamocco*, or if they refused, to do his best Endeavours to make Reprizals on them.

and recover our Seamen from them.

11. By other Instructions from Her Majesty, dated the 7th of *May*, he was farther ordered, that when he had seen the Merchant Ships as near to *Lisbon*, *Genoa*, *Livorne*, and such other Ports as might be necessary for their Safety, and allotted particular Convoys to *Smyrna*, *Constantinople*, and *Scanderoon*, he should proceed with the Remainder of the Fleet, *English* and *Dutch*, to the Coasts of *Naples* and *Sicily*, and there call a Council of War of the Flags of both Nations, and also of the Colonels, or Commanders in Chief of the Regiments of Marines and Land-Forces, and with them consider how he might best assist the Emperor's Forces in those Parts, not only with the Ships, but the said Marine Soldiers, Mortars, and Guns, in any Attempts the said Forces of the Emperor, or others in favour of the House of *Austria* should make, and to join, and co-operate with them in annoying the Enemy according to what should be agreed.

To proceed to Naples and Sicily,

and

assist the Troops of the House of Austria.

12. It was also recommended to him to take all Opportunities of attacking *Cadiz*, *Thoulon*, or any Place on the Coast of *France*, or *Spain*, as also their Ships, Gallies, or Magazines, provided such Attempts might not interrupt the principal Service he was going upon.

To do his utmost in attacking Cadiz, Thoulon, &c.

13. If he got Intelligence that the *French* had any considerable Magazines near *Genoa*, and a Council of War should agree that by landing Marines at *Porto Spezza*, (a little Town belonging to the Republick of *Genoa*) or elsewhere, they might be destroy'd, he was to further the Attempt, by giving all possible Assistance and Protection to the Men, in their landing, and reimbarking, so far as the same might be consistent with the Safety of the Ships.

To endeavour to destroy French Magazines near Genoa.

14. He had liberty to apply any Prize, Provisions, or Stores, to the use of the Seamen, with the Privity of the Prize-Officer in the Fleet, but to keep an exact Account thereof.

Power to dispose of Prizes.

15. If he should want Water, or other Refreshments, he was empowered to make a Truce, and to treat with the Enemy for a Supply; and he had liberty to give Rewards to deserving Persons for extraordinary Services done in the Expedition, out of the Money advanced for defraying the Contingencies of the Fleet.

To make a Truce upon occasion, and reward deserving Persons.

16. It was recommended to him to treat the Subjects of the *Grand Seignior*, and all other Princes and States in Amity with Her Majesty, or the States-General, in a friendly manner, and to take the best care he could that the *Dutch* did not molest any of our said Allies, though not in Friendship with them. But if he happen'd to meet with ill Treatment from any Neuter Nation, or that they assisted the Enemy, and refused the like to him when he might have occasion, he was to demand Satisfaction, and to take it by Force if refused;

To treat the Subjects of Allies in a friendly manner.

To demand Satisfaction if ill treated by Neuters.

CHAP. XIV. *from the Year* 1698, *to* 1712. 649

refused; though this was only to be done in his Passage down the *Streights*.

17. When he had performed such Services as he was able for the Advantage of Her Majesty, and Her Allies, he was to consider at a Council of War the most proper time for returning home, and of the best means of taking on board the Guns, Mortars, small Arms, and Ordnance-Stores, and also the Marine Soldiers, unless he should find it necessary, and for the Service of Her Majesty's Allies, to leave the Guns or Mortars, Carriages, small Arms, or Ordnance-Stores, or any part of them on shore. And he was also to consider what Services might be done by annoying the Enemy in his Return home, but to have a regard to join the Ships detached for Convoys, or on particular Services, and to bring with him all the Trade that could be gotten together. *To consider what Services might be done before his return home.*

18. If he received good Intelligence that any *French* Ships were in the *Adriatick* Sea, molesting the Emperor's Convoys for *Italy*, and it should be judged safe, after the Detachments were made, he was empowered to send thither such a Number of Ships as a Council of War should think expedient, for burning or destroying the Enemy, in any Place or Port within that Gulph, except the Roads and Ports of the *Grand Seignior*. *To take, or destroy French Ships in the Adriatick.*

19. He was directed to communicate to the *Dutch* Admiral his Instructions, and to desire him to do the like to him, as a Matter which might conduce very much to the carrying on the Service. *To communicate his Instructions to the Dutch Admiral.*

20. In Consideration of the Distance which might be between him and home, he was empowered to exchange Prisoners for such of Her Majesty's Subjects as had or should be taken by Ships of the Enemy, or otherwise detained, and therein to proceed by the Rule directed to be observed in *England*, until a Cartel could be concluded, *viz.* Man for Man, and Quality for Quality; but yet it was left to his Discretion to do otherwise upon any special Occasion. *Power to exchange Prisoners.*

And now the twelve Ships of the States-General being joined him, and no Prospect of any more from *Holland*, he was ordered, on the 16th of *June*, to set sail with the first Opportunity of Wind and Weather, and to do his utmost to put his Instructions in Execution, to perform which (how practicable soever the Services ordered might be) would have required a much longer time than he had to remain abroad with the Fleet.

It was thought necessary to strengthen him by eight *English* Ships more, and the 29th of *June* he was ordered to take them with him in the Condition they were, that so no Delay might be made. But if the *French*, when he was in the *Mediterranean*, should find themselves inferior to him in Strength, and therefore attempt to repass the *Streights*, he was to have a careful Eye on them, and endeavour by all possible means to hinder their coming towards *Portugal*, or these Seas: Or if they should happen to get through the *Streights*, he was to follow them, first making a Detachment of so many Ships as should be thought requisite, and he could spare, for Services towards *Italy*, mentioned in the aforegoing Instructions. *The Squadron strengthened.* *To prevent the French Ships passing the Streights.*

O o o o By

By what hath been said it appears that there was Work more than enough cut out for Sir *Cloudesly Shovell*; for since he sailed not *Sir Cloudesly Shovell sails.* from St. *Helen*'s before the 1st of *July*; that he was required by Orders from the Lord High-Admiral, (agreed to in Council) to return down the *Streights* some time in *September*, and that the *Dutch* Admiral was obliged by the States General, his Masters, to be at home with the Squadron under his Command in *November*, there was not Opportunity of complying with many things contained therein. However, that it may appear how far he endeavoured so to do, I refer to the following Account of his Proceedings.

Having received his final Instructions both from Her Majesty, and his Royal Highness, he set sail from St. *Helen*'s the 1st of *July*, early in the Morning, but since several of the Ships which were appointed for the Expedition could not timely get ready, he desired that the strictest Orders might be given for their proceeding after him to the Rock of *Lisbon*, the Place of Rendezvous, that so the Service might not be delay'd by his staying there in Expectation of them.

He endeavour'd to beat it out of the Chanel, but being got as far Westward as *Fowey*, with a Fleet of about two hundred and fifty Sail, of all sorts, *English* and *Dutch*, the Wind came about from the South to the S.W. and W.S.W. so that it was impossible for him to keep the Sea with the Merchant Ships, and therefore he bore up for *Torbay*, from whence he sent his clean Ships to cruise in several Stations against the Enemy, and to protect the Trade,

Obliged to bear up for Torbay.

Captain *John Norris* of the *Orford*, who had been cruising with the *Mountague* in the *Soundings*, joined the Admiral in *Torbay*, having after an Hour's Dispute taken the *Phelipeaux* of 36 Guns, 12 Patereroes, and two hundred and forty Men. Her Captain behaved himself well, and surrender'd not until he had near fifty Men killed and wounded, and his Ship much torn. The *Orford* had eight Men wounded, and some of them very desperately too; and her Mizen-mast, Fore-mast, and Main-yard being shot through, were wholly disabled. The *Mountague*, commanded by Captain *William Cleveland*, had also the good Fortune to take the Ship she chased, of 18 Guns, and one hundred and ten Men, but in the Pursuit the *French* Captain threw most of her Ordnance over-board; and the *Orford* soon after took another *French* Ship which had 16 Guns mounted.

A French Ship taken by Captain Norris.

Another taken by Captain Cleveland,

and a third by Captain Norris.

The Admiral sailed from *Torbay* the very first Opportunity which offered, and on the 13th of *July* the *Grafton* joined him, as Sir *Thomas Hardy* did in the *Bedford* two Days after, who having been on the S.W. of the Fleet, took a Ship of the Enemy's from the *West-Indies* of about one hundred and twenty Tuns, loaden with Sugar. And about this time Captain *Robert Bokenham*, who commanded her Majesty's Ship the *Chatham* of 50 Guns, being ahead of the Admiral, about Two in the Morning, fell in with two *French* Ships of War called the *Jason*, and the *Auguste*, which getting between him and the Body of the Fleet, he engaged them, at the Distance of about Pistol-shot, but when it was broad Day-light, they

The Admiral sailed again.

Sir Thomas Hardy takes a Ship.

seeing

CHAP. XIV. *from the Year* 1698, *to* 1712.   651

seeing our Strength left him, and endeavoured to make their Escape, whereupon he chased them, and coming within Gun shot about Noon, they exchanged their Broadsides at each other, mean while several other Ships of the Fleet had an Opportunity of getting near him. At Five in the Afternoon the *French* Ships separated, and about Eight at Night the *Worcester* of 50 Guns, commanded by Captain *Thomas Butler*, engaged the *Jason*, while the *Chatham* was in fight with the *Auguste*, but it proving little Wind, she rowed from her at some Distance. At Nine at Night the *Greenwich* came along side of the *Auguste*, and engaged her until One a Clock, at which time she being much disabled, and the *Medway*, another Ship of 50 Guns, commanded by Captain *James Littleton*, coming up, she struck, *A French* having 54 Guns mounted, and four hundred and twenty Men, com- *Ship called* manded by the Chevalier *Nesmond*; and being a very good Ship, *taken.* not above twelve Months old, she was added to our Royal Navy.

The 16th the Admiral had sight of Cape *Finisterre*, to which Station the Wind continued Easterly, and from thence he sent a proper Convoy with the Trade bound to the several Ports in *Portugal*.

The 22d Vice-Admiral *Leake*, with five Ships from *England*, *Vice-Admiral* joined the Fleet, and the 24th the Admiral sent two of our Frigates *the Fleet.* with the *Dutch* to strengthen their St. *Ubes* Convoy, arriving him- self in the Evening at *Cascais*, the Entrance into the River of *Lis-* *The Fleet ar-* *bon*, with all the Fleet and Merchant Ships, having gather'd up his *bon.* Cruisers in his Passage. From thence he sent a Letter to the King of *Portugal* by Vice-Admiral *Fairborn*, and several of the Nobility and Gentry came on board the Fleet, among whom it was reported was, *incognito*, the King himself.

The 25th a Council of War was held of *English* and *Dutch* Flag- *A Council of* Officers, by whom it was resolved to remain at *Cascais* until the *War called* 29th, to take in Water, and then to proceed into the *Streights*, the Place of Rendezvous being *Altea* Bay, but in case of a hard East- erly Wind, that of *Almeria* in *Granada*; and the Flags at this Council of War were,

English,

The Admiral,
Vice-Admiral *Leake*,
Vice-Admiral *Byng*.

Dutch,

Admiral *Allemonde*,
Vice-Admiral *Vandergoes*,
Rear-Admiral *Wassenaer*.

Being joined the 27th by the *Orford*, *Monmouth*, *Hampton-Court*, *Other Ships* *Pembroke*, and *Litchfield*, and by the *Nassau* the 29th, he un- *joins the Fleet.* moored the 30th, in order to prosecute his Voyage, but some time before he formed his Line of Battel, wherein the *Dutch* (as usual)

were

were to lead with their Star-board, and the *English* with their Larboard Tacks on board.

The Strength of the *English*.

Line of Battel.

N°.	Guns each.	Total of Guns.
4 of	96	
7	80	
17	70	2514.
3	60	
4	50	

besides five small Frigates, four Fireships, four Bomb-Vessels, and a Pink.

The *Dutch*.

N°.	Guns each.	Total of Guns.
1 of	94	
2	90	
3	72	862.
5	64	
1	52	

besides two small Frigates, three Fireships, and three Bomb-Vessels. So that there were forty seven Ships of the Line of Battel, with twenty two others, and the Number of Guns of the said Ships of the Line were 3376.

The Admiral sails, and received Advices of the Enemy's Ships. With this considerable Fleet, and the Trade, the Admiral sailed from *Cascais* the 31st of *July*, and came off Cape *Spartell* the 4th of *August*, where he met with a fresh *Levant* Wind. Here Captain *Norris* joining him, gave him an Account that there were twelve *French* Gallies at *Cadiz*, but none of their Men of War on the *Spanish* Coasts; and he had also Intelligence by Sir *Thomas Hardy* that twenty two great Ships had passed by *Faro* from *West-France* into the *Streights*, and that the Consul there was informed they had above forty Ships of War at *Thoulon*.

The strong *Levant* Winds forced him into *Tangier* Road the 9th of *August*, but sailing again the 12th, he arrived in *Altea* Bay, the Place of Rendezvous, the 31st; and having pretty well watered the Fleet, (wherein he met with Assistance rather than Interruption from the *Spaniards*) he sailed the 3d of *September*, and not having Intelligence of any *French* Ships in those Seas, he sent forward the *Turky Trade sent forward.* Trade to *Smyrna* and *Constantinople*, with a Third and Fourth Rate, and that for *Scanderoon* with two Ships of the like Strength, ordering both Convoys to keep Company as far as their way lay together, and accordingly they parted from the Fleet the 9th off of the Island of *Formentera*.

Two Days after there was a Meeting of the Flag-Officers, both *English* and *Dutch*, when Admiral *Allemonde* declared he was obliged by his Instructions to be in *Holland* by the 20th of *November*,

and

CHAP. XIV. *from the Year* 1698, *to* 1712. 653

and that since his Ships were victualled for no longer time, it was fit for him to be looking homeward. Our Admiral let him know that his Orders required his going to *Livorne*; that a Separation might be of ill Consequence, and that the Queen and Council ex- *Dutch Admi-* pected he should remain about the Coast of *Italy* until the 20th of *ral pressing to* September: To which Monsieur *Allemonde* answered, that though *return.* there was not any Prospect of doing Service, yet he would keep Company until the 15th, and then make the best of his way home, if the Wind came up Easterly.

On the 14th Sir *Cloudesly Shovell* represented to him, by Letter, the ill Consequences of parting, in case the *French* should come out *Dutch pressed* too strong, for he had an Account that he resolved to repair down *to stay some* the *Streights*; and withal he promised Admiral *Allemonde*, that if *time longer* the Winds did not come up fair for their proceeding to *Livorne* before the 30th of *September*, he would, with the Advice of his Flag-Officers, turn his Head homewards, rather than divide the Fleet. Upon what afterwards pass'd between the two Chiefs, a Council of *A Consulta-* War of the *English* Flags was called, where were present the Admi- *tion of the* ral, Sir *Stafford Fairborn*, *John Leake*, and *George Byng*, Esquires, *English Flags.* and Captain *James Stewart*, the Admiral's Captain; by whom it was resolved, that since Monsieur *Allemonde*'s Instructions required him to be at home the 20th of *November*, if they could not reach *Livorne* by the last of *September*, a Convoy should be sent thither with the Trade, and the whole Fleet return home: However, the Winds coming up Westerly, they arrived in *Livorne* Road the 19th, *The Fleet* where the Admiral found neither Letter nor Message from Prince *comes to Li-* *Eugene*, or General *Staremberg*; but there came to him an Ecclesiastical *vorne.* Person, who brought several printed Declarations from the Emperor, importing that the *Sicilians* should enjoy all their former Privileges, and the Clergy all the Spiritual Benefits of that Island, provided they would abandon the Interest of the Duke of *Anjou*. This Priest had also a Letter from the Count *de Lemberg*, by which he seemed to depend wholly on the Arms of *England* and *Holland* for reducing the Kingdoms of *Sicily* and *Naples*.

The 22d in the Morning the two Frigates returned which were sent into the Bay of *Narbonne*, where they arrived the 17th, and stood into the Shore between Port *Cette* and *Peccais*, the *Tartar* in ten Fathom Water, and the bigger Ship, the *Pembroke*, within two Miles of the Shore. The former first made the Signals as directed, as the other did some time after, but met not with any Returns. They observed several Guns fired along Shore, supposed to be to alarm the Coast, and they also saw two Gallies at Port *Cette* which rowed towards them, but retired again as soon as they made our *No Communi-* Ships; and there being not any Possibility of putting Arms or other *cation with* things on shore for the People of the *Cevennes*, the Captains, with *the Ceven-* the Advice of the Pilots, made the best of their way to *Livorne*. *nes.*

Another Council of War was held the 23d, of *English* and *Dutch* Flags, and, for the Reasons afore-mentioned, it was resolved that the Fleet should proceed homeward the 26th, if possible, or the next *Resolution to* Day at farthest, Wind and Weather permitting; but I will leave them *return home.*

for

for a while, and give some Account of what passed at *Livorne* during the Admiral's being there.

He anchored in the Road the 19th of *September*, in the Night, (as I have already acquainted you) and next Day in the Afternoon the Town fired five Guns, soon after which the Governor sent off some Officers to welcome Sir *Cloudesly Shovell* into those Parts, and to acquaint him that the five Guns from the Town was intended a Salute to the Queen of *England*'s Flag. This not giving Satisfaction, he sent him Word he was much surprized at it, and that he could not receive any Compliment, nor admit of any Visit, until due Honour was paid to Her Majesty in this Point. Answer was made that they gave no more Guns to Sir *John Narbrough*, the Duke of *Grafton*, nor Admiral *Aylmer*, who all bore the same Flag. But here it is to be observed, that the Case was very different; for although Sir *Cloudesly Shovell*'s Flag was the same with those they bore, yet it was accompanied with several others, both *English* and *Dutch*, whereas their's were single.

Dispute about Salutes at Livorne.

Next Day Sir *Lambert Blackwell*, Her Majesty's Envoy, came on board the Admiral, and informed him that several Couriers had passed to and from *Florence*, in relation to the Salute, and it took up three Days before any Resolution was taken by the Grand *Duke*; but on the 24th the *English* Vice-Consul, with the Captain of the Port, came aboard from the Governor of *Livorne*, who promised, that the Citadel, from whence all Salutes are made, should fire eleven Guns, if the Admiral would engage to return Gun for Gun, which he assured them should be done, whereupon they went immediately ashore, and the Salute was accordingly made, and answered, soon after which the *Dutch* Admiral saluted the Citadel with eleven Guns, they returning the same Number.

Salutes agreed upon.

The 28th the Count *de Lemberg*, Ambassador from his Imperial Majesty at *Rome*, came on board the Admiral, and acquainted him that the Arch-duke was proclaimed King of *Spain*, whereupon he and the rest of our Flag-Officers fired twenty one Guns each, and all the other Ships fifteen; the *Dutch* firing likewise, soon after the Ambassador had rowed along the Side of their Admiral, for he did not go on board of his Ship.

Guns fired upon the Archduke's being proclaimed King of Spain.

The Winds continued Westerly, and Southerly, with hard Gales, which obliged Sir *Cloudesly Shovell* to remain at *Livorne* until the 2d of *October*, when a Levant springing up he sailed, but it failing soon after, he met with great Difficulty in getting Westward of *Corsica*, where he arrived not before the 10th of *October*: And before he sailed from *Livorne* he writ to the Great Duke, demanding Satisfaction, in Her Majesty's Name, as he was directed, who promised fair, but performed little.

The Fleet proceeds homewards.

The Day he parted from the said Port of *Livorne*, he gave Orders to Captain *Swanton** of the *Exeter* to proceed with several Ships to *Tunis* and *Tripoli*, and commissioned him and Captain *Arris*, together with the Consuls at those Places to renew and confirm, in Her

Captains deputed to treat with Tunis and Tripoli.

---

* *Since Comptroller of the Navy.*

Majesty's

CHAP. XIV. *from the Year* 1698, *to* 1712.   655

Majesty's Name, the Treaties of Peace and Commerce with them, and to deliver Her Majesty's Presents. When that was done Capt. *Swanton*, together with the *Tartar*, was ordered to join the *Smyrna* Convoy at that Place, and Captain *Arris*, with the *Flamborough*, and *Terrible* Fireship, to sail to *Cyprus* and *Scanderoon*, to strengthen the Convoy to the Trade there; but the *Exeter* and *Tartar* met not those they were sent in Search of.

The Admiral being got as low as the Island of *Corsica* beforementioned, he ordered Rear-Admiral *Byng*, with five Third Rates to proceed to *Algier*, and renew the Peace with that Government; and after he had so done to join the Fleet, if possible, before he got through the *Streights*, otherwise to make the best of his Way to *England*. *Rear-Admiral Byng appointed to treat with the Algerines.*

On the 12th, between Nine and Ten at Night, there arose a sudden Storm of Wind, with Lightning, Rain, and Thunder, which did considerable Damage to the Ships in their Masts, Sails, and Rigging, but it lasted not long; so that the Fleet jogging down the *Streights*, they were off *Altea* the 22d, where they anchored, and landed between three and four hundred Marines, to protect the Men employed in filling Water. *The Fleet comes to Altea.*

The Admiral having promised the Alcayd of *Alcazar*, that when he returned down the *Streights* he would offer to him Articles for Peace between Her Majesty and the Emperor of *Morocco*, he accordingly empower'd Mr. *Tertius Spencer*, a Merchant in *Barbary*, to present them, and by Letter to the Alcayd excused his not calling on him: for being obliged to proceed forthwith home, he ordered Sir *Thomas Hardy* in the *Bedford*, together with the *Somerset*, and *Lizard*, to stretch a-head, and having put the Papers ashore at *Tangier*, to make the best of his Way to *England*, if he could not timely join the Fleet. *Deputation to treat with the Emperor of Morocco.*

The 27th the Admiral met with a Ship of *Algier*, of 26 Guns, becalmed in the *Streights* Mouth; and since the *Dutch* had War with that Government, he protected her until such time as they were all past by; and being informed that there were several Merchant Ships in the Ports of *Portugal*, which waited for Convoy to *England*, he ordered Sir *Andrew Leake* in the *Grafton*, with another Third Rate, a Fourth, a Fifth, and a Fireship, to proceed to *Lisbon*, and to protect the said Trade to the *Downs*. *The Admiral protects an Algerine from the Dutch.*

The Fleet arrived off of the Isle of *Wight* the 16th of *November*, the *Dutch* having crouded away for their Ports, and soon after the Admiral came to an Anchor in the *Downs*, who during the whole Voyage met with such favourable Weather (except the short Storm beforementioned) that the Ships were little the worse for the Expedition, but many of the Men were sick and weak, and not less than fifteen hundred died; but before he made the Land Captain *Norris* in the *Orford*, a Ship of the Third Rate, together with the *Warspight* of 70 Guns, and the *Litchfield* of 50, being a-head of the Fleet, gave Chase to a *French* Ship of War, and beginning to engage about Eight at Night, the Dispute continued until Two in the Morning, when having lost her Fore-top-mast, and all her Sails, *The Fleet arrives in the Downs.*

and

A French Ship called the Hazardous taken.

and her standing and running Rigging being much shattered, she struck. This Ship came from *Newfoundland*, was commanded by Monsieur *de la Rüe*,, was named the *Hazardous*, and had 50 Guns mounted, with three hundred and seventy Men, but had more Ports, and was larger than any of our 60 Gun Ships, so that she was register'd in the List of our Royal Navy.

CHAP. XV.

Containing an Account of the Damages done by the violent Storm in 1703.

AS it hath too often happened to Merchants, that when their Ships have been almost in View of the design'd Port, some unlucky Accident hath dashed all their hopes, and entirely deprived them of the longed-for Loading, so it almost fared with Sir *Cloudesly Shovell*, and the Ships of War which sailed with him from the *Downs* towards the River, which were the *Triumph, Association,* and *St. George,* Second Rates, and the *Cambridge, Russel, Dorsetshire, Royal Oak,* and *Revenge,* of the Third Rate; for on the 27th Day of *November,* between the Hours of Two and Five in the Morning, when he was at Anchor at the *Gunfleet,* a violent Storm arose at W. S. W. the like whereof hath scarcely happen'd in the Memory of Man. To describe the many unhappy Accidents which attended this Tempest, is altogether impossible; and therefore since those who were both Ear and Eye-Witnesses to it on shore, must doubtless retain a lively Sense of its Fury, I shall only relate what Damages the Publick sustained at Sea, without particularizing the great Losses of the Merchants in their Shipping, and of the Nation, by the unhappy drowning of so considerable a Number of our Seafaring People.

Damages sustained in the Storm.

Sir *Cloudesly Shovell* himself veered out more than three Cables of his best Bower, but it was not long before the Anchor broke. Soon after the Tiller of the Rudder gave way, and before the Rudder itself could be secured, it was torn from the Ship, which shook her Stern-Post so much, that she proved very leaky, insomuch that four Chain, and one Hand Pump were constantly employ'd to keep her free. This obliged them to let go the Sheet-Anchor, and to veer out to it all the Cables, but even that did not ride the Ship, for she continued driving near a Sand called the *Galloper,* the Breach whereof was in their View. In this Extremity the Admiral ordered

The Admiral cuts away his Main-mast.

the Main-mast to be cut by the Board, by which the Ship being much eased, she rid fast; but four of the eight which came out of the *Downs* with him were missing, namely the *Association, Russel, Revenge,* and *Dorsetshire,* of which I come now to give an Account.

Sir

CHAP. XV. *from the Year* 1698, *to* 1712.   657

Sir *Stafford Fairborn*, Vice-Admiral of the Red, had his Flag *Association* flying in the *Association*, and her Cable parting about Four in the *forced from* Morning, the Pilot let go the Sheet-Anchor, and veer'd out a Cable *and gets to* and a half, but the Ship not looking towards it, she drove about Se- *Gottenburgh.* ven in the Morning over the North End of the *Galloper*, in eight Fathom Water, where there broke against her so great a Sea, that it made her lie along for some time, without any hopes of her righting again. The Ship soon drove into deeper Water, and dragged her small Bower Anchor, with the best Bower, and Sheet Cables; but at length, by the help of a Piece of the Sprit-sail, (the Wind being too violent for more) they wore her, and brought her to with her Head Northward.

The 27th at Night they drove with Yards and Top-masts down, and the next Morning judged themselves drawing near the Coast of *Holland*, some of the other Ships being then in sight making the best shift for themselves they could. In fine, it was not without the greatest Difficulty and Hazard, that the Vice-Admiral got away with her at length into the Harbour of *Gottenburgh*, towards which Place he sometimes drove, and sometimes sailed, as Winds and Weather would permit. He arrived there the 11th of *December*, having for some time being given over as lost, for there was not any News of him until I received his Letter, which bore that Date, he having lost three Anchors, and five Cables, together with the Long-boat and Pinnace; and the great want of Provisions, and other Necessaries in that cold Country, mightily pinched the poor Men who had suffered so much before.

Being furnished from *Copenhagen* (and that in a very friendly manner) with what Anchors, Cables, and other things were necessary for the Security of the Ship in her Passage home, he arrived at the *Gunfleet* the 15th of *January* (the Place he was driven from in the violent Storm) with several Merchant Ships under his Convoy; where he had not been long at an Anchor, e'er another severe Gale of Wind happen'd, which might have been well accounted a Storm, had not the prodigious Violence of the other, and its dreadful Effects, been fresh in Memory; but it pleased God the Ship rid fast without farther Damage.

The *Revenge*, commanded by Captain *William Kerr*, was like- *The* Revenge wise forced from her Anchors, and drove over the North End of the *in great dan-* *Galloper* in less than four Fathom Water, as her Captain gave an *ger.* Account; and as soon as Day appear'd, the *Association*, *Russell*, and *Dorsetshire* were in sight of her, driving with their Heads to the Southward. Captain *Kerr* some time after put for *Helvoet-Sluys*, on the Coast of *Holland*, having neither Anchors nor Cables, but the Wind dullering, he could not reach that Harbour, so that he stood off again, and some time after meeting with the *Nottingham*, (which Ship, as well as others, was sent out with Anchors, Cables, &c. to assist those in Distress) he by that means chop'd to an Anchor in *Southwold* Bay, and afterwards brought his Ship safe into the River *Medway*.

The *Russell* was in like manner forced from the *Gunfleet*; for *The* Russell between Twelve and One at Night her best Bower Cable parted; where- *Coast of* Hol-
upon land.

Pppp

upon Captain *Isaac Townsend* *, her Commander, let go the Sheet-Anchor, and small Bower, but those could not sustain the Violence of the Wind. At Four in the Morning he was obliged to cut away his Long-boat, and immediately after lost his Rudder, which caused a Leak in the Stern-Post, and much Water came into the Bread and Fish Rooms. In this Distress the Poop and Quarter-Deck Guns were thrown overboard, the better to draw the Water to the Pumps, by poising the fore part of the Ship, which was much lightned by the want of the Anchors and Cables; and this had, in a great measure, its desired Effect. On Sunday the Wind was at W. N. W. and N. W. and it being judged that the Ships drew near to *Goree*, it was concluded that she must unavoidably drive on shore by Midnight. The Captain therefore ordered two Guns to be slung with the Top-Chains, and made them fast to the Sheet Cables, that so her Drift to the Land might be the slower; and at Six at Night falling into twelve and fourteen Fathom Water, he had sight of a Light, which he took to be either the Island of *Goree*, or of *Schowen*. At half an Hour past Ten the Ship came into seven Fathom Water, and then her Commander let go his Stream, and frapt it to a Kedge Anchor, in hopes the Cable which the Guns were made fast to, and this veered to the better end, would ride her in so shoal Water, but she came Head to Wind in five Fathom, and, dragging all home, tailed into four, when she struck twice, but not violently. The Water deepen'd to five, six, seven, and eight Fathom, and it was very smooth, but the Stream Cable soon broke, and cast the Ship Northward, so that she drove with the Wind on the Beam, and a great Breach was seen right to Leeward; whereupon they cut away the Cables, and set her Fore-sail and Fore-top-sail, with all possible Diligence, by which they were in four Fathom and a half, and immediately the Ship struck, but swimming still by the Stern, the Blow put her right before the Wind, and so she miraculously got over the Shoal, after she had touched several times. The Water soon deepen'd from four to twelve Fathom, and then became gradually lower, until they pitched her on shore on the Ouze, about two Miles below *Helvoet-Sluys*, a little after Three in the Morning; from whence, by the great Pains, and particular Industry of her Commander, she was gotten off, and put in a Condition to come to *England* in little time.

The Dorsetshire in very great danger.

The fourth Ship which was thus driven from the *Gunfleet* was the *Dorsetshire*, mounted with 80 Guns. Captain *Edward Whittaker* †, her Commander, found himself under such Circumstances as not to be able to set any Sail, but was forced to lie at the Mercy of the Sea, and Wind, which drove him directly upon the Tail of the *Galloper*, where she struck three times, but received little or no Damage. He made a very hard shift to keep the Sea, and arrived at the *Nore* the 15th of *December*, having in his Passage taken up a small Bower Anchor and Cable which belonged to another Ship,

---

* *Since a Commissioner of the Navy.*
† *Since Knighted, and a Flag-Officer.*

and

CHAP. XV. *from the Year* 1698, *to* 1712.

and were of very great Service to him, for he had lost most of his own.

These Ships, and those which rid fast at the *Gunfleet*, miraculously escaped, but it fared not so well with the Men of War and Merchant Ships in the *Downs*. Of the former there were lost on the *Goodwin* Sands the *Mary*, a Ship of 60 Guns, and the *Northumberland*, *Restauration*, and *Sterling-Castle*, each of 70; nor were there more than eighty Men saved of the whole Number which belonged to them. Rear-Admiral *Beaumont*, whose Flag was flying in the *Mary*, perished among the rest: A Gentleman who was very much lamented, and that deservedly too; for he was not only every way qualified to serve his Country, but was thus unhappily snatch'd away even in the Prime of his Years. *Ships lost in the Downs, where Rear-Admiral Beaumont perished.*

Although the *Prince George*, where Vice-Admiral *Leake*'s Flag was flying, as also the *Essex*, *Shrewsbury*, *Eagle*, *Content*, *Chatham*, *Assistance*, *Mary* Gally, and *Hunter* Fireship, happily rid it out in the *Downs*, with all their Masts standing, yet the *Nassau*, a Ship of 70 Guns, cut away her Main-mast, the *Guardland* and *Dunwich* all their Masts, as the *Postillion-Prize* did her Main and Mizen; and there were five great Ships, with two small ones, seen riding to the Northward with all their Masts by the Board. *Other Misfortunes from the Storm.*

It was a miserable Sight to behold many of the Ships in the *Downs*; for as they were almost torn in pieces by the Violence of the Wind, so was it not possible to give them any help from the Shore, even when they were in the greatest Extremity, and continually firing Guns for Relief; besides the Wind was at W.S.W. and they could not possibly carry a Knot of Sail to enable them to cling the Shore, so that many of them perished on the *Goodwin* Sands, and of about one hundred sixty Sail, of all sorts, which were in the *Downs* the Day before, not more than seventy were seen the next Morning, and many of them were only floating Bottoms, for all their Masts were gone by the Board; but several of the Merchant Ships and Vessels missing were afterwards heard of either in *Holland*, *Norway*, or the Ports of this Kingdom. *Great Damage done in the Downs.*

Among the Ships at *Spithead*, the *Vesuvius* Fireship was stranded near *Southsea-Castle*, but her Men were all saved, and she was afterwards got off with great Difficulty. The *Firebrand* Fireship lost her Main-mast, and the *Jefferies* Hospital Ship knock'd her Rudder off upon the Sand called the *Spit*. The *Newcastle*, of 50 Guns, as also the *Litchfield-Prize*, a Fifth Rate, were forced on shore, the latter being afterwards got off, but there was not more than twenty four of the Men belonging to the former saved, of which Number the Carpenter was the only Officer. The *Burlington*, a Fourth Rate, lost all her Masts, and the Merchant Ships and Vessels which were at *Spithead* suffered greatly, insomuch that the Coast thereabouts was almost cover'd with dead Bodies. *Mischiefs done at Spithead.*

Several Ships of War were at this time in *Yarmouth* Roads, namely the *Portland*, *Advice*, and *Triton*, all Fourth Rates, and the *Nightingale* a Fifth, which rid out the Storm without much Damage; but the 27th, about Eight in the Morning, the *Reserve*, a Fourth *Damage in Yarmouth Roads.*

Fourth Rate, was seen with all her Masts gone, and only her Ensign-Staff standing, firing Guns for help, which it was impossible to give her, so that about twelve a Clock she founder'd, and not one Soul belonging to her was saved. The *Lynn* and *Margate*, by other Ships driving on board them, were obliged to cut away their Masts, and rid in no little Danger near St. *Nicholas* Sand. A rich Merchant Ship, bound for the *Scaw*, was drove on the said Sand, and sinking within three Hours, the Sea broke over her, but the *Lynn* fortunately took up her Men; and of a considerable Fleet of Merchant Ships and Vessels which were in the Road, but few were seen the next Day, some of them being driven out to Sea, and others Shipwreck'd on the Sands.

To particularize all the Disasters which happen'd by this dreadful Tempest, would almost of itself require a just Volume, so numerous were the dismal Effects of it all along the Coast; nay the very Ships in our Harbours escaped not its Violence; for, among other Accidents the *Vantguard*, of 90 Guns, was forced from her Moorings in *Chatham* River, and by that means render'd unfit for farther Service; but this Loss, indeed, as it happen'd, was inconsiderable, since she was so weak before as to require rebuilding.

A Second Rate driven on shore at Chatham.

Rear-Admiral *Beaumont* had, all the preceding Summer, to the time of his unfortunate Loss lately mentioned, been employ'd with a Squadron of Ships which were particularly appointed to look after those at *Dunkirk* and *Ostend*, of whose Proceedings on that Service it will be proper in this Place to give some Account.

Rear-Admiral Beaumont's Proceedings off of Dunkirk, and elsewhere, for some Months before he perished in the Storm.
1703.

The 29th of *May* he sent Advice to the Lord High-Admiral of the *Dunkirkers* being at Sea, he having seen them in the Road the Afternoon of the 28th, but though he had even discover'd them going out, it would have been impossible for him at that time to have got up his Anchors.

Upon this Intelligence several Orders were sent by Express, giving Caution to all the Sea-Ports, and for stopping the Convoys which were Northward, and the Rear-Admiral proceeding in search of the Enemy, got sight of them from the Mast head, the 6th of *June*, at Four in the Morning, in the Latitude of 56^d. He had little Wind until eleven a Clock, and then they making what Sail they could from him, he chased them all that Day, but could not come nearer than four Leagues, and at Nine the next Night lost sight of them, so that returning to the *Downs*, he sailed again from thence the 20th of *June*, and anchored off of *Newport*, where he joined a Squadron of thirteen *Dutch* Ships under Command of Admiral *Callemberg* and Vice-Admiral *Evertsen*. About this time there was a Design of besieging *Ostend*, and the *English* and *Dutch* were to block it up, and attack it by Sea; but it was found impracticable to anchor with the smaller Ships nearer the Place than four Miles, or with the Fourth Rates nearer than eight, with any manner of Safety; nor could it have been bombarded without a Number of small Frigates to have opposed the Attempts from their Gallies; and as there would have been great Difficulties met with in landing the Artillery, so did not the *Dutch* care much for the Guns of the Gallies, being

Rear-Admiral Beaumont gets sight of the Dunkirkers,
but
returns to the Downs.

CHAP. XV. *from the Year* 1698, *to* 1712. 661

being apprehensive that they might sink the Frigates at a very considerable Distance, because they could throw a Shot much farther than the Cannon on board the Men of War; so that this Design was given over.

The 26th of *July* at Night the Rear-Admiral arrived in the *Downs*, and soon after was ordered to cruise for the *Russia* and *East-Country* Trade expected from those Parts, on which Service (pursuant to Orders afterwards sent him) he proceeded as far as *Gottenburgh*, where he arrived the 19th of *September*, with six Fourth Rates, and two Fifths. There he found the four Convoys to the *East-Country* Trade, whose Captains had been at *Maelstrand* or *Masterlandt*, (in the Neighbourhood of that Place) and met in that Port with six *French* Ships of War, three of them of 50 Guns, one of 40, one of 36, and one of 32; but under the Cover of the Guns, neither one nor the other were permitted to do any Act of Hostility. They had been there six Weeks, and were commanded by Monsieur *St. Paul*, with whom and his Officers our Captains had spoken, who, by what they could gather, expected to be joined by others, and then were to look out for the *Dutch Greenland* Ships, and our *Russia* Trade; but although ours had the good Fortune to escape them, the *Dutch* suffered very considerably in theirs, as their Fishery to the North, and their Convoys, had done from some *French* Privateers not long before. The Rear-Admiral received Advice that these Ships of the Enemy sailed from *Masterlandt* the 23d of *September*, which it was altogether impossible for him to prevent, as being in no Condition to put to Sea, for he was in want of Water and divers other Necessaries: But having furnished himself in the best manner he could, he left *Gottenburgh* the 8th of *October* with seventy four Merchant Ships under his Convoy, and arrived in the *Downs* the 19th, having appointed the *Triton* and *Lynn* to protect home those which were not ready to accompany him; and on this Service against the *Dunkirkers* he continued, until himself and many more Officers and Men unhappily lost their Lives, as is before related.

Rear-Admiral Beaumont proceeds to Gottenburgh, and heard of the French at Masterlandt.

The Dutch Fishing Ships seized by the French.

Rear-Admiral Beaumont comes to the Downs.

And now if we take a View of the Disposition of our Naval Strength this last Year, it may not be unnecessary to make some Remark on our Affairs at home, when such a Force was sent so remote with Sir *Cloudesly Shovell*, as four Second Rates, twenty four Thirds, and seven Fourths, and other Ships and Vessels of less Force. When this is consider'd, and that there were nine Third Rates, thirty four Fourths, and ten Fifths, actually in the *West-Indies*, and other foreign Parts, and not more in Pay for guarding the Chanel, and protecting the Trade, between the Months of *July* and *October*, than forty one Ships of the Line of Battel, *viz.* two First Rates, three Seconds, nine Thirds, and twenty one Fourths, some of which were on the Coast of *Ireland* with Rear-Admiral *Dilkes*, others dispersed up and down the Chanel, and employ'd as Convoys to the Colliers, and on divers necessary Services; I say, when these Circumstances are considered, it cannot but appear somewhat strange that the Enemy did not endeavour to insult us; and the rather, for that, by all

Remark on our sending so great a strength abroad, and leaving the Nation exposed.

Accounts

Accounts which were received of them, they had near sixty Ships of the Line of Battel at *Brest*, Port *Louis*, *Rochefort*, *Dunkirk*, and other Ports in these Seas, and possibly might have set them forth before we could have got our divided Fleet together, or mann'd other Ships in our Harbours whose Hulls were fit for Service, which were no more than three First, as many Seconds, eight Thirds, and two Fourth Rates, and they would have required eight thousand seven hundred and eighty five Men: Nor was there any Prospect at this time of our being strengthened by any of the Ships of War of the States-General, the twelve they sent with Sir *Cloudesly Shovell* being all that joined our whole Fleet this Year, which were in Number two hundred and seventeen, whereof one hundred and sixteen were from 100 to 50 Guns; and (according to their Complements) required at least fifty two thousand Men, reckoning those in Service at home, and in the *Streights* at their highest Number, and those in the *West-Indies*, and other remote Parts, at no more than their middle Complements.

Chap. XVI.

Containing an Account of Sir George Rooke's *carrying to* Lisbon *the Arch-Duke of* Austria, *and of his Proceedings afterwards to, and engaging the* French *Fleet in the* Mediterranean, *when joined by Sir* Cloudesly Shovell.

1703.

THE Arch-Duke of *Austria*, second Son to his Imperial Majesty, being proclaimed King of *Spain* at *Vienna*, took his Journey towards *Holland* soon after, in order to his Majesty's embarking, with his Ministers and Retinue, on board some *English* and *Dutch* Ships of War appointed to attend him to *Lisbon*, where he was expected with great Impatience, that so both he and his Ally, the King of *Portugal*, might timely take the Field with their Forces against the Duke of *Anjou*, who had been advanced to the *Spanish* Throne by his Grandfather the *French* King.

Sir *George Rooke*, Vice-Admiral of *England*, and Admiral of the Fleet, was appointed by Her Majesty to conduct this young King to *Lisbon*, and setting sail for *Holland*, in order to receive his Majesty on board, arrived in the *Maes* the 16th of *October*, where the King was expected the Night following.

The Admiral sent back the *Northumberland*, a Third Rate, (one of those afterwards unhappily lost in the Storm on the *Goodwin*) because she was too big to go into *Goree*, and the *Panther*'s Masts being sprung, she was ordered to *Portsmouth* to be refitted; so that he kept with him only the *Tiger*, *Newport*, and a few other Ships; but since the *Woolwich*, *Swallow*, *Vigo*, and *Swan* were designed on this Service, he press'd their being sent over without Delay, for

that

CHAP. XVI. *from the Year* 1698, *to* 1712.

that the Retinue of his Catholick Majesty would, for want of them, be very much incommoded, especially since no more than two of the twelve *Dutch* Ships were yet ready.

The Forces began to embark on board the Transport-Ships the 26th, and Count *Wratiflaw*, the Emperor's Envoy to our Court, but then in *Holland*, defiring to know whether the Admiral would answer for the Security of the Person of the King of *Spain* from the *Dunkirk* Ships, in his Paffage to *Spithead*, in regard there was yet but few *English* and *Dutch* Ships of War to convoy his Majesty as far as the *Downs*, he judged this a Matter of so much Confequence as to advife with the *English* Captains then prefent, who were all of Opinion that if the Convoy could be made up to eight Ships of War, either by the *Dutch*, or by the Arrival of any from *England*, it might be a fufficient Force to secure His Majesty, as well as the Transport Ships, to the *Downs*, where they would meet with an additional Force to accompany them to *Spithead*.

Neither the Ships from *Zeeland*, nor thofe expected from *England* were arrived the 5th of *November*, and therefore the States-General agreed that Admiral *Callemberg*, with thofe from the *Texel*, fhould come before the *Maes*, and join the Ships and Yachts from *Goree*, but in this the faid Admiral was prevented, for in his Paffage from the *Texel*, he was driven by the violent Storm far Northward, which feparated, and much fhattered his Squadron, as well as the Transport Ships, infomuch that he did not arrive at *Spithead*, in a confiderable time after. *Ships wanting to convoy His Majefty from Holland.*

The Troops being embarked, and the King of *Spain* on board, the Admiral failed, but the Winds taking him contrary, and blowing hard, his Majesty thought it convenient to go on Shore the 11th of *November*, and accordingly was carried up to *Rotterdam*, from whence he went to the *Hague*, but took very few of his Retinue, and little of his Baggage with him, that fo he might be in the greater Readiness to put to Sea upon the firft Opportunity, which the *English* and *Dutch* Officers were of Opinion they ought not to do with the Wind farther Southerly than the S. E. or E. S. E, confidering the Seafon of the Year, and the Number of Transports they were to take Care of. *The King comes on board, but goes on Shore again.*

Before the King left *Holland*, the Storm (which I have already given an Account of) put both the Ships of War and Transports in very great Diforder. The *Vigo*, a Ship of the Fourth Rate, (formerly our *Dartmouth*, and taken from the *French* at *Vigo*) was driven afhore just upon the Weft Pier-head of *Helvoet-Sluys*; but all the Officers and Men, as well as thofe who belonged to the King of *Spain* were fortunately faved. *Several Ships in Holland fuffer by the great Storm.*

The *Rochefter*, a Fourth Rate, loft her Main and Fore-top-mafts, and by another Ship's driving athwart her Hawfe, fhe narrowly efcaped being on fhore. Many of the Transport Ships were on the Ground, but the *Woolwich, Swallow, Tiger*, and *Greenwich* had the good Luck to ride it out. Some of them drove on board the *Newport*, a fmall Frigate, and carrying away her Bowfprit, fhe was forced to cut all her Mafts away, but was brought fafe into the

Pier;

Pier; and the *Swan* was forced on Shore, but afterwards got off again.

This much delayed the King of Spain's Passage.

To make good these Misfortunes the States-General caused the utmost Assistance to be given, but by reason of Damages sustained, especially by the Transport Ships, it was almost impossible to be in a Readiness to prosecute the Voyage in less time than a Month, for there was a Necessity of digging out of the Mud those that were on Shore; but since several of them could not with all Endeavours be gotten off, others were hired in their room and fitted in the best manner that could be.

Sir George Rooke comes to Spithead.

When every thing was in a Readiness, their sailing was for some time prevented by Fogs and Calms, but at length the Admiral got out, and joined Rear-Admiral *Vanderdussen* with five *Dutch* Ships of War, having four Fourth Rates, and one Fifth of ours, with which he arrived at *Spithead*. There came out but thirteen Transport Ships, the rest being left behind, for the Admiral was expressly ordered by the Queen to sail with the first fair Wind, and to take with him such of those Vessels as should then be ready.

Prince George and others, went to compliment His Catholick Majesty. His Majesty came to Windsor, and from thence returned to Portsmouth.

The Duke of *Somerset*, Master of the Horse to the Queen, and the Duke of *Marlborough*, Captain-General of Her Majesty's Forces, were appointed to go on board the Squadron at *Spithead*, and to wait on His Catholick Majesty on Shore; and His Royal Highness the Prince of *Denmark* met him on the Road to *Windsor*, where the Queen, and many of the Nobility came some time before to receive him. His Majesty remained a small time at Court, where he was not only entertained in every respect suitable to his Dignity, but very much to his Satisfaction, and then taking leave of the Queen, he set forward for *Portsmouth*, in order to prosecute his Voyage to *Lisbon*, where His Majesty was altogether as impatient to be as the King of *Portugal* and his People were for His Presence.

The Fleet sails again.

There was a Necessity of remaining some time at *Spithead* to receive on board the Marines, to shift the King's Retinue, and to make Draughts of Men from other Ships to put those designed to accompany His Majesty in a sailing Condition; but on the 4th of *January* the Admiral was unmoored, and on the 6th stood towards the Back of the Isle of *Wight* to join the Transport Ships which went thorough the *Needles*.

Next Morning he was off of the *Start*, having sent the *Swallow* before to *Plimouth* to call the Ships from thence; and on the 12th he reached the Latitude of 46^d and 21^m, where he met with Westerly Winds and very bad Weather, insomuch that he was obliged to bring to about Eleven that Night with his Head to the Northward, and the Storm continued until Saturday Noon, when it somewhat abating, in the Evening it was quite calm. The Squadron was the 15th drove back into the Latitude of 48^d 42^m, and next Morning there appeared some Hopes of a fair Wind, but at Ten a Clock it came again to the S. W. giving great Suspicions of bad Weather. The *Cornwall* was at this time missing, as well as the *Expedition*, *Norfolk*, and *Lancaster*, four Ships of the Third Rate, as were many

Chap. XVI. *from the Year* 1698, *to* 1712.

of the Transports, and Merchant Ships; and the Admiral being apprehensive that it would be a tempestuous Night (as indeed it proved) he, with the Advice of Admiral *Callemberg*, bore away for *Torbay*, the Place of Rendezvous, that so he might the better get together the scattered Fleet. *Bad Weather forced them out of the Sea to Torbay.*

About Midnight it blew so very hard at W. and W. by N. that the Ships were obliged to strike their Yards and Top-masts, and the *Humber* making twelve Foot Water in a Watch, she was sent away to *Spithead* to be refitted, and lucky it was she continued not longer at Sea, for in all likelihood she would have founder'd.

The Admiral, pursuant to Orders, came to *Spithead* with the Squadron, but the King of *Spain* was very desirous to have proceeded on his Voyage with the Ships which were together in *Torbay*. His Majesty went on Shore at *Portsmouth*, where he remained some time, and the Wind coming up to the N. E, the 1st of *February*, he designed, had it continued, to have embarked the next Day in the Afternoon, but it proved calm all Night, and the Morning following. *The Squadron comes to Spithead.*

Her Majesty considering of what Consequence it was that the King of *Spain* should be in *Portugal* as soon as it was possible, and with how much Earnestness His Majesty did press to proceed on his Voyage, was pleased to send Orders to the Admiral the 1st of *February*, to sail as soon as such a Number of Transport Ships could be got ready as might carry six thousand of the Troops. Hereupon he called a Council of War, where were present, Vice-Admiral *Leake*, and Captain *Wishart*, and of the *Dutch*, Admiral *Callemberg*, and Rear-Admiral *Vanderduffen*. They determined that since all the Transport Ships might be ready, whenever the Wind should permit them to sail, it was necessary to proceed with as many Ships of War for their Security as could possibly be spared from other Services, and that since there would be left behind no other Transports than those which were in *Holland*, it was judged that eight Men of War, and such other Ships of the *English* Quota for Service on the Coast of *Portugal*, as could be timely put into a Condition, would be a sufficient Convoy for them. *The Queen press'd Sir George Rooke to put to Sea again.*

They also represented it to be absolutely necessary, that all possible Diligence should be used in sending to *Lisbon* the Remainder of the thirty eight *English* Ships which were to join the nineteen *Dutch*, then at, and going to *Portugal*; for there was reason to apprehend the Enemy would get a strong Squadron together early in the Spring, and endeavour to block up our Ships in the *Tajo*, by which they would have had it in their Power to have intercepted all such as should be bound from *England*, and to disappoint the whole Summer's Service; whereas if the Fleet rendezvous'd early at *Lisbon*, it was judged they might be able to prevent the Enemy's joining their Fleets of the *Mediterranean* and *Ocean*, and to perform other Services on the Coast of *Spain*. *The Flag officers desired to be reinforced at Lisbon.*

After a very fine Passage of thirteen Days, the Squadron and Transports arrived in the River of *Lisbon* on the 25th of *February*, without so much as one ill Accident, and the Ceremonies for the Reception *The Squadron arrives at Lisbon.*

ception of the King of *Spain* being adjusted, which took up some time, the King of *Portugal*, with the young Princes, and many of the Nobility, came on board the 27th, and accompanied his Catholick Majesty on shore to the Apartment prepared for him in the Palace, where he was entertained with very great Magnificence, and all Expressions of Joy.

King of Portugal comes on board.

Among other Debates about settling the Ceremonies, the Business of the Flag was considered, the King of *Portugal* desiring that upon his coming on board in his Vessel of State, and striking his Standard, the *English* Flag might be struck at the same time, and that when His Catholick Majesty with himself should go off from the Ship, his Standard might be hoisted, and the Admiral's Flag continue struck until they were on shore. This Proposition was made from the King of *Portugal* by the King of *Spain*, to which the Admiral reply'd, that His Majesty, so long as he should be on board, might command the Flag to be struck when he pleased, but that whenever he left the Ship, he was himself Admiral, and obliged to execute his Commission, by hoisting his Flag; this, and some other Reasons, satisfied the King of *Spain*, as well as his *Portuguese* Majesty, so that the Flag of *England* was no longer struck than the Standard of *Portugal*.

Some Overtures made about striking the English Flag.

It was particularly recommended to the Admiral to endeavour to secure the *Turky* Trade in their Passage from the *Levant*, and to intercept the Ships from *Buenos Ayres* suddenly expected in some Port of *Spain*, one of which was already arrived at *Cadiz*, and the *Dutch* Cruisers had the good Fortune to force a *Spanish* Vice-Admiral on shore near *Lagos*, which Ship carry'd 60 Guns, and was richly loaden.

It was recommended to the Admiral to secure our Turky Trade, &c.

A Council of War was held on board the *Royal Katharine* at *Lisbon* the 29th of *February*, where were present the Admiral, Admiral *Callemberg*, Rear-Admiral *Dilkes*, Vice-Admiral *Wassenaer*, Rear-Admiral *Wishart*, and Rear-Admiral *Vanderdussen*. They considered of the Orders from his Royal Highness, dated the 16th of *November*, which directed that all possible Endeavours should be used to intercept Monsieur *D'Arteloire* in his Passage from *Cadiz* to the *West-Indies*, and hindering any Ships joining him at that Port; as also Her Majesty's Orders of the 1st of *January*, for securing the *Turky* Fleet in their Passage through the *Streights*, and the Earl of *Nottingham*'s Letter of the 2d of *February*, advising that three *Spanish* Ships were suddenly expected from *Buenos Ayres*. Upon the whole it was resolved that, for the Performance of the aforesaid Services, the Countenance and Protection of our Trade in general, the intercepting and disturbing the Enemy, and hindering them from sending their Ships of War by small Squadrons either to or from *East* or *West-France*, ten or eleven *English*, and six or seven *Dutch* Men of War should be sent to cruise between Cape St. *Vincent*, Cape St. *Mary*'s, and Cape *Spartell*, and on that Service to continue thirty Days, unless Circumstances of Affairs should render it necessary for them to repair sooner to the Squadron.

A Council of War held.

Agreed to send a Squadron off of Cape Spartell, &c.

The

CHAP. XVI. *from the Year* 1698, *to* 1712.   667

The 2d of *March* Vice-Admiral *Leake* arrived at *Lisbon* with the *Newark, Tyger, Guardland*, and the Transports with the Remainder of the Troops, and with these Ships sailed the Trade bound to *Portugal* that could not have an Opportunity of going with Sir *George Rooke*. Three Days after a Council of War was called, where were present the Admiral, Vice-Admiral *Leake*, Rear-Admiral *Dilkes*, and Rear-Admiral *Wishart*, and of the *Dutch*, Admiral *Callemberg*, and Vice-Admiral *Waffenaer*. They read several Advices of the Preparations the Enemy were making, and adhered to what had been determined at the former Council of War of the 29th of the last Month, for they were of opinion, that a Squadron of Ships appearing in the Sea would give great Countenance and Protection to our Commerce, and that several of our Ships which were clean might probably intercept small Squadrons of the Enemy's passing from one Sea to the other; and it was likewise judged there could be no Risque run from a greater Squadron of *French* Ships so early in the Year: Besides, it was hoped that at their Return from the Cruise, they might be enabled, by the Arrival of Ships from *England*, to form a Squadron of sufficient Strength to meet and oppose the Enemy's Fleets, either of *West-France*, or the Ports of the *Mediterranean*.

Vice-Admiral Leake arrives at Lisbon.

Another Council of War confirms the first.

The Detachment consisted of twenty two Ships, of which there were of the *English* six of 70 Guns, one of 60, four of 50, one of 40, one of 32, and one of 24; and of the *Dutch*, one of 92, two of 72, one of 68, one of 64, one of 62, one of 60, and one of 36, but the Winds hung contrary until the 7th, at which time the Admiral was not gotten clear of the Entrance of the River of *Lisbon*, at which Port he left Orders with Vice-Admiral *Leake* to remain with the rest of the Fleet, and to send the *Expedition* and *Advice* home with the Transport Ships and Trade.

Strength of the cruising Squadron.

The *Exeter* and *Tartar* arrived the 8th, having missed the Convoys which they were appointed, by Sir *Cloudesly Shovell*, to join from *Smyrna*, as hath been before observed; the former of which Ships the Admiral sent with the homeward-bound Convoy, and kept the latter with him, for he was in want of nimble Frigates.

The 9th of *March* he put to Sea, stretching away S. S. W. and next Day, a little before Noon, as he was hauling in towards Cape St. *Vincent*, a *Dutch* Privateer joined him from the Southward, which had seen the Night before a *Spanish* Ship of about 60 Guns, another with upwards of 50, and one of about 30, with a small Dogger, bearing then (as the Captain of the said Privateer judged) South, about ten Leagues distant. Hereupon the Admiral made all the Sail he was able, and sent away the *Suffolk, Panther*, and *Lark*, S. by E. and S. S. E. himself standing S. E. with the rest, being in hopes that by this means they could not escape him, or the *Dutch*, who came out the same Evening he did, but had not yet joined him. By the Signals the *Suffolk* and *Panther* made in the Evening, it was believed they had sight of them, and therefore Rear-Admiral *Dilkes* was sent to, to continue the Chase with the *Kent, Bedford*, and *Antelope*, the two former of 70 Guns, and the other 50, the Admiral

The Admiral puts to Sea, and receives Advice of some Spanish Ships.

Q q q q 2   letting

letting him know he would himself stand with the rest towards Cape *Spartell*, that by cruising from thence to *Cadiz*, and covering the *Streights* Mouth, he might the better intercept any thing which should escape the Ships with the said Rear-Admiral.

Next Morning it blew very hard at W. S. W. and continued so all Day and Night, so that the Ships were forced to try under a Mizen, but it being more moderate Weather on Sunday, he made the Capes *Spartell* and *Trafalgar*, and cruised off those Places until Thursday Morning, without seeing any thing, except a small *Spanish* Ship of about 70 Tuns, which the *Mountague* took under Cape *Spartell*, loaden with Horse-shoes, Nails, and some Rozin, (Materials much wanted by the *Spaniards*) the Master whereof gave an Account, that he came from St. *Sebastian*'s seventeen Days before, in Company of three new *Spanish* Men of War, which he left about twenty five Leagues from *Cadiz*, and that they had in them Bombs, Carcasses, and other Ordnance-Stores.

A farther Account of the Spanish Ships.

The 17th in the Evening the Admiral was off of Cape St. *Mary*'s, where the *Swallow* joined him, as the *Leopard* and *Charles*-Gally did the Day before, which two Ships had only met with, and forced on shore a *French* Ship of 30 Guns, and of about 300 Tuns, upon a Sand Bank near *Ayamonte*.

Dutch Ships disabled in a Storm.

The Storm had so disabled the *Dutch* Ships which were on this Cruise, that Baron *Wassenaer* acquainted the Admiral he had not more than three, and those their worst Sailers, in a Condition to keep the Sea, and that he was returning to *Lisbon* to repair the rest for the Summer's Service; but Sir *George* himself determined to continue out until the end of this Month, or at least to the time agreed on at the Council of War of the 29th of *April*, and then to go, or send to *Tangier* for Intelligence of our *Turky* Ships, which (if they were got down towards the *Streights* Mouth) he judged might be put into *Tetuan* Bay for Provisions. And here I shall leave him for the present, and give some Account of Rear-Admiral *Dilkes* his Proceedings in chasing the afore-mention'd Ships of the Enemy.

Rear-Admiral Dilkes chases the Spanish Ships.

On the 12th of *March*, between Eight and Nine in the Morning, he discovered four Sail on his Weather-Bow standing towards the North-East, which he chased W. by S. with the Wind at N. W. by W. having then in Company the *Kent*, *Bedford*, *Suffolk*, *Antelope*, and *Panther*, the three first Third Rates, and the other two Fourths. By Eleven he came up with them, they being three *Spanish* Ships, and the *Panther*, which was the headmost of ours, engaged them; the *Suffolk* getting the Wind of them did the same, as also the *Antelope* and the *Dutch* Privateer; insomuch that she of 60 Guns struck, after exchanging several Broadsides.

They come up and engage.

The Rear-Admiral could not get his own Ship in reach of them until Noon, and then engaging the Commadore, which was a Ship also of 60 Guns, she struck to him in a little time, as the third did soon after, which was a Merchant Ship of 24 Guns; and in this Action the *Panther* had her Fore-top-mast shot by the Board, the *Suffolk* her Main-mast, and the *Antelope*'s Masts and Yards were wounded. The two Ships before-mentioned of 60 Guns were Galleon

Spanish Ships taken.

CHAP. XVI. *from the Year* 1698, *to* 1712.   669

Men of War, one called the *Porta Cœli*, and the other the *St. Therefa*, and came from St. *Sebaſtian*'s with Bombs, Guns, Iron Bars, &c. being bound for *Cadiz*, where (as 'twas reported) they were to be fitted out for the *Weſt-Indies*, the Commadore Don *Diego Bicuna* having a Commiſſion to command all the Fleet deſigned thither; and in theſe Ships were taken near ſeven hundred Priſoners.

By reaſon of bad Weather, Calms, and contrary Winds, the Rear-Admiral arrived not with his Prizes at *Lisbon* until the 25th of *March*, and, as he was going in, the *St. Thereſa* was unfortunately loſt on the *North Catchup*, but ſeveral of the Men which were in her, both *Engliſh* and *Spaniſh*, were ſaved, amongſt whom was the Lieutenant of the *Suffolk*, who commanding the Prize, miſtook (as was ſuppoſed) the Light of St. *Julian*'s Fort for the Flag's own Light, and ſhaped his Courſe accordingly.

The Admiral being now return'd to *Lisbon*, and having received Orders from Her Majeſty to proceed up the *Streights*, he determined to ſail in few Days, and to leave Directions for the Ships of War, Victualling, and Storeſhips, expected from *England*, how to join him. In the mean while he ordered Rear-Admiral *Wiſhart* to lie off of Cape St. *Vincent* for Intelligence, with ſix Frigates and a Fireſhip, where, or at *Lagos*, he might be ready to join the reſt of the Fleet, if ordered ſo to do. *Sir George Rooke ordered to proceed up the Streights.*

A Council of War was held on board the *Royal Katharine* the 18th of *April*, where were preſent of the *Engliſh*, Vice-Admiral *Leake* of the Blue, and Rear-Admiral *Dilkes* of the White, and of the *Dutch*, Admiral *Callemberg*, Vice-Admiral *Waſſenaer*, and Rear-Admiral *Vanderduſſen*. Her Majeſty's Orders of the 24th and 28th of *March*, and Mr. Secretary *Hedges*'s Letter of the ſame Date, were read, whereupon it was determined to proceed up the *Streights* according to the Reſolution of the 12th Inſtant. But if the *Portugueſe* Troops deſigned under Command of the Prince of *Heſſe* for *Catalonia*, could be embarked in eight or ten Days, it was thought convenient to ſtay for them, and that Orders ſhould be left for the Ships expected from *England* to join the Fleet in *Altea* Bay, but not finding it there, to repair to *Algier* for their better Security. 1704. *A Council of War held.*

It was farther reſolved that, when in the *Streights*, a Frigate ſhould be ſent to *Nice* for Intelligence from Mr. *Hill*, our Reſident at the Court of *Savoy*, of the Preparations and Deſigns of the *French* Fleet, and that if he ſuppoſed there was any Proſpect of their inſulting *Villa Franca*, or *Nice*, it ſhould then be conſider'd how to execute Her Majeſty's Orders of the 14th of *March* for the Relief of thoſe Places. But the Flag-Officers thought it proper to repreſent, that by the want of the major part of our Quota of Ships, the others might poſſibly be extremely expoſed in that Service, and render'd uncapable, in many reſpects, to perform what Her Majeſty expected from them; and the Admiral having received ſome Advice of the Preparations the *French* were making both at *Thoulon*, and in *Weſt-France*, deſired that he might be timely and effectually ſtrengthened, to prevent the ill Conſequence of a Surprize, or any other unforeſeen Accident. *The Admiral deſired to be ſtrengthened.*

The

He is reinforced at Lisbon.

The 21st of *April* he was joined in the Bay of *Wares*, near *Lisbon*, by one Second Rate, four Thirds, and two Fireships, and some few Days after he detached for *England* with the Transports and Merchant Ships, the *Expedition, Exeter,* and *Advice.*

A Council of War, at the Desire of the King of Spain.

The 25th a Council of War was called, at the Desire of the King of *Spain*, upon a Paper delivered by the Almirante of *Castile*, where were present the several Flag-Officers who assisted at the former Council. His Catholick Majesty's Proposals by the said Almirante, as also Her Majesty's Orders of the 14th and 24th of *March* were read, relating to the Relief of *Nice*, and *Villa Franca*, together with the Resolutions taken at the said Council, and a Letter from the Earl of *Nottingham* of the 10th of *April*, advising that the Enemy were preparing to attack those two Places by Sea. It was

Agreed to proceed to the Relief of Nice *and* Villa Franca.

thereupon agreed that the Fleet should proceed to their Relief, according to the former Resolutions, but first sail to the Northward of the Islands of *Majorca* and *Minorca*, and, if the Winds would permit, as near the Coast of *Catalonia* as might be convenient, for gaining Intelligence; but that if they met with certain Advice that neither of the two Places before-mentioned were attacked, the Fleet should stop at *Barcelona*, and give his Catholick Majesty's Affairs all possible Countenance and Assistance in those Parts.

If certain Intelligence could not be gained, and that when the Fleet arrived at *Nice*, or *Villa Franca*, it should be found they were not besieged, it was resolved to return without loss of time to *Barcelona*, and as soon as the Service on the Coast of *Catalonia* should be over, to act farther as might be judged most advantagious by a Council of War for the Service of the King of *Spain*, and the Common Interest; and the Flag-Officers were likewise of opinion, that four of the Ships expected from *England* might be sufficient to convoy to the Fleet the Victuallers and Transports.

Since the Proposals of his Catholick Majesty by the Almirante of *Castile* are mentioned in the aforegoing Council of War, it may be expected that I let the Reader know what those Proposals were, for which reason I have hereafter inserted a Translation of them from the *Spanish* Original, viz.

The Proposals of the Almirante of Castile.

" The 6th of *May*, N. S. 1704, the Almirante of *Castile* propo-
" sed, by Order from his Catholick Majesty, to Admiral *Rooke*, and
" the other Flag-Officers of the *English* and *Dutch* Fleet, that in
" their Voyage to the *Mediterranean*, their chief Design should be
" to go *Barcelona*, to execute there what had been resolved on,
" and which would be of so great a Benefit not only to the Com-
" mon Cause, but to the Success of the Enterprize upon *Spain*, as
" well as easily be put in Execution, according to what had alrea-
" dy been represented to Admiral *Rooke*.

" When at *Barcelona*, if Advice should come from the Duke of
" *Savoy* that *Nice* was besieged, then the Admiral might go to the
" Relief of it according to his Orders; but if no such Advice should
" come, that then the Enterprize upon *Barcelona* might be execu-
" ted to the Good of the Common Cause, and without the Admi-
" ral's

CHAP. XVI *from the Year* 1698, *to* 1712. 671

"ral's being wanting in his due Obedience to the Orders he had
"from Her Majesty of *Great Britain*.

"But if his Royal Highness the Duke of *Savoy* should press to
"have the Fleet go up thither, and it might thereupon be judged
"necessary to appoint a Rendezvous, all that his Catholick Majesty
"desired was, that it might be at *Barcelona*, since even that alone
"would be of great Benefit to the Enterprize upon *Spain*, and con-
"sequently very advantagious to all the Allies.

"The Almirante of *Castile* said also, that his Catholick Majesty
"desired to know, if when the Fleet was on the Coast of *Piedmont*,
"and *Nice* not besieged, nor that Coast invaded by Sea by the
"*French*, by what time it might return to execute the Enterprize
"upon *Catalonia*.

"He also demanded whether, when the Service of *Catalonia* be-
"ing ended, (which it was supposed would soon be) the Fleet could
"proceed to the Coasts of *Naples* and *Sicily*, to give Life to his
"Catholick Majesty's Party in those Kingdoms, and to the Dispo-
"sitions there might be in them for the Benefit of the Common
"Cause, and the universal Good.

Having thus given you an Account of what the Almirante proposed to Sir *George Rooke* from the King of *Spain*, I will in the
next Place let you know what the Strength of the Fleet, both *English* and *Dutch*, would have been, when joined by the Ships of War,
and small Vessels expected from *England*, *viz*.

Intended Strength of the Fleet.

English.

	N°
90 Guns	2
80	7
74	1
70	14
60	1
50	5
Small Frigates	5
Fireships	4
Hospitals	2
Bombs	2
Yacht	1
	44

Dutch.

	N°.
90 Guns	1
72	3
66	1
64	6
60	2
52	2
50	3

Small

	N°.
Small Frigate	1
Fireship	1
Bombs	3

$$\begin{array}{rr} \textit{Dutch} & 23 \\ \textit{English} & 44 \\ \hline & 69 \end{array}$$

Of which of the Line of Battel,

$$\begin{array}{rr} \textit{English} & 30 \\ \textit{Dutch} & 18 \\ \hline & 48 \end{array}$$

Sir Cloudesly Shovell appointed to look out for a French Squadron.

I shall here leave Sir *George Rooke*, for some time, and give you an Account of Sir *Cloudesly Shovell*'s Proceedings, with a Squadron sent to Sea under his Command, for intercepting that designed from *Brest* with the Count of *Thoulouse*, High-Admiral of *France*, and the rather, for that he afterwards joined the Body of the Fleet.

Instructions to Sir Cloudesly Shovell.

Her Majesty having received Advice that the Enemy were setting forth a considerable Naval Force in *West-France*, directed that Sir *Cloudesly Shovell* should be ordered to repair forthwith to *Spithead*, to take under his Command a Squadron of Ships which were particularly appointed for him, and his Royal Highness, Lord High-Admiral, also ordered him to use all possible Diligence in the getting them together, and in a Readiness to proceed on Service, but, in the mean while, to appoint some of the smallest to cruise Westward, in such Stations where they might most probably gain Intelligence of the Enemy's Proceedings and Preparations.

If by this means, or any other, he got Advice that the *French* had been seen at Sea, and were coming into the Chanel with a greater Strength than he should have together, he was directed to retire among the Sands, even as far as the *Gunfleet*, if occasion were, for his greater Security, that so he might be the more readily join'd by Ships from the River, *Holland*, or other Parts, and in such Retreat he was to bring with him the Victuallers, Storeships, and Trade bound to *Lisbon*, unless he could have an Opportunity to secure them in *Portsmouth* Harbour.

When ready to sail he was to proceed off of *Brest* with his Squadron, and the Trade, Storeships, and Victuallers designed to Sir *George Rooke*; and if he perceived, or had certain Intelligence, that the *French* Squadron was there, he was to send the said Trade, Storeships, &c. to *Lisbon*, under the Convoy of two such Ships, or more, as a Council of War should judge proper, by whom he was to transmit an Account to Sir *George Rooke* where he was, and what he intended to do.

CHAP. XVI. *from the Year* 1698, *to* 1712. 673

If he found the Enemy in *Brest*, he was to use his best Endeavours to prevent the Junction of the Ships there with those of *Rochefort*, and Port *Louis*, if a Council of War should think it practicable; and if they attempted to come to Sea from any of those Ports, to do his utmost to take, sink, burn, or otherwise destroy them, if it should be judged he had a sufficient Strength to attempt it; but if the Enemy came out too strong, and followed him, he was then to retire into the Chanel, in such manner as he should think might most conduce to the Service, and endeavouring to join Her Majesty's Ships which might be there, repair among the Sands, as far as the *Gunfleet*, for his Security, if he found there might be occasion for his so doing, as is before-mentioned.

But if he learnt, when off of *Brest*, that the Enemy were gone from thence, and that he could not inform himself whither, or if he should have good Grounds to believe they had bent their Course to the *Streights*, and that, with the *Thoulon* Squadron, (which was said to consist of twenty five Sail of the Line of Battel, they might be superior to the Fleet with Sir *George Rooke*, (of which a List was sent him) he was either to go with, or send the Ships designed for *Lisbon*, (which were eight Third Rates, an Hospital, two Bomb-Vessels, and a Yacht) as also the Storeships, Victuallers, and Trade, together with such an additional Strength of the biggest Ships with him, as a Council of War, upon due Consideration, should judge proper, to make Sir *George Rooke* superior to the Enemy, supposing a Junction of their Ships from *West-France* and *Thoulon*.

It was Her Majesty's Pleasure that not more than twenty two Ships of War (including the eight designed for *Portugal*) should proceed with the Storeships, &c. to *Lisbon*, and therefore if he found it necessary that so many as eighteen, or the greater part of his Squadron should proceed thither, he was to go with them himself, and send the Remainder into the Chanel, under the Command of a Flag-Officer, with Orders to him to cruise there for the Security of the Trade; but he was to come into the Chanel himself, if such a Number only proceeded to *Lisbon* as might not require his commanding them thither.

Either himself, or the Flag, or Flag-Officers, he should send to *Lisbon*, were to put themselves under Command of Sir *George Rooke*; and if in his Passage to *Brest* he met the *Expedition*, *Exeter*, or *Advice* from *Portugal*, and found them in a Condition for Service, he was empowered to take such of them with him as he judged proper, but no farther than off of *Brest*; and if any thing of Consequence happened during his being abroad, which was not provided for in the aforegoing Instructions, he was to govern himself as should be agreed at a Council of War.

These Instructions prepared by order of his Royal Highness, Lord High-Admiral, were read at the Committee of Council the 25th of *April*, and being agreed unto, were signed and dispatched to Sir *Cloudesly Shovell* the same Night, and a Copy thereof to Sir *George Rooke* by the Packet Boat, that so he might have as early Information thereof as possible.

The Instructions approved of at a Committee of Council.

R r r r   Pursuant

Sir Cloudesly Shovell *sails.* 1704.

Pursuant hereunto he sailed from St. *Helen's*, and arrived off of *Plimouth* the 12th of *May* 1704, where Rear-Admiral *Byng* (who was afterwards Admiral of the Fleet, and one of the Lords Commissioners of the Admiralty) was making all possible Dispatch in getting Ships ready to join him; and here it may not be improper to insert the Line of Battel, which was as follows, *viz.*

The Line of Battel.

The *St. George* to lead with the Starboard, and the *Revenge* with the Larboard Tacks on board.

The Line of Battel.

Frigates, Fireships, &c.	Rate.	Ships.	Men.	Guns.	Division.
	2	St. George,	680	96	
	4	Moderate,	365	60	
Bridgwater,	3	Torbay, —	500	80	Vice-Admiral
Lightning Fire-ship,		Shrewsbury,	540	80	of the Red, Sir
		Essex, —	440	70	Stafford Fairborn.
Terror Bomb.	4	Glocester, —	365	60	
	3	Royal Oak,	500	76	
	4	Monk, —	365	60	
	3	Boyne, —	500	80	
Roebuck,		Warspight,	540	70	
Vulcan Fire-ship,	4	Triton, —	280	50	Admiral of the
	3	Orford, —	440	70	White, Sir
William and	2	Barfleur, —	710	96	Cloudesly Shovell.
Mary Yacht,		Namur, —	680	96	
Princess Anne	4	Medway, —	365	60	
Hospital.	3	Swiftsure,	440	70	
		Lenox, —	440	70	
		Nassau, —	440	70	
		Rupert, —	440	70	
Vulture Fire-ship,		Norfolk, —	500	80	Rear-Admiral
		Ranelagh,	535	80	of the Red,
Star Bomb.		Dorsetshire,	500	80	George Byng, Esq;
	4	Kingstone,	365	60	
		Assurance,	365	60	
		Revenge, —	440	70	
			11635	1514	

A Council of War held.

The 15th of *May* he was between the *Fourn-head* and the *Lizard*, his first Rendezvous, and then calling a Council of War of the Flag-Officers, and several of the senior Captains, upon Intelligence sent him from the Admiralty-Office that the Count of *Thoulouse* would be ready to sail the beginning of this Month, as also other Advices that he actually sailed from *Brest* the 2d; and from

a Frigate

CHAP. XVI. *from the Year* 1698, *to* 1712. 675

a Frigate sent to look into the said Port, that there was but one Ship of War seen in the Road, it was determined to leave the Station they were in immediately, and to sail to the second Rendezvous, which was in the *Soundings* W. S. W. or S. W. by W. about twenty Leagues from *Scilly*, and leaving a Ship there forty eight Hours to give notice to those wanting, forthwith to proceed with the Fleet to a Station West, or W. S. W. a hundred and forty, or a hundred and fifty Leagues from *Scilly*, if they could get thither, or if not, to part with the *West-India* Squadron, then under Command of Captain *Kerr*, a hundred and fifty Leagues from *Scilly*, as also with Sir *Stafford Fairborn*, and the Ships with him, and each Squadron to make the best of their way, according to the Instructions those Officers had received.

At this Council of War some of the Officers were for the Admiral's taking all the Ships with him, but since he was by his Orders restrain'd to twenty two, he determined to send back two of the Third Rate, five of the Fourth, and one of the Fifth, with Directions to Sir *Stafford Fairborn* to call in at *Kinsale* in *Ireland* for the homeward bound Trade, and see them to *Plimouth*, and wait there for the Orders of the Lord High-Admiral.

In his Passage out of the Chanel he took four Prizes, two of which were small Privateers, and on the 28th of *May*, when he was about 140 Leagues S. W. by W. from *Scilly*, he called a Council of War, where it was resolved, that since the Fleet had been traversing in the *Soundings*, and the Mouth of the Chanel, near a Fortnight, with Southerly and South-West Winds, and that they saw not the *French* Squadron, for which reason they judged they might be gone Southward, the Admiral should the next Morning send Sir *Stafford Fairborn* home, the *West-India* Squadron forward, and with the rest of his Ships make the best of his way to *Lisbon*, and join Sir *George Rooke*, of whose Proceedings both before and after the said Junction I will now give an Account.

That Admiral, pursuant to the Resolutions before-mentioned, setting sail from *Lisbon* for the *Mediterranean*, he came on the 29th of *April* off of Cape St. *Vincent*, when he had with him of *English* Ships two of the Second Rate, fifteen of the Third, four of the Fourth, one of the Fifth, one Sixth, and four Fireships, and of the *Dutch* Ships of War fourteen, all of the Line of Battel; and Orders were left at *Lisbon* for another of the Fourth Rate, and one of the Fifth to follow him.

On the 8th of *May*, about Two in the Afternoon, the Weather being then hazey, six *French* Ships of War fell in with him off of Cape *Palos*, (a little to the Eastward of *Carthagena*) to chase which he detached six Third Rates, one Fourth, and a Fifth, and they ran the Fleet out of Sight before it was Night. On the 10th in the Evening he anchored in *Altea* Bay, where the Squadron which he sent to chase the Enemy joined him that Night, having not had the good Fortune of coming up with them.

At the pressing Instances of the Prince of *Hesse*, he proceeded with the Fleet to *Barcelona* Road, who said that he had Assurances

Some Prizes taken.

Another Council of War.

Some of the Squadron sent back to England.

Sir Cloudesly Shovell proceeds to join Sir George Rooke at Lisbon.

Sir George Rooke proceeds to the Mediterranean.

Some French Ships of War fall in with the Fleet.

The Fleet before Barcelona.

R r r r 2 from

from the Deputies of *Catalonia*, and the principal Men of the City, that if some few Forces were landed, and a Shew made of a Bombardment, they would declare for King *Charles* the Third, and receive him the said Prince into the Town. Hereupon, on the 19th of *May*, about Noon, the Admiral caused to be landed about twelve hundred Marine Soldiers, and the *Dutch* about four hundred; but when they had been one Night on shore, and the *Dutch* had bombarded the Town from the Sea, the Prince was convinced of his Mistake, so that he himself proposed the re-imbarking of the Men; not but that the People were inclinable to rise, and would have done it, had they seen a Prospect of sufficient Force to support them. On the 18th Rear-Admiral *Wishart* joined the Fleet, who had met with the six *French* Ships before-mention'd much about the same Place, and they finding themselves too strong for him, (for he had only two Third Rates, two Fourths, and a Fireship) gave chase to him, but continued not their Pursuit, though some of them visibly gained on him.

A Number of Marine Soldiers landed to no purpose.

Rear-Admiral Wishart chased by the six French Ships.

On the 21st the Admiral steered away for the Isles of *Hieres*, but in crossing the Gulph had a hard Gale of Wind at N. N. W. and N. W. which dispersed the Fleet, and most of the Sails of our Ships flew away like Paper; but being joined again by the absent Ships, on the 27th, at Eight at Night, his Scouts made the Signal of seeing a Fleet, which he judged were the Enemy, and that they would make the best of their way to *Thoulon*, so that tacking, he stood to the Northward all Night, and on the 28th in the Morning, soon after Day, the *French* Fleet were in view, consisting of forty Sail, at which time it was calm. The Admiral called a Council of War, where were present Sir *John Leake*, Vice-Admiral of the Blue, Rear-Admiral *Dilkes* of the White, Sir *James Wishart*, Rear-Admiral of the Blue, and of the *Dutch*, Lieutenant-Admiral *Callemberg*, Vice-Admiral *Waffenaer*, and Rear-Admiral *Vanderduffen*. It was agreed that since the Enemy seem'd to avoid engaging, by making all the Sail they possibly could, our Fleet should continue the Chase as long as they could keep sight of them, or until they had reached the Coast of *Thoulon*, and that if a Junction with the Ships at that Port could not be prevented, they should then repair to *Lisbon*, as had been before determined. Accordingly the Enemy were chased until the 29th in the Evening, when being within thirty Leagues of *Thoulon*, where there were fifteen or sixteen Ships ready to join them, it was unanimously agreed to repair down to the *Streights* Mouth; and even by so doing they ran some hazard of being followed by the *French* with a superior Strength, for Sir *Cloudesly Shovell* had not yet joined the Admiral, and the Ships he had with him were but in a bad Condition, especially as to Sails, Topmasts, and Stores.

The Admiral discovers the French Fleet.

Our Fleet chase the French towards Thoulon.

The 14th of *June* our Fleet passed through the *Streights* Mouth, and off of *Lagos* were joined by Sir *Cloudesly Shovell* two Days after, when a Council of War being called, it was agreed, that the best Service which could be done, was to proceed up the *Mediterranean* in search of the *French* Fleet; and the Flag-Officers were of Opinion that they might co-operate in the Siege of *Cadiz*,

Resolution to proceed up the Streights in search of the French.

or

4

CHAP. XVI. *from the Year* 1698, *to* 1712. 677

or any Attempt on *Barcelona*, if sufficient Land-Forces were appointed for such a Service; but that till the Sentiments of the Courts of *Spain* and *Portugal* were known, it was most proper for the Fleet to lie in such a Station as might prevent the Enemy's getting to *Cadiz*, yet so as to be near to *Nice*, and *Villa Franca*, should they make any Attempts on those Places. It was also resolved that, upon the Desire of the King of *Portugal*, some Ships should be sent to the *Tercera* Islands for protecting his Majesty's Fleets expected from *Brazil*.

Some time after this the Admiral received Orders from the Queen, requiring him not to undertake any thing on the Coast without the Approbation of the Kings of *Spain* and *Portugal*, whose Proposals he received the 16th of *July*, when he was advanced up the *Streights*, for attempting somewhat on the Coast of *Andalusia*; whereupon a Council of War was called, at which were present, besides the Admiral himself, Sir *Cloudesly Shovell*, Sir *John Leake*, Rear-Admiral *Byng*, and Sir *James Wishart*, as also the three *Dutch* Flags before mentioned; and since it was concluded not to be practicable to attempt *Cadiz*, without an Army to assist therein, they resolved to land the Marine Soldiers, *English* and *Dutch*, under Command of the Prince of *Hesse*, in the Bay of *Gibraltar*, to cut off that Town from any Communication with the Main, and at the same time to bombard and cannonade the Place, and endeavour to reduce it to the Obedience of the King of *Spain*. *The Admiral ordered not to attempt any thing without the Consent of the Kings of Spain and Portugal. Agreed not to attempt Cadiz. Prince of Hesse and the Marines landed at Gibraltar.*

The 20th in the Night the Admiral pushed from the *Barbary* Shore over to *Gibraltar*, and the next Day, at Three in the Afternoon, landed the Marines, with the Prince of *Hesse* at the Head of them, who marched to the Mills near the Town, and sent a Summons to the Governor to surrender the Place, to which he received an Answer, That the Garrison had taken an Oath of Fidelity to their natural Lord, King *Philip* the Fifth, and that, as faithful and loyal Subjects, they would sacrifice their Lives in the Defence of the City. Hereupon the Admiral, on the 22d in the Morning, order'd twelve Third Rates, and four Fourths, with six Ships of the States-General, all under Command of Rear-Admiral *Byng*, to cannonade the Town, which was done with great Fury the next Day, so that the Enemy were beaten from their Guns at the South Mole Head. The Boats were then mann'd and arm'd, and sent with Captain (now Sir *Edward*) *Whittaker* to possess themselves of that Fort, which was very gallantly performed, and as our Men got on the great Platform, so some of them enter'd the Castle; but the Enemy having laid a Train to the Magazine, it blew up, and killed and wounded above one hundred of them; however they kept Possession of the Platform, and advanced, and took a Redoubt, or small Bastion, half way between the Mole and the Town. *The Place summoned. Rear-Admiral Byng cannonades Gibraltar. Some Outworks taken.*

It being *Sunday*, all the Women were at their Devotion in a little Chapel, about four Miles distant from the Town, so that our Men were between them and their Husbands, which was a very great Inducement to the Citizens to oblige the Governor to capitulate, whereupon the 24th in the Evening the Prince of *Hesse*, with the Marines,

The Town delivered up.

Marines, marched into the Town. They found there but two *Spanish* Regiments, of about forty Men each, but on the Walls above 100 Guns mounted, all facing the Sea, and the two narrow Passes to the Land; and in this Action we had sixty one Men killed, and two hundred and six wounded.

Dutch Admiral sends home six Ships.

The *Dutch* Admiral soon after sent to *Lisbon* the Rear-Flag with six Ships, whence they were to proceed home, intending himself to follow them in a little time; and the 9th Day of *August* Sir *George Rooke* returning from the Coast of *Barbary* (where he had been for Water) to *Gibraltar*, his Scouts made the usual Signals of seeing a

The French Fleet discovered.

strange Fleet, several Leagues to Windward, consisting, as their Commanders soon after said, of sixty six Sail; and a Council of War being thereupon called, it was determined to lay to the Eastward of *Gibraltar*, to receive and engage them; but it being judged from their Signal Guns in the Night, that they wrought away from our Fleet, the Admiral followed them in the Morning with all the Sail he could make, and continued so to do till the 12th, not hearing their Guns that Night, nor seeing any of their Scouts in the Morning.

This gave him a Suspicion that they might make a Double, and, by the help of their Gallies, slip between him and the Shore to the Westward, wherefore it was determined at a Council of War to repair to *Gibraltar*, if the Enemy should not be discover'd before Night; but standing in towards the Shore, the *French* Fleet were seen about Noon, with their Gallies, to the Westward, near Cape

Our Fleet chase the French.

Malaga, going away large, upon which our Admiral made what Sail he possibly could after them, and continued so to do all Night.

On Sunday the 13th, in the Morning, he was within three Leagues of them, when they brought to with their Heads to the Southward, the Wind being Easterly, and, forming their Line, lay in a Posture

Strength of the French Fleet.

to receive him. They were fifty two Ships, and twenty four Gallies, very strong in the Centre, but weaker in the Van and Rear, to supply which most of their Gallies were placed in those Squadrons. In the Centre was the Count of *Thoulouse*, High-Admiral of *France*, with the White Squadron; in the Van the White and Blue Flag, and in the Rear the Blue, each Admiral having his Vice and Rear-Admiral.

Strength of the English and Dutch.

Our Fleet consisted of fifty three Ships, but the Admiral order'd the *Swallow* and *Panther*, two Fourth Rates, with a Fifth and a Sixth, and two Fireships, to lay to Windward of him, that if the Enemy's Van should push through our Line, with their Gallies and Fireships, they might have given them some Diversion.

He bore down on the *French* Fleet until somewhat after Ten a Clock, when they set all their Sails at once, and seem'd as if they designed to stretch a-head and weather him; soon after which he caused the Signal to be made for Battel, and the Enemy keeping

The Battel begun.

themselves in a Posture to receive them, it began, and was smartly continued on both sides, wherein, among others, the Lord *Dursley*, then about three and twenty Years of Age, who commanded the

Boyne,

CHAP. XVI. *from the Year* 1698, *to* 1712.   679

Boyne, a Ship of 80 Guns, behaved himself with remarkable Resolution and Bravery.

In less than two Hour's time the Enemy's Van, which were pressed by ours, commanded by Sir *Cloudesly Shovell,* and led by Sir *John Leake,* gave way in no little Confusion, as their Rear did to the *Dutch* towards Evening. Their Centre being strong, and several Ships of the Admiral's own Division, as well as those of Rear-Admiral *Byng*'s, and Rear-Admiral *Dilkes*'s being forced to go out of the Line for want of Shot, (which it seems were not equally distributed throughout the Fleet, after the great Expence thereof in the Action of *Gibraltar*) the Battel fell very heavy on some of the Admiral's own Squadron, particularly the *St. George,* commanded by Sir *John Jennings* [*], and the *Shrewsbury* by Captain *Josiah Crowe:* And between six and seven at Night, when there was but little firing on either side, a Ship which was one of the Seconds to the *French* Admiral, and a-head of him, advanced out of the Line, and for some time engaged the *St. George,* but was so roughly handled, that she retreated back to the Fleet, after both her Captains, and many of her Men were killed. And as the *St. George* had before fought singly some Hours not only with this Ship, but with Count *Thouloufe* himself, and his other Second, neither our Admiral, nor any of the Ships nearest to her being in a Condition to come to her Assistance, by reason of their being disabled as well in their Rigging, as otherwise, so before Sir *John Jennings* engaged the afore-mention'd Ship after the Brunt of the Battel was over, he had at least twenty five Guns dismounted on that side he fought, and was obliged to bring others over from the opposite side in the room of them.

The Enemy at length went away to Leeward by the help of their Gallies, but the Wind shifting in the Night to the Northward, and in the Morning to the West, they by that means became to Windward, both Fleets lying by all Day, within three Leagues of each other, repairing Damages, but at Night the *French* fill'd their Sails and stood Northward.   *The French towed away to Leeward.*

On the 15th in the Morning they were gotten four or five Leagues to the Westward of our Fleet, and a little before Noon Sir *George Rooke* had a Breeze of Wind Easterly, with which he edged towards them until Four in the Afternoon, but it being judged then too late to engage, he brought to, and lay by with his Head Northward all Night.

The Wind continuing Easterly the 16th, with hazy Weather, and the Enemy not being seen, nor any of their Scouts, our Fleet bore away to the Westward, the Admiral supposing they might have been gone for *Cadiz;* but being advis'd from *Gibraltar,* and the Coast of *Barbary,* that they had not pass'd the *Streights,* he concluded they were retired to *Thoulon*; and as he was not wrong in his Judgment, so is it not unreasonable to think, that had they known how much several of our Ships of the Line of Battel were in want of Am-

---

[*] *Since Admiral of the White, and one of the Lords Commissioners of the Admiralty.*

munition

munition and Shot, or otherwise disabled from farther Action, they would not have made so great haste home, but rather have tried the Event of a second Engagement.

Remarks. The *English* and *Dutch* Ships began this Fight with manifest Disadvantage; for although their Strength and that of the *French* were near an Equality, yet had the Enemy their Ports at hand upon occasion, whereas the others, for want of such Shelter, would have been obliged, if overcome, to have wander'd about the Seas with their disabled Ships without proper Materials for repairing them, or to have destroyed them, that so they might not have fallen into the Hands of the Victors. But notwithstanding this Advantage on the side of the *French*, to which may be added that of their Gallies, they did not think it adviseable to renew the Fight; nor had the *English* and *Dutch* any great reason to value themselves on their Success, otherwise than that, by putting a good Face on it, they shewed themselves ready to try their Fortune a second time, while the *French* were retreating towards their Ports, as hath already been observed.

A Council of War resolve to proceed to Gibraltar. A Council of War being call'd, it was determined to repair with the Fleet to *Gibraltar*, there to secure the disabled Ships, and to repair their Masts, Yards, Sails, and Rigging, where arriving, and the best Assistance being given to that Garrison that possibly could be, it was resolved that all such Ships as were in a Condition for Winter Service should be put under the Command of Sir *John Leake*; that such as were not so, but might safely proceed to *England*, should repair thither, and that those in the worst Condition should go to *Lisbon* to be refitted.

Sir John Leake sent with a Squadron to Lisbon. Accordingly the Fleet sail'd from *Gibraltar*, and being out of the *Streights* Mouth the 26th of *August*, the Admiral gave Orders to Sir *John Leake* to take under his Command two Ships of the Third Rate, nine of the Fourth, four of the Fifth, one Sixth, and a Fireship, and proceed with them to *Lisbon*, from whence he was to send four to *England* with the Trade. He was also to take under his Command such Ships of the States-General as should be appointed for Winter Service in those Parts, and to employ the whole in guarding the Coasts of *Portugal* and *Spain*, and for the Security of our Trade, and the Garrison of *Gibraltar*. With the rest which were in a Condition to come home, the Admiral repaired towards *Sir George Rooke arrives in England.* *England*, where he arrived the 24th of *September* 1704, which Ships were five of the Second Rate, twenty five of the Third, four Fourths, six Fireships, two Hospital Ships, and a Yacht.

And here it may not be improper to give the Reader some Account of the Number of Officers and Men killed and wounded in the Engagement, which is as follows, *viz.*

Officers.

CHAP. XVII. *from the Year* 1698, *to* 1712.   681

	Officers.		Men.	
	Slain,	Wounded.	Slain,	Wounded.
In the Admiral's Division ——	6	2	219	508
Sir *Cloudesly Shovell*'s —	1	7	105	303
Sir *John Leake*'s ——		7	89	211
Rear-Admiral *Byng*'s —	1	5	155	361
Rear-Admiral *Dilkes*'s —		10	119	249
	8	31	687	1632

Officers and Men of the *English* kill'd and wounded — 2368
Of the *Dutch* —— —— —— 400

　　　　　　　　　　　　　　　　　　　　　　　　　　2768

CHAP. XVII.

Containing an Account of Sir John Leake's *relieving* Gibraltar, *and of his destroying several* French *Ships of War.*

HAVING brought home the Admiral of the Fleet from the *Mediterranean*, I shall return to Sir *John Leake*, and give an Account of his Proceedings during the time he commanded abroad.

The 30th of *September* Sir *John Leake* received a Letter from the Prince of *Hesse*, and another from Captain *Fotherby*, who commanded the *Larke*, by which he was informed that on the 4th of *October* in the Evening, a Squadron of the Enemy's Ships, in Number nineteen, great and small, came into *Gibraltar* Bay, and that there was a Design of besieging the Place both by Sea and Land, for which reason his Highness earnestly desired him to repair to their Relief with all possible Diligence.

1704. A Squadron of French Ships comes to Gibraltar.

Hereupon Sir *John* caused the utmost Dispatch to be made in the refitting the Ships, and some others joined him from *England* and *Holland*; but soon after he received another Letter from the Prince of *Hesse*, letting him know that the *French* Squadron was gone Westward, having left in the Bay of *Gibraltar* only six light Frigates from 40 to 20 Guns; but that they had landed six Battalions, so that the *French* and *Spanish* Troops might amount to about seven thousand Horse and Foot, and that they had open'd their Trenches against the Town. Sir *John* on this called a Council of War, and it was resolved to proceed to the Relief of the Place with three Third Rates, nine Fourth, and two Fifth Rates of the *English*, and of the *Dutch* six Ships of the Line of Battel.

Sir John Leake receives an Account that most of them were gone Westward, but that the French were attacking the Town by Land.

S f f f　　　　　　　　　　　Arriving

Sir John *Leake comes to* Gibraltar.

Arriving in the Bay of *Gibraltar*, a confiderable Number of Men were landed from the Fleet to affift in the Works; but upon Advice of a ftrong Squadron of *French* Ships being defign'd from *Cadiz* to attack him, it was thought reafonable that all the Men fhould embark again, except the Gunners and Carpenters, and the Marine Soldiers.

Our Ships wanting Provifions return to Lisbon, *but return and furprize French Ships at* Gibraltar,

Our Ships, by riding at the Weft fide of the Bay with a ftrong Eafterly Wind, having loft fome of their Anchors and Cables, and the *Dutch* moft of theirs, it was refolved to put to Sea, as foon as it fhould fpring up Wefterly, and to keep as near to *Gibraltar* as the Weather would permit; but Sir *John Leake* finding it abfolutely neceffary to proceed with the Squadron to *Lisbon*, for a Supply of Provifions, he repaired thither, and departed from thence again towards *Gibraltar* the 25th of *October*, with three Ships of the Third Rate, nine of the Fourth, two Fifths, and a Firefhip, together with fix *Dutch*, and arriving there the 29th, furprized two of the Enemy's Ships of 34 Guns each, one of 12, a Firefhip, a Tartan, and two *Englifh* Prizes, all which they ran on fhore and fet on fire; and another Ship of 30 Guns which had juft got out of the Bay, was alfo taken by one of ours. Had not the Vice-Admiral luckily arrived as he did, it was generally believed the Town muft have furrendered, or that the Enemy would have ftorm'd it, they being not only very numerous by Land, but had a Defign to put on fhore at the New Mole three thoufand Men, in Boats which they had got together from *Cadiz*, and other Places; and five hundred being difcover'd on the top of the Hill which overlooks the Town, the Granadiers, with Colonel *Borr*, (fince a Brigadier in the Army) very gallantly attack'd them, and kill'd about two hundred, taking moft of the reft Prifoners.

and relieved the Town.

Colonel Borr *kills feveral of the* Spaniards.

At a Council of War, held the 21ft of *December*, it was refolved to remain in *Gibraltar* Bay while the Wind continued Wefterly, and with the firft Eafterly Wind to proceed to *Lisbon*, to clean and refit the Squadron, the Garrifon being now reinforced by two thoufand Men. Before they failed the Enemy had much abated in their cannonading, and bombarding the Town; and, as the Deferters faid, defpair'd of taking it, fince Monfieur *Ponty* had not, as they expected, attempted our Ships in the Bay, with a Squadron from *Cadiz*, to which Place Sir *John Leake* had fome time before propos'd to go, in order to have attack'd them; but it was not confented to by the Prince of *Heffe*, and the Land-Officers, left, in his Abfence, the Town might have been loft to the Enemy.

The Garrifon of Gibraltar *reinforced.*

1705. *Sir* John Leake *has an Account of Monfieur* Ponty's *coming to* Gibraltar.

On the 21ft of *February*, at Seven at Night, he received a Letter from the Prince, giving him an Account that Monfieur *Ponty* was come into the Bay of *Gibraltar* with fourteen Ships of War, and two Firefhips, and preffed his coming to the Affiftance of the Town, againft which they intended a general Affault; whereupon it was determined to proceed thither, as foon as they could poffibly be furnifhed with fome Ordnance-Stores, and Soldiers for the Ships, in the room of a confiderable Number of Seamen which were wanting. Mean while Sir *Thomas Dilkes* arrived from *England* with five Ships of the Third Rate, and on the 3d of *March* part of the Troops embark'd

Sir Thomas Dilkes *arrives from* England.

CHAP. XVII. *from the Year* 1698, *to* 1712.

embark'd which were design'd for *Gibraltar*, towards which Place Sir *John Leake* sailed the 6th of the same Month, and on the 9th got sight of Cape *Spartell*, but not having Day-light enough to reach the Bay of *Gibraltar*, he lay by to prevent his being discover'd from the *Spanish* Shore, intending to surprize the Enemy early in the Morning; but by bad Weather was prevented in making Sail as soon as he intended. About half an Hour past Five he was within two Miles of Cape *Cabretta*, when he discover'd only five Sail making out of the Bay, and a Gun fir'd at them from *Europa Point*; whereupon concluding the Garrison was safe, he gave Chase to the Ships, they being the *Magnanime* of 74 Guns, the *Lis* of 86, the *Ardent* of 66, the *Arrogant* of 60, and the *Marquise* of 56.

Sir John Leake proceeds towards Gibraltar.

He chases several French Ships.

At first they stood over for the *Barbary* Shore, but seeing our Ships gained upon them, they stretched over to that of *Spain*, and at nine a Clock Sir *Thomas Dilkes*, in the *Revenge*, with the *Newcastle*, *Antelope*, *Expedition*, and a *Dutch* Man of War, got within half Gunshot of the *Arrogant*, which, after some small Resistance, struck; and before one a Clock the *Ardent* and *Marquise* were taken by two Ships of the States-General. The *Magnanime* and *Lis* ran on shore a little to the Westward of *Marvelles*, on board of the former of which was Monsieur *St. Paul*, and she came on the Ground with such Violence, that all her Masts fell by the Board, so that the Enemy burnt her, as they did the *Lis* next Morning.

French Ships taken or destroyed.

This Service being over, Sir *John* look'd into *Malaga* Road, where one of our Frigates had chased a Merchant Ship of the Enemy's on shore, of about three hundred Tuns, which they set on fire, as two others had done another of about two hundred and fifty Tuns, near *Almeria*, which was destroyed in the same manner; and there is reason to believe that the rest of the *French* Ships of War which got out of *Gibraltar* before our Squadron arrived, hearing the Guns there while they lay in *Malaga* Road, cut their Cables, and ran to *Thoulon*.

Sir John Leake proceeds to Malaga.

Other Ships destroyed on the Coast of Spain.

Sir *John Leake* arriving at *Lisbon* the 12th of *April*, appointed a Convoy to some *Portuguese* Troops design'd for *Gibraltar*, (which Garrison he had thus happily reliev'd a second time) and another to accompany our *Virginia* Trade well into the Sea; but soon after those Troops were countermanded, and marched to the Frontiers; and the *Swiftsure*, a Ship of the Third Rate, being much disabled in her Masts in the Engagement with the *French*, he sent her and three Fourth Rates to *England* with the loaden Merchants.

Sir John Leake arrives at Lisbon.

Some Ships sent home.

During his being in the River of *Lisbon* all possible Diligence was used in cleaning and refitting the Squadron; but the Provisions and Stores, as well as the additional Strength from *England*, not arriving as soon as was expected, he was not in a Condition to go to Sea, to prevent the Junction of the Ships fitting out in *West-France* with those in the *Mediterranean*, should they endeavour it, wherefore leaving him there for some time, we will now look homewards.

Chap. XVIII.

Containing an Account of Sir Cloudesly Shovell's *Proceedings to, and in the* Mediterranean, *when appointed joint Admiral of the Fleet with the Earl of* Peterborow *and* Monmouth; *the landing of the King of* Spain *at* Barcelona, *and the Reduction of that important City.*

SIR *Cloudesly Shovell* being appointed Admiral of the Fleet, he repaired on board the *Britannia* at the *Nore*, and on the 7th of *April* gave Orders to Sir *John Jennings* to proceed to *Spithead* with three First Rates, two Seconds, and as many Thirds: And at the time that he was thus appointed Admiral, (which was in Conjunction with the Earl of *Peterborow* and *Monmouth*, who was nam'd first in the Commission) Sir *George Byng* was nominated to Command in the *Soundings*, and Sir *Thomas Dilkes* off of *Dunkirk*.

Sir George Byng appointed to command in the Soundings, and Sir Thomas Dilkes off of Dunkirk. 1705.

Sir *Cloudesly Shovell* arrived at *Spithead* the 13th of *May*, and having, with all possible Dispatch, got the Ships as well there, as at *Portsmouth*, in a Readiness, and embarked the Troops designed for Service abroad; and the Ships of War being joined him from the *Downs*, in Company of which came those with Ordnance-Stores, he was unmooring the 21st of *May*, and the 22d in the Morning the Earl of *Peterborow* arrived at *Portsmouth*; but the Wind being out of the way, the Admirals were forced to come to an Anchor at St. *Helen's* that Night; however, all being now in a Readiness to proceed on their Voyage to the *Mediterranean*, it may not be improper here to give an Account of the Strength of the Fleet they carry'd with them, with which the Squadrons abroad were to join, *viz.*

Earl of Peterborow arrives at Portsmouth.

Rate.	N°.	
1	3	
2	6	29 of the Line of Battel;
3	12	
4	8	

besides Ships of the Fifth and Sixth Rates, Fireships, Bombs, and small Craft.

The 25th of *May* the Fleet came off of *Plimouth*, where they lay for some Ships of War, and Transports, which were to join them from thence, and the first Rendezvous the Admiral appointed was seven Leagues South from the *Lizard*, where they arrived two Days after, from whence they sent Orders to the Ships of War, and the Transports with Forces in *Ireland* to proceed directly to *Lisbon*.

Upon

CHAP. XVIII. *from the Year* 1698, *to* 1712. 685

Upon Intelligence from Sir *George Byng* and Sir *John Jennings*, as also the Account given by the Prisoners, that the Enemy had in *Brest* about eighteen Ships of War, it was resolved at a Council of Flag-Officers to leave Sir *George Byng* in the *Soundings*, with one First Rate, two Seconds, seven Thirds, and two Fourths, a Frigate, and a Fireship, and to proceed with the rest to *Lisbon*, which were two First Rates, four Seconds, and five Thirds. To Sir *George Byng* the Admirals gave Instructions to cruise off of *Ushant* and the *Fournhead*, and that if, when he got Intelligence the Enemy were sail'd from *Brest*, he was satisfied they had not any Design of coming into the *Soundings*, or infesting our Coast, he should send Sir *John Jennings* to the Bay of *Wares*, with the Ships intended for the Fleet, and himself put in Execution such Orders as he had or should receive from the Lord High-Admiral. But since it is proper to follow the Admirals of the Fleet in their Proceedings, that so their Transactions may appear at one View, I shall do that first, and then give an Account of Affairs at home. *Sir George Byng left in the Soundings, as also Sir John Jennings.*

The 11th of *June* the said Admirals were in the River of *Lisbon*, where they found the Ships with Sir *John Leake* (of which I have before given an Account) in want of Provisions, but issued Orders for furnishing them out of what was carried from *England*, so that they were all supplied with near four Months at whole Allowance; and some of the Ships of the States-General joined our Fleet at this Place, of which they expected nineteen or twenty of the Line of Battel. *The Fleet arrives in the River of Lisbon, where they met Sir John Leake, and some Dutch Ships.*

The 15th of *June* at a Council of Flag-Officers, where were present, besides the joint Admirals, Sir *Stafford Fairborn*, Sir *John Leake*, Sir *Thomas Dilkes*, and *John Norris*, Esq; first Captain to the Admiral of the Fleet; and of the *Dutch*, Admiral *Allemonde*, Vice-Admiral *Wassenaer*, Rear-Admiral *Vanderdussen*, and Rear-Admiral *de Ionge*; it was determined, since the Land-Forces from *Ireland* were not arrived, nor those which *Portugal* was to furnish in a Readiness, to put to Sea with about forty six, or forty eight Ships of the Line, *English* and *Dutch*, and to place them in such Station between Cape *Spartell* and the Bay of *Cadiz*, as might best prevent the Junction of the *French* Ships from *Thoulon* and *Brest*, until the Arrival of those from *Ireland*, but not to go into the *Streights* if it could possibly be avoided. *A Council of War held.* *Resolved to put to Sea with part of the Fleet.*

Five Days after another Council of War was held of the *English* Flag-Officers only, where it was agreed not to be adviseable to detach any Ships, in regard the Fleet was proceeding on Action, and that there was a Probability of the Junction of the Enemy's Ships of the *Ocean* and *Mediterranean*. *Agreed not to detach any Ships to Portugal.*

And now a Line of Battel was formed, which was composed of the following Strength, *viz.*

Rates.

	Rates.		Nº.	
Strength of the Line of Battel.	1	——	2	⎫
	2	——	4	⎬ *English.*
	3	——	22	⎭
	4	——	10	
	Of the Line	——	20	*Dutch.*

58 in all;
besides small Frigates, Fireships, Bomb-Vessels, Hospital-Ships, and other small Vessels.

Ships from Ireland join.   The 22d of *June* Sir *Cloudesly Shovell* getting out of the River of *Lisbon*, met with the Ships from *Ireland*, and the 24th a Frigate coming into the Fleet from *Gibraltar*, brought the Prince of *Hesse*, who was going to that Place, or to meet the Earl of *Peterborow* coming from thence with the Forces; and off of Cape *Spartell* the Fleet was to cruise until his Lordship arriv'd, with whom there were ten Ships from 50 Guns upwards, and some small Frigates.

King of Spain landed at Barcelona.   His Lordship coming on board the Fleet in *Altea* Bay, and his Catholick Majesty being desirous to land near *Barcelona*, since he thought himself assured of the Loyalty of the People of *Catalonia*, it was resolved to proceed thither with the first Opportunity of a Wind, and his Majesty with the Forces being landed there, it was judged necessary to attempt something of Moment, though with Hazard, for the Honour of the Queen's Arms, and the Service of the King.

Resolution upon some Questions of the Earl of Peterborow's.   The 24th of *August* the Earl of *Peterborow* desired, at a Council of War, to be informed whether, after eighteen Days, the Fleet could accompany the Army in any Enterprize on shore, and that if the Forces could be embarked in seven Days, the time would admit of their proceeding towards the Relief of the Duke of *Savoy*, and the Performance of Services recommended to them in *Italy*. Upon debating this Matter by the *English* and *Dutch* Flags, (his Lordship present) it was determined, that if it should be resolved to attack *Barcelona*, according to the King of *Spain*'s Letter of the 2d of *September*, N. S. all possible Assistance should be given therein by the Fleet, and that if the Troops marched towards *Tarragona*, it should attend them, and assist on any Enterprize. That if it was not found practicable to attempt *Barcelona*, otherwise than with apparent Ruin to the Army, and the Generals at Land should desire the Troops might embark, the Boats belonging to the Fleet should be employed in taking them from the Shore; and that when there was found but little Prospect of doing more Service in *Spain*, the Fleet might accompany the Troops as far as *Nice*, or thereabouts, provided they could embark in a Week's time.

On the 27th the Earl of *Peterborow* sent a Proposal, by Brigadier *Stanhope*, that a Number of Men might be landed from the Fleet, to assist in the Attempt against *Barcelona*, and it was determined by the Admiral, and the rest of the Flag-Officers, to land

CHAP. XVIII. *from the Year* 1698, *to* 1712. 687

two thousand five hundred Men, well arm'd, including those already *Agreed to* on shore, the doing whereof would reduce the Ships to their mid- *land Men* dle Complements, the *Dutch* Admiral agreeing also to assist with six *at Barcelona.* hundred Men: However, if the *French* Fleet approached, it was deemed necessary the said Men, as well as the Marine Soldiers, should immediately come on board again.

But considering the Winter Season was advancing, it was judged *Determined* too late for the Fleet to proceed to the Coast of *Italy*, insomuch *the Coast of* that it was determined to return towards *England* the first fair Wind *Italy.* after the 20th of *September*, yet since the Army had got Possession of *Mont Joui*, and all the Out-works, the Number of Men beforemention'd were put on shore, for the more speedy Reduction of *Barcelona*, and the Gunners, and Carpenters, desired by the Earl of *Peterborow*, were in a Readiness, when it might be thought necessary, to land them. It was also determined that eight Ships of War *Resolved to* should not only cannonade the Town, under the Command of Sir *land Men,* *Stafford Fairborn*, Vice-Admiral of the Red, but cover the Bomb- *nade Barce-* Vessels which were appointed to bombard it. Now although it had *lona.* been resolved some time before to be drawing homeward after the 20th of *September*, it was, on the 19th of that Month, agreed to remain before the Place with the Fleet, and to give all possible Assistance, since 'twas hoped it might in little time be reduced to Obedience; and Cannon, Powder, and Shot, were sent on shore for the Batteries, as well as for the Garrison of *Lerida*.

This important Place being reduced, it was, at a Council of War, *Barcelona re-* held the 1st of *October*, judged not to be convenient to continue *duced, and it* longer in the *Mediterranean*, since the Ships were in want of Pro- *ed to proceed* visions and Stores, which could not be had in those Parts, nor was *home with* there any Port for refitting them; wherefore it was resolved to ap- *the Fleet,* point fifteen *English* Ships of the Line, and ten *Dutch*, with Fri- *to appoint a* gates, Fireships, Bomb-Vessels, &c. for a Winter Squadron; and *a Winter* since the States-General were sending from *Holland* to *Lisbon* five *Squadron.* Ships of War, it was proposed that ten might be dispatched from *England*, which would make forty of the Line, that being judged sufficient until they could be strengthened towards the end of *April*.

A farther Quantity of Powder was put on shore from the *English* and *Dutch* Ships: with eight Brass Guns, carrying a six Pound Ball, and it was resolved that when the Ships design'd to continue abroad with Sir *John Leake* were reduced to seven Weeks Provisions at Short-Allowance, he should proceed to *Lisbon* to refit and victual them, and that two Fourth Rates, three Fifths, and one of the Sixth *Resolved to* should be left to follow the Orders of the Earl of *Peterborow*; *leave some* so that the whole were divided as follows. *the Earl of Peterborow.*

To proceed to *England* with Sir *Cloudesly Shovell*,

Rate.	Nº.
1	1
2	3

The manner how the Fleet was divided.

Rate.

Rate.	N°.
3	13
4	2
5	4
6	1
Bomb-Veffels	3
Firefhips	4
Yacht	1

To remain with Sir *John Leake*,

2	2
3	8
4	4
5	3
Bomb-Veffels	2
Firefhips	2
Hofpital	1
Yacht	1

With the Earl of *Peterborow*,

4	2
5	3
6	1

Left at *Gibraltar*.

6	2

To cruife for the *Brafil* Fleet.

3	1
4	1

Sir Cloudefly Shovell arrives at Spithead.

Accordingly Sir *Cloudefly Shovell* fail'd, and getting out of the *Streights* the 16th of *October*, appointed fome Ships to convoy the Trade home from *Lisbon*, himfelf arriving at *Spithead* the 26th of *November*.

CHAP. XIX.

Containing an Account of Sir John Leake's *Proceedings on the Coast of* Portugal, *and in the* Mediterranean, *(the Earl of* Peterborow *continuing still Admiral of the Fleet, and General of the Forces in* Spain*) and of the Relief of* Barcelona *when besieged by the* French : *As also of the yielding of* Carthagena *by the* Spaniards, *the taking of the Town and Castle of* Alicant, *and the Surrender of* Yviça *and* Majorca.

AFTER a tedious Passage of thirteen Weeks, Sir *John Leake* arrived in the River of *Lisbon* from the Coast of *Catalonia*, with one Second Rate, two Thirds, three Fourths, one Fifth, and a Fireship, having left the *Dutch* (for they had heavy Sailers among them) off of *Carthagena*, who were then reduced to two Pounds of Bread a Man a Week, of which they had not for above five Weeks, nor were our Ships much better provided; but off of Cape *St. Vincent* he met the *Pembroke*, *Roebuck*, and *Faulcon*, with a welcome Supply of Provisions from *England*.

The 16th of *February* a Council of War took into Consideration the Orders of the Lord High-Admiral, together with my Letters to Sir *John Leake*, of the 3d, 26th, and 31st of *December*, with an Account of the Enemy's Naval Preparations, and other Papers relating to the Disposition of the People of *Cadiz*, and to the Galleons which were going thence to the *Spanish West-Indies* ; and thereupon it was resolved to proceed directly to *Cadiz* with all the Ships then ready, *viz.* nine Third Rates, one Fourth, two Frigates, two Fireships, and one Bomb-Vessel of the *English*, and of the *Dutch*, six of the Line of Battel, one Frigate, two Fireships, and a Bomb ; and if they found the Galleons in the Bay, they were, if Wind and Weather would permit, to go directly in, and endeavour to take or destroy them. There were at this time some Ships of War and Transports expected with Forces from *England* for *Catalonia*, and it was determined, if they timely arrived, to take the former, and to leave the Transports at *Lisbon*, since it was not safe to send them up the *Streights* without a Convoy capable to protect them.

Three Days after another Council of War took into Consideration a Memorial of the King of *Portugal's* to the Lord-Ambassador Methuen, and the Minister of the States-General at *Lisbon*, as also the pressing Orders of the Lord High-Admiral for succouring *Barcelona*, whereupon it was determined to proceed according to the Resolutions of the former Council, and when that Service should be over, to appoint as many Ships as could be spared for the Security of the

Sir John Leake comes to Lisbon.

Provisions arrive from England.

170⅞.
A Council of War held,

and

resolved to attempt the Port of Cadiz.

A second Council of War agree to the Resolutions of the former.

Tttt *Portugal*

Portugal Brasil Fleet, and with the rest to repair to and remain at *Gibraltar*, until they should be join'd by the Ships and Transports expected from *England*.

Sir John Leake *under sail, but stopp'd by the Portuguese in the River of Lisbon.*

The 24th of *February* the *Dutch* Ships join'd ours in the Bay of *Wares*, and next Morning Sir *John Leake* got under Sail, but when he was near the Bar at the Entrance of the River of *Lisbon*, several Shot were fired at him from St. *Julian*'s Castle and some of the Forts, which obliged him to come to an Anchor; the Commanding Officer in the Castle acquainting him that he had Orders from the Duke of *Cadaval* not to suffer any Ship of War, or Merchant Ship to pass the Bar; so that, being thus delayed, he could not get out until next Morning.

The 27th he reached the length of the Cape St. *Vincent*, where he met the Wind Easterly, and towards Noon it fell calm, but then springing up Westerly, it veered not long after to the N. and N. by E.

He endeavours to intercept the Galleons from Cadiz.

which carry'd him by next Morning the length of Cape St. *Mary*'s, when it came to the N. E. and N. E. by E. with which he stood to the Southward, so as that he might lie in a fair way for intercepting the Galleons, should they get out before the Wind would permit his reaching *Cadiz*.

The same Night he received Advice, by a Letter from Vice-Admiral *Wassenaer*, that the Galleons and Flota sailed the 10th of *March*, N. S. in the Morning, with a hard Gale Easterly, and that they were in all about thirty five, or thirty six, of which ten or twelve of 40, 46, and some of 56 Guns, most of them Privateers, which were detained, by order of the *French* Court, to conduct them some part of their way. Sir *John* on this steer'd away S. W. by S. and S. W. all Night, though with little hopes of coming up with them, unless the Easterly Wind had left them when they got the length of the Cape St. *Vincent*. Next Morning he saw two Sail a head, the Wind being still fresh at E. N. E, and at six a Clock Vice-Admiral *Wassenaer* took one of them, as our Ship called the *Northumberland* did the other, they being *Spaniards* bound first to the *Canary Islands*, and thence to the *West-Indies*, and since they sailed from *Cadiz* the Day after the Galleons, it was judged to no purpose to follow them longer.

Sir John Leake *by being stopp'd by the Portuguese misses the Galleons.*

But here it is not improper to observe, that the same Day Sir *John* resolved to sail from *Lisbon* to *Cadiz*, he desired the Lord-Ambassador *Methuen* that an Embargo might be laid on all Ships and Vessels, that so no Advice might be given to the Enemy; and although what he thus desired was granted by the Court of *Portugal*, yet they suffered five to go over the Bar the next Day, two of which were supposed to be *Danes* bound up the *Streights*.

Advice of the Count of Thouloufe his being sailed to Barcelona.

The 19th of *March*, off of Cape *Spartell*, Sir *John Leake* spoke with an *English* Runner, nam'd the *Godolphin*, from *Genoa*, whose Master inform'd him, that the Count de *Thoulouse*, High-Admiral of *France*, sail'd the 23d of *April*, O. S. from *Thoulon*, with seventeen Ships of War for *Barcelona*, nine of which had three Decks, and that they had Forces on board; that Monsieur *Du Quesne* had been

CHAP. XIX. *from the Year* 1698, *to* 1712. 691

been there with nine others some time before, and that six more were daily expected to join them.

In the mean time, up the *Streights*, on this very Day, one of our Ships, the *Resolution*, of 70 Guns, commanded by Mr. *Mordaunt*, youngest Son to the Earl of *Peterborow*, falling in with six Ships of the Enemy near Cape *delle Melle*, in her Passage to *Genoa*, about Five in the Morning, some of which were mounted with 80 Guns, and others 70; they gave chase to her, whereupon Captain *Mordaunt* put his Ship before the Wind, hoping he should be able so to alter his Course in the Night as that the Enemy might not discover the same, but at six a Clock they had a fresh Gale of Wind Easterly, while at the same time he had but small Breezes, insomuch that they got within a League's Distance of him. Upon this the Earl of *Peterborow*, and his Catholick Majesty's Envoy to the Duke of *Savoy*, who were on board the *Resolution*, were, as they desired, removed into a small Frigate, named the *Enterprize*, in order to their being landed, if possible, at *Oneglia*.

The Resolution attack'd by some French Ships, and burnt by our own People.

About half an Hour after Nine, the *Milford*, a Ship of the Fifth Rate, which was also in Captain *Mordaunt*'s Company, stood away to the Northward, without being so much as followed by any of the Enemy's Ships, for they still made all the Sail they were able after the *Resolution*; at which time it beginning to blow very hard in Squalls, she was disabled in her Main-top-sail, and by that means the headmost of the *French* Ships got within Gun-shot of her.

About Twelve at Noon that Ship came up within Pistol-shot, making several Signals to the others which were in Sight, and by the Variety of Winds part of them were gotten somewhat to the Southward; whereupon Captain *Mordaunt* demanded the Opinion of his Officers, what was most proper to be done, who advised the running the Ship on shore on some part of the Territories of *Genoa*, rather than suffer her to be taken, and carried off by the Enemy.

Next Day, being the 20th, it was squally Weather, with the Wind almost round the Compass, and the Enemy continuing their Chase, there was but little hopes of escaping; however all possible care was taken to keep at as great a distance from them as might be, not but that one of their Ships of 70 Guns came, at Seven in the Morning, within Pistol-shot of the *Resolution*'s Larboard-Quarter, and there happen'd thereupon a sharp Engagement between them.

At eight a Clock the Land was so plainly seen, that the Town and Castle of *Vintimiglia*, about five Leagues to the Eastward of *Nice*, were discovered, and it was determined to make the best of their way to the said Place, in hopes of meeting Protection from the *Genoese*, but the Wind veering to the S. S. W. and the Enemy's Ship still continuing her Fire, and the rest of them outsailing the *Resolution*, they approach'd very near to her, insomuch that by ten a Clock two of their Ships of 70 Guns were within Gun-shot, and that of like force before-mentioned seldom out of the reach of a Shot from a Pistol, so that in an Hour's time after she received very much damage in her Masts, Sails, and Rigging.

Tttt 2 At

At Three in the Afternoon Captain *Mordaunt* ran her on shore on a sandy Bay close under the Castle of *Vintimiglia*, within a third of a Cable's length to the Land, and then one of the *French* Ships, which lay with her Broadside against her Stern, fired very smartly on her, as did the *Resolution*, in return, with all the Guns which could be brought to bear on her, insomuch that in an Hour and a half she tack'd, and lay by with her Head to the Southward within Gun-shot, the rest of the *French* Ships being at much the same Distance.

At half an Hour after Four Captain *Mordaunt* was carried on shore, having received a large Wound by a Cannon-shot in the back part of his right Thigh, and about Five several Signals were made by the *French* Commadore; on which all their Boats were mann'd, and sent to lay the *Resolution* on board, under the Protection of one of their Ships of 70 Guns, which made a continual Fire on the Approach of the Boats; but the warm Reception which they found constrained them to return to respective Ships.

On the 21st, about half an Hour past Six in the Morning, one of the Enemy's Ships of 80 Guns, weighing her Anchor, brought too under the *Resolution*'s Stern, and about nine a Clock, a Spring being put under her Cable, she lay with her Broadside towards her, while she at the same time looked with her Head right into the Shore, so that it was not possible to bring any more Guns to bear upon the *French* Ship than those of her Stern-Chase, and the others being within less than Gun-shot, and the Water coming into the *Resolution* as high as her Gun-Deck, Captain *Mordaunt* sent to his Officers for their Opinion what was fitting to be done, and, pursuant to their Advice, he gave them Directions to set her immediately on fire, which they did about eleven a Clock, after the Men were all put on shore, and by Three in the Afternoon she was burnt to the Water's Edge.

Earl of Peterborow orders the Fleet and Troops to the Coast of Valencia, but the great Ships to Barcelona.

On the 24th of *March* Sir *John Leake* received Orders from the Earl of *Peterborow*, who was then in *Valencia*, to come with the Fleet off of that Coast, and to send the small Frigates near to the Shore with the Men, Mony, Ammunition, and Artillery which were to be disembark'd, or else to land them at *Altea*, or *Denia*, that so he might repair with a Body of Horse to join them; and since there was a Squadron of twenty *French* Ships in *Barcelona* Road, his Lordship recommended it to him to proceed thither with the great Ships, and endeavour to attack and destroy them; but he receiving Advice the 19th of *April* that Sir *George Byng* was approaching him with twenty Ships from *England*, resolv'd to cruise off of *Altea* till he should be join'd by him, which was the next Day, and then it was determined not to stay for the Ships and Transports from *Ireland*, but to proceed to *Tarragona*; and if by the Scouts he sent for Intelligence, it should be found the *French* were in the Road of *Barcelona*, and not too strong, to give them Battel. It was determined to proceed Northward of *Majorca*, that so they might timely arrive to relieve the City, which they understood was in great danger, and that each Ship should make the best

Sir George Byng joins Sir John Leake.

Resolved to proceed to the Relief of Barcelona.

of

CHAP. XIX. *from the Year* 1698, *to* 1712. 693

of her way thither, without losing time by staying one for another; mean while the Earl of *Peterborow* came off to the Fleet with several Barks, on board of which were about fourteen hundred Land-Forces, and hoisted his Flag, as Admiral, on the *Prince George*, where Sir *John Leake* also bore his. Sir *George Byng* and Sir *John Jennings*, with several Ships which were the best Sailers, got into *Barcelona* Road on the 8th of *April*, in the Afternoon, some Hours sooner than the rest, who discovered the Rear of the *French* Fleet going thence in no little Disorder. *Earl of Peterborow hoists his Flag on board the Fleet. 1706. Sir George Byng and Sir John Jennings come first to Barcelona. French Ships retire, and our Forces put on shore.*

The Appearance of the *English* and *Dutch* Ships caused an exceeding Joy in the Inhabitants, and immediately the King sent off an Officer, desiring that the Land-Forces might be put on shore, for that he was in hourly Expectation the Enemy would make an Assault at the Breach, which was judged to be then practicable, so that all the Troops, together with the Marine Soldiers, were with all possible Diligence landed from the Fleet.

The *French* nevertheless continued their Attack on the 9th and the 10th, but the next Day their Fire abated very much; and great Numbers of Peasants and Miquelets coming down from the Mountains, they, with several Voluntiers from the City, endeavoured to dislodge the Enemy from the Post they had taken. These Skirmishes continued until Eleven at Night, and then the *French* fired two Guns from a Battery on an Hill, which proved to be the Signal for a general Retreat. The young Prince of *Hesse Darmstat*, who commanded at the Breach, sent out a Party to view the Fort *Mont Joui*, and to discover the Enemy's Mines; which they had the good Fortune to do just when the Matches were almost consumed, not but that one of them blew up some part of the Fort. *The French continued their Attacks. The French prepare to retreat from before the Town.*

The *French* set great part of their Magazines on fire, but the neighbouring Peasants saved some of them, as several Miquelets, and Soldiers, who sally'd out from the City, did a considerable Quantity of Powder, by timely putting out the lighted Matches; and these People at Break of Day, supported by some Horse, very much harrassed the Enemy's Rear, with whom they skirmished until Nine in the Morning, when a total Eclipse of the Sun held them both in Suspense for some time; but as soon as it was over, the *Catalans* fell on them with more Fury; mean while others went out of the Town to the Enemy's abandon'd Camp, where they found above a hundred Pieces of Brass Cannon, a great Number of Bombs and Granadoes, Powder, Cannon, and Musket-Balls, Lead, Spades, Shovels, and many other things, which in the Hurry and Confusion they were in they had left behind, and in the Camp were one hundred and fifty sick and wounded Men. *Set fire to their Magazines. The Miquelets, &c. harrass the French. An Eclipse of the Sun. The French leave many things in their Camp.*

This important Place being thus preserved, the Fleet sailed from thence the 18th of *May*, with all the Forces on board the Ships of War and Transports which could be spared from the Service of *Catalonia*, and arrived on the Coast of *Valencia* the 24th, where they were landed the next Day. *The Fleet arrives on the Coast of Valencia.*

On the 30th of the same Month, at the Instance of the Earl of *Peterborow*, a Council of War was called, where were present Sir *A Council of War held, and it was determined to attack Alicant.*

Sir *John* Leake, Sir *George* Byng, Sir *John* Jennings, and Captain *Price*; and of the *Dutch*, Vice-Admiral *Waſſenaer*, Captain *Moſſe*, and Captain *Somerſdike*, by whom it was reſolved to proceed to *Alicant*, but if the Town, upon Summons, refuſed to ſurrender, to repair to *Altea*, and remain there until they ſhould be join'd by the Bomb-Veſſels from *Gibraltar*, with the Ships of War expected from *England* and *Holland*, and that the Land-Forces arrived near *Alicant* to co-operate with the Fleet.

When they were the length of *Altea* two Gentlemen came off, who acquainted Sir *John* Leake that the People of *Carthagena* would, upon the Appearance of the Fleet, declare for King *Charles* the Third, but that Major-General *Mahoni* being gotten into *Alicant* with five hundred Horſe, it would require a formal Siege to reduce that Place. Hereupon he proceeded to *Carthagena*, and the *Spaniards* yielding, when they ſaw in what Condition we were to attack them, a Garriſon of ſix hundred Marines was put into the Place, under Major *Hedges*, who was appointed Governor, and Sir *John* Jennings was left to ſettle the Affairs of the City. Soon after Sir *John* Leake being informed that there was at *Altea* two Gallies going over to *Oran*, on the Coaſt of *Barbary*, with Mony to pay that Garriſon, he ordered the *Hampton-Court* and *Tyger* thither, upon the Appearance of which Ships they came off, and declared for King *Charles*.

Carthagena yields.

Two Spaniſh Gallies yield.

The Fleet arriving off of *Alicant* the 26th of *June* in the Afternoon, the Admiral ſent a Summons to the Garriſon, but was anſwer'd by *Mahoni*, that he was reſolved to defend it to the laſt Extremity, and that to enable him to do it, he had near one thouſand Horſe and Foot, beſides the Inhabitants, having turn'd out of the Place all the uſeleſs People.

Alicant ſummoned.

After remaining fourteen Days for the Troops in order to carry on the Siege, they were on the 10th of *July* within three Leagues of the Place, but in the whole they exceeded not one hundred and fifty *Spaniſh* Horſe, and thirteen hundred Foot. Brigadier *Gorge* commanded them, who was of opinion that not leſs than three thouſand were ſufficient for the intended Service, for he had not any Dependance on the two thouſand Militia; and it was now judged that there were not Forces ſufficient in *Spain* to aſſiſt the Duke of *Savoy*, they being in all not above two thouſand five hundred Foot; and (as the Earl of *Peterborow* repreſented) Affairs were much embarraſſed, by the King's reſolving to go to *Saragoſa*, inſtead of taking the readieſt way to *Madrid*.

Brigadier Gorge approaches Alicant with the Troops.

However, ſince it was determined to attack *Alicant*, all the Marines left at *Carthagena* were ſent for, my Lord *Peterborow* having appointed another Garriſon for that Place; and Brigadier *Gorge* marching from *Elche*, encamped the 21ſt within a Mile of the Town. The ſame Day, and the next Morning, all the Marines in the Fleet were landed, and eight hundred Seamen, and at Night the Town was bombarded.

Marines and Seamen landed, and Alicant bombarded.

Next Day at Noon Sir *George* Byng hoiſted his Flag on board the *Shrewsbury*, and with her, and four more Third Rates, anchored in

CHAP. XIX. *from the Year* 1698, *to* 1712.

in a Line so near to the Town, that they soon dismounted some of their Guns facing the Sea, which were above one hundred and sixty, and drove the Enemy from them.

The 24th Sir *John Jennings* arrived with the Ships from *Carthagena*, when the Marines he brought from thence were landed; and four Days after the Troops having, early in the Morning, made themselves Masters of the Suburbs, all the Boats being mann'd and arm'd, they repaired along the side of the *Shrewsbury*, to receive Orders for sustaining them, or to make an Attack on the Town. At Nine in the Morning the Ships had made a Breach in the round Tower at the West End of the Town, and another at the middle of the Curtain, between the Mole and the Eastermost Bastion, when the Land-Forces marching up towards the Wall of the City, fifteen Grenadiers with an Officer and Serjeant advancing, without order so to do, to the Breach at the round Tower, all the Boats under Command of Sir *John Jennings* went directly to sustain them, but e'er the Men landed, the Grenadiers were beaten back. However the Boats proceeded, and all the Men getting on shore, Captain *Evans* of the *Royal Oak* mounting the Breach first, got into the Town with two or three of the Boat's Crews; Captain *Passenger* of the *Royal Anne* followed, and next to him Captain *Watkins* of the *St. George*, with some Seamen. Sir *John Jennings*, with the rest of the Seamen and Forces who were in Possession of the Suburbs, mov'd on to support them, who coming into the Town, secur'd the Posts, and made proper Dispositions until the rest got in, when *Mahoni* retiring into the Castle, left them in Possession, with the Loss of but very few Men; but Colonel *Petit* was kill'd in the Suburbs, when standing Arm in Arm with Sir *John Jennings*, by a small Shot out of a Window, as they were viewing the Ground for raising a Battery against the Wall of the Town, besides whom there were not above thirty killed, either of the Sea or Land, and not more than eighty wounded, notwithstanding the *Spaniards* had a continued Communication from one House to another, and fired on our Men from the Windows, and Holes made for that purpose.

Next Day Brigadier *Gorge* sent a Summons to the Castle, but *Mahoni* answer'd, he was resolved to defend it to the last, although our Ships had then dismounted all their Cannon towards the Sea, beat down part of the Wall, and that the Shells thrown from the Bombs annoy'd them very much. Notwithstanding this Resolution of *Mahoni*, the Castle surrender'd the 25th of *August*, though it might have held out longer; but great part of the People who were in it being *Neapolitans*, and many of them Officers, they obliged the Governor to yield; for by a continued cannonading from the Ships, as well as from the Batteries, and by the *Coehorn* Mortars, which play'd on them both Day and Night, they had but little time to rest, and a considerable Number of Men were kill'd and wounded.

The 29th of *August* there was Intelligence that the *French* were beaten in *Italy*, and the Siege of *Turin* rais'd, so that it was resolved to proceed to *Altea* to take in Water, and to send the Transports to *England* with four Ships of the Third Rate, not in a Condition

Sir George Byng drives the Spaniards from their Guns.

Sir John Jennings arrives with the Marines from Carthagena. The Suburbs taken.

The Boats with Sir John Jennings sustain the Land-Forces. Some Officers and Seamen mount the Breach.

The Town taken, and Mahoni retires to the Castle. Colonel Petit killed.

Brigadier Gorge summons the Castle.

The Castle surrenders.

Advice that the Siege of Turin was raised.

dition to stay abroad, and the next Day the *Dutch* Admiral detach'd for *Holland*, by order of the States-General, six Ships of the Line, and soon after two more to *Lisbon*.

Some Dutch Ships sent home.

The 2d of *September* the Fleet came to *Altea* Bay, being one First Rate, two Seconds, twelve Thirds, one Fourth, and three Fireships of the *English*, and of the *Dutch* ten of the Line, which Day Sir *John Jennings* sail'd to *Lisbon* with six Third Rates, four Fourths, two Fifths, and a Fireship, there to refit and victual them for their intended Voyage to the *West-Indies*; and the Earl of *Peterborow* gave Orders to Sir *John Leake* to repair to *England*, leaving Sir *George Byng* to command the Winter Squadron, but first to proceed to *Yviça* and *Majorca*, and oblige those two Islands to submit.

Sir John Jennings proceeds with a Squadron design'd for the West-Indies to Lisbon. Sir John Leake order'd home, and Sir George Byng to remain abroad. Yviça surrender'd to Sir John Leake, and Majorca.

He sailing from *Altea* the 6th of *September*, came before *Yviça* the 9th, the Governor of which Island saluted him before he anchored, and sent Deputies to tender his Obedience. Five Days after he came to *Majorca*, but the Vice-Roy, and others in the Interest of the Duke of *Anjou*, declared, upon being summoned, that they would defend it to the last Extremity; however, when two *Dutch* Bomb-Vessels came near to the Town of *Palma*, the Capital of the Island, and had thrown in two or three Shells, the Inhabitants obliged the Vice-Roy to retire to the Palace, and to desire a Capitulation; but this Island, with several Places which had been taken from the *Spaniards*, was restored to King *Philip*, upon the ensuing Peace, the Crown of *England* keeping Possession only of *Minorca* and *Gibraltar*.

Sir *John Leake* leaving a Garrison of one hundred Marines, with a Captain and Lieutenant, to secure the Castle of *Porto Pin*, and two Ships to bring away the Vice-Roy, and disaffected Persons, he sailed from thence the 23d, and being off of *Alicant*, he received Orders from the Lord High-Admiral for his leaving all the Ships in a Condition to remain abroad under Command of Sir *George Byng*, and to repair home with the rest; pursuant to which he got through the *Streights* the 2d of *October* with the *Prince George*, a Ship of the Second Rate, the *Royal Oak*, *Hampton-Court*, *Dorsetshire*, and *Grafton*, of the Third, and a Fireship, with six *Dutch* Ships under Command of Admiral *Wassenaer*, some Days after which he was separated from them by a severe Storm, but arrived at *St. Helen's* the 17th of *October*, where he struck his Flag, which was that of Admiral of the White; but before he left the *Spanish* Coast, his Catholick Majesty was pleas'd, by Letter, to acknowledge the Zeal he had shewn for his Service, and to return him Thanks in a very obliging manner.

Sir John Leake arives in England.

The Orders he left with Sir *George Byng* were as follows, *viz.* to take under his Command one First Rate, one Second, ten Thirds, four Fourths, one Fifth, one Sixth, and two Fireships, and when he should make the Signal, to repair with them to *Lisbon*, where having clean'd, and refitted them, he was to appoint them to cruise in such Stations as that they might be most capable of annoying the Enemy, and of guarding the Coast of *Portugal*, according to the Treaty with that Prince, but nevertheless to have them all in Readiness

Sir John Leake's Instructions to Sir George Byng.

dineſs to proceed on any Service, with the Squadron of *Dutch* Ships which were to join him from *Holland.* If the Earl of *Peterborow* ſhould deſire it, and he had no particular Orders from the Queen, or the Lord High-Admiral to put in Execution, he was either to proceed with a part, or the whole Squadron to the Coaſt of *Spain,* and to that of *Catalonia,* if the ſame ſhould be thought adviſeable by a Council of War; and if the Miniſters of *England* and *Holland* at *Lisbon,* or the Earl of *Gallway* ſhould deſire it, he was to aſſiſt any of the Garriſons on the Sea-Coaſt not in Poſſeſſion of the Enemy, and to ſend Men, Ammunition, or Mony to them; and from time to time to ſupply the Garriſon at *Gibraltar* with what they might ſtand in need of.

Here we will leave Sir *George Byng,* until ſome Account is given of what happen'd in the *Weſt-Indies,* not only during Sir *John Jennings's* commanding in thoſe Parts, but even before his Arrival there, when Rear-Admiral *Whetſtone,* and, after him, Commadore *Kerr,* were at the Head of Squadrons at *Jamaica.*

CHAP. XX.

Containing an Account of Sir William *Whetſtone's Proceedings in the* Weſt-Indies; *with what happened afterwards while Commadore* Kerr, *Sir* John Jennings, *and Mr.* Wager *commanded in thoſe Parts, and particularly of the taking a Galleon, and other Ships by the latter; as alſo of the taking another Galleon, and ſeveral* French *Ships with Mr.* Littleton.

SIR *William Whetſtone* in his Paſſage from *England* arrived at the *Maderas* the 2d of *April* with one Ship of the Third Rate, four of the Fourth, and two of the Fifth, where taking in a Supply of Wine for the Men, (as is uſually done on ſuch Voyages, and of abſolute Neceſſity to preſerve their Healths) he proceeded on, and ſaw the Merchant Ships in Safety firſt to *Barbadoes,* then to the *Leeward-Iſlands,* and with the reſt repair'd to *Jamaica,* where he arrived the 17th of *May.* Having Intelligence that ſome *French* Ships were on the Coaſt of *Hiſpaniola,* he made all poſſible Diſpatch in getting the Squadron in a Readineſs to proceed to Sea, that ſo he might endeavour to intercept others which were coming from *Carthagena* and *Porto Bello.* The 6th of *June* he ſail'd, leaving thoſe at *Jamaica* which were to return to *England* with the Trade, and the 13th making the High-land of *Carthagena,* he came to an Anchor the next Day, but for Intelligence, kept two Frigates cruiſing to Windward. The 17th he chaſed a Ship that was

1705.

Sir William Whetſtone comes off of Carthagena.

discovered at a considerable Distance, which in the Night ran in among the *Sambay* Keys, where were very uncertain Soundings, and Shoal Water, insomuch that the *Bristol*, a Ship of 50 Guns, came on Ground, but was gotten off with little or no Damage; however, they came up with the *French* Ship, and after two Hours Dispute with those that were nearest to her, she submitted. She had 46 Guns mounted, and carried out with her three hundred and seventy Men, but bury'd all but one hundred and fifty, unless it were a few they had put into Prizes. She brought six hundred and forty Negroes from *Guinea*, of which two hundred and forty died, and most of the rest were set on shore at *Martinica*, the Island of St. *Thomas*, and *Santa Martha*, for they had heard that a Squadron of *English* Ships was in the *West-Indies*.

A French Ship of 46 Guns taken.

The Rear-Admiral plying to the Eastward, discover'd off of the Rivet *Grande* two Sail close in with the Land, one of which being forced on shore, was burnt by her own Men, being a Privateer fitted out at *Martinica* to disturb our Trade. The Coast being thus alarm'd, and no Prospect of any immediate Service, he returned to *Jamaica*, but appointed three of the best Sailers to cruise twenty Days off of *Anigada*, in the Windward Passage, for the *French* in their return home, it being the usual time for them to go from *Petit-Guavas*, *Port de Paix*, and other Places, but those Ships joined him again without any Success.

A French Privateer burnt.

Sir William Whetstone returns to Jamaica.

About the beginning of *August* he sent the *Mountague* and *Hector*, which were clean'd just before, to cruise between *Porto Bello* and *Carthagena*, for a rich Ship expected about that time to be in her Passage to Port *Louis*, which two Frigates took a *French* Ship of 24 Guns, bound to Cape *François*, with Sugar, Indigo, and between four and five thousand Hides.

A Ship of 24 Guns taken.

As it is usual for the Galleons, when they are to lade any considerable Quantity of Plate, to touch at some of the Windward Ports first, and then repair to *La Vera Cruz*, there to take in their Wealth, and about the Months of *March* or *April* to sail to the *Havana* for Water, and Refreshments, and thence to proceed home; so the most probable way for intercepting them is by a Squadron's cruising in the Bay of *Campeche*; but should they meet with Success, they must return to *England* through the Gulph of *Florida*, because it is very difficult to turn up to *Jamaica*, when they are so far to Leeward; not that the Rear-Admiral was strong enough to do this, even tho' he had left that Island, (which he was directed to have a particular Eye to) without any Guard by Sea.

The most probable way of intercepting the Galleons when returning home.

The 16th of *August* he sailed from *Jamaica* with the *Suffolk*, *Bristol*, and *Folkston*, together with the *Reserve*, which Ship he sent soon after to cruise on the North side of that Island. The 19th he got fair up with *Hispaniola*, and at Six in the Evening the Wind was at N. N. E. which shifted soon after to the S. S. E. with much Wind and Rain, so that most of the Ships were disabled in their Masts, Sails, and Rigging, and in such a Condition some of them were, especially that Ship where he bore the Flag, by the Weight of Water which made its way into them, that they were in the greatest danger

The Rear-Admiral comes off of Hispaniola, but much disabled by bad Weather, he returns to Jamaica.

CHAP. XX. *from the Year* 1698, *to* 1712. 699

danger of being founder'd; however, in this lamentable Case, they had the good Fortune to reach *Jamaica*, where they continued a considerable time before they could be put in a Condition for farther Service.

The *Mountague*, a Ship of 60 Guns, some time after met with on the Coast of *Hispaniola*, one of 48, and another of 36, both loaden, and bound to *France*, which after engaging about an Hour, and Night coming on, she lost sight of, but saw them fairly next Morning. The Officers were not then willing to renew the Fight, nor were the Seamen less backward, so that the Enemy slipt through their Fingers, of which the Commander complaining to the Flag, the Officers were dismissed, and his Conduct being examin'd into at a Court-Martial, he was honourably acquitted, it plainly appearing that neither his Officers nor Men had any Inclination to stand by him. *The Mountague engaging two French Ships, they escape.*

The Rear-Admiral, however, thought it proper to send two Fourth Rates in quest of these Ships that had escaped the *Mountague*, which meeting them, with Merchant Ships in their Company, they were so intent on seizing the latter, that they gave Opportunity to the others to escape, so that they only brought in five; but the Senior Captain, who had of Course the Command, was broke for his ill Conduct by a Court-Martial. *Some of our Ships meeting the aforesaid two Ships, take the Merchants, and let them escape.*

At this time there was a great want of Stores and Provisions in the Squadron, nor could the Island of *Jamaica* furnish what was necessary; in Addition to which Misfortune there happen'd another, for (by what Accident was not known) the *Suffolk*, where Rear-Admiral *Whetstone*'s Flag was flying, happen'd to blow up in the Gun-room, and as most of the Men there were kill'd, so were seventy more burnt to that degree in their Hammocks between the Gun-Decks, that most of them died soon after; and had the Ports been open when this unhappy Accident happen'd, the Ship must have run the greatest Hazard of being destroyed. *The Rear-Admiral's Ship blows up in the Gun-room.*

The Flag had an Account of no more than five *French* Ships at *Martinica*, which had some time before plunder'd the South side of St. *Christopher*'s, four of them from 66 to 50 Guns, and one of 32; besides which they had several Sloops; and towards the latter end of *March* he stretched over again to the Coast of *Hispaniola*, taking with him a Sloop, appointed by the Governor of *Jamaica* to carry the King of *Spain*'s Declarations to the Commander in Chief at *Carthagena*, in which Port the *Spanish* Galleons were arrived ten Days before he came on the Coast, but not being able to do any Service there, he return'd: And it is somewhat remarkable that this Year the *Barlovento* Ships, four in Number, went away from *La Vera Cruz* in *December*, which was sooner than had been known before, and arrived at *Puerto Rico* in *February*. 1705.

In the beginning of *June* the Rear-Admiral had Advice that some French Ships were at *Petit-Guavas*, three or four of them Men of War, and that they were to be join'd by the like Number from Cape *François*, whereupon he immediately put to Sea with one Ship of the Third Rate, two of the Fourth, two of the Fifth, and a Fire-ship, *Advice of some French Ships, and Sir William Whetstone goes to Sea.* 1706.

Uuuu 2

ship, in hopes of attacking them before they could join, but a strong Lee Current frustrated his Design; nor was it long e'er he heard that Monsieur *Du Casse* was gone to *Carthagena* with eight stout Ships of War, and that he was design'd from thence to *Porto Bello*, and afterwards (as was given out) for *La Vera Cruz*; besides, it was reported, that those to Windward would go to the *Havana*, and stay there until Monsieur *Du Casse* joined them from *La Vera Cruz*, so that they would then be in all sixteen.

Advice of Monsieur Du Casse, &c.

The 7th of *July*, pursuant to Orders from the Lord High-Admiral, he sent the *Mountague* and *Folkston* to *Newfoundland*, there to join other Ships which might be expected from *England*, and the 25th of the same Month Commadore *Kerr* arrived at *Jamaica*, upon which a Council of War was call'd, where it was agreed to send those Frigates back to *Barbadoes* and the *Leeward-Islands*, which he had brought from thence upon notice that *Jamaica* was in danger. The Ships that came from *England* with Mr. *Kerr* were one of the Third Rate, five of the Fourth, two of the Fifth, two Sixth Rates, and a Fireship; and Sir *William Whetstone* having Advice that some of the Enemy's Ships and Galleons were at *Carthagena*, it was resolved to proceed thither, pursuant to the Instructions of the High-Admiral, which required their acting together if they found any Prospect of doing Service.

Commadore Kerr arrives at Jamaica.

Rear-Admiral *Whetstone* and Captain *Kerr* sailed from *Jamaica* the 8th of *August*, and coming before the Harbour of *Carthagena* the 18th, a Letter was sent to the Governor of the Place, with some printed Papers, declaring the Success of Her Majesty's Arms, in Conjunction with those of Her Allies, and inviting him to submit to King *Charles* his lawful Prince; to which he made evasive Answers and withal told them, that he knew no other King than *Philip* his rightful Sovereign. In the Port there were fourteen Galleons, all lying close in with the Town, and unrigg'd, and as the *Spaniards* would not suffer any Ships to enter there, or at *Porto Bello*, so did not the Pilots in the Squadron think it proper to force a Passage, by reason of the Narrowness of the Port, and the Shoals, unless we were first in Possession of *Bocca Chica* Castle, and the other Forts, since there was no turning in for Ships of such Draught of Water; wherefore Sir *William Whetstone* returning to *Jamaica*, he, when the Trade was ready, made the best of his way from thence to *England*, where he arrived the 23d of *December*, having left Mr. *Kerr* to command the Ships design'd for farther Service at the aforesaid Island; and of what happen'd during his being there, as well as in his Passage thither, I shall in the next Place give an Account.

The Squadron comes before Carthagena,

but

judged not practicable to attempt the Galleons there.

Sir William Whetstone sails for England, and leaves Mr. Kerr at Jamaica.

In his Voyage from *England* he saw the Trade bound to *Virginia*, and *Newfoundland*, about one hundred Leagues into the Sea, and calling at *Barbadoes*, and the *Leeward Islands*, (at the latter whereof the *French* had some little time before done considerable Mischief, by landing Men from their Ships, and Sloops, and carrying off great Numbers of *Negroes*) it was resolved that his Squadron (which was one Third Rate, five Fourths, two Fifths, one Sixth, and a Fireship) should be re-inforced by the two Fourth Rates attending

Commadore Kerr's Proceedings before he joined Sir William Whetstone at Jamaica.

CHAP. XX. *from the Year* 1698, *to* 1712.

ing on *Barbadoes*, and the Fifth Rate Frigate at the *Leeward-Islands*, which were to be returned to their Stations as soon as they could be spared; for it was now judged that the *French* were gone to *Jamaica*, and that those Squadrons commanded by Monsieurs *Chabrenac* and *D'Iberville*, were to be join'd by another with Monsieur *Du Casse*, who, as it was reported, was first to touch at the Island of *Tabago*, lying almost as far to the Eastward as *Barbadoes*, in about 11^d and 16^m Latitude.

Stretching over from *Jamaica* to the Coast of *Hispaniola*, he appointed the Isle of *Ashe* for his Rendezvous, which is on the South West Coast of *Hispaniola*, just within which the *French* have a great Settlement call'd Port *Louis*, and thence plying over to *Terra Firma* to the Bay of *Gayra*, there the Squadron wooded and water'd, and the Men were refresh'd, whence departing the 4th of *September* for his aforesaid Rendezvous, the Isle of *Ashe*, the Winds hanging Northerly, he was forced to Leeward, and making the West End of *Hispaniola*, he held a Council of War, to consider whether it was practicable to attempt Port *Louis* by Surprize before they sailed to *Petit-Guavas*, but the Pilots not being well acquainted with the Entrance into the Port, it was determined forthwith to proceed to the latter Place, and to go to the Northward of the Island *Guanava*, the better to carry on the Design without being discover'd. *Not thought practicable to attempt Port Louis.*

The 13th of *September* he gave Orders to Captain *Boyce* to proceed with a small Frigate called the *Dunkirk-Prize*, and the Boats of the Squadron, mann'd and arm'd, and to range in the Night along the Bays of *Logane* and *Petit-Guavas*, with all possible Care and Secrecy, and so to dispose of them as that they might destroy the Enemy's Ships in either of those Roads, and to return to the Squadron next Morning upon the Signal which should be made. But if he got notice at *Logane* that there were any Number of *French* Ships at *Petit-Guavas*, he was, without proceeding farther, to come off and join the Commadore. On this Service the Frigate and Boats proceeded, but some of them straggling from the rest, alarm'd the Coast, so that the Attempt was render'd impracticable. *Capt. Boyce sent with Boats to destroy Ships at Logane and Petit-Guavas. They fail in the Attempt.*

There was such a Mortality among the Men belonging to the Ships, that for a considerable time the whole Squadron lay at *Jamaica* altogether useless; and on the 2d of *January* Sir *John Jennings* arrived with the Ships detached from the *Streights*, of whose Proceedings thither, and while he was in those Parts, I come now to give an Account. *Sir John Jennings arrives at Jamaica.*

As it hath been already said, he was directed to repair to *Lisbon* to refit and victual his Squadron, and although he was much interrupted therein by bad Weather, yet he sail'd from thence the 15th of *October*, but contrary Winds preventing his reaching the *Madeiras*, he bore away for *Teneriffe*, one of the *Canary* Islands, and stood close in to the Bay of *Santa Cruz* the 27th, where he discover'd five Ships near to the Fortifications. Some of the smaller Frigates were sent in to endeavour, by their Boats, to cut their Cables, and turn them on shore, but the *French* and *Spaniards* fired so hotly from the Platforms they had rais'd, that it was not practicable to make *Endeavour'd in his Passage to destroy some Ships at Santa Cruz.*

make any Attempt with the Boats, without laying some Ships so as that their Broadsides might batter the Forts; so that proceeding towards the Cape *Verde* Islands, he arrived the 4th of *November* at St. *Jago*, the chief of them, where he water'd the Ships, and supplied them with fresh Provisions, which he purchased by the Consent of the *Portuguese* Governor.

Sir John Jennings *comes to Barbadoes, and the* Leeward-Islands, *and* Jamaica, *as aforesaid.*

From thence he sail'd the 12th, and arrived in *Carlisle* Bay at *Barbadoes* the 29th, where he stay'd until the 5th of *December*, having put on shore the Guns and Ordnance-Stores appointed for the better Security of that Colony, as he did at the *Leeward-Islands*, when he arrived there.

On his Arrival at *Monserat*, he ordered the *Mary, Roebuck*, and *Faulcon* to run down the *Spanish* Coast, as low as *Carthagena*, to gain Intelligence in what Port the Galleons were, and then to join him at *Jamaica*; and he having touched at other of the *Leeward-Islands*; and sent some of the Ships of his Squadron to the rest, with the necessary Supplies, he arrived at *Jamaica* the 2d of *January*, as is before-mention'd. There he found Commadore *Kerr*'s Pendant of Distinction flying in the *Sunderland*, a Ship of the Fourth Rate, the rest of his Squadron, *viz.* the *Breda, Windsor*, and *Assistance*, being in the Harbour refitting, having buried a great many Men, but by the Assistance of General *Handasyde*, Governor of the Island, who furnished as many Soldiers as could be spared, he got the three first in a Condition for Service, and by the said Governor was informed, that, according to the last Advices he had received, the Galleons were still at *Carthagena*, all unrigg'd, having no part of their Loading on board, and that in all Probability they would not be ready to sail in less than nine Months.

Sir John Jennings *sends a Letter to the Governor of* Carthagena, *with an Account of our Success in Spain.*

By one of his Ships, the *Mary*, he sent a Letter to the Governor of *Carthagena*, letting him know that the Queen his Mistress having espoused the Interest of *Charles* the Third of *Spain*, had by her own Arms, and those of her Allies, reduced the greatest part of that Kingdom, and thereby redeem'd them from the intended Slavery of the *French*. That he was order'd into those Parts by Her Majesty, with the Concurrence of the Catholick King, to assure all his Subjects there of Her Majesty's Friendship and Protection;

Offers to conduct the Galleons to Spain.

and that if the General of the Galleons should think fit to accept of the Offer, he was directed to yield them all possible Assistance, and to see them in Safety to *Spain*, for that, in all likelihood, not only *Cadiz*, but *Sevil*, and St. *Lucar*, had declared for the King, and that a powerful Strength, both by Sea and Land, was going from *England* to countenance his Affairs. To this he desired an Answer with all convenient Speed, and particularly to be informed whether he might be permitted to enter the Port, having with his Letter transmitted to the Governor several of the King's Declarations, and some printed Papers of News.

The Governor receiv'd a contradictory Account.

The Governor answer'd him thus. That as to the News, it was entirely contradicted by a *Spanish* Advice-Boat, which arrived in forty Days from *Cadiz*, and brought him not only Orders from his Master, King *Philip*, but an Account that he was return'd to his

Court

CHAP. XX. *from the Year* 1698, *to* 1712.   703

Court at *Madrid*, had regain'd all those Towns which were in Possession of his Enemies, and totally routed them, so that himself, and the General of the Galleons, would shed the last Drop of their Blood in his Service.

The 15th of *January* it was determined at a Council of War to proceed with all the Ships, except the *Northumberland*, of the Third Rate, disabled by the Sickness of her Men, to the Bay of *Carthagena*, that so the Admiral might know the final Resolution of the Governor of that Place, and the aforesaid General of the Galleons. There he arrived the 24th of the same Month, but both the one and the other adhering to their former Resolutions, he departed thence, and coming into *Blewfields* Bay, at *Jamaica*, caused the Squadron to be water'd and fitted in the best manner that could be, whence sailing the 25th of *February*, he got through the Gulph of *Florida*, and with a prosperous Wind arrived at *Spithead* the 22d of *April*.

Sir John Jennings arrives at Carthagena, but returns to Jamaica, and to England.

1705.

Commadore *Kerr* being left at *Jamaica*, he gain'd Intelligence by Letters taken in a Prize, that a strong Squadron was expected in those Parts from *France*, under Command of Monsieurs *Cotlongon* and *Du Casse*, to convoy home the Galleons, but that as yet they were in no Readiness to accompany them; and a Supply of Provisions coming to *Jamaica* from hence, the Commadore sail'd the latter end of *November* for *England*; who being succeeded in the *West-Indies* by Mr. *Wager*, I shall in the next Place give an Account of his Proceedings there from the time he sailed from hence, and then return to Sir *George Byng*, who (as hath been said before) was left with a Squadron on the Coast of *Portugal*, and after that treat of Transactions at home, that so the several Services may appear as entire together as it is possible.

Commadore Kerr succeeded by Mr. Wager in the West-Indies.

Commadore *Wager* sailed with the Squadron under his Command, which consisted of one Third Rate, four Fourths, two Fifths, and a Fireship, and came to the *Maderas* the 26th of *April*, where taking in Wine for the Men, he departed from thence the 5th of *June*, and arrived at *Antegoa* the 9th, whence sailing next Morning, he water'd the Ships at *Monserat* the 11th, and came the Day following to *Nevis*.

Mr. Wager proceeds towards Jamaica.

1707.

Departing from that Island, he proceeded to *Jamaica*, where he found Commadore *Kerr*, whose Orders he was to observe during their Stay there together, which was not to be more than two or three Days after the 24th of *August*; and at this time there was not any Intelligence of the Enemy's Squadrons in those Parts, but their Privateers had done so much damage to our Trade, that the Loss was esteem'd to be Ten thousand Pounds.

The Privateers in the West-Indies much damage our Trade.

The 28th of *August* Mr. *Wager* called a Council of War, and it was agreed that for the Security of the Island of *Jamaica*, one Ship should be left in *Port Royal* Harbour, and another cruise on the East part of it; that two Frigates should be employed six Weeks, or two Months, or longer, if he thought fit, upon the Coast of *Carthagena* and *Porto Bello*, against the Enemy's Privateers there; and that the rest of the Ships, (for Mr. *Kerr* was then sail'd for *England*)

A Council of War held.

land) viz. the *Expedition, Windsor, Kingston, Portland, Assistance*, and *Dunkirk's Prize*, should proceed to Windward, and cruise six Weeks, or two Months upon the Coast of *Hispaniola*, and in the Windward Passage, but that if he received Advice of a *French* Squadron in those Parts, or of the sailing of the Galleons from *Carthagena*, it should be considered at a Council of War what farther Measures to take.

He was much hinder'd by the Rains in getting the Ships ready to proceed according to this Resolution, but on the 28th of *November* he sailed, and sent the *Severn* and *Dunkirk's Prize* a-head of him, to discover the Posture of the Galleons, and to gain Intelligence. Those Ships joining him the 5th of *December*, gave him an Account that the Galleons were not in a Readiness to sail; but by Letters found in a Sloop, taken in her Passage from *Porto Bello* to *Carthagena*, he understood that Monsieur *Du Casse* was come with a Squadron to *Martinica*, with a Design of convoying the Flota and Galleons from the *Havana*, which Squadron was much stronger than that under his Command.

Mr. Wager has an Account of Monsieur Du Casse.

Being the 10th of *December* off of *Carthagena*, he received a Letter by a Sloop from Brigadier *Handasyde*, Governor of *Jamaica*, with one enclosed to him from Colonel *Parkes*, who presided at the *Leeward-Islands*, dated the 18th of *November*, informing him that on the 11th of that Month Monsieur *Du Casse* arrived at *Martinica*, with ten Ships of War, eight of them from 70 to 86 Guns, and several large Privateers, and that they expected eighteen more. This Colonel *Parkes* believ'd too great a Strength, they having Land-Forces on board, to be design'd against the *Leeward-Islands*, and therefore dispatched notice of it to *Barbadoes*, and *Jamaica*, that they might be timely upon their Guard.

Farther Account of Monsieur Du Casse.

That very Night he left the *Spanish* Coast, and stood over for *Jamaica*, where arriving the 22d, he examin'd three Persons that had made their Escape from *Petit-Guavas*, who assured him it was generally reported that Monsieur *Du Casse* was at Port *Louis* with twenty Ships, so that apprehending they would attempt *Jamaica*, it was determined to place our Squadron at the Entrance of Port *Royal* Harbour, in such a manner as that, with the Assistance of the Fort, they might be able to give them a warm Reception; but other Prisoners, who came from St. *Domingo*, informed him that they had heard nothing of this *French* Squadron, although they had had the Liberty of walking the Streets, and conversing with the People of that Place.

By a Sloop sent to the Coast of *Hispaniola*, which took another off of Port *Louis*, he had an Account the 16th of *January* from the Prisoners, that Monsieur *Du Casse* stay'd but eight Days there, and then sail'd to the *Havana* (which was on the 19th or 20th of *December*) with nine Ships of War, the biggest mounted with 66, and the least with 50 Guns, together with a Fireship, in order to convoy the Flota and Galleons from thence, and that to hasten them he had sent a Ship of 50 Guns before him.

Advice of Monsieur Du Casse his being at Havana.

The

CHAP. XX. *from the Year* 1698, *to* 1712. 705

The Merchants at *Jamaica* (who were pretty well acquainted *The Merchant's Opinion about the Galleons.*
with the Affairs of the *Spaniards*) were of Opinion that the Galleons could not be at the *Havana* before *May*, but that if those they call the *Spanish* Men of War (which were four) should be hasten'd away with the King's Mony, and leave the Galleons behind, they might be there a Month sooner at least: Nor did they believe the Flota from *La Vera Cruz* could arrive before *April* or *May*, though there was a Probability the *French* Squadron might quicken both one and the other.

Receiving Advice, some time after this, that the *Spanish* Galleons were gone to *Porto Bello*, he sailed the 16th of *February*, and coming to the Isle of *Pines*, remain'd there until the 24th of *March*, during which time he received two Letters from Captain *Pudner* of the *Severn*, who was with our trading Sloops near *Porto Bello*, giving him an Account that the Galleons would not sail before *May*; and considering that his Provisions would be very short by that time, it was resolved at a Council of War to return to *Jamaica*, where he arriv'd the 5th of *April*, and another Council being call'd the 13th of that Month, it was judged not practicable to attempt the Ships in the Harbour of *Porto Bello*, by reason ours were inferior in Strength, so that it was resolved to proceed over to the *Spanish* *Resolved to proceed in quest of the Galleons.* Coast, and watch their Motion; but as our Ships could not lay there undiscover'd, it was thought most proper to endeavour to prevent their coming out of the Port; and at this time the Commadore expected to be join'd by the *Assistance*, *Scarborough*, and *Dunkirk's Prize* from *Hispaniola*.

The 23d of *May* he received a Letter from Captain *Pudner*, then *Captain Pudner sends an Account of the Galleons.* at the *Bastamentos*, that the Galleons, and other Vessels, in all thirteen, were the 19th of that Month under Sail off of that Place, in their way to *Carthagena*, which appearing not in three Days, though the Winds had hung Westerly, Mr. *Wager* suspected they had notice he was on the Coast, and were gone for the *Havana*: But the 28th at Noon there were discover'd from his Top-mast Head *Mr. Wager discovers the Galleons, and chases them.* seventeen Ships, the same he look'd for, and they considering his small Strength, (for then he had with him no more than the *Expedition*, *Kingston*, *Portland*, and *Vulture* Fireship) were resolved to push their way.

To these Ships, which bore South, and S. by W. from him, he gave Chase, with fair Weather, and very little Wind at S. S. E. and the same Evening discover'd them to be really the Galleons from *Porto Bello*, which did not endeavour to get from him, but finding they could not Weather the *Baru*, a small Island, so as to stand in for *Carthagena*, they stretched to the Northward with an easy Sail, and drew into an irregular Line of Battel, the Admiral, who wore a white Pendant at the Main-top-mast Head, in the Centre, the Vice-Admiral, with the same Pendant at the Fore-top-mast Head, in the Rear, and the Rear-Admiral, who bore the Pendant at the Mizen-top-mast Head, in the Van, about half a Mile from each other, there being other Ships between them. Of the seventeen, two were Sloops, and one a Brigantine, which stood in for the Land;

X x x x two

two others of them were *French* Ships, which running away, had no Share in the Action, the rest *Spaniards*.

The Commadore having been inform'd that the three Admirals (as they were call'd) had all the Money on board, it is not to be wonder'd at that he made his utmost Efforts against them, and coming near, he order'd the *Kingston* to engage the Vice-Admiral, he himself making Sail up to the Admiral, while a Boat was sent to the Captain of the *Portland* to attempt the Rear-Admiral, and since there was no present occasion for the Fireship, she was placed to Windward.

Mr. Wager attacks the Galleons, which lay by for him.

The Sun was just setting when Mr. *Wager* came up with the Admiral, and then beginning to engage, in about an Hour and half's time (it being dark) she blew up, not without great Danger to the *Expedition*, from the Splinters and Plank which fell on board her on fire, and the great Heat of the Blast. Hereupon the Commadore put abroad his Signal by Lights for keeping Company, and endeavour'd to continue Sight of some of the Enemy's Ships; but finding after this Accident they began to separate, and discovering but one, which was the Rear-Admiral, he made Sail after her, and coming up about Ten a Clock, when he could not judge which way her Head lay, it being very dark, he happen'd to fire his Broadside, or many Guns at least, into her Stern, which did so much Damage, that it seem'd to disable her from making Sail, and being then to Leeward, he tacking on the *Spaniard*, got to Windward of him, and the *Kingston* and *Portland* (which had by reason of the Darkness of the Night, or the blowing up of the Admiral, which made it very thick thereabouts, lost Sight of the other Ships) following his Lights, soon after came up with him, and assisted in taking the Rear-Admiral, who called for Quarter about Two in the Morning.

The Admiral of the Galleons blows up.

The Rear-Admiral of the Galleons chased, and taken.

On board of this Ship he sent his Boats to bring to him the chief Officers, and before the rising of the Sun he saw one large Ship on his Weather Bow, with three Sail upon the Weather Quarter, three or four Leagues off, ours lying then with their Heads to the North, the Wind being at N. E. an easy Gale. Then he put out the Signal for the *Kingston* and *Portland* to chase to Windward, not being able himself to make Sail, being much disabled; and as he had a great part of his Men in the Prize, so were there no less than three hundred Prisoners on board his own Ship.

The Kingston and Portland ordered to chase other Ships.

On Sunday the 30th, the Wind being from the N. E. to the N. N. W. and but little of it, the *Kingston* and *Portland* had left off Chase, but he made the Signal for their continuing it, which they did, and ran him out of Sight, the Fireship still continuing with him; and he having lain by some time not only to put the Prize in a Condition for Sailing, but to refit his own Rigging, made Sail Eastward the 31st, when the *Kingston* and *Portland* joined him, and gave him an Account that the Ship they chased was the Vice-Admiral, to which, as they said, they came so near as to fire their Broadsides at her, but were so far advanced towards the *Salmadinas*, a Shoal off of *Carthagena*, that they were forced to tack and leave her. Thus escaped that very rich Carrack; and though it is reasonable

to

CHAP. XX. *from the Year* 1698, *to* 1712. 707

to imagine, that when so fair a Prospect offered to those who were in Pursuit of her of making their Fortunes, nay such an one as could not have been hoped for again in an Age, the utmost would have been done to prevent her slipping thus through their Fingers; yet the Commadore not being satisfied with their Conduct, and the Officers and Men making great Complaints, he caused the same to be strictly enquired into at a Court-Martial, when he returned to *Jamaica*, and thereupon they were dismissed from their Commands.

By a small *Swedish* Ship which had been trading at the *Baru*, Mr. *Wager* had an Account that one of the large Galleons ran in there, whereupon he gave Orders to the Captain of the *Kingston* to take with him the *Portland* and Fireship, and endeavour to bring her out, or if that could not be done, to burn her, if possible, there being no considerable Fortifications at that Place. *An Account of a Galleon at the Baru, and the Kingston and Portland sent to seize her.*

Tuesday the first of *June* it was for the most part calm, and he endeavouring on Wednesday to get to the Eastward, found the Ship drove away to the S.W. when enquiring of the Prisoners the Strength and Riches of the Galleons, they gave him the following Account, *viz.* that the Admiral was a Ship of 64 Guns, with six hundred Men, called the *Joseph*, and had on board, as some said, five Millions of Pieces of Eight, others seven, in Gold and Silver. That the Vice-Admiral mounted 64 Brass Guns, and had between four and five hundred Men, with four, or, as some said, six Millions; and that the Rear-Admiral was mounted with 44 Guns, having eleven more in her Hold, with about three hundred Men, but that upon some Difference between the Admiral and him at *Porto Bello*, Orders were given that no more Money should be shipped on board her, so that thirteen Chests of Pieces of Eight, and fourteen Piggs, or Sows of Silver, was all that could be found, which were privately brought on board her in the Night, and belonged to some of the Passengers, except what others might have about them, or were in Trunks, of which they could give no Account. They also informed him that the other Ships had little or no Money on board, but were chiefly loaden with Coco, as the Rear-Admiral was. *An Account of the Riches on board the Galleons.*

Provisions and Water growing short, and the Commadore, by reason of contrary Winds, not being able to get Eastward, he bore up, and put the Prisoners on shore at the great *Baru*, with a Flag of Truce, and the Rear-Admiral also with the rest at his earnest Entreaty, where he understood from the *Spaniards*, (who were very civil) that one of the Galleons of 40 Guns was going out from thence towards *Carthagena* when the *Kingston* and *Portland* appeared, but that upon sight of them they went in again, and ran her on shore, when setting her on fire she soon blew up. *Advice that one of the Galleons ran on shore and was blown up.*

Mr. *Wager* having Intelligence at *Jamaica* that nine Ships were seen at an Anchor in the Bay of *La Guarda*, on the West side of *Porto Rico*, as also that others were ready to sail from *Cadiz* to *La Vera Cruz* in *April* last, he sent out the *Windsor* and *Scarbrough*, which were all the Ships he had ready to go to Sea, directing their Commanders to join the *Assistance*, and endeavour to intercept them off of Cape St. *Nicholas*, on *Hispaniola*, the Course which *Some Ships sent to intercept these of the Enemy.*

X x x x 2

which the *Spaniards* conſtantly ſteer; and having received Advice of the *French* Squadrons in thoſe Parts, and of the Galleons, he tranſmitted the ſame to *England*, that, if poſſible, Ships might be particularly appointed to look out for them in their Paſſage home.

Captain Hutchins has an Account of ſome Ships at the Baſtimentos.

Captain *Hutchins* of the *Portland* being, as hath been already ſaid, at the *Baſtimentos*, with the trading Sloops, he had Advice, juſt upon his Arrival on the Coaſt, that four of the Enemy's Ships were at Anchor there, two of them with *Dutch* Colours, of about 50 Guns each, one of the other with the Colours of *Denmark*, and the fourth ſhewing none at all. The next Morning he ſtood in for the *Baſtimentos*, and when he was about two Miles from the aforeſaid Ships, they all hoiſted *French* Colours, and drew up in a Line at the Entrance of the Harbour, whereupon he laid his Head off to Sea, and viewing them ſome time, judged them to be two of 50 Guns, and the other two of about 30 each. By a Cannoa which he diſpatched from the *Samblas*, he was informed that the two largeſt were the *Coventry*, (a Fourth Rate the *French* had ſome time before taken from us) and the *Minion*, both from *Guinea*, one of the other a *French* Trader of 36 Guns, and the Fourth a *Dutch* Ship they had taken at the *Baſtimentos*, and that the two laſt went down to *Porto Bello* the Day after he appeared off of that Place, the other two, namely the Ships from *Guinea*, being ready to proceed.

1708.

The 25th of *March* he ſailed from the *Samblas*, and the 27th arriving at the *Baſtimentos*, the *Spaniards* who came off aſſured him that the two *Guinea* Ships would ſail in a Day or two; and his Boat, which he kept in the Night off of the Harbour of *Porto Bello*, coming off the 1ſt of *April*, gave him an Account that they were ſailed the Evening before; whereupon he immediately ſtood to the Northward till the 3d, and then ſaw them about Eight in the Morning. At Noon he diſcover'd their Hulls very plain, and they being to Windward, bore down to him, firing ſome Guns as they paſſed by, ſoon after which they wore as if they deſign'd to engage in the Evening, but did not. It was little Wind, and about ſix a Clock he tack'd upon them, and keeping ſight all Night, near Eight in the Morning came up within Piſtol-ſhot of the *Minion*, but was obliged to fight her to Leeward, becauſe he could not poſſibly carry out his Lee-Guns, though the Ships of the Enemy did. The *Coventry*, after he had been warmly engaged, got on his Lee-Bow, and firing very ſmartly at his Maſts, did them no little Damage; but he being not willing to be diverted from the *Minion*, ply'd her very ſmartly, nor could ſhe get from him until they had ſhot his Main-top-ſail Yard in two, when both of them ſhot a-head, he creeping after them as faſt as poſſible in that crippled Condition, in the mean while ſplicing his Rigging, bending new Sails, and repairing other Damages in the beſt manner he could.

Captain Hutchins diſcovers two Ships.

About Four in the Morning a Boat was perceived going from the *Minion* to the *Coventry*, ſo that he believed he had much diſabled the former, and that by the frequent paſſing of the Boat between them, ſhe was ſending the beſt of her Loading on board the other.

By

CHAP. XX. *from the Year* 1698, *to* 1712.   709

By Ten at Night he had compleated all his Work, and the next Morning was ready for a second Encounter, but it proving little Wind, he could not come up with them until the 6th, when, before Seven in the Morning, he was close in with the *Coventry*, which Ship hauled up her Main-sail, and lay by for him. Coming nearer to her, it was observed she had many small Shot Men, so that he durst not clap her on board, as he had designed, but plied her with his Guns, mean while he received but little Damage from the *Minion*. Between Eleven and Twelve he brought the *Coventry*'s Main-mast by the Board, and then her Fire was much lessened; however, continuing to do what they could, at half an Hour past Twelve she struck, the first Captain being killed, the second wounded, and a great Slaughter made among the Men, many of them being those who belonged to the *Minion*, whereas of ours there were but nine killed, and twelve wounded, most of whom recover'd, and in the Prize there were about twenty thousand Pieces of Eight, great part whereof were found among the *French* Seamen. *Captain Hutchins engages the Coventry. The Coventry taken.*

Towards the latter end of *July* Mr. *Wager* received a Commission from his Royal Highness, appointing him Rear-Admiral of the Blue Squadron, with an Order for sending home six of the Ships under his Command, Captain *John Edwards* being arrived at *Jamaica* with the *Monmouth* of the Third Rate, the *Jersey* of the Fourth, and the *Roebuck* of the Fifth; with Orders to bring home with him the *Expedition*, *Windsor*, *Assistance*, *Dolphin*, *Dunkirk's Prize*, and *Vulture* Fireship; and by the last Intelligence the Rear-Admiral receiv'd of the *Spanish* Flota, they sailed from the *Havana*, with a *French* Squadron, commanded by Monsieur *Du Casse*, the latter end of *June* 1708, the *Flotilla*, which lately arrived from *Cadiz*, being gone to *La Vera Cruz*. *1708. Mr. Wager receives a Commission to be Rear-Admiral of the Blue. Advice of the Flota's sailing.*

The Vice-Admiral of the Galleons, with the others that got into *Carthagena*, were in that Port in the Month of *August* unrigg'd, and by all Accounts from the *South-Sea*, the *French* were very numerous in those Parts, many of them having begun to settle among the *Spaniards* at *Lima*, (the Capital of *Peru*) which not only made them very uneasy, but spoil'd our Trade on this side for Plate, except for what might come from *Mexico* to *La Vera Cruz*. *The French very numerous in the South-Seas.*

The latter end of *September* the Ships before-mention'd sailed towards *England*, except the *Dunkirk's Prize*, which Frigate not being in a Condition to be trusted home in the Winter, the Rear-Admiral sent her out on a short Cruise with the *Monmouth*, (the Ship whereon he was to hoist his Flag) under the Command of his first Lieutenant when in the *Expedition*, Captain *Purvis*, and they brought in two *French* Merchant Ships, one of 100, the other of 150 Tuns, loaden with Wine, Brandy, and other Goods from *Rochelle*, bound to *Petit-Guavas*; but cruising soon after on the North side of *Hispaniola*, the *Dunkirk's Prize* chased a *French* Ship until she ran on shore near *Port François*, and following her too near, the Pilot not being well acquainted, she struck upon a Ledge of Rocks, where, being a very weak Ship, she soon bulged. *Two French Merchant Ships taken. The Dunkirk's Prize lost, but*

Captain

Captain Purvis takes the Ship she chased.

Captain *Purvis* with some of his Men got upon a small Key, or Island, within Shot of the *French* Ship, and though she had 14 Guns, and sixty Men, and fired smartly upon them, yet he having gotten his Boats, with a Cannoe he had taken, and made a Stage, from whence he was ready to attack them, the *French* asked for Quarter, and surrender'd the Ship, upon Agreement that her Commander and Men should be put on shore, and with this Ship Captain *Purvis* arrived at *Jamaica* with all his Company, except twenty one who refused to assist in the Attempt, believing it to be altogether impossible to succeed therein.

A Council of War held, upon Advice of an intended Attack on Jamaica.

The 1st of *December* 1708, a Council of War was called, where were present, besides Rear-Admiral *Wager*, Captain *Trevor* of the *Kingston*, Captain *Pudner* of the *Severn*, Captain *Hutchins* of the *Portland*, Captain *Vernon* of the *Jersey*, and Captain *Charles Hardy* of the *Roebuck*. It was occasioned upon Intelligence sent the Rear-Admiral from the Admiralty-Office, with an Extract of a Letter from *Paris*, that Monsieur *Du Gue Trovin* was designed on an Expedition against *Jamaica*; and it being judged that if they made such an Attempt it would be to gain the Harbour of *Port Royal*, 'twas determined that all Her Majesty's Ships there, except such as it might be necessary to send to Windward for Intelligence, or on any other extraordinary Occasion, should be drawn up in a Line at the Entrance of the said Harbour, so as that, with the Assistance of the Fort, they might in the best manner defend it, and most annoy the Enemy.

1708/9. *Another Council of War, none of the Enemy's Ships appearing.*

The 18th of *January* another Council of War was called, and since the Letter of Advice before-mentioned was dated almost six Months before, it was consider'd whether the Squadron should be kept any longer together, since the Enemy's Ships had not appear'd, and determined that they ought to be employ'd on necessary Services.

The Portland takes a French Ship, and others taken by Captain Vernon and Captain Hardy.

Accordingly the Rear-Admiral appointing the *Portland* to see some Merchant Ships through the Windward Passage, she returned with a *French* Prize, taken near Cape St. *Nicholas*, worth about six thousand Pounds. Captain *Vernon* also, of the *Jersey*, took in *January* a *Spanish* Sloop loaden with Tobacco, and retook from two *French* Sloops a *Guinea* Ship with four hundred Negroes. Captain *Hardy* of the *Roebuck* brought in a Brigantine, partly loaden with Indigo, taken in at *Petit-Guavas*, which he met on the North side of *Hispaniola*, as she was going from thence to *Port de Paix*, or *Port François*, her Master pretending he belong'd to *Curaçoa*, and produced a Paper from the *Dutch* Governor there, empowering him to trade any where in the *West-Indies*: Nor was it long before this, when a Ship of War of ours called the *Adventure*, of 42 Guns, commanded by Captain *Robert Clarke*, was taken by the Enemy, about fourteen Leagues from *Monserat*, after her Commander and Lieutenant were killed, and near a hundred of her Men slain and wounded.

An English Ship called the Adventure taken.

1709.

About the latter end of *May*, Mr. *Wager*, upon the earnest Application of the Merchants, sent the *Severn* and *Scarbrough* to England

CHAP. XX. *from the Year* 1698, *to* 1712. 711

England with the Trade, for as they were but very weakly mann'd, *A Convoy* so had he Orders from the Lord High-Admiral, that when any of *sent with the* the Ships under his Command were so far reduced by Sickness, as *Trade to Eng-* that they should have no more Men than what might be sufficient *The Rear-Ad-* to sail them, to send them home; for an Act of Parliament was *miral ordered* passed, forbidding the Captains of our Ships of War employ'd in the *to send Ships* *West-Indies*, to impress any Men from Privateers, or Merchant Ships, *but weakly* as they had formerly done, when in want, to render them in a bet- *manned.* ter Condition for Service.

During Rear-Admiral *Wager*'s Stay at *Jamaica* little or nothing else of Moment happen'd; and he receiving Orders from the Lord High-Admiral to return to *England*, arrived at St. *Helen*'s the 20th *Rear-Admi-* of *November*, leaving the Command of the Ships which remained *ral Wager* at the Island with Captain *Tudor Trevor*. *arrives in England, and*

When Orders were sent for Mr. *Wager* to return to *Great Bri-* *Capt. Trevor* *tain*, Captain *Jonathan Span* was appointed to command a small *left abroad.* Squadron in the *West-Indies*, who sailed with the *Rupert*, and two *Captain Span* Ships of the Fourth Rate, the 30th of *January*, and when he had *sent with* seen the Trade to *Barbadoes* and the *Leeward Islands*, proceeded *some Ships to* from thence to *Jamaica*; but during his commanding in Chief in *Jamaica.* those Parts, not any thing more remarkable happen'd than the tak- 17½. ing a *French* Ship and a Sloop off of Cape *Mayz*, on the Island of *Cuba*, and forcing on shore between two Rocks on the South side of *Tuberon* Bay, at the West End of *Hispaniola*, another Ship of 30 Guns, and one of 14, to the biggest of which he sent his Lieu- tenants with the Boats armed, after he had by his Fire forced the *Some Prizes* Officers and Men to quit her and go on shore, but she blew up be- *taken.* fore they got on board, yet were her Guns, with part of the Fur- niture, brought away, but the smaller Ship being sunk, not any thing could be saved which belonged to her.

Captain *Span* was succeeded in the Command of Her Majesty's *Captain Lit-* Ships in the *West-Indies* by *James Littleton*, Esq; *, who with *tleton sent to* the *Jersey*, *Weymouth*, and *Medway Prize*, sailed from St. *Helen*'s *command in* the 24th of *August*, and in his way to *Plimouth* the *Medway Prize* *dies.* took a small Privateer of 4 Guns and thirty three Men. Calling at 1710. *Plimouth* for the Trade, he proceeded on his Voyage, and came to *Maderas* the 12th of *September*, where having taken in Wine for the Use of the Ships Companies, he arrived at *Barbadoes* the 18th of *October*, and at *Jamaica* the 2d of the next Month, leaving the *He arrives at* *Jersey* and *Medway Prize* to cruise off of *Hispaniola*. *Jamaica.*

Those two Ships joined him at *Port Royal*, after they had forced *A French* one of St. *Malo* on shore a little to the Eastward of *Port Louis*, *Ship forced* which they set fire to when they had taken out of her what they *on shore.* could, she being loaden chiefly with Bale-Goods. Mr. *Littleton* being informed that there were six Ships of War at *Carthagena*, he sent the *Nonsuch* and *Roebuck* over to that Coast, that so he might *The Nonsuch* know the Certainty of it, and if Captain *Hardy*, who commanded *and Roebuck* the said Ship *Nonsuch* found it was so, he was forthwith to send the *thagena.*

* *Since a Flag-Officer, and Commissioner of the Navy.*

Roebuck

Roebuck with Notice of it to *Jamaica*, and himself to join the *Windsor*, then on the aforesaid Coast with some trading Ships, and both of them to return to the Commadore as soon as it was possible, who intended, when he should be so joined, to sail with the *Rupert*, *Windsor*, *Nonsuch*, *Jersey*, *Weymouth*, *Roebuck*, and *Medway Prize*, and to use his best Endeavours to intercept the Enemy; but if the Report happened not to be true, the Captain of the *Nonsuch* was to leave the *Windsor* with the Merchant Ships on the Coast, and return to *Jamaica*.

Captain Hardy sends an Account of what he had discovered.

The 8th of *December* he sent home the *Falkland* with the Trade, and Captain *Hardy* having been on the *Spanish* Coast, sent an Account by the *Roebuck* that he had made the Land, and came to an Anchor at the *Great Baru*, where he found a *Jamaica* Trader, who had sailed from that Island five or six Days before him, the Master of which Vessel assured him, that, besides the Galleons, there was only one *Guinea* Ship, and a Packet-Boat of *Carthagena*, which Intelligence he had from the *Spaniards*, and from the Commander of a *Paraguay* Privateer from *Jamaica*, who had been several Months in those Parts.

The Falmouth arrives from England.

The *Falmouth* arrived at *Jamaica* in *January* from *England*, with the Tender to the *Star* Bomb, but the Bomb-Vessel her self was missing, having been seen by a Trader from *New England* without her Masts, and since the Merchant Ships bound home would be ready to sail by the 4th of *April*, Mr. *Littleton* intended to send the *Rupert*, *Dragon*, *Falmouth*, and *Roebuck* as their Convoy, pursuant to the Instructions he had received from the Lords of the Admiralty, which Ships had for some time before been at *Jamaica* under the Command of Captain *Span*, as I have already acquainted you, and the *Star* Bomb-Vessel being arrived, he designed to send her home also with the first Convoy.

Advice of Monsieur Du Casse his coming towards Carthagena.

In the Month of *May* he was informed by the Masters of some Vessels from the *Maderas*, that Monsieur *Du Casse* had been seen from that Island, and that he came very near to them as they were at an Anchor in the Road. A Sloop of *Jamaica* taking also another from *Carthagena*, there was found in her a Letter from the Governor of that Place to the Vice-Roy of *Mexico*, by which he gave him an Account that Monsieur *Du Casse* was daily expected there with a Squadron of seven Ships, whereupon Mr. *Littleton* sent a Sloop to the Coast of *New Spain* to call in the *Nonsuch*, expecting the *Windsor* and *Weymouth* every Moment from the *Havana*, and the *Jersey* was cruising to the Windward of *Jamaica*.

The Jersey takes a French Ship, and brings an Account of Du Casse; as Captain Hardy did.

The said Ship *Jersey* arriving the 23d of *May*, brought in with her a *French* Merchant Ship which sailed from *Port Louis* three Days before, in Company of Monsieur *Du Casse*, who (as the Master of the *French* Vessel said) was gone for *Carthagena*, with only a Ship of 74 Guns, another of 60, one of 50, one of 24, and one of 20; but the Commadore was assured by Captain *Hardy*, who came in from the Coast of *New Spain* on the 27th of *May*, that two of his Ships arrived at *Carthagena* ten Days before, and that they waited there for him, one of which was the *Glocester* of 50

Guns,

CHAP. XX. *from the Year* 1698, *to* 1712. 713

Guns, formerly taken from us, and the other of 44, and that as soon as the Galleons could be got ready, he designed for the *Havana*, and from thence to *Cadiz*.

The aforesaid Ship which Captain *Vernon* of the *Jersey* took belonged to *Brest*, and had 30 Guns, and a hundred and twenty Men. She came from trading on the Coast of *New Spain*, but had put all her Money on shore at *Port Louis*, so that there was found in her only a little Cocoa, and some few odd things, she being bound to *Petit-Guavas* to take in her Loading for *France*.

The *Jersey* was sent over again to the Coast of *New Spain*, to observe the Strength of the Enemy at *Carthagena*, and returned the 4th of *July*, her Commander having looked into that Port the 28th of *June*, where he saw twelve Ships and five Sloops, six of them rigged, and six not. Of the Ships which were rigged he judged, according to the Intelligence before received, that one was Monsieur *Du Casse* his own, named the *St. Michael*, of 74 Guns, another the *Hercules*, of 60, together with the *Griffin* of 50, and two Frigates, of about 20 Guns each, with the Vice Admiral of the Galleons of 60; and of the Ships which were unrigg'd, there were two at the upper End of the Harbour preparing for the Sea, one of which he thought might be the *Minion* of 50 Guns, another of about 40, the rest seeming to be Merchant Ships. *The Jersey sent out, and brings fresh Intelligence.*

The 11th of *July* the Trade from *Great Britain* arrived at *Jamaica* with their Convoy, and four Days afterwards Mr. *Littleton* was under Sail with one Third Rate, four Fourths, and a Sloop, towards *Carthagena*, with a Design to intercept Monsieur *Du Casse*, he having received Advice that the *Windsor* and *Weymouth*, which had been a considerable time absent beyond what he had limited for their Cruise, were at *New England* with three Prizes. *Mr. Littleton puts to Sea, with a design to intercept Monsieur Du Casse.*

On the 26th of *July* he arrived on the Coast of *New Spain*, and discover'd five Ships to Leeward, between him and the Shore, which he gave chase to, being then not far from *Bocca Chica*. They made the best of their way from him, and got into that Place, which is at the Entrance of *Carthagena* Harbour, whereupon he stood off to Sea the greatest part of the Night, but stretching in to the Shore next Morning, chased four Ships, and about Six at Night came up with the Vice-Admiral of the Galleons, and a *Spanish* Merchant Ship; and as Monsieur *Du Casse* had taken most of the Money out of the Galleon, having some Suspicion of the commanding Officer on board her, so was this very Carrack the same which had escaped from Mr. *Wager*, as hath been before related; and coming from *Carthagena* in Company of some *French* Ships of War, it happened she was separated from them, and believing our Ships to be those with Monsieur *Du Casse*, (as her Commander said) lay by the greatest part of the Day; and when Mr. *Littleton* came near, hoisted *Spanish* Colours, and a Flag at the Fore-top-mast Head, so that between Five and Six at Night, the *Salisbury Prize*, commanded by Captain *Robert Harland*, engaged her, soon after which the *Salisbury*, commanded by Captain *Francis Hosier*, did the same. The Commadore being within Pistol-shot, was just going to fire into her, when they *He comes up with the Vice-Admiral of the Galleons, and takes her. Captain Harland and Captain Hosier take another great Ship.*

Y y y y *and*

they ſtruck their Colours, and the *Jerſey* going after one of the Merchant Ships, took her, but the *Nonſuch* chaſing the other, ſhe eſcaped in the Night. The Vice-Admiral of the Galleons being wounded by a ſmall Shot, died ſoon after.

the Jerſey *a Merchant Ship.*

The Priſoners, by the Deſcription given to them of the Ships which were ſeen by the Commadore the Day he came off of *Carthagena,* aſſured him they were thoſe with Monſieur *Du Caſſe,* and that he had been out of *Carthagena* but two Days, being ſeparated from the *Spaniſh* Vice-Admiral, and nine Merchant Ships the Day after he came out; and ſince Mr. *Littleton* was well aſſured that he intended to touch at the *Havana,* it was determined to cruiſe a little to Leeward of *Point Pedro* Shoals, as the moſt proper Place for intercepting him, until ſuch time as farther Intelligence could be gained from Captain *Hook* of the *Jamaica* Sloop, who was ſent over to the Coaſt with ſome *Spaniſh* Priſoners.

Mr. Littleton *cruiſes for Monſieur Du* Caſſe.

Monſieur *Du Caſſe* (as the Commadore informed me by his Letter, and as I have mentioned before) had taken moſt of the Money out of the Galleon, except what was found in ſome Boxes, which belonged to private Perſons. She had 60 Braſs Guns mounted, and three hundred and twenty five Men, and the Ship which the *Jerſey* took was a *Spaniard,* belonging to the Merchants, of about 400 Tuns, and 26 Guns, loaden for the moſt part with Cocoa and Wool.

In the Month of *Auguſt* there being ſome Trade ready to proceed to *Great Britain,* Mr. *Littleton* ſent the *Nonſuch* as their Convoy, in which Ship Lieutenant-General *Handaſyde,* late Governor of *Jamaica,* took his Paſſage, and on the 23d of the ſaid Month, being in his appointed cruiſing Station, he received an Account from the Captain of the *Medway's Prize,* whom he had ſent into *Blewfields* Bay, that the Maſter of a Veſſel had made Oath before the Lord *Archibald Hamilton,* then Governor of *Jamaica,* that there were eighteen Sail of *French* Ships of War, and a conſiderable Number of Tranſports with Soldiers lately arrived at *Martinico,* and that their Deſign was to invade the ſaid Iſland of *Jamaica,* upon which, he made the beſt of his way thither; and acquainting the Governor with the Intelligence he had received, his Lordſhip aſſured him there was no Truth in it, and that he believed it to be a Story raiſed by ſome of the People of the Iſland.

The Nonſuch *brings the Trade and Lieutenant-General* Handaſyde *home.*

A falſe Account of the Enemy.

Captain *Hooke* of the *Jamaica* Sloop joined him off of the Weſt End of the Iſland the 25th, and brought an Account that Monſieur *Du Caſſe* ſailed from *Carthagena* three Days after he had left that Coaſt, but that he took no Merchant Ships with him; ſo that by the falſe Intelligence given to the Captain of the *Medway Prize,* Mr. *Littleton* in all Probability miſſed the Opportunity of meeting with him in his way to the *Havana.*

An Account of Du Caſſe *his ſailing from* Carthagena.

About the beginning of *October* he had an Account from the Captain of a Privateer Sloop belonging to *Jamaica,* that on the 8th of *September* he ſaw eight large Ships between that Iſland and *Cuba,* which he judged to be Monſieur *Du Caſſe's* Squadron going down that way to the *Havana*; and the *Defiance, Salisbury,* and *Jerſey* returning

CHAP. XX. *from the Year* 1698, *to* 1712. 715

returning to *Jamaica* the 17th of *October*, the latter brought in a
Ship she had taken on the North side of *Cuba*, bound from *Petit-* *A French*
Guavas to *France*, her Burthen of about 100 Tuns, and her Load- *Ship taken by*
ing chiefly Indigo, and Sugar. *the* Jersey.

The 25th of *November* the *Thetis*, a French Ship of War taken *The* Thetis
by the *Windsor* and *Weymouth*, arrived at *Jamaica*. She came out *taken by the*
from *New England* in Company of the *Weymouth*, but was sepa- Weymouth.
rated from her three Days after in bad Weather, and, as Mr. *Little-*
ton heard, Sir *Hovenden Walker* had carry'd the *Windsor* home
with him, after his Expedition was over towards *Quebeck*, of which
I shall shortly give an Account, as also of his relieving Mr. *Lit-*
tleton in the Command of Her Majesty's Ships in the *West-Indies*.

This Prize, the *Thetis*, was a very good Ship, being bored to
carry 44 Guns, and was not above five Years old, so that the Commadore, in behalf of himself and the Captors, offered to sell her for
the Queen's Service, but the Lords Commissioners of the Admiralty
did not think fit to have her purchased.

The 6th Day of *December* the *Weymouth*, commanded by Cap- *The* Wey-
tain *Leslock*, arrived with a small Privateer of 6 Guns, and forty Men *mouth takes*
belonging to *Porto Rico*; and with the Trade bound to *Great Bri-* *a Privateer.*
tain the Commadore sent the *Anglesey* and *Fowey*, as also the *Scar-* *A Convoy*
borough, the latter of which Ships was taken by the two former from *sent to Eng-*
the Enemy on the Coast of *Guinea*, where they had some time be- land.
fore taken her from us.

In *January* the *Defiance*, *Salisbury*, *Jersey*, and *Weymouth*, 17 11/12.
were cruising to Windward of *Hispaniola*, in different Stations, the
Salisbury Prize being daily expected in from the Coast of *New*
Spain; and the *Medway Prize* having been sent to cruise off of
Petit-Guavas, she returned with a *French* Sloop bound to *Havana*,
loaden with *Madera* Wine, Flower, and Cocoa. The *Salisbury* al-
so came in the 20th of *February* with a French Merchant Ship of *Other Prizes*
150 Tuns, loaden with Sugar from Cape *François*, on the North *taken.*
side of *Hispaniola*, and in few Days after she was sent to cruise in
her former Station. The *Jersey* arrived also the same Day, whose
Commander, Captain *Vernon*, being off of *Porto Rico*, saw a Sail
at an Anchor very near the Shore, and steering directly towards her,
found her to be a *French* Ship of about 20 Guns. He came to an
Anchor by her, and having fired several Shot, she breaking loose,
ran on shore, when the fresh Sea Breeze occasioning a great Swell, *A French*
she immediately fell in pieces. *Ship run on*
shore.

About the middle of *May* the Commadore designed to send the
Jersey hence with the Trade, and the *Star* Bomb, she not being in
a Condition to continue longer abroad, but she left not the Island
until the 18th of *May*. The *Defiance*, *Salisbury*, and *Salisbury*
Prize, which had for some time been cruising, returned into Port
without any Purchase; and about this time the *Weymouth* and *Tryal*
Sloop were, at the Request of the Merchants, appointed to convoy
the Vessels bound to the Bay of *Campeche* for Log Wood, which is
a very beneficial Trade to the Island, but was entirely interrupted
by the Enemy the Year before; and here we will leave Mr. *Lit-*
Yyyy 2 tleton

Commadore Littleton sent home in the Defiance, and Sir Hovenden Walker arrives at Jamaica.

tleton coming home in the *Defiance*, by Order of Sir *Hovenden Walker*, who arrived at *Jamaica* the beginning of *July* 1712, and of whose Proceedings, first on the Expedition to *Quebeck*, and in the *West-Indies* afterwards, I shall give some Account, when I have related what happened at home, and in the *Mediterranean*, before the said Expedition to *Quebeck* was so unadvisedly projected, and undertaken; and this will oblige me to look some Years backward, having (as hath been already observed) chosen to give these Accounts entire, to render the whole much less perplexed than otherwise they would have been.

Chap. XXI.

Containing an Account of Sir Thomas Hardy's *Proceedings in and about the* Chanel, *till order'd to the* Mediterranean; *as also of some of our Ships being taken in their Passage from the* Downs *Westward, and others in the* Soundings.

1706.

SIR *Thomas Hardy* being appointed to command a Squadron in the *Soundings*, which was designed not only to protect our Trade, but to annoy that of the Enemy, and intercept their cruising Frigates and Privateers, he got under Sail from *Plimouth* the 17th of *October*, and the 27th took a *French* Ship, with a Letter of Marque, of 20 Guns, after she had made some Resistance with great and small Shot. This Ship belonged to *Bourdeaux*, was loaden with Sugar, Cocoa, and Indigo, and had taken two *English* Vessels before, one of them bound to *Guinea*, the other in her Passage from *Oporto* into the *British* Chanel.

Ranging up and down the *Soundings*, he on the 21st of the next Month met with an *English* Ship of War named the *Dover*, commanded by Captain *Thomas Matthews*, about thirteen Leagues West from *Scilly*, who in his Passage from *New England* had lost Company with all his Convoys, about six hundred Leagues from the Land's End. Whether this was occasion'd by the Carelesness of the Masters of the Merchant Ships, (which but too often hath happened) I shall not determine, or whether from bad Weather at such a Season of the Year; but this I may venture to say, that let the Commander of a Convoy be never so careful, it is almost next to an Impossibility to keep the Trade together, especially in the Winter time, and when he has so great a Run as from *New England* to *Great Britain*.

Sir Thomas Hardy goes to Cork to convoy home some East-India Ships.

Some straggling Ships of ours Sir *Thomas Hardy* met with, during his continuing in the *Soundings*, and coming to *Plimouth* to refit and victual his Squadron, there he received Orders to proceed

CHAP. XXI. *from the Year* 1698, *to* 1712.

to *Cork* to conduct from thence some homeward bound *East-India* Ships. He lay Wind-bound at *Plimouth* until the 24th of *December*, but then sailing, came off of *Kinsale* the 27th, from whence he order'd Captain *Cock*, who commanded the Convoy to the *East-India* Men, to join him in *Cork* Harbour.

There he waited for a Wind until the 5th of *February*, when he put to Sea, but met with such bad Weather, as obliged him to repair to *Milford Haven*, where he was detained until the 22d, when he sailed with five Fourth Rates, one Fifth, and one of the Sixth, having in Company fifty three Merchant Ships, (those from *India* included) and steering for *Cape Cornwall*, designed to put through between the Islands of *Scilly* and the Main. Next Morning he made the Land, but it blowing hard at E. N. E. he durst not attempt to put through, as he intended, but bore away for *Cork* again, from whence sailing as soon as possibly the Winds would permit, he arrived in the *Downs* the 4th of *March*. Returning to *Plimouth*, he retook a Merchant Ship of *Topsham*, but as she was going into Port, she had the Misfortune of falling into the Enemy's Hands again, and while he continued in *Hamoze*, two *French* Privateers from *Dunkirk* came into *Plimouth* Sound, and carried away an *English* Runner, although four *Dutch* Capers were at Anchor in Sight, which might, had they so pleased, have preserved her.

Forced to Milford Haven,

and

to Cork again.

Comes to the Downs, and returns to Plimouth.

An English Ship taken in Plimouth Sound.

Being ordered with his Squadron to *Spithead*, he received Directions there, about the middle of *June*, to proceed towards *Lisbon*, for protecting the Transports, Storeships, and Victuallers bound from hence to the Fleet in the *Mediterranean*, as also the Trade designed to *Virginia*, *New England*, and other foreign Parts, as far as his and their way should lie together.

1707.

The 8th of *July* he put to Sea, having under his Care two hundred and five Merchant Ships, but contrary Winds obliged him to return to St. *Helen*'s. The 3d of the next Month he reached the length of the *Start*, but was forced back to *Torbay*, from whence he was not able to accompany the Ships bound to *Lisbon* as far on their way as he was directed until the last of *August*, such Difficulties are there often met with in getting out of our Chanel.

Sir Thomas Hardy proceeds with the Trade into the Sea.

Being in the Latitude of 49^d and 36^m, *Scilly* bearing North, 63^d East, distant about twenty six Leagues, and finding a Ship with our Naval Stores, which had been taken by the Enemy, and re-taken by a *Dutch* Privateer, he thought it adviseable to see her safe to *Plimouth* with his whole Squadron, the Stores on board her being of great Consequence, until another Opportunity could be met with for her proceeding to the Port whereto she was designed, since it was not certain whether Monsieur *Du Gue Trovine* was at Sea, or gone into *Brest*.

He brings a re-taken Ship with Naval Stores to Plimouth.

I may not omit acquainting you, that before Sir *Thomas Hardy* parted with the Ships bound to *Lisbon*, he, in the Latitude of 46^d and 54^m North, the *Lizard* bearing N. E. distant about ninety three Leagues, discovered, as it was believed, Monsieur *Du Gue Trovine*'s Squadron, which, as he had before understood, were two Ships of G

Sees Ships, which he believed were those with Monsieur Du Gue Trovine.

of 70 Guns, two of 60, one of 50, and one of 40. They brought to to the Westward, bearing N. E. of him, and being then at a great distance, wore round some time after, and stood upon the other Tack Eastward, under their Topsails and Courses, with a small Gale at N. W. Upon this a Council of War was called, and considering that the Prince's Orders to Sir *Thomas Hardy* were thus; That if in his Passage into the *Soundings* he should get sight of the aforesaid *French* Squadron, Captain *Kirktown* of the *Defiance* should, with the Ships of War under his Command, and the Transports, Storeships, and Victuallers, make the best of their way to *Lisbon*, and he give Chase to the Enemy, but that if he could not come up with them, he should return to a proper Station in the *Soundings*, and there cruise for the Security of our Trade; and he finding that the Enemy's Squadron were Hull to, almost in the Wind's Eye; that it being near Night, our Ships would soon lose Sight of them, so that it was to no purpose to continue the Chase; and considering that the Ships with Captain *Kirktown* were not of sufficient Strength to deal with them, it was determined to keep Company with him until he should be about one hundred and twenty Leagues from the Land's End, lest the Enemy should, by getting by our Squadron in the Night, take or destroy many of the Merchant Ships; and a sufficient Strength was kept in the Rear of the Fleet to prevent Accidents.

Proceeds farther into the Sea, for Security of the Trade, &c.

Parting with the Ships bound to *Lisbon*, he cruised in the Latitudes of 49^d, and 46^d and 30^m, for protecting our Trade coming from the aforesaid Port of *Lisbon*, under the Convoy of three Third Rates, and the 26th of *September* he came into *Plimouth* to refit and victual, where being detained by contrary Winds until the 2d of *January*, he then received Orders to accompany Sir *John Leake* to the *Mediterranean*.

Receives Orders to go to the Streights. 170⅘.

Here let me inform you of an unlucky Accident which befel two of our Ships of War in their Passage from the *Downs* Westward, which was as follows, *viz.* the *Royal Oak*, *Hampton-Court*, and *Grafton*, (the first of 76, the other two mounting 70 Guns each) sailing thence on the 1st Day of *May*, with several Merchant Ships and Vessels under their Convoy, all of them under the Command of Captain *Baron Wylde* of the *Royal Oak*, were attack'd about six Leagues to the Westward of *Beachy*, by nine Ships of War fitted out from *Dunkirk*, of between 50 and 56 Guns each, with which there were also several Privateers, and some of them of Force, being in all about twenty Sail. After a very sharp Engagement, wherein divers Officers and Men were killed on both sides, and the Ships very much shattered in their Hulls, Masts, and Rigging, the *Grafton*, commanded by Captain *Edward Acton*, and the *Hampton-Court* by Captain *George Clements*, (the former of whom was slain in Fight, and the latter soon after died of his Wounds) were constrained to yield, which (together with great part of the Trade) the *French* carried into *Dunkirk*. Captain *Wylde* finding those Ships in the Enemy's Possession, and having before engaged with two of theirs, made the best shift he could to save the *Royal Oak*, by running her

The Grafton *and* Hampton-Court *taken by a French Squadron, and the Royal Oak forced on shore.*

on

CHAP. XXI. *from the Year* 1698, *to* 1712.   719

on shore to the Eastward of *Dungeness*, having at that time, as he gave an Account, eleven Feet Water in the Hold, occasioned by several Shot she had received under Water, which he stopp'd in one Tyde, and getting her on float again, brought her to the *Downs* three Days after the Action.

Thus were two of our Ships of the Third Rate lost, and another in great danger of being so. The Enemy were indeed much superior in Number, and, according to the Magnitude of their Ships, much better manned; but since ours were more lofty, it may not be unreasonable to conjecture, that had they been drawn into a close Line, and, instead of lying by to receive the Enemy, kept constantly under Sail, and fought in that manner, the *French* would have met with very great difficulty (had they thus mutually assisted each other) in boarding them; whereas by their lying almost motionless, at too great a distance one from the other, they had better Opportunities of attacking them, being single, with Numbers of their Ships, and not only of raking them fore and aft with their Ordnance and small Shot, but of gauling them on their Broadsides also. *Observations upon the aforegoing Action.*

Nor let us here pass by an Accident that happened to some other of our Ships of War this Year, which were bound out of the Chanel. It was thus. On the 24th of *September* Orders were sent to Captain *Richard Edwards* * of the *Cumberland*, mounted with 80 Guns, to take under his Command the *Devonshire*, of like Force, the aforesaid Ship *Royal Oak* of 76, and the *Chester* and *Ruby* of 50 Guns each, with which he was to proceed for the Security of such Merchant Ships as had Horses on board for the King of *Portugal*, forty or fifty Leagues beyond *Scilly*, and then to leave them to go forward to *Lisbon* with the *Ruby* and *Chester*, their proper Convoy.

Sailing pursuant to those Orders, he had not long parted with the Land e'er he unluckily fell in with twelve Ships of the Enemy's, being the Squadron commanded by Monsieur *Du Gue Trovine*, joined by that of Monsieur *Fourbin*'s, both employed on private Accounts, although all, or most of them, were Ships of the *French* King's Navy, one of 72 Guns, others upwards of 60, some of 50, and none of them of less than 40. With these Ships they engaged a considerable time, while those under their Convoy secured themselves to Leeward; but being much overpowered, the *Cumberland*, (whose Commander was sorely wounded) as also the *Chester* and *Ruby*, (after having received from, and done very considerable Damage to the Enemy) fell at length into their Hands; the *Devonshire* blew up, as she maintained a running Fight against several Ships which pursued her, and the *Royal Oak*, steering another Course, a second time escaped. These Ships of ours were of very great Force; and had they kept together under Sail, (as I have observed in the Case before-mentioned) must have made a very formidable Battery, whereas (either by Accident, or otherwise prevented) it is likely, in *Monsieur Du Gue, and Monsieur Fourbin's Squadrons take the Cumberland, Chester, and Ruby. The Devonshire blows up, and Royal Oak escapes.*

* *Afterwards a Commissioner of the Navy.*   doing

doing it) the *French* Ships, being many more in Number, had Opportunities of attacking each of them singly with two, three, or more at a time, and so got the Advantage.

I now return to Sir *Thomas Hardy*, who coming to *London* to equip himself for his Voyage to the *Mediterranean*, took his Journey by Land to *Plimouth*, where he had Expectations of meeting the Fleet, but heard at *Exeter* that Sir *John Leake* was sailed the Day before. Arriving at *Plimouth*, he met with the *Burford*, a Ship of the Third Rate, and in her proceeded to *Lisbon*, where he came before the Fleet reached that Port; and here we will leave him going with the Admiral up the *Mediterranean*, until he returned in the Year 1711 to *England*, and give some Account of the Proceedings of the Lord *Durfley* in the *Chanel*, and *Soundings*, who was at this time Vice-Admiral of the Blue Squadron of the Fleet.

Chap. XXII.

Containing an Account of the Lord Durfley's *Proceedings with a Squadron in the* Soundings, *and of several* French Ships *taken during his Lordship's commanding there.*

1708.

THE Lord *Durfley* the beginning of *June* had been off of *Ushant* to inform himself of the Enemy's Naval Preparations at *Brest*, and determined when he had seen the outward bound Trades well into the Sea, to cruise in a proper Station in the *Soundings*, and from thence to send three Ships to *Ireland* to convoy to *England* the homeward bound *East-India* Ships.

This done, and his Lordship being off of *Kinsale* the 17th of *June*, under Orders to intercept a *French* Squadron which had been discovered off of *Gallway*, he determined to proceed within twenty Leagues of the Port of *Brest*, and to lie in a fair way between that Station and Cape *Clear*, in hopes of meeting with them, but after cruising thus some time, to proceed off of *Kinsale* for Intelligence whether they were yet on the *Irish* Coast. Not seeing the Enemy in his Station, he accordingly stretched off of *Kinsale*, and there meeting the three Ships he had appointed to protect the *East-India* Men, he ordered Captain *Owen* to proceed with them to *Plimouth*, and his Lordship himself joining the Trade from *New England*, accompanied them off of *Scilly*, sending them from thence into the said Port of *Plimouth* with two Ships of War, besides their proper Convoy, which he ordered to return and join him ten Leagues S. W. from the *Lizard*.

The

CHAP. XXII. *from the Year* 1698, *to* 1712.

The 26th of *June* his Lordship chased three Ships which he discovered near the Land's End, one of them of about 40 Guns, or between 40 and 50, the other two of about 30 Guns each, but they shewing *French* Colours, stood away South East for their own Coast; our Ships, which were most of them foul, not being able to come up with them; a Misfortune that often happened both before, and after; for the Enemy coming out of their Ports clean, to prey chiefly on our Trade, were, generally speaking, in a Condition either to take or leave, as they themselves pleased; whereas our Ships were frequently foul, and consequently could not have the like Advantage. Nor was this Inconvenience to be avoided so often as otherwise it might have been, had there been less occasion in a time of so great Action, to vary the Stations of our Ships, by appointing them sometimes to this, and then taking them off for other necessary Services, which could not possibly be foreseen when they were first pitched upon to cruise in the *Soundings*, or elsewhere against the Enemy; for since there was a Necessity to employ so great a part of our Naval Strength abroad, as well in the *Mediterranean*, as to guard our foreign Plantations and Trade, and to station others along the Coast of this Kingdom, as well as *Ireland*, it would seldom admit of such a Number in the *Soundings*, so as that while some were cruising, others could be from time to time cleaning to relieve them; and since there, and in the Chops of the Chanel, the *French* attempted to do us the most Prejudice, and had the fairest Opportunities for it, it were to have been wished that more nimble, and consequently the most proper Ships, could have been oftener spared for Service in those Parts.

His Lordship chases some French Ships.

Reasons why our Ships were not constantly cleaner.

The Lord *Dursley*, (who but too often experienced this Misfortune) proceeded from *Plimouth*, and crouded all the Sail the Ships could bear to get timely into his Station, which was between the Latitudes of 48 and 50^d, and West from *Scilly* between forty and fifty Leagues, where he cruised as long as his Beer and Water would permit. The *Salisbury*, one of the Ships under his Lordship's Command, took a *French* Merchant Ship bound to *Placencia*, whose Master assured him, that Monsieur *Du Gue Trovine* sailed with a Squadron from *Brest* two Months before, and that he was gone a foreign Voyage, having taken on board ten Months Provisions; but whither he was bound, this Master either could not, or would not tell.

His Lordship returns to his appointed Station.

The Salisbury takes a French Merchant Ship.

The Squadron returning, and being victualled and refitted at *Plimouth*, his Lordship sailed the 28th of *September* with five Ships of War, and was joined next Day by the *Hampshire*, which had taken a small Privateer. Another was taken by my Lord himself of 24 Guns, set forth from St. *Malo*, and the *August* retook a *Dutch* Merchant Ship, all which were sent to *Plimouth*.

Lord Dursley takes a Privateer, and the Hampshire another.

The 7th of *November* his Lordship returned to the said Port of *Plimouth*, and the *Hampshire* brought in a Privateer of 16 Guns, with a *French* Merchant Ship bound to the *West-Indies*. The *Salisbury* also brought in two Prizes, the Captain of one of which gave an Account that Monsieur *Du Gue Trovine* was at *Corunna*

The Hampshire and Salisbury take Prizes.

Z z z z with

with eleven Ships of War, which Intelligence he had from a *Dutch* Privateer that had taken a Storeship out of his Squadron.

His Lordship appointed three Frigates to cruise between the *Lizard* and *Ushant* till the 22d of this Month of *November*, and on the 11th the *Plimouth* brought in two Prizes, one from *Martinico*, and the other a Banker, which Ship had also met with two Privateers between the *Deadman* and the *Lizard*, and engag'd them for some time, but it being almost calm, they got away, one of them mounting 34, and the other 26 Guns.

The Plimouth brings in two Prizes.

The Prince being dead, and the Queen taking into her own Hands for a little while the Affairs of the Admiralty, wherein I had the Honour to serve Her Majesty, she was pleased to send Orders by Express, to the Lord *Durfley* at *Plimouth*, which he received the 12th of *November*, to proceed into the *Soundings*, and to use his utmost Endeavours to protect the Trade coming from the Plantations, and other remote Parts; and although his Lordship was apprehensive that Monsieur *Du Gue Trovine*'s Squadron was come to *Brest*, and that if he should be joined there by Ships from *Dunkirk*, his Force would be much superior to what he had a Prospect of having under his Command; yet on the 30th Day of *November* he put out from the Port of *Plimouth*, but was forced back by contrary Winds, as he was soon after to *Torbay*, whence his Lordship attempted to sail the beginning of *December*, mean while the *Salisbury* took a *French* Privateer of 20 Guns; and the Earl of *Pembroke* being now a second time appointed Lord High-Admiral, the Lord *Durfley* desired his Squadron might be cleaned, in order to his being more capable of doing Service against the Enemy.

The Prince dies, and the Queen for some time keeps the Admiralty in her own Hands, and Lord Durfley sent into, but forced back from the Soundings.

The Earl of Pembroke appointed a second time Lord High-Admiral.

The 29th of *December* his Lordship saw two Ships, which chased him, but, when they came near, bore away. He followed them until he was within Gun-shot, when their Commanders lighten'd them by heaving many things over-board, and so escaped, one of them being of 60 Guns, and the other 50, and had our Ships been clean, they might in all Probability have given a good Account of them; but all that his Lordship was able to do during this short Cruise, was the taking a *French Newfoundland* Banker.

Lord Durfley chases two French Ships of Force, but they escaped.

Returning to *Plimouth*, he received a Commission from the Lord High-Admiral, by which he was appointed Vice-Admiral of the White, and the 18th of *January* had Orders to cause all the Ships of his Squadron to be cleaned. His Lordship sailed the 14th of *February* with one Third Rate, and three Fourths, and off of the *Start* the *Medway* took a *French* Privateer of 12 Guns. On the 17th he was joined by two other Ships of the Fourth Rate, and one of the Fifth, and the *Dartmouth* taking another Privateer of 12 Guns, she was ordered with her to *Plimouth*, where if the Leak she complained of could be stopp'd, she was to proceed to the *Downs* with the Trade.

His Lordship appointed Vice-Admiral of the White. 170 4/7.

Prizes taken.

The 22d of *February* his Lordship fell in with eleven Sail, about twelve Leagues from *Scilly*, having then with him no more than the *Kent*, *Plimouth*, *Monk*, and *Litchfield*. This happened about Three in the Morning, and their Lights being discovered, he caused the

Lord Durfley falls in with eleven French Ships in a Fog.

the Signal to be made for Wearing, which was done, but not without hazard of falling among the Enemy, and the *Plimouth* and *Litchfield*, not seeing the Signal, stood on. It was such thick Weather that it could not be discerned what they were; however his Lordship designed, by clapping on a Wind, to get to Windward of them, that so, if possible, he might join the Ships and Trade coming from *Lisbon*, and thereby make himself strong enough to engage them, but missing of them in the Night, and stretching in for *Plimouth*, Captain *Stuart* of the *Dartmouth*, who not long before had been sent in thither with his Prize, (as hath been already mentioned) acquainted his Lordship that he had been chased by nine large Ships off of the *Lizard*, which he judged to be the very same he met with, and that had fallen in with, and engaged Captain *Tollet* in his Passage from *Ireland*, which Action being somewhat remarkable, I shall, in this Place, give the following Account of it.

A smart Dispute between some of our Ships with Captain Tollet, and the French.

On the 25th of *April*, in the Afternoon, the said Captain *Tollet* set sail from *Cork* with his own Ship, the *Assurance*, of 70 Guns, the *Sunderland* of 60, and the *Hampshire* and *Anglesey* of 50 Guns each, being join'd by the *Assistance*, another Ship of the like force, and the Trade from *Kinsale*. In his Passage the *Anglesey* and *Sunderland* lost Company, and on the 6th in the Morning, about Five a Clock, he saw four Sail standing after him, as he was steering away E. by N, the *Lizard* bearing N. N. E. near eight Leagues distance. About Seven they came within random Shot, and then brought to, whereupon he made the Signal for drawing into a Line of Battel, and another for the Merchant Ships to bear away for their Security, which (according to usual Custom) they took no notice of, but straggled some one way, and some another. About Eight the Enemy bore down, having drawn themselves into a Line, and when they were come within Musket-shot, they hoisted *French* Colours. The Commander in Chief, who was in a Ship of 70 Guns, or upwards, came ranging along the Larboard side of the *Assurance*, commanded by Captain *Tollet*, and fell on board of him, so that they engaged Yard-Arm and Yard-Arm for almost half an Hour, during which time the *French* Ship plying him with small Shot, cut off most of the marine Soldiers, and the Seamen quartered upon the Deck, after which she fell off, and came on board again on the Lee side, first ranging on his Bow, and then on his Quarter, whereupon he fired into her his upper Deck, and lower Deck Guns, insomuch that he obliged her to quit him, and then she stood away a-head after the Merchant Ships. The other three, of 40 and 50 Guns each, came ranging along his side, firing many Shot into him, and after that bore away as the other Ship had done. The Damage the *Assurance* received was very great, her sides being in many Places shot through and through; her Shrouds and Backstays, as also her main and false Stay cut in pieces; her Fore-sail and Fore-top-sail very much torn, the best Bower Anchor carried away with a Shot, one of the Flukes of the spare Anchor likewise Shot away, and the small Bower, by the *French* Ship's boarding her, forced through her Bowes.

When her Commander had made good these Damages as well as time would permit, all the Ships of War bore down to secure those of the Merchants, and expected a second Engagement, but the Enemy declining it, stood away to cut off some of the Convoys, which might, had they regarded his Signal, have gotten safe in with the Shore. Some of them he brought into *Plimouth*, and while he was engaged he saw others bear away for *Falmouth*, so that it could not then be known how many had fallen into the Enemy's Hands.

The Dispute lasted about two Hours, in the beginning of which Captain *Tollet* was wounded upon the Deck, where (having been ill before) he was carried in a Chair. The first Lieutenant was shot in the Leg, which he got dressed, and then returned to his Charge. The second Lieutenant was killed, as were several of those *French* Officers which were brought from *Ireland*, but more of them wounded; and in the whole the *Assurance* had twenty five killed, and fifty three maimed, some of whom died; for the Enemy making their chief Attempt on her, she was severely handled, the *Hampshire* having no more than two Men killed, and eleven wounded, and the *Assistance* but twenty one wounded, and eight slain.

1709.

Let us now return to the Lord *Dursley*, who the 20th of *March* ordered three Ships off of *Brest* for Intelligence, one of which was to bring him the same to *Plimouth*, and the other two to cruise off of *Scilly* till his Lordship joined them; mean while the *Salisbury* took a *French West-India* Ship, which proving very leaky, most of the valuable Goods were taken out of her, left she should founder before she got into Port.

The Salisbury takes a French West-India Ship.

The 29th of *March* his Lordship received Orders to conduct the Ships bound to *Lisbon* well into the Sea, and much about this time he had an Account that Monsieur *Du Gue Trovine* had been seen the 25th of the same Month with seven Ships, in the Latitude of 49^d, Westing from *Scilly* about thirty five Leagues; which being confirmed by the Master of a Ship of 20 Guns, taken and brought in by the *Romney*, his Lordship purposed to leave the Transports and Trade bound to *Lisbon* to the Care of some Ships of the States-General suddenly expected from *Portsmouth*, and to have proceeded to Sea immediately in search of the Enemy, but they not timely arriving, he took under his Protection the aforesaid Transports and Trade, and had no sooner parted with them in Safety, than he discovered two *French* Ships of War, which had that very Morning taken one of ours called the *Bristol*, of 50 Guns, the Captain of her being in Search of our Squadron from *Plimouth*. To these Ships his Lordship gave Chase, and retaking the *Bristol*, (ready to founder by reason of a Shot in her Bread-room) he ordered the two sternmost Ships to lie by her.

Lord Dursley retakes our Ship the Bristol.

and chases some of the French Ships.

His Lordship followed the Enemy from Six in the Morning until Nine at Night, but finding the biggest Ship outsailed him, which he afterwards understood was the *Achilles*, commanded by Monsieur *Du Gue Trovine*, he made the Signal for the headmost Ships to leave off chasing her. On the other, called the *Gloire*, of 44 Guns, he y gained, and the *Chester*, commanded by Captain *Thomas Matthews*,

CHAP. XXII. *from the Year* 1698, *to* 1712.

Matthews, coming up within Gun-shot, continued so near as to keep Sight of her all Night, and by false Fires shewed our other Ships what Course he steer'd, so that she surrender'd, after engaging some time. *The Gloire taken.*

The 26th of *April* two small Ships were taken; as was on the 7th of *May* a Privateer carrying 14 Guns and one hundred Men; but the Provisions in the Squadron growing very short, his Lordship was obliged to return to *Plimouth* the 13th, with one Third, and seven Fourth Rates, and there he had an Account that the *Sweepstakes*, a Ship of 32 Guns, had been taken, in her Passage Westward, by two of the Enemy's Privateers, each of which had more Men than were on board the said Frigate. *1709. Some other Prizes. Our Sweepstakes taken.*

The Lord *Dursley* coming from *Plimouth* to *London*, went down to the *Nore* the 16th of *July*, and on the 21st sailed from thence with a Squadron off of *Schouwen* in *Zeeland*, in order to intercept some Ships with Corn, coming from the North, for Supply of the Enemy's Army in *Flanders*, but not having the good Fortune of meeting with any of them, he proceeded to *Ouzly* Bay. *Lord Dursley comes to Town, and afterwards commands a Squadron of Zeeland.*

The 5th of *October* his Lordship repaired to *Spithead*, and sailing from thence, came to *Plimouth* three Days after, with one Third Rate, and two Fourths, from whence he dispatched three Ships of 50 Guns to cruise in *Bristol* Chanel, and Captain *Vincent* with six others to cruise in the Latitude of 48^d and 30^m, and 50^d, Westing from *Scilly* from twenty to thirty Leagues, for the Security of a considerable Fleet of Merchant Ships expected from the *West-Indies*, and some time after he himself sailed to join them. *His Lordship returns to command the Western Squadron.*

When his Lordship was off of *Scilly* the 31st of *October*, he took a *French* Ship from *Guadalupe*, and a small Privateer, and meeting the Fleet from *Barbadoes* the 2d of *December*, he appointed some Ships to strengthen that Convoy, and sent two Frigates off of *Brest* for Intelligence. *Two Prizes taken.*

The latter end of *November* Captain *Hughes* of the *Winchester* chased a Ship, which proved to be a *Dutch* Privateer, whose Commander being required to strike, he, instead of paying that due Respect to the Flag of *England*, fired both great and small Shot into him, but being answered in the same manner, after an obstinate Dispute, (though it was known the *Winchester* was an *English* Ship of War) the Commmanding Officer was killed, and between thirty and forty of the *Dutch* Seamen. *The Winchester and a Dutch Privateer have a Scuffle.*

On the 9th of *December* the Lord *Dursley* (who was then Vice-Admiral of the Red) order'd Captain *Hartnol* of the *Restauration* to cruise with that Ship, and four more, between the Latitudes of 49 and 50^d, Westing from fifteen to twenty Leagues from *Scilly*, to protect several *East-India* Ships and their Convoys from *Ireland*, and the 2d of *January* was going from *Plimouth* with seven clean Frigates to relieve them; but being ordered to accompany Sir *John Norris* in his way to *Lisbon*, his Lordship lay some time after that in the appointed Station, e'er he was forced from thence by contrary Winds, and during his being on this Service, he took a Privateer *Lord Dursley made Vice-Admiral of the Red.*

Prizes taken. teer of 20 Guns, and retook the *St. Peter* of *Dublin*, which had been seized by the Enemy off of *Cape Clear*.

Other Prizes taken. The *East-India* Trade being not yet arrived from *Ireland*; his Lordship appointed three of the Ships under his Command to see them in Safety from thence, and the 21st of *February* the *Kent* brought into *Plimouth* a small Privateer, and a *French* Merchant Ship, as the *Restauration* and *August* did the next Day four more, which were bound from *Nantz* to *Martinico*; and not many Days after his Lordship appointed the *Restauration* and *August* to see two *East-India* Ships well into the Sea, but by contrary Winds they were forced back again.

1710.

Other Prizes taken, and Lord Durfley comes to Town The 10th of *March* the *Mountague* took a Privateer of 10 Guns, and his Lordship having seen the *East-India* Ships, and those bound to the Isle of *May*, a hundred and fifty Leagues from *Scilly*, returned to *Plimouth* the 9th of *May*; seven Days after which the *Lyon*, *Colchester*, and *Litchfield* brought in four Prizes, two of them Privateers, the others Merchant Ships, when his Lordship leaving the Squadron, he came to Town by Consent of the Lord High-Admiral.

CHAP. XXIII.

Containing an Account of Sir John Norris *his Proceedings towards the intercepting some* French *Ships of War, and Merchant Ships with Corn from the* Baltick.

UPON Advice that the Enemy expected a very considerable Quantity of Corn from the *Baltick*, and that the Vessels were to be convoyed by four or five Ships of War, Sir *John Norris*, then Admiral of the Blue, was ordered with six *English* Ships to proceed to the *Sound*, and to endeavour to place himself in such a Station where he might most probably meet with them upon their coming from thence. He was directed in his Passage to endeavour to gain the best Intelligence he could concerning them from any Ships or Vessels he might meet with; and if by this means, or otherwise, he should be assured they were sailed, and that he had not any Prospect of coming up with them, he was to return to *Yarmouth* Roads, and there expect farther Orders.

A Council of War held, and These Instructions he received by a small Frigate called the *Experiment*, the Commander whereof informed him, that he had seen on the 13th of *June*, off of the *Galloper*, six *French* Men of War, standing N. N. E. with all the Sail they could make, and that he judged them to be bound to the *Baltick*. Thereupon he called a Council of War, where it was determined to keep in their Company a Ship of the Third Rate, and another of the Fifth, which

CHAP. XXIII. *from the Year* 1698, *to* 1712.   727

which had just before joined him, and to strike Ground on the *Juts Riff* Bank (which lies on the Coast of *Jutland*) in twenty Fathom Water, as being judged the most proper Station to meet the Enemy coming from the *Sound*, or others going thither; and after having lain there some time, to proceed between the *Scaw* and *Maesterlandt*, and there, and at the Mouth of the *Sound*, to continue until the Provisions of the Ships should be reduced to three Weeks at whole Allowance. *Stations agreed upon.*

The 19th of *June* he arrived between the *Scaw* and *Maesterlandt*, and sent on shore for Pilots skilled in the *Categat* and *Sound*. Our homeward bound Convoy at *Maesterlandt* informed him they sailed from *Elsinore* the 15th of *June*, where they left three *French* Privateers, of 22, 16, and 10 Guns, loaden with Corn, but had not heard of any others in those Parts. Sir *John Norris* made the best of his way to that Port, seizing on a *Dane* which had been cleared there as a *French* Ship, and there he was informed that the Enemy intended to convoy their Corn in Neutral Ships, and that there was near a hundred *Dutch* Vessels taking in their Loading, which the Envoy from the States-General was apprehensive they would carry to *France*. Calling a Council of War thereupon, it was determined to strengthen the Convoy bound from *Maesterlandt*, and to endeavour to stop all Ships whatever loaden with Corn from proceeding out of the *Sound*, until the *Dutch* Convoy arrived to carry their Vessels directly to *Holland*, *Sir John Norris sails to Elsinore. A Council of War held.*

The 2d of *July* he had Advice the three *French* Ships beforementioned, which sailed from *Elsinore*, were at *Hammer Sound* in *Norway*, and consequently a Neutral Place, but not fortified, and thither he sent four Frigates to look out for them, or on the Coasts thereabouts, but they had not the good Fortune of meeting them. Several *Swedish* Ships he stopp'd loaden with Corn, bound, as they pretended, to *Holland* and *Portugal*, and this under a Pretence lest the Enemy should meet them at Sea; but the Court of *Denmark* took Umbrage thereat, and the Governor of *Elsinore* let him know, that if he continued to stop Ships from passing the *Sound*, he should be obliged to force him to desist. *He sends Ships to Hammer Sound to intercept the Enemy, and stops several Swedish Ships with Corn.*

At this time Sir *John Norris* was between the two Castles at *Elsinore* and *Cronenburgh*, one belonging to the *Dane* and the other to the *Swede*, both of which, at his Arrival, had answered his Salute, from whence he ordered one of the Ships under his Command to go out of the *Sound*, and to endeavour to prevent all Vessels from passing; soon after which he received Orders from the Lord High-Admiral, with the Queen's Approval of what he had done; and on the 12th of *July* Rear-Admiral *Convent* arriving with twelve *Dutch* Ships of War to convoy home their Vessels loaden with Corn, and the *French* Ships being sailed, it was determined at a Council of War, that he should return to *England* with the Squadron, and take the Trade from *Maesterlandt* in Company with him, if they were not gone from that Port. *He is saluted by both the Castles at the Entrance of the Sound. He returns to England.*

CHAP.

C H A P. XXIV.

Containing an Account of Sir Cloudesly Shovell's *Proceedings to, in, and from the* Mediterranean, *with the beating of our Army in* Spain; *the unsuccessful Attempt on* Thoulon *by the Duke of* Savoy, *and the bombarding that Place soon after; together with the Loss of Sir* Cloudesly Shovell, *and several of our Ships on the Islands of* Scilly.

1706.
Sir Cloudesly Shovell with the Fleet, and Earl Rivers with Land-Forces going to assist the King of Spain.

HAving related what was done in the *Soundings,* as well as in the North Sea, and up and down in the Chanel, let us look back and give some Account of the Fleet which was fitting out in the Year 1706 for Service in the *Mediterranean,* under the Command of Sir *Cloudesly Shovell,* who had Orders the 12th of *July* to make all possible Dispatch in getting them ready; and on this Expedition went the Earl *Rivers,* and the Earl of *Essex,* with between nine and ten thousand Land-Forces, *English* and *Dutch,* who were to be employed in assisting the King of *Spain* towards the Recovery of his Kingdom from the Duke of *Anjou.*

When Sir *Cloudesly Shovell* arrived at *Lisbon,* he was to take under his Command the Squadron left there by Sir *John Leake* when he came from the *Mediterranean,* under the Conduct of Sir *George Byng,* who in the Interim had detached a Convoy home with the empty Transports and Trade, and sent some Ships of War off of *Carthagena,* at the Request of the Governor of that Place, the better to support him, should he be attack'd by the Militia of *Murcia,* who, since the Retreat of the Troops from thence, had advanced, and obliged *Origuela,* a neighbouring Town, to declare again for the Duke of *Anjou.*

The 6th of *September* Sir *Cloudesly Shovell* came to *Torbay,* where the greatest dispatch was made in getting off Corn and Hay for the Horses, and Water and Necessaries for the *English* and *Dutch* Transports, and being in the *Soundings* the 10th of the said Month the *Barfleur,* a Ship of the Second Rate, sprung a dangerous Leak so that he was forced to send her home, the Earl *Rivers* going then on board the Admiral's own Ship the *Association*; and many of the Ships of the Fleet, as well as those for Transportation, were not only separated, but received much damage by the Extremity of the Weather, insomuch that he arrived in the River of *Lisbon* with no more than four Ships of War, and about fifty Transports; but meeting most of the rest there, he sent out Cruisers to look for, and assist such as were missing. Here he found several empty Transport Ships, into which he removed those Troops from such others as were render'd unserviceable, and sent two of the Ships of Sir *George Byng's*

The Fleet separated by a Storm.

CHAP. XXIV. *from the Year* 1698, *to* 1712. 729

Byng's Squadron to *Alicant* with Money and Neceſſaries for the Army then under Command of the Earl of *Gallway*.

The 28th of *November* the Admiral had Orders not only to take under his Command all Her Majeſty's Ships which he ſhould find at *Lisbon*, but alſo ſuch others as he might meet with, not employed on any immediate and preſſing Service; and much about this time the King of *Portugal* dying, things were in no ſmall Confuſion at that Court. *King of Portugal dies.*

Colonel *Worſley* being ſent to the King of *Spain* at *Valencia*, returned to *Lisbon* with Letters from His Majeſty, and the Earl of *Gallway*, repreſenting the great danger he was in by the Superiority of the *French* and *Spaniards*, unleſs the Troops with the Earl *Rivers* came ſpeedily to His Majeſty's Aſſiſtance, inſomuch that it was feared things would be reduced to ſo great Extremities as in the laſt Winter; whereupon it was reſolved to proceed with the Forces to *Alicant* with the utmoſt Diſpatch; but it required much time and pains to put all things in a Readineſs, at a Port where but little could be had for making good the great Damages received in their Paſſage from *England*. *King of Spain preſſes for the Troops.*

Before the Month of *December* was expired, a very extraordinary Accident happened, which was thus. The Admiral having appointed ſome cruiſing Ships to proceed to Sea, as they were going out of the Mouth of the River the *Portugueſe* Forts fired at leaſt threeſcore Shot at them, to bring them to an Anchor, which he perceiving, ſent Orders to our Captains to puſh their way through, and accordingly they did ſo, without ſo much as returning one Shot at the Forts. The Court of *Portugal*, upon his repreſenting to them this barbarous Uſage, pretended that the Officers of the Forts had done it without Orders, for that they were only directed to fire at, and detain a *Genoeſe* Ship whoſe Maſter was indebted to the King. But the Admiral being certainly informed that this very Ship was at the ſame time lying before the Walls of the City of *Lisbon*, and that the Maſter of her was on ſhore tranſacting his Buſineſs, he let them know, in a manner which became a Perſon in his Poſt thus affronted, that if they offered to attempt any ſuch thing again, (for they had done it before to Sir *John Leake*, as hath been already related) he would not ſtay for Orders from his Miſtreſs, but take Satisfaction from the Mouths of his Cannon. *Portugueſe Forts fire at our Ships.*

And here it may not be improper to take Notice of ſome very handſome Actions performed by ſome of the Ships which Sir *Cloudeſly Shovell* thus ſent out to cruiſe, *viz.* the *Romney*, of 50 Guns, commanded by Captain *William Cony*, being with the *Milford* and *Fowy*, two Ships of the Fifth Rate, in *Gibraltar* Bay, on the 12th of *December*, they had Intelligence that a *French* Ship of 16 Guns, which had about 30 Pieces of Braſs Cannon on board, part of thoſe which belonged to the Ships of Monſieur *Ponty* which Sir *John Leake* had forced on ſhore, lay at an Anchor under the Guns of *Malaga*, whereupon Captain *Cony*, with the Ship he commanded only, proceeded thither, (one of the Fifth Rates being diſabled, and the other having accidentally ſeparated from him) and, notwithſtanding *A handſome Action of Captain Cony, and others ſent to cruiſe with him.*

A a a a a

withstanding the continual Fire of the Town, took her, and brought her off.

The 26th following he gave chase to, and came up with another *French* Ship, which proved to be the *Content*, of 64 Guns, which, to secure her self, got close under a Castle, about eight Leagues to the Westward of *Almeria*; but Captain *Cony* anchoring, and ordering the *Milford* and *Fowy* to do the same, one a-head, and the other a-stern of him, they plied their Guns on her upwards of two Hours, when she took fire, and after burning about three Hours, blew up, losing thereby great part of her Men. This Ship Monsieur *Villars*, who cruised with a *French* Squadron between Cape *Palos* and Cape *de Gates*, had detached to bring out to him the aforesaid Ship with Brass Ordnance from *Malaga*.

On the 8th of *July*, between Twelve and One at Night, Captain *Cony* discovered, and gave chase to another Ship, which was called the *Mercury*, carrying 42 Guns, and two hundred and fifty Men, but was lent by the *French* King to the Merchants, which Ship submitted to him, after her Commander was slain, and several of her Men were killed and wounded.

1705.

The beginning of *January* Earl *Rivers* received Orders from *England* to land the Troops at *Lisbon*, upon Assurances given by the Envoy from *Portugal* at our Court, and the Marquis *Montandre*, that the King would join a considerable Body to penetrate into *Spain*, and march to *Madrid* by way of *Toledo*. But since it was found that the Ministry of *Portugal* would have divided our Army, one half to go to *Valencia*, and the other to the Frontiers of *Portugal*, it was at a Council of War judged impracticable for either of them, in such case, to make any considerable Progress in *Spain*; and there-

It was resolved to land the Troops at Alicant.

fore it was resolved to land them at *Alicant*, for doing whereof Orders were some little time after received from *England*.

Accordingly the Fleet and Transports proceeded, and when the Troops should be put on shore, the Admiral determined to return to *Lisbon*, there to put the Fleet in a Condition for Service, but to leave six or seven Ships on the *Spanish* Coast, to assist on all Occasions.

The Admiral returns to Lisbon.

Leaving *Alicant* the 17th of *February*, he arrived at *Lisbon* the 11th of the next Month; but in his Passage down the *Streights* the *Burford* met with several Transports which had lost the Fleet in its outward bound Voyage, and he had ordered three Third Rates to follow him from *Alicant* with other Transports, when unloaden, that by their being sent from thence to *England*, the Government might be eased of their Charge as soon as 'twas possible.

The Army in *Spain* being in great want of Money, Cloaths, Provisions, and other Necessaries, he order'd Sir *George Byng* to proceed to *Alicant* with Supplies, and to take with him one First Rate, one Second, seven Thirds, and one Fourth, together with the nine Ships of the States-General, and some small Frigates and Fire-

Earl Rivers and the Earl of Essex return to Lisbon.

ships; and on the 23d of *March* Earl *Rivers* and the Earl of *Essex* came thither from *Alicant*, with several Officers who were returning for *England* after the Army was landed; the reason whereof I know

CHAP. XXIV. *from the Year* 1698, *to* 1712.   731

know not, unless it was that they had no Inclination to serve with the Earl of *Gallway*, who was a Senior Officer.

Sir *George Byng* sailed the 30th of *March*, who, when he had put on shore the Necessaries for the Army, was to employ the Ships under his Command so as that they might be of most Service to the Allies; and the Admiral was making the utmost Dispatch with the rest of the Fleet to follow him, which were one Ship of the Second Rate, eleven of the Third, four of the Fourth, as many of the Fifth, besides Fireships, Bombs, and other small Vessels.

1707. *Sir George Byng goes with a Squadron to Alicant.*

With these Ships he sailed, and when he was off of Cape St. *Vincent* he had the melancholy News of the Defeat of our Army in *Spain* at the Battel of *Almanza*, great part of the Foot being killed, or taken Prisoners, the Lord *Gallway* having desired Sir *George Byng* that what he had brought with him for their Use might be carried to *Tortosa* in *Catalonia*, to which Place his Lordship designed to retreat, and that, if possible, he would save the sick and wounded Men at *Denia*, *Gandia*, and *Valencia*, where it was intended the Bridges of Boats, Baggage, and all things that could be got together should be put on board. Accordingly he took care of the sick and wounded Men, and arriving at *Tortosa*, there the Lord *Gallway* propos'd to make a Stand with the poor Remains of the Army. This Service employed Sir *George Byng* almost the whole Month of *April*, and then he was in daily Expectation of being joined by Sir *Cloudesly Shovell* from *Lisbon*, either on that part of the Coast of *Spain*, or at *Barcelona*, whither he was designed.

Our Army in Spain beaten.

The Admiral arriving at *Alicant* the 10th of *May*, he sailed from thence the next Day, and joined Sir *George Byng* at *Barcelona* the 20th, whence he proceeded to the Coast of *Italy*, and the latter end of *June* anchored between *Nice* and *Antibes*, where he hourly expected his Royal Highness the Duke of *Savoy*, with the Army which was to attempt *Thoulon*, consisting, as it was represented to him, of thirty five thousand Men, all extraordinary good Troops, whereas that of the Enemy amounted not to thirty thousand, and most part of them new raised, not but that they were getting together the *Ban*, and the *Arriere Ban* of the Country, which might make as many more.

Sir Cloudesly Shovell joins Sir George Byng, and sails for the Coast of Italy.

The 29th of *June* the Duke of *Savoy* and Prince *Eugene* arriving, his Royal Highness came on board the Admiral, when he was at an Anchor about a League from the *Var*, where the Enemy were entrenched with part of their Troops. His Highness resolved to attempt the Pass before the rest of them came up, and the Admiral undertook to destroy their Works next to the Sea, for he could place his Ships in less than Musket-shot, so as to have them open to him. From thence he forced the Enemy, and Sir *John Norris* landing with five or six hundred Seamen and Marines, took Possession of them, insomuch that about half an Hour after his Royal Highness passed without Opposition, and the 4th of *July* decamped and marched towards *Thoulon*, while the Fleet made way to the Isles of *Hyeres*, the Admiral engaging to the Duke that if the Place was taken, and he

Duke of Savoy comes on board the Fleet, and the Enemy's Retrenchments upon the Var attacked.

Our Fleet goes to the Isles of Hyeres.

A a a a a 2

he could not retreat safely by Land, to convoy himself and the Army by Sea.

Four Third Rates, and five *Dutch* Ships joined him towards the latter end of *July*, as did those he had sent to *Genoa* and *Livorne*, with the Transports that were loaden with Ammunition and Provisions for the Army; and he appointed some Frigates not only to keep open the Communication by Sea, but to protect the Duke of *Savoy*'s Boats passing to and fro, and to awe the Enemy in *Villa Franca* and *Monaco*; besides which others were sent on proper Services.

Ships appointed on proper Stations.

One hundred Cannon were landed from the Fleet for the Batteries, with two hundred Rounds of Powder and Shot, and a considerable Number of Seamen to serve as Gunners; and Cordage, Nails, and Spikes, with all other things wanting for the Camp, (for indeed they were but poorly furnished) were supply'd from the Ships; so that Affairs had a very good Face till the 4th of *August*, when, early in the Morning, the Enemy making a vigorous Sally, forced most or all of the People out of the Works, and took Possession to the Right, where they continued all Day, and upon their going off, destroyed them, drawing away eight or ten Guns into the Town, in which Action there were killed and wounded on the Duke of *Savoy*'s side above eight hundred Men, among whom were the Prince of *Saxe Gotha*, and some Officers of Distinction.

Cannon, &c. landed from the Fleet.

The French make a successful Sally.

This Attempt being made with such Numbers, it put the Troops under great Apprehensions, and the Generals were of Opinion it would not be proper to carry on the Siege, since while the Duke of *Savoy*'s Army decreased, the Enemy rather gathered Strength; insomuch that on the 6th of *August* his Royal Highness desired the Admiral would immediately embark the Sick and Wounded, and take off the Cannon, in order to his raising the Siege, which from this time was turned only to a Cannonading and Bombardment. His Royal Highness also informed him that he purposed to decamp the 10th in the Morning, and desired that the Fleet might accompany the Army as far as the *Var*; which being done, it was proposed to the Duke, and Prince *Eugene*, to carry with the Fleet to *Spain* any Troops which could be spared for Service in that Country; but since there was not any thing determined in this Affair, the Admiral soon after shaped his Course down the *Streights*.

The Siege of Thoulon raised.

When the Army were withdrawn from *Thoulon*, our Bomb-Vessels played so warmly on the Town, that they set it on fire, which continued to burn furiously all Night, nor was it extinguish'd the next Day, but at length the Enemy brought both Guns and Mortars against the Vessels, and forced them to retire, not a little mangled.

Thoulon bombarded.

Before the *French* made their Sally, they were in such a Consternation, that they sunk about twenty of their Ships of War in the Harbour, ten, or more of them, with three Decks, and did it in such a manner, as render'd them unfit for any farther Service ever since.

French sink their Ships.

Thus

Chap. XXIV. *from the Year* 1698, *to* 1712. 733

Thus ended an Expedition, attended with so much Charge, against the most considerable Port the *French* have in the *Mediterranean*, and Sir *Cloudesly Shovell* being not a little mortify'd at the Miscarriage, though he contributed all in his Power towards the reducing it, he bent his Course homewards (as hath been already said) with one Ship of the First Rate, two of the Second, seven of the Third, two of the Fourth, one of the Fifth, two of the Sixth, four Fireships, one Sloop, and one Yacht, leaving at *Gibraltar* Sir *Thomas Dilkes* with nine Ships of the Line of Battel, three Fifth Rates, and one of the Sixth, for Service on the Coast of *Italy*. *Sir Cloudesly Shovell repairs down the Streights, and leaves some Ships with Sir Thomas Dilkes.*

Coming into the *Soundings* the 23d of *October*, he had ninety Fathom Water, which was in the Morning of that Day, and in the Afternoon he brought the Fleet to, and lay by, with a very fresh Gale at S. S. W. but hazey Weather. At Six at Night he made sail again, and stood away under his Courses, believing, as 'tis presumed, he saw the Light at *Scilly*; soon after which several of the Ships made the Signal of Danger, as he himself did. Sir *George Byng* was not then half a Mile to Windward of him, who saw the Breaches of the Sea, and soon after the Rocks of *Scilly* above Water, on one of which the Admiral struck, and in less than two Minutes there was not any thing of his Ship seen. The Ship where Sir *George Byng* bore his Flag was providentially saved chiefly by his own Presence of Mind in this imminent Danger, even when one of the Rocks was almost under her Main-Chains, and Sir *John Norris* and the Lord *Dursley* with very great difficulty disentangled themselves from the threatning Fate, besides whom several others ran no small hazard among these dangerous little Islands. *Sir Cloudesly Shovell among the Islands of Scilly. He is lost. Several Ships happily escaped.*

It cannot be imagined but that this sad Accident occasioned a very great Surprize at home, especially since so experienced a Seaman, and so good an Officer as Sir *Cloudesly Shovell* was had the conducting of the Fleet, and that there were other Flags, as well as private Captains, with him of undoubted Knowledge. As I cannot undertake to give the true Cause of this unhappy Miscarriage, I shall leave it with this common Observation, that upon approaching Land after so long a Run, the best Looker out is the best Sailer, and consequently the lying by in the Night time, and making sail in the Day is the most safe, which I think this unhappy Gentleman did not do, and might principally occasion not only the Loss of himself and all his Ships Company, but also of all the Officers and Men of the *Eagle*, a Ship of 70 Guns, and of the *Romney*, mounted with 50, the former of which was commanded by Captain *Robert Hancock*, and the other by Captain *William Cony*. The *Firebrand* Fireship was also lost, but Captain *Francis Percy*, and most of her Company saved, and the *Phœnix* Fireship, commanded by Captain *Sansom*, ran on shore, but was luckily got off again. *An Observation on this unhappy Accident. Other Ships lost.*

I cannot but have a lively Idea of the danger Fleets are exposed to upon entering the *British* Chanel, when coming from foreign Parts, but more especially when their Officers have not the Advantage of knowing their Latitude by a good Observation; for being sent from *Cadiz* by the Earl of *Orford*, (then Admiral *Russell*) to whom *An Observation of the danger which the Author ran near Scilly.*

whom I had the Honour to be Secretary, as I had been for several Years before, to take on me my present Employment of Secretary of the Admiralty, I had at that time no other Convenience of a Passage than on a *Dutch* Ship of War of 70 Guns, the Captain whereof was in Years, and had long commanded in the Service of the States-General, I will not say with how good Success.

Meeting a tedious Passage in the Winter Season, wherein we were exposed to no little Extremities both for want of Water and Provisions, the Trade which accompanied us from *Cadiz* were joined, when we approached the *English* Chanel, by several other *Dutch* Ships of War, and all other Merchant Ships bound from *Portugal*, so that there were in Company between three and four hundred Sail.

The Captain of the Ship on which I embarked, being the Senior Officer, led the whole, but was so far mistaken in his Reckoning, that had it not been for a Gentleman who accompany'd me in my Voyage, and who, near four a Clock in the Evening, the latter end of *December*, went into the Main top to look out, suspecting we were, by our Course, very near Land, the greatest part of the Fleet would infallibly have been lost, for at that very time we were all stemming directly on the Rocks of *Scilly*, and with the utmost difficulty got clear of them; so positive was the rash old Commander in his own Judgment, nor would he believe the happy Warping which was given him by the cautious Gentleman, till even he could almost see, at that time of Night, the danger he was running into from the Deck of his Ship

Chap. XXV.

Containing an Account of Sir Thomas Dilkes's *Proceedings while he commanded in the* Mediterranean.

1707.

I Now return to Rear-Admiral *Dilkes*, who, as hath been mention'd before, was left with a Squadron of Ships in the *Mediterranean*, to be employ'd in the Service of the King of *Spain*, with which he sailed from *Gibraltar* the 5th of *October*, (being seven Third Rates, three Fourths, and one Fifth of ours, and four Ships of the Line, with a Fireship, of the *Dutch*, in order to join some other of our Ships coming from *Italy* with a considerable Transport for *Catalonia*.

When he was some Leagues Westward of *Barcelona*, he received a Letter by Express from the King of *Spain*, another from the Earl of *Gallway*, and a third from our Envoy, Mr. *Stanhope*, desiring him to call at *Barcelona*, his Majesty having some Affairs of Importance to communicate to him. Being there, the King let him know that he was informed he had Orders to stop at *Livorne*, and

The King of Spain confers with Sir Thomas Dilkes,

to

CHAP. XXV. *from the Year* 1698, *to* 1712. 735

to carry from thence the Succours from *Italy* to *Catalonia*; then to employ the Squadron under his Command as might be best for his Service, until the middle of *January* next; and after that to repair to *Lisbon* to refit the Ships, and for a Supply of Provisions. His Majesty represented to him how highly prejudicial it would be to the Common Cause, and to himself in particular, if a Squadron did not constantly remain in the *Mediterranean*, not only to protect his Transports with Corn, but to bring the Queen from *Italy* when she should be ready to embark; and therefore proposed that the Ships with him might be thus divided. Part of them to attend the Queen, others to strengthen the Convoy from *Italy*, and the Remainder to endeavour to reduce the Kingdom of *Sardinia*, his Majesty having appointed the *Conde de Cifuentes* his Lieutenant-General there: But it was thought necessary that some Ships might be first sent to *Italy* to take in a Body of Men for this Service. His Majesty also let the Rear-Admiral know, that should he leave those Seas, all *Catalonia* would be much exposed to the Enemy, as well as his own Person to the hazard of a Siege, especially if *Lerida* should be lost, for which Reasons he earnestly pressed his stay.

and presses that a Squadron might remain in the Mediterranean.

King of Spain's Proposals for dividing the Ships.

Upon this a Council of War was called, and considering the Condition of the Ships, as to Stores and Provisions, it was judged absolutely necessary they should be at *Lisbon* by the middle of *January*; nor was it thought that the Flag was at liberty by his Instructions to divide the Squadron. But it was concluded, that if when he came to *Livorne*, he should find the Enemy had not a Strength at Sea to molest the Convoy with the Troops designed to *Catalonia*, he should then sail to the Island of *Sardinia*, as his Majesty had desired.

A Council of War held.

The King pressed him again to proceed to that Island, and assured him the Inhabitants wanted only an Opportunity of declaring for him, which when they had done, himself and Troops might from thence be furnished with Bread, at this time very much wanted; and his Majesty, as a farther Motive for his Proceeding on this Service, let him know that he had reason to believe the Transports from *Italy* were already on their way.

The King presses Sir Thomas Dilkes to proceed to Sardinia.

Since the Care of that Embarcation was particularly recommended to him by his Instructions, he sailed from *Barcelona* the 2d of *November*, but meeting with hard Gales of Wind, the Ships were separated, nor had they joined him again the 14th, when he was about twelve Leagues from Cape *Corsica*, where he was informed by a Letter from the King of *Spain* of the Loss of *Lerida*, so that it was absolutely necessary the Troops should be in *Spain* as soon as possible, especially since *Tortosa* and *Tarragona* were in great danger.

Lerida lost.

He arrived at *Livorne* the 19th of *November*, in which Road he met with so violent a Storm, that all the Ships suffered very much; and here he had notice from *Genoa* that all the Transports were ready to sail for *Final* to take in eight thousand Foot, besides some Horse, where he intended to join them with his whole Squadron, to

Sir Thomas Dilkes comes to Livorne.

to prevent Accidents from the Enemy, who had a confiderable Strength at Sea, and in all Probability might have a Defign to way-lay them.

The 1ft of *December* he had not any notice of the Tranfport Ships being arriv'd at *Final,* and fince the Commadore of the Convoy had informed him that by the ftrong South-Weft Winds the Cables of the Ships were very much damaged in the Port of *Genoa,* he thought they could not well be trufted at fuch a Seafon of the Year at *Final,* and therefore earneftly defired of our Envoy that the Troops might embark at *Vado,* a little Town about a League to the Weftward of *Savona,* where they might fafely be carried off in the worft Weather; but foon after this he died of a Fever after some Days Illnefs, during which time he committed the Care of the Squadron to Captain *Jafper Hicks,* who was the next Senior Officer.

Sir Thomas Dilkes dies, and Captain Hicks commands.

It may not be improper here to inform you, that upon Sir *Thomas Dilkes*'s coming into the Road of *Livorne,* he demanded a Salute of feventeen Guns, which being refufed, he writ to our Envoy at the *Grand Duke*'s Court, who was anfwer'd by the Secretary of State, that fince Sir *Thomas Dilkes* was not more than a Rear-Admiral, what he had demanded could not be granted, for that the Caftle at *Livorne* never had faluted the Flag of any Crowned Head firft, but fuch as were either Admirals, or Vice-Admirals; and that as to the Number of Guns he demanded, Sir *Cloudefly Shovell,* though Admiral of the Fleet of *Great Britain,* was contented with eleven, and anfwer'd the Salute with the fame.

A Difpute about the Salute at Livorne.

Captain *Hicks,* as I have faid, being at the Head of the Squadron, he took care to conduct the Tranfports to *Spain,* and coming to *Lisbon* the 7th of *March,* there he received Orders to put the Ships under his Command into the beft Condition he could againft the Arrival of Sir *John Leake,* Admiral of the Fleet, from *England,* of whofe Proceedings I fhall give an Account, after I have looked homeward for fome time, and informed you what was done in the *Chanel, Soundings,* and off of *Dunkirk.*

CHAP.

CHAP. XXVI.

Containing an Account of Sir Stafford Fairborn's *Expedition to the River* Charente; *as also of his Proceedings with a Squadron off of* Ostend, *when part of our Army laid siege to that Place; and what was done by Sir* Thomas Hardy *in the* Soundings.

WHEN Sir *Stafford Fairborn,* Vice-Admiral of the Red, had in the Month of *April* been hastening out Ships from the River *Medway,* he came to *Spithead,* and there making all possible Dispatch in getting the Squadron ready with which he was to proceed into the *Soundings,* he was under Sail the 24th of the aforesaid Month of *April* with two Third Rates, three Fourths, and one Fifth, being to join two other Third Rates at *Plimouth,* as also the *Centurion* of 50 Guns, if there, and another of 40, he having order'd the *Milford* to follow him. His Instructions from the Lord High-Admiral were to proceed, with all possible Secrecy, to the Mouth of the River *Charente,* and to use his utmost Endeavours to take, or destroy such Ships or Vessels as the Enemy might be fitting out from *Rochefort,* which commonly lie before the Mouth of the said River to take in their Guns, Stores, and Provisions.

1706.

Sir Stafford Fairborn *sent with a Squadron off of* Rochefort.

When he had done his utmost in this Attempt, he was to consider at a Council of War what farther Service might be performed against the Enemy in the *Bay,* or on the *French* Coast elsewhere, and to endeavour to put in Execution what should be agreed on, so as to return by the middle of *May* to *Plimouth,* in regard there might by that time be occasion for the Ships under his Command for other Services.

By contrary Winds he was obstructed a considerable time from putting these Instructions in Execution, but at length he got off of the River *Charente,* and had a fair Prospect, if the Winds would have permitted, to have burnt the Enemy's Ships before *Rochelle,* a Disposition being to that purpose made; but, thus frustrated, he returned to *Plimouth* the 17th of *May,* with some small Prizes taken between the Isles of *Rhé* and *Oleron,* where with their Boats they also took and destroyed ten trading Vessels.

He returns to Plimouth *with some Prizes.*

He lay not long at *Plimouth* e'er he had Orders to come to the *Downs,* where, on the 30th of *May,* he received Instructions to repair off of *Ostend,* with four Ships of the Third Rate, three of the Fourth, four of the Fifth, one Fireship, two Bomb-Vessels, two Brigantines, and as many Sloops. And since part of the Army in *Flanders* was to be detached to *Ostend,* in order to oblige that Garrison to declare for King *Charles* the Third of *Spain,* he was to employ the Ships in such manner as might best conduce to the Reduction of the said Place, holding Correspondence with the Commander in Chief of the Forces before it. And if the Duke of *Marlborough* should

Sir Stafford Fairborn *sent off of* Ostend.

should be present, he was to follow his Orders, in case his Grace should think it proper to employ the Squadron on any other Service besides that of *Ostend*.

Pursuant to these Instructions Sir *Stafford Fairborn* proceeded over to *Ostend*, and stood in so near that the Town fired upon him; but after he had answer'd them in the same manner, he came to an Anchor within two Miles of the Place, which was as near as the Banks would permit, when sending his Lieutenant on shore, he brought him an Account that the Duke of *Marlborough* was at *Thielt*, and that Monsieur *Auverquerque* was marching the 6th of *June* with a Body of fifteen thousand Men to cut off all Communication between *Newport* and *Ostend*, as also that some Battalions were marching down to the Water side, Westward of the Town, so as to make themselves Masters of all the Sluices.

Newport attempted.
The first Attempt was made on *Newport*, to which Place, at the Desire of Monsieur *Auverquerque*, Sir *Stafford Fairborn* sent three small Frigates, to prevent their being supply'd with Provisions by Sea, and kept in the mean while his lesser Ships in constant Motion on the Windward Tides, to prevent any thing going into, or coming out of the Harbour of *Ostend*; but soon after it was thought most proper to block up *Newport*, while the Siege of *Ostend* was *Ostend besieged.* carrying on, where Monsieur *Auverquerque* lay encamped with his first Line within random Shot, the second Line fronting *Newport*, and his Quarters were at Fort *Albert*.

The Entrance of the Harbour being long, narrow, and crooked, whatever Ship or Vessel attempted to go in would be much exposed to the Platform of Guns, so that there seemed but little hopes of attempting any thing against the Ships by Sea, which lay all in a Cluster close to the Key, on the back side of the Town; but there were Letters in the Camp which insinuated, that as soon as the Trenches were opened, the Batteries raised, and some Bombs thrown into the Place, the *Spaniards* in Garrison, assisted by the Seamen and Burghers, would oblige the *French* Battalions to yield.

Monsieur *Auverquerque* acquainting Sir *Stafford Fairborn* that the Enemy had drawn some of their Troops together at *Furnes*, under the Marshal *Villeroy*, and that he was of Opinion two or three Frigates might be of Service, by hindering their Foot or Horse from passing the *Gut* at *Newport*, he accordingly dispatched some small Ships thither, not but that he was of Opinion the Sands which lay off would prevent their Shot reaching the Shore.

The Trenches opened.
It was now the 16th of *June*, and the Trenches were not opened, for want of a sufficient Number of Fascines, but that was done next Day within Pistol-shot of the Counterscarp, the Enemy killing and wounding about forty Men, and the Colonel of the Train was shot through the Thigh.

Some Boats get into Ostend.
The 19th, before break of Day, three Shallops, supposed to come from *Dunkirk*, got into *Ostend*, notwithstanding there were six of our small Frigates and Vessels close with the Shore to the Westward, and eight Boats upon the Guard. The Wind being from off the Land, by the help of that, and a strong Tide in their favour, they shot

shot to the Eastward of the Boats, through the Fire of several of them, and of a whole Battalion drawn up along the Shore; but had there been a Battery to the Eastward of *Ostend*, which Sir *Stafford Fairborn* proposed when the Army came first before the Place, we might have had as much Command of the Entrance of the Port as the Enemy, who had already flung against the Army and Trenches near nine thousand Shot, and two hundred Shells, and made such a continued Fire with their small Arms, that it was to be wonder'd there was not more Mischief done.

Our Batteries being finished we began to play upon the Enemy at once with forty five great Cannon, twenty smaller, and thirty six Mortars, as did our two Bomb Vessels, so that the Town was on fire in several Places within a quarter of an Hour. This made them more slack in their firing than before; but the Duke of *Marlborough* the Lord *Raby*, (now Earl of *Strafford*) Count *Corneille*, the Prince Prince *d'Auvergne*, and the Prince of *Hesse*, making a Visit to Monsieur *Auverquerque*, and in the Afternoon entering the Trenches, they fired for some time faster than ever, believing the Duke to be there, by the Salutes given to his Grace by all our Ships; and while he was in the Camp, (which was open to the Town) where he exposed himself very much, a Detachment of Grenadiers lodged themselves, with but little Loss, upon an Angle of the Counterscarp. The 24th of *June* our Batteries were advanced to the first Parallel, and a great Number of Troops were sent to make the aforesaid Lodgment larger, so that on the 25th, when the Town was on fire in many Places, they hung out a Flag to capitulate.

The Town on fire in many Places.

A hot fire when the Duke of Marlborough and others were in the Trenches.

The Garrison capitulates.

When the Army began first to fire from their Batteries, Sir *Stafford Fairborn* ordered all the small Frigates to get under Sail, and stand as close in with the Shore as possibly they could, and fire their Broadsides into the Town, which they effectually did, receiving themselves little damage; and this he intended they should daily have done, but they were prevented by the Badness of the Weather.

The Garrison surrendering upon such Conditions as were thought reasonable, the 17th in the Morning Count *La Motte* with the *French* Troops (amounting to about two thousand three hundred and sixty Men) marched out of the Town, and the two *Spanish* Regiments breaking, every one went to his respective home, when Baron *Spar*, with four *Dutch* Battalions, took Possession of the Place, which was in a manner a heap of Rubbish. This Affair being over, Sir *Stafford Fairborn* proceeded to *Spithead* with the *English* and *Dutch* Transport Ships, and Troops designed for *Spain* with the Earl *Rivers*, of which I have already given an Account.

After Sir *Thomas Hardy* had been with Sir *Stafford Fairborn* in the Expedition to *Rochefort*, and that against *Ostend*, he was appointed to command a Squadron in the *Soundings*, where he cruised from time to time for the Protection of our Trade, and annoying the Enemy, wherein he had not only the good Fortune to secure our homeward bound Fleets, but to take divers Prizes; and there being several Ships from *India* arrived in the Harbour of *Cork*, he

Sir Thomas Hardy commands a Squadron in the Soundings.

Bbbbb 2 proceeded

He brings East-India Ships from Cork.

1706.

proceeded thither, and brought them from thence, after he had lain there a considerable time Wind-bound; but in his Passage to *England* he met with a violent Storm, which not only separated and damaged the Ships, but forced him to bear up for *Milford Haven*, insomuch that though he sailed from *Plimouth* towards *Cork* the 24th of *December* 1706, he arrived not in the *Downs* before the 4th of *March* following, having with him five Ships of War, and sixty three Merchant Ships, from whence he returned Westward.

CHAP. XXVII.

Containing an Account of Sir George Byng's *Proceedings Northward, after a Squadron of* French *Ships that sailed from* Dunkirk *with the Pretender, and a Body of Land-Forces which were intended to land in Scotland.*

1707. Advice of the Pretender's Design to invade the Kingdom.

The Naval Preparations made thereupon.

IN the Month of *February* 170⅞, there was certain Advice that the Pretender, with a Squadron of Ships, and armed Troops, intended to make an Attempt on Her Majesty's Dominions, and thereupon Orders were given to Sir *John Jennings*, Vice-Admiral of the Red, to go down the River, and hasten the Ships fitting out to the *Downs*, as well as others in the River *Medway*. The like Orders were given the same Day to Captain *Christopher Myngs* at *Portsmouth*, to send away those which were at *Spithead*, and Sir *George Byng* was also, on the 17th of *February*, order'd to *Portsmouth*, to quicken the Ships from thence by two or three at a time, as they should be ready, and to take Men (if he found occasion for it) from those in the Harbour, and from Merchant Ships.

Mr. *Baker*, Rear-Admiral of the White, was, on the same Day, ordered to proceed with the Ships at the *Nore* to the *Downs*, with all possible Dispatch, and when there, to keep one or two off of *Dunkirk* for Intelligence; and if the Enemy got out of that Port, he was directed to follow, and endeavour to intercept, or destroy them; but if a superior Flag-Officer came to the *Downs*, he was to communicate these Orders to him, that so he might put them in Execution.

The 22d of *February* Sir *John Jennings* was order'd immediately to repair to the *Downs*, and from thence off of *Dunkirk*; and when he had discovered what the Enemy were doing there, he was, as Winds and Weather might permit, to repair to the Flats of the *Foreland*, the *Downs, Rye-Bay*, or such other Station as he should judge most proper for intercepting them, if he found they proceeded either Westward, Northward, or up the River of *Thames*, but to return off of *Dunkirk* when the Weather would permit, and in the mean

CHAP. XXVII. *from the Year* 1698, *to* 1712. 741

mean while to leave proper Ships there to bring him early Intelligence. If he had Advice they were got out to Sea, he was to follow them as far as they should go, and endeavour to take or destroy them; and it was also recommended to him to inform himself from *Holland*, what Ships of the States-General were in a Readiness to join with Her Majesty's, and to acquaint the Commander of them with his Instructions and Rendezvous: But if Sir *George Byng*, then Admiral of the Blue, arrived timely in the *Downs* from *Spithead*, he was to serve under his Command, and he to put these Orders in Execution.

The next Day, being the 23d of *February*, the Lord High-Admiral, Prince *George* of *Denmark*, sent Instructions to Sir *George Byng*, to leave Orders with the Lord *Durfley*, that if the *French* Squadron appeared in Sight of *Spithead*, with an Easterly Wind, he with the Ships under his Command should endeavour to go through the *Needles*, in order to join those coming from *Plimouth* with Captain *Hovenden Walker* *, either at that Port, or in *Torbay*, and, when so joined, to come Eastward, and do his utmost to take, sink, or otherwise destroy them, should they attempt any thing at *Portsmouth*; and on the 24th Orders were sent to Sir *John Jennings*, that if the Enemy got out with an Easterly Wind, and stood Westward, before the Ships from *Portsmouth* could join him, and that they were too strong for those under his Command, he should endeavour not only to keep between them and our Ships at *Spithead*, but to join them as soon as possible, sending one of his best Sailers thither, with notice of his Approach, that so they might be in an immediate Readiness.

Sir *George Byng* arriving in the *Downs* the 2d of *March* 1707, and there being reason to believe that the Enemy's Ships were bound to *Scotland*, Orders were sent him next Day to consider at a Council of War where he might best come to an Anchor, or cruise for intercepting them, if they proceeded Northward, or attempted to come on the Coast of *England*, or to go Westward through the Chanel. And when he should be joined by Captain *Walker* from St. *Helen*'s, he was to consider if he had Strength sufficient to divide the Ships into two Squadrons, and if so, how they might be best employed for preventing the Enemy's getting out of *Dunkirk*, and intercepting those which it was apprehended were coming to that Port from *Brest*, wherein he was to govern himself according to what should be determined.

It was judged the French Ships were bound with the Pretender to Scotland.

Having thus given an Account of what was done towards getting a Number of Ships together to oppose the Designs of the Pretender, and his Friend the *French* King, and brought Sir *George Byng* to the Head of the Squadron, it remains that I acquaint you with his Proceedings before and after the Enemy got out of *Dunkirk*.

The 26th in the Morning, (having then with him three Ships of the Third Rate, twelve of the Fourth, six of the Fifth, three of the Sixth, and a Fireship) he called a Council of War, and 'twas re-

---

* *Afterwards a Flag-Officer.*

solved

Sir George Byng's Proceedings after the Pretender to the Coast of Scotland, and before he got out of Dunkirk.

solved to proceed immediately with all the Ships into *Gravelin Pits*, or off of *Dunkirk*, to take the best View, or gain the best Intelligence that possibly might be of the Enemy; and not knowing whether any Ships were joined from *Brest*, he desired to be strengthened, especially with some of Force.

It falling calm on the Ebb in the Evening, he was obliged to anchor within the *South Foreland*, but next Morning, at four a Clock, he weighed again, with very little Wind at South, and stretched over to *Gravelin Pits*, where he got Advice of the Enemy's Strength by the Men of a Fishing-Boat taken near the Shore, and that the 27th in the Evening, after he came to an Anchor, the King of *England* (as they called him) came to *Gravelin* with two Post Chaises, in his way to *Dunkirk*, where they daily expected Ships from *Brest*.

Upon consulting the Flag-Officers with him, who were Sir *John Jennings*, Vice-Admiral of the Red, the Lord *Durfley*, Vice-Admiral of the Blue, and *John Baker* Esq; Rear-Admiral of the White, it was judged adviseable, while the Winds were Westerly, and likely to blow, to ride in *Gravelin Pits*, both for the Security of the Squadron, and that they might lie in the way of the Ships from *Brest*, mean while to send a Frigate to *Holland*, with notice to the Deputies of the States that he was there, if they should think it proper to send any Ships to join him.

With a small Frigate he went within two Miles of *Flemish* Road, and had a good Sight of the Enemy's Ships, which he counted to be twenty seven in all, small and great, one of which he took to be a Ship of 60 Guns, and three of about 50, the rest smaller, all lying with their Topsails loose, the usual Sign of their being ready to sail; besides which he saw between forty and fifty within the Heads above the Forts, two or three of which seemed to be pretty large Ships, but discovered not more in the *Basin* than three, one of them unrigg'd, and another with a White Flag at her Main-topmast Head.

If not any of the Enemy's Ships appeared from the Westward, and the Weather was favourable, he had thoughts of shifting Roads, and to lie for a Day or two off of *Dunkirk*, in the fair way for the other Chanel, to observe their Motions should they come out, which if they did not attempt in that time, the Spring was so far over, that he judged they could not do any thing until the next, insomuch that he then intended to proceed to the *Downs*, a Road of much greater Security; but in this, and all other Movements he made, he resolved to take the Opinion of the Flag-Officers; and since the Enemy were not joined by any Ships from *Brest*, (at least he judged so from their Strength at *Dunkirk*) he had not yet sent to *Holland* for a Re-inforcement.

The 1st of *March* the Wind coming more Westerly, and it seeming as if it would be dirty Weather, he, pursuant to the Opinion of the Flag-Officers, plied out of *Gravelin* Roads to the Westward, and the next Day stood over to the *Downs*; for as the Squadron was fitted out in a Hurry, and consequently wanted Provisions, Stores, Water,

Water, and other Necessaries to enable them to follow the Enemy, he took the Opportunity of coming to our own Coast, that so they might be supplied. Before he left *Gravelin* he saw the same Number of Ships in *Flemish* Road, and in the Harbour within the Peers, as he had done before, the latter whereof he judged could not come out until the next Spring-Tides, especially the bigger Ships, but that those in *Flemish* Road might go to Sea from the Eastern Chanel, so that there was no Chance of preventing them, but by lying on the backside of the Sands of *Dunkirk*, where it was thought the Squadron would be too much exposed to the Weather so early in the Year; besides, should any Ships come from *Brest*, he judged himself in a fairer way in the *Downs* to intercept them, having placed three Scouts, one without the other, from the *Nesse* over to *Boulogne* Bay, with Orders to make Signals, so as that he might have timely notice. Besides which, he had sent two Ships of 50, one of 40 Guns, and two Sixth Rates off of the back of the Sands of *Dunkirk*, to look into the Road that way, and withal to observe if there were any Cruisers of theirs on that Station, and after they had made what Discoveries they could to join him; and three Days before he had sent a Frigate to *Holland* to acquaint the Deputies of the States that he was off of *Gravelin*, that so what Ships they intended to add to our Squadron might be ordered to repair to him; and he desired that Advice might be also sent to *Holland* by the way of *Harwich*, that he was in the *Downs*.

One of his Scouts spoke with a Dogger that came six Days before from *Nantes*, whose Master said, it was there reported the Armament at *Dunkirk* was designed for *Scotland*, and that many *Irish*, and others, were gone from that part of the Country to embark in it, so that he was of opinion that what the Fishermen, who were some Days before taken on the *French* Coast, said relating to the Pretender, was true; for at the same time they affirmed he went through *Gravelin*, he himself saw them fire the Guns round the Town.

By a Letter of the 2d of *March* he gave an Account that the Wind was come about to the East, and that he was of opinion the Ships in *Flemish* Road could not proceed on any Design very soon, should it so continue, for which reason he thought the Service no ways obstructed by his remaining in the *Downs*, until he could have the Prince's Orders for his farther Proceedings; and the next Day it blew very fresh at North-East, with drisling Weather.

The 5th of *March* he owned the Receipt of Orders from his Royal Highness to govern himself as a Council of War should think most adviseable, and Captain *Walker* having joined him with some Ships from the Westward, as also the *Bedford*, a Third Rate, from *Portsmouth*, himself and the other Flag-Officers were of opinion, *A Council of* that for the better preventing any of the Enemy's Ships joining *War held.* those at *Dunkirk*, and observing such as were at that Port, the whole Squadron should proceed over to *Gravelin Pits* the 8th Day of this Month, the Tides beginning then to lift, and after having viewed the Posture of the Enemy there, either to lie with the greatest part of the Ships off of the North Chanel of *Dunkirk,* or to keep under sail, as should be thought most safe, and that at the same time some others should be sent to cruise between *Beachy* and *Dieppe,* to intercept the Enemy's Ships which might come from *West France,* or to give him notice if they got sight of them, that so he might endeavour to prevent their joining those at *Dunkirk.*

Advice of the Pretender from General Cadogan.

The 6th in the Morning one of his Scouts made the Signal of seeing Ships Westward, upon which he immediately unmoored, and got under Sail; and as he was dispatching his Letter to give an Account of this to the Lord High-Admiral, he received Advice from Major-General *Cadogan,* by his *Aid de Camp,* who left *Ostend* the 4th at Night in a Sloop, that the Pretender arrived at *Dunkirk* the 10th, N. S. and that fifteen *French* Battalions, commanded by the Count *de Gace,* being to embark for *Scotland,* he had, in pursuance of Her Majesty's Commands, provided Shipping at *Bruges,* for ten Battalions, which should be ready to sail by the 18th, or 19th, N. S. and desired he would appoint such a Convoy as he judged necessary to see them safe to *Great Britain.* He also acquainted him that he was informed from the Pensionary of *Holland* eight of their Ships were ready to join him, whose Rendezvous was *Schoon-Velde,* on the Coast of *Zealand;* and with this Letter the Major-General sent him an Account of the Enemy's Ships at *Dunkirk,* which he assured him he might depend upon.

Besides this, the Gentleman who brought these Dispatches acquainted him, that after he had parted from the General, he was informed by the Governor of *Ostend* that the Enemy had embarked all their Troops, but that when our Squadron appeared off of *Gravelin,* they put them on shore again; that since his sailing thence, they were ordered to embark a second time, and, as he believed, might in a Day or two be all ready to sail.

When Sir *George Byng* received this Intelligence, the Wind blew fresh at S. W. by W. and he intended to proceed immediately to *Dunkirk,* or to govern himself as the Weather would permit, so as that he might be able to do the best Service; but it blew so very fresh South-Westerly all that Day, and the next Morning, as to put by the Cruisers he had stationed Westward, which in thick Weather,

Our Ships fall in with some of the Enemy's.

at Six in the Morning, had fallen in with eleven Sail, and were within Gun-shot of some of them. They judged them to be five from 50 to 60 Guns, the others of smaller Force, and were chased by them till they came in sight of our Squadron. Upon the Signal which these Cruisers made, Sir *George Byng* immediately weighed, and stood over towards the Enemy's Ships, which stretched away for *Gravelin Pits,* and were so far a-head, that he judged it to no purpose to pursue them, so that he purposed to lie off the North Chanel of *Dunkirk,* to prevent their proceeding to Sea from thence.

When it was Night he came to an Anchor between *Dover* and *Calais,* it being then dead Calm; but before it was Day a very fresh Gale sprung up at E. N. E. which obliged him to continue at an Anchor until the Windward Tide was made, when he got under Sail,

but

CHAP. XXVII. *from the Year* 1698, *to* 1712.   745

but it blew so hard, that he could not fetch into the *Downs*, wherefore standing for *Dover* Road, and finding the Sea run very high, and that it was likely the Wind would encrease, he bore away with the Fleet, and for their greater Security came to an Anchor under *Dungeness*.

By a Letter dated the 8th of *March*, at Night, he gave me an Account, for the Information of the Lord High-Admiral, that being in Expectation of somewhat better Weather, though the Wind was still fresh at E. N. E. he was preparing to sail the next Flood, and that, if possible, he should ply to Windward to the North Chanel of *Dunkirk* to watch the Motions of the Enemy; and by another Letter, dated the 9th, at Nine in the Morning, he informed me that four Ships of War of the States-General had joined him, and that he was standing, with a fine Gale at S. by West, along the back of the Sands between *Calais* and *Dunkirk*, where he hoped to discover the *French* Ships in the Afternoon: But upon his coming off of that Port, he had Advice they sailed the 7th at Night, and the Master of a Packet-Boat gave him an Account that the next Night he anchored by them in *Newport Pits*, about which time they made Signals, and shewed many Lights, so that he believed they sailed then from thence, for continuing at an Anchor until Day-light, he saw no more of them, but passing by *Flemish* Road discovered nine with their Sails loose.   *Notice of the sailing of the Enemy.*

A Council of War being called, they considered the Advice Sir *George Byng* had received from Major-General *Cadogan*, with that from my self by Command of the Prince, and they were of opinion the Enemy were designed for *Scotland*; but since they had no particular Account at what Place in that Kingdom they intended to land, it was unanimously determined to leave Rear-Admiral *Baker*, with his Division, behind them, together with four Ships of War that had just joined the Fleet, that so he might correspond with Major-General *Cadogan* at *Ostend*, and either with the whole Squadron, *English* and *Dutch*, and such other Ships as should join him, convoy the Troops which might be designed for *England* or *Scotland*, or appoint such part of them to do the same as he should judge sufficient, and with the rest to repair after the Fleet, as, upon considering Circumstances of Affairs, should be thought most adviseable. And it was farther resolved to proceed with the Remainder of the Ships in Pursuit of the Enemy, first to the Road of *Edenburgh*, and from thence according to such Intelligence as should be gained of them.   *A Council of War held.*   *Resolved to proceed to Scotland after the Pretender.*

The 13th of *March* in the Morning the *French* Fleet were discovered in the Mouth of the *Frith* of *Edenburgh*, off of which Place Sir *George Byng* anchored the Night before, and sent a Boat on shore to the Isle of *May*, from whence he had an Account that they came to an Anchor the 12th in the Afternoon; that they had sent one Ship up to *Leith* with a Flag at Main-top-mast-head, but that by the time she could get before the Town, they heard Guns fired in the manner of Salutes, which were ours for coming to an Anchor.   *The French discovered in the Frith of Edenburgh.*

Ccccc   This

This Ship came down in the Morning, and was within two Leagues of our Squadron, being, as it was judged, of about 60 Guns, but she had then no Flag abroad: Not but that when the Enemy weighed, a Flag was seen at Main-top-mast-head on board one of their Ships, and as they stood from Sir *George Byng*, he made the best of his way after them, with all the Sail he could; but this Advantage they had of him, that all their Ships were clean, and most of ours foul.

The Enemy chased to Buchanness.

He chased them as far Northward as *Buchanness*, and sometimes with reasonable hopes of coming up with them, but having no clean Ships, except the *Dover*, commanded by Captain *Thomas Matthews*, and the *Ludlow Castle* by Captain *Nicholas Haddock*, they were the first which came up with part of the Enemy's Squadron, passing by some of their smaller to reach their bigger Ships, in hopes of stopping them until they could be strengthened. These two Ships engaged two or three of the *French*, one of which was the *Salisbury*, of 50 Guns, formerly taken from us, nor parted they with them until more of ours came up in the Night, but worked in a very handsome manner so as to cut them off from the rest; yet when it was very dark they lost Sight of all but the *Salisbury*, and she falling in amongst the headmost of ours, the *Leopard*, commanded by Captain *Thomas Gordon*, sent his Boat first on board, and took Possession of her, where there were found the Persons hereafter mentioned, *viz.*

The Salisbury taken, with several Officers, &c.

The Marquis *de Levi*, Lieutenant-General, and his *Aid de Camp*.
The Marquis *de Mens*, Colonel of the Regiment of *Agenois*.
Monsieur *Faverolles*, Lieutenant-Colonel of the Regiment of *Auxerrois*.
Monsieur *Monteron*, Lieutenant-Colonel of the Regiment of *Luxembourg*.
Monsieur *du Guay Secqueville*, Captain of the Regiment of *Luxembourg*.
Monsieur *de Beaufort*, Captain of the Regiment of *Bearn*.
Monsieur *de Clerval*, Captain of the Regiment of *Bearn*.
Monsieur *de Blieux*, Captain of the Regiment of *Bearn*, and Adjutant.
The Sieur *Ouchan*, Lieutenant of the Regiment of *Bearn*.
The Sieur *d'Engny*, second Lieutenant of the Regiment of *Bearn*.
Monsieur *de Salmon*, Captain in the Regiment of *Thierache*.

Besides fifteen *Irish* Lieutenants of the Regiment of *O Brian*, formerly Lord *Clare's*.
Five Companies of the Regiment of *Bearn*, and other inferior Officers.
Monsieur *de Segent*, Commissary of War,
The Chevalier *de Nanges*, Captain of the Ship, and several Sea-Officers.
The Lord *Clerimont*, Colonel in the Regiment of *Lee*.
Mr. *Middleton*, Captain in the Regiment of *Nugent*.
The Lord *Griffin*.

CHAP. XXVII. *from the Year* 1698, *to* 1712. 747

All that the Admiral could learn from them was, that there were twelve Battalions on board their Squadron, commanded by the Count de Gace, a Marshal of *France*, and that the Pretender, the Lord *Middleton*, Lord *Perth*, the *Mac Donells*, Captain *Trevanion*, and several other Officers and Gentlemen, were on board the *Mars*, in which Ship Monsieur *Fourbin*, who commanded the Squadron, was. *What Persons were with the Pretender.*

The Morning after this Chase there were but eighteen of the Enemy's Ships seen, and they as far off as they could be discovered from the Mast-head, in the E. N. E. of our Squadron, so that the Admiral having no Prospect of coming up with them, he lay off and on, near *Buchanness*, all Day the 14th, to gather his Ships together. The next Morning it blew hard North Easterly, which made a great Sea, and he judging the *French* could not seize the Shore to make any Attempt, bore up for *Leith*, which was thought most reasonable, not only to secure, but to give Countenance and Spirit to Her Majesty's faithful Subjects, and discourage those who had, without doubt, a Design to side with the Enemy. There himself, Sir *John Jennings*, and the Lord *Dursley* determined to remain until he could have an Answer to the Letter he wrote to *England*, which he sent by Express, unless they had Intelligence, or should have reason to believe the *French* were on the Coast. *Our Squadron returns to Leith.*

The 16th a Council of War was held in the Road of *Leith*, when the Wind was coming about to the S. W. and the Flags considering where the *French* might probably attempt to land, or which way our Squadron might proceed, with most Probability of preventing any Design they might have, it was their opinion that if they should go Northward, and the Wind come up strong Westerly, it might hinder their gaining the *Firth* of *Forth*, and that since the Enemy were probably driven to the Southward of it, (which they thought was of the greatest Importance to secure) and were at first found at Anchor in the said *Firth*, it was reasonable to believe they intended for *Edenburgh*, the Metropolis; so that it was determined to remain in *Leith* Road until there should be Advice of their returning on the Coast, or that an Answer could be received to the Express dispatched to the Lord High-Admiral, but that, in the mean while, Scouts should be kept out between the *Firth* and *Aberdeen*, and all possible means used to gain Intelligence from the Shore, in order whereunto the Admiral desired the Earl of *Leven* to send some trusty Persons Northward towards the *Firth* of *Murray*.

The 23d of *March* he received Orders, dated the 19th, to send two Fourth Rates, and three Fifths with the Prisoners into the River of *Humber*, and the *Downs*, and with the rest of the Squadron to proceed to Sea, and guard the Coast of *Scotland*; whereupon calling a Council of War, it was resolved that as soon as the Prisoners could be removed, the Squadron should proceed off of *Buchanness*, and that there th Admirale should send on shore for Intelligence of the Enemy, but that if there could not be any Account gained of them by that means, or by his Scouts, he should ply it up again towards the *Firth* of *Edenburgh*.

Ccccc 2   Not

748　*Naval Tranſactions of the* Engliſh, Book V.

Sir George Byng receives Orders to come to the Downs.

Not being able to get any Advice, either by Sea or Land, of the *French* Squadron, and the Proviſions in that under his Command growing very ſhort, he received Orders the beginning of *April* to return to the *Downs*, but to leave three Ships to cruiſe on the Coaſt of *Scotland*, to prevent Correſpondence between diſaffected Perſons of that Kingdom and *France*. Accordingly he appointed the *Bonadventure*, *Mermaid*, and *Squirrel* for that Service, and arrived in the *Downs* the 16th of *April*, with three Third Rates, thirteen Fourths, (of which the *Salisbury Prize* was one) two Fifths, a Sixth, and a Fireſhip, having appointed ſome Frigates to convoy Recruits from *Scotland* to *Holland*.

Remarks.

Thus was the Chevalier *de St. George* (as the *French* have ſince termed him) prevented in landing in a Kingdom to which he doubtleſs had ſtrong Invitations from ſome, who, too much inclined to Novelties, (avoiding a more harſh Expreſſion) diſreliſhed Her Majeſty's Government, and who afforded not themſelves leiſure to conſider, that the Meaſures they were thus blindly taking, would have deprived them of thoſe valuable Rights and Liberties they enjoyed under a Proteſtant Prince, and infallibly have ſubjected them, in little time, to a mean and abject Slavery: For it is not to be imagined the *French* King at this time beſtirred himſelf thus purely in favour of the Pretender, but that by introducing into Her Majeſty's Realms an ungenerous, as well as an unnatural War, he had hopes of paving himſelf a way to the Conqueſt not only of *Scotland*, but of *England* and *Ireland* too, and thereby of fixing a more ſolid Foundation for his inſatiable Ambition.

Troops ready in England on this Occaſion.

But that the Monarch of *France* might be convinced we were not aſleep while he was making theſe Preparations for the pretended Service of the Chevalier, there were (beſides the Ships appointed to obſerve his Motions) ten Battalions ſhipped off from *Bruges*, to be commanded by Lieutenant-General *Withers*, and being conducted by Rear-Admiral *Baker* to *Tinmouth*, they lay there in a conſtant Readineſs to be tranſported to *Scotland*, or to any other part of Her Majeſty's Dominions where the Troops ſent from *France* might be put on ſhore.

1708.

The Pretender returns to France.

When the *French* Squadron had beat to and fro at Sea, until they judged ours were gone off the Coaſt, they made the beſt of their way to *Dunkirk*, and on the 25th of *March*, in the Morning, ſome of our Ships, which were cruiſing near to that Port, under the Command of Captain *Griffith*, got Sight of them, being fourteen in Number, one with a White Flag at Main-top-maſt Head; but they drawing into a Line of Battel when our Ships ſtood towards them, and being much ſuperior in Strength, ours kept their Wind, ſo that getting into the Harbour, they landed the Pretender, that ſo he might be at hand when the *French* King ſhould judge it for his own Advantage to ſend him on a ſecond Expedition of the like Nature.

CHAP.

CHAP. XXVIII.

Containing an Account of Sir John Leake's *Proceedings with the Fleet in the* Mediterranean; *his landing the Queen of* Spain *and Troops at* Barcelona; *the Surrender of* Sardinia; *as also the taking the Town and Castle of* Mahon, *while Sir* Edward Whitaker *was at the Head of a Squadron, with the Troops under the Command of General* Stanhope.

HAving related what of Consequence happened at home, (for to enumerate all things here which happened in the Chanel between single Ships of ours and the Ships of War or Privateers of the Enemy, would be too tedious) I come now to the Fleet, which was equipping for Service abroad under the Command of Sir *John Leake*, who on the 27th of *March* arrived therewith at *Lisbon*, having in his way thither seen the Merchant Ships bound to *Virginia*, and the *Canaries*, with their respective Convoys, well into the Sea, and taken care for the Security of others designed to the Ports in *Portugal*. Here he found the Ships with Captain *Hicks*, which were fourteen of the Third Rate, besides small Frigates and Bomb-Vessels, and at a Council of War it was resolved, that as soon as the Transports were ready to receive the Horse on board, the Fleet should proceed to *Vado*, and that such of the Ships of War as could not be got ready by that time, should follow to *Barcelona*, where there would be Orders left how they should farther proceed: But as for the *Dutch* Ships, they were all separated in bad Weather between *England* and *Lisbon*. It was also determined, at the Desire of the King of *Portugal*, to appoint the *Warspight*, *Rupert*, and *Triton* to cruise off of the *Tercera* or *Azores* Islands, for the Security of His Majesty's Fleet expected from *Brasil*; nor was there care wanting to guard the Streights Mouth, left otherwise our Trade should suffer by the Enemy's Cruisers, or Privateers.

Sir John Leake arrives with the Fleet at Lisbon.

The procuring Transport Ships, and putting them into a Condition for receiving the Horse, took up a considerable time, but on the 23d of *April* the Admiral was ready to sail with as many as could carry fifteen hundred, with one Second Rate, twelve Thirds, two Fourths, a Fireship, Bomb Vessels, &c. together with twelve Ships of the Line of Battel of States-General; and upon Advice from Colonel *Elliot*, Governor of *Gibraltar*, and from other hands, that some *French* Ships of War were seen cruising off of the *Streights* Mouth, one Third, and one Fourth Rate, and another of the *Dutch*, were appointed to strengthen those before ordered to ply up and down in that Station.

The 28th of *April* the Admiral sailed from the River of *Lisbon*, and being off of *Gibraltar* the 4th of *May*, he expected to be joined there

Sir John Leake sails from Lisbon.

there by the *Burford* and *Nassau*, two Ships of the Third Rate, which he had sent to land the Ambassador from the Emperor of *Morocco*, and after they had so done, to cruise about the *Streights* Mouth; but some Days before he got thither they met with, and engaged, off of Cape *Spartel*, a Ship of 50 Guns, called the *Happy Return*, (which the *French* had some time before taken from us) she being convoy to some Trade bound from *Marseilles* to *West France*. The said Ship they took, but those of the Merchants made their Escape, and the *Burford* and *Nassau* were so disabled, the former in springing her Bowsprit, and the latter in her Rigging, that the Admiral found it necessary to send them into Port to refit; but while they were on the Station, they forced a Privateer on shore of 24 Guns, which the *French* burnt, and took another with a Letter of Mart of 30 Guns.

The Happy Return *taken from the* French.

In his Passage up the *Streights* he appointed three Ships of the Third Rate to proceed a-head to *Alicant*, which, after they had landed some Money there for the use of the Army, were to repair to *Barcelona*, that by them the King of *Spain* might have notice the Fleet was advancing up the *Streights*.

When he was about twelve Leagues from *Alicant* he had Sight of several Vessels, which at first he took to be Fishing-boats, till seeing some Guns fired, he made the Signal for chasing, but there being little Wind the remaining part of the Day, and all Night, our Ships could not then come up with any of them. Next Morning he had Advice that the small Vessels, about ninety in all, were *Saëtias* and *Tartans*, bound with Wheat, Oil, and Barly to *Peniscola*, for the Use of the Enemy's Army, under Convoy of three small Frigates, the biggest of 44 Guns, which by the Assistance of their Oars in a Calm, got away, being likewise favoured by the Duskiness of the Night; but the small Vessels were not so fortunate, for seventy two of them were taken, most of them by the Ships of the Fleet, which continued the Chase, the rest by *Spanish* Privateers.

Seventy two Vessels with Provisions taken from the Enemy.

The Admiral arriving at *Barcelona* the 15th of *May*, he there found the *Defiance, Northumberland, Sorlings,* and *Faulcon*, the last of which, mounted with 32 Guns, had a little before met with a *French* Frigate of 22, and a hundred and sixty four Men, with which she had a very sharp Dispute, insomuch that Captain *Delaval* was slain, and forty of her Men killed and wounded. Here the Admiral received a Letter from the King of *Spain*, by which his Majesty represented to him the Consequence of guarding that Coast, but more especially of hindering the Enemy from conveying by Sea the Necessaries for their Troops on the side of *Tortosa*, and in the *Lampourdan*, as well as for the Preservation of his own Person, should the Enemy have a free Passage by Sea.

Captain Delaval *of the* Faulcon *kill'd.*

Several Ships desired by the King of Spain *upon the Fleet's coming to* Barcelona.

His Majesty also desired that seven or more Frigates, with Bomb-Vessels, might remain before *Barcelona*, at his Disposal, and that the rest of the Fleet going to the Coast of *Italy*, might with all possible Speed conduct the Troops designed for his Service from thence, the Enemy being so superior in *Catalonia*, that those his Majesty then had were not able to make head against them; and it was

CHAP. XXVIII. *from the Year* 1698, *to* 1712.   751

was also recommended to him to bring the Queen with him, in case she should be ready to embark by the time the Troops were put on board, for by Her Majesty's not coming to *Barcelona* as soon as was expected, disaffected Persons gave out that the King himself designed to leave *Spain*; however the timely bringing the Troops was what his Majesty chiefly insisted on.

The Reduction of the Island of *Sardinia* his Majesty also recommended to his Consideration, in regard his Army was then in great want of Provisions, which might be furnished from thence, and that he had hopes the People were very much inclined to render Obedience to him, could they be supported in throwing off the Yoke of *France*.

His Majesty also put him in mind of an Expedition to *Sicily*, which Kingdom he judged might be recovered with the Troops under the Command of Count *Daun*, who only wanted the Assistance of some Ships; but if this did not succeed according to his Majesty's Expectation, yet he judged this good Consequence might attend it, the driving from the *Phare* of *Messina*, and the adjacent Parts, the Embarcations which the Enemy had there, and the hindering the Passage of Provisions for the Supply of *Naples*.

Thus this young Monarch, almost shut up in the principal City of *Catalonia*, was contriving how he might not only enlarge himself, but be in a Condition to oppose his Enemies; and the Admiral calling a Council of War, where were present, besides himself, Sir *John Norris*, Sir *Edward Whitaker*, Sir *Thomas Hardy*, and three *English* Captains, as also the Baron *Wassenaer*, and two of the *Dutch*, it was determined to leave with the King three Third Rates, one Fourth, and one Fifth of ours, and two Ships of the States-General, and with the rest of the Fleet to proceed forthwith to the Port of *Vado*, in order to the transporting the Horse and Foot from thence to *Barcelona*, as also her Majesty the Queen of *Spain*, if she should be ready. *A Council of War held.*

According to this Resolution the Admiral sailed, and arrived in *Vado* Bay the 29th of *May*, but finding above a third part of the Hay and Corn for the Horses was still at *Livorne*, he was constrained to send two Transport Ships with a Convoy for the same; and the Number of Troops designed from *Italy* to *Spain* were near two thousand Horse, and four thousand Foot. *Sir John Leake arrives at Vado.*

By one Mr. *Campbell*, who had been Master of a Ship of *Glascow*, and was released from Imprisonment at *Thoulon*, he had an Account that there were in that Port the Ships following, *viz.* in the *Basin* fifteen of three Decks, and about twenty more from 30 to 50 Guns, but all unmasted; in the Harbour three Frigates armed, of 40 and 32 Guns, two of which were Convoy to the Corn-Vessels taken near *Alicant*, and that all the Ships in the *Basin* were prepared to be sunk upon occasion, but that they could not sink them in above three Foot Water more than they drew; and that the Garrison consisted of about four thousand disciplined Troops, including Marines, *Advice of Ships at Thoulon.*

The

The Fleet returns to Barcelona with the Queen of Spain and the Troops.

The 26th of *June* the Ships of War and Transports joined him which he sent to *Livorne* for Forage, and the other Transport Ships with the Troops arriving soon after, together with the Queen of *Spain*, he reached *Barcelona* the 14th of *July*, fourteen Days after the unfortunate Loss of *Tortosa*. Here he received a Letter from the King, by which his Majesty again recommended to him the Reduction of *Sardinia*, and the clearing the Coasts of *Sicily* from the Enemy's Privateers, that so a Passage might be opened for the Troops in the Kingdom of *Naples* to undertake the designed Expedition against *Sicily*, reserving some Ships and Transports to bring Corn to *Barcelona*, and to be at hand on all occasions which his Majesty might have for them.

A Council of War held.

A Council of War was held the 2d of *July*, when it was, at the earnest Instance of our Merchants, resolved to appoint three Frigates to cruise for some time between *Corsica* and *Livorne*, to protect the Trade in those Parts from the Insults of the Enemy; and upon

Another.

reading the King's Letter at another Consultation the 21st of the same Month, it was determined to leave four *English* and three *Dutch* Ships on the Coast of *Spain*, with some Transports, and that as soon as our Marine Soldiers came from *Tarragona*, and a Regiment of five hundred Men should be embarked, which were all that could be

Resolved to reduce Sardinia.

spared from *Catalonia*, the Fleet should proceed to *Sardinia*, and endeavour to reduce that Island to his Majesty's Obedience, and there to consider what Ships might be spared for clearing the Coasts of *Naples* and *Sicily*.

The first of *August* the Admiral arriving before *Cagliari*, the Metropolis of *Sardinia*, summon'd it, but not receiving a satisfactory Answer, he bombarded the Place all Night, and next Morning, by break of Day, landing Major-General *Wills* with the Marines, and the *Spanish* Regiment, which he designed should be followed by about nine hundred Seamen, they soon after thought it convenient to

Sardinia yields,

capitulate; and here he received Letters from the King of *Spain*, and Lieutenant-General *Stanhope* *. As his Majesty was pleased to thank him, in a very obliging manner, for the many good Services he had done him, so was the latter preparing all things which could be got in *Catalonia* for the Reduction of *Port Mahon*, and the Island of *Minorca*, designing suddenly to embark for that Port with the Troops, Cannon, Powder, &c. on the Ships left with the King of *Spain*, and the Transports.

The Admiral sailing from *Cagliari* the 18th of *August*, arrived before *Port Mahon* the 25th, but not finding Lieutenant-General *Stanhope*, nor any Troops there, he sent two Ships of the Third Rate to *Majorca*, to hasten the Embarcation of those which were to be furnished from that Island, which returned the first of *September*, with some *Saëtias* loaden with Materials of War for the Army; nor was it more than two Days before the *Milford* and three *Dutch* Ships

General Stanhope arrives with Forces before Port Mahon.

of War arrived with the Lieutenant-General, being followed by five Third Rates, Convoy to fifteen Transports that had on board them

---

* *Since Earl Stanhope.*

the

CHAP. XXVIII. *from the Year* 1698, *to* 1712.

the Land Forces, whereupon a Council of War was held of the Sea-Officers, and it was resolved that the Ships designed to return to *Great Britain* should leave behind them, to assist in the Attempt, all the Marine Soldiers above the middle Complement of each of them, and that the Squadron of *English* and *Dutch* designed to be continued abroad with Sir *Edward Whitaker* should remain at *Port Mahon*, to assist with their Marines and Seamen in the Reduction of that Place, so long as the Lieutenant-General should desire it, regard being had to the Season of the Year, the time their Provisions might last, and the transporting from *Naples* to *Barcelona* four thousand of the Emperor's Troops for the Service of his Catholick Majesty.

It was also resolved that the *English* Ships should spare the Forces as much Bread as they could, and both they, and the *Dutch*, all their Cannon-shot, except what might be necessary for their own Defence, and that when every thing should be landed which was necessary for the Siege, the Admiral should proceed to *England* with one Second Rate, and six Thirds of ours, and eight *Dutch* Ships of the Line; but some time after this he sent home two *English* and two *Dutch* Ships of War, with the empty Transports of both Nations, in order to their being discharged.

Having watered the Ships at *Majorca*, he sailed from thence the 17th of *September*, and being informed, when off of *Gibraltar*, that four *French* Men of War from *Cadiz* had taken near *Cape Spartel*, and sent into that Port, some of our Merchant Ships which run without Convoy, he left two Third Rates, one Fourth, and a Fifth, to cruise in that Station, under Command of Captain *Hartnoll*, and arrived at St. *Helen*'s the 19th of *October*, having met in the *Soundings* with the Squadron cruising there under the Command of the Lord *Dursley*, of whose Proceedings I have already given an Account.   *Sir John Leake arrives in England, Sir Edward Whitaker being left abroad.*

While the Artillery, and all things necessary were putting on shore for attacking the Castle of *Port Mahon*, Sir *Edward Whitaker* ordered a Ship of 70, and another of 50 Guns to *Port Fornelle*, in order to reduce the Fort there, which they did, after four Hours Dispute, it being a strong Place with 4 Bastions, 12 Guns, and garrisoned by forty *French*, but the least of our Ships was much damaged in her Masts and Yards, and had six Men killed and twelve wounded; and to this Harbour all the Transport Ships, with the Bomb-Vessels, were sent, the Admiral having not had any convenient Place before to secure them in.   *The Fort at Port Fornelle reduced.*

Some little time after the General sent a Detachment of about a hundred *Spaniards*, with three hundred or more of the Marquis *Pisaro*'s Regiment to *Citadella*, the chief Town of the Island, on the West side thereof, and Sir *Edward Whitaker* dispatched two Ships of War thither; which Place put them to no great Trouble, for the Garrison immediately surrendering, were made Prisoners of War, being a hundred *French*, and as many *Spaniards*.   *Citadella surrendered.*

The 17th of *September* our People began to play on the Enemy's Lines on the South side of the Harbour of *Mahon*, from a Battery of 10 Guns, and after about four Hours Dispute, making themselves

D d d d d   Masters

Masters of all their Out-works, lodged under the very Walls of the Castle of St. *Philip*, in which Dispute we lost but six Men, one of whom was Captain *Stanhope* of the *Milford*, as he was going on with his Brother the General.

The Castle of Mahon capitulates.
Next Day the Enemy offering to capitulate, Articles were in a little time agreed on, by which the Garrison were permitted to march out with all the Marks of Honour, carrying six Cannon, and four Mortars; the *French* to be transported to *Thoulon*, or the Islands of *Hyeres*, and the *Spaniards* to *Valencia*. There were about five hundred Marines in the Place, commanded by a Brigadier, and almost the same Number of *Spaniards*; and as they had upwards of a hundred Guns mounted, so were there between two and three thousand Barrels of Powder in store, with all things necessary, together with a considerable Quantity of Provisions; but the Wives and Children of the *Spaniards* flying into the Fort, they made almost an equal Number with the Garrison, which probably might occasion their capitulating so soon, for our Army did not consist of above two thousand four hundred Men.

Being thus possessed of this Island, we had thereby the Advantage of a goodly Harbour, which during the War was exceeding useful to us (as it may hereafter be when there shall be occasion to make use of it) in the cleaning and refitting such of our Ships as were employed in the *Mediterranean*; and not only Magazines of Stores were lodged there for that purpose, but such Officers appointed to reside on the Place as were judged requisite.

The Squadron comes to Livorne,
Sir *Edward Whitaker* leaving *Mahon* the 29th of *September*, proceeded with the Squadron to *Livorne*, having appointed a Convoy to General *Stanhope* and the Troops to *Catalonia*. There he received a Letter from Mr. *Chetwynd*, our Minister at *Genoa*, giving

and
an Account that a Body of a thousand Troops were ready at *Final* to embark for the Service of the King of *Spain* in *Catalonia*, and

a Convoy sent to Naples.
as a Convoy was immediately appointed for them, so was it agreed at a Council of War, that since the Squadron could not suddenly sail to *Naples*, for want of the Provisions and Stores which were getting ready at *Livorne*, the *Defiance*, *York*, and *Terrible* Fireship should proceed to *Piombino*, and their Commanders there consider with the chief Officers of the Imperial Troops, what might be most effectually done to secure the *Stato delli Presidi*, (a small Territory on the Coast of *Tuscany*, which with the foresaid *Piombino* on the same Coast, belongs to the Crown of *Spain*) as also towards reducing *Porto Longone* and *Porto Hercole*, on which Service they were ordered to continue eight Days, and then to proceed directly to *Naples*.

Upon a Letter from Cardinal *Grimani*, Vice-Roy of *Naples*, and another from the Marquis *de Prié*, Minister of his Imperial Majesty at the Court of *Rome*, giving an Account of the Commotions of the said Kingdom of *Naples*, from whence Troops could not possibly be spared, at this time, for the Service of the King of *Spain*, and desiring therefore that the Squadron might continue some time in those Parts, and endeavour to intercept the Pope's Gallies, and others expected

CHAP. XXVIII. *from the Year* 1698, *to* 1712. 755

expected from *France*, with a considerable Number of Men and Arms, which his Holiness was then in great want of, as also to countenance the Negotiations of the said Marquis *de Prié* at the Court of *Rome*, it was determined at a Council of War, held in *Livorne* Road the 30th of *October* 1708, to remain in those Seas a Month longer, if the Service should require it, and that Ships should be kept cruising in the *Bocca* of *Piombino*, or thereabouts, to intercept the aforementioned Gallies. *Agreed to appoint some Ships to intercept the Pope's Gallies.*

Notwithstanding three of our Ships had been employed off of *Porto Longone*, on the Island of *Elba*, ever since Sir *Edward Whitaker* arrived at *Livorne*, the *German* General had not made any Attempt against it, nor so much as embarked any Troops for that Service; but the Ships obliged the Enemy to retire from *Orbitello*, which they were bombarding, and had taken three Towers, which very much annoyed the Place; during which time four of the Pope's Gallies passing by *Livorne*, the *York* and *Firme* pursued them, but there being little Wind, they got away by the help of their Oars. *Some of the Pope's Gallies pursued.*

The Imperial Troops were on their March about the middle of *November*, within forty Miles of *Rome*, so that there was hopes of a speedy Accommodation at the Pope's Court; but at this time the Imperialists had nothing so much at heart as the Reduction of *Sicily*, so that it was likely the King of *Spain* would be disappointed of the promised Troops from *Italy* for Service in *Catalonia*; but during Sir *Edward*'s stay at *Livorne*, he received a Letter from his Majesty, giving him an Account that the Enemy had not only besieged *Denia* in *Valencia*, but given out that they would, after that, attack *Alicant*, having fifteen Ships of the Line of Battel to favour their Designs; for which reason, and lest they should block up the King in *Catalonia*, his Majesty earnestly pressed him not to pass the *Streights*, as required by Orders left him by Sir *John Leake*, but to remain on the Coasts of *Spain*, for that otherwise he would charge to him all the Misfortunes which might happen to his Affairs. The King also acquainted him that four of the Ships left with his Majesty were sailed to *Final*, to bring the Troops from the *Milanese*, and desired that in his return he would call at that Port, and accompany them, for their greater Safety. *The Enemy besiege Denia.*

This Letter of the King of *Spain*'s was inforced by one from General *Stanhope*, who let him know the great Misfortunes which might attend his leaving the Coasts of *Spain* unguarded, since the *French* by returning might prevent all Communication, and thereby expose the Army in *Catalonia* to a total want of Provisions, that Country being so far exhausted as not to be able to furnish sufficient for a Fortnight, so that, in such case, they should be obliged to give up the Country to any who would demand it. *General Stanhope presses the Squadron's remaining in the Streights.*

Upon these two pressing Letters it was determined, notwithstanding the late Resolutions taken at a Council of War, that as soon as the Squadron could be furnished with Provisions and Necessaries at *Livorne*, it should immediately proceed and join the Ships at *Vado*, and thence sail to *Barcelona*, in order not only to drive the Enemy *Result of a Council of War.*

Ddddd 2

Enemy from those Parts, but to secure the Country, and his Majesty the King of *Spain* from the imminent Danger which threaten'd them.

The 27th of *November* Sir *Edward Whitaker* got under Sail from *Livorne*, and arriving at *Barcelona*, the King by Letter acquainted him, that according to what had been agreed at a Council of War, held in his Royal Presence, the most considerable Service the Squadron under his Command could do at that Juncture of time, was to return to the Coast of *Italy*, and convoy the Troops designed from thence for *Catalonia*; but withal recommended to him not only the convoying the Transports with Corn from *Majorca*, and their being afterwards seen to *Sardinia* for a farther Supply, and for Horses to mount the Cavalry, but that when he should be on the Coast of *Italy*, he would appoint such Ships as Cardinal *Grimani* might desire, to secure the Passage of the *Phare* of *Messina*, which might conduce to the more speedy Accommodation of Affairs that were negotiating at *Rome*.

The King desires the Squadron may return to the Coast of Italy, &c.

Hereupon it was agreed that the *Dutch* Ships should proceed directly to *Majorca*, and convoy the Transports to *Barcelona*, and from thence to *Cagliari*, as soon as they should be unloaden, while the rest of the Squadron made the best of their way to *Livorne*, where arriving, he met with very bad Weather, but had Advice that Matters were accommodated at *Rome*, the Pope having owned *Charles* the Third King of *Spain*; and from the Marquis *de Prié*, that three thousand effective Men should be ready to embark at *Naples* as soon as he arrived there: And here we will leave Sir *Edward Whitaker*, that so we may give some Account of Sir *George Byng*, who was expected from *England* to command abroad.

The Pope owns Charles the Third of Spain.

Chap. XXIX.

Containing an Account of Sir George Byng's *Proceedings while he commanded in the* Mediterranean, *with the Attempt made to relieve* Alicant *by the Fleet, and the Troops under the command of General* Stanhope.

1708.

Sir George Byng arrives at Lisbon, and goes to Sea to protect the Brasil Fleet.

SIR *George Byng* being Admiral of the Blue, and appointed to to carry the Queen of *Portugal* to *Lisbon*, arrived at that Port the 14th of *October*, where being informed that the homeward-bound *Brasil* Fleet had been separated, the Commander in Chief on his sailing from *Bahia*, having not given them any Signals, nor so much as appointed a Place of Rendezvous, and several *French* Ships being lately seen about the *Burlings*, on the Coast of *Portugal*, he proceeded with his Squadron thither in quest of the Enemy, and to protect the Trade of that Kingdom, which were straggling on the

Coast

CHAP. XXIX. *from the Year* 1698, *to* 1712.   757

Coast, but meeting with bad Weather, was forced to return to *Lisbon* to refit some of the Ships which had received Damage, and to get ready a small Squadron to protect our Trade in and about the *Streights* Mouth from those Ships of the Enemy, which cleaned at *Cadiz*, and had taken several Prizes. With two of them, one of 56, and the other of 60 Guns, one of our Fourth Rates, named the *Winchester*, happened to meet, and being much ruffled, came to *Lisbon* with three more which had been cruising in that Station.

Sir *George* advising with Sir *John Jennings*, who had been with a Squadron some time before at *Lisbon*, appointed three Ships of the Third Rate, which were in the worst Condition for continuing abroad, to convoy home the Transports arrived from the *Mediterranean*, they being joined by four Ships of War of the States-General: And since the *Brasil* Fleet was not arrived, but daily came dropping in, he appointed some Frigates to cruise off of the Mouth of the *Tajo* for their Security, and the 13th of *November* the *Berwick*, of 70 Guns, arrived with the Rear-Admiral of *Portugal*, together with our Ships which were sent to the *Tercera* Islands to look out for the aforesaid *Brasil* Fleet. *A Convoy sent home with the empty Transports.*

About the middle of *November* the Admiral received Orders from the Lord High-Admiral to proceed to *Port Mahon*, and winter in the *Mediterranean*, and to leave Sir *John Jennings* at *Lisbon*, with two Ships of the Third Rate, and one of the Fifth, to whom he was to send such other Ships as were over and above the sixteen, which he was to have under his Command; and on the 29th of *November* he received Orders from the Queen to wear the Union-Flag in the *Mediterranean*, the Prince (through whose Hands it should otherwise have gone as Lord-High-Admiral) being dead; and by his Letter to my self, dated the 1st of *December*, he gave an Account that the *Portuguese* Ships of War were arrived with the Remainder of the *Brasil* Fleet, except two of their *East-India* Ships which put back, and some few left in that Country. *Sir George Byng ordered to Mahon, and Sir John Jennings to remain at Lisbon.*

The 27th of *December* he got under Sail with one First Rate, five Thirds, two Fireships, an Hospital Ship, Storeship, and the *Arrogant* Hulk, leaving Orders with Sir *John Jennings* to appoint the first Ships he should have clean to guard the Mouth of the *Streights*; and having sent two Third Rates, two Fourths, and a Fifth a-head of him to *Alicant*, to assure the Governor of the Castle there of his Assistance, he arrived himself about *Cape Palos* the 3d of *January*, whence standing in for *Alicant*, the Wind came off from the Land so fresh at N.N.W. that he could not fetch the Bay, so that he bore away for *Port Mahon*, but when he had got within four Leagues of that Place, which was on the 5th, the Wind came to the North, and N.N.E. blowing extreme hard, with much Snow, and the next Day it was so very tempestuous, that it separated most of the Squadron, forcing him almost as high as *Sardinia*, but on the 12th he got into *Port Mahon*, where he found most of the Squadron. *Sir George Byng arrives at Port Mahon.* 170 4/5.

The *Ipswich* being sent in search of the *Boyn*, she found her with all her Masts gone by the Board, except her Fore-mast. The Ship
with

with Ordnance-Stores came safe into Port, but the *Arrogant* being still missing, in which were the principal part of the Naval Stores, Sir *George Byng* sent some Ships to *Majorca*, and others to *Cagliari*, in quest of her, dispatching Orders at the same to Sir *Edward Whitaker*, on the Coast of *Italy*, to join him with the Ships under his Command, in case the Emperor's Troops intended for *Catalonia* were not ready to embark.

Sir Edward Whitaker ordered to join him from Italy.

Being in very great want of Stores, through the Loss of the *Arrogant*, he was put to no small Difficulties in putting the Ships into a Condition for Service, and having but a small Strength with him, he proposed that if the Enemy fitted out a Fleet, Sir *John Jennings* might join him from *Lisbon*, for Sir *Edward Whitaker* was still on the Coast of *Italy*, concerning whom, and the Troops he was to bring from thence, General *Stanhope* came to *Mahon* to consult with Sir *George Byng* the 14th of *February*; but on the 19th of *March* he arrived with the said Land-Forces, which were about three thousand five hundred effective Men.

General Stanhope comes to Mahon.

With these Troops, and the General, he put to Sea with eleven Ships of the Line of Battel, designing, if possible, to relieve the Castle of *Alicant*, having left others at Port *Mahon* to clean and refit, and employed some on Services desired by the King of *Spain*, so that he was not able yet to send any additional Strength to Sir *John Jennings*. The 5th of *April* in the Morning he stood into the Bay of *Alicant*, anchoring against the Batteries and Lines which the Enemy had thrown up along the Coast, and while the Cannon were playing against those Works, the General intended to push on shore, but the Wind coming up South-Easterly, and blowing very strong, occasioned a great Sea, which render'd it impracticable, and some of the Ships being in less than four Fathom Water, nay divers of them in little more than three, the *Northumberland* and *Dunkirk* struck several times, so that they were obliged before it was Night to ply farther out into the Road.

The Works at Alicant cannonaded.

The Weather continuing very bad till the 7th, and it being not known what Extremities the Garrison might be under, and the Enemy encreasing considerably in Strength, the General sent a Flag of Truce on shore, with Proposals for surrendering the Castle, which being agreed to, and our Men embarked, the Admiral proceeded with the Troops towards *Barcelona*, having detached some Ships to cruise for the *Turky* Fleet, others with Transports for Corn to *Barbary*, and the *Suffolk*, *Humber*, and *Ipswich*, which he left to clean at *Port Mahon*, were under Orders to proceed to *Genoa* and *Final*, for transporting the *German* Recruits from those Places to *Catalonia*.

The Castle of Alicant surrendered to the Enemy.

In his way to *Barcelona* he landed General *Stanhope* with the Troops at *Tarragona*, and returning with the Garrison of the Castle of *Alicant* to *Port Mahon*, joined some other Ships to those he first intended for *Genoa* and *Final*, and sent them thither under Command of Sir *Edward Whitaker*, but directed him first to proceed to *Livorne* for a Supply of Provisions, which was at this time very much wanted. The few Ships he had with him at *Port Mahon* he

General Stanhope landed at Tarragona.

was

CHAP. XXIX. *from the Year* 1698, *to* 1712. 759

was cleaning as fast as possible, that so they might cruise against the Enemy, who had taken the *Faulcon*, a Ship of 32 Guns, off of Cape *de Gates* in her Passage to *Lisbon*, from whence he had ordered Sir *John Jennings* to join him with the Ships under his Command, who was off of *Gibraltar* the 21st of *May*, with sixteen Men of War, *English* and *Dutch*, and about forty Transports, loaden with Corn, as also Provisions and Stores for the Fleet in the *Mediterranean*, and arrived at *Port Mahon* the 28th, from whence he guarded the Corn Ships to *Barcelona*, and was joined the 8th of *June* by Sir *George Byng*, with the rest of the *English* and *Dutch* Men of War, and there Sir *Edward Whitaker* arrived with his Squadron from *Italy*, and above two thousand Recruits for the Army in *Catalonia*.

1709.

All the Fleet join at Barcelona.

A Council of War being called, it was determined, that since the King of *Spain*, as the Posture of Affairs then were, could not come to any Resolution relating to the Fleet's assisting in the Reduction of those Parts of *Spain* still in the Possession of the Enemy, to sail to a Station ten Leagues South of Cape *Thoulon*, not only for intercepting their Trade, but to alarm them all that might be; but since it was necessary that a Squadron should be on the Coast of *Portugal*, Sir *John Jennings* was sent thither with one Ship of the Second Rate, four of the Third, five of the Fourth, and three of the Fifth.

Sir John Jennings sent back to Lisbon.

They both sailed together from *Barcelona* Road, and Sir *George Byng* arrived before *Thoulon* the 21st of *June*, in which Harbour he saw only eight Ships, which were rigged, and their Sails bent, and one large Man of War on the Careen, the rest being disarmed, which confirmed the Accounts he had before, that they did not intend to come to Sea with a Fleet, but only to guard their Transports for Corn with small Squadrons; so that after cruising there some time longer, he returned to *Barcelona* Road, where he found most of the Ships arrived from the Services whereon he had sent them, and the *Dunkirk* and *Centurion* were come from the Coast of *Barbary*, being obliged to leave twelve Prizes, loaden with Corn, which the former and the *Defiance* had taken, in *Porto Farina*, for want of Men to sail them.

Sir George Byng comes before Thoulon.

He returns to Barcelona.

Upon his Arrival at *Barcelona*, he found the Court of *Spain*, at the Instance of Cardinal *Grimani*, very desirous to have the Reduction of *Sicily* attempted, and was informed by General *Stanhope*, that it was Her Majesty's Pleasure part of the Fleet should assist in the Design upon *Cadiz*; but the *Dutch* Ships having been separated in bad Weather, and ours being too few to answer these, and many other Services the Court proposed, he suspended for some time the coming to any Resolution, being every Day in Expectation of the Ships of the States-General; but at length he formed a Disposition of Her Majesty's Ships, and appointed Sir *Edward Whitaker* for the Service of *Sicily*, while he himself designed to proceed on the other with General *Stanhope*.

Some Thoughts of attempting Sicily, and attacking Cadiz.

The 26th of *July* the Court of *Spain* having notice of the Enemy's penetrating into the *Ampourdan*, with Intention, as was apprehended,

prehended, to besiege *Girone*, and there being a want of Ships to protect the Coast of *Catalonia*, and hinder the Enemy's having Supplies by Sea, as also a Squadron to bring over the Prizes with Corn from *Porto Farina*, which they were in great want of in that Principality, and some Ships to go to *Italy* for Money for subsisting the Troops, the Court seemed to lay aside the Design on *Sicily*, and the Admiral sent five Ships for the aforesaid Vessels with Corn.

The Dutch not able to assist against Cadiz.

The *Dutch* arriving the 27th from *Livorne*, Sir *George Byng* called a Council of War, and laid before them Her Majesty's Orders, together with the Services which the King of *Spain* desired might be performed, and proposed to the Commander in Chief of the Ships of the States General his detaching part of them with him on the Expedition against *Cadiz*, but he excused himself, alledging their Provisions would not last longer than the end of *August*, N. S. yet offered to assist on any Service upon the Coast of *Catalonia* until the 20th Day of that Month. However, it was agreed that Sir *George Byng* should proceed to *Cadiz*, with six *English* Ships of the Line of Battel, and that two other Frigates should follow him when they arrived from *Genoa*, the rest, both *English* and *Dutch*, to be left under the Command of Sir *Edward Whitaker*, to perform such Services as the King of *Spain* might have for them.

Prizes taken, one of them the Fame.

Since the cleaning of the Ships at *Port Mahon*, they took thirty one Prizes, twenty two whereof were loaden with Corn, three from *Turky*, as many from *Marseilles*, and the like Number from *Carthagena*, the *Dutch* having seized on three more. Among our Prizes was the *Fame*, formerly a *Dutch* Privateer, of 24 Guns, which the Admiral bought of the Captors for the Queen, and employed against the Enemy. The *Antelope* and *Worcester* having been cruising up the *Levant*, took three *French* Merchant Ships; and when Sir *Edward Whitaker* appeared with his Squadron off of *Roses*, he discovered there about forty Embarcations which were

Several Vessels of the Enemy's taken with Provisions.

employed to transport Provisions to the Enemy's Army in the *Ampourdan*, thirty of which he took, whereby they were put to no little straits for want of the Supplies they hoped for by Sea.

Sir George Byng comes to Gibraltar.

Arriving at *Gibraltar* he expected to have met there with Rear-Admiral *Baker*'s Squadron, and the Troops designed for the Attempt on *Cadiz*, but not gaining any Intelligence of him, or of Sir *John Jennings*, he sent away the *Torbay*, *Colchester*, and *Hawk* Fireship, with Colonel *Du Bourguay* to *Lisbon*, and directed them to remain there for such Intelligence as he might receive, and then to bring him back to the Fleet.

CHAP. XXX.

Containing an Account of Sir Edward Whitaker's *Proceedings while he commanded in the* Mediterranean, *and what was done in those Parts by Vice-Admiral* Baker; *together with an Account of Admiral* Aylmer's *Proceedings with the Fleet at home; and of the Expedition to, and Reduction of* Port Royal *in* Nova Scotia.

SIR *George Byng* being now designed for *Great Britain*, and it having been determined at a Council of War to leave a Squadron of Ships in the *Streights* under the Command of Sir *Edward Whitaker*, he gave him Directions the 29th of *July*, with ten Third Rates, two Fourths, three Fifths, and one Sixth, to use his best Endeavours to protect the Coast of *Catalonia*, in Conjunction with such *Dutch* Ships as should be appointed to join him, and by cruising off of the Coast of *Roses*, or thereabouts, to prevent the carrying to the Enemy any Supplies of Provisions or Ammunition, and so to dispose of the Ships under his Command, from time to time, as that they might intercept their Vessels with Corn from the *Levant*, and the Coast of *Barbary*. And the Design against *Cadiz* being now wholly laid aside, the Admiral appointed the *Essex* and *Firme*, with a Sloop, and two Bomb-Vessels, to proceed to *England* with the empty Transports and other Vessels, to ease the Expence of keeping them unnecessarily in Pay; and the Horses with General *Stanhope* were so ill provided with Forage, that he was obliged to send them to the Earl of *Gallway* at *Lisbon*, to prevent their being starved.

But since it was necessary that the Troops with the aforesaid General, which were short of Provisions, should be seen in Safety to *Barcelona*, the Admiral proceeded with them up the *Streights*, till meeting with a strong *Levant* Wind off of Cape *de Gates*, he was obliged to return to *Gibraltar*, where consulting with the General, he was of opinion, grounded upon the Advice he had from the King of *Spain*, that the Troops should remain at *Gibraltar*, until Vice-Admiral *Baker* arrived from *Ireland*, with those expected from thence, and that then he should protect them to *Barcelona*; so that the Admiral, taking the Opportunity of a Wind, put through the *Streights* the 22d of *September*, and arrived at *Spithead* the 25th of the next Month with one Ship of the First Rate, two of the Third, and two of the Fourth, from whence he sent me an Account, for the Information of the Lord High-Admiral, which he had from a Vessel the Enemy took some time before, and was retaken from them, of the Station where Monsieur *Du Gué Trovine* cruised, and of the Strength of his Squadron, that so our Ships in the *Soundings*, then under the Command of the Lord *Dursley*, might endeavour to attack him, or to intercept the Trade they expected to meet with coming from the *West-Indies*; and of his

1709.

The Design against Cadiz *laid aside.*

Sir George Byng arrives in England.

Eeeee Lordship's

Lordship's Proceedings during his cruising there I have already given an Account.

While Sir *George Byng* was at *Port Mahon*, Sir *Edward Whitaker* failing from *Livorne* towards *Naples* with the Transport Ships, arrived there the 3d of *February*, when bad Weather setting in, they could not begin to embark the Troops till the 1st of *March*; and since General *Stanhope* had (as hath been before related) concerted Matters with Sir *George* for the Operation of the Troops and Ships of War, he sent Orders to Sir *Edward Whitaker* to repair to him to *Port Mahon* with all possible Dispatch, where he arrived the 18th of *March*, from whence he was sent with a Squadron, and some Transports, to *Final* for *German* Troops, designed for Service in *Spain*, and Money for the King from *Genoa*.

Sir Edward Whitaker sent off of the Coast of Roses, &c.

Having performed this Service, he was ordered to take under his Command ten Third Rates, three Fourths, two Fifths, and two Sixths of Her Majesty's, and seven *Dutch* Ships of War, and with such of them as were then at *Port Mahon*, leaving Orders for the rest to follow him, to proceed and cruise off of the Coast of *Roses*, *Collivre*, and in the Gulph of *Narbonne*, to prevent the Enemy their having any Supplies of Provisions, or Ammunition by Sea, and to intercept their Shipping, and annoy their Coasts. He was also directed to hold frequent Correspondence with Her Majesty's Ministers at the Courts of *Spain* and *Savoy*, and, at the desire of those Princes, to assist them on Services which a Council of War should judge practicable.

Sir Edward Whitaker takes several Vessels with Provisions.

The same Day he received these Orders, which was the 29th of *July* 1709, he sailing with her Majesty's Ships the *Boyne*, and *Suffolk*, of the Third Rate, and seven *Dutch* Ships of War, arrived the 3d of *August* off of the Bay of *Roses*, where he had the good Fortune to intercept thirty small Vessels, employed in carrying Bread and Meal from thence to the *French* Army, which was composed of between twelve and fourteen thousand Men, under Command of the Duke *de Noyelles*, encamped at a Place called *Tervel*, but he could not understand whether or not they were provided with Ammunition and Ordnance for the Siege of *Gironne*.

Sir Edward Whitaker comes to Port Mahon.

Off of this Coast he continued until the 16th of *August*, preventing the Enemy's receiving any Supplies by Sea, when receiving a Letter from Sir *George Byng*, and another from General *Stanhope*, by which they represented it was necessary he should make the best of his way to *Barcelona*, to convoy the Transports from thence to *Port Mahon*, as also the Storeships, and Victuallers, and then to proceed with them to *Algier* for Corn for the Army, which they were in great want of, he arrived at *Port Mahon* towards the latter end of *August* from *Barcelona*, but before he left that Place, our Troops had passed the *Segre*, and obliged the Enemy to retire on the other side the *Noguera*. They had also taken *Balaguer*, on the Banks of the River *Segre*, and in it three Battalions, two of them *Switzers*, and the other of *Badajoz*, with a very considerable Magazine of Barley.

With

CHAP. XXX. *from the Year* 1698, *to* 1712.   763

With the Transport Ships he proceeded to *Algier*, whence he returned to *Port Mahon*, and arrived at *Barcelona* with the Supply of Corn the 28th of *September*, from which Port the *Dutch* Ships were gone to *Majorca* for Provisions, but their return being suddenly expected, he left a Lettter for their Commadore to follow him to *Port Mahon*, whither with the Consent of the King of *Spain*, he was going to refit the Ships under his Command, but took care to have Cruisers on the *Barbary* Coast to intercept Supplies bound to the *French*.

He proceeds to Algier, thence to Port Mahon, &c.

The victualling Ships expected from *England* not being arrived the 23d of *October*, it was agreed at a Council of War to proceed to *Livorne* for what could be had there, and on the 11th of the next Month he sailed accordingly, leaving Rear-Admiral *Somerſdyke* at *Port Mahon*, refitting the *Dutch* Ships under his Command. In his Passage he met with extreme bad Weather, and lying off of *Thoulon* eight Days, he took several Barks, in one of which were Letters, giving an Account of the great Straits the Enemy were driven to for want of Corn, and Trade; and now receiving Advice from Vice-Admiral *Baker* that he was arrived at *Port Mahon* with the Victualling Ships from *England*, he returned thither, and on the 1st of *December* it was agreed at a Council of War, upon reading a Letter from the King of *Spain*, to appoint a Convoy, and a Number of Transport Ships in Her Majesty's Pay, to bring Corn for the Army in *Catalonia* from *Tarento* in the Kingdom of *Naples*.

The Squadron goes to Livorne for Provisions.

Vice-Admiral Baker arrives at Port Mahon.

Proceeding to Sea in order to intercept the *French* Transports, he had Advice the 23d of *December*, that the said Vessels, bound to *Thoulon* and *Marseilles*, with six Ships of War, had passed through the *Bocca di Bonifacio* the 25th in the Evening, and that they were got into St. *Tropez, Antibes,* and *Villa Franca*; whereupon it was considered whether there might be any probability of attacking them with Success, but it was determined not to be practicable, since they were fortified Places, and that the six *French* Men of War were almost equal to the Strength of ours; besides, there were several Merchant Ships of Force, some of them of between 40 and 50 Guns; so that it was resolved to proceed to *Livorne*, or *Port Mahon*, according as the Winds would permit.

Not practicable to attempt French Ships at Antibes, &c.

In the Road of *Livorne* he arrived the beginning of *January*, where he found the *Dutch* Rear-Admiral with all his Ships; and here he received a Letter from Captain *Evans* of the *Defiance*, giving him an Account that on the 8th of *November* he, with the *Centurion*, commanded by Captain *Mihill*, met with two *French* Ships of War of about equal Strength, between *Almeria* and *Malaga*, with which they began to engage about Eight in the Morning, and continued so to do until Twelve at Noon. The Fight was bloody on both sides, for the *Defiance* had twenty five Men killed, and sixty six wounded, nor fared it better with the *Centurion*; besides their Rigging was so disabled, and their Masts and Yards so much gaul'd, that they were not in a sailing Condition. However, the *French* leaving them about twelve a Clock, they made the best speed

English and Dutch Squadrons join at Livorne.

A warm Dispute between two English and two French Ships

Eeeee 2

speed they could after them till towards Evening, the least of the Enemy's Ships having the other in a Tow; but at length they sheltered themselves in the Port of *Malaga*, having, as was generally reported, lost a hundred Men, where they would not suffer those who were wounded to go on shore, lest the real damage they had received should be discover'd.

Sir *Edward Whitaker* arriving at *Port Mahon*, received a Letter from the King of *Spain*, and another from General *Stanhope*, by which he was desired to appoint two *English* Ships of War, and some Transports, to go up the *Archipelago*, and to other Places for Corn, the Army being in so very great want, that if not timely supplied, according to the Contract made by the General with the Merchants, they must of necessity abandon all *Catalonia*; whereupon it was determined, that Vice Admiral *Baker* should with nine Ships of the Line of Battel, one Frigate, and a Fireship, proceed with several Transport Ships into such a Latitude in the *Meridian* of *Tarento*, as he should judge most proper, and that from thence two *Dutch* Ships of War should convoy those bound to *Tarento*, and then the Vice-Admiral himself with the rest of the Ships accompany the other Transports as far as Cape *St. Angelo*, where he was to leave them to be seen by a Fourth and Fifth Rate as far as *Chio*, *Fochia Nova*, or farther up the *Arches* if thought fit, and when they should be loaden, to conduct them to the Port of *Navarino*, upon the *Morea*, and thence to *Port Mahon*, or *Barcelona*, according as the Winds might be. It was also resolved that when Mr. *Baker* had parted with the said Convoy, he should proceed to *Navarino*, and that when he received Advice there by what time the Transports, with the *Dutch* Ships, might be ready to sail from *Tarento*, he should govern himself either by cruising on the Coast to annoy the Enemy, or proceed directly to that Port, and convoy the Transports to *Port Mahon* or *Barcelona*.

Vice-Admiral Baker appointed to guard Ships for Corn up the Arches, &c.

These Orders being dispatched, and Sir *Edward Whitaker* having received Directions to return to *England*, he left *Port Mahon* the 27th of *March*, and arrived at *Lisbon* the 4th of *April* with three Ships of the Third Rate, where making some stay for our Trade, he sailed the 29th of that Month, and arrived in the Chanel, in Company of the *Dutch Portugal* Fleet and their Convoys, the first Day of *June* 1710. But before I enter on the Account of Vice-Admiral *Baker's* Proceedings in the *Mediterranean*, I will give a short Relation of what happened at home this Year; and of the Reduction of *Port Royal* in *Nova Scotia*.

Sir Edward Whitaker returns to England.

The Admiral of the Fleet, *Matthew Aylmer* Esq; being in the *Soundings* with several of Her Majesty's Ships, and a considerable Number of those belonging to the Merchants, with their Convoys outward-bound, he sent them forward on their respective Voyages the 27th of *July*, when he was about sixty eight Leagues S.W. by W. of the *Lizard*, in the Latitude of 48^d and 13^m. The rest of that Day, and the next he lay by, but seeing on the 29th at Noon thirteen Sail in the North-East of him, he ordered the *Kent*, *Assurance*, and *York* to chase a-head, himself following with the rest of the Ships under

Admiral Aylmer in the Soundings.

CHAP. XXX. *from the Year* 1698, *to* 1712. 765

under his Command, and kept a preffed Sail the whole Night; but the Weather proving very hazey, he could not difcover next Morning more than one Merchant Ship a-head, another Ship a great way to Windward, which he found afterwards to be the *York*, and three Sail more to Leeward, as far as it was poffible to difcern them.

The Admiral fending his Boats on board a *French* Merchant Veffel, which had been taken by the *Affurance*, the Mafter of her acquainted him, that the Ships which he had feen the Day before were fourteen in the Merchants Service, bound for the Bank of *Newfoundland* and *Martinica*, under Convoy of the *Superbe*, a *French* Ship of War of 56 Guns, and the *Concord* of 30, the former whereof, after having feen them into the Sea, was to cruife in the *Soundings*, and the latter to proceed to *Guinea*; that upon difcovering our Ships, they feparated in the Night, the *Concord* with all the Merchant Ships proceeding on their Voyage, (which were the Ships to Leeward) and that the Ship a-head which our Cruifers were in purfuit of, was the *Superbe*.

Soon after this the *Kent*, commanded by Captain *Robert Johnfon*, came up with, and engaged her for the Space of an Hour, when fhe ftruck, in which Action the faid Captain *Johnfon* behaved himfelf like a gallant Officer, and an experienced Seaman, for as he attack'd this *French* Ship in a very handfom manner, fo was fhe taken by him without any Affiftance, although fhe had a greater Number of Men than the *Kent*. Both of them were very much fhatter'd in the Fight, but fo good a Sailer was the *Superbe*, that had fhe not been three Months off of the Ground, fhe would in all probability have efcaped. This Ship had taken feveral valuable Prizes from us before, and our Cruifers had often chafed her without Succefs; but becoming thus in our Poffeffion, fhe was regifter'd in our Royal Navy, being very beautiful, and not above eighteen Months old. *A French Ship, the Superbe, taken.*

There having been a Project formed about the beginning of this Year, for taking from the *French Port Royal*, on the the Coaft of *Nova Scotia*, the feveral Ships hereafter mentioned were appointed to be employed on that Expedition, *viz.* the *Dragon*, commanded by Captain *George Martin*, the *Falmouth* by Captain *Walter Ryddell*, the *Loweftoff* by Captain *George Gordon*, the *Feverfham* by Captain *Robert Pafton*, and the *Star* Bomb-Veffel by Captain *Thomas Rochfort*, the two firft of them of 50 Guns each, and the other two of 32 and 36; but in regard the *Loweftoffe* and *Feverfham* were bound to *New England*, Captain *Martin*, who was appointed to command them all, had Inftructions to proceed thither, and join them, as alfo the *Chefter* of 50 Guns, commanded by Captain *Thomas Matthews*. And Colonel *Nicholfon* being appointed General by Land for this Expedition, he, with his Servants, were carried to *Bofton* from hence, as alfo a Body of Marine Soldiers, with proper Officers, and a Veffel loaden with Ordnance Stores. *The Expedition againft Port Royal.*

At *Bofton* it was to be confidered what additional Troops might be proper, or could be added to the Marine Soldiers, by the Governors of the Provinces in thofe Parts, which was to be determined by a Council of War, to confift of Colonel *Nicholfon*, the
Governors

Governors of *New England* and *New Hampshire*, Colonel *Vetch*, the eldest Colonel of the Land Forces raised in those Parts, as also the Major of the Marines, and Captain *Martin* himself, with three others of the Senior Sea-Captains.

And since the Queen, by Her Majesty's Instructions to Colonel *Nicholson*, had been pleased to direct, that when the Quotas of the aforemention'd Provinces were ready to embark, it should be consider'd at a Council of War, how it might be most proper to attack, and reduce *Port Royal*, the Lords of the Admiralty enjoined the Commadore of the Squadron carefully to put in Execution what should be so resolved, by proceeding with the Ships accordingly, and giving his best Assistance in the landing, and transporting the Troops, and in the taking them on board again when there should be occasion; and, if it should be found necessary, he was to cause the Marine Soldiers belonging to the Ships to be put on shore, in addition to the four hundred carried from hence in the Transports.

When the Place was reduced, or that it should be found that all was done which possibly could be with the Ships and Land-Forces, he was to order the *Chester*, *Lowestoff*, and *Feversham*, to return to their proper Stations at *New England* and *New York*, and himself with the other Ships and the *Star* Bomb-Vessel to repair to *Jamaica*, together with the two Transports, and the Marine Officers and Soldiers, that so the Commander in Chief of the Squadron there might endeavour by them to man the *Kingston* and *Coventry*, with which, and the other Ships under his Command, he was to repair without loss of time to *England*.

Pursuant to these Instructions Captain *Martin* sailed on his Voyage, and all things being settled at *New England* for the Attempt of *Port Royal*, he proceeded from *Nantasket* Road the 18th of *September*, with the *Dragon*, *Falmouth*, and *Lowestoffe*, *Feversham*, *Star* Bomb-Vessel, the Province Gally, two Hospital Ships, thirty one Transports, and two thousand Land-Forces, having sent the *Chester* before, to endeavour to intercept any Supplies which the Enemy might attempt to send to *Port Royal*, and on the 24th in the Afternoon he anchored at the Entrance of that Harbour, from whence standing soon after nearer in towards the Fort, between *Goat* Island and the North side of the said Harbour, a Council of War was called, and pursuant to what was agreed, the small Embarcations, and Boats were gotten ready to receive the Men, and put them on shore.

On the 25th, about Six in the Morning, Colonel *Vetch* and Colonel *Reding*, with fifty Men each, together with Mr. *Forbes*, the Engineer, went on shore to view the Ground for landing the Troops, and soon after Colonel *Nicholson* himself was with the Body of the Men landed, the Enemy firing at the Boats in which they were, from their Cannon and Mortars, but with no great Success.

Colonel *Vetch*, with five hundred Men on the North side, so lined the Shore, as that he protected the landing of the Cannon, Ammunition, and Stores; and the Mortar being fixed on board the

Bomb-

CHAP. XXX. *from the Year* 1698, *to* 1712.   767

Bomb Veffel, fhe driving up with the Tide of Flood within Cannon-fhot of the Fort, both that Day, and the next, bombarded the Enemy therein, which did in a great meafure induce them to capitulate fooner than otherwife they would have done, not but that they were very much gauled in the Attempts made on them, and the many Shot from the Artillery on fhore; but the 28th, 29th, and 30th the Bomb-Veffel was not able to throw any Shells, by reafon of the hard Gales of Wind.

The 1ft of *October*, at a Council of War held in the Camp, two Letters which were received from Monfieur *Subercaffe*, directed to Colonel *Nicholfon*, were taken into Confideration, together with the Anfwers which he had made thereunto, and the Preliminaries being agreed on, the Governor marching out of the Fort with the Garrifon, our Troops took Poffeffion of it foon after, with Drums beating, and Colours flying, where hoifting the Union Flag, they, in Honour of Her Majefty, called the Place *Annapolis Royal*, and a fufficient Number of Men being left therein, the Ships and Troops proceeded to *New England*, as foon as all things neceffary were fettled; from whence Captain *Martin* departed not long after, in order to his putting in Execution the remaining part of his Inftructions for his return to *England*. And now we return to Vice-Admiral *Baker*.

That Officer having conducted the Tranfports to the feveral Ports whereto they were bound, and arriving with them loaden at *Barcelona*, got Sight of four Ships off of the *Phare* of *Meffina*, and as many *Saëtias*, to which he gave Chafe, but could not fpeak with them that Night. Next Morning, being the 3d of *May*, the *Fame*, commanded by Captain *Mafters*, took one of the Ships; the *Suffolk*, Captain *Cleaveland* Commander, another of 56 Guns, called the *Galliard*, though fhe had no more than 38 mounted, but the other two, being fmall Gallies, with the *Saëtias*, efcaped. *Vice-Admiral Baker returns to Barcelona.*

Two French Ships taken.

The Vice-Admiral having feen the Tranfports fafe to *Barcelona*, joined Sir *John Norris* at *Tarragona* the 24th of *June*, of whofe Proceedings from *England*, in order to his commanding in the Mediterranean, before this Junction, and after it, it is neceffary in the next Place to give fome Account. *Vice-Admiral Baker joins Sir John Norris.*

CHAP.

Chap. XXXI.

Containing an Account of Sir John Norris's *Proceedings while he commanded in the* Mediterranean; *with an Attempt made on* Cette *and* Agdé *on the Coast of* Languedoc, *and the beating of the Spanish Army near* Saragosa.

1709/10.

Sir John Norris arrives at Port Mahon from England.

SIR *John Norris* sailed from *Plimouth* the 12th of *January*, and having seen the *Virginia* and *West-India* Trades, with their Convoys, well into the Sea, arrived at *Port Mahon* the 13th of *March*, where joining Sir *Edward Whitaker* and Rear-Admiral *Somersdyke*, he found that seven of Her Majesty's Ships, and two of the States-General, were gone into the *Arches* with Vice-Admiral *Baker*, to protect the Merchant Ships and Vessels with Corn for Supply of the Army in *Catalonia*, as hath been before related, while others were appointed on various Services; and from hence he sent three *English*, with two *Dutch* Ships to *Barcelona* with the Publick Money, Recruits, &c. and to receive His Majesty's Commands, who had by Letter desired him to come with the whole Fleet to that Port.

A Council of War held.

The 22d of *March* calling a Council of War, it was determined to send home four Ships of the Third Rate, which were in the worst Condition to remain abroad, pursuant to the Orders he had received from the Lords of the Admiralty, as also to detach one Fourth and two Fifth Rates to fetch General *Stanhope*, and the Money for the Army from *Genoa*, so that the Ships which would remain abroad under his Command were at this time disposed of in the manner following,

The Disposition of the Ships in the Streights.

viz. two Fifth Rates were order'd to *Lisbon* to clean, and then to join him at *Port Mahon*; one Third Rate, and one of the Fifth were sent by Sir *Edward Whitaker*, before he arrived, to *Oran* in *Barbary*, to convoy from thence Vessels with Corn to *Barcelona*, and another Frigate on the like Errand to *Algier*. Five Third Rates, one Fourth, one Fifth, a Sixth, and a Fireship were with Vice-Admiral *Baker* in and about the *Arches*, which, with two *Dutch* Ships, were to convoy Corn from thence. One Third Rate, and another of the Fourth were by Sir *Edward Whitaker* order'd to cruise in the *Phare* of *Messina*, and one of the Sixth sent by him to *Genoa*. A Fifth Rate was going to *Sardinia*, and a Fourth with two Fifths to *Genoa* for General *Stanhope*, (as is already mentioned) and four Third Rates, two of the Fourth, three Bomb-Vessels, and two Hospital Ships were going with Sir *John Norris* himself to *Barcelona*.

While he remained at *Port Mahon*, he had an Account that the *Pembroke*, a Ship of 64 Guns, and the *Faulcon* of 32, saw the 29th of *December*, seven Leagues to the Southward of *Nice*, five Sail of Ships, which their Commanders believing to be part of Sir *Edward Whitaker's*

CHAP. XXXI. *from the Year* 1698, *to* 1712. 769

Whitaker's Squadron, they hauled upon a Wind, and stood towards them, but perceiving they had *French* Colours, and that two of them were standing in for *Antibes*, while the other three went away with an easy Sail, our Ships made the Signal appointed by Sir *Edward Whitaker*, which they answered, one of them hoisting *Dutch*, and the other two *English* Colours, and bore down. Our People then judging them to be Ships belonging to the Enemy, the *Pembroke* edged towards the *Faulcon*, and as the *French* advanced nearer, they appeared to be large Ships, so that Captain *Rumsey* of the *Pembroke* made all the Sail he could from them, but they having a fine Gale, and ours but little Wind, the 70 Gun Ship soon came up, and attack'd the *Pembroke*, and in less than half an Hour after the other two, of 60 and 54 Guns, came within Gun-shot, and engaged her also, in which Action Captain *Rumsey* was killed. In the *Pembroke* there were one hundred and forty Men slain and wounded, and since her Mizen-mast was shot by the Board, and all her Rigging torn in pieces, the Officers agreed to surrender. Captain *Constable*, who commanded the *Faulcon*, was wounded by a small Shot in the right Shoulder, but left not his Post; and as she was also very much disabled, so were many of her Men killed and maimed. *The French take the Pembroke and Faulcon from us.*

About sixteen Days before this Accident happened, the *Warspight* and *Breda*, each mounted with 70 Guns, the former commanded by Captain *Josias Crow*, and the latter by Captain *Thomas Long*, being about forty Leagues S. W. by W. from *Cape Roxent*, gave chase to a Ship which was discovered at a considerable distance. The *Breda* getting up with her a little after eleven a Clock, had a short, but a very warm Dispute, in which her Commander was slain; but when the *Warspight* came up close under her Quarter, and was ready to lay her on board, she surrendered. This Ship had 54 Guns mounted, was called the *Moor*, and by that Name she was register'd in the List of our Royal Navy.

The 7th of *April* Sir *John Norris* sailed from *Port Mahon*, and the 11th arrived at *Barcelona*, where having assisted at Council with the King of *Spain*, he was informed by his Majesty, that he had Advice the Enemy intended to attempt *Cagliari* with twenty Gallies, five Ships, other small Vessels, and about three thousand five hundred Men, and therefore desired him to do his utmost to frustrate them, or if, instead of *Sardinia*, they should have a Design on *Naples*. *Sir John Norris arrives at Barcelona.*

A Council of War was called upon a second Letter from the King of *Spain*, and it was determined to proceed to *Sardinia* with the Vice-Roy, the Count *de Cifuentes*, and to land him, with such others as his Majesty should appoint, at *Cagliari*, but if they found not the Enemy there, to repair to *Vado*, in order to the convoying from thence to *Barcelona* the Imperial Troops ready to embark; and since Vice-Admiral *Baker* was suddenly expected on the Coast of *Catalonia*, it was agreed that Orders should be left for him to act as might be most for the Service of the King of *Spain*, but first to repair to *Port Mahon* to revictual. *A Council of War determine to proceed to Sardinia.*

Fffff   Having

Sir John Norris proceeds from Sardinia to the Coast of Italy.

Having conducted the Vice-Roy to *Sardinia*, where all things were quiet, he returned to the Coast of *Italy*, and was at *Livorne* the 6th of *May*, where he order'd Corn to be bought up for the Troops, and receiving an Account that Monsieur *de L'Aigle*, with his cruising Ships, very much annoyed our Trade, a Squadron was appointed to go in quest of him, but they had no greater Success than the taking a Ship called the *Prince of Frieze*.

Agreed to send a Squadron in quest of some French Ships.

Advice being received from Mr. *Crow*, Consul of *Barcelona*, that eight *French* Ships of War, and their Convoys, were about the latter end of *April* at *Scio*, laden, and ready to sail with Corn to *Thoulon*, a Council of War was held in *Vado* Bay the 24th of *May*, and upon considering the said Letter, and other Intelligence, it was resolved that six *English* and four *Dutch* Ships should be sent to cruise off of *Cape Thoulon*, for intercepting the Enemy, and to continue until Sir *John Norris* arrived at *Barcelona*, and then to join him, which they were to do, if they had certain Advice the *French* Ships were gone into the Harbour of *Thoulon*.

Agreed to send some Ships with Troops to Sardinia.

Another Council of War was held three Days after, upon Intelligence that the *French* Ships were sailed from *Porto Longone*, with two thousand Men, for the Island of *Sardinia*; and the King of *Spain* having desired, that when the Troops should be embarked, they might be conducted thither, it was at this Council of War, and another held the next Day, determined, that as soon as three thousand Soldiers were embarked, four *English* Ships and six *Dutch* should proceed with them to the aforesaid Island, and there adjust with the Vice-Roy whether the whole, or part of them should be landed, if the Enemy made a Descent on *Sardinia*, otherwise to repair to *Barcelona*. It was also agreed that two Ships of War should convoy four hundred Horse to *Catalonia*, and then cruise along the Coast from *Carthagena* to *Gibraltar*, to protect the Trade;

Ships appointed to several Stations.

that three of ours and four of the *Dutch* should be stationed off of *Thoulon*, to intercept the Enemy's Convoys with Corn, and that the Senior Captain should take the three Frigates with Captain *Stuart* under his Command, if he met with them in those Parts; but if they found the *French* were harboured at *Thoulon*, they were to join Sir *John Norris* at *Cagliari*, or, if not there, at *Barcelona*. It was farther resolved to send Orders to Vice-Admiral *Baker*, by the Ships which convoyed the Horse to *Barcelona*, to appoint two of the Ships to join those cruising off of *Thoulon*, or to proceed himself thither with three, if he judged it more proper, leaving the rest at *Barcelona*, until Sir *John Norris* himself should arrive there; and two Days after he appointed a Ship of the Third Rate, and another of the Fourth, to cruise to and fro near the *Streights* Mouth, for protecting our Trade.

A French Ship forced on shore.

Pursuant to these Resolutions Sir *John Norris* sailed the 1st of *June*, and his Cruisers which were a-head of him chasing a *French* Ship, forced her on shore at *Bastia*, the principal City of *Corsica*, where he had Advice that the Duke of *Turfis* was sailed with his Gallies from that Island, in order to make a Descent on *Sardinia*. In his way thither he crossed the *Bocca di Bonifacio*, and so on to the

Gulph

Gulph of *Terra Nova*, on the North-East side of *Sardinia*, where sending his Boat on shore, he had Intelligence that four of the Enemy's *Saetias* were in that Gulph, which he seized, two of them belonging to *France*, and the other to *Sicily*. The chief Commanders, and the four hundred Troops which were in them, had taken the Town of *Terra Nova*, situate at the Head of a Lake, six Miles farther than the Ships of War could go, whereupon the Troops were landed as soon as it was Day, under Command of General *Brown*, to whom the Town surrender'd. They embarked the next Day, as it was resolved, for *Cagliari*; but having Advice that the Duke of *Turfis*, who intended to land his Men near *Saffari*, hearing of the Approach of our Ships was sailed away to the Northward, towards *Adjazzo* in *Corsica*, it was concluded to follow him, and to destroy his Gallies, even though they were under the Cover of the Cannon of any Place in that Island.

Four Saetias seiz'd in the Gulph of Terra Nova.

Terra Nova retaken from the Enemy.

Resolv'd to proceed after the Duke of Turfis's Gallies.

On the 9th of *June* Sir *John Norris* was informed the Duke was gone with his Gallies the Night before from the Gulph of *Adjazzo* towards *Cape Calvi*, about twelve Leagues farther to the Northward, but that his seven *Saetias* were at an Anchor with six hundred Men, and his Ammunition, near *Adjazzo*, upon which it was proposed to the *Dutch* Flag to attempt them there, but he declined it, since it was a Neutral Port. However Sir *John Norris* let the Governor know that he was in Pursuit of the Enemy, and desired he would not permit them to land, assuring him that if he endeavour'd to hinder his attempting them, by firing on his Ships from the Castle, he should esteem it as an Act of Hostility; but this the Governor promised he would not do.

It was now but little Wind, and before he could reach the Port, the Enemy, who were gotten on shore, had betaken themselves to the Mountains, but he seized on their Vessels and Provisions. The Governor sent to Sir *John Norris*, and desired he would not land the Troops, assuring him that the Enemy should not be admitted into any of their Towns, nor be furnished with Subsistance; and since the pursuing them would have been very difficult, had our Men been put on shore, it was resolved to proceed to *Barcelona*, where he arrived the 18th of *June*, and the King of *Spain* desiring that part of the Troops might be landed in *Valencia*, and that the Fleet might be as soon as possible at *Tarragona*, it was resolved to proceed thither, and that Vice-Admiral *Baker* should follow.

The Vessels with the Duke of Turfis's Provisions seized.

Sir John Norris arrives at Barcelona.

The 20th he arrived at *Tarragona*, and the King having recommended it to him that, after the Troops were landed, an Attempt might be made on *Vineros*, a small Town on the Coast of *Valencia*, and the Magazines which the Enemy had therein, as also that a Convoy might be appointed to three hundred Horses from *Sardinia*, and that then the Fleet might be divided, so as that one part might appear on the Coast of *Valencia*, while the other lay on that of *Roussillon* at the same time, he sailed from *Tarragona*, and joining Vice-Admiral *Baker*, with five Ships of the Third Rate, and a Fireship, he order'd as strong a Detachment as he could spare from the Fleet, together with the Boats, and sent in the small Frigates to cover

The Fleet comes off of Tarragona.

Fffff 2

cover their landing near *Vineros*, but there being at that time a swelled Sea, all the Officers were of opinion it was not safe to attempt the putting the Men on shore; besides, the Master of a Ship of *Genoa*, who had the King of *Spain*'s Pass, affirmed that the Enemy had not any Magazine there; wherefore it was determined to range a Day or two along the Coast of *Valencia*, to alarm them, and then to proceed to *Barcelona*, where arriving the 30th of *May*, he received a Letter from General *Stanhope*, then at *Tarragona*, letting him know the King had consented the Regiment of Colonel *Stanhope* should be embarked, with three hundred Men from *Port Mahon*, to be employed on a Design in the Gulph of *Lyons*, with a Gentleman sent on purpose from *England* by the Queen's particular Order. This Enterprize was intended on *Cette*, on the Coast of *Languedoc*, and all things being ready, it was determin'd at a Council of War, held the 6th of *July*, to send by Express to his Royal Highness the Duke of *Savoy* an Account of the Design; and sailing from *Barcelana* the 9th, they arrived on the Coast of *Cette* the 13th, where the Troops were put on shore. The next Morning, at break of Day, they marched to the Town, and some Ships were appointed to batter the Fort at the *Mold-Head*, whereupon the Inhabitants betaking themselves to the Church, after a small firing the Town surrender'd, as did the Fort, on which were mounted eighteen Pieces of Cannon. A Detachment of three hundred Men were left to secure the Place, and Major-General *Seissau*, with the Regiment of *Stanhope*, and above three hundred Marines, marching to the Town of *Agde*, took a Post before it which makes the Isle of *Cette*, and that Night the Town capitulated without any Resistance.

An Attempt intended on the Town of Cette, and the Troops landed there.

The Town and Fort of Cette surrender.

The 15th there was Advice that the Duke *de Roquelaure*, who commanded in the Province of *Languedoc*, designed to make a Descent by Boats over the Lake on the Island of *Cette*, and the Major-General acquainted Sir *John Norris* that he would endeavour to oppose it, desiring the Assistance of the Boats belonging to the Fleet on the Lake, whereupon he, with the *Dutch* Flag, mann'd and arm'd all the Boats the next Morning, and going on the said Lake, prevented the intended Attempt; but our Troops, left to guard the Post of *Agde*, by some Mistake quitted the same, and were coming away in *Saetias*. The Major-General proposed marching back to regain the Pass, and accordingly it was resolved so to do, but being soon after informed that a great Body of Troops were coming down, it was thought proper to embark our Men, part of whom were left in the Fort of *Cette* to cover the Retreat.

Our Troops driven from the Posts they had taken.

The Enemy pursued so hard, that they took our advanced Guard, when the Fort surrendered to them, and as soon as they understood the Major-General was employed in this Enterprize, (who had shewn great Zeal and Bravery, and was a Native of that Country) they not only imprisoned his Family, but exposed them to very great Hardships.

Hardships done by the French to the Family of Lieutenant-General Seissau.

This Affair ending thus, Sir *John Norris* sailed the 19th, and shewed himself off of *Thoulon* and *Marseilles*, some Days after which he stood into the Road of *Hyeres*, where discovering a Ship,

Flyboat

CHAP. XXXI. *from the Year* 1698, *to* 1712.   773

Flyboat built, of about 50 Guns, under three Forts upon the Island *An Attempt*
of *Port Cros*, he ordered some *English* and *Dutch* Frigates, under *made on a*
the Command of Captain *Stepney*, to attack the said Flyboat, and *at the Isles of*
Forts, which, after a considerable Fire, beat the Men out of her, *Hyeres.*
and the lowermost of those Forts; but as our Boats boarded the
Ship, she took fire by a Train the Enemy had laid, and blowing up,
thirty five of our People were killed and wounded.

Our Cruisers off of *Thoulon* unluckily miss'd the *French* Convoy,
for being in great want of Water they were obliged to seek a Supply, mean while they got into Port. On the 14th of *August* Sir
John Norris came off of *Mahon*, and arrived in *Barcelona* Road *Sir John Nor-*
three Days after, where he met with the good News of our Army's *ris comes to*
having entirely defeated that with the Duke of *Anjou*, near *Sara-* *The Enemy's*
gosa, which might justly be attributed to the Advice, Conduct, and *Army beaten*
Bravery of General *Stanhope*, who had pressed the King and Mar- *fa.*
shal *Staremberg* to attack them, and from which he deservedly received Thanks from his Majesty at the Head of the Army.

The *Dutch* intending about this time to return home, Sir *John*
Norris would have had no more Ships with him, after such a Separation, than nineteen, besides two of 40 Guns; however, at the
Desire of the King of *Spain*, he was proceeding on an Enterprize
on the Coast of *Valencia*, his Majesty with his Army being within
eight Days March of *Madrid*, and the Duke and Duchess of *Anjou*
retired to *Valladolid*, but this Design was not put in Execution, the
Horse not being ready to embark, and the Provisions in the Ships
growing very short, so that it was resolved to proceed to *Port Ma-* *The Dutch*
hon, and the *Dutch* Vice-Admiral sailed homewards. *Vice-Admiral returns home.*

The Squadron being cleaned, Sir *John Norris* sailed from *Port*
Mahon the 30th of *October*, and proceeding down the *Streights*,
he took on the 6th of the next Month three *French* Ships from *Three French*
Newfoundland. The 9th he arrived at *Gibraltar*, when by the best *Newfoundland Ships ta-*
Intelligence he could gain, the Enemy had not above five or six Ships *ken.*
cruising without the *Streights*, whereas our Squadron consisted of
seven under the Command of Captain *Mighils* *. Sir *John Norris*
had no more than nine with him, with which he determined to proceed up the *Mediterranean*, as high as *Port Mahon*, with the *Turky*
Convoy and Trade, and there to consider how to protect them
farther.

After having touched in *Almeria* Bay, he arrived the 5th of *De-* *Sir John Nor-*
cember with the *Turky* Ships at *Mahon*, as did also Captain *Mighils* *ris proceeds up*
with those which he had been cruising with without the *Streights* *the Streights.*
Mouth, and being informed by the Queen of *Spain* that the Enemy
intended to attack *Girone*, he resolved to strengthen the *Turky* Convoy as high as the Chanel of *Malta* by five Ships of War, and
when he was joined by others which he expected, to proceed to
Barcelona, and concert Matters with his Catholick Majesty. Accordingly he arrived there the 4th of *January*, and understanding, *The Enemy*
when assisting at Council, that the Enemy had made a Breach at *Gi-* *attack Girone.*

---

* *Since a Flag-Officer.*   *rone,*

rone, which in a few Days would be practicable; that the Armies with the Duke *de Noielles* in *Catalonia*, and with the Dukes of *Anjou* and *Vendome* about *Saragofa* were either of them superior in Strength to that in *Catalonia*; and the King desiring that since the Troops were not ready to embark from *Italy*, the Fleet might proceed to the Coast of *Rofes* to annoy the Enemy, and then return to *Barcelona*, he failed accordingly, but by a violent Storm, which continued several Days, the Ships were separated, and forced to *Port Mahon*, most of them being disabled in their Masts and Sails, and the Cables of the *Refolution* parting in a strong Easterly Wind, which caused a great Sea, she drove on shore on the Coast of *Barcelona*, where she was lost.

The Fleet separated going to the Coast of Rofes.
The Refolution stranded.

There being a Necessity of convoying some Transports with Troops from *Italy* to *Barcelona*, the Admiral arrived the 19th of *March* in the Bay of *Vado*, and on the 22d following the *Severn*, *Lyon*, and *Lyme*, being Scouts, made the Signal of seeing four Ships, whereupon he ordered the *Naffau* and *Exeter* to slip and give them Chase. About Nine in the Morning Guns being heard, like Ships engaging, he made the Signal for the *Dartmouth* and *Winchelfea* to chafe also, and the *Elizabeth*, *Captain*, and *Northumberland* to slip both Cables, while the rest of the Ships were endeavouring to unmoor, but the Wind coming out of the Sea obliged them to ride fast.

The 27th the *Severn* and *Lyme* came into the Road, and Captain *Pudner*, who commanded the former, gave Sir *John Norris* an Account, that he had the Day before, with those two Ships, and the *Lyon*, of 60 Guns, engaged four belonging to *France* from 60 to 40, and that after two Hours firing, the Enemy seeing others of ours advancing, made what sail away they possibly could, as all but the *Severn* did after them, which Ship was too much disabled to follow, but they lost sight of them in the Night. The said Ship *Severn* had twenty three Men killed and wounded, the *Lyon* forty, Captain *Walpole* her Commander losing his right Arm by a Cannon Ball, and the *Lyme* had six Men slain and hurt. The *Exeter*, commanded by Captain *Raymond*, came up with one of these Ships of the Enemy's the 23d, and engaged her two Hours, when, being much disabled, he brought to. This Ship was formerly one of ours, named the *Pembroke*, and used to be mounted with 60 Guns, but at this time she had no more than 50.

An Engagement between fome English and French Ships off of Vado.

1711.

At a Council of War held in *Vado* Road the 28th of *March*, it was judged adviseable to send five Ships to cruise between that and *Cape Corfo*, for six or eight Days, to protect our Trade, and then to return and accompany the Fleet and Troops to *Barcelona*, which were embarked the 15th of *April*, and waited only a Wind; and there Sir *John Norris* received a Letter from Sir *John Jennings*, advising him that he was arrived in *England* from *Port Mahon*, in order to his commanding in the *Mediterranean*.

Sir John Jennings arrives to command in the Mediterranean.

Sailing with the Transports, and being off of *Cape delle Melle*, a violent Gale of Wind at S. W. forced both Men of War and Transports,

ports, in all about one hundred and twenty Sail, into the Road of *Araffio*, where with great difficulty Forage was procured for the Horses. There Sir *John Norris* lay Wind bound till the 4th of *May*, when he sailed, and arrived at *Barcelona* the 8th; and since the King of *Spain* could not come to any Resolutions about opening the Campaign till the Duke of *Argyle* arrived with Money for the Army, his Majesty desired him to stay there to assist in Council, when his Grace should arrive, and to send the Ships to *Mahon* with Vice-Admiral *Baker*. *Sir* John Norris *comes to* Barcelona.

The Duke of *Argyle* came to *Barcelona* the 18th of *May*, when Sir *John Norris* sent two Frigates to *Genoa* for the Publick Money; and the *French* having declared they would seize all *Genoese* Ships employed in transporting Troops, he dispatched with them to *Port Mahon* one Third Rate, one Fourth, and one Fifth, for their better Security; and coming himself to that Port, he accompanied Captain *Cornwall* with the *Turky* Trade to *Gibraltar* and *Lisbon*, from whence sailing the 15th of *September*, he arrived off of the Isle of *Wight* the 8th of the next Month with four Ships of the Third Rate, seven of the Fourth, three of the Fifth, two Bomb-Vessels, two Storeships, and an Hospital Ship, and from thence held on his Course to the *Downs*. *Duke of* Argyle *arrives at* Barcelona.

Sir John Norris *arrives in* England.

CHAP. XXXII.

Containing an Account of the unsuccessful Expedition against Quebec, *with a Squadron under the Command of Sir* Hovenden Walker, *and a Body of Troops commanded by General* Hill.

SIR *John Jennings* being arrived in the *Mediterranean*, as hath been already observed, we will leave him there for some time, until an Account is given of Sir *Hovenden Walker*'s Proceedings with a Squadron of Ships, and Land-Forces, on an Expedition against *Quebec*, lying far up in the River *Canada*, and of what was done by him after he arrived in *England*, and was sent to command the Ships at *Jamaica*, when we will return to Sir *John Jennings*, and close the War by bringing him home from the *Mediterranean*, after he had transacted several Services in those Parts for the Good of the Princes in Alliance with *Great Britain*.

The Queen's Instructions to Sir *Hovenden Walker*, Rear-Admiral of the White, were dated the 11th Day of *April* 1711, by which he was ordered to take under his Command the *Torbay*, a Ship of 80 Guns, the *Edgar*, *Swiftsure*, and *Monmouth*, of 70, and the *Dunkirk*, *Sunderland*, *Kingston*, and *Mountague*, each of 60 Guns, with two Bomb-Vessels, as also the *Leopard*, and *Saphire*, one of 1711. *Sir* Hovenden Walker *appointed to proceed with a Squadron to* Quebec.

50,

50, and the other of 30 Guns, sent before to *North America*.

Instructions to Sir Hovenden Walker.

With all these, except the two last, together with the Storeships and Transports designed on the Expedition, he was, as soon as might be, to rendezvous at *Spithead*, and when Mr. *Hill*, General and Commander in Chief of the Forces, should be embarked, and the Troops on board, he was with the first Opportunity of a Wind to proceed to *Boston* in *New England*, without touching at any Island, Country, or Place, if it could possibly be avoided; and as he was required to appoint proper Signals, and Places for Rendezvous, in case of Separation, so was he to give strict Orders to the Captains of the Ships under his Command, that if they happened to be so separated, they should not inform the Enemy, or any other, on what Design they were going.

In his Passage to *Boston*, the chief Town in *New England*, he was, when himself and the General should judge it most proper, to detach one Ship of War, or more, to convoy directly to *New York* the Transport Ships, on which were loaden Artillery, Stores, Cloaths, and Accoutrements, with other things for the Use of the Forces to be raised there, as well as in the *Jerzyes* and *Pensilvania*, the same to be delivered as the General should direct, and then the Ships of War were to be order'd to return to *Boston*. But if it should not be judged proper to make such a Detachment, the Transports were to be sent to *New York*, under a sufficient Convoy, when he arrived at *Boston*, and the said Convoy to bring thither such Necessaries and Stores as should be provided for the Squadron and Forces.

When he arrived at *New England* he was to take the *Leopard* and *Saphire* under his Command, and consider whether it might be necessary to make any Addition to the Squadron, by the Convoy to the *New England* Mast Ships, or others stationed on the Coast of *America*, which he was empowered to do; and if the General should, upon advising with him, think it practicable to send any Transports, with some of the new raised Troops in *New England*, to garrison *Annapolis Royal*, lately called *Port Royal*, and to bring from thence the Marines left there, or any part of them, or of the Artillery, or Stores of War, he was to appoint a sufficient Convoy, with Directions to them to return forthwith to *New England*.

He was, when at *Boston*, to take under his care all Transport Vessels, Ketches, Hoys, Boats, and other Necessaries provided in *New England*, and as soon as the Forces from hence, and those raised there, should be on board, he was to sail with them all into the River of St. *Lawrence*, up to *Quebeck*, in order to attack that Place, and being arrived, to make a proper Disposition of the Ships for that purpose, as well of such as might be fit to employ before the Town, as others, upon consulting with the General, to pass the Place, and proceed up the River towards the Lake, not only to prevent any Communication with *Quebec*, but to protect the *Canoas* and Boats with the Forces from *New York*; to which end he was empowered to convert some of the small Vessels sent from hence, or

New

New England, into Frigates, suitable to the Navigation of the upper part of the River, and to man and arm them accordingly.

At *New England*, or elsewhere, he was to assist the General with Vessels and Boats proper for landing the Forces, and embarking them again, but more especially upon his Arrival at *Quebec*, or for transporting them from Place to Place.

He was also ordered to send to the General such Marine Soldiers as should be on board the Squadron, when he should demand the same, which he was to have the chief Command of while employed on shore; besides which, he was to aid him with such a Number of Seamen, Gunners, Guns, Ammunition, and other Stores from the Ships, as he should demand for the Land Service, which Seamen were to assist in drawing and mounting the Cannon, or otherwise as should be found necessary.

He was strictly required to lose no time in proceeding to *New England*, and from thence to the River of St. *Lawrence*, nor in putting in Execution the Service at *Quebec*, but that, on his part, all Expedition should be used in the Reduction of the Place, and of the Country of *Canada*, or *New France*, and in the seasonable Return of the Squadron and Transports.

Her Majesty empowered him to direct the Commissary of the Stores to deliver to any Ship or Vessel, whether of War, or otherwise, any Provisions, or Liquors under his Care; and he had Liberty to provide any other Naval Stores for the use of the Squadron; and in case of Success, if it should be found necessary by him and the General to have a Naval Force left in the River of St. *Lawrence*, he was to appoint such part of the Squadron to remain there as might be judged proper, he taking care to make suitable Provision for the Maintenance and Repair of such Ships; and the like Liberty was given as to any of the smaller Vessels, such as Transports, or otherwise, or to make use of any of the Enemy's Ships which might be taken, if proper, to bring into *Europe* such Governors, regular Troops, religious Persons, or others, whom the General by his Instructions was directed to send away from *Canada*, with Commissaries, Stores, and Provisions for their Transportation.

These Services being directed, he was to take on board the General, if he should think fit to return, and such of the Forces as might not be left in *Canada*, and hasten with the Squadron and Transports out of the River; and if the Season of the Year would permit, he was to proceed to, and summon, and attack *Placentia* in *Newfoundland*, in such manner as General *Hill* should direct; which Service being over, he was to order such Ships of War as did not properly belong to the Squadron under his Command, to return to their several Stations, directing the Masters of the Transports which he should have no farther occasion for, to go and seek Freight either upon the Continent of *America*, or in the Islands, to ease the Publick of the farther Charge of them, and for the Benefit of the Trade of *Great Britain*.

Lastly, It was recommended to him, as it was to the General of the Land-Forces, to maintain a constant good Understanding and Agreement,

Agreement, and on all Occasions to render each other all necessary and requisite Assistance; and if any Difference should arise between them, upon any Construction of Command, or the Nature of Command in the Service, or otherwise howsoever, the Queen was pleased to reserve the Determination of the same to her self, at their return to *Great Britain*, without Prejudice to either of them, in submitting to each other for the Good of Her Majesty's Service. And that he might be sufficiently informed of Her Majesty's Design upon *Canada*, and of the Preparations directed to be made for carrying it on, Copies of the Instructions were sent to him which were dispatched to the Governors of *New York*, the *Massachuset's Bay*, and *New Hampshire*, as also of the additional Instructions to the Governors of *New York*, and of those to *Francis Nicholson* Esq; and the several Governors of the Colonies of *Connecticut*, *Rhode Island*, *Providence Plantation*, and *Pensilvania*.

Observations on the Instructions.

These were the Contents of the Queen's Orders to Sir *Hovenden Walker*, prepared without so much as consulting the then Lords Commissioners of the Admiralty, either as to the Fitness of the Ships appointed for the Expedition, or the Nature of the Navigation; but, on the contrary, the Design on which they were bound was rather industriously hid from them, as may appear by some Letters to Sir *Hovenden Walker* before he sailed from *Spithead*, by which a certain Person seemed to value himself very much that a Design of this Nature was kept a Secret from the Admiralty; who, had they been consulted, would not, I am apt to think, have advised the sending Ships of 80 and 70 Guns to *Quebec*, since the Navigation up the River of St. *Lawrence* was generally esteemed to be very dangerous. Nor were their Lordships permitted to know any thing of this Matter, at least not in form, until Advice was received that the *French* were equipping a considerable Squadron at *Brest*, which some of the Ministry were apprehensive might be designed to intercept Sir *Hovenden Walker*; but it was too late to take any proper Measures for preventing it, if the Enemy had really had any such Intentions.

Having thus given a brief Account of what Steps were taken to set forth this Squadron, which, e'er it returned, put the Nation to a very considerable Expence, it remains that we accompany them on the Expedition, and I shall give as particular an Account of their Proceedings as the Papers which I have before me will enable me to do.

Sir Hovenden Walker *sails.*

Sir *Hovenden Walker* was under sail with the Ships of War and Transports, off of *Dunose* the 29th of *April* 1711, but coming off of the *Start* the 1st of the next Month, a Westerly Wind obliged him to put in at *Plimouth*. Being the length of the *Deadman* the 4th, he met with the *Kent*, *Essex*, and *Plimouth*, which Ships he took with him some Leagues into the Sea, and then left them to their former Service of cruising in the *Soundings*.

He arrives at New England.

The 24th of *June* he arrived at *Nantasket*, near *Boston* in *New England*, having then with him five Ships of the Third Rate, six of the Fourth, one of the Fifth, and two Bomb-Vessels, but not meeting

CHAP. XXXII. *from the Year* 1698, *to* 1712. 779

meeting with that ready Affiftance which was expected from the Government and People of that Country, it was the 30th of *July* before he failed from thence, and then he was on his way to *Quebeck* with the *Britifh* and *New England* Forces.

The 14th of *Auguft* he got the length of the *Bird-Iflands*, which lie about two hundred and fifty Leagues from *Cape Anne*, and having fent the *Chefter*, *Leopard*, and *Sapphire* to cruife between *Placentia* and *Cape Breton*, on an Ifland oppofite to *Newfoundland*, expected their joining him in his Paffage to *Quebec*, the former of which Ships had taken, and fent into *Bofton*, before he failed thence, a Ship of about one hundred and twenty Tuns, with 10 Guns, that had feventy Men on board, whereof thirty were Soldiers for the Garrifon of *Quebec*. *Comes to the Bird-Iflands.*

The *Loweftoff*, *Feverfham*, *Enterprize*, and *Triton's Prize*, all fmall Frigates, which were ftationed at *New York*, and *Virginia*, he ordered to join him off of *Cape Breton*, being empowered by Her Majefty's Orders fo to do, if he fhould find it neceffary, and this he the rather did, becaufe of the Ufe they might be to him in his proceeding up the River to *Quebec*, which Navigation moft of the People with whom he had fpoken reprefented to be very dangerous, and therefore he rightly judged the *Humber* and *Devonfhire*, which mounted 80 Guns each, too big to be ventured thither, for which reafon he fent them home, and fhifted his Flag on board the *Edgar*, a Ship of 70 Guns, General *Hill* removing into the *Windfor*, which carry'd ten lefs; but fince he had Information that a Ship of 60 Guns and another of 30, were expected from *France* very fuddenly, he ordered the aforefaid Ships *Humber* and *Devonfhire* to cruife in the opening of the Bay of St. *Lawrence* until the laft of *Auguft*, and then to purfue their Voyage home. *Takes ftationed Ships at New York and Virginia with him.* *Sends home the Humber and Devonfhire.*

He had very fair Weather until he got into the aforefaid Bay, when it became changeable, fometimes thick and foggy, and otherwhiles calm, and little Winds, and the Navigation appeared to be intricate, and hazardous. The 18th of *Auguft*, when he was off of *Gafpé Bay*, near the Entrance of the River *Canada*, it blew frefh at N. W. and left the Tranfports fhould be feparated, and blown to Leeward, he anchored in that Bay, where ftaying for an Opportunity to proceed up the River, he burnt a *French* Ship which was fifhing, not being able to bring her off. *He arrives in the Bay of St. Lawrence.* *Anchors in Gafpé Bay.*

The Wind veering Wefterly the 20th of *Auguft*, he had hopes of gaining his Paffage, but the next Day, after Noon, it proved foggy, and continued fo all Night and the Day following, with very little Wind, till the Afternoon, when there was an extreme thick Fog, and it began to blow hard at E. and E. S. E. which rendering it impoffible to fteer any Courfe with Safety, having neither fight of Land, nor *Soundings*, or *Anchorage*, he, by the Advice of the Pilots then on board him, both *Englifh* and *French*, who were the beft in the Fleet, made the Signal for the Ships to bring to with their Heads Southward, at which time it was about Eight at Night, believing that in that Pofture they fhould not come near the North Shore, but rather have driven with the Stream in the Mid-Chanel; but, *Brings to with his Head Southward.*

Ggggg 2

In danger on the North Shore among Rocks and Iſlands. Eight Tranſport Ships loſt.

but, on the contrary, as they lay with their Heads Southward, and the Winds Eaſterly, in two Hours time he found himſelf on the North Shore, among the Rocks and Iſlands, at leaſt fifteen Leagues farther than the *Log-Line* gave, where the whole Fleet had like to have been loſt, the Men of War eſcaping the danger with the utmoſt difficulty, but eight Tranſport Ships were caſt away, and almoſt nine hundred Officers, Soldiers, and Seamen periſhed.

The *French* Pilot (who, as it was ſaid, had been forty Voyages in this River, and eighteen of them in Command) informed him that when it happens to be ſo foggy as to prevent the ſight of the Land, it is impoſſible to judge of the Currents, or to ſteer by any Courſe, for that he himſelf had loſt two Ships, and been another time caſt away upon the North Shore when he judged himſelf near the South, inſomuch that it was extreme difficult to procure Men in *France* to proceed on ſo dangerous a Navigation, ſince almoſt every Year they ſuffered Shipwreck.

Obſervation.

Thus it appeared how much things had been miſrepreſented in *Great Britain*, by thoſe who pretended to aver that Fleets of Ships might ſafely proceed up the River to *Quebec*, and it was demonſtrable that the People of *Boſton* knew not any thing of what they propoſed, when Schemes were laid for ſuch an Expedition.

A Council of War called.

Judg'd impracticable to get up to Quebec.

After this unhappy Diſaſter, and when Sir *Hovenden Walker* had plied two Days with very freſh Gales between the Weſt and the South, to ſave what Men, and other things he could, he called a Council of War, and upon enquiring of the Pilots, (who had been forced on board the Ships by the Government of *New England*) and duly examining into every Circumſtance, it was judged impracticable for a Fleet to get up to *Quebec*, ſince there were ſo many apparent Dangers, and no Pilots qualified to take the Charge; beſides, it was the Opinion of them all, both *Engliſh* and *French*, that had the Squadron been higher up the River, with the hard Gales they met with, all the Ships would inevitably have been loſt. At this Council of War there were, beſides the Rear-Admiral, Captain *Joſeph Soanes*, Captain *John Mitchel*, Captain *Robert Arris*, Captain *George Walton*, Captain *Henry Gore*, Captain *George Paddon*, Captain *John Cockburn*, and Captain *Auguſtine Rouſe*.

The Conſultation being over, the *Sapphire* was ſent to *Boſton* with an Account of the Misfortune, and the *Mountague* to find out the *Humber* and *Devonſhire*, and to ſtop all Ships bound up to *Quebec*; and the *Leopard* being left with ſome Sloops and Brigantines, to take any Men from the Shore that might be ſaved, and to endeavour to weigh ſome Anchors left behind, he proceeded to *Spaniſh* River in the Iſland of *Breton*, the Rendezvous he had appointed, there to be perfectly informed of the State of the Army and Fleet, and to ſettle Matters for their farther Proceedings, but all the Ships did not join till the 7th of *September*.

Sir Hovenden Walker repairs to Spaniſh River.

A Council of Sea and Land Officers.

The 8th Day, by Conſent of the General, he called a Council of War of Sea and Land-Officers, where it was conſidered whether, under their preſent Circumſtances, it was practicable to attempt any thing againſt *Placentia*, which all of them very much inclined to;

to; but upon examining into the State of the Provisions on board the Men of War and Transports, it was found there was but ten Weeks at short Allowance in the former, and in the latter much less, so that it was unanimously agreed not any thing of that kind could be undertaken, but that it was necessary the Squadron and Transports should proceed to *Great Britain*, since they had but barely Provisions sufficient for the Voyage, and that there was not any Prospect of a Supply from *New England*, the Season of the Year being too far advanced for navigating safely in those Parts of the World. At this Council of War there were, besides the Sea-Officers of the last, General *Hill*, Colonel *Charles Churchill*, Colonel *William Windresse*, Colonel *Campenfelt*, Colonel *Clayton*, Colonel *Kirke*, Colonel *Disney*, Colonel *Kane*, together with Colonel *Vetch*, and Colonel *Walton*, who commanded the Forces raised in *New England*.

Agreed not practicable to attempt Placentia.

Pursuant to what was thus determined in *Spanish River*, he sailed the 16th of *September*, and arrived at St. *Helen's* the 9th of *October*; and thus ended an Expedition so chargeable to the Nation, and from which no Advantage could reasonably be expected, considering how unadvisedly it was set on Foot by those who nursed it up upon false Suggestions, and Representations; besides, it occasioned the drawing from our Army in *Flanders*, under Command of his Grace the Duke of *Marlborough*, at least six thousand Men, where, instead of beating up and down at Sea, they might, under his auspicious Conduct, have done their Country Service. Nay, there may be added to the Misfortunes abroad, an unlucky Accident which happen'd even at their Return on our own Coast; for a Ship of the Squadron, called the *Edgar*, of 70 Guns, had not been many Days at an Anchor at *Spithead*, e'er (by what Cause is unknown) she blew up, and all the Men which were on board her perished.

Sir Hovenden Walker arrives in England.

Observation.

CHAP. XXXIII.

Containing an Account of Sir Hovenden Walker's *Proceedings with a Squadron in the* West-Indies; *with the Attempts made by the* French *on our Plantations of* Antegoa *and* Montserat, *and an Account of a terrible Hurricane at* Jamaica.

Having already acquainted you that some time after Sir *Hovenden Walker* returned from the before-mentioned unfortunate Expedition, he was sent out with a Squadron to the *West-Indies* to relieve Commadore *Littleton*, it may not be improper in this Place to accompany him from, and to *Great Britain* again, after which I shall treat of what happen'd remarkable in the *Channel*, and last of all

all in the *Mediterranean*, while Sir *John Jennings* commanded Her Majesty's Ships in those Parts.

1712.

Sir *Hovenden Walker* sailing from St. *Helen*'s the 28th of *April*, with one Ship of the Third Rate, two of the Fourth, three of the Fifth, and one Sixth, arrived off of *Plimouth* the next Day, having in his Company about one hundred Merchant Ships, but the Wind taking him short, he was obliged to go into Port; however he sailed thence next Morning, when the *Southsea-Castle*, commanded by Captain *Temple*, chased, and took a Privateer of 14 Guns, and one hundred Men.

He comes to the Maderas.

On the 4th of *May*, being about fourteen Leagues from *Cape Finisterre*, which bore S. E. by S. he parted with the *Litchfield* and *Southsea-Castle*, and the Trade bound to *Portugal*, and arriving at the *Maderas* the 20th, with the *Monmouth*, *August*, *Centurion*, *Scarborough*, *Roebuck* and *Jolley*, one of which was of the Third Rate, two of the Fourth, two of the Fifth, and the other a Frigate of about 20 Guns, it was determined to leave the *Barbadoes* Trade, which he met with here, under the Care of their proper Convoy, the *Woolwich*, *Swallow*, and *Lime*, and to proceed as soon as the Ships had taken in Wine, as usual; but before this could be accomplished the *Barbadoes* Convoy was ready, and they all sailed together the 28th.

Comes to the Leeward-Islands.

The 24th of *June* he arrived at *Antegoa*, where he was desired by the General of the *Leeward Islands* so to dispose of the Ships of War in the *West-Indies*, as that they might be ready to succour him, if another Insurrection should happen, which he assured him he would do, by sending some Ships from *Jamaica*, upon the first notice from him that there was any Disturbance, and left Orders with Captain *Archibald Hamilton*, who commanded the Ships at *Barbadoes*, to come to the Governor's Assistance at *Antegoa* in case of any mutinous Attempts.

SirHovenden Walker *arrives at* Jamaica.

At that Island he found the *Diamond* and *Experiment*, two Ships of the Fifth Rate, which had taken a considerable Prize, and sailing from thence the 26th of *June*, he arrived at *Jamaica* the 6th of the next Month, where he was informed that Captain *Mabbot* of the *Mary* Gally, with his Lieutenant, and Master, after having very bravely behaved themselves, were killed on the Coast of *Guinea*, Captain *Ryddell* of the *Falmouth*, and he, having there met with two *French* Ships, which, after a sharp Engagement, got away from them.

Upon Sir *Hovenden Walker*'s coming to *Jamaica*, he was informed by Commadore *Littleton* how the Ships which had been under his Command were disposed of in several cruising Stations, who by Orders from the Lords Commissioners of the Admiralty was to return to *England* with the *Defiance* and *Salisbury Prize*, together with the Trade, as soon as they should be ready to sail; but some time after he sent him home a Passenger in the former Ship, for she only accompanied those of the Merchants.

Some Prizes taken.

The 15th of *July* the *Salisbury* and *Defiance* came in from cruising, and brought with them a Prize which they took out of the Harbour

CHAP. XXXIII. *from the Year* 1698, *to* 1712. 783

Harbour of *Santa Martha*, loaden with Bale-Goods, after she had been sunk by a Hole the *French* had made in her bottom; and the same Day the *Salisbury Prize* came to *Jamaica* from cruising on the North side of that Island with a Sloop she had taken, whose Commander gave him an Account that the *Star* Bomb-Vessel, which sailed from *Jamaica* with the *Jersey*, was lost upon the Island of *Heneago*.

The 3d of *August* Captain *Thompson* of the *August* sent in a Vessel which he had taken, and the *Weymouth* and *Tryal Sloop* came in the next Day with a *French* Ship the latter had seized in the Latitude of 28^d, in their return to *Port Royal* from the Bay of *Campeche*, whither they had been sent by Commadore *Littleton* with the Sloops to cut Log-Wood. The Prisoners gave an Account that soon after Sir *Hovenden Walker* sailed from *Antegoa*, Monsieur *Caffard* with eight Ships of War, seventeen or eighteen Sloops, and about five thousand Men, had taken that Island and *Monserat*; that they had been at, and plundered St. *Jago*, (one of the Cape *Verde* Islands) and attempted the *Dutch* Settlements at *Surinam*, but were beaten off. But this being the Report only of the *French* Prisoners, it may not be improper to give a more particular Account of it, as related by Captain *Hamilton*, who (as hath been said before) commanded the Ships stationed at *Barbadoes*, and that being done, I shall return to the Squadron with Sir *Hovenden Walker*.

Other Prizes brought in.

News of the taking Antegoa and Monserat.

On the 13th of *July* a Vessel arrived at *Barbadoes* from Colonel *Douglas*, Governor of the *Leeward-Islands*, with Advice that a Fleet of *French* Ships and Sloops had attempted to land Men on the Island of *Antegoa*, and next Morning Captain *Constable* of the *Panther* came also thither, who informed Captain *Hamilton* that on the 2d of *July* he had been chased by ten Ships, five of which seemed to be larger than his, which mounted 50 Guns, and four Days after he himself chased a *French* Ship, whose Boat he took up with two Men, by whom he was informed that the Ships he had seen were seven Men of War from *Thoulon*, commanded by Monsieur *Caffard*, from 50 to 76 Guns, and that their Design was to attack the *Leeward Islands*. The same Day another Advice-Boat came in, with an Account that the Enemy had attacked *Monserat*, whereupon the Governor of *Barbadoes* called a Council, and desired the Captains of the Ships of War to assist thereat, which were the *Woolwich*, Captain *Archibald Hamilton*, the *Swallow*, Captain *Drake*, the *Panther*, Captain *Constable*, *Burlington*, Captain *Clarke*, and the *Experiment*, Captain *Matthew Elford*.

A more particular Account of the Enemy's attempting Antegoa and Monserat.

As soon as the Ships could possibly be put into a Condition, Captain *Hamilton*, who commanded in Chief, proceeded with them to *Antegoa*, where he arrived the 20th, and next Day the Captains meeting at a Council of War, they resolved to sail early the 22d directly for *Monserat*. In their Passage they met with an Advice-Boat, sent from *Antegoa* some Days before, whose Master said the *French* had plundered *Monserat*, and quitted it the 18th, whereupon our Ships returned to St. *John's* in *Antegoa*, and their Commanders proposed to go after the *French*, and appear off of their Ports, but to that the
Governor

Governor of the *Leeward-Islands* was not confenting, apprehending they might return and make a fecond Attempt.

On the 25th *Thomas Richards*, Mafter of a Veffel belonging to *Exeter*, came to *Antegoa* from *Monferat*, and gave an Account that the *French* Ships were the *Neptune* of 64 Guns, and eight hundred and fifty Men, commanded by Monfieur *Caffard*, the *Temeraire* of 56 Guns, the *Ruby* of 54, the *Parfait*, *Veftale* and *Valeur*, each of 44, the *Medufa* of 36, and the *Prince of Frieze* of 28, all of them doubly mann'd. That he was taken by them the 23d of *April* out of the Road of the Ifle of *May*, and that on the 25th they took St. *Jago*, from whence they proceeded to and attempted *Surinam*, but were beaten off. That then they failed to *Martinica* and *Guadalupe*, where they took in Men, muftering at leaft three thoufand five hundred, and from thence made the beft of their way to *Antegoa*, but miffing landing there, attack'd *Monferat*, when having Intelligence of our Ships coming to relieve it, they left it in a hurry, and intended for *Martinica*, from which Place three of them were to proceed to the *Havana*; fo that after our Ships had ftaid fome Days at *Antegoa*, they returned to their refpective Stations.

The Strength of the French Ships with Monfieur Caffard.

But on the 21ft of *Auguft* in the Evening a Sloop arrived at *Barbadoes*, with a Letter from the Governor of the *Leeward-Iflands*, fignifying his Apprehenfions that the Enemy would again attempt to land on *Antegoa*. Mr. *Lowther*, Governor of *Barbadoes*, acquainted Captain *Hamilton* and Captain *Conftable* of this, and they, with the other Commanders, refolved to proceed to the Relief of the Ifland. Accordingly they failed from *Carlifle* Bay the 25th in the Morning, and arriving the 30th, they were informed by the Governor that the Enemy ftood to the N. E. the 17th, with nine Ships and eight Sloops, and that he had fent out two Veffels to difcover their Motions.

Here the Ships of War remained till the 4th of *September*, and then getting under fail, they ftood away for *Guadalupe*, looking into the Enemy's Harbours there, and at *Martinica*; but finding they were not at thofe Places, made the beft of their way to *Barbadoes*.

News of the French Squadron, after they left the Leeward-Iflands.

The Mafter of a Sloop which came in, gave them the following Account. That on the 18th of *September*, in the Latitude of 28^d, he was chafed by a *French* Squadron, but Night coming on, got clear of them; and that not above three Days after he faw feveral Ships in the Latitude of 26^d, ftanding Southward, which he fuppofed were the fame that had chafed him; fo that the *Panther* being ready to fail with a confiderable Number of Merchant Ships from *Barbadoes* to *Great Britain*, Captain *Hamilton* accompanied them into the Latitude of 26^d, with the Ships under his Command, left the Enemy fhould endeavour to intercept them in their Paffage

Advice in the Leeward-Iflands of a Ceffation of Arms.

Returning to *Antegoa*, that there, if poffible, he might get Advice of the *French* Squadron, he met with the Queen's Proclamation for a Ceffation of Arms; but when he came to *Barbadoes*, and heard that feveral of our Merchant Ships and Veffels were carried into

into *Martinica*, contrary to the Agreement between both Nations, he sent a Ship to demand them of Monsieur *Phelypeaux*, General of the *French* Islands, upon which they were forthwith restored; and there being several *French* Prisoners at *Barbadoes*, which were taken on the Coast of *Guinea*, they were sent to the said General.

Having made this short Digression, I return now to the Squadron at *Jamaica*, where, on the 29th of *August*, there happened a terrible Hurricane, which encreasing from Nine at Night, abated not till near Twelve, doing a very great deal of Mischief. Most of the Shingles of the Houses were blown away, some of the Roofs were torn off, and a great part of the Walls laid flat with the Ground. The Lightening was very dreadful, seeming like a continued Flame, while the Wind roared like Thunder. The Morning discovered a dismal Scene of Houses ruined, Trees blown up, the Streets of the Town filled with Shingle and Rubbish, the People in great Consternation, condoling one another's Misfortunes, and the West End of the Church with the Walls were entirely ruined; the Governor's House suffered also very much, nor were there many that escaped without considerable Damage.

A terrible Hurricane at Jamaica.

Several People were drowned on the Shore in this Tempest, the Sea forcing the Boats and Canoes a great way into the Land at *Spanish Town*, and washed away the Houses, so that what with the Wind and the Water there were not above two standing, and few or none of the Ships of War but what were either driven on shore, lost their Masts, or were otherwise disabled. The Hospital was blown down to the Ground, and several of the sick People killed; and on the 1st of *September* a Third Rate Ship, the *Monmouth*, which had been on the Coast of *Hispaniola*, came in with Jury Masts, having lost her proper Masts in the Violence of the Weather, and had not her Main mast given way, she must (as her Commander believed) have instantly overset.

After this not any thing of Moment happen'd till the Proclamations for the Cessation of Arms were brought into those Parts; for to enlarge on the Disputes which frequently happen'd between the Sea and Land-Officers, the unjustifiable Desertion of the Seamen, tempted away by the Commanders and Owners of Privateers, and the intolerable Insolence of those People, would be too tedious to receive Place in these Sheets. Suffice it therefore that I acquaint you, when the Damages were repaired which the Ships received in the Hurricane, Sir *Hovenden Walker*, pursuant to the Orders he received from the Lords of the Admiralty, repaired homewards, and arrived off of *Dover* the 26th of *May* 1713.

Proclamation for a Cessation of Arms at Jamaica.

Sir Hovenden Walker returns to England.

Hhhhh

CHAP.

Chap. XXXIV.

Containing an Account of Sir Thomas Hardy's *Proceedings off of* Dunkirk, *and in the* Soundings; *as also of the delivering up of* Dunkirk *when Sir* John Leake *commanded the Fleet.*

1711.

Leaving Affairs in remote Parts for some time, I proceed to give an Account of what was done at home. Sir *Thomas Hardy*, Rear-Admiral of the Blue, being appointed to command a Squadron of Ships to observe the Motions of those of the Enemy at *Dunkirk*, he hoisted his Flag the 2d of *May* on board the *Canterbury*, a Ship of 64 Guns, and having examined the Master of a Prize belonging to the aforesaid Port, he was informed by him that there had sailed thence within ten Days eight Privateers, one of 28, one of 26, and one of 10 Guns, and another of 6, the other four open Boats, and that as eight more were fitting out from 30 to 10, so were the Carpenters at work in making the *Grafton*, (a Ship of 70 Guns taken from us) and four others ready for the Sea.

The 21st of *May* he sailed from the *Downs*, and came off of *Dunkirk* with four Fourth Rates, two Fifths, and two of the Sixth, when sending in three of the said Ships to *Flemish* Road, they forced into the Port two Privateers of about 20 Guns each, and a Dogger which carried 8, while the Enemy fired at them from the Platforms at the Peer-heads. He discovered six Ships in the *Basin*, four of which were of about 50 or 60 Guns, and the other two small ones, all unrigg'd; thirty Vessels were in the Peer not ready for the Sea, and he was informed that Captain *Saus* was fitting out a Ship of 50 Guns, with three Privateers of 24, 26, and 28, so as to be ready to sail in fourteen Days.

Having farther Advice the 28th of their Naval Preparations at *Dunkirk*, he took care to keep good looking out with three Ships he had with him, the others being then absent, but three of them *Some small* came in the 1st of *June* from cruising, having taken eight small *Prizes taken.* Prizes, which were not worth the Charge of condemning; and soon Prussians per- after he received Orders to permit the Subjects of *Prussia* to trade *mitted to* to *France* without Molestation. *Trade to France.*

The 11th of *May* he had with him in the *Downs* one Ship of the Third Rate, four of the Fourth, one of the Fifth, one Sixth, and a Sloop; and receiving Advice that the *Ruby*, of 50 Guns, formerly taken from us, was coming from *Morlaix*, in *Bretagne*, to *Calais*, and *Dunkirk*, with five other loaden Ships of about 20 Guns each, he appointed some of his Squadron to cruise for them on the *French* Coast, but they had not the good Fortune to meet with them.

The

CHAP. XXXIV. *from the Year* 1698, *to* 1712.   787

The 26th of *June* one of our Ships called the *Advice*, a small Fourth Rate, commanded by *Kenneth* Lord *Duffus*, was chased near *Yarmouth* by several *French* Privateers, which he engaged a considerable time, and even until his Sails and Rigging were almost torn in pieces, and many of his Men killed and wounded, so that at length he was constrained to yield, after he had himself received eight Wounds. Being carried into *Dunkirk*, the Officers and People of that Place treated him very civilly, but those who belonged to the Privateers stripped both his Lordship and his People of all they had, even their wearing Apparel. *An English Ship called the Advice taken.*

The 17th of *July* the *Dunwich and Whiteing* Sloop ran one of the *French* coasting Convoys, of about 16 Guns, on shore, and the *Hampshire, Cruiser*, and *Discovery* Dogger brought into the *Downs* the 31st five Prizes which they met with off of *Cape Antifer*. *Other Prizes taken.*

Sir *Thomas Hardy* being in *Yarmouth* Roads the 8th of *August*, he received Orders to proceed as far Northward as the Islands of *Orkneys* with the Trade bound to *Russia*, and to send some of the Ships that were with him to the *Downs*, there being Advice that Monsieur *Saus* was gone out from *Dunkirk*; and with these Orders he received others, requiring him to protect all Neutral Ships which might have Goods on board belonging to Her Majesty's Subjects.

Being joined by the *Russia* Trade, he guarded them as far as *Schetland*, and sending them forward from thence with their proper Convoy, he returned to the *Downs*, where receiving Orders to proceed Westward, he arrived at *Plimouth* the 23d of *October*, and being required, towards the latter end of *December*, to look out for Monsieur *Du Casse*, he determined to put to Sea with such four Ships of his Squadron as should be first ready. *Sir Thomas Hardy sees the Russia Trade as far as Schetland, and then proceeds Westward.*

The 6th of *January* the *York* brought into *Plimouth* a Privateer of 28 Guns, and two Days after the *Kinsale*, a Ship of the Fifth Rate, came to that Port, which had met with and engaged a *French* Frigate of 44, an Hour and half, near the Islands of *Jersey* and *Guernsey*, her Masts, Yards, and Rigging being very much disabled. $17\frac{11}{12}$. *The York takes a French Privateer.*

On the 8th of *January* Sir *Thomas Hardy* sailing from *Plimouth* with six Ships of War, came off of *Ushant*, when crossing the Bay for Cape *Finisterre*, he cruised between the Latitudes of 43 and 45^d North, and thirty and forty Leagues Westing from the said Cape, each Ship within View of the other, at least spreading every Day, sixteen Leagues. The 3d of *February* he took the *Peter* Gally, of about 120 Tuns, which sailed from St. *Domingo* the 12th of *December*, the Master whereof assured him that Monsieur *Du Casse* was not ready to come from *Martinico*, when a Sloop which he had spoken with before he left St. *Domingo* sailed from thence, but when that was his Memory did not serve him to tell with any Certainty. *Sir Thomas Hardy proceeds into the Soundings.*

The 13th of *February* he took a Privateer from *Dunkirk* of 20 Guns, which had been cruising with four more between Cape *Finisterre* and the Rock of *Lisbon*; and on the 21st of *March* the Master *A Privateer taken.*

Hhhhh 2

Master of a small Prize informed him that Monsieur *Du Gue Trovine* was at *Paris*; that three of his Ships from the *West-Indies* were not arrived, one of 70, one of 60, and another of 54 Guns, and that the *Mars*, which had lost all her Masts, was put into some Port of *Gallicia*.

Advice of Monsieur Du Caffe at the Groyne.

Having got four Ships of his Squadron refitted and victualled at *Plimouth*, (to which Port he was obliged to return) he put to Sea with them, and had Intelligence that Monsieur *Du Casse* arrived at the *Groyne* the 7th of *February*, with only one Ship of 60 Guns in his Company, and that as soon as the *Spanish* Money was landed, he was to repair to *Madrid*, but that the Ships following would be ready to sail the 18th, namely, the *St. Michael* of 76 Guns, the 60 Gun Ship before-mentioned, and one of 40, together with the *Mars* of 60 Guns, which was one of Monsieur *Du Gue Trovine*'s Squadron, and being disabled, they would take her in a Tow.

Other Intelligence of Monsieur Du Casse.

This made him use his utmost Endeavours to get off of *Brest*, in hopes of meeting them, but speaking with the Master of a Vessel on the 23d belonging to *Hamburgh*, which came from *Bourdeaux*, he gave an Account that the *S. Michael*'s Boat had been on board him some Days before, about thirty Leagues Westward of *Belle Isle*, and he exactly described the other Ships before-mentioned, which, as he said, stood N. E. to go through the *Race* of *Fontenay*, insomuch that he believed they got into *Brest* the 21st.

A French Squadron discovered, and the Griffin taken.

Sir *Thomas Hardy* had but little Success against the Enemy before the beginning of *August*, when chasing six Ships and a Tartan, one of them hoisted a broad white Pendant at Main-top-mast Head, shortened Sail, and making the Signal for a Line of Battel, tacked, and stood towards him, believing (as it was afterwards owned) that our Ships were Privateers of *Flushing*, with two Prizes; but when they came nearer, and found themselves deceived, they kept their Wind, and made all the Sail they could, as our Ships did after them, every one endeavouring to come up as soon as it was possible. At Five in the Afternoon Sir *Thomas* coming near one of them, which was the *Griffin*, a Ship of the King's, but lent out to the Merchants, of 44 Guns, with two hundred and fifty Men, commanded by the Chevalier *D'Aire*, Knight of the Order of *St. Louis*, she shortened sail, and brought to, when sending some of his Officers on board our Flag, he let him know by them that he was bound with Bale Goods to *La Vera Cruz*, and that before he sailed from *Brest*, he received Letters from *Paris*, assuring him he might in few Days expect the Queen of *Great Britain*'s Pass, but that his Friends advised him not to lose an Opportunity of a Wind by staying for it; to which he was answered, that if he had not the Pass on board the Ship was lawful Prize, whereupon he submitted without any Resistance.

Sir *Thomas Hardy* sent his Lieutenant to the Ship nearest him, with Directions to her Commander to assist in taking Possession of the Prize, and not shortening Sail himself, with the rest of the Ships under his Command chased the remainder of the Enemy, who made

all

CHAP. XXXIV. *from the Year* 1698, *to* 1712.

all the Sail that possibly they could, two of them, with the Tartan, keeping their Wind, and the other two going away large. The *Berwick* chased to Windward, while Sir *Thomas*, in the *Kent*, where he bore his Flag, and the *Windsor*, stood after the other two; but as the Wind dullered, and was sometimes quite calm, the *Windsor* now lay across him, and then had a Gale of Wind when he had none at all. However the said Ship *Windsor*, about Eleven at Night, came within random Shot of the *St. Esprit*, of 36 Guns, and one hundred and seventy five Men, bound with Bale-Goods to *Cadiz*, and after they had engaged near an Hour, she blew up, just at the time when, as her Commander said, he was going to strike, but he, with thirty of her Men, were saved by our Boats. *A French Ship blows up.*

The *Berwick* took the *Adventure* of *Havre de Grace*, carrying 12 Guns, and forty Men, bound to *Newfoundland*, but her Master producing the Queen's Pass, she was permitted to proceed on her Voyage. The said Ship took also the *L'Incomparable*, of 16 Guns, designed for *Martinica*; but the other of 8 Guns, and the Tartans made their Escape; however the *Ruby* was towed by her Boats to the Ship of 12 Guns, which she took, being also called the *Ruby*, and was bound to St. *Domingo*. *A French Ship taken by the Berwick.*

The before-mentioned Ship *Griffin* being brought into Port, and the Persons concerned in her soliciting a considerable time very earnestly for her Release, as Sir *Thomas Hardy* did for her Condemnation, that so she might, with her Loading, be divided between himself and the Captors, they were at length constrained to quit their Pretensions for a Sum of Money which was very short of her real Value.

Sir *John Leake*, as Admiral of the Fleet, commanding in the Chanel in the Year 1711, little or nothing remarkable happen'd; for since the Defeat given the *French* the preceding War off of Cape *Barfleur* by the Earl of *Orford*, and the Destruction of so many of their capital Ships then forced on shore at *La Hogue* and *Cherbourg*, and the Wounds they otherwise received in their Naval Force, they did not think it adviseable to come forth with any considerable Numbers in these Seas, but have either divided them into small Squadrons, or the *French* King hath contented himself in lending his Royal Ships to Merchants, to serve as Privateers, or on trading Voyages, in either of which Cases he hath had a Proportion of the Profit; or if any Number of his Ships hath been set forth together in a warlike manner, they were chiefly employed to annoy our foreign Islands and Plantations, and the Trade in those Parts; for never after the Defeat before-mention'd would they encounter us with a Fleet, unless it was when Sir *George Rooke* engaged them off of *Malaga*, of which I have given an Account in its proper Place. 1711.

The next Year Sir *John Leake* received a Commission from the Lords of the Admiralty to command again in the Chanel, and it was upon occasion of *Dunkirk*'s being to be delivered up to some of the Troops of *Great Britain*, under the Conduct of Lieutenant-General *Hill*, which having seen effected, he returned to the *Downs*, leaving the Troops in that Garrison to take care that what remained 1712. *Dunkirk delivered up to the English Troops.*

to

to be performed was put in Execution, namely, its Demolition after the Peace should take place.

We will therefore thus end our Naval Affairs at home, and conclude the whole of this Work with Vice-Admiral *Baker*'s Proceedings while he commanded a Squadron on the Coast of *Portugal*, and then of what happen'd remarkable during Sir *John Jennings*'s being at the head of our Ships of War in the *Mediterranean*.

Chap. XXXV.

Containing an Account of Vice-Admiral Baker's *Proceedings while he commanded a Squadron on the Coast of* Portugal.

17 11/12.

Vice-Admiral *Baker* being on the Coast of *Portugal* in *January*, with five Ships of the Third Rate, one of the Fourth, and two of the Fifth, pursuant to a Treaty of Alliance between Her Majesty and that Crown, for protecting not only the Coast, but the *Portuguese* Trade, it was on the 4th of *February* determined at a Council of War, upon considering Orders which he had received from the Lords of the Admiralty, to proceed with all the Ships under his Command as a Guard to the Storeships, Victuallers, and Transports, bound to *Port Mahon* for Supply of the Fleet, off of *Cape Spartell*, or into the *Streights* Mouth, and thence to send two Men of War with them to *Gibraltar*, and that then the rest of the Squadron should cruise either in sight of the said Cape, or that of St. *Mary*'s, or between both, for intercepting the Enemy's homeward bound Ships, there being a Report that Monsieur *Du Casse* (whom we have lately had occasion to mention) was expected in some Parts in *France* with the *Spanish* Galleons; but that however the Squadron should return, so as to be at *Lisbon* by the 1st of March, O. S.

Vice-Admiral Baker proceeds to cruise from Lisbon.

Pursuant to this Resolution the Vice-Admiral sailed the 8th of *February*, and on the 25th was informed by two *Dutch* Runners, which came in six Weeks from the Island of St. *Thomas*, that two Days before they came away they had an Account Monsieur *Du Casse* was sailed from *Martinico* with his Squadron, and about fourteen Merchant Ships. On the 16th of *February*, e'er he received this Advice, he chased a Ship about twelve or thirteen Leagues from Cape St. *Mary*'s, which ran on shore and sunk on a Bank, as they afterwards found, when the Weather would permit them to look nearer in towards the Land, and the *Portuguese* having taken Possession, rifled her all they could, her Loading being Sugar, Cocoa, Snuff, and Hides, and (as it was reported) she had Plate on board to the value of twenty thousand Dollars. This was a Ship of 60

Guns,

CHAP. XXXV. *from the Year* 1698, *to* 1712.   791

Guns, termed a *Patache* to the Galleons; and as she was forced on on shore by ours, the Vice-Admiral, by a Memorial to the King of *Portugal*, demanded the Effects belonging to her; but the same being privately secured in various Hands, he could not have any Redress.

Seeing some other strange Ships the 22d in the Morning, he came up with them close under the *Barbary* Shore, and one of them, loaden with Salt, some Wool, and Cochinele for *Martinica*, was taken, the other escaped. The Prize had 26 Guns, but her People threw eleven of them overboard, who confirmed the aforemention'd Report about Monsieur *Du Casse*'s Squadron, with this Addition, that he sailing from *Martinica*, lost Company with his Convoys in ten Days time, so that they doubted not but he was arrived in *France*, or some other Port in *Biscay*. *A French Ship taken.*

The Vice-Admiral arriving at *Lisbon* the 8th of *March*, received Orders from *England* to cruise with five Ships of War for the Security of the homeward bound *Brasil* Fleet, on which Service the Court of *Portugal* desired he might be ready to sail the 20th of *April*, N. S. as also that two Frigates might be appointed to see their outward bound *East-India* Trade to the *Maderas*; and at the same time he was under Orders from the Lords of the Admiralty to detach two Ships to cruise in the *Streights* Mouth, so that in this case he could have no more than three with his Flag, but had hopes the *Dutch* Commander in Chief would take care of the *India* Men. *Vice-Admiral Baker ordered to cruise for the homeward bound Brasil Fleet.*

The Convoy with Stores and Provisions from *England* arrived the 1st of *April*, and since the *Dutch* disappointed him in convoying the *Portuguese East-India* Ships, he determined to send a Fourth Rate Frigate with them to the Western Islands, which Ship might join him in the Station where he designed to place himself for the *Brasil* Fleet; and as for guarding the *Streights* Mouth, he had determined to order Captain *Maurice* to cruise there with a small Squadron.

The 6th of *May* the Vice-Admiral arrived in the Road of *Fayal*, and was then going to cruise with Five Third Rates, together with the *Pembroke*, between ten and twelve Leagues West of the *Tercera* Islands, for the aforemention'd Ships from *Brasil*, having taken a Ship of 22 Guns of Monsieur *Cassard*'s Squadron, bound to *Canada* with Wine and Brandy, which Ship left him the 20th of *April*, N. S. without the *Streights* Mouth, standing Westward, but her Commander did not certainly know whither he was bound. He said there were with him fifteen hundred Soldiers, forty flat bottomed Boats ready framed, with scaling Ladders, and all things proper for a Descent, and that his Squadron consisted of one Ship of 76 Guns, one of 60, one of 54, two of 44, one of 42, one of 24, and a Ketch, which agrees with the Account I have already given of him when he came to, and attempted our *Leeward Islands*. *Vice-Admiral Baker takes a Ship of Monsieur Cassard's Squadron.*

On the 9th of *July* Vice-Admiral *Baker* was informed by some Prisoners, that the Squadron was first designed for the *Canaries* to take in Wine, or to force some Provisions at St. *Jago*, (which, as hath

hath been already said, he plundered) and that then Monsieur *Cassard* was to proceed to *Bahia*, so that possibly he might arrive there before the *Brasil* Fleet sailed, unless they came away by the end of *May*; but he had hopes, from Intelligence he had received, that they might have reached that Place by the 18th of that Month, N. S. because they were under sail from *Rio de Janeiro* the 30th of *April*.

The Provisions of the Ships under his Command being reduced to five Weeks, at short Allowance, it was almost time for him to think of drawing towards *Portugal*; however, being apprehensive that if the *Brasil* Fleet were sailed before the *French* Squadron arrived, they would follow them to the *Terceras*, where they were obliged to call, he determined to remain in his Station as long as it was possible, and in order thereunto prevailed with the *Portuguese* to furnish him with fresh Provisions for three Weeks.

Off of the Islands of *Tercera* he continued cruising until the 11th of *September*, when meeting a *Portuguese* Frigate, her Commander informed him that he left the Fleet three Days before, twenty Leagues from *Corvo*, and that he believed they would be that Day at *Angra*, the chief Town of the Island *Tercera*. Soon after he had this Advice, a violent Storm arose, which very much shattered the Ships, and drove him so far away that he could not fetch the Island again; and judging that it must also have the same Effect on the *Brasil* Fleet, he made an easy Sail towards *Lisbon*, in order to pick up such as should be straggling from their Convoys, but had no Sight, or Intelligence of them, till he came off of the Rock, when he found they arrived the very Day before he made the Land; and since the Cessation of Arms soon after happened, the Squadron of Ships under his Command was called home, and the Expence of the Naval Officers at *Lisbon* retrenched.

Advice of the Brasil Fleet.

A violent Storm shatters the Squadron.

The Brasil Fleet arrive, and Vice-Admiral Baker called home.

CHAP.

CHAP. XXXVI.

Containing an Account of Sir John Jennings's *Proceedings, while he commanded in the* Mediterranean, *till the Cessation of Arms. His carrying the Emperor from* Barcelona *to* Vado, *and the Empress to* Genoa. *The People of* Barcelona *declare War against King* Philip, *and after they are constrained to submit, are inhumanly treated. His carrying the Duke and Duchess of* Savoy *to their Kingdom of* Sicily. *A Comparison between our Naval Loss and that of the* French *during this War.*

IN the last Place we come to the Admiral of the White, Sir *John Jennings*, who was appointed to command the Fleet in the *Mediterranean*, and, besides the Instructions he received from the Lords Commissioners of the Admiralty, he had Orders, in pursuance of the Queen's Pleasure signified to them, to follow such Commands as he might receive from Her Majesty; for whenever there is a Lord High-Admiral, or Commissioners for executing that Office constituted, the Prince investing the executive part of Naval Affairs in that Commission, frequently gives Orders to them to direct the Admiral of the Fleet, or the Commanders of particular Squadrons, to follow such Instructions as he may think necessary to give them.

Sir *John Jennings* sailed from *St. Helen's* the 7th of *January*, and arrived at *Lisbon* the 23d, where he waited the coming of the Ships of the States-General, and others with Transports from *Ireland*; but they not timely joining him, it was determined at a Council of War, held the 6th of *February*, to remain some few Days longer, and then to proceed to *Gibraltar* with such Transports as should be with him, and the Troops, and from thence to *Barcelona*, leaving Orders for the rest to follow, since the King of *Spain's* Affairs were then very pressing.

On the 20th of *March* he arriving at *Barcelona*, found Sir *John Norris*, with the Ships under his Command, was gone to *Vado*, to guard the Troops from thence to *Catalonia*, so that leaving Orders for him to repair to *Port Mahon*, he, at the Instance of the King of *Spain*, appointed a Convoy to several Transports with Troops, which his Majesty desired might be landed at *Tarragona*, or at *Salo Bay*.

In *April* he received Orders from the Lords Commissioners of the Admiralty to detain Sir *John Norris* with him in the *Mediterranean*, until he should receive farther Instructions concerning him, and he appointed some Ships, under the Command of Captain *Swanton*[*], to join the *Turky* Convoy at the appointed Rendezvous, and accom-

Since Comptroller of the Navy.

1711. Sir John Jennings proceeds towards the Streights.

He arrives at Barcelona.

Sir John Jennings ordered to keep Sir John Norris with him. He strengthens the Turky Convoy, &c.

pany

pany them in their homeward bound Voyage well out of the *Streights*; besides which he strengthened the Convoy with Troops and Corn from *Sardinia*, the King of *Spain* informing him that there had been lately seen off of *Barcelona* five large Ships, with the Colours usually born by those belonging to the Government of *Algier*.

Sir John Norris *comes to* Barcelona, *and Vice-Admiral* Baker *to Port Mahon.*

Sir *John Norris* arrived at *Barcelona* with the Troops from *Vado* the 8th of *May*, and on the 19th of that Month Vice-Admiral *Baker* joined Sir *John Jennings* at *Port Mahon* with greatest part of the Squadron, Sir *John Norris* himself continuing in *Barcelona* Road, at the Desire of the King of *Spain*, with the *Boyn*, and some other Ships, as hath been before observed, where Sir *John Jennings* arrived the 1st of *June*, from whence he proceeded to cruise off of

Sir John Jennings *proceeds off of* Thoulon.

Thoulon, and the Coast of *Province*, to intercept the Enemy's Convoy with Corn from the *Levant*, and sent three Ships to *Genoa* to strengthen the like Number which were coming from that Place with Money for the Troops in *Catalonia*, then almost in a starving Condition, having no other Credit than what the Duke of *Argyle* procured for them.

The Admiral ordered to carry the King of Spain *to* Genoa, *upon the Death of the Emperor.*

The Emperor *Joseph* being lately dead, the Admiral received Orders the beginning of *June*, while off of *Thoulon*, to carry the King of *Spain* to *Genoa*, or where else his Majesty should desire, in case he thought fit to go to his Hereditary Countries, as also to give *Naples* what Assistance he could, upon any Commotions which might happen at this Juncture of Affairs; whereupon it was determined at

Some Ships sent to Naples.

a Council of War to send two Ships of the Third Rate, one of the Fourth, and another of the Fifth, with two of the States-General's Ships, to the aforesaid Kingdom of *Naples*, as also to assist in case any Attempts should be made on the Garrisons of *Orbitello*, or *Piombino*, and to add another Frigate to that which was going with Dispatches to the King of *Spain*, and the Duke of *Argyle*.

The King was not inclinable to go to *Italy* until he received an Account that he was declared Emperor, nor was he willing that the Body of the Fleet should be out of Sight of his Capital in *Catalonia*; and now the Admiral having received farther Orders relating to Sir

Sir John Norris *ordered home, and Sir* John Jennings *repairs to* Mahon.

John Norris, it was determined to send him to *Great Britain* with three Ships of the Third Rate, as many of the Fourth, and two Fifth Rate Frigates, with the empty Storeships, Victuallers, and Transports: And there being a Necessity for Sir *John Jennings* to proceed with the Ships under his Command to *Port Mahon*, not only to refit them, but for a Supply of Provisions, he sailed from *Barcelona* the 13th of *July*, and arrived there the 18th.

The Turky *Trade sent home with Sir* John Norris.

Next Day the *Turky* Fleet appearing off of that Port, he gave Captain *Cornwall*, Commadore of that Convoy, Orders to proceed to *Majorca*, the Place of Rendezvous for the Storeships, and other Vessels bound home, from whence he sailed in Company of Sir *John Norris* the 26th of *July*, and Sir *John Jennings* himself proceeded to *Barcelona*. The Ships ordered for *Great Britain* being thus separated from the Fleet, it may not be improper to inform you how those which remained in the *Mediterranean* were at this time disposed of, which was as follows, *viz*.

At

CHAP. XXXVI. *from the Year* 1698, *to* 1712.   795

At *Barcelona* there were with Sir *John Jennings* one Second *How those*
Rate, five Thirds, one Fourth, and seven *Dutch*, under the Com- *which re-*
mand of Vice-Admiral *Peitersen*. There were cleaning at *Port* *were disposed*
Mahon one Fourth and two Fifth Rates; and two of the Third *of.*
Rate, with one of the Fifth, were gone to *Port Mahon* for Money, and to protect the *Genoese* Ships employed in the King of
Spain's Service. Two Fourth Rates were ordered to *Genoa,* and
there were expected from *Naples* two Ships of the Third, one of
the Fourth, and one Fifth of ours, with three *Dutch* Frigates; besides which there were gone to *Lisbon* one Third Rate, one Fourth,
and another of the Fifth.

The King of *Spain* embarking the 16th of *September,* arrived in
Vado Bay in ten Days, being attended by the Admiral, and twenty *The King of*
four Ships of War, and sailing thence, was soon after landed at *San* *Spain carried*
Pietro di Arena, a Suburb of *Genoa*; but to guard the Coast of *Ca-* *to Italy.*
talonia in the Absence of so great a part of the Fleet, there were
left four *English,* and two *Dutch* Ships of War.

There being a very great want of Cables, and other Stores, the
Admiral proceeded to *Livorne,* in order to procure what could be
had there, and the 18th of *October* the *Superbe* and *Tartar,* the
first commanded by Captain *Monepenny,* and the latter by Captain *Two rich*
Ogle, brought in two rich Prizes coming from the *Levant.* *Prizes taken.*

The 2d of *November* the Admiral sailed from *Livorne,* and in
two Days arrived in *Vado* Bay, where by the 10th there were embarked
seven hundred and twenty Horse, and upwards of two hundred and *Horse and Foot*
forty Foot; but since the Winter Season was so far advanced, it was *embark'd at*
not thought safe for the whole Fleet to go to *Barcelona,* so that the *convoy'd to*
Transports were put under the Protection of five Ships of War, and *Barcelona.*
two Fireships, commanded by Captain *Swanton,* and three of the
Ships of the States-General, which were to accompany the Admiral
as far Westward as *Cape Roses,* and then, upon a Signal, to separate,
at which time the Body of the Fleet proceeded towards *Port Ma-* *The Admiral*
hon, whither the others were ordered to repair when they had seen *proceeds to*
the Transports in Safety, that so the Admiral might make a Detach- *Port Mahon.*
ment to guard the Coast of *Portugal,* pursuant to the Orders he had
received; and some Cruisers were sent to the *Streights* Mouth for
Security of our Trade, but more especially that of the *Levant* Company.

When he had made the Island of *Minorca,* the Wind came up at *A hard Gale*
N. E. and blew extreme hard, insomuch that he was constrained to *of Wind.*
come to an Anchor on the West side of it, but most of the Ships
Sails blew away from the Yards; however he got into *Port Ma-*
hon the next Day, and the Captains of the two Ships which he
found there informing him that he had heard many Guns fired the
Night before, he sent out the *Chatham* and *Winchelsea* to see what
they could discover, which returning next Day, brought him an Account that the *Dutch* Vice-Admiral, with his Squadron, (who was
driven to Leeward when he anchored) was in the *Offing,* as also
Captain *Mighils* in the *Hampton-Court,* with the *Sterling-Castle,*
Nottingham, Charles Gally, and *Lynn,* which Ships of ours came
from

from the Coast of *Catalonia*, and had fallen in with two *French* Men of War, called the *Thoulose*, and *Trident*, of 50 Guns, and four hundred Men each.

The Hampton-Court takes a French Ship of War.

The *Hampton-Court* came up with the first of them, and engaged her two Hours, to whose Commander by the time the *Sterling-Castle* was within Musket-shot, (which was about Ten at Night) she struck; but by the Advantage of little Winds the *Trident* got away with her Oars. The *Hampton-Court's* Masts being much wounded in the Fight, they, by the Violence of the Weather, came next Day all by the board, so that she was towed into Port by the *Sterling-Castle*.

The Restoration lost.

About the same time the *Restoration*, a Ship of 70 Guns, was lost on the back-side of the *Mallora*, off of *Livorne*, but all her Officers and Men saved; nor fared it better with a *Saetia*, that had on board to the Value of about four thousand Crowns, which she was bringing from one of the Ports of *Corsica*.

The first Captain of the *Thoulose* was Monsieur *Le Grand Prié*, and the second Captain *Rigby*, an *Englishman*, who had formerly bore Command in our Fleet. From the former of them the Admiral accepted his Parole of Honour for six Months, but the latter he detained, although Monsieur *Le Grand Prié* assured him he was naturalized in *France*, and was become a *Roman* Catholick; but some way or other he found means to escape, and it was believed he got into a Ship of *Genoa*, which lay in the Harbour of *Mahon*.

Vice-Admiral Baker proceeds to the Coast of Portugal.

At length Vice-Admiral *Baker*, who had been detained by contrary Winds, sailed with the Ships appointed to be under his Command to the Coast of *Portugal*, of whose Proceedings, while there, I have already given an Account; and now *(viz.* in the Month of *January)* the Disposition of the Ships was as follows, *viz.* at *Port Mahon* one Second Rate, one Third, one Fireship, two Bomb-Vessels, two Hospital Ships, and six *Dutch* Men of War. Gone to *Lisbon*, five Third Rates, one Fourth, two Fifths, and a Fireship. A Third and Fourth Rate were sent to *Naples*, and four *Dutch* Ships were expected from thence. Two Fourth Rates were on the Coast of *Italy*, and one Fifth sent to *Barcelona*, as were also to that Coast one Ship of the Third, one of the Fourth, and two *Dutch*, with the Duke of *Argyle*. Two Fifth Rates, and one of the Ships of the States-General were gone to *Tarragona*, and a Third Rate, a Fourth, and a Fifth, sent to convoy a Ship with Naval Stores from *Gibraltar*. One Fourth Rate was dispatched to *Cagliari*, and thence to *Livorne*, and one of the Third, and another of the Fourth, were ordered on a short Cruise.

$17\frac{11}{12}$.

How the Ships were divided.

Advice of some Ships fitting out at Thoulon.

The Admiral receiving Advice, while at *Port Mahon*, that the Enemy were fitting out at *Thoulon* eight Ships from 70 to 60 Guns, with three of 40 each, and that they were bound to *Cadiz*, and thence to the *West-Indies*, he called a Council of War the 21st of *February*, and it being found that the Ships under his Command could not go to Sea, until they had Supplies of Provisions from *Italy*, it was determined to send a Frigate with this Intelligence to Vice-Admiral *Baker* at *Lisbon*, that so he might strengthen the Convoy

CHAP. XXXVI. *from the Year* 1698, *to* 1712. 797

voy from thence with the Storeships and Victuallers, and that as soon as the *English* and *Dutch* Ships arrived from *Italy*, the Admiral should cruise between *Port Mahon* and *Cape de Gates*, not only to protect the said Convoy, but to intercept the Enemy.

The Convoy being safely arrived at *Port Mahon*, and the Admiral receiving farther Intelligence of the Enemy's Naval Preparations, not only by my Letter, but from Mr. *Chetwynd*, Resident at *Genoa*, and Consul *Crow* at *Livorne*, it was resolved at a Council of War, both of the *English* and *Dutch*, the 11th Day of *March*, to proceed to Sea with one Second Rate, three Thirds, two of the Fifth, and two Fireships of ours, together with nine Ships of the States-General, and cruise ten or twelve Leagues S.S.W. from *Cape Thoulon*, until more certain Advice could be gained of the Enemy's Proceedings; but Captain *Wallpole* of the *Lyon* joining the Fleet from *Genoa*, and giving an Account that he saw from the Mast-head, the 22d of *March*, nine tall Ships steering to the Westward, with the Wind at E.S.E, the N.W. Point of the Island of *Minorca* then bearing S.W. by S. about ten Leagues off, it was resolved at a Council of War, held the next Day, to proceed to the Southward of *Majorca* and *Yviça*, and endeavour to intercept the Enemy between that and *Cape Martin*, in their Passage down the *Streights*. *Convoy with Transports and Victuallers from England arrive at Port Mahon. A Council of War determine to proceed off of Thoulon.*

Resolution about cruising for a French Squadron.

Gaining no farther Intelligence of the *French* Squadron, he came to an Anchor the 1st of *April* off of the Island of *Formentera*, from whence he sent two of the cleanest Ships to the Coast of *Valentia*, to look into the Bays of *Denia*, *Xabea*, and *Altea*, as also *Alicant* Road, and if they should not bring him any Advice, it was determined to sail between the Islands to *Barcelona*, where probably he might have some Account of them. Arriving there, and meeting with no farther News of them, it was resolved to detach a clean Frigate to look into *Thoulon*, and to proceed off of the Isles of *Hyeres*, to see what they were doing, and particularly whether the Squadron bound to *Cadiz* was still in that Harbour, which done, she was to join the Fleet in a Station S.S.E. ten Leagues from *Cape Thoulon*; and if no farther Intelligence could thus be gained, it was thought adviseable to repair to *Port Mahon* to revictual, and then to proceed to the Coast of *Italy*, as the Empress had desired, in order to the conducting the Transports with Troops from thence to *Catalonia*. *Ships sent for Intelligence.*

The Admiral being not able to procure any farther Account of the Enemy, arrived in *Vado* Bay the 1st of *May*, and finding Orders for embarking the Troops, he sent the Transport Ships into the *Mole*, and proceeded with the *English* and *Dutch* Ships to *Livorne* for Provisions, where he came the 7th of *May*, from whence he sent out clean Ships to cruise, and was preparing to return to *Genoa* with the rest, to concert Measures for the Embarcation, and, if possible, to prevent making two Voyages on that Service. But here it may not be improper to take notice that the *Winchelsea* joining him the 18th of *April*, her Captain gave an Account that while he was at *Gibraltar*, he saw a Squadron of *French* Ships pass through the *Streights*, whereupon he sent a Frigate to look into *Thoulon*, whose Commander, Captain *Haddock*, saw but four Ships in the *Basin* which were *Sir John Jennings arrives in Vado Bay, and thence proceeds to Livorne.*

Advice of French Ships being gone through the Streights.

were rigged; nor did they intend, by all the Advices which could be gained, to fit out more than six Ships from 80 to 50 Guns, which were to be sent, two and two, to *Smyrna* and *Scanderoon*.

Sir John Jennings looks in at Thoulon.

The 23d of *May* Sir *John Jennings* sailed from *Vado* with six *English* Ships, and looked in at *Thoulon*, where he saw but one Ship of War of 50 Guns ready for the Sea, with one or two of greater Force in the *Bafin*, for at this time the *French* were in great want of Naval Stores. From thence he proceeded and joined the *Dutch* Vice-Admiral, with the Tranfports that had on board them about six thousand five hundred Men, which were put on fhore in two Days time; and his Imperial Majefty and Count *Staremburgh*, urging, at a Conference, the Neceffity of bringing the Cavalry from *Italy*, it

Refolved to proceed to Vado, to conduct the Cavalry from thence.

was refolved to return to *Vado*; but fince the Enemy were tranfporting Provifions and Ammunition from *Carthagena* to *Penifcola*, it was thought neceffary to fend three *English* Ships, and two of the *Dutch*, to cruife upon the Coaft of *Valentia*, and after they had fo done for fome time, to lie either within, or without the *Streights*, to annoy the Enemy and protect our Trade, which Ships were put under the Command of Captain *Morrice* of the *Canterbury*.

The Tranfports conducted to Barcelona.
Sufpenfion of Arms.

The Admiral failing from *Vado* with the Tranfports the 27th of *July*, arrived at *Barcelona* the 7th of *Auguft*, and about the 7th of *September* he received the Queen's Orders for a Sufpenfion of Arms by Sea and Land, and a Letter from the Lord Vifcount *Bolingbroke*, then at *Paris*, fignifying to him Her Majefty's Commands that he fhould not moleft a great *French* Corn Fleet bound from the *Levant* to the Coaft of *Provence*, which he had for almoft ten Weeks been looking out for, and, in order to the intercepting them, had fo divided the Fleet on particular, and proper Stations, that it was next to an Impoffibility they could have efcaped.

The Emprefs carried to Genoa from Barcelona.

Continuing at *Barcelona*, in order to his tranfporting the Emprefs from thence, her Majefty (who had remained fome time in that Capital after the Departure of the Emperor) embarked with her Retinue, and being landed at *Genoa*, took her Journey towards the Imperial Court the 26th of *March*.

Catalonia being now in a great meafure evacuated, and there being now thirty thoufand Men in the Service of the Allies, who were encamped at *Oftalric* and *Blanes*, the Places the Duke of *Popoli* agreed they fhould poffefs till fuch time as they could be embarked for *Naples*, the Admiral took fuch extraordinary care and pains in that Affair, that he foon fent twelve thoufand of them away with a proper Convoy, and in few Days after failed himfelf, with the Tranfports that had the remainder of them on board, in the Performance of which Service, and others of like Nature, he faved Her Majefty a very confiderable Sum of Money on the Head of Victualling.

The People of Barcelona declare War againft King Philip.

The People of *Barcelona* foon after declared War, by beat of Drum, againft King *Philip*, in the Emperor's Name, but what they afterwards fuffered, by a long and infupportable Siege, and how they were wholly neglected at laft by thofe who had the moft reafon to exert themfelves in their behalf, hath been more amply explain'd by

others

CHAP. XXXVI. *from the Year* 1698, *to* 1712.

others than I am able to set forth here, and must be very fresh in every Man's Memory. It shall therefore suffice to say, that never did brave People endeavour more (from the Countenance they hoped to receive) to preserve their ancient known Rights and Liberties; nor hardly did ever a Number of Men, inclosed within the Walls of a City, suffer more in its Defence, or when they were, at the long run, constrained to submit, meet with more inhuman Treatment. *Barcelona yielded, and the People barbarously treated.*

But let us leave this melancholy Subject, and return to the Proceedings of our Admiral in those Seas, who having a Minister sent to him from the Duke of *Savoy*, to adjust Matters about his embarking, with his Duchess, for his Kingdom of *Sicily*, which was parcelled out to him upon the Peace, he accommodated those Matters so well, that he sailed with their *Sicilian* Majesties from *Villa Franca*, and landed them at *Palermo* the 30th of *September*, where they were received with very great Acclamations of Joy; so that having little or nothing more to do with the Fleet under his Command, and being left at liberty either to return home by Sea or Land, as it might suit best with his Convenience, he made choice of the latter, and arriving at *Paris* the 16th of *November*, came to *England* in few Days after. *Sir John Jennings carries their Sicilian Majesties to Palermo.*

Thus ended this second long and tedious War; and as I have at the close of the first summed up the Number of Ships which were either taken from us by the *French*, or lost, by their being forced on shore, or otherwise, as also what Losses they, in like manner, sustained in their Naval Force; so have I hereafter inserted the like Comparison, including therein such as have been retaken on either side, and those twenty great Ships the *French* precipitately sunk at the Siege of *Thoulon*, when Sir *Cloudesly Shovell* came off of that Port with the Fleet of *Great Britain*, which were never after fit for Service, as hath been before observed.

English.

Taken, or lost.

Guns.	Number.	Total of Guns.
80	2	160
70	4	280
60	2	120
50	8	400
48	1	48
40	2	80
36	1	36
32	4	128
30	1	30
28	1	28
24	11	264
22	1	22
	38	1596

French.

French.

Taken, or lost.

Guns.	Number.	Total of Guns.
100	4	400
90	8	720
86	8	688
74	1	74
70	3	210
64	1	64
56	1	56
54	4	216
50	2	100
48	1	48
40	1	40
36	2	72
34	1	34
32	1	32
30	2	60
28	1	28
24	8	192
20	3	60
	52	3094
		1596

The Loss of the *French* exceeded ours 1498

F I N I S.

AN
INDEX
OR

TABLE of the Names of Persons and Places, and of the principal Matters contained in the foregoing History.

A

ABantus, Licinius's *Admiral against* Constantine Page 181
Abdelmelich, *a Caliph or Emperor of the* Saracens 190
Abderames, *a Saracen General* 188
—— *Also a* Saracen *King in* Spain 311
Aberdeen, *a City in* Scotland 747
Aburman, *a Saracen Admiral* 311
Abydus, *a Town and Port on the* Asian *side of the* Hellespont 64, 87. vide 185
Acarnania (Despotato) *a Province of* Epire 72, 187
Achæans, *a People of* Peloponnesus 7
Achaia, *the Country so called* 145, 162
Achanis (Eziongeber) *a Port in the* Red Sea 9, 10
Achillas, *an Ægyptian (the Murderer of* Pompey) 160
Achradina, *an Island, part of the City* Syracuse 134
Acilius Glabrio, *a Roman General* 142
Acon & Acre, (Ptolemais) *a City and Port in* Phœnicia 197, 215, 239, 241, 313. 330
Acrothon, *a Town near Mount* Athos 75
Actium (Cape Figalo) *near* Lepanto 13
—— *where the* Corcyræans *beat the* Corinthians 66
—— *also* Octavius Marc Anthony 172
—— *and the* Venetians *the* Turks 228 *to* 233
Acton (Edward) *Captain of the* Grafton 718
Acunha (Peter) *a Spanish Admiral* 278
Adaulphus, *a Gothic Commander* 184
Adda, vide Adige
Addingus, *a Leader of the* Normans 133
Aden, *a Town and Port at the Entrance of the* Red Sea 258, 259

Adherbal, *a Carthaginian Admiral* 126
Adjazzo, *a Town and Port in* Corsica 771
Adige (Adda) *a River in* Italy 222
Admirals of England, *their Jurisdiction*, &c. 29, 32, 33, 318, 338, 339, 607, 608
—— vide Warwick *(Earl)* Buckingham *(Duke)* Howard, Pembroke *(Earl) and Prince* George, &c.
Admirals *of the* Cinque Ports 34
Admirals *of* France 310 *to* 318
—— *the Office suppress'd by* Richlieu 319
Adorni, *and* Fiesque, *two Genoese Nobles* 221
Adorni { Anthony, Raphael, Gabriel } *Doges of* Genoa 246, 249
Adrianople (Oresta) *a City of* Thrace 180, 233
Adriatic Sea *(the Gulph of* Venice) 11, 16, 96, 119, 159, 162, 197 *to* 201, 203, 237, 647, 649
Æantium, *a Town in the Hellespont* 181
Æetes, *King of* Colchis, *Father of* Medea 42
Ægean Sea (Archipelago) *on the East side of the* Morea 73, 96, 112, 175
Ægimurus (Zimbala) *an Island on the Coast of* Africa 127
Ægina, *an Island between* Athens *and the* Morea 7
Æginetans, *the People of* Ægina, *their Power at Sea*, &c. 7, 51, 52, 56, 90
Ægos, *and* Ægos-potamos, *a River of the* Thracian Chersonese 90, 91
Ægubius, vide Bussenus
Ægusa, *and* Æthusa (Favagnana) *an Island near* Lilybæum, *in* Sicily 127
Ægyptians, *improve Navigation* 3, 4
—— *their Dominion at Sea* 7
Ægypt, *subjected by* Cambyses 47, 48
—— *by* Alexander 98
vide Hercynion, *and* Tachus

Kkkkk Æmi-

INDEX.

Æmilius *and* Fulvius, Roman *Consuls, their vast Fleets* 13
Æmilius, *the* Roman *General* 113, 125
Æmonia *and* Emathla, Macedon *so called* 96
Ænaria (Ifchia) *an Island opposite to* Cumæ *in* Sicily 167
Ænobarbus, *a* Roman *of* Brutus*'s Party* 165
Æolian *Islands (the* Lipari *Islands so called)* 73
Æthalia, vide Elba
Ætna, *a flaming Mountain in* Sicily 135
Ætolia, *the Country so called* 187
Ætolians, *their Wars,* &c. 105, 112, 138
Afranius *and* Petreius, Pompey*'s Lieutenants in* Spain 157
Africa, *a Town near* Tripoli *in* Afric 196, 277, 309
Agatharcus, *a* Syracufan *Admiral* 81, 83
Agathocles, *Tyrant of* Syracufe 117
Agde, *a Port and Island on the Coast of* Languedoc, vide Cette 768, 772
Agefilaus, *the* Spartan *King* 93, 94
——*his Death* 95
Agincourt, *the Battle there* inter *the* French *and* English 334
Agis *the* Spartan, *Son of* Archidamus 74
——*his Acts.* &c. 85, 86
Agna, *a* Fort *in* America 549
Agricola, *the* Roman *Governor of* Britain 324
Agrigentum (Gergenti) *a City in* Sicily 115, 134
Agrigentines, *Confederates of the* Athenians 70
Agrippa, Auguftus*'s Admiral* 167
——*Defeats* Sext. Pompeius 169
Agron, *King of* Illyricum 130
Aguatulco, *a* Port *in* America 347
Ajan, *on the Coast of* Afric, *near the* Red Sea 255
Aigues Mortes, *a Port in* Languedoc 312
Aix la Chapelle, *the Peace there* 282
Alans, Goths, *and* Vandals vide 185
Albania (Scirwan *and* Zuirie) *a* Perfian *Province on the* Cafpian 151, 152
Albania (Dalmatia) *the West part of* Macedon *and* Illyrium, *bordering on the* Adriatick 130, 196, 222, 224
Albemarle *(Duke) Admiral of* England 399
Albert, *a Fort between* Newport *and* Oftend 300
Albohacen, *a* Moorifh *General* 269
Albuquerque (Francis) *a* Portuguefe *Admiral* 255, 256
Albuquerque *(Duke) a* French *General* 613
Albuquerque *(Duke, Vice-Roy of* Andalufia *and* Mexico 597
Alcamenes, *a* Spartan *Admiral* 85
Alcayd, *of* Alcazar 655
Alcazar, *a Town on the* Barbary *Coast* 254, 655
Alcibiades *the* Athenian *his Character,* &c. 77, 80, 85, 86, 87
Alcidas, *a* Peloponnefian *Admiral* 72
Alefio, vide Leffus.
Aleppo, *a City in* Syria 17
Alexander *destroys* New Tyre, &c. 5, 97, 98
——*his Death,* &c. 104, 106
Alexander, *Son of* Caffander 112
Alexander *the seventh* Pope 237
Alexandria *in* Ægypt *built,* &c. 103, 160, 161
Alexandria, Hieron*'s fam'd Ship so named* 137

Alexius Angelus, *and* } Greek *Emperors of* Conftantinople 213, 312
Alexius Comnenus,
Alfaques, *a Bay on the Coast of* Catalonia 505, 520
Alfred, *King of* Britain 326, 327
Algarve, *a part formerly of* Spain, *now of* Portugal 483
Algerines, vide *Pirates.*
Algezira, *a Town and Port in the Bay of* Gibraltar 269
Algier, *a Port Town in* Barbary 234, 309
——*bombarded by the* French, &c. 321, 322, 397, 401, 491, 510, 524, 763, 794
Algueri *and* Algeri, vide Larghes 240, 271
Alicant, *a City and Port Town in* Spain 510 *to* 518
——*besieged and taken by the Arch-Duke* 694, 695, vide 730, 731, 750, 755, 757, 758, 797
Alidas, *a* Gothic *Admiral* 187
Allemonde, *a* Dutch *Admiral* 437 *to* 440, 445, 465, 527, 540, 548, 583, 588, 611, 651, 652, 653, 675, 685
Allen (Sir Thomas) *an* Englifh *Vice-Admiral* 398
——*sent against the* Algerines, &c. 400, 401
Almada, *a City in* Portugal 253
Almanza, *a Town in* Spain; *the unfortunate Battel there* 731
Almeria, *a City and Port in* Granada *in* Spain 17, 239, 266, 544, 651, 683, 730, 763, 773
Alphonfus, *King of* Arragon 247
Alphonfus, *King of* Naples 222, 223, 272
Alta Vela *Cape in* Hifpaniola 579
Altea *Bay in the* Mediterranean *on the Coast of* Spain 506, 651, 655, 675, 686, 692, 694, 695, 696, 797
Alva *(Duke) Governor of* Flanders 285
Alvaredo, *a River of* New Spain 275
Amalfi (Melfi) *a Port Town on the Coast of* Naples 216
Amafis, *King of* Ægypt, Polycrates*'s Friend* 46
Ambleteufe, *a Sea Town in* France, inter Calais *and* Boulogne 341
Amboyna, *an Island in the* Weft-Indies, *one of the* Molucca*'s* 258, 292, 293, 294, 295, 369, 380
Ambracia, *a Country on the Gulf* di Larta 170
Ambraciots, *Allies of* Sparta 70
Ambulachus, *a* Saracen *Leader* 191
Amedee, *Duke of* Savoy 218
Ameland, vide Amiftrache
America, *aud* Americans 18, 24, 216, 275, &c.
Amilcar Senior, *the* Carthaginian 51
Amilcar Junior, *his Acts,* &c. 117, 124, 127
Aminias, *Admiral of the* Æginetans, *his Acts* 56
Aminocles, *the* Corinthian *Inventor of Gallies* 44
Amifius, *the* Roman *Embaffador so called* 175, 282
Amiftrache, *and* Auftrache, *Islands of* Friefland 309
Amphipolis, *a City of* Macedon 75
Amphoterus, *one of* Alexander*'s Admirals* 103
Amurath *the Second, a* Turkifh *Emperor* 223
Amurath *the Fourth, another* Turkifh *Emperor* 234
Amurath Dragut Rays, *a* Turkifh *Admiral at* Lepanto 230

Amynias

INDEX.

Amynias *the Æginetan Admiral, his Valour* 56
Amyntas, *a Greek Commander under Philip and Alexander* 97, 103
Amyrtæus, *a Prince of Ægypt* 61
Anactorians, *Allies of Sparta* 70
Ancalytes, *People in Britain* 156
Ancona, *a Port in Italy* 187, 192
Andalusia, *a Province of Spain* 525
Andri (Andros) *an Island of the Archipelago* 212, 214, 238, 244
Andronicus, *the Greek Emperor* 243
Angles, *a Tribe of the Saxons* 325
Anglesey (Mona) *an Island inter England and Ireland* 324
Anicetus, Vitellius's *Admiral, his new invented Ships* 176
Anigada *in the West-Indies* 698
Anjou (Duke) *made King of Spain* 662, 696
——*returns to Madrid* 703, 773
Annapolis *in Nova Scotia, vide Port Royal*
Annebault (Claude) *Admiral of France* 316, 340
Annius, *the Roman Admiral, defeats Sertorius* 148
Antandrus, *a City of Mysia* 75
Antegoa, *an Island in America* 453, 456, 552, 603, 703
——*attempted by the French* 782, 783, 784
Antibes *and Nice, two Ports in the Mediterranean* 731, 763, 768, 769
Antigonus *the Elder* 106, 107
Antigonus Doson 112
Antioch, *a City of Syria* 192
Antiochus, *King of Syria* 142
Antipachsu *and Pachsu, Islands lying between Corfu and Cephalenia* 229
Antipater, *one of Alexander's Captains* 105
Antipatris, *a City in Palæstina near Joppa* 239
Antisthenes, *a Sea Captain of Demetrius* 108
Antivari, *a City in Albania, on the Adriatic* 222, 224
Antonius, *Father of Marc Antony* 149, 150, 158, 159
Antonius (Marcus) *his Acts, &c.* 13, 160, 164 to 173, 233
Antonius Colonna, *Admiral of the Pope's Gallies* 228
Antwerp *in Flanders, its famous Siege* 285 to 290
Apocapses, vide Apolofarus
Apolliciarius, *one of Bellisarius's Officers* 185
Apollophanes, *one of Sext. Pompey's Sea Captains* 167
Apollonia (Spinarza) *a Town in Albania* 130, 138
Apolofarus *and Apocapses, two Saracen Leaders* 194
Appius Claudius, *the Roman Consul* 120, 134
Apulia 192 to 196
Aquileia, *a City in Italy* 16, 187, 188, 199
Aquilius, *a Roman, Metellus's Lieutenant* 148
Aradus, *the King thereof submits to Alexander* 100
Arassio, *a Road or Bay, near Cape delle Melle* 774, 775
Arcadius *and Honorius, Roman Emperors* 184

Archambert, *Chancellor to Charlemaign, and Admiral* 310
Archbishop *of Bourdeaux, a French Admiral* 320
vide *Bishops*.
Archduke *of Austria* 234
——*declared King of Spain* 645, 654, 662
——*his Voyage thither* ibid. 665, 700, 702, 769
——*declared Emperor* 794
——*leaves Spain* 793 *to* 798
Archelaus, Mithridates's *Admiral* 147
Archias, *a Corinthian Architect* 135
Archidamus, *a Spartan General* 70, 72, 74
Archimedes *the Syracusan, his wonderful Machines* 134
Archipelago (*the Ægean Sea*) *its Islands, &c.* 16, 17, 234, 235, 312, 764
Arelate, *the City Arles in France* 157
Argives, *a People of Peloponnesus* 7
Argonautes, *their Expedition to Colchis* 6, 42
Argyle (Duke) *at Barcelona* 775, 794, 796
Argynusæ, *Islands off Cape Malea* 89
——*the Fight there* 90
Ariamnes, *the Persian Admiral, slain* 55
Ariarathes, *a Son of Mithridates* 147
Arige, Peruca, *and Biscay, three Pirates about the Morea and Ægean* 224
Ariobarzanes, *King of Cappadocia* 147
Aristagoras, *Tyrant of Miletus, deserts the Persians* 48
Aristides, *the Athenian Admiral* 75
Aristo, *one of Alexander's Admirals* 98
Aristocrates *and Aristogenes, two Athenian Captains* 89, 90
Ariston *the Corinthian, his Advice to the Syracusans* 81
Aristonicus, *Tyrant of Methymnæ* 103
Ark *of Noah, the original of large Vessels* 2, 176
Armada *of Spain* 18, 350, 351, &c. 441, 492, 514, 517, 577, 709
Armiro, *the Gulf so called* 312
Arno, *a River of Italy* 248
Arragon, *a part of Spain, &c.* 244
Arrigon (Octavius) *a Sicilian Admiral* 278
Arrhiana, *a Town in the Hellespont* 87
Arris (Robert) *an English Sea Captain at Tunis, &c.* 654, 655
——*at Quebec* 780
Arsinoe, Alexander's *Daughter* 106
Arsinoe, *King Ptolemy's younger Sister* 161
Artabanes, *one of Justinian's Sea Commanders* 187
Artaphernes, *Darius's Nephew* 49
Artaxerxes, *King of Persia* 60, 61
——*Darius's Successor, &c.* 93, 95
Artemisia, *her Advice* 54
——*her Valour* 56
Artemisium, *a City; its Situation, &c.* 52
Arzille, *a Town on the Coast of Barbary* 254
Asafia, *a Town on the Coast of Barbary* 260
Asclepiodatus, Constantine's *Lieutenant* 179
Ascough (Sir George) *an English Admiral* 381, 397
Asdrubal, *the Carthaginian General* 115, 126, 132, 133
——*his Wife's Courage* 144, 145

Ashby

INDEX.

Ashby *(Sir* John) *an* English *Admiral* 445. 467, 468, 476
Ash *(the Isle of) near* Port Louis *in* Hispaniola 579, 580, 593, 701
Asoph, *a City on the* Palus Mæotis 307
Aspasia (Pericles's *Mistress) her Character* 65
Asprenas, vide Calpurnius
Aspropiti, *a Town in the Gulph of* Lepanto 229
Assyrians, *their Naval Armaments* 5
Assereto (Biugio) *a* Milanese *Admiral for* Genoa 248
Astactus, *a City in the Island* Cephalenia 70
Athanagild, *a* Gothic *King of* Spain 188
Athenæus *and* Cleodamus, *two Citizens of* Byzantium 135, -76
Athens *(now* Setines) 223
——*destroyed by the* Persians 54, 55, 92, 94, 106, 107
Athenians, *their Sea Dominion* 11, 48, 77
——*Cruelty to the* Æginetans 7, 90
——*declare War against* Persia, *and burn* Sardis 48
——*quarrel with the* Spartans. &c. 64, 66, 70, 74
——*and* Samians 65
——*aid the* Corcyræans 71
——*Jealousies of their Power* 69
——*their Allies,* &c. 70
——*their absolute Dominion* 77
——*invade* Sicily 78
——*but are miserably destroyed* 85
——*are beaten by the* Peloponnesians 91
——*their City taken,* &c. 92
——*rebuilt* 94
——*aid the* Thebans, &c. *and beat the* Lacedæmonians 95
——*submit to* Philip 97
——*rebel against* Alexander 105
——*their City taken by* Antipater 106
——*restored to Liberty* 107
——*subjected by* Demetrius 112
Athos (Cape di Monte Santo) *a high Promontory in* Macedon 49, 50, 75
Atlantic *Ocean, discovered by the* Phœnicians 4, 148
Atrius (Quintus) *a Sea Commander under* Cæsar 154
Attalus, *one of* Philip *of* Macedon's *Captains* 103
Attalus, *a* Roman *Citizen, made Emperor by the* Goths 184
Attamia *(the* Conde de). *Vice-Roy of* Sardinia 519
Attica, *the Country about* Athens, *so called* 59, 72, 73
Attila, *a King of the* Huns 16, 325
Attilius Varus, Pompey's *Lieutenant in* Africa 157
Attilianus, *a* Roman *General* 188
Avarians *united with the* Huns *(hence* Hungarians) 198
Auguste, *a* French *Ship taken* 651
Augustus, *Heir to* Julius Cæsar, *his stationary Fleets,* &c. 164
——*his Victories,* &c. 172
Aulis, *in* Bœotia, *the* Greeks *Expedition thence against* Troy, &c. 43, 112, 223
Aurelian, *the* Roman *Emperor* 177
Austrache, vide Amistrache

Austria *(Don* John) *Admiral of* Spain 228
Austria, vide *Archduke*
Auvergne *(Prince) at the Siege of* Ostend 739
Auverquerque *(Monsieur) General of the* Dutch *at* Ostend 738, 739
Auxerre *and* Bayonne, *the Bishops thereof, Admirals* 330
Aylmer *(an* English *Admiral)* 441, 446, 511, 512, 539, 564, 581, 764
Ayamonte, *a Port Town in* Spain 623
Azamor, *a Town in* Barbary 260
Azores *or* Tercera *(Islands in the* Atlantic *Ocean)* 17
——*possess'd by the* Portuguese, &c. 264, 278, 356, 590, 749

B

Babelmandel, *a Town near the* Streights *of the* Red Sea 229
Babylon, Alexander's *Death there* 104
Bachian *and* Machian, *two of the* Molucca *Islands* 260
Badur, *a King of* Cambaya 263
Bætis, vide Bœtis
Baffo (Mark) *a* Venetian *Admiral* 242
Bagne Point, *near the Isle of* Ash *in* America 579
Bagrada, *a River in* Afric 156
Bahama, *an Island in the Gulph of* Florida 274
Baharem, *an Island in the* Persian *Gulph* 259
Bahia *(St.* Salvadore) *in* Brasil 792
Bahus, *a Province in* Norway 303
Bajazet *the Second, a* Turkish *Emperor* 308
Baker (John) *an* English *Admiral* 740, 742, 748, 761, 767, 768, 769, 770, 771, 790, 791, 792, 794, 796
Baker, *an* English *Consul at* Algier 510
Balaguer, *a Town on the River* Segre *in* Spain 762
Baldus *and* Bartholus *cited* 26
Baldwin, *King of* Jerusalem 212
Baleares, *the Islands* Majorca, Minorca, *and* Yviça 145, 185, 191
——*reduced by the* Pisans, &c. 17, 132, 752
Balance of Power necessary 19
Baly, *an Island near* Java 290
Baltic *Trade* 381
Baltic *Sea, Property therein,* &c. 8, 9, 183, 302, 303, &c.
——*Sir* John Norris *there* 726, 727
Banda *and* Amboyna, *two of the* Moluccas 258, 260
Bankert, *a* Dutch *Admiral* 402
Bantam, *the King thereof* 298
Barault, *Vice-Admiral of* Guienne 317
Barbadoes 452, 459, 460
——*Sir* Francis Wheler *there* 447
——*Admiral* Nevil *there* 552, 559, 600
——*Sir* William Whetstone *there* 697, 700
——*Archibald* Hamilton 782, 783, 784
Barbarigo (Augustine) *a* Venetian *Captain at* Lepanto 228, 230 to 233, 336
Barbarossa (Frederick) *the Emperor* 213
Barbarussa, *a noted Pirate,* &c. 250, 277, 308

Barcelona,

INDEX.

Barcelona, *the Capital of* Catalona *in* Spain 247, 505 to 509, 513, 515, 518, 520, 521, 670, 675
——*reduced by the* English 686, 687
——*besieged by the* French, *and relieved* 689 to 693, 731
——*the King and Queen of* Spain *there* 749, 750 to 756, 758, 759, 762, 764, 767, 769, 770, 774, 775, 793, 795, 797, 798
Barfleur *Cape in* France 464, 467
Bari *and* Trani, *two Sea-Port Towns in* Apulia 195
Barrault (*Monsieur*) *a French Admiral* 317
Baru's, *two Islands in the* West Indies 705, 712
Baruth, *a City of* Syria 219, 239
Bassano (Alvarez) *Marquis of* Santa Cruz, *a Commander at* Lepanto 228
——*sent to recover the* Azores 278
Basilicate, vide Lucania
Basiliscus, *one of the Admirals of the Emperor* Leo 184
Basilius Macedo, *Emperor of the East* 192
Basque *Road on the Coast of* France 586
Bass, *an Island in* France 471, 476, &c. 545
Basse Terre, *a Fort*, &c. *at St.* Christopher's *in* America 454, 457, 458
Bastia, *the chief City of* Corsica 770
Bastimentos, *an Island in the* West Indies 705, 707, 708
Basterni, Tartars *of* Oxakow, *and about the Mouth of the* Nieper 152
Batavia, Holland, *and* Batavi, Hollanders 175, 176
Batavia *in* America, New Holland 297
Bay *of* Almeria 544
Bay *of* Altea, vide Altea
Bay *of* Bertheaume 496, 499, 514
Bay *of* Biscay 350
Bay *of* Bulls 493, 549, 611
Bays *of* Camaret *and* Carlisle, vide Camaret *and* Carlisle
Bay *of* Campeche 715
Bay *of* Conception 560
Bay *of* Colonas 632
Bay *of* Gara 701
Bay *of* La Guarda 707
Bay *of* Lagos, vide Lagos *Bay*
Bay *of* Placentia 632
Bay *of* Roses 762
Bay *of St.* Jeremy, *on the Barbary Coast* 494
Bay *of* Tangier 517
Bay *of* Tuberon 711
Bay *of* Verdon 643
Bay *of* Wares 690
Bayonne, *the Bishop thereof, an Admiral* 330
——*the Port there* 630
Beachy-head *in* Sussex, *the Fight near it* 425, 718
Bealieu, *a French Sea Commander* 317
Beaufort (Thomas) *the first Lord-Admiral of* England 34
Beaufort (*Duke* de) *a French Amiral* 400
Beaumont (Bazil) *an English Sea Captain and Rear-Admiral* 544, 545, 548, 635 *to* 641
——*lost* 659, 660, 661
Beckman (*Sir* Martin) *an English Engineer* 519, 521
Beeston (*Sir* William) *Governor of* Jamaica 556

Behol, *a Port Town in* America 276
Belisarius, Justinian's *General* 185 *to* 188
Belle Isle *in* France 438 *to* 442, 643
Belle Isle *in* America 560
Bellomont (*Earl*) *Governor of* New England 580
Bembo (Francis) *a* Venetian *Admiral* 221
Benavirus, *a Saracen General* 196
Benbow ( ) *an* English *Sea Captain* 539
——*and Admiral* 549, 564, 569, 570, 576, 588
——*his Death* 598, 610
Benevento, *a City of* Italy 194
Benjacob, *a King of* Morocco 246
Berkeley (*Sir* William) *an* English *Admiral* 296
Berkeley (*Lord* John) *an* English *Admiral* 495 *to* 500, *and* 226 *to* 531, 539, 546 *to* 549
Bernard, *King of* Italy 310
Bertheaume *Bay, on the* French *Coast* 496, 499, 544
Berwick *on the* Tweed 340
Bettumenus, *one of* Bossu's *Officers* 194
Bias *the Philosopher, his Advice to* Crœsus 45
Bibroci, *a People in ancient* Britain 156
Bibulus, *a Sea Captain of* Pompey's 159
Biervliet, *a Port Town in* Flanders 283
Bilboa, *a City and Port in* Spain 482
Billingsley (Rupert) *Captain of the* Lizard 586, 587
Bingley (*Sir* Ralph) *at* Rochelle 374
Bintam, *a City in the* East Indies 261
Bisagno, *a Suburb of* Genoa 252
Biscay Peter, vide Arige
Biscay, *its Bay*, &c. 320, 350
Biserta (Utica) *a City near* Carthage, *built* 4 vide 249, 277
Bisignano, *a Town in* Italy 194
Bishops (*Admirals*) 283, 320, 330
Bithynia, *a Province of* Asia Minor 146, 147, 149
Bivona, *a Town in* Italy 194
Bizaltia, *a Territory, near* Peloponnesus 75
Black Stakes, *in the River* Thames 538
Blackwell (*Sir* Lambert) *Consul at* Leghorn 482, vide 644
Blake, *an* English *Admiral* 294, 380, 382, 395
——*his great Character* 396
Blanes, *a Town and Port in the* Mediterranean vide 520, 798
Blanquet, *a French Commander* 316
Blavet, i. e. Port St. Lovis *in* Bretagne 318
Bleking, *a Province in* Sweden 303
Blewfields Bay *at* Jamaica 703, 714
Boabdelin, *a Saracen King of* Granada 192
Bocachiga *Castle in* America 555, 557
——*near the Harbour of* Carthagena 577, 700 vide 713
Boca Grande *Castle* ibid. 557
Boccanigra { Simon) *Doge of* Genoa 245
{ Giles) *a Genoese Admiral* 246, 269
{ Ambrose) *a Castilian Admiral* 270
Bocchoris *and* Psammis, *Kings of* Ægypt 7
Bodoaro (Ursus) *Doge of* Venice 198
Bodotria, *the Firth of* Forth 325
Bœotia, *the Country about* Thebes 70, 71, 75
Bœotians, *the Burthen of their Ships in* Homer 43
Bœtis (or Bætis) *the River* Guadalquivir *in* Spain 6, 9, 10, 148

Llll   Bokenham

INDEX.

Bokenham *(Captain) appointed for* Alicant, &c. 423, 425, vide 524, 564
Bokenham (William) *Captain of the* Aſſociation 627
Bokenham (Robert) *Captain of the* Chatham 650
Bolingbroke *(Viſcount)* 798
Boliſſus vide 86, &c.
Bombay, *an Iſland in the* Eaſt Indies 262, 397
Bomilcar, *a Carthaginian Commander* 116, 134
Bona, *a City near* Tunis *in* Africa vide 125, 250, 277, 516
Bonaviſta *in* America 613
Bonifacio, *a Town in* Corſica 247
Bonifacio *Harbour*, &c. 247, 248, 770
Boodes, *a Carthaginian Captain* 120
Bornholm, *an Iſland in the* Baltic 303
Borſdale (Henry) *Lord of* Vere, *a* Dutch *Admiral* 284
Boryſthenes, *the River* Nieper 174
Boſnia, *a Province North of* Dalmatia 130
Boſphorus Cimmerius, *the Streights of* Caffa, vide Caffa
Boſphorus Thracicus, *the inner Streights of* Conſtantinople 7, 62, 147, 150, 178, 180, 181
Boſſu (Roger) *a Norman General* 194
Boſton *in* New England 598, 765, 776, 778, 779
Boteler, *an Engliſh Sea Captain* 461
Botetort, *an Engliſh Admiral* 30, vide 331
Boucicaut, *a Marſhal of* France, *Admiral of the* Genoeſe 219
Bouckeld (William) *the Inventor of curing Herrings* 283, 284
Boulogne *in* France (Portus Iccius) 153, 340
Bourdeaux *River* 643
Bowles (Mr.) *Agent to the Commiſſioners for Victualling* 625
Boyce, *an Engliſh Sea Captain in* America 701
Bragadini, *Governor of* Famaguſta 227
Braganza *(Duke de) made King of* Portugal 264
Brancas (Andrew) *an Admiral of* France 316
Brandaris, *a Town on the Iſland* Schelling *in* Holland 400
Brandon *(Sir* Ch.*) an* Engliſh *Sea Commander* 337
Braſſidas, *a Spartan Admiral* 71, 75
Brava, *a City in the* Eaſt Indies 257
Braunſberg, *a Town in* Poliſh Pruſſia 302
Brazza, vide La Brazza
Brazile *in* America, *planted by the* Portugueſe 18
—— *accidentally diſcovered* 255, 264, vide 274
Breakhurſt, *an* Engliſh *Plantation in* America 549
Bredah, *the Treaty there* 37, 38, 297
Bremen *and* Ferden, *or* Verden, *Cities in* Germany 303
Breſcia, *a City in* Italy 222
Breſſello, *a Town on the River* Po 220
Breſt *in* France, *its Harbour*, &c. vide 338, 442, 495, 496, 499, 544, 741, 742, 788
Bretagne *in* France vide ibid.
Bridges (Sir Tobias) *his Acts in the* Weſt Indies 404
Briel, *a Town in the Iſle* Voorne 285
Brindiſi, vide Bronduſium
Brisbane, *an* Engliſh *Captain killed at* St. Chriſtopher's 454

Britain, vide Caſſiterides 4
—— *a Roman Province* 14
—— *invaded by the* Saxons 15
—— *by* Cæſar 153
—— *their Naval Affairs* 322, 324, &c.
Britiſh *Ocean, its Diviſion,* &c. 28
Britiſh *Fleet*. Temp. Eliz. & Jac. 1. vide 21
—— *See alſo Names of Ships,* &c.
Briton (Andrew) *a* Scottiſh *Pirate* 337
Broad Fourteens 551
Broad Sound 444, 554
Bromesbro, *a Peace there between the* Danes *and* Swedes 303
Brondolo, *a Town and Port in the* Adriatic 218
Brown *(General) in* Sardinia 771
Bructeri, *People about* Groningen 178
Brudenelle, *an* Engliſh *Collonel* 518
Brunduſium (Brindiſi) vide 157, 159, 175, 195
Brutius Surra, *a Roman Captain* 146
Brutus, Cæſar's *Admiral* 157, 158
Brutus *and* Caſſius vide 163 *to* 166
Bucephala, *a City built by* Alexander 103
Buchannels, *on the Coaſt of* Scotland 746, 747
Buchard, *a Conſtable of* France, *and Admiral* 310
Buckingham *(Duke) an* Engliſh *Admiral, his Expedition to* Rochelle, &c. 318
Budoa, *a Town and Port in* Albania 224
Budorus, *a Fort on* Cape Salamis 71
Buenos Ayres, *a Port in the River* Plata *in* America 666
Bugia, *a Town in* Afric 402
Bulgaria, *a Country on the* Euxine 176
Buoy *of the* Nore 541, 639
Burichus *and* Neon, *Sea Captains to* Demetrius 109
Burroughs (Sir John) *ſlain at* Rochelle 373, 374, 375
Buſſenus Ægubius, *a* Genoeſe *Admiral* 246
Butler (Thomas) *Captain of the* Worceſter 651
Byblis *(or* Byblus) *a City of* Ægypt vide 61, 100
Byng (Sir George) *an* Engliſh *Captain and Admiral* 640, 651, 653, 673, 677, 679, 684, 692 *to* 697, 703, 728, 731, 733, 740 *to* 748, 756 *to* 762
Byrſa *(the Citadel of* Carthage*) built by Queen* Dido 113, vide 145
Byzantium (Conſtantinople) Pauſanius *beſieged there* 60, 64
—— *it revolts from the* Athenians 86
—— *is beſieged by King* Philip *of* Macedon 97, vide 175, 180

C

Cabot (John) *a* Venetian, *makes Diſcoveries for* England 336
Cabot (Sebaſtian) *makes farther Diſcoveries* 341
Caccianimico de la Volta, *a* Genoeſe *Admiral* 240
Cacofogo, *a Ship ſo named* 347
Cadamuſtus, *a* Portugueſe, *his Diſcoveries,* &c. 255
Cadaval (Duke) *a* Portugueſe, *his Treachery to the* Engliſh 690
Cadiz, Gades *or* Cates *in* Spain, *built by the* Phœnicians 4, 148, vide Gibraltar Cadiz

INDEX.

Cadiz Bay 489, 492, 513, 514, 518, 796
Cadogan *(Major-General)* at Ostend 744, 745
Cæsar, vide Julius Cæsar
Cæsarea, *a City of Palestine* vide 239
Caffa, vide Capha
Cagliari, *a Sea-Port and Metropolis of Sardinia* 217, 268, &c. vide 519, 520, 552, 769, 796
Calabria, *now* Terre de Otranto 139, 176, 192, 193
Calis, *a Town and Port in* France, *bombarded* 530, 531, vide 539, 540, 541, 639
——*taken from the* English 342
Calbaruso (Naulochus) *near the North Cape of* Sicily 169
Cales *in* Spain, vide Cadiz
Calecut, or Calicut, *a Kingdom and City in the* East-Indies 255, 256, 262
Calecura, *a Country in the* East Indies 262
Calex, *a River falling into the* Euxine 75
Callemberg, *Vice-Admiral of the* Dutch 445, 472, 474, 493, 504, 505, 564, 621, 663, 665, 666, 667, 669, 676
Callicratidas, *a Spartan Admiral* 89
Callinicus, *an Ægyptian, his Invention of Wild-fire* 189
Calo Johannes *the Greek Emperor* 243
Calonymus *of* Alexandria, *Justinian's Admiral* 184, 185
Calpurnius Asprenas, *a Roman Admiral* 175
Calvi, *a Town in* Corsica 247
Calvisius, Sext. Pompeius's *Admiral* 167
Calycadnus, *a Promontory in* Natolia 143
Camarassa *(Marquis) General of the Spanish Gallies* ibid.
Camaret Bay *at the Entrance of* Brest *Harbour* 446, 472, 498 to 500, 544
Camarina, *a Town and River in* Sicily 126
Cambaya, *a Kingdom in the* East-Indies 262, 263
Cambyses, *Son of* Cyrus 10, 11
——*his Acts* 46, 47
Camicus, *a City in* Sicily 42
Campeachy Bay *in* America 698, 783
Campenfelt, *a Colonel at* Quebec 781
Campofulgoso (Dominic) *Doge of* Genoa 246
Campson, *Sultan of* Ægypt 257
Canada *in the* West Indies 775, 776, 777, 779
Cananor, *a Kingdom in the* East-Indies 255, 256, 262, 265
Canaries, *the Islands so called* vide 270, 271, 791
Cancale Point *near St.* Maloes 527
Candelora (Coracesium) 62, 150
Candia (vide Creet) *revolts from the* Venetians 217
——*attack'd by the* Turks 250
——vide 235, 237, 241
Candianus, *a Doge of* Venice *slain by the* Narentzes 198
Canea, *a City in* Candia *taken by the* Turks 235, 241
Canidius, Marc Antony's *General* 170
Cannæ, *the Battel there* 133, 138, vide 194
Cannefas, *a Battavian Admiral* 176
Canoba, *an American King* 274
Cantacuzenus, *a Greek Emperor* 242
Canville (Richard) *an English Admiral* 330
Canush (James) *a Portuguese Discoverer* 255
Caorle *and* Grado, *two Islands in the* Adriatic 197, 217, 243

Capello (Nicholas) *a Venetian General and Admiral* 224, 235
Capes, *a Town in* Afric 196
Capeland Bay *in* Newfoundland 559
Anne *in* New England 779
Antifer 687

Capes or Promontories.
Actium, vide Figalo 66
Alta Vela, vide A
St. Anthony, *the West End of* Cuba 599
St. Angelo 764
Barfleur 464, 467, 789
Baccalao 560
Bona (vide Hermea) 125, 516
Bona Esperanza, vide Goodhope infra
Breton *in* America 779
Cabretta 683
Calvi 771
Calycadnus, vide Supra
Cantin *in* Barbary 260, 345
Celidonia 62
Cheimerium 68
Clear 441, 439, 461, 549, 720
Comorin 256
Cornwall 717
Corsica 516
Corso 774
Dauzo 217
De Gates 544, 730, 761, 797
De la Hague 462
Delle Melle 691, 774
Di Istria 199, 218
Di Monte 221
Di Monte Santo 49
Donna Maria, *the West End of* Hispaniola 556, 594
Fair Promontory 140
Farrel, *or* Frehelle 472, 473, 527
Figalo, vide Actium
Finisterre 37, 544, 549, 787
Florida 537
Francis 536, 560, 600, 620
François 698 *to* 700, 715
Goodhope, vide G, *and* 104, 154, 290
Hermea, vide Bona
Lilybæum 126, 127
Lacinium 13
La Hogue 467, 468
Mahangulo 230
Malaga 678
Malea, *near* Lesbos 89
St. Martin, *near* Yviça 506, 797
St. Mary 504, 666, 690, 790
Matapan 173, 214
Mayze 593, 711
Metafuz vide 277
Micale 56
Misenium 13
St. Nicholas 707, 710
Ortegal 613, 614
Pachinnus, *or* Passaro *in* Sicily 202, 516
Palmas *in* India 225
Palos 675, 730, 757
Pine *in* Newfoundland 605
Prior 612, 613

Capes

INDEX.

Capes or Promontories. { Race, &c.	632, 634
Rizzuto	13
Rofes	795
Roxent	769
Roxo	255
Salamis, vide S	
Scyllæum (Schilli, *and* Sciglio)	167, 189
Sigæum	86
Spartel 504,505,517,544,652,666,690,753, 799	
Tempeftuous]	254
Thoulon	519, 797
Trafalgar	526
Tres Forcas	505
Tubaron	556
Verde	17, 702
Verde *Iflands*	273
St. Vincent 461, 483, 484, 492, 504, 544, 566, 567, 599, 625, 666, 675, 699, 690, 731	

Capha, *or* Caffa (Theodocia) *in* Little Tartary 17, 206, 246
Capitanate, *a Province of* Naples 222
Cappadocia 146, 147, 149, 151
Capral (Peter Alvarez) *a* Portuguefe *Difcoverer* 255
Caprara (Bernard) *a* Venetian *Admiral* 270
Capua vide 16
Caracozza, *a* Turkifh *Commander at* Lepanto 229
Caramania 223
Carantenus (Nicephorus) *the Emperor of* Conftantinople's *Admiral* 192
Caraus Hozias, *a* Turkifh *Pirate* 230
Caraufius (*in* Britain, &c.) *afpires to the Empire* 177, 178, 179
Carboniere, *a Port in* America 560, 561, 633
Carcerius (Rabanus) *a* Venetian *Sea Captain* 214
Carelfcroon *Harbour* 19
Carew *(Sir George) and the* Mary Rofe *loft* 240
Carew *(Sir George) and others attack* Cadiz 360
Caria *and* Carians, *their Sea Dominion* 7
——*fubjected by* Minos, &c. 6, vide 70 *and* 189
Caribbee *Iflands firft difcovered* 274, vide 452
Carina, *Cæfar's Admiral* 164
Carinus, *a* Roman *Emperor* 177
Carifta, *a Town and Port in* Negropont 216, 225
Carlifle *Bay at* Barbadoes 453, 456, 457, 460, 476, 702
Carlowitz, *the Peace there* 238
Carmania, *a Country fo called* 223
Carmarthen *(Marquis) a Sea Commander* 444
Carpafia, *a Town in* Cyprus 107
Carpentier, *difcovers* New Holland 299
Carrofo (Francis) *Admiral of* Arragon 268
Carrofo (Beringer) *his fon* ibid.
Carter, *an* Englifh *Rear-Admiral* vide 461 *to* 470 *and* 572
Carthage *in* Afric (Byrfa) *founded*, &c. 113, 119
——*invade* Sicily 57, 58
——*fend Ambaffadors to* Alexander 101, vide 103
——*their Wars with the* Romans 13, 119, 140
——*deftroyed* 145
——*repair'd by the* Vandals 184
Carthagena, New Carthage *in* Spain 132, 139, 505, 506, 520, 689, 694, 729, 770, 798

Carthagena *in* America, vide 553 *to* 558, 697, 698, 702 *to* 707, 712, 713, 714
Carthaginians, *their Sea Dominion*, &c. 11 vide Carthage
Cafal, *a Town in* Italy vide 519, 520
Cafcais, *a Port at the Entrance of the River* Lisbon 651, 652
Cafimir, *King of* Poland 295
Cafpian Sea vide 151, 307
Caffandria, *a City fo called* 112
Caffander, *one of* Alexander's *Succeffors* 106
Caffard *(Monfieur) a* French *Sea Commander in* America 783, 784, 791, 792
Caffiterides (Britifh *Iflands*) *difcovered* 4
Caffivellaunus, *one of the Kings of* Britain 156
Caffius, *a* Roman *Proconful* 146, vide **Brutus**
Caftile *and* Caftilians, *their Naval Affairs*, vide 266 *to* 272
Caftle Novo, *a Town in* Dalmatia 237
Catana, *a City in* Sicily 117
Catalonia, *a Province in* Spain. *Declares for King* Charles *the Third*, vide Barcelona *and* 509, 676, 770, 774, 793 *to* 798
Cato, *a* Roman *of* Pompey's *Party* 157
Cavala (Leo) *Admiral of the* Greek *Emperor* 214
Cavalca (John) *a* Pifan *Admiral* 240
Cave, *an* Englifh *Sea Captain* 359
Caudebec, *a Town in* Normandy 334
Cavendifh *(Captain* Thomas) *an* Englifh *Difcoverer*, &c. 349
Caulonia vide 81
Ceilon (Taprobana) *an Ifland in the* Eaft-Indies 256, 259
Celfi (Lawrence) *Doge of* Venice 217
Cenchrea, *a Port near* Corinth 85
Cenforinus, *a* Roman *General* 143
Centumcellæ, vide Civita Vecchia
Centurioni (Hippolytus) *a* Genoefe *Admiral* 251
Cephalonia, *an Ifland in the* Ionian *Sea* 70, vide 225, 229
Cephifus, *a River in* Bœotia 147
Cercurus, *a Gally fo named* 137
Cerigo, *an Ifland*, vide Cythera
Cette *in* Languedoc 646
——*attempted* 653, vide 768, 772
Cevennes, *People in* France 646, 653
Ceuta (Septa) *on the Coaft of* Barbary 185, 254, 269
Ceylon, *an Ifland in the* Eaft Indies (Taprobana) 256, 259
Cezimbra, *a Port of* Spain 367
Chabrias, *an* Athenian *Captain* 95
Chabrenac *(Monfieur) a* French *Sea Commander* 701
Chalard *(Monfieur) a* French *Admiral* 317
Chalcedon (Scutari) *over againft* Conftantinople 64, 149, 181
Chalcidica vide 96
Chancellour (Richard) *made the firft Voyage to* Archangel 341
Chapeau Rouge, *on the North of* Newfoundland 633
Charente, *a River in* France, *near* Rochelle 737
Charia, vide Loffina *and* 131

Charles

INDEX.

Charles *the First and Second, Kings* of England 369, 379
Charles *the Fifth*, &c. *Kings of* France 314, 315
Charles *the Third of* Spain, vide *Archduke, and* 756
Charles *the Ninth, King of* Sweden, *Father of* Gustavus Adolphus 300, 302
Charles *the Twelfth King of* Sweden 305
Charles Fort *at St.* Christopher*'s* 454, 455, 456
Charles Martel *and* Charlemaign, *Kings of* France 309, 310
Chateau Morant, *a* Genoese *Vice-Admiral* 220
Chateau Renault *(Monsieur) a* French *Admiral* 424, 544, 547, 566, 589, 592, 593, 610
Chaul, *a Town in the* East-Indies 262
Cheimerium, *a Promontory so called* 68
Cherbourg *in* France 339, 468, 789
Chersonesus { Taurica 190
{ Thracica 63, 90
{ Indica, vel Aurea 9
Chetwynd *(Mr.) an* English *Resident at* Genoa 756, 797
Chickens, *Rocks so called near* Brest *Harbour* 442
Chila, *a City in* New Spain 275
Chio, Chios *and* Scio, *an Island in the* Archipelago vide 17, 49, 66, 86, 764
Chiozza, *a small City in the* Adriatic 198, 217, 218, 243
Christian *the first and second Kings of* Denmark 301
Christina, *Queen of* Sweden 303
St. Christopher*'s, an Island in* America vide 453 to 456, 535, 699
Churchill, *an* English *Admiral* 642
Churchill (Charles) *an* English *Colonel at* Quebec 781
Cibao, *the Island* Hispaniola *in* America 273
Cicogna (Bernard) *a* Venetian *Admiral* 224
Cifuentes *(Count* de) *Vice-Roy of* Sardinia 769
Cilicia, *a Province of* Asia Minor 107
Cilician *Pirates, their Power,* &c. 14
——*reduced by* Pompey 145, 150
Cimbri *and* Saxons *invade* Britain, &c. 15
Cimon *the* Athenian, *Son of* Miltiades, vide 59 to 64
Cissa, *an Island,* vide Humago
Citadella, *the chief Town in* Minorca 752
Citium, *a Port in the* Mediterranean 108, 109
Citta, *or* Civita nuova, *in* Istria 198
Civilis *and* Cannefas, *Generals of the* Batavi 176
Civita di Chieti *in* Italy 194
Civita, vide Citta nuova supra
Civita Vecchia (Centumcellæ) *a City and Port in* Italy 191, 221
Claremont *(Monsieur) Admiral of the* Rochellers 316
Clark (Robert) *Captain of the* Adventure, *killed,* &c. 710
Clark ( ) *Captain of the* Burlington 783
Claudius *the Emperor, his Fleet in* Britain 14
Clayton, *an* English *Colonel at* Quebec 781
Clazomenæ, *a City of* Ionia *in* Asia Minor 85
Cleaveland (William) *an* English *Sea Captain, and Commissioner of the Navy* 601
Cleaveland *(Mr.) Captain of the* Suffolk 767

Cleippides, *an* Athenian *Sea Commander* 72
Clement *the Fifth (Pope)* 270
Clements (George) *Captain of the* Hampton-Court 718
Cleodamus, vide Athenæus
Cleombrotus, *King of* Sparta 95
Cleomenes, *King of* Sparta 48
Cleon, *an* Athenian *Sea Commander* 75
Cleone, *a Town near Mount* Athos 75
Cleopatra, *Queen of* Ægypt 160, 165, 172
——*her Chanel* 173
Cleveland (William) *Captain of the* Montague 650
Clodius, *a Roman Consul* 126
Clupea *(Castle* Gallipa) *a Town and Fort in* Afric 125, 140
Clyd Fryth, *the Gulph of* Glotta *in* Scotland 324
Cneius Pompeius, *Pompey's youngest Son* 163
Cnemus, *a Corinthian Admiral* 71
Cnidus, *a City and Port of* Caria *between* Rhodes *and* Cyprus 94
Cocalus, *a King of* Sicily 75
Cochin, *a Kingdom in the* East-Indies 255, 265
Cock *(Mr.) an* English *Sea Captain* 717
Cockburn (John) *an* English *Sea Captain at* Quebec 780
Codrington, *an* English *General in the* West-Indies 452, 453, &c. 552, 575, 599, 603, 604
Coetlogon *(or* Cotlogon*) a* French *Admiral* 587, 591, 592, 593, 643
Cohe, *an Island near* Margarita *in* America 359
Colæus *the* Samian vide 6
Colchis (Mengrelia) vide Argonauts 42
Coligny (Gaspar) *Admiral of* France 316
Colonna (Marc Antony) *the Pope's Admiral* 228
Colophon, *a Port or Haven near* Toron 75
Columbus (Christopher) *a* Genoese, *his Discoveries,* &c vide 18, 273, 274, 336
Coluri, vide Salamis
Comacchio, *a City in the* Adriatic 199
Comana, *a City of* Pontus 147
Comanagotta, *a Port in* America 592
Compass, vide *Mariner's Compass*
Congo, *a Kingdom in the* East-Indies 255
Connecticut *in* America 778
Conon, *an* Athenian *General, and Admiral* 88, vide 90 *to* 94
Conquest Bay, *near* Brest *in* France 338
Consilus, *a* Corinthian *Admiral* 71, &c.
Constable ( ) *Captain of the* Panther 783, 784
Constable *(Mr.*) *Captain of the* Faulcon 769
Constans, *and* Const. Pogonatus, *Emperors* 189
Constantinople (Byzantium) *built* vide 4
——*besieged by the* Saracens 189, vide 233
——*by the* Turks 308
——*taken by the* French 312
Constantine *the Great, Emperor* 174, 178, 179
Constantius, *Emperor* 177
Contareni (Paul) *the* Venetian *Governor of* Zant 229
Contarini (Andrew) *Doge of* Venice 217
Contarini ( ) *the* Venetian *Admiral at* Lepanto 195

Conta-

M m m m m

INDEX.

Contarini ( ) a Genoese *Admiral* 242
Convent *(Messieur)* a Dutch *Rear-Admiral* 727
Cony (William) *Captain of the* Romney, *his Actions* 729, 730
——*lost at* Scilly 733
Coote, *an* English *Colonel in the* West-Indies 518
Copenhagen, *its Basin, or Harbour* 19, vide 303, 304, 306, &c.
——*bombarded* 584, vide 657
Coracesium (Candelora) *in the Gulph of* Satalia 62, 150
Corcinus, *a Sea Commander for* Augustus 169
Corcyra, *the Isle of* Corfu 68
——*inhabited by the* Phæaces, &c. 44, vide 73, 95, 130, 187, 308
Corcyræans, *their War with the* Corinthians 66, 68, 72, 73
Corcyra Melæna (Curzola) *an Island near* Ragusa vide 157, 159, 200
Corinth, *a General Assembly of* Greece *there* 70, 96
——*destroyed* 145
Corinthians, *their Sea Dominion* 8
——*their Navigation,* &c. 10
——*Inventors of large Gallies* 44
——*War with the* Corcyræans, &c. 66, 72, 73
Cork, *a City and Port in* Ireland, vide 431, 461, 717, 739
Cornaro, *a* Venetian *General* 237
Corneille *(Count)* vide 739
Cornelius, *a* Roman *Admiral* 120, vide Gallus, &c.
Cornificius, *a Sea Captain of* Cæsar's *Party* 162, 163, 167, 168
Cornwall *(Captain) an* English *Sea Commander* 775, 795
Coron *and* Modon, *two Towns in the* Morea 214, 225, 249, 308
Corsica, *an Island in the Hands of the* Genoese, &c. 17, vide 129, 167, 239, 752
Cortez (Ferdinando) *his Conquests of* Mexico, &c. 275
Cortologi, *a* Turkish *Pirate of* Barbary 249
Corvariani (Raymond) *a* Milanese *Admiral* 248
Corunna, vide Groyne
Corvus, *an Engine to grapple Ships described,* &c. 121, 125
Cosenza, *a Town in* Italy 194
Cotlogon, vide Coetlogon
Cotrone, vide Crotona
Cotton ( ) *Captain of the* Salisbury 641
Courland *on the* Baltic vide 306
Cow and Calf *in* Norway 550
Coway Stakes, *near* Chertsey 156
Crabb *Island in the* East-Indies, *near* Porto Rico 579
Crœsus *vanquished by* Cyrus 45
Cranganor, *a Town in the* East-Indies 255, 265
Crassus, *his Combination with* Cæsar *and* Pompey 152
——*slain* 156
Craterus, *one of* Alexander's *Captains* 99
Craterus, *the Emperor* Michael's *Admiral* 191
Cremona, *a City of* Italy 221

Crete (vide Candia) *possess'd by the* Greeks, &c. vide 6, 42, 43
Cretans *invade* Sicily, *and settle in* Italy, &c. 42, vide 149
Crispus (John) *Lord of* Nixia Phermene, &c. 224
Crissæan *Gulf* (Lepanto) 70, 71
Critias, *a Captain of* Mithridates 146
Crosby *(Sir* Peter*) at* Rochelle 374
Croatia, *a Part of* Hungary vide 130, 212
Crommyon, *a Town on the East Coast of* Peloponnesus 74
Cronenburg *Castle* 19, 303, 304, 583, 727
Crotona (Cotrone) vide 192
Crowe (Josiah) *Captain of the* Shrewsbury 549, 679
——*of the* Warspight 697
Crowe *(Mr.) Consul at* Barcelona 770
——*and at* Leghorn 797
Cuba (Hispaniola) *an Island near Cape* Florida *in* America 275, 553 *to* 557, 711
Cue, *a Harbour or Creek in* Hispaniola 593, 603
Cul de Sac Royal *in* Martinica 477
Culeta, *a Port of* Calecute 260
Cumæ, vide Ænaria, *and* 167, 168
Cunha (Nunho, *and* Simon) Portuguese *Admirals in the* East-Indies 262
Curacoa, *an Island in* America 552, vide 710
Curco, *a Town in* Caramania 223
Curio, Cæsar's *Lieutenant in* Afric 157
Curzola (vide Corcyra) *and* 200, 241
Curzolarie *Islands* ibid.
Cutial, *Admiral of* Calecut 262
Cyanean *Islands, in the Mouth of the* Thracian Bosphorus 7, 62
Cyclades, *Islands in the* Ægean *Sea* 6, 147, 224
Cyclobium, vide Hebdomum
Cydnus, *a River of* Cilicia 165
Cydon (Cydonia) *the capital City of* Crete 71, 149
Cyme, *seems an Island or Promontory in the* Ægean 86
Cynægyrus, *an* Athenian *Captain, his noted Valour* 50
Cynos Sema vide 87
Cyprus, *an Island in the* Mediterranean, *when first inhabited* 3, vide 16
——*the* Persian *Fleet beaten there* 63, 64, vide 107
——*the* Venetians *Masters of it* 223, 224
——*the* Turks 226, 227, vide 233, 309
Cypriots, *their Sea Dominion,* &c. 7, vide 14
Cyrus *the Great wars with the* Ionians, &c. 10, 11
——*vanquishes* Crœsus 152
Cyrus *the Younger, Governor of* Ionia *and* Lydia 88
Cyrnus, *the Island* Corsica *so called* 114
Cythera (Cerigo) *an Island of the* Archipelago 75, 76, 147, vide 308
Cyzicus, *a small Island and a fam'd City in the* Propontis, *a Sea Fight there* 87
Czar *of* Muscovy, *his Genius, Power,* &c. 19, 307

D Da-

INDEX.

D

Dabul, *a City and Port in the Kingdom of Decan* 261
Dædalus, *his Improvement of Navigation* 42
D'aire *(Chevalier) a French Sea Commander* 788
D'aix, *an Island on the Coast of* France 586
Dalmatia *and* Dalmatians, *vide* 192, 196, 212, 218, 232, 235
Damagoras, *the Rhodian Admiral* 146
D'ambour, *a Fort near St.* Malo's 528
Damiata (Pelusium) *a City in* Ægypt 174, *vide* 283, 313
Danaus, *brought the first Ship into* Greece 3
Dandolo, *a* Venetian *Governor of* Cyprus 226
Dandolo (Reiner *and* Marc) *two* Venetian *Admirals* 241
Danes, *their Naval Force,* &c. 15, 19
——*Property in the* Baltic, vide B 18
——*Masters of* Sweden 300, 301
——*their Antiquity,* &c. 305, 306
——*their Wars,* &c. vide 582 *to* 585
Dantzick, *a City on the River* Embes 302, 303
Danubius (Ister) vide 174, 175, 176, 181
Dardagnus, *a* Turkish *Commander at* Lepanto 230
Dardanelles, *Castles at the Mouth of the Hellespont* 235, 236, 312
Dardania (Troy) *a Town on the Asian side of the* Hellespont 87
Dardanians, *reduced by* Philip *of* Macedon 97
Darien, *Sir* Francis Drake *there* 344
——*the* Scotch *Settlement three* 577
Darius, *King of* Persia, *his Anger against the Athenians* 48
——*his Death* 50
Darius *the Second* 88
Darius Nothus 92
D'arteloire, *a* French *Sea Captain* 643, 666
David, *King of* Israel, *his Riches, Fleets,* &c. 8, 9, 10
Decelea, *a Town in* Attica 80
De la Rue, *a* French *Captain taken* 656
Delaval *(Sir* Ralph) *an* English *Admiral, vide* 445, 451, 462, 463, 470, 472, 474
Delaval (George) *an* English *Flag-Officer* 582
Delaval, *Captain of the* Faulcon, *kill'd* 750
Delium, *a Town in* Bœotia 75
Delos, *an Island in the* Mediterranean, *taken by* Mithridates 146
Delphos, *its Oracles,* &c. *to the* Athenians 51
——Spartans 93, vide 94, 96
Delta, *the lower part of* Ægypt 51
Demaratus, *a* Spartan *King* vide 107
Demetrius, *Son of* Antigonus 130, 131
Demetrius *of* Pharia
Democares, *a Sea Captain of* Sext. Pompeius's 167, 168
Demosthenes, *an* Athenian *Admiral* 74, 81, 85
Dengynefs, *on the Coast of* England 463, 500
Denia, *a Town and Port in* Valentia *near* Altea 692, 731, vide 755, 797
Denmark, vide Danes, *and Prince* George

Deprie *(Marquis) the Emperor's Minister at* Rome 754, 756
Dercyllidas, *the* Spartan, *assists* Cyrus Junior 93
Desborow, *an* English *Sea Captain* 561, 562
De Relingue *(Monsieur) a* French *Sea Commander* 610
Deseada, *an Island near* Guadalupe 460
Despotato, vide Acharnania
D'estres *(Count) a* French *Admiral* 321, 402, 589, 610
D'Ibberville, *a* French *Sea Commander* 701
Diaz (John) *a* Spanish *Discoverer* 275
Didacus, *a Town in the* Hellespont 86
Dido, *Queen of* Carthage 113
Dieda (Anthony) *a* Venetian *Sea Captain* 222
Dieppe *in* France *bombarded by the* English 500, 501
Dilkes *(Sir* Thomas) *an* English *Sea Captain and Admiral* 559, 661, 666, 667, 669, 676, 679 *to* 686, 733
——*in the* Mediterranean 734, 735
——*his Death* 736
Dimalum, *a Town in* Illyricum 131
Dinham (John) *an expert Sea Commander* 334, 335
Dioclesian *the Emperor* 177, 325
Diomedon, *an* Athenian *Admiral* 89
Dionysius *the* Sicilian *Tyrant* 95, 115
Disney ( ) *an* English *Colonel at* Quebec 781
Diu, *an Island,* &c. *in the River* Indus, vide 309, &c.
Doggar Bank vide 550, 639
Dolabella, *a* Roman *of* Cæsar's *Party* 158, 159
Dominion *of the Sea in general, vide* lib. 1. ch. 10. and pag. 202 *to* 212
——*the* British *Kings Right thereto, vide* lib. 1. ch. 11.
——*of the Extent of that Dominion, vide* lib. 1. ch. 12. *and pag.* 30, 35
Dominion *of the* Adriatic *claim'd by the* Venetians 201, 202, 209, 237, &c.
——*of the* Mediterranean *acquired by the* Athenians, &c. 77, vide 7 *to* 20
——*of the* Baltic, *exercised by the* Danes, vide 18, 19, &c.
Domingo, *a City in* Hispaniola 535, 552, 787
Domitius, *a Sea Commander under* Pompey 157
Don (Tanais) *a River of* Muscovy 307
Doria (Aubert, Lambo, Philip, Peter, *and* Lucian) Venetian *Admirals* 218, 240 *to* 243, vide 315
Doria (Andrew *and* John) Venetian *Commanders at the Battel of* Lepanto 228, 229
Doria (Aiton *and* Gaspar) vide 268
Doria (Ansaldi) *a* Genoese *Admiral* 266
Doria (Pagan) *a noted* Genoese *Admiral* 242
Doria (Roger) *Admiral of* Arragon 267
Dorians, *the People inhabiting* Doris, *a part of* Achaia 70, 147
Dorilaus, *an Admiral of* Mithridates 147
Dorislaus *(Dr.) an* English *Ambassador at the* Hague 293
Dover Road 538, 539
Doughty (John) *a stout Seaman, beheaded* 346
Douſa

INDEX.

Doufa (Peter) *a Dutch Admiral* 290
Dowglafs *(Colonel) Governor of the Leeward Iflands* 783
Dowglafs, *an Englifh Captain, his refolute Act* 400, 401
Downs, *a Station of the* Englifh *Fleet* 539 *to* 541
Downing *(Sir George) Ambaffador in* Holland 297
Dragut-Rays, *a Pirate and* Turkifh *Sea Commander at* Lepanto, &c. 230, 277, 309
Drake *(Sir Francis) his Sea Difcoveries,* &c. 344, 345, 346
Drake ( ) *Captain of the* Swallow 783
Drepanum (Trepano del valle) *a Port and Town in* Sicily. *vide* Eryx 126
Drino, *a Gulf in* Albania 131
Dromones *(Runners) a fort of Gallies* 185
Drufus, *the* Roman *General* 174
Du Bart, *a French Admiral* 444, 541, 550
Dubourguay, *an Englifh Colonel at* Lisbon 760
Du Cafs, *a French Sea Commander* 558, 586, 593, 597, 700, 703, 704, 709, 712, 713, 714, 787, 788, 790
Dudley *(Colonel) Governor of* New England 598
Duffus (Kenneth, *Lord) Commander of the* Advice 787
Duilius, *a Roman General* 121
——— *bad the firft Naval Triumph* 122
Dulcigno, *a Town and Port in* Albania 224
Dunbar *(Captain) his daring Action* 500, 501
Dunkirk *vide* 36, 444
——— *Bombardment defigned* 501, 502, 503
——— *and attempted* 529, 530, *vide* 539 *to* 541, 635 *to* 640, 738, 740, 742, 786
——— *deliver'd up to the* Englifh 789, 790
Du Quefne, *and* Gennes, *two French Monfieurs* 321, *vide* 440, 690
Durazzo (Dyrrachium *and* Epidamnus) 66, *vide* 130, 195, 212, 224, 241, 308
Durley *(Mr.) Captain of the* Charles *Firefhip* 527
Durfley *(Lord) after Earl of* Berkeley (vide B)
——— *Commander of the* Litchfield 645
——— *and of the* Boyne 678, 679
——— *of a Squadron in the* Soundings 720 *to* 726
——— *in the* Mediterranean, *vide* 733, 742, 747, 761
Dutch, *their Naval Force,* &c. *vide* 18, *and* 282 *to* 299
Duyvelant, *a Town on the Coaft of* Zeeland 283
Dyme, *a Port of* Achaia 71
Dyrrachium, *vide* Durazzo

E

Ebro, *vide* Ibir
Ebubeker, *a Saracen Caliph or Emperor* 188
Eddiftone *Rock,* &c. *vide* 449
Edgar, *King of* England 327
Edinburgh, *in* Scotland, *burnt by the Englifh* 339
Edinborough Frith, *the Pretender,* &c. *there* 745, 746, 747
Edmund, *King of* England 328
Edrick, *the* Englifh *Traitor* 328

Edward *the Elder, and* Edward *the Confeffor, vide* 327, 328
Edward *the Firft, Second, and Third, Kings of* England 313, 331, *and* 335
Edwards (John) *Captain of a Squadron* 709
Edwards (Richard) *Captain of the* Cumberland, &c. 719
Egefta *and* Egeftans *vide* 79, 122
Egilochus, *one of* Alexander's *Admirals* 103
Eidonia, *a Country in* Greece 9, 15
Elæans, *Confederates of the* Argives, *againft the* Spartans 76
Elæus, *a City near the Mouth of the* Hellefpont 86
Elba (Æthalia) *an Ifland between* Piombino *and* Corfica 114, 241, 755
Elbe, *a River of* Germany 310
Elbing, *a Town in* Polifh Pruffia *vide* 302
Eleufis, *a Town near* Athens 93
Elford (Matthew) *Captain of the* Experiment 783
Elis, *a part of* Peloponnefus 70
Elizabeth, *Queen of* England, *her Naval Tranfactions* 342 *to* 367
Elliot, *an Englifh Captain at* Petit Guavas 557
Elliot, *an Englifh Governor at* Gibraltar 749
Elfinore, *a City and Port in* Denmark 585, 727
Emanuel, *Emperor of* Conftantinople 212
Emardus, *one of* Pepin's *Admirals* 310
Emathia, *vide* Æmonia *and* Macedon
Embarcations *before the Deluge* 1, 2
Embriachi (Hugh) *a Genoefe Admiral* 239
Embs, *a River, vide* Amifius 175
Engia, *an Ifland of the* Archipelago, *vide* 74, 224, 225, 308
England, *its Naval Power* 20
——— *Royal Navy Temp.* Eliz. & Jac. 1. *vide* 20, 21
——— *See alfo* Britain, *and from p.* 323 *to the End.*
Epaminondas, *the* Theban *General* 96
Ephefus, *a City in* Leffer Afia, *a Fight near it* 88, 106
Epicides, *the* Syracufan *Admiral* 133
Epidamnus, *vide* Durazzo
Epidaurus, *a City in* Peloponnefus 70, 74, 75
Epipolæ, *an Eminence near, and a part of* Syracufe 80, *vide* 124
Epirotes: *People of* Epire 138
Epire *(now* Leffer Albany) *vide* Naupactus, *and* 96, 196
Eræ, Teos, *and* Lebedus, *Cities of* Leffer Afia 86
Erafinides, *an* Athenian *Sea Captain* 89
Erefus, *a Town in* Lesbos 86
Eretria, *a City of* Eubœa, *a Fight near it* 86
Eretrians, *their Sea Dominion,* &c. 7
Ermengarius, *Governor of the* Baleares 191, *vide* 310
Erythræa, *a City of* Crete 149
Erythras (Efau *as fuppofed) a King of* Edom, *near the* Red Sea 3
Eryx, *a City in* Sicily (Trepano del monte) 115, 127
Esberne, *a Danifh Sea Commander* 306
Efiongeber *and* Eziongeber, *vide* Achanis

Efpernon

INDEX.

Espernon (Duke) besieges Rochelle 317
Essex (Earl) his Acts against the Spaniards 159, &c.
Essex and Rivers (Earls) vide Rivers
Esthodia in the Baltic vide 306
Eteonicus, a Peloponnesian Captain 89, 90
Ethelred and Ethelwolf, Kings of England 326, 327, 328
Evagoras, King of Cyprus 91
Evans (Mr.) Captain of the Royal Oak at Alicant 695
Evans (Mr.) Captain of the Defiance 763
Eubœa (the Island Negropont) three Sea Engagements vide 53
——the Peace there 65
——revolts from the Athenians 86
——subjected by Mithridates 147, 196, vide 214
Evertson, a Dutch Rear-Admiral 425, 505
——Vice-Admiral 519, 545, 551, 635, 637
Evertz, Admiral of Zeeland 296
Evertzon, Admiral of Zeeland 400
Eugene (Prince) of Savoy, in Spain 731
Eugenius the Fourth (Pope) 221
Eumenes, one of Alexander's Successors, &c. 105, 106
St. Euphemia vide 160
Euphenius, a Sicilian Traitor 191
Eurymedon, a River where Cimon beat the Persian Fleet 62
Eurymedon, an Athenian Admiral, his Acts, &c. 72 to 76, 81, 83
——slain 85
Eusebius, his Account of the Dominion of the Sea 7, 8, 9, &c,
Eustachius of Tesino, a Milanese Admiral 221
Eustatia, an Island and Fort near St. Christopher's 454
Euthymemes, a Native of Marseilles, his Discoveries 11
Euxine Sea (Pontus) Augustus's Guardfleet there 14
——Pompey's Dominion thereof 150
——Vespasian's Fleet there 175
——the Scythians and Franks there 176, 177, 184
Eyder, a River of Germany 584
Eziongeber, vide Achanis

F

Fabius and Buteo, Roman Consuls 127
Fabius Valens, a Sea Captain for Vitellius 176
Fairborne (Sir Stafford) an English Sea Commander and Admiral 581, 620, 625, 675, 685, 737, 738, 739
Fairfax (Robert) an English Sea Captain, &c. 643
Fair Promontory, vide Hermea
Famagusta, besieged and taken by the Turks 226, 227, vide 242
Faramida, a City or Port on the Coast of Ægypt 212
Favagnana, an Island, vide Ægusa 127
Fayal, one of the Azores 36, 791
St. Felix, a Town in Spain 523
Felton, kills the Duke of Buckingham 379

Ferdinand, King of Spain 225
Ferrars (Lord) an English Sea Commander 338
Ferrol, a Harbour near the Groyne 422
Fermozee and Ferryland in America, vide Renozee, and 549
Fez, a City and Kingdom in Afric, vide Marufians
Fierabras (William) a Norman Captain 194
Fiesque (Lovis) a Genoese Admiral 217
Final in Italy vide 517, 519, 554, 555
Firth of Forth, &c. on the Coast of Scotland 746, 747
Fitzpatrick, an English Sea Captain 545
Fitz Williams (Sir William) an English Sea Commander, his Character, &c. 339
Five Islands Bay at Antegoa 456
Flag, its Right and Duty paid anciently, &c. vide 35 to 39, 294, 295
——at Leghorn 736
Flavio of Amalfi, vide Gioia, or Goia
Fleets, vide Navy and Ships
Fleets of Pompey, Augustus, and Anthony, &c 13, 14
Flemish Road at Dunkirk 742, 786
Florida in the West Indies 703
Florus the Roman Commander 122
Flotilla of Spain, vide Armada
Fochia { Vecchia, in Natolia 215, 236, 241, 246
{ Nova vide 223, 246, 764
Foglietta (Lawrence) a Genoese Sea Commander vide 247
Fontarabia, a Town of Guipuscoa in Spain 320
Fontenay Race near Brest 788
Forbes (Mr.) an English Engineer at Port Royal 766
Forbisher (Martin) his Voyages to North America 344
Formentera, an Island between Spain and Yviça 513, 797
Formosa, an Island off of China 295
Forum Julii, Frejus in Provence vide 14
Foscolo, a Venetian Admiral 236
Fotherby ( ) Captain of the Lark 681
Foulis (Thomas) an English Sea Commander 693
Fourbin (Monsieur) a French Sea Commander 719
——attempts to invade Scotland 746, 747
Franks, Inhabitants on the Euxine 178
Francis the First, &c. Kings of France 315
Frawenbergh, a Town in Polish Prussia, vide 302
Frehelle Cape, vide Cape Farrel in C
French, the beginning and occasion of their Naval Force 20, vide 319
Frejus, vide Forum Julii
Friggots Bay at St. Christopher's 453
Fregose (Thomas) Doge of Genoa 247
Fregose (John Baptist) a Genoese Admiral 247, 248
Friuli, a City in Italy 218
Frotha, Third and Fourth, Kings of Denmark 305
Fuengirola, a City near Malago 493
Fulgose (Peter and Baptist) two Genoese Admirals 242, 248
Fulvia, the Wife of Marc Antony 165
Nnnnn Fulvius

INDEX.

Fulvius, *the* Roman *Consul* 131
Fundi, *a City on the Coast of* Naples, vide Nicolas *Count of* Fundi 246

G

Gabinius's *Law for* Pompey's *Government of the Sea* 150
Gace *(Count de) a Marshal of* France, *Commander of a French Squadron that attempted* Scotland 744, 747
Gades, Cadiz *and* Cales, vide C
Gaeta, *a City of* Naples 248, 271, 272, 311
Gaillard *(Monsieur) a* French *Protestant Sea Commander* 317
Galanga, *near* Lepanto 230
Galatia, *a Province of* Lesser Asia 146, 151, 175
Galba, *the* Roman *Emperor* 175
Galceranus, *Admiral of* Catalonia 266
Galerius, *a* Roman *Emperor* 179
Gallia Narbonensis, Languedoc *in* France 175, 179
Gallienus, *a* Roman *Emperor* 176
Gallies, first invented by the Corinthians 44
―― *when first built by the* Romans 12
Gallipa (Clupea) *a Castle, &c. in* Afric 125, 140
Gallipoli, *a City on the* Thracian *Bosphorus* 249
Galloper Sand, *about eight Leagues off the* Thames *Mouth* 571, 656, 657
Gallus (Cornelius) *a* Roman *General* 173
Gallway, *a Port in* Ireland 720
Galway *(Earl) an* English *General in* Spain 507, 519, 729, 734, 761
Gama (Vasquez de) *a* Portuguese *Vice-Roy of the* East-Indies 260
Gandia, *a Port in* Spain *near* Denia, *&c.* 731
Ganymedes, *an* Ægyptian, *opposes* Cæsar 161
Garda, *a Lake in* Italy, *and a considerable Town thereon* 222
Garonne, *a River in* France 193, 317
Gastanaga *(Marquis) a* Spanish *General* 518, 522
Gaspe Bay, *near the Mouth of the River* Canada 779
Gaza, *a City of* Palæstine *taken by* Alexander 103
Gedde *(Messieur) a* Danish *Admiral* 584
Gega, vide Kara
Geloan *Plains in* Sicily vide 117
Geloi, *People there inhabiting* vide 80
Gelon, *a King of* Sicily, *his Naval Power, &c.* 51
―― *assists the* Himerians 57
―― *beats the* Carthaginians, *and burns their Fleet* 58, vide 114
Gelon, *Son of* Hieron, *King of* Sicily 133
Genoa, *taken by the* Saracens 16
―― *the Coast there named* Liguria 129
―― *the City bombarded by the* French 321, &c. vide 515, 648, 732, 768, 775, 794, 795, 797, 798
Genoese, *subdue the* Pisans, *&c.* 17
―― *beat the* Saracens, *&c.* 214, 218
―― *their Wars with the* Venetians, *&c.* ibid. *and* 239 to 253
―― *their successive Doges, &c.* 245, 246, 247
Genseric, *a King of the* Vandals 184

Georgia (Iberia) *the Country so called* 152
Gergenti, vide Agrigentum
Germanicus, *a* Roman *General* 175
Germans *and* Germany vide 175
Gessoriacus Portus, Boulogne *in* France
Getæ, *People beyond the* Ister 174
Gibel, *a City of* Syria vide 239
Gibellines, vide Guelphs
Gibraltar, *a Town and Port at the Streights of* Cadiz, *or* Hercules Pillars, vide 4, 14, 104, 150
―― *taken by the* English 544
―― *besieged by the* French *and relieved*, vide 677 to 686
―― *possessed by the* English 696, 729, 734, 749, 761, 770, 773, 775, 793, 796
Gilbert *(Sir* Humphrey, *or Sir* Henry) *his Voyage to* Newfoundland 35, 348
Gilimer, *a King of the* Vandals 184, 185
Ginkle, *a Lieutenant-General in* Ireland 450
Gioia, *or* Goia (John) *Inventor of the Mariner's Compass* 216
Giorgi (Aloise) *a* Venetian *Sea Commander* 224
Girone, *a City of* Spain 760, 762, 773
Gisco, *a* Carthaginian *General* 115
Gizid *and* Marvan, *two* Saracen *Calips* 190
Glasii (Andrew *and* Henry) Venetian *Commanders* 214
Gnossus, *a City in* Crete 149
Goa, *a City and Island in the* East-Indies 257, 265
Godolphin *(Earl) Lord Treasurer of* England 575
Gogidiscus, *a* Gothic *Commander* 184
Goletta, *a Castle near* Tunis 250, 277, 278
Golf di St. Euphemia 160
Gondamore *(Count) the* Spanish *Ambassador* 368
Gordon (Thomas) *Captain of the* Leopard, *retakes the* Salisbury 746
Gordon (George) *Captain of the* Lowestoffe 765
Gore (Henry) *an* English *Sea Captain at* Quebec 780
Goree, *an Island* vide 658
Gorge, *an* English *Brigadier in* Spain 694, 695
Goselinus, *Admiral of the* Greek *Emperor* 195
Goths, *their Naval Wars, &c.* vide 175, 176, 182 *to* 188
Gottenburgh, *a City and Port in* Denmark 550, 584, 657, 661
Gozo, *an Island near* Malta 196, vide 309
Grado, *a Town in the* Adriatic 192, 198, 217, 218, 243
Grafton *(Duke) kill'd at* Cork 431
Granada, *a Kingdom and City in* Spain 239, 266
Granicus, *a River in* Asia 97, 149
Granville *in* France, *destroyed by the* English 528
Gravelin, *a Port in* Holland 538, 639, vide 742, 743
Graydon, *an* English *Vice-Admiral* 600 to 609, 625
Greeks, *their Naval Armaments*, *Sea Dominion, &c.* 6, 41 to 45, 48
Græcia propria vide 96
Græcian Sea, *a part of the* Ægean 96
Grestonia, *the Country so called* vide 75
Griffith *(Mr.) an* English *Sea Captain* 748
Grille

INDEX.

Grille (Steven) *a Genoese Admiral* 241
Grimaldi *and* Grimani, *Venetian Admirals* 224
Grimani, *a Venetian Admiral, drowned* 235
Grimani *(Cardinal) Vice-Roy of* Naples 754, 756
Grimbaldi, *a Genoese Admiral* 217
Grimbaltz, *a Genoese, the French King's Admiral* 29, vide 283
Grovais (Groy) *an Island on the Coast of* France 547
—— *off* Port Louis 644
Groyne (Corunna) *a Town and Port on the North Coast of* Spain 422, 599, 611 *to* 615
Guadalquivir, *a River in* Spain, vide Bœtis
Guadalupe, *a Town and Island in* America 456, 457, 458, 460, 535, 603, 604, 605, 725, 784
Guanahani, vide St. Salvadore
Guanava, *an Island in* America 701
Guelphs *and* Gibellines, *their Factions* 244, 245, 268
Guernsey *Island* 471
Guetaria, *a Port near St.* Sebastians 320
Guido, *Bishop of* Utrecht, *and* Guido, *Count of* Flanders 283
Guiercio (Baldwin) *a Genoese Admiral* 259
Guilford (Sir Henry) *an English Sea Commander* 337
Guiscard (Robert) *a Norman Leader* 194
Guldenlieu *(Count) Lord-Admiral of* Denmark
Gulfs, vide Bays [584
Gulfs *of* Strymon *and* Singus vide 50
Gumanapy, *an Island in the* East Indies 260
Gunfleet vide 657
Guns, *their first Invention* 218
Gustavus Adolphus, *King of* Sweden 302
Gustavus Ericson, *King of* Sweden 301
Gylippus, *a Spartan Admiral* 80, 86

H

Haddock (Sir Richard) *an English Admiral* 428 *to* 431
Haddock (Nicholas) *Captain of the* Ludlow Castle 746, vide 797
Haldan *the Second, King of* Denmark 305
Halissa, *a Cambayan Admiral* 262
Hamilton, *an English Brigadier at* Cadiz 621
Hamilton (Archibald) *an English Sea Commander at* Barbadoes 782
——*and Captain of the* Woolwich 783, 784
Hammer Sound, *in* Norway vide 727
Hamoze vide 717
Hancock (Robert) *Captain of the* Eagle, *lost* 733
Handasyde *(General) Governor of* Jamaica 702, 714
Hannibal, *the* Carthaginian *General* 114, 120, 131 *to* 138
Hanno *the* Carthaginian *doubled the Cape of* Good Hope 5, vide plus 12, 115, 116
Hansen (Monsieur) *a Danish Councellor of State* 584
Harbour Grace, *an Island in* America 561
Hardicnute, *a Danish King of* England 306, 328
Hardy (Sir Thomas) *an English Sea Captain in the* Bedford *at* Vigo, &c. 625, 650, 655, 716 *to* 720

——*at* Ostend, &c. 739, 751
——*before* Dunkirk, &c. 786 *to* 789
Hardy (Charles) *Captain of the* Roe Buck 710, 712
Harland (Robert) *Captain of the* Salisbury Prize 713
Harlow (Thomas) *an English Sea Commander* 559, 562, 563
Harold *the Third, King of* Denmark 365
Harold Graafield, *King of* Norway 193
Harold Harfager, *King of* England 318
Harpagus, Cyrus's *Lieutenant in* Ionia 11, vide 46, 47
Hartnol *(Mr.) Captain of the* Restauration 725
——*Commander in the* Mediterranean 753
Havana, *a Sea-Port and Town in* Hispaniola 553, 591, 593, 698, 704, 705, 715
Havre de Grace *in* France *bombarded,* &c. 462, 465, 501
Hawkins, *an English Sea Captain* 343, 357
Hazardous, *a French Ship, taken* 656
Hebdomium *and* Cyclobium, *two Suburbs of* Constantinople 189
Hedges *(Mr.) Secretary of State* 669
Hedges, *an English Major at* Carthagena *in* Spain 694
Hegesandridas, *a Spartan Admiral* 86
Hegesippus *of* Halicarnassus vide 108
Helepolis, *an Engine to batter Walls,* &c. 108
Helix, *an Engine to move vast Bodies,* &c. 135
Helias, *and* Hermione, *two Towns in* Peloponnesus 70
Hellen *and* Hesione, *their Rapes* 43
Hellespont vide 6
——Xerxes *Bridge thereon* 51
——*Actions therein,* &c. 80, vide 150, 180
Helsingberg, *opposite to* Cronenbergh 583
Helvoetsluice, *a Harbour of the States of* Holland 36, 639, 663, 658
Heneago, *an Island North of* Hispaniola *in* America vide 783
Hengist *and* Horsa, *two Saxon Leaders* 324
Henry *the Third, Fourth, Fifth,* &c. *Kings of* England 331 *to* 341
Hephestion, Alexander's *Favourite* 103
Heraclea, *a City on the* Euxine 75, 105, 149
Heraclea minor, *a City in* Sicily 123, 134
Heraclides, *a Syracusan General* 80
——*also a Syracusan Sea Captain* vide 83
Heraclius, *Emperor of the East* 188
Herbert *(Earl of* Torrington) *an English Admiral* 404, 405, 415
Herbesus, *a City in* Sicily 134
Hercules *goes against* Troy, &c. 42
Hercules Pillars, vide Gibraltar
Hercules Monceus (Monaco) *a Port so called* 176
Hercynion, *a King of* Ægypt 93
Hermea Promontory *(Cape* Bona, *and* Fair Promontory 125, 140
Hermocrates *of* Syracuse, *his Advice* 78
——*made General,* &c. 80, vide 114
Herrings, *the Invention of curing them*
Hesione, vide Hellen

Hesse

INDEX.

Hesse (Prince) the Emperor's General in Spain vide 581, 623, 625, 677
——at Ostend 739
Hesse (Prince) Junior, a Commander in Barcelona 693
Hetha, a warlike Swedish Lady 300
Heydic, vide Hovat
Hiarbas, King of Mauritania 113
Hicks (Jasper) an English Sea Commander 736, vide 749
Hieron, King of Sicily 114, 119
——his fam'd Ship vide 135 to 138
Hieronymus, Hieron's Successor, &c. 133
Hill (Mr.) an English Resident in Savoy 669
Hill, an English General at Quebec 766 to 781, 789
Himera, a River in Sicily 133
Himera, a City in Sicily, besieged by the Carthaginians 57
——by the Athenians 73, 80
Himilco the Carthaginian, his Voyage from Cales Northward 12, vide 114
Hippargetes, a Town between Utica and Carthage 144
Hippocrates the Syracusan Admiral 133
Hiram, King of Tyre, his Confederacy with David and Solomon 8, 10
Hirtius, and Pansa, the Roman Consuls 164
Hispaniola, vide Cibao, Cuba, Havana, &c. and 273, 535, 592, 594, 602, 603, 697, 698, 699, 701, 704, 711, 715
Holland and Hollanders, vide Batavia
Holstein and Holsteiners vide 303, 306, 307
Holmes, an English Commodore, &c. 295
——a Captain 557
Holmes (Sir Robert) an English Sea Commander vide 400, 401
Homer, his Account of the Grecian Ships 43
Honorat de Savoy, Admiral of France 316
Honosio (Villa Joisa) a Town in Spain 132
Hook (Mr.) Captain of the Jamaica Sloop 714
Hopson an English Vice-Admiral 484, 492, 493, 494, 588, 625, 626
Horsa, vide Hengist
Hosier (Francis) Captain of the Salisbury 713
Howard (Sir Edward and Sir Thomas) English Admirals, their Acts at Sea 337, 338, 339
Hovat and Heydic, two Islands on the Coast of France 547
Hudson's Bay discovered 291
Huen, an Island in the Baltic 584
Hugh, King of Italy 192
Hughes (Mr.) Captain of the Winchester, vide 725
Humago (Cissa) an Island near Istria 217, 243
Huns and Hungarians, vide Vandals, and 198
Hurricans, vide Storms, and Jamaica
Hutchins (Mr.) Captain of the Portland 708, 710
Hydaspes, a River in Persia 103
Hydruntum (Otranto) a City, &c. in Italy 119 vide 308
Hyeres (Stœchades) a Knot of small Islands on the Coast of Provence 176, 506, 519, 676
——the English Fleet there 731, vide 754, 772, 797

Hypalis, a River in Persia 503

I

Jackson and Pett, two Pilots, attempt a North Passage to China 347
St. Jago, one of Cape Verde Islands 783
Jamaica, an Island in the West Indies, vide 591, 622, 697 to 705, 710, 712, 715, 782, 783
——a terrible Hurricane there 785
Jambel (Frederick) an Italian Engineer 287
James the First and Second, Kings of England 21, 298, 299, 368, 369, &c. 470, 540
Japhet's Posterity, &c. 3
Iber (Ebro) a River of Spain 132
Icetes, a Prince of the Leontines 116
Ida, a Mountain near Troy 75
Idomeneus and Merion, Cretan Commanders against Troy 43
Jehosaphat, endeavours to restore Naval Affairs 10
Jennings (Sir John) Captain of the George, and Admiral 679, 684, 685, 693, 694, 695, 701, 740, 747, vide 757, 774, 775, 793 to 799
Jews, their Sea Affairs, &c. 8, 9, 10
Illyricum (Illyria) comprehends Dalmatia and Liburnia vide 96, 130, 162
Imbros, an Island in the Archipelago 86
Indian Ocean vide 104, 105
Indus, R. Semiramis's Victory thereon 5
——sail'd on by Alexander 104
Indutiomarus, a Gaulish Leader 156
Innocent the Tenth, Pope 250
Insula Batavorum (Holland) 282
Joan, Queen of Naples 271
John, an Admiral under Narses 187
Johnson (Robert) Captain of the Kent, takes the Superbe 765
Ionian Sea vide 96, 159
Ionians, their Sea Dominion 8
——War with Cyrus 10
——Vanquish'd, &c. 46, 48
Joppa, a Port near Jerusalem, &c. 10
Ischia, vide Ænaria
Isis, Queen of Ægypt, her Acts, &c. 3
Ismenias, a Theban Prince 92
Issa (Isle Grand) on the Coast of Italy vide 163
Issa (Lissa) a Town in Sicily 130, vide 163
Istone, a Hill near Corinth 73
Ister, vide Danubius
Istria and Istri, between the bottom of the Adriatic and the Danube 131, 192
Isthmusses (vide Peninsulas) of Leucas 73, 95
——of Corinth 70, 238
Ivica, vide Yvica
Juba, King of Mauritania 157
——vanquished by Cæsar 163
Julia (Cæsar's Daughter and Pompey's Wife) her Death 157
Julia, Marc Antony's Mother 166
St. Julian's Castle at the Mouth of the River of Lisbon 690
Julius Cæsar, his Acts, &c. 15, 148, 161, &c.
Julius the Eleventh, Pope 225, 226
Julius, an English Sea Captain 557

Jumper,

INDEX.

Jumper, *Captain of the* Lenox 620
Justiniani (Onuphrius) *a* Venetian *at* Lepanto 233
Justiniani (Pancratius) *a noble* Venetian 242
Justiniani (James) *a* Genoese *Sea Commander* 272
Juts Riffbank *on the Coast of* Jutland 727

K

Kalenus, *a Sea-Commander for* Cæsar *in* Achaia 162
Kane ( ) *an* English *Colonel at* Quebec 781
Kara *and* Gega, *two Islands on the Coast of* Ireland 418
Keigwin, *an* English *Sea Captain killed at St.* Christopher's 454
Kenneth, *King of* Scotland 327
Kenneth *Lord* Duffus, vide Duffus
Kerr (William) *Captain of the* Revenge 657, 675
———*Commadore* 697, vide 700, 702, 703
Keymish, *an* English *Sea Captain* 368
Kid *Captain) his Piracies*, &c. 576 to 580
Killigrew (James) *an* English *Captain, killed* 516
Killigrew, *an* English *Admiral* 422, 425
Kings *of* England, *their Dominion of the Sea anciently* 29
Kinsale, *a Haven*, &c. *in* Ireland 441, 720, 787
Kirk, *an* English *Colonel at* Quebec 781
Kirkby, *an* English *Colonel* 557
Kirktown *(Mr.) Captain of the* Defiance 718
Kittim, *Grandson of* Japhet 3
Kittim, *or* Chittim, *its Interpretation* 3
Knevett *(Sir* Thomas) *an* English *Sea Commander* 337
Knute, *Son of* Swaine *King of* Denmark, &c. 328
Koge *Bay, between* Copenhagen *and* Elsinore 585

L

Labbe *(Monsieur) a* Spaniard vide 553
Labienus, Cæsar's *Lieutenant in* Asia 156, vide 165
L'abrazza (Thauris) *an Island on the Coast of* Dalmatia 162
Lacedæmon, vide Sparta, *and* 74, 85, &c.
Lacedæmonians (Spartans) *their Sea Dominion* 7
——*besiege* Samos 46
——*War with the* Persians, Athenians, &c. 93
Laches, *the* Athenian *Admiral* 73
Lacinium *Promontory*, vide *Cape* Rizzulo
Laconia vide 74, 75, 81
Lada, *a small Island near* Miletus, *or* Maltha, *a Fight there* 48
Ladrones, *Islands in* America 276
Lælius, Pompey's *Admiral in* Asia, vide 140, 159
Lævinus, *a* Roman *Consul and Admiral* 138, 140
Lagos *Bay* vide 483, 484, 544, 666
Laguna, *a Town in the* Canaries 290
La Hogue *Fight between the* English *and* French 461 to 470, 789
L'aigle *(Monsieur) a* French *Sea Commander* 770

Lake di Gardi, vide Garda
Lamachus *the* Athenian, *his Advice*, &c 78, 79
La Motte *(Count) a* French *Governor of* Ostend 739
Lampourdan, *a Province in* Spain 750, 759, 760
Lampsacus *besieged*, &c. 90, 91
Lancerota, *one of the* Canaries vide 270
Landscroon, *near* Copenhagen 584, 585
Languedoc, vide Gallia Narbonensis, *and* 175, 772
Laqueximines, *Admiral of* Bintam 260, 261
Larache *and* Mahmora, *two Towns in* Barbary 278
Larghes *and* Larguero, vide Algueri
Larsus, *a Town in* Greece vide 223
Larta, *the Gulf so called* vide 225, 229
Lasthenes, vide Panares
La Valona, vide Valona
St. Lawrence *the Great and the Little) two Islands in* America 633
St. Lawrence, *a River there*, vide Quebec, *and* 776, 777, 778, 779
Lawson *(Sir* John) *an* English *Sea Commander* 296, vide 397
Leake *(Sir* Andrew) *Captain of the* Grafton 581, 665
Leake *(Sir* John) *after Admiral* 587, 641, 642, 651, vide 665, 667, 669, 676 to 684, 689 to 696, 720, 736
——*lands the Queen of* Spain, &c. *at* Barcelona 749 to 755, 789
Le Bebe, *a Town in the* Adriatic *near* Venice 218
Lebedus, vide Teos
Lecythus, *a Town in* Greece 75
Leeward Islands, vide 452, 453, 697, 700 to 705, 783, 791
Leganeze, *a* Spanish *Marquis* 519
Leghorn, *a free Port in* Italy, vide Livorne, *and* 240
Le Grand Prie *(Monsieur) Captain of the* Thouloufe 796
Leith, *and* Leith *Road, in* Scotland 745, 747
Lembero *(Count) the Emperor's Ambassador at* Rome 654
Lembro, *a Town in* Greece 223
Lemnos, vide Sta'imene, *and* 86
Leo *the Ninth (Pope) taken Prisoner* 194
Leo Cavala, *Admiral of the* Greek *Fleet* 214
Leonatus, *one of* Alexander's *Captains* 105
Leonidas, *King of* Sparta, *his Death at* Thermopylæ 54, 59
Leontium, *a Town in* Sicily 133
Lepanto, vide Naupactus (Sinus Crissæus) 70, 308, 309
Lepidus *the* Triumvirate 152, 164, 169
Leptis (Tripoli *in* Barbary) 4, vide Tripoli
Lercaro (Paul) *a* Genoese *Admiral* 247
Lerida, *a City in* Spain vide 687, 735
Lesbians, *their Sea Dominion* 7
——*beaten by* Polycrates 46
Lesbos, *an Island in the* Ægean *and* Lesbian 7, 17, 46
——*Allies of* Sparta 72, 85, 86

O o o o o Lesina

INDEX.

Lesina (Charia) *an Island in the Gulf of* Venice 131, 200
Lesina, vide Pharia
Lestock *(Mr.) Captain of the* Weymouth 715
Leucas Isthmus, *now the Island St.* Mawre 73, 95
Leucadia, *an Island, and* Leucadians, *near Samos, Allies of* Sparta 170
Leucopetra (Capo del Armi) *a Promontory in* Italy 168
Leven *(Earl) a* Scottish *Commander* 747
Lewis *the Twelfth, the* French *King* 225
Ley (Thomas) *an English Sea Captain* 621
Libya, *part of* Afric *next* Ægypt 150
——*the Coasts thereof first discovered* 45
Licinius, *a* Roman *Admiral* 180, 181
Liefkenshoeck, *a Fort on the River* Scheld 286
Liguria, *the Coast about* Genoa 129, 130
Lilybæum *(Cape* Marsalla) 126, 127, 132
——vide Marsala
Lima, *the Capital of* Peru 708
Limeric, *a strong City in* Ireland 449, 450, 451
Lipari *Islands (*Æolian *Islands) and* Lipara, vide 73, 120
Lisardo *(Baptist) a* Genoese *Admiral* 247
Lisbon *taken from the* Moors 253
——*the King of* Spain *there* 664, 665
——Sir John Jennings 757
——Sir John Norris 775
——*Admiral* Baker 790
——Sir John Jennings 793, 794, 796
Lisle *(Lord) Admiral of* England 339
Lissa, vide Issa
Lissus, Alesio, *a Town and River in* Albania 131
Littleton (James) *Captain of the* Medway, vide 582, 634, 651
——*in the* West Indies 711 to 715
——*Commadore* 781, 782
Livadia Albania *and* Epire, *Countries of* Greece 196, vide 238
Livius Salinator, *a* Roman *Consul* 131
Livorne (Leghorn) *a free Port in* Italy, vide 647, 648, 732, 736, 752 *to* 755, 763, 770, 795, 796, 797
Lizzard, *the farthest Southward Cape in* Cornwall 448, 545
Lloyd, *Captain of the* Falmouth 579
Loades (Edward) *an English Sea Captain* 608, 609
Loadstone, vide *Mariner's Compass*
Locrians, *Allies of* Sparta 70
Locri Opuntii vide 73
Locri Epizephyrii 74, 115
Logane, *a Bay or Gulph near* Cuba 537, 592, 593, 602, 701
Loire, *a River of* France 312
Long (Thomas) *Captain of the* Bredah 769
Longobardi (Lombards) vide 133
Loredano (Aloise) *a* Venetian *Admiral* 218, 221
Loredo, *a Town in the* Adriatic 218
Lotharius, *a* German *Emperor* 193
Loud's Cove, *a Port or Bay in* America 549
Lowther *(Mr.) Governor of* Barbadoes 784
Lucania (Basilicate) 176
St. Lucar *in* Spain, vide Tartessus

Lucius (Marc Antony's *Brother) Consul* 165
Lucullus, *a* Roman *General* 148, 149
Luna (Sarzana) *a City near* Porto Spezza 193
Lusitanians (Portuguese) vide 148
Lutatius, *a* Roman *Consul* 127, 128
Lycia *and* Lycians vide 70
Lycus, *a River of* Asia Minor 116
Lyctus, *a City in* Crete 149
Lydians, *their Sea Dominion* 6
Lysander, *a* Spartan *General* 88
——*made Admiral* 90
——*beats the* Athenians, &c. 91, 92
Lysias, *an* Athenian *Captain* 89
Lysias, *a* Syracusan *Orator* 92
Lysimachus, *one of* Alexander's *Captains*, &c. 106
Lytcot, *an* English *Sea Captain at* Petit Guavas 557

M

Mabbot (   ) *Captain of the* Mary Gally 782
Macedon, *and* Macedonians, vide Æmonia, *and* 96, 97, 112
Macella, *a Town in* Sicily 122
Machaneel Bay *on the North side of* Hispaniola 536
Mackarty, *an* English *Major General* 419
Madagascar, *an Island on the South-East Coast of* Afric. *The Race of* Abraham *there* 9
——*discovered by the* Portuguese 256, vide *Pirates*
Madera *Islands on the Coast of* Afric, *possessed by the* Portuguese 17, vide 148, 488, 551, vide 600, 604, 703, 712, 791
Madrid, *the Capital of* Spain vide 703, 773
Mæander, *a River in* Lesser Asia 311
Mæandrius, Polycrates's *Secretary* 47
Mægara *and* Mægarians, vide Megara
Maelstrand (or Maesterlandt) *a Port near* Gottenburgh 661, 627
Mæonia *and* Mæonians *of* Asia Minor
Mæotis Palus, *the Lake or Sea so called* 150, 184
Mæsia, vide Mœsia
Magadoxa, *a Town and Port on the Coast of* Ajan 255
Magellan (Ferdinand) *a* Portuguese, *his Discoveries and Death* 260, 261, 276
Magellan *Streights* vide 276, 346
Magna Græcia, *the South Parts of* Italy 44
Magnesia, *a City on the River* Mæander, vide 47
Mago, *a* Carthaginian *General* 115
Mahmora, vide Larache 278
Mahomet *the Impostor* vide 188
Mahomet *the first* Turkish *Emperor* 308
Mahon, vide Port Mahon
Mahoni, *an* Irish *Major General in* Spain 694
Maja, *a Town in* Italy 194
Maina, *a Town and Port near Cape* Matapan 224
Majorca, vide Baleares *and* Minorca
Malabar, *the Coast between the* Arabic *Sea and the Gulf of* Bengale 256, 262, 265
Malacca, *a Port in the East Indies* 258
Malaga

INDEX.

Malaga, *a City and Port in* Spain 489, 509, 763, 764, 789
Malamocco, *the Original of* Venice 310, vide 243, 199
Maldivies *Islands in the* East Indian Sea 256
Malea, *a Cape near* Lesbos 89
Maleus, *a Carthaginian General* 114, 115
Malfi, vide Melfi, *and* Amalfi
Mallora, *an Island off* Leghorn 17, vide 240, 796
St. Malo, *a Town and Port of* France *bombarded, &c.* 526, 527
Maltha (Miletus *and* Melita) *an Island in the* Mediterranean 20, vide Miletus, 235, 246, 277, 773
Mamertines, *a People in the North of* Sicily 119
Mancinus, *a Roman Admiral* 144
Maniaces, *the Emperor* Michael's *General* 194
Maniacium, *a Town in* Sicily *built by* Maniaces 195
Manlius, *a Roman Consul, &c.* 123, 144
Mansel *(Sir Robert) Vice-Admiral of* England 370
Mantineans, *Confederates of the* Argives, vide 76
Marabota (Frederic) *a Genoese Admiral* 245
Marano, *a Port and Island on the Coast of* Brasil
Marathon, *the* Athenians *beat the* Persians *there* 49, 51, 59
Marcellus, *a Roman General, &c.* 134, 138
Marcellus, *a Sea Captain of* Pompey's 159
Marchi (Thomas) *a Genoese Admiral* 246
Marcianopolis, *a City in* Mœsia 176
Mardonius, *a Persian General* vide 49, 60
Mareotis, *a Lake in* Ægypt *near* Alexandria, vide 103
Mari (Henry) *a Genoese Admiral* 240
Marigalante, *a French Island in the* West Indies 457
Mariner's Compass invented 216
Marine Regiments established in England 615 *to* 619
Marlborough *(Duke) an* English *Captain General* 639, 664, 737, 738, 739, 781
Marmora, *the Sea so called from an Island therein,* vide Propontis
Marsala (Lilybæum) *a City in* Sicily 126, 127, 132
Marsalquivir, *a Town on the Coast of* Barbary 272
Marseilles *(and* Massilians, *a City in* Provence) *built by the* Phoceans, *their Sea Dominion* 7, 11, vide 158, 159
——*taken by* Cæsar, *&c.* 158, vide 164, 271, 519, 772
Marsias, *a Sea Captain under* Demetrius 108
St. Martha, *an Island in the* West-Indies 698
Martinica, *a French Island in the* West-Indies 452, 457, 535, 591, 599, 698, 699, 784, 787
St. Martin's *Island,* vide Olonne
Martin, *an* English *Captain, dies at* Jamaica 593
Martin (George) *Captain of the* Dragon 765
Martius, *a Roman Admiral* 144
Martius, *a Roman Associate of* Mithridates 149
Martizano, *a Town in* Calabria *in* Italy 194
Marvan, vide Gizid

Marusians, *a People of* Fez *in* Afric 148
Mascarenhas (Peter) *a* Portuguese *Vice-Roy of* East-India 260, 261
Massanissa, *a King of* Numidia 141, 143
Massilians, *Inhabitants of* Marseilles, *their Sea Dominion* vide 11, 158
Masters *(Mr.) Captain of the* Fame 786
Masts and Sails of Ships, their Defects, &c. 454
Matan, *one of the* Philippine *Islands* 276
Matapan (Tænarium) *most Southern Cape of the* Morea 173, 224, 525
Mattagorda, *a Fort near* Cales 622
Matthews, *an* English *Brigadier* 621
Matthews (Thomas) *Captain of the* Dover 716
Matthews (Thomas) *Captain of the* Chester 724, 725, 765
Maurice *(Mr.) an* English *Sea Captain* 791
Mauritania, *a part of* Afric
St. Mawre *Island,* vide Leucas, *and* 250
Maxentius, Maximine, *and* Maximian, *Roman Emperors* vide 177, 180
Maximilian, *a German Emperor* 225
May *(Island) in* Edinborough *Frith* 745
Mazarine *(Cardinal) encreased the* French *Naval Power* 20
Meander, vide Mæander
Mecca *and* Medina, *Cities in* Arabia 258
Medea, *Daughter of* Æetes 42
Mediterranean *Sea* 14, 513, vide 793, &c.
——Sir Cloudesly Shovell *there* 728, 729
Medius, *a Sea Captain under* Demetrius 108
Meesters, *a Dutch Engineer,* vide 504, 527 *to* 530
Meeze (George) *an* English *Sea Captain* 549, 551
Meeze, *an* English *Rear-Admiral* 554, 555
Megabyzus, *Son of* Zopyrus, *a Persian Admiral* 60
Megara, *a City of* Greece vide 70, 71, 75
Megara, *a City in* Sicily 134
Megareans, *Allies of* Sparta, *&c.* vide 68 *to* 72
Melazzo (Olim Milæ) *a City in* Sicily, vide 121, 168, 194, 195
Melesander, *a Spartan Admiral, slain* 70
Melilla, *a Town in* Barbary 272
Melinda *in the* East Indies 256
Melita, vide Miletus *and* Maltha
Mellaria (Tariff) *in the* Streights *of* Gibraltar 148
Melo (Milo) *an Island in the* Ægean *Sea* 70, 73, 214
Memphis (Grand Cairo) *a City in* Ægypt, vide 61
Menander, *an* Athenian *Admiral* 83
Mencetius, *a Sea Captain under* Ptolemy 109
Menapii, *People of* Flanders *and* Brabant 177
Mende, *a Town in the* Peninsula *of* Pellene 75
Mendesium, *one of the Mouths of* Nile 61
Menecrates, *a Sea Commander under* Sext. Pompeius 167
Menelaus, *King of* Sparta 43
Menelaus, Ptolemy's *Governor of* Cyprus 107, 108
Mengrelia, vide Colchis

Meno-

INDEX.

Menodorus, Sext. Pompeius's *Admiral, his Advice* 166
——*revolts*, &c. 167, 168
Menzo, *a River in* Italy 222
Meſſalla, *a Roman Admiral* 139
Meſſana (Meſſina) *a City in* Sicily, vide 74, 80, 117, 120, 164, 194, 195, 751, &c.
——*See alſo* Sicily, *and* Phare *of* Meſſina
Meſſenians *of* Naupactus vide 70
Meſſenia, *a Country of* Greece 74
Metelino, *an Iſland in the* Archipelago 225, vide 308
Metellus, *a Roman General* 148, 149
Methone (Modon) vide 74, 120, 220, 308
Methwin, *an Engliſh Ambaſſador at* Lisbon, vide 628, 689
Methymnia, *a Town in the Iſland* Lesbos 72, 90, 103
Metrophanes, Mithridates's *Admiral* 146
Mexico, *a Province and City of* New Spain *in* America 275, 709
Micone, vide Mycone
Mighills, *Commander of the* Hampton-Court 773, 795
Mihill *(Mr.) Captain of the* Centurion 763
Milan, *a City of* Italy vide 220
Miletus, *the Iſland* Maltha, *ſack'd,* &c. *by the* Perſians 49
——*by the* Athenians 86
——*by* Alexander 97
——*by the* Romans 132
Mileſians, *their Sea Dominion,* &c. 7, 85
Milo, vide Melo
Miltiades, *an* Athenian *General* 49
——*Father of* Cimon 59
Milvius, *a Bridge near* Rome 180
Mindarus, *a* Peloponneſian *Admiral* 86, 87
Miolani, *a* French *Admiral* vide 249
Minorca, *one of the* Baleares, vide ibid. *and* 513, 520, 696, 752, 753, 754, 795, 797
Minos, *King of* Crete, *his Actions,* &c. 6, 42
Mira, *an Iſland in the* Eaſt Indies 260
Miſenum, Miſenium, *a Town and Promontory in* Italy 166, 175, 176
Miſiſtra, *a Town in* Greece 223
Mitchel (David) *an* Engliſh *Sea Captain and Admiral,* vide 519, 523, 524, 525, 548, 564 to 574
Mitchel (John) *an* Engliſh *Sea Captain at* Quebec 780
Mithridates, *King of* Pontus, *aſſiſted by the* Cilicians, &c. 14
——*beaten by the* Rhodians 146
——*and by the* Romans 147, &c.
——*his Sons* 147
Mithridates *of* Pergamus, *aſſiſts* Cæſar 161
——*made by him King of* Pontus 163
Mitylene (Lesbos) *a City and Iſland in the* Archipelago vide 72, 89, 90, 95
Mnaſippus, *a* Spartan *Admiral* 95
Mocenigo, *a* Venetian, *the firſt Governor of* Cyprus
Mocri, *a King of* Baharem 259
Modon, vide Methon, *and* 224, 225
Mœſia, *a Province of* Illyricum 176

Molucca's *Iſlands, in the* Eaſt-Indies 258, 261, 347
Monaco (vide Hercules Moncæus) *a Port near* Genoa 732
Monbaze *in the* Eaſt Indies 256
Monepenny *(Mr.) Captain of the* Superbe 795
Monford *(Sir Simon) Lord Warden of the five Ports* 335
Montague (William) *an* Engliſh *Admiral under* Edward the *Third* vide 34
Monſerrat, *an Iſland in North* America 453, 702, 703, 783, 784
Montandre *(Marquis) a* Portugueſe 730
Montezuma, *the* Indian *King of* Mexico 275
Montjovi, *a Caſtle near* Barcelona 687, 693
Montmorency, *Admiral of* France 316
Moore, *an* Engliſh *Captain at* Petit Guavas 557
Mordaunt *(Mr.) younger Son of the Earl of* Peterborow, *Captain of the* Reſolution 691
——*burns his Ship* 692
Morea, vide Peloponneſus, *and* 524
Mori, *a Town on the River* Adige 222
Morini, *a People of ancient* Gaul 153
Moroſini, *a* Venetian *Sea Commander* 235, 236, 237
——*and Admiral for the* Piſans 240
Moroſini (Roger) *a* Venetian *Admiral* 241
Morris *(Mr.) Captain of the* Canterbury 798
Mortemar *(Duke* de) *a* French *Sea Commander* 299
Moſchien, *an* Athenian *Captain* 135
Moſs ( ) *an* Engliſh *Sea Captain* 694
Motril, *a Port or Iſland in the* Mediterranean 544
Mozambique, *a City and Iſland on the Eaſt Coaſt of* Afric 234
Mucianus, Veſpaſian's *Admiral* 175
Muhavius, *a* Saracen *Caliph* 189
Muley Boahdelin, *King of* Granada 192
Munda (Rouda veja) *near* Malaga *in* Spain 163
Munden (Richard) *an* Engliſh *Sea Captain* 404
Munden *(Sir* John) *an* Engliſh *Admiral* 521, 582, 588, 611 to 615
Munychia, *a Fort near* Athens 106
Muræna, *the* Roman *General* 147
Murcia, *a Province in* Spain 728
Murcus, *a* Roman *of* Brutus's *Party* 165, 166
Murgantines, *an ancient People of* Sicily 117
Murzuphlus, *an Uſurper of* Conſtantinople 312
Muſactus, *a* Saracen *Leader* 239
Muſcovites, *their Naval Power,* &c. 19, vide 307
Muſtapha, *a* Turkiſh *General* 226, 227
Mutatio (John) *a* Venetian *Governor of* Tenedo 219
Mycale, *a Promontory in* Ionia 56
Mycenæ, *a City of* Peloponeſus *between* Argos *and* Corinth
Mycone, *an Iſland of the* Ægean, *one of the* Cylades 214
Mylæ, vide Melazzo
Myngs *(Sir* Chriſtopher) *an* Engliſh *Sea Captain* 296, 397, 740
Myſia, vide Mœſia, *and* 75, 146

N Nacſia,

INDEX.

N

Nacfia, vide Nicfia, *and* Nixfia, *and* 224, 308
Naez *of* Norway vide 639
Nambeadara, *a King of* Cochin 256
Names of Ships in the English *Navy and Squadrons* vide 21, 410, 413, 420, 429, 457, 481, 487, 488, 494, 541, 542, 543, 565, 674, 679
Names of English *and* Dutch *Admirals* 445, 474, 498, 499, 588, 624, 651, 674, 681
Names of Officers, &c. in the Navy 534, 535, vide 616, 617
Names of Prisoners taken in the Salisbury 746
Names and Numbers, &c. of French *Ships taken* vide 573, 627, vide 746, 799, 800
Nantasket *Road in* New England 766, 778
Naples, *a City of* Italy, vide 186, 272, 751, 794, 795, 796, *and* 798
Napoli di Romania (Nauplia) *a City on the East Coast of* Morea 238
Narborough (*Sir* John) *a Sea Commander at* Tripoli 404
Narenza (Narona) *and* Narenzans, *their Original, &c.* 198 to 201
Naron, *a River so called* vide 201
Narsames, *the Emperor* Basilius's *Admiral* 192
Narses, Justinian's *General in* Italy 187, 188
Nasidius, *a Sea Commander for* Pompey 158
Nassau, *a Dutch Rear-Admiral* 564, 565, 566
Natolia (Asia Minior *so called*) vide 236
Navarino (Pylus) *a Port in the* Morea, vide 74, 225, 308, 764
Navaza, *an Island in* America 556
Naucratis, *a City in* Ægypt, *built, &c.* 7
Navigation of the Ancients, &c. 2, 3
Navy (Royal) of England, Temp. Eliz. & Jac. 1. vide 21
Navy of England, vide *Names of Ships and Officers, and* 434, 435, 436, 481, 494, 497, 534, 565, 573, 574, 588, 652, 672, 674, 681, 684, 686, 688
Naulochus, vide Calbaruso, *and* 169
Naupactus (Lepanto) vide Actium, *and* 70, 71, 72
Naxos, *one of the* Cyclades, *and* Naxians, vide 7, 95, 138
Neapolis, *part of* Syracuse *so called* 134, vide 186
Nearchus, *a skilful Navigator under* Alexander 104
Nearchus, *a Commander under* Agathocles 117
Nebuchadnezzar *destroyed Old* Tyre 5
Negropont, Eubœa, *an Island of the* Archipelago 49, 214, vide 308
Neon, vide Burichus
Nero (Claudius) *the* Prøprætor 139
Nero, *the* Roman *Emperor; also a pretended* Nero 175
Nesmond (*Monsieur*) *a* French *Sea Commander* 443, 460, 461, 610
——*taken* 651
Neville, *an* English *Admiral* 491, 493, 495, 511, 519, 559 to 562, 567
Nevis, *an Island in* North America 605, 703
Neustria, Normandy *so called* 133

New England vide 755, 756, 776, 777, 778
Newfoundland 348, 601, vide 631 to 634, 700, 765, 773, 777, 779
New France, vide Candia, *and* Quebec
New Jersey *in* America 776
Newport, *near* Ostend, *attempted by the* English 738
New York *in* America 776, 779
Nicæa, *a City in* Persia, *built by* Alexander 103
Nicastro (Numistrum) *a City in* Calabria 139, 194
Nice, *a City of* Provence *in* France, vide 669, 670, 677, 691
Nicholochus, *a Spartan Admiral* 95
Nicholson, *an* English *Colonel at* Port Royal 765, vide 778
Nicias *and* Nicostratus, Athenian *Admirals* 75
Nicias *the* Spartan, *his Peace, &c.* 76
——*his Advice, &c.* 79
Nicomedes, *a King of* Bithynia vide 146
Nicon, *a* Tarentine vide 139
Nicopolis (Prevesa) *opposite to* Actium 173
Nicosia, *the capital City of* Cyprus vide 226
Nicostratus, *an* Athenian *Admiral* 72, 75
Nicotera, *a City and Port of* Calabria, *on the* Tyrrhene 196
Nicsia *and* Nixia, *an Island, one of the* Cyclades vide 214, 224
Nieper, vide Boristhenes, *and* 174
Nile, *the fam'd River of* Ægypt 161
Nimeguen, *the Peace there* 298
Nisæa, *a Port and Arsenal of* Sparta vide 71, 75
Noah, *his Ark and Posterity* 2, 176
Noailles (*Duke de*) *a* French *General in* Spain 762, 774
Noguera, *a River of* Spain 762
Nombre de Dios *in* America vide 276
Normans, *their Power, Wars, &c,* 16, 193 *to* 197
Norris (*Sir* John) *Captain of the* Orford, *and Admiral* 559, 560, 562, 650, 655, 685, 725, 726, 727, 731, 733, 751, 767 to 727, *and* 768 *to* 775, 793, 794
Norris (*Sir* William) *Ambassador to the* Mogul 582
Nottingham (*Earl*) *Secretary of State* vide 670
Nova Scotia, vide Port Royal
Numantia (Soria) *an ancient City of* Spain 145
Numerius, *a Roman Emperor* 177
Numistrum, vide Nicastro
Nutria, *a Town in* Albania *or* Epire 130

O

Obdam (*or* Opdam) *a* Dutch *Admiral* 295, 296, 398
Obelerius, *a Doge of* Venice 310
Ochus (Darius) *the* Persian *Successor of* Artaxerxes 95
Octavius *the* Roman *Emperor,* vide Augustus
Octavius, *a* Roman *Admiral* 140
——*under* Pompey 162
Octavia, Augustus's *Sister, and* Marc Antony's *Wife* 166
Oczakow, vide Basterni
P p p p p Oderzo

INDEX.

Oderzo (Opitergium) *in the Republick of* Venice 159
OEnias, *a City of* Acarnania 72, 138
OEta, *a high Mountain in* Thessaly 85
Officers and Offices of the Navy, vide 533, 534, 535, 616, 617
Olbia, *a Sea-Port of* Sardinia 122
Oleron, *an Island on the Coast of* France 316, 317, 737
Olonne *and St.* Martin's, *two French Islands* 547, 548
Olophixus, *a City near Mount* Athos 75
Oluz Aly, *Dey of* Algiers, *at* Lepanto 229, 230
Olympias, *Mother of* Alexander, *her Death* 106
Olympus, *a City of* Sicily 150
Oneglia, *a Port bordering on the State of* Genoa 691
Oneficritus, *a skilful Navigator under* Alexander 104
Onobola, *a River in* Sicily 168
Opdam, *a Dutch Admiral, blown up* 398
Ophir, *a Digression about it* 9, 10
Opitergium, vide Oderzo
Opitergians, *their desperate Act* 159
Opuntii, *a People of* Bœotia 73
Oquendo (Antonio de) *a Spanish Admiral* 279
Orætes *crucifies* Polycrates 47
Oran, *a City and Port on the Coast of* Barbary 272, 513, 695, 768
Orange *(Prince) opposes the Duke of* Alva 285
Orange *the Prince invited into* England, vide 299
Orbitello, *a Town in Italy on the Borders of* Tuscany 755, 794
Orcades, *the Islands of* Orkney 175
Orfacan, *a City in the* East Indies 257
Orford *(Earl)* vide Russel *(Admiral) and* 789
Orfordness vide 550
Oricum *(now* Val del orso) *in* Sicily 119
Origuela, *a Town near* Murcia *in* Spain 728
Oristagni, *a Town in* Sardinia 319
Orkneys, *Islands on the North of* Scotland 787
Ormond *(Duke) at* Cales and Vigo, vide 619 *to* 631
Ormus, *an Island in the* East Indies 257, 259, 260, 264
Oronoque, *a River in* New America 368
Ortegal, *a Cape on the Coast of* France 613, 614
Ossory *(Lord) an English Admiral* 404
Ossuna *(Duke) Vice-Roy of* Naples 278
——*and Admiral of* Spain 495
Ostalric, *a Town on the Coast of* Spain 523, 798
Ostend, *a Port in* Flanders, *the fam'd Siege thereof by the English Fleet,* &c 737, 738
——*surrender'd* 739
Ostia, *a Port and River in* Italy 187, 188
Ostrogoths, &c. vide 184
Osyris, *a King of* Ægypt 3
Otho *the* Roman *Emperor* 175
Otho *the First, a German Emperor* 192, 193
Otranto, vide Hydruntum, *and* Calabria 720
Ouzley *Bay* vide 725
Owen (   ) *an English Sea Captain* 720
Oxenstiern, *Chancellor of* Sweden 303
Oxenham (John) *an eminent English Seaman* 345
Oxydracæ, Alexander *wounded by them* 104

P

Pachsu, vide Antipachsu
Pachynus, *a* Promontory *(Cape* Passa*)* 202
Paddon (George) *an English Sea Captain at* Quebec 780
Padus, *the River* Po *in* Italy 175
Palamos *in* Spain *bombarded,* &c, vide 508, 509, 513, 520 to 523
Paland, *an English Brigadier at* Cales *and* Vigo 621
Paleologus (Michael) *Emperor of the East* 215
Palermo (Panormus) *in* Sicily 120, 126, 184, 185, 646, 799
Palestrina (Præneste) *a Town of Italy near* Venice 243, 310
Palinurus, *a Cape or Promontory in* Sicily 168
Palma *(Count) Nephew of Cardinal* Portocarrero 581
Palma, *the capital City of* Majorca 269, 696
Palus Mæotis vide 307
Pamphylia *and* Pamphylians, vide 14, 62, 150, 175
Panares *and* Lasthenes, *Admirals of* Cydon, vide 149
Panormus, vide Palermo
Pantalarea, *(or* Pandatarea*) an Island in the* Mediterranean 516
Paphlagonia *(and* Paphlagonians) *on the* Euxine 7, 146, 147
Paphos, *a City of* Cyprus 108
Papias, *one of* Pompey's *Lieutenants* 169
Parætonium, *a Mouth or Harbour of the River* Nile 173
Paraguai *in the* West-Indies 712
Parenzo, *a City of* Istria *on the Gulph of* Venice 199, 242
Pario, vide Paros
Parkes *(Colonel) Governor of the* Leeward Islands 704
Parmenio, *one of* Philip *of Macedon's Commanders* 97
Paros *(and* Pario*) an Island in the* Ægean *Sea* 95, 149, 214, 236, 308
Parthians, *join* Labienus 165
Particiatus, *Doge of* Venice 192, 197
Passagio, *a Town in* Natolia 223
Passaro, vide Pachynus
Passenger, *Captain of the* Royal Anne 695
Paston (Robert) *Captain of the* Feversham 765
Patane, *in the* East-Indies 161
Patara (Patera) *a City of* Lycia *in* Lesser Asia 146
Patræ *(and* Patras) *a City and Port in the* Morea 71, 170, 237
Pavia, *a City in* Italy
St. Paul *(Monsieur) a French Sea Commander* 641, 683
Paulini, Barberigo's *Secretary, hang'd* 236
Paulin de la Gard, *a French Sea Commander* 316
Paulus Æmilius *the* Roman *General,* &c. 113, 143
Pausanias, *a Spartan General* 60, 72

Pausa-

INDEX.

Pausanias, *a noble* Macedonian *who kill'd* Philip 97
Peccais, *a Town on the Coast of* Languedoc 646, 653
St. Pedro *Fort*, vide Gibraltar
Peirce, *an English Colonel at* Cales, &c. 620, 621
Peleg, *one of* Noah's *Descendants* 2
Pelion, *a Mountain in* Greece 52
Pellene, *a* Peninsula *in* Greece 75
Peloponnesus *(the* Morea *so called)* vide 237, 238
Peloponnesian *War, its Causes,* &c. 66, 69 to 95, 166, 167
Pelorus, *a City in* Sicily 134
Pelusium (Damiata) *a City in* Ægypt 161, 174
Pembroke *(Earl) Lord High-Admiral of* England 607, 619
──── *a second time* 722
Peninsula's *made Islands,* &c. 50, 51, 73, vide 76 and 161
Peniscola, *a Port in the* Mediterranean, vide 798
Penn, *an English Admiral,* vide Venables
Penn *(Sir* William) vide 398, 399
Pennington, *an English Admiral* 280, 369
Penon de Velez, *a Fort on the Coast of* Barbary 272, 277
Pensylvania *in* America vide 776, 778
Pepin, *King of* Italy, &c. 310
Pera, *a Suburb of* Constantinople 241, 242
Percey (Francis) *Captain of the* Firebrand 733
Perdiccas, *one of* Alexander's *Captains* 99
Perez (Ferdinand) *King of the* Canaries 271
Pergamus, *a City of* Mysia *in* Lesser Asia, vide 14, 147
Pericles *the* Athenian *Admiral* 64, 65
──── *takes* Samos, &c. 66, vide 69
Pericles Junior vide 89
Perseus, *King of* Macedon, *his Acts* 143
Persians *their Naval Power subject the* Ionians, &c. 46, 48
──── *conquer* Ægypt, &c. 47
──── *beaten by the* Athenians *at* Marathon 49
──── *conquer'd by* Alexander, vide Alexander
Pertauh Pasha, *a Turkish Commander at* Lepanto 229, 230
Perusia, *seiz'd by* Lucius Antonius 165
Peschera, *near the* Curzolarie *Islands,* vide 230
Peterborow *(Earl) joint Admiral,* &c. *with Sir* Cloudesly Shovell 684 to 688
──── *and General in* Spain 689 to 697
Peterson, vide Pieterson
Petit-Guavas *in* North America 537, 553, 556, 557, vide 602, 698, 699, 701
Petit, *an English Colonel kill'd at* Alicant 695
Petreius, vide Affranius
Pevensey *in* Sussex vide 197
Pharaoh Neco, *King of* Ægypt, *employs the* Phœnicians *on Discoveries,* &c. 4
Phare *of* Messina vide 756, 767, 768
Pharia, vide Lessina.
Pharnabazus, *a Persian Governor of* Hellespont
Pharnaces, *a King of* Pontus 163
Pharos, *a Tower and Island in* Ægypt 161, 174
Pharsalia (Philippi) *a Part of* Macedon 159, 160, 165

Phaselis, *a City of* Cilicia 156
Phelypeaux *(Monsieur) General of the* French *Islands in* America 785
Phermene, *one of the* Cyclades 224
Phideas, *a Roman Prætor* 148
Philantropenus, *a Greek Admiral* 312
Phileas, *a Sicilian Engineer* 137
Philip *of* Macedon 96, 97, 138
Philip *the Second,* &c. *Kings of* France 312, 313
Philip *the Second and Third, Kings of* Spain, vide 277, 278, 279
Philip *the Fifth of* Spain, vide Anjou *(Duke)*
Philippi, *a City of* Macedon 165, vide Pharsalia
Philocles, *an Athenian Admiral, his cruel Advice and Death* 90, 91
Philoctetes, *his Ships against* Troy 43, 44
Phocæa *and* Phocæans, *their Naval Affairs,* &c. 7, 11
Phocenses, *rob the Temple at* Delphos 96, 97
Phœnice, *the Capital of* Epire 130, 138
Phœnicia *and* Phœnicians, *improve Navigation, build Cities,* &c. 4
────*employ'd by* Pharaoh, *and* Semiramis 4, 5, 6
────*reduced by* Cambyses 47
────*beaten by the* Greeks 48, 64, vide 169
Phœnix, *a Port of* Caria 189
Phormio, *a* Peloponnesian *Admiral* 71
Photinus, *Governor of* Ægypt 160
Phrips *Bay at St.* Christopher's 454
Phrygia Minor vide 106
Phrygians, *their Sea Dominion* 7
Phylæ, *a Castle on the Frontiers of* Attica 92
Piccinini, *a* Milanese *General* 220
Pieterson, *a Dutch Admiral at* Cales, &c. 621, 795
St Pietro di Areno, *a Suburb of* Genoa 795
Piombino, *a City between* Orbitello *and* Leghorn 239, 754, 755, 794
Piræus, *the Port of* Athens, vide 71, 72, 92 *to* 95, 180, 181
Pirates *of* Cilicia, vide Cilicia, *and* 145, 148, 150, 164
Pirates *of* Narenza 198, 199
Pirates *of the* Adriatic vide 213, 224
Pirates *of* Algiers *and* Barbary, vide 251, 314, 317, 321, 360, 369, 397, 401, 404, 582
Pirates *of* Madagascar, &c. vide 277, 581
Pirates *in the* West Indies, vide Kidd
Pisa, *and* Pisans, *their Sea Dominion,* &c. vide 17, *and* 239, 240, 241
Pisander, *a Spartan General* 94
Pisani (Victor) *a Venetian Admiral* 217, 218, 243
Pisatello, vide Rubicon
Piso, *a Roman General* 144
Pityusa, *an Island, one of the* Baleares, vide Yviça
Pius Quintus, *Pope* 227
Placentia, *in* Newfoundland 606, 632, 633, 634, 777, 780
Plata, *a River of* South America
Platæa, *an ancient City of* Greece 72
Plemmyrium, *a Promontory near* Syracuse 81, 82

Plistia

INDEX.

Plistias *of* Cos, *one of* Demetrius's *Sea Captains* 109
Plistonax, *Father of* Pausanias 72
Po (Padus) *a River of* Italy 222
Point Pedro *in* America 555, 714
Pola, *a City of* Istria 199, 213, 217
Polani (Peter) *Doge of* Venice 212
Polemon, *a Sea Captain under* Alexander 103
Policandro, *an Island of the* Archipelago 214
Poliorcetes, *a Sirname of* Demetrius 111
Poliuchus, *a Syracusan Admiral* 83
Pollio, *a Commander under* Cæsar 157, 164
Pollis, *a Spartan Captain, his Acts* 95
Polybius, *his fine Observation* 129
Polycrates, *Tyrant of* Samos 8
——*his Naval Power*, &c. 10, 11
——*his strange Fortune*, &c. 46
——*circumvented by* Orætes, &c 47
Polyperchon, *one of* Alexander's *Successors* 106
Les Pomegues, *Islands before* Marseilles 158
Pompeipolis, vide Soli
Pompey *the Great, his Fleet*, &c. 13
——*his Acts* 15, vide 148, 150
——*his Triumphs* 151, 152
——*his Death* 160
——*his Sons* 163
Pomponius *the Civilian cited* 25
Pomponius, *one of* Cæsar's *Sea Commanders* 160
Pondicheri *on the Coast of* Cormandel 643
Pontenille, &c. French *Protestant Sea Commanders* 316
Ponte Vedra *on the Coast of* Spain 623
Pontochan, vide Vittoria
Pontus (*the* Euxine *Sea*) vide 14, 147, 149, 175, 176
Ponty (*Monsieur*) *the French Admiral*, vide 551 to 563, 682
Ponza, *an Island near* Gaeta 272
The Pope *owns the Archduke for King of* Spain 756
Popoli (*Duke* de) *a Spanish General* 798
Porca, *in the* East-Indies vide 262
Portmore (*Lord*) *an English General in* Spain 621
Porto Bello vide 553, 697, 698, 703 to 707
Porto Brondolo vide 218
Portocarrero (*Cardinal*) 581
Port Cros, *an Island, one of the* Hyeres 773
Port de Paix 536, 537, 603, 698
——i. e. François 710
Porto Farino, *in* Tunis *Bay* 395
Porto Fino *near* Genoa 221
Port Fornelle *in* Minorca 753
Port François *in* Hispaniola 709, 710
Port Hercole *in* Italy 754
Porto Longone *on the* Elba 754, 755, 770
Port Louis *in* France 586, 640, 644
Port Louis *in* Hispaniola 602, 698, 701, 704
Port Mahon *in* Minorca 513, 525, 752, 753, 754, 757, 763, 764, 768, 769, 773, 774, 775, 793, 795, 796, 797
Porto Morant vide 553
Port St. Mary *near* Cadiz 620
Port Passage *in* Biscay 320
Porto Pin 696

Porto Reale, *near* Cadiz 525, 621
Porto Rico *in* America 552, 699, 707, 715
Port Royal *in* Jamaica, *burnt* 598, vide 703, 710
Port Royal (Annapolis) *in* Nova Scotia 553, 764, 765, 766, 767
Porto Spezzo, *near* Genoa, *in* Italy 217, vide 648
Portus, *a Fort at the Mouth of the* Tyber 187, 188
Portus Achæorum vide 149
Portus Iccius *in* Britain vide 153
Portus Trutulensis (*for* Rutupensis) 234
Portugal Cove *near* Belle Isle *in* America 560
Portugal (vide Lusitania) *the King on bord the English Fleet* 666
Portuguese, *their Naval Power, Navigation*, &c. 17, 148, 254
——*and* Lib. 3. Ch. 8. per totum
——*stop the English Fleet at* Lisbon 690
——*See the like attempted* 729
Potidea, *and* Potideans vide 71, 95
Pozzuolo (Puteoli) *a Port in* Italy 168
Prætor, *his Power with the* Romans 26
Præveza (vide Nicopolis) *and* 173
Pregent, *a French Admiral* 315
Pretender, his Attempt on Scotland 740 to 748
Price, *an English Sea Captain* 694
Prienne, *a City of* Ionia 65
Prince (George) *of* Denmark, *Lord High Admiral of* England 610, 618, 619
——*his Death* 722, 741, 757
Probus, *a Roman Emperor* 177
Prodeno, *an Island near* Modon 224
Property, *observed by the* Americans, &c. 24 to 27
Propontis, *the Sea of* Marmora, *or* Constantinople 150, 180
Prosopitis, *an Island in* Nile 61
Protomachus, *an Athenian Admiral* 89, 90
Provence *in* France, *near* Languedoc 175, 794, 798
Psammis, *and* Bocchoris, *Kings of* Ægypt 7
Ptolemais, vide Acres
Ptolemy, Alexander's *Successor in* Ægypt 106, 108, 109
Ptolemy Philopator, *his great Ships* 137
Ptolemy, Cleopatra's *Brother* 160, 161
Ptolemy *the Astronomer* 203
Pudner (*Mr.*) *Captain of the* Severn 705, 710, 774
Puizar (*Marquis*) *a French Commander* 518
Punic *War, the first and second* vide 13, 119
Punta de la Guada vide 552
Punta di Salvori, vide Bahia
Puntals, *Forts near* Cadiz 510, 511, 515, 622
Purvis (*Mr.*) *Captain of the* Dunkirk *Prize* 709, 710
Pydius, *a River in the* Hellespont 87
Pygmalion, *Tyrant of* Tyre 113
Pylus (Navarino) *a Town of* Messina 74
Pyrrhus, *King of* Epire 112, 118, 120
Pythæas, *a Native of* Marseilles, *his Discoveries* 11
Pythes, *a Corinthian Admiral* 83

Pytho-

INDEX.

Pythodorus, *an Athenian Admiral* vide 73
Pyrrhus, *King of Epire* 112, 118, 120

Q

Quahutimoca, *the last King of* Mexico 275
Quarto (Simon) *a* Venetian *Admiral* 244
Quebec, *the unadvised Expedition thither* 479, 715, 716, *and* Lib. 5. Cap. 32. per totum
Queens of England (Mary I.) 341
——Elizabeth 342
——Anne 610, 722, 741
Queen of Spain *in* England 421
——*at the* Groyne, Barcelona, &c. vide Lib. 5. Ch. 28. *and* 36
Queen Christina *of* Sweden 202
Quesne, vide Du Quesne
Quiloa, *in the* East-Indies 255, 256
Quince Rock, *a Fort near* St. Malo 526, 527, 528
St. Quintin, *a City in* France *taken by the* English 342
Quintius, *a Roman Admiral* 139
Quirini (Marc Antoni) *a Commander at* Lepanto 229

R

Rabanus Carcerius, *a* Venetian *Commander* 214
Raby (Lord) vide Strafford (*Earl*)
Ragusa, *a small Republick in* Italy vide 131
Old Ragusa, vide Epidaurus
Raleigh (Sir Walter) *his Acts at Sea* 357, 359, 360 *to* 365, 368, &c.
Rametta, *a Town in the Plain of* Melazzo 195
Rapallo, *the Gulf so called* 221, vide 249
Rape of Helen *and* Hesione 43
Ravenna, *a Port in the* Adriatic 13, 176, 180, 188
Rausigiodus, *a King of the* Sauromati 180, 181
Raymond ( ) *Captain of the* Exeter 774
Reading (*Mr.*) *an* English *Colonel at* Port Royal 766
Reco, *a Port between* Genoa *and* Leghorn 221
Redondela, *a Town near* Vigo 626, 628
Red Sea vide 3, 4, 258, 259
Reggio, vide Rhegium
Regulus, *a Roman Consul* 123
Remonstrance against Admiral Grimbaltz, vide 29
Renooze, vide Fermooze
Retimo, *a Town in the Island* Candia vide 235
Rhe, *an Island on the Coast of* France 317, 737
Rhegium (Reggio) vide 73, 74, 79, 80, 164, 195
Rhegians, *their Actions* 115, 195
Rhenea, *an Island subdued by* Polycrates 11
Rhine, *the River so called* 175, 310
Rhium, *a Town in* Italy 71
Rhizon, vide Risine
Rhodes *and* Rhodians, vide 16, 100, 107, 111, 112, 146, 219, 308
Rhodian *Law* 211, 212
Rhode *Island in* America 778
Rhosne, Rhodanus, *a River in* France 11, 135
Richards (*Colonel* Commander *of the* Blaze *Fireship against* Calais 530

Richards (*Captain*) *an Engineer at* Newfoundland 562
Richlieu (*Cardinal*) *advances the* French *Naval Power* vide 20, 319, *and* 320
Rigby (*Captain*) *a Deserter*, &c 796
Rio de la Hacha *in* Hispaniola 597
Rio de Janeiro *in* Brasil vide 792
Rio de la Plata vide 276
Rio de Buenna Sennas 256
Risbank, *and other Forts near* Dunkirk 529
Risine (Rhizon) *a Town in* Dalmatia 130
Riva, *a Town on the Lake* di Garda 222
Riva (James de) *a* Venetian *Admiral* 236
Rivers *and* Essex (*Earls*) *goes with Sir* Cloudesly Shovel *to* Spain, &c. 728
——*and return* 730, vide 739
Rochefoucauld (*Monsieur*) *Admiral of* France 316
Rochefort, *a Port in* France 737
Rochelle, *a City and Port in* France, *its fam'd Siege*, &c. 270, 317, 318, 369 *to* 379, 737
Rochfort (Thomas) *Captain of the* Star *Bomb-Vessel* 765
Rohan (Duke) *at* Rochel 379
Rome *and* Romans, *their Naval War with the* Carthaginians, &c. 12, 13, 119 *to* 182
——*with the* Goths 186, 187
Roman *Emperors*, *Successors of* Tiberius 175
Romania vide 214
Romelia *and* Patras, *two Castles at the Entrance of the Gulf of* Lepanto 237
Ronda veja, vide Munda
Rooke (Sir George) *an* English *Admiral* 467
——*his Proceedings to* Cadiz 524
——*in the Soundings*, &c. 543, 564
——*in the* Baltic 582
——*and in the* Chanel 585
——*conducts the Forces to* Spain 619
——*carries the Archduke to* Lisbon 662, &c, vide 673
Roquelaure (Duke de) *a* French *Commander* 772
Rostoc, *a City on the* Baltic 306
Rota, *a Village near* Cadiz 620, 621
Roveredo, *a Town in* Italy vide 222
Rouse (Augustine) *an* English *Sea Captain at* Quebec 780
Roussillon, *a Province of* Catalonia 771
Rubicon (Pisitello) *a River of* Italy 157
Rugen, *an Island in the* Baltic 303, 306
Rumsey (*Mr.*) *Captain of the* Pembroke 769
Rupert (*Prince*) *Admiral of the* English *Fleet* 321, 340, 398, 399, 403, 404
Russell (*Admiral*) *Earl of* Orford, &c. *serves the Queen of* Spain *to the* Groyne 420
——*his Acts in the* Soundings 433, 434, &c.
——*engages the* French *off* La Hogue 462, 463, &c.
——*his Proceedings in the* Mediterranean 504 *to* 522, vide 733
Ruyter, *the* Dutch *Admiral* 295 *to* 298, vide 321, 394, 401 *to* 403
Ryddell (Walter) *Captain of the* Falmouth 764, 782

Ryswick,

INDEX.

Ryſwick, *the Treaty and Peace there* 38, 39, 575
Ryves (*Dr.*) *cited* 202, 203

S

Saba, a Turkiſh *Commander* 191, 192
Sacrifices of Mithridates 149
Saguntus, *or* Saguntum, *an ancient City of* Spain 131
St. Lawrence *River in* Canada, vide Quebec, *and* 776, 777, 778
Salamis (Coluri) *a City and Port in* Cyprus 54, 55, 56
——*the* Perſian *Fleet beaten* 59, 72, 107
Salisbury, *the Ship ſo named, taken by the* French 641
——*retaken with the Pretender's Friends on the Coaſt of* Scotland 746
Salley, *a City and Port in the Kingdom of* Fez 582
Salmadinas, *a Shoal off* Carthagena 706
Salo *Bay, near* Tarragona 793
Salonichi, vide Theſſalonica
St. Salvadore (Guanahani, *and* Cat Iſland) *one of the* Bahama's 273
Salvidienus, Octavius's *Admiral, beat by* Sextus Pompeius 164
Samana *Gulf, on the North of* Hiſpaniola 536
Samaudrachi, *an Iſland of the* Archipelago, vide 225
Sambay *Keys in the* Weſt Indies 698
Samblas *Iſlands near the Iſthmus of* Darien *in* America 708
Samians, *their Sea Dominion* 8, 10
——*quarrel with the* Athenians, &c. 65, vide 86
Samos, *an Iſland of the* Ægean *Sea* 8
——*fortified by* Polycrates 46
——*ſack'd,* &c. 49, vide 212
Sampayo, *a* Portugueſe *Vice-Roy of the* Eaſt-Indies 262
Samſon (*or* Sampſon) *an* Engliſh *Rear-Admiral* 296, 398
San Pietro di Areno, *a Suburb of* Genoa 795
Sandwich (*Earl*) *an* Engliſh *Admiral* 295, 397, vide 398 *to* 403
Sanſom (*Mr.*) *Captain of the* Phoenix 733
Santa Cruz *in* America 701
Santa Martha, vide Martha
Santi Quaranta, *a City in* Epire 196
Sanudo (Paul) *a* Genoeſe *Sea Captain* 220
Sanutus, *a* Venetian *Commander* 214
Sapienza, *an Iſland in the* Mediterranean *near* Candia vide 220, 242
Saraceni (Andrew) *a* Piſan *Admiral* 240
Saragoſa, *a City of* Arragon *in* Spain 694, 774
Saracens, *their Naval Force, Wars,* &c. 16 *and* 188 *to* 193
Sarca, *a River falling into the Lake* di Garda 222
Sardes, *the capital City of* Lydia 48
Sardinia, *an Iſland in the* Mediterranean, vide 11, 268, 269
——*reduced to King* Charles *the Third,* vide 519, 751, 752, 768, 769, 770, 771

Sardinians *vanquiſhed by the* Romans 133
Sarmati, *People beyond the* Viſtula 174, 181
Saſſari, *a City on the North of* Sardinia 771
Sarzana, vide Luna
Saſeno, *an Iſland in the* Archipelago vide 196
Satalia, *and Gulf of* Satalia vide 62, 150, 223
Savona, *an Iſland at the Eaſt End of* Hiſpaniola 535
Savona, *a City and Port near* Genoa 515, 736
Savoy (*Duke*) *joins in the Attempt on* Thoulon 731
——*declared King of* Sicily 799
Sauromati vide 174, 181
Saus (*Monſieur*) *a* French *Sea Captain at* Dunkirk vide 786, 787
Sax Gotha (*Prince*) *kill'd before* Thoulon 732
Saxons, *invade* Britain, &c. 15, vide 325
Scalimute, *a Town in* Natolia 143
Scandaroon *in* Turkey vide 143, 524, 798
Scandea, *a Town in the Iſland* Cythera 75
Scheld, *a River in* Holland vide 311
Schelling, *an Iſland on the Coaſt of* Holland 400
Schetland vide 787
Schilli, *and* Sciglio, vide Scyllæum
Schonen, *an Iſland in the* Baltic 303
Schonevelt, *a* Dutch *Harbour on the Coaſt of* Zealand 635, 744
Schowen, *an Iſland near the* Goree 658
Scilly, *Iſlands at the* Land's End 722
——*Sir* Cloudeſly Shovell, &c. *loſt there* 733
Scio, *an Iſland of the* Archipelago, vide Chio 212, *and* 223, 238, 770
Scione, *a City of* Greece 75
Scipio *the Elder, the* Roman *General and Conſul* 122, 131, 132
Scipo, *his Son, Conſul* 140
——*vanquiſhed by* Cæſar 163
Scirwan (Albania) *a Province of* Perſia 152
Scotland, *attempted by the* Pretender 740 *to* 748
Scutari (Chalcedon) *a Town on the* Propontis vide 149, 224
Scyllæum *Promontory* (*Cape* Schilli, *or* Sciglio) 167, 189
Scyro, *an Iſland of the* Archipelago, *one of the* Cyclades 214, 224
Scythians, *ſubdued by* Philip *of* Macedon 97
——*infeſt the* Roman *Empire* 176
Segeſta *and* Segeſtans, *in* Sicily 114
Segontiaci, *People about* Hampſhire 156
Segre, *a River in* Spain 762
Seine *River,* vide Sequana
Seiſſau, *a Major General at* Cette 772
Sejus Saturninus, *a* Roman *Admiral in* Britain 325
Selden's *Mare Clauſium cited* 21
Selechia, *a Town in* Caramania 223
Seleucia, *a City of* Syria, *near* Antioch 239
Seleucus, *one of* Alexander's *Succeſſors* 100, 112
Selim *the Second, Emperor of the* Turks 226
Selinus, *a City of the* Selinuntians *in* Sicily 58, 79, 80, 114
Selwyn (*Brigadier General*) *Governor of* Jamaica 591, 592
Semiramis, *Queen of* Aſſyria, *her Acts* 5, 6
Sempronius *the* Roman *Conſul* 132

Sentius

INDEX.

Sentius, *a Roman Prætor of* Macedon 147
Sequana, *the River* Seine *in* France 179, 310
Serapion, Cleopatra's *Lieutenant* 165
Serrana, *Note an unknown Shoal near it* 577
Sertorius *the Roman General* 148
Servilius *the* Roman *Admiral* 150
——— Cæsar's *Partner* 159
Servilius *the* Roman *Consul* 125
Servilius Geminus vide 132
Sesostris, *King of* Ægypt, *his Expedition* 4
Sesto (Sestos) *opposite to* Abydus 87, 90
Setines, vide Athens, *and* 223
Severus, *Son of* Galerius *the Emperor* 180
Sextus (Pompey's *Son*) *his Acts* 164
Seymore (William) *an* English *Brigadier at* Cadiz 614, 621
S'fax, *a Town in* Africa 196
Shannon, *a River in* Ireland, vide 438, 447, 450,
Sherrant, *a River in* France vide 1, 5. c. 26
Ships Names, vide *Names of Ships*
A Shoal (unknown) Eastward of the Serrana 577
Shoals, off Point Pedro 714
Shovell (Sir Cloudesly) *an* English *Admiral*, vide 430 *to* 434, 442, 470, 538, 542, 548, 551, 587, 588, 628 *to* 630, 656, 661, 662, 674, 677, 679, 684 *to* 688
——— *his Acts in the* Mediterranean, *at* Thoulon, &c. *with his Death* 728 *to* 733, 799
Sicambri, *Inhabitants near* Zutphen 156, 175
Sicanus, *a* Syracusan *Admiral* 80
——— *his Fireship* 84
Sichæus, *the Husband of* Dido 113, 114
Sicily, *an Island near* Naples, *invaded by the* Athenians 77, 78
——— *by the* Carthaginians, &c. 115
——— *by the* Romans, &c. 123 *to* 136
——— *seiz'd by* Sextus Pompeius 164, 166
——— *attempted by* Octavius 168
——— vide Messina
——— *Duke of* Savoy *King thereof* 799
Sicyon, *an ancient City of* Peloponnesus 75
Silly *Islands*, vide Scilly
Sidon, *an eminent City of* Phœnicia 4
Sidonians *save the* Tyrians *from* Alexander's *Massacre* 102
Segefrid, *a King of* Denmark 305
Sigæum *Promontory* vide 86, 149
Singus, *a Gulf near Mount* Athos 50
Sinope *and* Sinopoli, *a City and Port in* Paphlagonia *on the* Euxine vide 7, 245
Siroc (Mehemet) *a* Turkish *Commander* 229
Smith, *an* English *Sea Captain* 296
Smyrna, *a City of* Lesser Asia *on the* Propontis 212, 524, 798
Soames (Joseph) *an* English *Sea Captain at* Quebec 780
Sobians, *a People conquered by* Alexander 103, 104
Sofala, *the East Coast of* Africa *near* Madagascar 9, 254
Soli (Pompeipolis) *a City of* Cilicia 151
Solion, *a Town belonging to* Corinth 70
Solomon *and* David, *their Fleets, Navigation,* &c. 8, 9
Solyman *the* Turkish *Emperor* 308

Somersdyke, *a* Dutch *Sea Captain* 694
——— *and Admiral at* Port Mahon 763, 768
Somerset (Duke) *Master of the Horse* 664
Soria *in* Old Castile. vide Numantia, *and* 145
Soubieze (Duke) *the* Rocheller's *General* 317
Soundings, *Lord* Dursley *there* 720
——— *and* vide Jennings, Rooke, Russell
Sourius, *a River of* Italy 308
Spain *and* Spaniards, *their Naval Power,* &c. 18
Span (Jonathan) *Commander of a Squadron in the* West-Indies 711, 712
Spanish Armada *against* England 349, 350, 351, 352
——— *destroyed* 353, &c.
Sparr (Baron) *a* German *General in* Spain 620
——— *takes Possession of* Ostend 139
Sparta, vide Lacedæmon
Spartans, *their Actions,* &c. 60, 64, 65
Sphacteria, *an Island near* Navarino, *or* Pylus 74
Sphax, *or* S'fax, *a Town in* Afric 196
Spina, *a Town at the Mouth of the* Po, *and* Spinetans vide 11
Spinarza, vide Apollonia, *and* 130
Spinola, *a* Genoese *Admiral at* Lepanto 228
Spinola (Nicholas) *another* Genoese *Admiral* 241
Spinola (Francis, Peter, Conrade, *and* Nicholas) *four* Genoese *Admirals* 221, 240, 241, 242, 243, &c.
Spodriades, *a* Spartan *Captain* 95
Spragge (Sir Edward) *an* English *Admiral* 399, 401, 403, 404
Stackhover, *a* Dutch *Rear-Admiral* 296
Stalimene (Lemnos) *an Island of the* Archipelago 224, 236
Stanhope (Mr.) *an* English *Envoy at* Madrid 510, 734
Stanhope (Mr.) *Captain of the* Milford, *kill'd* 754
Stanhope (General *and* Earl) *his Acts in* Spain *and* Italy 749, 752, 753, 754, 755, 759, 761, 762, 768, 772, 773
The Start Point vide 545
Stato delli Presidi, *a Territory of* Tuscany 754
Staremberg (Marshal *and* Count) *an Imperial General in* Spain 773, 798
Stayner, *an* English *Sea Captain* 395
Stepney, *an* English *Sea Captain at the Islands of* Hieres 772
Steficleus, *an* Athenian *Admiral* 55
Stewart (James) *Captain of the* Dartmouth 539, 723
Stewart, *an* English *Colonel and Brigadier General* 518 *to* 522
Stercather, *a* Danish *Sea Commander* 305
Stives, vide Thebes
Stœchades, vide Hyeres
Storm, its Violence in 1693, &c. vide 448, 493, 494
——— *and in* 1713 vide 656 *to* 660, 785
Strafford (Earl) *Lord* Raby, *at the Siege of* Ostend 739
Stralsund *in the* Baltic 306
Stromboli (Strongyle) *an Island on the North of* Sicily 168
Strozza (John) *Podestat of* Genoa 244
Strozzi (Philip) *a* French *Admiral* 278
Strymon,

INDEX.

Strymon, *a Gulf near* Mount Athos 50
Suaco, *a Place near* Cales 621
Subercasse *(Monsieur) a* French *Governor of* Port Royal 767
Sueno, *a King of* Denmark 133
Suevi, *a People of ancient* Germany 3
Suiones (Swedes) *their Original, &c.* vide 299
Sulpitius, *one of* Cæsar's *Admirals against* Pompey 160
Sunda *Islands, in the* East-Indies, *attempted by the* French 262
Surinam, *in* America vide 783, 784
Surrey *(Earl) Lord High-Admiral* 339
Swaine, *King of* Denmark 328
Swanton *(Mr.) Captain of the* Exeter 654, 655, 793, 795
Swedes *and* Sweden, *their Naval Stores, Fleets, &c.* 18, 19, 183, 299 *to* 305
Sylla *the* Roman *General* 187
Syphax, *King of* Numidia 141
Syracuse, *its Situation and Haven* 81
———*beat the* Athenians 80 *to* 84
———*taken by the* Saracens 16, 74
———*by the* Romans 133, 134
Syria, *a Country near* Judæa 150, 239, 241

T

Tabago, *an Island in* America *possessed by the* English 404, vide 701
Tachus, *a King of* Ægypt 95
Tacitus, *a* Roman *Emperor* 177
Tænarium, *a Promontory, now* Cape Matapan 173
Tajo (Tagus) *the River of* Lisbon 757
Talmarsh, *an* English *Lieutenant General at* Brest 495, 499
Tamisis, *the River* Thames 156
Tanagra, *a City of* Bœotia 73
Tanais, *a River,* vide Don
Tangier *on the Coast of* Afric 254, 397, 405, 652
Taormina (Tauromenia) *a City in* Sicily 168
Taprobana, vide Ceilon
Tarento (Tarentum) *a City of* Naples 763, 764
———*and the chief City of the* Tarentines, vide 78, 139, 168, 176
Tarentines, *their Wars with the* Romans, &c. vide 11, 78, 139, &c.
Tariff, vide Mellaria
Tarragona, *a City and Port of* Spain 692, 752, 767, 771, 772, 793, 796
Tarshish, *and* Tarsus, *a Discourse thereon* 9
Tartessus (St. Lucar) *at the Mouth of the* Bætis vide 6, 9, 10
Tasso (Thasus) *an Island at the bottom of the* Archipelago 63
Tauromenia, vide Taormina
Tauromenites, *a kind of Gems* 136
Taurus, *a Sea Captain under* Augustus 168
Teias, *and* Totillas, Gothic *Kings in* Spain 186, 188
Temple *(Captain) Commander of the* South Sea Castle 782
Tenant (Matthew) *an* English *Sea Captain* 431

Tenedo, *and* Tenedos, *an Island in the* Archipelago 215, 218, 219, 236, 278
Teneriff, *one of the* Azores *or* Canary *Islands* 271, 290, 701
Tenths of Maritime Revenues consecrated 11
Teos, Lebedus, *and* Eræ, *Cities of* Lesser Asia 86
Tercera, *the principal Island of the* Azores 590, 677, 691, 692
Tergesta, vide Trieste
Ternate, *one of the* Molucca's *in the* East-Indies 260, 262, 278, 298, 347
Terovenne, *a City in* France 339
Terracina, *a City* Campania *in* Italy 246
Terra Firma, *a Province of* New Spain *on the Isthmus of* Panama 274, vide 592, 701
Terra Nova, *a Town in* Sardinia 771
Tervel, *a City of* Arragon *in* Spain 762
Tetuan, *a City of* Fez *in* Afric 513, 520
Teuta, *a Queen of* Illyricum 130
Thames, vide Tamisis
Thasus, vide Tasso
Thapsus, *a Peninsula near* Syracuse 80
Thauris *Island, vine* Labrazza
Thebes (Stives) *in* Bœotia, *built by* Phœnicians 4, vide 93, 96, 196
Themison, *one of* Demetrius's *Sea Commanders* 108
Themistocles, *an* Athenian *Admiral, his Character* 51, 56
———*his Death* 63
Theodoric, *a* Gothish *King in* Spain 188
Theodosia, Caffa *in Little* Tartary 17
Theodosius, *Emperor of the East* 325
Thera, *an Island of the* Ægean Sea 70
Theramenes *the* Athenian *put to Death* 92
Thermopylæ, *a narrow Pass at the Mountain* OEta *in* Thessaly 54, 59, 97
Thessaly, *a Province South of* Macedon, *and West of the* Archipelago 96
Thessalonica (Salonichi) *a City and Province of* Macedon 180, 181
Thielt, *a Village near* Ostend 738
St. Thomas, *an Island East of* Porto Rico 579
Thompson ( ) *Captain of the* August 783
Thornhill (Sir Timothy) *an* English *Commander at* Bass Terre 453, 454, 455
Thoulon, *a* French *City and Port in the* Mediterranean 512, 513, 520, 690
———*besieged and bombarded by the* English, &c. 732, 770, 772, 794, 796, 797, 799
Thoulouse (Count) *High-Admiral of* France 678, 690
Thracia *and* Thracians, *their Sea Dominion, &c.* 6, 96
Thracian Bosphorus, *the inner Streights of* Constantinople 7, 62
Thracian Chersonesus, vide Chersonesus, *and* 63, 90
Thrason *of* Thebes, *a Peloponnesian Admiral* 89
Thrasybulus *the* Athenian 87
———*exiled* 88
———*beats the Tyrants* 93
Thrasylus, *an* Athenian *Admiral* 86, 87, 89

6 Thronium

INDEX.

Thronium, *a Town belonging to* Corinth 70
Thyssa, *a City near* Mount Athos 75
Tiberius *the* Roman *Emperor* 174, 175
Tidore, *an Island, &c. in the* East-Indies 260, 261, 262, 276, 278
Tiepolo (Lawrence) *a Venetian Sea Commander* 415
Tigranes, *King of* Armenia 146
Timoleon, *the Corinthian Admiral, his Acts* 116
Timotheus, *(Son of* Conon) *an Athenian Admiral* 95
Tina, *an Island or City on the* Archipelago 214
Tindaris (Tindaro) *a Town in* Sicily 168
Tiptot (Robert) *an English Admiral* 313
Tirrick Hiddes, *Admiral of* Friesland 400
Tisienus Gallus, *one of Sext.* Pompeius's *Sea Commanders* 169
Tissaphernes, *the Persian General* 86, 87, 93
Tita, *a Town on the Coast of* Barbary 260
Titinius, *a Sea Captain under* Augustus 169
Toiras (Monsieur) *a French Commander at* Rochelle 373, 374, 375
Toll (Messieur) *a Dutch Sea Captain in* Ireland 440
Tollet (Mr.) *Captain of the* Assurance, *his smart Engagement* 723, 724
Toningen, *a Port, &c. on the River* Eyder 584
Toledo (Frederick de) *Admiral of* Spain 279
Torbay, *a noted Port in* England 414, 415, 444, 446, 545, 546, 717, 728
Torbole, *a Town on the Lake di* Garda 222
Torone, *taken by* Brasidas, *and recovered by* Cleon vide 75, 76, 95
Torra, *a Port of* Sardinia 268
Torrington (Earl) vide Herbert, *and* 446
Torstensohn (Leonard) *a Swedish Admiral* 303
Tortosa, *a City of* Catalonia 17, vide 239, 266
——— *Lord* Galway *retires thither* 731, vide 750
——— *taken by the* French, &c. 752
Totillas, *a King or General of the* Goths 185, 186, 188
Tour de Cordovan vide 311
Tourville, *a French Admiral* 466, 470, 485, 572
Tournay, *a City in* France *taken by the* English 339
Townsend (Isaac) *an English Sea Commander* 658
Trafalgar, vide Cape Trafalgar
Trani, vide Bari
Trapano, vide Drepanum, Eryx, *and* 214
Traspassy *Harbour* 632
Trapesus (Trebizond) *a City on the* Euxine 376
Traw, *a Town in* Dalmatia 212
Trebizond, *a City on the* Euxine vide 176, 308
Trebonius, Cæsar's *Lieutenant at* Marseilles 157
Treguier, *a Port in* France 314
Trelebais *and* Pontenille, &c. *French Protestant Sea Commanders* 317
Treport *in* France, *burnt by the* English 340, 341
Trevisano (John) *a Venetian Admiral* 214
Trevisiano (Nicholas) *another* Venetian *Admiral* 221
Trevor (Mr.) *Captain of the* Kingston 740
Triarius, *a Sea Captain of* Pompey 159
Tribonius, *a Sea Commander under* Augustus 159

Trieste (Tergesta) *a City and Port of* Istria *in the* Adriatic vide 192, 197
Tripoli *in* Barbary (Leptis) *built by* Phœnicians 4, vide 196, 309, 397, 491
Tripoli, *or* Tripolis, *in* Syria 98
Triumvirate *of the* Romans, vide 152, 164, 196, 397
Troezen, *a Town in* Peloponnesus 70, 74, 75
Tromp, vide Van Tromp
Tron, *a Doge of* Venice 198
Trovin (Monsieur Guie) *a French Admiral* 710, 717, 719, 721, 722, 724, 761, 788
Troy *in* Asia, *the City destroyed* vide 42, 43
Truccadero, *a Creek near* Cadiz *in* Spain 325
Tuditanus, *a Roman Proconsul* 138
Tunis, *a City on the Coast of* Afric 196
——— *taken by the* Turks 308, 309, vide 250, 278, 314, vide 397, 491
Turin, *the capital City of* Savoy 695
Turks, *their Naval Affairs*, vide 19, 20, 308, 309
Turky *Trade* vide 491, 518, 519
Tursis, *the Duke thereof* vide 771
Tuscany *(the Grand Duke thereof)* 736
Tycha, *a part of* Syracuse 134
Tyndaro, vide Tindaris
Tyrants *of* Athens vide 92, 93
Tyre *and* Sidon, *chief Cities of* Phœnicia 4
Tyre *destroyed, &c.* vide 5, 98 *to* 102, 212, 215, 241
Tyrrhenians, *People of* Tuscany, *their Sea Dominion, &c.* 11, 114
Tyrrhene *Sea* vide 203
Tzazon *the* Vandal, *Brother of* Gilimer 185

U

Vado, *a little Town and Port West of* Savona 736, 749, 751, 755, 769, 770, 774, 793, 794, 797, 798
Val del Orso, vide Oricum
Valens, *and* Valentinian *Emperors* 184
Valentia, *a City and Kingdom in* Spain 509, 698
——— *the Arshduke there* 729, 730, 754, 771, 772, 773, 798
Valerian, *an Admiral under* Narses 187
Valerius, *a Roman Admiral* 138, 140
Valerius, Cæsar's *Lieutenant* 167
Valerius Flaccus, *the Roman Consul* 147
Valerius Paulinus, Vespasian's *Admiral* 176
Valladolid, *a City in* Spain 773
Valois (Charles, *Count de*) *a French Admiral* 313
Valona (or La Valonna) *a large Town in* Albania vide 226
Vandals, *the* Vandals 184, 185, vide 306
Vanderdussen, *a Dutch Rear-Admiral* 637, 664, 665, 666, 669, 676, 685
Vandergoes, *a Dutch Vice-Admiral* 484, 485, 488, 571, 621, 652
Vander-Hulft, *Vice-Admiral of* Amsterdam 296
Vannes *in* Bretagne *inhabited by the* Veneti 15, vide 316
Vanstaten *Land, in* Norway 37
Van Tromp, *the Dutch Admiral* 279, 281 *to* 292, 398
Var, *a River near* Thoulon 731, 732
Varna,

INDEX.

Varna, *a Town in* Bulgaria 176
Varus, *a Roman General* 174
Vasques d'Gama, *a Portuguese High-Admiral* 260
Vatazi (John) *a Genose Sea Commander* 214
Vatican *at* Rome 191
Vatinius, *a Sea Commander for* Cæsar *at* Brundusium, &c 139, 162, 163
Udstedt, *a Port in* Denmark 585
Venables *and* Penn *sent to the* West-Indies 385 *to* 395
Venerianus, *the Emperor* Galienus *Admiral* 176
Vendosme *(Duke) a* French *Commander in* Spain 774
Veneti *of* Gaul, vide Vannes, *and* 153, 323, 324, 325
Venice, *its Original,* &c. 16, 17, vide 310
Venetians *beaten by the* Saracens 16
—— *master* Cyprus, Candia, &c. 17
—— *beat the* Turks 20
Veniere (Sebastian) *a* Venetian *Admiral* 228
Ventidius, M. Antony's *Lieutenant against the* Parthians 167
Vera Cruz *in the* West-Indies 591, 597, 699, 705, 707, 709, 788
Vercingetorix, *a* Gaulish *Commander* 156
Verden, vide Bremen
Vere *(Sir* Francis*) an* English *Sea Commander* 359
Verezano (John) *a* Florentine, *Discoverer of* New France 316
Vernon (Mr.) *Captain of the* Jersey 710, 713, 715
Verona, *a City of* Lombardy
Vespasian, *the* Roman *Emperor* 175, 324
Vetch ( ) *an* English *Colonel at* Port Royal *in* America 766
—— *and at* Quebec 781
Vetrani, *a famous* Genoese *Commander* 214
Ufford (William) *an* English *Admiral under* Edward *the Third* vide 33
Ugolin *(Count) a* Pisan *Sea Commander* 240
Viadri (James) *a* Venetian *Commander* 214
Vibo (Bivona) *a Port in* Calabria 160, 168
Vieste, *a City in* Italy *on the* Adriatic 222
Vigo, *the Action there* 623, 626 *to* 631
Vilikins, *a* Dutch *Admiral* 292
Villa Muerda, *a Town in* Portugal 253
Villa Nova *on the* French *Coast* 485
Villa Franca *on the Coast of* Spain 669, 670, 677, 732, 763, 799
Villars *(Monsieur) Commander of a* French *Squadron* 730
Villena *(Marquis) Vice-Roy of* Catalonia 507
Villeroy *(Marshal) a* French *General* 738
Villet *(Monsieur) a* French *Admiral* 485
Vincent ( ) *an* English *Sea Captain* 603, 725
Vineros, *a Town on the Coast of* Valentia 771, 772
Vintimiglia, *a City near* Genoa 691, 692
Virbius Geminus, Vespasian's *Admiral* 76, 171
Virginia *in* America 700, 779
Virgins *Islands at the East of* Porto Rico 579
Visigoths, *their Acts* 184
Visconti (Barnaby *and* John) *Dukes of* Milan 243, 446
Vistula, *a River of* Poland, *falls into the* Baltic, &c. 174
Visurgis, *the River* Weser 282, vide W
Vitalis (Michael) *Doge of* Venice 213
Vitellius *the Roman Emperor* 175
Vittoria (Pontochan) *a City of the* Americans vide 275
Uleckery, *a Harbour in* Norway 36
Ulit, *a* Sarazen *Leader* 190
Ulmerugi, *a People of* Germany 183
Umphrevill *(Sir* Robert) *Vice-Admiral of* England 334
Volga, *a River falling into the* Caspian *Sea* 307
Volo, *a City in* Thessaly vide 236
Voorue, *an Island in* Holland 285
Urania, *a Town in* Cyprus 107
Urphen, vide Ophir
Urseolus, *Doge of* Venice 200
Ursine (Paul) *a Commander at* Lepanto 232
Ursus Particiatus, *Doge of* Venice 192, 197
Ushant, vide 442, 443, 444, 471, 545, 642, 643, 644, 787
Utica, vide Biserta, *and* 140, 141
Utrect, *the Treaty,* &c. *there* 38, 39, 282
—— *the Bishop thereof a* Dutch *Admiral* 283
Vulterius, *the* Opitergian 159

W

Wager *(Sir* Charles*) an* English *Admiral* 641
Wager *(Mr.) Commadore in the* West-Indies, vide 703 *to* 711
Waldemar, *King of* Denmark 306, 307
Walker *(Sir* Hovenden*) Captain of the* Burford, &c. 599, 600, 605, 624, 715, 716
—— *and Admiral* 741, 742
—— *his Expedition to* Quebec, &c. 775 *to* 786
Walpole *(Captain) Commander of the* Lyon 774, 797
Walton (George) *an* English *Sea Captain at* Quebec 780
Walton ( ) *an* English *Colonel at* Quebec 781
Wamba, *a* Gothic *King in* Spain 188
Warna, *a River of* Germany 306
War declared against France *and* Spain 619
Warren (Thomas) *an* English *Sea Captain* 581, 582
Warwick *(Earl) Lord High-Admiral of* England 334, 335
Wassenaer, *a* Dutch *Rear-Admiral* 588, 624, 651, 666, 667, 669, 676, 685, 690, 694, 696, 751
Watchtmeister *(Count) Admiral, General of* Sweden 583
Waterford, *a City in* Ireland 432
Watkins, *Captain of the* St. George 695
Weissel *and* Elbe, *Rivers of* Germany 299
The Well, *a Shoal off* Lincolnshire 639
Westphalia, *the Peace there* 303
Wetheman, *a* Danish *Admiral* 306
Wheler *(Sir* Francis*) an* English *Admiral* 478, 479, 491, 494
Whetstone *(Sir* William*) an* English *Rear-Admiral* vide 592, 597, 598, 600, 602, 606
—— *his Proceedings to the* West-Indies 697 *to* 702
Whitaker *(Sir* Edward*) an* English *Admiral* 658, 677
—— *in the* Mediterranean 751 *to* 764, 768, 769
Wight

INDEX.

Wight *Isle* (Vectis) vide 462, 463, 664, 775
Wildfire, invented by Callinicus, &c. 189, vide 287, 288
William *the First and Second Kings of* England) 328, 329
William *the Third, King of* England, &c. *his Naval Affairs* vide 410 *to* 607
Wills *(Colonel) a Commander in the* West-Indies 604
Wills *(Major-General)* in Spain 752
Wilmot (Robert) *an* English *Sea Captain in the* West-Indies 531 *to* 537
Wimbleton *(Viscount) an* English *Admiral* 370
Windresse (William) *an* English *Colonel at* Quebec 781
Winter (William) *an* English *Sea Commander* 341
Wisheart (James) *an* English *Sea Captain and Vice-Admiral* 625, 643, 660, 665, 666, 667, 676, 677
Wismar, *a City of* Holstein *near* Rugen. *Yielded to the* Swedes 303, vide 306
Withers *(Lieutenant-General)* in Flanders, &c. 748
Witte, or De Witte, *a* Dutch *Vice-Admiral* 344
Wivell (Francis) *Captain of the* Bartleur, vide 486, 627, 630
Worsley *(Mr.) an* English *Colonel in* Spain 729
Wrangel, *a* Swedish *Admiral* 303
Wren (Ralph) *Captain of the* Norwich 459, 460
Wright (William) *an* English *Sea Captain at* La Hogue 466
Wright (Lawrence) *an* English *Sea Captain at the* West-Indies 451 *to* 458, 466
Wyat, *an* English *Sea Captain* 638
Wyld (Baron) *Captain of the* Royal Oak 718

X

Xabea, *a Town and Port near* Altea *and* Denia 797
Xaintogne, *a Province of* France 317
Xantippus, *a* Lacedæmonian *General* 125
Xeres, *a River near* Cadiz *in* Spain 621
Xerxes, *the* Persian *King, succeeds* Darius, *and reduces the* Ægyptians 50
——*invades* Greece, &c. 50, 51, 54
——*his Fleet and Army beaten* 55, 56
Ximenes (Rowland) *accuses* Columbus 274

Y

Yarmouth *Road* 639
York *, Duke) Commander of the* English *Fleet* 295,
Yviça (Ebusus *and* Pityusa) *one of the* Baleares, *reduced by the* Pisans 298, 321
——*seiz'd by* Sertorius 17
——*possess'd by King* Charles *of* Austria, vide 696, 799

Z

Zabaim, *a King of* Goa 257, 258
Zaffe Hibraim, *interpreted* 9
Zanguebar *in the* East-Indies 257
Zant, *the Island* Zacynthus 70, 74, 138, 224, 308
Zanzibar, *an Island of the* Æthiopic *Ocean in* Afric 255, 256
Zara, *a Town in* Dalmatia 213, 215, 220
Zarabis, *a* Mahometan *Prince* 245
Zeeland, *a part of* Holland 283
Zegna, *a Sea-Port of* Croatia 234
Zeila, *a Town on the* Afric *Coast of the* Red *Sea* 259, 261
Zembla, i. e. Nova Zembla 290
Zempoallan, *a Town in* Mexico 275
Zeni (Thomas) *a* Venetian *Admiral* 225
Zeno (Charles) *a* Venetian *Admiral* 217, 218, 219
Zeno (Renier) *a* Venetian *Admiral* 213
Zeno (Peter) *a* Venetian *Admiral, his Acts* 216 *to* 220
——*his Stratagem* 220
——*taken Prisoner* 222
Zerbi, *an Island near* Tripoli *in* Barbary 246, 277, 309
Zerfadin *the Second (a King of* Ormus) 257
Ziani (Sebastian) *Doge of* Venice 213
Zimbala, vide Ægimurus
Zocotora, *an Island near the Mouth of the* Red Sea 256, 257
Zopyrus, *Father of* Megabyzus
Zirickzee, *on the Coast of* Zeeland 283
Zuirie, vide Albania
Zullimin *(or* Solyman) *a* Saracen *Emperor* 190
Zurickzee, *the* French *King's Admiral there* 29, vide 283, 783

ERRATA

ERRATA.

PReface, Page 6. line 16. after *time*, add *(including also the Merchant Ships of the Kingdom)* Book, Page 10. line 26. read *of his Successors*. l. 32. dele *as*. P. 11. l. 31. for *Æguator* r. *Æquator*. P. 14. in the Margin, f. *Provenæ* r. *Provence*. P. 15. l. 17. insert a Comma after *Ports*. P. 28. l. 34. f. *Nergivian* r. *Vergivian*. l. 39. r. *challenged*. P. 33. l. 26. f. *the* r. *his*. P. 35. l. 5. r. *extend to the*. P. 37. l. 15. r. *far from being sufficient*. P. 38. in the Margin, f. *Treaty of Breda* r. *Treaty for a Suspension of Arms in 1712*. P. 42. l. 20. dele *Naval*. P. 44. l. 12. f. *Flegonus* r. *Telegonus*. P. 64. l. 43. f. *at* r. *as*. P. 66. in the Margin, f. *Conon's* r. *Cimon's*. P. 69. l. 8. f. *was* r. *were*. P. 83. l. 10. r. *taken and killed great Numbers of Men*. P. 84. l. 39. f. *Barks* r. *Beaks*. P. 85. l. 37. f. *them* r. *him*. P. 103. l. 34. r. *Gedrosians*. P. 112. l. ult. r. *Doson*. P. 113. l. 41. dele *that Princess*. P. 126. l. 45. r. *Drepanum*. In the Margin r. *Trapani*. P. 130. l. 39. after *commanded* r. *in Corcyra*. P. 132. l. 20. f. *and* r. *who*. In the Margin, f. *Miletus* r. *Melita*. P. 134. l. ult. f. *an Island* r. *and the Island*. P. 139. l. 20. f. *drew* r. *drove*. P. 141. l. 30. dele the Comma after *Ambassador*. l. 31, dele *and*. P. 161. in the first Note in the Margin, f. *Ganymedes* r. *Athillas*. l. 9. after *Eunuch* r. *who*. P. 168. l. 34. dele *but*. l. 36. r. *but* Agrippa's. l. 37. dele *so that*. P. 170. l. 38. r. *a-peek*. P. 180. l. 6. f. *on* r. *of*. l. 8. f. *and on* r. *and of*. P. 185. l. 31. r. *Prætorio*. P. 186. l. 32. f. *fixed* r. *fastened*. P. 219. l. 18. r. *Boucicaut*. P. 336. l. 20. r. *Tract*. P. 447. l. 48. f. *Dominica* r. *Guadalupe*. P. 518. l. 29. f. *ailsing* r. *sailing*. P. 619. l. 8. dele the Comma after *before*. P. 633. l. 13. r. *Gally*. P. 724. l. 50 f. *hey* r. *they*. P. 750. l. 44. f. *Lampourdan* r. *Ampourdan*. P. 773. l. 16. f. *from* r. *for*. P. 774. l. 46. r. *from* England *at Port* Mahon. P. 791. l. 8. f. *for* r. *from*. P. 794. l. 28. dele *that*. P. 797. l. 27. f. *of* r. *to*.

F I N I S.